DIGITAL CODING OF WAVEFORMS

PRENTICE-HALL SIGNAL PROCESSING SERIES

Alan V. Oppenheim, Editor

DIGITAL CODING OF WAVEFORMS
Principles and Applications
to Speech and Video

N. S. JAYANT

Bell Laboratories, Inc.
Murray Hill, NJ

PETER NOLL

Technical University of Berlin

PRENTICE-HALL, INC.   Englewood Cliffs, New Jersey   07632

Library of Congress Cataloging in Publication Data

Jayant, Nuggehally S., 1946-
  Digital coding of waveforms.

  Includes index.
  1. Signal processing—Digital techniques. 2. Coding
theory. I. Noll, P. (Peter), 1936-   II. Title.
TK5102.J39   1984   621.38′043   83-22170
ISBN 0-13-211913-7

Editorial/production supervision: *Shari Ingerman*
Cover design: *Edsal Enterprises*
Manufacturing buyer: *Tony Caruso*
Page layout: *Diane Koromhas*

Printed in the United States of America

10   9   8   7   6   5   4   3   2   1

ISBN 0-13-211913-7 01

Prentice-Hall International, Inc., *London*
Prentice-Hall of Australia Pty. Limited, *Sydney*
Editora Prentice-Hall do Brasil, Ltda., *Rio de Janeiro*
Prentice-Hall Canada Inc., *Toronto*
Prentice-Hall of India Private Limited, *New Delhi*
Prentice-Hall of Japan, Inc., *Tokyo*
Prentice-Hall of Southeast Asia Pte. Ltd., *Singapore*
Whitehall Books Limited, *Wellington, New Zealand*

To Amma, Anna
and Angelika

and to Julia

Contents

Items with asterisks (*) are special topics that can be skipped without loss of continuity.

Contents

Preface

Digital Coding is by no means a new subject. It has been practiced for the better part of fifty years, with the last twenty years witnessing an unprecedented amount of activity. The number of archival publications in this period is in the thousands. The momentum of this activity is expected to continue although there may be important shifts in emphasis. One such shift may be from concepts-type literature to implementation-type endeavors. As in many other subjects, fundamental innovations will probably, and hopefully, continue to be made in digital coding, leading to advances in bit rate reduction more impressive than those reported in this book. It may be fair to say, however, that our understanding of speech and image coding has now reached a very mature point, making the time ripe for a book of the type we are offering.

Emerging communications- and information networks require ubiquitous uses of digital speech, digital audio and digital video. Applications include transmission, storage, conferencing and many kinds of signal processing for information manipulation and display. Basic to all these systems are techniques for waveform digitization with acceptable levels of signal quality. This indeed is the topic of our book.

There have been outstanding books on specific aspects of waveform coding. These include pioneering works on Pulse Code Modulation and Deltamodulation. There have also been well-respected books on Speech and Image Processing with excellent special sections on Digital Coding. However, to our best knowledge, the present book is the first to offer a broad and in-depth coverage of waveform coding concepts and algorithms. This is also the first attempt to include both speech and image systems under one cover, not counting a reprint book on the subject edited by one of us about eight years ago.

The non-existence of a treatise on waveform coding was certainly a major motivation for our book, and its production has made possible the unification of a wealth of information that was hitherto scattered in diverse branches of literature such as Information Theory, Communications Technology and Signal Processing. The idea of a book that would treat both speech and image signals was not obvious since the authors of this book were much closer to speech coding than to image coding. But it became apparent at a fairly early stage of the project that the fundamental principles of most coding algorithms, as well as the notion of using statistical input models for coder analyses, were equally valid for speech and image waveforms. In fact, these principles could best be illustrated by invoking examples from both fields, and this is indeed the approach used in this book.

In the interest of a unified exposition, issues that are very specific to one type of signal are usually avoided in this book. Exceptions are extremely important and standardized systems such as logarithmic PCM coders for speech and run-length coders for two-level graphics images. In general, optimization of coding algorithms to a given signal involve attention to specific signal properties as well as specific issues in perception, and these result in finely tuned coding structures that may not be covered in our basic treatment. Practicing professionals seeking such information will therefore be expected to supplement the chapters of this book with speech-specific or image-specific reading, as the case may be. There are fairly long, although not exhaustive, lists of references at the end of each chapter to help the readers in this regard.

An example of a topic that is entirely out of the scope of our book is analysis-synthesis vocoding for speech. But there are many fundamental signal processing algorithms covered in this book that have direct application in the above specialized area as well. Examples of such basic algorithms are those for quantization and prediction.

As a text for a university course on waveform coding, this book is perhaps unique. It makes possible, for the first time, a complete one-semester or one-quarter graduate course on coding, instead of teaching coding as a small aspect of a signal-processing or communications systems course. The problems and the computer projects in the text have been chosen to provide a useful mix of drill-type exercises and perspective-providing tools, and a solutions manual for the problems is being offered to faculty desiring to teach this course. Included in the table of contents are asterisks reflecting optional or specialized topics that could be eliminated for the purposes of teaching the course. Needless to mention, some lecturers intending to use this book for a course will tend to exercise their own specific choices with regard to scope and emphasis. There is also the possibility of teaching the book in two companion semesters or quarters.

Parts of this book have been used by its authors as the bases for regular courses in universities, intensive courses for practicing professionals and courses in continuing education programs in professional environments such as Bell Laboratories. In its present form, the book was first used to teach a 40-hour one-semester graduate course at the University of California at Santa Barbara in the beginning of 1983. The background that was expected from the students in this course was basic knowledge of linear systems, probability and statistics, and familiarity with programming techniques for carrying out computer projects.

Synopsis

The following paragraphs summarize the purpose and content of each of twelve chapters in this book. Most of these chapters include problems for solution. There is a separate section on computer projects. There are seven appendices.

Chapter 1 defines the waveform coding problem and summarizes the accomplishments in the field of bit rate reduction. It introduces objective as well as subjective criteria for the measurement of digitized signal quality. It also addresses the issues of coder complexity and coding delay by identifying three broad classes of coding algorithms, examples of which are discussed at length in later chapters of the book.

Chapter 2 describes properties of speech and image waveforms that are relevant to the coding problem. It discusses quantitative statistical models that are used in later chapters to motivate quantization and coding algorithms, and to calibrate their performances with respect to the promises of Rate Distortion theory. The statistical descriptors used in modelling waveforms include the probability density function, the autocorrelation function, power spectral density and a special property thereof called the spectral flatness measure. Also discussed in this chapter are properties that are specific to speech and image waveforms, such as nonstationarity and quasi-periodicity.

Chapter 3 discusses the process of waveform sampling. This process is a basic prerequisite for digital coding systems, and most of the chapter is an attempt to recapitulate well-known fundamental results and theorems on uniform time sampling. The chapter also includes discussions that are specific to speech and image sampling. For example, it discusses the rationale behind specific anti-aliasing or prefiltering operations that are tacitly assumed in most of speech and image work.

Chapter 4 deals with amplitude quantization. It is the longest chapter in this book, and it could very well have been a monograph by itself. After a fairly complete description of uniform quantization and a derivation of a fundamental 6 dB/bit signal-to-noise ratio result, the chapter goes on to the extremely important refinements of nonuniform quantization, logarithmic companding and adaptive quantization of nonstationary inputs. The chapter includes a section on the statistical properties of quantization errors which helps to put in perspective commonly assumed error properties such as uniformity of its probability density function and whiteness of its power spectral density. The chapter also shows the benefits of variable-length entropy coding in bringing quantizer performance closer to the Rate Distortion bound. Vector Quantization, which has a similar potential, is discussed in a later chapter.

Chapter 5 is on pulse code modulation (PCM). This is the earliest and best understood technique for digital coding and 8-bit PCM coding provides a standard against which other algorithms are compared, in both speech and image work. In deference to the ubiquitous use of 8-bit logarithmic PCM for high-quality speech communication, a good deal of this chapter is devoted to discussions specific to this standard.

Chapters 6, 7 and 8 are very closely related. They discuss, respectively, differential PCM, noise feedback coding and deltamodulation.

Chapter 6 begins the discussion of differential PCM (DPCM) with the theory of linear prediction and the notion of prediction gain as a measure of redundancy removal in a sequence of correlated samples. Several examples illustrate the dependence of prediction gain on the number of waveform samples used in the prediction of a sample to be coded. Later sections of this chapter discuss adaptive algorithms needed for the efficient prediction of a nonstationary process with time-varying spectrum; and algorithms based on distant samples, for the predictions of a quasi-periodic signal such as voiced speech or a moving image. Adaptive Prediction is the basis of high quality speech and image coding systems using 4 bits per sample. Combinations of adaptive and distant-sample-based prediction produce some of the best results in bit rate reduction, and make possible high-quality digitizations of speech and video at coding rates as low as 1 to 2 bits per sample.

Chapter 7 deals with the notions of open-loop DPCM and noise feedback coding, and provides a formal discussion of noise shaping. Linear prediction, as discussed in Chapter 6, can provide a very useful utilization of redundancies inherent in waveform production. Suitable designs of prediction error quantizers in DPCM can also exploit some of the properties of the human perceptual mechanisms, and provide coding configurations that enhance perceived quality at a given bit rate. Noise feedback coding provides an additional degree of freedom in coder design and makes possible a more direct control of reconstruction noise spectrum. This kind of noise shaping can provide very powerful perceptual optimizations of DPCM-type coders.

Chapter 8 is on deltamodulation, the special case of DPCM with a two-level quantizer. Deltamodulation is the simplest form of digital coding, and like PCM, it has found wide applications in digital transmission as well as in signal processing. The coarseness of the one-bit quantizer usually necessitates the oversampling of the input waveform. The chapter therefore includes a discussion of prediction gain as a function of sampling frequency. For important classes of input spectra, the result is a 9 dB/octave result for the signal-to-noise ratio of deltamodulation with a single integrator or first-order predictor. After pointing out the advantages of double integration and delta sigma modulation, the chapter enters into a comprehensive discussion of adaptive step-size algorithms for nonstationary inputs. In particular, syllabically adaptive deltamodulation is well known for its transmission error resistance and this type of coder, usually known as continuously variable slope deltamodulation (CVSD), is discussed at length.

Chapter 9 discusses delayed decision coding, a class of algorithms that anticipate, or take into account by some means, the characteristics of the actual sequence being digitized. The mechanism for doing this involves the use of significant encoding delay by definition, and a search for a best output sequence, or a part thereof, as stored or generated in structures such as trees, trellises or codebooks. Coding algorithms based on codebooks are also known as vector quantizers. An interesting result of this chapter is that delayed decision coding is useful even when the input is a sequence of independent, identically distributed random variables. In fact, the technique provides an important approach to rate-distortion bounds with inputs such as gamma-distributed variables for which the performance of conventional scalar quantizers is very poor. Delayed decision coding is also a powerful technique for the encoding of correlated sequences. In this case, there are two alternative approaches. The first is based on the direct application of delayed decision coding to the correlated input sequence. The second method is based on redundancy removal as in differential coding, followed by delayed decision coding of the prediction error waveform. Examples from speech coding are used to illustrate the efficiency of these techniques at coding rates in the order of 1 bit per sample. Delayed Decision Coding also provides a natural framework for realizing fractional coding rates such as 0.5 bit per sample.

Chapter 10 deals with a very specific waveform, that of two-level graphics, or facsimile. Many important classes of two-level images are characterized by long clusters or runs of all-black or all-white pixels along a horizontal scan line. Run-length coding is a conceptually simple, and highly efficient technique for the error-free coding of such inputs. The techniques usually call for some kind of variable-length coding to account for the fact that the probability of a given run is a very nonuniform function of the run-length. Run-length coding techniques can also utilize vertical or inter-line correlations in the graphics input, for greater encoding efficiency in appropriate two-dimensional algorithms. Several run-length coding algorithms have been standardized internationally, and these standards are discussed at some length in this chapter. The more efficient examples of the run-length algorithms encode standard graphics documents using less than 0.1 bit per pixel on the average.

Chapters 11 and 12 return to the problem of encoding multi-level inputs with non-zero error. Unlike the predictive coding methods of earlier chapters, the last two chapters of the book use a frequency-domain or transform-domain approach.

In the sub-band coding approach of Chapter 11, an input such as speech is first split into contiguous sub-band signals which are encoded separately. The sub-band partition makes possible the use of variable bit allocation, so that input components that are deemed more important can be quantized with greater numbers of levels. The bit allocation may reflect differences in speech power in the various sub-bands, and/or differences in the perception of noise occurring in those sub-bands. Emphasis in Chapter 11 is on relatively simple designs for speech coding, characterized by a fairly small number of sub-bands, and a time-invariant design of the bit allocation algorithm.

Chapter 12 is on transform coding. This chapter generalizes the sub-band approach to include the possibility of splitting the input into a much larger number of frequency-domain, or more generally, transform-domain components. These components are in fact the transform coefficients that result from a linear operation on an input sequence block whose length equals the number of transform coefficients desired. Transform Coding performance increases with block length. The maximum performance of transform coding is shown to be identical to the maximum performance of a differential or predictive coding system. Transform coding and predictive coding are however very different in the perceived properties of their reconstruction error sequences, and in the perceived effects of transmission errors. Practical versions of transform coding use suboptimal but easily implementable transforms. Several examples of these transforms and their properties are discussed at length. Later sections of this chapter concentrate on applications to speech and image coding. In the case of speech coding, emphasis is on algorithms for adaptive bit allocation to track the time-varying nature of the input spectrum. In the case of images, an additional point of focus is the need for efficient approaches in two-dimensional and three-dimensional coding. In both cases, transform coding is shown to lead to very high quality digitizations at a bit rate in the order of 2 bits/sample, a result that is comparable with the best results with adaptive predictive coding.

Acknowledgements

The following colleagues were kind enough to review aspects of our book: B. P. Agrawal, W. R. Daumer, H. Fehn, A. Gersho, J. Gibson, J. F. Kaiser, R. Lippmann, J. B. O'Neal, D. Preuss, A. Tomozawa, T. Thomas, R. Zelinski and Ms. C. Volmary. We would like to thank them for their time and effort.

Many of the image coding illustrations in this book were made using original material supplied by respective authors. For this kind co-operation, we thank N. Ahmed, R. Baker, R. M. Gray, R. Hunter, K. Iinuma, T. Kummerow, M. Kunt, H. Landau, R. Lei, R. Lippmann, H. Musmann, W. Pratt, D. Preuss and R. Steele.

The line drawings for this book were prepared by Comprehensive Designers Incorporated, Union, New Jersey. For co-ordinating this effort, we thank Mr. Roy Anderson of the art studio at Bell Laboratories, Murray Hill, and his ever-helpful colleagues.

Several members of the text processing department at Bell Laboratories have contributed to the realization of this document. For their efforts and expertise, we thank Mrs. Beverly Heravi, Ms. Babe Hill, Mrs. Donna Manganelli, Ms. Joan McCarthy, Ms. Carmela Patuto and Mrs. Susan Tarczynski. In particular, we would like to acknowledge the sustained contributions of Ms. Hill and Mrs. Tarczynski, and the invaluable role played by the latter in the final phases of a time-worn project.

The editorial and production departments at Prentice Hall have done an excellent job of bringing out this book in its present form. We thank them for their contributions. In particular, it is a pleasure to acknowledge the help of the copy editor, the production editor Ms. Shari Ingerman and the college text editor, Mr. Bernard Goodwin. And our thanks to Prof. Alan Oppenheim for having this book in his distinguished series on Signal Processing.

Students at the University of Bremen and the Technical University of Berlin have used early versions of chapters of this book to carry out projects and thesis work, and thereby have contributed to this book in many ways. We would like to thank them for their contributions.

Prof. A. Gersho invited one of us to try out the book draft as the basis of a new graduate course offered by the University of California at Santa Barbara. The teaching of this course was extremely beneficial to the book. Our thanks to Prof. Gersho.

The endorsement of this book by Bell Laboratories has been a major factor in the realization of this book. We are grateful to Bell for our extensive use of its excellent facilities, especially the photography department, the art studio and the text processing facilities at Murray Hill.

Our involvement with this book has been long and sometimes difficult. Two individuals at Bell Laboratories have made the process a little easier. For their encouragement and inspiration, we thank Drs. J. L. Flanagan and L. R. Rabiner. Dr. Flanagan was instrumental in bringing together the authors of this book about ten years ago. In doing so, he also set the stage for the production of this work.

N. S. Jayant   Peter Noll

1

Introduction

1.1 Digital Coding of Waveforms

This book will discuss many techniques for representing analog waveforms by sequences of binary digits, or bits. *Digital coding* is the process, or sequence of processes, that leads to such digital representations. The benefits of digital representation are many and well known [Aaron, 1979]. Perhaps most significant is the fact that digital signals are less sensitive than analog signals to transmission noise; as a result, digital signals have offered the possibility of making better use of interference- and noise-limited communication media, although at the expense of greater bandwidth than that demanded in analog communications. To give a concise list of other advantages, digitized signals are easy to *regenerate* and *store*, to *error-protect* and *encrypt*, and to *multiplex, packetize* and *mix*. Digitization of waveforms also enables an efficient *unification of transmission and switching* functions in communications; it also permits an extensive application of *digital signal processing*. Time-shared digital signal processing, unlike analog processing, makes better use of new classes of technology, such as optical and millimeter wave devices, which excel in speed rather than in properties such as linearity. Digital processors and terminals also make better use of the rapid revolutions in microprocessor and integrated circuit technologies.

Digital representations of analog waveforms entail, however, the introduction of some kind of coding distortion; and a basic problem in waveform coding is to achieve the *minimum possible distortion for a given encoding rate* (bits per second, or bits per waveform sample) or, equivalently, to achieve a *given acceptable level of distortion with the least possible encoding rate*. The encoding rate is referred to as the *bit rate* in the rest of this book, and it is specified either as the number of bits per second, or as the number of bits per waveform sample. The distortion is specified either by an objective measure such as the *signal-to-noise ratio*, or by a subjective measure such as the *mean opinion score*. An additional parameter that enters the picture is coder complexity or cost, but the role of this parameter tends to diminish as advances in technology and signal processing bridge cost gulfs between the sophisticated and the simple.

Applications of digital representations are many and increasing. They include transmission and/or storage of speech, audio, video and graphics waveforms, satellite imagery, and geophysical and medical data, to mention important examples. Digital representations are also very helpful in the processing, copying, editing and displaying of the above-mentioned signals. This book focuses primarily on *telephone-bandwidth speech* and *monochrome video*. The digital coding of these signals will be referred to as *speech coding* and *image coding*, respectively. Our treatments of these topics can be generalized, sometimes in straightforward fashion, to apply to higher-bandwidth audio and color video. Chapter 10 provides a special discussion of two-level graphics.

The Basic Processes of Digital Coding. Figure 1.1 is a qualitative illustration of how analog waveforms, which are *time-continuous* and *amplitude-continuous*, enter the digital world by means of *time discretization (sampling)* and *amplitude discretization (quantizing)*. The waveform in (a) is *analog*, and that in (d) is its *digitized* version. Each of the time waveform samples in (d) has a finite number of allowed amplitude values, represented by appropriate groups of binary digits, such as the sequences 01, 10 and 11 in the illustration. The transformation from (a) to (d) can be via stage (b) or — as is more usual — via stage (c). Time discretization will be assumed for waveform sources in all of this book, unless otherwise mentioned. When performed with adequate resolution, time discretization will be seen to be an *information-preserving* operation. In contrast, amplitude quantization will be *information-lossy* by definition.

A *waveform encoder* typically accepts a time-discrete input such as (c) and provides a binary output sequence which is sufficient to derive the digitized

Figure 1.1 Four types of signals: (a) amplitude-continuous and time-continuous; (b) amplitude-discrete and time-continuous; (c) amplitude-continuous and time-discrete; and (d) amplitude-discrete and time-discrete.

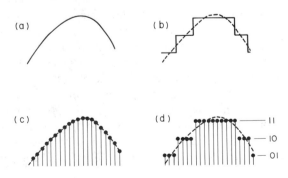

reconstruction (d). It is the function of a *waveform decoder* to accept that binary output sequence, or a version of it, at the output of a storage or transmission medium, and thence to deliver the reconstruction (d) — strictly, a lowpass filtered, or smooth version of it. The term *waveform coding* is sometimes used to suggest the encoding process alone. But throughout this book, as in most coding literature [Jayant, 1976] [Flanagan et al., 1979] [Netravali and Limb, 1980], the term will imply the combination of encoding and decoding processes. This is the notation in Figure 1.3, where the single box labeled *waveform coding system* signifies encoding as well as subsequent decoding.

1.1.1 The Digital Communication System

The overall digital communication scenario is shown in Figure 1.2, and most of this book focuses on the waveform encoder and waveform decoder boxes. The composite of these two boxes is sometimes called a *waveform coder* or *waveform codec* (*co*der + *dec*oder = *codec*). The latter terminology is especially used in the context where both coder and decoder are implemented within a single unit at transmitter and receiver terminals. A simple example of the waveform encoder box is a PCM encoder (Chapter 5), which involves an amplitude quantizer followed by a binary codeword generator.

Prefiltering and *sampling*, and the inverse operation of reconstruction filtering in the receiver, are procedures that are tacitly assumed in digital waveform ɔmmunication. The concept of information-lossless sampling of a *bandlimited*

Figure 1.2 (a) Digital communication of waveforms; (b) digital channel.

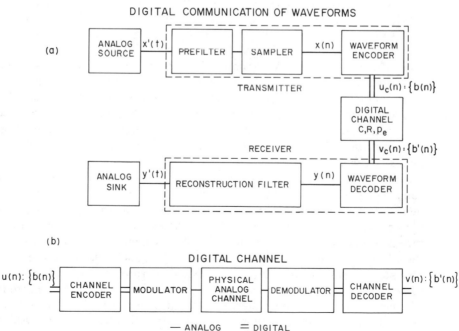

analog source is very significant and is discussed at length in Chapter 3. It is also shown there that coder design based on the signal-to-noise ratio (*SNR*), obtained by comparing $x(n)$ and $y(n)$ as in Figure 1.1, is equivalent to a design that would result by comparing the analog versions $x'(t)$ and $y'(t)$. It should also be noted that coder inputs can sometimes be amplitude-discrete. Examples are two-level graphics images and computer-stored multi-level waveforms used in coder simulations and implementations. In the former example, the aim is to transmit two-level graphics without introducing further degradation. In the latter situation, one has a sequence of multi-level signal samples (say, 8-bit or 256-level image samples and 12-bit or 4096-level speech samples); and the object is to reduce the bit rate for ease of transmission or storage, with a non-zero but hopefully minimum possible amount of signal degradation.

It must be emphasized that *digital* waveform communication still uses physical channels that transmit *analog* waveforms. Digital systems for waveform storage use analog media or "channels" as well. In Figure 1.2, double lines indicate digital signal paths, and the *modulator* and *demodulator* boxes provide the interface between analog and digital signals in the communication system.

In *binary* digital communication, which is assumed in this book, the output $\{b(n)\}$ of the waveform encoder, as well as the output of the channel encoder, are sequences whose elements are 1 or 0. Note that the binary code letters 1 and 0 are *logical* symbols and will be used as such in this book. Electrical signals that are used to convey the above binary information can be members of several binary or non-binary sets: for example, pulse, or sinusoidal signals with amplitude levels (S and 0) volts, or ($+S$ and $-S$) volts, or ($+S$, 0, and $-S$) volts. The choice of an electrical signal set is dictated by transmission requirements such as the need to avoid a dc or zero frequency component in the transmitted signal spectrum, ease of synchronization and automatic error detection [Bennett, 1978] [Shanmugam, 1979] [Schwartz, 1980]. An example of a practical electrical signal set is that in a *bipolar* system where a logical 0 is represented by 0 volts, and a logical 1 is represented alternately as $+S$ and $-S$, with the alternation taking place at every occurrence of a 1. With an equiprobable (1, 0) output from the digital waveform coder, the resulting ternary sequence does not have a dc component; further, the frequent zero crossings permit easy recovery, when needed, of the discrete-time information from the received channel signal; and finally, the $\pm S$ alternation property results in automatic error detection of any isolated error, which causes an immediate violation of the alternation rule.

Figure 1.2(a) has introduced the notion of a *digital channel*. The several components of such a channel are shown in Figure 1.2(b). The modulator in this figure maps the channel encoder outputs 1 and 0 into analog signals suitable for the physical transmission channel, while the demodulator uses an appropriate decision threshold to interpret received signals as corresponding to either 1 or 0. The role of the *channel encoder* is to add controlled redundancy into a bit stream so that its inverse, the *channel decoder*, can correctly interpret digital sequences even in the presence of some channel noise and consequent bit errors in the demodulator. The channel encoder, the modulator, the physical channel, the demodulator and the channel decoder are sometimes lumped into one ideal box, a *noiseless digital channel*; in this ideal case, $b'(n) = b(n)$ in Figure 1.2. However, in this book we allow the possibility of a *noisy digital channel* with a non-zero *bit error probability* p_e. This error probability is sometimes called the *bit error rate*. When $p_e \neq 0$, the bit sequence $b'(n)$ available to the waveform decoder is no longer identical to the sequence $b(n)$ provided by the waveform encoder.

In Figure 1.2, codewords at digital channel inputs and outputs, which are really sequences of R consecutive values of $b(n)$ and $b'(n)$, respectively, have been denoted by symbols $u_c(n)$ and $v_c(n)$. In succeeding chapters, we will consider the channel as a mapping between an amplitude-quantized input $u(n)$ and an amplitude-quantized output $v(n)$. The mapping from $u(n)$ to $u_c(n)$ and the mapping from $v_c(n)$ to $v(n)$ will be implicit in those discussions.

1.1.2 Signal-to-Noise Ratio and Transmission Rate

Figure 1.3 can be used to quantify the encoding rate and distortion parameters mentioned earlier. Inputs and outputs to the waveform coding system are represented by illustrative samples $x(nT)$ and $y(nT)$, where T is the *sampling interval* — the reciprocal of *sampling rate* f_s — and n is a discrete-time index. For simplicity, these samples will henceforth be denoted by $x(n)$ and $y(n)$. In

Figure 1.3 Waveform coding example: (a) block diagram of coding system; (b) input waveform $x(n)$; (c) output waveform $y(n)$; and (d) reconstruction error waveform $r(n) = x(n) - y(n)$.

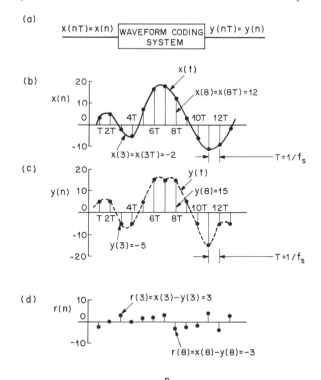

waveform communication, information needed to reconstruct the *digitized* signal $y(n)$ is conveyed to the receiver by means of a code sequence, usually a binary code sequence $\{b(n)\}$. The *reconstruction error* $r(n)$ is defined as the difference between $x(n)$ and $y(n)$:

$$r(n) = x(n) - y(n) \tag{1.1}$$

Let the variances of $x(n)$, $y(n)$, and $r(n)$ be denoted by σ_x^2, σ_y^2 and σ_r^2. These variances are formally defined in Chapter 2, but we note here that in the special case of zero-mean signals, variances are simply equal to respective mean square values measured over an appropriate sequence length M:

$$\sigma_u^2 = \frac{1}{M} \sum_{n=1}^{M} u^2(n) \quad \text{where} \quad u = x, y, \text{ or } r \text{ is a zero-mean signal} \tag{1.2}$$

A standard objective measure of coded waveform quality is the *ratio of signal variance to reconstruction error variance*, referred to for historical reasons as the *signal-to-noise ratio (SNR)*, usually expressed in decibels (dB):

$$SNR \ (\text{dB}) = 10 \log_{10} (\sigma_x^2/\sigma_r^2) \tag{1.3}$$

Unless otherwise specified, subsequent uses of the log $(\cdot)$ function in this book will imply $\log_{10} (\cdot)$, as in (1.3).

The use of a mean square function σ_x^2 to measure input signal level is convenient and mathematically tractable. In image coding work, input amplitudes are often considered to be all-positive quantities with a non-zero mean; and their maximum value $x_{\max}$ is sometimes used in the numerator of the *SNR* formula instead of the root-mean-square (rms) value σ_x used in (1.3). The values of *SNR* in such measurements will be much higher than the values obtained from (1.3), with a difference in the order of 10 dB.

The reconstruction error variance σ_r^2 is often referred to simply as the *mean square error* (mse) and coder designs that minimize this quantity are called *minimum mean square error* (mmse) designs.

The use of a mean square function for measuring waveform distortion implies that large values of reconstruction error are much more serious than smaller values thereof. The mean square formulation is also a time-honored one, and the signal-to-noise ratio (1.3) is the single most used criterion of coder performance. As we progress in this book, we shall make ubiquitous use of the above-defined *SNR*. But we shall also note, when appropriate, the inadequacy of *SNR* as a perceptually meaningful measure of digitized waveform quality. Very briefly, the inadequacy of *SNR* has to do with the fact that reconstruction error sequences in general do not have the character of signal-independent additive noise; and that therefore, the seriousness of the impairment cannot be measured by a simple power measurement. This can be illustrated by the simple example of a small geometric tilt of a picture signal. This kind of impairment can lead to a very large value of σ_r^2, and hence a very small value of *SNR*, although the slightly tilted image can be perceptually very acceptable. An example more relevant to digital coding is that of a thin but bright horizontal streak in an image (Chapter 6). In this case, σ_r^2 can be quite small and the *SNR* can be very high, but the perceived image quality can be quite unacceptable. Similar examples can also be given in the field of speech digitization. In fact, in both image and speech coding work, the truly definitive measures of coded signal quality are perceptual ones, as measured by careful subjective experimentation (Appendix F). However, subjective testing of coding systems can be very time-consuming; and several refinements of the *SNR* will therefore be invoked in the course of this book in an attempt to make this time-honored objective quantity subjectively meaningful (Appendix E).

The *transmission rate I* of the system of Figure 1.3 is the product of the *sampling rate* f_s and the number of *bits per sample R* used by the system to represent input amplitudes:

$$I = f_s R \quad bits \ per \ second \ \text{(b/s)} \tag{1.4}$$

The rate *I* may also be expressed in *kilobits per second* (kb/s) or *megabits per second* (Mb/s). For lowpass signals, and in fact also for bandpass signals under a simple constraint (Chapter 3), the sampling rate f_s (in *samples per second*) should be no less than $2W$, where W is the input signal bandwidth (in *hertz*, or Hz); in fact, in practice, $f_s > 2W$. Very often, when W and f_s are known and fixed, the transmission rate is simply specified by the *rate*

$$R \quad bits \ per \ sample \ (\text{or } bits/sample) \tag{1.5}$$

In coding literature, as well as in this book, the expression *bit rate* is used to represent both *I* and *R*. The units that are specified for the bit rate will indicate which of the two quantities is actually implied in a given context.

Several coding systems, including the simple example of PCM (Pulse Code Modulation) use a single 2^R-level quantizer for discretizing all amplitude samples. In such systems, the number of bits used to represent each sample is simply $\log_2 2^R = R$. In coding systems such as Sub-Band Coding and Transform Coding, the input signal is represented as a sum of several components each of which is separately digitized, with different values of sampling rate and/or bits per sample. The transmission rates *I* in these systems will be simple generalizations of the product in (1.4).

In the example of Figure 1.3, $R = 2$ bits/sample; each input amplitude is quantized to one of $2^2 = 4$ possible levels: $+15$, $+5$, -5 and -15. These levels could be digitally represented by using the set of four codewords 00, 01, 10 and 11. The coarseness of the quantization in Figure 1.3 is reflected by the occurrence of very large reconstruction error samples. For example, the magnitude of $r(3)$ in this example is actually greater than that of the corresponding input, $x(3)$.

Figure 1.4 is an example of much finer quantization; it is based on a speech input, $R = 8$ bits/sample and therefore $2^8 = 256$ levels. The speech waveform in the illustration is taken from the speech sound "Joe" which includes unvoiced speech (the left half of the waveform) as well as voiced speech (the right half of the waveform). It is one of the test waveforms used repeatedly in the course of this book. The output levels of the quantizer, unlike in Figure 1.3, are also non-

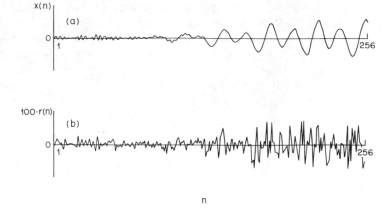

Figure 1.4 Waveform coding example with $R = 8$ bits/sample. Time-continuous versions of (a) speech waveform $x(n)$ and (b) reconstruction error waveform $r(n)$ in log-PCM coding (Chapter 5) magnified by a factor of 100 [Jayant, 1981].

uniformly spaced, a design that is characteristic of high-quality speech digitization (Chapter 4). The reconstruction error waveform has been magnified by a factor of 100 in order to bring out its characteristics. Notice also that this magnification makes the waveform in (b) roughly comparable in amplitude levels to the waveform in (a). According to (1.3), this would suggest an error variance that is smaller than the signal variance by a factor in the order of 10000, and hence an *SNR* in the order of 10 log 10000 = 40 dB. We will note in Chapter 4 that the *SNR* provided by the illustrated coding scheme is indeed very close to 40 dB — 38 dB, to be exact.

We will note later in this book that for PCM systems, the signal-to-noise ratio *SNR* increases at a rate very close to 6 dB per additional bit:

$$\sigma_r^2 = a\ 2^{-2R}\sigma_x^2\ ; \qquad SNR\ (\text{dB}) = 6R - 10 \log_{10} a$$

a is a constant in the order of 1 to 10 . (1.6)

Note finally that the waveforms in Figure 1.4 are really time-continuous versions of $x(n)$ and $r(n)$. In many future illustrations of waveforms in this book, the phrase "time-continuous" is often not stated, but implied.

1.1.3 Examples of High-Quality PCM Digitization

Table 1.1 puts the quantities f_s, R and I in perspective by invoking important signal examples. Many of the entries in Table 1.1 are order-of-magnitude values. For example, the bandwidth of telephone speech is usually 3.2 or 3.4 kHz, as in later chapters of this book, although the sampling rate is maintained at the standard value of 8 kHz. The 40 kHz rate for music is appropriate for studio-quality, 20 kHz bandwidth material. Lower bandwidths such as 15, or even 7 kHz are sometimes employed in audio systems. Corresponding sampling rates can be less than 40 kHz. Television signals may be sampled at 14.3 MHz or 13.5 MHz in

Table 1.1 Examples of high-quality digitization with a PCM (Pulse Code Modulation) coder.

Waveform to Be Digitized	Signal Bandwidth W (kHz)	Sampling Rate f_s (kHz)	PCM Bit Rate	
			R (bits/sample)	I (kb/s)
Telephone speech	4	8	8	64
Music	20	40	12	480
Videophone	1000	2000	8	16000
Television	5000	10000	8	80000

systems for color television; *component coding* systems include two separate signals for color information, each sampled at a lower rate such as 6.75 MHz [CCIR, 1982]. The bit rates in the corresponding PCM systems will be higher than the value cited in the table. Even higher sampling rates and bit rates may be used in the processing of studio television images.

The 2000 kHz or 2 MHz rate for videophone refers to a sampling of 2×10^6 *pic*ture samples or *el*ements (*pixels*) per second. For a 30 Hz frame rate, this implies a resolution in the order of $2 \times 10^6/30 \sim 0.067$ million pixels/frame. Indeed, a 225-line picture, with a 4:3 aspect ratio, has a total of $300 \times 225 \sim 0.067$ million pixels/frame. An image of this kind is not necessarily a well-accepted standard, but it will serve as a useful example in many discussions of this book. The resolution in a 5 MHz bandwidth television frame is much greater, in the order of $700 \times 525 = 0.37$ million pixels/frame. Some of the illustrations in this book are indeed based on this degree of resolution, and these images will appear sharper than the lower resolution examples. High-quality graphics transmission offers frame (page) resolutions exceeding that in commercial TV. A high-resolution CCITT standard, for example, calls for $2128 \times 1728 \sim 3.7$ million pixels/page.

1.2 Subjective Quality, Bit Rate, and Coder Complexity

In Section 1.1, we noted that an important problem in waveform coding is one of maximizing *SNR* for a given transmission rate I. We shall now amplify on this theme. In doing so, we shall introduce several additional parameters. All of these parameters will need to be considered before a specific waveform coder is selected for a given communications task. The first additional parameter to be considered in this section is *subjective quality*. Before discussing this notion, it will be useful to attempt a more critical description of the term *waveform coding*.

1.2.1 Waveform-Preserving Coders

Waveform coders can be defined as that class of analog signal coders where an input signal is approximated by mimicking the amplitude-versus-time waveform.

A viable alternative for digitizing waveforms such as speech and image signals consists in a signal-analysis procedure for extracting perceptually significant parameters from the input signal and using these parameters to synthesize an output signal that is useful to the human receiver, although not a waveform replica of the input speech or picture. Such *analysis-synthesis* procedures (for example, speech *vocoders)* provide the greatest economies in terms of bit rate, but they also entail fundamental limitations on subjective quality, and great expenses in terms of coder complexity and cost. Furthermore, the design and performance of such coders tend by definition to be highly input-specific, even while dealing with signals within one class. Excellent discussions of input-specific devices appear elsewhere, in contexts such as vocoding of speech [Flanagan, 1972] [Rabiner and Schafer, 1978] [Flanagan et al., 1979] and contour coding of images [Pratt, 1978] [Gonzalez and Wintz, 1977] [Rosenfeld and Kak, 1976].

The waveform coding principles discussed in this book are by contrast largely non-signal-specific. Although refined versions of certain waveform coders are intentionally tailored to input classes, they differ from analysis-synthesis systems in that the coder outputs are not synthesized from features, but rather, made to follow and preserve the input waveforms per se. Thus, in the waveform coding of speech, a basic criterion will still be the input-output difference $r(n)$, although a sophisticated mapping from the $r(n)$ sequence to a distortion measure may include facts about the perception of speech signals, and a coder that seeks to minimize this distortion may have to use facts or statistics about speech production in order to refine the basic blocks (for example, quantizer, predictor) of the waveform coding system.

1.2.2 Subjective Quality Versus Bit Rate in Speech Coding

In the coding of signals such as speech and video, subjective measures of quality are more relevant than objective measures such as the *SNR*. However, reliable values of subjective measurements are in general more difficult to obtain.

The dependence of digitized signal quality upon coder bit rate is well exemplified by subjective results from speech coding, as shown in Figure 1.5. Output speech quality in Figure 1.5 is measured by a *Mean Opinion Score* (MOS) (Appendix F) as obtained from formal subjective testing [Daumer, 1982]. Unlike objective *SNR* measurements (Section 1.1.2) and bounds (Section 1.3.2), subjective quality of digitized speech tends to saturate as the bit rate is increased, with a "knee" of the MOS versus bit rate curve that is coder-dependent. A score of 5.0 implies perfect quality. But this is hardly ever attained, even by an undigitized speech stimulus, as explained in Appendix F. A score approaching 4.5, on the other hand, may be regarded as a *necessary* condition for *toll quality*, the quality of commercial telephony. This quality roughly implies that digitized speech will be indistinguishable from the bandlimited input in a subjective test involving pairwise comparisons of stimuli. An MOS score in the order of 4.5 also implies that the *intelligibility* of the coded (digitized) speech is practically equal to that of the original. Toll quality thus defined is higher than *communications quality* [Flanagan et al., 1979] which is a term used to connote detectable distortion, but

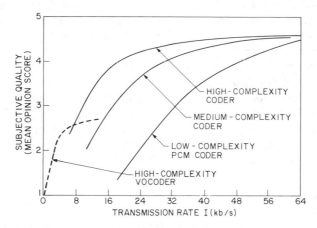

Figure 1.5 Subjective quality versus bit rate I in speech digitization [Daumer;©1982, IEEE] [Flanagan et al.;©1979, IEEE]. The three levels of waveform coder complexity are illustrated by several examples in later chapters.

still very little degradation of intelligibility. Toll quality will be more completely defined, using objective specifications by CCITT (International Telegraph and Telephone Consultative Committee), in Chapter 5. That discussion will include further *sufficient* conditions for a rigorous definition of toll quality. These conditions will reflect traditional communications network criteria such as coder performance with multiple stages of coding and decoding, and coder performance in the presence of impairments introduced by other parts of the network. Logarithmic PCM using $R = 8$ bits/sample ($I = 64$ kb/s) will be seen to be a toll quality coder in this traditional and rigorous sense (Chapter 5).

The upper solid curve in Figure 1.5 denotes the performance of the best waveform coder at a given bit rate, without regard to complexity or cost. In Figure 1.5, speech digitization with toll quality or almost toll quality is not realized at bit rates below $I = 16$ kb/s, or $R = 2$ bits/sample. In fact, even the high-complexity coders that achieve an MOS score approaching 4.5 at $I = 32$ kb/s, or $R = 4$ bits/sample, have to satisfy further criteria before they can be regarded as toll quality coders.

An important focus of continuing work in speech coding is to realize an upward shift of the topmost curve of Figure 1.5, and a leftward shift of the knee of that curve, implying improved performance in the range of $R = 2$ to 1 bits/sample, or less.

Lowest in the hierarchy of speech quality levels is *synthetic quality* that applies to vocoders. This quality is characterized by substantial loss of naturalness and robustness with respect to speakers and speaking environments. The broken curve in Figure 1.5 describes an optimistic estimate of the general performance of vocoders. These digitizers are appropriate for digitizations at very low bit rates, but their synthetic quality results in a ceiling of performance that is clearly well below the best performance of waveform coders. As indicated earlier, vocoders for synthetic speech are beyond the subject of waveform coding, and they will not be discussed henceforth in this book. For similar reasons, we will exclude formal discussions of very specific techniques such as those using *time compression* or *harmonic scaling*. Instead, we will cite some specific examples of the use of such techniques, as appropriate.

Also beyond the scope of this book are bit rate reduction techniques such as TASI (*time assignment speech interpolation*) [Flanagan, 1972] and DSI (*digital speech interpolation*) [IEEE, 1982], which exploit silences in speech to reduce the effective bit rate, and allow efficient time-sharing of digital channels. These techniques can be used in conjunction with conventional digital coders such as PCM, as well as with all classes of bit rate reducing coders, to provide further reductions of overall bit rate. Examples of such combinations will be cited as appropriate.

Subjective results such as MOS scores constitute an indispensable supplement to objective measurements of *SNR* or noise variance. For example, based only on objective *SNR* measurements, 16 kb/s speech coders, however complex, are inferior to 64 kb/s PCM by an order of magnitude. On the other hand, according to the subjective results of Figure 1.5, speech coders at 16 kb/s can be designed to provide an MOS quality that falls short of the 64 kb/s score by no more than a half point. The fact that non-PCM coders perform better in subjective assessments is due to the fact that the perceived annoyance of the reconstruction errors in these coders is less than that of PCM errors, for the same error variance σ_r^2 (or equivalently, for the same measured *SNR*). This will be illustrated repeatedly in this book for both speech and video coding, and for both the medium-complexity and high-complexity coder classes in each case.

Subjective results are critical for image coding as well, and criteria have been developed for different levels of quality, the highest of which is *broadcast quality* [Netravali and Limb, 1980]. Broad conclusions for image coding will be similar to those from Figure 1.5 after an appropriate rescaling of the transmission rate axis. The rescaling roughly involves multiplication of the bit rates on the x-axis of Figure 1.5 by a factor of 1200, the ratio of image bandwidth (5 MHz) to telephone speech bandwidth (4 kHz).

1.2.3 Impressionistic Results for Four Classes of Signals

The results of Figure 1.6 refer to very high quality digitizations of the four classes of signals mentioned in Table 1.1, and they utilize both ways of expressing coder bit rate: bits per second I and bits per sample R. Figure 1.6(a) uses an exponential bit rate axis to accommodate a six-orders-of-magnitude range of I. It shows that television is the most demanding system in terms of overall bit rate I, a natural consequence of the very high sampling rates in commercial video (see Table 1.1). On the other hand, Figure 1.6(b) indicates that studio-grade music is the most demanding signal in terms of bits per sample R.

1.2.4 Coder Complexity

Figures 1.5 and 1.6 have introduced the notion of coder complexity. Complexity is a continuous quantity with strictly an infinite range, but the figures use only

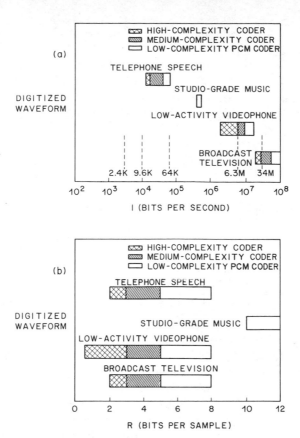

Figure 1.6 Exchange of coder complexity and transmission bit rate for very high quality digitizations of four signals [Jayant, 1981]. Bit rates are expressed as bits per second in (a), and as bits per sample in (b). An important focus of continuing research is the improvement of coder performance at bit rates lower than the limits indicated in this figure.

three levels of complexity for ease of illustration. The simplest of these levels would refer to *a low complexity coder* [such as PCM (Chapter 5) or DM (Chapter 8)]. The next level refers to a *medium complexity coder* such as DPCM with nonadaptive prediction (Chapter 6) or SBC with nonadaptive bit allocation (Chapter 11), which offers a significantly lower bit rate than PCM for a given quality. The last level denotes a *high complexity coder* [such as APC (Chapter 6) or ATC (Chapter 12)], which provides the very best results in bit rate reduction by utilizing highly adaptive algorithms and/or extensive use of long-term waveform memory.

The levels of coder complexity listed above can also be quantified by implementation criteria such as the number of multiply/add operations involved per waveform sample. Advances in technology tend to bridge the differences between algorithms of differing complexity, and they tend to make complex algorithms increasingly more practical. A factor that will continue to separate algorithms of different complexity, making some algorithms less useful than others, is the factor of encoding delay. The high-complexity coders of Figures 1.5 and 1.6 are also characterized by the highest levels of encoding delay.

1.2.5 Digital Hierarchies

The special values of I shown in Figure 1.6(a) by dashed lines are numbers that are standardized in practical digital systems. Examples of such systems are illustrated in the network hierarchy of Table 1.2.

Table 1.2 Digital Network Hierarchy.

	Level in Digital Hierarchy	1	2	3	4
United States	Number of 64 kb/s channels	24	96	672	4032
	Total bit rate (Mb/s)	1.544	6.312	44.736	274.176
Europe	Number of 64 kb/s channels	30	120	480	1920
	Total bit rate (Mb/s)	2.048	8.448	34.368	139.264
Japan	Number of 64 kb/s channels	24	96	480	1440
	Total bit rate (Mb/s)	1.544	6.312	32.064	97.728

Practical waveform coding systems assume an available bit rate I and seek to maximize coder performance with these constraints. Important numerical values of I depend on the digital system hierarchy in question (Table 1.2); for example, a rate of 1.544 Mb/s, which is the bit rate supported by the so-called T1 carrier system in the United States, can include 24 speech channels using 64 kb/s each. A television system in Europe may be required to have a bit rate equal to 34.368 Mb/s, while a television system in the United States may use a transmission rate of 44.736 Mb/s that fits into level 3 of Table 1.2. Coder rates slightly under $45/N$ and $35/N$, where N is integral, would also be attractive in respective situations; they would permit the multiplexing of N video channels. The sampling rate f_s depends on the input bandwidth, being at least twice that value. The value of f_s is typically 8 kHz for telephone speech, and 10 MHz or higher for TV images. In both speech and video, there will be systems that need to oversample the input (Chapter 8). In these systems, values of f_s will be significantly higher than the numbers cited above.

Submultiples of 64 kb/s, such as 32 kb/s and 16 kb/s, are of importance in so-called *low bit rate* systems for commercial telephony [IEEE, 1982]. Bit rates such as 9.6 kb/s and 2.4 kb/s [Figure 1.6(a)] have evolved from data communication practice. *Very low bit rate* speech coding, such as that with 2.4 kb/s, has been used for a long time in tactical speech communication systems. In these systems, the need for digital encryption has motivated the use of digitization at bit rates that are not high enough for high quality speech, but low enough for the output of the digital coder to be transmitted over conventional analog media such as a 4 kHz telephone line or a HF-band radio link.

Integrated Services Digital Networks (ISDN). We have seen from the numbers in Table 1.2 that 64 kb/s represents a standardized unit of bit rate. This unit, together with its multiples or sub-multiples, is also the basis of proposals for the designing of *Integrated Services Digital Networks* (ISDN) [Decina, 1982], which are networks providing end-to-end digital connectivity to support a wide range of services, including voice, data, audio, graphics and video. One important example of integration in such networks is the use of a 64 kb/s facility for the simultaneous transmission of graphics and voice. The bit rate allocated to voice coding in such a system would be in the range of 8 to 56 kb/s; for example, it may be one of the standard bit rates mentioned in the previous paragraph. The possibility of *variable rate coding* of the speech signal affords further flexibilities in the design of ISDN systems. Examples of such coding methods will be mentioned in this book when appropriate.

Circuit Switching and Packet Switching. The network architecture in digital systems may be based either on conventional *circuit switching* or *packet switching*. In circuit switching, a given pair of users (message sender and message receiver) have a dedicated connection for the length of their communication, with a guaranteed transmission rate. Time Division Multiplexing (TDM) is used to carry assemblies of lower-rate channels onto a single channel, such as a 64 kb/s facility, using appropriate padding/depadding techniques if necessary. In packet switching, messages from each user of the network are segmented into standard-sized smaller units, or *packets*, of appropriate length. The packets traverse the network as individual entities that are subsequently reassembled at the receiver in proper order. Packets from different parts of the message, as well as packets from several users, are statistically multiplexed before transmitting them over digital links that operate at a specific standard bit rate.

1.2.6 Waveform Properties and Encoding Delay

Coder complexity is a function of the signal processing involved. It is also related to *encoder delay* or *encoder memory*, which shows the extent to which a waveform has to be observed in order for the coder to exploit waveform structure for economical (digital) representation. Examples are listed in Table 1.3. This list attempts to grade quantizer and coder classes in order of increasing encoder memory or delay; and this hierarchy is closely matched to a similar hierarchy of waveform properties in Chapter 2. The utilization of these properties calls for increasing amounts of coder memory. The classifications in Table 1.3 are based on typical designs, but counter-examples are possible: for example, in speech coding, depending on the extent of memory utilized, sub-band coders, vector quantizers and tree coders may well be included in the class of coders with long-term memory.

The frame period in video is either 33.33 ms or 40 ms, depending on power line frequency, while the pitch period in speech can be in the range 3 to 15 ms, depending on speaker. The use of *long-term memory* in Table 1.3 indicates waveform observations over a duration in the order of the pitch period in speech, and the frame period in video. This implies transmission delays that can be several tens of milliseconds in both speech and image coding. Such delays can have important ramifications in aspects of waveform communications separate from coding per se, such as echo control in long-distance two-way transmissions.

Table 1.3 A listing of coding systems in terms of encoding delay.

Waveform Memory Used in Coding	Coding System Example
Zero Memory	• Instantaneous Quantizers: PCM
Short-term Memory	• Adaptive Quantizers • Differential PCM systems with near-sample-based predictions • Deltamodulators • Sub-Band Coders for Speech • Vector Quantizers, Tree- and Trellis Coders • Intraframe Transform Coders for Images
Long-term Memory	• Differential PCM systems with distant-sample-based predictions • Transform Coders for Speech • Interframe Transform Coders for Images

1.2.7 Irrelevancy and Redundancy

We have already noted that PCM coders are the simplest in principle; given a time-discrete input, they involve nothing more than quantization and an appropriate binary mapping. Quantizers are devices that remove the *irrelevancy* in this signal; they accomplish this through an irreversible, *information-lossy* procedure. For example, if a fractional resolution in image intensity that is smaller than 1/256 of the total amplitude range is visually unrecognizable or irrelevant, there is no need for digitized images to have more than 256 levels. If, indeed, the image has more levels (say, 1024 or infinity as with an analog image), this irrelevancy can be removed by passing the image signal into a quantizer with 256 output levels, each of which can be described by $R = \log_2 256 = 8$ bits/sample.

Quantization, as described above, is a zero-memory process, and is discussed as such in many parts of this book. However, there are important classes of quantizing systems which do depend on the utilization of waveform memory. Examples of such systems are adaptive quantizers and vector quantizers.

Non-trivial waveform coders (PCM will be the only trivial case) are designed to remove the *redundancy* in a signal for purposes of bit rate reduction. They do this through a reversible, *information-lossless* procedure that depends critically on the utilization of waveform memory. For example, consider an artificial $N \times N$ array of 8-bit picture elements (pixels) which is redundant in that every even pixel on a scan line (row of array) is identical in intensity to the odd pixel preceding it. A clever coding system exploits this redundancy by transmitting only odd pixels, and reduces the bit rate by a factor of 2. We will discover more realistic redundancies in video and speech, as we traverse this book, and learn about time- and frequency-domain systems which exploit these redundancies. Figure 1.7 formalizes the concept of reducing irrelevancy and redundancy. It indicates an interesting

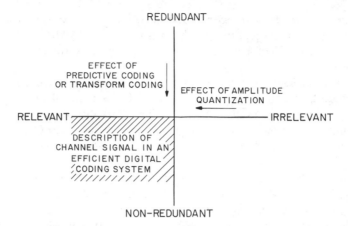

Figure 1.7 Irrelevancy and Redundancy [Schouten, 1957]. The distinction between quantization and coding is a convenient concept for most of the discussion in this book. There are examples of digitizing systems where the processes that reduce irrelevancy and redundancy cannot be clearly demarcated.

region that digital waveform coders seek to be in — a region where digitized signals are *perceptually relevant* and *statistically non-redundant*. In coding systems such as differential PCM and transform coding, there is significant and sometimes uncontrollable interaction between stages that reduce redundancy and irrelevancy; and in systems such as vector quantizers for correlated inputs, the stages that reduce redundancy and irrelevancy cannot be clearly demarcated.

1.2.8 Transmission Errors

The coders in Figures 1.5 and 1.6 have also been tested in the presence of binary transmission errors. Depending on the coder and the signal being digitized, *acceptable* values of random bit error probability p_e can be as demanding as 10^{-6} and less, or as high as 10^{-2} and more. Examples in this book will show that, in general, high quality image coding systems require lower values of p_e than high quality speech coding systems. *Actual* bit error rates can range from negligible values (say, less than 10^{-6}) in high-quality digital systems that may sometimes include explicit error control, to very high values (say, greater than 10^{-2}) in environments such as mobile radio. In the radio example, bit errors are also non-random and clustered in time. Most results in this book will refer to the simpler case of independent random errors, with the following order-of-magnitude descriptions of channel quality:

$$p_e < 10^{-6} \quad \text{in } high \ quality \text{ channels}$$

$$p_e > 10^{-2} \quad \text{in } very \ noisy \text{ channels} \qquad (1.7)$$

In this book, the quality of a digital channel is specified simply by the parameter p_e. In practice, digital channel performance may need additional characterization. An important performance parameter is the *percent of time intervals which have more than a specified error rate* [Johannes, 1983]. For example, in high quality speech transmission at 64 kb/s, a standard requirement is for at least 90% of 1 minute intervals to have an error rate of 10^{-6} or less [CCITT, 1980].

For the sake of better output quality, practical waveform coding systems often include some kind of explicit error protection, incurring a small penalty in transmission rate in the process. The gains due to such error protection can be significant for one of two reasons. First, if the value of p_e is very small to start with, the effect of error protection on the *intelligibility* of the digitized signal is very small, but the protection can enhance *quality* by increasing the mean time between (the already infrequent) bit errors. On the other hand, if p_e is objectionably high to start with, the impairment in the received output may be so significant that error protection coding may make the crucial difference between an unacceptable system and an acceptable one. While we shall illustrate gains due to explicit error protection whenever appropriate, the actual design or description of error-protection procedures [Berlekamp, 1974] will be beyond the scope of this book.

More relevant to this book is the fact that there are ways of making waveform coding systems inherently more *robust* to transmission errors. In other words, the effects of a given p_e can be rendered perceptually more acceptable or tolerable by careful designs of coder components such as quantizers and predictors. We shall comment on such designs repeatedly in the course of this book.

Because of its special relevance to this book, we illustrate a binary digital channel more explicitly in Figure 1.8(a) [Berlekamp, 1974]. An important class is the *memoryless binary symmetric channel* defined in Figure 1.8(b), where the bit error probability p_e is the same whether the input was 1 or 0, and it is independent of whether the previous input was received correctly or not. The error rate p_e is a monotonically decreasing function of analog channel quality, and Figure 1.8(c) provides a quantitative illustration of this dependence for the example of binary phase modulation or binary *phase shift keying* (PSK) over an additive Gaussian noise channel [Viterbi and Omura, 1979]. Channels used in waveform communication may indeed be non-Gaussian, and the signal impairments may indeed be non-additive in some cases; but the additive Gaussian model is simple, often approximately valid, and adequate for the points we wish to make. The illustration also assumes coherent detection, which means that a perfect reference carrier is available at the receiver for demodulation. Without channel encoding for error reduction, this modulation system realizes a p_e value of 10^{-6} with a *signal-to-channel-noise ratio per binary digit* (ratio of signal energy per bit to one-sided power spectral density of channel noise), denoted by s_n, of about 10.8 dB. With $s_n = 7$ dB, on the other hand, $p_e = 10^{-3}$, a value that can be seriously high for certain classes of waveform digitization, as we shall see in later chapters. Also shown in Figure 1.8(c) is the *Shannon limit*, which suggests the possibility of a zero error rate whenever s_n exceeds a mere -1.6 dB (Appendix C). This figure is only a bound, however. With an analog channel corrupted by Gaussian noise, the above bound can strictly be realized only with Gaussian input signals and infinite delays in channel encoding and channel decoding. The gap between the two curves

(a)

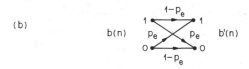

(b)

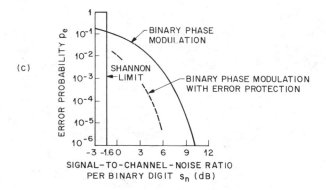

(c)

Figure 1.8 (a) Block diagram of a binary digital channel; (b) binary symmetric channel with bit error rate p_e; and (c) dependence of p_e on signal-to-channel-noise-ratio per binary digit [Forney;©1970, IEEE].

in Figure 1.8(c) can be significantly bridged by practical procedures for error protection. This is particularly appropriate for the better utilization of *power-limited* analog transmission media such as satellite communication channels. If power limitations are not serious, as in telephone lines, which are really *bandwidth-limited* media, better channel utilizations are also possible with more-than-two-level modulations (of phase and/or frequency and/or amplitude) [Lucky, Salz and Weldon, 1968] [Shanmugam, 1978] [Viterbi and Omura, 1979] [Schwartz, 1980]. Higher-level modulations, however, require greater values of s_n for a given p_e. For example, 16-level PSK requires an s_n of 18.7 dB for $p_e = 10^{-6}$, as against the 10.8 dB needed in 2-level PSK. The efficiency of a modulation scheme is also measured by the number of *bits per second per hertz (b/s/Hz)* of channel bandwidth that is characteristic of the scheme. This number is limited by considerations of intersymbol interference; upper bounds that are adequate for the present discussion are 1.0 *b/s/Hz* for two-level PSK and 4 *b/s/Hz* for 16-level PSK [Brodhage and Noack, 1979] [Oetting, 1979].

We shall now examine the relevance of the preceding discussions to digital waveform coding using the example of speech signals. Analog communication of speech with commercial quality will require, as discussed earlier, a channel quality given by a signal-to-channel-noise ratio of at least 30 dB. Digital speech coders, on the other hand, are very robust to error rates in the order of 10^{-6}, and with the modulation systems of the previous paragraph, they require signal-to-channel-noise ratios of only 10.8 dB and 18.7 dB for operating at this error rate. The saving in terms of required channel quality is, of course, accompanied by greater demands on bandwidth. In place of the 4 kHz bandwidth required for analog speech communications, digital speech systems employing the above-mentioned modulation systems will need bandwidths of at least $I/1$ and $I/4$ Hz respectively, where I is the coder bit rate in bits/second. For a 32 kb/s speech coder, these lower bounds on bandwidth are 32 kHz and 8 kHz, respectively, signifying respective bandwidth expansions of at least 8 and 2 over the analog system. With appropriate changes of numbers — 50 dB instead of 30 dB for output signal quality, and 10^{-8} instead of 10^{-6} for tolerable p_e — the above arguments can be repeated for image coding as well. In both cases, digital communication is based on an *exchange of bandwidth for (channel) signal-to-noise ratio*; this exchange constitutes a fundamental advantage of digital coding and leads to better utilization of interference-limited media.

1.3 Information Theoretical Limits

For a given transmission rate of I bits/second, or equivalently for a given value of R bits/sample, and for a given encoding delay, waveform coding systems seek to attain the smallest value of reconstruction distortion (for example, error variance σ_r^2), complexity permitting. If complexity is indeed of no concern, an interesting parameter is the minimum value of σ_r^2 over all coding systems. The value of this minimum in turn is a monotonically decreasing function of allowed encoding delay; and the *source coding* results of information theory specify the asymptotic infinite-encoding-delay values of minimum distortion, denoted by D. These results are derived using stationary stochastic signal models, and hence their application to real signals such as speech and video waveforms should always be appropriately qualified.

1.3.1 Source and Channel Coding

The performance of a waveform communication link can be put in perspective (subject to qualifications warranted by the complex nature of real-life waveforms) by the *noisy channel coding* and *source coding* theorems of information theory [Shannon, 1948] [Slepian, 1973] [Viterbi and Omura, 1979] [Wyner, 1981].

According to the *noisy channel coding theorem*, information can be transmitted reliably (i.e., without error) over a noisy channel at any source rate, say R, below a so-called *capacity* C of the channel (Appendix C):

$$R < C \quad \text{for reliable transmission} \tag{1.8}$$

According to the *source coding theorem*, there exists a mapping from the source waveform to codewords such that for a given *distortion D*, $R(D)$ bits (per source sample) are sufficient to enable waveform reconstruction with an average distortion that is arbitrarily close to D (Appendix D). Therefore, the actual *rate R* has to obey

$$R \geq R(D) \quad \text{for fidelity given by } D \quad\quad (1.9)$$

The function $R(D)$ is called the *rate distortion function* [Berger, 1971]. Its inverse, $D(R)$, is the *distortion rate function*.

Both C and $R(D)$ can be related to the as-yet-undefined concept of *mutual information* (Appendix C). Refer to the waveform communication link of Figure 1.2. Let **X** and **Y** refer to sufficiently long sequences of coder input and decoder output; and let **U** and **V** refer to sufficiently long sequences of channel input and channel output. With stochastic modeling of these sequences, the average information transmitted to the destination *per sample* is given by the average mutual information $I(X;Y)$, which is a measure of the statistical dependence of X and Y. Distortion D and $I(X;Y)$ will depend on the type of source coding. There is a minimum of $I(X;Y)$, however, that is needed for a reconstruction at the destination if the average distortion must not exceed the specified upper limit D. This *minimum value of $I(X;Y)$* is $R(D)$. The channel capacity C, on the other hand, is related to the average mutual information $I(U;V)$ *per sample* that characterizes channel input statistics and input-output mappings across the channel, as described by appropriate conditional probabilities. For example, if channel outputs do not depend on channel inputs, this information transfer is zero; while if the channel is perfect or error-free, the transfer is greatest, for any given statistics at the channel input. In fact, for a given channel, C is the *maximum of $I(U;V)$ over all channel input statistics*. Later sections will include several discussions involving the function $R(D)$, and Appendix C will discuss the capacity C as a function of channel quality. The point to be made right now is that theorems (1.8) and (1.9) above, put together, lead to the *information transmission theorem*:

$$C \geq R(D) \quad \text{for reliable transmission and fidelity } D \quad\quad (1.10)$$

This theorem states that waveform reconstruction with fidelity D is also possible after transmission over a noisy channel, provided that its capacity is greater than $R(D)$. The significance of this theorem is that it justifies the separation of *source coding* (source representation) and *channel coding* (information transmission) functions in waveform communication and provides a framework wherein the *channel controls the rate, but not necessarily the accuracy, of waveform reproduction.* Thus the only property of the channel that should concern the source coder is the single parameter C and the only requirement for the efficient utilization of the channel is that its input statistics (statistics at output of source coder) should be so as to maximize $I(U;V)$. *For the important case of a binary symmetric channel, this maximization merely requires that channel input symbols be an i.i.d. sequence (independent and identically distributed and hence equiprobable).* This defines a *necessary* property of an optimal source coder. Additionally desired features of a digital coder output are that the i.i.d. sequence is in some sense matched to the waveform at its input; and that the number of the *i.i.d.* input symbols (say for one second of input waveform) is as small as possible.

The above discussion also suggests the lumping of the channel coder, channel and channel decoder boxes of Figure 1.2 into one box, a "perfect digital channel," so that attention can be focused, if need be, on the source coding and source decoding boxes. This is indeed the approach used in most waveform coding literature. However, as mentioned earlier, because of an improper, or at best suboptimal use of an analog channel of capacity C, the binary digital channels in waveform communications will have non-zero bit error probability p_e.

1.3.2 Qualitative Distortion Rate Curves

The information transmission theorem is a very general statement. It applies to discrete-amplitude as well as continuous-amplitude sources, and to sources with or without memory (as defined in Chapter 2). The case to be discussed most in this book is that of continuous-amplitude sources with memory as indicated, for instance, by sample-to-sample correlations or, equivalently, non-flat power spectra. Discrete-amplitude sources will also be of interest in certain sections of this book. For example, facsimile systems involve two-level images; also, all quantizer outputs will be discrete-amplitude signals, by definition.

The plots in Figure 1.9 show that the rate distortion functions are monotonically non-increasing. It is reasonable that higher information-rate representations should lead to smaller (strictly, non-increasing) average distortions. It is also clear that the distortion at rate $R = 0$ should be finite if the input variance is finite. To appreciate this for the discrete-amplitude case, consider the binary signal generated by repeated tossings of an unbiased coin; let *heads and tails* signify signal amplitudes of 1 and −1, respectively (implying a variance of $\sigma_x^2 = 1$ for the zero-mean signal). Consider a zero-rate communication scheme where the receiver reproduces the binary signal by independent tossings of another unbiased coin; the

Figure 1.9 Qualitative sketches of rate distortion function for (a) a continuous-amplitude source, and (b) a discrete-amplitude source.

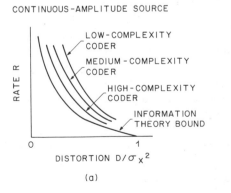
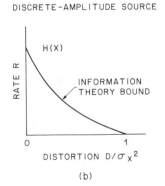

encoding error will be zero one-half of the time and ± 2 the other half of the time, and the average square distortion will be 2, and finite. The average square distortion will in fact be less, and equal to 1, as in Figure 1.9(b), if the zero-rate receiver has the option of constantly outputting the *neither-heads-nor-tails* amplitude of 0. The continuous-amplitude case is perhaps more interesting. Consider a zero-mean input sequence $\{x(n)\}$ with a variance (power) of σ_x^2. Regard, as the output of a zero-information-rate system, an all-zero sequence described by $y(n) = 0$; all n. The magnitude of the encoding error now equals that of the input for ail its samples. The error variance therefore equals the input variance, which again is finite in the present example, and with all practical sources. In summary, $D(R)$, the inverse of the function $R(D)$, is monotonically non-increasing, and $D(0)$ is finite, as in Figure 1.9.

Discrete-Amplitude Sources. The value of $R(0)$ is by far the most interesting feature in the plots of Figure 1.9. This value is finite only for *discrete-amplitude* sources. $R(0)$ is the value of information rate necessary for exact reproduction ($D = 0$) of the source. This number is the entropy $H(X)$ (average information content) of the discrete-amplitude source. As detailed in Appendix C, all sources with a finite number K of possible amplitudes will have a finite informational entropy that is no greater than $\log_2 K$ bits/symbol. For the coin-toss source, the entropy is upper bounded by $\log_2 2 = 1$ bit/sample, and the bound is attained if the coin is unbiased; and a coding system that is willing to transmit 1 bit, or one binary item of information (say, the correct value, *heads* or *tails*, for each input toss), can reproduce coin-toss outcomes with zero distortion or errors.

Noiseless entropy coding procedures which realize or approach the bound $R(0) = H(X)$ will be described in Appendix C and applied for exact reproductions of quantizer outputs and facsimile images. Due to unequal symbol probabilities and inter-symbol dependencies, the entropy of these sources will in general be less than the maximum possible value of $\log_2 K$. The idea of entropy coding will be to exploit unequal symbol probabilities as well as source memory to realize average bit rates approaching $H(X)$ bits/symbol. Entropy coding techniques include many varieties of fixed-length-to-variable-length and variable-length-to-fixed-length mappings of codewords, and we shall illustrate different specific procedures as and when appropriate. Clearly, such mappings can also include coding with distortion; but it should be remembered that non-exact reproductions are not inevitable for discrete-amplitude sources in the sense that $R(0) = H(X)$ is strictly finite. On the other hand, non-exact mappings may be necessary purely for implementation reasons, for example, to mitigate buffering problems in variable-rate encoding.

As discussed earlier, all quantizer outputs are discrete-amplitude sources. Special examples are sequences of 2^{12}-level or 12-bit speech samples and 2^8-level or 8-bit image samples. Such sequences are often used as coder inputs prior to bit rate reduction. The entropies of these signals are typically much less than the respective values of 12 and 8 bits/sample for speech and video.

Continuous-Amplitude Sources. The average information content or entropy $H(X)$ of a *continuous-amplitude* source is in fact infinite, reflecting the fact that each sample amplitude from such a source can have an infinite number of possible values. Another interpretation of the fact is that $R(0)$, the information rate needed for an exact reproduction of such a source, is infinite. More relevantly, no practical, i.e., finite-rate, coding procedure can reproduce a continuous waveform with perfect fidelity. Waveform coders therefore employ a value of R that is large enough so that the theoretical distortion D — or more relevantly, the actual reconstruction error variance σ_r^2 — is an adequately small fraction of input variance. The three practical coder curves in Figure 1.9(a) represent a complexity versus rate trade-off for any given value of σ_r^2. These coder classes have already been discussed in relation to Figures 1.5 and 1.6. The most complex of these coders is also the one that is closest to the rate distortion bound in Figure 1.9(a).

It will be noted in Appendix D that for a *memoryless Gaussian source*, the distortion rate function, for a mean square distortion measure, is

$$D(R)_G = 2^{-2R}\sigma_x^2 \qquad \leftrightarrow \qquad \max\{SNR\} \text{ (dB)} = 6R \qquad (1.11)$$

This can be shown to be an upper bound for the minimum distortion for *memoryless non-Gaussian* sources with representation rate R. In other words, smaller distortions than the above can be realized in digitizing non-Gaussian sources.

For *Gaussian sources with memory*, we shall note that

$$D(R)_G = 2^{-2R}\gamma_x^2\sigma_x^2 \; ; \qquad 0 \leqslant \gamma_x^2 \leqslant 1 \qquad (1.12)$$

where γ_x^2 is a *spectral flatness measure (sfm)* (Chapter 2) that measures redundancy as manifested in the structure and shape of the psd (power spectral density) function. For the special case of a white (flat) input spectrum, $\gamma_x^2 = 1$. Again, in the case of non-Gaussian sources, smaller distortions can be realized. Later chapters in the book will show how spectral redundancy can be removed by waveform coders with adequate encoding delay: specifically by recursive procedures called Differential or Predictive Coders, or by nonrecursive block-quantization schemes called Transform Coders.

References

M. R. Aaron, "The Digital (R)Evolution," IEEE Communications Magazine, pp. 21-22, January 1979.

J. C. Bellamy, *Digital Telephony*, John Wiley, New York, 1982.

G. H. Bennett, *PCM and Digital Transmission*, Marconi Instruments, 100 Stonehurst Court, Northvale, N.J., 1978.

T. Berger, *Rate Distortion Theory*, Prentice-Hall, Englewood Cliffs, N.J., 1971.

E. R. Berlekamp (ed.), *Key Papers in the Development of Coding Theory*, IEEE Press, New York, 1974.

H. Brodhage and W. Noack, "Planungsgrundlagen für den Einsatz von Richtfunksystemen," Siemens Telcom Report No. 2, pp. 123-127, 1979.

CCIR (International Radio Consultative Committee), "Encoding Parameters of Digital Television for Studios," Rec. 601, 1982.

CCITT (International Telephone and Telegraph Consultative Committee), "Error performance on an International Digital Connection forming part of an Integrated Services Digital Network," Rec. G.821, *Seventh Plenary Assembly Yellow Book,* Geneva, Switzerland, 1980.

W. R. Daumer, "Subjective Evaluation of Several Efficient Speech Coders," IEEE Trans. on Communications, pp. 655-662, April 1982.

M. Decina, "Managing ISDN through International Standards Activities," IEEE Communications Magazine, pp. 19-25, September 1982.

J. L. Flanagan, *Speech Analysis, Synthesis and Perception,* Springer-Verlag, New York, 1972.

J. L. Flanagan, M. R. Schroeder, B. S. Atal, R. E. Crochiere, N. S. Jayant and J. M. Tribolet, "Speech Coding," IEEE Trans. on Communications, pp. 710-737, April 1979.

G. D. Forney, "Coding and Its Application in Space Communications", IEEE Spectrum, pp. 47-58, June 1970.

R. G. Gallager, *Information Theory and Reliable Communication,* McGraw-Hill, New York, 1965.

R. C. Gonzalez and P. Wintz, *Digital Image Processing,* Addison-Wesley, Reading, Mass., 1977.

IEEE Transactions on Communications, Special Issue on Bit Rate Reduction and Interpolation, M. R. Aaron and N. S. Jayant (eds.), April 1982.

N. S. Jayant (ed.), *Waveform Quantization and Coding,* IEEE Press, New York, 1976.

N. S. Jayant, "Voice and Image Techniques," unpublished work, Bell Laboratories, 1981.

V. I. Johannes, "Performance Parameters for Digital Communications," Proc. IEEE, p. 539, April 1983.

R. W. Lucky, J. Salz and E. J. Weldon, Jr., *Principles of Data Communication,* McGraw-Hill, New York, 1968.

Members of Technical Staff, Bell Laboratories, *Transmission Systems for Communications,* Western Electric Company, Technical Publications, Winston-Salem, N.C., 1971.

A. N. Netravali and J. O. Limb, "Picture Coding: A Review," Proc. IEEE, pp. 366-406, March 1980.

J. D. Oetting, "A Comparison of Modulation Techniques for Digital Radio," IEEE Trans. on Communications, pp. 1752-1762, December 1979.

W. K. Pratt, *Digital Image Processing,* John Wiley, New York, 1978.

L. R. Rabiner and R. W. Schafer, *Digital Processing of Speech Signals,* Prentice-Hall, Englewood Cliffs, N.J., 1978.

A. Rosenfeld and A. C. Kak, *Digital Picture Processing,* Academic Press, New York, 1976.

J. F. Schouten, "Nachricht und Signal," Nachrichtentechnische Fachberichte, Bd. 6, pp. 1-2, 1957.

M. Schwartz, *Information Transmission, Modulation and Noise,* McGraw-Hill, New York, 1980.

K. S. Shanmugam, *Digital and Analog Communication Systems,* John Wiley, New York, 1979.

C. E. Shannon, "A Mathematical Theory of Communication," Bell System Tech. J., pp. 379-423 (Part I) and pp. 623-656 (Part II), 1948.

D. Slepian (ed.), *Key Papers in the Development of Information Theory,* IEEE Press, New York, 1973.

A. J. Viterbi and J. K. Omura, *Principles of Digital Communication and Coding,* McGraw-Hill, New York, 1979.

A. D. Wyner, "Fundamental Limits in Information Theory," Proc. IEEE, pp. 239-251, February 1981.

2

Waveform Characterization

2.1 Introduction

The topic of this book is the efficient transmission of waveforms over digital channels. These waveforms will typically be analog (time- and amplitude-continuous) and therefore time discretization and amplitude quantization are necessary prior to transmission.

Time discretization requires very little deliberation in that most waveform coding methods of interest use only one basic method for doing it, viz., uniform time-sampling. A very fundamental result in digital waveform coding is that a *bandlimited or bandpass signal* can be completely recovered from its samples provided that the sampling frequency is at least two times the highest frequency contained in the waveform (Chapter 3). In fact, the minimum sampling frequency will be two times the bandwidth if the lowest frequency is an integral multiple of the bandwidth. This includes the special case where the lowest frequency is zero, the case of a *lowpass* signal. The use of uniform time-sampling is so well-established in theory and practice that digital signal processing treatises tacitly assume the availability of time-discrete waveform samples. We shall do the same. In anticipation of sampling, *all waveforms in this book will be assumed to be bandlimited*. Also, in this book, the term *time discretization* will be used in a general sense that includes *space discretization* for two-dimensional image signals.

Efficient *amplitude quantization*, unlike time discretization, is more waveform-specific. For example, the theory of zero-memory quantizers, as discussed in Chapter 4, is related to the *probability density function* (pdf) for the amplitudes of input samples; while the design and performance of predictive coders (Chapters 6 to 10) and transform coders (Chapters 11 and 12) depend directly on the correlations amongst the amplitudes of waveform samples. A good part of Chapter 2 will therefore be devoted to characterizing the so-called univariate and multivariate distributions of waveform amplitudes; the latter, in particular, will characterize the *predictability* of waveforms as described by the *autocorrelation function* (acf), *power spectral density* (psd), and also by the *spectral flatness measure* (*sfm*), a compact description of waveform predictability.

The study of distributions implies a modeling of waveforms or waveform samples by random processes [Dunn and White, 1940] [Kretzmer, 1952]. This kind of modeling will be discussed in Section 2.2. The *model sources* of Section 2.4 will be random processes with special acf and psd functions that resemble the real-signal properties described in Section 2.2. In coding literature, deterministic waveforms usually play the role of test signals that describe real waveforms in an average or partial sense; for example, speech waveforms are sometimes modeled by a 800 Hz sinusoid, and edge transitions in an image waveform are often modeled by step functions. Deterministic signals, however, have zero information content, and for communications signals such as speech and images, random process models, if affordable, are definitely more appropriate.

Chapter 2 will begin with a non-mathematical review of speech and video waveform properties in Section 2.2, with emphasis on pdf, acf and psd descriptions. Section 2.3 will provide a summary of random process mathematics, formalizing notions of pdf, acf and psd. Section 2.4 will describe the model sources with special acf and psd functions. These sources will be invoked repeatedly in later chapters.

The information content of random waveforms can be quantified in terms of the *rate distortion function* $R(D)$ or its inverse, the *distortion rate function* $D(R)$ (Appendix D). The function $R(D)$ specifies the amount of information R, in bits per sample, that one will have to expend for communicating the waveform with a specified fidelity, as measured by a distortion D. Numerical results exist only for a few tractable waveform descriptions, and one result, involving the spectral flatness measure, has already been mentioned in Chapter 1. Rate distortion bounds provide a useful calibration for the performance of specific quantizers and coders for real waveforms. However, much of the analytical development in this book, while depending heavily on pdf, acf and psd models, will be independent of $R(D)$ concepts per se. This stand recognizes the fact that perceptually adequate $R(D)$ models are untractable, if not impossible, for speech and video signals.

In developing the formalism of Chapter 2, we shall assume that the reader is familiar with the basic concepts of random processes and linear system theory. Our mathematical material should be regarded as an attempt to make our discussions self-contained, and not as an alternative to existing standard literature.

2.2 Characteristics of Speech and Image Waveforms

2.2.1 Amplitude versus Time Plots

The simplest description of any waveform is an amplitude-versus-time plot that typifies it. Examples appear in Figures 2.1 through 2.3. They refer respectively to speech, two-level graphics and a multi-level, or gray-level image. These plots qualitatively indicate many significant waveform features, some of which are quantified in subsequent sections. These features include (a) the relative probabilities of different amplitudes, (b) the extent of sample-to-sample correlations and (c) the existence of macroscopic structure such as quasi-periodicity and non-stationarity. Some of the above descriptions have universal value and some, for example (c), may be signal-specific. Common to all the waveforms, however, is the important property [related to (b) above] that the waveform is appropriately bandlimited, as described by the values of W in Table 1.1 for speech and image examples.

Figure 2.1 shows a sentence-length speech waveform (a) (result of a male utterance "every salt breeze comes from the sea"), together with magnified waveforms (b) and (c) for the "A" and "S" segments in the word "salt". Notice that the low-frequency voiced waveform of "A" is more slowly varying than the high-frequency unvoiced fricative waveform of "S". Notice also that the voiced waveform is *quasi-periodic*, with slightly over four "periods" in 32 ms; this

Figure 2.1 Amplitude waveforms of speech for (a) a sentence-length (2.5 seconds) segment; (b) a short-time (32 ms) segment of voiced speech; and (c) a short-time (32 ms) segment of unvoiced speech [Flanagan et al.;©1979, IEEE].

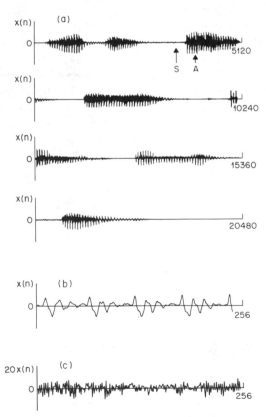

Waveform Characterization   2

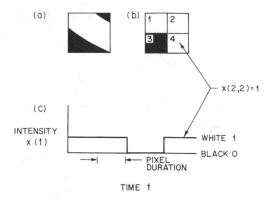

Figure 2.2 (a) Two-level image; (b) division of the image into pixels; and (c) intensity plot obtained by a systematic scan of the rows of (b). The amplitude levels 1 and 0, associated with white and black intensities, are sometimes rescaled to be +1 and −1, for analytical reasons.

corresponds to a *fundamental frequency* or *pitch frequency* that is somewhat less than $(8.0 \text{ ms})^{-1} = 125$ Hz in our example; the unvoiced waveform, on the other hand, is more noise-like. Also, its energy level is much lower than that of the voiced segment. Clearly, the speech waveform is extremely nonstationary, with significant inter-segment differences both in terms of amplitude level and spectral (frequency) content. Descriptions of locally stationary speech segments (of period in the order of 32 ms) will be formally termed *short-time* or *short-term* descriptions, while *long-time* or *long-term* descriptions will refer to speech waveform durations that are several orders of magnitude greater.

Figure 2.2(a) shows a tiny segment of a graphics image with two levels of intensity, *white* and *black*. The two black areas may be magnified versions, for example, of two nearly parallel black line segments on a weather-map. Figure 2.2(b) is a time-discrete, or space-discrete, representation of the sub-image in Figure 2.2(a) as a 2 × 2 array consisting of four picture elements, usually termed *pixels*, or *pels*. Note that only one of these pixels is black. The other three are white, suggesting predominantly white areas in corresponding portions (quarters) of the sub-image (a). For example, the pixel in row 2, column 2 is white. Using two-dimensional notation, and the convention that white = 1 and black = 0, $x(2,2) = 1$. The general intensity value is $x(m,n)$ for pixel location (m,n). Figure 2.2(c) shows an intensity-versus-time waveform obtained by scanning the four pixels — a left-to-right scan of the first row, followed by a left-to-right scan of the second row. The term *image waveform* will refer in this book to an *intensity* plot such as that in Figure 2.2(c), and pixel samples will have appropriate values of sample index and sample intensity. For example, in the present illustration, $x(4) = x(2,2) = 1$, while $x(3) = x(2,1) = 0$. In some analyses, it may be convenient to regard pixel amplitudes as zero-mean random variables, falling in the range −1 to +1. This can be realized by a simple rescaling and mean subtraction process. Thus, in the above example, we might have $x(4) = 2x(2,2)-1 = 1$, and $x(3) = 2x(2,1)-1 = -1$, instead of the values 1 and 0 cited earlier.

The two-level plot in Figure 2.2(c) is a very simple example; it will be discussed again in Chapter 10. More generally, we will be interested in image waveforms with many levels of intensity; gray-level monochrome images, as well as color images, belong to this general class.

Figure 2.3 shows three examples (a) (b) and (c) of multi-level monochrome images that include shades of *gray* between the white and black extremes. Such images are also called *gray-level* images. The image in (a) will be used for several future illustrations in this book.

In gray-level images, the function $x(m,n)$ takes on values in the continuous range $(0,1)$. Figure 2.3(d) is the intensity plot corresponding to a three-line row-by-row scan of part of the scene "Karen" in (c). Notice the bursts of high-intensity pixels for which $x(m,n) \rightarrow 1$, or $x(n) \rightarrow 1$ in the one-dimensional plot. This is the result of scanning an image segment with a predominance of white areas (the face of Karen). Notice also the presence of sharp intensity transitions. Such rapid transitions are typical of many classes of image waveforms. Notice, moreover, that as in the voiced waveform of Figure 2.1, the waveform of Figure 2.3 is quasi-periodic, with the "period" corresponding to the duration of one (horizontal) scan line. A second source of quasi-periodicity exists in moving pictures. This is due to pixel patterns that tend to repeat in successive *frames* in a moving image. Unlike the fluctuating pitch period in speech, the scan-line and frame periods in image

Figure 2.3 Gray-level images (a), (b) and (c); and (d) intensity waveform corresponding to three consecutive horizontal scans of the face in (c). The image (a) is used for several future illustrations in this book.

(a)

(b)

(c)

(d)

systems are constant numbers. Correlations and periodicities in image inputs are therefore more structured than in speech.

The speech waveform in Figure 2.1 is *one-dimensional* (1-D), or *scalar*; images may be regarded as *two-dimensional* (2-D) signals [Figure 2.2(b)], although the post-scanning intensity waveforms in Figures 2.2(c) and 2.3(b) are shown as being one-dimensional. Good examples of *multi-dimensional* waveforms are *vector* waveforms that occur in Adaptive Prediction, Transform Coding and Sub-band Coding systems. In Adaptive Prediction (Chapter 6) and Transform Coding (Chapter 12), the components of the vector signal are, respectively, predictor coefficients and transform coefficients of different order; in sub-band coding of speech (Chapter 11), the components correspond to the outputs from contiguous speech frequency bands.

2.2.2 Probability Density Functions

Consider a finite-length sequence $\{x(n)\}$; $n = 0,1,...,N-1$ obtained by observing a finite segment of a sampled continuous waveform. Very simple, but not complete, descriptions of the waveform are provided by the quantities

$$\mu_x = \frac{1}{N} \sum_{n=0}^{N-1} x(n); \qquad \chi_x^2 = \frac{1}{N} \sum_{n=0}^{N-1} x^2(n); \qquad \sigma_x^2 = \frac{1}{N} \sum_{n=0}^{N-1} [x(n)-\mu_x]^2 \quad (2.1)$$

called respectively the *mean value, mean square value (or average power)* and *variance* of that segment. The quantity σ_x, the square root of variance, is called the *standard deviation*. If the mean μ_x is known a priori, the third term in (2.1) is a so-called *unbiased* estimate of variance. When the mean is estimated by the first term in (2.1), an unbiased estimate of variance is obtained by replacing $1/N$ in the third term of (2.1) by $1/(N-1)$.

An interesting special case, one that is approximated in speech waveforms for large N, is that of a *zero-mean* sequence:

$$\mu_x = 0 ; \qquad \chi_x^2 = \sigma_x^2 \qquad (2.2)$$

A more informative description is provided by a *probability density function* (pdf). Consider an amplitude interval $\mathscr{I}_k$ defined by an amplitude range $\mathscr{I}_k:(x_k \leqslant x < x_{k+1})$. Out of the N samples in sequence $\{x(n)\}$, let n_k amplitudes fall in interval $\mathscr{I}_k$. A plot of the normalized count n_k/N shows the shape of the (non-negative) pdf $p_x(x)$, which is really defined as a continuous function whose area in interval $\mathscr{I}_k$ equals n_k/N. The pdf $p_x(x)$ specifies not only the average values (2.1) and (2.2), but also indicates other waveform features such as boundedness and peakiness.

The quantities μ_x, σ_x^2 and $p_x(x)$ above are *short-term* or *segment-specific* descriptions obtainable by indicated measurements with an observed waveform of length N samples. They are also useful as *estimates* of corresponding random process characteristics if the input waveform is *stationary* and *ergodic* and N is large; ergodicity implies that ensemble statistics can be equated to those of one sample sequence.

Experimental pdf Examples. The pdf of *speech* amplitudes depends on input bandwidth and recording conditions. With a high-quality microphone and telephone bandwidth (200 to 3200 Hz), a first approximation to the *long-term* pdf or *long-time-averaged* pdf ($N \rightarrow \infty$) is provided by a *two-sided exponential* or *Laplacian* model; a better fit is provided by the so-called *gamma* pdf as shown by dashed lines in Figure 2.4(a). The experimental speech pdf in the figure is based on measurements over 55 seconds of speech, spoken by five speakers [Zelinski and Noll, 1974]. Note the distinct peak at zero in the long-term pdf; this is a result of pauses and low-level speech segments. Note also the significant probability of high amplitudes such as $\pm 4\sigma_x$. *Short-time* pdf's of speech segments are also unimodal or single-peaked; but they are better described by a bell-shaped *Gaussian* pdf, irrespective of whether the speech segments are voiced or unvoiced.

An experimental long-time-averaged pdf of *video* amplitudes is illustrated in Figure 2.4(b) [Kummerow, 1972]. It is based on four image frames that include the low- and high-detail scenes "lady in a straw hat" and "playboy" in Figures

Figure 2.4 Typical long-time-averaged probability density functions for (a) speech amplitudes [Zelinski and Noll, 1974] and (b) image amplitudes [Kummerow, 1972].

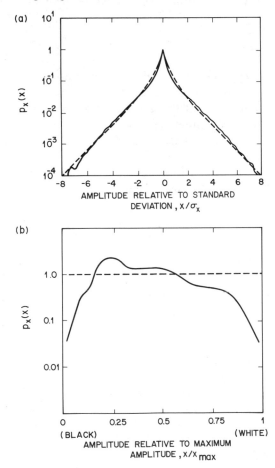

2.3(a) and (b); these examples will also be used in Section 2.2.3. Unlike the speech pdf, the video pdf is not unimodal. The average pdf of image material is crudely modeled (as shown by dashed lines) by a *uniform* pdf, where all luminances from black to white are equiprobable.

Waveforms are sometimes represented in terms of *adjacent-sample differences*. The pdf of the difference signal $x(n)-x(n-1)$ for an image waveform follows the *two-sided exponential* or *Laplacian* function. Neighboring pixels are very similar in amplitude since the signal is slowly changing. The difference pdf therefore has a significant peak at difference values near zero, corresponding to the situation $x(n) \sim x(n-1)$ (Problem 2.2). The pdf of the adjacent-sample difference in speech is qualitatively similar to the pdf of individual amplitudes themselves, and is again modeled best by the gamma distribution. The Laplacian and gamma models for adjacent-sample differences in image and speech waveforms are also applicable, respectively, to so-called linear prediction error signals in image and speech coding (Chapter 6).

Also significant for image coding is the pdf of the frame-to-frame differences of a given pixel. This pdf is also symmetrical and peaked at zero, but the actual shape is motion-dependent; increased motion results in increased probability content in the pdf tails, while smaller tails indicate greater interframe redundancy.

Model pdf's. Figure 2.5 and Table 2.1 are descriptions of the four model pdf's mentioned so far. For simplicity, we have set $\mu_x = 0$ in all cases, including the uniform pdf, although Figure 2.4(b) shows a positive mean; further, in Figure 2.5, all the pdf's have a variance $\sigma_x^2 = 1$. The four models will be invoked frequently in this book with the notations **U, G, L** and **Γ** used in Table 2.1. The *finite-support* uniform pdf **U** has been mentioned already as a model for image amplitudes. It will also be used as a model for quantization noise distribution in Chapter 4. The Gaussian pdf **G** in Table 2.1 will also be referred to sometimes as the zero-mean normal pdf $N(0,\sigma_x^2)$. The pdf **Γ** used in this book is a special case of a wider class of gamma pdf's [Richards, 1973]. A property that is common to the *infinite-support* models **G, L** and **Γ** is the fact that $p_x(x)$ monotonically *decreases* with $|x|$;

Figure 2.5 Four model pdf's with a mean value of zero [Zelinski and Noll, 1974].

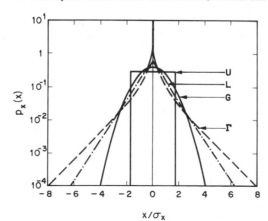

Table 2.1 Four model pdf's with a mean value of zero.

Name	Notation	$p_x(x)$
Uniform or Rectangular	U $(\sigma_x^2 = \Delta^2/12)$	$\dfrac{1}{\Delta}; \quad x \in (-\dfrac{\Delta}{2}, \dfrac{\Delta}{2})$ $0; \quad otherwise$
Gaussian or Normal	G $N(0,\sigma_x^2)$	$\dfrac{1}{\sqrt{2\pi\sigma_x^2}}\exp\left[-x^2/2\sigma_x^2\right]$
Laplacian or Two-sided Exponential	L	$\dfrac{1}{\sqrt{2}\sigma_x}\exp\left[-\sqrt{2}|x|/\sigma_x\right]$
Gamma	Γ	$\dfrac{\sqrt[4]{3}}{\sqrt{8\pi\sigma_x|x|}}\exp\left[-\sqrt{3}|x|/2\sigma_x\right]$

significant differences in pdf shape exist, of course, both at $|x| = 0$ and at the tails, $|x| \rightarrow \infty$. A model where $p_x(x)$ *increases* monotonically with x is the *arcsine* pdf (Problem 2.1), which describes the distribution of sine-wave amplitudes. This pdf is of interest because a sine-wave input serves as a standard test signal for coding algorithms (Section 5.3).

Nonstationarity of Speech Signals. The distinction between short-time and long-time pdf in speech is related to the fact that speech waveforms are nonstationary. Figure 2.6 quantifies one aspect of this nonstationarity. It shows the time-dependence of segment variance $\sigma_x^2(k)$ (2.1) measured over contiguous 32 ms segments of the speech of a single speaker. The number of speech segments used is

Figure 2.6 Time dependence of short-term speech variance for (a) the 2.3 second waveform of Figure 2.1(a) [Jayant, 1982], and for (b) a different speech waveform, of duration 1.4 seconds [Noll, 1974]. The segment length is 32 ms.

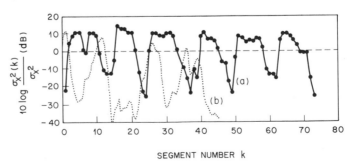

73 in example (a) and 44 in example (b). The 0 dB line corresponds to the average σ_x^2 of the 73 values of $\sigma_x^2(k)$ in example (a). Note that the dynamic range of short-time variance can exceed 40 dB over a time duration of no more than 1 second. Further, if one considers the variation of the average of short-term variance as a function of speaker, the resulting across-speaker distribution has an additional dynamic range of about 20 dB [Richards, 1973]. The above level variations are sometimes compounded by further level uncertainties in communication, resulting from ambient conditions and telephone connection efficiency. On the other hand, the 40 dB and 20 dB dynamic ranges mentioned above are not always additive (which would imply a dynamic range of 60 dB!). Also, when high-frequency pre-emphasis is present in telephone systems, the effect is to decrease the dynamic range of the speech signal significantly. Sustained performance over an input dynamic range in the order of 30 to 40 dB is therefore a well-accepted design criterion for coders and quantizers in high-quality speech communication.

2.2.3 Autocorrelation Functions

Successive sample amplitudes $x(n)$ and $x(n-1)$ of a slowly varying waveform are said to be highly correlated. As a result, the adjacent-sample difference (in general, a prediction error signal) has a much smaller variance than the original signal $x(n)$. This fact is exploited in redundancy-removing differential PCM (DPCM) coders for both speech and video.

A fundamental waveform property, therefore, is an *autocorrelation function* (acf) which quantifies the closeness of the amplitudes of two samples as a function of their time- or space-separation; it is a function that tells us how close, or similar, samples $x(n)$ and $x(n+k)$ are, on the average:

$$R_{xx}(k) = \frac{1}{N} \sum_{n=0}^{N-|k|-1} x(n)x(n+|k|) \qquad (2.3)$$

The acf $R_{xx}(k)$, as a function of k, is a deterministic descriptor of a waveform which itself may best be modeled by a random sequence. The use of $|k|$ in (2.3) makes $R_{xx}(\cdot)$ symmetric about $k = 0$; while the summation to $N - |k| - 1$ recognizes the fact that only $N - |k|$ pairs are available for the product operation if $\{x(n)\}$ is an N-sample sequence defined for $n = 0,1,...,N-1$. If $R_{xx}(k)$ is used as an estimate of correlation, it can be shown [Jenkins and Watts, 1968] that (2.3) provides a better result than a formula that uses $N - |k|$ instead of N in the denominator, especially if k is close to N. An *autocovariance function* results if the mean value μ_x is subtracted from the terms in the product of (2.3), but the distinction disappears for $\mu_x = 0$. For *zero-mean* sequences, it is clear from (2.1) that

$$R_{xx}(0) = \sigma_x^2 \qquad (2.4)$$

A *variance-normalized acf* is defined in the form

$$\rho_k = \rho_{xx}(k) = R_{xx}(k)/R_{xx}(0) ; \qquad \rho_0 = \rho_{xx}(0) = 1 \qquad (2.5)$$

The quantity ρ_k has values in the range $(-1, +1)$. A value of $\rho_k = 1$ implies perfect positive correlation such as that between any two samples of a constant waveform. A value of $\rho_k = -1$ suggests perfect negative correlation such as that between any pair of adjacent samples of a sinusoid sampled only at its (positive and negative) peaks. A value of $\rho_k = 0$ implies total decorrelation as between samples of a totally random white noise process. The *adjacent sample correlation* $\rho_1 = \rho_{xx}(1)$ is a very useful parameter. It corresponds to a sample separation of $k = 1$. This signifies a separation of one Nyquist interval, except in oversampled systems.

Figure 2.7 illustrates a *long-time-averaged* acf based on measurements [Noll, 1972] with a 55-second speech sample that is either lowpass-filtered (LPF: 0 to 3400 Hz) or bandpass-filtered (BPF: 300 to 3400 Hz). The sampling frequency is 8 kHz. In each set of curves, the upper and lower limits represent acf maxima and minima, respectively, over four speakers (two male and two female), and the middle curve gives the mean acf value (average over four speakers). Notice that in

Figure 2.7 (a) Long-time-averaged acf plots [Noll, 1972] for LPF and BPF speech waveforms. (b) Evolution of the short-term speech acf with time for the example of three consecutive 32 ms segments in Figure 2.1 [Jayant, 1982].

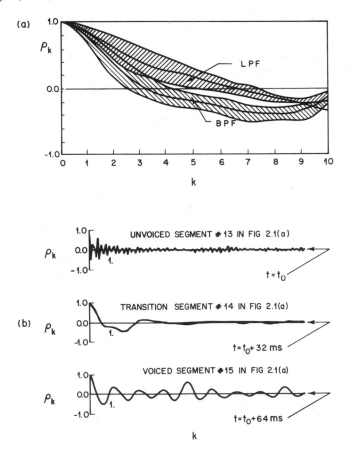

general ρ_1 has a value close to $+0.9$, and that the ρ_k crosses zero at a higher value of k for LPF speech than for BPF speech. The increased evidence of lower frequencies in LPF speech causes higher correlations for a given separation k.

Table 2.2 lists four sets of ρ_k values for 8 kHz-sampled speech, for $k = 0$ to 5. These results are taken from different sources in speech literature, including the source used in Figure 2.7(a).

Table 2.2 Values of acf for 8 kHz-sampled speech.

Speech Source	LPF Source Average from Figure 2.7(a) [Noll, 1972]	BPF Source Average from Figure 2.7(a) [Noll, 1972]	LPF Source [McDonald, 1966]	BPF Source with High-Frequency Emphasis [Grizmala, 1972]
ρ_0	1.00	1.00	1.0000	1.000
ρ_1	0.86	0.79	0.8644	0.825
ρ_2	0.64	0.38	0.5570	0.562
ρ_3	0.40	0.05	0.2274	0.308
ρ_4	0.26	-0.08	-0.0297	0.004
ρ_5	0.20	-0.16	-0.1939	-0.243

The acf plots in Figure 2.7(b) are measured over *short segments* (32 ms; $N=256$) of a single speech waveform, and successive acf plots in Figure 2.7(b) are results of acf recomputation once every 32 ms. The evolution in Figure 2.7(b) is from (i) an aperiodic acf (for an aperiodic fricative segment), to (iii) a periodic acf (for a periodic voiced segment); the intermediate case (ii) is a fast-decaying transitional acf (indicating a non-steady-state segment during unvoiced-to-voiced transition). The acf plots of Figure 2.7(b) follow (2.3), (2.4) and (2.5). In periodic speech, the envelope of $|\rho_{xx}(k)|$ decreases monotonically with k until k equals the fundamental period, at which point a second peak occurs in $\rho_{xx}(k)$, similar to that at $\rho_{xx}(0) = 1$.

Intraframe acf plots for 256×256 monochrome images are shown in Figure 2.8(a). The plots are those of $\rho_{xx}(k_h, k_v)$ as a function of horizontal separation k_h and vertical separation k_v. The acf is seen to decay at a similar rate in both horizontal and vertical directions for the images considered. There is, however, a significant difference in the acf values of the *low-detail* and *high-detail* examples, for a given (k_h, k_v). As expected, acf values are generally higher for the low-detail image.

Table 2.3 compiles experimental intraframe acf values for two 512×512 images, differing once again in image detail.

The presence of significant intraframe correlations, or redundancies, carries over to the case of two-level graphics images, and this can be demonstrated by acf functions that are nearly exponential in both vertical and horizontal directions. We shall note in Chapter 10 that an even more useful description of redundancy in two-level graphics is in terms of so-called *run-length* or cluster-length distributions.

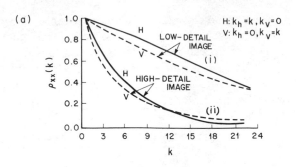

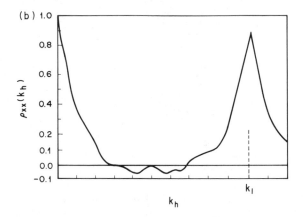

Figure 2.8 (a) Intraframe acf plots for gray-level images with (i) low detail (a face) and (ii) high detail (a crowd) [Habibi and Wintz;©1971, IEEE]. (b) An acf plot that includes values of horizontal spacing greater than the number of pixels/scan line. The input used in (b) is the image "Karen" in Figure 2.3 [O'Neal,1966,II; ©AT&T].

Table 2.3 Experimental values of intraframe acf for a low-detail image (Lady in straw hat) and for a high-detail image (Playboy). Values for the high-detail image are in parentheses. The parameters k_h and k_v refer to horizontal and vertical spacing (in pixels).

k_v \ k_h	0	1	2
0	1.000(1.000)	0.967(0.956)	0.926(0.892)
1	0.970(0.904)	0.954(0.884)	0.922(0.844)
2	0.934(0.816)	0.928(0.805)	0.907(0.783)

The Case of Large k. We have already mentioned that in voiced speech, the envelope of $|\rho_{xx}(k)|$ decreases monotonically with k at first; but when k is large enough to be equal to the pitch period k_p, a second peak appears in the acf function, after which the short-term acf pattern tends to repeat the behavior that characterized its first k_p values. We shall discuss this again in Chapter 6 in the context of acf-based pitch extraction. What is worth noting here is that the pitch period k_p is a *time-varying* quantity.

Figure 2.8(b) is a one-dimensional intraframe acf $\rho_{xx}(k_h)$ display for an image that includes values of horizontal spacing k_h up to and greater than k_l, the number of pixels per scan *line*. A horizontal separation of $k_h = k_l$ corresponds to a vertical separation of $k_v = 1$. The acf plot therefore has a secondary peak at $k_h = k_l$. Unlike in speech, this secondary peak always occurs at a *time-invariant* lag k_l that corresponds to the scan-line length.

Interframe acf's in video are motion- and activity-dependent. An average characteristic would have approximately an exponential shape for small values of *frame* separation k_f. The interframe acf decays from a typical value in the order of 0.85 to 0.90 for $k_f = 1$ (temporal spacing of 1/30 s) to a value in the order of 0.30 for $k_f = 10$ (temporal spacing of 1/3 s).

2.2.4 Power Spectral Density Functions

The concept of a *power spectral density* function (psd), which shows the power in a waveform as a function of frequency, is closely related to the acf concept discussed in Section 2.2.3. In Section 2.3 we shall note that for stationary signals, the psd and acf functions indeed form a *Fourier Transform* pair.

The psd is a non-negative quantity that can be measured by using an appropriate filter bank and measuring the average power at the output of each filter. If the waveform is available as a finite-length sequence $\{x(n)\}$; $n = 0,1,...,N-1$, various other techniques exist to estimate its psd. The psd $S_{xx}(e^{j\omega})$ is defined such that if (ω_1,ω_2) is an interval on the radian frequency axis, the average power $\chi_x^2(\omega_1,\omega_2)$ in that interval is

$$\chi_x^2(\omega_1,\omega_2) = \frac{1}{\pi} \int_{\omega_1}^{\omega_2} S_{xx}(e^{j\omega})d\omega \; ; \qquad \omega_1, \omega_2 \geqslant 0 \; ; \qquad \chi_x^2(-\pi, \pi) = \chi_x^2 \quad (2.6)$$

The definition implies a non-negative psd.

For a time-discrete waveform, the *periodogram*

$$P_{xx}(e^{j\omega}) = \frac{1}{N} |X(e^{j\omega})|^2 \tag{2.7}$$

may also serve as an estimate of $S_{xx}(e^{j\omega})$, with $X(e^{j\omega})$ signifying the Discrete Fourier Transform (DFT) of $\{x(n)\}$. A better estimate results if an N-sequence is divided into M non-overlapping subsequences, and corresponding periodograms are averaged. A totally different procedure for estimating $S_{xx}(e^{j\omega})$ is the so-called *autoregressive estimation* technique. This will be discussed in Chapter 6.

Figure 2.9(a) shows a *long-time-averaged* psd for two ensembles of speakers, together with the psd of the speech waveform of Figure 2.1(a). All the three plots show a *lowpass* characteristic in the frequency range above 500 Hz, signifying a preponderance in speech of low frequency segments such as sustained vowels. It is important to note, however, that high frequencies in speech waveforms, although

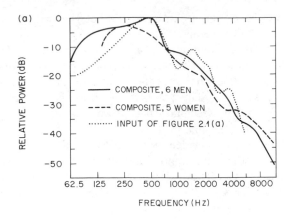

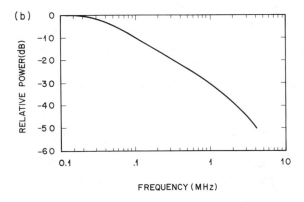

Figure 2.9 Long-time-averaged psd for (a) speech [Dunn and White, 1940] [Flanagan, 1972. Reprinted with permission] [Jayant, 1982] and (b) image waveforms [Connor, Brainard and Limb;©1972, IEEE].

having relatively less power, provide important information in the form of fricatives, stop sounds and unvoiced consonants.

A *long-time-averaged* psd for images is shown in Figure 2.9(b). The *lowpass* function is relatively flat for frequencies up to at least twice the line rate of about 15 kHz (corresponding to 525 lines in 1/30 s); it begins to fall at about 6 dB/octave in the middle region of the spectrum, and at about 12 dB/octave at very high frequencies. The prepondering low frequencies refer to the large area of constant brightness levels in an image frame. The power at high frequencies is comparatively small, but it provides the information about sharp changes in luminances.

Figure 2.10 shows *short-time-averaged* psd plots corresponding to the voiced and unvoiced segments "A" and "S" in Figure 2.1. In each case is shown a psd with low frequency resolution [Figures (a)(i) and (b)(i), obtained from a 64-point DFT analysis]; and a psd with high frequency resolution [Figures (a)(ii) and (b)(ii), obtained from a 256-point DFT analysis]. Note that while the short-time psd of "A" is *lowpass* as in the average plot in Figure 2.9(a), the psd for the fricative "S" is nearly flat, and in fact somewhat *highpass*, as expected. High-pass psd's also

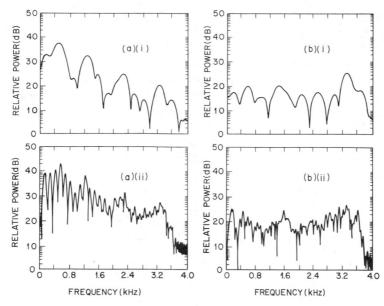

Figure 2.10 Short-time psd for the (a) voiced and (b) unvoiced speech examples in parts (b) and (c) of Figure 2.1 [Jayant, 1982]. In each case, the two psd's shown are results of analysis with (i) a low resolution in frequency [64-point DFT (Chapter 12 and Appendix A)] and (ii) a high resolution in frequency [256-point DFT].

occur in certain kinds of music material, for example, popular guitar. Moreover, in music, several lowpass and highpass sources (say, different instruments) can occur simultaneously at a given time, unlike in the speech of a single talker. As indicated earlier, lowpass and highpass segments in images are usually referred to as *low-detail* and *high-detail* segments.

Lowpass and highpass psd's are manifested, in the time domain, by different acf's — specifically by ρ_1 values that are positive and negative, respectively. The lowpass voiced speech psd (a) also exhibits four distinct resonances (*formants*) in the 0 to 4000 Hz band, corresponding to vocal tract resonances characteristic of the sound "A". The rapid oscillations in the voiced psd of part [(a)(ii)] of Figure 2.10 correspond to the fundamental frequency or pitch frequency, and they signify the quasi-periodic nature of voiced speech.

2.3 Mathematics of Random Waveforms

2.3.1 Random Processes

Although communication waveforms are not deterministic, their average properties (especially the long-time averages) are often regarded as deterministic and known a priori. Examples of such deterministic characterizations are those for long-time mean value and long-time acf. Further, the linear systems that communication waveforms are passed through during encoding and decoding processes are also deterministic. We have therefore summarized in Appendix A some basic mathematics that applies to deterministic signals and systems. The mathematics of the present section will apply specifically to the characterization of discrete-time *random* or *stochastic* signals, specifically those that are *stationary* in a way that will be defined presently. This is a natural framework in which to describe communication waveforms for which the signal-generating rule is either not known or is so complex as to make precise signal description impossible.

Each sequence (or waveform) from a random process is considered to be a member of an ensemble of discrete-time signals characterized by a set of *probability distributions* or *probability density functions*. Let us suppose that $\{x(n)\}$, $n = 0, \pm 1, \pm 2, \ldots$ is a sequence of sampled values of a waveform. Its value at a specific time instant n is $x(n)$. The sequence can be interpreted as a *realization* or *sample sequence of a random process*. It is one of the strictly infinite number of possible sequences which form the ensemble and it is regarded as being chosen randomly by nature. At a given time instant n, the value $x(n)$ of the

Figure 2.11 Random processes in (a) one and (b) two dimensions [Rosenfield and Kak, 1976. Reprinted with permission].

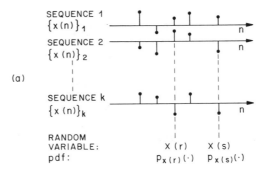

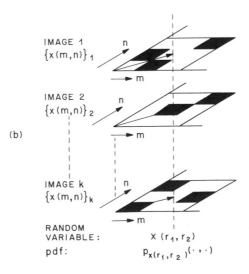

sequence $\{x(n)\}$ is a particular value of a *random variable (r.v.) X(n)*. The ordered set of r.v.'s $\{X(n)\}$ is the *random process* or *random sequence* [see Figure 2.11(a)]. At any time instant, the behavior of the random process can be described (at least conceptually) by a set of probability distributions or probability density functions. The above probability distributions are descriptors of multivariate statistics in general. We will therefore be able to characterize all the important properties of communication waveforms in the random process framework.

We can extend Figure 2.11(a) to the two-dimensional case, as in the simple example of Figure 2.11(b), which shows sample images with two levels of intensity, white and black. In characterizing two-dimensional images, we use the symbol $x(m,n)$ to denote an image element, or pixel intensity, at coordinates (m,n). The notation $\{x(m,n)\}$; $m,n=0,1,...,N-1$ is used to define an evolving 2-D sequence. This sequence $\{x(m,n)\}$ is a realization of an ensemble $\{X(m,n)\}$ of possible images. In the 1-D case, $\{X(n)\}$ was a random process, a r.v. $X(n)$ evolving in time. In the 2-D case, $\{X(m,n)\}$ is a *random field*, a r.v. $X(m,n)$ evolving in two spatial directions. Similarly, in the case of moving image sequences, we could describe an image element $x(m,n,o)$, where o is the time index, as a sample of a 3-D random sequence or field $\{X(m,n,o)\}$; this is alternatively describable as a r.v. $X(m,n,o)$ evolving in three directions.

Most of the material in the rest of Section 2.3 will refer to one-dimensional (scalar) random processes. Extensions to higher-dimensional (vector) random processes (see Section 2.2.1) will be invoked in the book as and when necessary.

2.3.2 Univariate Distributions

The value $x(n)$ of a sample sequence $\{x(n)\}$ of a random process can be interpreted as a particular outcome of a random variable $X(n)$. The r.v. $X(n)$ is a real-valued quantity; we assume that it is sufficiently well behaved so that the probability of the event $\{X(n) \leqslant x\}$ is defined for all real values of the dummy variable x. The probability of this event is termed the *probability distribution function* of the r.v. $X(n)$ and will be denoted by

$$P_{x(n)}(x) = P\{X(n) \leqslant x\} \tag{2.8}$$

We now assume that the distribution function is continuous and define a *probability density function* (pdf) as the derivative of the distribution function:

$$p_{x(n)}(x) = d/dx \; P_{x(n)}(x) \tag{2.9}$$

In general, with a nonstationary process, the pdf is a function of absolute time n as in Figure 2.11. Let us, however, consider the case where the statistical properties of the random process are independent of time. The minimum requirement for this to hold is that the univariate distribution and density functions are independent of time *(stationarity of first order)*. We may then simplify the notation by omitting the time index n:

$$p_x(x) = d/dx \; P_x(x) \tag{2.10}$$

From (2.8) it follows that the distribution function is monotonically nondecreasing, and that $P_x(-\infty) = 0$ and $P_x(\infty) = 1$. The probability that the r.v. X is in the range (a,b) is

$$P\{a < X \leqslant b\} = P_x(b) - P_x(a) = \int_a^b p_x(x)dx , \qquad (2.11)$$

the area of the shaded element in Figure 2.12(a). Also, by definition,

$$p_x(x) \geqslant 0 , \text{ all } x ; \qquad \int_{-\infty}^{\infty} p_x(x)dx = 1 \qquad (2.12)$$

Expectations of a r.v. Simple descriptions of a r.v. X are provided by *expectations*. Very generally, if $g(X)$ is a function of the r.v., the expectation of the new r.v. $g(X)$ is

$$E[g(X)] = \int_{-\infty}^{\infty} g(x)p_x(x)dx \qquad (2.13a)$$

In particular, the *mean value* is

$$\mu_x = E[X] = \int_{-\infty}^{\infty} xp_x(x)dx , \qquad (2.13b)$$

the center of gravity of the pdf of X. Also of interest are the expected values of the nth moment $g(X) = X^n$ and the nth central moment $g(X) = (X-\mu_x)^n$. With $n=2$, we obtain the *mean square value*

$$\chi_x^2 = E[X^2] = \int_{-\infty}^{\infty} x^2 p_x(x)dx \qquad (2.14a)$$

and the *variance*

$$\sigma_x^2 = E[(X-\mu_x)^2] = \int_{-\infty}^{\infty} (x-\mu_x)^2 p_x(x)dx \qquad (2.14b)$$

The variance is a measure of the spread of the distribution about the mean. The positive square root σ_x of the variance is called the *standard deviation* or *rms value*. From the last two equations, it follows that

$$\sigma_x^2 = \chi_x^2 - \mu_x^2 \qquad (2.14c)$$

Note that μ_x, σ_x^2 and χ_x^2 can be estimated using N-sample sequences as in (2.1).

Example 2.1. Distribution function of the normal pdf
   The *normal* probability distribution function is defined by

$$P\{X \leqslant x\} = P_x(x) = \frac{1}{2}\left[1 + \text{erf}\, \frac{x - \mu_x}{\sqrt{2}\sigma_x}\right] \; ; \quad \text{erf}\, x = \frac{2}{\sqrt{\pi}}\int_0^x e^{-t^2/2} dt \qquad (2.15)$$

The *error function* erf x is widely tabulated [Thomas, 1969] [Abramowitz and Stegun, 1964], and used to compute the probability that a r.v. X falls into a given range. For example,

$$P\{(-4\sigma_x + \mu_x) \leqslant X \leqslant (4\sigma_x + \mu_x)\} = 2\, P_x(4\sigma_x + \mu_x) - 1 = \text{erf}(2\sqrt{2}) = 0.999936$$

is the probability that a normally distributed r.v. has a magnitude not exceeding $4\sigma_x$. The closeness of this probability to 1.0 is the rationale for the so-called *four-sigma loading* in quantizer design. •

In the case of *nonstationary* processes, all expectations will be functions of time index n. In most sections of this book, we shall assume *wide-sense stationarity* which requires only that the first two moments of the distribution are independent of time:

$$\mu_x(n) = \mu_x(n+k) \; ; \qquad \sigma_x^2(n) = \sigma_x^2(n+k) \qquad (2.16)$$

Table 2.1 and Figure 2.5 have already provided a comparison of four model pdf's for amplitude-continuous sources. Another significant comparison of these models is in terms of two related pdf-specific properties, *differential entropy* and *entropy power*. These are discussed at length in Appendix C and Chapter 4.

The *characteristic function* $\Phi_x(j\Omega)$ of a random variable X is defined as

$$\Phi_x(j\Omega) = \int_{-\infty}^{\infty} p_x(x)e^{j\Omega x} dx \qquad (2.17a)$$

the complex conjugate of the Fourier transform of the pdf $p_x(x)$. The inverse Fourier transform expresses $p_x(x)$ in terms of the characteristic function

$$p_x(x) = \frac{1}{2\pi}\int_{-\infty}^{\infty} \Phi_x(j\Omega)e^{-j\Omega x} d\Omega \qquad (2.17b)$$

$\Phi_x(j\Omega)$ always exists because $p_x(x)$ is absolutely integrable in view of (2.12). Also, from (2.13), $\Phi_x(j\Omega)$ is identical with the expectation $E[e^{j\Omega X}]$.

Amplitude-discrete r.v.'s. An amplitude-discrete r.v. X can only assume one out of N possible values (outcomes) x_k; associated with each of these possible outcomes is a probability

$$P(x_k) = P\{X = x_k\} \qquad (2.18a)$$

and a pdf can be defined by using the Dirac delta-function $\delta(x)$:

$$p_x(x) = \sum_{k=1}^{N} P(x_k)\, \delta(x - x_k) \qquad (2.18b)$$

Note that the expectations defined earlier still apply. The mean and variance, for example, are found to be

$$\mu_x = \sum_{k=1}^{N} x_k P(x_k) \quad \text{and} \quad \sigma_x^2 = \sum_{k=1}^{N} (x_k - \mu_x)^2 P(x_k)$$

by using (2.18) in (2.13b) and (2.14b).

2.3.3 Bivariate Distributions

As a first step toward formalizing correlation functions, consider two r.v.'s X and Y whose mean values and variances are denoted by μ_x, σ_x^2, μ_y, σ_y^2, respectively. They have a *joint probability distribution* $P_{xy}(x,y)$ and a *joint pdf* [Figure 2.12(b)] defined, as in (2.8) and (2.10), by

$$P_{xy}(x,y) = P\{X \leqslant x, Y \leqslant y\}$$

$$p_{xy}(x,y) = \frac{\partial^2}{\partial x \, \partial y} P_{xy}(x,y); \qquad \int_{-\infty}^{\infty} \int_{\infty}^{\infty} p_{xy}(x,y) \, dx \, dy = 1 \qquad (2.19a)$$

Figure 2.12 (a) pdf of the amplitude of r.v. X; total area under $p_x(x)$ is unity; (b) joint pdf of the amplitudes of two r.v.'s X and Y; total volume under $p_{xy}(x,y)$ is unity.

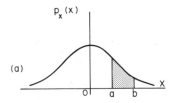

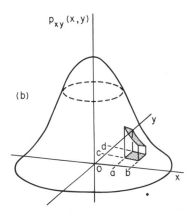

As in (2.11), the probability that the r.v.'s X and Y are jointly in ranges (a,b) and (c,d) is

$$P\{a < X \leqslant b, c < Y \leqslant d\} = \int_a^b \int_c^d p_{xy}(x,y)\,dx\,dy\ , \qquad (2.19b)$$

the volume of the shaded element in Figure 2.12(b).

Two zero-mean r.v.'s X and Y are *jointly normal* if

$$p_{xy}(x,y) = \frac{1}{2\pi\sqrt{1-\rho_{xy}^2}\,\sigma_x\sigma_y}\exp\left[-\frac{1}{2(1-\rho_{xy}^2)}\left\{\left(\frac{x}{\sigma_x}\right)^2 - \frac{2xy\,\rho_{xy}}{\sigma_x\sigma_y} + \left(\frac{y}{\sigma_y}\right)^2\right\}\right] \qquad (2.20)$$

where ρ_{xy} is the correlation coefficient to be defined in (2.26b).

Univariate pdf's can be derived from the joint pdf, in the form of *marginal pdf's*

$$p_x(x) = \int_{-\infty}^{\infty} p_{xy}(x,y)\,dy\ ; \qquad p_y(y) = \int_{-\infty}^{\infty} p_{xy}(x,y)\,dx \qquad (2.21)$$

That is, the value $p_x(x_1)$ of the pdf $p_x(\cdot)$ is the area under the profile of $p_{xy}(x_1,y)$ obtained by intersecting the surface $p_{xy}(\cdot,\cdot)$ by the plane $x = x_1$. The r.v.'s X and Y are said to be *statistically independent* if

$$p_{xy}(x,y) = p_x(x)p_y(y) \qquad (2.22)$$

The expectation of a function $g(X,Y)$ of the two r.v.'s X and Y is

$$E[g(X,Y)] = \int_{-\infty}^{\infty} \int_{-\infty}^{\infty} g(x,y)p_{xy}(x,y)\,dx\,dy \qquad (2.23)$$

We are mainly interested in the joint moments $E[X^m Y^n]$. It is easy to see that $E[X^m Y^n] = E[X^m]E[Y^n]$ if X and Y are statistically independent. In particular, X and Y are said to be *uncorrelated* if $E[XY] = E[X]E[Y]$; and *orthogonal* if $E[XY] = 0$. Clearly, if either of $E[X]$ or $E[Y] = 0$, a pair of uncorrelated r.v.'s is also orthogonal.

The mean of a sum of two r.v.'s is the sum of the means, regardless of statistical dependence:

$$\mu_{x+y} = E[X+Y] = E[X] + E[Y] = \mu_x + \mu_y \qquad (2.24)$$

The power of the sum is

$$\chi_{x+y}^2 = E[(X+Y)^2] = E[X^2] + 2E[XY] + E[Y^2]$$

Using (2.14) in the last equation, we see that

$$\sigma_{x+y}^2 = \sigma_x^2 + \sigma_y^2 \quad \text{for uncorrelated r.v.'s}\ , \qquad (2.25)$$

suggesting a simple *addition* of variances in this special case. Another value of interest is the *joint central moment*

$$\sigma_{xy} = E[(X-\mu_x)(Y-\mu_y)] , \qquad (2.26a)$$

the *covariance of the r.v.'s X and Y*. The normalized covariance of X and Y is

$$\rho_{xy} = \sigma_{xy} / (\sigma_x \sigma_y) \qquad (2.26b)$$

This quantity is also known as the *correlation coefficient*. Covariance and correlation coefficients are zero if X and Y are uncorrelated.

Conditional Distributions. The *conditional probability distribution function* of a r.v. X, *knowing* a single point event $\{Y = y\}$ [Papoulis, 1965], is

$$p_x(x|Y = y) = p_{xy}(x,y) / p_y(y) \qquad (2.27)$$

provided that $p_y(y) \neq 0$. The r.v.'s are *independent* when the occurrence of any value $X = x$ is in no way influenced by the occurrence of any value $Y = y$. The conditional pdf is then $p_x(x|Y=y) = p_x(x)$ and the joint pdf is simply that of (2.22). It turns out that independent r.v.'s X and Y are also uncorrelated, as seen by using (2.26), (2.22) and (2.23); the converse of this statement is not true in general. But the converse does apply in the case of Gaussian statistics. In the special case of jointly normal (2.20) r.v.'s, if X and Y are uncorrelated ($\rho_{xy}=0$), they are also statistically independent. (See Problem 2.4).

As a generalization of (2.13a), we can define a *conditional expectation*

$$E[g(X)|Y = y] = \int_{-\infty}^{\infty} g(x)p_x(x|Y = y)dx , \qquad (2.28)$$

the expectation of $g(X)$ knowing that event $Y = y$ has occurred.

In addition, we note that the *conditional* pdf of a r.v. X, given that event $\{X \in I\}$ has occurred, is

$$p_x(x|X \in I) = \begin{cases} p_x(x)/P\{X \in I\} & \text{if } X \in I \\ 0 & \text{otherwise} \end{cases} \qquad (2.29)$$

Linear and Nonlinear Estimation. Bivariate distributions can be used directly in the solution of fundamental problems in estimation or prediction. For example, given the value y of a r.v. Y, *the best linear estimate* $\hat{x}_{opt}$ of the value x of another r.v. X, and the associated minimum mean square error in estimation, are

$$\hat{x}_{opt} = c_{opt} y = (\rho_{xy}\sigma_x/\sigma_y) y ; \qquad \min\{E[X-\hat{X}]^2\} = \sigma_x^2(1-\rho_{xy}^2) \qquad (2.30)$$

For the same problem, the *best nonlinear estimate* is defined by

$$\hat{x}_{opt} = E[X|Y = y]; \qquad \min\{E[X-\hat{X}]^2\} \leqslant \sigma_x^2(1-\rho_{xy}^2) \qquad (2.31)$$

If X and Y are jointly Gaussian (2.20), the results of linear and nonlinear estimation are identical (Problem 2.8).

PDF of the Sum of Two Random Variables. We have already derived the mean value, power and variance of the sum of two r.v.'s, $Z = X + Y$. Events $\{Y = y\}$ and $\{X = z-y\}$ imply the event $\{Z = z\}$. Therefore the pdf of r.v. Z is

$$p_z(z) = \int_{-\infty}^{\infty} p_x(z-y|Y = y)p_y(y)dy = \int_{-\infty}^{\infty} p_{xy}(z-y, y)dy \qquad (2.32)$$

If X and Y are *statistically independent*, we can use (2.22) to obtain

$$p_z(z) = \int_{-\infty}^{\infty} p_x(z-y)p_y(y)dy = p_x(z)*p_y(z) \qquad (2.33)$$

where * denotes convolution.

The result of (2.33) can easily be extended to a sum of n variables. The *central limit theorem* states that, if these r.v.'s are independent of each other, the pdf of the sum of these r.v.'s approaches a Gaussian distribution very quickly as a function of n, regardless of the pdf's of the individual r.v.'s (Problem 2.5). In the case of a set of Gaussian r.v.'s, any linear transform (Chapter 12) yields another set of Gaussian r.v.'s, irrespective of whether they are independent or not.

2.3.4 Correlation Functions of Random Processes

We now come back to the description of properties of a random process $\{X(n)\}$; $n = 0, \pm1, \pm2$ by a simultaneous description of the behavior of two r.v.'s $X(m)$ and $X(n)$ of this process. These r.v.'s are illustrated by $X(r)$ and $X(s)$ in Figure 2.11(a). Equations (2.19a) and (2.28) have already defined joint and conditional pdf's. Partial descriptions of joint statistics are given by the *autocovariance function*

$$C_{xx}(m,n) = E[(X(m)-\mu_{x(m)}) \ (X(n)-\mu_{x(n)})] \qquad (2.34)$$

and the *autocorrelation function* (acf)

$$R_{xx}(m,n) = E[X(m) \ X(n)] = C_{xx}(m,n) + \mu_{x(m)}\mu_{x(n)} \qquad (2.35)$$

For zero-mean sequences, the expectations above are identical:

$$R_{xx}(m, n) = C_{xx}(m, n) \qquad \text{if} \qquad \mu_{x(m)} = \mu_{x(n)} = 0 \qquad (2.36)$$

Unless otherwise stated, we assume throughout the book that mean values are zero, and use the term acf *to signify* (2.36). Clearly, the acf and the autocovariance function depend on two time variables m and n or, alternatively, on absolute time instant m and time displacement or time lag $k = n - m$. A *wide-sense stationary process*, however, is defined by the fact that its first-order pdf $p_{x(n)}(x)$ is independent of time (implying a constant mean) and that its joint pdf $p_{x(m)x(n)}(x,y)$ depends only on time shift (implying that the acf depends only on $n-m=k$). Indeed, wide-sense stationarity refers only to first- and second-order statistics. In the *strict-sense stationary process*, on the other hand, none of the statistics is affected by a time shift. This book will mainly assume wide-sense stationarity. It can be shown, however, that Gaussian processes are stationary in the strict sense if they are stationary in the wide sense [Papoulis, 1965].

For wide-sense stationary processes, the acf and autocovariance function do not depend on the absolute instant of time; they may be rewritten as

$$C_{xx}(k) = E[(X(n)-\mu_x)(X(n+k)-\mu_x)]; \qquad R_{xx}(k) = E[X(n)X(n+k)] \quad (2.37)$$

It can be shown that $R_{xx}(k) = R_{xx}(-k) = R_{xx}(|k|)$ and $|R_{xx}(k)| \leqslant R_{xx}(0)$ for all k; note also that $R_{xx}(0) = \chi_x^2 = \sigma_x^2 + \mu_x^2$ [see (2.14c)]. We will also make use of the *variance-normalized acf* defined in (2.5):

$$\rho_k = \rho_{xx}(k) = R_{xx}(k)/R_{xx}(0) ; \qquad \rho_{xx}(0) = 1 \qquad (2.38)$$

The acf and autocovariance function are functions of time lag k; they are also *deterministic* since they describe average quantities of the process. Further, as we shall see presently, values of these functions cannot be chosen arbitrarily.

At this point it is convenient to introduce matrix terminology, which will be used extensively in Chapters 6 and 12. We denote an observation N-sequence and the associated r.v. sequence by column vectors

$$\mathbf{x} = \{x(k)\}; \qquad \mathbf{X} = \{X(k)\}; \qquad k = 0,1,...,N-1 \qquad (2.39a)$$

and the *autocorrelation* (or *mean square value*) *matrix* by

$$\mathbf{R}_{xx} = \{R_{xx}(|k-l|)\} ; \qquad (2.39b)$$

$$= R_{xx}(0) \{\rho_{xx}(|k-l|)\}; \qquad k,l = 0,1,...,N-1 ;$$

$$\mathbf{R}_{xx} = \begin{bmatrix} R_0 & R_1 & R_2 & \cdots & R_{N-1} \\ R_1 & R_0 & R_1 & \cdots & R_{N-2} \\ R_2 & R_1 & R_0 & \cdots & R_{N-3} \\ \cdot & \cdot & \cdot & \cdots & \cdot \\ R_{N-1} & \cdot & \cdot & \cdots & R_0 \end{bmatrix} = R_0 \begin{bmatrix} 1 & \rho_1 & \rho_2 & \cdots & \rho_{N-1} \\ \rho_1 & 1 & \rho_1 & \cdots & \rho_{N-2} \\ \rho_2 & \rho_1 & 1 & \cdots & \rho_{N-3} \\ \cdot & \cdot & \cdot & \cdots & \cdot \\ \rho_{N-1} & \cdot & \cdot & \cdots & 1 \end{bmatrix} \quad (2.40)$$

where we have used the notation

$$R_{|k-l|} = R_0 \, \rho_{|k-l|} = R_{xx}(|k-l|) = E[X(n+l)X(n+k)] \qquad (2.41)$$

for the element in the kth row and lth column. The autocorrelation matrix can also be described by

$$\mathbf{R}_{xx} = E[\mathbf{X} \, \mathbf{X}^T] \tag{2.42}$$

where T denotes the *transpose* of a vector. Similarly, the *covariance matrix* (or *variance matrix*) is obtained by taking into account mean values μ_x:

$$\mathbf{C}_{xx} = \mathbf{R}_{xx} - \boldsymbol{\mu}_x \boldsymbol{\mu}_x^T = \{ C_{xx}(|k-l|) \} ; \qquad k,l = 0,1,...,N-1 \tag{2.43}$$

where $\boldsymbol{\mu}_x$ is the mean-value vector with identical elements μ_x:

$$\boldsymbol{\mu}_x = E[\mathbf{X}] = \{ E[X(k)] \} ; \qquad k = 0,1,...,N-1 \tag{2.44}$$

Clearly, $\mathbf{R}_{xx} = \mathbf{C}_{xx}$ for a zero-mean vector r.v. $\mathbf{X}$. It is easy to see that $\mathbf{R}_{xx}$ and $\mathbf{C}_{xx}$ are *nonnegative definite*; i.e., the scalar quantities $\boldsymbol{\alpha}^T \mathbf{R}_{xx} \boldsymbol{\alpha}$ and $\boldsymbol{\alpha}^T \mathbf{C}_{xx} \boldsymbol{\alpha}$ are nonnegative for any arbitrary N-dimensional vector $\boldsymbol{\alpha}$. For example, in the case of $\mathbf{R}_{xx}$,

$$\boldsymbol{\alpha}^T \mathbf{R}_{xx} \boldsymbol{\alpha} = E[\boldsymbol{\alpha}^T \mathbf{X} \, \mathbf{X}^T \boldsymbol{\alpha}] = E[(\boldsymbol{\alpha}^T \mathbf{X})^2] \geqslant 0 \tag{2.45}$$

where the inequality holds because $\boldsymbol{\alpha}^T \mathbf{X}$ is a dot product. In the following we will assume that $\mathbf{R}_{xx}$ is *positive definite*, which implies that the equality in (2.45) is only achieved if $\boldsymbol{\alpha}$ is a zero-element vector. A positive-definite correlation matrix is also *nonsingular*, i.e., it has an *inverse*. This also implies that the psd and all *eigenvalues* (Section 2.3.5), which are measures of variances, are non-negative. (See the references in Appendix B). Finally, we note that

$$|\mathbf{R}_{xx}| > 0 \tag{2.46}$$

is a necessary and sufficient condition for $\mathbf{R}_{xx}$ to be a correlation matrix. For $N = 2$, (2.46) implies that $|\rho_1| < 1$. The case of $N = 3$ is illustrated in Problem 2.7 and Figure 2.13.

Figure 2.13 Constraints on ρ_1 and ρ_2 for $\mathbf{R}_{xx}$ to be a 3×3 correlation matrix.

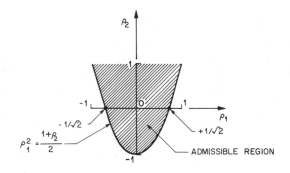

The correlation matrix is symmetric; also, elements along any diagonal in it are equal. Such a matrix is called a *symmetric Toeplitz* matrix. The elements $R_{xx}(k,l)$ of $\mathbf{R}_{xx}$ can refer either to N samples from a stationary scalar source (as in our context), or to N components of a vector source. In the latter case, the autocorrelation matrix can be non-Toeplitz. Elements along the main diagonal will now be mean square values of N different signal components, and these will differ in general.

A useful partial description of the dependencies between two random processes $\{X(n)\}$ and $\{Y(n)\}$ is the *crosscorrelation function*

$$R_{xy}(m,n) = E[X(m)Y(n)] \tag{2.47}$$

Again, if the processes are *jointly stationary* [i.e., $\{X(n)\}$ and $\{Y(n)\}$ are wide-sense stationary and the cross-correlation depends only on time shift], this function is a function of only one variable, the time lag k:

$$R_{xy}(k) = E[X(n)Y(n+k)] \tag{2.48}$$

It can be shown that $R_{xy}^2(k) \leqslant R_x(0) R_y(0)$ and $R_{xy}(k) = R_{yx}(-k)$ for all k. A *crosscovariance function* can be defined by including mean values in (2.48).

Effect of a Linear System on Mean and acf. Consider a linear, time-invariant and stable system with impulse response $h(n)$ and transfer function $H(e^{j\omega})$ (Appendix A). Consider a wide-sense stationary random process $\{Z(n)\}$ applied to its input. The mean value and acf of the output process $\{X(n)\}$ (Problem 2.10) are then given by

$$\mu_x = \mu_z H(0) \tag{2.49}$$

$$R_{xx}(k) = R_{zz}(k) * h(k) * h(-k)$$

$$= \sum_{i=-\infty}^{\infty} \sum_{j=-\infty}^{\infty} h(i)h(j)R_{zz}(i-j-|k|) \tag{2.50}$$

Therefore, the mean of $\{Y(n)\}$ is constant and its acf depends solely on time displacement k. Hence $\{Y(n)\}$ is also wide-sense stationary.

The Multivariate Gaussian Distribution. Descriptions of N r.v.'s by joint pdf's are too complex to be of practical use, and these pdf's are usually not known, nor are they easy to measure. One relatively simple model, however, is the multivariate Gaussian distribution; this is of great importance in applications, because, as we have already mentioned, many physical events can be modeled by Gaussian distributions.

The joint Gaussian pdf of a vector random variable $\mathbf{X} = (X_0, X_1,..., X_{N-1})^T$ is

$$p_\mathbf{x}(\mathbf{x}) = (2\pi)^{-N/2}|\mathbf{C}_{xx}|^{-1/2}\exp\left[\frac{1}{2}(\mathbf{x}-\boldsymbol{\mu}_\mathbf{x})^T\mathbf{C}_{xx}^{-1}(\mathbf{x}-\boldsymbol{\mu}_\mathbf{x}) \right] \tag{2.51}$$

in which $\mathbf{x} = [x_0, x_1, ..., x_{N-1}]^T$ is a vector of dummy variables, $|\mathbf{C}_{xx}|$ is the determinant of the covariance matrix $\mathbf{C}_{xx}$, and $\mathbf{C}_{xx}^{-1}$ is its inverse. Notice the important fact that the joint pdf in the Gaussian case is totally determined by the mean values of the elements of the vector r.v. $\mathbf{X}$ and by the covariances between its elements.

Second-order statistics are therefore sufficient for describing Gaussian processes. If the elements of $\mathbf{X}$ are uncorrelated, they are also statistically independent. In this special case,

$$p_\mathbf{x}(\mathbf{x}) = \prod_{k=0}^{N-1} p_{x_k}(x_k) \quad ; \quad p_{x_k}(x_k) = \frac{1}{\sqrt{2\pi}\sigma_k} \exp\left[-\frac{1}{2}(x_k-\mu_k)^2/2\sigma_k^2\right] \quad (2.52)$$

Finally, consider any *linear transform* $\mathbf{Y} = \mathbf{AX}$ (Appendix B and Chapter 12); if $\mathbf{X}$ is Gaussian, the vector r.v. $\mathbf{Y}$ also has a joint Gaussian pdf.

2.3.5 Eigenvalues and Eigenvectors

Associated with any correlation matrix $\mathbf{R}_{xx}$ is a set of *eigenvalues* λ_i and *eigenvectors* $\mathbf{l}_i$ defined by

$$\mathbf{R}_{xx}\mathbf{l}_i = \lambda_i \mathbf{l}_i \quad ; \qquad i = 0,1,...,N-1 \qquad (2.53)$$

Eigenvectors and eigenvalues will play an important role in the analyses of Transform Coding (Chapter 12).

Let $\mathbf{l}$ be an eigenvector of $\mathbf{R}_{xx}$. The corresponding eigenvalue λ is then defined by

$$\mathbf{R}_{xx}\,\mathbf{l} = \lambda\mathbf{l} \qquad \text{or} \qquad (\mathbf{R}_{xx} - \lambda\mathbf{I})\,\mathbf{l} = 0 \qquad (2.54)$$

This is a linear homogeneous system of equations for the unknown λ. In order to have a nonzero eigenvector, it is both necessary and sufficient that

$$|\mathbf{R}_{xx} - \lambda\mathbf{I}| = 0 \qquad (2.55)$$

The above equation is called the *characteristic equation* of $\mathbf{R}_{xx}$. This determinant, when expanded, is a polynomial in λ of degree N, and it will have N zeros λ_i with corresponding eigenvectors $\mathbf{l}_i$. The eigenvectors are of course determined only to within a scalar multiple. Recall that $\mathbf{R}_{xx}$ is a real symmetric matrix. It can be shown therefore that the characteristic equation has N distinct and real zeros (with multiplicities, in general); and consequently, it has exactly N distinct eigenvectors. In general, it is very difficult to find the eigenvalues of a matrix, and numerical techniques are needed.

Example 2.2.   Example of $N = 2$
Consider a stationary source with variance $\sigma_x^2 = 1$ and normalized autocorrelation ρ between neighboring samples

$$\mathbf{R}_{xx} = \begin{bmatrix} 1 & \rho \\ \rho & 1 \end{bmatrix} \qquad (2.56)$$

The eigenvalues λ are obtained from the characteristic equation (2.55):

$$\begin{vmatrix} 1-\lambda & \rho \\ \rho & 1-\lambda \end{vmatrix} = 0 ; \qquad \lambda_0 = 1+\rho ; \quad \lambda_1 = 1-\rho \qquad (2.57)$$

To find the eigenvector $\mathbf{l}_0$ we use (2.53):

$$\begin{bmatrix} 1 & \rho \\ \rho & 1 \end{bmatrix} \begin{bmatrix} l_0(0) \\ l_0(1) \end{bmatrix} = (1+\rho) \begin{bmatrix} l_0(0) \\ l_0(1) \end{bmatrix} ; \qquad l_0(0) = l_0(1) \qquad (2.58a)$$

Similarly, for $\mathbf{l}_1$, we find that $l_1(0) = -l_1(1)$. If we scale the vectors so that

$$l_0(0)^2 + l_0(1)^2 = l_1^2(0) + l_1^2(1) = 1 , \qquad (2.58b)$$

$$\mathbf{l}_0 = \frac{1}{\sqrt{2}} \begin{bmatrix} 1 \\ 1 \end{bmatrix} ; \quad \mathbf{l}_1 = \frac{1}{\sqrt{2}} \begin{bmatrix} 1 \\ -1 \end{bmatrix} \qquad (2.59)$$

The above equations show that the product of the eigenvalues λ_0 and λ_1 equals $1-\rho^2 = |\mathbf{R}_{xx}|$. In addition, the eigenvectors are *orthonormal*, i.e.,

$$\mathbf{l}_0^T \mathbf{l}_1 = \mathbf{l}_1^T \mathbf{l}_0 = 0 ; \qquad \mathbf{l}_0^T \mathbf{l}_0 = \mathbf{l}_1^T \mathbf{l}_1 = 1 \qquad (2.60) \quad \bullet$$

For $N > 2$, computations are tedious. However, so-called MA(1) and AR(1) processes (Section 2.4) will have explicit solutions.

Some Properties of Eigenvalues and Eigenvectors

(a) Eigenvectors are *orthogonal* ($\mathbf{l}_i^T \mathbf{l}_j = 0$ for $i \neq j$), and by choosing a proper scaling in $\mathbf{R}_{xx} \mathbf{l} = \lambda \mathbf{l}$, they can be made to be *orthonormal*:

$$\mathbf{l}_i^T \mathbf{l}_j = \delta_{ij} \qquad (2.61)$$

(b) Eigenvectors define $\mathbf{R}_{xx}$ (Problem 2.20) in the form

$$\mathbf{R}_{xx} = \sum_{i=0}^{N-1} \lambda_i \, \mathbf{l}_i \, \mathbf{l}_i^T \qquad (2.62)$$

(c) Eigenvalues have the properties

$$|\mathbf{R}_{xx}| = \prod_{j=0}^{N-1} \lambda_j ; \qquad \text{trace } (\mathbf{R}_{xx}) = \sum_{j=0}^{N-1} \lambda_j \qquad (2.63a)$$

Note that trace $(\mathbf{R}_{xx}) = N\sigma_x^2$ for zero-mean processes. Hence for any N, the average value of eigenvalues equals the variance of the process:

$$\sigma_x^2 = \frac{1}{N} \sum_{j=0}^{N-1} \lambda_j \tag{2.63b}$$

Since the eigenvalues are measures of variance, they are non-negative. In addition, if λ_j's are the eigenvalues of $\mathbf{R}_{xx}$, then the eigenvalues of $\mathbf{R}_{xx}^{-1}$ are given as λ_j^{-1}.

(d)   Let $S_{xx}(e^{j\omega})$ be the psd (see Section 2.3.6) of the process with correlation matrix $\mathbf{R}_{xx}$. Then

$$\lambda_j = S_{xx}(e^{j\Omega_j}) \tag{2.64}$$

i.e., eigenvalues are samples, although not equidistant ones, of the psd. Specific Ω_j-values, the *eigenfrequencies*, are usually not simply obtainable from the psd.

(e)   For any function $f(\cdot)$, the *Toeplitz distribution theorem (Szego-theorem)* [Grenander and Szego, 1958] states that for any function $f(\cdot)$,

$$\lim_{N \to \infty} \frac{1}{N} \sum_{j=0}^{N-1} f(\lambda_j) = \frac{1}{2\pi} \int_{-\pi}^{\pi} f[S_{xx}(e^{j\omega})] d\omega \tag{2.65}$$

For example, with $f(\cdot) = \log_e(\cdot)$, we have

$$\lim_{N \to \infty} \log_e \left[\prod_{j=0}^{N-1} \lambda_j \right]^{1/N} = \frac{1}{2\pi} \int_{-\pi}^{\pi} \log_e S_{xx}(e^{j\omega}) d\omega \tag{2.66}$$

Hence, with property (c),

$$\lim_{N \to \infty} |\mathbf{R}_{xx}|^{1/N} = \exp \left[\frac{1}{2\pi} \int_{-\pi}^{\pi} \log_e S_{xx}(e^{j\omega}) d\omega \right] \tag{2.67}$$

2.3.6 Power Spectral Density of Random Processes

Many results on stationary random processes, involving only second moments, can also be discussed in the frequency domain. Suppose that $\{X(n)\}$ is a discrete-time wide-sense stationary process with acf $R_{xx}(k)$ (2.37). The *power spectral density function* (psd) is defined to be the Fourier transform of the acf of the process; we thus obtain a Fourier transform pair

$$R_{xx}(k) = \frac{1}{2\pi} \int_{-\pi}^{\pi} S_{xx}(e^{j\omega}) e^{jk\omega} d\omega \; ; \tag{2.68a}$$

$$S_{xx}(e^{j\omega}) = \sum_{k=-\infty}^{\infty} R_{xx}(k) e^{-jk\omega} \tag{2.68b}$$

which is a statement of the *Wiener-Khinchine theorem*. The function $S_{xx}(e^{j\omega})$ exists if $R_{xx}(k)$ is absolutely summable. Also, using the fact that $R_{xx}(k)$ is a real-valued even function,

$$S_{xx}(e^{j\omega}) = R_{xx}(0) + 2 \sum_{k=1}^{\infty} R_{xx}(k)\cos k\omega \qquad (2.69a)$$

Hence, the psd is a real even function of frequency ω, i.e., $S_{xx}(e^{j\omega}) = S_{xx}(e^{-j\omega})$. As a result, the acf can also be rewritten in the form

$$R_{xx}(k) = \frac{1}{2\pi} \int_{-\pi}^{\pi} S_{xx}(e^{j\omega})\cos k\omega \, d\omega \qquad (2.69b)$$

Further, the area under the power spectral density function in the range $(-\pi, \pi)$ is 2π times the average power in the process [see (2.14a)]:

$$\chi_x^2 = E[X^2(n)] = R_{xx}(0) = \frac{1}{2\pi} \int_{-\pi}^{\pi} S_{xx}(e^{j\omega}) d\omega \qquad (2.70)$$

Specifically, the power of the process in the frequency range $(\omega_k - \Delta\omega/2, \omega_k + \Delta\omega/2)$ is approximately $S_{xx}(e^{j\omega_k})\Delta\omega/\pi$. Since the power cannot assume negative values, it is clear that we must have $S_{xx}(e^{j\omega}) \geqslant 0$ for all ω. This is the spectral equivalent to the requirement of a non-negative-definite $\mathbf{R}_{xx}$.

The *cross spectral density* of two jointly stationary processes $\{X(n)\}$ and $\{Y(n)\}$ is

$$S_{xy}(e^{j\omega}) = \sum_{k=-\infty}^{\infty} R_{xy}(k)e^{-jk\omega} \qquad (2.71)$$

This function exists if $R_{xy}(\cdot)$ is absolutely summable. Since $R_{xy}(k) = R_{yx}(-k)$, it can be shown that $S_{yx}(e^{j\omega}) = S_{xy}^*(e^{j\omega})$, where * denotes a conjugate. Note that the cross spectral density function is not necessarily even or real, or positive.

Effect of a Linear System on psd. Consider a process $\{Z(n)\}$ applied to a linear, time-invariant and stable filter with transfer function $H(e^{j\omega})$. The psd of output $\{X(n)\}$ is given by (Problem 2.10)

$$S_{xx}(e^{j\omega}) = S_{zz}(e^{j\omega}) |H(e^{j\omega})|^2 \qquad (2.72)$$

2.3.7 Spectral Flatness Measure

Consider a zero-mean process $\{X(n)\}$ with psd $S_{xx}(e^{j\omega})$. Its variance is

$$\sigma_x^2 = \frac{1}{2\pi} \int_{-\pi}^{\pi} S_{xx}(e^{j\omega}) d\omega \qquad (2.73)$$

We define the *spectral flatness measure (sfm)* [Makhoul and Wolf, 1972] as

$$\gamma_x^2 = \frac{\exp\left[\frac{1}{2\pi} \int_{-\pi}^{\pi} \log_e S_{xx}(e^{j\omega})d\omega\right]}{\frac{1}{2\pi} \int_{-\pi}^{\pi} S_{xx}(e^{j\omega})\,d\omega} = \frac{\eta_x^2}{\sigma_x^2} \tag{2.74}$$

Note that $\gamma_x^2 = 1$ if $S_{xx}(e^{j\omega}) = \sigma_x^2$, which is the psd that describes a *white noise* process. We will see presently that

$$0 \leqslant \gamma_x^2 \leqslant 1 \tag{2.75}$$

We will use *sfm* as an important tool to describe the shape of a psd by a single value. Indeed, the *sfm* bounds the performance of two classes of coding schemes, classes that exploit waveform redundancy (as shown by a non-flat psd) by *predictive coding* and by *transform coding*. In fact, we shall see later that η_x^2, the numerator in (2.74), can be interpreted as a *minimum prediction error variance*, or as the variance of a white innovations process that is modified by a linear filter to yield a process $\{X(n)\}$ that is colored and hence predictable.

The inverse of the *sfm*, γ_x^{-2}, is a measure of *waveform predictability*. This number is typically 3 and 16 for the long-term psd's of speech and video, respectively. Short-term psd's are sometimes characterized by much higher values of γ_x^{-2}, implying higher predictability. From Wiener theory, it is known further that processes with $S_{xx}(e^{j\omega}) = 0$ over finite intervals are predictable with zero error. For these cases, $\gamma_x^2 = 0$, $\gamma_x^{-2} = \infty$, and the predictability is infinite.

We now show that $0 \leqslant \gamma_x^2 \leqslant 1$, as claimed in (2.75). Let the psd $S_{xx}(\cdot)$ be divided into N sections of width $\Delta\omega = \pi/N$ within the interval $(0,\pi)$. The samples of the psd are

$$S_k = S_{xx}(e^{j\omega_k}) \quad \text{where} \quad \omega_k = \frac{\pi}{N}\left(k - \frac{1}{2}\right); \quad k = 1,2,...,N \tag{2.76}$$

The denominator of (2.74) then reads

$$\sigma_x^2 = \lim_{N\to\infty} \frac{1}{\pi} \sum_{k=1}^{N} S_k \Delta\omega = \lim_{N\to\infty} \frac{1}{N} \sum_{k=1}^{N} S_k$$

and the numerator is

$$\eta_x^2 = \lim_{N\to\infty} 2^{\frac{1}{N}\sum_{k=1}^{N} \log_2 S_k} = \lim_{N\to\infty} \left[\prod_{k=1}^{N} S_k\right]^{1/N} \tag{2.77}$$

Therefore, γ_x^2 is the ratio of the geometric mean and the arithmetic mean of the samples of the psd. This ratio, by definition, is not greater than unity. The value of unity is only obtained if all samples are equal. Later sections will give numerical examples to illustrate (2.75).

The spectral flatness measure is reflected directly in the *entropy power* Q (Appendix C). For a Gaussian source, $Q = \gamma_x^2 \sigma_x^2$. Also, the distortion rate function for this source (Appendix D) is $D(R)_G = 2^{-2R} \gamma_x^2 \sigma_x^2$. Thus, smaller γ_x^2 values signify lesser entropy, greater predictability, and a smaller theoretically possible mean square distortion D for given rate of R bits/sample.

2.3.8 Optimum Linear Predictions and Transforms

The significance of the acf and psd descriptions developed so far is in the fact that such second-order designs are adequate for optimal designs of *linear predictive* and *linear transform* coders. Prediction and transform operations serve to remove the redundancy in an input waveform, and thus permit bit rate-efficient digitizations thereof. Nonadaptive and adaptive versions of these coders remove input redundancy by utilizing long-time-averaged and short-time statistics, respectively. Further, predictive and transform coding techniques respectively use *time-domain* and *frequency-domain* approaches for redundancy removal, as we shall see in later chapters. A common feature is that because of the linear operations involved, both of these approaches are regarded as means for utilizing *linear redundancy*; and the performances of both coder classes are upper-bounded by a measure of this linear redundancy that we have already developed, the *spectral flatness measure* γ_x^2.

While discussing predictive and transform coders, we shall come across several parameters that depend directly on waveform properties. These parameters could therefore be discussed appropriately in this chapter on waveform characterization. However, purely for convenience, we shall defer detailed discussions of these to respective coding chapters. The properties we have in mind are *linear prediction coefficients*, *parcor coefficients* (Chapter 6) and *transform coefficients*, especially those resulting from a *Karhunen-Loeve Transform* (Chapter 12). The following is merely a brief introduction to these concepts, using the simple example of a 1-D input.

Linear prediction coefficients h_j are used in *one-step-ahead* predictions

$$\hat{x}(n) = \sum_{j=1}^{N} h_j \, x(n-j) \qquad (2.78)$$

For any given order of prediction N, the mean square value ${}^N\sigma_d^2$ of prediction error $d(n) = x(n) - \hat{x}(n)$ will be minimized by

$$\mathbf{h}_{\text{opt}} = \mathbf{R}_{xx}^{-1} \mathbf{r}_{xx} \qquad (2.79)$$

where $\mathbf{R}_{xx}$ is the correlation matrix and $\mathbf{r}_{xx}$ is a vector which has the first N acf values as its elements. If waveform sources are modeled as the output of a linear filter with a white noise or *innovations* process $\{Z(n)\}$ as its input, the asymptotic value of minimum mean square prediction error $d(n)$, as $N \rightarrow \infty$, merely given by the variance σ_z^2 of the innovations

$$\eta_x^2 = \min \{{}^\infty\sigma_d^2\} = \sigma_z^2 \qquad (2.80)$$

The optimum prediction error filter is in fact a *whitening filter* for the waveform at the input to a coder, and its transfer function is the inverse of the input psd. The decoder in a linear predictive system operates on a quantized version of $d(n)$ to recover an approximation to $x(n)$. The transfer function of this decoder in fact matches the input psd.

Autoregressive or Markov source models (Section 2.4) are very useful in the analysis of predictive coders. In this case, the reconstruction at the decoder is often performed with an infinite impulse response filter which is the inverse of the prediction error filter. An interesting special property is that for an AR(N) process, or a Markov process of order N, the optimum linear predictor has a finite order, N.

Linear transforms of an input random vector $\mathbf{X}$ of length N are defined by

$$\mathbf{Y} = \mathbf{AX} \qquad (2.81)$$

where $\mathbf{X}$ is the input column vector of length N, $\mathbf{A}$ is an $N \times N$ transform matrix, and $\mathbf{Y}$ is the random vector of transform coefficients.

Second-order statistics of $\mathbf{Y}$ are described by

$$\mathbf{R}_{yy} = E[\mathbf{YY}^T] = \mathbf{A}\,\mathbf{R}_{xx}\,\mathbf{A}^T \qquad (2.82)$$

If $\mathbf{A}$ is the so-called *Karhunen-Loeve Transform* (KLT) for the input process, $\mathbf{R}_{yy}$ will be diagonal. This special *covariance-diagonalizing* transform is input-process-specific by definition and therefore complex to implement. Suboptimum linear transforms such as the Discrete Fourier Transform (DFT) approach the above ideal of diagonalization for special input models or classes. We shall see later why the diagonalization of $\mathbf{R}_{yy}$ is an important ideal in transform coding. We shall merely note at this point that a side result of such diagonalization will be that the transform coefficient variances $R_{yy}(i,i) = \sigma_i^2$; $i = 0,1,...,N-1$ (the main diagonal elements of $\mathbf{R}_{yy}$) will be *unequal*, unlike the main diagonal elements in the Toeplitz matrix $\mathbf{R}_{xx}$, which are equal by definition. The success of Transform Coding depends in fact on this ordering of coefficient variances and the related strategy of *variable bit allocation*. In the KLT, the main diagonal elements of $\mathbf{R}_{yy}$ are called the *eigenvalues* λ_i that are characteristic of the input process. The *arithmetic mean* of λ_i; $i = 0,1,...,N-1$ is merely the input variance σ_x^2 [see (2.63b)]; and for $N \rightarrow \infty$, we can use (2.63a) and (2.67) to show that the *geometric mean* is the input-specific parameter η_x^2 defined earlier. This is the numerator of (2.74), a measure of input redundancy.

For a white input spectrum, $\eta_x^2 = \sigma_x^2$; in this special case, the linear redundancy is zero, the gains due to predictive coding and transform coding are both 0 dB, and efficient digitization can be realized by a simple PCM coder (Chapter 5).

2.4 Model Sources with Special Correlations and Spectra

In the preceding sections we have defined various quantities that give a partial description of a random process. The quantities of main interest are the pdf, the acf and the psd. Measurements of these properties are simplified if the process can be assumed to be ergodic. With such a process, statistics can be computed simply by averaging over a sample sequence. In the case of a stationary process, the psd is an equivalent description of the acf, and the spectral flatness measure is a compact description of waveform redundancy. Finally, in the case of a Gaussian process, probability distributions are completely defined by its mean and autocorrelation functions.

Waveforms such as speech are not Gaussian, ergodic, or stationary. However, *local stationarity* or *quasi-stationarity* makes random process models very meaningful for short-time descriptions. In fact, even long-time-averaged random process descriptions have demonstrated their value in terms of improving coder design and performance.

The purpose of this section is to describe model sources characterized mainly by special acf and psd functions; we shall subsequently use these as simple probabilistic models for the speech and image statistics described in Section 2.2. These simple models will be used to derive physical insight as well as to provide bases for analytical design. Some of the models are appropriate for globally averaged or *long-time-averaged* descriptions, while some models (for example, the autoregressive model for voiced speech) are excellent descriptions of *short-time* behavior.

2.4.1 Discrete-Time Models

Equations (2.49), (2.50) and (2.72) have specified the effect of linear filters on the mean, acf and psd of an input process. Interesting classes of discrete-time linear processes can be generated by passing *constant-psd* or *white-noise* sequences through a linear, time-invariant filter with impulse response $h(n)$ (Figure 2.14). A wide-sense-stationary zero-mean white-noise process $\{Z(n)\}$ is defined by

$$S_{zz}(e^{j\omega}) = \sigma_z^2 \qquad (2.83)$$

$$R_{zz}(k) = E[Z(n)Z(n+k)] = \sigma_z^2\, \delta(k) \; ; \qquad \delta(k) = \begin{cases} 1 & \text{for } k = 0 \\ 0 & \text{otherwise} \end{cases} \qquad (2.84)$$

In (2.84), $\delta(k)$ is the *Kronecker delta* function. For any nonzero time lag k there is zero correlation between the samples of the process. Suppose that this white-noise or *innovations* signal is passed through a linear time-invariant filter whose transfer function $H(z)$ is a rational function of z. Such a function can be represented as a ratio of two polynomials in z:

$$H(z) = \frac{A(z)}{B(z)} = \frac{\displaystyle\sum_{j=0}^{M} a_j z^{-j}}{1 - \displaystyle\sum_{j=1}^{N} b_j z^{-j}} \qquad (2.85)$$

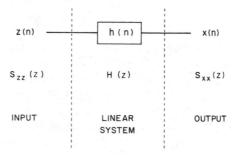

Figure 2.14   Linear system with wide-sense-stationary input and output.

with N poles (roots of the denominator polynomial) and M zeros (roots of the numerator polynomial). The output is given by the difference equation

$$X(n) = \sum_{j=0}^{M} a_j Z(n-j) + \sum_{j=1}^{N} b_j X(n-j) \tag{2.86}$$

If the filter impulse response is absolutely summable, the filter is stable and its output is a wide-sense stationary process $\{X(n)\}$ with an acf (Problem 2.10)

$$R_{xx}(k) = R_{zz}(k) * h(k) * h(-k) = \sigma_z^2 \sum_{j=0}^{\infty} h(j)h(j+|k|) \tag{2.87a}$$

with zero mean

$$E[X(n)] = 0 \tag{2.87b}$$

and a z-transform

$$S_{xx}(z) = \sigma_z^2 H(z) H(z^{-1}) \tag{2.88}$$

The average power in the output (Problem 2.10) is

$$E[X^2(n)] = R_{xx}(0) = \sigma_x^2 = \sigma_z^2 \sum_{j=0}^{\infty} h^2(j) \tag{2.89}$$

The ratio of the variances of the source and the innovations will be called the *power transfer factor*

$$\alpha = \sigma_x^2/\sigma_z^2 = \sum_{j=0}^{\infty} h^2(j) = \frac{1}{2\pi} \int_{-\pi}^{\pi} |H(e^{j\omega})|^2 d\omega \tag{2.90}$$

The factor α is the energy in the impulse response, and the right-hand equality in (2.90) is due to *Parseval's theorem*. Since $\{Z(n)\}$ is a white process, the coloring or non-flatness of the psd of $\{X(n)\}$ is due entirely to $H(z)$. In fact, for any rational $S_{xx}(e^{j\omega})$, *the sfm is just the inverse of the power transfer factor* (Problem 2.11) if $h(0)$ is normalized to unity:

$$\gamma_x^2 = \sigma_z^2/\sigma_x^2 = \alpha^{-1} \qquad (2.91)$$

In the specific models used in the rest of this section, the value of $h(0)$ is indeed unity. If this normalization is not ensured, the power transfer factor will include a gain or scaling factor that will be irrelevant to spectral shaping. In the degenerate case of $h(j) = 0$ for all $j \neq 0$, and $h(0) \neq 1$, the filter will not color the white input, but it will simply scale it by a factor $h(0) \neq 1$. The value of α will be $h^2(0) \neq 1$, but the value of *sfm* will continue to be unity, the value characteristic of a white psd according to (2.74). In other words, the *sfm* will *not* be the reciprocal of α in this un-normalized case.

From (2.86), each r.v. of the process can be generated from the input and linear combinations of previous inputs and outputs. It is useful to consider in some detail two special cases that have proven to be of importance in modeling waveform sequences: processes that result from filtering white noise with either an *infinite impulse response* filter or a *finite impulse response* filter. In the first case the process is called an *all-pole process*, an *autoregressive* (AR) *process* or a *Markov process*. In the second case, the process is called an *all-zero process*, or a *moving average* (MA) *process*. The process described by (2.85) and (2.86) includes AR and MA terms and is sometimes called an *autoregressive moving average* (ARMA) *process*.

2.4.2 Autoregressive or All-Pole Processes

An autoregressive (AR) process is generated by passing the *innovations* or *white-noise* process $\{Z(n)\}$ of psd $S_{zz}(z) = \sigma_z^2$ through a filter

$$B(z) = \cfrac{1}{1 - \sum\limits_{j=1}^{N} b_j z^{-j}} = \cfrac{z^N}{z^N - \sum\limits_{j=1}^{N} b_j z^{N-j}} \qquad (2.92)$$

This transfer function is termed *all-pole* since the N multiple zeros at $z = 0$ are trivial. The following is a difference equation which generates the AR process $\{X(n)\}$:

$$X(n) = Z(n) + \sum_{j=1}^{N} b_j X(n-j) \qquad (2.93)$$

The process $\{X(n)\}$ is called an AR(N) *process* or an *Nth order Markov process*. The sample sequences are also called *Markov-N* sequences or *autoregressive* sequences, and the b_j are called *autoregressive constants*. Figure 2.15 shows the filter that realizes the AR-process, with z^{-1} denoting unit delay.

The impulse response of an all-pole filter is not finite in general. However, the acf of the output process $\{X(n)\}$ can be calculated recursively for any given set of coefficients b_j; $j = 1,2,...,N$. This is seen by multiplying $X(n)$ in (2.93) with $X(n-k)$ and taking expectations on both sides of the equation; and by noting that $E[Z(n)X(n-k)] = 0$ for $k > 0$ because the innovations signal $Z(n)$ is by definition uncorrelated with past outputs. As a result of the above steps,

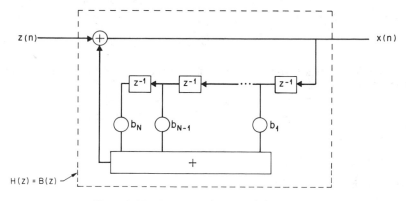

Figure 2.15 Generation of an AR(N) process.

$$\sigma_x^2 = R_{xx}(0) = \sum_{j=1}^{N} b_j R_{xx}(j) + \sigma_z^2 \qquad (2.94)$$

$$R_{xx}(k) = \sum_{j=1}^{N} b_j R_{xx}(k-j) ; \qquad k > 0 \qquad (2.95)$$

For a given set of AR constants b_j; $j=1,2,...,N$ (a given all-pole filter), the values $R_{xx}(k)$ for $k = 0,1,...,N$ can be solved recursively via fast algorithms [Atal and Hanauer, 1971]. For $k > N$, (2.95) can be used to calculate all needed acf-values $R_{xx}(k)$ successively as the linear combination of acf predecessors weighted by the set of coefficients b_j; $j = 1,2,...,N$. A very related problem is that of finding the set b_j; $j = 1,2,...,N$ of coefficients of a recursive filter whose first N output acf-values match a set of N given or measured acf-values. For $k = 1,2,...,N$, we obtain from (2.95) a set of N linear equations for those coefficients b_j, $j = 1,2,...,N$ in terms of given acf values. Chapter 6 will discuss the problem of solving this set of linear equations. The coefficients b_j will be shown to be numerically identical to a set of *optimum predictor coefficients*.

Example 2.3. First-order Markov or AR(1) process:
  The AR(1) process with zero mean, $N = 1$ and $b_1 = \rho$ is generated by

$$X(n) = Z(n) + \rho X(n-1) \qquad (2.96)$$

$$= Z(n) + \sum_{j=1}^{\infty} \rho^j Z(n-j) \qquad (2.97)$$

i.e., by passing white noise of variance σ_z^2 through a filter with impulse response

$$h(n) = \begin{cases} \rho^n & \text{for } n \geqslant 0 \\ \\ 0 & \text{for } n < 0 \end{cases} \qquad (2.98)$$

and frequency response

$$H(e^{j\omega}) = (1 - \rho e^{-j\omega})^{-1} \qquad (2.99)$$

which is that of a first-order all-pole filter. We shall now calculate the acf $R_{xx}(k)$. From (2.97),

$$X(n+k) = Z(n+k) + \sum_{l=1}^{\infty} \rho^l Z(n+k-l) \qquad (2.100)$$

Hence

$$R_{xx}(k) = E[X(n)X(n+k)]$$

$$= R_{zz}(k) + \sum_{j=1}^{\infty} \rho^j R_{zz}(k+j) + \sum_{l=n}^{\infty} \rho^l R_{zz}(k-l) + \sum_{j=1}^{\infty}\sum_{l=1}^{\infty} \rho^j \rho^l R_{zz}(k+j-l) \qquad (2.101)$$

With $R_{zz}(k) = \sigma_z^2 \delta(k)$, and the identity $1 + \sum_{j=1}^{\infty} \rho^{2j} = (1-\rho^2)^{-1}$,

$$\sigma_x^2 = R_{xx}(0) = \frac{\sigma_z^2}{1 - \rho^2} \; ; \qquad R_{xx}(k) = \sigma_x^2 \rho^{|k|} \qquad (2.102)$$

Note that acf values could also have been calculated recursively using (2.95):

$$\rho_k = \rho_{xx}(k) = \rho \, \rho_{xx}(k-1) = \rho^k \qquad (2.103)$$

The first part of (2.102) also implies that the *sfm* is

$$\gamma_x^2 = 1 - \rho^2 = \alpha^{-1} \qquad (2.104)$$

The spectrum is flat for $\rho = 0$ and $\gamma_x^2 \to 0$ for $\rho \to 1$. The special case of $\rho=1$ is the *Wiener process* to be discussed in Example 2.4.

The psd of the AR(1) process is

$$S_{xx}(e^{j\omega}) = \sigma_z^2 |H(e^{j\omega})|^2 = \frac{1 - \rho^2}{1 + \rho^2 - 2\rho \cos \omega} \sigma_x^2 \qquad (2.105)$$

and the reader may wish to verify (Problem 2.12) that this psd indeed has the *sfm* value of $\gamma_x^2 = (1-\rho^2)$. Note that the AR constant b_1 is the first normalized acf value of the AR(1) process, i.e., $b_1 = \rho = \rho_1$.

The process is stationary if the filter is stable; therefore we require that $|\rho| < 1$, since

$$\sum_{n=0}^{\infty} |h(n)| = (1 - |\rho|)^{-1} \qquad (2.106)$$

is then finite. Figures 2.16(a) and 2.16(b) discuss examples of $\rho = 0.9$ and $\rho = -0.9$, respectively. In each of the figures (a) and (b), (i) is a segment of a sample sequence, (ii) is the normalized acf, and (iii) is the psd. Note that the acf takes a long time to decay in the case of a large positive correlation $\rho = 0.9$. The smooth nature of $x(n)$ in this case is also reflected in the psd of Figure 2.16(a), which has a *lowpass* characteristic. In Figure 2.16(b), where $\rho = -0.9$, adjacent samples are highly negatively correlated and the acf oscillates; and the psd has a *highpass* characteristic.

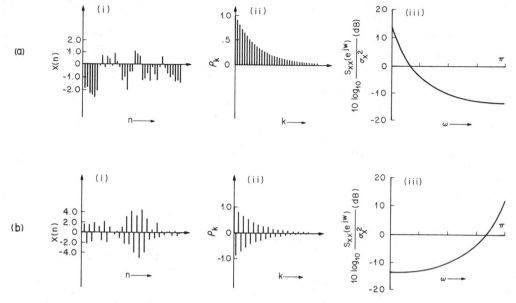

Figure 2.16 First-order Markov or AR(1) process: (i) typical sequence $x(n)$; (ii) acf ρ_k [Jenkins and Watts, 1968. Reprinted with permission]; and (iii) psd $S_{xx}(e^{j\omega})$; for (a) $\rho = 0.9$ and (b) $\rho = -0.9$.

Finally, the first-order Markov process has an Lth *order* correlation matrix $\mathbf{R}_{xx} = E[\mathbf{X}\,\mathbf{X}^T]$ with elements $R_{xx}(k-l) = \sigma_x^2\,\rho^{|k-l|}$:

$$\mathbf{R}_{xx} = \sigma_x^2 \begin{bmatrix} 1 & \rho & \rho^2 & \cdot & \cdot & \rho^{L-1} \\ \rho & 1 & \rho & & & \cdot \\ \rho^2 & \rho & 1 & \rho & \cdot & \cdot \\ \cdot & & \rho & 1 & \cdot & \cdot \\ \cdot & & & \rho & \cdot & \rho \\ \rho^{L-1} & \cdot & \cdot & & \cdot & 1 \end{bmatrix} \tag{2.107}$$

which is of course symmetric Toeplitz. Its eigenvalues are (Section 2.3) samples of the psd (2.105). They can be obtained as roots of the characteristic polynomial [Berger, 1971]. Also, see Example 12.3. For highly correlated processes ($\rho \to 1$), the eigenfrequencies Ω_k are uniformly distributed in $(0,\pi)$; and the eigenvectors are sampled sine waves with phases depending on Ω_k. ●

Example 2.4. Wiener process

We have stated that the process generated by (2.96) is stationary for $|\rho| < 1$. We will now show that a nonstationary process results if $\rho = 1$. Let the process start at $k = 1$. At time n,

$$X(n) = \sum_{k=1}^{n} Z(k) \tag{2.108}$$

If $\{Z(n)\}$ is assumed to be stationary with mean μ_z and variance σ_z^2, the output process then has a *linearly increasing* mean value and variance:

$$E[X(n)] = n\mu_z \; ; \qquad E[(X(n)-n\mu_z)^2] = n\sigma_z^2 \qquad (2.109)$$

The process $\{X(n)\}$ is called a *random walk* since the increment $X(n) - X(n-1) = Z(n)$ at time instant n is not correlated with increments at any other time instant. This process is also called a *Wiener process*. ●

Example 2.5. Second-order Markov or AR(2) process

The AR(2) process of zero mean is generated by

$$X(n) = Z(n) + b_1 X(n-1) + b_2 X(n-2) \qquad (2.110)$$

i.e., by passing white noise through a second-order all-pole filter with transfer function

$$H(z) = (1 - b_1 z^{-1} - b_2 z^{-2})^{-1} \qquad (2.111)$$

It can be shown that the impulse response and acf can both be described by oscillatory terms with exponentially damped amplitudes. Figure 2.17 is an example with $b_1 = 1.0$, $b_2 = -0.5$. It shows (a) an illustrative realization of $\{X(n)\}$, (b) the acf and (c) the psd. Note that unlike with an AR(1) process, it is now possible to produce spectra with a peak or a trough at an intermediate angular frequency. The psd is given (Problem 2.15) by

$$S_{xx}(e^{j\omega}) = \sigma_z^2 |H(e^{j\omega})|^2 = \frac{1}{1 + b_1^2 + b_2^2 - 2b_1(1-b_2)\cos\omega - 2b_2\cos 2\omega}\sigma_x^2 \qquad (2.112)$$

Figure 2.17 Second-order Markov or AR(2) process: (a) typical sequence $x(n)$; (b) acf ρ_k [Jenkins and Watts, 1968. Reprinted with permission]; (c) psd $S_{xx}(e^{j\omega})$ for $b_1 = 1.0$ and $b_2 = -0.5$; and (d) admissible regions for b_1 and b_2.

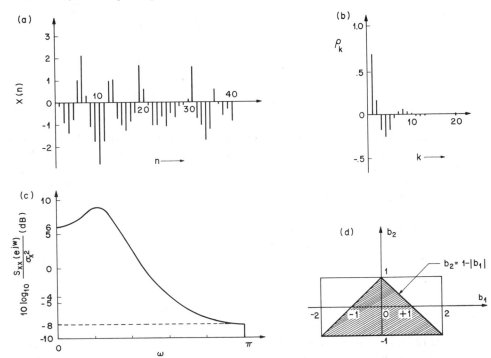

It has an extremum at a frequency $\omega = \arccos [b_1(b_2-1)/(4b_2)]$; the extremum is a maximum if $b_2 < 0$ (Problem 2.15). The roots of the denominator polynomial [the poles $z_{\infty1,2}$ of $H(z)$] may be real or conjugate complex. The filter is stable if the poles are inside the unit circle ($|z_{\infty1,2}| < 1$). It is not difficult to show that b_1 and b_2 are bounded by $b_2 + b_1 < 1$; $b_2 - b_1 < 1$, and $|b_2| < 1$. Figure 2.17(d) shows this stability region.

The acf values, obtained from (2.94) and (2.95), satisfy

$$\rho_k = b_1\rho_{k-1} + b_2\rho_{k-2}; \quad k > 0 \tag{2.113}$$

Therefore, since $\rho_0 = 1$ and $\rho_{-1} = \rho_1$, we have

$$\rho_1 = \frac{b_1}{1 - b_2}; \qquad \rho_2 = b_2 + \frac{b_1^2}{1 - b_2} \tag{2.114}$$

Note that all acf-values ρ_k; $k > 2$ can be determined recursively. Also, (2.114) can be solved for the AR coefficients:

$$b_1 = \frac{\rho_1(1-\rho_2)}{1 - \rho_1^2}; \qquad b_2 = \frac{\rho_2 - \rho_1^2}{1 - \rho_1^2} \tag{2.115}$$

Figure 2.17(d) has already shown the admissible region for these filter coefficients for stability. We may also calculate the admissible region for ρ_1 and ρ_2 from it. This will be the same as the admissible region for *positive semi-definiteness* of $\mathbf{R}_{xx}$, in Figure 2.13. For the example of Figure 2.17 ($b_1 = 1.0$, $b_2 = -0.5$), (2.114) shows that $\rho_1 = 2/3$ and $\rho_2 = 1/6$. Also, using (2.90), the spectral flatness measure is $\gamma_x^2 = 0.417$ (Problem 2.15). An AR(1) process with the same $\rho_1 = 2/3$, on the other hand, would have $\gamma_x^2 = 0.55$. $\quad\bullet$

The importance of AR processes lies in the fact that a wide variety of acf's (and psd's) can be produced from them, for modeling stationary processes. The AR(1) model is a good analytical tool for first-order prediction analysis; the AR(2) provides a good fit to the long-time-averaged second-order statistics of speech (damped sinusoidal acf and peaked psd); and AR(N) models with $N \geq 10$ are appropriate for adequate short-term descriptions of voiced speech [Markel and Gray, 1976] [Flanagan et al., 1979]. This is seen in the AR(N) simulations of a voiced speech spectrum in Figure 2.18, with $N = 6, 8, 10$ and 12. The five curves in the figure have been vertically separated out for clarity. The separation does *not* indicate differences in average power level across the different curves. The actual spectrum, the uppermost characteristic in the figure, includes the fine structure due to pitch periodicity. The characteristic also exhibits four peaks in spectral envelope, indicated by dark triangular spikes, and these peaks are well reflected in the AR(N) model spectra with $N = 10$ and 12. It will be interesting to compare the spectra of Figure 2.18 with that of Figure 2.10(a). In that spectrum, the zeros are more pronounced than the poles. This has to do with the fact that the Fourier transform operation used to obtain that spectrum is a *finite impulse response (all-zero)* operation, as implied in the transfer function (2.116) to be mentioned presently.

The importance of AR processes will become quite evident in Chapter 6 where DPCM coders and decoders will be matched to the psd of the waveform to be transmitted, by using an AR model of its psd. We will also see there that optimum

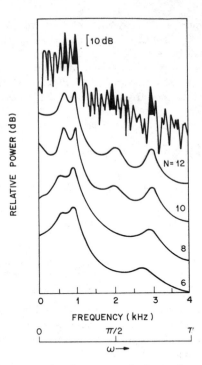

Figure 2.18 AR(N) spectrum models for short-term voiced speech example; $N = 6, 8, 10$ and 12 [Flanagan et al.;©1979, IEEE].

predictor coefficients $h_{j,opt}$ used for this matching are indeed equal to the autoregressive coefficients b_j. The redundancy of AR(N) waveforms can be completely removed by linear prediction of order N.

2.4.3 Moving Average or All-Zero Processes

A moving average (MA) process is generated by passing a white noise sequence $\{Z(n)\}$ with psd $S_{zz}(z) = \sigma_z^2$ through a filter with an *all-zero* transfer function

$$A(z) = \sum_{j=0}^{M} a_j z^{-j} \qquad (2.116)$$

The psd of the generated process $\{X(n)\}$ is

$$S_{xx}(z) = \sigma_z^2 A(z) A(z^{-1}) \qquad (2.117)$$

The MA(M) process is generated by the difference equation

$$X(n) = \sum_{j=0}^{M} a_j Z(n-j) \qquad (2.118)$$

and the structure of the filter is shown in Figure 2.19. The impulse response of the all-zero filter is

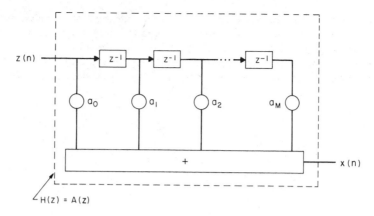

Figure 2.19 Generation of a MA(M) process.

$$h(n) = \begin{cases} a_n & \text{for } n = 0,1,...,M \\ \\ 0 & \text{otherwise} \end{cases} \tag{2.119}$$

The acf of the moving average process (Problem 2.18) will therefore be

$$R_{xx}(k) = \begin{cases} \sigma_z^2 \sum\limits_{j=0}^{M-|k|} a_j a_{j+k} & \text{for } |k| \leqslant M \\ \\ 0 & \text{otherwise} \end{cases} \tag{2.120}$$

$\{X(n)\}$ is a stationary process if the filter is stable, i.e., if its impulse response is absolutely summable:

$$\sum_{j=0}^{M} |a_j| < \infty \tag{2.121}$$

Note the important fact that for finite M, the impulse response is finite and therefore the acf is also finite.

Example 2.6. MA(1) process

The MA(1) process with zero mean and $a_0 = 1$ is generated by

$$X(n) = Z(n) + a_1 Z(n-1) \tag{2.122}$$

i.e., each output of the two-tap filter is a weighted sum of the actual input sample and its predecessor. It is easy to verify that

$$\sigma_x^2 = R_{xx}(0) = \sigma_z^2(1 + a_1^2) \tag{2.123}$$

$$\rho_{xx}(1) = \frac{a_1}{1 + a_1^2} \quad \text{and} \quad \rho_{xx}(k) = 0 \quad ; \quad |k| > 1 \tag{2.124}$$

Note that (2.122) causes correlations between neighboring samples, and that unlike in the AR process we have to solve a *nonlinear* equation to obtain a_1 from a specified $\rho_{xx}(1)$. Also unlike in an AR(1) process, the requirement of zero $\rho_{xx}(k)$ for $|k|>1$ in (2.124) is reflected in constraints on allowable $\rho_{xx}(1)$. In fact, by setting $\rho_{xx}(2) = \rho_2 = 0$ in Figure 2.13, we see that $\rho_{xx}(1) \leqslant 1/\sqrt{2}$ (also see Problem 2.16). Note that (2.124) signifies a matrix

$$\mathbf{R}_{xx} = \sigma_x^2 \begin{bmatrix} 1 & \rho_1 & 0 & \cdot & \cdot & 0 \\ \rho_1 & 1 & \rho_1 & \cdot & & \cdot \\ 0 & \rho_1 & 1 & \cdot & & \cdot \\ \cdot & & & & & \\ \cdot & & & & 1 & \rho_1 \\ 0 & & & & \rho_1 & 1 \end{bmatrix} \tag{2.125}$$

From (2.68), the psd is

$$S_{xx}(e^{j\omega}) = \sigma_z^2(1 + a_1^2 + 2a_1\cos \omega) \tag{2.126}$$

If $a_1 = 1$ *(sum filter)*, the psd is a simple *raised cosine, lowpass* characteristic. If $a_1 = -1$ *(difference filter)*, the spectrum is *highpass*.

The correlation matrix $\mathbf{R}_{xx}$ of order L can be used to determine its eigenvalues:

$$\lambda_k = S_{xx}(e^{j\Omega_k}) \; ; \qquad k = 0,1,...,L-1 \tag{2.127}$$

$$\Omega_k = \pi \frac{k+1}{L+1} \; ; \qquad k = 0,1,...,L-1 \tag{2.128}$$

i.e., the eigenvalues are equally spaced samples of the psd in this specific example. The eigenvectors have sampled sine-wave values as its elements:

$$\mathbf{l}_k = \{\sin(n+1)\,\Omega_k\}_{n-0,1,...,L-1} \; ; \qquad k=0,1,...,L-1 \tag{2.129a}$$

From (2.91) and (2.126) the *sfm* of the MA(1) process is

$$\gamma_x^2 = (1 + a_1^2)^{-1} \tag{2.129b} \quad \bullet$$

Constraints on acf values exist for higher-order MA processes as well. For example, the admissible region for (ρ_1, ρ_2) in a MA(2) process with $\rho_{xx}(k) = 0; |k|>2$, is a subset of the (ρ_1, ρ_2) admissible region of Figure 2.13, and its coefficients a_1 and a_2 have the same admissible region as b_1 and b_2 in Figure 2.17(d). The *sfm* of the MA(2) process is given in Problem 2.17.

2.4.4 First-Order Models for Two-Dimensional Sources

Consider a random field in which the mean does not depend on spatial coordinates, i.e.,

$$\mu_{x(m,n)} = \mu_x = constant \quad \text{for all } m,n \tag{2.130}$$

and in which the acf is translation-invariant. The acf can then be written as a function of two variables

$$R_{xx}(k_h, k_v) = E[X(m,n)X(m+k_h, n+k_v)] \qquad (2.131)$$

where h and v refer to *horizontal* and *vertical* directions. Random fields which obey the above two equations are called *homogeneous*. They are *wide-sense-stationary* random fields with a psd-acf description

$$S_{xx}(e^{j\omega_1}, e^{j\omega_2}) = \sum_{k_h} \sum_{k_v} R_{xx}(k_h, k_v) e^{-j\omega_1 k_h} e^{-j\omega_2 k_v} \qquad (2.132a)$$

$$R_{xx}(k_h, k_v) = \left(\frac{1}{2\pi}\right)^2 \int_{-\pi}^{\pi}\int_{-\pi}^{\pi} S_{xx}(e^{j\omega_1}, e^{j\omega_2}) e^{j\omega_1 k_h} e^{j\omega_2 k_v} d\omega_1 d\omega_2 \qquad (2.132b)$$

The interpretation of psd is very similar to that for 1-D signals. For example, if all values of $R_{xx}(k_h, k_v)$ are zero except $R_{xx}(0,0)$, the psd is white in both spatial directions:

$$R_{xx}(k_h, k_v) = \sigma_x^2 \delta(k_h, k_v) ; \qquad S_{xx}(e^{jw_1}, e^{jw_2}) = \sigma_x^2 \qquad (2.133)$$

According to experimental data, the acf of a large variety image data follow one of two models — the *separable* model appropriate especially to many artificial or man-made images; and the *isotropic* model appropriate especially to images of natural objects [Pratt, 1978]. Using earlier nomenclature, we shall discuss corresponding discrete-space models as *discrete-time* models.

The Separable acf Model. In continuous coordinates, an important acf model is the stationary first-order Markov model

$$R_{xx}(k'_h, k'_v) = \sigma_x^2 \exp(-\alpha|k'_h| - \beta|k'_v|) \qquad (2.134)$$

where k'_h and k'_v are the spatial shifts in horizontal and vertical image directions and α and β describe respective amounts of correlation. The model (2.134) is called *separable* because of the absence of terms like $k'^p_h k'^q_v$ $(p,q \neq 0)$ in the acf expression (2.134). Let us use a spatially discretized description, with

$$\rho_h = e^{-\alpha} ; \qquad \rho_v = e^{-\beta} \qquad (2.135)$$

Setting (2.135) in (2.134), and using integer-valued variables k_h and k_v,

$$R_{xx}(k_h, k_v) = \sigma_x^2 \rho_h^{|k_h|} \rho_v^{|k_v|} \qquad (2.136)$$

Adjacent rows and columns in a square grid of pixels (Figure 2.20) are separated by unit distances $k_h = 1$ and $k_v = 1$, respectively. Note the special case

$$R_{xx}(k_h, k_v) = \sigma_x^2 \rho^{|k_h| + |k_v|} \quad \text{if} \quad \rho_v = \rho_h = \rho , \qquad (2.137a)$$

which is a generalization of the 1-D expression in (2.102).

From (2.137a), the normalized correlation between *diagonal neighbors* [case of $k_h = 1$, $k_v = 1$ in (2.137a) as well as in Table 2.3] is

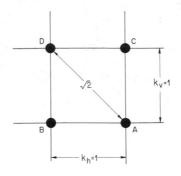

Figure 2.20 A (2 × 2) grid of pixels.

$$\rho_{AD} = \rho_{BC} = \rho_{xx}(1,1) = \rho^{1+1} = \rho^2 \qquad (2.137b)$$

whereas *horizontal and vertical neighbors* have the correlations

$$\rho_{AB} = \rho_{AC} = \rho_{CD} = \rho_{BD} = \rho^{0+1} = \rho^{1+0} = \rho \qquad (2.137c)$$

The separable model is matched to images wherein contours of equal autocorrelation are rectangles or squares with horizontal and vertical edges, as in Figure 2.21(a).

A discrete random field with a separable acf and with equal correlations in the two spatial directions can be represented by the difference equation

$$X(m,n) = b\ X(m,n-1) + c\ X(m-1,n) + d\ X(m-1,n-1) + Z(m,n) \quad (2.138)$$

$$b = c = \rho\ ; \qquad d = -\rho^2\ ; \qquad |\rho| \leqslant 1 \qquad (2.139)$$

where $\{(Z(m,n)\}$ is a 2-D zero-mean random field of uncorrelated r.v.'s with common variance σ_z^2. This yields a source variance (Problem 2.19)

Figure 2.21 Constant-acf contours in (a) separable and (b) circularly symmetric (isotropic) 2-D Markov processes.

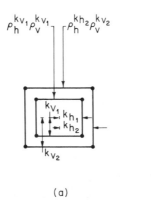

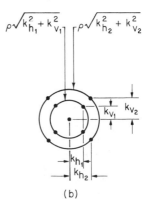

(a)

(b)

$$\sigma_x^2 = \sigma_z^2 \ (1-\rho^2)^{-2} \qquad (2.140a)$$

The recursive formula (2.138) can also be interpreted as the output of a 2-D recursive filter with $\{Z(m,n)\}$ as input. Its transfer function $H(e^{j\omega_1}, e^{j\omega_2})$ is given in (A.42), and conditions for its stability are given in Example 6.9. Using earlier nomenclature, $X(m,n)$ in (2.138) is an *autoregressive* or *Markov* process, a generalization of the 1-D process (2.96). From (2.140a), the *sfm* of the process (Problem 2.19) is

$$\gamma_x^2 = (1 - \rho^2)^2 \qquad (2.140b)$$

The Isotropic acf Model. The acf model

$$R_{xx}(k'_h, k'_v) = \sigma_x^2 \exp(-\alpha k') = \sigma_x^2 \exp[-\alpha(k_h'^2 + k_v'^2)^{1/2}] \qquad (2.141)$$

describes, with continuous co-ordinates, a 2-D acf model whose spatial behavior is describable by a single Euclidean distance term k'. The rotational symmetry of the model suggests that it is appropriate [O'Neal and Natarajan, 1977] for natural objects with no preferred orientation. The function in (2.141) is called *isotropic*; unlike (2.134), it is *non-separable*. Using discrete-space co-ordinates k_h and k_v for horizontal and vertical separation, and with

$$\exp(-\alpha) = \rho, \qquad (2.142)$$

$$R_{xx}(k_h, k_v) = \sigma_x^2 \ \rho^{(k_h^2 + k_h^2)^{1/2}} \qquad (2.143)$$

Contours of equal autocorrelation are circles, as in Figure 2.21(b). Normalized values of adjacent pixel correlations (Figure 2.20) are

$$\rho_{AB} = \rho_{CD} = \rho_{AC} = \rho_{BD} = \rho_{xx}(1,0) = \rho_{xx}(0,1) = \rho \qquad (2.144)$$

and the diagonal neighbor correlation (Figure 2.20) is

$$\rho_{BC} = \rho_{AD} = \rho_{xx}(1,1) = \rho^{\sqrt{2}} \qquad (2.145)$$

2.4.5 Models in the Continuous-Time Domain

Most communication signals are originally continuous-time signals; sampling leads to discrete-time sequences which are almost always assumed in this book. However, we will sometimes need a description of the original continuous-time process as well. One example is the traditional modeling of a correlated source by the output of a resistor-capacitor network driven by white noise (Chapter 8). A second application of continuous-time descriptions is in the discussion of the effects of bandpass filtering and sampling on analog signal reconstruction (Chapter 3).

The autocorrelation function (acf) of a stationary, continuous-time random process $\{X(t)\}$ is

$$R_{xx}(\tau) = E[X(t)X(t+\tau)] = \int_{-\infty}^{\infty} \int_{-\infty}^{\infty} xy \, p_{x(t)x(t+\tau)}(x,y)\,dx\,dy \qquad (2.146)$$

where τ is the time lag. The normalized acf is $\rho_{xx}(\tau) = R_{xx}(\tau)/R_{xx}(0)$, and the properties for acf's of discrete-time processes apply also to the continuous-time case. The psd is

$$S_{xx}(\Omega) = \int_{-\infty}^{\infty} R_{xx}(\tau) e^{-j\Omega\tau} d\tau \qquad (2.147)$$

provided that $R_{xx}(\tau)$ is absolutely integrable. The inverse operation yields

$$R_{xx}(\tau) = \frac{1}{2\pi} \int_{-\infty}^{\infty} S_{xx}(\Omega) e^{j\Omega\tau} d\Omega \qquad (2.148)$$

The mean power in the process is

$$\sigma_x^2 = R_{xx}(0) = E[X^2(t)] = \frac{1}{2\pi} \int_{-\infty}^{\infty} S_{xx}(\Omega) d\Omega \qquad (2.149)$$

Many techniques given in the literature on Digital Signal Processing can be applied if a discrete-time analogue of a continuous-time system or signal has to be designed. For example, the continuous time filter that generates an analog spectrum can be transformed into an equivalent digital filter. One approach is to replace the differentials in the generating equation for $X(t)$ with finite differences, in order to obtain a difference equation that approximates the differential equation. Another possibility is to make use of the *impulse-invariant transformation*: here we choose the impulse response of the digital filter as equally spaced samples of the impulse response of the analog filter. In this case, the values of the acf $\rho_{xx}(n)$ [resulting from passing white noise sequences through a digital filter with impulse response $h(n)$] will also be samples of the continuous-time acf $\rho_{xx}(\tau)$. This will be illustrated by the equivalence of the acf's in integrated power spectrum and AR(1) processes, in Example 2.7. It must be emphasized, however, that the psd in the digital domain is never identical with the psd in the analog domain. This is due to aliasing effects (Chapter 3) and the use of samples of the continuous-time acf whose Fourier transform (the psd) may not be bandlimited.

Example 2.7. Integrated power spectra
A widely used approximation to many spectra with *lowpass* character (i.e., with a main power contribution at low frequencies) is the *integrated power spectrum* obtained at the output of a resistor-capacitor integrator network with a transfer function of the form

$$H(j\Omega) = \frac{1}{1 + j\Omega/\Omega_C} \qquad (2.150)$$

and a white-noise input $\{Z(n)\}$ of spectral density

$$S_{zz}(\Omega) = \sigma_x^2(2/\Omega_C) \qquad (2.151)$$

$H(j\Omega)$ is also named a *first-order Butterworth* lowpass filter. The output psd is

$$S_{xx}(\Omega) = S_{zz}(\Omega)|H(j\Omega)|^2 = \frac{2}{\Omega_C} \frac{\sigma_x^2}{1 + (\Omega/\Omega_C)^2} \tag{2.152}$$

Note that the above represents a psd which tends to decrease very slowly with frequency until the *corner frequency* Ω_C, after which the psd falls rapidly with frequency, with an asymptotic decay of 6 dB/octave [Figure 2.22(b)(i)].

Using (2.148) and the standard integral

$$\int_0^\infty \frac{\cos ax}{1 + x^2}\, dx = \frac{\pi}{2} e^{-|a|}, \tag{2.153}$$

we obtain an exponential acf

$$R_{xx}(\tau) = \sigma_x^2 \exp(-\Omega_C|\tau|); \qquad \rho_{xx}(\tau) = \exp(-\Omega_C|\tau|) \tag{2.154}$$

That is, the spectral density is that of a process $\{X(n)\}$ whose acf has a Laplacian (two-sided) exponential characteristic [Figure 2.22(a)(i)]. The frequency Ω_C is the -3 dB point

Figure 2.22 Plots of (a) acf and (b) psd for (i) the integrated power spectrum with a 6 dB per octave roll-off, and (ii) a spectrum with 12 dB per octave roll-off.

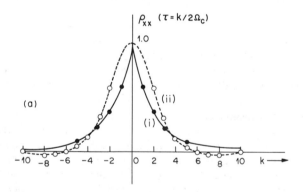

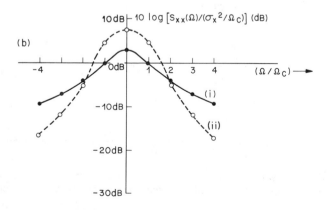

in the psd: $S_{xx}(\Omega_C) = S_{xx}(0)/2$. The acf $R_{xx}(\tau)$ could alternatively be obtained from a convolution of white noise acf and filter-acf, i.e.,

$$R_{xx}(\tau) = R_{zz}(\tau) * h(\tau) * h(-\tau); \qquad h(\tau) = \Omega_C \exp(-\Omega_C \tau); \qquad \tau \geqslant 0 \qquad (2.155)$$

We note in passing that random processes which are generated by passing a white noise process through a linear system are called *linear processes*. It can be shown that the generated process is stationary with finite variance if the impulse response is absolutely integrable. In our example, the linear process $\{X(t)\}$ can also be defined by a differential equation of the form

$$\frac{1}{\Omega_C} \frac{d}{dt} X(t) + X(t) = Z(t) \qquad (2.156)$$

which is a *continuous-time autoregressive* or *first-order Markov process*.

We will use the impulse-invariant transformation mentioned earlier to show that the integrated power spectrum process is indeed equivalent to the discrete-time Markov AR(1) process. The variance-normalized samples $\rho_{xx}(kT)$ from (2.154) define a normalized acf sequence

$$\rho_{xx}(kT) = \exp(-\Omega_C |k| T) \qquad (2.157)$$

Let ρ denote the first value of this sequence as in the discrete-time case, i.e., $\rho_{xx}(T) = \rho$. It follows immediately that

$$\rho_{xx}(kT) = \rho^{|k|} \qquad (2.158)$$

as in the acf of the AR(1) process (2.103).

Note, however, that the psd $S_{xx}(\Omega)$ cannot be reconstructed from samples $\rho_{xx}(kT)$ since it is not bandlimited; the discrete-time model can only approximate the psd $S_{xx}(\Omega)$. ●

Example 2.8. Bandlimited integrated power spectrum

The integrated power spectrum (2.152) is not bandlimited, although its power density decreases at 6 dB/octave at frequencies well above the −3 dB point. If a signal with this spectrum is to be the input to a discrete-time system, the signal has to be bandlimited to an upper frequency Ω_W which is no higher than the Nyquist frequency of the discrete-time system. Therefore the psd has to be multiplied by rect $(\Omega/2\Omega_W)$. The resultant acf is a convolution of the acf of (2.154) with $\Omega_W \operatorname{si}(\Omega_W \tau)/\pi$. An approximate result [O'Neal, 1966, I] for the normalized acf of the bandlimited signal is

$$\rho_{xx}(\tau) = \frac{\exp(-\Omega_C \tau) - \dfrac{2\Omega_C \tau}{\pi} \left[\dfrac{\cos \Omega_W \tau}{\Omega_W \tau} + \operatorname{Si}(\Omega_W \tau) - \dfrac{\pi}{2} \right]}{1 - \dfrac{2}{\pi} \dfrac{\Omega_C}{\Omega_W}} \qquad \text{for} \quad \begin{array}{l} \tau \to 0 \text{ and} \\ \Omega_C \ll \Omega_W \end{array}; \qquad (2.159)$$

$$\operatorname{Si}(x) = \frac{\pi}{2} - \int_x^{\infty} \frac{\sin t}{t} dt = \frac{\pi}{2} + \operatorname{si}(x) \qquad (2.160)$$

$\operatorname{Si}(x)$ is the *sine integral function*. The non-exponential term in (2.159) has a strong influence on the acf, especially at small values of the lag τ. Such values are particularly important in discussing the effect of oversampling a signal; the correlations between samples are then given by values $\rho_{xx}(\tau)$ close to $\tau = 0$ (Chapter 8). Table 2.4 illustrates the modeling [O'Neal, 1966, I] of three communication signals with a bandlimited integrated power spectrum. The numerical values of Ω_W and Ω_C in rows 3 and 1 of the table correspond closely with the values in the lowpass spectra of Figure 2.9.

Table 2.4 Integrated power spectrum modeling of three sources (Ω_W and Ω_C denote cutoff and corner frequencies).

Signal	$\psi = \Omega_W/\Omega_C$	$\Omega_W/2\pi$ (kHz)	$\Omega_C/2\pi$ (kHz)
Black- and- White TV	$\dfrac{2\pi}{.068}$	4500	49
Picturephone	$\dfrac{2\pi}{0.25} \sim 25$	1000	40
Telephone Speech	4	3.2	0.8

The parameter ψ is the ratio of cutoff frequency Ω_W to the corner frequency Ω_C. The numerical values of ψ in Table 2.4 will be utilized in Chapter 8 to characterize the performance of deltamodulation coders for speech and images.

The bandlimited signals above can be Nyquist-sampled at $T = f_s^{-1} = \pi/\Omega_W$. Let us compare acf values from (2.154) and (2.159) at $\tau = T$. For the picturephone example of Table 2.4, $\rho_{xx}(T) = \exp(-0.125) = 0.883$ using (2.154), and $\rho_{xx}(T) = 0.907$ using (2.159). The increase in the acf value reflects the higher relative contributions of low frequency components in the bandlimited case. One of the most significant consequences of the bandlimited model is that

$$\lim_{\tau \to 0} \rho_{xx}(\tau) \to 1 - \beta\tau^2 \; ; \qquad \beta = \Omega_W \Omega_C/\pi \tag{2.161}$$

This formulation will be very useful in prediction error analysis in differential coders, especially those involving input *oversampling*, so that $T \ll \pi/\Omega_W$ (Chapter 8).   ●

Example 2.9. 12 dB spectrum (second-order Butterworth characteristic)

Another spectrum of interest is one that falls off with a slope of 12 dB/octave at high frequencies. Its psd

$$S_{xx}(\Omega) = \frac{4\sqrt{2}\sigma_x^2}{\Omega_C} \frac{1}{1 + (\Omega/\Omega_C)^4} \tag{2.162}$$

is obtained by filtering white noise of variance $4\sqrt{2}\sigma_x^2/\Omega_C$ with a second-order Butterworth filter whose amplitude-squared frequency response is $[1 + (\Omega/\Omega_C)^4]^{-1}$.

As in the case of the integrated power spectrum, Ω_C is the 3 dB corner frequency. For speech, $\Omega_C/2\pi = 800$ Hz is a reasonable value (Figure 2.9). The acf of (2.162) is

$$\rho_{xx}(\tau) = \sqrt{2} \exp(-\Omega_C|\tau|/\sqrt{2})\sin\left[\frac{\pi}{4} + \Omega_C|\tau|/\sqrt{2}\right] \tag{2.163}$$

The psd and acf functions in (2.162) and (2.163) are shown along with those of the integrated power spectrum [equations (2.152) and (2.154)] in Figure 2.22. The relatively higher contributions of low frequency components in the 12 dB spectrum are reflected by higher values of acf for small values of delay k. Comparing these with statistics measured on speech (Figure 2.9a), one notes that neither of the two models predicts the non-monotonic nature of the speech psd. But in the frequency range of Ω_C to Ω_W (800 to 3200 Hz), the 6 dB per octave model is a better descriptor of average speech psd. On the other hand, a comparison with the LPF speech acf (Figure 2.7a) shows that the damped-cosinusoidal property (implying the presence of negative acf values) is better matched by the acf of the 12 dB model.

Bandlimitation does not affect the general shape of the acf as much as in the case of the 6 dB/octave psd—except, however, for extremely small values of time lag τ which will be of interest in oversampling (Chapter 8). ●

Example 2.10. Bandlimited white spectrum

Consider a spectrum that is uniformly distributed over a specified range (Ω_l, Ω_u) and zero outside. It is obtained by passing a white signal through a bandpass filter with center frequency $\Omega' = (\Omega_l + \Omega_u)/2$, and bandwidth $2\Delta\Omega = (\Omega_u - \Omega_l)$. The psd and acf are

$$
S_{xx}(\Omega) = \begin{cases} \pi\sigma_x^2/\Delta\Omega & \text{for } \Omega_l \leqslant |\Omega| \leqslant \Omega_u \\ 0 & \text{otherwise} \end{cases}
\tag{2.164}
$$

$$
\rho_{xx}(\tau) = \cos\left[(\Omega_l + \Omega_u)\tau/2\right] \text{ si } (\Delta\Omega\tau) = \cos \Omega'\tau \, \text{si}(\Delta\Omega\tau)
$$

Non-bandlimited *white noise* results if $\Delta\Omega \to \infty$:

$$
S_{xx}(\Omega) = \text{constant for all } \Omega \; ; \qquad \rho_{xx}(\tau) = \delta(\tau)
\tag{2.165}
$$

No two samples of this process have non-zero correlation, but the non-bandlimited process is unrealizable since its power is infinite. ●

Example 2.11. Raised cosine spectrum

A good model for voiceband data signals or modem waveforms is that described by a *raised cosine* psd:

$$
S_{xx}(\Omega) = \begin{cases} \dfrac{\pi}{\Delta\Omega} \, \sigma_x^2 \left[1 + \cos 2\pi \, \dfrac{|\Omega| - \Omega'}{2\Delta\Omega}\right] & \text{for } \Omega' - \Delta\Omega \leqslant |\Omega| \leqslant \Omega' + \Delta\Omega \\ 0 & \text{otherwise} \end{cases}
\tag{2.166}
$$

$$
\rho_{xx}(\tau) = \frac{\cos\dfrac{\Delta\Omega\tau}{2} \cos \Omega'\tau}{1 - \left[\dfrac{\Delta\Omega\tau}{\pi}\right]^2} \cdot \text{si}\left[\frac{\Delta\Omega\tau}{2}\right]
\tag{2.167} \quad ●
$$

The spectrum models discussed in Examples 2.10 and 2.11 are sketched in Figure 2.23, together with a Gaussian psd (Problem 2.21) whose center frequency is Ω', and whose four-sigma point equals the half-bandwidth $\Delta\Omega$. The psd's are

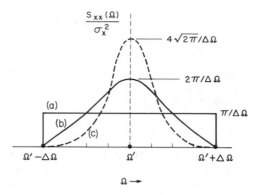

Figure 2.23 Positive-frequency halves of three psd's of equal variance σ_x^2: (a) bandlimited white- and (b) raised-cosine psd's with half-bandwidth $\Delta\Omega$; and (c) Gaussian psd with a four-sigma point of $\Delta\Omega$.

scaled such that all processes have identical variance σ_x^2. Note that these spectra are *non-lowpass* and *non-speech-like*. Digital coders designed for speech-like spectra consequently perform poorly when actual input spectra resemble those of Figure 2.23. This is the situation, for example, if voice-band data signals (analog modem waveforms, typically with a raised cosine psd) are encountered as inputs in switched telephone networks, and they are to be digitized using waveform coders designed for speech transmission.

Example 2.12. A highly structured, two-level psd

Figure 2.24 shows a *two-level* psd

$$S_{xx}(\Omega) = \begin{cases} (\pi/\Omega_W)(2-\alpha)\sigma_x^2 & \text{for } 0 \leqslant |\Omega| \leqslant \Omega_W/2 \\ (\pi/\Omega_W)\alpha\sigma_x^2 & \text{for } \Omega_W/2 \leqslant |\Omega| \leqslant \Omega_W \\ 0 & \text{for } |\Omega| > \Omega_W \end{cases} \quad (2.168)$$

with $\alpha \leqslant 1$. The psd has a variance σ_x^2 and an *sfm* given by $\gamma_x^2 = [\alpha(2-\alpha)]^{\frac{1}{2}} \sim \sqrt{2\alpha}$ if $\alpha \to 0$ (Problem 2.22). The special case of $\alpha = 1$ is simply the bandlimited white psd (with $\Omega_W = 2\Delta\Omega$). We shall see in Chapter 11 that sub-band coding with a two-filter bank is adequate to remove all the redundancy in this input process. ●

Figure 2.24 A highly structured two-level psd; bandlimited white spectra result when $\alpha = 0$ or 1.

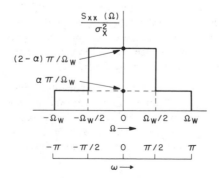

Problems

(2.1) Let $X = A \sin \phi$, where the phase ϕ has a uniform pdf $p(\phi) = \dfrac{1}{2\pi}$ in the interval $I: (0, 2\pi)$.

   (a) Show that the distribution of X is the arcsine pdf $\dfrac{1}{\pi\sqrt{A^2 - x^2}}$ for $|x| \leq A$.

   (b) Show that $\mu_x = 0$ and $\sigma_x^2 = A^2/2$.

(2.2) The pdf of an image signal can be approximately described by a uniform pdf in the interval $(0,a)$. In some differential coding systems, one considers the difference between neighboring samples as the message to be transmitted. Show that the pdf of this difference signal would be triangular in the interval $(-2a, 2a)$ if the samples of the waveform were statistically independent.

(2.3) Assume two statistically independent zero-mean Gaussian r.v.'s X and Y. Show that $Z = X+Y$ has the pdf $N(0,\sigma_x^2 + \sigma_y^2)$.

(2.4) Refer to the bivariate normal pdf (2.20).

   (a) Show that marginal pdf's $p_x(\cdot)$ and $p_y(\cdot)$ are those of $N(0,\sigma_x^2)$ and $N(0,\sigma_y^2)$ r.v.'s, respectively.

   (b) Show by computing appropriate expectations that
   (i) $E[X^2] = \sigma_x^2$
   (ii) $E[Y^2] = \sigma_y^2$
   (iii) $\rho_{xy} = E[XY]/\sigma_x \sigma_y$

   (c) Verify that the r.v.'s X and Y are statistically independent $[p_{xy}(x,y)=p_x(x)p_y(y)]$ if they are uncorrelated $(\rho_{xy}=0)$.

   (d) Show that the conditional pdf of X, assuming that $Y = y$, is

   $$p_x(x|Y=y) = \frac{1}{\sqrt{2\pi(1-\rho_{xy}^2)}\sigma_x} \exp\left[-\frac{1}{2\sigma_x^2}(1-\rho_{xy}^2)^{-1}(x - \frac{\sigma_x}{\sigma_y}\rho_{xy}y)^2\right]$$

   [Papoulis, 1965], which is the pdf of a Gaussian r.v., of mean $(\sigma_x/\sigma_y)\rho_{xy}y$, and variance $(1 - \rho_{xy}^2)\sigma_x^2$. Note that its mean depends linearly on the given value of y. The conditional expectation of x is simply $(\sigma_x\rho_{xy}/\sigma_y)y$, which in turn is simply $\rho_{xy}y$ if $\sigma_x = \sigma_y$.

(2.5) Show that the pdf of the sum of n identical independent r.v.'s with a uniform pdf in the range $(-A,A)$ approaches a $N(0,nA^2/3)$ pdf in the limit of large n. For finite n, the approximation is, of course, only valid for values well within the range $(-nA,nA)$ because the sum cannot exceed this range [Bennett, 1956]. (Hint: For independent r.v.'s, the characteristic function of the sum is the product of individual characteristic functions.)

(2.6) Let the real and imaginary components u and v of a complex r.v. (e.g., transform coefficient of Chapter 12) be zero-mean Gaussian variables with identical pdf's $N(0,\sigma^2)$. Show that the magnitude $x = \sqrt{u^2 + v^2}$ has the Rayleigh pdf $p(x) = (x/\sigma^2)\exp(-x^2/2\sigma^2)$, with $\mu_x = \sigma\sqrt{\pi/2}$, $\sigma_x^2 = (2-\pi/2)\sigma^2$. This pdf is sometimes used as a model for image amplitudes, instead of the simpler uniform pdf.

(2.7)   Show that (2.46) implies the following conditions for $N = 2,3$:

(a) $N = 2$: $|\rho_1| < 1$

(b) $N = 3$: $|\rho_1| < 1$; $|\rho_2| < 1$; $\rho_1^2 < (1+\rho_2)/2$

(2.8)   Verify the results of (2.30) and (2.31).

(2.9)   Show that the acf of $x(n) = \sin(2\pi f n)$ is cosinusoidal, also with frequency f. Use (2.3), $N \to \infty$, and assume a sampling rate that is an integral multiple of f.

(2.10)   Consider a linear, time-invariant, and stable system with impulse response $h(n)$ and a stationary random process $\{Z(n)\}$ of finite mean and variance applied to its input.

(a)   Show that the mean value of the output random process is

$$\mu_x = \mu_z \sum_{n=-\infty}^{\infty} h(n) = \mu_z H(0)$$

(b)   Use the simple case of $\mu_z = 0$ to show that

$$R_{xx}(k) = R_{zz}(k)*h(k)*h(-k) = \sum_{i=-\infty}^{\infty} \sum_{j=-\infty}^{\infty} h(i)h(j)R_{zz}(|k-i+j|)$$

$$S_{xx}(e^{j\omega}) = S_{zz}(e^{j\omega}) |H(e^{j\omega})|^2$$

(c)   Hence show that if the input $\{Z(n)\}$ is a white process,

$$R_{xx}(k) = \sigma_z^2 \sum_{j=-\infty}^{\infty} h(j)h(j+k) ;   \sigma_x^2 = \sigma_z^2 \sum_{j=0}^{\infty} h^2(j)$$

(2.11)   Let $S_{xx}(e^{j\omega})$ be a rational spectrum, i.e.,

$$S_{xx}(e^{j\omega}) = \sigma_z^2 \frac{\prod_i |e^{j\omega}-z_{oi}|^2}{\prod_i |e^{j\omega}-z_{\infty i}|^2}$$

where σ_z^2 is the variance of the "innovations" white noise process that is fed into the filter with zeroes z_{oi} and poles $z_{\infty i}$. Use the result $\int \log|e^{j\omega}-z|^2 d\omega = 0$ to show that [Bunin, 1969]

$$\gamma_x^2 = \sigma_z^2/\sigma_x^2$$

This is a very important result since it shows that the model sources of Section 2.4 have a value of *sfm* that is simply the ratio of the variances of innovations and source waveforms.

(2.12)   Verify that the psd (2.105) for an AR(1) process with $b_1 = \rho_1 = \rho$ has a spectral flatness measure $\gamma_x^2 = (1 - \rho^2)$.

Problems

(2.13)   Verify that for an AR(1) process [Grenander and Szego, 1958]

$$\mathbf{R}_{xx}^{-1} = \frac{1}{(1-\rho^2)\sigma_x^2} \begin{bmatrix} 1 & -\rho & 0 & . & . & 0 \\ -\rho & (1+\rho^2) & -\rho & 0 & . & 0 \\ . & & & & & \\ . & & & & (1+\rho^2) & -\rho \\ 0 & . & . & . & -\rho & 1 \end{bmatrix}$$

is indeed the inverse of (2.107).

(2.14)   Use the results of Problem (2.13) and (2.79) to show that the optimum predictor of an AR(1) process is simply a first-order predictor. This result will be mentioned again in Chapter 6.

(2.15)   Consider the AR(2) process (2.110).

(a)   Show that its psd is that in (2.112).

(b)   Show that the psd has an extremum at a frequency given by $\omega = $ arc cos $[b_1(b_2-1)/(4b_2)]$, assuming that $b_1^2(1-b_2)^2 < 16b_2^2$; and show that this extremum is a maximum if $b_2 < 0$.

(c)   Using (2.90) and (2.91), show that

$$\gamma_x^2 = \frac{(1+b_2)(1-b_1-b_2)(1+b_1-b_2)}{(1-b_2)}$$

(2.16)   Define a MA(1) process (2.122) by insisting that

$$R_{xx}(0) = \sigma_x^2 \quad ; \quad R_{xx}(\pm 1) = \alpha\sigma_x^2 \quad ; \quad R_{xx}(k) = 0 \quad ; \quad |k| > 1$$

Calculate its psd and show that we must have $|\alpha| \leq 1/\sqrt{2}$ for a nonnegative determinant $|\mathbf{R}_{xx}|$ of order 3. Note that the above constraint on α is satisfied for any value of a_1 in (2.122).

(2.17)   (a)   Calculate the acf and psd of the MA(2) process

$$X(n) = Z(n) + a_1Z(n-1) + a_2Z(n-2)$$

(b)   Show that the spectral flatness measure is

$$\gamma_x^2 = (1 + a_1^2 + a_2^2)^{-1},$$

using the results of (a), *and* by evaluating the power transfer factor α.

(2.18)   Show that the general MA process (2.118) has the acf described in (2.120).

(2.19)   Show that (2.138) and (2.139) can also be written as

$$X(m,n) = \sum_{i=0}^{\infty} \sum_{j=0}^{\infty} \rho^{i+j} Z(m-i,n-j)$$

which is the 2-D equivalent of (2.97). Show that this random field indeed has the normalized acf $\rho_{xx}(k_h,k_v) = \rho^{|k_h|+|k_v|}$ and that $\sigma_z^2 = \sigma_x^2(1-\rho^2)^2$. [Hint: Use the simplifying concept of the 2-D z-transform $X(z_1,z_2)$, although this is strictly valid only for a deterministic signal.]

(2.20)   The acf values $\rho_{xx}(k_h,k_v)$ in the following table have been measured for an interlaced picturephone image (128 lines and 120 pixels per line) [Habibi and Wintz, 1971]. With $\alpha = 0.124$ and $\beta = 0.110$ in (2.135), and with $\alpha = (0.124 + 0.110)/2 = 0.117$ in (2.142), compute the acf-values of a first-order source with separable and isotropic statistics. Verify that the latter one is a much better model of the above measured statistics, especially for the higher values of k_h and k_v in the table.

Table of measured acf values.

k_h $\quad$ k_v	0	1.000	2	3
0	1	0.896	0.808	0.725
1	0.883	0.857	0.793	0.725
2	0.776	0.778	0.748	0.702
3	0.691	0.700	0.692	0.661

(2.21)   Consider the Gaussian psd

$$S_{xx}(\Omega) = \frac{\sqrt{2\pi}}{\Omega_\sigma} \sigma_x^2 \exp(-\Omega^2/2\Omega_\sigma^2)$$

(a)   Show that $\pm\Omega_\sigma$ are the frequencies at which the value of the psd is -2.2 dB relative to its maximum value.

(b)   Show that the acf of the process is also Gaussian: $\rho_{xx}(\tau) = \exp(-\Omega_\sigma^2 \tau^2/2)$.

(2.22)   Consider the two-level psd of Figure 2.24 and (2.168).

(a)   Verify that the variance is σ_x^2.

(b)   Show that the continuous-time version of the spectral flatness measure (2.74) for a psd bandlimited in $(-\Omega_W, \Omega_W)$ is

$$\gamma_x^2 = \frac{\eta_x^2}{\sigma_x^2} = \frac{\dfrac{\Omega_W}{\pi} \exp\dfrac{1}{2\Omega_W} \displaystyle\int_{-\infty}^{\infty} \log_e S_{xx}(\Omega)\, d\Omega}{\dfrac{1}{2\pi} \displaystyle\int_{-\infty}^{\infty} S_{xx}(\Omega)\, d\Omega}$$

[Hint: Set $\omega = \pi\Omega/\Omega_W$, $d\omega = \pi d\Omega/\Omega_W$ and $S_{xx}(e^{j\pi\Omega/\Omega_W})$ $= S_{xx}(e^{j\omega}) = S_{xx}(\Omega)\Omega_W/\pi$.]

(c)   Use the result in (b) to show that the *sfm* of the two-level psd is $[\alpha(2-\alpha)]^{1/2} \sim \sqrt{2\alpha}$ if $\alpha \to 0$.

(d)   Derive the same result using (2.74), and the discrete-time version of the psd obtained upon replacing Ω_W by π in Figure 2.24.

(e)   Discuss the special cases of $\alpha = 0$ and $\alpha = 1$.

References

M. Abramowitz and I. A. Stegun, *Handbook of Mathematical Functions*, U.S. Dept. of Commerce, National Bureau of Standards, Applied Mathematics Series, June 1964.

B. S. Atal and S. L. Hanauer, "Speech Analysis and Synthesis by Linear Prediction of the Speech Wave," J. Acoust. Soc. Am., pp. 637-655, August 1971.

W. R. Bennett, "Methods of Solving Noise Problems," Proc. IRE, p. 609, May 1956.

T. Berger, *Rate Distortion Theory*, Prentice-Hall, Englewood Cliffs, N.J., 1971.

B. J. Bunin, "Rate Distortion Functions for Gaussian Markov Processes," Bell System Tech. J., pp. 2059-3074, November 1969.

D. J. Connor, R. C. Brainard and J. O. Limb, "Intraframe Coding for Picture Transmission," Proc. IEEE, pp. 779-791, July 1972.

H. K. Dunn and S. D. White, "Statistical Measurements on Conversational Speech," J. Acoust. Soc. Am., pp. 278-288, January 1940.

J. L. Flanagan, *Speech Analysis, Synthesis and Perception*, Springer-Verlag, New York, 1972.

J. L. Flanagan, M. R. Schroeder, B. S. Atal, R. E. Crochiere, N. S. Jayant and J. M. Tribolet, "Speech Coding," IEEE Trans. on Communications, pp. 710-737, May 1979.

U. Grenander and G. Szego, *Toeplitz Forms and Their Applications*, University of California Press, Berkeley, Calif., 1958.

F. R. Grizmala, unpublished work, Bell Laboratories, 1972.

A. Habibi and P. A. Wintz, "Image Coding by Linear Transformation and Block Quantization," IEEE Trans. on Communications, pp. 50-63, February 1971.

N. S. Jayant, unpublished work, Bell Laboratories, 1982.

G. M. Jenkins and D. G. Watts, *Spectral Analysis and Its Applications*, Holden-Day, San Francisco, 1968.

E. R. Kretzmer, "Statistics of Television Signals," Bell System Tech. J., pp. 751-763, July 1952.

T. Kummerow, "Statistics for Efficient Linear and Nonlinear Picture Coding," Int. Telemetering Conf., pp. 149-161, October 1972.

J. I. Makhoul and J. J. Wolf, "Linear Prediction and the Spectral Analysis of Speech," Bolt, Beranek and Newman, Inc. Technical Report, 1972.

J. D. Markel and A. H. Gray, Jr., *Linear Prediction of Speech*, Springer-Verlag, New York, 1976.

R. A. McDonald, "Signal-to-Noise and Idle Channel Performance of Differential Pulse Code Modulation Systems — Particular Applications to Voice Signals," Bell System Tech. J., pp. 1123-1151, September 1966.

P. Noll, "Non-adaptive and Adaptive DPCM of Speech Signals," Polytech. Tijdschr. Ed. Elektrotech./Electron (The Netherlands), No. 19, 1972.

P. Noll, "Adaptive Quantizing in Speech Coding Systems," Int. Zurich Seminar on Digital Commun., pp. B3.1-B3.6, March 1974.

J. B. O'Neal, Jr., "Delta Modulation Quantizing Noise — Analytical and Computer Simulation Results for Gaussian and Television Signals," Bell System Tech. J., pp. 117-141, January 1966.

J. B. O'Neal, Jr., "Predictive Quantizing Systems (DPCM) for the Transmission of Television Signals," Bell System Tech. J., pp. 689-719, May-June 1966.

J. B. O'Neal, Jr. and T. R. Natarajan, "Coding Isotropic Images," IEEE Trans. on Information Theory, pp. 697-707, November 1977.

A. Papoulis, *Probability, Random Variables and Stochastic Processes,* McGraw-Hill, New York, 1965.

W. K. Pratt, *Image Coding,* John Wiley, New York, 1978.

D. L. Richards, *Telecommunication by Speech,* Halsted Press, John Wiley, New York, 1973.

J. B. Thomas, *Introduction to Statistical Communication Theory,* John Wiley, New York, 1969.

R. Zelinski and P. Noll, "Optimale Quantisierung gedächtnisfreier Gammaquellen und Anwendungen für die PCM — Codierung von Sprache", Technischer Bericht Nr. 169, Heinrich Hertz Institut, Berlin, 1974.

3

Sampling and Reconstruction of Bandlimited Waveforms

3.1 Introduction

Refer to the waveform communication system of Figure 3.1(a). Tacitly assumed components of all digital waveform systems are the devices labeled *sampler* and *interpolation filter*. The latter is sometimes referred to as a *reconstruction filter*, as in Figure 1.3. The quantities $x(kT)$, denoted simply by $x(k)$ in the rest of the book, are *discrete-time samples* derived from a continuous-time signal $x(t)$ at times kT, where T is the *sampling period*. Note that T is the reciprocal of the *sampling frequency* or *sampling rate* f_s:

$$T = 1/f_s \tag{3.1}$$

The samples $x(kT)$ are equally spaced in time; this kind of *uniform sampling* is almost always assumed, for simplicity. The aim of the interpolation filter at the receiver is to derive a continuous waveform $y(t)$ from the decoder samples $y(kT)$ using an appropriate *interpolation* procedure. Under certain conditions we will show that sampling and interpolation operations are error-free for bandlimited $x(t)$. If this is true — and it is invariably assumed true in this book — the main source of reconstruction noise is in fact that caused by the waveform coder and waveform decoder boxes of Figure 3.1(a).

The simple example of a PCM communication system is shown in Figure 3.1(b). In this case, sampling and coding operations can be combined into a single box which is widely known as an *analog-to-digital* or A/D *converter*; and the PCM decoder can be simply represented as a *digital-to-analog* or D/A *converter*. An

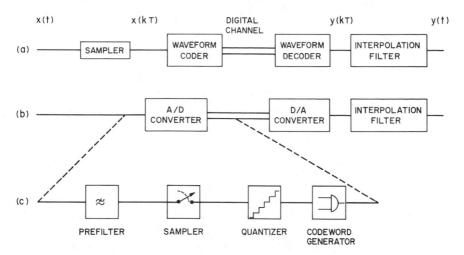

Figure 3.1 Sampling and reconstruction of analog waveforms: (a) a general waveform communication system; (b) a special example, PCM; (c) an expanded block diagram of A/D conversion.

expanded version of the A/D box appears in Figure 3.1(c). This diagram emphasizes that *prefiltering* or *bandlimiting* is a prerequisite for error-free sampling and interpolation, unless input $x(t)$ is already bandlimited. The prefilter of Figure 3.1(c) is also called an *anti-aliasing* filter, for reasons that will be apparent later in this chapter.

Section 3.6 will demonstrate quantitatively that prefiltering is a critical step in any digital coding system. Briefly, the purpose of prefiltering is to prevent or minimize *aliasing* effects which can be perceptually very objectionable in speech and image coding. The operation of prefiltering introduces its own distortion into the input signal, but this *bandlimiting* effect is generally less objectionable than aliasing if the nominal bandwidth is appropriately chosen, as in Table 1.1. *SNR* characterizations of coding systems are based on the comparison of *prefiltered waveforms* with *coded prefiltered waveforms*. These *SNR* characterizations will therefore not include the contribution of prefiltering error; rather, they will reflect only the distortions introduced into the prefiltered waveform in the coding process.

Coder inputs can either be the amplitude-continuous samples $x(kT)$ or finely amplitude-quantized versions thereof, as obtained at the output of an A/D converter preceding the coder box. The latter situation is true in computer simulations as well as in many implementations of coding systems where speech or image signals are stored as a sequence of finite resolution (say, 12-bit) numbers.

Once a certain desired value of nominal bandwidth is established, the need to prevent aliasing will allow very little flexibility in the design of prefilter or in the design of minimum sampling rate f_s; and the only way to reduce the transmission rate I of the digital coding system will be by controlling the parameter R in the equation $I = f_s R$.

The sampler in Figure 3.1 is often referred to as a *sample-and-hold* device, and Figure 3.2 is a schematic diagram of a sample-and-hold circuit. For purposes of implementation, a sample is a measure of the amplitude of a signal, evaluated over

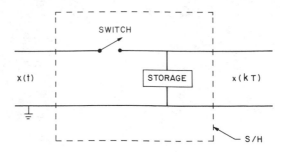

Figure 3.2 Sample-and-hold operation.

a short period of time during which the signal changes by only a negligible amount. However, even though a sample may be evaluated in the above fashion in an arbitrarily short time that is typically much smaller than T, there may be a need to retain its value for a longer period; for instance, to apply it to a waveform coder, which usually performs a sequence of operations rather than a single very rapid operation. The sample-and-hold process consists of charging a storage element (such as a capacitor, in the simplest case) to a potential which represents the sample amplitude over a small duration of time when the switch in Figure 3.2 is closed. When the switch is open, the charge is held or retained, except for the slow leakage through circuits of nominally infinite, and practically very high, impedance. An important problem in sampling is one of combining an adequately fast acquisition of the sample amplitude with an adequately steady holding of the acquired sample, maintaining adequate precision in both phases of the process. The degree of the problem is a function of the sampling rate. In the sampling of a multiplexed-speech system with 24 channels and a shared A/D converter, $T = 1/24 \,(8\text{kHz})^{-1} = 5.2\mu s$ [Damann, McDaniel and Maddox, 1972]. In sampling a single broadcast-quality video channel, $T = (10\text{MHz})^{-1} = 0.1\mu s$.

In the rest of this chapter, we assume *ideal coding* $[y(kT) = x(kT)]$ and concentrate on the process that recovers $x(t)$ from samples $y(kT) = x(kT)$. The waveform $x(t)$ will be either *deterministic* or a sample function of a continuous-time *random process*. The last section of this chapter will consider the problem of reconstructing $x(t)$ from *disturbed samples* $y(kT) = x(kT) + \epsilon(kT)$, where $\epsilon(kT)$ is an additive error term due to coding and/or transmission.

3.2 Deterministic Lowpass Signals

Consider a real-valued continuous-time signal $x(t)$ with finite energy

$$\int_{-\infty}^{\infty} |x(t)|^2 \, dt < \infty \tag{3.2}$$

and hence a Fourier integral pair representation

$$X(j\Omega) = \int_{-\infty}^{\infty} x(t)e^{-j\Omega t} \, dt; \quad x(t) = \frac{1}{2\pi} \int_{-\infty}^{\infty} X(j\Omega)e^{j\Omega t} \, d\Omega \tag{3.3}$$

Assume that $X(j\Omega)$ is a *lowpass* signal that is *bandlimited* to W hertz or $\Omega_W = 2\pi W$ radians/second (rad/s):

$$X(j\Omega) = 0 ; \quad |\Omega| \geqslant \Omega_W = 2\pi W \qquad (3.4)$$

3.2.1 The Sampling Theorem

Define, as in Figure 3.3, a periodic extension of $X(j\Omega)$:

$$X^*(j\Omega) = \sum_{k=-\infty}^{\infty} X[j(\Omega - 2k\Omega_W)] \qquad (3.5)$$

It is clear that $X(j\Omega)$ can be regenerated from $X^*(j\Omega)$ as follows:

$$X(j\Omega) = X^*(j\Omega)\text{rect}(\Omega/2\Omega_W) = \begin{cases} X^*(j\Omega) & |\Omega| \leqslant \Omega_W \\ 0 & \textit{otherwise} \end{cases} \qquad (3.6)$$

The periodic Fourier spectrum $X^*(j\Omega)$ can be described by its Fourier series

$$X^*(j\Omega) = \sum_{k=-\infty}^{\infty} c_k \exp(-jk\pi\Omega/\Omega_W) \qquad (3.7a)$$

Figure 3.3 Fourier representation of a bandlimited signal: (a) input spectrum $|X(j\Omega)|$; (b) periodic extension $|X^*(j\Omega)|$; and (c) bandlimiting of $|X^*(j\Omega)|$ to recover $|X(j\Omega)|$.

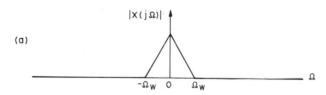

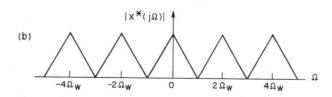

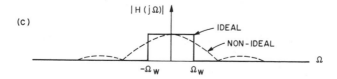

$$c_k = \frac{1}{2\Omega_W} \int_{-\Omega_w}^{\Omega_w} X(j\Omega) \exp (jk\pi\Omega/\Omega_W) \qquad (3.7b)$$

where c_k are the Fourier coefficients. Comparing this with (3.3), and noting that $X(j\Omega) = 0$ for $|\Omega| > \Omega_W$,

$$c_k = \frac{\pi}{\Omega_W} x(k\pi/\Omega_W) = T x(kT); \qquad T = \frac{\pi}{\Omega_W} \qquad (3.8)$$

i.e., the *Fourier coefficients are equal to scaled values of samples of the time waveform taken at multiples of time*

$$T = \frac{\pi}{\Omega_W} = \frac{1}{2W} \qquad (3.9)$$

The above sampling interval T is the *Nyquist interval*, and its reciprocal $f_s = 1/T = 2W$ *is the Nyquist rate* or *Nyquist sampling rate* for the bandlimited signal. The bandwidth W is the *Nyquist frequency* and $x(kT) = x(k/2W)$ are called the *Nyquist samples*.

Since the time samples $x(kT)$ give the Fourier coefficients c_k, we can reconstruct the complete waveform $x(t)$ from its samples taken at time instants kT. This is done by computing the periodic spectrum $X^*(j\Omega)$ from the c_k in (3.7) and by bandlimiting this spectrum to the interval $(-\Omega_W, \Omega_W)$ as in (3.6) [see Figure 3.3(c)]. An inverse Fourier transform yields $x(t)$ from $X(j\Omega)$.

We have thus shown that there exists a mathematical procedure for recovering a bandlimited waveform $x(t)$ from its samples $x(kT)$ taken at a sampling interval $T = 1/2W$. That is, it is possible to reconstruct the waveform from its samples if the sampling rate equals $2W$ samples per second. In other words, $2WT$ numbers are sufficient to represent a function of duration T and highest frequency W [Nyquist, 1928]. This *sampling theorem* is one of the most fundamental results in digital signal processing, and we shall presently extend it by noting that sampling frequencies *higher than* $2W$ also permit recovery of bandlimited $x(t)$. In the specific context of digital waveform transmission, the theorem implies that one needs to transmit accurately only the Nyquist samples of the bandlimited signal. Note that the theorem says nothing about the bit rate of the transmission system. This depends on the accuracy with which the Nyquist samples are represented for transmission, as measured by R, the number of bits/sample in (1.4).

The *frequency-domain* result of (3.7) and (3.8) can also be expressed in a different form that suggests a constructive *time-domain* interpolation procedure for recovering $x(t)$ from its Nyquist samples. Using (3.7) through (3.9),

$$X(j\Omega) = T \operatorname{rect} (\Omega/2\Omega_W) \sum_{k=-\infty}^{\infty} x(kT) e^{-jk\Omega T} \qquad (3.10)$$

The time signal $x(t)$ is the inverse transform in (3.3), with $X(j\Omega)$ defined in (3.10):

$$x(t) = \frac{1}{2\pi} \int_{-\infty}^{\infty} \left[T \operatorname{rect}(\Omega/2\Omega_W) \sum_{k=-\infty}^{\infty} x(kT)\, e^{-jk\Omega T} \right] e^{j\Omega t} d\Omega \qquad (3.11)$$

$$= \frac{1}{2\pi} \int_{-\Omega_W}^{\Omega_W} \left[T \sum_{k=-\infty}^{\infty} x(kT) e^{-jk\Omega T} \right] e^{j\Omega t} d\Omega \qquad (3.12)$$

$$= T \sum_{k=-\infty}^{\infty} x(kT) \left[\frac{1}{2\pi} \int_{-\Omega_W}^{\Omega_W} e^{j\Omega(t-kT)} d\Omega \right] \qquad (3.13)$$

The term in the square bracket can be evaluated using

$$\frac{1}{2\pi} \int_{-\Omega_W}^{\Omega_W} e^{ju\Omega} d\Omega = \frac{\sin(u\,\Omega_W)}{\pi u} \qquad (3.14)$$

This leads to an alternate, constructive version of the *sampling theorem* [Whittaker, 1935] [Shannon, 1949] [Jerri, 1977]:

$$x(t) = \sum_{k=-\infty}^{\infty} x(kT) \operatorname{si}\left[\frac{\pi}{T}(t-kT)\right]; \qquad \operatorname{si} x = \sin x / x \qquad (3.15)$$

Figure 3.4 Recovery of $x(t)$ in the time domain: (a) Nyquist samples; and (b) si-function-based reconstruction of $x(t)$. The bold-line waveform is the reconstructed, smoothed output. It is the sum of an infinity of weighted si functions. (c) Suboptimal staircase reconstruction of $x(t)$.

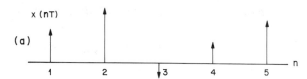

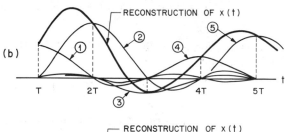

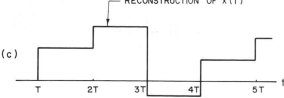

for waveform recovery in the *time domain*. Equation (3.15) signifies a superposition of shifted versions of the *sampling function* si(·), each of which is weighted by a respective sample value $x(kT)$. See Figure 3.4(b) for a simple illustration (Problem 3.1). Note that sampling functions overlap such that the space *in between* samples is filled up with proper original amplitudes. Samples $x(kT)$ themselves are not affected by the above overlaps. They already form points of the final waveform; si[$\pi(t-kT)/T$] has zeros for all $t = nT \neq kT$. The practically important but sub-optimal case of non-sin x/x interpolation will be discussed in Section 3.2.2.

The above sampling theorem has another interpretation: from *any* set of samples with $f_s = 1/T$ seconds, a continuous-time signal can be reconstructed with a bandlimitation $W = 1/2T$ Hz. Such a signal can be transmitted over an analog channel of bandwidth W (specifically, an ideal lowpass characteristic transfer function of width W) and resampled at the receiver. This implies that it is possible to transmit $2W$ independently chosen samples per second over a channel with ideal lowpass characteristic and bandwidth W.

3.2.2 Interpolation Filters

This subsection deals with the implementation of (3.15). The signal $x(t)$ is sampled by a train of impulses $s_p(t)$ to produce a modulated signal $\tilde{x}(t)$:

$$s_p(t) = \sum_{k=-\infty}^{\infty} s(t-kT) \; ; \quad \tilde{x}(t) = x(t)\, s_p(t) \tag{3.16}$$

In *ideal sampling*, $s_p(t)$ is a train of *dirac delta* impulses [Figures 3.5 and 3.6(a)]:

$$s_p(t) = T \sum_{k=-\infty}^{\infty} \delta(t-kT) \tag{3.17}$$

The modulated impulse train $x^*(t)$ with ideal sampling is

$$x^*(t) = \tilde{x}(t) = s_p(t)\, x(t) = T \sum_{k=-\infty}^{\infty} x(kT)\, \delta(t-kT) \tag{3.18}$$

Complete reconstruction is possible by passing $x^*(t)$ through an ideal lowpass filter with impulse response

$$h(t) = (1/T)\, \text{si}(\Omega_W t) \tag{3.19}$$

Figure 3.5 Ideal sampling and interpolation.

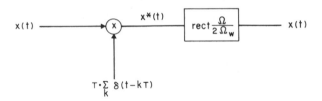

and hence a frequency response

$$H(j\Omega) = \text{rect } (\Omega/2\Omega_W) = \text{rect } (\Omega T/2\pi) \tag{3.20}$$

In the time domain the output is a convolution of impulse train $x^*(t)$ and impulse response $h(t)$:

$$x^*(t) * h(t) = \int_{-\infty}^{\infty} x^*(\tau) \, h(t-\tau) \, d\tau$$

$$= \sum_{k=-\infty}^{\infty} x(kT) \, \text{si}[\frac{\pi}{T}(t-kT)] = x(t) \tag{3.21}$$

where we have used the sampling theorem and the integral property of the delta function $\delta(t)$:

$$\int_{-\infty}^{\infty} \phi(t) \, \delta(t-\tau) \, dt = \phi(\tau) \tag{3.22}$$

for any function $\phi(\cdot)$ that is continuous at $t = \tau$.

In the frequency domain, the spectrum of the modulated impulse train $X^*(t)$ (3.18) is a repetition of $X(j\Omega)$ at intervals $2\Omega_W$ [Problem 3.2(a)]:

$$X^*(j\Omega) = \sum_{k=-\infty}^{\infty} X\left[j[\Omega-k\frac{2\pi}{T}]\right] \tag{3.23}$$

Therefore, $X(j\Omega)$ can be recovered from $X^*(j\Omega)$ by lowpass filtering, via (3.20).

From the above results, we conclude that *ideal sampling* followed by *ideal lowpass filtering* is just an implementation of the interpolation procedure suggested by the sampling theorem (3.15). According to (3.19), this filter is *non-causal* [$h(t) \neq 0$ for $t < 0$]. A non-causal ideal filter can be approximated in practice by allowing for a sufficiently delayed impulse response. In Figure 3.6(c), for example, $h'(t) \sim 0$ for $t < 0$.

Figure 3.6 (a) Dirac Delta impulse used in ideal sampling; and (b)(c) approximation of a non-causal ideal filter (b) by (c) a realizable filter and an adequate delay. The impulse response $h'(t)$ is forced to be zero for negative t.

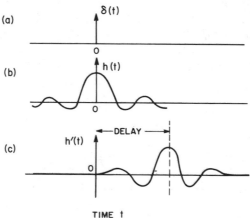

Note finally from (3.15) that non-si interpolations, such as straight-line interpolations or staircase interpolations, are sub-optimal. We shall presently note that si function interpolations are in fact necessary to provide the ideal *lowpass* bandlimiting of Figure 3.3(c).

The dashed-line filter response in Figure 3.3(c) corresponds to a non-ideal bandlimiting characteristic si$(\Omega T/2)$ that characterizes a *staircase* interpolator (hold circuit) with an impulse response $h(t) = $ rect $(t/T-1/2)$ [Figure 3.4(c) and Problem 3.2]. Indeed, the outputs of practical D/A converters are staircase reconstructions. As indicated in Figure 3.3(c), the staircase interpolator passes significant contributions of the multiples of the baseband spectrum. The out-of-band contributions can be damped by including a second, simple (non-ideal) lowpass filter; while the in-band damping can be corrected by a sinx/x — compensating highpass response that possesses a 4 dB gain (Problem 3.2) at $\Omega = \pi/T$. The above arrangement is often used for waveform reconstruction. A system without the compensating filter is simpler, and has a delay of only $T/2$ seconds; and its error performance may be adequate, especially if the signal is highly oversampled (Chapter 8).

The theory of sampling can be generalized in many ways [Jerri, 1977], but the procedures suggested in these generalizations will not be utilized in this book. One generalization, for example, refers to *nonuniform* time sampling with appropriate requirements on average sampling rate. Another generalization depends on a *transform* representation of $x(t)$ as a weighted sum of *orthonormal basis functions*. The *interpolation* formula (3.15), which is also called a *cardinal series* representation, is a special case with the property that the weights for the above summation are simply the samples of the waveform (Problem 3.3).

3.2.3 The Case of Slight Oversampling

Consider Figure 3.7, which is a generalization of Figure 3.3. The spectrum extension $X^*(j\Omega)$ in Figure 3.7 has a period Ω_S rather than the signal-specific $2\Omega_W$ in the earlier figure. It is clear that the periodic extension in Figure 3.7 leads to a simple non-overlapping repetition of $X(j\Omega)$ as long as $\Omega_S \geqslant 2\Omega_W$; and if this condition is satisfied, $X(j\Omega)$ can be recovered from $X^*(j\Omega)$ with a bandlimiting operation as in Figure 3.3(c). The above observation is the basis of a more general version [Papoulis, 1966] of the *sampling theorem* which says that a bandlimited signal can be adequately sampled with an interval $2\pi/\Omega_S$ that is *equal to or less than* the Nyquist interval π/Ω_W; or with a sampling frequency that is *equal to or greater than* the Nyquist rate $2W$:

$$T = \frac{2\pi}{\Omega_S} \leqslant \frac{\pi}{\Omega_W} ; \qquad f_s = T^{-1} \geqslant 2W \qquad (3.24)$$

This result is in contrast to (3.9). A good deal of the analysis of Section 3.2.1 can in fact be repeated routinely for the more general case of $f_s > 2W$ by simply replacing $2\Omega_W$ by Ω_S in expressions for the periodic spectrum and bandlimiting filter.

Reconstruction in the general case depends, for example, on a lowpass

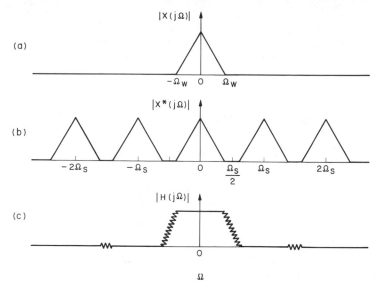

Figure 3.7 The case of $f_s > 2W$ or $T < \pi/\Omega_W$: (a) input spectrum $|X(j\Omega)|$; (b) periodic extension $|X^*(j\Omega)|$ and (c) bandlimiting of $|X^*(j\Omega)|$ to recover $|X(j\Omega)|$.

interpolating filter of bandwidth $\Omega_S/2 = \pi/T$. In fact, requirements on such a filter can be relaxed if $T < 1/2W$ (or $\Omega_W < \Omega_S/2$). As shown in the example of Figure 3.7, oversampling implies non-overlapping repetitions of $X(j\Omega)$ in the periodic version $X^*(j\Omega)$, and this leads to a "guard space" [the jagged edges of $H(j\Omega)$ in Figure 3.7(c)] where the interpolating filter can have arbitrary characteristics. In practice, this guard-space permits the use of finite roll-off characteristics (in lieu of a filter with an infinitely sharp cutoff at Ω_W). For example, in the CCITT-recommended commercial telephony filters of Figure 3.8,

Figure 3.8 A typical bandpass filter for digital coders in commercial PCM-telephony. The filter characteristic is compatible with international (CCITT) and North American standards, as shown by the hatched characteristics. The reconstruction filter in the decoder would have a similar lowpass characteristic, but it may include a sin x/x compensator discussed in Section 3.2.2 [Siemens AG, 1983].

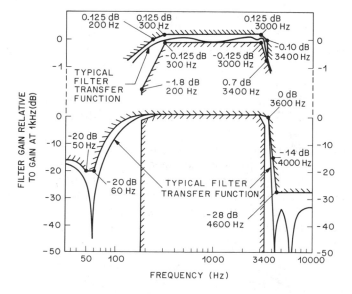

$W = 3.4$ kHz, $f_s = 8$ kHz, and the region between 3.4 to 4.6 kHz is a guard space. Notice that the typical filter response achieves a near-unity gain up to $W = 3.4$ kHz, and nearly 50 dB of attenuation at the 4.6 kHz guard-space edge.

3.3 Bandpass Signals

Consider a signal $x(t)$ that is bandlimited to the range (Ω_1, Ω_2)

$$X(j\Omega) = \begin{cases} 0 & |\Omega| \leqslant \Omega_1 = 2\pi W_1 \\ \\ 0 & |\Omega| \geqslant \Omega_2 = 2\pi W_2 \end{cases} \qquad (3.25)$$

where $0 < \Omega_1 < \Omega_2 < \infty$. The center frequency is $\Omega_C = (\Omega_1 + \Omega_2)/2$ and its bandwidth (in Hz) is

$$W = W_2 - W_1 = (\Omega_2 - \Omega_1)/2\pi = \Omega_W/2\pi \qquad (3.26)$$

A typical example is an FDM (frequency division multiplex) signal with twelve 4-kHz speech bands modulating carrier frequencies in the range 60 to 108 kHz. A more direct example of a bandpass signal occurs when speech is split into frequency-contiguous bandpass components for independent coding (Chapter 11).

The theory of Section 3.2 has shown that a sampling rate of $2W_2$ (Hz) or greater is adequate for a lowpass signal of highest frequency W_2. Therefore, by regarding (3.25) as a special case of such a lowpass signal, we conclude that a sampling rate of $2W_2$ is also adequate for the bandpass signal of (3.25). In this section we will note that in fact, under certain conditions, the bandpass signal (3.25) can be completely described by $2W$ (rather than $2W_2$) samples per second. To be precise, we will note that it is possible to reconstruct a bandpass signal $x(t)$ from its samples $x(kT)$ provided that the sampling rate $f_s = T^{-1}$ has a specific minimum value (to be defined presently) within the range

$$2W \leqslant f_s \leqslant 4W \qquad (3.27)$$

and that the rate of $2W$ can be adequate under the condition of an integral W_1/W. Even for conditions where $\min\{f_s\}$ exceeds $2W$, it will be upper-bounded by $2W_2$, as discussed at the beginning of this paragraph.

Recall that sampling of a lowpass signal of bandwidth W at or above the Nyquist rate $2W$ gives a periodic repetition of the spectrum (Figures 3.3 and 3.7) without an overlap of baseband spectrum elements. Very similarly, a bandpass spectrum will be periodic, as shown in Figure 3.9, and there will be certain conditions for the periodic extension to be overlap-free. In Figure 3.9, with $f_s = 2W$, the second right-hand repetition of the negative band ($N2$ in figure) is shifted just to the left of the positive spectrum P, while the third repetition ($N3$ in figure) is shifted just to the right hand side of P. There is no overlap of any repetition of N with P in this case, and this non-overlap has only been achieved

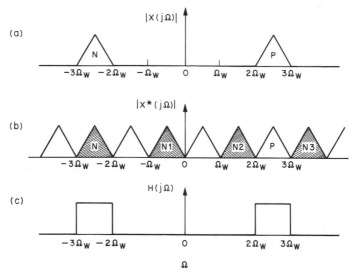

Figure 3.9 Fourier representation of a bandpass signal: (a) input spectrum $|X(j\Omega)|$; (b) periodic extension $|X^*(j\Omega)|$; and (c) bandlimiting of $|X^*(j\Omega)|$ to recover $|X(j\Omega)|$.

because we have considered a spectrum whose lowest value W_1 is just a multiple of the bandwidth W. This is in fact an important general result: a *sampling rate of* $2W$ is adequate if the ratio W_1/W of lowest frequency W_1 to bandwidth W is an exact integer $n=0,1,2...$. Note that $n=0$ refers to the special case of a *lowpass* signal.

A good example where the above result is used with non-zero n is in *integer-band sampling* as used in a sub-band coder (Chapter 11). In the simplest case, a lowpass signal of bandwidth B is divided into M contiguous sub-bands of equal width $W = B/M$. The W_1/W ratio for sub-band n is simply equal to the band number $n = 0,1,...,M-1$. Instead of sampling the full-band signal directly with rate $2B$, the bandpass outputs are sampled with rates $2W = 2B/M$ to permit independent coding operations. Since there are M sub-bands, the total sampling rate will again be $2MW = 2B$ samples/sec.

In general, for non-integral W_1/W, it can be shown [Kohlenberg, 1953] that the minimum sampling rate is

$$\min \{f_s\} = 2W \; \frac{1 + W_1/W}{1 + \lfloor W_1/W \rfloor} \; ;$$

$$\lfloor W_1/W \rfloor = \text{greatest integer in } W_1/W \tag{3.28}$$

Figure 3.10 sketches min $\{f_s\}$ as a function of W_1/W. Note that upper and lower limits in this curve are indeed $4W$ and $2W$ as in (3.27), and that the minimum value of $2W$ is attained when W_1 is an integral multiple of bandwidth W. Note that non-integral choices of W_1/W lead to higher sampling rate requirements; and that in particular, W_1 values slightly less than nW lead to worst-case results

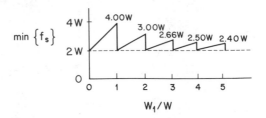

Figure 3.10 Minimum sampling rate for a bandpass signal.

corresponding to the peaks in Figure 3.10. Finally, it can be verified, as claimed earlier, that all values of $\min\{f_s\}$ in (3.28) and Figure 3.10 are upper-bounded by $2W_2$. Also see Problem 3.4.

3.4 Random Processes

Let $\{X(t)\}$ be a continuous-time wide-sense stationary process with bandlimited psd

$$S_{xx}(\Omega) = 0; \quad |\Omega| > \Omega_W = 2\pi W \tag{3.29}$$

The psd is the inverse Fourier transform of the acf $R_{xx}(\tau)$:

$$S_{xx}(\Omega) = \int_{-\infty}^{\infty} R_{xx}(\tau)\, e^{-j\Omega\tau}\, d\tau\,; \quad R_{xx}(\tau) = E[X(t)X(t+\tau)] \tag{3.30}$$

The power of the process is finite; it is an upper bound on the acf for nonzero τ:

$$E[X^2(t)] = R_{xx}(0)\,; \quad |R_{xx}(\tau)| \leqslant R_{xx}(0) \tag{3.31}$$

The condition that $R_{xx}(\tau)$ be *absolutely integrable* is sufficient for the existence of the Fourier transform $S_{xx}(\Omega)$. Note that the individual sample functions of the process do not possess Fourier transforms since their energies are not finite. Despite this fact, we will note a result that is close to the sampling theorem for deterministic finite-energy processes: *from samples $x(kT)$, a signal $x'(t)$ can be reconstructed* using

$$x'(t) = \sum_{k=-\infty}^{\infty} x(kT)\, \text{si}\, \frac{\pi}{T}\,(t-kT) \tag{3.32}$$

The signal $x'(t)$ can be viewed as a sample function of a random process $\{X'(t)\}$. The error function

$$e(t) = x(t) - x'(t) \tag{3.33}$$

has a mean square value given by

$$\sigma_e^2 = E[E^2(t)] = E[\{X(t) - X'(t)\}^2] = 0 \quad \text{if} \ \ T \leqslant 1/2W \qquad (3.34)$$

which we shall now evaluate.

From (3.32) and (3.34),

$$E\,[E^2(t)] = E\,[\{X(t) - \sum_{k=-\infty}^{\infty} X(kT) \ \text{si} \ \frac{\pi}{T} \ (t-kT)\}^2]$$

$$= R_{xx}(0) - 2E\,[X(t) \sum_{k=-\infty}^{\infty} X(kT) \ \text{si} \ \frac{\pi}{T} \ (t-kT)]$$

$$+ E\,[\sum_{j=-\infty}^{\infty} \sum_{k=-\infty}^{\infty} X(jT)X(kT) \ \text{si} \ \frac{\pi}{T} \ (t-jT) \ \text{si} \ \frac{\pi}{T} \ (t-kT)] \qquad (3.35)$$

By interchanging the order of expectation and summation, we find that

$$E\,[E^2(t)] = R_{xx}(0) - 2 \sum_{k=-\infty}^{\infty} R_{xx}(t-kT) \ \text{si} \ \frac{\pi}{T} \ (t-kT)$$

$$+ \sum_{j=-\infty}^{\infty} \text{si} \ \frac{\pi}{T} \ (t-jT) \sum_{k=-\infty}^{\infty} R_{xx}(jT-kT) \ \text{si} \ \frac{\pi}{T} \ (t-kT) \qquad (3.36)$$

However, $R_{xx}(\cdot)$ is a *deterministic bandlimited* function (with a nonzero psd only for $|\Omega| \leqslant \Omega_W$). Therefore the sampling theorem of Section 3.2 applies and the second term of (3.36) equals $2R_{xx}(0)$, since $R_{xx}(t-kT) = R_{xx}(kT-t)$, and since a time-shifted function $x(t-\alpha)$ can be reconstructed from its time-shifted samples $x(kT-\alpha)$. In addition, by applying the sampling theorem two times to the third term of (3.36), we find that this term is $R_{xx}(t-t) = R_{xx}(0)$, so that $E[E^2(t)] = \sigma_e^2 = 0$. Because of Tchebyscheff's inequality, $P\{E(t) > c\} \leqslant \sigma_e^2/c^2$ [which holds for any pdf of $E(t)$ and any c]. Note that $\sigma_e^2 = 0$ implies that the probability $P\{E(t) \neq 0\}$ vanishes for all t.

The above proof is non-rigorous to the extent that the error function is zero at specific instants, viz. the instants kT, and thus $\{E(t)\}$ is not wide-sense stationary. However, these zero points are a set of zero probability and thus do not affect the expectation. A more rigorous deviation [Brown, 1960] [Thomas, 1969] [Tretter, 1976] [Jerri, 1977] is based on introducing a relative non-zero random phase ν between sampling function and waveform $x(t)$, by assuming that ν is uniformly distributed in the sampling interval $(0,T)$, and by averaging over all phases. Note that $\nu = 0$ in our simple proof.

3.5 2-D and 3-D Signals

The intensity function $\{f(x,y)\}$ of a 2-D image can be regarded as a deterministic signal or as a sample field of an ensemble, a random field $\{F(x,y)\}$. In this section, we shall discuss the sampling theorem for a bandlimited 2-D

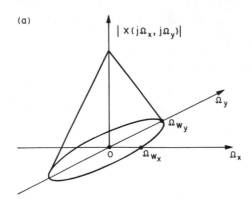

(a)

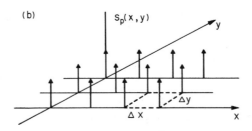

(b)

Figure 3.11　(a) Fourier representation of a 2-D bandlimited signal; (b) a 2-D sampling grid.

deterministic sequence [Figure 3.11(a)]. Extension to the case of a random field can be made following the random process material in the 1-D case (Section 3.4).

3.5.1 Sampling Theorem for 2-D Signals

The sampling of an image frame is actually a spatial operation, and the theory is best discussed by referring to a 2-D grid with sample (pixel) spacings of Δx and Δy in the two directions, as in Figure 3.11(b). In *ideal sampling*, the value of sample $f(k_h \Delta x, k_v \Delta y)$ is simply the gray level at the sample point $(k_h \Delta x, k_v \Delta y)$, and the sampling function $s_p(x,y)$ is an infinite array of Dirac delta functions of spacing Δx, Δy:

$$s_p(x,y) = \Delta x\, \Delta y \sum_{k_h=-\infty}^{\infty} \sum_{k_v=-\infty}^{\infty} \delta(x-k_h\, \Delta x, y-k_v\, \Delta y) \qquad (3.37)$$

It can be shown that the sampled function $f^*(x,y) = f(x,y)s_p(x,y)$ has the spectrum

$$F^*(j\Omega_x, j\Omega_y) = \sum_{k_h=-\infty}^{\infty} \sum_{k_v=-\infty}^{\infty} F[j(\Omega_x - k_h \frac{2\pi}{\Delta x}), j(\Omega_y - k_v \frac{2\pi}{\Delta y})] \qquad (3.38)$$

i.e., an infinite repetition of the baseband spectrum $F[j\Omega_x, j\Omega_y]$ in both directions of the frequency plane. Let Ω_{W_x} and Ω_{W_y} be the highest frequencies of the image. There is no spectral overlap if the sampling periods Δx and Δy satisfy

$$\Delta x \leqslant \frac{\pi}{\Omega_{W_x}}, \quad \Delta y \leqslant \frac{\pi}{\Omega_{W_y}} \tag{3.39}$$

with equality corresponding to *Nyquist sampling*. Obviously, the baseband can be reconstructed by a spatial filter with frequency response

$$H(j\Omega_x, j\Omega_y) = \text{rect}\frac{\Omega}{2\Omega_{W_x}} \text{ rect}\frac{\Omega}{2\Omega_{W_y}} \tag{3.40}$$

which is a rectangular block in the (Ω_x, Ω_y) plane. Its impulse response, also called a *point spread function*, is the product of two si functions, and we recover $f(x,y)$ from its samples $f(k_h\Delta x, k_v\Delta y)$ using the *ideal reconstruction* procedure

$$f(x,y) = \sum_{k_h=-\infty}^{\infty} \sum_{k_v=-\infty}^{\infty} f(k_h\Delta x, k_v\Delta y)\text{si}[\frac{\pi}{\Delta x}(x-k_h\Delta x)]\text{si}[\frac{\pi}{\Delta y}(y-k_v\Delta y)] \tag{3.41}$$

This is the *sampling theorem* for bandlimited 2-D signals, the counterpart of the 1-D result (3.15). The above theory can be extended to n dimensions [with a product of n si$(\cdot)$ terms in the interpolating operation corresponding to (3.41)], and to the sampling of random fields with a $\sigma_e^2 = 0$ result corresponding to (3.34).

3.5.2 Sampling of Moving Images

Section 3.5.1 provides a rigorous procedure for 2-D sampling and 2-D reconstruction. Practical image-sampling systems provide the resolutions Δx and Δy demanded by (3.39), but they do this through a *raster-scanning process* which is a means of sampling a 2-D signal in 1 dimension (the time dimension). The one-dimensional scanning process is often followed by 1-D reconstruction filtering, for example, with a 5 MHz cutoff. This filtering provides only horizontal interpolations in the resulting image. Vertical filtering in these systems is limited to the optical smoothing provided by factors such as the finite size of a spot on the cathode ray tube, and the lowpass characteristics of the human visual system. When explicit 2-D filtering is employed, it usually takes the form of approximations [Pratt, 1978] to the ideal si-function product in (3.41). See Problem 3.10.

An important consideration in moving images is the sampling of the third (temporal) dimension. It is typical to sample 2-D image matrices at 50 or 60 Hz, although this may sometimes constitute sub-Nyquist sampling, for scenes with very rapid motion (see Section 3.6). The 50 or 60 Hz is, however, sufficient to eliminate discernible flicker. The perceived resolution of the spatio-temporal sampling process is improved by an *interlacing* procedure; scan lines in successive matrices are staggered and because of the persistence of vision over a two-matrix period (1/25 s or 1/30 s), the impression is that of a single matrix with twice the number of scan lines. An individual matrix as defined above is called a *field*. Each

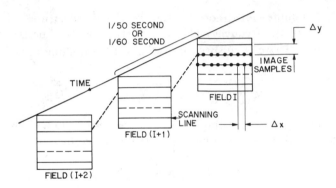

Figure 3.12 Sampling of the moving image in television [Netravali and Limb;©1980, IEEE].

complete image, composed of two spatially-interlaced fields, is called a *frame*. The frame rate (25 or 30 Hz) is clearly one-half of the field rate.

Figure 3.12 defines the conventional operations that convert a television signal from a scene into a sequence of pixels for subsequent image coding or image processing. This is done by first sampling the 3-D image in time to get the fields, followed by an adequate sampling of the 2-D image that defines pixels in each field. In this stage, the number of pixels/line determines the horizontal sample resolution Δx, while the number of lines per field determines the vertical resolution Δy. Also, in anticipation of interlace mentioned earlier, the distance Δx between two horizontally adjacent pixels in a field is smaller than the distance Δy between two vertically adjacent pixels.

3.6 Errors in Sampling — Aliasing Effects

The purpose of this section is to study errors due to non-ideal bandlimiting, i.e., non-ideal *prefiltering*. We have already noted instances of non-ideal *postfiltering*, or non-ideal reconstruction filtering. But errors due to these are perceptually less serious, and they will therefore not be discussed further. Errors such as those due to time jitter and certain other inaccuracies in the sampling process [Balakrishnan, 1962] [Landau, 1967] [Papoulis, 1966] can also be made small in practice, and hence are less serious than those due to insufficient prefiltering.

The bandlimitation assumed in Section 3.2 is never strictly realized. For example, real-world signals are time-limited, and as a consequence not strictly bandlimited. Moreover, practical presampling filters are non-ideal, leading potentially to inadequate sub-Nyquist sampling in systems designed on the basis of a "nominal" expected bandwidth in the input.

The result of inadequate sampling $(\Omega_S < 2\Omega_W$ or $f_s < 2W)$ is illustrated in Figure 3.13, which shows spectral overlaps from adjacent spectral segments in the periodic spectrum $X^*(j\Omega)$. Such *sideband overlap*, called *aliasing*, causes a distortion in the high-frequency range. The effect in the reconstruction $|X'(j\Omega)|$ is one of the spectrum folding back into the baseband with a reverse frequency

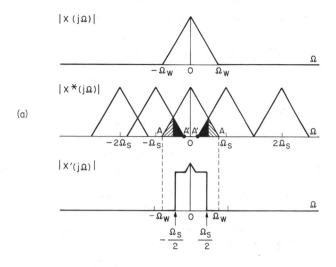

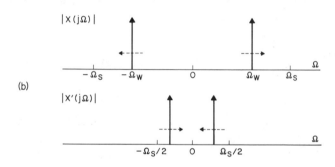

Figure 3.13 (a) Aliasing due to the undersampling of a bandlimited input; and (b) simple example of a cosinusoidal input.

direction. This foldover distortion can be mitigated by the use of a $\Omega_S/2$ cutoff lowpass filter (which is usually associated with an Ω_S sampling rate). The result is the dark triangular distortion areas adjacent to the points marked A'. A second effect of the above lowpass filter is the removal of high-frequency components of the signal, the cross-hatched triangular distortion areas adjacent to the points marked A. We will analyze these two types of distortion in detail very shortly. Let us note right now, however, that (a) the triangular regions corresponding to the above two types of distortion are equal in area, and that (b) the foldover distortion is perceptually more harmful than the lowpass distortion, both in speech and video applications.

It is interesting to note that an ideal reconstruction filter will have as its output a signal $x'(t)$ that is strictly bandlimited to $\Omega_S/2$, but that $x'(t)$ does not equal $x(t)$ because of aliasing. Samples $x'(kT)$, however, are equal to respective samples $x(kT)$.

3.6.1 Effect of Aliasing on Waveform Reconstruction

Example 3.1. Aliasing of a cosinusoidal input

The nature of aliasing can be understood better with the special example of a cosinusoidal input of frequency $\Omega_W > \Omega_S/2$ [Figure 3.13(b)]. This signal $x(t) = \cos \Omega_W t$ has a discrete line spectrum $X(j\Omega)$ with spectral lines at $\pm \Omega_W$. Sampling at $\Omega_S/2$ produces an infinite number of sum and difference frequencies in the periodic extension $X^*(j\Omega)$. When this spectrum is bandlimited to $\Omega_S/2$, the remaining frequency lines are at $\pm(\Omega_W - \Omega_S/2)$. In Figure 3.13(a), these locations are the points marked A'. The frequency $(\Omega_W - \Omega_S/2)$ in the reconstructed output is the *alias* frequency that is available to the user, in place of the original Ω_W. The perceptual annoyance of this alias frequency is related to the fact that input frequency Ω_W has a negative unity weight in the alias term — the higher the value of Ω_W, the lower is the value of the alias frequency.   •

Figure 3.14 Examples of aliasing with (a) unvoiced speech input [Jayant, 1978], and (b) 2-D image input [Pratt, 1978. Reprinted with permission].

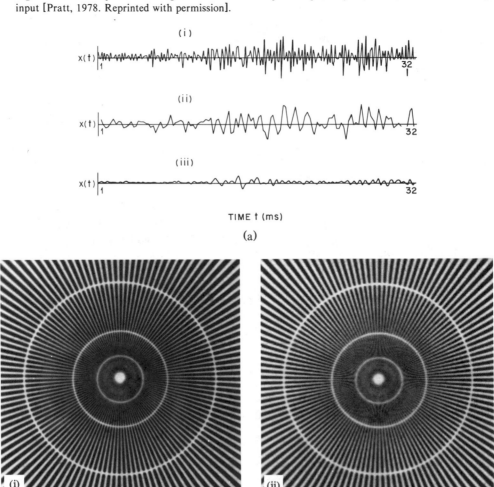

Example 3.2. Aliasing in speech and images

Figure 3.14 further illustrates aliasing with 1-D and 2-D waveforms. Unlike in Figure 3.13(a), we have selected highpass or high-detail inputs in both of the examples of Figure 3.14. This has been done to illustrate the effects of aliasing effectively.

Speech example. In the speech example (a), an unvoiced input (i) with $W = 3.2$ kHz is undersampled at 4 kHz and subsequently lowpass filtered to $f_s/2 = 2$ kHz. The result is the waveform in (ii). Also shown is the result of simply lowpass filtering the input (i) to 2 kHz. This result is the waveform in (iii). Note that in the undersampled case (ii), low frequency aliases appear that exist neither in (i) nor in the simply filtered version (iii). These aliases are caused by the foldover of high-frequency components into the (0, 2 kHz) band, and they have the pronounced effect of creating higher amplitudes in the waveform in (ii), as compared with (iii). Perceptually, both (ii) and (iii) have reduced intelligibility in comparison with (i). But while (iii) sounds smooth and perhaps acceptable in special applications, (ii) sounds harsh, annoying and generally unacceptable.

If (i) is approximated as a pure 3 kHz input, (iii) would be a zero signal, and (ii) would be a 1 kHz alias (corresponding to the alias term $(\Omega_W - \Omega_S/2)$ in Example 3.1. Since (i) is not a pure cosinusoid, the waveform (ii) contains a multiplicity of alias frequencies.

Image example. In the 2-D example of Figure 3.14(b), spatial undersampling of the image (i) similarly creates artificial low spatial frequency components in the reconstruction (ii), in both x- and y- directions. These patterns are particularly noticeable in the center of the reconstructed image (ii). In the field of optics, aliasing errors are known by the term *Moire patterns* that may involve multiple alias frequencies in general. Aliasing carries over to 3-D images as well. The so-called "stagecoach" effect in movies is an example: the frequency of 25 or 30 frames/second is sometimes inadequate for wheels of increasing rotating speed (or frequency); as a consequence, the wheels appear to decrease in speed, appear to stop, to accelerate again, and so on. ●

3.6.2 Ideal Prefiltering of a Non-Bandlimited Signal

We shall now compute the error variance σ_f^2 due to the prefiltering of a *non-bandlimited* stochastic signal $\{X(t)\}$ with psd $S_{xx}(\Omega)$.

In section 3.2, we have shown (3.23) that the sampling of an input waveform implies a periodic repetition of its spectrum. Similarly, sampling of the realizations of a random process implies a periodic repetition of its psd:

$$S_{xx}^*(\Omega) = \sum_{k=-\infty}^{\infty} S_{xx}(\Omega - k\,\Omega_S) \qquad (3.42)$$

Figure 3.15(a) is an example where $S_{xx}(\Omega)$ resembles the integrated power spectrum to be discussed presently, in Example 3.3.

The input process $\{X(t)\}$ is considered split into two processes: $\{X_l(t)\}$, which is passed through an *ideal* lowpass filter with cutoff frequency $\Omega_S/2$, and $\{X_u(t)\}$, which is suppressed. From Section 3.2, the lower frequency band component with psd $S_{xx}(\Omega)\text{rect}(\Omega/\Omega_S)$ can be sampled and reconstructed with zero mean-squared error. The upper band with psd $S_{xx}(\Omega)[1-\text{rect}(\Omega/\Omega_S)]$ is missing at the output of the system. The mse is

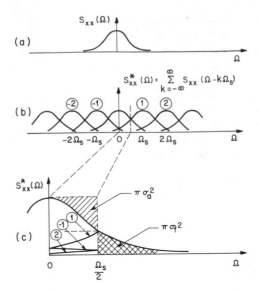

Figure 3.15 Analysis of prefiltering and aliasing error variances [Cattermole, 1969].

$$\sigma_f^2 = \frac{1}{2\pi} \int_{-\infty}^{\infty} S_{xx}(\Omega)[1 - \mathrm{rect}\,(\Omega/\Omega_S)]d\Omega = \frac{1}{\pi} \int_{\Omega_S/2}^{\infty} S_{xx}(\Omega)\,d\Omega \qquad (3.43)$$

which would be $1/\pi$ times the area of the cross-hatched tail in the magnified and slightly more general illustration of Figure 3.15(c).

Example 3.3. Prefiltering error with integrated power spectrum

For an integrated power spectrum (2.152) with corner frequency Ω_C:

$$S_{xx}(\Omega) = \frac{2}{\Omega_C} \frac{\sigma_x^2}{1+(\Omega/\Omega_C)^2}, \qquad (3.44)$$

the signal-to-prefiltering error ratio (σ_x^2/σ_f^2) has the simple form $\pi\Omega_S/4\Omega_C$ (Problem 3.8) for $\Omega_S(=2\Omega_W) \gg \Omega_C$, where Ω_W is a nominally selected bandwidth or *nominal cutoff* frequency. The ratio σ_x^2/σ_f^2, as given in the result of Problem 3.8, is plotted as a function of $(\Omega_S/2\Omega_C)$ in Figure 3.16(a). Note that its value is only 8.3 dB if the *half-Nyquist* rate, the *nominal* cutoff frequency $\Omega_W = \Omega_S/2$, is four times the corner frequency Ω_C. •

As noted in Table 2.4, the long-time-averaged spectrum of telephone speech (Figure 2.9) can be modeled after (3.44) with $\Omega_W = 4\,\Omega_C = 2\pi\,(3200)$ rad/s; the signal-to-prefiltering error ratio is therefore no more than 8.3 dB! Also of interest are the so-called *articulation index* (Appendix E) scores for lowpass filtered speech, shown in Figure 3.16(b) as a function of *nominal cutoff* Ω_W. Note that for $\Omega_W/2\pi = 3200$ Hz, this score is approximately 90%. Clearly as $\Omega_W \to \infty$, the articulation index tends to unity and σ_x^2/σ_f^2 tends to infinity. For the

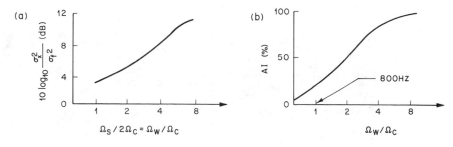

Figure 3.16 Prefiltering of speech. Effect of nominal lowpass cutoff Ω_W on (a) the signal-to-prefiltering ratio, and on (b) the articulation index score [Beranek, 1947].

nonstationary speech signal, the articulation index score is perceptually a better indicator for design of cut-off Ω_W.

A parallel result can be mentioned for the highest frequency of interest in video representation. This can be stated in terms of the number of pixels/frame that is necessary for preserving perceptually important detail. While the above number is scene-dependent, useful standards are in the order of 512×512 for broadcast TV quality and 256×256 for low quality videophone. The inadequacy of 128×128 resolution is demonstrated in Figure 3.17. A checker effect appears in the 128×128 example because pixels are repeated four times in each direction to maintain a uniform 512×512 output for display purposes. A similar effect exists, but less obviously, in the 256×256 example. Recall that with a temporal sampling of 30 frames/second, 256×256 resolution corresponds to an overall image sampling rate of 256×256×30 ~2 MHz, and a corresponding Nyquist bandwidth of 1 MHz. The sampling rate and bandwidth are both increased by a factor of 4 in the case of 512×512 resolution. Illustrations in this book are based either on 512×512 inputs or, as in some cases, on 256×256 inputs. These cases are usually quite distinguishable because of the greater sharpness in the 512×512 examples.

With an *ideal* prefilter with cutoff Ω_W, followed by corresponding Nyquist sampling with $f_s = \Omega_W/\pi$, the only source of error of interest to the present discussion is σ_f^2. With a *non-ideal* prefilter, on the other hand, a finite amount of power above Ω_W will be retained. This component will then cause fold-over or aliasing distortion (Figures 3.13 and 3.15), causing a second error component σ_a^2 which we shall presently analyze.

Example 3.4.   Prefiltering error with $6n$ dB/octave roll-off psd

Consider the equal-variance input spectra in Figure 3.18(a), which are flat up to Ω_C and decay thereafter at the rate of $6n$ dB/octave (Problem 3.9) with $n = 1,2,...,6$ and ∞. Also shown for comparison, in dashed lines, is an integrated power spectrum of equal variance. Values of (σ_x^2/σ_f^2) for this class of spectra are displayed in Figure 3.18(b) as a function of nominal prefilter cutoff Ω_W, with n as parameter. Note that the integrated power spectrum used in the calculations for Figure 3.16(a) is very close to the case of $n = 1$. Note also that as n increases, prefiltering error decreases for a given Ω_W; equivalently, for a given error, larger values of n permit lower values of Ω_W.   ●

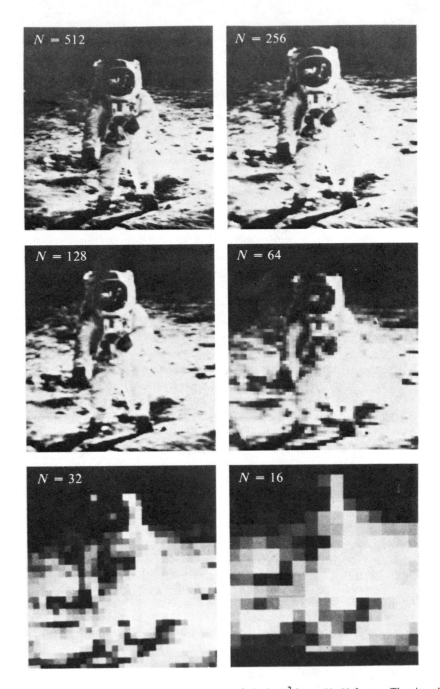

Figure 3.17 Image quality as a function of number of pixels N^2 in an $N \times N$ frame. The six values of N are 512, 256, 128, 64, 32 and 16 [Gonzalez and Wintz, 1977. Reprinted with permission].

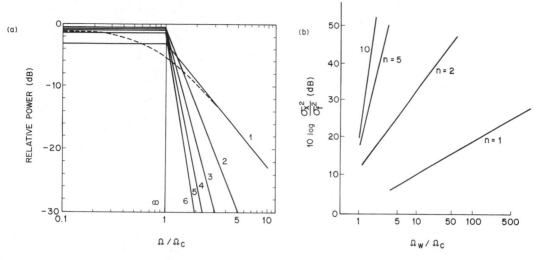

Figure 3.18 (a) Input spectra that are flat up to Ω_C, with a subsequent $6n$ dB/octave roll-off [Cattermole, 1969]. (b) Signal-to prefiltering error variance ratio σ_x^2/σ_f^2 as a function of prefilter cutoff Ω_W, normalized to Ω_C [Gagliardi, 1978. Reprinted with permission].

3.6.3 Aliasing Errors with Non-Ideal or No Prefiltering

Let us go back to Figure 3.15. In Section 3.6.2, we have noted that sampling of an input process implies a periodic repetition of its psd. Components in the periodic repetition of input spectrum $S_{xx}(\Omega)$ are numbered $\pm 1, 2, ...$ and respective contributions to foldover or aliasing distortion are shown by circled numbers in Figures 3.15(b) and (c). The contribution of component n is $S_{xx}(\Omega - n\Omega_S)$ and the total contribution due to all components is

$$S_{aa}^*(\Omega) = \sum_{n \neq 0} S_{xx}(\Omega - n\,\Omega_S) \tag{3.45a}$$

The contribution of this to the baseband forms the aliasing error, whose psd is

$$S_{aa}(\Omega) = S_{aa}^*(\Omega)\,\text{rect}(\Omega/\Omega_S) \tag{3.45b}$$

Figure 3.15 shows that repetitions corresponding to $n = \pm 1 \pm 2, ...$ contribute successively less to the aliased spectrum $S_{aa}(\Omega)$. The power is given by $(1/\pi)$ times the area under the sum of aliased contributions. By folding these contributions back to higher frequencies, we find that the shape and hence the area of the overall contribution equals that of the baseband above $\Omega_S/2$, the shaded area in Figure 3.15(c); so that the mse aliasing distortion σ_a^2 will simply be equal to the prefiltering error σ_f^2 which involves the same area in $S_{xx}(\Omega)$. Explicitly,

$$\sigma_a^2 = \frac{1}{2\pi} \int_{-\infty}^{\infty} S_{aa}(\Omega)d\Omega = \frac{1}{\pi} \int_{\Omega_S/2}^{\infty} S_{xx}(\Omega)d\Omega = \sigma_f^2 \tag{3.46}$$

Therefore, without prefiltering, the aliasing error variance equals that of ideal prefiltering; thus, the results of Figures 3.16(a) and 3.18 also show the aliasing mse. Note, however, that the types of distortion are perceptually quite different; as mentioned earlier, aliasing error is much more objectionable in speech and image coding.

Without prefiltering, the total error variance σ_t^2 has two components, one due to a σ_f^2 term because of the nominal cutoff of the reconstruction filter, and one due to the aliasing term σ_a^2. In fact, the total error variance *without prefiltering* is

$$\sigma_t^2 = \sigma_f^2 + \sigma_a^2 = 2 \, \sigma_f^2 = \frac{2}{\pi} \int_{\Omega_s/2}^{\infty} S_{xx}(\Omega) \, d\Omega \qquad (3.47)$$

which is *twice the error variance with prefiltering* (in which case the aliasing error is zero).

The above analysis shows the importance of prefiltering in that it can reduce the total error σ_t^2 by a factor of 2. In practice, the prefilter and the interpolation filter are both non-ideal. In fact, imperfect interpolation filters can be used to reduce aliasing effects somewhat by providing attenuation at higher baseband frequencies where aliasing effects tend to be the greatest. In video, such attenuation can be provided simply by defocusing of the moving spot on the picture tube screen.

In summary, we have seen in this section that prefiltering is a critical first step in a sampling process, and therefore a critical step in any digital coding system. In systems for speech and image coding, once a certain value of Ω_W is required from perceptual considerations [for example, Figure 3.16(b)], one cannot take many liberties in terms of either prefiltering or sampling rate; and the only way to reduce the transmission rate of the digital coding system is by reducing the bits/sample R in the equation $I = f_s R$. The coder inputs in the rest of the book are always assumed to be appropriately prefiltered versions. Aliasing is assumed to be zero $(\sigma_a^2 = 0)$ and the only error in the sampling process will be that due to prefiltering $(\sigma_t^2 = \sigma_f^2)$; since this error already exists in the input to the digital coding system, SNR characterizations of coding systems (comparison of *prefiltered waveform* with *coded prefiltered waveform*) will *not* include this parameter σ_f^2; rather, they will reflect only the further distortions introduced into the prefiltered waveform in the coding process, as noted in Chapter 1.

3.7 Discrete-Time Error and Continuous-Time Error

The rest of this book analyzes and optimizes coding schemes on the basis of discrete-time inputs $x(nT)$ and discrete-time outputs $y(nT)$, which will differ because of coding and digital transmission errors. The thesis of this section is that *minimization of the variance of reconstruction error $r(nT)$ in the discrete-time domain ensures minimization of the variance of error $r(t)$ between analog versions $x(t)$ and $y(t)$ as well; and that these two error signals indeed have equal variances.*

The reconstruction error in the discrete-time domain is described by

$$r(nT) = x(nT) - y(nT)$$

$$R_{rr}(kT) = E[R(nT)\,R((n+k)T)] \tag{3.48}$$

It is a good assumption that the discrete-time process is zero-mean (because positive and negative errors of any given magnitude are equiprobable in quantizing and coding systems that we will be studying). Hence the variance is

$$\sigma_r^2 = R_{rr}(0) = E[R^2(nT)] \tag{3.49}$$

This is the error variance minimized in future chapters of the book.

The analog output $y(t)$ is derived from its samples $y(nT)$ by passing them through an ideal lowpass filter with impulse response $h(t) = (1/T)\text{si}(\pi t/T)$ [see (3.19)]. This filters the reconstruction error as well. Hence the continuous-time error signal, in accordance with (3.20), is

$$r_A(t) = \sum_{k=-\infty}^{\infty} r(kT)\text{si}\,\frac{\pi}{T}\,(t - kT) \tag{3.50}$$

where subscript A denotes "analog". Note that $r(kT)$ can be viewed as a sample of a time-continuous process $\{R(t)\}$ whose psd may be quite wide as we will note in later chapters. Therefore, the strictly bandlimited version $r_A(t)$ will not resemble $r(t)$.

The psd of $\{R(t)\}$ is $S_{rr}(\Omega)$; its sampled version has a psd

$$S_{rr}^*(\Omega) = \sum_{k=-\infty}^{\infty} S_{rr}(\Omega - k\,\Omega_S) \tag{3.51}$$

and hence a variance in the baseband $(-\Omega_S/2,\ \Omega_S/2)$ given by

$$\sigma_{rA}^2 = \frac{1}{2\pi} \int_{-\Omega_s/2}^{\Omega_s/2} S_{rr}^*(\Omega)d\,\Omega \tag{3.52}$$

Insertion of (3.51) in (3.52) yields the important result

$$\sigma_{rA}^2 = \frac{1}{2\pi} \int_{-\infty}^{\infty} S_{rr}(\Omega)d\,\Omega = \sigma_r^2 \tag{3.53}$$

showing that discrete-time and analog-time errors have identical variances [Bennett, 1948] [Papoulis, 1966]. A coding system that minimizes σ_r^2 also minimizes σ_{rA}^2. The equality (3.53) may be surprising because the spectrum of the discrete-time error is much wider than that of the passband. However, this wideband error is effectively undersampled in the coding process. Aliasing occurs as a result, in a fashion very similar to the situation in Figure 3.15(b). This aliasing enhances the in-band component, and hence the analog error variance σ_{rA}^2, to a level that attains the equality in (3.53).

Problems

(3.1) Refer to the input samples in Figure 3.4(a). Derive $x(t)$ in the window $(T,5T)$ by using a $\sin x/x$ interpolation of the samples. Verify that the result is the bold-line waveform in Figure 3.4(b).

(3.2) Assume that a staircase approximation [as in Figure 3.4(c)] is used for reconstruction, rather than the optimal reconstruction in Figure 3.4(b).

(a) Show that an ideally sampled signal $x^*(t)$ (3.18) has the spectrum $X^*(j\Omega)$ of (3.23).

(b) Show that the staircase function has a spectrum

$$X_{st}(j\Omega) = T \text{ si } \frac{\Omega T}{2} \sum_{k=-\infty}^{\infty} X\left[j(\Omega - k\frac{2\pi}{T})\right]e^{-j\omega T/2}$$

which is the non-ideal spectrum in Figure 3.3(c).

(c) Show that the associated high-frequency damping of in-band components in the spectrum is characterized by an approximate 4 dB loss at $\Omega_W = \pi/T$, relative to $\Omega = 0$.

(3.3) Show that the *basis functions* $\psi_k(t) = \text{si}(\pi/T)(t-kT)$ in (3.15) are orthogonal over the interval $[-\infty,\infty]$, with

$$\int_{-\infty}^{\infty} \psi_k(t)\,\psi_l(t)\,dt = \begin{cases} T & k=l \\ 0 & \text{otherwise} \end{cases}$$

Therefore, sampling can be viewed as an orthogonal expansion of a bandlimited signal where the weights are just the samples of the signal.

(3.4) Consider a bandpass signal with a center frequency $2W$ and a bandwidth of W ($W_1 = 1.5W$; $W_2 = 2.5W$). Show that this signal can be ideally sampled and reconstructed

(a) if $f_s = 2.5W$,

(b) if $f_s > 5W$,

(c) but *not* if $f_s = 3.5W$.

(3.5) In a sub-band coding scheme for speech, the 0 to 3200 Hz band is split into 4 bands with frequency ranges following one of two designs below:

    (a)   [0-400] [400-800] [800-2000] [2000-3200]
    (b)   [0-800] [800-1600] [1600-2400] [2400-3200]

Show that the minimum overall sampling rates in (a) and (b) are 8800 Hz and 6400 Hz, respectively. Note that (b) is a better design because $W_1 = nW$ for all of its bands.

(3.6) A source of bandwidth 2500 Hz is to be amplitude modulated onto a subcarrier and then sampled at the rate of 10000 Hz. Indicate the permitted subcarrier frequencies that may be used for sampling at the minimal rate.

(3.7)   In an FDM (Frequency Division Multiplex) system, twelve 4 kHz speech bands modulate carrier frequencies in the range 60 to 108 kHz. Show that the minimum sampling rate for the resulting bandpass signal is $2.25W = 108000$ Hz.

(3.8)   Consider a process with integrated power spectrum of (3.44). Show that prefiltering with an ideal $\Omega_S/2$ rad/s lowpass filter causes a mean square filtering error σ_f^2 given by

$$\sigma_f^2/\sigma_x^2 = 1 - \frac{2}{\pi} \arctan \frac{\Omega_S}{2\Omega_C} \approx \frac{4\Omega_C}{\pi\Omega_S} \quad \text{for } \Omega_S/2 \gg \Omega_C$$

(3.9)   Assume a spectrum that is flat up to Ω_C and falls thereafter at $6n$ dB per octave [Figure 3.18(a)]:

$$S_{xx}(\Omega) = \begin{cases} A_n ; & |\Omega| \leq \Omega_C \\ A_n \left[\dfrac{\Omega_C}{\Omega} \right]^{2n} ; & |\Omega| > \Omega_C \end{cases} \quad \text{with } A_n = \frac{\pi}{\Omega_C}\left[1 - \frac{1}{2n} \right]\sigma_x^2$$

(a)   Show that the variance is σ_x^2.

(b)   For sampling frequency $\Omega_S \gg 2\Omega_C$, show that the prefiltering error variance is

$$\sigma_f^2 = \frac{1}{2n}\left[\frac{2\Omega_C}{\Omega_S} \right]^{2n-1} \sigma_x^2$$

Compare the $n=1$ case of this result with the approximate result of Problem 3.8.

(3.10)   The bell-shaped *cubic B-spline*

$$R(u) = (u)_+^3 - 4(u-T)_+^3 + 6(u-2T)_+^3 - 4(u-3T)_+^3$$

$$(u)_+^m = \begin{cases} u^m & \text{for } u > 0 \\ 0 & \text{for } u \leq 0 \end{cases}$$

is an attractive candidate for image interpolation because of its properties of continuity and smoothness at its extremities defined as $u = 0$ and $u = 4T$. Sketch the spline function in the range $u = 0$ to $4T$. Compare with the $\sin x/x$ function of Figure A.1. Sketch a cubic-spline interpolation of the samples in Figure 3.4(a), obtained by replacing the si function in (3.15) by $R(t-kT+2T)$, and compare it with the optimal si-function interpolation of Figure 3.4(b). Note, for example, that the sub-optimal spline-interpolated waveform has a positive value at sampling instant $3T$, unlike the waveform in Figure 3.4(b).

(3.11)   Consider the Nyquist sampling ($f_s = 2W$) of a unit-variance lowpass input of bandwidth W. Show that if the psd is symmetrical about $W/2$, the acf value is

$\rho_1 = R(f_s^{-1}) = 0$. Note that a white input is a special case, while typical speech and video inputs have psd's that are asymmetrical about $W/2$, resulting in non-zero acf values ρ_1 (Figures 2.7 and 2.8).

References

A. V. Balakrishnan, "On the Problem of Time Jitter in Sampling," IRE Trans. on Information Theory, pp. 226-236, April 1962.

W. R. Bennett, "Spectra of Quantized Signals," Bell System Tech. J., pp. 446-471, July 1948.

L. L. Beranek, "The Design of Communications Systems," Proc. IRE, pp. 880-890, September 1947.

J. L. Brown, Jr., "Mean Square Truncation Error in Series Expansions of Random Functions," J. SIAM, pp. 18-32, March 1960.

K. W. Cattermole, *Principles of Pulse Code Modulation,* American Elsevier, New York, 1969.

C. L. Damann, L. D. McDaniel and C. L. Maddox, "D2 Channel Bank: Multiplexing and Coding," Bell System Tech. J., pp. 1675-1699, October 1972.

R. M. Gagliardi, *Introduction to Communications Engineering*, John Wiley, New York, 1978.

R. C. Gonzalez and P. Wintz, *Digital Image Processing,* Addison-Wesley, Reading, Mass., 1977.

N. S. Jayant, unpublished work, Bell Laboratories, 1982.

A. B. Jerri, "The Shannon Sampling Theorem — Its Various Extensions and Applications: A Tutorial Review," Proc. IEEE, pp. 1565-1596, November 1977.

A. Kohlenberg, "Exact Interpolation of Bandlimited Functions," J. Applied Physics, pp. 1432-1436, December 1953.

H. J. Landau, "Sampling, Data Transmission and the Nyquist Rate," Proc. IEEE, pp. 1701-1706, October 1967.

A. N. Netravali and J. O. Limb, "Picture Coding: A Review," Proc. IEEE, pp. 366-406, March 1980.

H. Nyquist, "Certain Topics in Telegraph Transmission Theory," AIEE Trans., p. 617 ff, 1946.

A. Papoulis, "Error Analysis in Sampling Theory," Proc. IEEE, pp. 947-955, July 1966.

W. K. Pratt, *Image Coding,* John Wiley, New York, 1978.

C. E. Shannon, "Communication in the Presence of Noise," Proc. IRE, pp. 10-21, January 1949.

Siemens AG, Munich, Data Sheet SM 153, 1983.

J. J. Spilker, *Digital Communications by Satellite,* Prentice-Hall, Englewood Cliffs, N.J., 1975.

F. G. Stremler, *Introduction to Communication Systems,* Addison-Wesley, Reading, Mass., 1977.

J. B. Thomas, *Introduction to Statistical Communication Theory,* John Wiley, New York, 1969.

S. A. Tretter, *Introduction to Discrete-Time Signal Processing,* John Wiley, New York, 1976.

J. M. Whittaker, "Interpolatory Function Theory," *Cambridge Tracts in Mathematics and Mathematical Physics,* Chapter 4, Cambridge University Press, 1935.

4

Quantization

4.1 Introduction

Information-bearing waveforms are typically *continuous-amplitude* and *continuous-time* in nature. Hence *analog-to-digital (A/D) conversion* is needed to produce a discrete representation of the waveform. We have discussed *sampling* or *time discretization* in Chapter 3. Resulting samples are still continuous in amplitude, as in Figure 1.1(c), and the process of *amplitude quantization* is needed to limit the number of possible amplitudes to a finite value, as in Figure 1.1(d). The operations of sampling and quantization could be performed in either order; but in practice, sampling precedes quantization. Amplitude quantization is a crucial step in a digital communication link, since it determines to a great extent the overall distortion as well as the bit rate necessary to communicate the waveform to the receiver.

Amplitude quantization is the procedure of transforming a given signal amplitude $x(n)$ at time n into an amplitude $y(n)$ taken from a finite set of possible amplitudes. In many of the discussions in this chapter, we will assume the important simple situation of *memoryless* and *instantaneous quantization*, a procedure where the transformation at time n is not affected by earlier or later input samples. Such a scheme is simple, but it is not optimum, even if the input samples are statistically independent; this is discussed in Chapter 9. Memoryless quantization is particularly inefficient if the samples are statistically dependent; these dependencies are therefore typically eliminated prior to quantization in the coders to be discussed in later chapters.

Coding systems involving Entropy Coding or certain types of Adaptive

Quantization need the use of memory and encoding delay, but even in these systems, the process of quantization itself can be regarded as instantaneous. But this is not true of the Vector Quantization systems to be discussed in Chapter 9.

When dealing with memoryless quantizers, we will drop the time index, and use symbols such as x instead of $x(n)$. We shall see later that the quantizer input need not always be the amplitude of the primary waveform to be coded. It may as well be a function of this waveform, for example, a difference between neighboring samples or some type of spectral information about input samples; and the quantizing process may only be one component of the overall coding system.

A digital system consists of at least three mappings. At the transmitter, the real-valued amplitude x is mapped into an L-ary number k. The channel maps k into k, deterministically, if the transmission is error-free; if not, it maps k into another L-ary number k', probabilistically. At the receiver, the L-ary number k or k' is mapped into representation level y_k or $y_{k'}$. These mappings are shown in Figure 4.1. Technically, the mappings at the transmitter and receiver are performed by an *Analog-to-Digital (A/D) Converter* and a *Digital-to-Analog (D/A) Converter*, respectively (Appendix G). In the absence of transmission errors, the combination of A/D and D/A operations is exactly identical to the quantizer mapping $Q(\cdot)$.

As shown in Figure 4.2, the signal amplitude x is specified by index k if it falls into the interval

$$\mathscr{I}_k: \{x_k < x \leqslant x_{k+1}\} ; \quad k = 1,2,...,L \tag{4.1}$$

The L-ary number k is transmitted to the receiver, typically in binary format. Let $L = 2^R$; then a *bit rate* of

$$R = \log_2 L \quad bits/sample \tag{4.2}$$

is needed to inform the receiver about that index. At the receiver, the index k is transformed into an amplitude y_k that represents all amplitudes of the interval $\mathscr{I}_k$. The amplitudes y_k are called the *representation levels* or the *reconstruction values*, and the amplitudes x_k are called *decision levels* or *decision thresholds*. The

Figure 4.1 Digital communication system (a) with and (b) without transmission errors.

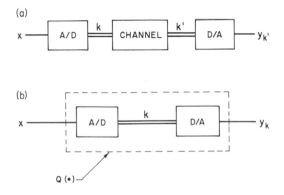

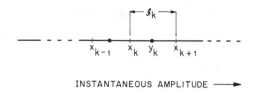

INSTANTANEOUS AMPLITUDE ⟶

Figure 4.2 Quantization of amplitude x.

number of intervals equals the number of possible outputs y_k and each of these equals the finite number L. The set of possible outputs is described by

$$y \in \{y_1, y_2,...,y_L\} \qquad (4.3)$$

Unless otherwise mentioned, we assume error-free transmission. We thus have an output

$$y = y_k \quad \text{if} \quad x \in \mathscr{I}_k \qquad (4.4)$$

For a close approximation to the input, one requires that $y_k \in \mathscr{I}_k$. The actual mapping

$$y = Q(x) \qquad (4.5)$$

is the *quantizer characteristic*, a staircase function by definition.

Several types of $Q(x)$ are shown in Figure 4.3 for $L = 8$ and $L = 7$. All of these characteristics are symmetric about zero. Unless otherwise stated, all future discussions will assume such symmetry. The quantizers in parts (a) and (c) of the figure are *nonuniform*, with decision level- and reconstruction level intervals being different in length and being functions of k. We will also be discussing at length

Figure 4.3 Quantizer characteristic types: (a) nonuniform midrise; (b) uniform midrise; (c) nonuniform midtread; and (d) uniform midtread.

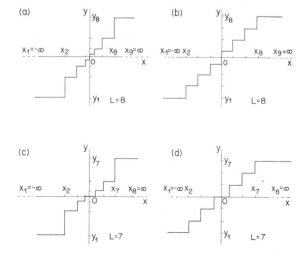

the special but important case of a *uniform* quantizer, shown in parts (b) and (d) of the figure:

$$\text{Uniform Quantizer:} \quad y_{k+1} - y_k = \Delta; \quad k = 1,2,...,L-1$$

$$(4.6)$$

$$x_{k+1} - x_k = \Delta; \quad \text{for finite } x_k, x_{k+1}$$

The characteristic $Q(x)$ can also be of *midtread* or *midrise* type, depending on whether zero is one of the output levels or not. For symmetry, L is chosen to be odd for midtread quantizers, as in parts (c) and (d) of Figure 4.3. Unless otherwise stated, we always assume midrise quantizers with even L.

Inherent in the quantization process is an error between input x and output y. This error is called *quantization error*, and we shall define it as the difference between x and y:

$$q = x - y = x - Q(x) \qquad (4.7)$$

where $y \in \{y_1, y_2, ..., y_L\}$. It is important to realize that the quantization error is totally deterministic for a given x because an input $x \in \mathcal{I}_k$ always leads to a single output y_k. Figure 4.4 shows this deterministic error as a function of x for an $L=8$ midrise example. However, if x is an outcome of a random variable X, it is reasonable to consider q as an outcome of another random variable Q; for this reason, we sometimes use the term *quantization noise* to describe the errors introduced by the quantizer. The use of the term "noise" is also motivated by an attempt to unify nomenclature, consistent with "channel noise" and "thermal noise" in analog systems. Indeed, quantization noise can often be modeled analytically as additive noise, especially if the quantization is very fine, as discussed in Section 4.7; in fact, with a technique known as dithering (Section 4.8), resulting errors in quantization can be modeled as input-independent additive noise even with coarse quantization. However, it must be remembered that unlike channel noise or thermal noise, quantization noise is deliberately introduced and in general it is signal-correlated.

Figure 4.4 Illustration of the deterministic nature of quantization error q in zero-memory quantization: (a) uniform quantization characteristic (step size $\Delta = 1$) and (b) nonuniform quantization characteristic (min $\{\Delta\} = 0.5$; max $\{\Delta\} = $ max $\{y_k - y_{k-1}\} = 1.6$).

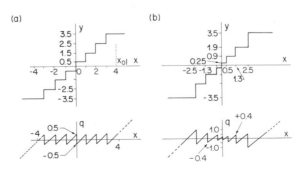

4.2 Calculation of Quantization Error Variance

4.2.1 Basic Formulas

Let X be a zero-mean random variable at the quantizer input, with variance σ_x^2 and pdf $p_x(\cdot)$:

$$\mu_x = E[X] = \int_{-\infty}^{\infty} x p_x(x)\,dx = 0; \qquad \sigma_x^2 = E[X^2] = \int_{-\infty}^{\infty} x^2 p_x(x)\,dx \qquad (4.8)$$

If the input X has a nonzero mean, we can remove it by subtracting $E[X]$ from the input, and add it back after quantization. Alternatively, we could interpret this procedure as a shift of the center of the quantizer to the mean value. A zero mean will therefore be assumed in our analytical studies without loss of generality.

A quantizer $Q(\cdot)$ maps X into the discrete-valued r.v. Y:

$$Y = Q(X) = y_k \quad \text{if } X \in \mathscr{I}_k \qquad (4.9)$$

Thus, the quantization error $Q = X - Y$ is also a random variable with pdf $p_q(\cdot)$ and variance

$$\sigma_q^2 = E[Q^2] = \int_{-\infty}^{\infty} q^2 p_q(q)\,dq \qquad (4.10)$$

Alternatively, as $Q = X - Q(X)$ is a function of X,

$$\sigma_q^2 = E[Q^2] = \int_{-\infty}^{\infty} [x - Q(x)]^2 p_x(x)\,dx \qquad (4.11)$$

By breaking up the region of integration into L intervals $\mathscr{I}_k$ (4.1) and by making use of (4.9), we obtain the expression

$$\sigma_q^2 = \sum_{k=1}^{L} \int_{x_k}^{x_{k+1}} (x - y_k)^2 p_x(x)\,dx \qquad (4.12)$$

Quantization error variance is the most important quantity for comparing the performances of quantizers, and we often use (4.12) to calculate this variance. Its calculation via (4.10) is possible only if the pdf $p_q(q)$ is known, which is typically not the case. However, we shall see in Example 4.1 and later in Section 4.7 that $p_q(q)$ may be approximated by a constant over a finite range in the case of uniform quantization.

Example 4.1. Uniform quantization of a bounded input

Consider the example of an input x with amplitudes in the range

$$x \in (-x_{\max}, x_{\max}) \qquad (4.13)$$

and a uniform quantizer with $-x_{max} = x_2 - \Delta$; $x_{max} = x_8 + \Delta$, as in the 3-bit example of Figure 4.3(b). In this case,

$$\Delta = 2x_{max}/2^R \qquad (4.14)$$

Quantization errors [as seen in Figure 4.4(a)] will have values in the range

$$-\Delta/2 \leqslant q \leqslant \Delta/2 \qquad (4.15)$$

If Δ is sufficiently small, it is reasonable to assume that they are uniform in the above range:

$$p_q(q) = \begin{cases} 1/\Delta & |q| \leqslant \Delta/2 \\ 0 & otherwise \end{cases} \qquad (4.16)$$

and (4.10) yields

$$\sigma_q^2 = \Delta^2/12 \qquad (4.17)$$

Using (4.14),

$$\sigma_q^2 = \frac{1}{3} x_{max}^2 \, 2^{-2R} \qquad (4.18)$$

Equation (4.17) shows that the standard deviation (rms value) of the noise increases linearly with step size, and (4.18) shows that the rms value decreases exponentially with increasing bit rate R. Since $L = 2^R$, an increase of R by 1 bit/sample implies a doubling of the number of steps L and hence, for a given x_{max}, a reduction in step size Δ by a factor of 2. Note finally that (4.15) and (4.16) are true only if the input is bounded. For example, if $|x| > 4$ in Figure 4.4(a), the error would increase linearly with $|x|$, as shown by the dashed extensions in the lower part of the figure.

Maximum Fractional Error. Consider the uniform quantization formula $\Delta = 2x_{max}/2^R$ (4.14). For a bounded input, we define the *maximum fractional error* as $(\Delta/2)/x_{max}$. For this number to be 1% and 0.1%, we respectively need $R = 7$ ($L = 128$) and $R = 10$ ($L = 1024$). •

The preceding example has shown that σ_q^2 can be obtained from (4.10). But (4.12) is also significant; it allows us to calculate σ_q^2 when the quantizer parameters (thresholds and representation levels) and the pdf of the input are given. Moreover, it also allows us to find quantizer parameters which result in the *minimum mean squared error variance (mmse)*. We shall discuss specific mmse designs in Sections 4.3 and 4.4.

Quantizer Performance Factor. It is useful to relate the error variance σ_q^2 to the input signal variance σ_x^2. The ratio

$$\epsilon_q^2 = \sigma_q^2/\sigma_x^2 \qquad (4.19)$$

will be called the *quantizer performance factor*. It is the quantization error variance for a unit-variance input signal. The inverse of ϵ_q^2 is the *signal-to-quantization noise ratio SNR*:

$$SNR \ (\text{dB}) = 10 \ \log_{10} \ (\sigma_x^2/\sigma_q^2) = 10 \ \log_{10} \ (1/\epsilon_q^2) \qquad (4.20)$$

It is sometimes useful to split the quantizer performance in the form

$$\sigma_q^2 = \epsilon_*^2 \ 2^{-2R} \ \sigma_x^2 \qquad (4.21)$$

The parameter ϵ_*^2 is in fact the reciprocal of the constant a in (1.6). We shall note presently that ϵ_*^2 is greater than unity for inputs with the four pdf's in Figure 2.5, except in some instances where a refinement called entropy coding is applied (Section 4.6).

The foregoing notation allows us to compute a general expression for the necessary bit rate for a given *SNR*:

$$R = \frac{1}{2} \ \log_2 \ (\sigma_x^2/\sigma_q^2) + \frac{1}{2} \ \log_2 \ \epsilon_*^2 \qquad \text{bits/sample} \qquad (4.22a)$$

For a given value of σ_q^2, the minimum bit rate as given by rate distortion theory (Appendix D) is of the form

$$\min\{R\} = \frac{1}{2} \ \log_2 \ (\sigma_x^2/\sigma_q^2) - \alpha_R \qquad \text{bits/sample} \qquad (4.22b)$$

where $\alpha_R = 0$ for a Gaussian i.i.d. source (D.19) and $\alpha_R > 0$ for a non-Gaussian i.i.d. source. The $\log_2 \epsilon_*^2$ term, on the other hand, is positive; but it can be made negative by employing entropy coding. Indeed, we will show in Section 4.6 that for all these sources, the second term can be made at least arbitrarily close to $0.25 - \alpha_R$, leading to a required bit rate R that is only 0.25 bit greater than min $\{R\}$.

4.2.2 Granular Noise and Overload Distortion

Let us go back to Figure 4.4. Recall that step size in that figure was $\Delta = 1$. The dashed extensions in the error plots refer to a region of input amplitude where the error q no longer has the finite range $(-\Delta/2, \Delta/2)$. The value $|x| = 4\Delta$ in Figure 4.4(a), for example, is called the *overload amplitude* x_{ol}, the region $|x| > x_{ol}$ is called the *overload region*, and samples of $|q|$ that exceed $\Delta/2$ are called *overload errors*. Errors in the finite $(-\Delta/2, \Delta/2)$ range are called *granular* errors. Granularity refers to the rapid oscillatory or "fine-grained" structure of the solid line part of the $q(x)$ function of Figure 4.4. This structure is also characteristic of the $q(n)$-versus-n waveforms that result when $x(n)$ values increase or decrease rapidly with n in an input waveform segment. Overload error waveforms, on the other hand, are characterized by bursts of $q(n)$ samples of identical polarity (Figure 4.5) that occur if the overloading input $x(n)$ is slowly varying, as most Nyquist-sampled and over-sampled waveforms are. The above distinction in the structure of the two types of errors is emphasized by the terms *granular noise* and *overload distortion*. The difference in corresponding error

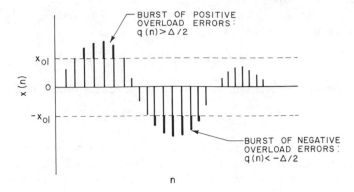

Figure 4.5 Overload error bursts. Heavy lines indicate overload error samples caused by bursts of $|x(n)|$ values that exceed $|x_{ol}|$.

spectra is reflected by significant differences in the perceptual annoyance of the two types of errors in the coding of physical signals, and we shall comment on this many times in this book. We note at this point that purely *from an error-variance viewpoint*, overload errors can be more serious, simply because these error samples are unbounded in the case of unbounded inputs, and these values are squared in computing σ_q^2.

Although overload errors can be unbounded, the *probability of overload* can be reduced by a proper design of the quantizer. In fact, this probability can be made zero if the input pdf is *bounded* to x_{max} and the quantizer overload amplitude x_{ol} is designed to equal or exceed x_{max}. In Figure 4.6(a), $L=4$ and $x_{max} = x_{ol} = 2\Delta$. Designs such as these will indeed be shown to be optimal for a uniform input pdf (Section 4.3). If the input pdf is *unbounded* $(x_{max} = \infty)$, there is always a non-

Figure 4.6 Four-level quantizers with (a) bounded and (b) unbounded inputs.

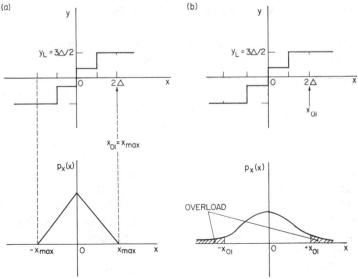

zero probability of overload. This is shown by the shaded area in Figure 4.6(b). The overload point x_{ol} has been defined in the midriser example in Figure 4.6(a) so that $|q| > \Delta/2$ for $|x| > x_{ol}$. The same definition of x_{ol} can also be applied to a midtread quantizer. In general,

$$x_{ol} = \begin{cases} 2^{R-1}\Delta & \text{for a uniform midrise quantizer} \\ (2^{R-1}- 0.5)\,\Delta & \text{for a uniform midtread quantizer} \end{cases} \quad (4.23)$$

An interesting type of non-uniform quantizer is one where step size Δ_k in interval $\mathcal{I}_k$ is an increasing function of k [Figure 4.3 (a) and (c)]. In this case, x_{ol} may be defined so that $|q| > \max\{\Delta_k\}/2$ for $|x| > x_{ol}$.

The total error variance (4.12) can be expressed for any quantizer characteristic as a sum of granular and overload error variances:

$$\sigma_q^2 = \sigma_{q(granular)}^2 + \sigma_{q(overload)}^2 \; ; \quad (4.24)$$

$$\sigma_{q(granular)}^2 = \sum_{k=2}^{L-1} \int_{x_k}^{x_{k+1}} (x-y_k)^2 p_x(x)\,dx + 2\int_{x_L}^{x_{ol}} (x-y_L)^2 p_x(x)\,dx \quad (4.25a)$$

$$\sigma_{q(overload)}^2 = 2 \int_{x_{ol}}^{\infty} (x-y_L)^2 p_x(x)\,dx \quad (4.25b)$$

Relative values of granular and overload noise components depend on x_{ol}, and hence on step size.

Figure 4.7 shows $SNR = 10 \log_{10} (\sigma_x^2/\sigma_q^2)$ as a function of x_{ol}/x_{max} for the example of a uniform quantizer (Problem 4.1) with a uniform pdf input

Figure 4.7   Uniform quantizer performance with uniform input pdf.

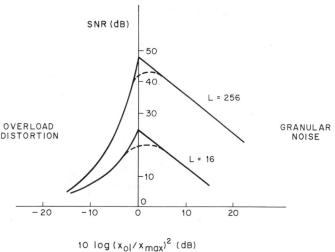

$(|x| \leq x_{max})$, using values $L = 16$ and 256 for illustration. The extreme left of the figure (small x_{ol}) is an overload-distortion-dominated region, while the right $(x_{ol} > x_{max})$ describes the effects of granular errors. The fact that SNR decreases more rapidly with increasing overload than with increasing granularity causes an asymmetry about the SNR-axis that will be observed repeatedly in similar future illustrations in this book.

The dashed lines in Figure 4.7 indicate qualitative results for unbounded inputs such as those with a Gaussian pdf. In this case, the transition between overload and granular regions will be a smooth one, and the maximum of the characteristic depends on the so-called *loading factor*; see Example 4.4 and Figure 4.8.

Example 4.2. Probability of overload

The probability of overload can easily be calculated for a random variable X with a Gaussian pdf. Following (2.15), the probability that the amplitude is above the overload point is

$$P\{|x| > x_{ol}\} = 2(1 - P_x(x_{ol})) = 1 - \text{erf }(x_{ol}/(\sqrt{2}\sigma_x)) \tag{4.26}$$

For $x_{ol} = 4\sigma_x$ (4σ-loading), we have a probability of overload given by $1 - \text{erf } 2\sqrt{2} = .000064$, a generally negligible value. With $x_{ol} = 2\sigma_x$ (2σ-loading), on the other hand, the overload probability will be $1 - \text{erf }\sqrt{2} = 0.046$. ●

4.3 Uniform Quantization

In *uniform quantizers*, the decision intervals $\mathscr{I}_k$ are of the same length Δ, and the reconstruction levels are the midpoints of the decision intervals. In the case of midrise quantizers,

$$x_1 = -\infty ; \quad x_{L+1} = \infty ; \quad x_{k+1} - x_k = \Delta ; \quad k = 2,...,L-1 \tag{4.27}$$

Figure 4.3(b) has already shown the transfer function of the uniform midriser quantizer for the example of $L=8$.

4.3.1 The Case of Zero or Negligible Overload

We assume an input random variable X of variance σ_x^2 where the amplitudes are bounded and the dynamic range of the input equals that of the quantizer. Following Figure 4.6(a),

$$|x| \leq x_{max} = x_{ol} = L\Delta/2 \tag{4.28}$$

As shown earlier on the basis of a uniform (granular) error pdf in the range $(-\Delta/2, \Delta/2)$ (which is a good assumption for $R \gg 1$),

$$\sigma_q^2 = \Delta^2/12 = (1/3) x_{max}^2 2^{-2R} \tag{4.29}$$

This error variance can be reduced by a factor of 4 by reducing the step size Δ by a factor of 2, i.e., by doubling L (for a given x_{max}). Let us define a *loading factor*

$$f_l = x_{ol}/\sigma_x = L\Delta/2\sigma_x \qquad (4.30)$$

This determines the half-amplitude range of the quantizer in multiples of the standard deviation of the signal to be quantized. From (4.29) and (4.30),

$$\sigma_x^2/\sigma_q^2 = 3L^2 \, \sigma_x^2/x_{max}^2 = 3L^2/f_l^2$$

$$SNR \ (dB) = 6.02R - 10 \log_{10} (f_l^2/3) : \quad R \gg 1 \qquad (4.31)$$

Example 4.3.   Uniform pdf input with $x_{max} = x_{ol}$

$f_l = x_{max}/\sigma_x$, which is equal to $\sqrt{3}$ for the uniform pdf ; $SNR \ (dB) = 6.02 R$ (4.32)

We will note presently (also see Figure 4.7) that the empirical design $x_{max} = x_{ol}$ is indeed optimal for the uniform pdf.   ●

Example 4.4.   Sine-wave input with $x_{max} = x_{ol}$

$f_l = x_{max}/\sigma_x$,   which is equal to $\sqrt{2}$ for the arcsine pdf; $SNR \ (dB) = 6.02 R + 1.76$ (4.33)

Quantization of sine-waves is of interest since they are useful as test signals in digital coding systems. Also see Problem 4.3.   ●

Example 4.5.   Unbounded input with negligible overload probability

The formulas derived above may also be used for *unbounded* inputs if x_{ol} is chosen such that the probability of overload $P\{|x| \geq x_{ol}\}$ is sufficiently small so that the corresponding overload errors can be neglected. A typical value of the loading factor is $f_l = 4$ (4σ-loading, as in Example 4.2). In this case,

$$f_l = 4 ; \qquad SNR \ (dB) = 6.02 R - 7.27 \qquad (4.34)$$

It will be seen in the next section that this choice of f_l *does not give the minimum overall (i.e., granular plus overload) noise*; the optimum value of f_l is pdf-and R-dependent. For Gaussian pdf's it is a monotonically increasing function of R, with values between 1.6 and 3.8 in the range of $R = 1$ to 8. This implies an overload probability (4.26) that increases with decreasing R.   ●

4.3.2 PDF-Optimized Uniform Quantizers

The preceding section has shown that it is easy to calculate the SNR under the assumption of zero overload. In general, σ_q^2-minimizing designs imply non-zero overload for any unbounded pdf. We find the optimum or *minimum mean squared error (mmse)* step size, and hence the *mmse uniform quantizer*, by minimizing the error variance as given by (4.12) with the uniform quantizer definitions given by (4.27):

$$x_k = \left[k - \frac{L+2}{2} \right] \Delta \; ; \quad k = 2,3,\ldots,L$$

$$y_k = \left[k - \frac{L+1}{2} \right] \Delta \; ; \quad k = 1,2,\ldots,L \qquad (4.35)$$

where we have assumed a midrise quantizer [Figure 4.3(b)] with an even number L of output levels ($x_1 = -\infty$; $x_{L+1} = \infty$). For minimizing σ_q^2 we require that $d\sigma_q^2/d\Delta = 0$. In general it is not possible to calculate the optimum step sizes Δ_{opt} explicitly. The simple cases of $L = 2$ and $L = 3$ will be seen to be exceptions. However, we can solve the minimization problem numerically with a computer [Max, 1960] [Paez and Glisson, 1972]. The resulting step size Δ_{opt} minimizes the total error variance, the sum of $\sigma_q^2{}_{(granular)}$ and $\sigma_q^2{}_{(overload)}$. Figure 4.8 shows an example of the dependence of these terms on f_l. The granular noise variance *increases* with f_l because of increasing step size, and the overload noise variance *decreases* with f_l because the probability of overload becomes smaller. The total noise σ_q^2 has a minimum with respect to f_l (near 3.05 in the 5-bit Gaussian example in the figure). Note that a similar minimum occurred in the uniform pdf example of Figure 4.7; although at a different value of f_l: specifically, at a value of f_l for which $x_{ol} = x_{max}$ i.e., at $f_l = x_{max}/\sigma_x = \sqrt{3}$ (see Example 4.3).

Table 4.1 gives the optimum step sizes and the corresponding *SNR*-values max$\{SNR\}$ of pdf-optimized symmetric uniform quantizers for various pdf's. The *SNR* values for the uniform pdf are those of (4.32). The other pdf's are those of unbounded random variables. Large step sizes have to be chosen in order to have a balance between granular noise and overload noise. A study of Table 4.1 reveals that for unbounded inputs the deviation of the *SNR* (in dB) from a simple 6.02 R formula increases with bit rate. In the term ϵ_*^2 of (4.21), this implies an increase of ϵ_*^2 with R. For example, for a gamma pdf we have $\epsilon_*^2 = 2.67$ for $R=1$ and $\epsilon_*^2 =$

Figure 4.8 Dependence of normalized overload and granular error variances on loading factor $f_l = x_{ol}/\sigma_x$ in the uniform 5-bit quantization of a Gaussian input.

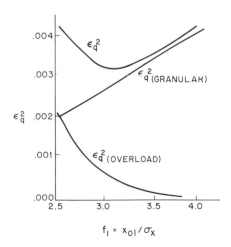

Table 4.1 Optimum step size and max{SNR} for uniform symmetric quantizers with different input pdf's (U: Uniform G: Gaussian L: Laplacian Γ: Gamma) [Max, 1960] [Paez and Glisson, 1972].

R (bits/sample)	Δ_{opt}/σ_x pdf				max {SNR} (dB) pdf			
	U	G	L	Γ	U	G	L	Γ
1	1.7320	1.5956	1.4142	1.1547	6.02	4.40	3.01	1.76
2	0.8660	0.9957	1.0874	1.0660	12.04	9.25	7.07	4.95
3	0.4330	0.5860	0.7309	0.7957	18.06	14.27	11.44	8.78
4	0.2165	0.3352	0.4610	0.5400	24.08	19.38	15.96	13.00
5	0.1083	0.1881	0.2800	0.3459	30.10	24.57	20.60	17.49
6	0.0541	0.1041	0.1657	0.2130	36.12	29.83	25.36	22.16
7	0.0271	0.0569	0.0961	0.1273	42.14	35.13	30.23	26.99
8	0.0135	0.0308	0.0549	0.0743	48.17	40.34	35.14	31.89

32.77 for $R=7$. On the other hand, rate distortion theory promises ϵ_*^2 values that are upperbounded by a value of 1.0. In this sense, we conclude that the relative performance of uniform quantizers becomes worse at high bit rates. Finally, we note from Table 4.1 that the step size values (Δ_{opt}/σ_x) can also be used to compute the optimum loading factor $f_{l,opt}$ and hence the SNR in (4.31). It turns out that $f_{l,opt}$ in general is not a constant but depends on $R = \log_2 L$. When using the approximate rule-of-thumb formula (4.34), this should be kept in mind. A special case is that of the uniform pdf for which $f_{l,opt} = \sqrt{3}$ for all R. This is easily verified from the numbers in Table 4.1. On the other hand, for the example of a Gaussian input, optimal values of f_l for $R = 1, 2, 3$ and 4 are 1.6, 2.0, 2.3 and 2.7, respectively.

4.3.3 One-Bit Quantization ($R = 1$)

One-bit quantization is depicted in Figure 4.9:

$$x_1 = -\infty; \quad x_2 = 0: \quad x_3 = +\infty$$

$$y_1 = -\delta = -\Delta/2 ; \quad y_2 = +\delta = \Delta/2 \tag{4.36}$$

The step size Δ and hence the absolute value δ of the reconstruction level can be optimized in closed form. From (4.12),

$$\sigma_q^2 = \sigma_x^2 + \delta^2 - 4\delta \int_0^\infty x p_x(x)\,dx \tag{4.37}$$

if the pdf is symmetric, and therefore

$$\delta_{opt} = 2 \int_0^\infty x p_x(x)\,dx \tag{4.38}$$

(a)

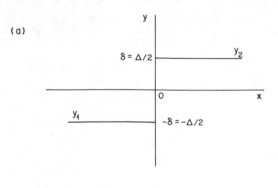

(b)

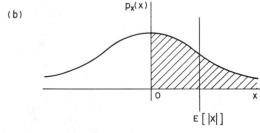

Figure 4.9 (a) One-bit quantization ($R = 1$, $L = 2$); (b) $\delta_{opt} = E[|X|]$ is the center of gravity of the right half of the input pdf, indicated by the shaded area.

$$\min\{\sigma_q^2\} = \sigma_x^2 \min\{\epsilon_q^2\} = \sigma_x^2 - \delta_{opt}^2 \qquad (4.39)$$

Note that the magnitude of the optimum reconstruction level is just the conditional mean of the random variable for positive or negative values, or the mean of the absolute value:

$$\delta_{opt} = \Delta_{opt}/2 = E[X|x > 0] = E[|X|] \qquad (4.40)$$

The optimum reconstruction level δ_{opt} and the minimum error variance depend on the pdf of the signal to be quantized: to be more exact, on the variance of the signal and on the functional form of the pdf (see Table 4.2 and Problem 4.3). If we had chosen a value $\delta \neq \delta_{opt}$, we would have

$$\sigma_q^2 = \sigma_x^2 + \delta^2 - 2\delta\delta_{opt} = \min\{\sigma_q^2\} + (\delta - \delta_{opt})^2 \qquad (4.41)$$

This could happen if we had chosen a specific value δ expecting the signal to have either a different variance than the actual one or a different unit variance pdf. Such effects of *variance mismatch* or *pdf mismatch* on the quantization error variance are small in the case of one-bit quantization. This is not true for quantizers with more than two levels (Section 4.4.3).

Closed-form optimizations can also be given for 3-level quantization (Problems 4.4 and 4.5). It can be shown that for a symmetrical midtread 3-level quantizer (Figure 4.10), the *SNR* gain over the optimized two-level midrise (Figure 4.9) is 1.8 dB for a Gaussian input. This gain is obtained by increasing R from $\log_2 2 = 1$ to $\log_2 3 = 1.59$ bits/sample.

Quantization   4

Table 4.2 Two-level quantization; dependence of δ_{opt} and min $\{\epsilon_q^2\}$ on pdf.

pdf	δ_{opt}/σ_x	min$\{\epsilon_q^2\}$	max$\{SNR\}$ (in dB)
U	$\sqrt{3}/2$	0.25	6.02
G	$\sqrt{2/\pi}$	0.363	4.40
L	$1/\sqrt{2}$	0.5	3.01
Γ	$1/\sqrt{3}$	0.667	1.76

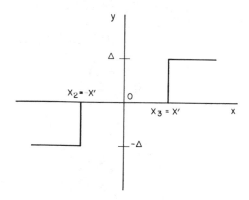

Figure 4.10 Three-level quantization.

Non-symmetric quantizers. The results of Table 4.1 apply to quantization characteristics that are symmetric with respect to zero, as in Figure 4.3(b). For the gamma pdf, as discussed again in Section 4.4, the optimum quantizer is non-symmetric. For example, if $R = 1$ bit/sample, the use of a decision threshold $x_2 = 0$ and reconstruction values $y_1 = -1.51\sigma_x$ and $y_2 = 0.27\sigma_x$, instead of the symmetric design of (4.36) and (4.38), will provide an SNR of 2.23 dB (which is nearly 0.5 dB higher than the value of 1.76 dB in Table 4.1) [Brehm and Trottler, 1983].

4.4 Nonuniform Quantization

Uniform quantization is the most common means for transforming an amplitude-continuous random variable into an amplitude-discrete variable. Equidistant decision and representation levels are simple conceptually, as well as for implementation. However, they do not necessarily represent the most effective conversion; it is possible, in general, to quantize a random variable with a smaller error variance. This can be attained by choosing smaller decision intervals where the probability of occurrence of the random variable X is high, i.e., where the pdf $p_x(x)$ is comparably high, and by choosing larger decision intervals otherwise, as seen in Figure 4.3(a) and (c). Note also that this procedure makes the magnitude of the quantization error depend strongly on that of input x.

There are two approaches to the problem of finding the sets of optimum decision and representation values x_k, y_k for a given pdf. One is an exact solution based on an iterative procedure, and another is an approximation that is good for quantizers with a large number of levels. Before we go into the details of this analysis, we will note that nonuniform quantization can be achieved by compressing the signal x using a nonuniform *compressor characteristic* $c(\cdot)$, by quantizing the compressed signal $c(x)$ employing a uniform quantizer, and by expanding the quantized version of the compressed signal using a nonuniform transfer characteristic $c^{-1}(\cdot)$ that is inverse to that of the compressor. Figure 4.11 shows a block diagram of this *companding* technique (*com*pressing and ex*pand*ing). The compressor characteristic $c(\cdot)$ is sometimes also called the *companding law*. Implementation of this type of nonuniform quantization is no longer common (See Chapter 5). The companding concept is, however, useful in analyzing and optimizing nonuniform quantizers with a large number of levels.

As in the figure, consider the example of a bounded input in the range $(-x_{\max}, x_{\max})$. The characteristic $c(x)$ analytically defines non-uniform intervals Δ_k via uniform intervals of length $2x_{\max}/L$ each. The slope of the compressor characteristic $c(\cdot)$ in interval $\mathscr{I}_k$ is

$$\frac{dc(x)}{dx} \approx \frac{2x_{\max}}{L\Delta_k} \qquad \text{for large } L \qquad (4.42)$$

The slope term $dc(x)/dx$ describes the *interval density*, and it is inversely proportional to the local step size in the equivalent non-uniform characteristic

Figure 4.11   The use of a compression function $c(x)$ to realize a nonuniform quantizer characteristic.

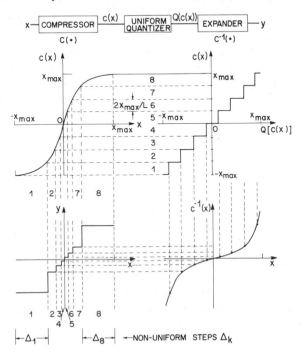

Quantization   4

$Q(x)$. Thus, with a saturating $c(x)$ characteristic as in Figure 4.11, the equivalent step size is smallest at $x = 0$, and greatest at $x = x_{max}$. *In the case of a uniform quantizer, $c(x) = x$ and $dc(x)/dx = 1$.* As in the sketch of Figure 4.11, a typical nonuniform characteristic has an approximately constant slope around the origin. Since this slope defines the density of inner step sizes, it turns out that the inner step sizes will be approximately uniform. In addition, these step sizes near the origin will be smaller than for a uniform quantizer $[dc(x)/dx=1]$. But for large signal values, we now find larger step sizes and fewer intervals. The term

$$G_C = \frac{dc(x)}{dx}\bigg|_{x \to 0} \geqslant 1 \qquad (4.43)$$

is called the *companding gain*. We will come back to this term in the section on log-quantizers. The interval density $dc(x)/dx$ can also be used to determine the ratio of maximum to minimum step size (See Example 4.7). From (4.42) and (4.43), this ratio is

$$\frac{\max\{\Delta\}}{\min\{\Delta\}} = \frac{dc(x)/dx\big|_{x \to 0}}{dc(x)/dx\big|_{x \to x_{max}}} = \frac{G_C}{dc(x)/dx\big|_{x \to x_{max}}} \qquad (4.44)$$

4.4.1 PDF-Optimized Nonuniform Quantizers: Iterative Solutions

The one-bit example has already shown that a quantizer can be optimized to yield the *minimum mean-squared error (mmse)* min $\{\sigma_q^2\}$. The mmse quantizer is frequently called the *Max quantizer* or *Lloyd-Max quantizer* [Max, 1960] [Lloyd, 1957, 1982]. Explicit solutions are possible in the case of $L=2$ and 3, as noted earlier. For $L > 2$, the mmse quantizer is nonuniform if the input pdf is itself nonuniform.

In the following we shall consider a stationary zero-mean random sequence $\{X(n)\}$ of variance σ_x^2 and give a non-explicit exact solution for *pdf-optimized quantizers* that minimize σ_q^2. Note that optimization with regard to pdf shape includes a match of quantizer to input variance σ_x^2. Mismatch relative to the shape or variance will be discussed later.

A general expression for quantization error variance has been given in (4.12) for any choice of the decision levels x_k; $k = 2,3,...,L$ and reconstruction levels y_k; $k = 1,2,...,L$. Necessary conditions for a minimum are

$$\frac{\partial \sigma_q^2}{\partial x_k} = 0 ; \quad k = 2,3,...,L; \qquad \frac{\partial \sigma_q^2}{\partial y_k} = 0 ; \quad k = 1,2,...,L$$

Note that these conditions may define a local optimum. However, if $p_x(x)$ is log-concave, i.e., if $\partial^2 \log p_x(x)/\partial x^2$ is negative, these conditions are also sufficient [Fleischer, 1964], and they lead to the important results [Lloyd, 1957,1982] [Max, 1960]:

$$x_{k,opt} = \frac{1}{2} (y_{k,\,opt} + y_{k-1,\,opt}); \qquad k = 2,3,...,L,$$

$$x_{1,opt} = -\infty, \quad x_{L+1,opt} = \infty \qquad\qquad (4.45a)$$

$$y_{k,opt} = \frac{\displaystyle\int_{x_{k,opt}}^{x_{k+1,opt}} x p_x(x)\,dx}{\displaystyle\int_{x_{k,opt}}^{x_{k+1,opt}} p_x(x)\,dx}; \qquad k = 1,2,...,L \qquad\qquad (4.45b)$$

The log-concave property holds for the pdf's **U**, **G** and **L** but not for the gamma pdf **Γ**. In this case, (4.45) will *not* define a global optimum.

The first of these equations shows that the optimum *decision levels are half-way between neighboring reconstruction levels*, and the second equation states that a *reconstruction level should be the centroid of the pdf in the appropriate interval*. Note that this centroid is the mean of the input signal on the given interval. Note also that (4.45) is true for previous results for $L = 2,3$. Various extensions can be drawn from (4.45). First, since the denominator equals $P_k = P\{X \in \mathscr{I}_{k,opt}\}$ and since $p_x(x) = P_k\, p_x(x|X \in \mathscr{I}_{k,opt})$ within interval $\mathscr{I}_{k,opt}$,

$$y_{k,opt} = \int_{-\infty}^{\infty} x\, p_x(x|X \in I_{k,opt})\,dx = E[X|X \in I_{k,opt}], \qquad\qquad (4.46)$$

a result that can also be anticipated from estimation theory. Further, the result (4.46) can be rearranged in the form

$$\int_{-\infty}^{\infty} (x - y_{k,opt}) p_x(x|X \in I_{k,opt})\,dx = E[Q|X \in I_{k,opt}] = 0 \qquad (4.47a)$$

i.e., the mean of the quantization noise in the interval is zero if the reconstruction level is chosen as the mean of the input in that interval. This last result implies that the unconditional mean of quantization error is zero:

$$E[Q] = \sum_k E[Q|X \in \mathscr{I}_{k,opt}]\, P_k = 0 \qquad\qquad (4.47b)$$

We can also multiply (4.47) with $y_{k,opt}$ and sum over all indices k, to obtain

$$E[QY] = 0 \qquad\qquad (4.48)$$

i.e., *the quantization noise is orthogonal to the output of the pdf-optimized quantizer.* However,

$$E[QX] = E[Q(Y+Q)] = E[Q^2] = \min\{\sigma_q^2\} \qquad\qquad (4.49a)$$

i.e., *input and quantization error are correlated*, so that a simple input-independent additive noise model is invalid. Finally, by an algebraic manipulation that employs (4.48) twice, we can show that

$$\sigma_y^2 = \sigma_x^2 - \min \{\sigma_q^2\} \tag{4.49b}$$

i.e., *the variance of the output is less than that of the random variable at the quantizer input* [Wood, 1969]. This is related doubtless to the non-zero probability of input values greater than the maximum output level y_L. Also, as $L \rightarrow \infty$, min $\{\sigma_q^2\} \rightarrow 0$ and $\sigma_y^2 \rightarrow \sigma_x^2$. The observation $\sigma_y^2 < \sigma_x^2$ is also true of the rate distortion-optimal $x \rightarrow y$ mapping as noted in Appendix D.

Two other corollaries of the above set of results are worth mention:

$$E[XY] = (1 - \epsilon_q^2) \, \sigma_x^2 \tag{4.50}$$

$$P_k E[Q^2 | X \in \mathscr{I}_{k,opt}] = P_j E[Q^2 | X \in \mathscr{I}_{j,opt}] \tag{4.51}$$

The last result shows that *error variance contributions from different intervals are identical*. This is true in spite of varying Δ_k, because of the equalizing role of interval probability values P_j and P_k. This result is formally derived in Section 4.4.2.

From the conditions in (4.45), the optimum values $x_{k,opt}$ and $y_{k,opt}$ can be calculated iteratively. Only positive values have to be calculated if $p_x(x)$ is symmetric. A special procedure is known for Laplacian inputs [Nitadori, 1965] [Noll and Zelinski, 1979].

One begins by choosing a value y_1, solves (4.45b) for x_2, solves (4.45a) for y_2, ..., and solves (4.45a) for y_L. One then checks if y_L is close enough to the right hand term of (4.45b). If not, one perturbs y_1 in an appropriate direction and continues the iteration. Table 4.3 lists the decision and reconstruction levels for various pdf's and for quantizers with $L = 2, 4, 8$ and 16 levels. The table uses a re-numbering scheme for x and y indices for convenience, and shows only positive values, recognizing symmetry about zero. Note that the $x_{k,opt}, y_{k,opt}$-values of Table 4.3 have to be multiplied with σ_x for inputs with a non-unity variance. Note also that in the case of a uniform input pdf, the Max quantizer will be uniform as well, as in Section 4.3.

Implied in Table 4.3, as in Table 4.1, is a *symmetry about zero* in the quantizer characteristic. This symmetry is an intuitively expected result when the input has a pdf that is symmetrical about zero. The four pdf's that we have considered are indeed symmetrical about zero. There are examples of zero-mean symmetrical pdfs for which the mmse quantizer is *not* symmetric. See Section 4.3.3, Problem 4.5 and [Abhaya and Wise, 1981].

Table 4.4 lists signal-to-noise ratios of Max quantizers for $R = 1, 2,...,7$ bits/sample. The results of the present table should be compared with those of Table 4.1, and with the rate distortion bounds of Table D.1. Notice that gains due to non-uniform quantization are most significant with a very "non-uniform" pdf such as the gamma pdf. With $R = 7$, the gain over uniform quantization is 2.7 dB for a Gaussian pdf, and 7.7 dB for a gamma pdf.

Table 4.3 Optimum decision values x_j and reconstruction values y_j for pdf-optimized nonuniform quantizers (U: Uniform G: Gaussian L: Laplace Γ: Gamma) [Max, 1960] [Paez and Glisson, 1972] [Noll and Zelinski, 1974]). Note that in this table, the quantizer characteristics are symmetrical about zero; $j = 1$ corresponds to the first non-negative value of x or y, and $j > 1$ to succeeding positive values. This notation is different from that in the rest of this chapter; the more usual notation is that of Figure 4.3.

R		1		2		3		4	
pdf	j	$x_{j,opt}$	$y_{j,opt}$	$x_{j,opt}$	$y_{j,opt}$	$x_{j,opt}$	$y_{j,opt}$	$x_{j,opt}$	$y_{j,opt}$
U	1	0.000	0.866	0.000	0.433	0.000	0.217	0.000	0.109
	2			0.866	1.299	0.433	0.650	0.217	0.326
	3					0.866	1.083	0.433	0.542
	4					1.299	1.516	0.650	0.759
	5							0.866	0.975
	6							1.083	1.192
	7							1.299	1.408
	8							1.516	1.624
G	1	0.000	0.798	0.000	0.453	0.000	0.245	0.000	0.128
	2			0.982	1.510	0.501	0.756	0.258	0.388
	3					1.050	1.344	0.522	0.657
	4					1.748	2.152	0.800	0.942
	5							1.099	1.256
	6							1.437	1.618
	7							1.844	2.069
	8							2.401	2.733
L	1	0.000	0.707	0.000	0.420	0.000	0.233	0.000	0.124
	2			1.127	1.834	0.533	0.833	0.264	0.405
	3					1.253	1.673	0.567	0.729
	4					2.380	3.087	0.920	1.111
	5							1.345	1.578
	6							1.878	2.178
	7							2.597	3.017
	8							3.725	4.432
Γ	1	0.000	0.577	0.000	0.313	0.000	0.155	0.000	0.073
	2			1.268	2.223	0.527	0.899	0.230	0.387
	3					1.478	2.057	0.591	0.795
	4					3.089	4.121	0.051	1.307
	5							1.633	1.959
	6							1.390	2.822
	7							3.422	4.061
	8							5.128	6.195

Figure 4.12 plots the quantity $\Delta SNR = 6.02R - \max \{SNR\}$ as a function of R. Solid curves are for pdf-optimized non-uniform quantizers, while dashed curves are for pdf-optimized uniform quantizers. Note that in the case of a uniform pdf, the optimum quantizer (which is also uniform) attains $\Delta SNR = 0$ for all R; one gains exactly 6.02 dB for every doubling of L. With other pdf's, ΔSNR increases with R, but rapidly attains a pdf-specific asymptote, as given in (4.68); uniform quantizers for these pdf's become increasingly inefficient with increasing R.

Table 4.4 Performance of pdf-optimized quantizers. Values of max{SNR} (in dB). (U: Uniform G: Gaussian L: Laplace Γ: Gamma) [Max, 1960] [Paez and Glisson, 1972] [Noll and Zelinski, 1974].

R (bits per sample)	pdf			
	U	G	L	Γ
1	6.02	4.40	3.01	1.76
2	12.04	9.30	7.54	6.35
3	18.06	14.62	12.64	11.52
4	24.08	20.22	18.13	17.07
5	30.10	26.01	23.87	22.85
6	36.12	31.89	29.74	28.73
7	42.14	37.81	35.69	34.67

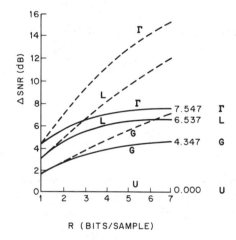

Figure 4.12 Values of $\Delta SNR = 6.02R - \max\{SNR\}$ in pdf-optimized quantizers. Solid and dashed curves are for nonuniform and uniform quantizers, respectively [Noll and Zelinski, 1974].

We will see in Section 4.6 that even smaller values of ΔSNR can be realized with Entropy Coding, if the quantizer input is stationary. On the other hand, with non-stationary inputs, logarithmic non-uniformity (Section 4.5) and adaptive techniques (Section 4.10) provide important means for robust quantization.

4.4.2 PDF-Optimized Nonuniform Quantizers: Approximate Formulas for Large R

Consider the high bit rate case where R and therefore L, the number of quantizer steps, are both sufficiently large; we can then assume that the pdf $p_x(x)$ of the input signal is *approximately flat in all intervals* $\mathcal{I}_k$; $k = 1,2,...,L$, which includes the outermost intervals 1 and L. We also assume that the input is bounded in practice to a value x_{max}, even if the pdf should have a long tail. We also assume that the pdf is symmetric. Let

$$p_x(x) = constant = p_x(y_k) \quad \text{for } X \in \mathcal{I}_k \tag{4.52}$$

where y_k is a value between x_k and x_{k+1}. Let Δ_k be the length of interval $\mathcal{I}_k$:

$$\Delta_k = x_{k+1} - x_k \tag{4.53}$$

The probability of finding X in the interval $\mathcal{I}_k$ is then

$$P_k = P\{X \in \mathcal{I}_k\} = p_x(y_k)\Delta_k; \quad \sum_{k=1}^{L} P_k = 1 \tag{4.54}$$

The error variance (4.12) is

$$\sigma_q^2 = \sum_{k=1}^{L} \frac{P_k}{\Delta_k} \int_{x_k}^{x_{k+1}} (x-y_k)^2 dx \tag{4.55}$$

and a necessary condition for a minimum is

$$\frac{\partial \sigma_q^2}{\partial y_k} = 0 ; \quad k = 1,2,...,L \tag{4.56}$$

which results in

$$y_k = \frac{1}{2}(x_k + x_{k+1}) \tag{4.57}$$

The representation level y_k lies in the middle of the interval $\mathcal{I}_k$; this is of course a direct consequence of the assumption of a flat pdf in the intervals, and y_k is the centroid of $p_x(x)$ in this interval $\mathcal{I}_k$ as in (4.45b). By combining (4.55) and (4.57) we obtain

$$\sigma_q^2 = \frac{1}{12} \sum_{k=1}^{L} P_k \Delta_k^2 \tag{4.58}$$

with $\Delta_k^2/12$ representing the error variance conditioned on interval $\mathcal{I}_k$. For uniform quantizers ($\Delta_k = \Delta$; all k), (4.58) reduces to $\Delta^2/12$ [as in (4.17)] since the summation over P_k values (4.54) equals 1. Note also that (4.58) does not depend on the y_k-values because these are defined by the decision levels (4.57). Therefore only these decision levels (or, equivalently, the lengths of the intervals) need to be optimized.

A first condition for optimality can be derived as follows. With (4.54) and (4.58),

$$\sigma_q^2 = \frac{1}{12} \sum_{k=1}^{L} p_x(y_k)\Delta_k^3 = \frac{1}{12} \sum_{k=1}^{L} \alpha_k^3 \tag{4.59}$$

However, we have the constraint that

$$\sum_{k=1}^{L} \alpha_k \simeq \int_{-x_{max}}^{x_{max}} \sqrt[3]{p_x(x)}\, dx \simeq constant \qquad (4.60)$$

since the above integral is a function only of its limits. Use of the Lagrange multiplier technique

$$\frac{\partial}{\partial \alpha_k}\left(\sigma_q^2 + \lambda \sum_{k=1}^{L} \alpha_k\right) = 0 \quad \text{for } k = 1, 2, ..., L$$

therefore results in

$$p_x(y_k)\,\Delta_k^3 = P_k \Delta_k^2 = constant \qquad (4.61)$$

An interval must be small if the probability is high that this interval is occupied, and vice versa. From (4.58) and (4.61) we see that *all quantizer intervals will produce identical quantization error variance contributions*; also see (4.51).

We shall now derive equivalent results in closed form using the $c(x)$ notation of Figure 4.11. From (4.58) and (4.42),

$$\sigma_q^2 \approx \frac{x_{max}^2}{3L^2} \sum_{k=1}^{L} P_k \left[dc(x)/dx\right]^{-2} \quad \text{for large } L \qquad (4.62)$$

Setting $P_k \simeq p_x(x)\,dx$ after (4.54),

$$\sigma_q^2 \approx \frac{x_{max}^2}{3L^2} \int_{-x_{max}}^{+x_{max}} p_x(x) \left[dc(x)/dx\right]^{-2} dx \quad \text{for large } L \qquad (4.63)$$

This result [Bennett, 1948] expresses the error variance in terms of input pdf and the compressor characteristic $c(\cdot)$ of the quantizer. Recall that $c(\cdot)$ determines the decision levels, and that the reconstruction levels are determined by the latter ones via (4.57).

We can now minimize the error variance by searching for the optimum companding law $c(x)$ under the constraint of a fixed area under the interval density:

$$\int_{-x_{max}}^{x_{max}} \left[dc(x)/dx\right] dx = constant \qquad (4.64)$$

The area under the interval density is a measure of the number of levels and should therefore be a constant. Note that without the constraint, $\sigma_q^2 \rightarrow 0$ for $dc(x)/dx \rightarrow \infty$. To use Lagrange multipliers, consider

$$p_x(x)\left[(dc(x)/dx)\right]^{-2} + \lambda\, dc(x)/dx \qquad (4.65)$$

The derivative with respect to dc/dx is set to zero and λ is eliminated by using (4.64). Then

$$\frac{dc_{opt}(x)}{dx} = \frac{x_{max}}{\int\limits_{0}^{x_{max}} \sqrt[3]{p_x(x)}\,dx} \sqrt[3]{p_x(x)} \qquad (4.66)$$

i.e., the optimum interval density is proportional to the cube root of the pdf of the quantizer input as in (4.61). By integrating (4.66) and choosing c such that $c_{opt}(x_{max}) = x_{max}$ (a boundary condition in Figure 4.11), we obtain the optimum compressor characteristic

$$c_{opt}(x) = x_{max}\left[\int\limits_{0}^{x}\sqrt[3]{p_x(x)}\,dx\right]\left[\int\limits_{0}^{x_{max}}\sqrt[3]{p_x(x)}\,dx\right]^{-1} \qquad (4.67)$$

From this result we can find the optimum decision levels $x = x_{k,opt}$ that result when $c_{opt}(x)$ takes on the values kx_{max}/L; $k = 1,2,...,L$.

Also, by combining (4.63) and (4.67), we obtain [Panter and Dite, 1951]

$$\min\{\sigma_q^2\} \approx \frac{2}{3L^2}\left[\int\limits_{0}^{\infty}\sqrt[3]{p_x(x)}\,dx\right]^3 \quad \text{for large } L \qquad (4.68)$$

If the pdf $p_x(x)$ is unbounded, (4.68) describes only the granular contribution for bounded inputs. For large L, SNR values corresponding to (4.68) agree well with the numbers already mentioned for different pdf's in the exact results section (Table 4.4 and Figure 4.12, which actually shows asymptotic values of $6.02 - \max\{SNR\}$). We must emphasize that (4.68) is valid for quantizers with many levels ($L \geqslant 32$). The assumption used in (4.63) and hence in (4.68), viz., constant input pdf over an interval, does not really hold for the outermost intervals, causing (4.68) to be inexact, especially for small L. Approximate SNR formulas that are closer to the exact result (4.12) have been proposed elsewhere [Algazi, 1966] [Roe, 1964] [Wood, 1969].

In later chapters, we shall mention nonuniform quantizers that minimize *noise audibility* or *noise visibility* rather than *noise variance*. Such quantizers are often designed on the basis of subjective experimentation. In principle, they can also be realized by replacing the probability function in (4.67) and (4.68) by appropriate subjective functions [Rubinstein and Limb, 1978].

Example 4.6. Uniform pdf
Using (4.67) and (4.68),

$$c_{opt}(x) = x; \qquad \min\{\sigma_q^2\} = 2^{-2R}\,\sigma_x^2 \qquad (4.69) \quad \bullet$$

Example 4.7. Laplacian pdf
The optimum compressor characteristic can be given in closed form [Smith, 1957] using (4.67):

$$m-law: \quad c_{opt}(x) = x_{max}\ \text{sgn}(x)\ \frac{1 - e^{-m|x|/x_{max}}}{1 - e^{-m}}; \qquad m_{opt} = \frac{\sqrt{2}}{3\sigma_x}\,x_{max} \qquad (4.70)$$

$$\min\{\sigma_q^2\} = (9/2)\ 2^{-2R}\sigma_x^2\ ;\quad SNR\,\text{(dB)} = 6.02R - 6.53\ ;\quad \max\{\Delta\}/\min\{\Delta\} = e^m \quad (4.71)$$

See Problem 4.7 for a numerical illustration. For a specified input-clipping level $x_{\max}$, the optimum performance is attained only if m is chosen as in (4.70); this will provide an optimal loading factor $f_{l,opt} = 3m_{opt}/\sqrt{2}$. Equivalently, for a given design of m and $x_{\max}$, the optimal input level is described by $\sigma_{x,opt} = \sqrt{2}\,x_{\max}/3m$. The quantizer-input mismatch that results otherwise can lead to drastic reductions in SNR from the value implied in (4.71). See Example 4.8. •

4.4.3 Quantizer Mismatch

Communication systems may have to carry signals of changing statistics; for example, inputs with different variances in telephony. Therefore, optimum quantizers are often not matched to the statistics of the actual inputs. Mismatches can be in terms of variance (with a known pdf shape at the input), or in terms of pdf shape as well [Mauersberger, 1979].

Of special interest is a *mismatch in variance*. It implies that suboptimum step sizes are employed, and if the input variance is higher than the design value, it changes the ratio of granular noise and overload noise. Figure 4.8 has shown that one-bit quantizers are rather insensitive to changes in variance (or, equivalently, improperly chosen step sizes). Variance mismatches can be much more serious with $R > 1$.

Example 4.8. 8-bit m-law quantization of Laplacian input with unknown variance σ_x^2
We have mentioned already that the best m-law performance is obtained if the Laplacian input has the σ_x value $\sqrt{2}x_{\max}/3m$ of (4.70), where $x_{\max}$ is the input clipping level, the saturation point in the $c(x)$ characteristic. Figure 4.13 shows the effect of a

Figure 4.13 Performance of 8-bit m-law quantization.

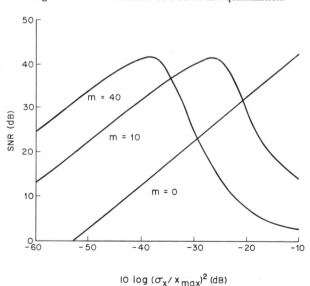

general σ_x value that is not necessarily equal to the optimum. The results of Figure 4.13 are precise ones, following (4.68) and (4.12) rather than (4.63). The $m = 0$ curve refers to uniform quantization. For $m = 10$, the optimum occurs for $f_{I,opt} = 30/\sqrt{2}$ which is the -26 dB point on the abscissa. •

In Figure 4.13, performance is a strong function of input standard deviation σ_x. We will note in Sections 4.5 and 4.10 that with *logarithmic quantization* or *adaptive step size* procedures, a performance that is nearly independent of σ_x can be attained over a wide range of input variance unlike in Figure 4.13.

Example 4.9.   4-bit quantization with known input variance, but mismatched pdf shape

Figure 4.14 shows *SNR*'s of optimum nonuniform and optimum uniform quantizers designed for uniform (**U**), Gaussian (**G**), Laplacian (**L**), and gamma ($\mathbf{\Gamma}$) pdf's. The *SNR*'s are shown for all combinations of input pdf and quantizer type. Thus, the *SNR* at abscissa point **G** of the $\mathbf{\Gamma}$-curve is the value that the gamma-optimized quantizer attains if the pdf of the input is actually Gaussian.

The following conclusions emerge from Figure 4.14:

(a)   The pdf-mismatch performance of the optimum uniform quantizers is very similar to that of optimum nonuniform quantizers; differences can be significant for $R > 4$.

(b)   Uniform quantizers, which are optimal for signals with a uniform pdf, are an extremely bad match for signals with different pdf's. The strong decrease in performance is caused by severe overload effects.

(c)   Uniform, Gaussian, and Laplacian quantizers show an improved performance if their inputs have a pdf with shorter tails; this is an improvement obtained even under pdf-mismatch conditions!

(d)   Gamma quantizers achieve a signal-to-noise ratio that is nearly independent of the type of pdf. For this reason, the most significant numbers in Table 4.3 are those referring to gamma quantization. The robustness of gamma quantizers is

Figure 4.14   Effects of quantizer mismatch in (a) optimum nonuniform and (b) optimum uniform quantizers. Letters on abscissa represent input pdf and letters on curves represent pdf's used in optimizing the quantizer. (**U**: Uniform, **G**: Gaussian, **L**: Laplace, $\mathbf{\Gamma}$: Gamma) [Noll and Zelinski, 1976].

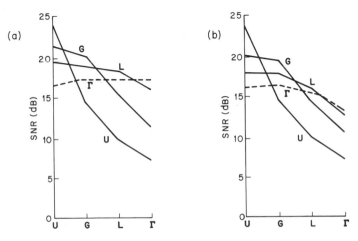

related to the fact that the quantization characteristic of the optimum gamma quantizer does not differ much from a logarithmic one. A logarithmic characteristic has the well-known property (Section 4.5) of giving a performance nearly independent of the shape of the input pdf. Logarithmic quantization can also provide a performance that is nearly constant over a very wide variation of input variance. •

4.5 Logarithmic Quantization

4.5.1 Basic Formulas

We have seen that for uniform quantizers the quantization noise is $\sigma_q^2 = \Delta^2/12$, i.e., it is independent of the variance of the input signal, assuming that the signal does not exceed the range of the quantizer. This implies an *SNR* that decreases with a decrease of the signal level (see Figure 4.13 for $m = 0$). In the case of pdf-optimized quantizers we have seen that the *SNR* is only at its maximum for one specific variance; any deviation from this specific value leads to a significant decrease in *SNR* (see Figure 4.13 for $m = 10,40$).

In situations such as speech coding, the exact value of the input variance is not known in advance; and in addition, it tends to change with time (Figure 2.6). In such situations, a signal-to-quantization noise ratio that is constant over a broad range of input variances can be obtained by using a logarithmic companding law [Holzwarth, 1949].

The benefits of logarithmic companding are illustrated in the dynamic range curves of Figure 4.15, which refer to the performance of an 8-bit $\mu 255$ quantizer

Figure 4.15 Dependence of *SNR* on σ_x^2 in 8-bit log- and uniform quantization of a bounded Laplacian input. The dashed line refers to a pdf-optimized quantizer.

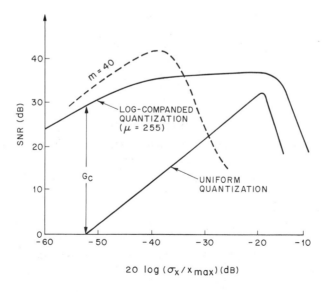

with a Laplacian input assumed bounded to x_{max}. Note that as in Figures 4.7 and 4.13, the uniform quantizer has a performance that is highly input-dependent. The logarithmic quantizer, on the other hand, has a *dynamic range* of about 30 dB (−15 dB to −45 dB on the abscissa) over which its *SNR* is within 3 dB of the maximum value of 38 dB. Also shown in the figure is the companding gain for small inputs, the parameter G_C of Section 4.4. Note that this gain is about 30 dB, which implies that the smallest step size min $\{\Delta\}$ is about 32 times smaller than the step size of a corresponding uniform quantizer with identical x_{max} and R. We will presently define the $\mu 255$ law and note that indeed $G_C \approx 30$ dB for this companding function. Note also that a pdf-optimized quantizer (broken curve in the figure) has a higher maximum *SNR* than the log-quantizer, but a smaller dynamic range; the pdf-optimized quantizing system is the $m = 40$ system of Figure 4.13.

For large values of x_{max}, or for truncated pdf's, the value of σ_q^2 in (4.63) leads to a signal-to-noise ratio

$$SNR = \frac{\sigma_x^2}{\sigma_q^2} = \frac{3L^2}{x_{max}^2} \frac{\int_{-\infty}^{\infty} x^2 p_x(x)\,dx}{\int_{-\infty}^{\infty} p_x(x) \left[dc(x)/dx\right]^{-2} dx} \tag{4.72}$$

Thus we can obtain a constant *SNR* if the interval density $dc(x)/dx$ is inversely proportional to x:

$$dc(x)/dx = (Kx)^{-1} ; \quad K = \text{constant} \tag{4.73}$$

$$SNR = \sigma_x^2/\sigma_q^2 = 3L^2/K^2 x_{max}^2 \tag{4.74}$$

From (4.73),

$$c(x) = K^{-1} \log_e x + \text{constant} ; \quad x > 0 \tag{4.75}$$

and because $c(x) = x_{max}$ for $x = x_{max}$ (Figure 4.11),

$$c(x) = \left[\frac{1}{K} \log_e \frac{|x|}{x_{max}} + x_{max} \right] \text{sgn}(x) \tag{4.76}$$

The characteristic (4.76) implies a negative infinite $c(x)$ value at the specific point $x = 0$. In order to attain a practically implementable boundary condition $c(x) = 0$ for $x \rightarrow 0$ as in Figure 4.11, we have to correct the companding law. Two proposals will be discussed in the following. In both proposals we find a linearization of $c(\cdot)$ near the origin.

4.5.2 A-Law Companding

The A-law compression characteristic [Cattermole, 1969] is based on a linear companding characteristic near the origin $(|x| \leqslant x_{max}/A)$ and a logarithmic

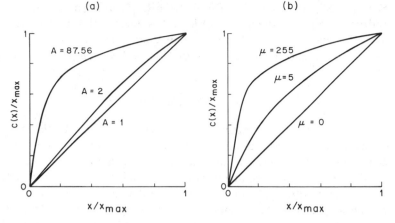

Figure 4.16 Logarithmic compression characteristics (shown for $x > 0$): (a) A-law and (b) μ-law.

companding characteristic for large x [Figure 4.16(a)]:

$$
c(x) = \begin{cases}
\dfrac{A|x|}{1+\log_e A}\,\text{sgn}(x)\; ; & 0 \leqslant \dfrac{|x|}{x_{\max}} \leqslant \dfrac{1}{A} \\[4mm]
x_{\max}\dfrac{1+\log_e\,(A|x|/x_{\max})}{1+\log_e A}\,\text{sgn}(x)\; ; & \dfrac{1}{A} < \dfrac{|x|}{x_{\max}} \leqslant 1
\end{cases}
\tag{4.77}
$$

From (4.73), (4.74) and (4.77), we find that for *large signals*,

$$
K = (1+\log_e A)/x_{\max}; \quad \sigma_x^2/\sigma_q^2 = 3L^2/(1+\log_e A)^2 \tag{4.78}
$$

$$
SNR_{A\text{-}law}\ (\text{dB}) = 6.02R + 4.77 - 20\log_{10}\,(1+\log_e A) \tag{4.79}
$$

The companding gain is

$$
G_C = dc(x)/dx\big|_{x\to 0} = A/(1+\log_e A) \tag{4.80}
$$

and, using (4.63), we find that for *small signals*

$$
\sigma_x^2/\sigma_q^2 = 3L^2(\sigma_x^2/x_{\max}^2)G_C^2 \tag{4.81}
$$

Recall that the *SNR* of a uniform quantizer with negligible overload (4.31) is

$$
\sigma_x^2/\sigma_q^2 = 3L^2(\sigma_x^2/x_{\max}^2)\; ; \qquad |x| \leqslant x_{\max}
$$

Comparison of the above two results implies that the step size in the linear part of $c(x)$ is reduced by the companding gain G_C. The equivalent increase of *SNR* for *small signals* is described by

$$
SNR_{A\text{-}law}\ (\text{dB}) = SNR_{uniform}\ (\text{dB}) + 20\log_{10} G_C\; ; \qquad |x| \to 0 \tag{4.82}
$$

For $A = 87.56$, this increase is 24.08 dB. A uniform quantizer would need four additional bits for the same SNR at low levels; although its SNR at high levels would be higher than that of the A-law quantizer.

It can be shown (Problem 4.10) that A-law companding provides a step size ratio

$$\max\{\Delta\}/\min\{\Delta\} = A \qquad (4.83)$$

The ratio increases linearly with A; recall that in Laplacian-optimized m-law companding, the ratio is an exponential, e^m. Figure 4.16(a) demonstrates A-law compression characteristics and Figure 4.17(a) shows the effect of compression on a sine-wave input. Notice how smaller amplitudes are effectively amplified relative to higher amplitudes. The effect of the logarithmic compressor can also be described by the way it changes the input pdf. The general tendency, for any input pdf, is to obtain an output pdf that more closely resembles the uniform pdf $\mathbf{U}$. For example, with a Laplacian input, the effect of μ-law or A-law compression is to produce a

Figure 4.17 (a) Modification of sine-wave by A-law and μ-law compression ($A = 87.56$, $\mu = 255$) [Steele, 1975. Reprinted with permission]. (b) Modification of Laplacian pdf by A-law and μ-law compression ($A = 87.56$, $\mu = 100$) [Sundberg and Rydbeck, 1976. Reprinted with permission].

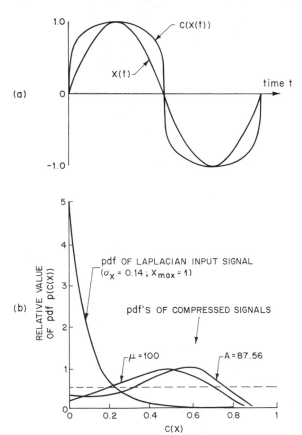

compressed signal pdf $p[c(x)]$ that is much flatter; with a mode, or $p[c(x)]$-maximizing value that is no longer at $c(x) = 0$ [Figure 4.17(b) and Problem 4.9; also see Problem 4.8]. *SNR* curves for A-law quantization, as a function of input power, will be similar to the μ-law dynamic range curve in Figure 4.15. Further comparisons of A-law and μ-law characteristics will appear in Chapter 5.

Example 4.10. $A = 87.56$ [European PCM standard (Chapter 5)]

$$SNR_{A\text{-}law} \ (dB) = 6.02R - 9.99$$

$$G_C = 24.08 \ dB \ ; \quad \max\{\Delta\}/\min\{\Delta\} = 87.56 \quad \bullet$$

4.5.3 μ-Law Companding

The μ-law compression characteristic [Holzwarth, 1949] [Panter and Dite, 1951] [Smith, 1957] is

$$c(x) = x_{\max} \frac{\log_e \ (1+\mu|x|/x_{\max})}{\log_e \ (1+\mu)} \ \text{sgn} \ x \tag{4.84}$$

This characteristic (Figure 4.16(b)) is quasi-logarithmic; it is linear for small x-values [$\log_e \ (1+ax) \approx ax$]. For *large signals* $(\mu|x| \gg x_{\max})$, it is logarithmic:

$$c(x) = \frac{x_{\max}}{\log_e \ (1+\mu)} \ \log_e (\mu|x|/x_{\max}) \ \text{sgn} \ x \tag{4.85}$$

From (4.73) and (4.85),

$$K = \log_e \ (1+\mu)/x_{\max} \tag{4.86}$$

and we find, using (4.74), that the *SNR* is again independent of the statistics of the input signal:

$$\sigma_x^2/\sigma_q^2 = 3L^2/[\log_e \ (1+\mu)]^2 \quad \text{for} \ \mu|x| \gg x_{\max} \tag{4.87}$$

$$SNR_{\mu\text{-}law} \ (dB) = 6.02R + 4.77 - 20 \ \log_{10}(\log_e \ (1+\mu)) \tag{4.88}$$

For *small signals* we obtain the companding gain

$$G_C = dc(x)/dx \big|_{x \to 0} = \mu/\log_e \ (1+\mu) \tag{4.89}$$

It can be shown (Problem 4.11) that μ-law provides a step size ratio

$$\max\{\Delta\}/\min\{\Delta\} = 1+\mu \tag{4.90}$$

Example 4.11. $\mu=255$ [North American PCM standard (Chapter 5)]

$$SNR_{\mu\text{-}law} \ (dB) = 6.02R - 10.1$$

$$G_C = 33.25 \text{ dB} ; \quad \max\{\Delta\}/\min\{\Delta\} = 256 \quad \bullet$$

The log-quantizer results of Examples 4.10 and 4.11 are primarily applicable to speech coding, and they can be summarized, as in (1.6), in the form

$$SNR \text{ (dB)}_{log-quantized \ speech} = 6.02R - 10.1 \qquad (4.91a)$$

This should be contrasted with (4.32), the uniform quantizer and uniform pdf result that is more representative of image coding:

$$SNR \text{ (dB)}_{uniformly \ quantized \ image} = 6.02 \ R \qquad (4.91b)$$

Image SNR results are sometimes defined as peak-to-peak-signal to rms-noise ratios. These numbers are higher than the values in (4.91b) by about 10.8 dB (Problem 5.2).

4.5.4 Quantizer-Input Mismatch

We have shown in Figure 4.15 that the logarithmic quantizer is very insensitive to a *quantizer mismatch relative to variance.* For example, consider a Laplacian pdf. The pdf-optimized quantizer has an SNR of 6.02 $R - 6.53$ (dB) as given in (4.71), whereas the log-characteristic (e.g., $\mu = 255$) results in a smaller SNR of 6.02 $R - 10.1$ (dB). On the other hand, the pdf-optimized quantizer can be very sensitive to a mismatch in variance or pdf shape (Figures 4.13 and 4.14). It is obvious that the log-quantizer is extremely robust. The log-quantizer is also very insensitive to a mismatch in relative shape of the pdf, for a given variance. Differences in the quantization of different pdf's are only significant in the overload region. This is indicated by the dashed overload-region skirt in Figure 4.15.

The illustration in Figure 4.15 is for the example of $R = 8$ bits/sample, an example of great practical importance (Chapter 5). For much coarser designs such as $R < 4$ bits/sample, the approach of adaptive quantization (Section 4.10) will be seen to be even more efficient than time-invariant log-quantization.

4.6 Entropy-Coded Quantization

4.6.1 Entropy Coding — Concept and Implementation

In our previous discussion we have concentrated on the quantizer characteristic $Q(\cdot)$ and on its corresponding quantization error. An input random variable X is represented at the quantizer output as a discrete-valued random variable $Y = Q(X)$ such that

$$Y = y_k \quad \text{if} \quad X \in \mathscr{I}_k \quad \text{for} \quad k = 1,2,...,L \qquad (4.92)$$

Clearly, y_k is a member of an L-ary alphabet of capacity $\log_2 L$ (Appendix C). Actually, it is the L-ary index k of representation level y_k that is transmitted to the receiver. The channel maps k into k if the channel is error-free and the receiver maps k into representation level y_k.

The L-ary index of the chosen output is typically encoded in a binary format with

$$R \geqslant \log_2 L \quad \text{bits/sample} \tag{4.93}$$

R has to be an integer: the smallest integer that is needed to describe L numbers in a binary format. For example, $R=3$ for $L=8$, and also for $L=5$. When L is not a power of 2, transmission with about $\log_2 L$ bits/sample is still possible by appropriate *block coding* where *sequences* of L-ary indices are converted into sequences of binary digits. For example, consider $5^3=125 \sim 128=2^7$; there are 125 possible 5-ary letter blocks of length 3; these can be encoded very efficiently by binary sequences that are 7 bits long. Table 4.6 and Problem 4.12 discuss other examples where L is not a power of 2.

The quantizer output can be viewed as a discrete-valued information source (Appendix C) with an L-ary alphabet. The average information content of this source is given by the *zeroth-order entropy* of the quantizer output:

$$H_Q = - \sum_{k=1}^{L} P_k \log_2 P_k \tag{4.94}$$

P_k is the probability of an occurrence of quantizer output y_k:

$$P_k = P\{X \in \mathcal{I}_k\} = P\{Y = y_k\} = \int_{x \in \mathcal{I}_k} p_x(x)\,dx \tag{4.95}$$

Note that H_Q represents the average information content only if the quantizer outputs are statistically independent. In optimized coding schemes such as DPCM with optimal prediction (Chapter 6), this is always an approximately valid assumption. The importance of H_Q stems from the *noiseless coding theorem* for discrete sources (Appendix C): a discrete-valued source can be encoded with an average bit rate $\overline{R}$ that is arbitrarily close to H_Q:

$$\min \{\overline{R}\} = H_Q + \epsilon \quad \text{bits/sample;} \quad \text{arbitrary } \epsilon > 0 \tag{4.96}$$

such that perfect reconstruction is possible at the receiver. There are at least two techniques that can realize this ideal, *permutation coding* [Berger, 1982] and the approach used in this book, *entropy coding*. Entropy coding is obtained by means of a *variable length coding* procedure which assigns codewords of variable lengths to the possible outcomes y_k such that highly probable outcomes are assigned shorter codewords, and vice versa. If the entropy coding is ideal, the bit rate at the output of the L-level quantizer can be reduced by

$$\Delta R = \log_2 L - H_Q \tag{4.97}$$

In fact, ΔR is the *redundancy* of the discrete-valued source. For example, if $L = 4$, $P_1 = P_4 = 1/8$ and $P_2 = P_3 = 3/8$, and if we assume statistically independent quantizer outputs, $\log_2 L = 2$, $H_Q = 1.81$, and $\Delta R = 0.19$ bit/symbol. It is obvious that no reduction is possible if all outcomes are equally probable, i.e., $P_k = 1/L$. Indeed, from (4.94), $H_Q = \log_2 L$ in that case, i.e., the entropy equals the capacity of the alphabet. In all other cases, a savings of ΔR is possible by entropy coding: here, indices of the quantizer outputs which occur with probability P_k; $k = 1,2,...,L$ are coded with codewords of different lengths.

Let y_k be assigned a codeword of n_k bits which may be smaller, equal to or greater than $\log_2 L$. The average length of the binary codewords also defines the *average bit rate*:

$$\overline{R} = \sum_{k=1}^{L} P_k\, n_k \quad \text{bits/sample}$$

and the obtained reduction is

$$\log_2 L - \overline{R} \quad \text{bits/sample} \tag{4.98}$$

The *optimum code* is given for

$$n_k = -\log_2 P_k \tag{4.99}$$

We then have $\overline{R} = H_Q$ and hence the bit rate reduction equals ΔR, as given by (4.97). This optimal code can only be reached if the probabilities satisfy the Shannon-Fano integer constraint

$$P_k = 2^{-n_k} \tag{4.100}$$

In all other cases, the average length $\overline{R}$ that results from entropy coding will be slightly higher than H_Q. Appendix C shows that it may be useful to use entropy coding on sequences (rather than on single outputs) in order to make the term ϵ of (4.96) as small as possible. This is true even for independent, identically distributed samples. The effect of coding in sequences is to provide a better approach to the *Shannon-Fano integer constraint*. Appendix C further demonstrates the constructive procedure of Huffman coding [Huffman, 1952], which seeks to realize the existence results just summarized.

Appendix C also discusses discrete sources with memory. If the source memory is significant, entropy coding can be quite complex since it must be based on processing long blocks and since joint probabilities must be known to construct the codebook. *In the practical approaches emphasized in this book, linear redundancies are removed by linear filtering prior to quantizing.* The quantizer outputs are then uncorrelated and the minimum rate to convey the information about the output sequence to the receiver is again given by the zeroth-order entropy H_Q.

Table 4.5 demonstrates the benefits of entropy coding for an example with $L = 4$ and $H_Q = 1.49$. As discussed in Appendix C, variable-length codes need special properties or structure to be useful. The reader should verify that code EC1 is useless, being *not uniquely decipherable*; code EC2 is decipherable but *non-instantaneous* (in terms of decoding); codes EC3 and EC4 are *instantaneous* in

Table 4.5 Codes for a 4-level quantizer (NBC: Natural Binary Code, FBC: Folded Binary Code, EC1 to EC4: Entropy Codes).

output	P_k	NBC	FBC	EC1	EC2	EC3	EC4
y_1	0.60	00	00	0	0	0	0
y_2	0.25	01	01	1	01	10	10
y_3	0.10	10	11	01	011	110	110
y_4	0.05	11	10	10	111	111	1110
$\bar{R}$		2	2	1.15	1.55	1.55	1.6

that their codewords can be decoded as soon as the last digit of a codeword has been received; and code EC4 is *self-synchronizable* in that each codeword ends with a specific terminating symbol or *comma*, 0.

Buffer Considerations. The source, and hence the quantizer, produces samples at a constant rate. If these samples are mapped into codewords of variable length, these encoder outputs must be initially fed into a buffer, to accommodate a communication channel that accepts symbols at a constant rate. The buffer tends to fill when a succession of long codewords is generated. This is the case if the random variable assumes improbable values on several successive samples. A long buffer must be employed to prevent *buffer overflow* that would cause a loss of samples and hence a large distortion. On the other hand, the buffer tends to empty if highly probable codewords (which have short lengths) are generated with a local probability that exceeds the average probability. This is the situation of *buffer underflow*. In this case the transmitter must resort to *bit stuffing*, and transmit a dummy signal to mark time until it has enough non-trivial information to put out.

It can be shown [Jelinek, 1968] that any buffer will eventually overflow with probability 1 in the case of stationary signals. Nonstationary signals are even more difficult to encode since the local entropy may be quite different from the long term entropy. For example, in image coding, *high entropy* or *high detail* areas of the image cause the buffer to become full. High entropy areas are the *busy* areas characterized by frequent changes of brightness. There is no such problem in *low entropy* or *low detail* areas which are also called the *quiet* areas of the image. Anyway, buffer overflow will occur whenever the information rate is higher than the transmission rate for a long enough period of time. The easiest way of preventing overflow is to have a buffer-feedback control of the quantizer, as in Figure 4.18. In speech applications, where *adaptive quantization* is often employed, the quantizer range is expanded whenever the buffer tends to overflow. It is also possible to conceive designs which change only the quantizer thresholds, and keep the reconstruction values fixed. Such systems have the advantage that the decoder at the receiver will be the same as that of a system without entropy coding. In image coding, the quantizer is typically fixed, and the easiest way to change quantizing characteristics is to switch between two quantizers. We shall mention these entropy coding systems again in Chapter 6, in the context of DPCM coding of speech and images.

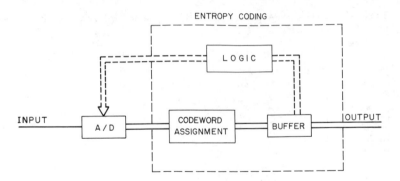

Figure 4.18 Entropy coding with quantizer control.

So far we have mentioned nothing about the receiver buffer. The status of the transmit buffer need not be transmitted provided that the channel is error-free. This is because transmit and receive buffers are strongly related. When the transmit buffer is approximately full the receiver buffer is nearly empty, and vice versa, and the total number of samples in the two buffers equals a constant.

Synchronization Problems. A single channel error can cause loss of codeword synchronization which leads to a long sequence of erroneous receiver outputs. This problem can be minimized by proper code selection which will permit re-acquisition of synchronization quickly. An example is the self-synchronizing code EC4 in Table 4.5. Codeword synchronization is obtained as soon as a 0 appears. In fact, the 0 is the synchronizing symbol or *comma*. Decoding is simply a matter of counting the 1's before the comma.

An alternative solution is a *variable-length input to fixed-length output code*. For this code, each final codeword of given fixed length may represent a different number of source output symbols. Table 4.6 is an example for 3-level quantizers [Cohn and Melsa, 1975] and three possible outputs A, B, and C, where B is the output of highest probability. The code accumulates a sequence of source symbols until a message in the output dictionary is formed. Note that in this code, all channel codewords have the same length so that channel errors do not lead to long losses of codeword synchronization.

Table 4.6 Fixed-length code for variable-length input from ternary source. B: center level of high probability. A,C: outer levels of low probability [Cohn and Melsa, 1975].

Source Word	Codeword
BBB	000
BBA	001
BBC	010
BA	011
BC	100
A	101
C	110

4.6.2 Entropy Coding of Quantizer Outputs

We shall now re-examine the bit rate reduction parameter ΔR in (4.97). We shall show that $\Delta R_{pdf-opt}$, the value of ΔR that results in mmse pdf-optimized quantization (Section 4.4) is *not* the best value achievable by entropy coding; and that at high bit rates, the best value of ΔR is in fact given by $\max\{\Delta R\} = (3/2)\Delta R_{pdf-opt}$. Further, this best configuration will involve a *uniform threshold* quantization characteristic with $L \to \infty$ for any $\bar{R}$; and at high bit rates $\bar{R}$, its performance falls short of the rate distortion bound by 1.53 dB for any input pdf, whereas at low bit rates $\bar{R}$, its performance approaches this bound [Berger, 1982].

Table 4.7 shows the results of Huffman-coding of pdf-optimized minimum mean square error (mmse) quantizers, for the example of a Gaussian input pdf. Note that the entropy H_Q of the quantizer output symbols is only slightly lower than the capacity $\log_2 L$ of the alphabet. We will show presently that the above gap can be made even smaller if the quantizers are re-optimized such that efficient entropy-coding is possible. The re-optimization results in a redistribution of the probabilities P_k in such a way that there are only few symbols with comparatively high values of the probability (and therefore short codewords) and a majority of symbols with small probabilities. The problem of designing an optimum quantizer will be reformulated as that of obtaining decision and reconstruction levels to minimize the entropy, subject to a constraint on the mean square error σ_q^2. Such entropy-coded quantizers are sometimes called *entropy-constrained* quantizers. This is in contrast to *level-constrained* quantizers discussed hitherto, whose bit rate is $R = \log_2 L$.

A quantitative description of entropy coding bounds is given in Figure 4.19(a). For any σ_q^2 and L, there is one quantizer characteristic $Q(\cdot)$ that has minimum output entropy. In Figure 4.19(a) the curve marked $L = 8$ describes the (minimum) H_Q versus σ_q^2 performance of eight-level quantizers. Point a refers to the pdf-optimized mmse quantizer. This is the level-constrained quantizer with $H_Q = 2.825$ (Row 2 of Table 4.7). The output entropy in this case is H_a and the bit rate reduction that is possible with entropy coding is $\Delta R_{pdf-opt}$. We note that for a given L, H_Q can be reduced at the cost of a higher σ_q^2. The absolute minimum is $\min\{H_Q\} = 1$ since we have assumed an even number L of levels, which means that at least one bit is needed to assign codewords to positive and negative outputs. We shall see shortly that smaller values of entropy can be

Table 4.7 Huffman coding of the output of a Gaussian-pdf-optimized quantizer. (H_Q: output entropy; SNR: that of Gaussian Max quantizer, in dB; $\bar{R}$: average length of codewords with Huffman coding based on single outputs) [Zelinski and Noll, 1972].

L	$\log_2 L$	H_Q	$\bar{R}$	SNR
4	2	1.911	1.989	9.30
8	3	2.825	2.884	14.62
16	4	3.765	3.809	20.22
32	5	4.730	4.771	26.01

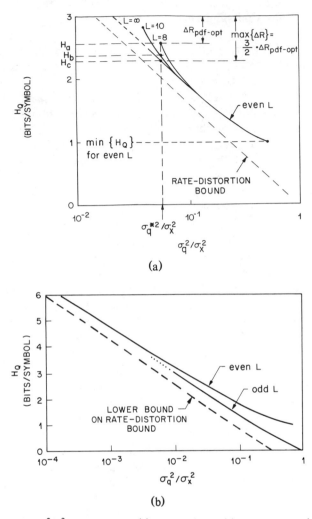

Figure 4.19 H_Q versus σ_q^2/σ_x^2. Results for (a) a quantizer with an even number of levels and a Gaussian-pdf input [Zelinski and Noll, 1972]; and (b) for gamma-pdf inputs [Granzow and Noll, 1983].

realized by employing an odd number of levels L. On the other hand, consider a fixed $\sigma_q^2 = \sigma_q^{*2}$. It is seen that the entropy can be reduced at this distortion level by increasing the number of levels. With $L = 10$, we obtain H_b, and by letting $L \to \infty$, an absolute minimum H_c is obtained. The savings in bit rate is then $\max\{\Delta R\} = \log_2 L - H_c$. Note also that this falls short of the rate distortion bound by 0.25 bit, as shown by the $H_Q = 2^{-2R}\sigma_x^2$ curve in Figure 4.19(a). We will note presently that at high bit rates, $\max\{\Delta R\} = (3/2) \Delta R_{pdf-opt}$.

We see that the numbers of quantizer steps can be made arbitrarily high in the case of entropy coding: outer steps will have a very small probability of occurrence so that their contribution to the *average* length of codewords will be very small. On the other hand, for a given entropy, we obtain a decrease in distortion because even very high-valued input samples can be coded without overload distortion. The following sections will analyze the savings obtainable from entropy coding the quantizer outputs with or without quantizer reoptimization. In the case of high entropies (high average bit rates) we will obtain results in closed form using the large-L approximation (4.63) for σ_q^2. The main result will be that for a given distortion, a *uniform-threshold* quantizer will yield the minimum entropy, and that this minimum is higher than the rate distortion bound (the absolute minimum) by only about 1/4 bit (as in Figure 4.19); a uniform-threshold quantizer is one that has uniform intervals between decision levels. In the case of small values of entropy, we will present results as obtained from iterative computer procedures. The main result is again that of a uniform-threshold quantizer, but analyses will be based on the exact σ_q^2 result (4.12) and solutions will be computer-based and non-explicit.

Entropy Coding at High Average Bit Rates. When the number of quantizer steps is sufficiently high, we may use the approximation formulas of Section 4.4 based on the companding law $c(x)$.

The entropy of the L-level quantizer output (4.94) can be split into two terms if we make use of the result $P_k = p_x(y_k)\Delta_k$:

$$H_Q = -\sum_{k=1}^{L} p_x(y_k)\Delta_k \log_2 p_x(y_k) - \sum_{k=1}^{L} p_x(y_k)\Delta_k \log_2 \Delta_k \qquad (4.101)$$

For large L and statistically independent inputs, the first term becomes the *differential entropy* of the quantizer input

$$h(X) = E[-\log_2 p_x(X)] = -\int_{-\infty}^{\infty} p_x(x) \log_2 p_x(x)\,dx \qquad (4.102)$$

The differential entropies are given in Table 4.8 for various pdf's. Using (4.42) to relate Δ_k to $c(x)$, and using (4.101) and (4.102),

$$H_Q = h(X) + \log_2 \frac{L}{2\,x_{\max}} + \int_{-\infty}^{\infty} p_x(x) \log_2 \frac{dc(x)}{dx}\,dx \qquad (4.103)$$

This result gives the entropy for any companding law as given by its interval density dc/dx. It can be verified (Problem 4.13) that in the special case of a uniform pdf input and zero overload, H_Q in (4.103) reduces to $\log_2 L$.

The entropy of the quantizer output can be reduced (by an amount no greater than $\max\{\Delta R\}$ of Table 4.8) by taking into account the fact that one can employ an arbitrary number of quantizer levels in the case of entropy coding; and it can be shown then (Problem 4.14), as in columns 4 and 5 of Table 4.8, that

$$\max\{\Delta R\} = (3/2)\,\Delta R_{pdf-opt} \qquad (4.104)$$

A practical approach will be to seek a minimum of the output entropy for a given distortion σ_q^2; i.e., we choose the companding law $c(x)$ such that H_Q of (4.103) is minimized subject to the constraint of a fixed mse as given by the large-L

Table 4.8 Entropy Coding with different input pdf's (U: Uniform, G: Gaussian, L: Laplace, Γ: Gamma) [Noll and Zelinski, 1978]. C = 0.5772 is the Euler Constant. Values in the last column are maximum SNR gains due to entropy coding.

pdf	$h(X)$	ϵ_*^2	$\Delta R_{pdf-opt}$ (bits/sample)	$\max\{\Delta R\}$ (bits/sample)	$\Delta SNR_{EC} =$ 6.02 $\max\{\Delta R\}$ (dB)
U	$\frac{1}{2}\log_2 12\sigma_x^2$	1.00	0.000	0	0
G	$\frac{1}{2}\log_2 2\pi e\sigma_x^2$	2.71	0.312	0.467	2.81
L	$\frac{1}{2}\log_2 2e^2\sigma_x^2$	4.50	0.623	0.934	5.62
Γ	$\frac{1}{2}\log_2 \frac{4\pi}{3e^{C-1}}\sigma_x^2$	5.68	1.138	1.707	10.28

approximation (4.63). We use the Lagrange multiplier technique. Consider

$$p_x(x)\, \log_2 \frac{dc(x)}{dx} + \lambda p_x(x) \left[\frac{dc}{dx}\right]^{-2} \tag{4.105}$$

Setting the derivative with respect to dc/dx to zero,

$$dc_{opt}(x)/dx = (-\lambda/3)^{1/2} = constant \tag{4.106}$$

and with the boundary conditions $c(x_{max}) = x_{max}$ and $c(0) = 0$ of Figure 4.11, we obtain

$$c_{opt}(x) = x \tag{4.107}$$

This means that *uniform quantization* leads to *a minimum of the output entropy for a given distortion*, provided that the step size is small enough to support the assumption of constant pdf used in (4.63). Using (4.107) in (4.103), we obtain [Wood, 1969]

$$\min\{H_Q\} = h(X) - \log_2 \Delta = h(X) - (1/2)\log_2 12\sigma_q^2 \tag{4.108}$$

where $\Delta = 2x_{max}/L$ is the quantizer step size and $\sigma_q^2 = \Delta^2/12$.

Comparison with the Rate Distortion Bound. We will now compare this minimum average bit rate $\bar{R} = \min\{H_Q\}$ with the rate distortion lower bound ^LR that applies to a memoryless source of pdf $p_x(x)$ and differential entropy $h(X) = E[-\log_2 p_x(X)]$ [(D.22) and Table C.2]:

$$^LR = h(X) - (1/2)\log_2 2\pi e\sigma_q^2 \tag{4.109}$$

$$\min\{H_Q\} = {}^LR + (1/2)\log_2 \pi e/6 = {}^LR + 0.255 \tag{4.110}$$

Thus we find that entropy coding with $\bar{R} = \min \{H_Q\}$ bits/sample based on a uniform quantizer is only $(1/2) \log_2 (\pi e /6)$ bits or 0.255 bits above the lower bound, irrespective of the pdf of the signal. This result has been derived for Gaussian signals both experimentally [Goblick and Holsinger, 1967] and theoretically [Gish and Pierce, 1968]. Recall that the above statement assumes very small step sizes and hence high average bit rates. At these high rates the rate distortion function is asymptotically close to the lower bound $^L R$. The small difference of 0.255 bits translates to an approximate 1.5 dB difference on the basis of the $6.02R$ formulas noted repeatedly in this chapter. The above difference from the theoretical bound is the price paid for having the simplicity of single-letter or memoryless quantization.

In summary, a non-entropy-coded L-level quantizer can perform with an error variance of $\min\{\sigma_q^2\} = \epsilon^2 \sigma_x^2 / L^2$ if it is pdf-optimized [$c(x) = c_{opt}(x)$ of (4.67)]. Its bit rate is then $R = \log_2 L$. A re-optimized (and hence uniform) quantizer can perform with same variance $\min\{\sigma_q^2\}$ with (average) bit rate $\bar{R} = \min\{H_Q\}$ as given in (4.110). The maximum obtainable bit rate reduction with single-letter quantizing systems followed by entropy coding is

$$\max\{\Delta R\} = \log_2 L - \min\{H_Q\} = (1/2) \log_2 12\epsilon^2 \sigma_x^2 - h(X) \qquad (4.111)$$

These are the values listed in column 5 of Table 4.8. With a Gaussian pdf, the gain is only 0.467 bit/sample. But in the case of the gamma pdf, about 1.7 bits per sample can be saved by entropy coding. Alternatively, for a given average bit rate, entropy coding will increase the SNR by $\Delta SNR_{EC} = 6.02 \max\{\Delta R\}$ dB over that of a non-entropy-coded Max quantizer. These values are also listed in Table 4.8. By comparing these with the values given in Figure 4.12 for large R, we find that SNR values for Gaussian and Laplacian inputs are now much closer to the value of $6.02 R$; and for gamma sources, they are actually higher than $6.02 R$, by 2.73 dB. The improvements in entropy coding are, of course, a consequence of employing an arbitrarily high number of quantizer levels. It is important to mention again that these additional levels of the quantizer are *not* used to increase the resolution in the region where the pdf of the input is significant (this would cause a significant increase in entropy), but they are used to assign representation levels to the outer parts of the pdf where they do not contribute significantly to entropy.

The result $\min\{H_Q\} = h(X) - \log_2 \Delta$ in (4.108) has a simple information-theoretical interpretation. The differential entropy $h(X)$ of the random variable at the quantizer input is a measure of the average information of the source. The information at the input of the quantizer is partly destroyed by the effect of quantization. However, the quantization error Q is uniformly distributed in the interval $(-\Delta/2, \Delta/2)$ since we have assumed small step sizes Δ, and a high number of levels that prevents overload. Its differential entropy is

$$h(Q) = E[-\log_2 p_q(Q)] = \log_2 \Delta \qquad (4.112)$$

Assuming that X and Q are statistically independent, we obtain $\min\{H_Q\}$, the average information of the quantized output, as the difference between $h(X)$ and $h(Q)$. This is the difference in (4.108).

Entropy Coding at Low Average Bit Rates. The discussion of the preceding section was based on the assumption of a sufficiently high (average) bit rate. The derivation used (4.63) which assumed that the pdf is approximately constant over any of the intervals; however, this will not be true if the average bit rate is low. A different approach has to be used in order to find the optimum entropy-encoded quantizers.

We minimize the exact expression for quantization error variance in (4.12), subject to the constraint of a given entropy H_Q (4.94): The necessary conditions for a minimum in error variance are [Berger, 1972] [Zelinski and Noll, 1972]:

$$\frac{\partial \sigma_q^2}{\partial y_k} + \lambda \frac{\partial H_Q}{\partial y_k} = 0 \quad ; \quad k = 1,2,...,L \qquad (4.113a)$$

$$\frac{\partial \sigma_q^2}{\partial x_k} + \lambda \frac{\partial H_Q}{\partial x_k} = 0 \quad ; \quad k = 2,3,...,L \qquad (4.113b)$$

where λ is the Lagrange multiplier. However, H_Q does not depend on the reconstruction levels y_k; hence, from (4.113a), we obtain again the result of the pdf-optimized quantizer: the reconstruction level should be the centroid of the pdf in its interval. The minimization problem can be solved iteratively on a digital computer. The minimization results in a H_Q-versus-σ_q^2 performance as given for Gaussian memoryless sources in the quantitative result of Figure 4.19(a). Figure 4.19(b) shows the H_Q-versus-σ_q^2 performance for a memoryless gamma source, for entropy-coded quantizers with both even and odd numbers of levels L. Note the significant reduction in distortion, for a given entropy, in the case of odd L. This is because successive samples of the source will have values close to zero with high probability. The midtread characteristic of an odd-L quantizer will then lead to long clusters, or sequences of zero-value outputs that can be assigned the shortest possible codeword of length 1. Longer codewords, signifying sequences including one or more non-zero outputs, will have much smaller probabilities with the gamma pdf input.

Example 4.12. Entropy coding of a gamma source with $R = 1$ bit/sample

Consider a midtread quantizer with an odd number of levels L. As noted in the first row of Table 4.9, an *SNR* of 7.80 dB can be obtained using a step size of $\Delta = 2.003\sigma_x$. Experiments have shown that a quantizer with the specific design of $L = 9$ yields a very close result, 7.79 dB. We will now show how the output of this system can indeed be entropy coded for the rate of 1 bit/sample.

Consider the coding of sequences of three successive output samples. Of the $L^3 = 9^3 = 729$ possible sequences, the sequence of three (midtread) zeros has a probability of 0.536, and it is assigned a codeword of length 1. Note that this nearly satisfies the Shannon-Fano integer constraint (4.100) because $2^{-1} \sim 0.536$. All other codewords have lengths of at least 4 bits. These codewords all have probabilities in the neighborhood of 0.055; once again, this follows the Shannon-Fano integer constraint closely, because $2^{-4} \sim 0.055$. As a result, the encoding system is very efficient. However, to realize a synchronous output rate of 1 bit/sample, buffer lengths needed are in the order of 800 to 1000 bits [Granzow and Noll, 1983]. Also see Problem 4.15. ●

Table 4.9 Maximum *SNR*-values (in dB) and corresponding threshold step sizes for entropy-coded memoryless Γ-sources [Granzow and Noll, 1983]. Also included for comparison are *SNR* values with pdf-optimized (Max-) quantizers (Table 4.4) and RDF-bounds (Table D.1).

$\bar{R}$ bits/sample	Max - quantizers *SNR*	Entropy-coded quantizers				RDF- bounds
		L even		*L* odd		
		SNR	Δ/σ_x	*SNR*	Δ/σ_x	
1	1.76	1.76	∞	7.80	2.003	8.53
2	6.33	11.60	0.965	14.15	0.816	15.21
3	11.47	18.78	0.400	20.36	0.370	21.59

Table 4.9 lists maximum *SNR* values in the entropy coding of a gamma source, and compares them with the performance of a Max-quantizer, and with rate distortion bounds.

Figure 4.20 shows the gain ΔSNR_{EC} obtained by entropy-coding the Γ-source, instead of using a Max-quantizer. The figure is based on the values of Table 4.9. Note that the maximum gain $\Delta SNR_{EC} = 10.28$ dB of Table 4.8 can be obtained only for $\bar{R} \rightarrow \infty$. From that table, it is also clear that **L**- and **G**-sources have significantly smaller asymptotic values. Entropy coding with even L-quantizers and finite $\bar{R}$-values have been given elsewhere [Noll and Zelinski, 1978] for **U**, **G**, **L** and **Γ** sources.

The above bounds for single-letter quantization refer to quantizers with a theoretically infinite number of levels. A finite number of levels has to be used in practical applications. In practice, it has been shown that even for small *L* values,

Figure 4.20 Maximum gain in *SNR* over Max-quantization due to entropy coding of a memoryless gamma-pdf source [Granzow and Noll, 1983]. The dashed curve is the rate distortion bound, also expressed as a gain over Max-quantizer performance [Noll and Zelinski, 1978].

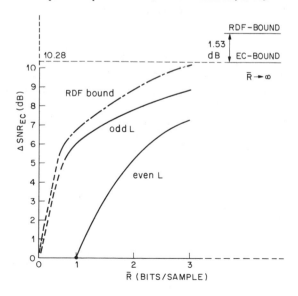

entropy coding performance is very close to the best possible entropy coding results. See Example 4.12.

Note that the gap between the RDF bound and entropy-coding performance decreases with decreasing R until it vanishes at rate zero. Also, see [Berger, 1982] for Gaussian and Laplacian examples. For large R, there is the 1.53 dB difference implied in the 0.255 bit gap of (4.110). Other sections of this book discuss the bridging of this residual gap by *delayed decision coding* (Chapter 9, for the case of Gaussian and gamma pdf's).

4.7 Statistical Properties of Quantization Errors

Previous sections have concentrated on computing the variance of the quantization error. We recall that, for a given input x, the output y is deterministically given as $y = x-q$, where q is the quantization error. However, if x is a realization of a random variable X, then q can be considered as a realization of a random variable Q. This section will discuss some of the statistical properties of Q; in particular, its pdf and its acf (and hence its psd). The discussions will show that the assumption of a uniform pdf for q is valid if $R \geqslant 2$, and that the assumption of a white quantization error is valid if $R \geqslant 2$, and if the adjacent sample correlation of the input, $\rho_{xx}(1)$, is not too close to $+1$.

4.7.1 Probability Density Functions

Figure 4.4 has shown the nature of quantization error. In uniform quantization [Figure 4.4(a)], the input intervals are of constant length Δ. The error is then bounded to $\pm \Delta/2$ provided that the representation values are midway between decision thresholds. It seems reasonable in this case to assume that all amplitude samples within the range of $\pm \Delta/2$ occur with the same probability. This means that the pdf $p_q(q)$ is constant over the interval $-\Delta/2 \leqslant q \leqslant \Delta/2$, as noted in (4.16).

A more rigorous discussion can be used to justify the above model. Consider a (not necessarily uniform) quantizer with $L = 2^R$ levels. The errors produced in each of the decision intervals $\mathscr{I}_k$ contribute to the total quantization error, and the contributions depend on the probability $P_k = P\{X \in \mathscr{I}_k\}$ that we find the amplitude of the input signal in this interval. The total pdf $p_q(\cdot)$ is thus the sum of L conditional pdf's weighted by the corresponding probabilities, since the events $\{X \in \mathscr{I}_j\}$ and $\{X \in \mathscr{I}_k\}$ are mutually exclusive:

$$p_q(q) = \sum_{k=1}^{L} P_k \, p_q(q|X \in \mathscr{I}_k) \, ; \qquad p_q(q|X \in \mathscr{I}_k) = p_x(q+y_k|X \in \mathscr{I}_k) \quad (4.114)$$

However, from (2.29),

$$p_x(x|X \in \mathscr{I}_k) = \begin{cases} (1/P_k)p_x(x) \, ; & X \in \mathscr{I}_k \\ 0 & \text{otherwise} \end{cases} \qquad (4.115)$$

Thus, $p_q(q)$ is just a superposition of sections of the input pdf $p_x(x)$. These sections are given by the decision intervals $\mathcal{I}_k$ and they are recentered by a shifting of $\mathcal{I}_k$ by a distance y_k. Figure 4.21 shows an example: the input has a bounded pdf and it is quantized by a 4-level uniform quantizer. Note that the resulting pdf

Figure 4.21   Justification of the uniform pdf model for quantization errors.

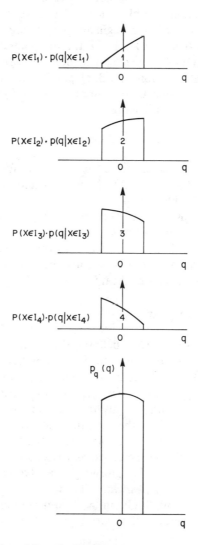

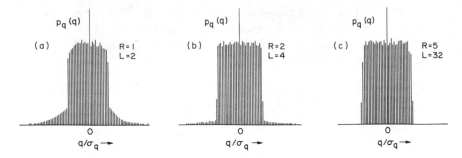

Figure 4.22 Quantization error pdf for Gaussian inputs and uniform quantization with (a) 2, (b) 4 and (c) 32 output levels [Koerber, 1979].

of the quantization error is almost flat-topped even if certain individual sections are not quite flat. In fact, an exactly flat $p_q(q)$ is exactly guaranteed for all symmetric input-pdf's if the pdf within a segment is a straight line, if the quantization is uniform, if the reconstruction levels are the midpoints of the corresponding decision intervals, and if the input is bounded in amplitude. In Figure 4.21, these conditions are not satisfied, and therefore the final pdf is not exactly flat. Even if the input random variable is unbounded, a flat-topped pdf $p_q(q)$ is a useful approximation if the number of output levels is large:

$$p_q(q) = (1/\Delta)\text{rect}(q/\Delta) \quad \text{for large } L \quad (4.116)$$

Figure 4.22 shows experimental error pdf's for uniform quantization of a Gaussian input with $L=2,4$ and 32. Note the rapid evolution of a uniform pdf as L increases. Also see Problem 4.16.

A precise condition can be given for a flat-topped error pdf if $L\rightarrow\infty$. This result is part of what is sometimes known as the *Quantization Theorem* [Widrow, 1956] [Sripad and Snyder, 1977]. This theorem states conditions under which the pdf of an input can be recovered from that of its quantized version, so that statistical measurements can be meaningfully based on quantized signals.

4.7.2 Power Spectral Densities

Let $Q(m)$ and $Q(n)$ be r.v.'s defining the quantization errors at times m and n. We arc interested in the acf $R_{qq}(m-n) = E[Q(m)Q(n)]$ and its Fourier transform, the psd $S_{qq}(e^{j\omega})$. It is clear that these quantities can be determined if the joint pdf $p_{q(m)q(n)}[q(m), q(n)]$ is known. Instead of attempting analytical results, we note some intuitive arguments. Figure 4.23 shows a segment of a random waveform as well as the quantization error waveform. If the number of quantizer levels is sufficiently large, as it is in the figure, there are many changes in sign in the error waveform, and it seems reasonable that error samples taken from it at a sufficiently low rate (as given by the Nyquist frequency illustrated in the figure) are *statistically independent*. This will not be true (i) if the waveform does not change much in amplitude in a Nyquist interval $[\rho_x(1)\rightarrow+1]$, (ii) if the waveform has periodicities that correlate distant error samples, or (iii) if the

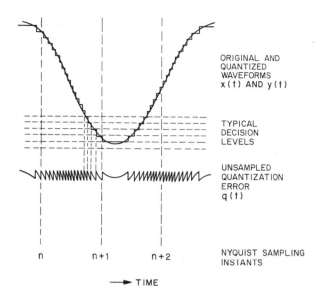

ORIGINAL AND
QUANTIZED
WAVEFORMS
x(t) AND y(t)

TYPICAL
DECISION
LEVELS

UNSAMPLED
QUANTIZATION
ERROR
q(t)

NYQUIST SAMPLING
INSTANTS

n   n+1   n+2

⟶ TIME

Figure 4.23   Unsampled signal and quantization error waveform [Cattermole, 1969].

quantizer has only a few levels so that error oscillations such as those of Figure 4.23 do not exist.

One of the consequences of statistical independence of successive error samples $q(m)$ and $q(n)$ is that their joint pdf is the product of individual pdf's, so that with the uniform univariate model (4.116),

$$
p_{q(m)q(n)}[q(m), q(n)] = \begin{cases} 1/\Delta^2 & -\Delta/2 \leqslant q(m), q(n) \leqslant \Delta/2 \\ \\ 0 & otherwise \end{cases}
\tag{4.117}
$$

which represents a square probability box of constant height $1/\Delta^2$.

Another consequence of statistical independence is that the quantization noise is *white*:

$$
R_{qq}(m-n) = \sigma_q^2 \, \delta_{mn}
\tag{4.118}
$$

We can also invoke a spectral interpretation to support (4.118). The unsampled error waveform has a spectrum that is much broader than the signal spectrum. Sampling of the quantized signal implies an undersampling of the error waveform (see Figure 4.23) and hence aliasing. (Quantizing of the samples gives equivalent results.) The total noise spectrum has many components that would be folded back into the baseband as in Figure 3.15(b). Consequently we have two results: (i) the noise spectrum flattens, and (ii) its baseband power equals the variance of the unsampled error waveform. We have already discussed (ii) in Chapter 3. The flattening of spectrum (i) is shown by the dashed spectrum in Figure 3.15(b). Graphically, it is not very different from the pdf-flattening process in Figure 4.21.

The nature of quantization noise spectrum can also be discussed by looking at the equivalent description by means of quantization noise acf, as in the following example.

Example 4.13. Measurements with an AR(1) Source

Consider a Gaussian AR(1) source with normalized adjacent sample correlation $\rho_{xx}(1)$, and quantizers with numbers of levels $L=2,4,...,32$. Figure 4.24(a) demonstrates that there are significant correlations $\rho_{qq}(1)$ only if the quantization is coarse (say $L \leqslant 4$) and/or $\rho_{xx}(1) \rightarrow 1$. For $\rho_{xx}(1)$ values of practical significance ($\rho_{xx}(1) < 1$), $\rho_{qq}(1)$ values are insignificant for $L=32$.

Figure 4.24(b) shows the entire acf sequence $\rho_{qq}(n)$ for quantization error with $L=2$ and $\rho_{xx}(1)=0.95$. Notice that $\rho_{qq}(n)$ decays exponentially with n; $\rho_{qq}(1)$ is, of course, the value 0.56 on the $\rho_{xx}(1)=0.95$ point of Figure 4.24(a).

Figure 4.24 Quantization of a Gaussian AR(1) input: (a) $\rho_{qq}(1)$ versus $\rho_{xx}(1)$; (b) $\rho_{qq}(n)$ versus n; and (c) $\rho_{qx}(0)$ versus $\rho_{xx}(1)$ [Koerber, 1979].

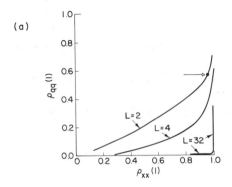

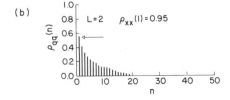

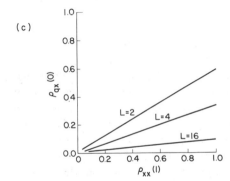

Figure 4.24(c) shows the crosscorrelation value $\rho_{qx}(0) = E[Q(n)X(n)]/\sigma_q\sigma_x$ as a function of $\rho_{xx}(1)$. In very coarse quantization $(L = 2)$, a significant crosscorrelation exists between quantization error and input for $\rho_{xx}(1) \rightarrow 1$. Also see Problem 4.17(a). •

4.7.3 The Gain-Plus-Additive-Noise Model

We have noted that it is reasonable to assume that the quantization noise is white and that its pdf is flat. We shall now characterize this noise a little further. Since $Y=X-Q$, by squaring and taking expectations,

$$\sigma_y^2 = \sigma_x^2 + \sigma_q^2 - 2E[XQ] \tag{4.119}$$

A simple *additive input-independent noise* model would imply that

$$E[XQ] = 0; \qquad \sigma_y^2 = \sigma_x^2 + \Delta^2/12 \tag{4.120}$$

In the above model, therefore, the variance of the quantizer output is greater than that of the input by the amount $\Delta^2/12$ [Figure 4.25(a)].

We have already seen, however, that with *the noise in pdf-optimized quantizers*, $\sigma_y^2 < \sigma_x^2$. In fact, in that case we have shown (4.49) that

$$E[XQ] = \min\{\sigma_q^2\}; \qquad \sigma_y^2 = \sigma_x^2 - \min\{\sigma_q^2\} \tag{4.121}$$

A better model for quantization is therefore not a purely additive independent noise model, but one with a less-than-unity *gain* component and an *additive* component. This is shown in Figure 4.25(b) where the gain is $\alpha_g < 1$, and the additive component is described by a r.v. N. If N is additive and input-independent, $E[XN] = 0$, $E[XQ] = E[X(X-\alpha_gX-N)] = \sigma_x^2(1-\alpha_g)$, and for (4.121) to hold

$$\alpha_g = 1-\min\{\sigma_q^2\}/\sigma_x^2 = 1 - \min\{\epsilon_q^2\} \tag{4.122}$$

Clearly, $\alpha_g \rightarrow 1$ as $L \rightarrow \infty$. This has been noted in the gain-plus-additive-noise model of rate distortion theory, Appendix D. Also see Problem 4.18 and Figure D.2.

Figure 4.25 Quantization noise models: (a) purely additive noise model; and (b) model with non-unity gain and additive noise.

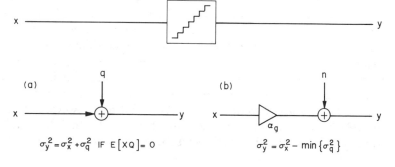

It is clear from the above that a careful analysis of quantization noise must take into account the fact that the noise is not additive, and not uncorrelated with the input. In particular, at low bit rates, especially at $R = 1$ bit/sample, the errors in quantization must necessarily be considered as belonging to two classes: one caused by a change in level and one caused by uncorrelated noise. It is obvious why these types of distortions must often be considered separately. In speech communication, for example, a change only in level will have very little perceptual significance, unless the change exceeds about 3 dB [Richards, 1973]. In coarse quantization, α_g values can be small enough to cause an attenuation of 2.5 dB; this is seen by using $\min\{\epsilon_q^2\} = 0.25$ from Table 4.2 in (4.122), and computing $20 \log \alpha_g$. But the main source of perceptual degradation is not this attenuation, but rather the additive noise component N.

4.8 The Use of Dithering in Coarse Quantization

Figure 4.24 has shown that when quantization is coarse (for example, $L=2$), $\rho_{qq}(n)$ and $\rho_{qx}(1)$ values are quite significant, suggesting a colored and input-correlated error sequence. Equation (4.121) has shown that $E[XQ]=\min\{\sigma_q^2\}$; this shows again that quantization error and input are correlated in pdf-optimized quantization, and that this correlation increases as L decreases, causing a higher $\min\{\sigma_q^2\}$. The above autocorrelation and crosscorrelation properties are reflected by perceptually undesirable signal-dependent patterns in the error sequence. By adding appropriate high-frequency signals to a waveform prior to quantization, it is possible to break up these undesirable patterns. The high-frequency perturbation signal can be a pseudorandom signal; it can also be a carefully designed deterministic signal; in either case, it is referred to as a *dither* signal, and the refinement of *dithering* is particularly useful with coarse quantizers [Goodall, 1951] [Jaffe, 1959] [Roberts, 1962] [Furman, 1963]. We shall begin with a study of dithered quantizers from a statistical viewpoint. At a later point in this section, we will discuss the dithering of speech and image signals [Thompson and Sparkes, 1967] [Limb and Mounts, 1969] [Wood and Turner, 1972] [Jayant and Rabiner, 1972] and relate the respective perceptual phenomena to the statistical viewpoint.

Figure 4.26 illustrates the principle of dithering with the example of a 9-sample input sequence and a uniform one-bit midrise quantizer. Figure 4.26(a) shows the conventional two-level output and the conventional reconstruction error $r(n) = x(n)-y(n)$. Note how the error pattern mimics the input in the left and right skirts as well as in the concave segment in the middle. Note also that the output $y(n)$ shows sustained artificial *contours* of amplitude ± 0.5. In Figure 4.26(b), the addition of a high-frequency dither signal $\partial(n)$ prior to quantization results in an error sequence that is more oscillatory and less input-like. For example, the extreme right skirt of the error waveform is now falling, unlike the rising input; and the input-like concavity in the error waveform of (a) is also broken up by zero crossings at samples 5 and 6. However, the error waveform in (b) clearly has a larger variance than that in (a). In (c), on the other hand, the additional final operation of dither subtraction at the receiver seems to restore the

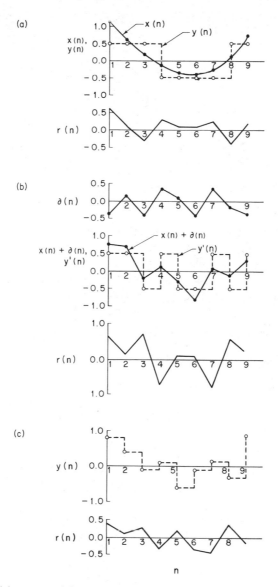

Figure 4.26 Input $x(n)$, output $y(n)$ and reconstruction error $r(n)$ in quantizing systems: (a) without dithering; (b) with dither $\partial(n)$, but without subsequent subtraction of dither; and (c) with dithering, followed by subtraction of dither at the receiver.

variance of the reconstruction error waveform without losing its oscillatory character. The reconstructed output $y(n) = y'(n) - \partial(n)$ (see Figure 4.27) tracks the input very closely, unlike the waveform $y'(n)$; *further, the number of possible levels in $y(n)$ is no longer limited to two, the number of actual quantizer levels, as in the output sequences in (a) and (b).* The implementation in (c) requires knowledge of the dither signal at the receiver with full sample-to-sample synchrony with the $\partial(n)$ used at the transmitter. The simpler system of (b) is therefore used

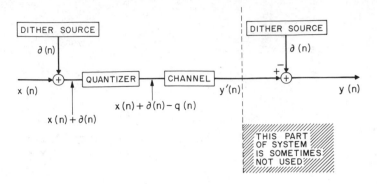

Figure 4.27 Block diagram of a dithered quantization system. The section to the right of the dashed line represents an operation that is sometimes uncritical; for example, in image quantization.

quite often. The increase in error variance in (b) is more than offset by the perceptual gain in terms of a non-input-like error pattern.

Figure 4.27 is a block diagram of a dithered quantizer system. As stated, the subtraction of the dither signal $\partial(n)$ at the receiver is sometimes uncritical and not done, especially in picture quantizers. In such systems, the final output is $y'(n)$, not $y(n)$. Usual operations of codeword assignment and D/A conversion are implied in Figure 4.27.

4.8.1 A Statistical Interpretation

Consider the reconstruction error variance

$$\sigma_r^2 = E[R^2] = \int_x \int_y p_{xy}(x,y)(x-y)^2\, dxdy \qquad (4.123)$$

By setting $x-y = x-Q(x)$, and noting that the integral of the joint pdf over y is $p_x(x)$, (4.123) reduces to the earlier (4.11). For simplicity, $x(n)$, $y(n)$, and later the dither signal $\partial(n)$ will be denoted by x,y and ∂; and subscript indices will be dropped from all pdf's. From earlier discussions, we know that $E[R^2] = \Delta^2/12$ for uniform quantizers (4.17), if there are no overload effects.

Let $E[Y|x]$ denote the conditional mean of the output for a given input x:

$$E[Y|x] = \int_y yp(y|x)\, dy \qquad (4.124)$$

It will be interesting to split $E[R^2]$ into three components, each of which involves the conditional mean $E[Y|x]$:

$$E[R^2] = \int_x \int_y p(x,y)(x-E[Y|x]+E[Y|x]-y)^2\, dxdy$$

$$= \int_x \int_y p(x,y)(x-E[Y|x])^2\, dxdy + \int_x \int_y p(x,y)(E[Y|x]-y)^2\, dxdy$$

$$+ \int_x \int_y p(x,y)\, 2(x-E[Y|x])(E[Y|x]-y)\, dxdy$$

$$= I_1 + I_2 + I_3 \qquad (4.125)$$

The third integral can be rewritten as the sum of two components:

$$2 \int_x \int_y p(x,y)(x E[Y|x]-xy)dxdy + 2\int_x \int_y p(x,y)(y E[Y|x]-(E[Y|x])^2)\,dxdy$$

It can be seen that both these components vanish by definition, so that the third integral in (4.125) equals zero. The fact that $E[Y|x]$ is a function only of x enables us to express the first integral as a single integral

$$I_1 = \int_x p(x)(x-E[Y|x])^2\,dx \qquad (4.126a)$$

The second integral is

$$I_2 = \int_x \int_y p(x)\,p(y|x)(y-E[Y|x])^2\,dx\,dy \qquad (4.126b)$$

The quantity I_2 has been termed *apparent noise*: it represents the variation in y relative to the conditional mean output value; and the component I_1 has been called the *tonal quality*: it shows the deviation of the conditional mean output value from the true input [Roberts, 1962]. In coarse quantization of an image, for example, a slowly varying or constant gray tone would be displaced, if $I_1 \neq 0$, into a different average shade or tone of gray in the output. Thus, the quantities I_1 and I_2 are descriptors of orthogonal effects, both statistically and perceptually, and since $I_3 = 0$,

$$\sigma_r^2 = E[R^2] = I_1 + I_2 \qquad (4.127)$$

In refining coarse quantizers for speech and image inputs, a central notion is that the degradation represented by I_1 is perceptually more annoying than that given by I_2. A good quantizer should seek to decrease I_1, at the cost of I_2, if necessary, while keeping the total error σ_r^2 as low as possible. Before proceeding to show how I_1 can be decreased by dithering, we should mention that the perceptual importance of I_1 is augmented by statistical interpretations. First, $I_1 = 0$ in (4.126b) implies that $E[Y|x] = x$ for all x because the integrand is a product of two nonnegative terms. Thus if $I_1 = 0$, *the expected value of reconstruction equals that of input, for all values thereof.* Note also that $E[Y|x] = x$ implies that $E[R|x] = 0$, because $Y = X - R$. Further, if $\eth(n)$ is a zero-mean, input-independent signal, $E[Y|x] = E[Y'|x]$ and $E[R|x] = E[R'|x]$, where $R' = R + \eth$; so that $I_1 = 0$ implies that $E[Y'|x] = x$ and $E[R'|x] = 0$. Thus, for any given value of the input, the conditional mean values of the reconstruction errors R and R' are both zero. Finally, a value of $I_1 = 0$ *is a necessary and sufficient condition for the reconstruction errors R and R' to be statistically independent of the input X* [Schuchman, 1964]. Therefore the object of dithering will be to render $I_1 = 0$ and equivalently, to make R and R' independent of X.

The fact that $E[R|x] = 0$ with dithering, *for any input x*, is very significant. Recall from Section 4.4 that in a pdf-optimized quantizer without dithering $E[R|\mathcal{I}_k] = 0$, for *any input interval $\mathcal{I}_k$*.

The Effect of Dithering on I_1, I_2 and σ_r^2. To get some perspective about the quantities I_1 and I_2, we shall use the example of a uniform pdf input. As noted in Chapter 2, this is a good model for image inputs.

Example 4.14.   Uniform quantization of a bounded input

Consider a midrise R-bit quantizer with step size Δ. Assume for simplicity that the maximum input magnitude is

$$\max\{|x|\} = x_{\max} = (2^{R-1}-1/2)\Delta = x_{ol} - \Delta/2 , \qquad (4.128)$$

a value smaller than that of the bounded input in (4.28) where $x_{\max}$ was equal to x_{ol}. The present special assumption about $|x|_{\max}$ is not critical for realizing the benefits of dithering. It is merely used for analytical simplicity in this example. Figure 4.28 represents the quantization of a random input of the form

$$x = (k+1/2) \Delta + s ; \quad 0 < s < \Delta/2 \qquad (4.129)$$

where k is an integer in the range $(-2^{R-1},2^{R-1})$ and the requirement of positive s is for convenience. The ensuing discussion will extend to negative s also, in a very straightforward fashion. The arrows in Figure 4.28 represent adjacent reconstruction values in the quantizer characteristic, and the interval $\mathcal{I}_k$ from earlier notation includes the reconstruction value $(k+1/2) \Delta$. Three situations are of interest: (i) quantization without dither (ii) quantization with random dither, and no subsequent subtraction of it at the receiver, and (iii) quantization with pseudo-random dither which is eventually subtracted from the quantizer output, as in Figure 4.27.

i.   **Quantization without dither**

From earlier notation, $r(n) = q(n) = s$ showing how the error is strongly dependent on the input. Therefore $\sigma_r^2 = \Delta^2/12$ and $I_2 = 0$ because, for any given value of input $x(n)$, there is no variation in the output $y(n)$, the latter being uniquely specified by the transfer function of the quantizer. From (4.126) and (4.127), therefore,

$$I_2 = 0 ; \quad I_1 = \sigma_r^2 = \Delta^2/12 \qquad (4.130)$$

Figure 4.28   Notation used for dither analysis in Example 4.1. Arrows indicate adjacent reconstruction values in the quantizer output.

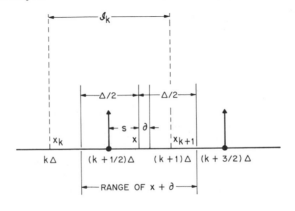

ii. **Quantization with unsubtracted random dither**

As in Figure 4.28, let the random zero-mean dither ∂ have a range $(-\Delta/2, \Delta/2)$ and a pdf

$$p_{\partial}(\partial) = 1/\Delta \ \text{rect} \ (\partial/\Delta) \tag{4.131}$$

Two sub-cases can be distinguished, keeping in mind that $s > 0$:

(a) $-\Delta/2 < \partial < \Delta/2 - s$ or $x + \partial \in \mathscr{I}_k$: In this case the quantizer input is $(x + \partial) < (k+1)\Delta$, the output is $(k+1/2)\Delta$ and the reconstruction error is s.

(b) $\Delta/2 - s < \partial < \Delta/2$ or $x + \partial \in \mathscr{I}_{k+1}$: This is the range of ∂ for which the quantizer output is $(k+3/2)\Delta$, and the reconstruction error is $s - \Delta$. In this case, the effect of dithering is to shift quantizer input from interval $\mathscr{I}_k$ to I_{k+1}, although coder input X is in $\mathscr{I}_k$.

Expressions for $E[Y'|x]$ and reconstruction error variance $\sigma_{r'}^2$ result from averaging the results in (a) and (b), first over ∂ and then over the variable s. The probabilities of the ∂-ranges in (a) and (b) are $(1-s/\Delta)$ and (s/Δ), because of the uniform distribution (4.131). Consequently,

$$E[Y'|s] = (1-s/\Delta) \ (k+1/2) \ \Delta + (s/\Delta) \ (k+3/2)\Delta \ ;$$

$$E[R'^2|s] = (1-s/\Delta) \ (s)^2 + (s/\Delta) \ (s-\Delta)^2$$

With a uniform model for input pdf,

$$p_s(s) = 2/\Delta \ ; \quad 0 < s < \Delta/2 \tag{4.132}$$

We now average $E[Y'|s]$ and $E[R'^2|s]$ over r, using (4.132), to obtain

$$E[Y'|s>0] = (k+1/2) \ \Delta + \Delta/4 \ ; \quad E[R'^2|s>0] = \Delta^2/6$$

Similarly, it can be shown that for negative s,

$$E[Y'|s<0] = (k+1/2) \ \Delta - \Delta/4 \ ; \quad E[R'^2|s<0] = \Delta^2/6$$

so that expected values over all s $(-\Delta/2 \leqslant s \leqslant \Delta/2)$ are

$$E[Y'|x] = (k+1/2)\Delta x \ ; \quad \sigma_{r'}^2 = \Delta^2/6$$

Using (4.126) and (4.127),

$$I_1 = 0 \ ; \quad I_2 = \sigma_{r'}^2 = \Delta^2/6 \tag{4.133}$$

Note from (4.130) and (4.133) that unsubtracted dithering decreases I_1 and increases I_2; it also doubles the total error variance. We now examine a means of keeping a zero I_1, while reducing the error variance to the original minimum value of $\Delta^2/12$.

iii. **Quantization with subsequently subtracted pseudo-random dither**

If a known dither signal is eventually subtracted at the receiver from the quantizer output, the analysis of (ii) above will have to include the effect of this subtraction in evaluating $E(Y|s)$ and $E[R^2|s]$. With dither subtraction, the final output decreases by ∂, and the reconstruction error consequently increases by the same amount ∂. Consequently, reconstruction errors for subcases (a) and (b) [defined in (ii)] will be $s + \partial$ (instead of s) and $\Delta - s + \partial$ (instead of $\Delta - s$), respectively. Note that for the extreme example of $s = \Delta/4$ and $\partial = \Delta/2$ [values just satisfying the requirement of subcase (b) in (ii)], the error with dither subtraction is zero; while without dither subtraction, the final error would be $-\Delta/2$.

The properties of a quantizer with dither subtraction can be analyzed as in case (ii), and the results are

$$I_1 = 0 ; \quad I_2 = \sigma_r^2 = \Delta^2/12 \qquad (4.134)$$

Table 4.10 Effect of dithering on σ_r^2, I_1 and I_2 for uniform quantization with a non-overloading input $x_{max} = x_{ol} - \Delta/2$.

Quantizing scheme	σ_r^2	I_1	I_2
No dither	$\Delta^2/12$	$\Delta^2/12$	0
Unsubtracted random dither	$\Delta^2/6$	0	$\Delta^2/6$
Subtracted pseudo-random dither	$\Delta^2/12$	0	$\Delta^2/12$

The benefits of dithering, as summarized in Table 4.10, reflect the breaking up of signal-dependent patterns in the granular error region, as already illustrated in Figure 4.26. The most important effect of non-zero overload is to render the zero I_1 values in the table non-zero as well; resulting I_1 values will in fact be equal to $\Delta^2/12$ weighted by the probability of quantizer overload.

Independence of Error and Input with Uniform Dither. We can also show that in cases (ii) and (iii) above, the pdf of reconstruction noise is independent of the value of input. For example, for case (iii), we express the probability distribution function as a weighted sum of two terms, corresponding to subcases (a) and (b):

$$P\{R < t|s\} = P\{-\Delta/2 \leqslant \partial \leqslant \Delta/2-s\} P\{s + \partial < t\}$$
$$+ P\{\Delta/2-s \leqslant \partial \leqslant \Delta/2\} P\{s - \Delta + \partial < t\}$$

Using the uniform dither pdf (4.131), and considering a specific fixed value of s,

$$P\{R < t|s\} = \frac{\Delta-s}{\Delta} \cdot \frac{t-s+\Delta/2}{\Delta} + \frac{s}{\Delta} \cdot \frac{t-s+\Delta+\Delta/2}{\Delta} = \frac{1}{\Delta}(t + \Delta/2)$$

which depends on t and Δ, but is *independent* of s. In fact, the above distribution is simply that of a uniform pdf with support $(-\Delta/2, \Delta/2)$; the reconstruction error follows this pdf *irrespective* of the value of s, and hence irrespective of the value of x. ●

4.8.2 Results for Speech and Images

Speech Quantization. Figure 4.29 shows the effect of dithering on the normalized error-input crosscorrelation $\rho_{rx}(0) = E[R(n)X(n)]/\sigma_r\sigma_x$ in speech quantization.

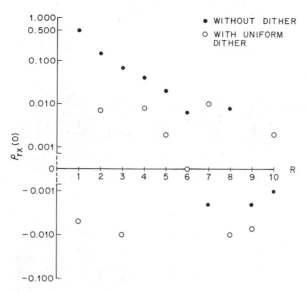

Figure 4.29 Measured signal-to-error correlation $\rho_{rx}(0)$ versus R in uniform quantization of speech. In the dither example, the dither signal was eventually subtracted at the receiver [Jayant and Rabiner;©1972, AT&T].

Note the nonlinearity of the y-axis scale. The effect of dithering is to make the crosscorrelation very small for all values of R, the number of quantizer bits. In the absence of dithering, the magnitude of the crosscorrelation is a monotonically decreasing function of R in the range $R = 1$ to 6; and a significant correlation exists in coarse quantization (say $R \leqslant 2$). The correlation value of 0.5 for $R=1$ is very close to that for the AR(1) input with $R=1$ and the speech-typical $\rho_{xx}(1)=0.85$ [Figure 4.24(c)].

Figure 4.30 shows waveforms of speech input $x(n)$ and reconstruction error $q(n) = r(n) = x(n) - y(n)$ for the three values of R in Figure 4.29, and for the cases of dither (b) and no dither (c). The error waveforms are magnified (by a factor 2^R) to highlight their features. Note that (i) the signal-dependence in $r(n) = q(n)$ is a monotonically decreasing function of R in the absence of dithering; and (ii) dither serves to decorrelate $r(n)$ and $x(n)$ even for the worst case $R=1$.

Perceptual studies of speech dithering with fixed uniform quantizers [Rabiner and Johnson, 1972] serve to supplement the analytical and graphical results noted above. The tests involve a set of ten sentences and several subjects, and the following are the main observations:

(i)   strong preferences for dithered quantization for bit rates $R=2$ to 6;

(ii)   for $R=2,3$ and 4, a preference for dithered quantization even when it had one less bit per sample than the undithered quantizer;

(iii)   an increase in word intelligibility with dithering for $R=4,5$ and 6; and

(iv)   a decrease in word intelligibility with dithering for $R = 2$ and 3.

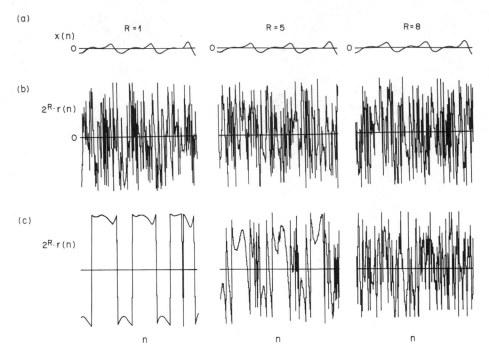

Figure 4.30 Waveforms of (a) speech input $x(n)$; and reconstruction error $r(n)$ in uniform quantization using R bits/sample (b) with dither and (c) without dither. In (b), dithering is followed by eventual subtraction of it at the receiver. The error waveforms have been magnified by a factor 2^R [Jayant and Rabiner;©1972, AT&T].

The difference between *preference* results and *intelligibility* results at $R=2$ and 3 is interesting, although these bit rates are academic for high-quality speech coding (Chapter 5) unless sophisticated redundancy reducing techniques are employed (Chapters 6 to 12). The loss of word intelligibility in (iv) has been attributed to the masking of low-energy, high frequency consonant information by reconstruction noise [Miller and Nicely, 1950]. Dithering tends to whiten the error spectrum and to produce more high-frequency error components than are present in the signal-dependent error signal of an undithered quantizer; and this results in increased consonant masking of low-level consonants by the errors. The masking and intelligibility loss noted above can be reduced in conditional dithering systems [Wood and Turner, 1972] [Chen and Turner, 1973] where the dithering process is halted whenever input speech amplitudes are in the innermost quantizer levels, indicating a high zero-crossing probability that is characteristic of consonant inputs.

Image Quantization. Video examples from a pioneering work on dithering [Roberts, 1962] appear in Figure 4.31. Note that with $R=3$, input-error dependencies in conventional quantization manifest themselves in the form of *contouring*, which is the result of abrupt changes of output level in a slowly changing gray area of the input scene. Such contouring is also indicated from the conventional (undithered) reconstructions of a slowly varying input in Figure

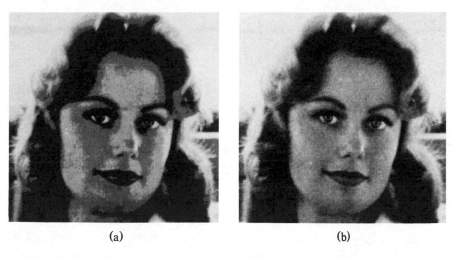

(a)   (b)

Figure 4.31 Examples of 3-bit image quantization: (a) without dithering and (b) with dithering. In (b), the dither signal was eventually subtracted at the receiver [Roberts;©1962, IRE].

4.26(a). The use of uniform dither breaks up these contours and provides an image smoothness similar to that in undithered quantization with $R=6$. An important factor in image dithering is the lowpass filtering action of the eye. This gives a smooth appearance to the oscillatory outputs of dithered system reconstructions, even those with unsubtracted dither and consequently higher-than-conventional error variance $\Delta^2/6$ [as in Figure 4.26(b)]. The absence of such lowpass filtering in speech perception makes dither subtraction more critical in speech work; this is one reason why implementations of dithering in video work have been more extensive than in speech coding [Limb, 1969] [Lippel and Kurland, 1971] [Jarvis, Judice and Ninke, 1976].

4.8.3 Useful Forms of the Dither Signal

In the quantization of bounded inputs, where overload effects do not exist, there is a class of dither signals [Schuchman, 1964] that renders the reconstruction error $R(n)$ statistically independent of the input $X(n)$; the most useful member of this class is one whose pdf is uniform over the support $(-\Delta/2, \Delta/2)$. This was already demonstrated in Example 4.13. Also, as stated earlier, a necessary and sufficient condition for Q to be independent of X is that I_1 be zero [Schuchman, 1964].

Amplitude-Quantized and Deterministic Dither Signals. Practical systems need to employ amplitude-quantized dither signals. As long as the resolution in the dither signal is fine compared with that of the quantizer input, one expects that the error-decorrelating properties of dither should be unaffected. Indeed, experiments with speech signals indicate that an adequate design is to make the step size in the quantized dither signal no greater than *one-fourth* the step size of the speech quantizer [Jayant and Rabiner, 1972]. In fact, this is precisely the design that was used in the illustration of Figure 4.26 where the quantizer step size was $\Delta = 1$, and

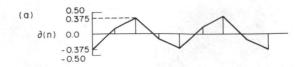

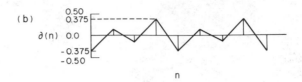

Figure 4.32 Periodic four-level dither sequences [Limb, 1969].

$\partial(n)$ randomly assumed one of four levels ($-3/8$, $-1/8$, $1/8$ and $3/8$), with an adjacent level spacing that was one-fourth of the quantizer step size. It is reasonable to insist, of course, that the dither signal be a symmetrical zero-mean quantity, with a uniform distribution of (discrete) amplitude in the range ($-\Delta/2$, $\Delta/2$).

Dither signals can go a step further in terms of simplicity in that they can be *deterministic*. The motivation for a deterministic dither signal, besides simplicity, is to force negative correlations in the quantizer input $x(n) + \partial(n)$. When $x(n)$ is constant, as in the slowly varying areas of a picture, this is simply achieved by adding to it a dither sequence that rapidly oscillates about a zero mean. The ultimate perceptual result is an error waveform that is not only independent of the input, but also spectrally shaped in a perceptually desirable fashion — meaning specifically an error spectrum that is rich in the relatively less visible high-frequency components. Such a spectrum is the result of negative correlations induced in the error sequence. We recall from the simple AR(1) model of Figure 2.16(b) that a negative value for adjacent sample correlation results in a highpass psd. Error shaping can be illustrated by considering the amplitude-quantized deterministic dither sequences of Figure 4.32:

$$\partial(n):\{-3/8,\ 1/8,\ 3/8,\ -1/8...\} \quad \text{and} \quad \partial(n):\{-3/8,\ 1/8,\ -1/8,\ 3/8...\} \quad (4.135)$$

When used with a constant gray level input $x(n)=0.5$ and a two-level quantizer ($y=1$ if $x>0.5$; $y=0$ otherwise), the respective values of error acf $\rho_{rr}(1)$ are 0 and -1, respectively (Problem 4.19). The dither signal in Figure 4.32(b) [the right-hand half of (4.135)] is the suggested design if one seeks a highpass error spectrum in constant-brightness areas of a picture. A visibility analysis [Limb, 1969] shows that this sequence has perceptual properties that are in fact better than those of random dither.

Dither Matrices. A natural extension of the 1-D sequence (4.136) is to a 2-D deterministic *dither matrix* with an oscillatory, or negatively-correlated $\partial(n)$ pattern in both dimensions. There is a systematic procedure for generating such dither matrices. One starts with a well designed 2×2 matrix such as [Limb, 1969]

$$^2\mathbf{D} = \begin{bmatrix} D_{00} & D_{01} \\ D_{10} & D_{11} \end{bmatrix} = \begin{bmatrix} 0 & 2 \\ 3 & 1 \end{bmatrix} \qquad (4.136)$$

and for larger matrices, one uses a recursion relationship of the form [Jarvis, Judice and Ninke, 1976]

$$^n\mathbf{D} = \begin{bmatrix} 4 \cdot {}^{n/2}\mathbf{D} + D_{00}\lambda & 4 \cdot {}^{n/2}\mathbf{D} + D_{01}\lambda \\ 4 \cdot {}^{n/2}\mathbf{D} + D_{10}\lambda & 4 \cdot {}^{n/2}\mathbf{D} + D_{11}\lambda \end{bmatrix}; \quad \begin{array}{l} \lambda \text{ is an all} - one \\ \text{matrix of order } n/2 \end{array} \qquad (4.137)$$

For example, the first recursion produces (Problem 4.21) a 4×4 matrix

$$^4\mathbf{D} = \begin{bmatrix} 0 & 8 & 2 & 10 \\ 12 & 4 & 14 & 6 \\ 3 & 11 & 1 & 9 \\ 15 & 7 & 13 & 5 \end{bmatrix} \qquad (4.138)$$

Dither matrices have a perceptually optimal size $n \times n$ in image coding. Very small n represents inadequate randomness in dithering and insufficient quantization of dither amplitudes; while with very large n, the repetition of dither pattern produces signal-masking effects at a very low spatial frequency (given by f_s/n; f_s being the sampling frequency). A good design is an (8×8) dither matrix [Bayer, 1973].

4.9 Transmission Error Effects

In this section, we shall consider the effect of a noisy channel on the uniform and nonuniform quantization systems of Sections 4.3, 4.4 and 4.5. We shall assume that random errors are introduced in the bits that convey information about quantizer output level. As in Figure 1.9, we assume a *binary symmetric channel*, which implies that information about quantizer output level will be transmitted as a sequence of $R = \log_2 L$ bits; and we denote the random *bit error probability*, or *bit error rate*, by p_e. The above channel is assumed to be a *stationary memoryless channel*. *Stationarity* implies that channel properties do not change with time. A *memoryless* channel is one where the mapping between input and output at any given time is independent of previous outcomes.

In what follows we assume statistically independent inversions of message bits, signifying a totally random error pattern. This is a good model not only for channels without memory (where the fates of successive message bits are indeed independent) but also in systems where channel memory is rendered ineffective by bit-rearranging procedures such as interleaving or scrambling—procedures that tend to randomize channel error patterns that may be bursty or clustered [Jayant, 1975].

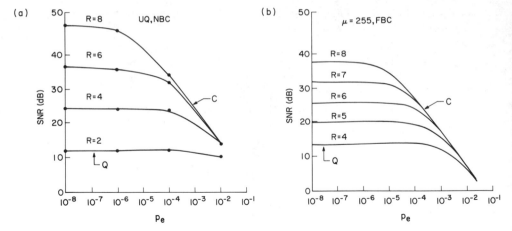

Figure 4.33 Illustration of quantizer-limited performance and channel-limited performance in digital transmission. The two limits are indicated by letters Q and C. (a) Uniform quantization of a uniform pdf input, followed by NBC coding of the output. (b) Quantization of a Laplacian pdf input with log companding ($\mu = 255$) and FBC coding of the output [Rydbeck and Sundberg, 1975]. The NBC and FBC coding systems are defined in Figure 4.35.

Further, most of our analyses will assume a bit error probability p_e that is small enough to justify consideration of only *single-error* patterns in received codewords.

Before proceeding with channel error analyses, let us put the effects of quantization errors and channel errors in perspective by means of the sketches of Figure 4.33. The results in (a) refer to the uniform quantization of a uniform pdf input. The performance of this system with channel errors will presently be derived (4.174). The results in (b) refer to the $\mu 255$ log-quantization of a Laplacian input [Rydbeck and Sundberg, 1975]. Figures 4.33(a) and (b) both suggest that at high bit rates, the quantizer system is more sensitive to very high values of p_e, and we shall see later that this is typical. The figures also suggest that when we are operating in the *channel-limited region* rather than in the *quantizer-limited region* of p_e, it pays to design the system with a coarser quantizer; and perhaps allocate some of the transmission capacity for explicit bit protection.

4.9.1 Error Definitions and Channel Codes

Referring to Figure 4.34, we find that in the presence of transmission errors, reconstructed output signal $y(n)$ will include the effects of *both quantization error*

Figure 4.34 Transmission of quantized amplitudes over noisy channels. In a noiseless channel, $v(n) = u(n)$.

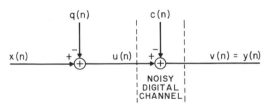

Quantization   4

$q(n)$ *and channel error* $c(n)$, resulting in a total reconstruction error $r(n)$ that is the sum of $q(n)$ and $c(n)$:

$$q(n) = x(n) - u(n) \qquad (4.139a)$$

$$c(n) = u(n) - v(n) \qquad (4.139b)$$

$$y(n) = v(n) = u(n) - c(n) = x(n) - q(n) - c(n)$$

$$r(n) = x(n) - y(n) = q(n) + c(n) \qquad (4.140)$$

We will see presently that there are important classes of systems in which $\sigma_r^2 = \sigma_q^2 + \sigma_c^2$, or at least approximately so.

For example, refer to the midrise quantizer in Figure 4.35(a) with $L = 8$ levels and $R = 3$ bits per codeword. This quantizer maps each input sample $x(n)$ into one of a set of eight rational numbers $u(n) \in \{y_k\}$; $k = 1, 2, ..., 8$. The representation level y_k is chosen if $x_{k+1} \geqslant x(n) > x_k$. The index k of input symbol y_k of the transmission system is transmitted to the receiver in a binary format, as the *channel codeword*; the received *channel codeword* is interpreted as one of the eight output symbols $v(n) \in \{z_k\}$; $k = 1, 2, ..., 8$, with $z_k = y_k$ [Figure 4.35(b)]. A change in amplitude $\Delta_{kj} = |y_k - z_j|$ results if the transmitted quantizer index k is changed to j because of channel errors. If this happens for input sample n, the corresponding channel error is $c(n) = \Delta_{kj}$.

Several *binary codes* are shown in Figure 4.35(a): the *natural binary code*, NBC; the *folded binary* code, FBC (also known as a *sign-magnitude* code, SMC); the *two's complement* code (TCC), where the codeword for amplitude y complements, bit by bit, the codeword for amplitude $-y$; and the *Gray* or *reflected binary* code (RBC), where every pair of adjacent codewords has exactly one bit position where the codewords differ.

The codewords in NBC are merely the so-called *binary representations* of decimal numbers 0 to $2^R - 1$:

$$\text{codeword: } [b_1 \, b_2 \, b_3 \, ... \, b_R]; \quad \text{decimal equivalent: } \sum_{r=1}^{R} 2^{R-r} b_r \qquad (4.141)$$

For example, if $R = 3$, the 3-bit word 110 represents a quantizer output of $4 \cdot 1 + 2 \cdot 1 + 1 \cdot 0 = 6$ in decimal notation, which is y_7 in Figure 4.35. The bit with the highest weighting in (4.141) is b_1, the *most significant bit* (MSB). The *least significant bit* (LSB) is b_R. The most significant bit b_1 in Figure 4.35(a) is a *sign bit*. The remaining bits constitute an $(R-1)$-bit NBC code used to convey magnitude information. Bit b_2 is the *most significant magnitude bit*.

If the channel input is y_2, an error in the most significant bit causes the reception of z_6 with NBC coding ($001 \rightarrow 101$), and of z_7 with FBC ($010 \rightarrow 110$). In general, an error in the most significant bit causes a displacement equal to $2^{R-1}\Delta$ (half the quantizer range) in NBC and TCC, and a displacement that is

(a)

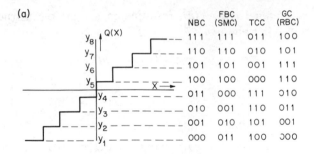

	NBC	FBC (SMC)	TCC	GC (RBC)
y_8	111	111	011	100
y_7	110	110	010	101
y_6	101	101	001	111
y_5	100	100	000	110
y_4	011	000	111	010
y_3	010	001	110	011
y_2	001	010	101	001
y_1	000	011	100	000

(b)

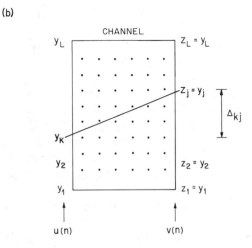

Figure 4.35 (a) Symmetric midrise quantizer with eight output levels, and four binary codes. (b) Effect of transmission errors on y_k.

proportional to input amplitudes in FBC and RBC. If signal amplitudes near zero are more probable than those away from zero (as in speech), the FBC code would clearly lead to a smaller channel error variance than the NBC code (see Problem 4.31).

It is possible to optimize a channel code to minimize channel error variance. Such a code would be constructed so that errors in the most probable codewords make only a small contribution to error variance. This, in turn, is achieved if codewords resulting from an error are close to the original codeword — in other words, this would lead to a *minimum distance code*, MDC. At least for one example of an input pdf with a high probability of small amplitudes, viz., the Laplacian pdf, the FBC is identical to the MDC for $R=2$ and 3 [Sundberg and Rydbeck, 1976].

With an R-bit code, the *probability of no error* in the received codeword is equal to the probability of R correctly received bits:

$$P_0 = (1-p_e)^R \simeq \exp(-p_e R) \quad \text{for small } p_e \qquad (4.142)$$

The probability of *one or more errors* in the received codeword is

$$P_{>0} = 1-P_0 \simeq 1-\exp(-Rp_e) \simeq Rp_e \quad \text{for small } p_e \qquad (4.143a)$$

The probability of *exactly one error* in the received codeword is the probability of $(R-1)$ correct bits and one incorrect bit (with R possible positions in the codeword):

$$P_1 = \binom{R}{1} p_e (1-p_e)^{R-1} = Rp_e (1-p_e)^{R-1} \qquad (4.143b)$$

$$\simeq Rp_e \simeq P_{>0} \quad \text{for small } p_e \qquad (4.143c)$$

Thus, for $p_e \to 0$, most error patterns imply single errors per codeword.

A useful tool in channel error analyses is the *Hamming distance D_{kj}*, the number of codeword letters that are different in the representation of intended output level y_k and actual output level y_j. It can be seen (Problem 4.22) that with a binary symmetric channel, and an R-bit code, the conditional probability P_{kj}, the probability that y_j will be received when y_k was sent, is given by

$$P_{kj} = P\{V(n)=y_j | U(n)=y_k\} = p_e^{D_{kj}}(1-p_e)^{R-D_{kj}} \qquad (4.144)$$

Note that if $p_e < 0.5$, P_{kj} decreases monotonically with D_{kj}.

The Hamming distance D_{kj} between y_k and y_j depends on the binary coding scheme. For example, from Figure 4.35, D_{26} is 1 for NBC, and 3 for FBC. Based on (4.144), the corresponding values of conditional probability P_{26} are $p_e(1-p_e)^2$ for NBC and $(1-p_e)^3$ for FBC. Also see Problem 4.30. Conditional probabilities P_{kj} are completely described for $k,j = 1,2,...,L$ by a *channel transition matrix*

$$\mathbf{P}_c = \{P_{kj}\}; \quad k,j = 1,2,...,L \qquad (4.145)$$

with the special characterizations

$$p_e = 0: \quad \mathbf{P}_c = \mathbf{I}, \qquad (4.146)$$

$$p_e = 0.5: \quad \mathbf{P}_c = \{P_{kj}\} = \{2^{-R}\} ; k, j = 1,2,...,L . \qquad (4.147)$$

for *error-free* ($p_e=0$) and *totally noisy* ($p_e=0.5$) binary channels.

With a noisy channel, the *mean-squared reconstruction error* is given by

$$\sigma_r^2 = E[(X(n)-V(n))^2] = E[Q(n) + C(n)]^2 \qquad (4.148)$$

$$= \sigma_q^2 + \sigma_c^2 + 2\sigma_m^2 \qquad (4.149)$$

where σ_q^2, σ_c^2 and σ_m^2 are *quantization error*, *channel error* and *mutual error* components defined by

$$\sigma_q^2 = E[(X(n)-U(n))^2] = E[Q^2(n)] \qquad (4.150)$$

$$\sigma_c^2 = E[(U(n)-V(n))^2] = E[C^2(n)] \qquad (4.151)$$

$$\sigma_m^2 = E[Q(n)\ C(n)] \qquad (4.152)$$

The *mutual error* is the crosscorrelation between quantization and channel errors. This mutual correlation arises in the process which maps channel noise into reconstruction noise. The mutual error term in (4.152) will be seen in general to be non-zero, although the noise on the channel that causes channel error $C(n)$ is quantizer-independent.

4.9.2 Reconstruction Error Variance

The total reconstruction error variance (4.148), skipping time index n, is

$$\sigma_r^2 = E[(X-V)^2] = \int_{-\infty}^{\infty} \int_{\infty}^{\infty} (x-v)^2 p_{xv}(x,v)dxdv \qquad (4.153)$$

and since

$$p_{xv}(x,v) = p(v|x)p_x(x) ; \text{ and } p(v|x) = \sum_{k=1}^{L} P\{V = y_k|x\}\delta(v-y_k) , \quad (4.154)$$

$$\sigma_r^2 = \sum_{j=1}^{L} \sum_{k=1}^{L} P_{kj} \int_{\mathscr{I}_k} (x-y_j)^2 p_x(x)dx \qquad (4.155)$$

Note that for $p_e = 0$, $\mathbf{P}_c = \{P_{kj}\}$; $k, j = 1,2,...,L = \mathbf{I}$, as in (4.146); for this case, (4.155) reduces to that for the error-free system, the familiar (4.12). The channel contribution to error variance is

$$\sigma_c^2 = E[(U-V)^2] = \sum_{k=1}^{L} \sum_{j=1}^{L} (y_k-y_j)^2 P\{y_k, y_j\}$$

$$= \sum_{k=1}^{L} \sum_{j=1}^{L} (y_k-y_j)^2 P_{kj} \int_{\mathscr{I}_k} p_x(x)dx \qquad (4.156)$$

Using the quantization error result of (4.12) and the identity $\sum_{j=1}^{L} P_{kj} = 1$, the mutual error term is

$$\sigma_m^2 = E[Q(n)\ C(n)] = \sum_{k=1}^{L} \sum_{j=1}^{L} P_{kj}(y_k-y_j) \int_{\mathscr{I}_k} (x-y_k)p_x(x)dx \quad (4.157)$$

The mutual error vanishes if (i) $p_e = 0$ so that $P_{kj} = \delta_{kj}$, or if (ii) the quantizer has been chosen such that its reconstruction values y_k are the centroids of intervals $\mathscr{I}_k$ (4.45b) so that the integral in (4.157) vanishes [Totty and Clark, 1967]. This is the Max-quantizer condition, and we will denote the quantizer characteristic by $Q_*(\cdot)$ and its mmse by $\min\{\sigma_q^2\} = \sigma_{q*}^2$. Thus

$$\sigma_r^2 = \sigma_{q*}^2 + \sigma_c^2 \qquad \text{for Max-quantizers } Q_*(\cdot) \qquad (4.158a)$$

Experience shows that σ_m^2 can be neglected in general for small p_e, even if the quantizer is not $Q_*(\cdot)$; while σ_c^2 depends on the chosen decision and reconstruction values, and (through P_{kj}) on error probability *and* chosen channel code.

The approximate relation

$$\sigma_r^2 = \sigma_q^2 + \sigma_c^2 \qquad (4.158b)$$

will be used in many of the later sections. Note that $\sigma_q^2 \geqslant \sigma_{q*}^2$ if the quantizer is non-Max. However, σ_c^2 may be much smaller in that case, so that the overall mse can be smaller than that of (4.158a). Such re-optimizations of the quantizer will be discussed in Section 4.9.4.

4.9.3 One-Bit Quantization

Closed-form solutions are possible in the case of $R=1$. The one-bit quantizer of a zero-mean random variable has only one finite decision level $x_2 = 0$ and two reconstruction values which will be denoted by

$$y_1 = -\delta \; ; \; y_2 = \delta \qquad (4.159)$$

The quantization error variance is

$$\sigma_q^2 = 2\int_0^\infty (x-\delta)^2 p_x(x)dx = \sigma_x^2 + \delta^2 - 2\delta \, \delta_* \; ; \qquad (4.160)$$

$$\delta_* = \left[\int_0^\infty x p_x(x)dx\right] \bigg/ \left[\int_0^\infty p_x(x)dx\right] = E[X|x \geqslant 0] \qquad (4.161)$$

where δ_* is the mean absolute value of X, equal to the centroid of the area under positive $p_x(x)$. This is the mmse reconstruction value that was pdf-optimal for $p_e = 0$ and was therefore called δ_{opt} in that context (Section 4.3). We have already seen that this value minimizes σ_q^2 and that [see (4.39) and (4.41)]

$$\sigma_{q*}^2 = \min\{\sigma_q^2\} = \sigma_x^2 - \delta_*^2 \; ; \qquad \sigma_q^2 = \sigma_{q*}^2 + (\delta_* - \delta)^2 \; , \qquad (4.162)$$

which shows that quantization error variance increases by the square of the deviation of step size δ from δ_*. Values of optimal step size δ_* are listed in Table 4.11 for several $p_x(x)$ models. The δ_* and ϵ_{q*}^2 values are the same as the δ_{opt} and $\min\{\epsilon_q^2\}$ values of Table 4.2.

Table 4.11 Optimum step size, minimum quantization error variance, and channel coefficients of one-bit quantizers. (U: Uniform, G: Gaussian, L: Laplacian, Γ: Gamma).

pdf	δ_*/σ_x	$\epsilon_{q*}^2 = \sigma_{q*}^2/\sigma_x^2$	ξ_*
U	$\sqrt{3}/2$	0.25	3.0
G	$\sqrt{2/\pi}$	0.363	2.55
L	$1/\sqrt{2}$	0.50	2.0
Γ	$1/\sqrt{3}$	0.667	1.33

The *channel error variance* is simply obtained by noting that the magnitude of a possible channel error contribution is $|y_1 - y_2| = 2\delta$ and errors $\pm 2\delta$ occur with probability $p_e/2$ each. Thus,

$$\sigma_c^2 = 4\delta^2 p_e/2 + 4\delta^2 p_e/2 = 4\delta^2 p_e , \qquad (4.163)$$

a variance that increases linearly with p_e and squared step size.

The *mutual error variance* can be derived from (4.157) to be

$$\sigma_m^2 = E[Q(n)C(n)] = 2\delta \, p_e \, (\delta_* - \delta) , \qquad (4.164)$$

and it increases linearly with step size deviation $(\delta_* - \delta)$. The *total reconstruction error variance* for the one-bit quantizer, using (4.149), is

$$\sigma_r^2 = \sigma_x^2 + \delta^2 - 2\delta\delta_* (1 - 2p_e) \qquad (4.165)$$

resulting in an optimal step size and minimum variance given by setting $\partial \sigma_r^2/\partial \delta = 0$:

$$\delta_{**} = \delta_* (1 - 2p_e) ; \qquad \min\{\sigma_r^2\} = \sigma_x^2 - \delta_{**}^2 \qquad (4.166)$$

Note the special results for the extreme cases of $p_e = 0$ and 0.5:

$$p_e = 0: \qquad \delta_{**} = \delta_*; \qquad \min\{\sigma_r^2\} = \sigma_x^2 - \delta_*^2 \qquad (4.167)$$

$$p_e = 0.5: \qquad \delta_{**} = 0; \qquad \min\{\sigma_r^2\} = \sigma_x^2 \qquad (4.168)$$

Clearly, a bit error probability of 0.5 suggests a degenerate situation where the optimum strategy is not to transmit at all. Formally, this corresponds to a redesign involving a vanishing quantizer characteristic, i.e., step sizes $\delta_{**} \rightarrow 0$. For more realistic channels $(0.5 > p_e > 0)$, we will note that the redesign (4.164) will involve step sizes δ_{**} that do not tend to zero but are nevertheless smaller than the Max-quantizer values δ_*. The problem in utilizing (4.166) is that in many practical situations, the exact value of p_e may be unknown.

When $\delta \approx \delta_*$, the mutual error variance (4.164) vanishes, and from (4.163)

$$\sigma_r^2 = \sigma_{q*}^2 + \sigma_c^2 = (\epsilon_{q*}^2 + \xi p_e)\sigma_x^2 ; \qquad \xi = \xi_* = 4\delta_*^2/\sigma_x^2 \qquad (4.169)$$

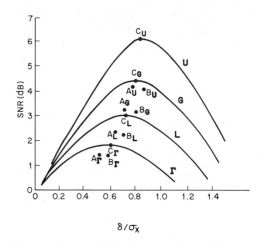

Figure 4.36 One-bit quantizer results. *SNR* versus step size δ for $p_e = 0$, and effects on *SNR* of random bit errors; $p_e = 5 \cdot 10^{-2}$ (U: Uniform, G: Gaussian, L: Laplacian, Γ: Gamma) [Noll, 1976].

The parameter ξ will be called the *channel coefficient* [Noll, 1975]. Its values ξ_* for $\delta = \delta_*$ are listed in Table 4.11. The gamma pdf, which has the highest value of ϵ_{q*}^2 in the table, also has the lowest value of ξ.

As an example for the use of Table 4.11 and (4.169), consider a Laplacian unit variance input for which $\xi = 2.0$. The error variance will increase from 0.5 with an error-free channel ($p_e = 0$) to 0.7 with a bit error rate of 10% ($p_e = 0.1$). An interesting interpretation of ξ_* is that it can be simply related to p_{eqc}, the error probability threshold for which $\sigma_c^2 = \sigma_{q*}^2$ (Problem 4.26):

$$p_{eqc} = (1/\xi_* - 1/4) \qquad (4.170)$$

Figure 4.36 shows the dependence of *SNR* on step size for the pdf models of Table 4.11. The pdf models are denoted by usual subscripts **U**, **G**, **L** and Γ. The points labelled C show the optimum step size and corresponding maximum *SNR* for $p_e = 0$. In addition, points A and B show the effect on (σ_x^2/σ_r^2) of 5% ($p_e = 0.05$) random errors; point A corresponds to a quantizer redesign $\delta = \delta_{**}$ based on (4.166), while B is the performance for $\delta = \delta_*$ (optimum step size for $p_e = 0$). Note that the improvement due to quantizer redesign is very small. The gains due to quantizer redesign (step size reduction) will be more significant for higher error rates (Problem 4.28). They will also be seen to be more significant, for any given p_e, for multilevel quantizers ($L > 2$). As mentioned earlier, these gains can only be realized if the bit error rate p_e is indeed known exactly, or at least approximately.

4.9.4 Multilevel Quantizers

Uniform pdf Input. Closed-form solutions for σ_r^2 are generally not available for $R > 1(L > 2)$. An interesting exception is the transmission error performance of a coding scheme that transmits signals with a *uniform pdf input* and employs a *uniform quantizer*. In this case, $\epsilon_q^2 = 2^{-2R}$ and $\xi_* = 4(1-\epsilon_q^2)$.

Assume that the step size is $\Delta_* = 2x_{\max}/L$, which implies an optimum (Max-) quantizer $Q_*(\cdot)$ for $p_e = 0$ from (4.28). From (4.158a),

$$\sigma_r^2 = \sigma_{q*}^2 + \sigma_c^2 \; ; \quad \sigma_{q*}^2 = \sigma_x^2/L^2 = \Delta_*^2/12 \tag{4.171}$$

With NBC coding of the quantizer output (Figure 4.35), an error in the ith most significant bit causes a displacement of $2^{R-i}\Delta_*$. If the error rate is small, the probability of more than one error per codeword is negligible, and single errors in the R bit positions are equally likely, with probability p_e, and

$$E[C^2(n)|U(n)\in \mathscr{I}_k] = \sum_{i=1}^{R} p_e \, (2^{R-i}\Delta_*)^2 = p_e\Delta_*^2(2^{2R}-1)/3 \tag{4.172}$$

because of the independence of the contributions. The quantizer level probabilities P_k are also equal, with probability $1/L$, and

$$\sigma_c^2 = \sum_{k=1}^{L} P_k E[C^2(n)|U(n)\in \mathscr{I}_k] = \Delta_*^2 p_e (2^{2R}-1)/3 \tag{4.173}$$

The reconstruction error variance [Viterbi, 1966] is

$$\sigma_r^2 = \sigma_{q*}^2 + \sigma_c^2 = (2^{-2R} + \xi_* p_e)\sigma_x^2 \; ; \quad \xi_* = 4(1-2^{-2R}) \tag{4.174}$$

The channel error contribution σ_c^2 increases linearly with p_e. But it decreases as quantization becomes coarser (Figure 4.33). The special case of $\xi_* = 3$ for $R = 1$ corresponds to the ξ_* value in the first row of Table 4.11.

Re-optimization of Multilevel Quantizers. Gains due to re-optimizing a two-level quantizer were noted to be very modest in Figure 4.36. Re-optimization of a 3-bit ($L=8$) quantizer is described numerically in Figure 4.37 for the example of a Gaussian input. As with $R = 1$, re-optimization is based on minimizing the sum $\sigma_r^2 = \sigma_q^2 + \sigma_c^2$ by reducing σ_c^2, while using a quantizer with $\sigma_q^2 > \sigma_{q*}^2$. Such re-optimization is possible if p_e is high, and can be considered constant and known.

The figure demonstrates differences for two nonuniform 3-bit quantizers with NBC coding. Note the significant decrease in *SNR* with increasing p_e for the Max-quantizer $Q_*(\cdot)$. The re-optimized $Q_{**}(\cdot)$ is more robust for high error rates, but it is suboptimal if the actual error rate is small because $Q_{**}(\cdot)$ is optimized for a specific p_e value, namely 2.5%. It is therefore suboptimal for $p_e \neq 0.025$, but it still performs better than Q_* for high values of p_e. A comparison of quantizer characteristics Q_* and Q_{**} would reveal significant shrinkage (about 30%) in quantizer range, as opposed to a much smaller shrinkage (about 5%) in one-bit quantization, as given by the $(1-2p_e)$ factor in (4.166).

In general, if $p_e > 0$, system performance is maximized by setting partial derivatives of σ_r^2 [see (4.155)] (rather than σ_q^2) with respect to x_j and y_j to zero. This leads to an optimum quantizing characteristic $Q_{**}(\cdot)$ [Kurtenbach and Wintz, 1969]:

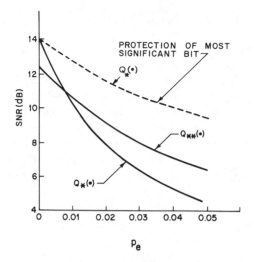

Figure 4.37 *SNR* versus p_e for $R = 3$ and Gaussian inputs, for Max-quantizer Q_* and re-optimized quantizer Q_{**} (optimized for $p_e = 2.5 \cdot 10^{-2}$) [Noll, 1975,II; ©AT&T].

$$y_{k**} = \frac{\sum\limits_{j=1}^{L} P_{kj} \int\limits_{\mathscr{I}_k} x p_x(x)\,dx}{\sum\limits_{j=1}^{L} P_{kj} \int\limits_{\mathscr{I}_k} p_x(x)\,dx} \; ; \qquad x_{k**} = \frac{\sum\limits_{j=1}^{L} y_j^2 (P_{k-1,j} - P_{k,j})}{2 \sum\limits_{j=1}^{L} y_j (P_{k-1,j} - P_{k,j})}$$

$$k = 1,2,...,L \qquad\qquad k = 2,3,...,L$$

$$(4.175)$$

Note again that without errors, earlier designs result, as in (4.45). Also see Problem 4.24.

Channel Coefficients for Multi-level Quantizers. The transition probability P_{kj} was defined in (4.144). Using this expression, the channel error variance σ_c^2 (4.151) can be written as [Noll, 1975,II]

$$\sigma_c^2 = \sigma_x^2 \sum_{j=1}^{R} \xi_j p_e^j \qquad\qquad (4.176)$$

where ξ_j are *channel coefficients* that reflect the effects on σ_c^2 of the quantizer characteristic, the chosen binary code and the source statistics. These coefficients give only global information about channel error variance. If the individual effects on each possible codeword are needed, *digital error coefficients* must be introduced to take into account all possible error sequences [Rydbeck and Sundberg, 1976].

If p_e and R are sufficiently small, the channel contributes to σ_c^2 only through single errors. With $P_{kj} = p_e(1-p_e)^{R-1} \sim p_e$, terms involving p_e^2, p_e^3 ,... can be neglected. The mutual error term can also be neglected as before. Therefore, with $\xi_1 = \xi$, the error variance σ_r^2 reduces to a form similar to the one-bit result (4.169):

$$\sigma_r^2 = \sigma_q^2 + \xi p_e \sigma_x^2 = (\epsilon_q^2 + \xi p_e)\sigma_x^2 \qquad (4.177)$$

Note that although (4.177) is functionally similar to (4.169), ξ (as well as σ_q^2) are functions not only of input pdf, but also of R.

Table 4.12 lists channel coefficients for various pdf models, and for two types of quantizers, nonuniform Max-quantizer Q_* and uniform Max-quantizer Q_{L*}. The values for $R = 1$ are those from Table 4.11, and the NBC values for uniform pdf were obtained in closed form from (4.175). Note that coefficients for a uniform quantizer are in general less than those for a nonuniform quantizer. This is due to the fact that displacements Δ_{ij} are in general smaller, for given i and j, with uniform quantizers. For example, with $R = 2$ and mmse quantization of a gamma-input, the output levels in Q_* are proportional to ± 0.313 and ± 2.223 (Table 4.3), while in Q_{L*}, they are proportional to ± 0.5 and ± 1.5. With a most significant bit in error and an NBC code, the displacement Δ_{ij} is always half the quantizer range, which is 2.536 for Q_* and 2.0 for Q_{L*}. Table 4.12 also indicates that channel coefficients are the least for a uniform pdf for $R > 2$, and that for nonuniform pdf sources and $R \geqslant 2$, FBC outperforms NBC.

In the one-bit example, we saw that quantizer re-optimization decreased the value of ξ by a factor $(1-2p_e)$ (Problem 4.28). This was directly related to quantizer shrinkage by a factor $(1-2p_e)$. Re-optimizations of multibit quantizers lead to similar step size shrinkage. In multibit quantization, it is also more important to choose an appropriate channel code.

Figure 4.38(a) shows ξ_* as a function of R (1 to 8), input pdf and binary code. Note that for the speech-typical gamma pdf, the set of three solid curves shows that the FBC code has better ξ_* values than the NBC code and that the FBC values are very close to those for MDC. In the case of image inputs, a uniform input pdf is typical, and thus the NBC code is optimal, as seen from the pair of dashed curves.

Figure 4.38(a) also shows the values of ξ in log-quantization of a Laplacian input. Results are shown for $R = 8$, FBC and MDC, and for two levels of input power, -17 dB and -40 dB relative to the level that would begin to cause overload

Table 4.12   Channel coefficients ξ_* [Noll, 1976].

R pdf		1	2		3	
			NBC	FBC	NBC	FBC
U		3.0	3.75	4.50	3.94	4.88
G	Q_*	2.55	4.97	4.65	6.91	5.75
	Q_{L*}		4.96	4.57	7.21	5.57
L	Q_*	2.00	7.08	5.30	12.67	7.50
	Q_{L*}		5.91	4.29	11.22	6.39
Γ	Q_*	1.33	9.07	6.28	18.55	9.11
	Q_{L*}		5.68	3.62	13.31	6.64

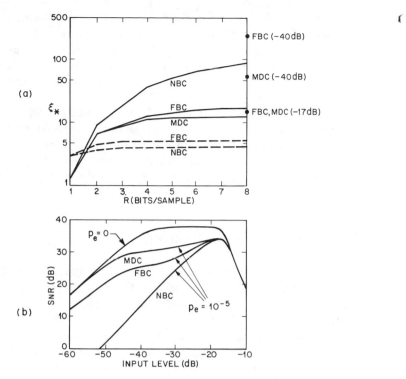

Figure 4.38 Effect of binary code on channel error performance of quantizers. (a) Channel coefficients ξ_* as a function of R, input pdf and binary code [Zelinski;©1979, IEEE] [Rydbeck and Sundberg, 1976]. Solid curves refer to a gamma input pdf and dashed curves to a uniform input pdf. Quantizers are optimized for mmse in each case. The black dots refer to log-quantization of a Laplacian input for two input levels, −40 dB and −17 dB, relative to the level that begins to introduce overload. (b) Dynamic range characteristics of A 87.56 quantization for a Laplacian input, $R = 8$ bits/sample and $p_e = 10^{-5}$ [Rydbeck and Sundberg, 1976. Reprinted with permission].

[Rydbeck and Sundberg, 1976]. With companded quantizers, the importance of selecting a channel code is very significant if the system is underloaded (as shown by the −40 dB example).

The relative performances of NBC, FBC and MDC are also shown by the dynamic range curves of Figure 4.38(b) for the example of A 87.56 quantization, $R = 8$ and $p_e = 10^{-5}$. Note that the range of the Laplacian input signal over which the *SNR* of the companded system is at least 30 dB is 10, 12 and 28 dB respectively, for NBC, FBC and MDC.

Effect of Bit Protection. In multi-bit quantization, it is realistic to protect the more significant bits from transmission error (for example, by the use of increased transmitter power or by redundant transmissions), because most of the contribution to σ_c^2 is due to the large displacements δ_{ij} caused by bit errors in the first and second most significant bits. For example, with $R = 3$ and NBC, protection of the most significant bit will prevent displacements of the form δ_{15}, δ_{26}, δ_{37} and δ_{48} (Figure 4.35). Setting corresponding displacement terms to zero in (4.156) leads to a smaller value for σ_c^2 and hence for the channel coefficient ξ. Figure 4.37 shows the effect of protecting the most significant bit when the input is Gaussian and $p_e = 0.025$ (Also see Problem 4.29). Finally, there are instances (for example, gamma pdf, FBC, $R=4$) where protection of the second most significant bit (most significant magnitude bit) is more advantageous than protection of the first most significant (sign) bit.

The reduction in ξ by means of error protection will of course have to be interpreted carefully because the protection of the significant bits involves in general an increase of transmission capacity, or a reduction in the number of quantizer bits for a given total transmission capacity. As seen in Figure 4.33, such reallocation of bits is a very logical thing to do in the channel-limited region of operation.

4.10 Adaptive Quantization

Quantizer adaptations to changing input conditions can take several forms, and three important cases are illustrated in Figure 4.39. In each of these cases, we see two pairs (i) and (ii) of sample input sequence $x(n)$ and an input-matched quantization characteristic $Q(x)$.

In (a) we show adaptation of $Q(x)$ to the *dynamic range* (or *variance*) of $x(n)$. The range of $Q(x)$ as well as that of $x(n)$ increase by a factor of 1.5 as we go from (i) to (ii). There is no change in the shape of the input pdf, and no change of the functional form of $Q(x)$, which happens to be a uniform characteristic.

In (b) we show adaptation of $Q(x)$ to a change of *shape in input pdf*, without any change in dynamic range of either $x(n)$ or $Q(x)$. As we go from (i) to (ii), very small values of $x(n)$ become more likely and $Q(x)$ matches this condition by allowing for a minimum step size in (ii) that is smaller than that in (i). Thus $Q(x)$ is uniform in (i), but nonuniform in (ii).

In (c) we show the result of adaptation of $Q(x)$ to a changing *mean of the input*. As we go from (i) to (ii), the mean changes from zero to a non-zero positive

Figure 4.39 Three ways of adapting $Q(x)$ to changing input statistics, to match (a) input dynamic range or variance; (b) shape of input pdf; and (c) mean value of input.

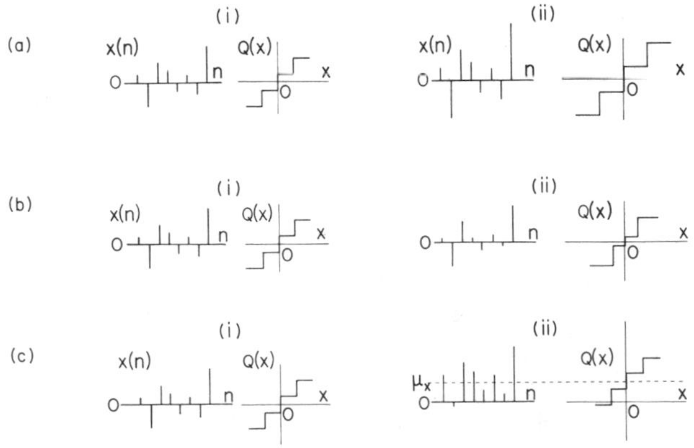

value μ_x, and the quantizer matches this condition by simply shifting or displacing $Q(x)$ vertically, by an amount μ_x. The shape of $Q(x)$ as well as the dynamic range remain unchanged.

The logarithmic companding technique of Section 4.5 was already shown to enhance the performance of a quantizer with an input that has a large dynamic range. A log-quantizer is still *time-invariant*, however; and in that sense, it is not the ideal device for quantizing nonstationary inputs; and although log-quantization has proven to be extremely useful in speech quantization with $R = 8$ bits/sample (Chapter 5), speech coding systems for lower bit rates will be seen invariably to use adaptive quantization of some kind. The better performance of adaptive quantization at low bit rates will be demonstrated by examples with $R \leqslant 4$ bits/sample (Figure 4.43 for $R = 3$, and Figure 6.21). The price paid for using an adaptive algorithm will be a very modest amount of encoding delay, which in speech work can range from a fraction of a millisecond to several milliseconds, depending on the logic.

A logical arrangement for such inputs is *switched quantization*; this consists in providing a bank of B fixed quantizers, and switching among them as appropriate, in response to changing input statistics. As shown in Figure 4.40(a), the quantizers in the bank may be either uniform or nonuniform, zero-mean or non-zero mean,

Figure 4.40 Block diagrams of (a) switched quantization and (b) (c) adaptive quantization.

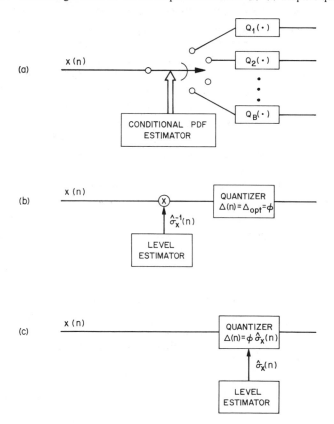

with large step size or small step size [Schlink, 1972] [Cohen, 1972,1973] [Zschunke, 1977]. The choice of quantizer characteristics is dictated by conditional input statistics; the conditioning is based on the entire past of the input in the ideal case, but in practice only based on the state of recent input or output samples. Switched quantizing systems have been used in both speech and video applications, and gains over fixed quantization have been noted with as few as $B = 2$ quantizers in a bank. In the important special case of *symmetrical zero-mean pdf's* of known shape, adaptation to input statistics consists merely in matching quantizer dynamic range to input variance, as in Figure 4.39(a). With *non-independent inputs*, conditional pdf's have strictly non-zero means in general, even if the unconditional pdf is a zero-mean function, as in Figure 4.39(c). These non-zero means can be simply taken into account by prediction procedures (Chapter 6) that essentially provide quantizer shifts. The zero-mean symmetrical pdf model for quantizer input is therefore quite useful in a wide class of applications.

The *adaptive quantizers* of this section correspond to the limiting case of $B \rightarrow \infty$, at least in principle. We shall concentrate on the important case of a zero-mean input pdf of known shape and unknown level (standard deviation σ_x); and although we mention nonuniform quantizers when appropriate, most of our discussion will relate to the case of a uniform $Q(x)$, with adaptive size, as in Figure 4.39(a). As shown in Figures 4.40(b) and (c), the output of the level estimator in these systems is expected to provide an essentially continuous adaptation of quantization characteristic. In Figure 4.40(b), the goal of this adaptation strategy is to offer a unit level input to a fixed quantizer for all time n. In Figure 4.40(c), the idea is to adapt the quantizer step size to an input-matched value for all n.

We will note presently (Figure 4.43) that adaptive quantization (especially for low values of R) can provide a better quantization error performance than companded quantization if the input is nonstationary. This fact will be significant particularly in the context of coarse quantizers for the low bit rate encoding of speech (Chapters 6 to 8, 11 and 12). There are several other reasons why adaptive quantizers are attractive. First, time-varying quantizing systems can be designed to be even less signal-specific than a time-invariant companded device. Second, there is an increased interest in the coding of individual speech signals, as distinguished from multiplexed inputs; and in a per-channel codec environment, step size adaptations to individual user waveforms (based on their separate histories) is simpler to implement than in a multiplex environment. A third attraction of time-varying quantizers is that they provide *code trees* with less structure than those of time-invariant quantizers. This will be explained presently in the context of Figure 4.42. The desirability of destructuring code trees will be explained further in Chapter 9.

In the interest of uniformity, the term *adaptive quantization* will henceforth refer always to quantizers that operate with a time-varying step size $\Delta(n)$ as in Figure 4.40(c). Furthermore, the adaptive quantizer, at any given time, will be assumed to have a uniform transfer characteristic unless otherwise mentioned. The basic problem then is to adapt step size $\Delta(n)$ to changing input variance $\sigma_x^2(n)$. Ideally, the time-varying step size would continuously follow the value Δ_{opt} that a fixed quantizer would employ if the input were stationary, or at least locally stationary, and the variance σ_x^2 were known. We know from previous sections that Δ_{opt} is related to σ_x via a parameter, say ϕ, that depends only on input pdf and number of bits per sample R. For example, if $R = 2$, if $p_x(x)$ is Gaussian and if $Q(x)$ is uniform, $\phi = .996 \sim 1.0$ from Table 4.1. The operation of an adaptive quantizer can therefore be defined in the form

$$\Delta(n) = \phi \hat{\sigma}_x(n) ; \quad \phi = \text{constant} \tag{4.178}$$

The quantizer loading factor $f_l = \Delta/\sigma_x$ (Section 4.3) therefore tends to be *independent* of σ_x in an ideal adaptive quantizer. A future example (Figure 4.49) will show the dependence of f_l on σ_x in quantizers with different degrees of adaptation.

For a nonstationary input, σ_x is *time-variable*, and the problem of adaptive quantization, according to (4.178), is one of estimating it continuously. The problem is very similar if the input is stationary, or locally stationary, with *unknown* variance σ_x. Subsequent sections will describe how to estimate σ_x or related measures of input level such as $E[|X|]$ or $|x|_{max} = \max\{|X|\}$; and how these estimates can be derived from observations on $\{x(n)\}$, and very often from observations on the quantizer output $\{y(n)\}$; as the number of bits/sample R increases, estimates of σ_x based on quantizer output samples get increasingly closer to estimates of σ_x based on unquantized input samples. *A significant result of this section is that for an exponentially weighted variance estimate, based on the entire available past of $y(n)$, is exactly equivalent to one that is possible with an explicit memory of only the latest value of $y(n)$ when $R \geqslant 2$.*

A subject of great interest is the distinction between the *static* performance of an adaptation logic [as given by the matching of step size to a locally stationary value of $\sigma_x(n)$], and its *dynamic* performance [as measured by how quickly the changing step size sequence can respond to a changing $\sigma_x(n)$ and exhibit a narrow short-term distribution centered on the local mean value of step size]. Adaptation logics generally exhibit a compromise between the static and dynamic responses, and these two properties have associated perceptual ramifications in speech and image coding.

Our theoretical discussions will refer mainly to the example of independent and identically distributed (i.i.d.) input samples. Many results on level estimation are available for such i.i.d. inputs. Also, in many important situations (such as the differential encoding of speech and video), the quantizer input can be modeled to a fair approximation as an i.i.d. sequence.

4.10.1 "Forward" and "Backward" Adaptations — AQF, AQB

We assume a zero-mean input $x(n)$, and the problem will be one of estimating input level in terms of σ_x or related parameters $E[|X|]$ or $|x|_{max}$. We shall consider *forward* estimates based on unquantized samples $x(n)$, as well as *backward* estimates derived from samples $y(n)$ of the quantizer output. Respective systems are denoted by AQF (*adaptive quantization with forward estimation*) and AQB (*adaptive quantization with backward estimation*). The AQF system has also been known by the term *block companding* [Croisier, 1974]. Block diagrams of these procedures appear in Figure 4.41.

Forward estimates of step size are unaffected by quantization noise. Step size estimates $\Delta(n)$ in AQF are therefore more reliable than those in AQB. The AQF technique implies, however, that level information is to be explicitly transmitted to a remote decoder using typically about 5 to 6 bits per step size sample; and this translates to a corresponding amount of *side information* that needs to be additionally transmitted to the receiver. The AQF technique, however, permits special protection of step size information in transmission because this information is typically only a small fraction of the overall transmission rate; adding a certain percentage of redundancy to this information increases overall transmission rate by a much smaller percentage. Forward estimation also implies an estimation delay in the encoding operation. We shall use equivalent terms "learning period" or "AQF block length" for this parameter N (number of learning samples). The encoding delay, which may be in the order of 16 ms for speech (see Table 4.13), is a significant transmission parameter — unacceptable in some systems, but uncritical in some. Finally, AQF also requires a buffering of "unquantized" input samples — practically, a buffering of samples quantized an order of magnitude finer than the resolution of the AQF system quantizer itself.

The learning period N allowed for a forward level estimator is an interesting issue. When the input signal is locally stationary, the best learning period is a compromise among several factors: (i) the need to minimize the encoding delay, (ii) the need to keep down the information rate in level-transmission and (iii) the need

Figure 4.41 Adaptive quantization with (a) forward estimation of input level (AQF), and (b) backward estimation of input level (AQB).

(a) AQF

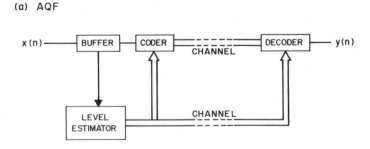

(b) AQB

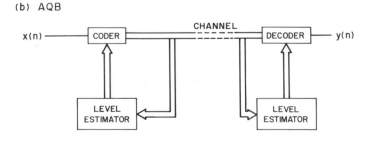

Table 4.13 *SNR* (dB) values in 3-bit quantization of speech with forward adaptation (AQF) [Noll, 1974].

Nonuniform Quantizers	Nonadaptive	Adaptive $N = 128$ (16 ms)	Adaptive $N = 1024$ (128 ms)
μ-law ($\mu=100$; $x_{max}=8\sigma_x$)	9.5	-	-
Gaussian	7.3	15.0	12.1
Laplacian	9.9	13.3	12.8
Uniform Quantizers			
Gaussian	6.7	14.7	11.3
Laplacian	7.4	13.4	11.5

to track the changing statistics of speech with an appropriate speed. Learning periods in the order of 16 ms ($N = 128$ samples with 8 kHz speech) are appropriate in speech communication [Noll, 1974] [Jayant, 1975]. *SNR* losses in going from 16 ms to, say 128 ms, can be as high as 3 dB. This is seen in the *SNR* results of Table 4.13. As noted in Chapter 2, the input pdf to the quantizer is Gaussian if the AQF block length is short enough to ensure local stationarity (say 16 ms); with a 128 ms block length, the pdf tends to the Laplacian. If the block length is much less than 16 ms, the side information for step size can become excessive (Problem 4.32), and the assumption of a zero-mean input becomes decreasingly valid [Esteban, Menez and Temime, 1976]. In that case, quantizer adaptations should include an adaptation to input mean, as in Figure 4.39(c).

Shorter learning periods such as $N = 16$ have been recommended in image coding applications; the side information in these systems is still kept at a reasonable level by employing a relatively small dictionary of step sizes. In one example, where the AQF technique is used as part of a DPCM coder (Chapter 6), $N = 16$; but the allowed number of step sizes is only four, so that the side information for step size is only 1/8 of a bit per pixel [Habibi and Batson, 1978].

Backward estimators extract step size information $\Delta(n)$ from the recent history of the quantizer output, and thus avoid the problems of estimation delay and level transmission. Quantization noise in estimator samples clearly degrades level-tracking performance in AQB; and this degradation increases with the coarseness of quantization. An adaptive quantizer with backward estimation is a nonlinear system with feedback, and it is not obvious that it will be stable. It can be shown, however, [Stroh, 1974], that the system is indeed stable in at least one sense: if the input $x(n)$ is bounded, so are the backward standard deviation estimate $\hat{\sigma}_x$, step size and the estimation error.

Figure 4.42 shows a speech input $x(n)$, output waveforms $y(n)$ in typical AQF and AQB systems, and also step size variations in AQF and AQB. Note that the AQF system illustrated is *blockwise-adaptive*, or *periodically adaptive*; its step size $\Delta(n)$ gets updated once every (locally stationary) block, and remains constant over the duration of the block. Note also that the AQB is stable in the bounded $\Delta(n)$-sense. The $y(n)$ waveform with the fixed quantizer uses a total of 4 possible amplitudes by definition. On the other hand, $y(n)$ waveforms in AQF and AQB systems have the flexibility to use a much greater number of amplitude levels, as

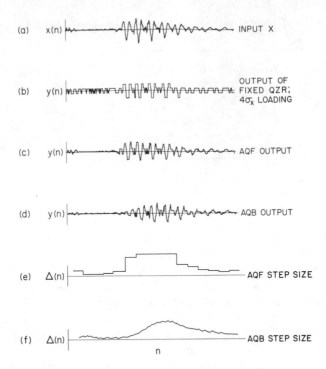

Figure 4.42 Two-bit quantization with fixed and adaptive quantizers: (a) input speech $x(n)$; and output $y(n)$ in (b) fixed quantizer with $4\sigma_x$ loading and in (c) AQF-type and (d) AQB-type adaptive quantizers. Variations of step size $\Delta(n)$ are shown in (e) for AQF and in (f) for AQB [Noll, 1975,I; ©AT&T].

indicated in parts (c) and (d) of the figure. This is the "destructuring" of the code tree that we mentioned earlier. The concept will be re-invoked in Chapter 9.

The results of Figure 4.43 refer to the 3-bit quantization of a bandlimited (300-3400 Hz) speech waveform sampled at 8 kHz [Noll, 1974]. The measures of quantizer performance used in the illustration are *SNR*, *SNR* (m) and *SNRSEG* = E[*SNR* (m)]. The first quantity is the conventional signal-to-quantization-error ratio averaged over the entire speech utterance, and expressed in dB. Temporal variations of signal-to-noise-ratio can be studied by computing the ratio once for every segment of 128 samples (16 ms), to give the short-term quantity *SNR* (m), where m is the segment number. The last measure of performance, *SNRSEG* or the *segmental SNR* (Appendix E) [Noll, 1974], is the average of the *SNR* (m) (dB) values, as computed over the total length of the speech waveform. Bursts of low *SNR* (m) values that are typical in the nonadaptive quantization of low-level speech segments leave the conventional *SNR* unaffected, but they are better reflected in the value of *SNRSEG*.

Figure 4.43 shows plots of short-term input speech $\sigma_x^2(m)$ and *SNR* (m) for several 3-bit quantizers. The nonadaptive quantizer is a fixed nonuniform quantizer matched to the speech pdf. For the specific illustrated waveform, this quantizer in fact performs better, on the average, than a μ-law log-quantizer, and realizes slightly higher values of *SNR* and *SNRSEG*. However, the weak-signal

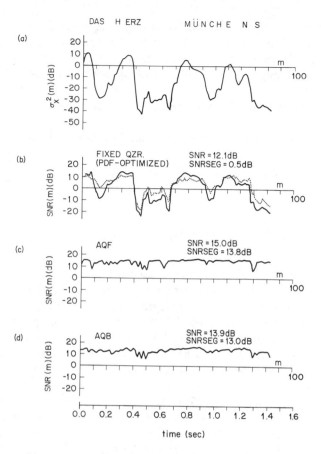

Figure 4.43 Plots of (a) short-term speech variance $\sigma_x^2(m)$ and short-term signal-to-noise ratio $SNR\ (m)$ in 3-bit quantization with (b) time-invariant- (c) AQF- and (d) AQB algorithms [Noll, 1974].

performance is better with the μ-law quantizer. Its $SNR(m)$ characteristic is indicated by the dotted waveform in (b). The adaptive quantizers use nonuniform quantizing characteristics optimal for the Gaussian pdf. The AQF estimator is based on a learning buffer of 128 samples, while the backward estimator uses a one-word memory logic to be described in Section 4.10.3. The benefits of adaptive quantization are evident from the waveforms of Figure 4.43 and the associated SNR values that appear alongside those waveforms. Note especially the 13 dB $SNRSEG$ gain in adaptive quantization! This is due to the fact that unlike the nonadaptive systems, AQF and AQB systems maintain a fairly constant and *non-negative* SNR-versus-time characteristic for all input speech segments in the illustration.

The Special Case of $R = 1$. In a one-bit quantizer, magnitude information is available only at the quantizer *input*; the output preserves only (two levels of) sign information. For this reason, backward step size adaptation is possible in one-bit quantization only in the context of highly correlated input sequences. In this case, magnitude information is reflected by the structure in the output bit stream. This structure is indeed the basis of many classes of adaptive deltamodulation (DM-AQB, or simply, ADM) used for both speech and image coding (Chapter 8).

4.10.2 Estimators of Input Variance or Input Level

As mentioned earlier, step size adaptations can follow input variance via

$$\text{AQF:} \quad \Delta(n) = \phi \hat{\sigma}_x(n) \; ; \quad \hat{\sigma}_x(n) = [(1/N) \sum_{i=0}^{N-1} x^2(n+i)]^{1/2} \quad (4.179a)$$

$$\text{AQB:} \quad \Delta(n) = \phi \hat{\sigma}_x(n) \; ; \quad \hat{\sigma}_x(n) = [(1/N) \sum_{i=1}^{N} y^2(n-i)]^{1/2} \quad (4.179b)$$

The input window for variance estimation contains N samples in each case; it extends from input sample n to $n+N-1$ in AQF; and from output sample $n-N$ to $n-1$ in AQB. For a stationary, uncorrelated input, the *learning period* N that is necessary for good estimation is at least an order of magnitude less than the value (say $N = 128$) that is needed for learning the variance of a correlated quasi-stationary input such as 8 kHz sampled speech. Furthermore, the convergence to input variance will be somewhat slower in the AQB mode, where the estimation is based on noisy quantized samples.

The estimator in (4.179b) requires an explicit memory of N samples. We now show that it is possible to estimate the variance with a shorter explicit memory of samples if we allow the x^2 (or y^2) terms in the estimate to be suitably weighted; and that the resulting estimate can be still nearly optimal in a certain sense. The weighting of interest is *exponential* and the magnitude of the weighting decreases monotonically with the age of the x^2 (or y^2) term in question. For example, if the estimate is based on $y(n)$ values,

$$\hat{\sigma}_y^2(n) = (1-\alpha_l) \sum_{i=1}^{\infty} \alpha_l^{i-1} y^2(n-i) \; ; \quad 0 < \alpha_l < 1 \quad (4.180)$$

The term α_l^{i-1} provides the desired weighting, and $(1-\alpha_l)$ is simply a normalizing term which makes the sum of weights equal to unity.

Note that for values of α_l close to 1, the weighting of adjacent x samples is very nearly equal; and as $\alpha_l \to 1$ the *learning period* $N = (1+\alpha_l)/(1-\alpha_l)$ (Problem 4.33) tends to ∞. In this sense, an exponentially weighted estimator with $\alpha_l \to 1$ is basically equivalent to the unweighted logic with large N. Values of α_l closer to zero imply an estimator that is based heavily on the most recent samples $y(n-1), y(n-2),\dots$. In fact, the more nonstationary the input, the closer should α_l be to zero. It can be shown that (4.180) can be written in the recursive form (Problem 4.34)

$$\hat{\sigma}_y^2(n) = \alpha_l \hat{\sigma}_y^2(n-1) + (1-\alpha_l) y^2(n-1) \quad (4.181a)$$

$$[\hat{\sigma}_y^2(n)/\hat{\sigma}_y^2(n-1)] = \alpha_l + (1-\alpha_l)\, y^2(n-1)/\hat{\sigma}_y^2(n-1) \qquad (4.181\text{b})$$

The step size $\Delta(n)$ is proportional to $\hat{\sigma}_x(n) \simeq \hat{\sigma}_y(n)$, assuming adequately fine quantization. We can therefore interpret the left hand side of (4.181b) as a ratio of successive squared step sizes, or as the square of a *step size multiplier* $M(n-1) = \Delta(n)/\Delta(n-1)$. Note that $y^2(n-1)$ is the corresponding squared output $[H(n-1)\Delta(n-1)/2]^2$ of a midrise quantizer where $\pm H(n-1) = 1,3,5,\ldots$; and assume that the best guess of $\Delta(n-1)$ is $\phi\hat{\sigma}_x(n-1)$ as per (4.178). With these assumptions, it can be shown that the step size multiplier for an adaptive quantizer with a *one-word memory* is

$$M(n-1) = \left[\alpha_l + (1-\alpha_l)\, H^2(n-1)\phi^2/4\right]^{\tfrac{1}{2}} \qquad (4.181\text{c})$$

This type of adaptive quantization will be discussed at length in Section 4.10.3.

The parameter α_l determines the *time constant* of adaptation: the time taken for $\hat{\sigma}_y$ to decay to a fraction e^{-1} of the initial value when $y(n)$ has become an all-zero sequence. If the sampling rate is f_s, this time constant will be (Problem 4.35)

$$\tau = 2(f_s \log_e \alpha_l^{-1})^{-1} \qquad (4.182)$$

Figure 4.44 shows the effect of α_l on the speed of adaptation to a speech waveform segment. The value of (a) $\alpha_l = 0.90$ causes fairly rapid changes of $\hat{\sigma}_x$ that follow

Figure 4.44 Speech variance estimates in (a) instantaneous and (b) syllabic adaptation. Values of $\hat{\sigma}_x(n)$ have been magnified for clarity, but the scaling factors are the same in (a) and (b) [Barnwell et al., 1974. Reprinted with permission].

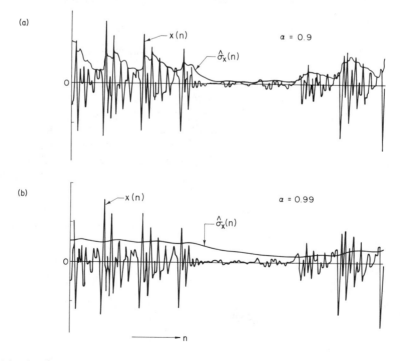

the local peaks in the input waveform, with a time constant $(f_s \log_e \alpha_I^{-1})^{-1}$ of 2.6 ms; this kind of adaptation is called *instantaneous adaptation*. The value of (b) $\alpha_I = 0.99$ causes slower changes in $\hat{\sigma}_x$ that do not follow local waveform peaks, but only their envelope, with a time constant of 25.0 ms; this kind of adaptation is called *syllabic adaptation*. These two types of adaptation have clear distinctions in terms of the *dynamic* and *static* performances mentioned earlier.

Level Estimates Based on Maximum- and Average-Magnitude Statistics. A simple approach to adaptive quantization [Golding and Schultheiss, 1967] is to use local values of peak output magnitude $|y|_{max} = \max\{|y(n)|\}$ to vary the overload level in image quantization. The adaptations can be done in an AQB mode; prior to the quantization of every horizontal line i, the overload level $|y|_{max}$ is set equal to the peak output from the N samples of the previous line. In fact, the lower saturation level of the quantizer is also varied independently, and matched to local minima $|y|_{min} = \min\{|y(n)|\}$, but the adaptation based on maximum value is more critical in that it controls overload errors, which tend to be dominant contributors to total quantization noise. The scheme achieves a typical 2 dB of *SNR* gain in 4-bit quantization, as compared with a nonadaptive scheme.

Adaptive quantizers for speech have also employed the maximum-input criterion [Croll, Moffat and Osborne, 1973] [Duttweiler and Messerschmitt, 1975], [Jayant, 1975] [Noll, 1975], but strictly in an AQF mode. The correlations in typical speech waveforms are much less than those between the adjacent image lines: and this makes backward estimation based on extremal statistics relatively less reliable in speech quantization.

Maximum-magnitude logics can be summarized in the form

$$\text{AQF:} \quad \Delta(n) = \theta_1 |x|_{max}; \quad |x|_{max} = \max\{|x(n+i)|\}; \quad i = 0,1,2,...,N-1 \quad (4.183a)$$

$$\text{AQB:} \quad \Delta(n) = \theta_1 |y|_{max}; \quad |y|_{max} = \max\{|y(n-i)|\}; \quad i = 1,2,...,N \quad (4.183b)$$

where θ_1 is a scaling constant whose best value can usually be related to the constant ϕ of (4.178) for a given pdf [Jayant, 1975]. Adaptive logics based on maximum-magnitude logics are particularly appropriate when an important criterion is the control of overload distortion; and for simultaneous control of overload distortion as well as long term mse in high-quality PCM systems for speech, it is imperative to use extremely small values of learning period (say, 2 ms); the 8 ms that was recommended earlier for variance estimators is more typical of low bit rate differential PCM (Chapters 6 and 8) and transform coding (Chapter 12) systems, where the use of AQ is more common than in PCM.

Another simple indicator of signal level is the *average magnitude* function, and resulting adaptation logics can be summarized in the form

$$\text{AQF:} \quad \Delta(n) = \theta_2 [(1/N) \sum_{i=0}^{N-1} |x(n+i)|] \quad (4.184a)$$

$$\text{AQB:} \quad \Delta(n) = \theta_2 [(1/N) \sum_{i=1}^{N} |y(n-i)|] \quad (4.184b)$$

where θ_2 is a pdf-specific scaling factor. For a given pdf, the ratio of θ_2 to the factor ϕ in (4.178) is simply the reciprocal of a corresponding (δ_{opt}/σ_x) value from the theory of one-bit quantization (Table 4.2).

A properly weighted average-magnitude (Problem 4.36) estimate permits a recursive computation, and this makes the average-magnitude function very attractive for practical adaptation procedures [Castellino et al., 1974]. We have seen in (4.181) that a similar recursive realization is possible for a weighted variance estimate as well.

4.10.3 Adaptive Quantization with a One-Word Memory

The recursive variance estimator (4.181b) suggests that effective adaptations can be realized with an explicit memory of only one sample $x(n-1)$ (or a quantized version $y(n-1)$ of it), assuming that all valuable information in the quantizer history is available in condensed form in a slowly varying parameter $\hat{\sigma}_x^2(n-1)$ or the corresponding step size $\Delta(n-1)$. We shall now explore such an adaptive logic. It is instructive to begin with an intuitive description of the adaptation strategy, and introduce the notion of step size multipliers. These multipliers have been introduced already in (4.181) as square roots of the ratio $\hat{\sigma}_x^2(n)/\hat{\sigma}_x^2(n-1)$. This interpretation will apply to any kind of quantizer, but the specific adaptation procedure of this chapter will apply only to quantizers where the number of levels exceeds 4 $(R \geqslant 2)$. In such quantizers, the output contains both sign and magnitude information, and the latter part is the one that is exploited in step size modifications. The procedure to be described has been referred to as *adaptive quantization with a one-word memory* [Jayant, 1973]; the term "one word" refers to the latest R-bit output of the quantizer; this is the word that carries information about the latest sample $y(n-1)$. In the case of $R = 1$, more than one word of memory is needed for backward step size adaptation (Chapter 8).

Step Size Adaptations. Figure 4.45 explains adaptive quantization for the example of $R = 3$ bits/sample, $L = 8$, and a set of $L/2 = 4$ step size multipliers M. Only 4 distinct multiplier values are shown in view of the symmetry of zero-mean quantization, and with the notion that step size multipliers should depend only on the magnitude (not the sign) of the quantizer output. If the latest output level from the midrise quantizer is

$$y(n-1) = H(n-1)\,\Delta(n-1)/2; \quad \pm H(n-1) = 1,3,5,...,2^{R-1}; \quad R \geqslant 2 \quad (4.185a)$$

the adaptation logic derives the next step size $\Delta(n)$ as the product of $\Delta(n-1)$ and a multiplier $M(\cdot)$ that is a time-invariant function of the latest *magnitude index* $|H(n-1)|$:

$$\Delta(n) = M(|H(n-1)|)\,\Delta(n-1) \quad (4.185b)$$

In the example of Figure 4.45, the four possible values of $|H(n-1)| = 1,3,5$ and 7 lead to the respective multipliers M_1, M_2, M_3 and M_4.

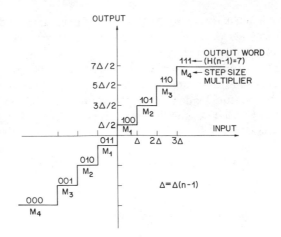

Figure 4.45 Adaptive 3-bit quantization (AQB) with a one-word memory. The figure shows a snapshot of quantizer characteristic $Q(x)$ at time $(n-1)$ [Jayant;©1973, AT&T].

A reasonable design of multipliers is of the form

$$1 > M_1 \leqslant M_2 \leqslant M_3 \leqslant M_4 > 1 \qquad (4.186)$$

In this algorithm, an output sample of $\pm 7\Delta(n-1)/2$ (NBC codeword 000 or 111) will indicate that the quantizer is probably in *overload*, and the step size is therefore *increased* by a factor $M_4 > 1$. On the other hand, an output of $\pm \Delta(n-1)/2$ tends to serve as an *underload* cue, and the step size is *decreased* in this case by a factor $M_1 < 1$. Intermediate conditions of quantizer loading suggest suitable intermediate modifications M_2 and M_3. Note that step size increases and decreases imply that the entire transfer function $Q(x)$ is expanded and contracted, like an accordion; and in the example of Figure 4.45, the uniform nature of the quantization characteristic is maintained for all time n as in Figure 4.39(a). Figure 4.45 is actually the snapshot, at time $n-1$, of a variable-range (variable step size) quantizer. As a trivial case, if all the multipliers are unity, the result is a time-invariant uniform quantizer.

It is important that in practice, the adaptations (4.185) are subject to constraints on the maximum and minimum values of step size. Formally,

$$\Delta_{\min} \leqslant \Delta(n) \leqslant \Delta_{\max} \qquad (4.187)$$

The value of $\Delta_{\min}$ controls the level of idle-channel noise (granular noise with a zero, or near-zero input), while the value of $\Delta_{\max}$ controls the level of overload distortion. Optimum values of $\Delta_{\min}$ and $\Delta_{\max}$ are functions of R (for example, see Figures 6.12 and 8.20), and examples will be mentioned as appropriate. For a given variance of the coder input, the maximum step size tends to be smaller in DPCM coding (Chapter 6) than in PCM coding (Chapter 5). This is because of the presence of a prediction process in DPCM. This process leads to a quantizer input variance that is usually smaller than the coder input variance, thus permitting smaller values of $\Delta_{\max}$ for a given degree of overload.

The algorithm (4.185) assumes an initial step size $\Delta(0)$. In principle, this can be any empirical value in the allowed range of step size values. It is often meaningful, however, to set $\Delta(0) = \Delta_{\min}$. This is particularly appropriate when the beginning portion of the input being quantized is expected to be of low amplitude, as in the silence segments that precede speech activity.

Three other parameters will be of interest in characterizing the adaptation logic:

$$\Delta_{\mathrm{mid}} = [\Delta_{\min}\Delta_{\max}]^{\frac{1}{2}} ; \quad \Delta_{\mathrm{range}} = [\Delta_{\max}/\Delta_{\min}] \tag{4.188}$$

and, finally, an optimal step size Δ_{opt} which a nonadaptive quantizer would use if the input variance σ_x^2 were constant and known [see (4.178)]. Let us consider that we are quantizing such a stationary input, without knowledge of Δ_{opt} (or σ_x). The object now is to study quantizer performance as a function of its intrinsic range Δ_{range}, and the disposition of its central step size Δ_{mid} with respect to Δ_{opt}. Note that for a nonadaptive logic, $\Delta_{\mathrm{range}} = 1$ and $\Delta_{\mathrm{mid}} = \Delta$, a time-invariant value.

Results for the 4-bit quantization of a stationary Gaussian input appear in Figure 4.46. The maximum SNR is that of a uniform pdf-optimized quantizer (19.38 dB, as in row 4, Table 4.1). The advantage of adaptation consists in increasing the *dynamic range of the quantizer* rather than the maximum possible value of SNR. The dynamic range of the quantizer is the range of variation in σ_x which the quantizer can handle; equivalently, the range of Δ_{mid} which a given stationary input can tolerate, for a specified minimum signal-to-noise ratio. Note that with $\Delta_{\mathrm{range}} = 100$, which implies a step size dynamic range of $20\log_{10}100 = 40$ dB, the dynamic range of the quantizer, as defined in the last sentence, is also about 40 dB. This is a nearly adequate match to the dynamic range that may be encountered in the speech input of a single speaker (Figure 2.6). Note also that the flattening of the performance curve in Figure 4.46 corresponds to a constant, input-independent loading factor f_l. In the case of nonadaptive quantization, Δ is constant and f_l is inversely proportional to σ_x by definition (4.30). The asymmetrical SNR - versus - step size profile for the nonadaptive case ($\Delta_{\mathrm{range}}=1$) in Figure 4.46 should be familiar from earlier discussions (see Figure 4.7).

Figure 4.46 Measured dynamic range curves for a 4-bit adaptive quantizer for a stationary Gaussian AR(1) input with $\rho_1 = 0.5$. The numbers 1, 10 and 100 on the three curves are respective values of Δ_{range} [Jayant;©1973, AT&T].

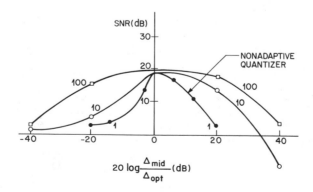

The value of 100 cited above for Δ_{range} is typical of many quantizing systems, as an order-of-magnitude number. Values which are multiples of 2, such as 128, 256, 512 or 1024 are also frequently encountered. The last value implies a dynamic range of nearly 60 dB. It is also the value used in a standardized DPCM coder design for high quality speech (Section 6.5.3). Transmission error sensitivity, however, is an increasing function of Δ_{range}.

Relative Values of the Step Size Multipliers and the Steady-State Behavior of the Adaptation Logic. More can be said about desirable multipliers than the simple constraints in (4.186). An intuitive stability criterion [Jayant, 1973] would be of the form

$$\prod_{i=1}^{2^R-1} M_i^{P_i} = 1 \; ; \qquad M_1^{P_1}M_2^{P_2} = 1 \quad \text{if} \quad R = 2 \; ;$$

$$M_1^{P_1}M_2^{P_2}M_3^{P_3}M_4^{P_4} = 1 \quad \text{if} \quad R = 3 \qquad (4.189)$$

where the probability P_i represents the probability of output magnitude level i (and hence the probability of using multiplier M_i) in the *steady-state*, i.e., after the adaptive logic has essentially learned the variance σ_x^2 of a stationary input. The argument is that if a requirement such as (4.189) did not apply, the step size Δ would eventually decay to zero [if the product in (4.189) were less than 1], or blow up [if that product were greater than 1]; and these would represent an unstable adaptive logic in the presence of a stable input.

Example 4.15.   2-bit quantization of Gaussian inputs
    Let us illustrate the above notion more quantitatively with the example of $R=2$ for stationary Gaussian inputs. In uniform mmse quantization of a Gaussian input with step size Δ, the probabilities of the two output magnitudes $3\Delta/2$ and $\Delta/2$ are approximately $P_2 = 0.33$ and $P_1 = 0.67$ (a result of setting $\Delta = \Delta_{opt}=0.996\sigma_x$; see row 2 of Table 4.1 and Problem 4.37). The above probabilities are also the respective multiplier probabilities by definition, so that from (4.189),

$$R = 2: \qquad M_1^{0.67}M_2^{0.33} \sim M_1^2 M_2 = 1 \qquad (4.190)$$

One example of a multiplier-pair that closely satisfies (4.190) is [$M_1=0.8;M_2=1.6$], and a pair that clearly violates the requirement is [$M_1=0.5,M_2=2.0$]. It indeed turns out, in computer simulations with an uncorrelated Gaussian sequence, that the former multiplier-pair outperforms the latter. Corresponding steady-state signal-to-noise ratios differ by about 2 dB [Jayant, 1973].   ●

Example 4.16.   3-bit quantization of Gaussian inputs
    For the 3-bit quantization of i.i.d. Gaussian sequences, an equation corresponding to (4.190) results from an earlier result ($\Delta_{opt}=0.586\sigma_x$ if $R=3$; row 3 of Table 4.1), and the resulting probabilities P_1 through P_4 (Problem 4.37):

$$R = 3: \qquad M_1^{0.47}M_2^{0.30}M_3^{0.14}M_4^{0.09} = 1 \qquad (4.191) \quad ●$$

The selection of multiplier values for $R = 3$ according to (4.191) is more difficult than for $R = 2$ [from (4.190)]. The problem can be simplified by associating more structure with multiplier sets $\{M_i\}$ and the probabilities P_i; a theoretically, as well as practically, useful way of doing this is by insisting [Mitra, 1974], [Goodman and Gersho, 1974] that multipliers be expressed in the canonical form

$$M_i = \gamma^{k_i} ; \quad \gamma > 1 , \quad \pm k_i = 0,1,2,...$$ (4.192)

so that the constraint (4.189) can be rewritten as

$$\sum_{i=1}^{2^{R-1}} P_i k_i = 0 \quad \text{(for some } \gamma > 1\text{)}$$ (4.193)

The problem of multiplier selection now becomes one of selecting integer sets $\{k_i\}$ that satisfy (4.193) closely. It is easy to see that with $R = 2$, there is only one simple $\{k_i\}$ pair that satisfies (4.193) for the Gaussian probabilities (0.67 and 0.33); while for the four probabilities for $R = 3$ in (4.191), there are more degrees of freedom, permitting the choice of alternative $\{k_i\}$ sets [Mitra, 1974]. The following numbers are illustrative:

$$R = 3; \quad \{k_i\} = \{-1,-1,2,5\} \quad \text{or} \quad \{-1,0,1,4\}$$ (4.194)

The steady-state SNR performance of the second multiplier set for $R = 3$ is better by about 0.5 dB [with $\gamma=1.04$ in (4.192)]. Compare this with the more significant 2 dB difference for the two multiplier-pairs mentioned earlier for $R = 2$. This difference of 2 dB relates to the fact that one of the multipliers-pairs for $R = 2$ clearly did not satisfy (4.190) or (4.193); while both the multiplier sets in (4.194) satisfy the corresponding stability requirement closely [with respective values of -0.4 and $+0.03$ for the sum in (4.193)].

A quite striking property of all multiplier sets discussed in this subsection is that step size *increases* are always designed to be faster than step size *decreases*. The property carries over to larger values of bits ($R > 3$) [Jayant, 1973] and it is related to the fact that the Gaussian pdf leads to a monotonically decreasing set of probabilities P_i in mmse uniform quantization. Fast increases of step size, while preserving such a probability configuration, serve the related physical purpose of mitigating overload noise in relation to granularity. This is desirable from an SNR point of view, as noted earlier. Furthermore, fast step size increases and slow decreases are also matched to the envelope characteristics of speech waveforms (Figures 2.1 and 2.6).

We have so far concentrated on the steady-state performance of the adaptation logic, as determined by the steady state probabilities P_i and the constraints they impose on a desirable set of k_i values. The latter, in turn, specify only the relative values of the multipliers M_i, and not their absolute magnitudes. These magnitudes are determined by γ, and the choice of γ describes the dynamic response of the adaptive logic.

Absolute Values of Step Size Multipliers and the Dynamic Response of the Adaptive Logic. When step size adaptations are used for learning the variance of a stationary input, or for tracking a very slowly changing variance, there are many (not unrelated) reasons for selecting multipliers M_l that are close to unity, or equivalently, for selecting a value of γ very close to unity. An interesting observation is that for such γ, the ratio of two multipliers M_i and M_j is linearly related to the difference between integers k_i and k_j. Another property is that as γ tends to unity, the effective variance-estimator weight α in (4.181) tends to unity as well. Finally, as γ approaches 1, the variance of the estimator $\hat{\sigma}_x^2$ (i.e., the oscillation of step size in the steady state) approaches zero [Mitra, 1974]. This is illustrated by the results in Figure 4.47 which refer to 2-bit adaptive quantization of an i.i.d. Gaussian input [Goodman and Gersho, 1974]. Plots A and B show $\hat{\sigma}_x(n)$ as a function of sample number n for two pairs of multiplier values. The multiplier-pairs in these figures correspond to $\gamma = 1.20$ (plot A) and $\gamma = 1.05$ (plot B) and the k-values $\{-1,2\}$ from (4.193). The larger value of $\gamma = 1.20$ provides faster dynamic response. The lower value of $\gamma = 1.05$ provides an estimate with smaller oscillations, or a smaller variance about the mean. Adaptations with differing dynamic responses have also been illustrated earlier in Figure 4.44, for the example of a real-speech input, as a function of α.

Also shown in Figure 4.47 is the nature of step size variation that may characterize a *training-mode* quantizer where all multiplier values converge to 1.0 after the adaptation logic has been trained adequately by a stationary input signal of unknown variance (plot C). When the input of unknown variance is known to be stationary (as in the case of voiceband data waveforms), emphasis is on minimal steady-state oscillation after an appropriate training phase. Step-size multiplier functions for such a system can be expressed in the form $[M(|H(n-1)|)]^{a_n}$ with an appropriately converging $\{a_n\}$ sequence [Gersho and Goodman, 1974]. One

Figure 4.47 Variance estimate $\hat{\sigma}_x^2(n)$ versus n in the adaptive 2-bit quantization of a stationary Gaussian i.i.d. input. Plot A refers to the case of $M_1 = 0.83$, $M_2 = 1.44$, $\gamma = 1.2$; plot B to the case of $M_1 = 0.95$, $M_2 = 1.10$, $\gamma = 1.05$; and plot C to a case where γ decreases with time, and M_1 and M_2 eventually converge to 1.0 [Goodman and Gersho;©1974, IEEE].

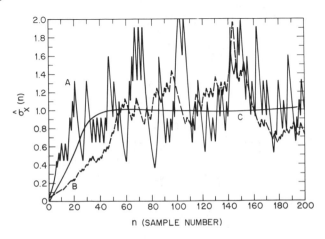

n (SAMPLE NUMBER)

example of such a sequence, used in Figure 4.47(c) [Gersho and Goodman, 1974] is

$$\{a_n\}: 1, 1/2, 1/2, 1/4, 1/4, 1/4, 1/8,... \qquad (4.195)$$

A somewhat different approach to the quantization of a stationary signal of unknown variance is the *dynamic locking quantizer* described in Section 6.5.3. This system does not need prior knowledge of the fact that the input is stationary; it detects this property automatically, and freezes the step size to an appropriate fixed value.

Adaptive Quantization of Speech with a One-word Memory. Preceding sections have considered adaptive quantization using two different approaches, one exemplified by the recursive variance estimator (4.181), and the other by a set of step size multipliers (4.192). Both formulations have independent means of specifying the dynamic response of the adaptive quantizer (via α and γ respectively), as well its static properties (via the pdf-specific quantities ϕ and k_i). In fact, by equivalent settings of α_l, γ and of ϕ and k_i, very similar multiplier sets result in both approaches (Problem 4.38).

Figure 4.48 and Table 4.14 illustrate multiplier functions recommended [Jayant, 1973] for the adaptive quantization of speech waveforms in PCM (Chapter 5) and first-order prediction error waveforms in DPCM (Chapter 6). Note, in both cases, that step size increases are relatively faster than step size decreases, as noted in earlier discussion.

Figure 4.48 Nature of the step size multiplier function in adaptive quantization of speech with a one-word memory [Jayant;©1973, AT&T].

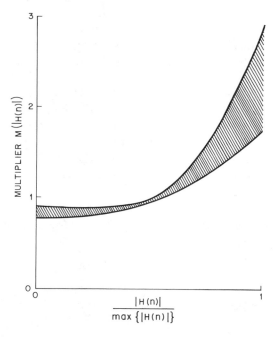

Table 4.14 Step-size multipliers for AQB with a uniform quantizer and speech inputs [Jayant, 1973].

Coder	PCM			DPCM		
R	2	3	4	2	3	4
M_1	0.60	0.85	0.80	0.80	0.90	0.90
M_2	2.20	1.00	0.80	1.60	0.90	0.90
M_3		1.00	0.80		1.25	0.90
M_4		1.50	0.80		1.75	0.90
M_5			1.20			1.20
M_6			1.60			1.60
M_7			2.00			2.00
M_8			2.40			2.40

Approximations of Multiplier Functions. The number and possible resolution of multiplier values increases with the number R of quantizer bits, and approximate values are often desirable for implementation purposes. Implementations often use a *read-only-memory* (ROM) arrangement where the ROM input address is a function of the quantizer output history ($|H(n-1)|$, for example), and the ROM output directly gives step size. Variance estimations and step size multiplications discussed so far are built into such ROM designs, sometimes with practical approximations.

In variance-estimating quantizers, a useful approximation to optimal design results by constraining the speed parameter in the form

$$\alpha_l = 1 - 2^{-J} \quad ; \quad J = 1,2,... \tag{4.196}$$

The negative power of 2 is easily realizable by a shift register circuit with binary entries.

In implementations based on explicit step size multiplication, multiplier values have already been simplified in the form γ^k. A hardware implementation of a 3-bit quantizer for DPCM uses, for example, $\gamma = \sqrt[4]{2}$ and $\{k\} = -1, -1, 1, 3$ [Cummiskey, Jayant and Flanagan, 1973]. Corresponding M_l values are 0.84, 0.84, 1.19 and 1.68, and these follow the numbers in column 5 of Table 4.14. Further simplifications result by setting some of the integers k equal to zero as in the second set in (4.194). Experiments have shown that useful adaptations, with SNR losses often no more than a fraction of 1 dB [Noll, 1974] [Johnston and Goodman, 1978], result even with maximally simplified logics such as the ones below for $R = 3$:

$$k_1 < 0, k_4 > 0; \; k_2 = k_3 = 0 \; \leftrightarrow \; (M_1 < 1, M_4 > 1; \; M_2 = M_3 = 1) \tag{4.197}$$

$$k_1 = k_2; \; k_3 = k_4 \; \leftrightarrow \; (M_1 = M_2 < 1; \; M_3 = M_4 > 1) \tag{4.198}$$

The multiplier design (4.197) has three distinct multipliers while (4.198) has only two distinct multipliers. The two-multiplier design is the basis of an ROM implementation of adaptive quantization on a digital signal processor chip [Boddie et al., 1981]. The two-multiplier design also has very good resynchronization properties in situations where step sizes at transmitter and receiver may end up being different, for example, due to transmission errors.

The use of a log-step size concept converts step size *multiplications* to log-step size *additions*, and thus provides another approach for simple implementation. This method will be presently elaborated in (4.199b).

Although most of our discussion has assumed a uniform quantization characteristic $Q(x)$, it is to be expected that pdf-optimized $Q(x)$ functions can be used in adaptive quantization, provided that the pdf at the quantizer input is known, as in Figure 4.40(c); or can be determined from the coder input pdf, as in Figure 4.40(b). Nonuniform $Q(x)$ functions have therefore been proposed for speech coding systems with AQB [Noll, 1974] [Qureshi and Forney, 1975] [Cohn and Melsa, 1975] with noticeable *SNR* gains. It should be mentioned, however, that the perceptual gains due to a nonuniform $Q(x)$ function have usually fallen short of the objectively measured *SNR* gains in AQB systems; and the refinement of a nonuniform $Q(x)$ is of a second order of importance compared with the refinement of a time-varying step size logic.

Robust Adaptive Quantization for Noisy Channels. In Section 4.9, the performance of nonadaptive quantizers with transmission errors was shown to improve as a result of a subdued quantization strategy involving a modified $Q(x)$ characteristic with smaller step sizes. Adaptive quantizers can also be subdued to increase transmission error robustness, and we will show this with the example of a one-word memory adaptation rule.

When a step size sample $\Delta(n)$ is recovered erroneously because of a bit error affecting $y(n-1)$, the effect propagates into future step sizes $\Delta(n+l)$; $l = 1,2,...,$ because of the memory in the logic (4.185b).

An effective means of reducing this error propagation is by using a simple generalization of (4.185b). This leads to the *robust adaptive quantizer* [Goodman and Wilkinson, 1975] [Mitra and Gotz, 1978]:

$$\Delta(n) = M(|H(n-1)|)\Delta^{\beta}(n-1); \qquad \beta = 1 - \epsilon^2; \epsilon^2 \to 0 \qquad (4.199a)$$

The use of the *leakage factor* $\beta < 1$ helps the system to "forget" the effect of a wrong step-size $\Delta(n-1)$ (Problem 4.39). However, it also implies imperfect, or sluggish adaptations that may slightly diminish coder performance over an error-free channel (and with channels where the error probability p_e is less than the error rate for which a given β is appropriate). But the intent is to improve coder performance with a noisy channel over which the $\beta = 1$ performance can be very inadequate due to step size error propagation. The zero-error-rate performance of the sluggish logic (4.199a) can be boosted somewhat by compensatory devices such as selecting multiplier values farther away from unity (compared to a $\beta=1$ design); or by an *interleaved* adaptation logic where the decay factor β is not used for every sample n, but rather infrequently, in a periodic fashion. The latter refinement also has advantages in terms of finite-precision arithmetic in implementation [Mitra and Gotz, 1978].

An important consequence of (4.199a) is that the multiplier is no longer the ratio of $\Delta(n)$ to $\Delta(n-1)$; instead, it is that ratio modified by a factor $[\Delta(n-1)]^{\epsilon^2}$. In other words, the step-size multiplier is not independent of input variance, as implied hitherto in this chapter. In practice, multiplier values may be required to be time-invariant for simplicity. In such applications, the multipliers should at least be re-optimized in some fashion to compensate partially for the compromise of a time-invariant design (See Section 6.5.3).

In log-step size notation, (4.199a) can be rewritten

$$\log \Delta(n) = \beta \log \Delta(n-1) + \log M(|H(n-1)|) \qquad (4.199b)$$

With $\beta < 1$, (4.199) represents a leaky integration procedure which has been directly utilized in robust quantizer implementations. The time constant of the leaky adaptation logic can be defined as the time taken for a channel-error-induced log-step-size offset to decay to a fraction e^{-1} of its original value. This time constant can be shown to be $(f_s \log_e 1/\beta)^{-1}$ where f_s is the sampling rate (Problem 4.39). As in the case of α (4.196), β values are generally chosen in the form

$$\beta = 1 - 2^{-J} \; ; \; J = 1,2,... \qquad (4.200)$$

for easy implementation.

The performance of the robust adaptive quantizer is further illustrated in Figures 4.49 and 4.50 and Table 4.15.

Dependence of loading factor on β. The following discussion refers to 4-bit adaptive quantization of Gaussian signals with the multiplier set [0.8, 0.8, 0.8, 0.8, 1.25, 1.25, 2.0 and 3.0]. Consider the *loading factor* f_l of (4.30), the ratio of quantizer overload point x_{ol} to input standard deviation σ_x, for $R = 4$ and $x_{ol} = 4 \Delta_0$; Δ_0 is a mean value of step-size which, along with σ_x, is determined over a sufficiently long segment (say, 1000 of step-size samples of a stationary input). Figure 4.49 plots experimental values of f_l as a function of $\hat{\sigma}_x/\sigma_x$ for different values of β. Three classes of plots are evident: (i) *nonadaptive* quantization ($\beta=0$) where f_l is inversely proportional to σ_x by definition, so that a given dB-increase in σ_x causes an identical dB-decrease in f_l, as with the dashed line in the figure; (ii) *perfect adaptation* ($\beta=1$) where f_l is independent of σ_x. The value of f_l is 1.23, corresponding to a step size $\Delta_0 = (1.23/4) \sigma_x = .31 \sigma_x$, a value that is very close to the Max-value $0.33 \sigma_x$ (Row 4 of Table 4.1) for $R = 4$; and (iii) *robust adaptations* ($\beta<1$, $\beta \to 1$) where f_l does decrease with σ_x, but very slowly (for example, by 4.5 dB for a 40 dB variation of σ_x, with $\beta=63/64$).

Example 4.17 Performance of robust adaptive quantizer in 3-bit PCM-AQB coding
Figure 4.50 illustrates output speech waveforms in PCM-AQB systems with $\beta = 1$ and $\beta = 63/64$, for error rates of 0 and 1%, in each case. The step-size multiplier set is [0.8, 1.0, 1.0, 1.5], as in Table 4.14. With $p_e = 0$, there is very little difference between the output waveforms [parts (b) and (c) of the figure] or between SNR values, for $\beta = 1$ and $\beta = 63/64$. With $p_e = 1\%$, the robust quantizer ($\beta = 63/64$) mitigates the scale changes in the output waveform due to bit errors [parts (d) and (e) of the figure], and produces substantial improvements in SNR and $SNRSEG$. ●

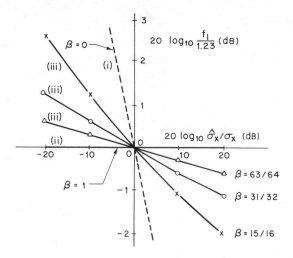

Figure 4.49 Loading factor f_l versus $\hat{\sigma}_x/\sigma_x$ in (i) nonadaptive, (ii) perfectly adaptive and (iii) robust adaptive 4-bit quantizers for a Gaussian input [Goodman and Wilkinson;©1975, IEEE].

Figure 4.50 Performance of robust adaptive quantizer in 3-bit PCM-AQB coding of speech: (a) input waveform $x(n)$, from Figure 1.4(a); and outputs $y(n)$ with (b) $\beta = 1$, $p_e = 0$; (c) $\beta = 63/64$, $p_e = 0$; (d) $\beta = 1$, $p_e = 0.01$; and (e) $\beta = 63/64$, $p_e = 0.01$. [Thomas and Noll, 1983].

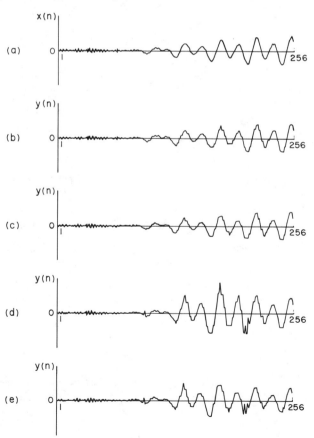

Example 4.18. Performance of robust adaptive quantizer in 3-bit DPCM-AQB coding

The effect of β on decoded waveform quality is shown in Table 4.15 for the example of DPCM coding of speech (Chapter 6) with adaptive quantization using the multiplier set [0.9, 0.9, 1.25 and 1.75]. The signal-to-noise ratios *SNRT* and *SNRR* refer to values at the transmitter and receiver. These ratios were computed in a simulation with a bandlimited (female) speech input, "The boy was mute about his task". The random bit error probability in the simulation was $p_e = 0.023$. Note that $\beta = 1$ maximizes *SNRT* ($= SNRR$ for $p_e = 0$), $\beta = 31/32$ maximizes *SNRR* for $p_e = 0.023$, while $\beta = 63/64$ maximizes [0.5(*SNRT* + *SNRR*)], suggesting a design that may be appropriate in general for a class of channels given by $(0 \leqslant p_e \leqslant 0.023)$.

Table 4.15 Effect of β on speech quality at transmitter (*SNRT*) and at receiver (*SNRR*); R = 3 and p_e = 2.3% (Multiplier values for step size are 0.9, 0.9, 1.25 and 1.75) [Jayant, 1975].

β	*SNRT* (dB)	*SNRR* (dB)	0.5[*SNRT*+*SNRR*] dB
1	17.9	3.7	10.8
63/64	16.2	6.9	11.6
31/32	14.3	7.1	10.7
15/16	10.7	6.7	8.7
7/8	5.4	4.4	4.9

Problems

(4.1) Consider a uniform R-bit midrise quantizer with $L = 2^R$ levels and a uniform input pdf in the range $(-x_{max}, x_{max})$. Let the overload point be x_{ol} as in (4.23). Show that

(a) $\sigma_x^2 = x_{max}^2/3$

(b) $\sigma_q^2 = x_{ol}^2/3L^2$ if $x_{max} \leqslant x_{ol}$

(c) $\sigma_q^2 = \dfrac{x_{ol}^2}{3L^2} \left[\dfrac{x_{ol}}{x_{max}} \right] \left[1 + L^2 \left(\dfrac{x_{max}}{x_{ol}} - 1 \right)^3 \right]$ if $x_{max} > x_{ol}$

(d) Sketch $SNR = 10\log_{10}\sigma_x^2/\sigma_q^2$ as a function of (x_{max}/x_{ol}) for $L = 16$ and $L = 256$. Verify that the result is that of Figure 4.7.

(4.2) Verify analytically that with $L \rightarrow \infty$, $(x_{ol}/x_{max})_{opt} = 1$ for a uniform pdf. Note therefore that the empirical design of Example 4.3 is indeed optimum.

(4.3) One-bit quantization of sine-waves is of interest in the analysis of deltamodulation schemes (which use two-level quantizers and are often tested with sine waves). Verify, using the arcsine pdf of Problem 2.1(a) for instantaneous amplitude x, that

$$\delta_{opt}/\sigma_x = \sqrt{8}/\pi \sim 0.9; \quad \min\{\epsilon_q^2\} = 1 - 8/\pi^2 \sim 0.19$$

Note that the *SNR* is 7.23 dB and that the approximate result of (4.33) yields a slightly higher value. Note also that the performance above is better than that for all other pdf's in Table 4.2. This has to do with the very small peak-to-rms ratio of the arcsine pdf.

(4.4)   (a)   Consider the midtread 3-level quantizer of Figure 4.10. Consider the uniform case defined by $\Delta = 2x'$. Show that the mean square error is

$$\epsilon_q^2 = \sigma_q^2/\sigma_x^2 = 1 - 8x' \, \phi_{x'} \, (M_{x'}-x')/\sigma_x^2 \; ;$$

$$\phi_{x'} = P \, \{X > x'\} \; ; \qquad \text{and } M_{x'} = E \, [X|X > x']$$

Hence show, using the erf function of (2.15), that for a Gaussian input, σ_q^2 is minimum at $x' \sim 0.6\sigma_x$ and min $\{\epsilon_q^2\}) \sim 0.23$, indicating a 1.8dB again over optimum two-level quantization of a Gaussian input.

(b)   Unlike in the uniform example of Problem 4.4(a), consider a nonuniform characteristic. Show that the mean square error for a Gaussian input is minimized for $\Delta = M_{x'}$ and min$\{\epsilon_q^2\} = 1 - 2M_{x'}^2\phi_{x'}/\sigma_x^2$ which in turn is minimized by $x'=0.61\sigma_x$, for a minimum normalized mse of 0.19, an SNR gain of 2.8 dB over the optimum two-level case; and a gain of 1 dB over the optimum uniform 3-level case.

(4.5)   Consider a r.v. X that assumes values $\pm a$ with probability P_1 each, and a value of zero with probability P_0. For the case of $P_0 = 0.5$ and $P_1 = 0.25$,

(a)   show that the *symmetric* 1-bit mmse quantizer is defined by output levels of $\pm 0.5a$, and an mse of $a^2/4$.

(b)   show that the *non-symmetric* 1-bit quantizer with output levels $-a/3$ (for $x \leqslant 0$) and $+a$ (for $x > 0$) has a smaller mse, equal to $a^2/6$ [Denker, 1983].

(4.6)   Use the Panter-Dite result (4.68) to show that SNR values for pdf-optimized 7-bit (128-level) quantizers with

(a)   uniform

(b)   Gaussian and

(c)   Laplacian inputs

are approximately 42, 37.7 and 35.5 dB.

(4.7)   (a)   Sketch the m-law compression characteristic (4.70) for the specific examples of $m = 0$ and 10.

(b)   Verify that for $x = 0.5 \, x_{max}$, respective $|c(x)|/x_{max}$ values are 0.5 and 0.99 respectively.

(4.8)   For any one-to-one mapping $y = c(x)$, the pdf of y is given, in terms of that of x, by the formula

$$p_y(y) = \frac{p_x(x)}{\left|\dfrac{dc(x)}{dx}\right|}\Bigg|_{x \,=\, c^{-1}(y)}$$

(a)   Show that an input with $p_x(x)$ can be transformed to a new r.v. y with a uniform pdf in the range (0, 1) by the mapping $y = \displaystyle\int_{-\infty}^{x} p_x(x)dx$.

(b)   Let X be a Gaussian r.v. $N(0,1)$ and let $Y = -3X+2$. Show that Y is a Gaussian r.v. $N(2,3)$.

(4.9)   Derive the pdf of $x' = c(x)$ where $c(x)$ is the μ-law characteristic (4.84) with $\mu = 255$, and the input pdf $p_x(x)$ is Laplacian. To simplify notation, set $x_{max} = 1$ and assume 4σ-loading ($x_{max} = 4\sigma_x$). Note that the pdf $p_{x'}(\cdot)$ is "flatter" or "more uniform" than the input pdf.

(4.10)   Show that for A-law companding (4.77), the ratio of maximum to minimum step size (ratio of maximum to minimum interval density dc/dx) is equal to A.

(4.11)   Consider the μ-law characteristic (4.84). For large L,

    (a)   show that the characteristic has a step size ratio

$$\max\{\Delta\}/\min\{\Delta\} = 1+\mu \approx \mu$$

    (b)   show that the ratio of sample value x to its corresponding step size is

$$|x|/\Delta = \begin{cases} c & \text{if } x \text{ is large} \\[2mm] c\mu|x|/x_{max} & \text{if } x \text{ is small} \end{cases} \quad ; \quad c = L/[2\log_e(1+\mu)]$$

(4.12)   Consider the variable rate coding of a 3-level quantizer with probabilities P_o, P_i and P_o, where i and o refer to inner and outer levels.

    (a)   Show that if output codewords have lengths n_o, n_i and n_o, the average codeword length $\bar{n} = n_o - P_i(n_o - n_i)$.

    (b)   Hence, show that if $n_o = 2$, $n_i = 1$, $\bar{n} \leqslant 1.5$ bits/symbol as long as $P_i \geqslant 0.5$.

(4.13)   (a)   Consider the output entropy result (4.103). For the special case of no companding [$c(x) = x$], a uniform pdf, and zero overload ($f_l = \sqrt{3}$) show that the output entropy reduces to $\log_2 L$.

    (b)   Consider a uniform quantizer and a Laplacian input. Compute and plot output entropy and mse σ_q^2 versus step size Δ for $L = 4$.

(4.14)   Use the results of Section 4.4.2 to show that the output entropy of pdf-optimized quantizers is [Wood, 1969]

$$H_Q|_{pdf-opt} = \frac{2}{3} h(X) - \frac{1}{3} \log_2 \frac{12 \min\{\sigma_q^2\}}{L} \quad \text{for large } L$$

Hence show (as noted in Figure 4.19) that

$$\Delta R|_{pdf-opt} = \log_2 L - H_Q|_{pdf-opt} = (2/3)\max\{\Delta R\}$$

(4.15)   Consider a uniform 9-level midtread quantizer with step size $2.0\,\sigma_x$ (Example 4.12) and a memoryless zero-mean gamma input.

    (a)   Determine the probabilities of the zero output level y_5 and of its neighboring levels y_4 and y_6.

    (b)   Determine the probabilities of sequences of length 2, 3 and 4 involving all possible permutations of y_4, y_5 and y_6.

(c)   Estimate the entropy of the quantizer output. Compare with the result of Example 4.12.

(4.16)   Compute numerically the pdf's of quantization errors for Gaussian inputs and optimum uniform quantization with $L = 2$ and 4 levels. Compare results with those of Figure 4.22.

(4.17)   ˇConsider a one-bit quantizer with a Gaussian AR(1) input.

(a)   Show that the cross-correlation between input and quantization error is

$$\rho_{xq}(0) = (\sigma_x^2 - \Delta E[|X|])/\sigma_x (\sigma_x^2 + \Delta^2 - 2\Delta E[|X|])^{1/2} .$$

For $\Delta = \Delta_{opt}$, the mmse value of Section 4.3, note that $\rho_{xq}(0) \sim 0.6$, as in Figure 4.24(c). Note also that $\rho_{xq}(0) = 0$ at $\Delta \sim 1.25\,\sigma_x$.

(b)   Derive the autocorrelation $\rho_{qq}(1)$ as a function of Δ; show that for $\rho_{xx}(1) = 0.85$, $\rho_{qq}(1)$ equals 0.85 at $\Delta = 0$, 0.65 at $\Delta = \infty$, and a minimum value of 0.45 at $\Delta = 1.25\,\sigma_x$.

(4.18)   Consider the gain-and-noise quantization model of Figure 4.25(b) with $\alpha_g = 1 - \min\{\epsilon_q^2\}$ (4.122). Compute α_g values for

(a) $L=2$ and a Gaussian input, as well as for

(b) $L=2,4$, and 8 and a uniform pdf input.

(4.19)   Consider the periodic 4-step dither sequences in (4.135) and Figure 4.32. Assume a constant input $x(n)=0.5$ and a quantizer defined by the transfer function: (output $= 1$ or 0 depending on whether input is greater than or less than 0.5). Show that the following are the respective values of $\rho_{qq}(1)$ for the dither sequences in Figures 4.32(a) and (b):

(a)   0

(b) -1

(4.20)   Show that the (4 × 4) dither matrix obtained by using (4.136) in (4.137) is that in (4.138).

(4.21)   Let p_e be the bit error probability in a BSC, and let R be the number of bits in a codeword that represents one of 2^R levels at a quantizer output. Show that

(a)   the probability of no error in the reception of a codeword is $P_0 = (1-p_e)^R$,

(b)   the probability of at least one error in a codeword is $P_{>0} = 1-(1-p_e)^R$

(c)   the probability that exactly E bits are in error is
$$P_E = \begin{pmatrix} R \\ E \end{pmatrix} p_e^E(1-p_e)^{R-E},$$

(d)   the probability that any *given* bit is in error is $P_{1g} = p_e(1-p_e)^{R-1}$

(4.22)   Consider a BSC with $p_e=0.05$. Show that the probability of no error in the reception of an R-bit codeword is 0.8145 for $R = 4$ and 0.6634 for $R = 8$.

(4.23)   Verify that the results of (4.175) reduce to those of the Max-quantizer if $p_e = 0$.

(4.24)   Consider the quantizer reoptimization results (4.175). For a totally noisy channel with $p_e = 0.5$ and $P_{kj} = 2^{-R}$ (all k,j), show that $x_{k**} = y_{k**} = 0$, so that the minimum reconstruction error variance is $\min\{\sigma_r^2\} = \sigma_x^2$.

(4.25) Based on the data of Table 4.11, show that the use of δ_* instead of δ_{**} will result in an increase of σ_r^2 by a factor

$$[\sigma_x^2 - \delta_*^2(1-4p_e)/\sigma_x^2 - \delta_*^2(1-2p_e)^2] \sim 1 + 12p_e^2 \text{ for } p_e \ll 1 \text{ with a uniform pdf}$$

(4.26) Show that the error probability threshold p_{eqc} where channel error variance σ_c^2 equals the minimum quantization error variance σ_{q*}^2 is given by

$$p_{eqc} = (1/\xi_* - 1/4)$$

with values of $1/12$ and $1/2$ for uniform and gamma pdf's (Table 4.11).

(4.27) Sketch the transmission error performance (4.174) for the Max-quantization of a uniform pdf input as a function of p_e and L.

(a) Show that this is the result of Figure 4.33.

(b) Show that the critical error rate for which $\sigma_c^2 = \sigma_{q*}^2$ is given by $p_{eqc} = [1/4(L^2-1)]$.

(4.28) Show that the quantizer redesign (4.166) by a factor $(1-2p_e)$ causes a decrease in channel coefficient ξ by the factor $(1-4p_e)$ if $p_e \ll 1$:

$$\xi_{**} = \xi_*(1-4p_e)$$

(4.29) For a uniform pdf and an NBC code, show that when $i < R$ most significant bits are error-protected, the resulting channel coefficient is $\xi^{(i)} = 4(2^{-2i} - 2^{-2R})$ [Zelinski, 1979].

(4.30) Define the Hamming distance between two codewords as the number of positions in which they differ. For $R=3$ and an FBC code show that the Hamming distance matrix is

$$\begin{bmatrix} 0 & 1 & 1 & 2 & 3 & 2 & 2 & 1 \\ 1 & 0 & 2 & 1 & 2 & 3 & 1 & 2 \\ 1 & 2 & 0 & 1 & 2 & 1 & 3 & 2 \\ 2 & 1 & 1 & 0 & 1 & 2 & 2 & 3 \\ 3 & 2 & 2 & 1 & 0 & 1 & 1 & 2 \\ 2 & 3 & 1 & 2 & 1 & 0 & 2 & 1 \\ 2 & 1 & 3 & 2 & 1 & 2 & 0 & 1 \\ 1 & 2 & 2 & 3 & 2 & 1 & 1 & 0 \end{bmatrix}$$

(4.31) Consider a 2-bit uniform quantizer and symmetrical input pdf models where relative quantizer slot occupancies are simple integers. For example, in an "$n:1$" pdf, the probability of the inner level is n times that of the outer levels. Assume an input variance of $\sigma_x^2 = 1$, a single bit error per word, and an equal probability of the error being in any of the two positions in the codeword. Show that normalized error variance $\sigma_c^2/\Delta^2 p_e$ for different binary codes are the values listed in the following table. Assuming a mmse step size of $\Delta_{opt} = 0.996$, which is optimal for a Gaussian input (Table 4.1) and $R = 2$, and assuming that $p_e = 5\%$, show that the normalized σ_c^2 value of 2.5 for the NBC and TCC codes in the table corresponds to a signal-to-channel-noise ratio of 9 dB. Show that the ratio increases to 16 dB for all the pdf's in the table if the most significant bit (MSB) is totally error-protected. Note that the above noise reductions are only upper bounds because error protection is never ideal with realistic constraints on the side information required for it.

pdf	$\sigma_c^2/\Delta^2 p_e$	
	FBC, GC	NBC, TCC
1:1	3.0	2.5
2:1	2.33	2.5
3:1	2.0	2.5

(4.32) Consider an R-bit AQF system for speech with explicit transmission of step size information once every N samples, using an r-bit codeword for step size.

(a) Derive the fractional increase of transmission rate as a function of r, R and N.

(b) Assume that 16 levels of $\hat{\sigma}_x^2$ are allowed and that the 4-bit variance information is redundantly transmitted five times in anticipation of a noisy channel, which introduces random bit errors with a probability of 0.025. Assume that the variance estimate is updated once every 256 samples.

  (i) Show that the overall transmission rate is increased by $(7.8/R)\%$ due to variance-transmission.

  (ii) Show that variance-detection based on a majority-count-in-five logic is going to be erroneous (more than 2 errors in the 5 transmissions of any of the 4 variance bits) with a probability of about 6 in 10000.

(4.33) Show that, for an i.i.d. input, (4.180) is equivalent to (4.179b), with respect to the first and second moments of $\hat{\sigma}_x^2(n)$, if, in (4.179b), the learning period $N = (1+\alpha_l)/(1-\alpha_l)$; $N \gg 1$.

(4.34) Show that the variance estimate (4.180) can be written in the recursive form (4.181a).

(4.35) Show that the time constant τ of the adaptation logic (4.181) is $2(f_s \log_e 1/\alpha)^{-1}$. Hence show that with $f_s = 8$ kHz, τ values of 1/4, 2 and 10 ms can be realized with $\alpha = 0.370$, 0.883, and 0.975, respectively.

(4.36) Consider a weighted average AQB step size rule

$$\Delta_n = \phi_3 \, E[|Y(n)|] = \theta_2(1-\alpha_l) \sum_{i=1}^{\infty} \alpha_l^{i-1} \, |y(n-i)|$$

where θ_2 is defined in (4.184), and $0 < \alpha_l < 1$. A good value for speech quantization is $\alpha_l = 0.75$ [Castellino et al., 1974]. Show that Δ_n can be written in a recursive form involving only $E[|Y(n-1)|]$ and $|y(n-1)|$.

(4.37)   Consider the mmse uniform midrise quantizer for Gaussian inputs with $R=2$ and 3. Using the results of Table 4.1, and the erfc function in (2.15), show that the probabilities of output magnitudes are

(a)   0.67 and 0.33 ($R=2$) and

(b)   0.47, 0.30, 0.14, and 0.09 ($R=3$).

(4.38)   (a)   Derive step size multipliers for an adaptive 3-bit quantizer assuming a Gaussian pdf ($\phi=0.586$ for $R=3$) and a value of $\alpha = 0.5$ in (4.181c).

         (b)   Show that these multipliers correspond closely to those obtained from (4.192) with $\gamma = 1.12$, and $\{k\}$ values from the first set in (4.194), and that both multiplier sets are approximated by $\{M_i\} = 0.9, 0.9, 1.25$ and 1.75. Note that the $H(n-1)\Delta(n-1)/2$ term leading to (4.181c) ignores overload effects; and therefore leads to slightly smaller values for multiplier M_4.

(4.39)   Assume that in AQB-type adaptive quantization, the effect of a bit error on $y(n-1)$ is to change the multiplier value from M_t at the transmitter to M_r at the receiver. Assuming no further channel errors up to sample time $n + l$, show that the ratio of received and transmitted versions of $\Delta(n+l) = \Delta_{n+l}$ is

$$(M_r/M_t) \quad \text{if} \quad \beta = 1 \; ; \quad (M_r/M_t)^{\beta^l} \quad \text{if} \quad \beta < 1$$

Note the log-step size offset is $\beta^l \log_e (M_r/M_t)$. For this to decay to a fraction $(1/e)$ of the original value $\log_e (M_r/M_t)$ at sample n, show that

$$l_{(1/e)} = \frac{1}{f_s \log_e \beta^{-1}} \text{ ms}$$

where f_s is the sampling frequency in kHz. This can be interpreted as the time constant of a leaky integration logic for log step size. Show that if $f_s = 8$ kHz, β values of 31/32 and 63/64 provide time constants of approximately 4 and 8 ms.

(4.40)   Consider a robust adaptive quantizer (4.199) for $R=2$ and NBC code. Assume that the input is described by $x(n)=0$ ($n<5$), $x(n) = 20(4 \leqslant n \leqslant 13)$, $x(n) = 0(13<n)$ and that at $n=0$, $\Delta(0) = \Delta_{min} = 2$ and output codeword $\{b(0)\} = 00$. Sketch $x(n)$, $y(n)$ and $\Delta(n)$ for (i) $\beta = 1$ and (ii) $\beta = 7/8$.

References

E. Abhaya and G. L. Wise, "Some Notes on Optimal Quantization," Proc. Int. Conf. on Communications, pp. 30.7.1-30.7.5, Denver, June 1981.

V. L. Algazi, "Useful Approximations to Optimum Quantizing," IEEE Trans. on Communications, pp. 297-301, June 1966.

T. P. Barnwell, A. M. Bush, J. B. O'Neal and R. W. Stroh, "Adaptive Differential PCM Speech Transmission," Report No. RADC-TR-74-177, Rome Air Development Center, July 1974.

B. E. Bayer, "An Optimum Method for Two-Level Rendition of Continuous-Tone Pictures," Proc. Int. Conf. on Communications, pp. 26-11 to 26-15, Seattle, June 1973.

W. R. Bennett, "Spectra of Quantized Signals," Bell System Tech. J., pp. 446-472, July 1948.

T. Berger, "Optimum Quantizers and Permutation Codes," IEEE Trans. on Information Theory, pp. 759-765, November 1972.

T. Berger, "Minimum Entropy Quantizers and Permutation Codes," IEEE Trans. on Information Theory, pp. 149-157, March 1982.

J. R. Boddie, J. D. Johnston, C. A. McGonegal, J. W. Upton, D. A. Berkley, R. E. Crochiere and J. L. Flanagan, "Digital Signal Processor: Adaptive Differential Pulse Code Modulation," Bell System Tech. J., pp. 1547-1561, September 1981.

H. Brehm and K. Trottler, "Vector Quantization of Spherically Invariant Random Processes," Proc. European Signal Processing Conference, pp. 383-386, 1983.

P. Castellino, G. Modena, L. Nebbia and C. Scagliola, "Bit Rate Reduction by Automatic Adaptation of Quantizer Step Size in DPCM Systems," Proc. Int. Zurich Seminar on Digital Communications, pp. B6.1-B6.6, March 1974.

K. W. Cattermole, *Principles of Pulse Code Modulation*, Iliffe Books, London, 1969.

M. Chen and L. F. Turner, "Zero Crossing Preservation in the Low-Bit Rate Pseudorandomly Dithered Quantization of Speech Signals," Technical Report, Imperial College of Science and Technology, London, 1973.

F. Cohen, "A Switched Quantizer for Non-linear Coding of Video Signals," Nachrichtentech. Z., pp. 554-559, December 1972.

F. Cohen, "A Switched Quantizer for Markov Sources Applied to Speech Signals," Nachrichtentech. Z., pp. 520-522, November 1973.

D. L. Cohn and J. L. Melsa, "The Residual Encoder: An Improved ADPCM System for Speech Digitization," IEEE Trans. on Communications, September 1975.

A. Croisier, "Progress in PCM and DM: Block Companded Coding of Speech Signals," Int. Zurich Seminar on Digital Commun., pp. B1.1-B1.4, March 1974.

M. G. Croll, M. E. B. Moffat and D. W. Osborne, "Nearly Instantaneous Compander for Transmitting Six Sound Program Signals in a 2.048 Mb/s Multiplex," Electronics Letters, July 1973.

P. Cummiskey, N. S. Jayant and J. L. Flanagan, "Adaptive Quantization in Differential PCM Coding of Speech," Bell System Tech. J., pp. 1105-1118, September 1973.

T. Denker, private communication, 1983.

D. L. Duttweiler and D. G. Messerschmitt, "Nearly Instantaneous Companding for Non-Uniformly Quantized PCM," IEEE Trans. on Communications, pp. 864-873, August 1976.

D. J. Esteban, J. E. Menez and J. Temime, "Optimum One-Bit Quantizing," Proc. 91st Meeting of Acoust. Soc. Am., April 1976.

P. E. Fleischer, "Sufficient Conditions for Achieving Minimum Distortion in a Quantizer," 1964 IEEE Int. Conv. Rec., pt. 1, pp. 104-111, 1964.

G. G. Furman, "Improving the Quantization of Random Signals by Dithering," Rand Corporation Memo RM-3504-PR, May 1963.

A. Gersho, "Principles of Quantization," IEEE Transactions on Circuits and Systems, pp. 427-436, 1978.

A. Gersho, "Asymptotically Optimal Block Quantization," IEEE Trans. on Information Theory, pp. 373-380, July 1979.

A. Gersho and D. J. Goodman, "A Training Mode Adaptive Quantizer," IEEE Trans. on Information Theory, pp. 746-749, November 1974.

H. Gish and J. N. Pierce, "Asymptotically Efficient Quantizing," IEEE Trans. on Information Theory, pp. 676-683, September 1968.

T. J. Goblick and J. L. Holsinger, "Analog Source Digitization: A Comparison of Theory and Practice," IEEE Trans. on Information Theory, pp. 323-326, April 1967.

L. S. Golding and D. M. Schultheiss, "Study of an Adaptive Quantizer, Proc. IEEE, pp. 293-297, March 1967.

W. M. Goodall, "Television by Pulse Code Modulation," Bell System Tech. J., pp. 33-49, January 1951.

D. J. Goodman and A. Gersho, "Theory of an Adaptive Quantizer," IEEE Trans. on Communications, pp. 1037-1045, August 1974.

D. J. Goodman and R. M. Wilkinson, "A Robust Adaptive Quantizer," IEEE Trans. on Communications, pp. 1362-1365, November 1975.

A. Habibi and B. H. Batson, "Potential Digitization/Compression Techniques for Shuttle Video," IEEE Trans. on Communications, pp. 1671-1681, November 1978.

H. Holzwarth, "Pulse Code Modulation und ihre Verzerrungen bei logarithmischer Amplitudenquantelung," Archiv der elektrischen Übertragung, pp. 277-285, January 1949.

D. Huffman, "A Method for the Construction of Minimum Redundancy Codes," Proc. IRE, pp. 1098-1101, September 1952.

R. C. Jaffe, "Causal and Statistical Analysis of Dithered Systems Containing Three-Quantizers," S.M. thesis, Dept. Elec. Eng., MIT, August 1959.

J. F. Jarvis, C. N. Judice and W. H. Ninke, "A Survey of Techniques for the Display of Continuous Tone Pictures on Bilevel Displays," Computer Graphics and Image Processing, pp. 13-40, 1976.

N. S. Jayant, "Adaptive Quantization with a One Word Memory," Bell System Tech. J., pp. 1119-1144, September 1973.

N. S. Jayant, "Step-Size Transmitting Differential Coders for Mobile Telephony," Bell System Tech. J., pp. 1557-1581, November 1975.

N. S. Jayant and L. R. Rabiner, "The Application of Dither to the Quantization of Speech Signals," Bell System Tech. J., pp. 1293-1304, July-August 1972.

F. Jelinek, "Buffer Overflow in Variable-Length Coding of Fixed Rate Sources," IEEE Trans. on Information Theory, pp. 490-501, May 1968.

J. D. Johnston and D. J. Goodman, "Multipurpose Hardware for Digital Coding of Audio Signals," IEEE Trans. on Communications, pp. 1785-1788, November 1978.

W. Koerber, "Spectral Analysis of Nonadaptive and Adaptive Coding Schemes" (in German), Masters thesis, University of Bremen, 1979.

A. J. Kurtenbach and P. A. Wintz, "Quantizing for Noisy Channels," IEEE Trans. on Communications, pp. 291-302, April 1969.

J. O. Limb, "Design of Dither Waveforms for Quantized Visual Signals," Bell System Tech. J., pp. 2555-2582, September 1969.

J. O. Limb and F. W. Mounts, "Digital Differential Quantizer for Television," Bell System Tech. J, pp. 2583-2599, September 1969.

B. Lippel and M. Kurland, "The Effect of Dither on Luminance Quantization of Pictures," IEEE Trans. on Communications, pp. 879-888, December 1971.

S. P. Lloyd, "Least Squares Quantization in PCM," Institute of Mathematical Statistics Meeting, Atlantic City, N.J., September 1957; also IEEE Trans. on Information Theory, pp. 129-136, March 1982.

W. Mauersberger, "Experimental Results on the Performance of Mismatched Quantizers," IEEE Trans. on Information Theory, pp. 381-386, July 1979.

J. Max, "Quantizing for Minimum Distortion," IRE Trans. on Information Theory, pp. 7-12, March 1960.

G. A. Miller and P. E. Nicely, "Analysis of Perceptual Confusions among Some English Consonants," J. Acoust. Soc. Am., pp. 338-352, March 1955.

D. Mitra, "Mathematical Analysis of an Adaptive Quantizer," Bell System Tech. J., pp. 867-898, May-June 1974.

D. Mitra and B. Gotz, "An Adaptive PCM System Designed for Noisy Channels and Digital Implementations," Bell System Tech. J., pp. 2727-2763, September 1978.

K. Nitadori, "Statistical Analysis of DPCM," Electron. Commun. (Japan), February 1965.

P. Noll, "Adaptive Quantizing in Speech Coding Systems," Int. Zurich Seminar on Digital Communications, pp. B3.1-B3.6, March 1974.

P. Noll, "A Comparative Study of Various Quantization Schemes for Speech Encoding," Bell System Tech. J., pp. 1597-1614, November 1975.

P. Noll, "Effects of Channel Errors on the Signal-to-Noise Performance of Speech-Encoding Systems," Bell System Tech. J., pp. 1615-1636, November 1975.

P. Noll, unpublished work, Bell Laboratories, 1976.

P. Noll and R. Zelinski, "A Contribution to the Quantization of Memoryless Model Sources" (in German), Technical Report, Heinrich Hertz Institut, Berlin, 1974.

P. Noll and R. Zelinski, "Effects of Quantizer Mismatch," Archiv für Elektronik und Übertragungstechnik, Bd. 30, pp. 373-374, 1976.

P. Noll and R. Zelinski, "Bounds on Quantizer Performance in the Low Bit Rate Region," IEEE Trans. on Communications, pp. 300-305, February 1978.

P. Noll and R. Zelinski, "Comments on Quantizing Characteristics for Signals Having Laplacian Amplitude Probability Density Function," IEEE Trans. on Communications, pp. 1259-1260, August 1979.

M. D. Paez and T. H. Glisson, "Minimum Mean Squared Error Quantization in Speech PCM and DPCM Systems," IEEE Trans. on Communications, pp. 225-230, April 1972.

P. F. Panter and W. Dite, "Quantization Distortion in Pulse Count Modulation with Nonuniform Spacing of Levels," Proc. IRE, pp. 44-48, January 1951.

S. U. H. Qureshi and G. D. Forney, Jr., "A 9.6/16 kb/s Speech Digitizer," Proc. Int. Conf. Commun., pp. 30-31 to 30-36, San Francisco, June 1975.

L. R. Rabiner and J. A. Johnson, "Perceptual Evaluation of the Effects of Dither on Low Bit Rate PCM Systems," Bell System Tech. J, pp. 1487-1494, September 1972.

D. L. Richards, *Telecommunication by Speech; The Transmission Performance of Telephone Networks,* Butterworth, London, 1973.

L. G. Roberts, "Picture Coding Using Pseudo-random Noise," IRE Trans. on Information Theory, pp. 145-154, February 1962.

G. M. Roe, "Quantizing for Minimum Distortion," IEEE Trans. on Information Theory, pp. 384-385, 1964.

C. B. Rubinstein and J. O. Limb, "On the Design of Quantizers for DPCM Coders: The Influence of the Subjective Testing Methodology," IEEE Trans. on Communications, pp. 565-573, May 1978.

N. Rydbeck and C. E. W. Sundberg, "Techniques for Introducing Error-Correcting Codes into TDMA Satellite Communication Systems," Ericsson Technics, pp. 217-246, 1975.

N. Rydbeck and C. E. W. Sundberg, "Analysis of Digital Errors in Nonlinear PCM Systems," IEEE Trans. on Communications, pp. 59-65, January 1976.

W. Schlink, "A Redundancy Reducing PCM System for Speech Signals," Proc. 1972 Zurich Seminar on Communications, pp. F4.1-F4.3, March 1972.

L. Schuchman, "Dither Signals and Their Effect on Quantization Noise," IEEE Trans. on Communication Technology, pp. 162-164, December 1964.

B. Smith, "Instantaneous Companding of Quantized Signals," Bell System Tech. J., pp. 653-709, May 1957.

A. B. Sripad and D. L. Snyder, "A Necessary and Sufficient Condition for Quantization Errors to be Uniform and White," IEEE Trans. on Acoustics, Speech and Signal Processing, pp. 442-449, October 1977.

R. Steele, *Delta Modulation Systems,* John Wiley, New York, 1975.

R. W. Stroh, "Differential PCM with Adaptive Quantization for Voice Communications," Proc. Int. Conf. Communications, pp. 130.1-130.5, June 1974.

C. E. Sundberg and N. Rydbeck, "Pulse Code Modulation with Error-Correcting Codes for TDMA Satellite Communication Systems," Ericsson Technics, pp. 3-56, 1976.

T. Thomas and P. Noll, Technical University of Berlin, unpublished work, 1983.

J. E. Thompson and J. J. Sparkes, "A Pseudo-random Quantizer for Television Signals, Proc. IEEE, pp. 353-355, March 1967.

R. E. Totty and G. C. Clark, "Reconstruction Error in Waveform Transmission," IEEE Trans. on Information Theory (Correspondence), pp. 336-338, April 1967.

A. J. Viterbi, *Principles of Coherent Communications*, McGraw-Hill, New York, 1966.

C. Volmary and P. Noll, Technical University of Berlin, unpublished work, 1983.

B. Widrow, "A Study of Rough Amplitude Quantization by Means of Nyquist Sampling Theory," IRE Trans. on Circuit Theory, pp. 266-276, December 1956.

R. Wood, "On Optimum Quantization," IEEE Trans. on Information Theory, pp. 248-252, March 1969.

R. G. Wood and L. F. Turner, "Pseudorandomly Dithered Quantization of Speech Samples in PCM Transmission System," Proc. IEEE, pp. 512-518, May 1972.

R. Zelinski and P. Noll, "Investigations on Quantization of Memoryless Gaussian Sources" (in German), Technical Report No. 159, Heinrich Hertz Institut, Berlin, 1972.

R. Zelinski, "Effects of Transmission Errors on the Mean-squared Performance of Transform Coding

5

Pulse Code Modulation

5.1 Introduction

In Figures 1.5 and 1.6, *Pulse Code Modulation* (PCM) was noted to be the most bit-consuming digitizing system. We will presently see (Section 5.4) that PCM is also a very demanding system in terms of bit error rate on the digital channel; and that for speech inputs, there are other techniques (such as Delta-modulation) which are much more tolerant to bit errors. In spite of the above observations, PCM is the best established, the most implemented (Section 5.3) and the most applied of all digital coding systems. One reason for this is simply the fact that PCM is the earliest developed and also the best understood coding system. It is also the conceptually simplest system; further, most versions of PCM coders are *instantaneous*, implying a coding delay of no more than one sample period. Another reason for the importance of PCM is that, unlike the techniques of later chapters, it is *not signal-specific*; rather, it is versatile: for example, PCM is not mismatched to voiceband data waveforms in a way speech-specific DPCM coders are (Section 6.3.3). For this reason, PCM is widely accepted as a standard against which to calibrate other approaches to waveform digitization. Finally, all waveform coders, with the possible exception of Deltamodulation (Chapter 8), involve stages of PCM coding and decoding. In this sense, PCM is more than just one example of a digital coding system; parts of this chapter are relevant to succeeding chapters of this book as well.

A PCM coder is nothing more than a waveform sampler followed by an amplitude quantizer [Figure 5.1(a)]. In this sense, the underlying principles for PCM coding have already been described in Chapters 3 and 4. Chapter 4 has also

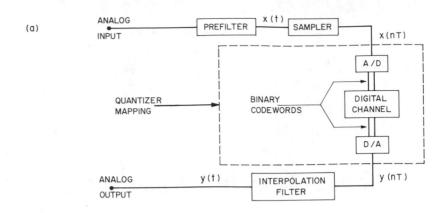

Figure 5.1 PCM system schematics: (a) explicit representation; and (b) a representation where the A/D stage includes the operation of sampling.

discussed refinements that are important in practical PCM systems; for example, log-companding, adaptive quantization, and dithering.

Appendix G will describe the principles behind important techniques used in the A/D and D/A conversion stages of Figure 5.1. Often, A/D implementations include the operation of sampling. In these cases, the block diagram of Figure 5.1(b) is more appropriate. The conversion principles discussed in Appendix G will apply not only to PCM, but also to coders in later chapters.

The sampling rate f_s for a PCM system follows the considerations of Chapter 3. The number of bits/sample R is related to the SNR versus R results of Chapter 4 [in particular, the 6 dB-per-additional bit results of (1.6) and (4.91)]:

$$SNR\,(dB)|_{PCM} = \begin{cases} 6.02R - 10 & \text{for speech} \\ 6.02R & \text{for images} \end{cases} \tag{5.1a}$$

The quality of images is sometimes measured as a peak-to-peak signal to rms-error ratio. The resulting numbers will be 10.8 dB higher (Problem 5.2) than the $6.02R$ value from (5.1a). The transmission rate I of a PCM system, as for any other coding system, is the product in (1.4):

$$I = f_s\, R \quad \text{bits/second} \tag{5.1b}$$

The term *code* in Pulse Code Modulation refers to the fact that the R bits of information per sample are transmitted as a special *codeword*. This is illustrated with the example of $R=4$ in Figure 5.2. There are actually $2^R!$ ways of assigning codewords to the 2^R possible quantizer output levels. Four of these binary codes

Pulse Code Modulation 5

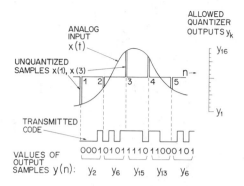

Figure 5.2 Signals in a PCM system.

were illustrated in Figure 4.35. One of these four codes is the NBC code; this is also the code used in Figure 5.2. The terms *pulse* and *modulation* in PCM are common to a large class of pulse modulation systems (such as pulse amplitude modulation, pulse width modulation). Books on modulation theory [Hancock, 1961] provide a formal comparison of modulation techniques. Digital modulation techniques such as PCM have the important feature of "trading bandwidth for increased signal-to-noise ratio", as compared with analog modulation [Oliver, Pierce and Shannon, 1948]. This concept was briefly explained in the last part of Section 1.2. In the case of PCM, and related techniques such as DPCM (Chapter 6), the transmission rate (5.1b) and hence the required channel bandwidth (Section 1.2) increase linearly with R; on the other hand, digital signal quality increases exponentially, as reflected by the linear increase with R in the expression (5.1a) for *SNR* (dB).

PCM has proven to be the most useful among the class of pulse modulation systems; and this is related to the fact that the bits in a PCM codeword are capable of periodical, essentially error-free, regeneration in the process of long-distance waveform communication over a noisy analog channel. For a given analog channel quality, parameters such as non-discretized pulse amplitude or pulse width are more sensitive and prone to irreversible modification. The long-distance transmission robustness of PCM applies to the other coding systems of this book, all of which in fact involve PCM coding stages. These waveform coding techniques, with the exception of differential PCM and Deltamodulation, have shed the term *modulation* in their names, while retaining the word *coding*: for example, TC stands for *transform coding* (Chapter 12).

An important early application of PCM coders has been in the context of multiplexed speech. Here, several speech communication channels (typically 24 or 30; see Table 1.2) share a common PCM coder, using *time division multiplexing* (TDM) [Members of Technical Staff, Bell Laboratories, 1971] [Van Trees, 1979] [Bellamy, 1982] [Owen, 1982]. Shared PCM coders result in *analog multiplexing*; the prospect of inexpensively implemented coders is, however, providing system designers with the option of subscriber-dedicated per-channel coding and *digital multiplexing*, with resulting gains in cross-talk performance. Figure 5.3 illustrates the operation of a 4-channel TDM system.

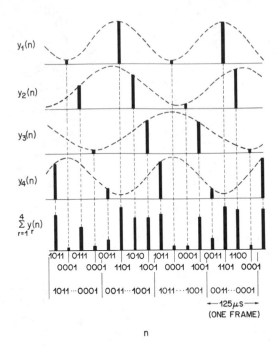

$y_1(n)$

$y_2(n)$

$y_3(n)$

$y_4(n)$

$\sum\limits_{r=1}^{4} y_r(n)$

| 1011 | 0111 | 0011 | 1010 | 1011 | 0001 | 0011 | 1100 | |
| 0001 | 0001 | 1101 | 1001 | 0001 | 1001 | 1101 | 0001 |

| 1011···0001 | 0011···1001 | 1011···1001 | 0011···0001 |

←—125 μs —→
(ONE FRAME)

n

Figure 5.3 Multiplexing of four channels in a PCM system [Bennett, 1978].

5.2 PCM Coding of Speech, Video and Audio Waveforms

Chapter 1 has already defined sampling and quantization designs appropriate for PCM coding of different waveforms. These numbers are valid for both transmission and storage applications. Figure 1.6, for example, has noted that for high quality representation, the minimum value of R is 8 bits/sample for speech and video. It should be emphasized that speech can be encoded with high quality using 8-bit PCM only if log-companding (or some kind of adaptive step size logic) is included in the PCM quantizer, so that the coder can cope with expected variations in input level (Section 2.2.2). In the PCM coding of video, although some amount of companding may be advantageous [Schreiber, 1978], associated gains are much less than in speech, and 8-bit linear (i.e., uniformly quantized) PCM is sufficient to provide very high output quality. An 8-bit linear format implies a maximum-intensity to minimum-intensity ratio of $2^8 = 256$. Video scenes can have much higher perceptible intensity ratios, but practical video displays make better-than-8-bit intensity representations irrelevant except in special signal processing environments such as those in studio television [Netravali and Limb, 1980]. The input range problem is most significant in high quality audio material that includes music waveforms. As indicated in Figure 1.6, high quality PCM coding of audio material requires at least 10- to 12- bit quantization, even if the quantizer is companded or adaptive, as we shall note at the end of this section.

5.2.1 Speech Waveforms

Figure 5.4 demonstrates PCM performance with a speech input sampled at $f_s = 8$ kHz, and quantized with $R = 8, 4, 2$ and 1 bits/sample. The quantizers use log-companding with $\mu = 255$. The 8-bit log-quantizer is equivalent in dynamic range (ratio of maximum output magnitude to minimum output magnitude) to a 13-bit uniform quantizer. A PCM system with either of the above quantizers provides toll quality digitized speech, and this topic will be amplified in Section 5.3, where 8-bit log-quantization will be used for communication of high-quality telephone speech at a transmission rate of $I = 64$ kb/s. The lower bit rate outputs in Figure 5.4 show the effect of *amplitude overload* or *clipping*; resulting reductions in speech intelligibility are surprisingly small, even in the worst case of *infinite clipping* ($R = 1$). However, output speech quality falls rapidly with decreasing R. In particular, the quality of the $R = 4$ log-quantizer is not very useful. It has an MOS score of about 3, as compared with the score of 4.5 typical of 8-bit PCM (Figure 1.5). The coding techniques of later chapters will provide significant gains over PCM for speech coding with 4 bits/sample.

Figure 5.4 Log-PCM coding of speech with a continuous μ-law quantizer (Chapter 4, $\mu = 255$) and bit rate $R = 8, 4, 2$ and 1 bits/sample. The coder input is the waveform of Figure 1.4(a) [Jayant, 1982].

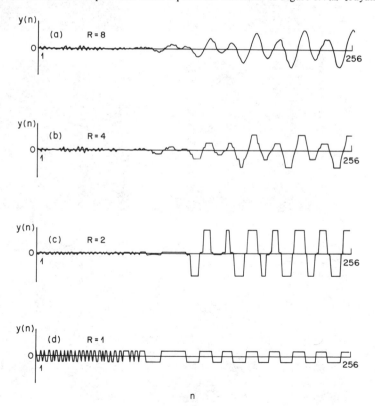

5.2.2 Image Waveforms

Figure 5.5 demonstrates PCM performance with an image input for $R = 8, 4, 2$ and 1 bits/sample. The uniform quantizer results in parts (a) to (d) show the rapid degradation of quality for R values of 4 bits/sample or less. Parts (e) and (f) illustrate the benefits of nonuniform quantization in low bit rate PCM coding, using the example of $R = 2$ bits/sample.

Figure 5.5 PCM coding of images: (a)(b)(c)(d) uniform quantizer with $R = 8, 4, 2$ and 1 bit/sample [Gonzalez and Wintz, 1977. Reprinted with permission]; (e) uniform versus (f) nonuniform quantizer, $R = 2$ bits/sample [Rosenfeld and Kak, 1976. Reprinted with permission].

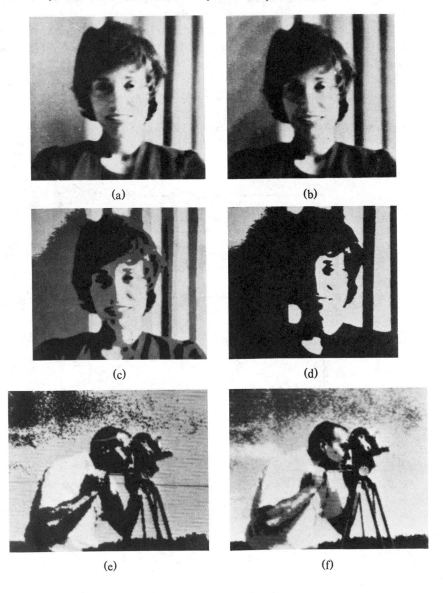

(a)

(b)

(c)

(d)

(e)

(f)

As seen in the 4-bit example of Figure 5.5(b), the poor quality of medium bit rate PCM is due mainly to *contouring*, in the near-constant gray areas of the image. This is the effect of sudden jumps from one quantizer level to the next in the context of a slowly changing input intensity function. However, as noted in Figure 4.31, such contouring can be eliminated by the use of dithering prior to quantization. Although the resulting quality still falls short of 8-bit PCM quality, a 4-bit PCM system with dither can be useful in applications where requirements on quality are modest, the need for bit conservation is severe, and the need for simplicity suggests the use of PCM, rather than, say, DPCM or Transform Coding. One such application may be in image storage; see Problem 5.1. The perceived output quality in PCM systems for video can also be improved somewhat by high frequency pre-emphasis prior to encoding; see Chapter 7 (Example 7.9).

The 8-bit/sample coder provides a very high quality gray-level output. If the black-and-white image is sampled at $f_s = 10$ MHz, the corresponding bit rate I would be 80 Mb/s.

PCM Coding of Color Video. Eight-bit representations are also adequate for high quality digitization of color images [Limb, Rubinstein and Thompson, 1977]. The total bit rates are, however, much higher than for a black-and-white image, especially in *studio* television. For example, in studio systems based on 13.5 MHz sampling of the luminance signal [CCIR, 1982], and 6.75 MHz sampling of each of two color-difference signals, the total transmission rate I would be 8 (13.5 + 6.75 + 6.75) = 216 Mb/s. Standard sampling and transmission rates will be lower in *broadcast* television.

5.2.3 Audio Waveforms

Applications of digitized audio are in digital recording and in the distribution of broadcast music material. As noted in Figure 1.6, digitizers for music require extremely high values of R for high-quality representation. This is due to the very large dynamic range of audio signals. However, in many applications of music digitization, the PCM coder input is pre-recorded music with a dynamic range no greater than that of the recording tape. This range is in the order of 75 dB [Blesser and Kates, 1978]. As a result, 14-bit uniform resolution (output magnitude range of $20 \log_{10} 2^{13} = 78$ dB for a zero-mean input) is then an adequate design goal. However, in intra-studio applications, 16-bit resolution may be called for, to allow a sufficient quality margin in the presence of subsequent signal-processing operations such as mixing. A 16 bit/sample format is also standard for *compact disc* recordings that offer a signal-to-noise ratio of more than 90 dB. The sampling rate used in this recording system is 44.1 kHz.

The minimum adequate value of number of bits R can be decreased as in the case of video, by preemphasis and dithering techniques [Blesser and Kates, 1978], but the greatest reductions in R are those due to companding (for example, piecewise linear A-law log-quantization; see Section 5.3), and/or adaptive quantization. In fact, one of the first investigations of AQF systems was in the encoding of music material [Croll, Moffat and Osborne, 1973]. Resulting useful values of R are typically in the range of 12 or even 10, and the side information for AQF step size is a small fraction of 1 bit/sample for an updating time in the order of 1 ms (Problem 5.3).

Transmission systems for digital audio are designed to operate at bit rates that are multiples of 64 kb/s. Examples of such systems are a 12 bit/sample, 32 kHz sampling rate system with $I = 384$ kb/s, and a 12 bit/sample, 16 kHz sampling rate system with $I = 192$ kb/s. The respective sampling rates are appropriate for bandwidths in the order of 15 and 7 kHz.

The bit-economical coding systems of later chapters have been developed mainly for speech and video; they can be adapted to music coding as well, resulting in digitizing systems with R values much less than 12 bits/sample. We shall note at least one such example in the context of sub-band coding (Chapter 11).

5.3 PCM Systems for High-Quality Speech Coding

The adaptive quantizers discussed in Chapter 4 have been applied widely in low bit rate speech coding systems using techniques such as DPCM, SBC and TC. At these low bit rates (say, $R \leqslant 4$ bits/sample), as we have noted in Figure 4.43, adaptive quantization provides a significant performance gain over time-invariant nonuniform quantization. Commercial PCM systems, on the other hand, are based on the use of 8 bits/sample; at these higher bit rates, a time-invariant quantizer can provide *toll quality* speech, provided an appropriate form of log-companding is employed. As noted in Chapter 4, log-companding increases the range of input level variation over which a specific level of SNR can be maintained; and, in particular, ensures an adequate SNR for the frequently occurring low-level segments in speech communication. The term toll quality will be defined more completely in terms of a CCITT specification of dynamic range in Figure 5.10. This specification implies, among other things, that an SNR of nearly 34 dB is maintained over a range of input signal variation slightly exceeding 30 dB. We will be discussing two digital companding systems for 8-bit PCM in this section, and both of these will meet the CCITT specifications for toll quality speech. The CCITT 30-channel system approximates A-law companding, and typifies European PCM practice. The CCITT 24-channel system approximates μ-law companding and typifies North American and Japanese PCM practice [Bennett, 1978] [Bellamy, 1982] [Owen, 1982]. We shall also note in Figure 5.11 that 8-bit PCM systems have a sufficient "safety margin" in quality to accommodate several stages of coding and decoding in tandem.

With a speech sampling rate of $f_s = 8$ kHz, and coding with $R = 8$ bits/sample, the transmission rate is $I = 64$ kb/s. As pointed out in Chapter 1, this is a very important number in digital transmission practice. The bit rate of 64 kb/s is the smallest unit for the well-established digital hierarchies listed in Table 1.2. This unit continues to be an important standard rate for emerging digital networks. This includes *Integrated Services Digital Networks* (ISDN) where a channel rate of 64 kb/s, or multiples or sub-multiples thereof, may be allocated not only for digital speech subscribers, but for digital transmission of other signals such as data, graphics and video.

5.3.1 PCM Multiplex Systems

In the CCITT 30-channel A-law system, each TDM frame is made up of a set of 32 channel time slots (0 to 31). Each channel time slot comprises 8 digit time slots with a duration of 125 μs/32 = 3.9 μs. Each digit time slot has a duration of 3.9μs/8 = 0.488 μs. The overall bit rate of the system is 8000 × 32 × 8 = 2048 kb/s. Voice channels are numbered 1 to 30, and are allocated to channel time slots 1 to 15 and 17 to 31, all 8 bits in each time slot being used for encoding speech samples. Time slot 0 contains frame synchronization and alarm indication information, while slot 16 is devoted exclusively to "signaling", which relates to control and switching information for telephone exchange equipment.

The CCITT 24-channel μ-law system uses a different format wherein frame synchronization information is obtained by the addition of a special bit at the end of the 125 μs TDM frame. Each frame thus contains (8 × 24) + 1 = 193 bits. The digit slot duration is 125 μs/193 = 0.648 μs. The overall bit rate of the system is 8000·193 = 1.544 Mb/s. Signaling information is provided by periodic stealing of the least significant bit from 8-bit codewords representing speech samples (Problem 5.4).

5.3.2 Digitally Linearizable Log-Companding

Early PCM systems [Damann, McDaniel and Maddox, 1972] made use of the nonlinear properties of diodes to approximate the quasi-logarithmic μ-law and A-law characteristics of Chapter 4. Contemporary versions, such as the CCITT-recommended systems just mentioned, are based on *digitally linearizable* companding which permits a precise control of quantization characteristics. As we shall presently see, digital companding also implies direct digital conversion from a uniform PCM format to a log-PCM format, and vice versa. The compression and expansion characteristics in these digital companding systems are piecewise linear approximations to μ- and A-law characteristics. Recall from Chapter 4 that the slope of the companding law (the interval density) is a measure of the number of levels. Therefore, in these piecewise linear systems, the quantizer step size as well as the number of quantizer intervals are constant quantities within each linear segment. *Step-sizes in consecutive segments are related by powers of 2.*

Digitally linearizable PCM with a bit rate of R = 8 bits/sample is a widely accepted standard for speech digitization. Lower bit rate systems are often designed to be compatible with the above standard even if they are not equivalent to it in performance. These systems include lower rate PCM systems such as *Nearly Instantaneous Companding* [Duttweiler and Messerschmitt, 1975] as well as lower rate systems based on differential PCM (Chapter 6) or related procedures [Adoul, 1982].

The standard values of μ = 255 and A = 87.56 are designed to provide a good approximation to respective piecewise characteristics for R = 8 bits/sample. These standard values also have other interesting properties. For example, in the μ-law system, the ratio of maximum to minimum step size is $1 + \mu$ in the continuous law (last column of Table 5.1), and of the form 2^{2^K}, where K is an integer, in the piecewise law. The value of μ which has the form $2^{2^K} - 1$ and is also in the order

Table 5.1 Properties of Companding Laws (See Section 4.5).

Type of Law	Defining equation for positive x	Companding Gain G_C	$\dfrac{\text{max. slope in } c(x)}{\text{min. slope in } c(x)}$
A-law: Logarithmic with linear tangential segment	$c(x) = \dfrac{Ax/x_{max}}{1+\log_e A};\ 0 \leqslant \dfrac{x}{x_{max}} \leqslant \dfrac{1}{A}$ $= x_{max}\dfrac{1+\log_e Ax/x_{max}}{1+\log_e A};\ \dfrac{1}{A} < \dfrac{x}{x_{max}} \leqslant 1$	$\dfrac{A}{1+}\log_e A$	A
μ-law: Quasi-logarithmic	$c(x) = x_{max}\dfrac{\log_e (1+\mu x/x_{max})}{\log_e (1+\mu)}$	$\dfrac{\mu}{\log_e (1+\mu)}$	$1+\mu$

of $\mu = 100$ (Section 4.5) is indeed 255. In the case of the A-law, the value of $A = 87.56$ has the property of providing a companding gain of exactly 24.08 dB, or 4 bits (Section 4.5).

Figure 5.6 shows a piecewise linear compressor characteristic designed to provide a good approximation to the $\mu 255$ and $A\,87.56$ compression laws in Figure 4.16 and Table 5.1. The term V on the y-axis is a scaling factor which can be set, if needed, to ensure that $c(x_{max})/x_{max} = 1$ as in Table 5.1. The linear segments in the characteristic are identified by a *segment number* s; $s = 0, 1, 2, ..., s_{max}$. The approximation to the $\mu 255$ law consists of a 15-segment characteristic; there are $s_{max} + 1 = 8$ segments on each side of zero and the innermost two segments are collinear, as shown in Figure 5.6. This results in $16 - 1 = 15$ segments of distinct slope. The approximation to the $A\,87.56$ law has four innermost segments that are collinear, resulting in $16 - 3 = 13$ segments of distinct slope. In each case, segment information is conveyed by $\log_2 16 = 4$ bits. Further, the amplitudes within any given segment are quantized to 16 *levels*, or 4 additional bits of information, resulting in the following overall 8-bit representation of the compressed input:

Bit 1: *sign* ;   Bits 2 to 4: *segment* ;   Bits 5 to 8: *level* .

The nonuniform step size $\Delta(s)$ in Figure 5.6 corresponds to the Δ_k in Figure 4.11. If the smallest step size $\Delta(0)$ is set equal to 1, the maximum value of input magnitude for which there is no quantizer overload, which is also beginning point $B(s_{max}+1)$ of the last segment, is nearly 2^{12} in the 15-segment characteristic, and nearly 2^{11} in the 13-segment characteristic. On the other hand, the total number of output levels [number of quantized values of $c(x)$] is only $256 = 2^8$ in each 8-bit system.

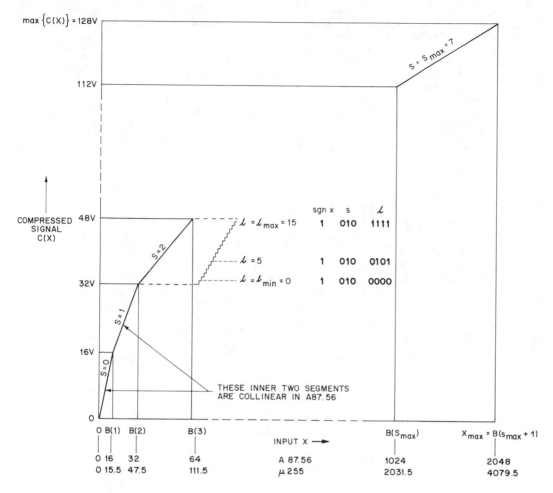

Figure 5.6 The positive half of a piecewise linear compression characteristic for $R = 8$ bits/sample; $s_{max} = 7$ and $\ell_{max} = 15$. The illustration is not drawn exactly to scale, for purposes of clarity. The listed values of $B(s)$ on the x-axis are the same as those listed in boldface in Tables 5.2 and 5.3 for the case of $\Delta(0) = 1$. The $B(s)$-versus-s curve is essentially exponential in both $\mu255$ and $A87.56$ laws. The quantity V on the $c(x)$-axis is a scaling factor that can be set so that max $\{c(x)\} = c(x_{max}) = x_{max}$, as in Figure 4.11. The listed values of $c(x)/V$ correspond to values of decoded level number in column 5 of Tables 5.2 and 5.3.

Explicit Quantization Characteristics. Tables 5.2 and 5.3 show explicit input-to-output mappings in (midtread) $\mu255$ and (midrise) $A87.56$ 8-bit systems. Input and output magnitudes are shown in the first and last columns of these tables, and quantizer mappings for negative inputs are simply obtained by including minus signs in both columns. The boldface entries in the first columns correspond to the $B(s)$ values in Figure 5.6. It can be seen that if the scaling factor in Figure 5.6 is $V = 32$ (μ-law) or $V = 16$ (A-law), max$\{c(x)\} = x_{max}$, as in Figure 4.11.

Table 5.2 Encoding/Decoding table for $\mu 255$ PCM. Boldface entries are the $B(s)$ values listed in Figure 5.6 [Bellamy, 1982. Reprinted with permission].

Input Magnitude Range			Step size Δ	Segment Code s	Level Code ℓ	Decoder Level Number	Decoded Magnitude
0	–	0.5			0000	0	0
0.5	–	1.5			0001	1	1
			1	000			
⋮					⋮	⋮	⋮
14.5	–	**15.5**			1111	15	15
15.5	–	17.5			0000	16	16.5
⋮			2	001	⋮	⋮	⋮
45.5	–	**47.5**			1111	31	46.5
47.5	–	51.5			0000	32	49.5
⋮			4	010	⋮	⋮	⋮
107.5	–	**111.5**			1111	47	109.5
111.5	–	119.5			0000	48	115.5
⋮			8	011	⋮	⋮	⋮
231.5	–	**239.5**			1111	63	235.5
239.5	–	255.5			0000	64	247.5
⋮			16	100	⋮	⋮	⋮
479.5	–	**495.5**			1111	79	487.5
495.5	–	527.5			0000	80	511.5
⋮			32	101	⋮	⋮	⋮
975.5	–	**1007.5**			1111	95	991.5
1007.5	–	1071.5			0000	96	1039.5
⋮			64	110	⋮	⋮	⋮
1967.5	–	**2031.5**			1111	111	1999.5
2031.5	–	2159.5			0000	112	2095.5
⋮			128	111	⋮	⋮	⋮
3951.5	–	**4079.5**			1111	127	4015.5

Binary Channel Codes. Note that a *natural binary code* (NBC) has been used in Tables 5.2 and 5.3 for representing segment s as well as level ℓ. With the use of the same NBC representation for both positive and negative magnitudes, and the use of a separate bit for sign information, the resulting overall system is a *folded binary code* (FBC). With an input pdf that is typical of speech [Figure 2.4(a)], this coding system implies that the density of 0's in the coder output is higher than the density of 1's. In transmission practice, PCM codewords are often manipulated in reversible one-to-one mappings, to increase the density of 1's in the channel input [Bennett, 1978]. These manipulations may involve the complementing of either entire PCM codewords, or of every other letter in the PCM codewords.

Table 5.3 Encoding/Decoding table for A 87.56 PCM. Boldface entries are the $B(s)$ values listed in Figure 5.6 [Bellamy, 1982. Reprinted with permission].

Input Magnitude Range			Step size Δ	Segment Code s	Level Code ℓ	Decoder Level Number	Decoded Magnitude
0	–	1			0000	0	0.5
1	–	2			0001	1	1.5
	$\vdots$		1	000	$\vdots$	$\vdots$	$\vdots$
15	–	**16**			1111	15	15.5
16	–	17			0000	16	16.5
	$\vdots$		1	001	$\vdots$	$\vdots$	$\vdots$
31	–	**32**			1111	31	31.5
32	–	34			0000	32	33
	$\vdots$		2	010	$\vdots$	$\vdots$	$\vdots$
62	–	**64**			1111	47	63
64	–	68			0000	48	66
	$\vdots$		4	011	$\vdots$	$\vdots$	$\vdots$
124	–	**128**			1111	63	126
128	–	136			0000	64	132
	$\vdots$		8	100	$\vdots$	$\vdots$	$\vdots$
248	–	**256**			1111	79	252
256	–	272			0000	80	264
	$\vdots$		16	101	$\vdots$	$\vdots$	$\vdots$
496	–	**512**			1111	95	504
512	–	544			0000	96	528
	$\vdots$		32	110	$\vdots$	$\vdots$	$\vdots$
992	–	**1024**			1111	111	1008
1024	–	1088			0000	112	1056
	$\vdots$		64	111	$\vdots$	$\vdots$	$\vdots$
1984	–	**2048**			1111	127	2016

Table 5.4 summarizes features of the piecewise linear versions for 8-bit quantization. Note that as a result of the approximation to the ideal companding characteristics, the ratio of maximum to minimum step size is less than ideal in the μ-law approximation (128 instead of $\mu + 1 = 256$), as well as in the A-law approximation (64 instead of $A = 87.56$). The μ-law approximation has a smaller value of $\Delta(0)$ (relative to maximum speech input) than the A-law approximation (1/4096 instead of 1/2048), and this is reflected in somewhat superior idle-channel noise performance. The A-law, on the other hand, has slightly better performance for middle to upper signal levels. These small differences between the two piecewise linear systems are reflected in the performance curves of Figure 5.7.

Table 5.4 Properties of Digitally Linearizable Approximations to 8-bit μ- and A-law Quantizers (Δ (s) = step size in segment s)

Piecewise Linear Compression Law	15-segment (μ255)	13-segment (A 87.56)
Number of non-collinear chords on either side of zero	8	7
$\dfrac{\Delta(s_{max})}{\Delta(0)} = \dfrac{\Delta_{max}}{\Delta_{min}}$	128	64
$\dfrac{\text{Maximum non-overloading input}}{\Delta(0)}$	~4096	~2048

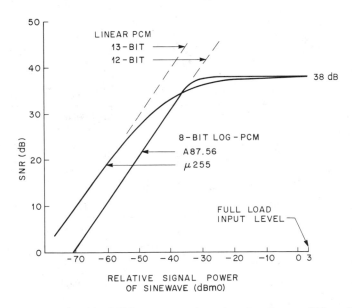

Figure 5.7 Comparison of 8-bit PCM systems using piecewise linear μ255 and A87.56 law approximations [Bellamy, 1982. Reprinted with permission]. Input level is specified in terms of decibels relative to 1 milliwatt (dBm0). The 0 in dBm0 indicates that the signal level is measured at the reference point or 0 dB transmission level point in the network [Members of Technical Staff, Bell Laboratories, 1971]. Recall that the *SNR* formula $6R-10$ (dB) in (5.1a) indeed predicts 38 dB, which is the highest *SNR* value in this figure.

These curves refer to a 400 Hz sine-wave input. We shall say more about *SNR* measurement in Section 5.3.4.

The numbers 4096 and 2048 in Table 5.4 correspond to peak-to-peak signal-to-Δ_{min} ratios of $8192 = 2^{13}$ and $4096 = 2^{12}$. In this *dynamic range* sense, the μ-law and A-law companded PCM systems above are equivalent to 13-bit and 12-bit uniform PCM. The *maximum SNR* in Figure 5.7 corresponds, however, to $6R-10$ dB [see (4.91a) and (5.1a)] with $R = 8$, and *not* with $R = 13$ or 12.

The peak *SNR* of a 13-bit quantizer (as obtained by completing the leftmost broken-line characteristic in Figure 5.7) is in the order of 70 dB. This can also be predicted by using (4.34) with $R = 13$. This peak value is, of course, realized only for a specific input level [Shenoi and Agrawal, 1980]. Nevertheless, the value is much higher than the peak value of 38 dB in 8-bit log-quantization; there is therefore an irreversible degradation, in general, when one converts from a 13-bit uniform to 8-bit log-format. A similar degradation occurs in the conversion from 12-bit uniform PCM to 8-bit log-PCM. These *SNR* losses will of course be academic in situations where *SNR* values exceeding 38 dB are irrelevant.

5.3.3 Conversions Between Input Amplitudes and 8-Bit Codes

The mapping from 8-bit logarithmic code to 13- or 12-bit amplitude (Tables 5.2 and 5.3) can be defined analytically. The mapping from 13- or 12-bit (or analog) amplitude to 8-bit code is more difficult to formulate in closed form.

We denote threshold and output amplitudes by x and y, respectively, the compressed input amplitude by $c(x)$ and the quantized compressed input amplitude by $\bar{c}(x)$. We use the notation of Figure 5.6. Note once again that characteristics are symmetrical about zero, so that most formulations need to be derived only for one input polarity, specifically for positive x in what follows. However, because of the many differences in detail between the systems of Tables 5.2 and 5.3, the following analytical formulation will have to be involved in appearance, although simple in concept [Kaneko, 1970].

The quantities sgn x, s and ℓ are functions of bits in an 8-bit word

$$[b_1]\ [b_2 b_3 b_4]\ [b_5 b_6 b_7 b_8] \tag{5.3}$$

The *b*'s are all 0 or 1, and

$$\text{sgn } x = 2b_1 - 1$$

$$s = \text{decimal (NBC) representation of } [b_2 b_3 b_4]$$

$$\ell = \text{decimal (NBC) representation of } [b_5 b_6 b_7 b_8] \tag{5.4}$$

The step size in segment s is given by

$$\Delta(0) = 1; \qquad \Delta(s) = 2^s \qquad\qquad \text{for } s > 0 \qquad (\mu 255)$$

$$\Delta(0) = 1; \qquad \Delta(1) = 1; \qquad \Delta(s) = 2^{s-1} \quad \text{for } s > 1 \qquad (A\,87.56) \tag{5.5}$$

Segment s begins at input level $B(s)$. For positive inputs, $B(s)$ values are recursively determined by

$$B(0) = 0$$

$$B(1) = B(0) + 16\Delta(0) - 0.5 = 15.5 \qquad\qquad (\mu 255)$$

$$\quad = B(0) + 16\Delta(0) = 16 \qquad\qquad (A\,87.56)$$

$$B(s) = B(s-1) + 16\Delta(s-1) \qquad \text{for } s > 1 \qquad (5.6)$$

$$= 16(2^s-1) - 0.5 \qquad (\mu 255)$$

$$= 16 \cdot 2^{s-1} \qquad (A\,87.56)$$

Values of $B(s)$ for negative inputs are simply obtained by multiplying values in (5.6) by -1.

The quantizer half-range x_{max} is determined by the beginning point $B(s_{max} + 1)$ of the last segment, which is the ending point of the next-to-last segment:

$$x_{max} = B(s_{max} + 1) = 16(2^8-1) - 0.5 = 4079.5 \qquad (\mu 255)$$

$$= 16 \cdot 2^7 = 2048 \qquad (A\,87.56) \qquad (5.7)$$

The above values of x_{max} are very close to 2^{12} and 2^{11}, respectively, the half-ranges in 13-bit and 12-bit resolution.

Mapping from 8-Bit Code to 13-Bit or 12-Bit Amplitude. If ℓ is the level number within a segment ($\ell = 0$ to 15), the output signal amplitude y, *for positive input x,* is

$$y = \begin{cases} B(0) + \ell\Delta(0) = \ell & (\mu 255) \\ & \text{for } s = 0 \\ B(0) + (\ell+1/2)\Delta(0) = \ell + 0.5 & (A\,87.56) \end{cases} \qquad (5.8)$$

$$y = B(s) + (\ell+1/2)\Delta(s) \qquad \text{for } s \geqslant 1$$

$$= 2^s(\ell+16.5) - 16.5 \qquad (\mu 255) \qquad (5.9)$$

$$= 2^{s-1}(\ell+16.5) \qquad (A\,87.56) \qquad (5.10)$$

Corresponding equations can be derived for negative x also, but these values can most easily be determined as the negatives of positive y values that correspond to an appropriate reflected code.

It can be verified that the above formulations for $B(s)$, Δ and y provide results that are identical to the numerical values in columns 1, 2 and 6, respectively, in Tables 5.2 and 5.3. As an example, in the $\mu 255$ midtread characteristic, 8-bit codes corresponding to innermost and outermost positive levels can be shown, using (5.8) and (5.10), to map into 13-bit amplitudes 0 and 4015.5, respectively (Problem 5.5).

The compressed signal along the $c(x)$-axis of Figure 5.6 has a 8-bit rather than 13-bit resolution. The general formula for the quantized compressed output $\tilde{c}(x)$, correct to the scaling factor V, is

$$|\tilde{c}(x)| = 16s + (\ell + 1) \qquad (5.11a)$$

so that with $\ell_{max} = 15$ and $s_{max} = 7$,

$$\max\{|\tilde{c}(x)|\} = 112 + 16 = 128 = 2^7 ; \quad 2\max\{|\tilde{c}(x)|\} = 2^8 \qquad (5.11b)$$

Mapping from 13-Bit or 12-Bit Amplitude to 8-Bit Code. The mapping from 13-bit or 12-bit uniform format to 8-bit logarithmic code cannot be given in simple explicit form. It can be given in tabular form as in Tables 5.2 and 5.3 with quantizer output values following equations (5.8) to (5.10), and quantizer threshold values being displaced from the former by corresponding values of $\Delta(s)/2$. Left and right threshold amplitudes x_l and x_r on either side of output y are $y - \Delta(s)/2$ and $y + \Delta(s)/2$. Given a 13-bit or 12-bit input x, one determines the appropriate (x_l, x_r) pair that includes x; this in turn specifies output y, and a corresponding 8-bit codeword.

The above mapping can also be directly performed using appropriate modifications of the A/D conversion procedures to be described in Section 5.5. In this approach, the 13-bit format is considered to be the "analog" amplitude input to the A/D device. In practice, however, the mapping from analog input to 8-bit representation is best implemented with an intermediate stage of 13- or 12-bit linear PCM, followed by a digital linear-to-log code conversion.

5.3.4 Digital Conversion between Log- and Uniform PCM

Figure 5.8 shows how a practical PCM system may use 8 bit/sample coding for speech transmission although 13-bit or 12-bit uniform resolution speech formats may exist both at transmitter and receiver. The uniform (or linear) formats may be the result of an initial A/D conversion at the transmitter. It may also be a desired format both at transmitter and receiver for signal-processing operations such as those in digital switching [Shenoi and Agrawal, 1980] and conferencing. A fundamental advantage in using the piecewise linear $\mu 255$ and $A 87.56$ laws is the ease with which they can be *digitally linearized*.

Figure 5.8 PCM transmission system using direct digital conversion between uniform (linear) and logarithmic quantization formats.

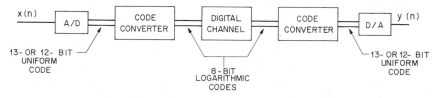

Table 5.5 Direct conversion between μ-law and linear PCM codes [Bellamy, 1982. Reprinted with permission].

(a) μ-Law Encoding

Biased Linear Input Code	Compressed Code
0 0 0 0 0 0 0 1 w x y z a	0
0 0 0 0 0 0 1 w x y z a b	0 0 1 w x y z
0 0 0 0 0 1 w x y z a b c	0 1 0 w x y z
0 0 0 0 1 w x y z a b c d	0 1 1 w x y z
0 0 0 1 w x y z a b c d e	1 0 0 w x y z
0 0 1 w x y z a b c d e f	1 0 1 w x y z
0 1 w x y z a b c d e f g	1 1 0 w x y z
1 w x y z a b c d e f g h	1 1 1 w x y z

(b) μ-Law Decoding

Compressed Code	Biased Linear Output Code
0 0 0 w x y z	0 0 0 0 0 0 0 1 w x y z 1
0 0 1 w x y z	0 0 0 0 0 0 1 w x y z 1 0
0 1 0 w x y z	0 0 0 0 0 1 w x y z 1 0 0
0 1 1 w x y z	0 0 0 0 1 w x y z 1 0 0 0
1 0 0 w x y z	0 0 0 1 w x y z 1 0 0 0 0
1 0 1 w x y z	0 0 1 w x y z 1 0 0 0 0 0
1 1 0 w x y z	0 1 w x y z 1 0 0 0 0 0 0
1 1 1 w x y z	1 w x y z 1 0 0 0 0 0 0 0

Direct Conversion between $\mu 255$ and Linear Formats. The simplicity of converting from a linear code to a compressed code is most evident if the linear code is biased by adding the value 16.5 to the magnitude of all samples. Notice that this bias shifts the encoding range (column 1 of Table 5.2) from (0 to 4079.5) to (16.5 to 4096). The addition process can be performed directly on the analog samples before encoding or with digital logic after encoding. In either case, the general form of all biased linear code patterns and the corresponding compressed codes are shown in Table 5.5a.

It can be seen from the table that all biased linear codes have a leading 1 that indicates the value of the segment number s. Specifically, the value of s is equal to 7 minus the number of leading 0's before the 1. The value of ℓ is directly available as the four bits (w, x, y, z) immediately following the leading 1. All trailing bits (a through h) are merely ignored when generating a compressed code.

Table 5.5b indicates how one can generate a biased linear code from a compressed code. An unbiased output can be obtained by subtracting 16.5 from the biased code.

Direct Conversion Between $A 87.56$ and Linear Formats. Table 5.6a shows the conversion of a 12-bit linear code directly into a compressed A-law code. The algorithm is basically the same as for the $\mu 255$ conversion except that biasing the linear code is unnecessary and a first segment code does not have a leading 1.

Table 5.6 Direct conversion between A-Law and linear PCM codes [Bellany, 1982. Reprinted with permission].

(a) A-Law Decoding

Linear Code	Compressed Code
0 0 0 0 0 0 0 $w\,x\,y\,z\,a$	0 0 0 $w\,x\,y\,z$
0 0 0 0 0 0 1 $w\,x\,y\,z\,a$	0 0 1 $w\,x\,y\,z$
0 0 0 0 0 1 $w\,x\,y\,z\,a\,b$	0 1 0 $w\,x\,y\,z$
0 0 0 0 1 $w\,x\,y\,z\,a\,b\,c$	0 1 1 $w\,x\,y\,z$
0 0 0 1 $w\,x\,y\,z\,a\,b\,c\,d$	1 0 0 $w\,x\,y\,z$
0 0 1 $w\,x\,y\,z\,a\,b\,c\,d\,e$	1 0 1 $w\,x\,y\,z$
0 1 $w\,x\,y\,z\,a\,b\,c\,d\,e\,f$	1 1 0 $w\,x\,y\,z$
1 $w\,x\,y\,z\,a\,b\,c\,d\,e\,f\,g$	1 1 1 $w\,x\,y\,z$

(b) A-Law Decoding

Compressed Code	Linear Output Code
0 0 0 $w\,x\,y\,z$	0 0 0 0 0 0 0 $w\,x\,y\,z$ 1
0 0 1 $w\,x\,y\,z$	0 0 0 0 0 0 1 $w\,x\,y\,z$ 1
0 1 0 $w\,x\,y\,z$	0 0 0 0 0 1 $w\,x\,y\,z$ 1 0
0 1 1 $w\,x\,y\,z$	0 0 0 0 1 $w\,x\,y\,z$ 1 0 0
1 0 0 $w\,x\,y\,z$	0 0 0 1 $w\,x\,y\,z$ 1 0 0 0
1 0 1 $w\,x\,y\,z$	0 0 1 $w\,x\,y\,z$ 1 0 0 0 0
1 1 0 $w\,x\,y\,z$	0 1 $w\,x\,y\,z$ 1 0 0 0 0 0
1 1 1 $w\,x\,y\,z$	1 $w\,x\,y\,z$ 1 0 0 0 0 0 0

Thus, the segment number s can be determined as 7 minus the number of leading zeros, as before. The ℓ data are obtained as the four bits ($wxyz$) immediately following the leading 1, except when $s = 0$, in which case the ℓ data are contained in the 4 bits following the 7 leading 0's.

Table 5.6b provides the means of generating a linear code word directly from a compressed codeword. The output value corresponds to the middle of the quantization interval designated by s and ℓ.

5.3.5 Measurement of Reconstruction Noise and SNR

The SNR formula in (1.2) is easy to evaluate in computer simulations of coding where all samples $x(n)$, $y(n)$, and therefore $q(n)$ are available. Practical evaluations of coder SNR differ in two respects. First, simpler test signals such as sine-waves and narrow-band noise are used, rather than real speech. This is in the interest of standardization and repeatability of tests at different times and places. Second, instead of the sampled approach in (1.2), approximations to input and error power are obtained by direct average power measurements using the scheme illustrated in Figure 5.9.

The input test signal in Figure 5.9(a) is a narrowband Gaussian random input with bandwidth 200 Hz and center frequency 450 Hz. The coding noise spectrum has a broader spectrum (say 200 to 3400 Hz in a speech system application, as in Figure 3.8). When the switch S is connected to the filter F1 (position 1), the

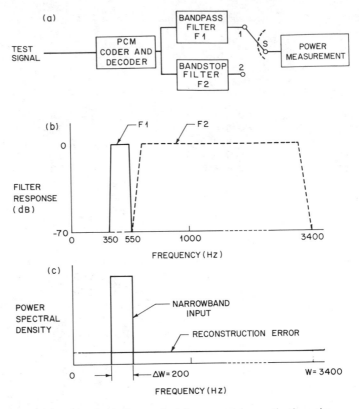

Figure 5.9 Notch-filter method for measuring quantization noise.

measured power is approximately that of the narrowband input, because the noise power that is passed by F1 is a small fraction of the total noise power (which in turn is a small fraction of the signal power in high-quality applications). When the switch S is connected to the bandstop filter F2 (position 2), the power measured is the noise power in the rest of the band. Since the eliminated band in $F2$ corresponds to the narrow spectrum of the test signal (the characteristic of filter $F1$), the above noise power is approximately equal to the total noise power in the speech band. In fact, if the noise spectrum can be assumed to be white as in Chapter 4, Figure 5.9(c) shows that the total noise power can be more exactly estimated from the approximate value above by using a correction factor $=(1-\lambda)^{-1}$ where $\lambda = \Delta W/W$ is the ratio of eliminated bandwidth to the full speech bandwidth. In the example of Figure 5.9, this correction factor is 1.067, or 0.23 dB.

Figure 5.10 illustrates SNR characteristics of a PCM coder obtained as explained above. The coder maintains an SNR of 38 dB over a wide range of input variance. A very similar SNR characteristic is also obtained with a real speech input. Values of the segmental measure $SNRSEG$ (Appendix E) are 4 to 6 dB lower for speech inputs, and this will be mentioned again in Chapter 6 in the context of PCM-DPCM comparison.

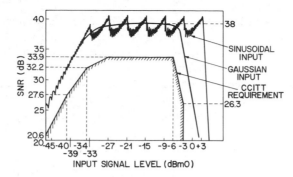

Figure 5.10 *SNR* characteristics in 8-bit $\mu 255$ PCM with sinusoidal and Gaussian inputs. See Figure 5.7 for a definition of the dBm0 unit for input level. The minimum *SNR* requirement is that specified in CCITT document Rec. G.712.

Figure 5.10 also illustrates the *SNR* characteristic obtained with a sinusoidal test signal. The earlier droop in strong-signal *SNR* with the narrowband Gaussian input is related to the fact that quantizer overload in this case sets in earlier than with a sinusoidal signal of equal power. This, in turn, is because the infinite-support Gaussian pdf (Figure 2.5) has a longer tail than the finite-support arcsine pdf. For the same reason, the dynamic range curve for real speech droops much earlier than that for the sinewave test signal in Figure 5.10. The oscillations in the sine-wave *SNR* characteristic are, however, informative. They correspond to the jerky use of contiguous segments (of different step size) that occurs as the input peak level ($\sqrt{2}$ times input rms level) varies with changing input power level. This jerkiness is not present with speech or Gaussian inputs to the coder. The reason is that with these signals, the power level (rms value) and "peak" value are more decoupled, not being simple deterministic functions of each other.

Figure 5.10 also shows the CCITT specification for minimum *SNR* as a function of input level. Although this dynamic range characteristic refers to measurements with a narrow-band noise input, it is used as a standard specification for a *toll quality* PCM speech coder.

Toll Quality Coding. Log-PCM at 64 kb/s is a time-honored basis for speech coding because it is a low-complexity technique with zero delay [Cattermole, 1969] [Owen, 1982]. It also provides *toll quality* in a strict communication network sense, a property not always possessed by the *high quality* speech coders of future chapters. The motivation for these coders of course is that they offer better speech quality at bit rates considerably lower than 64 kb/s. For example, Figure 1.5 has shown that at 32 kb/s, the subjective quality (Mean Opinion Score) provided by log-PCM drops to a value of less than 3, on a scale of 1 to 5; while the quality offered by *medium-* and *high complexity* coders is in the neighborhood of 4.0.

As noted in Chapter 1, toll quality coding implies an MOS score of nearly 4.5 on a scale of 1 to 5. We will note this presently in Figure 5.11. It should be emphasized, however, that an *SNR* of 38 dB and an MOS of 4.5 are to be regarded only as necessary conditions of toll quality coding. For example, one additional condition that may be demanded in communication networks is that the speech coder can pass voiceband data signals with very few penalties in received data error rate (for example, an error rate less than 10^{-6} with voiceband data waveforms at data rates up to 4800 b/s). This condition is also met by 64 kb/s log-PCM speech coders with $\mu = 255$ or $A = 87.56$ [Raulin et al., 1982]. Further conditions for toll quality can be specified in terms of idle channel noise and performance with multiple stages of coding and decoding.

5.3.6 Idle Channel Noise and Tandem Coding

A complete characterization of PCM coding noise in speech networks depends on at least two other specifications: *idle channel noise* and performance with *multiple coding.*

Idle channel noise is the coding noise with a zero input. Strictly speaking, this noise power equals $\Delta^2/4$ for a midtread quantizer (which encodes zero or near-zero amplitudes by one of the innermost output levels $\pm \Delta/2$); and it equals zero for a midrise quantizer (whose output for a zero input is supposed to be zero, by definition). In practice, however, the idle channel input is never exactly zero, due to finite amounts of background noise or crosstalk [Shenoi and Agrawal, 1980]. In addition, practical quantizer characteristics can be non-ideal. As a consequence, the idle channel noise with midtread quantization will also be in the order of, although less than, $\Delta^2/4$. This $\Delta^2/4$ value, together with the peak input-to-minimum step size ratios in Table 5.4, and typical peak-to-rms ratios in speech, suggests idle channel noise levels in the order of 60 dB in the toll quality coder (Problem 5.6).

Multiple or *tandem codings*, with D/A conversion at the output of each coding stage, are important in speech communication networks involving a mixture of analog and digital components. The quality of a coder then depends on the nature of a function $SNR(n)$, the signal-to-noise ratio at the output of the nth encoding stage. On the basis of identical PCM coders in each stage, each of which adds a constant amount of signal-independent and previous-stage-independent noise, the function $SNR(n)$ can be shown to have the recursive forms (Problem 5.7)

$$SNR(n) \text{ (dB)} = SNR(1) \text{ (dB)} - 10 \log_{10} n \qquad (5.12a)$$

$$= SNR(n-1) \text{ (dB)} - 10 \log_{10}[n/(n-1)] \qquad (5.12b)$$

It should be emphasized that (5.12) is merely a simplified model; real PCM 1982].

An even better characterization of tandeming performance is in terms of subjective speech quality as a function of n. This is shown in Figure 5.11 in terms of Mean Opinion Scores (on a scale of 1 to 5). These MOS ratings are for asynchronous encodings, implying D/A conversion at the output of each coding stage. The MOS ratings are shown for three coders — $\mu 255$ PCM, and two lower bit rate DPCM coders to be discussed in Chapter 6. It is seen that the performance gap between 64 kb/s PCM and the contending coders is an increasing

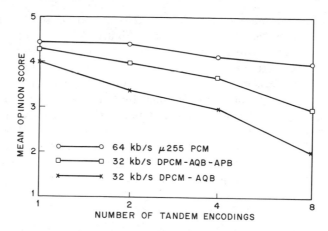

Figure 5.11 Subjective effect of coding noise with multiple "asynchronous" encodings, implying D/A conversion at the output of each coding stage. The DPCM-AQB coder uses robust adaptive quantization with a one-word memory, and fixed first-order prediction (Section 6.4). The DPCM-AQB-APB system uses adaptive algorithms for quantization as well as prediction (Section 6.5.3) [Petr, 1982].

function of number of encodings n. The fact that the MOS rating in the PCM system goes down by no more than 0.5 even after 8 encodings suggests a significant factor of safety built into the 64 kb/s PCM design. The slopes of the characteristics in the figure also suggest that 64 kb/s PCM is inherently more robust in the context of repeated encodings.

5.4 Transmission Error Effects

In Chapter 4 we discussed the effects of random bit errors on quantizer performance. We expressed channel error variance σ_c^2 as a product of bit error rate p_e and a channel coefficient ξ that was a function of quantizer and binary code, and we expressed the total reconstruction error variance σ_r^2 as the sum of quantization error variance σ_q^2 and channel error variance σ_c^2 (4.158b):

$$\sigma_r^2 = \sigma_q^2 + \sigma_c^2 = \sigma_q^2 + \xi\, p_e\, \sigma_x^2 \tag{5.13}$$

In the special case of a uniform pdf input (a good model for images), and uniform quantization with NBC coding, the channel coefficient can be analytically expressed (4.174):

$$\xi = 4(1 - 2^{-2R}) \tag{5.14}$$

Setting this in (5.13), and using (4.31) to obtain σ_q^2 with $f_l = \sqrt{3}$ (Example 4.3), we obtain a closed-form *SNR* result for $R \gg 1$:

$$SNR \text{ (dB)} \approx 6.02\, R - 10 \log_{10}(1 + 2^{2(R+1)}p_e) \text{ for images ;} \qquad R \gg 1 \tag{5.15}$$

According to the last equation, if $R = 8$ and $p_e = 10^{-4}$, the *SNR* loss due to channel errors is 14.3 dB (also see Figure 4.33a). We also demonstrated that quantizing and coding systems can be made more robust in the sense of designing them for an optimum ξ. We will note presently, in Figures 5.13 and 5.14(b), that perceptual effects of $p_e = 10^{-4}$ can be quite serious in image coding.

For speech applications we noted that values of ξ are smaller in log-quantizers as a class, compared with uniform quantizers, for given binary code and R [Figure 4.38(a)]. We also showed [Figure 4.33(b)] that if $R = 8$, the *SNR* loss at $p_e = 10^{-4}$ is over 10 dB; and at $p_e = 10^{-2}$, the *SNR* loss is about 30 dB: this is the channel-limited region in Figure 4.33(b). The *SNR* loss of 30 dB is indeed reflected by the perceptual effects of $p_e = 10^{-2}$ in speech coding, as reflected in an MOS score that drops to 2.0, from a value of 4.3 at $p_e = 0$ (Figure 5.14a).

The purpose of the present section is to emphasize the perceptual effects of bit errors on PCM systems for audio and video applications; and to discuss additional techniques for the mitigation of error effects when p_e values are too high for the quantizer refinements in Section 4.9 to be effective. The higher values of error rate (say, $p_e > 10^{-3}$) may be encountered in digital radio systems. High quality speech systems conforming to CCITT standards are actually switched off when $p_e > 10^{-3}$.

5.4.1 Effects of Random Bit Errors on Speech and Image Waveforms

Figures 5.12 and 5.13 demonstrate the effect of bit errors on speech and image PCM systems with $R = 8$, FBC coding and error rates of $p_e = 0.5\%$ for speech, and 0.6% for images. These are clearly unacceptable error rates for both examples. Based on illustrative perceptual tests, the MOS score with these error rates drops, from the best value of 4.5 to a value of 2.2 in speech coding [Figure 5.14(a)], and from 4.8 to an extrapolated value of less than 2.0 in image coding [Figure 5.14(b)]. The most harmful events in both cases are those where the higher order bits (say, the first and second most significant bits in the 8-bit word) are received in error; these are the error types that produce the greatest contributions $|y_k - z_j|^2$ (Figure 4.35) to channel error variance. They are also the perceptually most serious error types. The spikes in Figure 5.12 and the dark and bright spots in Figure 5.13 are significant. They represent channel error effects that are localized in time and

Figure 5.12 Effects of bit errors on 8-bit log PCM coding of speech ($\mu\,255$; FBC coding): (a) decoder output with $p_e = 0$; and (b) decoder output with $p_e = 5 \cdot 10^{-3}$ [Jayant, 1982].

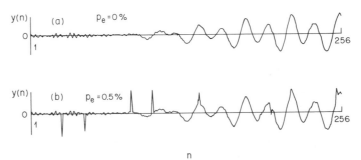

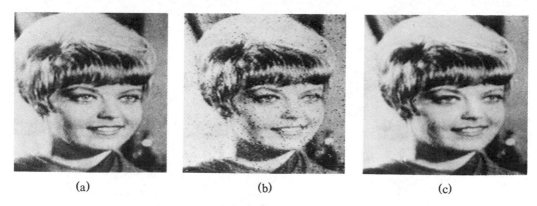

(a)   (b)   (c)

Figure 5.13 Effects of bit errors on 8-bit PCM coding of a 128×128 image (FBC coding): (a) decoder output with $p_e = 0$; (b) decoder output with $p_e = 6 \cdot 10^{-3}$; and (c) result of error-detection in (b) followed by interpolation estimates of error-corrupted samples [Ngan and Steele;©1982, IEEE].

space. This localization occurs because PCM encoding and decoding operations are memoryless. In the DPCM chapter we will note the contrasting situation of non-localized error effects due to decoder memory. In the coding of images, DPCM errors manifest as streaks which could be more visible and degrading than the spots of Figure 5.13. But in the case of speech waveforms, the localized error spikes in PCM are perceptually more degrading than the smeared-out effects in a coder with memory.

The above differences in the channel error sensitivities of PCM-coded speech and images are further demonstrated by the subjective results in Figure 5.14. The error-sensitivity of PCM-coded speech is demonstrated in the comparison with two differential coders in Figure 5.14(a). These coders will be described in Chapters 6 and 8. Contrast this result with the comparison of Figure 5.11 where PCM was shown to be maximally robust in the context of tandem encoding. On the other hand, in image coding, differential coders perform worse as a class than PCM, in the context of channel errors. This is shown in Figure 5.14(b). Recall, finally, the concept of quantizer-limited and channel-limited regions of operation introduced in Figure 4.33. From the subjective viewpoint, very significant channel error degradation is evident at $p_e = 10^{-3}$ in speech transmission [Figure 5.14(a)], and at $p_e = 10^{-4}$ [Figure 5.14(b)] in image transmission. At these error rates, respective MOS ratings of output quality drop by more than 1 point on a scale of 1 to 5.

The discrete spikes and spots in Figures 5.12 and 5.13 also suggest a simple rule-of-thumb for estimating acceptable levels of p_e. Assuming that the most perceived channel errors are those affecting the first s most significant bits, and assuming *one spot or spike per t seconds* as an empirical threshold of acceptability, the tolerable error rate will be $(stf_s)^{-1}$, where f_s is the waveform sampling rate (see Problem 5.8). Consider the example of $s = 4$ and $t = 1$. For telephone speech and broadcast video, this rule corresponds (using Table 1.1) to acceptable error rates of approximately 10^{-4} and 10^{-7}, respectively. Criteria for digital music fidelity are much more stringent ($t \gg 1$), and such levels of high fidelity are maintained by explicit error protection procedures (Section 5.4.2).

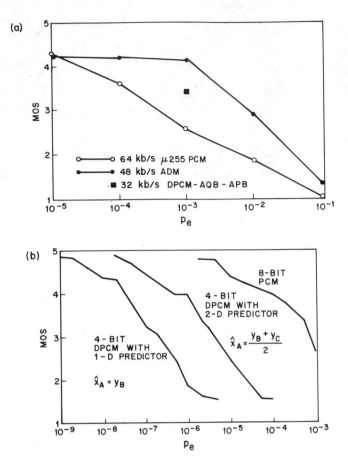

Figure 5.14 (a) MOS ratings for different speech coders as a function of random bit error rate p_e. The DPCM coder is similar, but not identical to that defined in Figure 5.11. The ADM coder is a DM system with syllabic adaptation of step-size using a (4, 4, 1) logic (Chapter 8) [Daumer and Cavanaugh,©1978, AT&T] [CCITT, 1983]. (b) MOS ratings for different image coders as a function of bit error rate [Kummerow, 1981].

5.4.2 Signal Protection Based on Explicit Redundancy

Some of the coder refinements of Chapter 4 affected the transmitter; they in fact compromised coder performance with $p_e = 0$, being matched only to one specific error rate $p_e > 0$. PCM redesigns involving substantial error protection coding are an extreme example of compromising coder capabilities in anticipation of bad channels. For example, if the least significant 2 of the 8 bits in a PCM system are stolen for algebraic error-protection [Rydbeck and Sundberg, 1975, 1976] [Sundberg and Rydbeck, 1976], the maximum possible SNR is reduced by 12 dB, and the error-protected 6-bit system performs better than an unprotected 8-bit system only in the channel-noise-dominated situation [Figure 4.33(a)] described by $p_e > p_{eqc}$, an appropriately defined threshold probability. Problem 4.26 discusses the value of p_{eqc} analytically. Estimates of p_{eqc} based on perceptual evaluations will in general be smaller in PCM coding because channel errors are much more noticeable than quantization errors of identical variance. For example, the measured SNR difference between the images in Figures 5.13(a) and 5.13(b) is 12 dB, suggesting a 2 bit difference; but the image in Figure 5.13(b) will be much less acceptable than a 6-bit PCM output with $p_e = 0$.

Explicit error protection is extremely critical in the PCM transmission of *digital audio* with high fidelity. If the expected error rate p_e is in the order of 10^{-5} or more, and if the total bit rate is fixed, it is useful to steal 1, or even 2 least significant bits, in order to provide parity checks on the more significant PCM bits; this is done although stealing of 2 bits may result in a perceptible increase of quantization noise.

In the *compact disc* application, the 16-bit codewords are error-protected using a Reed Solomon code. This increases the total number of bits in the ratio 4:3, but corrects many classes of error patterns expected in the system. For example, error bursts with lengths up to 4000 bits (corresponding to a 2.5 mm track length on the disc) are completely correctable. Error-affected samples that cannot be corrected can still be detected and replaced by using an enhancement procedure (see the next section). The undetected error rate is 1 every 750 hours, if the original bit error rate p_e is 10^{-3} [Hoeve, Timmermans and Vries, 1982].

5.4.3 Signal Enhancement Based on Natural Redundancy

The fact that the PCM decoder is a memoryless device suggests relatively simple techniques for detecting channel errors in its output, which can be followed by appropriate enhancement procedures. The efficacy of this approach is illustrated in Figure 5.13(c). Error detection in this system is based on an algorithm for detecting unexpected differences in the video output $y(n)$. The rms value $\sigma_{\Delta y}$ of adjacent pixel differences is evaluated once for each block of 64 pixels. Whenever the magnitude of an instantaneous difference $y(n) - y(n-1)$ exceeds $m\sigma_{\Delta y}$ ($m = 5$ in the design of the illustrated scheme), $y(n)$ is deemed to be in error. This amplitude is then re-estimated by *second-order nearest neighbor interpolation*: simply as the average of two past (corrected) and two future (yet uncorrected) pixel amplitudes [Ngan and Steele, 1982]. Similar techniques have proved useful for enhancing speech as well [Steele and Goodman, 1977] [Steele, Ngan and Goodman, 1978].

Detection of amplitude errors can also be accomplished by *soft-zone decisions*. Here the input to the PCM decoder is no longer binary (1 and 0), but includes a third "erasure" symbol which is outputted by a receiver (the demodulator of Figure 1.2b) when it is in doubt, suggesting a high probability of bit inversion in a hard binary decision [Sundberg, 1978] [Jayant et al., 1980]; and hence a high probability of an amplitude error in PCM output $y(n)$. Correction of detected amplitude errors can likewise follow many approaches. For example, it may be adequate sometimes to use a *first-order interpolator* or a *zero-order extrapolator*. In the former case, re-estimation involves the averaging of one past and one future sample. In zero-order extrapolation, one simply replaces a suspect amplitude by that of the previous sample.

The interpolation approach has also been proposed for digital audio applications [Blesser and Kates, 1978]. In the *compact disc* system, an explicit error protection algorithm indicates uncorrectable errors. Corresponding signal samples are then replaced by linear first order interpolations using past and future neighbors, if these neighbors are detected as being reliable samples. If this is not possible, as in the case of certain burst error patterns, the audio signal is electronically muted for an appropriate length of time [Hoeve, Timmermans and Vries, 1982].

A very efficient technique for error correction is the nonlinear approach of *median filtering* [Rabiner, Sambur and Schmidt, 1975] [Jayant, 1976] [Steele and Goodman, 1977]. With highly correlated signals and impulsive errors, median filtering offers the possibility of detecting and correcting improbable amplitude peaks without at the same time destroying legitimate signal peaks and patterns, which is a problem encountered in many classes of linear filtering. (See Problem 5.9 for a simple example).

Common to all the enhancement techniques discussed above is the property that they are optional refinements of the PCM receiver. They leave the PCM transmitter unaffected. This is a good philosophy when the PCM coder is expected, with a high probability, to operate in a clean environment.

Problems

(5.1)   Consider a waveform storage system with 64 kbytes of memory (1 byte = 8 bits). Assume that high-quality coders are available that can represent either audio or video inputs with 8 bits/sample.

    (a)   Calculate the maximum resolution N of an $N \times N$ square pixel array that can be stored in this system.

    (b)   Calculate the length of speech (in seconds) that can be stored in this system assuming a sampling frequency of 8 kHz.

(5.2)   The quality of image coding systems is sometimes measured as the ratio SNR' of peak signal to rms error. Assuming a uniform pdf at the input of the image coder, show that

$$SNR' \text{ (dB)} = 6.02R + 10.8$$

instead of the SNR (dB) $= 6.02R$ result of (5.1a).

(5.3)   In a PCM-AQF system for music, $f_s = 40$ kHz and $R = 10$ bits/sample. The quantizer step size is recomputed once every millisecond, and it is encoded for transmission (over an error-free channel) using 5 bits or 32 levels. Show that the effective transmission rate is 10.125 bits/sample.

(5.4)   Assume that in an R-bit PCM system, the least significant bit is stolen once every M samples for signaling purposes. Show that the SNR loss due to bit stealing is $10 \log_{10} (1+3/M)$ dB, assuming the exponential performance characteristic implied in (4.74) and (4.91a). For example, if $M = 6$, the SNR loss is 1.77 dB [Bellamy, 1982].

(5.5)   Consider the piecewise linear system of Figure 5.6 with

$$s_{max} = 7, \, l_{max} = 15 \, ; \quad s_{min} = l_{min} = 0 \, .$$

Show, by using (5.8) and (5.10), that in the μ 255 law,

(a)   the innermost output levels (corresponding to 8-bit codes [10000000] and [00000000] are ± 0.0; and that

(b)   the outermost output levels (corresponding to 8-bit codes [11111111] and [01111111] are ± 4015.5.

(5.6)   Assume an idle channel noise power of $\Delta^2(0)/4$. Assume a peak-to-rms ratio in speech in the order of 15 dB. Use the results of Table 5.4 to show that the signal-to-idle channel noise ratios in 15-segment μ 255 and 13-segment A 87.56 systems (both with $R = 8$) are 63 and 57 dB, respectively.

(5.7)   Show that under the assumption of equal amounts of signal-independent encoding noise during every encoding stage, the coder SNR as a function of number of encoding stages n follows the relations

(a) $SNR(n)$ (dB) $= SNR(1)$ (dB) $- 10 \log_{10} n \, (n > 1)$

(b) $SNR(n)$ (dB) $= SNR(n-1)$ (dB) $- 10 \log_{10} (n/(n-1)) \, (n > 1) \, .$

(5.8)   Consider a PCM system for waveform communication. Let the sampling rate be f_s kHz. Assuming that a threshold of acceptability corresponds to errors affecting either of the first two most significant bits in the PCM word, once in t seconds, show that the acceptable random error rate is $\max\{p_e\} = (2000 t f_s)^{-1} \, .$

(5.9)   Consider the non-increasing input $\{20, 18, 16, 14, 12, 10, 8, 6, 4, 2, \ldots \}$. Assume that a random transmission error alters the value of the sixth sample from 10 to 50.

(a)   Show that smoothing of the output input using a running mean with a 3-sample window leads to a non-monotonic output with a maximum residual error of 17.8.

(b)   Show that smoothing of the output using a running median with a 3-sample window leads to a monotonically non-increasing result (as in the original input), with a maximum residual error of 4.0.

References

J. P. Adoul, "Backward Adaptive Re-encoding: A Technique for Reducing the Bit Rate of μ-Law PCM Transmissions," IEEE Trans. on Communications, pp. 581-592, April 1982.

J. C. Bellamy, *Digital Telephony,* John Wiley, New York, 1982.

G. H. Bennett, *PCM and Digital Transmission,* Marconi Instruments, 100 Stonehurst Court, Northvale, N.J., 1978.

B. Blesser and J. M. Kates, "Digital Processing in Audio Signals," Chapter 2 in A. V. Oppenheim (ed.), *Applications of Digital Signal Processing,"* Prentice-Hall, Englewood Cliffs, N.J., 1978.

R. A. Bruce, "Optimum Pre-emphasis and De-emphasis Networks for Transmission of Television by PCM," IEEE Trans. on Communication Technology, pp. 91-96, September 1964.

K. W. Cattermole, *Principles of Pulse Code Modulation*, Iliffe, London, 1969.

J. R. Cavanaugh, private communication, Bell Laboratories, 1982.

CCIR, "Encoding Parameters of Digital Television for Studios," Rec. 601, 1982.

CCITT Study Group XVIII, Ad Hoc Group on 32 kb/s ADPCM Algorithms, Temporary Document, July 1983.

M. G. Croll, M. E. B. Moffat and D. W. Osborne, "Nearly Instantaneous Compander for Transmitting Six Sound Program Signals in a 2.048 Mb/s Multiplex," Electronics Letters, July 1973.

C. L. Damann, L. D. McDaniel and C. L. Maddox, "D2 Channel Band: Multiplexing and Coding," Bell System Tech. J., pp. 1675-1699, October 1972.

W. R. Daumer and J. R. Cavanaugh, "A Subjective Comparison of Selected Digital Codecs for Speech," Bell System Tech. J., pp. 3119-3166, November 1978.

D. L. Duttweiler and D. G. Messerschmitt, "Nearly Instantaneous Companding and Time Diversity as Applied to Mobile Radio Transmission," Proc. Int. Conf. on Communications, pp. 40-12 to 40-15, San Francisco, June 1975.

R. C. Gonzalez and P. Wintz, *Digital Image Processing*, Addison-Wesley, Reading, Mass., 1977.

J. C. Hancock, *Introduction to the Principles of Communication Theory*, McGraw-Hill, New York, 1961.

H. Hoeve, J. Timmermans and L. B. Vries, "Error Correction and Concealment in the Compact Disc System," Philips Technical Review, pp. 166-172, 1982.

N. S. Jayant, "Average- and Median-Based Smoothing Techniques for Improving Digital Speech Quality in the Presence of Transmission Errors," IEEE Trans. on Communications, pp. 1043-1045, September 1976.

N. S. Jayant, unpublished work, Bell Laboratories, 1982.

N. S. Jayant, R. Steele, N. W. Chan and C. E. Schmidt, "On Soft Decision Demodulation for PCM- and DPCM-Encoded Speech," IEEE Trans. on Communications, pp. 308-311, February 1980.

H. Kaneko, "A Unified Formulation of Segment Companding Laws and Synthesis of Codecs and Digital Companders," Bell System Tech. J., pp. 1555-1588, September 1970.

T. Kummerow, "Der Einfluss von Übertragungsfehlern bei der DPCM-codierten Übertragung von Farbfernsehsignalen," Technischer Bericht Nr. 214, Heinrich Hertz Institut, Berlin, May 1981.

J. O. Limb, C. B. Rubinstein and J. E. Thompson, "Digital Coding of Color Video Signals — A Review," IEEE Trans. on Communications, pp. 1349-1385, November 1977.

Members of Technical Staff, Bell Laboratories, *Transmission Systems for Communications*, Western Electric Company, Technical Publications, Winston-Salem, N.C., 1971.

A. N. Netravali and J. O. Limb, "Picture Coding," Proc. IEEE, pp. 366-406, March 1980.

K. N. Ngan and R. Steele, "Enhancement of PCM and DPCM Images Corrupted by Transmission Errors," IEEE Trans. on Communications, pp. 257-265, January 1982.

B. M. Oliver, J. R. Pierce and C. E. Shannon, "The Philosophy of PCM," Proc. IEEE, pp. 1324-1331, November 1948.

F. Owen, *PCM and Digital Transmission Systems*, McGraw Hill, New York, 1982.

D. W. Petr, "32 kbps ADPCM-DLQ Coding for Network Applications," Proc. IEEE Globecom Conference, pp. 239-243, December 1982.

W. K. Pratt, *Image Coding,* John Wiley, New York, 1978.

L. R. Rabiner, M. R. Sambur and C. E. Schmidt, "Applications of a Nonlinear Smoothing Algorithm to Speech Processing," IEEE Trans. on Acoustics, Speech and Signal Proc., pp. 552-557, December 1975.

J.-M. Raulin, G. Bonnerot, J.-L. Leandot and R. Lacroix, "A 60 Channel PCM-ADPCM Converter," IEEE Trans. on Communications, pp. 567-573, April 1982.

A. Rosenfeld and A. C. Kak, *Digital Picture Processing,* Academic Press, New York, 1976.

N. Rydbeck and C. E. W. Sundberg, "Techniques for Introducing Error-Correcting Codes into TDMA Satellite Communication Systems," Ericsson Technics, pp. 217-246, 1975.

N. Rydbeck and C. E. W. Sundberg, "Analysis of Digital Errors in Nonlinear PCM Systems," IEEE Trans. on Communications, pp. 59-65, January 1976.

K. Shenoi and B. P. Agrawal, "Selection of a PCM Coder for Digital Switching," IEEE Trans. on Acoustics, Speech and Signal Proc., pp. 545-550, October 1980.

W. F. Schreiber, "Image Processing for Quality Improvement," Proc. IEEE, pp. 1640-1651, December 1978.

R. Steele and D. J. Goodman, "Detection and Selective Smoothing of Transmission Errors in Linear PCM," Bell System Tech. J., pp. 399-409, March 1977.

R. Steele, K. N. Ngan and D. J. Goodman, "Adaptive Difference Detection and Correction System for Partial Correction of Transmission Errors in Linear PCM," Electronics Letters, pp. 381-382, June 1978.

R. Steele, N. S. Jayant and C. E. Schmidt, "Statistical Block Protection Coding," Bell System Tech. J., pp. 1647-1657, September 1979.

C. E. W. Sundberg, "Soft Decision Demodulation for PCM Encoded Speech Signals," IEEE Trans. on Communications, pp. 854-860, June 1978.

C. E. W. Sundberg and N. Rydbeck, "PCM with Error Correcting Codes for TDMA Satellite Communication Systems," Ericsson Technics, pp. 3-56, 1976.

H. L. Van Trees (ed.), *Satellite Communications,* IEEE Press, New York, 1979.

6

Differential PCM

6.1 Introduction

In Chapter 2, we characterized speech and image signals as redundant waveforms. In this and in the two succeeding chapters, we describe *differential coding* or *predictive coding* systems where waveform redundancy is utilized in time-domain operations to realize straightforward reductions in bit rate, for a specified quality of digitization. *Differential PCM* (DPCM) coders, which are based on the notion of quantizing a prediction error signal, are important examples of predictive coding systems [Cutler, 1952] [Oliver, 1952] [Elias, 1955]. DPCM systems with one-bit quantizers constitute an important subclass, *deltamodulation* (Chapter 8).

The *linear predictors* mentioned in Section 2.5 constitute a central topic of discussion in the present chapter. The complexity of a DPCM system is directly related to that of the predictor algorithm. Predictors based on recent waveform history and time-invariant predictor coefficients (Section 6.4) lead to a class of coders which constitutes one example of the *low-to-medium-complexity* designs in Figures 1.5 and 1.6. These coders utilize *time-invariant* or *fixed* speech predictors and *intraframe* image predictors for high-quality digitizations at bit rates in the order of $R = 3$ or 4 bits/sample, in each case. DPCM systems of *high complexity* are characterized by the use of *adaptive predictors* matched to short-time input spectrum (Section 6.5), and/or the use of *distant-sample-memory* for utilizing waveform periodicities (Section 6.6). Examples of the latter are *pitch predictors* for speech and *interframe* predictors for video. These complex approaches are necessary for high-quality coding with $R = 2$ or 1 bits/sample.

The quantizer refinements discussed in Chapter 4 are also applicable to the *prediction error quantizers* of DPCM systems. For example, nonuniform and adaptive quantizers are taken for granted in DPCM systems for video and speech, respectively; and in both cases, entropy-coded quantizers lead to significant gains, especially at lower bit rates. Quantizer designs used specifically in DPCM systems will be cited as and when appropriate.

6.1.1 DPCM versus PCM: The Prediction Gain

By representing a correlated waveform in terms of appropriate difference samples, or prediction error samples, one can achieve an increased *SNR* at a given bit rate; or equivalently, a reduction of bit rate for a given requirement of *SNR*. This can be appreciated at least qualitatively for the simple but important case where the correlation ρ_1 between adjacent samples approaches unity. In this case, assume that the encoder represents the waveform as a succession of adjacent sample differences $\{x(n)-x(n-1)\}$; that these difference samples are quantized for transmission; and that a decoder recovers an approximation to the input essentially by integrating quantized adjacent sample differences. With $\rho_1 \rightarrow 1$, the variance of the quantizer input is much smaller than that of the coder input $x(n)$; and since quantization error variance is proportional to quantizer input variance for a given number of bits/sample R (Chapter 4), the above reduction of quantizer input variance leads directly to a reduction of reconstruction error variance σ_r^2 for a given value of R. In general, the quantizer input in a DPCM coder is a *prediction error* or *difference signal*

$$d(n) = x(n) - \hat{x}(n) \tag{6.1}$$

where $\hat{x}(n)$ is a *prediction* of $x(n)$, and the ratio

$$G_P = \sigma_x^2/\sigma_d^2 \tag{6.2}$$

is a corresponding *prediction gain*. With some qualifications to be noted presently, the prediction gain will be seen to represent the *SNR* improvement in going from PCM to DPCM [McDonald, 1966]. For the important sub-class of *linear predictors*, the prediction gain is upper-bounded by the inverse of spectral flatness measure γ_x^2 defined in Chapter 2. The performance of DPCM systems will be bounded by the following expression for minimum mean square value of reconstruction error $r(n) = x(n) - y(n)$:

$$\min\{\sigma_r^2\} = \epsilon_q^2 \gamma_x^2 \sigma_x^2 ; \quad \gamma_x^2 \leqslant 1 \tag{6.3}$$

Note in contrast that the distortion in a PCM system is $\epsilon_q^2 \sigma_x^2$. Thus, by exploiting input signal redundancies, DPCM coding will realize a decrease of error variance by a factor that could be as much as γ_x^2. As noted in Chapter 2, typical values of γ_x^2 for long-term speech and image spectra are in the order of 1/8 and 1/16 respectively. Much smaller values are realized in short-term voiced speech spectra (say, $\gamma_x^2 \leqslant 1/256$) and in the spectra of low-activity images.

6.1.2 Closed-Loop DPCM with Feedback around Quantizer

Consider a prediction $\hat{x}(n)$ based on many previous input samples $x(n-1)$, $x(n-2)$, ... The best possible prediction of $x(n)$, for a minimum mean square error (mmse), is the conditional expectation

$$\hat{x}(n) = E[X(n)|X(n-1), X(n-2),...] \tag{6.4a}$$

The above predictor is impractical for two reasons. First, the conditional (or joint) pdf needed to evaluate (6.4a) will in general not be available; and DPCM systems, unless otherwise mentioned, will use linear prediction algorithms whose design and performance depend only on second-order statistics. Second, in order that the transmitter and receiver parts of the DPCM system track (and reconstruct) input waveforms in synchrony, it will be desirable, if not essential, that the prediction $\hat{x}(n)$ depend on previous quantized values $y(n) = \tilde{x}(n)$ rather than on previous unquantized inputs $x(n)$. Incorporation of this property leads to the *closed-loop* or *feedback-around-quantizer* structure of Figure 6.1.

The DPCM coder uses linear prediction of the input in the form

$$\hat{x}(n) = \sum_{j=1}^{N} h_j \, \tilde{x}(n-j) \tag{6.4b}$$

where $\mathbf{h} = \{h_j\}$; $j = 1,2,...,N$ is a set of predictor coefficients. Borrowing from the notation of (2.85), (2.86) and Figure 2.15, we will refer to the predictor in (6.4b) as an *all-pole predictor*. The DPCM decoder filter will have the structure of Figure 2.15, and the all-pole property is really a characterization of this filter (Section 6.3.4). It is also possible to define an *all-zero predictor* in the form

$$\hat{x}(n) = \sum_{j=1}^{M} g_j \, u(n-j) \tag{6.4c}$$

The corresponding decoder filter will have the structure of Figure 2.19. This structure has good properties in the presence of transmission errors, and it is in fact used as part of a specific, but important DPCM system, in Section 6.5.3. However, unless otherwise mentioned, our discussions will refer to the more widely understood all-pole structure in (6.4b) and Figure 6.1. Also, unless otherwise mentioned, DPCM coding will imply the closed-loop operation used in this figure; and, except in Sections 6.5 and 6.7, the channel for transmitting quantized prediction error information is assumed error-free, as noted in Figure 6.1.

The coder of Figure 6.1 can be regarded as a generalized quantizer whose zero- or center-point keeps getting shifted to the latest value of $\hat{x}(n)$ [Cattermole, 1969]. This shifting aligns the quantizer with the amplitude range(s) most likely to be occupied by $x(n)$, and enables the encoder to use finer quantization (than in PCM) for a given number of quantization levels. Clearly, quantizer shifting implies predictability of $x(n)$. In the trivial case of an uncorrelated or i.i.d. input, the best possible estimate $\hat{x}(n)$ is simply the unconditional mean value (typically zero) for all n; and the best encoding strategy merely uses a zero-mean quantizer for all n

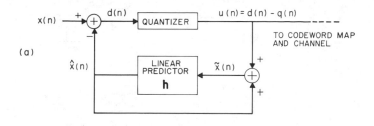

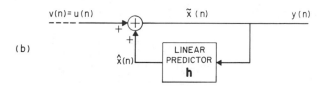

Figure 6.1 Block diagram of DPCM: (a) coder; and (b) decoder.

(non-differential PCM, as in Chapter 5). The quantizer-shift interpretation was already anticipated in Figure 4.39(c).

The block diagram of Figure 6.1 is merely a schematic. Implementations of DPCM may produce several variations. Two possibilities for the DPCM coder are illustrated in Figure 6.2. In (a) and (b) the signal paths are mostly analog, except for the parts between the A/D and D/A boxes. In (b) and (c) many of the coder paths are digital. The adaptive quantizer in (b) is typical of speech practice. In (c) all the signals of the coder circuit are digital, including the input $x(n)$, which, for example, may be an 8-bit number, as in video practice. The classifier in (c) is merely a nonlinear quantizer with a finite-resolution input and the weighter in the feedback loop is needed to provide a linear representation $\tilde{x}(n)$ at the predictor input. The predictor itself is shown as an analog filter in (a), and as a digital filter in (b). In the simplest version of DPCM in Section 6.1.1, this filter is merely a one-sample delay.

The basic equations describing DPCM are, from Figure 6.1,

$$d(n) = x(n) - \hat{x}(n) \tag{6.5}$$
$$u(n) = d(n) - q(n) \tag{6.6}$$
$$\text{and} \quad y(n) = \hat{x}(n) + v(n) \tag{6.7}$$

where $y(n)$ is the DPCM approximation to coder input $x(n)$, $d(n)$ is the prediction error, $q(n)$ is the quantization error, $u(n)$ is the quantized prediction error, and $v(n)$ is the receiver version thereof. Notice that with error-free reception of $u(n)$ [i.e., $v(n) = u(n)$] the predictor input at the transmitter is

$$\tilde{x}(n) = \hat{x}(n) + u(n) = \hat{x}(n) + v(n) = y(n) \tag{6.8}$$

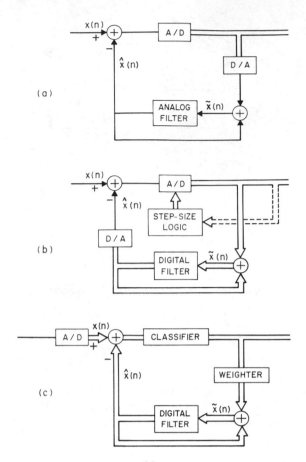

Figure 6.2 Variations of a DPCM coder: (a) an "analog" implementation with a fixed uniform quantizer; (b) a "digital" implementation with an adaptive quantizer; and (c) a "digital" implementation with a fixed nonuniform quantizer.

The fact that $y(n) = \tilde{x}(n)$ is available at the transmitter (as a "locally decoded" value) means that both transmitter and receiver can use the same prediction algorithm:

$$\hat{x}(n) = f[y(n-1), y(n-2),...] \tag{6.9}$$

An alternative algorithm such as

$$\hat{x}(n) = f[x(n-1), x(n-2),...] \tag{6.10}$$

would have the advantage of better predictions at the encoder, based on uncorrupted input samples rather than on quantization-noise-corrupted samples as in (6.9). However, in this case, the receiver would still be forced to employ (6.9), and differing prediction values at the encoder and decoder would result in an overall poorer mse performance. The *open-loop* structure implied in (6.10) can, however, provide better performance with certain types of frequency-weighted error criteria. This will be demonstrated in Chapter 7.

The Case of $\hat{x}(n) = x(n-1)$. The simplest DPCM predictor is the unit delay operator defined by $\hat{x}(n) = x(n-1)$, or $h_1 = 1$. In this case, the DPCM decoder is simply a *perfect integrator*:

$$y(n) = \hat{x}(n) + u(n) = \tilde{x}(n-1) + u(n) = y(n-1) + u(n) \qquad (6.11)$$

With a more general predictor in the DPCM coder, the DPCM decoder takes on a more general form as well. The more general DPCM decoder is sometimes referred to as a *leaky integrator*.

Reconstruction Error in DPCM. We shall now show that in DPCM the *reconstruction error $r(n)$* for sample n is identical to the *quantization error $q(n)$* defined in (6.6). The coding error or reconstruction error is defined as

$$r(n) = x(n) - y(n) \qquad (6.12a)$$

It follows from (6.5), (6.6), (6.7) and (6.11), and simple algebra, that *with error-free transmission of $u(n)$* [i.e., $v(n) = u(n)$],

$$r(n) = q(n) \qquad (6.12b)$$

The above formula [Gish, 1967] reflects an important property of the "closed-loop" predictive coding scheme of Figure 6.1, the property that quantization noise does not accumulate [in the sense of contributing to future samples of reconstruction error $r(n)$]. The mse performance of DPCM is thus described completely by

$$\sigma_r^2 = \sigma_q^2 \qquad (6.13)$$

The term $\sigma_q^2 = E[Q^2(n)]$ depends on the conditions at the quantizer input, and on the quantizer itself. Thus

$$\sigma_r^2 = \sigma_q^2 = \epsilon_q^2 \sigma_d^2 \qquad (6.14)$$

where $\sigma_d^2 = E[D^2(n)]$ is the *difference-signal (prediction error) variance* and ϵ_q^2 is the quantizer performance factor (noise variance for unit input variance), which depends on the type of quantizer used, the number of levels therein, and the pdf of the quantizer input.

The fact that $r(n) = q(n)$ [see (6.12)] also implies that the spectrum of the reconstruction error equals that of the quantization error. Thus if $S_{qq}(e^{j\omega})$ is white, which is a good model in the case of optimal prediction (Section 6.3.1) and adequately fine quantization ($R > 2$, Section 4.7), $S_{rr}(e^{j\omega})$ will be white as well. We shall comment on the statistical properties of $r(n)$ again in Section 6.3.4, and in the context of speech and image examples.

6.1.3 Slope Overload and Granular Noise

The operation of a DPCM coder is illustrated by the waveform examples in Figure 6.3. The example uses the simplest predictor, which is the unit delay mentioned earlier.

Figure 6.3 also demonstrates the two types of reconstruction error already mentioned in Chapter 4: overload distortion and granular noise. Note, however, that we are no longer quantizing $x(n)$, as in PCM, but we are quantizing the difference signal $d(n)$. As a result, overload errors in DPCM are characterized not as amplitude overload, but as *slope overload*. As shown in Figure 6.3, slope overload occurs whenever the largest step size of the quantizer is too small for local values of $d(n)$, resulting in a lag of the staircase function $y(n)$ with respect to a fast-changing input — for example, the rapid increase of speech amplitude at the onset of a pitch period (see Figure 2.1), or the rapid change of image intensity at a high-contrast edge (see Figure 2.3). The opposite situation of *granular noise* occurs when the input variations are too small in comparison with the smallest step size of the quantizer. Examples are in the coding of silences in speech, or of constant or nearly constant gray areas in images. A third kind of DPCM error is identifiable with image coding. This occurs in the coding of low contrast edges, where the quantizer output oscillates in a *random* fashion, and takes on slightly different values from line to line or from frame to frame. This spatio-temporal effect is called *edge-busyness*. The types of error mentioned above have different perceptual annoyance values, and they make DPCM errors perceptually different from PCM errors for a given objective mse σ_r^2.

Figure 6.3 Illustration of waveform coding by DPCM and of different types of reconstruction error. Granular noise is caused by the coarseness of the minimum quantizer step in the coding of a slowly changing waveform. Slope overload distortion is caused when the maximum quantizer step is insufficient to track a rapidly changing input. Edge-busyness is a distortion specific to image coding. It is a spatio-temporal effect that is associated with the coding of low-contrast edges [Netravali and Limb;©1980, IEEE].

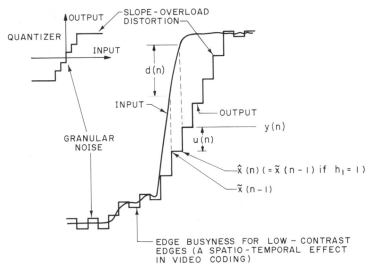

6.1.4 Analyses and Designs of Linear Predictors

Based on (6.14), and a corresponding PCM equation (4.19), the *SNR* gain in going from PCM to DPCM is

$$\sigma_{rP}^2/\sigma_{rD}^2 = (\epsilon_{qP}^2 \sigma_x^2)/(\epsilon_{qD}^2 \sigma_d^2) = (\epsilon_{qP}^2/\epsilon_{qD}^2)(\sigma_x^2/\sigma_d^2) \qquad (6.15a)$$

where subscripts P and D denote PCM and DPCM, respectively.

The first term on the right hand side of (6.15a) is in general not equal to unity. A good example is from the encoding of image signals. As seen in Chapter 2, the pdf of pixel amplitudes tends to be uniform while that of pixel differences tends to be Laplacian; and for quantizers with a large number of levels, corresponding values of ϵ_{qP}^2 and ϵ_{qD}^2 (from Chapter 4) are 2^{-2R} and $2^{-2R}(9/2)$, respectively. The ratio $\epsilon_{qP}^2/\epsilon_{qD}^2$ tends to be closer to unity in the case of speech signals where both pdf's in question tend to be gamma; and in fact there are at least two instances where the ratio $\epsilon_{qP}^2/\epsilon_{qD}^2$ is close to unity: Gaussian sources (which produce Gaussian difference signals with linear prediction), and logarithmic quantization with a large number of levels, say at least 16 (with a performance that is relatively insensitive to changes in input statistics). In these cases, (6.15a) simplifies to

$$\sigma_{rP}^2/\sigma_{rD}^2 = \sigma_x^2/\sigma_d^2 = G_P \qquad (6.15b)$$

The prediction gain G_P is typically greater than 1, as will be seen in many examples to follow. Also, since the *SNR* in PCM and DPCM are given by σ_x^2/σ_{rP}^2 and σ_x^2/σ_{rD}^2, respectively, use of (6.15b) leads to

$$SNR|_{DPCM} \text{ (dB)} = SNR|_{PCM} \text{ (dB)} + 10 \log G_P \qquad (6.16)$$

In view of the 6 dB-per-bit *SNR* results of Chapter 4, this implies that DPCM coding provides a $(10\log G_P)/6$-bit advantage over PCM; for a given *SNR* requirement, the bit rate needed in DPCM is smaller by an amount $(10\log G_P)/6$ bits/sample. Later results in this chapter will imply minor modifications of this last statement, reflecting the influence of other parameters of the DPCM system, such as quantizer performance and quantization error feedback.

Even in cases where $\epsilon_{qP}^2/\epsilon_{qD}^2$ is expected to be significantly different from unity, it is useful, as a first approximation, to assume that $\epsilon_{qD_1}^2/\epsilon_{qD_2}^2$ is 1, where subscripts refer to two contending differential schemes: in other words, it is useful, while optimizing predictor design, to maximize the second term on the right hand side of (6.15a) although a rigorous procedure would be to seek a design that maximizes the product therein.

The rest of this chapter will indeed adopt this simplification. We shall therefore use, as a criterion of DPCM performance, the prediction gain G_P, and evaluate it for many input and predictor examples to follow. Furthermore, as mentioned earlier, we shall confine our discussion to all-pole linear prediction of order N defined by

$$\hat{x}(n) = \sum_{j=1}^{N} h_j y(n-j) = \sum_{j=1}^{N} h_j [x(n-j) - q(n-j)] \qquad (6.17)$$

with $y(n) = \tilde{x}(n)$, as in (6.1b) and Figure 6.1(a). The weighting factors h_j, $j = 1,2,..., N$ will be called *predictor coefficients*. We note from (6.17) that $\hat{x}(n)$ — and hence also the quantizer input $d(n)$ — includes a term $\sum h_j q(n-j)$. This implies that quantization noise is first filtered or colored by the predictor and is then fed back to the input of the quantizer. This *quantization error feedback* implies that prediction is based on noisy samples; this increases the prediction error variance. It also implies that if $S_{qq}(e^{j\omega})$ is white (See Section 4.7), the error that is transmitted is non-white; but it gets recolored at the decoder, so that the final reconstruction error spectrum is white and equal to $S_{qq}(e^{j\omega})$, as implied in (6.12b).

A case of great importance is that of "fine" quantization, a term that will have a special working definition for the purposes of DPCM analyses: $R > 2$ in nonadaptive prediction (Figure 6.11), or $R \geqslant 2$ in adaptive prediction (Figure 6.11). With these values of R, equation (6.17) can be usefully *approximated* as

$$\hat{x}(n) \simeq \sum_{j=1}^{N} h_j x(n-j) \qquad (6.18)$$

Effects of $q(n-j)$ terms in (6.17) also tend to decrease as the order of prediction N decreases, making the approximation (6.18) more valid. Most of our predictor analyses will indeed use this approximate algorithm (6.18) for simplicity, and the subject of quantization error feedback, or prediction from noisy past samples (6.17) will be deferred to the one-bit quantizer case in Chapter 8.

We emphasize once again that many of the analyses in this chapter will be based on two sets of reasonable but strong assumptions that are made mainly for simplicity. One set of assumptions concerns the notion of "fine" quantization just discussed, leading to the non-consideration of quantization error feedback. The other set of assumptions is the ideal model of a white quantizer input and a white reconstruction error sequence.

The maximum value of prediction gain ${}^N G_P$ obtainable using the Nth order prediction of (6.18) is the asymptotic maximum as $N \to \infty$; this is also the reciprocal of the spectral flatness measure [(Chapter 2) and (6.52)]:

$$\max_{N \to \infty} \{ {}^N G_P \} = (\gamma_x^2)^{-1} \qquad (6.19)$$

Before proceeding with DPCM analyses, we reiterate that our sources are modeled by a random sequence $\{X(n)\}$, with mean $\mu_x = E[X(n)] = 0$ unless otherwise mentioned; variance $\sigma_x^2 = R_{xx}(0)$; acf $R_{xx}(k)$ and psd $S_{xx}(e^{j\omega})$; and normalized acf values

$$\rho_k = R_{xx}(k)/\sigma_x^2; \quad k = 0, 1, 2, ... \qquad (6.20)$$

The acf, while being only a partial description of source-sample dependencies, is adequate for the optimal design of the subclass of linear predictors (6.18). Linear predictors, as seen in Chapter 2, are indeed optimal from the mse viewpoint (and thus for the minimization of σ_d^2) in the case of Gaussian sources.

6.2 Linear Predictors of Order $N = 1$, 2 and 3

In this section, we will illustrate how the prediction error and gain vary as a function of N for $N = 1,2$ and 3. We will be able to give closed-form expressions for these values of N, and for acf descriptions that follow speech and image models from Chapter 2. As in (6.18), we will uniformly assume predictions based on past unquantized samples, for analytical simplicity.

6.2.1 First-Order Prediction

Consider the prediction $\hat{x}(n) = h_1 x(n-1)$. The difference signal is

$$d(n) = x(n) - h_1 x(n-1) \tag{6.21}$$

and its variance, by taking squares and expectations, is

$$\sigma_d^2 = (1 + h_1^2 - 2\rho_1 h_1)\sigma_x^2 \tag{6.22}$$

Setting $\partial \sigma_d^2 / \partial h_1 = 0$ yields the optimum h_1 and the corresponding minimum prediction error variance:

$$h_{1,opt} = \rho_1 ; \quad \min\{^1\sigma_d^2\} = (1 - \rho_1^2)\sigma_x^2 \tag{6.23}$$

The maximum prediction gain for $N = 1$ is therefore

$$\max\{^1 G_P\} = (1 - \rho_1^2)^{-1} \tag{6.24a}$$

The dependence of (6.24) on ρ_1 can be illustrated using ρ_1 values typical in long-term characterizations of bandpass filtered speech (column 5 and row 2 of Table 2.2) and images (Table 2.3):

$$\max\{^1 G_P\} = \begin{cases} 0.319^{-1} = 3.13 & (5.0 \text{ dB}) & \text{if } \rho_1 = 0.825 \\ 0.0975^{-1} = 100.26 & (10.1 \text{ dB}) & \text{if } \rho_1 = 0.950 \end{cases} \tag{6.24b}$$

Note that the variance (6.23) is less than σ_x^2 for all non-zero values of ρ_1. By contrast, the first-difference predictor $\hat{x}(n) = x(n-1)$ considered in Section 6.1 has a prediction error variance that provides a positive prediction gain only for $\rho_1 > 0.5$ (Problem 6.1; also see Problem 6.6). This is easily seen because

$$\sigma_d^2 = 2(1 - \rho_1)\sigma_x^2 \quad \text{if } h_1 = 1 \tag{6.25}$$

Long-time-averaged ρ_1 values for Nyquist-sampled speech and television signals are indeed characterized by $\rho_1 > 0.5$ although short-term averaged values of ρ_1 can vary over the entire admissible range $(-1 \leqslant \rho_1 \leqslant 1)$. Thus, while short-time-optimized adaptive predictors (see Section 6.4) necessarily follow (6.23) with ρ_1 updated periodically, time-invariant predictors for speech and images are often based on the long-term acf and sometimes, even the sub-optimal design $h_1 = 1$ of

Section 6.1. Associated losses in mse performance, given by $[2(1-\rho_1)/(1-\rho_1^2)]$ are less than 1 dB if $\rho_1 > 0.6$, and less than 0.5 dB if $\rho_1 > 0.78$ (Problem 6.3).

The optimum value of h_1 was obtained by minimizing the explicit form (6.22) with respect to h_1. Alternatively, one could differentiate an unexpanded form of the square of (6.21) with respect to h_1 to obtain

$$E[\ \{X(n) - h_{1,opt}\ X(n-1)\}\ X(n-1)] = 0 \qquad (6.26)$$

This would lead to the same value for $h_{1,opt}$ as in (6.23). The condition (6.26) is a simple case of an *orthogonality principle* (Section 6.3.1) which states that the minimum prediction error is orthogonal to all the data [in this case, $x(n-1)$] used in the prediction.

An interesting property of linear prediction systems is the acf of the prediction error sequence $d(n)$. Redundancy removal in DPCM is related to the decorrelation of the input prior to quantization; complete decorrelation implies a whitened sequence $d(n)$ (Section 6.3.4). In the above sense, first-order predictors, even when optimized for minimum mse, are useful but inadequate for speech and image signals. This is illustrated, for example, by non-zero prediction-error correlations $\rho_{dd}(1)$ in first-order predictors for speech (Problem 6.4); and by the residual structure (non-whiteness) in the prediction error signals in Figure 6.4 for first-order horizontal and vertical predictions, based respectively on the horizontal and vertical neighbors of the pixel being predicted. With horizontal prediction, most of the residual structure is in the form of vertical edge preservation in $d(n)$ [for example, the subjects' left ear in Figure 6.4(b)]; and with vertical prediction, most of the residual structure is in the form of horizontal edge preservation [for example, the subjects' eyebrows in Figure 6.4(c)]. The horizontal and vertical predictors in Figure 6.4 are simple examples of *intraframe* predictors that remove spatial redundancies. Later sections will consider examples of *interframe* predictors for removing temporal redundancies in moving images.

An input for which a first-order predictor is adequate, in the sense of a whitened prediction error $d(n)$, is a first-order Markov or AR(1) source (Problem 6.5).

Figure 6.4 First-order predictions of image samples: (a) input image; (b) prediction error sequence with previous sample prediction; and (c) prediction error sequence with previous line prediction [Harrison;©1952, AT&T].

 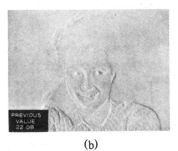 

(a)   (b)   (c)

6.2.2 Second-Order Prediction

Consider the linear predictor of order two given by

$$\hat{x}(n) = h_1 \, x(n-1) + h_2 \, x(n-2) \qquad (6.27a)$$

$$d(n) = x(n) - h_1 \, x(n-1) - h_2 \, x(n-2) \qquad (6.27b)$$

Optimal values of h_1 and h_2 are obtained by setting partial derivatives of $E[D^2(n)]$ with respect to h_1 and h_2 to zero, or by requiring that $d(n)$ is orthogonal to the data used for the prediction:

$$h_{1,opt} = \rho_1(1-\rho_2)/(1-\rho_1^2) \; ; \qquad h_{2,opt} = (\rho_2-\rho_1^2)/(1-\rho_1^2) \qquad (6.28a)$$

$$\min\{^2\sigma_d^2\} = \left[1-\rho_1^2 - \frac{(\rho_1^2-\rho_2)^2}{1-\rho_1^2}\right]\sigma_x^2 \qquad (6.28b)$$

The above equation shows that the error variance is almost always less than the minimum value (6.23) that is characteristic of first-order prediction. The exception occurs if $\rho_2 = \rho_1^2$ [an AR(1) source] in which case there is no gain in using a second-order predictor. In fact, (6.28b) can be rewritten in the form

$$\min\{^2\sigma_d^2\} = \min\{^1\sigma_d^2\} \, (1-\pi_2^2) \qquad (6.29)$$

where pre-scripts 2 and 1 refer to prediction order, and π_2 is the second *parcor (partial correlation) coefficient* [see (6.75)]. In the AR(1) case, $\pi_2^2 = 0$.

Example 6.1. Second-order prediction of speech
Using acf values from Table 2.2, $\rho_1 = 0.825$ and $\rho_2 = 0.562$. Using these in (6.28), $h_{1,opt} = 1.13$, $h_{2,opt} = -.371$ and $\min\{^2\sigma_d^2\} = 0.281 \; \sigma_x^2$. This represents a gain of only 1.13, or 0.51 dB over the first-order predictor in (6.24b).   ●

Consider a general version of (6.27) in the form

$$\hat{x}_A = b x_B + c x_C \qquad (6.30)$$

where x_A, x_B and x_C are adjacent waveform samples that are not necessarily equally spaced. Let the normalized acf values for the set (A, B, C) be ρ_{AB}, ρ_{BC} and ρ_{AC}. Optimal prediction is then a generalization of (6.28) and it is given by

$$b_{opt} = (\rho_{AB} - \rho_{AC}\rho_{BC})/(1-\rho_{BC}^2) \; ; \qquad c_{opt} = (\rho_{AC} - \rho_{AB}\rho_{BC})/(1-\rho_{BC}^2)$$

$$\min\{^2\sigma_d^2\} = \left[1 - \frac{\rho_{AB}^2 + \rho_{AC}^2 - 2\rho_{AB}\rho_{AC}\rho_{BC}}{1-\rho_{BC}^2}\right]\sigma_x^2 \qquad (6.31)$$

The result (6.31) shows how the prediction error is a function not only of the correlations between predicted samples and samples used for the prediction, but also of mutual correlations between the latter set of samples.

In the special case where x_A, x_B and x_C are equally-spaced adjacent waveform samples, $\rho_{AB} = \rho_{BC} = \rho_1$ and $\rho_{AC} = \rho_2$. With these special settings, (6.31) reduces to (6.28).

6.2.3 Two-Dimensional Second-Order Prediction

An important application of second-order prediction is in the prediction of pixel intensity values in an image frame; specifically, the prediction of an intensity value $x(i,j)$ based on a previous sample on the same scanning line $x(i,j-1)$, as well as a previous line neighbor $x(i-1,j)$. In the notation of Figure 6.5, it is the prediction of sample A based on sample values B and C. The mathematics of this (linear) prediction problem is contained in (6.30) and (6.31). Two special cases are of interest, corresponding to the *isotropic* and *linearly separable* acf models discussed in Chapter 2. We shall assume for simplicity that $\rho_{AB} = \rho_{AC}$, and we shall separately consider ρ_{BC} values that are appropriate to each model.

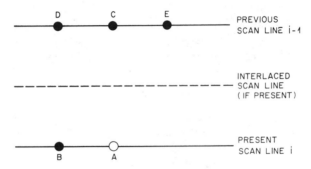

Figure 6.5 Two-dimensional predictions of image samples. Pixel A is the sample whose intensity value x_A is to be predicted; B, C, D and E are neighbors used for the prediction of x_A.

Example 6.2. Isotropic acf $(\rho_{AB} = \rho_{AC} = \rho;\ \rho_{BC} = \rho^{\sqrt{2}})$
Using the general results of (6.31),

$$b_{opt} = c_{opt} = \rho/(1 + \rho^{\sqrt{2}}) ; \quad \min\{^2\sigma_d^2\} = \left[1 - \rho^2\left(\frac{2}{1+\rho^{\sqrt{2}}}\right)\right]\sigma_x^2 \qquad (6.32)$$

For $\rho = 0.95$, $b_{opt} = c_{opt} = 0.492$, and (6.32) constitutes a 1.78 dB gain over optimal first-order prediction. As $\rho \to 1$, the gain over optimal first-order prediction tends to 1.89 dB (Problem 6.7). ●

Example 6.3. Separable acf $(\rho_{AB} = \rho_{AC} = \rho;\ \rho_{BC} = \rho^2)$
Once again, using the general results of (6.31),

$$b_{opt} = c_{opt} = \rho/(1 + \rho^2) ; \quad \min\{^2\sigma_d^2\} = \left[(1-\rho^2)\frac{1}{1+\rho^2}\right]\sigma_x^2 \qquad (6.33)$$

For $\rho = 0.95$, $b_{opt} = c_{opt} = 0.499$, and (6.33) represents a 2.8 dB gain over optimal first-order prediction. For $\rho \to 1$, an approximate design

$$b = c = 0.5 \tag{6.34}$$

yields a σ_d^2 value very close to (6.33) (Problem 6.8). However, a two-element predictor using pixels B and E and weights 0.5 each does significantly worse (Problem 6.9). In spite of its obvious sub-optimality in a mse sense, this averaging predictor is sometimes used in image coding because of its perceptual benefits — for reducing quantization noise visibility as well as for reducing effects of transmission errors (Section 6.7). A very simple but perceptually effective two-dimensional *intraframe* predictor system is the *switched predictor* described as follows: $\hat{x}_A = 0.5(x_B + x_E)$ or $\hat{x}_A = x_B$ according as $|x_B - x_D| < |x_E - x_D|$ or otherwise. •

The mathematics of prediction is the same as in (6.33) if one had a 1-D waveform where sample A was being estimated in terms of past and future nearest neighbors B and C; this is in fact the *first-order interpolation* problem in one dimension. As seen in (6.33), the mse with optimum first-order interpolation is smaller than the mse in optimum first-order prediction by a factor $(1+\rho^2)$ if the input is Markovian, with adjacent-sample correlation ρ.

6.2.4 Third-Order Prediction in One and Two Dimensions

We shall consider two examples for the general third-order scheme

$$\hat{x}_A = bx_B + cx_C + dx_D \tag{6.35}$$

As in second-order prediction, we will note that objective gains over a lower order predictor are modest for speech and for an image with an isotropic acf, but significant for an image with a separable acf.

Example 6.4. One-dimensional speech predictor
Let A, B, C, and D denote adjacent speech samples. With the long-time-averaged acf values of the last column of Table 2.2, the mse with optimal third-order prediction ($b_{opt} = 1.18$, $c_{opt} = -0.28$, $d_{opt} = -0.08$) is about 1 dB better than with optimal first-order prediction (Problem 6.10). The design and performance numbers just cited follow the formal analysis of Section 6.3. •

Two-Dimensional Image Predictors. Refer again to Figure 6.5. Consider the prediction of pixel A using the three neighbors B, C and D. Let $\rho_{AB} = \rho_{BD} = \rho_{CD} = \rho_{AC} = \rho$, and $\rho_{AD} = \rho_{BC} = \rho^J$. The optimal third-order prediction is described by (Problem 6.16)

$$b_{opt} = c_{opt} = \frac{\rho(1-\rho^J)}{1+\rho^J-2\rho^2} \; ; \qquad d_{opt} = \rho^J - \frac{2\rho^2(1-\rho^J)}{1+\rho^J-2\rho^2} \tag{6.36a}$$

$$\min\{{}^3\sigma_d^2\} = [1+2b_{opt}^2(1+\rho^J)+d_{opt}^2+4b_{opt}\rho(d_{opt}-1)-2d_{opt}\rho^J] \, \sigma_x^2 \tag{6.36b}$$

Two special cases are of interest:

Example 6.5. Third-order 2-D predictors for isotropic and separable acf models
Isotropic ACF ($J = \sqrt{2}$). Let $\rho = 0.95$. It follows from (6.36a) that $b_{opt} = c_{opt} = 0.52$, and $d_{opt} = -0.058$. Also,

$$\min\{^3\sigma_d^2\} = 0.65(1-\rho^2)\sigma_x^2 \qquad (6.36c)$$

which is less than the mse in optimal first-order prediction by 1.9 dB.   •

Separable ACF (J = 2). Once again, from (6.36a), $b_{opt} = c_{opt} = \rho$ and $d_{opt} = -\rho^2$. The minimum prediction error variance is now

$$\min\{^3\sigma_d^2\} = (1-\rho^2)^2\sigma_x^2 \qquad (6.36d)$$

For $\rho = 0.95$, this is less than the mse in optimal first-order prediction by 10.1 dB!   •

An approximation to the predictor in Example 6.5 is the easily implemented *planar* predictor [Harrison, 1952] defined by

$$b = c = 1; \quad d = -1 \qquad (6.37a)$$

In this predictor, if magnitudes of pixels x_B, x_D and x_C (Figure 6.5) are represented by three vertices of a parallelogram, in that order, the fourth vertex that completes the parallelogram in the same *plane* will determine the magnitude of the prediction $\hat{x}_A$. Interesting interpretations of $\hat{x}_A$ are obtained by rewriting (6.37a) in the explicit forms

$$\hat{x}_A = x_B + (x_C - x_D) \,; \qquad \hat{x}_A = x_C + (x_B - x_D) \qquad (6.37b)$$

In other words, $\hat{x}_A$ can be interpreted as x_B plus an estimate of horizontal intensity transition; or as x_C plus an estimate of vertical intensity transition.

An interesting property of all the predictor examples of this section is that the magnitude of the sum of predictor coefficients is less than unity (*leaky prediction*). In the image examples, this sum is in fact usually very close to unity, reflecting the fact that the acf values involved in the calculation of these coefficients are themselves close to +1. This design minimizes prediction error variance, and also provides robustness in the presence of transmission errors (Section 6.7). Also, see [Pirsch, 1982].

It is also clear from these image examples and corresponding examples in Section 6.1.3 that higher-order prediction provides much greater objective benefits in the case of 2-D sources describable by separable acf models. It turns out, however, that the acf's of typical images, especially of natural objects and scenes, are closer to being isotropic; and prediction gains (as in the case of one-dimensional speech prediction) saturate pretty fast as a function of predictor order (unless one employs distant-sample-based predictions or adaptive predictions, as in Sections 6.4 and 6.5). In an isotropic model with $\rho = 0.95$, the asymptotic value of G_P in 2-D prediction can be shown to be no more than 3 dB higher than that for previous sample prediction [O'Neal, 1972].

As mentioned earlier, two-dimensional, higher-order predictors in image coding are used not so much for better *SNR* performance in the coder but (a) for better subjective performance, as indicated for example by better edge rendition; and (b) for better tolerance to transmission error effects. The transmission error performance of 2-D predictors will be discussed at length in Section 6.7.

6.3 Linear Predictors of Order N

The low-order predictors discussed so far, with $N \leqslant 3$, have been the basis of low-complexity DPCM coding systems (Section 6.4) that can provide high quality digitizations of speech and video with bit rates in the range of $R = 4$ or 3 bits/sample. These systems are of low complexity for two reasons. First, the low order of prediction implies a correspondingly low amount of storage — up to three Nyquist samples in speech, and up to one scan-line worth of pixels in intraframe coding of video. Second, these DPCM systems use time-invariant predictor coefficients based on long-time-averaged signal statistics, and this feature simplifies predictor design while still providing a significant amount of G_P, and hence a significant improvement over PCM (which needs $R=8$ bits/sample for high-quality digitizations of speech and video).

We shall now consider linear prediction of general order N, and we shall derive general expressions for optimum coefficients and minimum prediction error variances. This section will show the effect of increasing N (to values greater than three, the largest value considered in Section 6.2), the asymptotic result for $N \rightarrow \infty$ (the maximum obtainable prediction gain), and the nature of prediction and reconstruction error spectra. Predictors of high order will be especially meaningful in adaptive prediction (Section 6.5).

6.3.1 General Expressions for Optimum Prediction

We are interested in *one-step-ahead* linear prediction of the form

$$\hat{x}(n) = \sum_{j=1}^{N} h_j x(n-j) \tag{6.38a}$$

which is a weighted sum of N previous samples. The weights h_j are *linear predictor coefficients*. The linear prediction problem above is a special case of the general linear filtering problem [Kolmogoroff, 1941] [Wiener, 1949]. As mentioned earlier, (6.38a) represents only a model for DPCM studies where predictions are actually based on quantized samples $y(n) = \tilde{x}(n)$ rather than on input samples $x(n)$ as in (6.38a); related inadequacies in the model (6.38) are, however, negligible for $R > 2$.

Figure 6.6 shows the structure of a *linear predictor* or order N. Its transfer function is

$$H(e^{j\omega}) = \sum_{k=1}^{N} h_k e^{-jk\omega} \tag{6.38b}$$

We note, therefore, that the DPCM decoder of Figure 6.1(b) has a transfer function

$$H_{DEC}(e^{j\omega}) = \frac{1}{1-H(e^{j\omega})} \tag{6.38c}$$

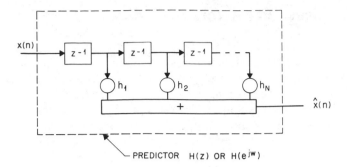

Figure 6.6 Linear predictor of order N. The input to the predictor box is shown as $x(n)$ for purposes of analytical simplicity. Unless otherwise mentioned, this input is actually $\tilde{x}(n) = y(n)$ in DPCM coding systems, as in Figure 6.1.

We shall show later that an optimum predictor $H_{opt}(e^{j\omega})$ leads to a magnitude-squared response $|H_{DEC,opt}(e^{j\omega})|^2$ that is usually an approximate match to the psd of the coder input.

To optimize the filter $H(z)$ in a mean squared sense, we minimize

$$\sigma_d^2 = E[D^2(n)] = E[(X(n) - \hat{X}(n))^2] \qquad (6.39)$$

Clearly, σ_d^2 is a function of all filter coefficients h_i and

$$\partial\sigma_d^2/\partial h_i = 0 \; ; \quad i = 1,2,...,N \qquad (6.40)$$

is a necessary condition for minimum mse. One way of performing the operation in (6.40) is to start by expanding the square in (6.39) explicitly. We have done this in Section 6.1. A simpler procedure, especially useful for large N, is to evaluate the derivative of (6.39) without explicit squaring, in the form

$$E[2\{X(n) - \hat{X}(n)\} \; \partial/\partial h_i \{-\hat{X}(n)\}]$$

Equating this to zero yields, with (6.38),

$$E[\{X(n) - \hat{X}_{opt}(n)\}X(n-i)] = 0 \; ; \quad i = 1,2,...,N \qquad (6.41)$$

Thus the minimum error $X(n) - \hat{X}_{opt}(n)$ must be orthogonal to all the data used in the prediction, which is the *orthogonality principle* (also known as *Hilbert space projection theorem*). Expansion of (6.41) gives the following conditions for optimum h_j:

$$R_{xx}(k) = \sum_{j=1}^{N} h_{j,opt} R_{xx}(k-j) \; ; \quad k = 1,2,...,N \qquad (6.42)$$

or

$$\begin{bmatrix} R_{xx}(1) \\ R_{xx}(2) \\ R_{xx}(3) \\ \cdot \\ R_{xx}(N) \end{bmatrix} = \begin{bmatrix} R_{xx}(0) & R_{xx}(1) & R_{xx}(2) & \cdot & R_{xx}(N-1) \\ R_{xx}(1) & R_{xx}(0) & R_{xx}(1) & \cdot & R_{xx}(N-2) \\ R_{xx}(2) & R_{xx}(1) & R_{xx}(0) & \cdot & R_{xx}(N-3) \\ \cdot & & & \cdot & \cdot \\ R_{xx}(N-1) & R_{xx}(N-2) & R_{xx}(N-3) & \cdot & R_{xx}(0) \end{bmatrix} \begin{bmatrix} h_{1,opt} \\ h_{2,opt} \\ h_{3,opt} \\ \cdot \\ h_{N,opt} \end{bmatrix} \quad (6.43)$$

In matrix notation,

$$\mathbf{r_{xx}} = \mathbf{R_{xx}}\mathbf{h}_{opt} \quad (6.44a)$$

$$\mathbf{h}_{opt} = \mathbf{R_{xx}^{-1}}\,\mathbf{r_{xx}} \quad (6.44b)$$

where $\mathbf{r_{xx}^T} = \{R_{xx}(i)\}$; $\quad \mathbf{R_{xx}} = \{R_{xx}(|i-j|)\}$; $\quad i, j = 1,2,...,N \quad (6.44c)$

The equations are called *normal equations*, *Yule-Walker prediction equations*, or *Wiener-Hopf equations*.

The solution of (6.44a) can be considerably simplified in general if the matrix $\mathbf{R_{xx}}$ is expressed as the product of a lower triangular matrix $\mathbf{T}$ (with positive diagonal elements) and its transpose, resulting in a pair of more easily solvable equations [Nash, 1979]:

$$\mathbf{Ta} = \mathbf{r_{xx}} ; \quad \mathbf{T^T}\mathbf{h}_{opt} = \mathbf{a} \quad (6.44d)$$

The $\mathbf{h}_{opt}$ may also be solved for by a special recursive algorithm for symmetric Toeplitz matrices [Levinson, 1947] (See Section 6.5.1) or, even more efficiently, by an algorithm that recognizes that there are $(N-1)$ identical elements in the vectors $\mathbf{R_{xx}}$ and $\mathbf{r_{xx}}$ [Durbin, 1960]. The algorithms calculate in successive steps the solutions $^k\mathbf{h}_{opt}$ for predictors of order k, with k ranging from 1 to N. In this computation, the mmse terms min $\{^k\sigma_d^2\}$ are calculated as by-products [Rabiner and Schafer, 1978].

The mmse

$$\min\{\sigma_d^2\} = E[(X(n)-\hat{X}_{opt}(n))^2] \quad (6.45)$$

follows directly from the orthogonality condition:

$$E[(X(n)-\hat{X}_{opt}(n))\hat{X}_{opt}(n)]=0; \quad \text{or } E[X(n)\hat{X}_{opt}(n)]=E[(\hat{X}_{opt}^2(n)]$$

so that

$$\min\{\sigma_d^2\} = E[X^2(n)]-2E[X(n)\hat{X}_{opt}(n)] + E[\hat{X}_{opt}^2(n)]$$

$$= \sigma_x^2 - E[X(n)\hat{X}_{opt}(n)] = \sigma_x^2 - \sum_{i=1}^{N} h_{i,opt} R_{xx}(i) \quad (6.46)$$

$$= \sigma_x^2 - \mathbf{h}_{opt}^T \mathbf{r_{xx}} = \sigma_x^2 - \mathbf{r_{xx}^T}\mathbf{R_{xx}^{-1}}\mathbf{r_{xx}} \quad (6.47)$$

It can also be shown [by applying Cramer's rule to (6.47)] that the mmse is

$$\min \{{}^N\sigma_d^2\} = |{}^{N+1}\mathbf{R}_{xx}| / |{}^N\mathbf{R}_{xx}| \qquad (6.48)$$

in which $|{}^{N+1}\mathbf{R}_{xx}|$ is the determinant of the $(N+1) \times (N+1)$ correlation matrix of $\{X(n)\}$. Note that we may express this determinant by a product of prediction error variances, and perform the operation repeatedly:

$$|{}^{N+1}\mathbf{R}_{xx}| = \min \{{}^N\sigma_d^2\} \; |{}^N\mathbf{R}_{xx}|$$

$$= \min \{{}^N\sigma_d^2\} \min \{{}^{N-1}\sigma_d^2\} |{}^{N-1}\mathbf{R}_{xx}| ,...$$

with the end result

$$|{}^{N+1}\mathbf{R}_{xx}| = \sigma_x^2 \prod_{i=1}^{N} \min \{{}^i\sigma_d^2\} , \qquad (6.49)$$

which will be used in Chapter 12.

We make use of a result on Toeplitz determinants [Grenander and Szego, 1958]:

$$\lim_{N \to \infty} \frac{|{}^{N+1}\mathbf{R}_{xx}|}{|{}^N\mathbf{R}_{xx}|} = \exp \left[\frac{1}{2\pi} \int_{-\pi}^{\pi} \log_e S_{xx}(e^{j\omega}) d\omega \right] \qquad (6.50)$$

By comparing this with (6.48) we find the minimum of the obtainable prediction error variance:

$$\min \{{}^\infty\sigma_d^2\} = \exp \left[\frac{1}{2\pi} \int_{-\pi}^{\pi} \log_e S_{xx}(e^{j\omega}) d\omega \right] \qquad (6.51)$$

This result is one of the rare examples where the performance of a causal optimal linear filter can be given explicitly [Kolmogoroff, 1941]. Recall from Chapter 2 that the right-hand term equals $\gamma_x^2 \, \sigma_x^2$ (Also see Problem 2.11). Thus the spectral flatness measure γ_x^2 is the reciprocal of the maximum prediction gain:

$$\gamma_x^2 = \min \{{}^\infty\sigma_d^2\}/\sigma_x^2 = [\max\{{}^\infty G_P\}]^{-1} \qquad (6.52)$$

6.3.2 Further Examples from Speech and Image Prediction

Speech Prediction. We have already shown long-time-averaged acf sequences of speech signals in Figure 2.7. Prediction gains that can be obtained using these values in (6.43) are illustrated in Figure 6.7 for lowpass and bandpass speech [Noll, 1972]. In each case, the spread in G_P is due to speaker differences, and middle curves give mean values (over four speakers used in the experiment). These mean values are not very different from the numerical results of Section 6.2 for $N \leqslant 3$. It is also interesting that the value of G_P typically saturates for predictions of order $N = 2$, as predicted in Section 6.2. Notice also that the prediction gains are higher

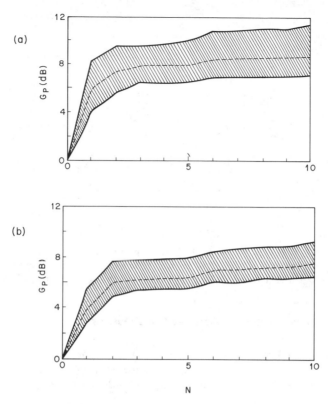

(a)

(b)

N

Figure 6.7 Maximum prediction gain versus predictor order N for (a) lowpass-filtered speech; and (b) bandpass-filtered speech [Noll, 1972].

for speech that is *not* bandpass-filtered. This is expected because lowpass-filtered speech has greater low-frequency energy, and hence greater adjacent sample correlations. We shall note in Section 6.5 that prediction gains in adaptive prediction often saturate much later, say at $N=10$; and that values of G_P at saturation can be much higher than corresponding saturation values in Figure 6.7.

Image Prediction. The prediction gain characteristics of Figure 6.8 refer to an *intraframe* predictor for a low-detail image with a 208 × 250 pixel grid [Habibi, 1971]. They show, once again, an early saturation of performance with increasing predictor order. Most of the prediction gain is realized with $N = 3$. The gain in going from $N = 1$ to $N = 3$ [2-D predictor (6.35)] is seen to be about 4 dB. This gain is higher than what is predictable by an isotropic model with $\rho = 0.971$ (average of ρ_{AB} and ρ_{AC} values in Figure 6.8). But it is less than what is predictable with a separable acf model with the same value of $\rho = 0.971$. Following the procedures of Examples 6.4 and 6.5, but with $\rho = 0.971$ instead of $\rho = 0.95$, the gains in the two models would be 1.8 dB and 12.2 dB, respectively. Gains in higher-order prediction ($N > 1$) [Habibi, 1971] are significantly less if the predictor designs are based on acf measurements not matched to those of an image being coded.

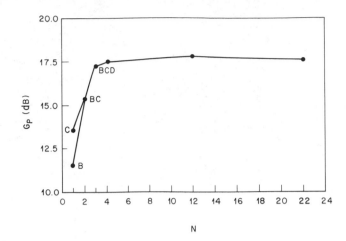

Figure 6.8 Example of maximum prediction gain versus predictor order N in intraframe image coding. Points marked B, C, BC and BCD refer to prediction algorithms given by $\hat{x}_A = 0.965x_B$, $0.977x_C$, $(0.379x_B + 0.617x_C)$ and $(0.746x_B + 0.826x_C - .594x_D)$, respectively [Habibi;©1971, IEEE].

6.3.3 Suboptimum and Mismatched Predictors

Polynomial Predictors of Order N. The importance of careful predictor design is best appreciated by noting the obviously poorer performance of an empirical acf - independent prediction scheme such as *polynomial prediction*:

$$h_j = (-1)^{j+1} \binom{N}{j} ; \quad j = 1,2,...,N \tag{6.53}$$

The simplest case is the *zero-order* ($N=1$) polynomial predictor $[\hat{x}(n) = x(n-1)]$. This predictor was studied earlier. The prediction gain was noted to be $2(1-\rho_1)$ which exceeds 1 only if $\rho_1 > 0.5$. This predictor is clearly suboptimal in comparison with the acf-matched scheme ($h_1 = \rho_1$) whose prediction gain $(1-\rho_1^2)^{-1}$ is always greater than 1. It can be shown that the suboptimality of polynomial prediction increases as a function of order N. In fact, the prediction gain in polynomial prediction is not guaranteed to be an increasing function of N. This can be verified by computing the magnitude square frequency response $|H_{DEC}(e^{j\omega})|^2$ of the decoder filter with (6.38c). It will provide a decreasingly adequate match to typical speech or image spectra as N is increased. This can be illustrated by the example of a first-order Markov input (Problems 6.18 to 6.20).

Mismatched Predictors. Polynomial extrapolation is one example of *predictor-source mismatch* in the sense that the polynomial coefficients are not acf-based. Section 6.2 has also noted examples of non-acf-based predictors for images — for example, the second-order averaging predictor (6.34) and the third-order planar predictor (6.37). These predictors were not very suboptimal in an mse sense in Section 6.2, but we shall note that in the context of transmission errors, these special predictors are severely suboptimal (Section 6.7). This is because the sum of predictor coefficients will need to be less than unity for mitigating channel error propagation, and this condition is not satisfied in the above predictor designs.

Another example of mismatched prediction would be the case of a speech-optimized predictor used in the DPCM coding of a data signal waveform, or vice versa.

Subtler types of mismatch occur when predictor parameters derived from a sample set of source statistics are used in the encoding of new source material. In typical image and speech coding applications, such mismatches can easily cause SNR degradations of a few (say 1 to 4) dB. The purpose of this section is to note a simple formula for prediction error variance when the prediction vector is $\mathbf{h}_{opt} + \boldsymbol{\delta}$ instead of $\mathbf{h}_{opt}$. The perturbation $\boldsymbol{\delta}$ can be either an implementation error, or the result of an attempt to accommodate different source statistics.

From analyses similar to those earlier in this section, (6.39) generalizes to

$$\sigma_d^2 = \sigma_x^2 - 2\mathbf{h}^T\mathbf{r}_{xx} + \mathbf{h}^T\mathbf{R}_{xx}\mathbf{h} \tag{6.54}$$

Setting

$$\mathbf{h} = \mathbf{h}_{opt} + \boldsymbol{\delta} \tag{6.55}$$

where $\mathbf{h}_{opt}$ is given by (6.44), we have

$$\sigma_d^2 = (\sigma_x^2 - 2\mathbf{h}_{opt}^T\mathbf{r}_{xx} + \mathbf{h}_{opt}^T\mathbf{R}_{xx}\mathbf{h}_{opt}) + (-2\boldsymbol{\delta}^T\mathbf{r}_{xx} + \boldsymbol{\delta}^T\mathbf{R}_{xx}\mathbf{h}_{opt} + \mathbf{h}_{opt}^T\mathbf{R}_{xx}\boldsymbol{\delta}) + \boldsymbol{\delta}^T\mathbf{R}_{xx}\boldsymbol{\delta}$$

Using (6.44) and (6.47), we note that the terms in the first pair of parentheses represent the minimum obtainable $\min\{\sigma_d^2\}$. The terms in the second pair of parentheses add to zero, once again using (6.44); so that

$$\sigma_d^2 = \min\{\sigma_d^2\} + \boldsymbol{\delta}^T\mathbf{R}_{xx}\boldsymbol{\delta} \tag{6.56}$$

The additional prediction error variance thus depends on the difference of the actual vector from the optimal one, as well as on the signal acf.

For the special case of $N = 1$, with $h_1 = \rho_1 + \delta_1$, (6.56) simplifies [instead of the simpler (6.22)] to

$$\sigma_d^2 = \min\{\sigma_d^2\} + (h_1 - \rho_1)^2\sigma_x^2 = (1 - \rho_1^2 + \delta_1^2)\sigma_x^2 \tag{6.57}$$

A good example of spectral mismatch is the use of a predictor based on a speech design such as (6.24b) in the coding of pre-emphasized speech. For example, if $h_1 = 0.825$ but $\rho_1 = 0.7$, the loss in G_p is at least 2 dB [Problem 6.14(b)]. The problem of encoding data signal waveforms with a predictor matched to speech illustrates an extreme example of spectral mismatch (Problem 6.21). The bandpass raised-cosine input spectrum example in Problem 6.21 reveals many important characteristics of the data signal. For example, a first-order predictor is useless for this data spectrum. First-order predictors are very effective if the input spectrum is highly lowpass ($\rho_1 \rightarrow 1$, as with image and speech inputs), or very highpass ($\rho_1 \rightarrow -1$), but not if the spectrum is bandpass. In fact, as also seen in Problem 6.21, a third-order predictor can provide a much better spectral fit (and hence, a significant prediction gain) for the bandpass spectrum in question.

The above discussion suggests several approaches for designing coders in communication systems that are hoped to handle waveforms with varying statistics. For example, a DPCM encoder can be switched into a non-predictive PCM mode upon detection of low input correlations, as with unvoiced speech or data inputs. Alternatively, in *switched prediction*, one could switch to different predictors in a bank, once again depending on which input is detected or expected. A third, time-invariant approach, one that does not require input classification, is that of a *compromise predictor* [O'Neal and Stroh, 1972] which is matched to an acf that is the weighted average of component acf's (as in the speech-and-data example, Problem 6.22). The most complete solution to the mismatch problem is that of *adaptive prediction*, and this will be discussed at length in Section 6.5.

In interpreting predictor performance, it is good to bear in mind that the signal-to-noise ratio is a useful but not ultimate criterion of encoding quality. The subjects of speech and image quality are being discussed at great length in this book; in the case of data signal waveforms, the defining criterion of quality should be the message error rate in the data communication systems. This is a monotonically increasing, but not simple, function of reconstruction noise.

6.3.4 Analysis of the Prediction Error Sequence

As in previous analyses, the following results will be based on a predictor process with an unquantized input $\{X(n)\}$. The prediction error signal is therefore a discrete-time random process $\{D(n)\}$ obtained by passing the input process $\{X(n)\}$ through the *prediction error filter* [Figure 6.9(a)] with transfer function $1-H(e^{j\omega})$. The acf of $\{D(n)\}$ depends clearly on the coefficients of the prediction error filter. An important result can be obtained for the case where the predictor has been optimized, with the number of coefficients N being infinity. Using the orthogonality principle that the error signal must be orthogonal to all previous inputs, a prescript ∞ to indicate $N \rightarrow \infty$, and the notation $D_{opt}(n)$ to indicate use of $\mathbf{h}_{opt}$,

$$E[D_{opt}(n)X(n-i)] = 0 ; \quad i = 1,2,... \qquad (6.58)$$

Since

$$X(n-i) = D_{opt}(n-i) + \hat{X}_{opt}(n-i) ,$$

$$R_{d_{opt}d_{opt}}(i) = -\sum_{j=1}^{\infty} h_{j,opt} \ E[D_{opt}(n)X(n-i-j)]; \quad i = 1,2,... \qquad (6.59)$$

which implies that

$$R_{d_{opt}d_{opt}}(i) = \min\{^{\infty}\sigma_d^2\}\delta(i) \qquad (6.60)$$

which is the acf of a white noise process. Indeed, the acf of $D_{opt}(i)$ is zero for all nonzero lags because of the orthogonality principle (6.58). Note, however, that the result only holds in general for $N = \infty$.

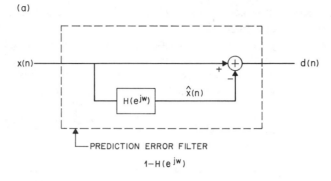

(a)

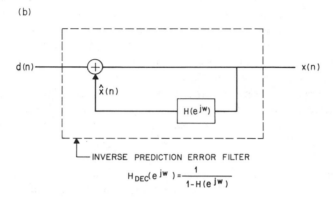

(b)

INVERSE PREDICTION ERROR FILTER

$$H_{DEC}(e^{jw}) = \frac{1}{1-H(e^{jw})}$$

Figure 6.9 Simplified schematics of DPCM: (a) encoder; (b) decoder.

We have shown that the output of an optimized linear prediction error filter with transfer function $1 - {}^{\infty}H_{opt}(e^{j\omega})$ is a white noise process. The prediction error filter is sometimes known as a *whitening filter* for this reason. It is also known as an *inverse filter* since its magnitude-squared frequency response $|1 - {}^{\infty}H_{opt}(e^{j\omega})|^2$ must be the inverse of the psd of the input

$$S_{xx}(e^{j\omega})|1 - {}^{\infty}H_{opt}(e^{j\omega})|^2 = S_{d_{opt} d_{opt}}(e^{j\omega}) = \min\{{}^{\infty}\sigma_d^2\} \tag{6.61a}$$

$$|1 - {}^{\infty}H_{opt}(e^{j\omega})|^2 = \min\{{}^{\infty}\sigma_d^2\}/S_{xx}(e^{j\omega}) \tag{6.61b}$$

The DPCM decoder must have a transfer function that is the inverse of that of the prediction error filter:

$$|{}^{\infty}H_{DEC}(e^{j\omega})|^2 = \frac{1}{|1 - {}^{\infty}H_{opt}(e^{j\omega})|^2} = \frac{S_{xx}(e^{j\omega})}{\min\{{}^{\infty}\sigma_d^2\}} \tag{6.62a}$$

However, the decoder is an all-pole filter. Therefore, the DPCM design can be regarded as an *input identification process* whereby an all-pole model (Section 2.4) is calculated which matches the input spectrum best. In our analysis, the match is based on an mse measure. In the example of ideal mmse prediction, the unquantized difference signal $D(n)$ will be a good estimate of $Z(n)$, the innovations process in Section 2.4.

The equality in (6.62a) holds only if the predictor (and therefore the decoder filter) has an infinite number of coefficients, unless the input is an $AR(M)$ process in which case M coefficients are adequate for the equality.

In general, when using a predictor of order k defined by ${}^k\mathbf{h}_{opt}$ instead of ${}^\infty\mathbf{h}_{opt}$,

$$\min\{{}^k\sigma_d^2\}\ |{}^kH_{DEC}(e^{j\omega})|^2 = \frac{\min\{{}^k\sigma_d^2\}}{|1-{}^kH_{opt}(e^{j\omega})|^2} = \hat{S}_{xx}(e^{j\omega}) \qquad (6.62b)$$

is an *estimate* of input spectrum $S_{xx}(e^{j\omega})$. In this case, we use $k+1$ measured values $\hat{R}_{xx}(0)$, $\hat{R}_{xx}(1),...,\hat{R}_{xx}(k)$ to compute ${}^k\mathbf{h}_{opt}$ and then we obtain $\min\{{}^k\sigma_d^2\}$ via (6.47). The above estimate is an *all-pole* or *autoregressive* estimate $\hat{S}_{xx}(e^{j\omega})$. This estimate defines the psd of an $AR(k)$ process whose first k acf values equal the measured ones. Successive acf values $\hat{R}_{xx}(j)$ are not assumed to be zero, but they are implicitly given by the recursive rule (2.95). Conventional psd estimations are based on making use of a finite number of acf values. In the AR-method for psd estimation, however, an infinite set of acf values is implicitly used. For Gaussian statistics, the above procedure also has the property that the estimate $\hat{S}_{xx}(e^{j\omega})$ is the one with the *maximum entropy power* of all psd's with the same given acf values.

In the case of nonadaptive prediction, $\mathbf{h}_{opt}$ is computed from acf values measured with long-time-averaged statistics. The decoder magnitude-squared frequency response will then describe the long-term psd of the process. Figure 6.10 shows the long-time frequency response of a DPCM decoder for speech, optimized for an average of four speakers [data of Figure 2.7(a)]. Also shown are the spectra of two short-time speech segments, a voiced segment (b) and an unvoiced segment (c). It is clear that the non-adaptive DPCM coder is not well-matched to these spectra. We shall come back to this example in Section 6.5.

Special Case: Mth Order Markov Source. Let $\{X(n)\}$ be an Mth order Markov source. We have shown (2.95) that its acf-values $R_{xx}(\cdot)$ can be computed recursively:

$$R_{xx}(j) = \sum_{j=1}^{M} b_j R_{xx}(j-i) \ ; \ j > 0 \qquad (6.63a)$$

Let N be an optimum linear predictor operating on this process, and let $N \geqslant M$. A direct comparison of (6.42) and the above equation leads to

$$h_{i,opt} = \begin{cases} b_i & i = 1,2,...,M \\ 0 & i = M+1,...,N \end{cases} \qquad (6.63b)$$

Hence we obtain the important result that *the optimum linear predictor $H_{opt}(z)$ for Mth order Markov sources has a finite number M of predictor coefficients.* This is intuitively obvious, since we have shown already that the error signal is a white noise process in the case of optimum prediction. An Mth order Markov

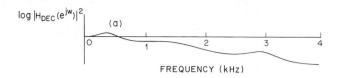

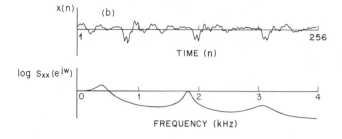

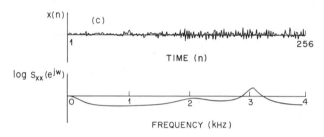

Figure 6.10 (a) Magnitude-squared frequency response of DPCM decoder optimized for long-time-averaged speech statistics; and waveforms $x(n)$ and their short-term spectra $S_{xx}(e^{j\omega})$ for (b) voiced speech and (c) unvoiced speech. The waveform duration is 32 ms. [Noll, 1973].

process is obtained by passing white noise through an all-pole filter $B(z)$ with M coefficients. Its inverse is just an Mth order prediction error filter, and accordingly, the error signal must be identical to the white noise which is used for generating the Markov process, implying that

$$1 - H_{opt}(z) = [B(z)]^{-1} \qquad (6.63c)$$

From the above (also see Problem 6.17), it is clear that

$$\min\{{}^{\infty}\sigma_d^2\} = \min\{{}^M\sigma_d^2\} \qquad (6.63d)$$

6.3.5 Predictions Based on Quantized Samples

The analyses of this section, as well as those in the preceding section for $N \leqslant 3$, have utilized the idealized coder model of Figure 6.6. In the non-idealized structure of Figure 6.1, there is a certain feedback of quantization error; and in general this feedback will be expected to influence DPCM design (selection of **h**) as

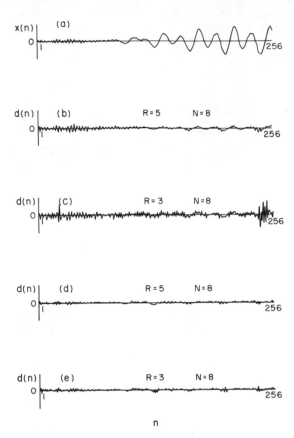

Figure 6.11 Waveforms of (a) input and prediction error with log quantization and bit rate R equal to (b) 5 bits/sample and (c) 3 bits/sample. Also shown in (d) and (e) are prediction error waveforms for $R = 5$ and 3 and adaptive prediction (Section 6.5). The input speech waveform is the same as that in Figure 1.4(a) [Volmary and Noll, 1983].

well as DPCM performance (value of σ_d^2). Clearly, the finer the quantization, the less important are these effects, and the more realistic will be the simplified quantities used hitherto. The prediction error waveforms in Figure 6.11 include the effects of quantization noise feedback, and they indicate that feedback effects may influence the performance for $R \leqslant 3$. These effects can be mitigated by making N smaller and by using adaptive quantization. The use of adaptive quantization is helpful, in particular, in minimizing slope overload errors during the onset of a pitch period in speech.

First-Order Gauss-Markov Processes. Analytical evaluations of quantization noise feedback have proved tractable at least with a first-order Gauss-Markov model for coder input. In this case, a striking result is that quantization error feedback has very little effect on the optimal value of predictor coefficient, *however coarse the quantization*. Formally,

$$h_{1,opt} = \rho_1 \qquad (6.64)$$

It is interesting to compare the above result with the situation where predictions are based on samples that are affected by additive white noise, rather than quantization errors. The effect of additive white noise is to make the mmse coefficient $h_{1,opt}$ less than ρ_1 (Problem 6.12).

While we will not derive (6.64) rigorously, we can mention at least two sets of results that support the use of that design. The first set comprises experimental results (computer simulations) from DPCM encoding of first-order Gauss-Markov sequences with $R \geqslant 1$ [Arnstein, 1975]. There is also a body of analytical results which leads, even more categorically, to (6.64) [Stroh, 1970]. An interesting side result from this analysis is that the quantizer output is white with optimal prediction but the quantizer input (prediction error signal) is non-white as a result of noise feedback. Contrast this with the white prediction error, or white quantizer input result of Problem 6.5, where prediction was on the basis of unquantized data. Another important result of this body of analyses is that the quantization noise is not white but has the acf of a first-order Markov source:

$$R_{qq}(k) = \sigma_q^2 [\epsilon_q^2 \rho_1]^{|k|} \tag{6.65}$$

For the simple example of a first-order Markov input source, if one assumes (6.64) tacitly, it can be shown that the SNR decrease in DPCM due to error feedback is approximately given by $10 \log (1-\epsilon_q^2\rho_1^2)^{-1}$ [Nitadori, 1965] (Problem 6.23). The term ϵ_q^2 is the quantizer performance factor. For a Gaussian input and $\rho_1 = 0.85$ (as in speech), this represents a degradation of more than 1 dB for $R=1$, but less than 0.4 dB for $R=2$. A detailed discussion will be given in Chapter 8.

It is obvious from (6.65) that with fine quantization ($\epsilon_q^2 \to 0$), the quantization noise can be considered to be white; and from (6.12), the reconstruction noise is white as well. This is true in spite of the coloring action of the DPCM decoder filter, because the error sequence at its input is already colored in an inverse sense by the feedback process in the DPCM encoder: the error sequence transmitted over the channel in a DPCM system is not $q(n)$ but the filtered version

$$q_c(n) = q(n) - \sum_{j=1}^{N} h_j q(n-j) \tag{6.66}$$

The result (6.66) can be derived as follows:

$$u(n) = d(n) - q(n) = x(n) - \hat{x}(n) - q(n)$$

$$= x(n) - \sum_{j=1}^{N} h_j [x(n-j) - q(n-j)] - q(n)$$

$$= [x(n) - \sum_{j=1}^{N} h_j x(n-j)] - [q(n) - \sum_{j=1}^{N} h_j q(n-j)] \tag{6.67}$$

The term in the first square bracket is the prediction error without quantization error feedback. The term in the second square bracket is quantization noise that is colored by the prediction error filter. This coloring is undone at the receiver and in the case of fine quantization, the end result is white reconstruction noise.

6.4 Low Complexity DPCM Systems

6.4.1 Speech Coding

Discussions in this section will refer to DPCM-AQB, a DPCM system with adaptive quantization. This system is often referred to as ADPCM where "A" stands for adaptation of the quantizer [Jayant, 1976]. In some examples of coding literature, "A" is used to denote adaptations of both quantizer and predictor (as in Section 6.5.3). For clarity, discussions in this book will use a longer terminology in which adaptations of quantizer and predictor are separately identified.

Figure 6.12 Waveforms in DPCM-AQB coding of speech: (a) Input speech waveform $x(n)$; reconstruction waveforms $y(n)$ with (b) $R = 4$, (c) $R = 3$ and (d) $R = 2$ bits/sample; and reconstruction error waveforms $r(n)$ with (e) $R = 4$, (f) $R = 3$ and (g) $R = 2$ bits/sample. The first-order predictor is defined by $h_1 = 0.85$ and the AQB logic is that of Table 4.14. The maximum speech input was $x_{max} = 2048$. The minimum step size of the quantizer Δ_{min} was $5-R$, and the maximum step size was $\Delta_{max} = 128\Delta_{min}$. All error waveforms have been magnified by a factor of 6.25. The input speech waveform is the same as that in Figure 1.4(a) [Jayant, 1982].

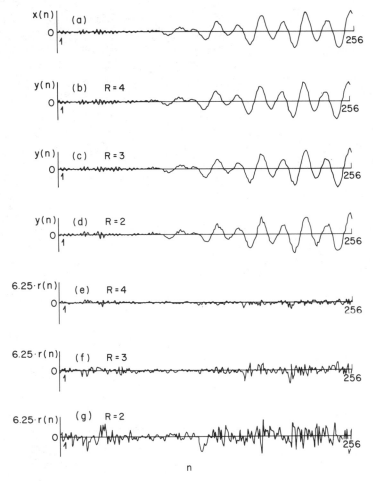

Figure 6.12 illustrates speech and reconstruction waveforms obtained in DPCM-AQB coding with $R = 4$, 3, and 2 bits/sample using a fixed first-order predictor optimized for the long-time-averaged speech spectrum ($h_1 = 0.85$); and an adaptive quantizer with a one-word memory (Section 4.10). The outputs with $R = 4$ and $R = 2$ [parts (b) and (d) of the figure] should be compared with corresponding log-PCM outputs [parts (b) and (c) of Figure 5.4]. The advantage in using DPCM is obvious in each case. The quality of 2 bit DPCM-AQB is limited however by quantization effects that are evident in Figure 6.12(d). Section 6.6 will discuss a 2-bit DPCM system that includes adaptive spectrum prediction, adaptive pitch prediction and noise shaping (Chapter 7) to realize high-quality digitization at 16 kb/s. The error waveforms in parts (e) (f) and (g) of Figure 6.12 will be useful in comparing the DPCM-AQB coder with an adaptive transform coder in Chapter 12.

The performance of DPCM systems is characterized not only by the prediction gain G_P and SNR (6.16), but also by the shape of the reconstruction error spectrum. Figure 6.13 compares reconstruction error spectra in log-PCM and DPCM-AQB speech coders of identical SNR [Cummiskey, Jayant and Flanagan, 1973]. Note that the DPCM noise spectrum is more speech-like (lowpass) than the PCM noise spectrum, which is quite white. The non-whiteness of the DPCM error spectrum is due to suboptimal prediction ($N = 1$) and slope overload in the quantization, and it is also evident in the error waveforms of Figure 6.12, especially in part (g). In subjective tests involving 3-bit and 4-bit DPCM-AQB, and PCM coders of identical SNR, the DPCM noise spectrum is the preferred shape, and this leads to a higher ranking for the DPCM coder in spite of an SNR that is no greater than that of PCM.

Figure 6.13 Comparison of log-PCM and DPCM-AQB speech coders. Log spectra of (a) speech input and of reconstruction errors in (b) DPCM-AQB ($R = 4$ bits/sample) and (c) log-PCM ($R = 7$ bits/sample) [Cummiskey, Jayant and Flanagan;©1973, AT&T].

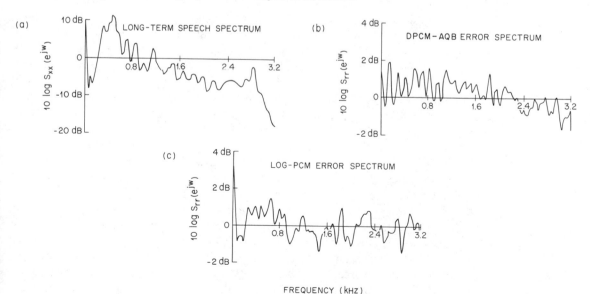

A comprehensive comparison of the coders across a wide range of R is included in Table 6.1. The comparison shows the inadequacy of SNR as a criterion of perceived coder quality. It shows, specifically, that the 4-bit DPCM coder, although inferior to 6-bit log PCM in an SNR sense, is ranked higher from a subjective viewpoint. Discrepancies between objective and subjective rankings can be made smaller by the use of an objective measurement that is perceptually more meaningful. One example of such a measurement, found to be useful in the specific context of DPCM-PCM comparisons, is the segmental signal-to-noise ratio $SNRSEG$ (Appendix E). Values of $SNRSEG$ are 4 to 6 dB less than SNR values in log-PCM; while in DPCM-AQB, values of SNR and $SNRSEG$ are much closer. In the range of speech quality represented in Table 6.1, $SNRSEG$ tends to be a better indicator of perceived quality than SNR.

Table 6.1 Objective and subjective rankings of DPCM-AQB and log-PCM speech coders [Cummiskey, Jayant and Flanagan;©1973, AT&T].

Objective Ranking (SNR)	Subjective Ranking (Preference)	
7 bit PCM	7 bit PCM	(high)
6 bit PCM	4 bit DPCM-AQB	
4 bit DPCM-AQB	6 bit PCM	
5 bit PCM	3 bit DPCM-AQB	
3 bit DPCM-AQB	5 bit PCM	
4 bit PCM	4 bit PCM	(low)

We shall comment again on the tolerance of slope overload (Chapter 8), and on the perceptual desirability of a speech-like reconstruction error spectrum (Chapter 7). The two phenomena are inter-related in DPCM operation; and the preference of these conditions to white noise of equal variance is due to a *masking effect* in speech perception: error components accompanied by sufficiently strong signals in the same frequency regions (for example, at or near formant peaks) are simply not heard.

As anticipated in Figure 6.2(b), adaptive quantization of $d(n)$ is almost always assumed in DPCM coding of speech. The nonstationarity of the DPCM quantizer input is related to two factors — the nonstationarity of the coder input itself, and the changes in predictor error variance, caused in this case by nonadaptive prediction of an input with changing psd or acf. Both AQF and AQB systems are possible. However, AQF requires buffering which is complex and also causes delay; low-complexity DPCM systems therefore use AQB logics where there is the additional advantage of not needing extra bits for explicit transmission of step size information. Both instantaneous and syllabic adaptations have been used [Qureshi and Forney, 1975] [Castellino et al., 1974] [Cohn and Melsa, 1975] [Noll, 1974] [Jayant, 1975] [McDermott, Scagliola and Goodman, 1978]. In both cases, the intent is to provide a perceptually best mix of slope overload distortion and granular noise. DPCM quantizer design is also dictated by the need to provide adequate transmission error resistance (Section 6.5), and the robust adaptive quantizer with a one-word memory [4.199(a)] is often used [Johnston and Goodman, 1978] [Adelman, Ching and Gotz, 1979] [Boddie et al., 1981].

DPCM-AQB Coders for 32 kb/s and 24 kb/s Speech Coding with Communications Quality. The DPCM coders just described are appropriate for certain types of applications at 32 kb/s and 24 kb/s. They operate with a fixed first-order predictor for simplicity. Resulting speech quality, as seen in Table 6.1, is less than conservatively defined toll quality (that of 8-bit log-PCM). Nevertheless, 32 kb/s DPCM-AQB quality may be considered acceptable for certain speech transmission applications, especially those which do not require too many multiple encodings (see Figure 5.11). On a subjective quality scale of 1 to 5, the mean opinion score for this coder is very close to 4.0 at 32 kb/s [Daumer, 1982].

Voice storage systems, such as those for recorded announcements, have even less stringent demands on quality. Consequently, they can use a smaller speech bandwidth (say 0 to 2700 Hz), and achieve 24 kb/s coding with 4-bit quantization ($f_s = 6$ kHz, $R = 4$) [Rosenthal et al., 1974]. The quality of a conventional bandwidth 24 kb/s system ($f_s = 8$ kHz, $R = 3$) is less; the greater quantization noise with $R = 3$ (instead of 4) is more objectionable than the loss of bandwidth in going from 3.2 to 2.7 kHz. It is possible, however, to enhance the quality of 3-bit DPCM-AQB speech quite significantly by adaptive postfiltering procedures which capitalize on the fact that the short-time speech cutoff frequency is often less than the nominal 3.2 kHz limit [Smith and Allen, 1981] [Jayant, 1981,II]; see Problem 6.11.

Section 6.5.3 will discuss a standardized class of DPCM coders for toll quality coding at 32 kb/s. These coders include adaptive quantization as well as adaptive prediction.

6.4.2 Image Coding

Figure 6.14 illustrates the performance of a 3-bit DPCM system for image coding [Musmann, 1979,I]. The predictor used is a low-order intraframe predictor of order $N = 3$. As in the speech example, notice the remarkable improvement in going from 3-bit PCM to 3-bit DPCM. Notice once again, however, that the quality of the illustrated DPCM system falls short of 8-bit PCM quality. Slope-overload effects, although more tolerable than granular noise of equal variance, cause visible losses in edge- and contrast-rendition. The quality of 4-bit DPCM, on the other hand, is very close to that of 8-bit PCM. On a subjective quality scale of 1 to 5, intraframe DPCM coding with 4 bits/sample can realize an MOS rating in the order of 4.0 [Yamagata et al., 1981] or higher (Figure 5.14). Note that an MOS score in the order of 4.5 can be considered to be a necessary condition for broadcast-quality television coding.

DPCM coding using 3 to 4 bits/sample can be the basis of broadcast quality digitizations of moving images at rates such as 34 Mb/s and 45 Mb/s. This is the range of bit rates used in the third levels of the digital hierarchies in Table 1.2. The present section discusses general principles relevant to the design of coding systems for the above range of bit rates.

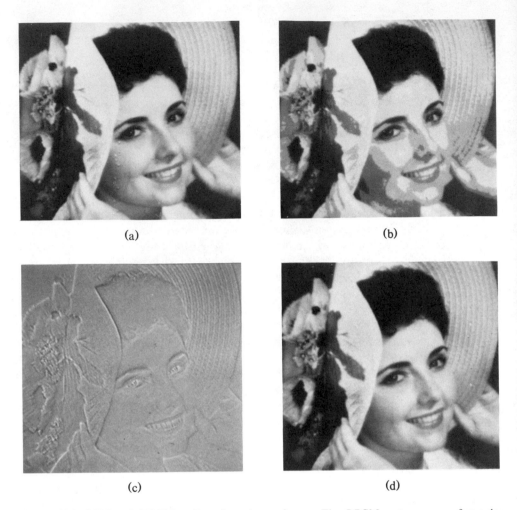

(a)   (b)

(c)   (d)

Figure 6.14 PCM and DPCM coding of an image frame. The DPCM system uses a first-order predictor based on previous pixel B on the same scan line. (a) 8-bit PCM input $x(n)$; (b) 3-bit PCM output; (c) difference signal $d(n)$ in 3-bit DPCM; and (d) 3-bit DPCM output $y(n)$ [Musmann, 1979,I. Reprinted with permission].

Because of the high sampling rates in video systems, low-complexity approaches are highly desirable, and the *intraframe* techniques described in this section reflect that fact. The *interframe* techniques of Section 6.6 demand higher levels of complexity and storage. They also lead to the effective use of lower bit rates such as 1 bit/sample or less.

Quantizers for the difference signal in video use tapered quantization both for intraframe and interframe applications, with the intention of representing relatively smaller spatial and temporal changes with greater resolution, to match viewer preferences. The use of tapered quantization is a general characteristic of DPCM coders, for monochrome as well as color video. The ideal intent in the design of these quantizers is to minimize *noise visibility* rather than mean square error

[Musmann, 1979,I] [Rubinstein and Limb, 1978] [Limb and Rubinstein, 1978] [Netravali and Limb, 1980] [Pirsch, 1981]. The end result, however, is typically either a tapered quantizer (as in the case of algorithms that minimize the mse with the assumption of a monotonically decreasing pdf), and/or an adaptive or switched quantization procedure.

Nonuniform Quantization and Noise Visibility. The exact nature of recommended quantizer nonuniformity depends on several factors such as the number of levels and on quantizer type (midtread or midrise). At bit rates in the order of 3 to 4 bits/sample, the nonuniformity tends to be slightly less than that of the Laplacian characteristic in Table 4.3, with a smallest quantizer interval in the order of one-hundredth of the peak-to-peak input amplitude, and a largest quantizer interval that is at least an order of magnitude wider than the smallest interval [Netravali and Limb, 1980] [Lukas and Kretz, 1983].

Analytical studies of noise visibility have been well complemented by direct perceptual assessments of quality. These assessments are sometimes based on a four-fold categorization of DPCM errors — *slope overload* and *edge-busyness* that occur at sharp edges (Figure 6.3); and *granularity* (Figure 6.3) and *contouring* [Figure 4.31 and Figure 6.14(b)] that occur in flat areas of near-constant brightness. Edge-busyness is most easily noticeable as an interframe, or spatio-temporal effect, while the other types of distortion can be observed within a single frame. Also, as discussed in Chapter 4, contouring effects predominate with very coarse quantization and dithering provides a suitable remedy.

Designs that formally minimize noise visibility, or seek to make it zero, generally follow two steps. The first is the experimental determination of the *noise visibility threshold*, the maximum allowable noise that is *masked* and therefore irrelevant in perception. This threshold is determined as a function of an input parameter such as the *instantaneous* first difference or the instantaneous prediction error [Thoma, 1974]. The visibility threshold is typically a monotonically increasing function of prediction error, with a positive nonzero value at the origin [Musmann, 1979,I]. The second part of the design involves the matching of the quantizer characteristic to this threshold function.

A straightforward and systematic procedure exists for designing a quantizer with the minimum number of output levels, under the constraint that the maximum magnitude of the error introduced by this quantizer is upper bounded by the visibility threshold for any value of quantizer input (the prediction error, correct to quantization feedback effects) [Sharma and Netravali, 1977]. The resulting quantizer is nonuniform because of the increasing nature of the threshold function. With simple types of intraframe prediction, a nonuniform quantizer designed as above needs 16 to 32 levels (4 to 5 bits/sample) to provide reconstruction error patterns of near-zero, or zero visibility [Netravali and Limb, 1980].

Further refinements consist in considering noise masking as a function of image detail *surrounding* a pixel to be coded. High contrast detail implies decreased sensitivity in perception, or the masking of errors with greater magnitudes. Detail, or activity, can be defined in many ways that involve measurements on a set of pixels surrounding the one to be coded. For example, it can be measured as the weighted average of several vertical and horizontal intensity gradients [Netravali and Prasada, 1977] or as the maximum prediction error in the 2-D neighborhood [Musmann, 1979,I]. The value of the activity can also be used to switch to a perceptually appropriate characteristic in a *switched quantization* algorithm.

Switched Quantization. A simple way of adapting quantizers for the difference signal in video is to switch to low- and high resolution modes depending on whether an edge is detected or not. For example, in the notation of Figure 6.5, a horizontal edge is detected if $|x_B - x_D|$ is large, a vertical edge is detected if $|x_C - x_D|$ is large; both transmitter and receiver can make these detections in synchrony and use them for switching to a low resolution quantizer characteristic. In some examples of edge-adaptive differential coding, the quantizer is fully *adaptive*, with an AQB logic. This structure has been developed mostly for the case of one-bit quantization. It will accordingly be described in the chapter on deltamodulation (one-bit DPCM) (Chapter 8).

We shall conclude the discussion of quantization by mentioning a very specific switched quantization strategy for mitigating slope overload noise [Musmann, 1971,I]. Assume a bounded input $x(n) \leq x_{max}$ as in an 8-bit PCM format, and consider its predicted value $\hat{x}(n)$ as shown in Figure 6.15. We have already mentioned that DPCM operation is equivalent to shifting the quantizer mid-point to $\hat{x}(n)$. This is indeed shown in Figure 6.15(a). However, in this case, quantizer levels 6, 7 and 8 are useless, and the use of nearest level 1 to quantize $d(n)$ results in a significant value of reconstruction error $r(n)$. If, however, levels 6, 7 and 8 are used to *extend* the quantizer characteristic downward (away from x_{max}) as in Figure 6.15(b), the reconstruction error $r'(n)$ could be made much smaller. In the illustration, this is realized by use of level 7 in its new position 7'. Note that the quantizer extension is based on $\hat{x}(n)$; since this is also available at the decoder, no side information is needed to effect it at the receiver. The above procedure is an attempt to align the quantization characteristic with a conditional pdf of input $x(n)$ given the past reconstruction values. Because of the reflection of part of the quantizer characteristic in the above system, the use of an optimum nonuniform characteristic as described in previous discussions is never assured. Further, the principle of quantizer extension is clearly most relevant for *bounded inputs*, such as image inputs with a finite-support pdf. Some realizations of extended quantization make use of a *set* of quantizers and an appropriate switching strategy [Bostelmann, 1974].

Figure 6.15 A switched quantization strategy for bounded inputs [Musmann, 1971,I].

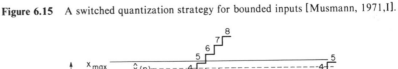
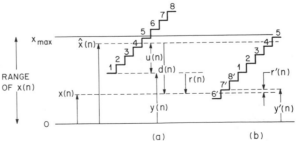

Switched Prediction. A simple example of an *intraframe* switched prediction algorithm was mentioned in Example 6.3. In that example, the alternative predictors in the system were a first-order 1-D predictor and a second-order 2-D predictor; and the switching was based on a comparison of the prediction gains to be expected from the alternative arrangements in a given localized area of the image. The design of an optimal switched prediction algorithm depends on several factors such as the bit rate and the quantization algorithm in use [Zschunke, 1977]. Switched prediction can also be extended to include an *interframe* or *interfield* predictor as one of the alternatives in the predictor system [Yamamoto, Hatori and Murakami, 1981].

An illustrative example of intraframe switched prediction is one where the predicted value of x_A (see Figure 6.5) is one of four possible values x_B, x_C, x_D or x_E, depending on the most likely direction of the image 'contour'. The determination of this most likely direction is made on the basis of reconstructed values of the previous neighbors of pixel A, and therefore represents information that need not be separately transmitted to the receiver. Predictor switching can therefore be as frequent as warranted; for example, on an instantaneous, pixel-by-pixel basis. Gains over a third-order fixed predictor $[\hat{x}_A = x_B + 0.5 \, (x_C - x_D)]$ can be in the order of 4 dB, but more significant are the perceptual gains over fixed prediction in the encoding of specific classes of images [Zschunke, 1977].

Switched prediction that includes interframe or interfield prediction, as alternatives to intraframe prediction, provides the possibility of robust performance over a wide range of grades of motion. Still images tend to favor interframe or interfield prediction while images with violent motion favor the use of an intraframe predictor. In composite color coding, for example, significant gains over fixed prediction are realized with simple third-order configurations for the intraframe and interfield alternatives, a conditional replenishment algorithm (Section 6.6.3) and a maximum updating frequency of one switch for every block of eight pixels. The subjective quality of a 30 Mb/s DPCM coder with this kind of switched prediction is an MOS rating (Appendix F) in the order of 4.5 on a scale of 1 to 5, and this represents broadcast-quality digitization [Yamamoto, Hatori and Murakami, 1981]. The MOS rating decreases to about 3 with a random bit error rate of 10^{-7}, as in Figure 5.14.

6.4.3 Entropy Coding

The output of a DPCM coder is ideally a quantized innovations process. Even with non-ideal prediction, the output process has fewer temporal or spatial dependencies than a typical coder input, suggesting that entropy coding is less crucial in DPCM than in nondifferential PCM. This is indeed true [Goyal and O'Neal, 1973]. The motivation for using entropy coding in DPCM is to take advantage of residual output structure; in the simplest implementations, the structure that is exploited is merely the nonuniform univariate pdf of the output, or the unequal probabilities of different output words. In general, the better the prediction in DPCM, the less the gain expected from entropy coding, if it is based on conditional entropies obtained from coding output samples in sequences

(Appendix C); and the less the variability of output data rate, suggesting shorter buffers for evening out data flow.

The bit-saving potential of entropy coding is used to increase the number of quantizer levels, and thus to realize a specified output quality at a given *average* bit rate. Typical buffer requirements needed in speech coding are tens of bits with 7-level quantization used in 16 kb/s DPCM-AQB coding, and hundreds of bits with 5-level quantization used in 9.6 kb/s DPCM-AQB coding [Qureshi and Forney, 1975]. Designs for lower average bit rates also call for buffer control of allowed quantizer resolution, and high quality applications include adaptive prediction as an additional refinement. In buffer-controlled quantization, quantizer *threshold* values are changed if the probability of overflow or underflow of the buffer is high. There is no need to modify the decoder if the *reconstruction* levels are fixed.

Buffers for video DPCM coders are typically thousands of bits long. A good example of buffer control is that in a *dual-mode coder* [Goyal and O'Neal, 1973] where buffer overflow causes the quantizer to switch to the coarser of two characteristics. One example of a convenient, yet perceptually acceptable procedure is to allow quantizer switching no more frequently than once per scan line. Coarsely quantized image lines are less degrading during "active scene," or "high entropy" periods which produce long codewords, than during "stationary scene" or "low entropy" periods. The procedure has been used for a DPCM coder using 6 MHz sampling, 4-bit quantization, fixed previous element prediction and a typical output *average* transmission rate of 18 Mb/s. The characteristics of this *dual-mode* coder are summarized in Table 6.2. Note that with the full buffer, the system switches from a 16-level characteristic to a 6-level characteristic (last column of table) with output levels ± 1, ± 3 and ± 6.

Table 6.2 Characteristics of an entropy-coded dual-mode DPCM coder for video.

Quantizer Level Number	Normal Buffer (4016 bits)			Full Buffer (4048 bits)		Quantizer Level Number
	DPCM Code	Entropy Code	Code Length	Entropy Code	Code Length	
1	0000	11	2	11	2	1
2	0001	011	3	010	3	3
3	0010	1000	4	010	3	3
4	0011	10011	5	010	3	3
5	0100	101100	6	011	3	6
6	0101	101110	6	011	3	6
7	0110	0100110	7	011	3	6
8	0111	1010	4	011	3	6
−8	1000	01000	5	000	3	−6
−7	1001	0100111	7	000	3	−6
−6	1010	101111	6	000	3	−6
−5	1011	101101	6	000	3	−6
−4	1100	010010	6	001	3	−3
−3	1101	10010	5	001	3	−3
−2	1110	0101	4	001	3	−3
−1	1111	00	2	10	2	1

6.4.4 Variable-Rate Coding

The price paid for the bit rate efficiency in entropy coding is the variability in transmission rate, and the complexities and delays associated with buffer memories and logics. There are special digital communication networks, however, where one explicitly designs a coder for an elastic or variable output rate. Such *variable-rate coding* usually implies *variable-quality* coding. For example, in packet transmissions of speech (Section 1.2.5), one attempts to handle the overloading of a packet transmission facility by reducing the coder bit rate rather than by discarding whole packets. The procedure is particularly appealing if speech silence statistics in a multi-user system are jointly exploited to minimize the bit rate penalties incurred by active speakers. Similarly, in *Digital Speech Interpolation*, it is desirable to have the flexibility of switching to a lower bit rate instead of clipping parts of active speech [Sciulli and Campanella, 1973] [IEEE, 1982]. The bit allocation for a given speech signal should ideally be determined by the short-term speech activity (short-term speech variance) in that signal, as well as by the local demands on the communication channel [McPherson, O'Neal and Stroh, 1977] [Yatsuzuka, 1982]. For a given average transmission rate, variable-rate coding with speech-silence exploitation can have significant gains in average bit rate over a corresponding fixed-rate coder. For example, in a variable-rate simulation of DPCM-AQB [Cox and Crochiere, 1980], average values of these gains were in the order of 1 bit per sample or more in a single-user system, with input-buffering of a few hundred (say, 200 to 500) milliseconds; with multiple users (say, 4 to 12), the average gains were up to 2 bits/sample even for zero input buffering on individual channels (zero encoding delay).

Embedded coding systems have the feature that bit rate reductions can be effected at any point along the communication network; also, this can be done without the transmitter and receiver knowing about these changes, as long as the number of bits dropped is not too many for a given coder design. In fact, embedded coding implies, by definition, a packet or block of bits within which is embedded a sub-packet or sub-block which by itself is sufficient for producing decoded speech of useful quality, although full quality is achieved only upon reception of the entire packet or block. Embedded coding thus implies a hierarchy of sub-blocks where least crucial sub-blocks are discarded first, as the channel gets overloaded. This hierarchical concept is a natural one for many classes of speech and image coders [Knowlton, 1980] [Bially, Gold and Seneff, 1980] [O'Leary et al., 1981]. This class includes the special case where component sub-blocks in the coder output have equal significance [Jayant and Christensen, 1981] [Jayant, 1981,I].

PCM coding of speech is an embedded system in that the quantizer output is a hierarchy of bits of differing significance — least significant bits of all users of an R-bit system can be discarded, for example, to achieve an embedded $(R-1)$ bit system. Indeed, periodic *bit stealing* (Problem 5.4) is used in the North American PCM system for purposes of signaling.

The DPCM coder of Figure 6.1 is *not* an embedded system. Discarding of less significant bits by the network implies (after a customary addition of random dummy bits prior to receiver decoding) that the predictors at coder and decoder have different inputs. This leads, in general, to a large reduction in the quality of output speech $y(n)$, the exact amount of the degradation depending of course on the original number of bits R and the number of bits discarded by the channel, R_C. Fortunately, however, the DPCM coder can be adjusted to provide a robust embedded system by the simple expedient of deleting R_B bits from the inputs to the feedback loops both at transmitter and receiver, where R_B is greater than or equal to $\max\{R_C\}$, the largest expected value for the number of bits dropped by the channel [Ching, 1973]. The effect of coarse feedback is to provide *subdued prediction*, as in the context of transmission errors (Section 6.7) and in the context of *open-loop* DPCM (D*PCM) (Chapter 7). The use of coarse feedback makes the system inferior to a conventional R-bit system with an ideal channel ($R_C = 0$); but with a non-ideal channel ($R_C > 0$), the performance is very close to that of a conventional $(R-R_C)$-bit coder [Goodman, 1980].

An alternative approach to realize an embedded DPCM system involves explicit coding of DPCM reconstruction noise using R_n bits/sample. This can be the basis of an embedded variable-rate system with a minimum bit rate of R, the bit rate of the basic DPCM coder; and a maximum bit rate of $R + \max\{R_n\}$. In this approach, the resulting quality at the higher bit rates $R + R_n$ can in fact be designed to be better than that of conventional DPCM at the same bit rate $R + R_n$. This is a result of *adaptive bit allocation* that makes possible the quantization of the more significant noise samples with a greater number of bits, for a given constraint on the average noise coding rate R_n. The adaptive bit allocation requires the use of encoding delay in the order of 4 ms, but no additional side-information is needed to inform the receiver about it if the bit allocation is based on observations of previous quantizer outputs [Jayant, 1983].

6.5 Adaptive Prediction

Previous sections have specified predictor designs as functions of input statistics as given by acf descriptions, or equivalent psd descriptions. In these prediction algorithms, benefits saturated early with predictor order N, in the order of 3 or 4. Maximum values of prediction gain were in the order of 10 dB for illustrative speech data (Figure 6.7) and in the order of 18 dB for illustrative image data (Figure 6.8). Such gains indicate a less than 2-bit advantage over PCM in the case of speech, and a 3-bit advantage in the case of images, if mean square error is used as a criterion of performance.

The next two sections of this chapter will discuss DPCM coders that are more complex but also more bit-efficient. These coders will provide toll-quality speech at $R = 4$ bits/sample, and useful digitizations at bit rates as low as $R = 2$ and less. These systems are based on adaptive prediction, including schemes for exploiting periodicities in speech and video (Section 6.6). In low bit rate speech coding, the generic term *Adaptive Predictive Coding* (APC) (Sections 6.5.1, 6.5.2, 6.5.3 and 6.6.1) is used to describe a large class of coding systems using adaptive prediction [Atal and Schroeder, 1970] [Gibson, 1980]. The term APC includes coder classes with and without pitch prediction. In low bit rate image coding, the generic term *Interframe Coding* (Section 6.6) describes a large category of efficient predictive coders [Haskell, Mounts and Candy, 1972] [Habibi, 1977] [Netravali and Limb, 1980]. Adaptations for image predictions typically use the simpler structure of *switched prediction* (Section 6.4.2). For simplicity in high-speed implementation, image predictor designs favor simply implemented coefficients such as 0, 1, 1/2 or 15/16, but seek for each pixel, or sub-image, the best (out of a small dictionary of) predicting pixel sets.

Input statistics such as acf and psd are time-varying in the case of nonstationary signals and, as a consequence, best predictor designs for inputs such as speech should be time-varying, or adaptive, as well. Figure 2.7 has shown a typical sequence of normalized short-term acf's of speech to illustrate the problem of nonstationarity. The acf evolves from an aperiodic one (top of figure) to a highly periodic pattern (bottom of figure), reflecting a similar evolution of the input waveform. Figure 2.10 has illustrated nonstationarity in the psd domain, with examples of voiced-speech and unvoiced-speech spectra. These acf and psd descriptions suggest that severe *spectral mismatches* are inherent in nonadaptive speech prediction, which is based on long-time-averaged statistics. Such a mismatch has also been illustrated in Figure 6.10. Corresponding to these mismatches are losses in DPCM performance in terms of less than maximum possible prediction gain G_P. Figures 6.16 and 6.17 show waveforms of coder input $x(n)$ and prediction error $d(n)$ for voiced and unvoiced speech, together with G_P values, for both adaptive prediction (of the APF type to be described presently) and nonadaptive prediction with $N = 8$. The examples use a 5-bit nonadaptive quantizer for $d(n)$. The benefits of adaptive prediction are clearly higher for the unvoiced speech, for which G_P increases from -7 dB to $+3$ dB.

The next two subsections will discuss strategies for predictor adaptation. As in adaptive quantization, adaptation information can be either explicitly transmitted to the DPCM receiver (forward adaptation, APF, the system used in Figures 6.16 and 6.17), or derived from the history of recent quantized data (backward adaptation,

Figure 6.16 DPCM coding of a 32 ms segment of voiced speech with $N = 8$, and a 5-bit log-quantizer. Waveforms of (a) speech $x(n)$; and difference signal $d(n)$ in (b) nonadaptive and (c) adaptive prediction [Noll, 1973]. The speech waveform is that in Figure 6.10(b).

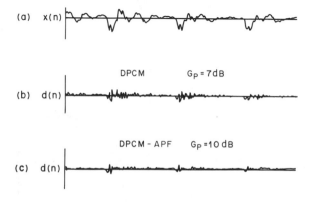

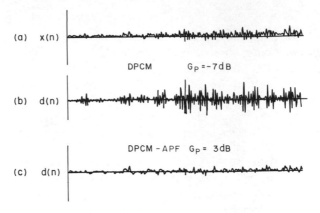

Figure 6.17 DPCM coding of a 32 ms segment of unvoiced speech with $N = 8$, and a 5-bit log-quantizer. Waveforms of (a) speech $x(n)$; and difference signal $d(n)$ in (b) nonadaptive and (c) adaptive prediction [Noll, 1973]. The speech waveform is that in Figure 6.10(c).

APB). The results of the next two subsections will be highly speech-specific. The analyses will be appropriate to the adaptation of coefficients in *near-sample-based* (spectrum) predictors; *distant-sample-based* (pitch) predictors are also inherently adaptive but in a slightly different sense, as we shall see in Section 6.6.

Figure 6.18 shows the structure of DPCM coders using forward and backward estimations of adaptive predictor coefficients. Quantizer adaptation is not shown, but is assumed unless otherwise stated. Sections 6.5.1 and 6.5.2 will respectively discuss the designs of the APF and APB systems in Figure 6.18.

Figure 6.18 Block diagram of DPCM with (a) forward-adaptive prediction (APF); and (b) backward-adaptive prediction (APB).

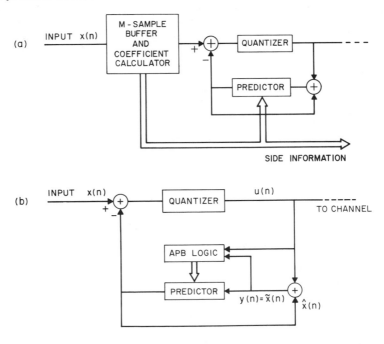

Differential PCM   6

6.5.1 Forward Adaptation — APF

In Figure 6.18(a), M input values are buffered, and are released after a set of N predictor coefficients has been optimized for the buffered segment. We have already seen that the optimum prediction gain is a monotonically increasing function of predictor order N. A good choice of N should correspond to adequate prediction gain together with a manageable amount of side information. The choice of learning period or buffer length M likewise involves a compromise, reflecting three considerations: (i) the frequency with which predictor information will have to be updated and transmitted; (ii) the rate at which input statistics change; and (iii) the block size needed for reliable learning of (locally stationary) statistics. As in AQF systems, an intrinsic property of APF algorithms is that they may imply a significant amount of encoding delay, which may be objectionable in certain classes of communication networks.

For speech, a good choice of M corresponds to a 16 ms buffer, while a value of $N = 10$ ensures adequate use of short-term predictability with a sampling rate of 8 kHz. Figure 6.19 shows time-dependencies (assuming 16 ms-averaged values in

Figure 6.19 Time dependencies of (a) input speech level and of prediction gain G_P in (b) nonadaptive prediction and (c) adaptive prediction. All three waveforms are 1440 ms long and are sampled once every 16 ms. The points M, N and N refer to nasal sounds (in the word "München"), which are characterized by very high values of G_P, in the order of 20 dB [Noll, 1973].

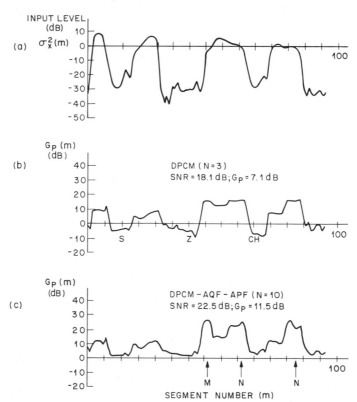

each case) of speech power and prediction gains in nonadaptive and adaptive systems. Note that the prediction gain G_P is sometimes negative in the non-adaptive system. As seen in Figure 6.17, negative values of G_P occur mainly during severe spectral mismatches in the coding of low-level unvoiced segments. With adaptive prediction, G_P is always positive. Figure 6.19 also shows, as in Figure 6.16, that averaged values of G_P (over the sentence-length input) are 7 and 11 dB respectively for nonadaptive and adaptive prediction, indicating a $4/6 = 0.67$ bit per sample advantage due to APF in this example.

Finally, the gain G_P is plotted as a function of the order N of adaptive prediction in Figure 6.20. Results are given for a population of four speakers, and for both lowpass and bandpass inputs, the same inputs that were used in the nonadaptive prediction example of Section 6.3 and Figure 6.7. The smallest value of G_P for $N = 8$ is about 10 dB, the value noted for $N = 8$ in the voiced speech example of Figure 6.16. The value of G_P for unvoiced speech is much less, as noted in Figure 6.17. Note also that prediction gains saturate much slower with increasing order N than in the nonadaptive prediction example of Figure 6.7 (also see [Dunn, 1971]). A comparison of asymptotic values in Figures 6.7 and 6.20

Figure 6.20 Maximum prediction gain versus order N of adaptive predictor for (a) lowpass-filtered speech; and (b) bandpass-filtered speech [Noll, 1973].

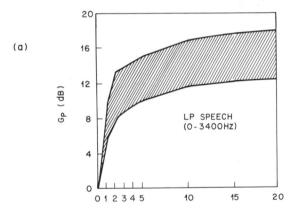

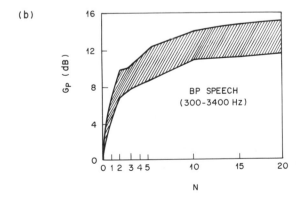

indicates a typical 6 dB/sample or 1 bit/sample advantage for APF over fixed-predictor DPCM.

A Comparison of PCM and DPCM Speech Coders at 24 kb/s. Figure 6.21 provides a summary of DPCM performance with speech at 24 kb/s ($f_s = 8$ kHz, $R = 3$); the y-axis on the left hand side is coder *SNR* in dB, while that on the right hand side is the gain over 3-bit log-PCM. Note that contributions due to adaptive quantization (AQF in this case) and adaptive prediction (APF) are both significant, and with the inclusion of entropy coding, the *SNR* in DPCM is 18 dB better than that of 3-bit log-PCM, corresponding objectively to 6-bit log PCM. The simplest DPCM coder in Figure 6.21 is the one-bit quantizer system, *deltamodulation* (DM-AQB), operating at $f_s = 3 \cdot 8$ kHz $= 24$ kHz. Even this simple system has a gain of nearly 10 dB over log-PCM at 24 kb/s.

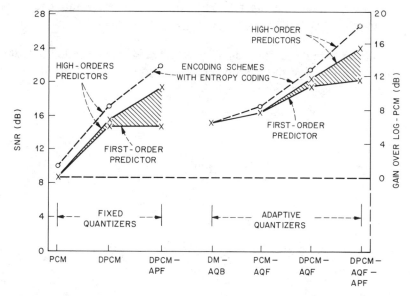

Figure 6.21 Performance of several 24 kb/s DPCM coding schemes for speech inputs, and gains over 24 kb/s log PCM [Noll,I;©1975, AT&T].

Predictor Optimization in APF. As in Sections 6.2 and 6.3, adequate insight into predictor design can be derived from a simplified analysis that neglects quantization noise. Thus, the predicted value is approximated as in (6.38a). The power of the difference signal $d(n) = x(n) - \hat{x}(n)$ for an M-block (starting with $n=1$) is

$$\chi_d^2 = \sum_{n=1}^{M} d^2(n)/M \qquad (6.68)$$

This is minimized by setting $\partial \chi_d^2 / \partial h_i = 0$; $i = 1, 2, ..., N$; it results in a set of equations

$$\sum_{j=1}^{N} h_{j,opt} \hat{R}_{xx}(i,j) = \hat{R}_{xx}(0,i); \quad i = 1,2,...,N ; \qquad (6.69a)$$

$$\hat{R}_{xx}(i,j) = \frac{1}{M}\sum_{n=1}^{M} x(n-i)x(n-j) ;$$

$$\min\{\chi_d^2\} = \hat{R}_{xx}(0,0) - \sum_{j=1}^{N} h_{j,opt}\hat{R}_{xx}(0,j) \qquad (6.69b)$$

The hats on the acf $R_{xx}(\cdot,\cdot)$ reflect the fact that in adaptive prediction, acf values are block-specific estimates. They are estimates of an acf of an input sequence $\{X(n)\}$ that is assumed to be at least locally stationary. In what follows, we describe two procedures for producing these block-specific estimates. Associated with these procedures are the terms *autocorrelation* and *covariance*. Unfortunately, this well-accepted terminology is confusing. The difference between the two procedures is *not* related to the fundamental difference between the terms autocorrelation and covariance as explained in Chapter 2.

A Simple Estimation Procedure for R_{xx}: The Autocorrelation Solution. Assume that the only data used to determine $\mathbf{h}_{opt}$ for a given segment are the $x(n)$ values in that segment [Figure 6.22(a)]

$$x(n) = 0 ; \quad M < n \leqslant 0 \qquad (6.70)$$

so that

$$\hat{R}_{xx}(i,j) = \frac{1}{M}\sum_{n=1}^{M-|i-j|} x(n)x(n+|i-j|) = \hat{R}_{xx}(|i-j|) \qquad (6.71)$$

With $|i-j| = k$, and with

$$\hat{R}_{xx}(k) = \frac{1}{M}\sum_{n=1}^{M-k} x(n)x(n+k) ; \quad k = 0,1,...,N,$$

(6.69) will read

$$\sum_{j=1}^{N} h_{j,opt}\hat{R}_{xx}(|i-j|) = \hat{R}_{xx}(i) ; \quad i = 1,2,...,N \qquad (6.72)$$

Figure 6.22 Input data windows used in (a) autocorrelation and (b) covariance solutions of APF.

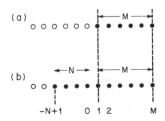

Thus, instead of the nonadaptive design $\mathbf{r}_{xx} = \mathbf{R}_{xx}\mathbf{h}_{opt}$, we now have

$$\hat{\mathbf{r}}_{xx} = \hat{\mathbf{R}}_{xx}\mathbf{h}_{opt} \; ; \qquad \mathbf{h}_{opt} = \hat{\mathbf{R}}_{xx}^{-1}\hat{\mathbf{r}}_{xx} \; ;$$

$$\hat{\mathbf{r}}_{xx}^T = \{\hat{R}_{xx}(i)\} \; ; \qquad \hat{\mathbf{R}}_{xx} = \{\hat{R}_{xx}(|i-j|)\} \; ; \qquad i, j = 1,2,..., N \qquad (6.73)$$

In other words, the observed samples in Figure 6.22(a) are used to define the first row of the acf matrix $\hat{\mathbf{R}}_{xx}$, and no new terms are needed to define the entries in the other rows. Instead, the entries in the first row are used to construct a Toeplitz matrix $\hat{\mathbf{R}}_{xx}$ where entries along any diagonal are equal. The matrix $\hat{\mathbf{R}}_{xx}$ is therefore symmetric and Toeplitz, and the equations (6.73) are *normal equations* of the form (6.44). We have already mentioned that the $\mathbf{h}_{opt}$ may be solved for by a recursive algorithm. That algorithm also gives the variance of the prediction error as a side result. This variance can directly be used to control an AQF algorithm that may be used in the DPCM coder.

The above solution is also called the *autocorrelation solution* [Itakura and Saito, 1968] [Markel and Gray, 1976]. Besides the imposed Toeplitz property mentioned above, the autocorrelation solution has the advantage that the recursive filter that uses $\mathbf{h}_{opt}$, and hence the DPCM decoder, will also be stable (Problem 6.24).

A Second Estimation Procedure for R_{xx}: The Covariance Solution. This procedure assumes that the last N samples of a previous M-block are also available for computing the optimum predictor. This is a reasonable procedure considering that these samples are after all used in predicting the beginning samples of the current block. Thus, as in Figure 6.22(b),

$$x(n) = 0 \; ; \qquad M < n \leqslant -N \qquad (6.74)$$

The solution can be derived from (6.69a). The resulting matrix $\hat{\mathbf{R}}_{xx}$ will be symmetric but *non-Toeplitz* because each row of the acf matrix is independently defined by the observations of each of N sliding windows of M samples each (Problem 6.27). Because of the absence of the Toeplitz structure, this method has a significant computational disadvantage. It is called a covariance matrix by speech researchers [Makhoul and Wolf, 1972], and the procedure based on (6.74) is called the *covariance solution*.

Comparison of the Two Estimation Procedures. The autocorrelation solution is usually preceded by a windowing of input data [Rabiner and Schafer, 1978], so that $x(n)$ values at the beginning and end of a block are tapered to zero. Such windowing makes the artificial zero-setting in (6.70) less discontinuous. No such windowing is necessary in the covariance solution: input values for predicting the early samples of a block are made available from the previous block.

Performance differences between the autocorrelation and covariance solutions are small for large M. The autocorrelation solution is more robust in the context of coarse quantization, although the peak performance is better with the covariance method [Markel and Gray, 1976] [Gibson, 1980].

Use of Polarity Correlation. The computational task in APF is significantly reduced if one uses so-called *polarity correlations* in place of $\hat{R}_{xx}(k)$: for example, the *two-sided polarity correlation* $\hat{R}''_{xx}(k) = (1/M)\sum \text{sgn } x(n) \text{ sgn } x(n+k) = (2/\pi)\arcsin \rho_{xx}(k)$ (Problem 6.26) instead of $\hat{R}_{xx}(k)$. Resulting filters are stable. However, the achievable gain G_P is often significantly reduced in this suboptimal approach. Similar statements are true for the *one-sided polarity correlation* $\hat{R}'_{xx}(k) = \sum x(n) \text{ sgn } x(n+k)$. But the polarity correlation functions have found useful applications in APB designs seeking minimal complexity (Section 6.5.3).

The Lattice Solution. Both the covariance and the autocorrelation methods consist of two steps: (i) computation of a matrix of correlation values, and (ii) solution of a set of linear equations. In another class of methods, called *lattice* methods, the above two steps are combined into a recursive algorithm for determining the linear predictor parameters. Byproducts of the lattice methods are the *parcor*, or partial correlation coefficients [Itakura and Saito, 1968] to be discussed presently.

Transmission of Side Information. For a given choice of N and M, the amount of side information in APF is determined by the extent to which $\mathbf{h}_{\text{opt}}$ values are quantized for transmission. It is implied that predictors, both at the transmitter and at the receiver, use the same quantized predictor vector $Q(\mathbf{h}_{\text{opt}})$, ignoring possible transmission error effects. The direct transmission of predictor coefficients would include the following steps:

$$\text{Coder:} \quad \{x(n)\} \rightarrow \hat{\mathbf{r}}_{xx} \rightarrow \mathbf{h}_{\text{opt}} \rightarrow Q(\mathbf{h}_{\text{opt}})$$

$$\text{Side Information:} \quad Q(\mathbf{h}_{\text{opt}})$$

Clearly, side information can be kept small by quantizing $\mathbf{h}_{\text{opt}}$ values coarsely. However, coarse quantizations of coefficients can cause a stability problem in the all-pole decoder filter. When the decoder filter attempts to mimic the spectrum of the source (Figure 6.10), the calculated coefficients $\mathbf{h}_{\text{opt}}$ may represent a psd with poles close to unity. Round-off and truncation errors may then cause some of the zeros of $[1-H_{opt}(z)]$ to lie outside the unit circle, although the least-squares predictor equations always lead to a stable solution [Robinson and Wold, 1963]. One safeguard against the above problem is inherent in windowing techniques. Windowing of the data of the analysis segment or windowing of calculated acf values increases the bandwidths of the poles, and hence their distances to the unit circle.

Partial Correlation Coefficients as Side Information. An elegant solution to the coefficient quantization problem consists in representing $\mathbf{h}$ values in terms of equivalent *partial correlation (parcor) coefficients* (Problem 6.28).

We have already mentioned that in the autocorrelation solution a recursive algorithm computes successively, $^k\mathbf{h}_{\text{opt}}$ and min $\{^k\sigma_d^2\}$, for $k = 1,2,...,N$ using the acf-values of the process $\{X(n)\}$. In every step k, the highest-numbered predictor-coefficient denoted by $^k h_{k,opt} = \pi_k$ is of particular importance. It is called a *reflection coefficient* or, in the statistical literature, partial correlation coefficient (*parcor* coefficient). The parcor coefficients have the properties:

$$\pi_k = {}^k h_{k,opt} \; ; \quad \min \{{}^k \sigma_d^2\} = \min \{{}^{k-1} \sigma_d^2\}(1 - \pi_k^2) \tag{6.75}$$

Since

$$\min \{{}^k \sigma_d^2\} \leqslant \min \{{}^{k-1} \sigma_d^2\} , \tag{6.76}$$

this implies that

$$|\pi_k| \leqslant 1 \quad \text{for all } k \tag{6.77}$$

A repeated use of (6.75) yields

$$\min \{{}^k \sigma_d^2\} = \sigma_x^2 \prod_{j=1}^{k} (1 - \pi_j^2) \tag{6.78}$$

In addition, from (6.75) and Section 6.3.4, we find that in the case of a *M*th *order Markov process,*

$$\pi_{M+j} = 0 \; ; \quad j = 1,2,... \tag{6.79}$$

The fact that the magnitudes of π_k are bounded means that quantization effects can be easily studied and, if necessary, compensated for, thus providing a simple stability check. The steps involved if $\boldsymbol{\pi}_{opt}$-values are used for transmission (and as a stability check) can be summarized as below, with $Q(\cdot)$ representing quantization:

$$\text{Coder:} \; \{x(n)\} \rightarrow \hat{\mathbf{r}}_{xx} \rightarrow \mathbf{h}_{opt} \rightarrow \boldsymbol{\pi}_{opt} \rightarrow Q(\boldsymbol{\pi}_{opt}) \rightarrow Q(\mathbf{h}_{opt}) \tag{6.80}$$

$$\text{Side Information:} \; Q(\boldsymbol{\pi}_{opt}) \tag{6.81}$$

$$\text{Decoder:} \; Q(\boldsymbol{\pi}_{opt}) \rightarrow Q(\mathbf{h}_{opt}) \tag{6.82}$$

It is possible to avoid the last step $[Q(\boldsymbol{\pi}_{opt}) \rightarrow Q(\mathbf{h}_{opt})]$ in (6.80) and (6.82) by using a *lattice network* as predictor [Markel and Gray, 1976] [Goldberg, Freudberg and Cheung, 1976] [Makhoul, 1977] [Friedlander, 1982]. Otherwise, a short-form algorithm has to be used for the mapping $Q(\boldsymbol{\pi}) \rightarrow Q(\mathbf{h})$ both at coder and decoder to provide identical predictions. This algorithm regenerates ${}^k h_j$ (at the kth iteration) by using the recursion [Levinson, 1949]

$${}^k h_{j,opt} = {}^{k-1} h_{j,opt} - {}^{k-1} h_{k-j,opt} \pi_k \; ; \quad j = 1,2,...,k-1 \; ; \quad k = 2,3,...,N \tag{6.83a}$$

$${}^k h_{k,opt} = \pi_k = \frac{R_{xx}(k) - \sum_{j=1}^{k-1} R_{xx}(|k-j|) \; {}^{k-1} h_{j,opt}}{R_{xx}(0) - \sum_{j=1}^{k-1} R_{xx}(j) \; {}^{k-1} h_{j,opt}} \; ; \quad k = 1,2,...,N \tag{6.83b}$$

The initial value in (6.83b) is obviously

$$\pi_1 = {}^1h_{1,opt} = R_{xx}(1)/R_{xx}(0) = \rho_1 \qquad (6.83c)$$

We have explained earlier that there are certain constraints on allowable values of acf. Indeed, if $k - 1$ values of acf have been given, $R_{xx}(k)$ can only lie in a specific region that is described by π_k. A value of acf outside that region would indicate that the correlation matrix $\mathbf{R}_{xx}$ is not non-negative definite, and that the psd would have negative values. In this sense, parcor coefficients describe only the admissible sections of the acf. The *log-area coefficients*

$$c_k = \log \frac{1+\pi_k}{1-\pi_k} \qquad (6.84)$$

provide still another representation of **h**-values in APF. They were devised first in the context of vocoders for synthetic speech [Makhoul, 1975] [Markel and Gray, 1976]. One of the advantages of this representation is that efficient *uniform* quantizers can be designed for log-area coefficients [Viswanathan and Makhoul, 1975].

Efficient Quantizers and Coders for h and π Vectors. The simplest approach for efficient quantization of coefficient values is to match quantizers to simple individual statistics such as the means and standard deviations of h_j or π_j; and to distribute the available quantizer bits equally among the N coefficients.

More efficient encoding results if the available bits of transmission in a given block are distributed more equitably, to reflect coefficient-variance characteristics. Specifically, if all of the N mean square distortions D_j; $j = 1,2,...,N$ are required to be equal, the bit allocation procedure will be one that allots more bits to coefficients of higher variance [Viswanathan and Makhoul, 1975]. The topic of variance-dependent bit allocation is discussed at length in the context of block quantizers for transform coding of waveforms (Chapter 12).

The **h** vectors cannot be efficiently quantized due to lack of a convenient method to ensure that $Q(\mathbf{h})$ will result in stable all-pole filter operation. Recall from Chapter 2 that only in the case of $N = 2$ have we been able to derive the admissible region (h_1, h_2) of an all-pole filter (Figure 2.17). To ensure decoder stability, components of **h** would require at least a 12 bit/sample quantizer. For a block length of 20 ms and predictor order $N = 10$, the resulting side information of $50 \cdot 10 \cdot 12R = 6000$ bits/second would be prohibitive for low bit rate application. With π vectors, on the other hand, adequate bit rate allocations for $N = 10$ may be in the order of

$$\{5, 5, 4, 3, 3, 3, 3, 3, 3, 3\} \quad \text{or} \quad \{8, 7, 6, 6, 5, 5, 5, 5, 4, 4\}$$

corresponding to totals of 35 or 55 bits/block. If we add 5 bits/block for AQF step size, respective side information rates are 2000 or 3000 bits/sec with 20 ms blocks. Further decreases of side information will be possible in lower order predictor systems ($N = 4$, for example) which may be used at very low bit rates such as 8 kb/s; at these bit rates, quantization noise feedback may in fact limit useful predictor order to low values such as $N = 4$.

Gains in the coding of side information can also be realized by exploiting dependencies that exist *within* and *between* coefficient vectors. Techniques that do this include differential or transform coding of coefficient vectors [Sambur, 1975].

Switched Prediction. A suboptimal but simple approach to APF consists in *switched prediction* where both the transmitter and the receiver have a bank of L_P possible predictors, and adaptations consist in switching to one of these predictors based on appropriate procedures that we shall presently discuss. The advantages of the procedure are: (i) all L_P predictors are predetermined, obviating the need to solve for, or quantize, predictor coefficients during coder operation; (ii) the side information transmitted is simply the index of the predictor picked by the coder for a given input block; and (iii) the amount of side information, $\log_2 L_P$ bits/block, is much smaller than the numbers cited at the end of the last section.

For communications-quality speech coding at bit rates such as 24 or 32 kb/s, rather simple switched predictor procedures may be adequate. An illustrative system is the switched second-order four-predictor system of Table 6.3 where the predictor switches, once for every block of 256 samples, to one of $L_P = 4$ possible states as dictated by observations only on the first normalized acf value ρ_1. The system provides significant gains over a time-invariant second-order predictor matched to the long-time-averaged speech spectrum [Evci, Xydeas and Steele, 1981]. For example, in the coding of speech blocks involving voiced-to-unvoiced transitions, the *SNR* gain can be as high as 4 to 5 dB. The performance of the switched predictor system can itself be improved further by using it in conjunction with APB procedures (Section 6.5.2) where, for each block, *initial* predictor values h'_j ($j = 1, 2$) in a given state are one of the four coefficient-pairs of Table 6.3; and these coefficients are continuously updated for every sample of the block by procedures to be discussed in Section 6.5.2.

In image coding, various algorithms for switched prediction have been proposed. In particular, these techniques can provide better edge response in intraframe DPCM coding using less than 3 bits/sample [Musmann, 1979]. A simple example of switched prediction has also been given in Example 6.3.

Table 6.3 A second-order, four-state, switched predictor for speech [Evci, Xydeas and Steele, 1981].

State Number	Range of ρ_1			h_1	h_2
1	0.7	to	1.0	1.53	-0.72
2	0.4	to	0.7	0.95	-0.34
3	0.0	to	0.4	0.48	-0.21
4	-1.0	to	0.0	-0.63	-0.36

Vector Quantization. For low bit rate speech applications, more complex switched predictor procedures are appropriate. In these systems, the value of L_P is much greater than the value $L_P = 4$ in Table 6.3. Further, the selection of predictor may also follow a different strategy involving a complex, sometimes exhaustive, *search* rather than a simple input *classification* as in Table 6.3. The performance of these *vector quantization* procedures has been studied as a function of L_P for speech inputs similar to those used in the nonadaptive and adaptive predictions of Figure 6.7 and Figure 6.20. For a given predictor order N, the values of G_P in these figures provide lower and upper bounds, respectively, for the prediction gain in a vector quantization approach for switched prediction. With $L_P = 16$, the prediction gains are close to, but smaller than those in Figure 6.20.

The vector quantization approach [Smith, 1963] [Adoul, Debray and Dalle, 1980] [Buzo et al., 1980], is based on a *codebook* that contains the side information in the form of a large number L_P of typical $\mathbf{r}_{xx}$ vectors, which we will call $\mathbf{r}_{cc}$ vectors. This codebook can be generated by means of iterative procedures [Linde, Buzo and Gray, 1980] using a sufficiently large sample of typical input blocks. Let codeword $\mathbf{r}_{cc}(k)$ describe the kth entry in the codebook. For each $\mathbf{r}_{cc}(k)$ there is also the corresponding $\mathbf{h}_{opt}(k)$-vector which is computed and stored. Therefore, at the encoder, a codebook

$$\mathscr{R} = \{\mathbf{r}_{cc}(k)\} ; \quad k = 1,2,...,L_P$$

and a codebook

$$\mathscr{H} = \{\mathbf{h}_{opt}(k)\} ; \quad k = 1,2,...,L_P$$

are available. The decoder only needs the codebook $\mathscr{H}$.

The coding procedure involves computation of $\hat{\mathbf{r}}_{xx}$ as in Section 6.5.2, a comparison of $\hat{\mathbf{r}}_{xx}$ with all reference vectors $\mathbf{r}_{cc}(k)$; $k = 1,2,...,L_P$ in $\mathscr{R}$; and determination of the nearest neighbor to $\hat{\mathbf{r}}_{xx}$, for example, on a squared error basis. The error energy will be

$$E_k = [\hat{\mathbf{r}}_{xx} - \mathbf{r}_{cc}(k)]^T [\hat{\mathbf{r}}_{xx} - \mathbf{r}_{cc}(k)]$$

The next step is the transmission of the entry number l of the best of L_P possible codewords, using a sequence of $\log_2 L_P$ bits. Encoder and decoder operation involves using this index to switch to the best filter $\mathbf{h}_{opt}(l)$ by reading its parameters from codebook $\mathscr{H}$. Note that there is no computation of predictor coefficients in the coding process, and that the accuracy of $\mathbf{h}_{opt}$-vectors is no longer determined by side information considerations but by the read-only-memory representation. This implies that no explicit quantization of the side information is needed in the coding process. Only the following steps are involved [compare with (6.80) to (6.82)]:

$$\text{Coder:} \quad \{x(n)\} \rightarrow \hat{\mathbf{r}}_{xx} \rightarrow \left[\mathscr{R} = \{\mathbf{r}_{cc}(k)\} \right] \rightarrow l \rightarrow \mathbf{h}_{opt}(l) \qquad (6.85)$$

$$\text{Side Information:} \quad l$$

$$\text{Decoder:} \quad l \rightarrow \mathbf{h}_{opt}(l)$$

The main disadvantage of this approach is the substantial amount of computation required for the exhaustive searching of the codebook: the exhaustive search requires the computation of L_P dot products. However, there is a suboptimal but much simpler technique, a nonexhaustive *binary tree search*, which can reduce computational complexity by a factor $L_P/2\log_2 L_P$ (Section 9.3).

In the vector quantization scheme, the side information is given by $\log_2 L_P$ bits/block. With $L_P = 1024$, this side information is $\log_2 1024 = 10$ bits/block. Assuming 5 bits for AQF and 20 ms blocks as before, the total side information would now be 750 bits/second. With $L_P = 16$, this number decreases to 300 bits/second. These numbers are orders of magnitude smaller than the 6000 bits/second cited for **h**-quantization and the 2000 to 3000 bits/second cited for π-quantization.

6.5.2 Backward Adaptation — APB

The main disadvantages of APF are (i) coding delay and data buffering and (ii) the extra channel capacity needed for side information. These disadvantages may not be very significant in certain types of communications, like those on packet-switched networks, especially if the delay and side-information are both within reasonable limits. On the other hand, if optimal predictor coefficients can be estimated on the basis of quantized and transmitted data $y(n)$, there is the possibility of updating the coefficients $\mathbf{h}(n)$ as frequently as desired; for example, from sample to sample. This kind of a (linear) predictor is also called a *sequentially adaptive backward predictor* [Gibson, 1978], and various algorithms for adapting such a predictor appear profusely in estimation theory literature [Sage and Melsa, 1971] [Widrow et al., 1976] [Gibson, 1980] [Honig and Messerschmitt, 1982]. In most cases, the algorithms are based on the method of *steepest descent* or *gradient search*. The general structure of an APB-based DPCM coder appears in Figure 6.18(b), where the predictor-updating algorithm is labeled APB logic.

An expression was derived earlier [see (6.54)] for the minimum mean square prediction error σ_d^2 in DPCM without consideration of feedback effects. More generally, the mse as a function of **h** will be a quadratic function of the weights:

$$\epsilon^2(\mathbf{h}) = \sigma_d^2(\mathbf{h}) = \sigma_x^2 - 2\mathbf{h}^T\mathbf{r}_{xx} + \mathbf{h}^T\mathbf{R}_{xx}\mathbf{h} \tag{6.86}$$

Geometrically, the above performance function is a bowl-shaped surface, as shown for the examples of first- and second-order predictors in Figure 6.23. The bottom of the concave surface defines $\mathbf{h}_{opt}$ in each case. Given any **h**, adaptation implies a bottom-seeking procedure, and the desired direction of approach is given by the gradient of the performance surface $\epsilon^2(\mathbf{h})$. The gradient at any point is defined by

$$\nabla\epsilon^2 = d\epsilon^2(\mathbf{h})/d\mathbf{h} \tag{6.87}$$

Therefore the optimum $\mathbf{h}_{opt}$ is given by $\nabla\epsilon^2(\mathbf{h}_{opt}) = 0$, which, via (6.86), leads again to the Wiener-Hopf equations of (6.44):

$$\mathbf{h}_{opt} = \mathbf{R}_{xx}^{-1}\mathbf{r}_{xx} \tag{6.88}$$

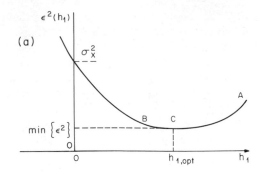

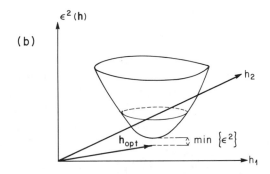

Figure 6.23 Prediction error variance versus coefficient vector for predictor order $N = $ (a) 1 and (b) 2.

Also, from (6.86),

$$\nabla \epsilon^2 = 2\mathbf{R}_{xx}\boldsymbol{\delta} \; ; \quad \boldsymbol{\delta} = \mathbf{h} - \mathbf{h}_{\text{opt}} \tag{6.89}$$

showing that the gradient depends on source statistics as well as on the difference between $\mathbf{h}$ and its optimum value $\mathbf{h}_{\text{opt}}$. In the simple case of a first-order predictor, the gradient is simply $2\sigma_x^2 \rho_1 (h - h_{1,opt})$. For given values of σ_x^2 and ρ_1, the gradient is proportional to $h - h_{1,opt}$. Thus, in Figure 6.23(a), the gradients at points A, B and C are respectively *positive* and *negative* and *zero*. The corrections needed to drive h_1 toward its optimal value are therefore respectively *negative* and *positive*, i.e., in a direction that is *opposite to that of the gradient*.

The Method of Steepest Descent. In a sequentially adaptive scheme based on the method of steepest descent, a given vector $\mathbf{h}(n)$ at time n is readjusted from sample to sample. Each adjustment is proportional to the negative of an *estimate* of the gradient:

$$\mathbf{h}(n+1) = \mathbf{h}(n) - \alpha(n)\hat{\nabla}\epsilon^2(n)/2 \tag{6.90a}$$

In view of (6.89), each such adjustment is proportional to $-\boldsymbol{\delta}$, as it should be. Note that an efficient design is based on having a proper estimate of the gradient.

The true gradient of (6.89) cannot be obtained since neither $\mathbf{R}_{xx}$ nor δ is known. The term $\alpha(n)$ is a normalizing *gradient coefficient* which controls the rate of adaptation and stability. It is often chosen to be a constant α. Large values of α signify fast adaptation, but greater steady-state estimation noise, signifying oscillations of $\mathbf{h}$ around $\mathbf{h}_{opt}$. For stationary signals, a convergence criterion can be given [Widrow et al., 1976] that involves α and the trace of the matrix $\mathbf{R}_{xx}$ that appears in (6.89); specifically, for convergence,

$$0 < \alpha < 1/\lambda_{max} \tag{6.90b}$$

where λ_{max} is the largest eigenvalue of the acf matrix $\mathbf{R}_{xx}$.

Adaptation algorithms designed for nonstationary (strictly, locally stationary) signals such as speech invariably include appropriate counterparts of (6.90b) for α-design.

The LMS Method. There is one extremely simple solution to the gradient estimation problem, the *least mean square* (LMS) algorithm [Widrow et al., 1976]. This method is based on using the square of the *instantaneous* difference signal $d(n)$ as the error criterion, instead of an average over many samples as implied in (6.86). Further, a basic problem in APB procedures is that the gradient estimate has to be made only on the basis of data available at the receiver as well, i.e., quantized data. For example, quantized data that are available at the receiver are values of quantized difference signal $u(n)$ and the elements of the vector $\mathbf{y}(n) = \{y(n-r)\}$; $r = 1,2,...,N$. Consider therefore the quantized difference sample

$$u(n) = d(n) - q(n) = x(n) - \mathbf{h}^T(n)\mathbf{y}(n) - q(n) = y(n) - \mathbf{h}^T(n)\,\mathbf{y}(n)$$

and the gradient of the instantaneous squared error

$$\hat{\nabla}\epsilon^2(n) \simeq \nabla u^2(n) = 2u(n)\nabla u(n) = -2u(n)\mathbf{y}(n) \tag{6.91}$$

Setting (6.91) in (6.90a) specifies an updating algorithm that uses only quantized data:

$$\mathbf{h}(n+1) = \mathbf{h}(n) + \alpha(n)\mathbf{y}(n)u(n) ; \quad \text{or} \tag{6.92a}$$

$$h_j(n+1) = h_j(n) + \alpha_j(n)\,u(n)\,y(n-j) ; \quad j = 1,2,...,N \tag{6.92b}$$

The $[u(n)\,y(n-j)]$ correction in (6.92b) is a crosscorrelation term which vanishes by definition in the steady state, because of the orthogonality principle (6.41), if prediction is optimal and quantization effects are small.

In practice, the update term $u(n)\mathbf{y}(n)$ will never exactly vanish. Therefore with *stationary signals* in the steady-state situation, the mse min$\{\epsilon^2\}$ will not really be reached. However, by using a small α or a function $\alpha(n)$ that decreases with time n, the mse may come close to the minimum. *Nonstationary signals* differ in that the center and shape of the bowl in Figure 6.23 change with time. The gradient coefficient α has to be chosen to be small enough so that the fluctuations of

$h(n)$ about the intended values are acceptable, and large enough so that the algorithm can track changes in input statistics. Further, as implied in (6.90b), $\alpha_j(n)$ will have the dimensions of the inverse of input variance (Also see Example 6.6).

Suboptimal versions of (6.92b) use polarity crosscorrelations in the update term for implementation simplicity, and a non-unity weighting of the $h(n)$ term for recovering from the effects of transmission errors:

$$h_j(n+1) = \lambda_j h_j(n) + \alpha_j(n) \text{ sgn } u(n) \text{ sgn } y(n-j)$$

$$j = 1,2,...,N ; \quad \lambda_j = 1-2^{-k_j} ; \quad k_j \gg 1 ; \quad \alpha_j(n) = 2^{-l_j} ; \quad l_j \gg 1 \quad (6.92c)$$

Note that with the use of polarity correlations, $\alpha_j(n)$ is a dimensionless quantity. The values of k_j and l_j are chosen to make the λ_j close to unity and the values of $\alpha_j(n)$ very small compared to unity. Typical values of k_j and l_j would be in the range of 5 to 8 (See Example 6.6 and Section 6.5.3). The specific forms of λ_j and $\alpha_j(n)$ in (6.92c) facilitate implementation since a negative power of 2 can be simply realized by a shift operation.

Adaptation algorithms for an all-zero predictor. The analysis for the LMS algorithm (6.92) can be extended in a straightforward fashion to the case of the all-zero predictor (6.4c). The final result is the use in (6.92a) of an update term that is proportional to $\mathbf{u}(n)u(n)$, rather than $\mathbf{y}(n)u(n)$ [Nishitani et al., 1982]. This is a consequence of using $u(n)$ rather than $y(n)$ in the prediction. In this case, the correction term $[u(n)u(n-j)]$ is an autocorrelation which vanishes by definition in the steady state, once again because of the orthogonality principle. The all-zero adaptation equations that correspond to (6.92c) will have the form

$$g_j(n+1) = \lambda_j g_j(n) + \alpha_j(n) \text{ sgn } u(n) \text{ sgn } u(n-j) \quad (6.92d)$$

where, once again, $\lambda_j \rightarrow 1$ and $\alpha_j(n) \ll 1$.

Example 6.6.   Robust LMS algorithm for noisy channels.

An illustrative algorithm for predictor updates is that used in a 9600 b/s speech coding system designed for noisy channels [Cohn and Melsa, 1975]:

$$h_j(n+1) = ah'_j + (1-a)[h_j(n) + \alpha(n)u(n)y(n-j)] ; \quad j = 1,2,...,N \quad (6.93a)$$

where h'_j are fixed predictor values to be defined presently, $\alpha(n) = b/(E[|y(n)|])^2$, and $E[|y(n)|]$ is an exponentially biased time average of $|y(n)|$:

$$E[|y(n)|] = (1-d) \sum_{i=0}^{\infty} d^i |y(n-i)| + c \quad (6.93b)$$

The fact that $\alpha(n)$ is inversely proportional to local variance makes h changes in (6.93) independent of local input variance. Also, unlike in (6.92), memory and weighting are included in the updates of (6.93). The parameters a, b and d determine the memory in the updating process. Recommended values are

$$a = 0.01; \quad b = 0.02; \quad c = \max\{|x(n)|\}/40 ; \quad d = 0.90 \quad (6.93c)$$

These provide a memory time that is slightly less than what is optimal for the speech process. The use of a decreased memory time is intentional; it is in anticipation of non-ideal transmission media and resulting error-propagation effects in the predictive decoder (Section 6.6). The parameters h'_j represent the quiescent values of the coefficients h_j; for example, $h'_1 = 0.85$ and $h'_j = 0$ for $j > 1$. During silences, the predictor coefficient vector $\mathbf{h}^T = \{h_1, h_2, ..., h_N\}$ tends to track back to its quiescent value $\mathbf{h'}^T = \{0.85, 0, 0, ..., 0\}$ so that transmitter-receiver differences, caused by channel errors, decay toward zero. The bias term c prevents $\alpha(n)$ from becoming very large during silences $[y(n) \rightarrow 0]$. It represents the minimum value of $E[|y(n)|]$; this in turn affects both the adaptive predictor and the adaptive quantizer used in the coder. The parameter has to be matched to the dynamic range of the speech input.   ●

Many sophistications have been proposed for APB design. These include modifications of memory and weighting, and modifications for ease of implementation [Gibson, 1980] [Qureshi and Forney, 1975]. One of them involves the use of a generalized weighted error performance criterion such as

$$\epsilon^2(n) = \sum_{k=0}^{K-1} [u(n-k)]^2 w(k)/K$$

where $w(k)$ is a weighting sequence, instead of $\epsilon^2(n)$ in (6.91) which is the special case of $K = 1$. A second class of sophistications involves the use of *Kalman-filtering* with one or both of two objectives: (i) recursive filtering in the prediction loop to mitigate effects of quantization noise feedback which makes the gradient search difficult because it is based on noisy samples, and (ii) replacement of the *stochastic gain* term $\alpha(n)\mathbf{y}(n)$ (6.94a) by a vector Kalman gain for better tracking of unknown statistics [Gibson, Jones and Melsa, 1974] [Gibson, 1978].

Comparison of APF and APB. On the basis of the most optimistic examples of APB performance, APB can provide prediction gains that are only 1 dB short of the gains in APF with the same order of prediction. Note, on the other hand, that the additional transmission of side information in APF can be roughly equivalent to an *SNR* loss of the same order because if $f_s = 8$ kHz, 8 kb/s is worth 6 dB and 2000 b/s (6.84) is worth 1.5 dB. This implies that for a given total bit rate, APB and APF are very close in performance [Gibson, 1980] [Noll, 1973]. Note, however, that the APF class is expected to perform better at low bit rates where APB gains are limited by quantization effects. All APB designs employ AQB as well, and the resulting interaction is such that (i) robust quantizers are needed, and (ii) the number of predictor coefficients needs to be limited to a range of about four to six. As seen in Figure 6.15, this does not realize a prediction gain close to the maximum possible value.

6.5.3 DPCM-APB-AQB for Toll Quality Speech at 32 kb/s

We noted in Section 6.4.1 that low-complexity DPCM coding can provide communication quality speech at bit rates in the order of 24 to 32 kb/s. Even at 32 kb/s, that quality is significantly less than that of 8-bit log PCM, as illustrated in Table 6.1. We will now describe a class of more complex DPCM schemes that can digitize speech with toll quality (8-bit log PCM quality) at 32 kb/s. In order to realize this level of quality with a 4-bit quantizer, these schemes necessarily employ adaptive quantization together with adaptive prediction of sufficiently high order; and to keep encoding delay at the minimum possible value, these coders use backward estimation procedures for adapting the quantizer and predictor parameters. Several such coders have been proposed with the common terminology ADPCM with "A" denoting adaptation of both quantizer and predictor algorithms [Raulin et al., 1982] [Nishitani et al., 1982] [Petr, 1982]. A primary common objective is the satisfaction of the CCITT requirements of Figure 5.10 together with the realization of a subjective MOS rating that is in the order of 3.5 or higher, even after four successive, asynchronous stages of coding and decoding. Other objectives are the possibility of stable operation with bit error rates as high as 10^{-3}, and the capability of digitizing the waveforms of 4800 b/s voiceband data with a decoding error rate in the range 10^{-6} to 10^{-5} after four stages of coding and decoding. We now describe the components of a specific coding system [Petr, 1982] [Nishitani, 1982] [CCITT, 1983] that is proposed as a CCITT standard for toll quality DPCM at 32 kb/s.

The AQB algorithm. The adaptive quantizer is a *dynamic locking quantizer* (DLQ) [Petr, 1982, 1983] which stops adapting in the presence of a stationary input. This feature enhances DPCM performance with voiceband data signal inputs.

Figure 6.24a shows a block diagram of the quantizer adaptation algorithm. The *unlocked* step-size component $\Delta_u(n)$ follows an expression similar (but not identical) to the robust algorithm [Cummiskey, Jayant and Flanagan, 1973] [Jayant, 1973] [Goodman and Wilkinson, 1975] of (4.199a):

$$\Delta_u(n) = \Delta^\beta(n-1) \, M(|H(n-1)|) \; ; \quad \beta = 31/32 \qquad (6.94a)$$

In the purely unlocked state of the quantizer, as explained below, the term $\Delta(n-1)$ in (6.94a) reduces to $\Delta_u(n-1)$). In this case, (6.94a) will be identical in form to the robust algorithm (4.199a); and as in that case, the effective step size multiplier will be M, modified by a factor $[\Delta_u(n-1)]^{\beta-1}$.

The eight possible values of multiplier M are

$$\begin{array}{llll} M_1 = 0.984 & M_2 = 1.006 & M_3 = 1.037 & M_4 = 1.070 \\ M_5 = 1.142 & M_6 = 1.283 & M_7 = 1.585 & M_8 = 4.482 \end{array} \qquad (6.94b)$$

Note that the above multiplier set is quite different from the one recommended in Table 4.14 for a DPCM system with nonadaptive prediction, uniform quantization with $\beta = 1$, and only speech signals as its input. But (6.94) is still qualitatively similar to the characteristic of Figure 4.48. The *locked* step-size component is $\Delta_l(n)$ generated by lowpass filtering $\Delta_u(n)$. If the logarithms of the step size components are $\nabla_u(n)$ and $\nabla_l(n)$,

$$\nabla_l(n) = (63/64) \, \nabla_l(n-1) + (1/64) \, \nabla_u(n) \qquad (6.95a)$$

The final step size $\Delta(n)$, with logarithm $\nabla(n)$, is obtained as an adaptive linear combination of the locked and unlocked components:

$$\nabla(n) = w \, \nabla_u(n) + (1-w) \, \nabla_l(n) \; ; \qquad \nabla(n) = \log \Delta(n) \qquad (6.95b)$$

This step-size $\Delta(n)$ is used in a nonlinear quantizer whose characteristic is very close to the Gaussian pdf-optimized Max quantizer of Table 4.3.

The quantizer is in a purely locked state if $w = 0$, and in the purely unlocked state if $w = 1$. The value of the weighting parameter w $(0 \leqslant w \leqslant 1)$ is obtained by the sequence of operations in the lower half of Figure 6.24(a). The input to this process is the magnitude of the quantizer output level, whose value ranges from 1 to 8 in a 4-bit quantizer. In the notation of Section 4.10, the quantity in question is the value of $0.5 \, |H(n-1)| + 0.5$. Comparison of the short-term and long-term averages of this quantity provides a measure of the constancy of the variance of the quantized prediction error $u(n)$. The sequence of nonlinear operations following the above comparison ensures that the quantizer unlocks quickly when the coder input is low-level noise (the idle channel), allowing for fast attack at the beginning of the speech bursts.

The maximum and minimum step sizes in the system are defined by

$$\Delta_{max}/\Delta_{min} = 1024 \; ; \qquad \Delta_{min} = \Delta(0)\big|_{log-PCM} \qquad (6.95c)$$

$\Delta(0)$ is the smallest step-size in 8-bit log-PCM (Chapter 5), which is expected to be a standard interface to the low bit rate DPCM coder in an all-digital network. The step size limits (6.95c) and the multiplier set (6.94b) are both designed assuming a peak input magnitude of $|x|_{max} = 4096$, as in 13-bit uniform PCM with a step size of unity.

The APB algorithm. The adaptive predictor uses a *pole-zero* configuration [Nishitani et al., 1982], a combination of all-pole and all-zero components, defined in (6.4b) and (6.4c). The structures of corresponding decoder circuits follow the AR- and MA-process generators in Figures 2.15 and 2.19. The pole-zero predictor design is motivated in part by the need for decoder stability in the presence of transmission errors. The APB system (6.93) based on sequential updates of predictor coefficients is quite sensitive to error rates in the order of 10^{-3}, although the leaking effect [provided by λ_j in (6.92c) and by $(1-a)$ in (6.93)] mitigates error effects. Error-sensitivity is particularly evident with all-pole prediction of very high order. The all-pole predictor in the proposed system (Figure 6.24b) is therefore designed as a second-order predictor, with specific constraints on coefficient values h_1 and h_2. Adequate matches to the input spectra of speech and non-speech signals are facilitated by the inclusion of a sixth-order all-zero predictor which is more stable in the presence of transmission errors. The prediction of input $x(n)$ is now a sum of all-pole and all-zero components, denoted by subscripts ap and az:

$$\hat{x}(n) = \hat{x}_{ap}(n) + \hat{x}_{az}(n) = \sum_{j=1}^{2} h_j(n)y(n-j) + \sum_{j=1}^{6} g_j(n)u(n-j) \qquad (6.96a)$$

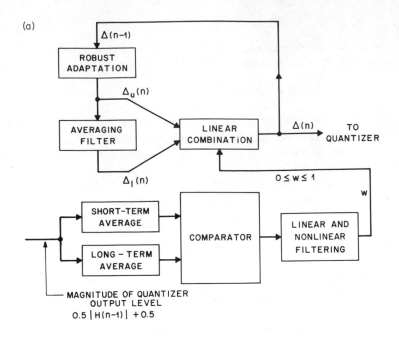

(a)

$\Delta(n-1)$

ROBUST
ADAPTATION

$\Delta_u(n)$

AVERAGING
FILTER

LINEAR
COMBINATiON

$\Delta(n)$ TO QUANTIZER

$\Delta_l(n)$

$0 \leq w \leq 1$

w

SHORT-TERM
AVERAGE

COMPARATOR

LINEAR AND
NONLINEAR
FILTERING

LONG-TERM
AVERAGE

MAGNITUDE OF QUANTIZER
OUTPUT LEVEL
$0.5 |H(n-1)| + 0.5$

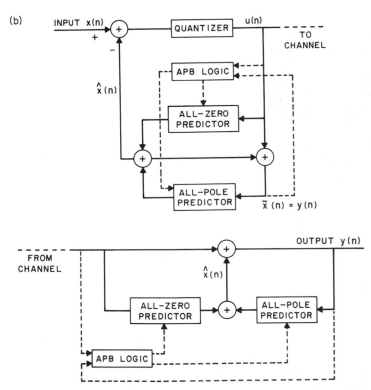

(b)

INPUT x(n)
+
+
−

QUANTIZER

u(n)

TO
CHANNEL

$\hat{x}(n)$

APB LOGIC

ALL-ZERO
PREDICTOR

ALL-POLE
PREDICTOR

$\tilde{x}(n) = y(n)$

OUTPUT y(n)

FROM
CHANNEL

$\hat{x}(n)$

ALL-ZERO
PREDICTOR

ALL-POLE
PREDICTOR

APB LOGIC

Figure 6.24 Block diagrams of quantizer and predictor systems that provide toll quality speech coding at 32 kb/s: (a) dynamic locking quantizer [Petr;©1982, IEEE]; and (b) coder and decoder with a combination of all-pole and all-zero predictors [Nishitani et al.;©1982, IEEE]. The adaptation processes for the predictor coefficients are indicated by broken lines.

The adaptation of the all-zero coefficients $g_j(n)$ follows (6.92d) with $\lambda_j = 255/256$ and $\alpha_j(n) = 1/128$ for all j:

$$g_j(n+1) = (255/256)g_j(n) + (1/128) \text{ sgn } u(n) \text{ sgn } u(n-j) \qquad (6.96b)$$

The adaptation of the all-pole coefficients is defined by a more complicated algorithm [CCITT, 1983] [Miller and Mermelstein, 1984] that involves polarity correlations of the partial output $y'(n) = u(n) + \hat{x}_{az}(n)$:

$$h_1(n+1) = (255/256)h_1(n) + (3/256)\text{sgn } y'(n)\text{sgn } y'(n-1)$$

$$h_2(n+1) = (127/128)h_2(n) + (1/128)\text{sgn } y'(n) \text{ sgn } y'(n-2)$$

$$- (1/128)f[h_1(n)]\text{sgn } y'(n)\text{sgn } y'(n-1)$$

$$f[h_1(n)] = \begin{cases} 4h_1(n) & \text{if } |h_1(n)| \leqslant 1/2 \\ 2 \text{ sgn } h_1(n) & \text{if } |h_1(n)| > 1/2 \end{cases} \qquad (6.96c)$$

The algorithm for updating the all-pole predictor is designed to provide adequate response to specific narrow-band inputs in the telephone network [CCITT, 1983]. The performance with speech inputs is very close to that provided by the more conventional algorithm in (6.92c). The values of λ_j and $\alpha_j(n)$ in (6.96b) and (6.96c) are order-of-magnitude designs rather than critically optimum numbers.

Decoder stability in the presence of transmission errors is ensured by the following explicit constraints on the values of all-pole predictor coefficients:

$$-0.75 \leqslant h_2 \leqslant 0.75 ; \qquad |h_1| \leqslant 15/16 - h_2 \qquad (6.96d)$$

Note that the above constraints eliminate only a very small portion of the triangular allowed region for all-pole filter coefficients (b_1, b_2) in Figure 2.17(d).

Performance of the ADPCM System. The coder described in this section [CCITT, 1983] satisfies formal requirements for toll quality, some of which were defined in Chapter 5 and in the beginning of this section. For example, the SNR performance of the system exceeds the CCITT template of Figure 5.10 with the standard bandlimited noise input mentioned in Section 5.3. However, unlike log-PCM, the performance of the DPCM system is very signal-dependent. With speech, its SNR performance is in the order of 25 to 30 dB, which is much lower than the value of 38 dB in Figure 5.10, because bandlimited noise with a 200 Hz bandwidth and a center frequency such as 450 Hz is significantly oversampled in a 8 kHz system, and this provides greater amounts of prediction gain G_P (Section 8.2). However, the DPCM system maintains an MOS score in the order of 3.5 after four stages of asynchronous tandem coding and decoding, with D/A conversion at the output of each coding stage (also see Figure 5.11); it retains its maximum score of about 4.0 after any number of stages of synchronous encodings involving itself, or 64 kb/s PCM; and unlike 8-bit log-PCM, it provides an MOS score of about 3.5 with a random bit error rate of 10^{-3} [Figure 5.14(a)].

6.6 Distant-Sample-Based Predictions for Periodic Signals

The predictions mentioned in preceding sections have utilized adjacent or neighboring samples for the prediction of a waveform sample. Thus in speech prediction, amplitudes $y(n-k)$; $k = 1,2,...$, or quantized versions thereof, were used to predict $x(n)$; while in image prediction, amplitudes $\{y(i-k_h,j-k_v)$; $k_h, k_v = 0,1,2,...$; k_h, k_v not simultaneously $= 0$, within a frame, were used to predict $x(i,j)$. We shall refer to the above types of prediction [adjacent-sample-based speech prediction (also called *spectrum prediction*), intraframe image prediction] as *near-sample-based* predictions. This will enable us to characterize the special predictors of the present section [pitch predictors for speech, interframe predictors for images] as *distant-sample-based* predictors. The nomenclature of near- and distant-sample-based prediction is not well known, but it is convenient as well as physically well-founded. The smallest "distances" involved in distant-sample-based predictions can be in the range of 20 to 100 samples in speech and in the order of 50,000 to 500,000 samples in image examples. These numbers respectively reflect pitch and frame periodicities (Section 2.2) in speech and image signals, and these periodicities suggest distant-sample-based prediction.

Speech and image waveforms are not strictly periodic. In speech, the time-varying nature of the pitch period necessitates adequately frequent updates of the same [Atal and Schroeder, 1970]. Techniques that ignore slow variations of the pitch period can lead to very low bit rate coding systems [Frei et al., 1973] which offer useful *intelligibility,* but not necessarily high *quality* (Appendix F). Periodicity updates in image signals can take the form of a relatively complex temporal prediction process called *motion compensation* [Netravali and Limb, 1980]. Simpler versions of temporal predictions are based on the tacit use of the frame period as a crude estimate of periodicity [Haskell, Mounts and Candy, 1972].

6.6.1 Speech Predictions Based on Quasi-Periodicity

Figure 2.1 has demonstrated quasi-periodic voiced speech segments, and Figure 2.10(a) has shown a short-term log-spectrum of voiced speech. The pitch excitation that produces quasi-periodicity in the amplitude-time waveform of Figure 2.1 also causes the fine structure in the spectrum of Figure 2.10(a) (ii). This fine structure is not utilized in the transfer functions of near-sample-based prediction; these predictors only exploit redundancies in the spectral envelope; they result in a prediction error sequence (Figure 6.25b) that will not be white (as expected from the theory of Section 6.3.5), but instead structured because of speech periodicity. Removal of this periodic structure calls for a second stage of prediction, one that exploits correlations between the speech sample being encoded and a sample, or set of samples, one pitch period away. The result of this second stage of prediction is a prediction error sequence (Figure 6.25c) that is more nearly white. In general, the samples providing the pitch prediction can also be an integer number of pitch periods away.

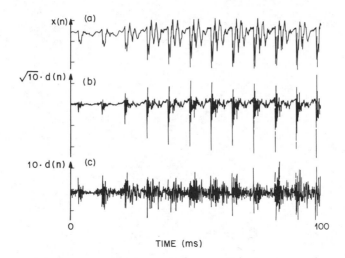

Figure 6.25 Waveforms of (a) speech input; and prediction error with (b) spectrum prediction of order 16 and (c) spectrum prediction of order 16 plus pitch prediction of order 3. Waveforms (b) and (c) have been magnified by $\sqrt{10}$ and 10, respectively [Atal;©1982, IEEE].

Figure 6.26(a) shows the structure of a speech predictor that includes both distant- and near-sample-based predictions, with transfer functions $H_1(z)$ and $H_2(z)$. Predictor 2 operates on the reduced waveform $d_1(n)$, the prediction error due to predictor 1. Figure 6.26(b) shows a version of this predictor that is realizable in the DPCM feedback configuration, because of the explicit presence of an output $\hat{x}(n)$.

The order of spectrum and pitch prediction is not critical if the combination is carefully optimized. However, in applications where the short-term spectrum predictor of speech is needed anyway (instead of a spectrum predictor operating on the output of the pitch predictor), it makes sense to let $H_2(z)$ be the pitch predictor, as in Figure 6.25. One such application is Noise Feedback Coding (Chapter 7). The predictor in each case can be described by the transfer function

$$H(z) = H_1(z) + [1-H_1(z)]H_2(z) \tag{6.97}$$

Note that the input in Figure 6.26 is in practice the reconstruction sample sequence $\tilde{x}(n) = y(n)$, as in all DPCM schemes.

The transfer function (6.97) is quite general in that it will be uncritical, to a first approximation, which of the two types of prediction is carried out first. However, the prediction gain in a system that combines the two types of prediction is always less than the sum of gains in systems employing $H_1(z)$ and $H_2(z)$ in isolation. In the former system, the first predictor of the combination, whether it is $H_1(z)$ or $H_2(z)$, provides the bulk of the prediction gain (for example, 10 to 13 dB out of 16 dB if carefully optimized [Flanagan et al., 1979]). Furthermore, to be maximally effective for nonstationary speech signals, both types of prediction need to be adaptive, and typical additional prediction gains are at least 3 dB, in comparison with the value for either $H_1(z)$ or $H_2(z)$ used alone. Actual values depend on speech material and predictor algorithm.

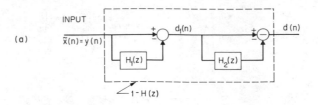

(a)

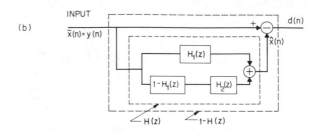

(b)

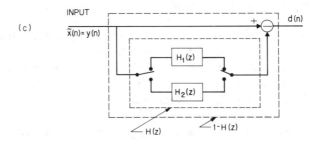

(c)

Figure 6.26 Coders that include both near- and distant-sample-based predictors: (a) a tandem predictor realization that isolates the two stages of prediction in Figure 6.25; (b) an equivalent predictor that can be realized in the DPCM feedback configuration; and (c) switched predictor approximation of (b).

Assume for convenience that $H_1(z)$ refers to distant-sample predictions. The simplest structure for a distant-sample-based predictor is that given by

$$H_1(z) = a z^{-k_p}; \qquad \hat{x}_1(n) = a y(n-k_p) \qquad (6.98)$$

where k_p is the pitch period. The "pitch gain" coefficient a indicates that there is either a gain change from one pitch period to the next, or that speech is not perfectly correlated with period k_p. The difference between $y(n)$ and $\hat{x}_1(n)$ is a pitch prediction error $d_1(n)$ (Figure 6.26a).

Inclusion of near-sample predictions will lead to the prediction of $d_1(n)$ based on N previous samples of it:

$$\hat{x}(n) = ay(n-k_p) + \sum_{j=1}^{N} h_j d_1(n-j)$$

$$= ay(n-k_p) + \sum_{j=1}^{N} h_j [y(n-j) - ay(n-k_p-j)] \qquad (6.99)$$

with three predictor parameters $(a, k_p, \mathbf{h})$ in place of the single parameter $\mathbf{h}$ of Sections 6.2 and 6.3. A DPCM scheme which is based on (6.99), and adaptive quantization of $[x(n)-\hat{x}(n)]$, has a 4-bit gain over log-PCM if predictor parameters are appropriately designed, as demonstrated in an example with $R = 1$ bit/sample, or $I = 8$ kb/s [Atal and Schroeder, 1968]. This is nearly 6 dB higher than the maximum gain of 18 dB in Figure 6.21. The side information in this APC system consists of that for $\mathbf{h}$, as in Section 6.4, plus information about a and k_p. This extra side information will at least be about 10 extra bits per block, including 4 bits for a and 6 to 7 bits for k_p [Daumer, 1982]. For 20 ms blocks, this leads to a side information increase of about 200 b/s. Inclusion of pitch prediction also makes the APC system more sensitive to transmission error effects.

Predictor Optimization. Predictor design is based on minimizing the energy of the difference signal

$$E = \sum_{n \in \mathcal{W}} [x(n)-\hat{x}(n)]^2 \tag{6.100}$$

where $\mathcal{W}$ includes all samples of a speech segment during which a, k_p and $\mathbf{h}$ are assumed fixed. A suboptimum solution is obtained by minimizing the total energy in two steps and by expressing $\hat{x}(n)$ in terms of previous input samples $x(n)$ instead of reconstructions $y(n)$ [Atal and Schroeder, 1968].

In the *first step*, one considers $\hat{x}_1(n)$ of (6.98) and minimizes

$$E_1 = \sum_{n \in \mathcal{W}} [x(n)-\hat{x}_1(n)]^2 \tag{6.101}$$

By setting $\partial E_1/\partial a$ to zero, we find the optimum value

$$a_{opt}(k_p) = \frac{\displaystyle\sum_{n \in \mathcal{W}} x(n)x(n-k_p)}{\displaystyle\sum_{n \in \mathcal{W}} x^2(n-k_p)} \quad \text{for any } k_p \tag{6.102}$$

For a stationary input, a_{opt} has the interpretation of a normalized acf with values in the range $(-1, 1)$. For a nonstationary input, a_{opt} will have the interpretation of a gain whose magnitude could exceed 1. The parameter a_{opt} will be close to unity for sustained vowels, and will be close to zero for sustained noise-like sounds. Methods for determining k_p will be summarized in a separate sub-section. For the present, it is assumed that an optimal $k_{p,opt}$ is known, so that $a_{opt} = a_{opt}(k_{p,opt})$.

In the *second step*, one finds the optimum coefficients of the short-term predictor. This prediction is based on samples of the difference signal $d_1(n)$, and following Section 6.3, the predictor design is based on

$$\mathbf{h}_{opt} = \mathbf{R}_{d_1 d_1}^{-1} \, \mathbf{r}_{d_1 d_1} \tag{6.103}$$

A suboptimal solution is obtained by assuming that the spectrum *envelope* appropriate to the residual $d_1(n)$ after pitch prediction is close to the spectrum *envelope* of the input speech $x(n)$, so that

$$\mathbf{h}_{\text{opt}} \sim \mathbf{R}_{xx}^{-1}\mathbf{r}_{xx} \qquad\qquad (6.104)$$

Windowing techniques used in the solution of (6.103) or (6.104), as well as sequential procedures for determining $\mathbf{h}_{\text{opt}}$, were described in earlier sections.

Modifications. A generalization of (6.98) is one that uses more than one distant sample for pitch prediction:

$$H_1(z) = \sum_{k=-I}^{J} a_k z^{k-k_p} ; \qquad \text{typically } I = J = 1 \qquad (6.105)$$

One motivation for the three-coefficient predictor (6.105) is that the sampling process may not necessarily include the true pitch distance as a single sample (describable by a single parameter k_p). The refinement (6.105) becomes especially appropriate for low sampling rates (say, 6 kHz instead of the standard 8 kHz). The three coefficients a_k also help provide a more general frequency-dependent "pitch-period gain" (compared to only one coefficient a), and this is very desirable since voice periodicity does not show up as strongly at higher frequencies in speech. The set $\mathbf{a}_{\text{opt}}$ can be determined using techniques discussed earlier if one uses the suboptimal strategy of minimizing E_1 separately (from E_2). In computer simulations, third-order pitch prediction $H_1(z)$ based on (6.105) has provided average prediction gains of about 3 dB over the first-order pitch predictor (6.98) [Flanagan et al., 1979].

A simplification of coder design results if one takes the option of switching as appropriate between the upper branch and the simplified lower branch. The resulting *switched predictor* approximation appears in Figure 6.26(c). Clearly, this structure is appropriate only if we decide that during highly *periodic* segments, a significant amount of prediction can be provided by pitch prediction alone [$H_2(z)=0$], and that during aperiodic segments, the pitch gain vanishes [$a=0$; $H_1(z)=0$]. Implementation of such a scheme will clearly depend on reliable indications of periodicity, and resulting switches to distant-sample or near-sample-based predictions with respective coefficients $\mathbf{a}$ and $\mathbf{h}$. The decision about whether a speech segment is deemed to be very periodic or not is explained in the next section on pitch detection.

Example 6.7. Switched Predictor System with Spectrum and Pitch Prediction
In one application of the above switched predictor approach [Grizmala, 1972] [Jayant, 1977], $H_1(z)$ was adaptive, as it always should be, to accommodate time-varying pitch; while a fixed three-coefficient design based on long-time-averaged statistics was used for $H_2(z)$. *SNR* gains in this medium-complexity APC procedure can be at least 3 dB in 16 kb/s or 24 kb/s DPCM-AQ coding of speech. Speech waveforms abound in highly periodic segments and the idea is that the use of this periodicity may provide a prediction potential that is substantial enough to obviate the need for adaptive short-term prediction. Design of $H_2(z)$ depends on certain thresholds used to hypothesize pitch-periodicity. If these thresholds are very high [implying that $H_1(z)$ is switched in only if the periodicity is very strong], the "aperiodic" class will include a substantial amount of voiced (but not very periodic) speech, and the optimal $H_2(z)$ will reflect the above mix of voiced and unvoiced segments in "aperiodic speech." If, on the other hand, the periodicity thresholds are quite

low, most of the "aperiodic" class will be unvoiced, and $H_2(z)$ will be accordingly different: typically, a highpass characteristic. ●

Variations of APC systems differ in predictor order, parameter quantization and implementation procedure. High-quality speech digitization requires APC bit rates in the order of 24 to 32 kb/s without pitch prediction and 16 to 24 kb/s with pitch prediction. APC systems with pitch prediction can digitize speech with communications quality at bit rates as low as 9.6 kb/s. A quantitative study of *quality* versus bit rate for a pitch-predicting NFC system (a DPCM-type system to be defined in Chapter 7) with a ten-coefficient spectrum predictor, a three-coefficient pitch predictor (6.105) and an *adaptive noise shaping* system shows that the mean opinion score (MOS), on a scale of 1 to 5, is 4.25 at 24 kb/s, 3.9 at 16 kb/s, but drops to 3.4 at 12 kb/s [Daumer, 1982]. MOS values without noise-shaping are expected to be slightly lower in each case. APC coders at bit rates lower than 16 kb/s are expected to have fairly low values of MOS rating, as indicated above, but they can still digitize speech with adequate levels of *intelligibility* to suit many communications applications.

Example 6.8. APC System with Spectrum and Pitch Prediction
A 6.4 kb/s implementation [Goldberg and Shaffer, 1975] of APC is based on a combination of fourth-order spectrum prediction and pitch prediction, a 5200 Hz sampling rate, and 1 bit/sample coding of residual signal $d(n)$ using 5200 b/s. The 1200 b/s side information includes 30 bits in every 25 ms frame. These 30 bits include 6 bits for pitch period k_p, 3 bits for gain, 4 bits for quantizer step size, $4 + 4 + 3 + 3 = 14$ bits for the four parcor coefficients and 3 bits for a normalization needed for a fixed-point arithmetic implementation. The processing time for each 25 ms frame is about 8 ms at the encoder and 2 ms at the decoder. The coder has a DRT word intelligibility score (Appendix F) of 87%. ●

6.6.2 Pitch-Measurement Algorithms

Several pitch-measurement algorithms have been discussed in speech literature [Rabiner et al., 1976], [Rabiner and Schafer, 1978]. In the DPCM context, unlike in vocoder techniques, the success of pitch-adaptive DPCM does not depend critically on accurate pitch detection, for two reasons. First, pitch-measurement errors are now part of a difference signal and are thus transmitted and corrected. Second, problems such as detection of a double-pitch periodicity are quite harmless: it does not matter whether a good prediction of $x(n)$ is provided by $x(n-k_p)$ or, on occasion, by $x(n-2k_p)$. What we attempt in this section, therefore, is not a systematic discussion of pitch measurement for speech signals; rather, a summary of two simply implemented approaches for periodicity detection, both of which are adequate in the context of DPCM encoding. We also assume that pitch detection logics use unquantized speech samples $x(n)$. Use of quantized samples $y(n)$ will obviate the need to transmit pitch information to the receiver, but it also leads to inferior DPCM performance in situations of interest (which involve coarse quantization). Note, however, that the actual prediction process is always based on reconstructed samples $\tilde{x}(n) = y(n)$.

Pitch analyses will be based, in general, on a window containing $\mathcal{W}$ contiguous speech samples. The pitch period k_p is assumed to have minimum and maximum values $k_{p,min}$ and $k_{p,max}$, respectively (typical values of 16 and 160 cover the pitch frequency range, assuming 8 kHz samples). A rather important requirement is that the analysis window $\mathcal{W}$ is in the order of 256 samples, well in excess of the maximum anticipated pitch $k_{p,max}$. Parameters G_1 and G_2 below are thresholds that can be used to hypothesize waveform periodicity with varying degrees of confidence.

Autocorrelation-Based Pitch Measurement. By substituting the value of $a_{opt}(k_p)$ (6.102) in E_1 (6.101), and after rearrangement of terms,

$$E_1 = \sum_{n \in \mathcal{W}} x^2(n) - \frac{[\sum_{n \in \mathcal{W}} x(n)x(n-k_p)]^2}{\sum_{n \in \mathcal{W}} x^2(n-k_p)} \tag{6.106}$$

which is minimized by maximizing the second term, or equivalently by maximizing

$$\rho(k_p) = \frac{\sum_{n \in \mathcal{W}} x(n)x(n-k_p)}{[\sum_{n \in \mathcal{W}} x^2(n) \sum_{n \in \mathcal{W}} x^2(n-k_p)]^{\frac{1}{2}}} \tag{6.107}$$

In other words, $k_{p,opt}$ is obtained as the non-zero integer value that maximizes the normalized acf of the input speech. Note that unlike the quantity a in (6.102), the magnitude of $\rho(k_p)$ is less than or equal to unity.

It turns out that a simpler version of (6.107), one that is based on the acf of sgn x (Problem 6.26) is also adequate for periodicity detection, provided that certain refinements, as described below, are included.

Consider the two-sided polarity acf

$$C(k_p) = \frac{1}{N_0} \sum \text{sgn } x(n)\text{sgn } x(n-k_p) \; ; \quad k_p = k_{p,min,}\ k_{p,min}+1,...,k_{p,max} \tag{6.108a}$$

where N_0 is the total number of pairs $(n,n-k_p)$ such that both $x(n)$ and $x(n-k_p)$ are in $\mathcal{W}$ and furthermore, both $|x(n)|$ and $|x(n-k_p)|$ exceed an appropriate speech-clipping level [Rabiner et al, 1976]

$$x_{clip} = 0.64 \; \text{max}\{(^1|x|_{\text{max}}, ^3|x|_{\text{max}})\} \tag{6.108b}$$

where $^1|x|_{\text{max}}$ and $^3|x|_{\text{max}}$ are the maximum speech magnitudes in the first and last one-third parts of $\mathcal{W}$.

The pitch detector estimates the pitch-period k_p to be

$$k_p = k_{p,opt} \quad \text{if} \quad C(k_{p,opt}) > C(k_p) \tag{6.109a}$$

for all k_p in the range of $(k_{p,min}, k_{p,max})$ with the exception of $k_{p,opt}$, and if

$$C(k_{p,opt}) > G_1 \qquad (6.109b)$$

The parameter G_1 is the periodicity-detecting threshold mentioned earlier, with a typical useful setting $G_1 = 0.2$. The non-zero value of $k_{p,min}$ excludes the obvious maximum $C(0) = 1$ at $k_p = 0$.

The center-clipping operation (6.108) serves to mitigate spurious peaks in the $C(k_p)$ functions, such as peaks representing a low first-formant frequency. A further useful refinement is the lowpass filtering (say to 900 Hz) of $x(n)$ prior to pitch-analysis.

AMDF-based Pitch Measurement. Consider the *average magnitude difference function*

$$AMDF(k_p) = \frac{1}{N'_0} \sum |x(n) - x(n-k_p)| \;\; ; \;\; k_p = k_{p,min}, k_{p,min}+1, ..., k_{p,max} \quad (6.110)$$

where N_0 is the total number of all pairs $(n, n-k_p)$ such that both $x(n)$ and $x(n-k_p)$ are in $\mathcal{W}$.

The pitch detector estimates the pitch period k_p to be

$$k_p = k_{p,opt} \qquad (6.111a)$$

if $AMDF(k_{p,opt}) < AMDF(k_p)$ for all k_p in the range $(k_{p,min}, k_{p,max})$ with the exception of $k_{p,opt}$, and if

$$AMDF(k_{p,opt}) < G_2 \, E[|X(n)|] \qquad (6.111b)$$

for all n in $\mathcal{W}$. The parameter G_2 is also a periodicity-detecting threshold, with a typical setting $G_2 = 0.5$, and $E[|X(n)|]$ is a time average, taken over all n in $\mathcal{W}$. The operation (6.111b) serves to check that the minimum at k_p actually corresponds to a voiced segment, and is not a spurious minimum from an unvoiced or silent segment. The parameter $k_{p,min}$ excludes the obvious minimum $AMDF(0)$ at $k_p = 0$.

During voiced speech, the multiply-free AMDF method, [unlike the multiply-free polarity correlation method (6.108a)], gives exactly the same value of $k_{p,opt}$ (and hence of a_{opt}) as the true autocorrelation method (6.107). Figure 6.27 shows an illustrative plot of the time-variation of $k_{p,opt}$ [obtained using (6.111a)] and a_{opt} [obtained using (6.102)]. The plots refer to the speech input from a male speaker. The estimated pitch period (or multiple of it) varies from 25 to 150 samples, but there are many runs of near-constant $k_{p,opt}$. During sustained quasi-periodic vowel activity, a_{opt} is often in the neighborhood of unity; values of $a_{opt} < 1$ and $a_{opt} > 1$ correspond to regions where the speech envelope decreases or increases, respectively, from one pitch period to the next. Values of a_{opt} that are significantly different from unity correspond to unvoiced speech and to regions of transition between voiced and unvoiced segments.

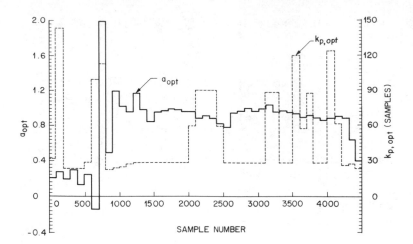

Figure 6.27 Illustrative time variations of $k_{p,opt}$ and a_{opt} [Melsa et al., 1980. Reprinted with permission].

6.6.3 Interframe Predictions of Images

Distant-sample prediction is in principle simpler with moving images in that unlike the pitch period, the frame-to-frame or field-to-field delays, which are approximate measures of periodicity, are constant and always known a priori. In the following discussion, we shall refer to techniques that utilize frame-to-frame, rather than field-to-field redundancies. As seen in Figure 3.12, corresponding pixels in successive frames (fields I and I+2) are spatially closer, although temporally farther, than corresponding pixels in successive fields (I and I+1, for example). However, considerations in color coding may necessitate the use of interfield techniques [Brainard, Pearson and Netravali, 1982] [Yamamoto, Hatori and Murakami, 1981].

The simple techniques for interframe coding utilize temporal correlations that exist at a delay of *exactly* one frame period. They also capitalize on the fact that observers are more tolerant of distortions in moving images. This permits reduced resolutions in amplitude quantization as well as in spatial sampling [Haskell, Mounts and Candy, 1972].

Interframe DPCM Coders. Predictor coefficients used in DPCM coding of images are usually time-invariant, and take on simply implementable values such as 0 and 1, and sometimes 1/2. Once again, this is the interest of simple implementation at the high sampling rates in image coding. Fortunately, the structure of video signals and the subjective criteria for moving image coding are such that significant gains result even with these simple structures, both in intraframe and interframe DPCM.

The simplest interframe coder for images is a frame-to-frame DPCM coder (Figure 6.28) where the difference signal is the difference between pixel x_A to be coded and corresponding quantized pixel y_{AF} that is one frame, or k_f samples, away:

$$\hat{x}_A = y_{AF} ; \quad d = x_A - y_{AF} ; \tag{6.112}$$

320

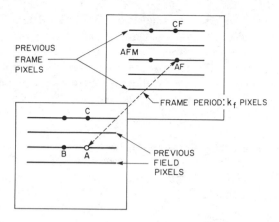

Figure 6.28 Pixel notation for frame-to-frame differential coding and motion-compensation coding.

For an $N \times N$ frame size, $k_f = N^2$ and a storage of N^2 pixels is therefore needed for the interframe coder. It has been shown that with the above scheme, a 6-bit quantizer is adequate for excellent (8-bit PCM-equivalent) reproduction of videotelephone scenes, while a 4-bit quantizer can provide good reproduction except with very rapid movement [Haskell, Mounts and Candy, 1972] [Haskell, 1975] [Netravali and Limb, 1980]. In either case, best results are obtained with a tapered quantizer which reproduces small changes more accurately than large ones, to exploit the fact that viewers are less sensitive to distortion in active areas. A bit rate reduction from 8 to 6 bits per sample is equivalent objectively to a 12 dB increase of SNR for a given bit rate. In this sense, the above distance-sample-based predictions are no more efficient than the near-sample-based predictions in Figure 6.8 which need at most the storage of one line of pixels, rather than a frame. Subjectively, however, the coding distortions in the two classes of prediction are different. Intraframe DPCM coding results in poor rendition of high spatial detail, whereas interframe coding results in poor rendition of areas with high temporal detail. Besides, further improvements in interframe coding performance can be realized by using intraframe DPCM coding of the interframe difference signal in (6.112). We shall define this presently in (6.113).

A more sophisticated, but not much more complex, prediction algorithm is one where the quantized difference signal is the *line-to-line* difference of a *frame-to-frame* difference. In the notation of Figures 6.6 and 6.28,

$$\hat{x}_A = x_{AF} + x_C - x_{CF}$$
$$d = (x_A - x_{AF}) - (x_C - x_{CF}) \tag{6.113}$$
$$H(z) = z^{-k_f} + z^{-L} - z^{-(k_f + L)}$$

With $N \times N$ image frames, $k_f = N^2$ as in (6.112), and $L = N$. Thus, it is a linear predictive interframe coder whose differential signal does not depend on the previous pixel or on any pixels in the previous field. This allows the use of subsampling along the line as well as the dropping of alternate fields without affecting the performance of the predictive coder.

Low-activity videophone images are natural candidates for DPCM systems that exploit temporal redundancy. These signals have a sampling rate of 1 to 2 MHz (Table 1.1), and for coding these images at bit rates in the order of 1 bit per sample, neither interframe DPCM (6.112) nor a hybrid with intraframe DPCM (Section 6.5.1) is adequate. Solutions depend on a much more selective allocation of bits — for better rendering of parts of a moving image where perceptual tolerance of errors is the least.

Exchange of Spatial and Temporal Resolution. Sophisticated differential techniques in interframe coding [Haskell, Mounts and Candy, 1972] [Haskell, 1975] depend on classifying pixels into stationary and moving classes; and on the use of sampling procedures, predictors, interpolators and quantizers that are appropriate to each class. Pixels that change by less than, say, 1.5% of maximum signal amplitude can be regarded as *unchanged* pixels, without impairing image quality. These pixels are *redundant* and the corresponding non-zero interframe differences $x_A - x_{AF}$ are *perceptually irrelevant*. With this 1.5% criterion, less than 10% of the pixels change in one frame *on the average* during normal videophone motion (Figure 6.29a). These pixels can accept reduced *temporal resolution*. On the other hand, pixels with significant changes or motion cannot accept any lessened temporal resolution. The interframe difference may need 4- to 6-bit quantization so that fast-moving edges may not appear jagged. But these segments can accept significant reductions in *spatial resolution* [such as 2:1 horizontal subsampling followed by nearest-neighbor interpolation: $\hat{y}(n) = 0.5y(n-1) + 0.5y(n+1)$].

Conditional Replenishment Coders. In these interframe coders, transmission capacity is used only to replenish those pixels which have changed significantly since the previous frame [Mounts, 1969]. Reconstruction values y_A for *unchanged* or *inactive* pixels, for which $|x_A - y_{AF}|$ is less than the threshold mentioned earlier, are simply set equal to corresponding y_{AF}. The coding of *active* pixels is based on quantizing and transmitting a difference signal, using the interframe predictor in (6.112), for example. Typical results with such techniques have been the encoding of low-activity videophone material using an average rate R in the order of 1 bit/pixel, as in video-conferencing systems operating at 3 Mb/s [London and Menist, 1981]; and the use of even lower rates in the order of 0.1 to 0.05 bit/pixel for the encoding of graphics-type material with little or no motion or even in the encoding of moving scenes in applications where significant amounts of blurring are acceptable. Corresponding transmission rates can be as low as 64 kb/s [Musmann and Klie, 1979] or less [Wallis and Pratt, 1981].

Conditional replenishment systems need to transmit addressing information to tell the DPCM receiver which of the $(N \times N)$ pixels in a frame are active, and thus in need of replenishment. The amount of this side information increases with image activity, as well as the frequency with which activity status is updated within frame (Problem 6.30).

The amount of this side information can be reduced, however, by *cluster-coding*: changed pixels tend to occur in *clusters* or *runs*, and economies in side information result by signaling only the beginning and ending addresses of each cluster; or equivalently the beginning address and *cluster-length*, or *run-length*.

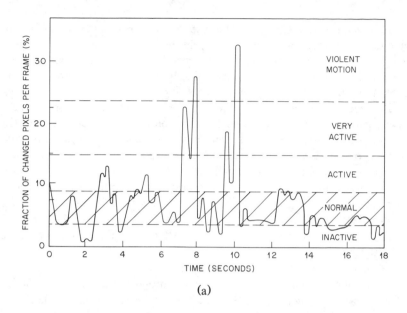

(a)

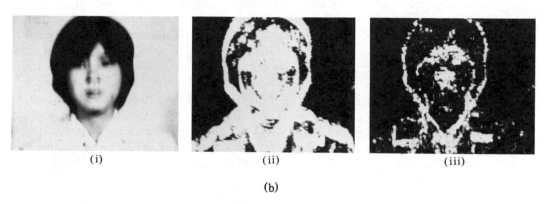

(i)   (ii)   (iii)

(b)

Figure 6.29 (a) Illustration of the amount of movement in an 18-second videotelephone scene. The total number of pixels per frame is 67,000 [Candy et al.;©1971, AT&T]. (b) Illustration of the effect of motion compensation on interframe differences: (i) original image; and significantly changed pixels (white areas) in interframe systems (ii) without motion compensation and (iii) with motion compensation [Ishiguro and Iinuma;©1982, IEEE].

Run-length coding is discussed at length in the context of two-level graphics (Chapter 10).

Conditional replenishment coding implies the use of a buffer to adapt a variable-rate output (see Figure 6.29a) to a channel that accepts a constant bit rate. Buffer size is determined by statistics of image activity. A useful buffer size is in the order of the number of pixels per frame. The probability of buffer overflow can be reduced by the spatial subsampling technique described earlier, or by using a feedback from the buffer to the coder for replacing the 1.5% movement criterion with a higher threshold.

Motion Compensated Coders. The use of the frame period as an indicator of periodicity is clearly a simplification, in general. In moving images, an image element $x(i,j,k)$ is not maximally correlated with a corresponding element $x(i,j,k-1)$ from the previous frame. In the notation of Figure 6.28, pixel A may not be maximally correlated with pixel AF, but rather with pixel AFM. This would indeed be the case if the object in the moving scene had a spatial *translation* equivalent to one vertical unit and two horizontal units in the image grid. Optimal predictors of moving scenes will thus have to incorporate some kind of *movement detection* or *motion compensation* [Limb and Murphy, 1975] [Netravali and Robbins, 1979] [Stuller, Netravali and Robbins, 1980] [Ishiguro and Iinuma, 1982]. Interframe coders that incorporate this refinement in order to reduce prediction error are called *motion compensated interframe coders*. These coders have excellent potential for high-quality digital videoconferencing at 1.5 Mb/s. For sampling rates in the order of 5 to 10 MHz, this implies a bit rate in the order of 0.15 to 0.3 bit/pixel.

The complexity of a motion compensated coder is directly related to the complexity of the algorithm that makes a time-variant, and space-variant estimate of the translation vector. As in adaptive quantization and adaptive prediction, there are two classes of algorithms — backward estimation procedures requiring no side-information and forward estimation procedures that explicitly transmit translation vector information. The backward algorithms can afford to estimate translation vectors individually for each pixel, while the forward procedures need to use a single translation vector for an entire sub-image, for economies in side-information. In both cases, improvements over a non-motion-compensated coder can be dramatic for scenes typical in videoconferencing applications (Figure 6.29b). These improvements have also been demonstrated by measurements of output entropy [Netravali and Robbins, 1979] [Ishiguro and Iinuma, 1982], and by measurements of subjective quality. On an image impairment scale of 1 to 5 (Appendix F), motion compensation can provide MOS gains of up to one point in videoconference images, depending on the type of motion involved [Koga et al., 1983].

6.7 Transmission Error Effects

Differential PCM systems are affected differently by bit errors than PCM systems because the DPCM decoder loop causes an error propagation, while a PCM error does not propagate in time. The next section is primarily concerned with a calculation of the total mean-squared reconstruction error of DPCM systems, as well as a demonstration of perceptually important error effects in speech and video coding. We will note that from an objective mse viewpoint, DPCM can perform equal to or even better than PCM for a given bit error rate. Subjectively, DPCM is more error-robust than PCM in speech coding [Yan and Donaldson, 1972], but less robust than PCM for image coding [Kummerow, 1981]. These results were indicated earlier in Figure 5.14.

6.7.1 Error Definitions and Propagation Effects

We will now show that channel errors are no more serious for DPCM than for PCM under an mse criterion when a predictor as specified by linear prediction theory is used. We will also see that the total SNR for a DPCM system with re-optimized predictor is considerably higher than for a PCM system operating on the same digital channel [Chang and Donaldson, 1972].

Differences between error-prone PCM and DPCM systems can be understood with reference to Figure 6.30. In both cases a channel error sample

$$c(n) = u(n) - v(n) \tag{6.114}$$

changes channel input $u(n)$ to a wrong value $v(n)$. In PCM, the erroneous reconstruction value $y(n)$ is simply equal to $v(n)$. In DPCM, however, $v(n)$ is the input to the DPCM decoder. Due to the linearity of the decoder filter, the correct computation of output [corresponding to correct decoder input $v(n)$] is superposed by an error output caused by an input $c(n)$ to the decoder loop.

If the decoder is an all-pole filter, there will be an infinite sequence of error samples at the output, with decaying amplitudes in the case of stable filters. Transmission errors therefore *accumulate* or *propagate* in the reconstructed DPCM waveform. In the case of first-order prediction, the effect, on a future reconstruction value, at time $m \geqslant n$, is described by

$$c(m) = c(n)h_1^{m-n}; \quad m \geqslant n \tag{6.115}$$

Error propagation will also be present in the case of an all-zero predictor (6.4c) but the decoder memory would be finite in this case, and equal to the predictor order itself. This was in fact an important motivation for using the combination of all-pole and all-zero components in the specific system of Figure 6.24(b) for toll-

Figure 6.30 Definitions of sequences in (a) PCM and (b) DPCM.

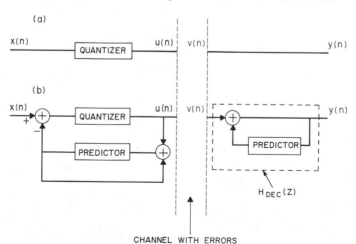

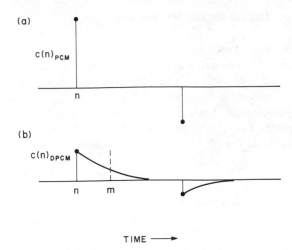

(a)

$c(n)_{PCM}$

n

(b)

$c(n)_{DPCM}$

n   m

TIME ⟶

Figure 6.31 Error propagation in DPCM decoder. The effect of a channel noise component c(n) remains impulsive in the PCM output (a), but it gets attenuated in the DPCM output (b).

quality speech. The rest of this section will, however, deal only with the more widely understood case of an all-pole DPCM predictor.

Transmission error propagation in DPCM is shown qualitatively in Figure 6.31. Because of the prediction process at the encoder, the channel inputs, and therefore channel error samples in DPCM [Figure 6.31(b)] are smaller than in PCM [Figure 6.31(a)]. But successive reconstruction error samples in DPCM are highly correlated because of the error propagation that results from decoder memory.

This kind of error smearing is perceptually desirable in *speech* communication where a PCM error spike [impulse $c(n)$ at time n] of large magnitude is more

Figure 6.32 Transmission error patterns in speech decoding with $p_e = 10^{-2}$: (a) input speech waveform of duration 256 samples (32 ms); (b) output of μ255 log PCM ($R = 8$ bits/sample); and (c) output of DPCM-AQB ($R = 4$ bits/sample). The arrows in (c) indicate segments with channel error propagation due to decoder memory [Jayant, 1982].

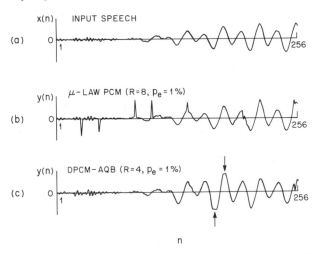

(a) $x(n)$ INPUT SPEECH

0
1   256

(b) $y(n)$ μ-LAW PCM (R=8, p_e=1%)

0
1   256

(c) $y(n)$ DPCM-AQB (R=4, p_e=1%)

0
1   256

n

annoying than a low-amplitude error waveform smeared over a long duration (as seen in samples at time $m \geqslant n$). Figure 6.32 is a 32 ms sequence of output samples in log-PCM and DPCM-AQB with the same $p_e = 1\%$. The predictor in the DPCM system is all-pole and of first order, with $h_1 = 0.85$. Notice the spiky speech output in the PCM example and the persistence of incorrect outputs in the DPCM case.

In *image* coding, on the other hand, error propagation is perceptually very undesirable, taking the form of very visible streaks or blotches with one- and two-dimensional predictors, respectively. Figure 6.33(a) and (b) show outputs from a

Figure 6.33 (a) and (b) Transmission error propagation in DPCM encoding of an image with $R = 4$ bits/sample and bit error rates of (a) $p_e = 5 \cdot 10^{-4}$ and (b) $p_e = 10^{-3}$. (c) Result of using an error-robust hybrid of PCM and DPCM schemes with the input of (a) [Kummerow, 1981. Reprinted with permission]. (d) Result of receiver enhancement of output of (b) by explicit error detection followed by the replacement of a corrupted 1-D segment by a corresponding segment from a previous line [Ngan and Steele;©1982, IEEE].

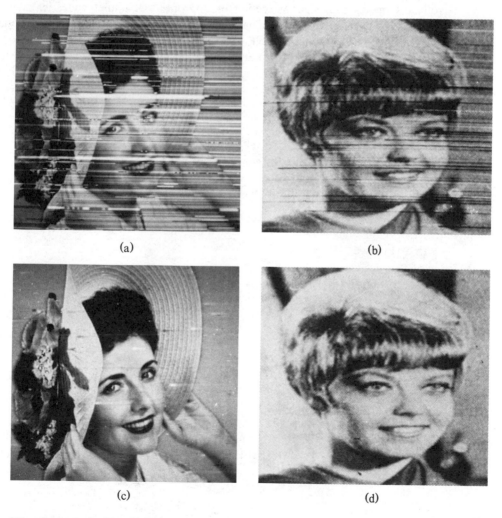

(a)

(b)

(c)

(d)

DPCM decoder with a one-dimensional predictor of the all-pole type discussed in the examples of Section 6.2. Unlike in PCM [Figure 5.13(b)], channel errors are manifested as streaks instead of spots. The error patterns of course decay with stable decoder filters. Figure 6.33(c) is the effect [on the input in (a)] of an error-robust scheme called *hybrid DPCM* (Section 6.7.4) that includes an *implicit* PCM component in the coder output *without increasing the bit rate*. Figure 6.33(d) is the result of post-processing the output of (b) in a scheme where 1-D image segments that are detected to be in error are replaced by corresponding segments from the previous scan line (Section 6.7.4). The error detection in this example is provided by *explicit* PCM components that are periodically inserted in the coder output, *resulting in an increase in bit rate*.

6.7.2 Error Analysis

The effect of channel errors on quantizers and ways of making quantizers more robust (smaller step sizes, selection of appropriate channel code, leakage in AQ logic) have been discussed in Chapter 4. These observations extend to quantizer design in DPCM systems as well. The purpose of the present section is to discuss the dependence of error patterns and of mse on predictor design.

The output of the decoder filter (Figure 6.30) with impulse response $h_{DEC}(n)$ is

$$y(n) = v(n) * h_{DEC}(n) = u(n) * h_{DEC}(n) - c(n) * h_{DEC}(n) \qquad (6.116)$$

The output without channel errors is simply

$$u(n) * h_{DEC}(n) = x(n) - q(n) \qquad (6.117)$$

Therefore the reconstruction noise with channel errors is

$$r(n) = x(n) - y(n) = q(n) + c(n) * h_{DEC}(n) \qquad (6.118)$$

with a variance

$$\sigma_r^2 = E[R^2(n)] = \sigma_q^2 + 2 \sum_{k=0}^{\infty} h_{DEC}(k) E[Q(n) \, C(n-k)]$$

$$+ \sum_{k=0}^{\infty} \sum_{l=0}^{\infty} h_{DEC}(k) h_{DEC}(l) E[C(n-k) C(n-l)] \qquad (6.119)$$

Note that the channel error is defined by an incorrect mapping between quantizer outputs and its reconstruction at the receiver. Hence a memoryless channel does not necessarily imply that $E[C(m)C(n)] = 0$ for $m \neq n$.

However, certain simplifications of (6.119) are still meaningful. If the channel is memoryless and if the samples of the difference signals are statistically independent, it can be shown that [Chang and Donaldson, 1972]

$$E[Q(n)C(n-k)] = 0 \, ; \quad k \neq 0 \qquad (6.120)$$

and

$$E[C(n)C(n-k)] = 0 \; ; \quad k \neq 0 \tag{6.121}$$

The above correlations are in fact known to be insignificant even if difference signal samples are weakly correlated (as in practical DPCM). Using (6.120) and (6.121), (6.119) simplifies to

$$\sigma_r^2 = \sigma_q^2 + 2E[Q(n)C(n)] + \sigma_c^2 \sum_{k=0}^{\infty} h_{DEC}^2(k) \tag{6.122}$$

where $\sigma_c^2 = E[C^2(n)]$. Earlier discussions (Section 4.9) have shown that the second term in (6.122) is a *mutual error* term which is nearly equal to zero if the quantizer characteristics are close to that of an optimum quantizer. For this case (6.122) simplifies again to

$$\sigma_r^2 = \sigma_q^2 + \alpha \; \sigma_c^2$$

$$\alpha = \sum_{k=0}^{\infty} h_{DEC}^2(k) = \frac{1}{2\pi} \int_{-\pi}^{\pi} \left| H_{DEC}(e^{j\omega}) \right|^2 d\omega \tag{6.123}$$

which differs from earlier PCM results [see (4.158)] in that the channel error variance σ_c^2 has to be multiplied by the term α. This term is the energy of the impulse response. It is also the *power transfer factor* (2.90) of the decoder network, the value by which the power of a white noise input signal is increased by the network. With the notation

$$\sigma_q^2 = \epsilon_q^2 \sigma_d^2; \quad \sigma_c^2 = \epsilon_c^2 \sigma_d^2; \quad G_P = \sigma_x^2/\sigma_d^2 \tag{6.124}$$

(6.123) can be rewritten

$$\sigma_{r,DPCM}^2 = (\epsilon_q^2 + \alpha \epsilon_c^2) \sigma_x^2 G_P^{-1} \tag{6.125}$$

Recall that for PCM,

$$\sigma_{r,PCM}^2 = (\epsilon_q^2 + \epsilon_c^2) \sigma_x^2 \tag{6.126}$$

Thus in DPCM the quantization noise contribution is smaller than in PCM by a factor G_P, the prediction gain; and *the channel error contribution is smaller than in PCM by a factor G_P/α.* This assumes that ϵ_q^2 and ϵ_c^2 are not significantly different for PCM and DPCM, i.e., there are no significant differences in quantizer input pdf.

Recall that ϵ_c^2 is the channel error variance for a unit-variance input, and $\epsilon_c^2 = \xi p_e$ for single bit errors in codewords. For example, if the input is Gaussian and $R = 2$ bits/sample, $\xi = 4.65$ from Table 4.12. Thus if $p_e = 5\%$, $\sigma_c^2 = 0.23$ in the above example.

The case of $h_1 < \rho_1$, or $\alpha < \max \{G_P\}$. It is always possible to design a decoder such that $\alpha < G_P$. Hence, in DPCM, the channel error contributions can be made smaller than those of PCM schemes for any channel. For a first-order predictor with identical coefficient h_1 at transmitter and receiver,

$$\alpha = \sum_{k=0}^{\infty} h_{DEC}^2(k) = 1 + h_1^2 + h_1^4 + \ldots = (1 - h_1^2)^{-1}, \qquad (6.127)$$

a result that can also be derived in the frequency domain. Further, from earlier results in this chapter,

$$G_P = (1 - 2h_1\rho_1 + h_1^2)^{-1} \qquad (6.128)$$

and it can be seen that

$$\alpha < G_P \quad \text{if } h_1 < \rho_1 \qquad (6.129)$$

The case of $h_1 = \rho$, or $\alpha = \max \{G_P\}$. With *optimum (mmse) prediction*, the difference signal is uncorrelated and has a variance smaller than that of the input by a factor $\max\{G_P\}$. This power reduction is compensated at the decoder with power transfer factor

$$\alpha = \max\{G_P\} \qquad (6.130)$$

and the channel error variance then becomes equal to that of PCM provided the two systems have the same normalized error variances ϵ_q^2 and ϵ_c^2 (because $\alpha/G_P = 1$) [Chang and Donaldson, 1972] [Noll, 1978]. Specifically, (6.125) reduces to

$$\sigma_{r,DPCM}^2 = \left[\frac{\epsilon_q^2}{\max\{G_P\}} + \epsilon_c^2 \right] \sigma_x^2 ; \qquad (6.131)$$

$$\sigma_{c,DPCM}^2 = \sigma_{c,PCM}^2 \quad \text{for } \textit{optimal prediction} \qquad (6.132)$$

Although DPCM does not contribute more to the channel error than PCM, a comparison of (6.126) and (6.131) shows that the effect of channel errors, *relative to quantization errors*, is much more serious in DPCM than in PCM.

Example 6.9. First-order prediction with $\rho_1 = 0.95$.
    If $h_1 = \rho_1 = 0.95$,

$$\alpha = \max\{G_P\} = (1 - \rho_1^2)^{-1} = 10.3 \qquad (6.133a)$$

On the other hand, if $h_1 = 7/8$,

$$\alpha = 4.27, \quad G_P = 9.70, \quad \alpha/G_P = 0.44 \qquad (6.133b)$$

The prediction gain loss factor is only $10.3/9.7 = 1.06$, but the error contribution is reduced by a factor $1/0.44 = 2.3$. ●

Example 6.10. Two-dimensional prediction of orders 2 and 3.

Prediction of order three. For the *two-dimensional* predictor of Figure 6.5, with $\hat{x}_A = bx_B + cx_C + dx_D$, it can be shown (A.43) [Jung, 1979] that

$$\alpha = \frac{1}{[(1+b)^2 - (c-d)^2]^{1/2}[(1-b)^2 - (c+d)^2]^{1/2}} \tag{6.134}$$

The filter will be *stable* if [Huang, 1972]

$$|b| < 1 \quad ; \quad \left|\frac{c+d}{1-b}\right| < 1 \quad ; \quad \left|\frac{c-d}{1+b}\right| < 1 \tag{6.135}$$

Violations of this condition will cause diverging outputs for infinite-length inputs; in the case of finite-length inputs, the output may not diverge. For optimal prediction with a separable acf (Section 6.2.4), $b_{opt} = c_{opt} = \rho$ and $d_{opt} = -\rho^2$. For this case

$$\alpha = (1-\rho^2)^{-2} = \max\{G_P\} \tag{6.136a}$$

A comparison with (2.140) shows that such a predictor is optimum for the 2-D Markov source described in Section 2.4.4.

Prediction of order two. For the special case of prediction with two samples, $\hat{x} = bx_B + cx_C$, (6.134) can be used with $d = 0$. It is also easy to show that

$$G_P = \frac{1}{[1 + b^2 + c^2 - 2\rho(b + c - bc\rho)]} \tag{6.136b}$$

We have already shown in (6.33) that $\max\{G_P\} = (1+\rho^2)/(1-\rho^2)$ for the separable-acf-optimal second-order predictor with $b_{opt} = c_{opt} = \rho/(1+\rho^2)$. Note that for this optimal case, α (from 6.134) reduces to $\max\{G_P\}$. For example,

$$\alpha = \max\{G_P\} = 19.5 \quad \text{if} \quad \rho = 0.95 \tag{6.137}$$

If, for ease of implementation, $b = c = 1/2$, $\alpha \to \infty$ from (6.134), suggesting a non-converging transmission error pattern. On the other hand [Chang and Donaldson, 1972], if $b = 3/8$ and $c = 1/2$, [so that $|c| < |1-b|$ in (6.135)],

$$\alpha = 2.08, \quad G_P = 15.0; \quad \alpha/G_P = 0.139 \tag{6.138}$$

Comparison with (6.137) suggests a prediction gain loss factor of only 1.3, but an error effect reduction factor of more than 7. ●

   Subjectively, the use of 2-D prediction provides better resistance to bit errors than 1-D prediction; and the use of hybrid PCM-DPCM coding (Section 6.7.4) further improves that bit error resistance.

Image Coding Illustrations. We have already seen in Figure 5.14b that for a given value of p_e, DPCM has a much poorer subjective performance for images than PCM. In image coding, it is the pattern of an error that is perceptually significant, rather than the mse. So far, we have used $\alpha = \sum h_{DEC}^2(k)$, with the summation from $k = 0$ to ∞, to analyze DPCM error performance in the 1-D case. To study

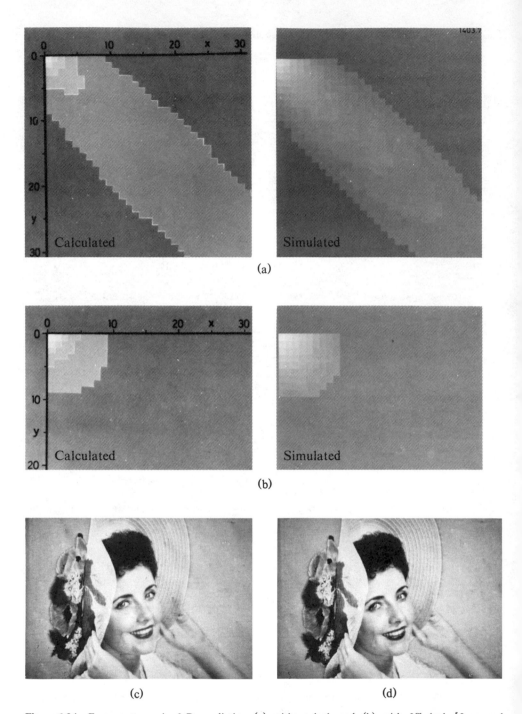

Figure 6.34 Error patterns in 2-D prediction (a) without leak and (b) with 3% leak [Jung and Lippmann, 1975. Reprinted with permission]. These patterns are the impulse responses of corresponding decoder filters Reconstructed images with 2-D predictors (c) without leak and (d) with 1.5% leak, for an error rate of $p_e = 5 \cdot 10^{-4}$ [Kummerow, 1981. Reprinted with permission].

the error pattern generated in image coding by a channel error, illustrations of the 2-D impulse response $h_{DEC}(k_h,k_v)$ are quite helpful.

Two-dimensional predictions can provide error patterns (hazy spots) which are less annoying than the error patterns (streaks) characteristic of one-dimensional DPCM filters. Consider the third-order 2-D predictors

$$\hat{x}_A = (3/4)\, x_B - (1/2)\, x_D + (3/4)\, x_C \qquad (6.139a)$$

$$\hat{x}_A = (3/4)\, x_B - (17/32)\, x_D + (3/4)\, x_C \qquad (6.139b)$$

Figures 6.34(a) and (b) show the corresponding impulse response functions. The impulse response of the decoder filter in the first scheme above is a converging one [Figure 6.34(b)], while that in the second scheme is only slowly converging [Figure 6.34(a)]. In each case, the numbers on the illustrations show the horizontal and vertical separations k_h and k_v for the impulse response function $h_{DEC}(k_h,k_v)$. Both patterns are *diagonal*, as opposed to *horizontal* patterns that characterize 1-D previous sample prediction. Notice also that the first scheme is a 2-D predictor *without leak* ($|b+c+d| = 1$) while the second is a 2-D predictor *with leak* ($|b+c+d| = 0.97 < 1$, implying a 3% leak); and that in both cases predictor coefficients have the easily implementable form $1-2^{-J_1}-2^{-J_2}$ where J_1 and J_2 are integers. Figures 6.34(c) and (d) show reconstructed images for predictors similar to those in (6.139a) and (6.139b), for the example of $p_e = 5\cdot10^{-4}$. The improvement due to leaky prediction is not as easy to perceive as in the comparison of parts (a) and (b) of the figure. On the other hand, the errors in both (c) and (d) are far less perceptible than the horizontal streaks with a 1-D predictor at the same error rate [Figure 6.33(a)].

It can also be seen that with the leaky predictor design (b) mentioned above, $G_P = 84$ and $\alpha = 7 < G_P$ for a separable acf model and $\rho = 0.95$. For the predictor (a) with no leak, $G_P = 80$ but $\alpha = \infty$!

6.7.3 Optimum Prediction for Noisy Channels

We shall see in this section how predictor redesign can improve channel error performance in DPCM. The redesign decreases prediction gain G_P compared with that of an optimum predictor for a clean channel, but also decreases the overall reconstruction error variance σ_r^2 when the bit error rate p_e is nonzero.

First-Order Prediction. We have already noted with a first-order predictor h_1 that

$$\alpha = (1-h_1^2)^{-1}; \qquad G_P = (1-2h_1\rho_1+h_1^2)^{-1} ; \qquad (6.140)$$

Hence, using (6.125),

$$\sigma_r^2 = \left[\epsilon_q^2 + \epsilon_c^2/(1-h_1^2)\right](1-2h_1\rho_1+h_1^2)\sigma_x^2 \qquad (6.141)$$

Thus for an *error-free* channel

$$h_{1,opt} = \rho_1; \qquad \min\{\sigma_r^2\} = \epsilon_q^2(1-\rho_1^2)\sigma_x^2 \quad \text{if } p_e = 0 \qquad (6.142)$$

Ideal integration $(h_1 = 1)$ is sub-optimal for $p_e = 0$ in that G_P for this case is $[2(1-\rho_1)]^{-1}$ instead of $(1-\rho_1^2)$. With a nonzero p_e, on the other hand, ideal integration can be disastrous in that $\alpha = \infty$ for $h_1 = 1$, signifying infinite error propagation. In fact, if p_e is nonzero, $h_{1,opt} < \rho_1$. An analytically tractable situation is for *very high error rates* which cause the channel error variance to dominate in σ_r^2:

$$\epsilon_c^2 \gg (1-h_1^2)\epsilon_q^2 \qquad (6.143)$$

In this case, DPCM performance can be improved by (i) decreasing the quantizer step size, to reduce ξ as noted in Section 4.9.4, and more significantly (especially in low bit rate systems where the effect of quantizer reoptimization on ξ can be very modest), by predictor reoptimization. In fact, setting (6.143) in (6.141), this optimization is provided by minimizing $\alpha/G_P = (1-2h_1\rho_1+h_1^2)/(1-h_1^2)$. The results are [Chang and Donaldson, 1972]

$$h_{1,opt} = \rho_1^{-1}(1 - \sqrt{1-\rho_1^2}) \; ;$$
$$\min\{\sigma_c^2\} = \sqrt{1-\rho_1^2} \; \epsilon_c^2\sigma_x^2 \; ; \qquad \text{for large } p_e \qquad (6.144)$$

Note that the above indicates a channel error variance that is less than that in PCM by a factor $(1-\rho_1^2)^{1/2}$. The choice in (6.144) is suboptimal for small channel error probabilities, but the resulting reconstruction error variance increase (which is simply the loss in G_P for $p_e \to 0$) is never more than 3 dB (Problem 6.33). On the other hand, the design can considerably increase the overall *SNR* over that of PCM.

Example 6.11. Gaussian AR(1) source, $p_e = 5\%$.

Figure 6.35 refers to the example of DPCM coding of a Gaussian AR(1) input $(\rho_1 = 0.85)$ with two-bit quantization, and an FBC binary code. The bit error rate is $p_e = 5\%$ and we have $\epsilon_q^2 = 0.118$ and $\epsilon_c^2 = \xi p_e = 0.233$ with $\xi = 4.65$ (Table 4.12). The solid-line theoretical results for error variance are those corresponding to (6.141); they have been modified to account for quantization noise feedback and a loss of G_P given by $(1-\epsilon_q^2 h_1^2)$ as in Chapter 8. Note that there is an improvement over PCM, and that $h_{1,opt} = 0.57 < \rho_1$ for the noisy channel. Reducing h_1 to 0.57 (from 0.85) decreases the 1% error decay time to 8 (from 30) samples (Problem 6.31). Included is a D*PCM curve (Chapter 7) with

$$\sigma_{r,D^*PCM}^2 = (\epsilon_q^2 + \epsilon_c^2)\alpha \, G_P \, \sigma_x^2$$

D*PCM (Chapter 7) is a scheme that quantizes a difference signal $d^*(n)$ *without feedback around the quantizer*. The quantization errors then affect the performance in the same way as channel errors. Therefore, at high values of error rate, D*PCM results can be used to estimate the error performance of DPCM. In the case of high p_e, DPCM would be optimized in a total mse sense if the predictor is chosen such that $\{d(n)\}$ is *half-white* which implies that the decoder filter has a magnitude-squared frequency response that follows $|H_{DEC}(e^{j\omega})|^2 \sim \sqrt{S_{xx}(e^{j\omega})}$ rather than $S_{xx}(e^{j\omega})$. The value of $h_{1,opt}$ [see (6.144)] is an approximation to the half-whitening design. ●

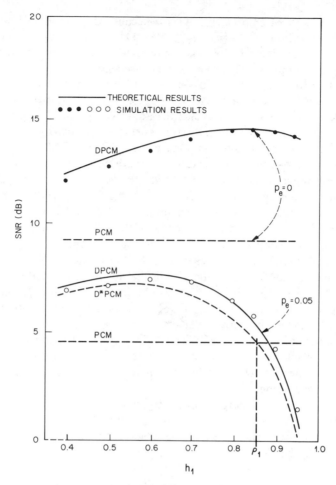

Figure 6.35 2-bit coding of a Gaussian AR(1) source. SNR versus h_1 in PCM and DPCM for $p_e = 0$ and $5 \cdot 10^{-2}$ [Noll;©1978, AT&T].

6.7.4 Error Protection

Previous sections have shown how the DPCM predictor can be designed to be robust to transmission errors. We shall next discuss three classes of explicit error protection techniques that have proved useful in DPCM operation over noisy channels.

Hybrids between PCM and DPCM. In order to avoid extreme error propagation, it is useful to reset predictor coefficients periodically to zero. For example, a PCM representation may be used, instead of DPCM, for reconstructuring the first pixel of every Mth line in image coding. This is equivalent to restarting the decoding process periodically with a PCM word. The technique of *leaky integration* ($h_1 < h_{1,opt}$) in Figure 6.35 can also be interpreted as a DPCM approach that includes a PCM component. This is because the quantizer input $[x(n)-h_1 y(n-1)]$ can be rewritten as $[x(n)-h_{1,opt} y(n-1)] + [h_{1,opt}-h_1]y(n-1)$. The first term in the above sum is an innovations or prediction error term, correct to the quantization error at sampling instant $n-1$. The second term is simply a scaled version of output $y(n-1)$. The inclusion of the second term increases transmission error resistance but it also increases quantization error variance.

A coding system that avoids the above compromise, while still retaining a PCM component for transmission error-resistance, is *hybrid DPCM* [van Buul, 1978]. This scheme is explained in Figure 6.36. The "PCM" amplitude is $y'(n)$, and in general, it has a higher accuracy representation than $u'(n)$, the conventional channel input in DPCM. In hybrid DPCM, a "PCM" component is added to the channel input as follows. To each R-bit binary codeword $u'(n)$, the R most significant bits $[a'(n)$, as given by a quantizer $Q*]$ of the previous reconstructed codeword $y'(n-1)$ are added modulo-2^R, which implies that the carry of the last addition is suppressed. Thus, the sum $u'(n) + a'(n)$ still has an R-bit representation. At the receiver $a''(n)$ is subtracted. With error-free transmission, the scheme has no effect on DPCM performance. In the case of channel errors, $u''(n) = u'(n) - c(n)$, which would imply an error propagation into the next sample times $n + 1, n + 2,...$. In this case, the hybrid scheme has the potential of improving the error performance. An error $c(n) = u'(n) - u''(n)$ in transmission at time n will lead to a difference $a'(n + 1) - a''(n + 1)$ at time $n + 1$ which is a reasonable measure of that error $c(n)$. The effect of $c(n)$ therefore nearly gets canceled out in hybrid DPCM at sample $n+1$, thus avoiding error propagation.

In order to illustrate the mitigation of error propagation, assume that the addition operations above are not modulo-2^R but include a carry of all bits. Further assume that the mmse predictor operation is a simple one-sample delay, signifying that $h_{1,opt} = 1$. Then the decoder outputs at times n and $n+1$ are

$$y''(n) = y'(n) - c(n)$$

$$y''(n+1) = u''(n+1) + y'(n) - c(n)$$

$$= u'(n+1) + a'(n+1) - a''(n+1) + y'(n) - c(n)$$

$$\simeq u'(n+1) + y'(n) = y'(n+1)$$

Figure 6.36 Schematic block diagram of hybrid DPCM [van Bull;©1978, IEEE].

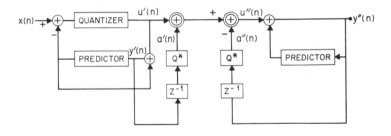

i.e., the channel error is compensated for. Practically, the modulo-2^R operation makes error-compensation imperfect, and the design of quantizer and predictor, together with the statistics of the input signal, influence the overall performance.

With image signals, use of hybrid DPCM provides significant improvement over conventional DPCM in the context of channel errors, and this improvement is particularly valuable in the context of one-dimensional prediction. This is shown by the comparison of images (a) and (c) in Figure 6.33. The benefits noticed in Figure 6.33 are also accompanied by significant gains in subjective quality as measured by MOS figures [Kummerow, 1981]. In Figure 5.14(b), the MOS curve for hybrid-DPCM with a *first-order* predictor would lie between the characteristic shown for a *second-order* conventional DPCM system and the characteristic shown by the PCM system. Thus, for a given predictor, the improvement provided by the hybrid technique is such as to increase tolerable error rate for given subjective quality by at least an order of magnitude.

Use of Natural Redundancies. As in the case of PCM, it is possible to utilize *natural redundancies* that are present in video and speech signals to enhance error-corrupted DPCM-decoder outputs [Steele, Esdale and Goodman, 1977] [Steele, Goodman and McGonegal, 1979]. The channel outputs in DPCM systems correspond, however, to prediction error signals $d(n)$ which are less redundant (Problem 6.4) than the channel outputs $y(n)$ in PCM. As a consequence, simpler types of receiver-end refinement such as 1-D median filtering and 1-D interpolation produce less dramatic gains in DPCM than in PCM.

In image coding, however, the presence of substantial, and simply structured, interline redundancy is very useful in designing very effective 2-D enhancement algorithms. For example, in *line-averaging* techniques [Connor, Pease and Scholes, 1971], pixels on a line that is detected to be error-corrupted are simply replaced by averaging corresponding neighbors from previous and future lines. Reliable detection of errors may, however, need, in general, the use of additional redundancy or side-information.

Use of Explicit Redundancies. Error-moderation techniques in DPCM systems for speech typically require the use of *explicit redundancy*, implying that additional error-protection information of some kind is to be transmitted. In severe burst error environments such as mobile radio, with $p_e = 5\%$ and correlated errors, this may involve protection of significant DPCM bits with redundancies in the order of 25 to 50% [Noll, 1975] [Jayant, 1975].

In one experiment with a burst-error channel with *average* bit error rate $\bar{p}_e$, protection of the most significant bit in DPCM-AQF ($R = 3$), provided an *SNR* gain of nearly 3 dB in the range $(.01 < \bar{p}_e < .05)$; while protection of the two most significant bits provided a gain that increased with $\bar{p}_e$, reaching a value of 9 dB at $\bar{p}_e = .05$ (Figure 6.37). Note that *ideal* error protection is assumed in this illustration, and no correction of the curves is made for the side information needed for error protection.

In random error environments with p_e in the order of 1%, significant enhancement can result by the use of *statistical block protection coding* procedures

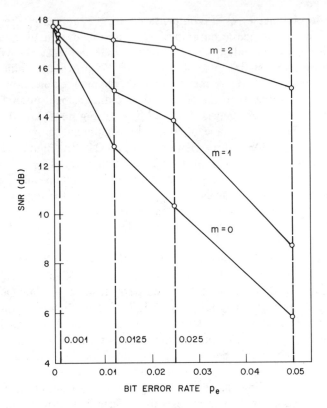

Figure 6.37 Effects of protecting the first m bits in DPCM-AQF transmission of speech over burst error channels; $h_1 = 0.6$ and $R = 3$ bits/sample. Ideal error protection is assumed when $m > 0$ [Noll,II;©1975, AT&T].

that need no more than 10% of side information [Steele, Jayant and Schmidt, 1979]. These techniques use statistical features of an input block such as the average and maximum magnitudes of the reconstructed first difference $y(n) - y(n-1)$; the maximum statistic is used to detect the most seriously affected *samples* in the received waveform block (rather than *all erroneous bits*), and the average statistic is used to correct these samples approximately.

A good example for the use of natural *and* explicit redundancy is the image coding system that produces the result of Figure 6.33(d). This system is based on the division of each scan line into eight segments, explicit transmission of a PCM word once for each segment for purposes of error detection [Ngan and Steele, 1982], and the replacement of a segment deemed to be in error by a corresponding segment from the previous row. As seen by the comparison of Figures 6.33(b) and (d), this technique works very well if the natural inter-line redundancy is significant (as in the test image in question). The explicit redundancy for (error-protected) PCM transmissions is in the order of 10% of the total transmission rate [Ngan and Steele, 1982].

Problems

(6.1) Consider the sub-optimal first-order predictor defined by $h_1 = 1$. Show that this produces a prediction gain equal to $[2(1-\rho_1)]^{-1}$ which exceeds unity only if $\rho_1 > 0.5$.

(6.2) For an input with mean m and first autocovariance value ρ_1 show that mmse first-order linear prediction is defined by $\hat{x}(n) = \rho_1 x(n-1) + (1-\rho_1)m$.

(6.3) (a) Show that if $h_1 = 1$ instead of ρ_1, the loss in mse performance in first-order prediction is less than 1 dB if $\rho_1 > 0.6$ and less than 0.5 dB if $\rho_1 > 0.78$.

(b) Consider the first-order prediction of pixel A (Figure 6.5) using a same-line pixel that is two samples to the left of A, instead of the immediate neighbor B. The above design is simpler for real-time implementation but it also involves a reduction in prediction gain G_P. With an AR(1) input model, and $\rho = 0.95$, show that the loss in G_P is nearly 3 dB. This loss can be compensated for if one uses higher order 1-D prediction involving B and other pixels to the left of it [Yamagata et al., 1981].

(6.4) (a) Show that the first normalized acf value for the adjacent-sample difference signal $d(n) = x(n)-x(n-1)$ is $\rho_{dd}(1) = (2\rho_1-\rho_2-1) \, / \, 2(1-\rho_1)$.

(b) With $\rho_1 = 0.825$ and $\rho_2 = 0.562$, show that $\rho_{dd}(1) = 0.25$.

(c) Show also that with an AR(1) source, $\rho_{dd}(1) = (\rho_1-1)/2$.

(6.5) (a) Show that the first normalized acf value for the prediction error signal in mmse first-order prediction is given by $\rho_{dd}(1) = [\rho_1(\rho_1^2 - \rho_2)/(1 - \rho_1^2)]$.

(b) Note that this acf vanishes for a first-order Markov input for which $\rho_2 = \rho_1^2$.

(c) With the $\rho_1 = 0.825$ and $\rho_2 = 0.562$, as in Problem 6.4, show that the first acf value of optimal prediction error is 0.306.

(6.6) Show that the prediction gain in first-order prediction is greater than 1 as long as $h_1(h_1-2\rho_1) < 0$. Thus if $\rho_1 = 0.85$, $^1G_P > 1$ as long as $0 < h_1 < 1.7$ (Figure 6.23a).

(6.7) Consider the two-pixel image predictor (6.30) and an isotropic acf model. Show that as $\rho \to 1$, (6.32) represents an asymptotic 1.895 dB gain over optimal first-order prediction (6.23) (Hint: Use L'Hospital's rule).

(6.8) Consider a two-pixel image predictor (6.30), a separable acf model, and an approximation to the design (6.33): $b = c = 0.5$, corresponding to an averaging predictor $\hat{x}_A = 0.5(x_B+x_C)$.

(a) Show that the prediction gain is $[(1-\rho)(3-\rho)/2]^{-1}$.

(b) Show that this is better than the gain of an optimum previous-pixel-based predictor if $\rho > 1/3$.

(c) Show that for $\rho \to 1$, the prediction gain is very close to the optimum 2-D prediction gain obtained by (6.33).

(6.9) Consider the image predictor $\hat{x}_A = 0.5(x_B+x_E)$ (see Figure 6.5). With a separable acf model $(\rho_{AB} = \rho, \rho_{AE} = \rho^2, \rho_{BE} = \rho^3)$, show that the resulting prediction gain with $\rho = 0.95$ is 1.8 dB worse than that provided by the averaging predictor of Problem 6.8.

(6.10)   Let A,B,C,D in (6.35) denote adjacent speech samples with acf values of $\rho_1 = 0.825$, $\rho_2 = 0.562$ and $\rho_3 = 0.308$.

     (a)   Show that optimal values for b,c and d are 1.10, -0.28 and -0.03.

     (b)   Show that the prediction gain from this third-order scheme is about 0.8 dB higher than that from optimal first-order prediction $(b=\rho_1; c=d=0)$.

(6.11)   The quality of digitized speech in adaptive differential PCM (ADPCM) can be significantly improved by passing the output speech through a reconstruction lowpass filter that is matched to an appropriately defined short-time speech cut-off frequency $f_c(t)$. Practically, the adaptive procedure involves switching the decoder output into one of a bank of N lowpass filters whose cut-off frequencies f_{cn}, $n=1$ to N, span the expected range of input speech bandwidth, 0 to W. For any given segment of speech, the switching is made to the filter with the smallest value of f_{cn} that is greater than the local block-specific bandwidth $W(t)$. The result is the rejection of quantization noise in the frequency band $[f_{cn},W]$. For the case of equally spaced filter cut-offs $f_{cn} = W/N$, and with uniform psd and pdf models for the quantization noise spectrum and the cut-off frequency f_{cn}, with constant values $1/W$ in each case in the range $(0,W)$, show that

     (a)   the gain in segmental SNR due to adaptive filtering is

$$G_{AF}(N) = [10 \log N - (10/N) \sum_1^N \log n]\ \mathrm{dB}$$

     (b)   Show also that more than one-half of the maximum adaptive filtering gain $G_{AF}(\infty)$ (in dB) is realizable by a bank of four filters.

(6.12)   Consider an input $\{X(n)\}$ of variance σ_x^2 and normalized adjacent sample correlation ρ_1, contaminated by additive white Gaussian noise of variance σ_n^2. Show the mmse first-order prediction of $x(n)$, based on the previous sample $x(n-1)$, is described by

$$h_{1,opt} = \frac{\rho_1}{1 + (\sigma_n^2/\sigma_x^2)}$$

(6.13)   Compute $h_{1,opt}$ and $h_{2,opt}$ in second-order prediction

     (a)   directly (6.43).

     (b)   via $\mathbf{R}_{xx}^{-1}$ (6.44).

     (c)   Compute min $\{\sigma_d^2\}$

          (i)   directly.

          (ii)   by using (6.46) and (6.47) .

          (iii)   by using (6.48).

     (d)   Discuss the special case of $\rho_2 = \rho_1^2$.

(6.14)   (a)   Show that for any given vector $\mathbf{h}$ of predictor coefficients, the prediction error variance is given by $^N\sigma_d^2 = \sigma_x^2 - 2\mathbf{h}^T\mathbf{r}_{xx} + \mathbf{h}^T\mathbf{R}_{xx}\mathbf{h}$. Verify that for first-order prediction, $^1\sigma_d^2 = \sigma_x^2(1 - 2h_1\rho_1 + h_1^2)$.

       (b)   Consider the use of the usual speech design $h_1 = 0.825$ [see (6.24b)] for pre-emphasized speech with $\rho_1 = 0.7$. Show that the resulting G_P is 2.8 dB rather than 4.96 dB, the value in (6.24b). If, on the other hand, h_1 is set equal to $\rho_1 = 0.7$, show that $G_P = 2.9$ dB.

(6.15)   Consider three random variables A, B and C and the acf example $[\rho_{AB} = 0.95, \rho_{AC} = 0.90]$. Show that the admissible region for the third acf value ρ_{BC} is the interval $[0.72, 0.99]$. If B and C are used in a second-order linear prediction of A, show that the minimum prediction error as a function of ρ_{BC} has a maximum at $\rho_{BC} = 0.95$.

(6.16)   Derive the result of (6.36).

(6.17)   A general result for the mmse of an Mth order predictor has been given by (6.48). Show that for the Mth order Markov process

$$\min \{^\infty\sigma_d^2\} = \lim_{M \to \infty} \frac{|^{M+1}\mathbf{R}_{xx}|}{|^M\mathbf{R}_{xx}|} = \frac{|^{M+1}\mathbf{R}_{xx}|}{|^M\mathbf{R}_{xx}|} = \min \{^M\sigma_d^2\}$$

so that an optimum predictor for an Mth order Markov source needs M coefficients to yield the mmse.

(6.18)   Compute and sketch the magnitude-squared frequency response of DPCM decoder filters with coefficients given by the polynomial predictors of order N [see (6.53)], for $N = 1, 2$ and 3.

(6.19)   (a)   Show that straight-line extrapolation ($N = 2$: $h_1 = 2$, $h_2 = -1$) has a prediction error variance of $2(3-4\rho_1+\rho_2)\,\sigma_x^2$.

       (b)   For a first-order Markov source ($\rho_2 = \rho_1^2$), show that the prediction error variance for this extrapolator is at least a factor of 2 higher than that of a zero-order scheme (first-order prediction with $h_1 = 1$).

(6.20)   (a)   Show that quadratic extrapolation ($N = 3$: $h_1 = 3$, $h_2 = -3$ and $h_3 = 1$) has a prediction error variance of $2(10-15\rho_1+6\rho_2-\rho_3)\sigma_x^2$.

       (b)   For a first-order Markov source ($\rho_2 = \rho_1^2$), show that the prediction error variance for this extrapolator exceeds that of a zero-order polynomial (first-order prediction with $h_1 = 1$) by a factor not smaller than 4.

(6.21)   Consider the raised cosine spectrum of (2.166) which is a data signal whose center frequency and half-bandwidth are given by $\Omega'/2\pi = 1800$ Hz and $\Delta\Omega/2\pi = 1200$ Hz.

       (a)   Verify that the first three acf values of this signal are $(0.148, -0.750$ and $-0.261)$.

       (b)   Show that the maximum prediction gain possible with this signal is not higher than 0.1 dB for $N = 1$ (first-order prediction), but that the maximum possible gain is about 5.5 dB for $N = 3$.

(c) Also, show that a first-order predictor optimized for speech ($h_1 = \rho_1 = 0.825$) has almost a 5 dB gain in *SNR* over PCM, but that the same predictor would produce a negative gain (about -1.5 dB) over PCM with the data signal input.

(d) Finally, verify that the third-order predictor optimized for the data signal would provide a prediction gain of about -1.3 dB with a speech input [O'Neal and Stroh, 1972].

(6.22) Assume two inputs with statistics distinguished by subscripts u and v. For a given predictor $\mathbf{h}$, let respective difference signal variances be σ_{du}^2 and σ_{dv}^2, as defined in (6.54). Consider the weighted sum

$$\sigma_d^2 = \lambda \sigma_{du}^2 + (1-\lambda)\sigma_{dv}^2$$

where λ ($0 < \lambda < 1$) is an input-weighting parameter. Show that σ_d^2 is minimized by $\mathbf{h}_{\mathrm{opt}} = \mathbf{R}^{-1}\mathbf{r}$ where the elements of $\mathbf{R}$ and $\mathbf{r}$ are obtained from

$$\rho(i) = \lambda \rho_{uu}(i) + (1-\lambda)\rho_{vv}(i)$$

The above result defines a *compromise predictor*, one that is matched to an acf which is the weighted average of component acf's. In the speech and data problem (Problem 6.21), a value of $\lambda = 0.5$ leads to positive prediction gains for both input classes, with prediction order $N = 3$ [O'Neal and Stroh, 1972].

(6.23) (a) Show that the quantizer input in DPCM is $[x(n)-h_1x(n-1)] + [h_1q(n-1)]$ where the last term is due to quantization noise feedback.

(b) If the coder input is an AR(1) process with adjacent sample correlation ρ_1 and if $h_1 = \rho_1$, show that the mean square value of the quantizer input, assuming vanishing correlations between $x(n)$ and $q(m)$ for all n and m, is $\sigma_x^2(1-\rho_1^2)(1-\epsilon_q^2\rho_1^2)^{-1}$.

(c) Hence show that the *SNR* degradation due to error feedback is given by $10 \log (1-\epsilon_q^2\rho_1^2)^{-1}$.

(6.24) Show that in the autocorrelation method for APF, $\hat{\mathbf{R}}_{xx} = \{\hat{R}_{xx}(|i-j|)\}_{i,j\,=\,1,2...N}$ is positive semidefinite, i.e., show that $\mathbf{a}^T\hat{\mathbf{R}}_{xx}\mathbf{a} \geqslant 0$ for any non-zero vector $\mathbf{a}$. This is a necessary and sufficient condition for the stability of the inverse filter.

(6.25) Consider an APF system for speech with the following features: sampling frequency of 7.0 kHz, block length of 20 ms, and a forward-adaptive one-bit difference-signal quantizer. Assume that all side information (for quantizer step size and parcor coefficients) uses 4-bit representation, and that the predictor order is 4. Show that the total transmission rate is 8 kb/s.

(6.26) Show that for stationary Gaussian signals, the normalized two-sided polarity correlation function is related to input acf $\rho_{xx}(k)$ via the equations

$$R_{xx}''(k) = E[\mathrm{sgn}\,X(n)\,\mathrm{sgn}\,X(n+k)]/E[\mathrm{sgn}\,X(n)]^2 = (2/\pi)\arcsin \rho_{xx}(k)$$

(6.27) Consider the covariance solution for APF, as defined by (6.69a), (6.74) and Figure 6.22(b). Using the simple example of $N = M = 3$, and a specific input sequence $\{x(-2), x(-1),..., x(3)\}$, show that the resulting matrix $\mathbf{R}_{xx}$ is symmetric but non-Toeplitz.

Differential PCM   6

(6.28)   Assume a source with $\rho_1 = 0.825$, $\rho_2 = 0.562$ and $\rho_3 = 0.308$ as in Problem 6.10.

    (a)   Compute the mmse for predictors of order 1, 2 and 3.

    (b)   Compute the mmse predictor coefficients directly from (6.44b).

    (c)   Compute the mmse coefficients using the recursive algorithm (6.83).

    (d)   Compute the *parcor* coefficients π_1, π_2 and π_3, and the corresponding *log-area* coefficients c_1, c_2 and c_3.

    (e)   Confirm the result of (6.78): $\max\{{}^3 G_P\} = \left[\prod_{j=1}^{3} (1 - \pi_j^2) \right]^{-1}$.

(6.29)   Consider a conditional replenishment coder. Assume that 8-bit PCM is used for amplitudes, 8-bit addresses for positioning along the line and a negligible amount of information for vertical addressing, because of the systematic scanning procedure. Assuming that the average fraction of changed pixels is 9% [Figure 6.29(a)], show that the *average* data rate generated would be approximately 1.44 bits per picture element. The *peak* data rate may, however, be an order of magnitude greater [Haskell, 1975] [Haskell, Mounts and Candy, 1972].

(6.30)   Consider conditional replenishment coders for $N \times N$ image frames. Each frame is divided into subimages of size $M \times M$, and each subimage classified as either active or not. The addresses of active subimages are transmitted to the receiver as PCM words of appropriate size. If the average probability of an active subimage is P_A, show that the average amount of addressing information is $(N^2 P_A / M^2)$ $\{[\log_2 (N^2/M^2)]+1\}$ bits per frame, where [·] represents "greatest integer in".

(6.31)   With first-order prediction,

    (a)   Show that the number of samples $n(f)$ needed for an error to decay to a fraction f, is given by

$$n(f) = \log_e (1/f)/\log_e (1/h_1) \ .$$

    (b)   Hence note that for a decay to 1%, $n(f)$ values with $h_1 = 0.95$, 0.85, 0.74 and 0.57 are 90, 29, 16 and 9 samples, respectively.

(6.32)   Calculate values of α [see (6.134)] and $\max\{G_P\}$ for the predictors in (6.139), assuming a separable acf model with $\rho = 0.95$.

(6.33)   (a)   Show that the predictor design in (6.144) implies a decrease in prediction gain G_P by a factor

$$\left[(2/\rho_1^2) \left(1 - \sqrt{1-\rho_1^2} \right) \right]$$

    (b)   Note that this reduction is greatest, and equal to 3 dB, when $\rho_1 = 1$.

(6.34)   For the example of a first-order Markov sequence of acf $R_{xx}(k) = \rho^{|k|}\sigma_x^2$, show that the reduction in mse for DPCM over PCM for high error rates [Noll, 1978] [see (6.156)] is

$$\left(\frac{\pi}{2} \right)^2 \left[\frac{1}{1-\rho^2} \right] \left[F\left(\frac{\pi}{2}, \rho \right) \right]^{-2} = \frac{1}{1-\rho^2} \left[1 + \frac{\rho^2}{4} + \frac{9\rho^4}{64} + ... \right]^{-2}$$

where $F(\cdot)$ is the complete elliptical integral of the first kind. For $\rho = 0.9625$, this improvement is a factor of 7.2. Recall that a simple reoptimization (6.144) of a first-order predictor leads to a gain of $(1-\rho^2)^{1/2} = 5.2$.

(6.35)   Consider the highly-structured two-level psd of Figure 2.24, (2.168) and Problem 2.22.

   (a)   Compute the acf $R_{xx}(k)$ and show that it vanishes for even values of k.

   (b)   Compute the values of minimum prediction error $\min\{{}^k\sigma_d^2\}$ for $\alpha = 2/17$ and $k = 1, 2$ and ∞.

References

H. W. Adelman, Y. C. Ching and B. Gotz, "An ADPCM Approach to Reduce the Bit Rate of μ-Law Encoded Speech," Bell System Tech. J, pp. 1659-1672, September 1979.

J. P. Adoul, J. L. Debray and D. Dalle, "Spectral Distance Measure Applied to the Optimum Design of DPCM Coders with L Predictors," Proc. ICASSP, pp. 512-515, 1980.

D. Anastassiou, J. L. Mitchell and W. B. Pennebaker, "A High Compression DPCM-based Scheme for Picture Coding," Proc. Inter. Conf. on Communications, pp. B.4.5.1-B4.5.5, June 1983.

D. Arnstein, "Quantization Errors in Predictive Coders," IEEE Trans. on Communications, pp. 423-429, April 1975.

B. S. Atal, "Predictive Coding of Speech at Low Bit Rates," IEEE Trans. on Communications, pp. 600-614, April 1982.

B. S. Atal and M. R. Schroeder, "Predictive Coding of Speech Signals," Bell System Tech. J., pp. 1973-1986, October 1970.

B. S. Atal and M. R. Schroeder, "Predictive Coding of Speech Signals and Subjective Error Criteria," Proc. ICASSP, pp. 573-576, 1978.

T. Bially, B. Gold and S. Seneff, "A Technique for Adaptive Voice Control in Integrated Packet Networks," IEEE Trans. on Communications, pp. 325-333, March 1980.

J. R. Boddie, J. D. Johnston, C. A. McGonegal, J. W. Upton, D. A. Berkley, R. E. Crochiere and J. L. Flanagan, "Digital Signal Processor: Adaptive Differential Pulse-Code-Modulation Coding," Bell System Tech. J., pp. 1547-1562, September 1981.

G. Bostelmann, "A High-Quality DPCM System for Videotelephone Signals Using 8 Mb/s," Nachrichtentech. Z., pp. 115-117, February 1974.

R. C. Brainard, D. E. Pearson and A. N. Netravali, "Predictive Coding of Composite NTSC Color Television Signals," SMPTE J., pp. 245-252, March 1982.

A. Buzo, A. H. Gray, Jr., R. M. Gray, and J. D. Markel, "Speech Coding Based upon Vector Quantization," IEEE Trans. on Acoustics, Speech and Signal Proc., pp. 562-574, October 1980.

J. C. Candy, M. A. Franke, B. G. Haskell and F. W. Mounts, "Transmitting Television as Clusters of Frame-to-Frame References," Bell System Tech. J., pp. 1889-1918, July-August 1971.

P. Castellino, G. Modena, L. Nebbia and C. Scagliola, "Bit Rate Reductions by Automatic Adaptation of Quantizer Step Size in DPCM Systems," Proc. Int. Zürich Seminar on Digital Communications, pp. B6.1-B6.6, March 1974.

K. W. Cattermole, *Principles of Pulse Code Modulation*, Iliffe Books, London, 1969.

C.C.I.T.T. Report, Study Group XVIII, Temporary Document 18, Draft Recommendation G.7zz, Geneva, November 21-25, 1983.

K. Chang and R. W. Donaldson, "Analysis, Optimization, and Sensitivity Study of Differential PCM Systems Operating on Noisy Communication Channels," IEEE Trans. on Communications, pp. 338-350, June 1972.

Y. C. Ching, "Differential Pulse Code Communications Systems Having Dual Quantization Schemes," U.S. Patents 3,781,685; 3,781,686, December 25, 1973.

D. L. Cohn and J. L. Melsa, "The Residual Encoder — An Improved ADPCM System for Speech Digitization," Proc. Int. Conf. on Communications, pp. 30-26 to 30-31, June 1975.

D. J. Connor, R. F. W. Pease and W. G. Scholes, "Television Coding Using Two-dimensional Spatial Prediction," Bell System Tech. J., pp. 1049-1061, March 1971.

R. V. Cox and R. E. Crochiere, "Multiple User Variable Rate Coding for TASI and Packet Transmission Systems," IEEE Trans. on Communications, pp. 334-344, March 1980.

P. Cummiskey, N. S. Jayant and J. L. Flanagan, "Adaptive Quantization in Differential PCM Coding of Speech," Bell System Tech. J., pp. 1105-1118, September 1973.

V. M. Cuperman, "Efficient Waveform Coding of Speech Using Vector Quantization," Ph.D. dissertation, University of California, Santa Barbara, February 1983.

C. C. Cutler, "Differential Quantization for Communication Signals," U.S. Patent 2,605,361, July 29, 1952.

W. R. Daumer, "Subjective Evaluation of Several Efficient Speech Coders," IEEE Trans. on Communications, pp. 567-573, April 1982.

W. R. Daumer, Bell Laboratories, private communication, 1983.

J. G. Dunn, "An Experimental 9600 bits/second Voice Digitizer Employing Adaptive Prediction," IEEE Trans. on Communication Technology, pp. 1021-1032, December 1971.

J. Durbin, "The Fitting of Time-Series Models," Rev. Inst. Int. Statist., pp. 233-243, 1960.

P. Elias, "Predictive Coding," IRE Trans. on Information Theory, pp. 16-33, March 1955.

C. C. Evci, R. Steele and C. S. Xydeas, "DPCM-AQF Using Second-Order Adaptive Predictors for Speech Signals," IEEE Trans. on Acoustics, Speech and Signal Proc., pp. 337-341, June 1981.

C. C. Evci, C. S. Xydeas and R. Steele, "Sequential Adaptive Predictors for ADPCM Speech Encoders," Proc. Nat. Telecom. Conf., pp. E8.1.1-E8.1.5, November 1981.

J. L. Flanagan, M. R. Schroeder, B. S. Atal, R. E. Crochiere, N. S. Jayant and J. M. Tribolet, "Speech Coding," IEEE Trans. on Communications, pp. 710-736, April 1979.

A. H. Frei, H. R. Schindler, P. Vettiger and E. Von Felten, "Adaptive Predictive Speech Coding Based on Pitch-Controlled Interruption/Reiteration Techniques," Proc. Int. Conf. on Communications, pp. 46.12-46.16, June 1973.

B. Friedlander, "Lattice Filters for Adaptive Processing," Proc. IEEE, pp. 829-867, August 1982.

J. D. Gibson, "Sequentially Adaptive Backward Prediction in ADPCM Speech Coders," IEEE Trans. on Communications, pp. 145-150, January 1978.

J. D. Gibson, "Adaptive Prediction in Speech Differential Encoding Systems," Proc. IEEE, pp. 488-525, April 1980.

J. D. Gibson, S. K. Jones and J. L. Melsa, "Sequentially Adaptive Prediction and Coding of Speech Signals," IEEE Trans. on Communications, pp. 1789-1797, November 1974.

H. Gish, "Optimum Quantization of Random Sequences," Defense Agency Report AD-656042, 1967.

A. J. Goldberg, R. L. Freudberg and R. S. Cheung, "High Quality 16 kb/s Voice Transmission," Proc. ICASSP, pp. 244-246, 1976.

D. J. Goodman, "Embedded DPCM for Variable Bit Rate Transmission," IEEE Trans. on Communications, pp. 1040-1046, July 1980.

D. J. Goodman and R. M. Wilkinson, "A Robust Adaptive Quantizer," IEEE Trans. on Communications, pp. 1362-1365, November 1975.

A. J. Goldberg and A. Shaffer, "A Real-time Adaptive Predictive Coder Using Small Computers," IEEE Trans. on Communications, pp. 1443-1451, December 1975.

S. K. Goyal and J. B. O'Neal, "Entropy Coded Differential Pulse Code Modulation Systems for Television," IEEE Trans. on Communications, pp. 660-666, June 1973.

U. Grenander and G. Szego, *Toeplitz Forms and Their Applications,* University of California Press, Berkeley, Calif., 1958.

F. Grizmala, "Application of Linear Predictive Coding to Long Haul Facilities — Results of a Simulation Study," unpublished Bell Laboratories report, 1972.

A. Habibi, "Comparison of nth Order DPCM Encoder with Linear Transformations and Block Quantization Techniques," IEEE Trans. on Communications, pp. 948-956, December 1971.

C. W. Harrison, "Experiments with Linear Prediction in Television," Bell System Tech. J., pp. 764-863, July 1952.

B. G. Haskell, "Entropy Measurements for Nonadaptive and Adaptive, Frame-to-Frame, Linear Predictive Coding of Videotelephone Signals," Bell System Tech. J., pp. 1155-1174, August 1975.

B. G. Haskell, F. W. Mounts and J. C. Candy, "Interframe Coding of Video Telephone Pictures," Proc. IEEE, pp. 792-800, July 1972.

M. L. Honig and D. G. Messerschmitt, "Comparison of Adaptive Linear Prediction Algorithms," IEEE Trans. on Communications, pp. 1775-1785, July 1982.

T. S. Huang, "Stability of Two-Dimensional Recursive Filters," IEEE Trans. on Audio and Electroacoustics, pp. 158-163, June 1972.

IEEE Transactions on Communications, Special Issue on Bit Rate Reduction and Interpolation, (M. R. Aaron and N. S. Jayant, eds.), April 1982.

J. Isailovic, "Possible Improvements in Television Signal Prediction Due to Interframe Correlations," Electronics Letters, pp. 427-428, September 1973.

T. Ishiguro, K. Iinuma, Y. Iijima, T. Koga and H. Kaneko, "NETEC System: Interframe Encoder for NTSC Color Television Signals," Proc. Third Inter. Conf. on Digital Satellite Communication, Kyoto, November 1975.

T. Ishiguro and K. Iinuma, "Television Bandwidth Compression Transmission by Motion-Compensated Interframe Coding," IEEE Communications Magazine, pp. 24-30, November 1982.

F. Itakura and S. Saito, "Analysis-Synthesis Telephone Based Upon the Maximum Likelihood Method," Proc. 6th Int. Congress on Acoustics, pp. C17-20, Tokyo, 1968.

A. K. Jain, "Image Data Compression," Proc. IEEE, pp. 349-389, March 1981.

N. S. Jayant, "Adaptive Quantization with a One-Word Memory," Bell System Tech. J., pp. 1119-1144, September 1973.

N. S. Jayant, "Step-Size Transmitting Differential Coders for Mobile Telephony," Bell System Tech. J., pp. 1557-1581, November 1975.

N. S. Jayant (ed.), *Waveform Quantization and Coding,* IEEE Press, New York, 1976.

N. S. Jayant, "Average and Median-Based Smoothing Techniques for Improving Digital Speech Quality in the Presence of Transmission Errors," IEEE Trans. on Communications, pp. 1043-1045, September 1976.

N. S. Jayant, "Pitch-Adaptive DPCM Coding of Speech with Two-Bit Quantization and Fixed Spectrum Prediction," Bell System Tech. J., pp. 439-454, March 1977.

N. S. Jayant, "Subsampling of a DPCM Speech Channel to Provide Two 'Self-Contained' Half-Rate Channels, Bell System Tech. J., pp. 501-509, April 1981.

N. S. Jayant, "Adaptive Postfiltering of DPCM Speech," Bell System Tech. J., pp. 707-717, May-June 1981.

N. S. Jayant, unpublished work, Bell Laboratories, 1982.

N. S. Jayant, "Variable Rate ADPCM Based on Explicit Noise Coding," Bell System Tech. J., pp. 657-677, March 1983.

N. S. Jayant and S. W. Christensen, "Effects of Packet Losses in Waveform-Coded Speech and Improvements Due to an Odd-Even Interpolation Procedure," IEEE Trans. on Communications, pp. 101-109, February 1981.

J. D. Johnston and D. J. Goodman, "Multipurpose Hardware for Digital Coding of Audio Signals," IEEE Trans. on Communications, pp. 1785-1788, November 1978.

P. Jung, "Statistical Comparison of Additive Error Effects in DPCM Image Coding with Two-Dimensional Prediction" (in German), NTZ Archiv, H.12, pp. 259-262, 1979.

P. Jung and R. Lippmann, "Error Response of DPCM Decoders," Nachrichtentechnische Z. (NTZ), pp. 431-436, 1975.

K. Knowlton, "Progressive Transmission of Grey-Scale and Binary Pictures by Simple, Efficient and Lossless Encoding Schemes," Proc. IEEE, pp. 885-896, July 1980.

T. Koga, A. Hirano, K. Iinuma, Y. Iijima and T. Ishiguro, "A 1.5 Mb/s Interframe Codec with Motion Compensation," Proc. Int. Conf. on Communications, pp. D8.7.1-D8.7.5, June 1983.

A. N. Kolmogoroff, "Interpolation and Extrapolation of Stationary Random Sequences," Bull. Acad. Sci., USSR, Ser. Math, pp. 3-14, 1941.

T. Kummerow, "Der Einfluss von Übertragungsfehlern bei der DPCM-codierten Übertragung von Farbfernschsignalen", Technical Report, Heinrich Hertz Institut, Berlin, May 1981.

N. Levinson, "The Wiener RMS (Root Mean Square) Error Criterion in Filter Design and Prediction," J. Math. Phys., pp. 261-278, 1947.

J. O. Limb and C. B. Rubinstein, "On the Design of Quantizers for DPCM Coders: A Functional Relationship between Probability, Visibility and Masking," IEEE Trans. on Communications, pp. 573-578, May 1978.

J. O. Limb and J. A. Murphy, "Estimating the Velocity of Moving Images from Television Signals," Computer Graphics and Information Processing, pp. 311-327, 1975.

Y. Linde, A. Buzo and R. M. Gray, "An Algorithm for Vector Quantizer Design," IEEE Trans. on Communications, pp. 84-95, January 1980.

H. S. London and D. B. Menist, "A Description of the A.T.& T. Video Teleconferencing System," Proc. Nat. Telecom. Conference, November 1981.

F. Lukas and F. Kretz, "DPCM Quantization of Color Television Signals," IEEE Trans. on Communications, pp. 927-932, July 1983.

J. Makhoul, "Linear Prediction: A Tutorial Review," Proc. IEEE, pp. 561-580, April 1975.

J. Makhoul, "Stable and Efficient Lattice Methods for Linear Prediction," IEEE Trans. on Acoustics, Speech and Signal Proc., pp. 423-429, October 1977.

J. Makhoul and J. J. Wolf, "Linear Prediction and the Spectral Analysis of Speech," Bolt Beranek and Newman, Inc., Cambridge, Mass., NTIS AD-749066, Report No. 2304, August 1972.

J. D. Markel and A. H. Gray, Jr., *Linear Prediction of Speech*, Springer-Verlag, New York, 1976.

B. J. McDermott, C. Scagliola and D. Goodman, "Perceptual and Objective Evaluation of Speech Processed by Adaptive Differential PCM," Bell System Tech. J., pp. 1597-1618, May-June 1978.

R. A. McDonald, "Signal-to-Noise and Idle Channel Performance of DPCM Systems with Particular Application to Voice Signals," Bell System Tech. J., pp. 1123-1151, September 1966.

T. R. McPherson, Jr., J. B. O'Neal, Jr., and R. W. Stroh, "PCM Speech Compression via ADPCM/TASI," Proc. ICASSP, pp. 184-187, 1977.

J. L. Melsa et al., "Design and Implementation of a Speech Coding Algorithm at 9600 b/s," Final Report DCA-100-79-C-0005, Dept. of Elect. Eng., University of Notre Dame, Notre Dame, Ind., April 30, 1980.

D. Miller and P. Mermelstein, "Prevention of Predictor Mistracking in ADPCM Coders," Proc. Int. Conf. on Communications, Amsterdam, May 1984.

F. W. Mounts, "A Video Encoding System with Conditional Picture-Element Replenishment," Bell System Tech. J., pp. 2545-2554, September 1969.

H. G. Musmann, "Codierung von Videosignalen," NTZ, Bd. 24, pp. 114-116, February 1971.

H. G. Musmann, "Predictive Image Coding," in *Advances in Electronics and Electron. Physics,* Suppl. 12, pp. 73-112, Academic Press, New York, 1979.

H. G. Musmann, "Bildübertragung auf einem Fernsprechkanal," Mitteilungen der DFG, 3, pp. 8-11, 1979.

H. G. Musmann and Klie, "TV Transmission Using a 64 kb/s Transmission Rate," Proc. Inter. Conf. on Communications, pp. 23.3.1-23.3.5, June 1979.

J. C. Nash, *Compact Numerical Methods for Computers: linear algebra and function minimization,* John Wiley, New York, 1979.

A. N. Netravali and J. O. Limb, "Picture Coding: A Review," Proc. IEEE, pp. 366-406, March 1980.

A. N. Netravali and B. Prasada, "Adaptive Quantization of Picture Signals Using Spatial Masking," Proc. IEEE, pp. 536-548, April 1977.

A. N. Netravali and J. D. Robbins, "Motion Compensated Television Coding — Part I," Bell System Tech. J., pp. 631-670, March 1979.

K. N. Ngan and R. Steele, "Enhancement of PCM and DPCM Images Corrupted by Transmission Errors," IEEE Trans. on Communications, pp. 257-265, January 1982.

T. Nishitani, S. Aikoh, T. Araseki, K. Ozawa and R. Maruta, "A 32 kb/s Toll Quality ADPCM Codec Using a Single Chip Signal Processor," Proc. ICASSP, pp. 960-963, April 1982.

K. Nitadori, "Statistical Analysis of DPCM," J. Inst. Electron. Commun. Eng. Japan, pp. 4-6, 1965.

P. Noll, "Non-adaptive and Adaptive DPCM of Speech Signals," Polytech. Tijdschr. Ed. Elektrotech./Elektron (The Netherlands), No. 19, 1972.

P. Noll, "Speech Transmission with Methods of Adaptive Differential Pulse Code Modulation," (in German), Technical Report No. 164, Heinrich Hertz Institut, Berlin, 1973.

P. Noll, "Adaptive Quantizing in Speech Coding Systems," Proc. Int. Zurich Seminar on Digital Communications, pp. B3(1)-(6), 1974.

P. Noll, "A Comparative Study of Various Quantization Schemes for Speech Encoding," Bell System Tech. J., pp. 1597-1614, November 1975.

P. Noll, "Effects of Channel Errors on the Signal-to-Noise Performance of Speech Encoding Schemes," Bell System Tech., J., pp. 1615-1636, November 1975.

P. Noll, "On Predictive Quantizing Schemes," Bell System Tech. J., pp. 1499-1532, May-June 1978.

G. C. O'Leary, P. E. Blankenship, J. Tierney and J. A. Feldman, "A Modular Approach to Packet Voice Terminal Design," Proc. National Computer Conference, pp. 183-189, AFIPS Press, Virginia, 1981.

B. M. Oliver, "Efficient Coding," Bell System Tech. J., pp. 724-756, July 1952.

J. B. O'Neal, "Predictive Quantizing Systems for the Transmission of Television Signals," Bell System Tech. J., pp. 689-719, May-June 1966.

J. B. O'Neal, Jr., in "Noise Considerations in Bit Rate Compression," *Picture Bandwidth Compression*, T. S. Huang and and O. J. Tretiak (eds.), Gordon and Beach, New York, 1972.

J. B. O'Neal, Jr., and R. W. Stroh, "Differential PCM for Speech and Data Signals," IEEE Trans. on Communications, pp. 900-912, October 1972.

D. W. Petr, "32 kb/s ADPCM-DLQ Coding for Network Applications," Proc. IEEE Globecom Conf., pp. A8.3.1-A8.3.5, December 1982.

D. W. Petr, Bell Laboratories, private communication, August 1983.

P. Pirsch, "Design of DPCM Quantizers for Video Signals Using Subjective Tests," IEEE Trans. on Communications, pp. 990-1000, July 1981.

P. Pirsch, "Stability Conditions for DPCM Coders," IEEE Trans. on Communications, pp. 1174-1184, May 1982.

W. K. Pratt (ed.), *Image Transmission Techniques,* Academic Press, New York, 1979.

S. U. H. Qureshi and G. D. Forney, Jr., "A 9.6/16 kb/s Speech Digitizer," Proc. Int. Conf. on Communications, pp. 30-31 to 30-36, June 1975.

L. R. Rabiner and R. W. Schafer, *Digital Processing of Speech Signals,* Prentice-Hall, Englewood Cliffs, N.J., 1978.

L. R. Rabiner, M. J. Cheng, A. E. Rosenberg and C. A. McGonegal, "A Comparative Performance Study of Several Pitch Detection Algorithms," IEEE Trans. on Acoustics, Speech and Signal Proc., pp. 399-418, October 1976.

J. M. Raulin, G. Bonnerot, J.-L. Jeandot and R. Lacroix,, "A 60 Channel PCM-ADPCM Converter," IEEE Trans. on Communications, pp. 567-573, April 1982.

E. A. Robinson and H. Wold, "Minimum Delay Structure of Least Squares and EO-OPSO Predicting Systems for Stationary Stochastic Sources," in *Time Series Analysis* (ed., M. Rosenblatt), John Wiley, New York, 1963.

L. H. Rosenthal, L. R. Rabiner, R. W. Schafer, P. Cummiskey and J. L. Flanagan, "A Multiline Computer Voice Response System Utilizing ADPCM-Coded Speech," IEEE Trans. on Acoustics, Speech and Signal Proc., pp. 339-352, October 1974.

C. B. Rubinstein and J. O. Limb, "On the Design of Quantizers for DPCM Coders: Influence of Subjective Testing Methodology," IEEE Trans. on Communications, pp. 565-573, May 1978.

A. P. Sage and J. J. Melsa, *Estimation Theory with Applications to Estimation and Control,* McGraw-Hill, New York, 1971.

M. R. Sambur, "An Efficient Linear Prediction Vocoder," Bell System Tech. J., pp. 1693-1724, December 1975.

J. A. Sciulli and S. J. Campanella, "A Speech Predictive Encoding Communication System for Multi-channel Telephony," IEEE Trans. on Communications, July 1973.

D. K. Sharma and A. N. Netravali, "Design of Quantizers for DPCM Coding of Picture Signals," IEEE Trans. on Communications, pp. 1267-1274, November 1977.

C. P. Smith, "Voice Communications Method Using Pattern Matching for Data Compression," Jour. Acous. Soc. America, p. 805(A), 1963.

J. O. Smith and J. B. Allen, "Variable Bandwidth Adaptive Deltamodulation," Bell System Tech. J., May-June 1981.

R. Steele, N. S. Jayant and C. E. Schmidt, "Statistical Clock Protection Coding for DPCM-Coded Speech," Bell System Tech. J., pp. 1647-1657, September 1979.

R. Steele and N. S. Jayant, "Statistical Block Protection Coding for DPCM-AQF Speech," IEEE Trans. on Communications, pp. 1899-1907, November 1980.

R. Steele, D. J. Esdale and D. J. Goodman, "Partial Correction of Transmission Errors in DPCM Without Recourse to Error Correction Coding," Electronics Letters, May 1977.

R. Steele, D. J. Goodman and C. A. McGonegal, "DPCM with Forced Updating and Partial Correction of Transmission Errors," Bell System Tech. J., pp. 721-728, March 1979.

R. W. Stroh, "Optimum and Adaptive Differential Pulse Code Modulation," Ph.D. dissertation, Polytechnic Inst. Brooklyn, N.Y., 1970.

J. A. Stuller, A. N. Netravali and J. D. Robbins, "Interframe Television Coding Using Gain and Displacement Compensation," Bell System Tech. J., pp. 1227-1240, September 1980.

W. Thoma, "Optimizing DPCM for Video Signals Using a Model of the Human Visual System," Proc. Int. Zürich Seminar on Digital Communications, pp. C3.1-C3.7, March 1974.

M. C. W. van Buul, "Hybrid D-PCM, a Combination of PCM and DPCM," IEEE Trans. on Communications, pp. 362-368, March 1978.

R. Viswanathan and J. Makhoul, "Quantization Properties of Transmission Parameters in Linear Predictive Systems," IEEE Trans. on Acoustics, Speech and Signal Processing, pp. 434-446, June 1975.

R. H. Wallis and W. K. Pratt, "Video Teleconferencing at 9600 Baud," Proc. Int. Conf. on Communications, pp. 22.2.1-22.2.3, Seattle, June 1981.

B. Widrow, J. M. McCool, M. G. Larimore, and C. R. Johnson, Jr., "Stationary and Nonstationary Learning Characteristics of the LMS Adaptive Filter," Proc. IEEE, pp. 1151-1162, August 1976.

N. Wiener, *The Extrapolation and Smoothing of Stationary Time Series, with Engineering Applications,* John Wiley, New York, 1949.

J. Yamagata, H. Takashima, N. Bando and T. Doi, "Asynchronous Intraframe Coding with One-dimensional Prediction," Proc. Int. Conf. on Communications, pp. 62.1.1-62.1.5, Seattle, June 1981.

H. Yamamoto, Y. Hatori and H. Murakami, "30 Mb/s Codec for the NTSC Color TV Signal Using an Interfield-Intrafield Adaptive Predictor," IEEE Trans. on Communications, pp. 1859-1867, December 1981.

J. Yan and R. W. Donaldson, "Subjective Effects of Channel Transmission Errors on PCM and DPCM Voice Communication Systems," IEEE Trans. on Communications, pp. 281-290, June 1972.

Y. Yatsuzuka, "High-Gain Digital Speech Interpolation with ADPCM Encoding," IEEE Trans. on Communications, pp. 750-761, April 1982.

W. Zschunke, "DPCM Picture Coding with Adaptive Prediction," IEEE Trans. on Communications, pp. 1295-1301, November 1977.

7

Noise Feedback Coding

7.1 Introduction

Chapter 6 has discussed techniques for minimizing reconstruction error by means of efficient input prediction. We have also mentioned when appropriate that the spectrum of reconstruction error is perceptually very significant. If the prediction is such that the quantizer input is nearly white, and if the quantization is adequately fine, the reconstruction error in DPCM will also be nearly white, based on the results of Section 4.7. Whitening of the reconstruction error is, however, not always perceptually optimum. In this chapter we shall take a closer look at the reconstruction error spectrum, its relation to input spectrum, and the perception-oriented notion of *frequency-weighted* errors. We shall thus motivate two variations of DPCM coding: a special case that we will call D*PCM; and a generalized coding technique called *Noise Feedback Coding* (NFC) that is very useful in low bit rate applications in both speech and image work. Chapter 8 will resume the DPCM discussion of Chapter 6 for the special case of $R = 1$ bit/sample.

The quantizer input $d(n)$ in DPCM coding was defined by (6.5) and (6.17):

$$d(n) = x(n) - \hat{x}(n) = x(n) - \sum_{j=1}^{N} h_j \, y(n-j)$$

$$= x(n) - \sum_{j=1}^{N} h_j x(n-j) + \sum_{j=1}^{N} h_j q(n-j) \tag{7.1}$$

where $q(n)$ is the quantization error. The quantizer input thus consists of two parts: (i) the prediction error $d*(n)$ of undisturbed prediction with a linear predictor error filter $1-H(z)$ [first two terms in (7.1)] and (ii) the third term in (7.1), which is the quantizer error signal filtered by the linear predictor network $H(z)$. The quantizer input description in (7.1) suggests an interesting alternative description of the DPCM block diagram, as shown in Figure 7.1(a). Note that in this description, coder input $x(n)$ and quantizer error $q(n)$ have their own separate filters, $1-H(z)$ and $H(z)$, respectively [Cattermole, 1969].

An important property of the DPCM coders of Figures 6.1 and 7.1(a) is that the reconstruction error $r(n)$ is identical to the quantizer error $q(n)$ [see (6.12)]. Using z-transform notation,

$$r(n) = q(n) ; \quad S_{rr}(z)|_{DPCM} = S_{qq}(z) \tag{7.2}$$

A special predictive coder that results when the error feedback is eliminated is shown in Figure 7.1(b) [Oliver, 1952]. This coder is sometimes referred to as *open-loop* DPCM [Flanagan, 1972]. In this book, we shall refer to it as a D*PCM coder [Noll, 1978]. Note that this coder can also be regarded as PCM with pre-filtering and post-filtering operations. The properties of this coder are discussed at length in Section 7.2. Significant to the present discussion is that

$$S_{rr}(z)|_{D*PCM} = S_{qq}(z) \ \frac{1}{|1-H(z)|^2} \tag{7.3}$$

since $|1-H(z)|^{-1}$ is the decoder transfer function.

Figure 7.1(c) shows a generalized predictive coder with an error feedback or noise feedback function $F(z)$. Such a scheme will be called error feedback coding, or *noise feedback coding* (NFC). This will be described at length in Section 7.3 in the context of low bit rate coding of speech using APC-NF. Significant to the present discussion is that in this system

$$S_{rr}(z)|_{NFC} = S_{qq}(z) \ \frac{|1-F(z)|^2}{|1-H(z)|^2} \tag{7.4}$$

In the following derivation of (7.4), all summations are from 1 to N, and h_j and f_j; $j = 1,2,...,N$ are the coefficients of recursive filters $H(z)$ and $F(z)$:

$$
\begin{aligned}
r(n) &= x(n) - y(n) \\
&= x(n) - \left[\sum h_j \, y(n-j) + u(n) \right] \\
&= x(n) - \sum h_j \, y(n-j) - [d*(n) - n(n)] \\
&= x(n) - \sum h_j \, y(n-j) - \left[x(n) - \sum h_j \, x(n-j) - n(n) \right] \\
&= \sum h_j \, r(n-j) + n(n) \\
&= \sum h_j \, r(n-j) + \left[q(n) - \sum f_j \, q(n-j) \right] \tag{7.5a}
\end{aligned}
$$

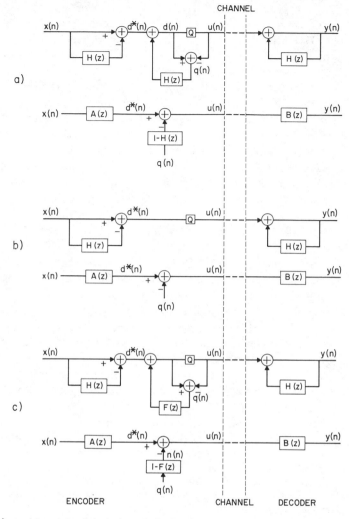

Figure 7.1 (a) An alternative description of the DPCM circuit of Figure 6.1. (b) The special case (D*PCM) obtained by eliminating noise feedback. (c) The general noise feedback coder (NFC) obtained by replacing the feedback filter $H(z)$ in (a) by a more general feedback filter $F(z)$.

Therefore, if the z-transforms of sequences $r(n)$ and $q(n)$ are $R(z)$ and $Q(z)$,

$$r(n) - \sum h_j\, r(n-j) = q(n) - \sum f_j\, q(n-j) \,, \tag{7.5b}$$

and

$$R(z) = Q(z)\, \frac{1 - \sum f_j z^{-j}}{1 - \sum h_j z^{-j}} = Q(z)\, \frac{1 - F(z)}{1 - H(z)} \tag{7.5c}$$

which leads to (7.4). The filter $F(z)$ has been assumed to be also of order N, for simplicity. Practical NFC systems often employ noise feedback filters of order

$N' < N$, the order of $H(z)$ [Atal and Schroeder, 1979] [Makhoul and Berouti, 1979]. Clearly, the DPCM and D*PCM equations (7.2) and (7.3) are special cases of (7.4), with $F(z) = H(z)$ and $F(z) = 0$, respectively.

If the quantizer error spectrum is white (a reasonable assumption, particularly if the prediction error is white and the quantization of it is adequately fine), the reconstruction noise spectrum would also be white in DPCM, $H(z)$-dependent and typically input-like in D*PCM, and $H(z)$- and $F(z)$-dependent in NFC. These situations are sketched in Figure 7.2, which compares input and noise psd's for the three coders of Figure 7.1. The noise variances σ_r^2, the areas under the noise psd's, are in general different when the three coders are individually optimized, as explained later in this chapter. The input psd that is illustrated is that of voiced speech and $H(z)$ is chosen to be the mmse predictor filter $H_{opt}(z)$. The feedback filter $F(z)$ assumed for the NFC example in Figure 7.2(c) is a design that may be also related to $H_{opt}(z)$, but in a more general fashion than in Figure 7.1(a) (Example 7.10). It exemplifies low bit rate APC-NF systems for speech [Atal and Schroeder, 1979].

The importance of the NFC coder is that the feedback filter $F(z)$ provides an additional parameter which can be used to control the shape of the noise spectrum for improved performance [Kimme and Kuo, 1963]. This is on top of the performance improvement due to $[1-H(z)]$ shaping of input, which also exists in DPCM and D*PCM. In the coding of real signals such as speech and video, the extreme situations of DPCM and D*PCM do not provide perceptually optimum noise spectra when their filters are designed to minimize prediction error variance; while NFC, in principle, can optimize the noise spectrum to an extent limited only by our understanding of the perceptual mechanism. In speech coding, for example, occurrence of the sharp peaks of the noise spectrum of Figure 7.2(c) near the speech formants is a desirable feature in view of noise-masking properties in the hearing mechanism. Note that noise shaping does not add complexity to the

Figure 7.2 Comparisons of coder input spectrum (solid curves) and coding noise spectrum (dashed curves) for the three coders of Figure 7.1: (a) DPCM; (b) D*PCM; and (c) NFC. The input is a segment of voiced speech and $H_{opt}(z)$ is the transfer function of the mmse predictor for this input. [Atal and Schroeder;©1979, IEEE].

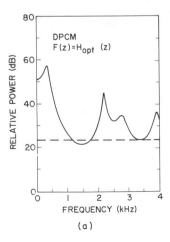

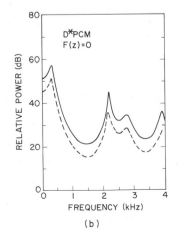

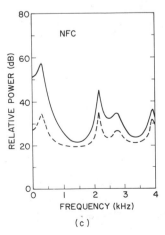

(a) (b) (c)

decoder but only to the encoder. One implication is that highly complex and adaptive shaping procedures may be implemented in the encoder since *the decoder need not be informed about shaping parameters.* Indeed, Figures 7.2(b) and (c) have tacitly assumed a noise shaping that is adaptive, and dependent on short-time psd. The noise variance is not constant in the examples of Figure 7.2. In fact, the D*PCM and NFC coders exhibit an *increase* in noise variance. The benefits of D*PCM and NFC have to do with a decrease in *perceived noise.* However, such a subjective improvement is only realized if the original noise level is adequately low, as in Figure 7.2(a).

A useful way of modeling perceptual effects is to use a frequency-weighted noise power criterion in optimizing coder design. Specifically, the idea is to minimize a *frequency-weighted* noise power (Figure D.8 and Section E.4)

$$\sigma_{rw}^2 = \frac{1}{2\pi} \int_{-\pi}^{\pi} S_{rr}(e^{j\omega}) \, S_{ww}(e^{j\omega}) d\omega \qquad (7.6a)$$

where $S_{ww}(e^{j\omega})$ is the frequency-weighting function. A small value of $S_{ww}(e^{j\omega})$ indicates that a high value of reconstruction error variance is acceptable at that frequency, and *vice versa.* The function $S_{ww}(e^{j\omega})$ can be regarded as a psd with variance σ_w^2. The noise-weighting operation can be normalized, without loss of generality, to obtain the unit variance

$$\sigma_w^2 = \frac{1}{2\pi} \int_{-\pi}^{\pi} S_{ww}(e^{j\omega}) d\omega = 1 \qquad (7.6b)$$

The frequency-weighted error spectrum is

$$S_{ss}(e^{j\omega}) = S_{rr}(e^{j\omega}) \, S_{ww}(e^{j\omega}) \qquad (7.6c)$$

As in Figure 7.3, the weighted error $s(n)$ can be regarded as the output of a *noise-weighting filter* $W(e^{j\omega})$ whose input is $r(n)$. The squared magnitude response of this filter is $S_{ww}(e^{j\omega})$. By comparison with (7.6a), the frequency-weighted noise power σ_{rw}^2 is also the variance σ_s^2, the variance of the output of filter $W(z)$. In the special case where the filter input $r(n)$ is white, the integration of (7.6a) leads to a special result:

$$\sigma_{rw}^2 = \sigma_r^2 \, \sigma_w^2 = \sigma_r^2 \quad \text{if} \ r(n) \ \text{is white} \qquad (7.6d)$$

The special case of a DPCM coder $[F(z) = H(z)]$ is optimum for unweighted noise $[W(z) = 1]$. In other words, DPCM and APC coders are the best non-frequency-weighted mmse designs as claimed in Chapter 6. The importance of a frequency-weighted design increases with decreasing bit rate. For example, in APC

Figure 7.3 Frequency weighting of reconstruction noise $r(n)$. The filter output $s(n)$ is the frequency-weighted noise.

systems for speech, the noise-shaping gains in NFC begin to be very significant at bit rates of $R \leqslant 2$ bits/sample $(I \leqslant 16$ kb/s). At these bit rates, typical subjective gains due to noise shaping can be equivalent to several dB. Section 7.3 will show that D*PCM $[F(z) = 0]$ is optimal for a noise weighting function that is the inverse of the input psd provided that $H(z) = H_{opt}(z)$ is the mmse predictor; and that the generalized NFC scheme of Figure 7.1(c), for any $H(z)$ and $F(z)$, is optimal for a noise weighting function of the form

$$W(z) = \frac{1-H(z)}{1-F(z)} \qquad (7.7)$$

7.2 D*PCM

D*PCM, which is the special case of $F(z) = 0$, can be viewed as a PCM scheme with prefilter $A(z)$ and postfilter $B(z)$. If we model the quantizer as an additive noise source, the optimization of D*PCM is almost identical to a joint optimization of pre- and postfilters in analog communication systems in which additive channel errors are present [Costas, 1952] [Bruce, 1964] [Berger and Tufts, 1967] [Chan and Donaldson, 1971] [Goodman and Drouilhet, 1966]. However, unlike in those references, our D*PCM analyses will be based on the assumption of small quantization error contributions, which will imply that $B(z) = A^{-1}(z)$.

A characteristic property of the open-loop scheme of Figure 7.1(b) is that predicted values $\hat{x}(n)$ at transmitter and receiver (unlike in closed-loop DPCM) are based on different predictor inputs and therefore differ. As a result, the reconstruction error $r(n)$ consists of two terms: the quantization noise term $q(n)$ as in Chapter 6, plus an additional term equal to the difference between predictor outputs at transmitter and receiver. Assume that the networks at encoder and decoder are reciprocal:

$$A(z) = 1/B(z) ; \qquad a(n)*b(n) = \delta(n) \qquad (7.8a)$$

where $\delta(n)$ is the Dirac delta function. Assuming further that quantization noise is additive, the D*PCM reconstruction error can also be written in the form

$$
\begin{aligned}
r(n) &= x(n) - y(n) = x(n) - u(n)*b(n) \\
&= x(n) - [d^*(n) - q(n)]*b(n) \\
&= x(n) - x(n)*a(n)*b(n) + q(n)*b(n) \\
&= q(n)*b(n) \qquad (7.8b)
\end{aligned}
$$

where $b(n)$ is the impulse response of the linear decoder network.

Quantization error samples $q(n)$ are approximately white noise samples if the number of quantizer levels L is sufficiently high. Hence in D*PCM, the reconstruction noise $r(n)$ is non-white, with each quantization error causing an infinite output sequence as indicated by (7.8). One consequence of this error propagation is that the SNR in D*PCM is always less than that of DPCM (unless a specific type of frequency-weighting is used in calculating the noise power).

We will see that when the predictor $H(z)$ of Figure 7.1(b) is an mmse predictor $H_{opt}(z)$ (one that minimizes prediction error variance), the SNR of the D*PCM system will be identical to that of PCM. However, D*PCM can perform better than PCM if $H(z)$ is re-optimized. Briefly, this re-optimization will result in a *half-whitening* of the input process rather than the *full-whitening* characteristic of the mmse prediction error filters of Chapter 6. Section 7.3 will then show that D*PCM based on a mmse predictor $H_{opt}(z)$ is an optimum coding scheme for a frequency weighting function that is the inverse of the psd $S_{xx}(e^{j\omega})$.

Reconstruction Error Variance σ_r^2. Recall that the reconstruction error variances in PCM and DPCM systems were given by

$$\min\{\sigma_{r,PCM}^2\} = \epsilon_q^2 \, \sigma_x^2 \qquad (7.9)$$

$$\min\{\sigma_{r,DPCM}^2\} = \epsilon_q^2 \, \eta_x^2 = \epsilon_q^2 \, \gamma_x^2 \, \sigma_x^2 \qquad (7.10)$$

where ϵ_q^2 is the quantizer performance factor, η_x^2 is the minimum achievable prediction error variance when feedback of $q(n)$ is neglected, and γ_x^2 is the spectral flatness measure, the inverse of the optimally obtainable prediction gain.

In D*PCM, the white noise quantization error of variance $\sigma_q^2 = S_{qq}(e^{j\omega})$ is filtered by the linear decoder network with frequency response $B(e^{j\omega}) = A^{-1}(e^{j\omega})$. Thus the reconstruction error variance is

$$\sigma_r^2 = \frac{1}{2\pi} \int_{-\pi}^{\pi} S_{rr}(e^{j\omega}) d\omega = \sigma_q^2 \frac{1}{2\pi} \int_{-\pi}^{\pi} |B(e^{j\omega})|^2 d\omega \qquad (7.11)$$

That is, the quantization error variance is increased by the power transfer factor

$$\alpha = \frac{1}{2\pi} \int_{-\pi}^{\pi} |B(e^{j\omega})|^2 d\omega \qquad (7.12)$$

of the decoder filter.

The variance of the quantization error is

$$\sigma_q^2 = \epsilon_q^2 \sigma_{d*}^2 = \epsilon_q^2 \frac{1}{2\pi} \int_{-\pi}^{\pi} S_{xx}(e^{j\omega}) |A(e^{j\omega})|^2 d\omega \qquad (7.13)$$

and from (7.11) and (7.12)

$$\sigma_r^2 = \alpha \sigma_q^2 = \epsilon_q^2 \, \alpha \, \sigma_{d*}^2 \qquad (7.14a)$$

$$SNR \mid_{D*PCM} (\text{dB}) = SNR \mid_{DPCM} (\text{dB}) - 10 \log \alpha \qquad (7.14b)$$

The total error variance of D*PCM is α times that of an equivalent DPCM coder (with $\sigma_d^2 = \sigma_{d*}^2$ in the case of fine quantizing and identical prediction filters).

If the impulse response of the postfilter $B(z)$ is given by $\{1, b_1, b_2, \ldots\}$,

$$\alpha = 1 + \sum_{k=1}^{\infty} b_k^2 \geqslant 1 \qquad (7.15)$$

signifying that DPCM outperforms D*PCM from an mse viewpoint, for *any* choice of the predictor network. This result also implies that the optimum mse performance of DPCM is better than the optimum mse performance of D*PCM [Noll, 1976].

Example 7.1. First-order predictor

With predictor coefficient h_1, the power transfer factor of the decoder network is

$$\alpha = 1 + h_1^2 + h_1^4 + \ldots = (1-h_1^2)^{-1} \qquad (7.16)$$

Thus the coding mse is (Problem 7.1)

$$\sigma_{r,D*PCM}^2 = \epsilon_q^2 \alpha \sigma_{d*}^2 = \epsilon_q^2 (1-h_1^2)^{-1} (1-2h_1\rho_1+h_1^2)\sigma_x^2 \qquad (7.17)$$

where ρ_1 is the variance-normalized value of acf value $R_{xx}(1)$. Note that mmse prediction ($h_1 = \rho_1$) results in the same mse as that of PCM, and that $\sigma_r^2 \to \infty$ for any ρ_1 if $h_1 \to 1$. The minimum of mse with respect to h_1 is obtained by setting $d\sigma_r^2/dh_1 = 0$ in (7.17). This is mathematically similar to the minimization of α/G_P in Section 6.10, and the minimization results in

$$h_{1,opt}|_{D*PCM} = \rho_1^{-1}(1-\sqrt{1-\rho_1^2}); \quad \min\{\sigma_{r,D*PCM}^2\} = \epsilon_q^2 \sqrt{1-\rho_1^2}\,\sigma_x^2 \qquad (7.18)$$

The gain over PCM in this case is $(1-\rho_1^2)^{\frac{1}{2}}$ rather than the familiar $(1-\rho_1^2)$ result in ideal DPCM (with negligible feedback). We shall note later that a gain of $(1-\rho_1^2)^{\frac{1}{2}}$ over PCM is also characteristic of block quantization or transform coding with blocklength 2 (Chapter 12).

Figure 7.4 compares the performances of DPCM and D*PCM systems with a first-order predictor. Included for comparison are results for PCM coding. The results are *SNR* plots as functions of predictor coefficient h_1. The input is a Gaussian first-order Markov source with correlation $\rho_1 = 0.9625$. The quantizer for each R value ($R = 1, 2$ and 4) is one that is optimized for Gaussian signals. Analytical results for D*PCM are based on (7.17). Those for DPCM follow results noted already in Chapter 6:

$$\sigma_{r,DPCM}^2 = \epsilon_q^2 (1-2h_1\rho_1+h_1^2)(1-\epsilon_q^2 h_1^2)^{-1}\sigma_x^2 \qquad (7.19)$$

$$h_{1,opt}|_{DPCM} \simeq \rho_1; \quad \min\{\sigma_{r,DPCM}^2\} = \epsilon_q^2 (1-\rho_1^2)(1-\epsilon_q^2\rho_1^2)^{-1}\sigma_x^2 \qquad (7.20)$$

Recall that the term $(1-\epsilon_q^2\rho_1^2)^{-1}$ is a correction that takes into account the effects of quantizer error feedback in the closed-loop circuit of Figure 7.1(a).

Note in Figure 7.4 that the agreement between theory and measurement improves with fineness of quantization (increasing R) and that, as expected, DPCM performance always upper-bounds the *SNR* obtainable in a corresponding D*PCM system. Also, note in part (b) of the figure that the gain over PCM is zero for the full-whitening design $h_1 = \rho_1$. Finally, Figure 7.4 shows that if $\rho_1 \to 1$, the performance with ideal integration ($h_1 = 1$) is

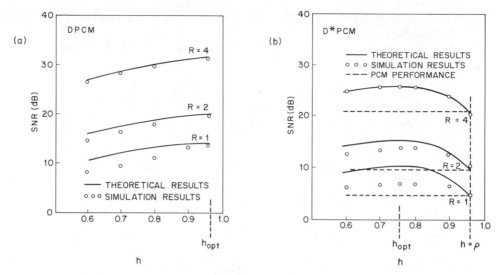

Figure 7.4 *SNR* versus first-order predictor coefficient in (a) DPCM coding and (b) D*PCM coding of a first-order Gauss-Markov input with $\rho_1 = 0.9625$ [Noll;©1978, AT&T].

only slightly suboptimal in DPCM, but severely so in the case of D*PCM. This is the so-called *noise accumulation* property of open-loop differential coding with $h_1 = 1$. •

In Example 7.1, quantizer performance was simply characterized by the factor ϵ_q^2 and minimization of mse was with respect to predictor coefficient. This approach will be adopted in all of the rest of this chapter, and expressions for mse will be minimized with respect to predictor parameters, as well as with respect to prefilter, postfilter and noise feedback filter parameters. Resulting observations will permit adequate relative comparisons of several coders. For absolute assessments of coder performance, it should be assumed that values of minimum mse in the above analyses are further minimized with respect to quantizer design, simply by setting $\epsilon_q^2 = \min\{\epsilon_q^2\}$, as in Chapter 4.

Analysis of General Predictors. We come back now to the mse equation (7.14). Explicitly,

$$\sigma_r^2 = \epsilon_q^2 \left[\frac{1}{2\pi} \int_{-\pi}^{\pi} S_{xx}(e^{j\omega})|A(e^{j\omega})|^2 d\omega \right] \left[\frac{1}{2\pi} \int_{-\pi}^{\pi} |A(e^{j\omega})|^{-2} d\omega \right] \qquad (7.21)$$

assuming that $B(z) = A^{-1}(z)$. Note that the term in the first brackets reduces to $\eta_x^2 = \min\{^{\infty}\sigma_{d*}^2\}$ if $A(z)$ is the full-whitening mmse prediction error filter. The difference signal $d*(n)$ is then white, and since the last term in (7.21) is the power transfer factor of the decoder for white noise inputs, it equals σ_x^2/η_x^2. Therefore, the total mse is $\sigma_r^2 = \epsilon_q^2 \sigma_x^2$, and thus equals that of PCM (assuming identical ϵ_q^2 values, an assumption that is valid at least with log-quantization and/or Gaussian inputs, as discussed in Chapter 6) [Bodycomb and Haddad, 1970] [Noll, 1976]. The error spectrum $S_{rr}(e^{j\omega})$ is, however, different, since the white-noise quantization error sequence is passed through $B(z)$ which, for mmse prediction error filters $A(z)$, resembles the psd $S_{xx}(e^{j\omega})$.

Let us now relate the mmse obtainable with D*PCM to those of DPCM and PCM. Consider Schwarz's inequality

$$\int_I f_1^2(x)\,dx \int_I f_2^2(x)\,dx \geqslant \left[\int_I f_1(x)f_2(x)\,dx\right]^2 \qquad (7.22)$$

with equality if $f_1^2(x)/f_2^2(x) = \text{constant}$ for any square-integrable functions $f_1(\cdot)$ and $f_2(\cdot)$. Applying this to (7.21), we obtain

$$\min\{\sigma_{r,DPCM}^2\} \geqslant \epsilon_q^2 \left[\frac{1}{2\pi}\int_{-\pi}^{\pi} \sqrt{S_{xx}(e^{j\omega})}\,d\omega\right]^2 \qquad (7.23)$$

Equality is obtained if

$$|A_{opt}(e^{j\omega})|^2 \sqrt{S_{xx}(e^{j\omega})} = \text{constant} \qquad (7.24)$$

We conclude that the squared-magnitude frequency response of the mmse D*PCM encoder filter has to be inversely proportional to the square root of the psd of the input (*half-whitening*). Therefore, the optimum frequency response $A_{opt}(e^{j\omega})$ is a mmse prediction error filter for a psd $\sqrt{S_{xx}(e^{j\omega})}$, but not for the input psd $S_{xx}(e^{j\omega})$. The corresponding minimum of the prediction error variance would be just the square root of that to be obtained from an optimum prediction of a process with psd $S_{xx}(e^{j\omega})$ [this can be verified from the η_x^2 equation (6.51)]:

$$|A_{opt}(e^{j\omega})|^2 \sqrt{S_{xx}(e^{j\omega})} = \eta_{\sqrt{x}}^2 = \eta_x \qquad (7.25)$$

Example 7.1 has shown that an improvement over PCM can be obtained with D*PCM. By appling Schwarz's inequality to the right-hand term of (7.23), we have

$$\epsilon_q^2 \left[\frac{1}{2\pi}\int_{-\pi}^{\pi} \sqrt{S_{xx}(e^{j\omega})}\,d\omega\right]^2 \leqslant \epsilon_q^2 \sigma_x^2 = \min\{\sigma_{r,PCM}^2\} \qquad (7.26)$$

with equality only if $\{X(n)\}$ is a white noise sequence, i.e., an improvement over PCM can be obtained for all non-white processes [Noll, 1978]. In addition, (7.14) has already indicated that DPCM outperforms D*PCM for any nonwhite psd $S_{xx}(e^{j\omega})$.

In Chapter 6, it was shown that for a Markov input of order M, a linear predictor of order M was sufficient to provide the maximum performance in DPCM. A similar result does not hold for D*PCM. The following example will discuss this for the case of $M = 1$.

Example 7.2. First-order Markov source
Consider a first-order Markov sequence as in (2.96), with an acf

$$R_{xx}(k) = \rho_1^{|k|}\sigma_x^2 \qquad (7.27)$$

The best DPCM performance is still obtained (as in Example 7.1) with a first-order predictor since $\{X(n)\}$ is Markov. The D*PCM reduction factor $\sqrt{1-\rho_1^2}$ (Example 7.1) is not optimal, however. Indeed, the value of $h_{1,opt}$ in (7.18) is a first approach to half-whitening, with the constraint of a one-tap filter realization. It is interesting to compare that one-tap D*PCM result with the upper bound obtainable without the constraint of prefilter realizability (Problem 7.2).

Using (7.23) and the Markov source psd (2.105),

$$\min\{\sigma_{r,D*PCM}^2\} \geq \epsilon_q^2 \beta \sigma_x^2 \tag{7.28}$$

$$\beta = (1-\rho_1^2)(2/\pi)^2 F^2(\pi/2,\rho_1) \tag{7.29}$$

where $F(\pi/2,\rho_1)$ is the complete elliptical integral of the first kind:

$$F(\pi/2,\rho_1) = \int_0^{\pi/2} \frac{d\phi}{(1-\rho_1^2\sin^2\phi)^{\frac{1}{2}}} = \frac{\pi}{2}\left[1+\left[\frac{1}{2}\right]^2\rho_1^2 + \left[\frac{1\cdot3}{2\cdot4}\right]^2\rho_1^4 + ...\right] \tag{7.30}$$

Therefore, the mse in D*PCM coding of a first-order Markov source is lower-bounded by a reduction factor

$$\beta = (1-\rho_1^2)\left[1+\frac{1}{4}\rho_1^2+\frac{9}{64}\rho_1^4+...\right]^2 \tag{7.31}$$

For $\rho_1 = 0.9625$, one-tap D*PCM coding results in a coding mse that is $(1-\rho_1^2)^{-1} = 3.7$ times greater than that of ideal DPCM [with negligible quantization error feedback, because of (7.18)], and it is lower bounded by a factor 3.0, as given by (7.31). For $\rho_1 = 0.85$, the corresponding values are 1.9 and 1.8, respectively, implying a decreased motivation for a higher-order prediction network. ●

The foregoing discussion has shown that D*PCM is a suboptimal coding scheme if the performance criterion is unweighted coding error variance. Section 7.3 will demonstrate that D*PCM is an optimum coding scheme for a specific frequency-weighted error criterion.

Transmission Error Effects in D*PCM and DPCM. Earlier chapters have derived the following expressions for total reconstruction noise in PCM and DPCM systems operating with a random bit error probability p_e:

$$\sigma_{r,PCM}^2 = (\epsilon_q^2+\epsilon_c^2)\sigma_x^2 \tag{7.32}$$

$$\sigma_{r,DPCM}^2 = (\epsilon_q^2+\alpha\epsilon_c^2)\sigma_d^2 \tag{7.33}$$

In D*PCM, transmission errors $c(n)$ contribute to the total reconstruction error in exactly the same way as quantization noise. The overall reconstruction error is a generalization of (7.8):

$$r(n) = [q(n) + c(n)]*b(n) \tag{7.34}$$

and it has a variance

$$\sigma_{r,D*PCM}^2 = (\epsilon_q^2 + \epsilon_c^2)\alpha\sigma_{d*}^2 \tag{7.35}$$

We recall that in all cases the normalized channel error variance is $\epsilon_c^2 = \xi p_e$ provided that the codewords are affected only by single bit errors of probability p_e. An optimized D*PCM scheme minimizes at the same time both error contributions in (7.35). The mean square errors are those given in earlier parts of this section if ϵ_q^2 is replaced with $\epsilon_q^2 + \epsilon_c^2$. Note therefore that the optimal filters in D*PCM do *not* depend on bit error rate p_e. We have seen that half-whitening of the input spectrum provides a D*PCM performance bound. From (7.23) we conclude that the minimum channel error variance is given as

$$\min\{\sigma_{c,D*PCM}^2\} = \epsilon_c^2 \left[\frac{1}{2\pi} \int_{-\pi}^{\pi} \sqrt{S_{xx}(e^{j\omega})} \, d\omega \right]^2 \tag{7.36}$$

Let us go back to the DPCM expression (7.33). With high bit-error probabilities $(\alpha\epsilon_c^2 \gg \epsilon_q^2)$, the total mse is minimized if the prediction network performance is close to that of an optimized D*PCM coder, and (7.36) provides a lower bound in channel error variance for DPCM in the case of noisy channels. For low bit error rates, the best re-optimized predictor will have a characteristic in between full-whitening (error-free transmission) and half-whitening (D*PCM bound for noisy channels). Therefore,

$$\min\{\sigma_{c,PCM}^2\} \geqslant \min\{\sigma_{c,DPCM}^2\} \geqslant \min\{\sigma_{c,D*PCM}^2\} \tag{7.37}$$

Example 7.4. Two-bit coding systems for Gaussian source ($p_e = 0$ and $p_e = 0.05$)
Figure 6.35 has already shown that at high error rates, D*PCM results bound DPCM performance (Problem 7.4). In addition, it has shown that D*PCM performance equals PCM performance if full-whitening is used ($h_1 = \rho_1$) and that the error performance can be improved by trying to half-whiten the input ($h_1 < \rho_1$).

The channel-optimal h_1 for DPCM, for high error probabilities, is also identical to the optimal D*PCM coefficient $h_{1,opt}$ as given in (7.18). See (6.144). •

7.3 Noise Feedback Coding

The preceding section has shown the sub-optimality of an open-loop coder for an mmse criterion. We will now pursue this discussion and show that the open-loop differential coder can be very advantageous with certain types of frequency-weighted error criteria. Open-loop coding will be particularly effective if input $x(n)$ and quantization error $q(n)$ can be processed with *separate* filters, as in Figure 7.1(c).

7.3.1 Noise Shaping

The fact that DPCM performs better than D*PCM for mmse coding of a nonwhite process is a result of feeding back, and adding to the input, a filtered version of quantization noise in a loop that is entirely missing in D*PCM. The linear filter in this feedback loop is $F(z) = H(z)$ in DPCM. In general, NFC is characterized by $F(z) \neq H(z)$ [Figure 7.1(c)] [Kimme and Kuo, 1963]. For stability, $F(z)$ should have a minimum delay of one sampling time. With this constraint, the object in NFC systems is to design $F(z)$ for a perceptually optimum reshaping of the reconstruction noise spectrum $S_{rr}(e^{j\omega})$. The NFC coder of Figure 7.1(c) has many equivalent circuits, one of which is a so-called *direct-feedback coder* [Brainard and Candy, 1969] [Brown, 1969]. All the derivations and examples to follow are based on the assumption of small quantization errors [Noll, 1978].

In order to consider the sensitivity of the receiver to reconstruction errors in different frequency ranges, we introduce a subjective *frequency-weighting function* $S_{ww}(e^{j\omega})$ whose inverse describes the sensitivity of the receiver to noise. A small value of $S_{ww}(e^{j\omega})$ indicates that a high coding error variance is acceptable in that specific frequency region, and vice versa. If the function $S_{ww}(e^{j\omega})$ is interpreted as a psd, it will have a variance (Chapter 2) given by

$$\sigma_w^2 = \frac{1}{2\pi} \int_{-\pi}^{\pi} S_{ww}(e^{j\omega}) d\omega \qquad (7.38)$$

which can be normalized to unity without loss of generality [see (7.6b), Example 7.7 and Problem 7.5]. We can also define, as in Chapter 2, a quantity

$$\eta_w^2 = \exp\left[\frac{1}{2\pi} \int_{-\pi}^{\pi} \log_e S_{ww}(e^{j\omega}) d\omega\right], \qquad (7.39a)$$

a minimum prediction error variance, and a spectral flatness measure

$$\gamma_w^2 = \eta_w^2/\sigma_w^2 ; \qquad \gamma_w^2 = \eta_w^2 \text{ if } \sigma_w^2 = 1 \qquad (7.39b)$$

Note, however, that the above definitions serve only as simple partial descriptors of $S_{ww}(e^{j\omega})$ which can in general be a fairly complex function.

The weighted reconstruction noise has a spectrum $S_{ss}(e^{j\omega}) = S_{rr}(e^{j\omega}) S_{ww}(e^{j\omega})$ with variance σ_{rw}^2 given in (7.6a). In the simple case of PCM, since $S_{rr}(e^{j\omega}) = \sigma_q^2 = \epsilon_q^2 \sigma_x^2$,

$$\sigma_{rw,PCM}^2 = \epsilon_q^2 \sigma_w^2 \sigma_x^2 ; \qquad \sigma_{rw,PCM}^2 = \epsilon_q^2 \sigma_x^2 \text{ if } \sigma_w^2 = 1 \qquad (7.40)$$

We will show presently that NFC coders provide a reduction in mse over PCM that is the product of a *source-shaping reduction factor* γ_x^2 (whose inverse is the optimum prediction gain) and the *noise-shaping reduction factor* γ_w^2:

$$\min\{\sigma_{rw,NFC}^2\} = \gamma_w^2 \gamma_x^2 \sigma_{rw,PCM}^2 \qquad (7.41)$$

The Basic Formula for NFC. Let us represent the quantizer as a device that adds signal-independent white noise of variance σ_q^2 and psd $S_{qq}(e^{j\omega})$. We can then replace the feedback-quantizer with a nonwhite noise source [see Figure 7.1(c)]

$$n(n) = q(n)*[\delta(n) - f(n)] \qquad (7.42a)$$

with a psd

$$S_{nn}(e^{j\omega}) = \sigma_q^2 |1-F(e^{j\omega})|^2 \qquad (7.42b)$$

The feedback acts as a linear filter on the open-loop quantizing noise, and the effective quantization noise is colored.

The mse in NFC is given by

$$\sigma_{rw}^2 = \epsilon_q^2 \left[\frac{1}{2\pi} \int_{-\pi}^{\pi} S_{xx}(e^{j\omega}) |A(e^{j\omega})|^2 d\omega \right] \left[\frac{1}{2\pi} \int_{-\pi}^{\pi} S_{ww}(e^{j\omega}) |B(e^{j\omega})|^2 |1-F(e^{j\omega})|^2 d\omega \right] \qquad (7.43)$$

using (7.6a) together with (7.4) and (7.13). Note that $A(e^{j\omega})$ and $B(e^{j\omega})$ are the pre- and postfilters of Figure 7.1. We are now free to choose linear filters $A(e^{j\omega})$, $B(e^{j\omega})$ and $F(e^{j\omega})$ such that the frequency-weighted error variance is minimized. This is obtained by a proper reshaping of the signal spectrum *and* the quantization noise prior to transmission [Kimme and Kuo, 1963].

If we restrict our attention to the case of small quantization noise variance,

$$S_{nn}(e^{j\omega}) \ll |A(e^{j\omega})|^2 S_{xx}(e^{j\omega}) \qquad (7.44)$$

it can be shown that

$$B_{opt}(e^{j\omega}) = 1/A(e^{j\omega}) \qquad (7.45)$$

suggesting a *reciprocal* postfilter for *any* prefilter $A(e^{j\omega})$. By applying Schwarz's inequality to (7.43),

$$\min\{\sigma_{rw}^2\} = \epsilon_q^2 \left[\frac{1}{2\pi} \int_{-\pi}^{\pi} \sqrt{S_{xx}(e^{j\omega}) S_{ww}(e^{j\omega})} |1-F(e^{j\omega})|^2 d\omega \right]^2 \qquad (7.46)$$

for any given $S_{ww}(e^{j\omega})$ and $F(e^{j\omega})$. This minimum is reached if

$$|A_{opt}(e^{j\omega})|^2 = C^2 \left[S_{ww}(e^{j\omega}) |1-F(e^{j\omega})|^2 / S_{xx}(e^{j\omega}) \right]^{1/2} \qquad (7.47)$$

where C is a constant.

Optimization of the NFC Coder. It can be shown that the square root term in (7.46) must be a constant. Note that the $1-F(e^{j\omega})$ term describes a prediction error structure. Therefore equality is obtained by choosing $F(e^{j\omega})$ to be the mmse predictor for a random sequence of psd $S_{xx}(e^{j\omega}) S_{ww}(e^{j\omega})$. With the formalism of Chapter 6,

$$S_{xx}(e^{j\omega}) S_{ww}(e^{j\omega}) |1-F_{opt}(e^{j\omega})|^2 = \eta_x^2 \eta_w^2 \qquad (7.48)$$

The right hand equality in (7.48) can be obtained from Kolmogoroff's result (the definition of η_x^2) by substituting $S_{xx}(e^{j\omega})$ with the frequency-weighted version $S_{xx}(e^{j\omega}) S_{ww}(e^{j\omega})$. Comparison of (7.46) and (7.48) shows that

$$\min\{\sigma_{rw,NFC}^2\} = \epsilon_q^2 \eta_x^2 \eta_w^2 = \epsilon_q^2 \gamma_x^2 \gamma_w^2 \sigma_x^2 \qquad (7.49a)$$

As stated earlier, comparison of (7.49) with the earlier PCM result shows that the weighted reconstruction error variance in NFC is smaller by a factor $\gamma_x^2 \gamma_w^2$. Thus, as a generalization of (6.16),

$$SNR|_{NFC}(\text{dB}) = SNR|_{PCM}(\text{dB}) + 10\log G_P + 10\log(1/\gamma_w^2) \qquad (7.49b)$$

where the last term is the *SNR* gain obtained by noise shaping.

We also see from (7.47) and (7.48) that $S_{xx}(e^{j\omega})|A_{opt}(e^{j\omega})|^2 = $ constant. This implies, however, that $|A_{opt}(e^{j\omega})|^2$ *is a filter that whitens* $S_{xx}(e^{j\omega})$. Thus a sufficient condition for an optimum NFC scheme is to choose as a prefilter an mmse optimized prediction error filter

$$A_{opt}(e^{j\omega}) = 1 - H_{opt}(e^{j\omega}) \qquad (7.50)$$

where $H_{opt}(e^{j\omega})$ is defined by

$$S_{xx}(e^{j\omega})|1 - H_{opt}(e^{j\omega})|^2 = \eta_x^2 \qquad (7.51)$$

We finally note from (7.4), (7.48) and (7.51) that *the weighted error spectrum*

$$S_{ss}(e^{j\omega}) = S_{rr}(e^{j\omega})S_{ww}(e^{j\omega}) = \min\{\sigma_{rw,NFC}^2\} \qquad (7.52)$$

is a constant, and thus equals the total error variance (7.49).

An important conclusion from the foregoing analysis is that overall performance is optimized if the prefilter is an mmse prediction error filter that whitens the input, and that this result holds for any choice of weighting function. To take noise weighting into account, we modify the quantization noise feedback loop, not the prefilter. We note that the result of (7.49) indicates that at least for Gaussian signals and small distortions, the NFC coder operates close to the distortion rate bounds (Appendix D). Indeed it can be shown that the minimum obtainable mse is [O'Neal, 1971] [Berger, 1971] [Noll, 1978] $D(R) = 2^{-2R}\eta_x^2\eta_w^2$. The difference between (7.49a) and the above expression for $D(R)$ is in the first term: recall that $\epsilon_q^2 > 2^{-2R}$ for scalar quantization. In the case of higher distortions, NFC analyses as well as rate distortion theory results suggest a division of spectrum to be coded into appropriate passbands and stopbands.

We shall now re-discuss briefly the special cases of DPCM and D*PCM.

Example 7.5. $S_{ww}(e^{j\omega}) = 1$ for all ω (DPCM)

Comparing (7.48) and (7.51), we see that $F_{opt}(e^{j\omega}) = H_{opt}(e^{j\omega})$ since $\eta_w^2 = 1$ (7.39). This results in the DPCM structure of Figure 7.1(a) and we have

$$\min\{\sigma_{rw}^2\} = \epsilon_q^2 \sigma_w^2 \eta_x^2 = \gamma_x^2 \sigma_{rw,PCM}^2 \qquad (7.53)$$

which implies a gain over PCM by a factor γ_x^2 only, i.e., we do not obtain any noise-shaping gain. More generally, if $S_{ww}(e^{j\omega}) = 1$, no frequency weighting of the quantization noise is possible for *any* choice of $H(e^{j\omega}) = F(e^{j\omega})$ (provided that pre- and postfilters are reciprocal), since the quantization noise passes through both the feedback filter with response $1 - H(e^{j\omega})$, and its inverse, the postfilter. ●

Example 7.6. $S_{ww}(e^{j\omega}) \propto S_{xx}^{-1}(e^{j\omega})$ **for all** ω **(D*PCM)**

A weighting function that is inverse to the input psd is a criterion that tends to avoid masking of a weak signal in specific frequency ranges by the quantization noise (Appendix E). For such a weighting, (7.48) shows that $|1 - F_{opt}(e^{j\omega})|^2$ has to be a constant. This means that $F_{opt}(e^{j\omega}) = 0$ for all ω. This is the D*PCM scheme of Figure 7.1(b). The prefilter, as for all optimal NFC coders, is a whitening filter. The D*PCM scheme is suboptimal if used in connection with any other weighting function (such as the unweighted error of Example 7.5 and Section 7.2). With the inverse noise weighting function and prefilter of this example, subjective gains of 6 to 10 dB are obtained in speech coding [Cattermole, 1969] [Schlink, 1976]. ●

Example 7.7. Noise-feedback PCM

Even without pre- and postfilters $[A(z) = B(z) = 1]$ there is a gain over PCM by the addition of noise-feedback (PCM-NF)

$$\min\{\sigma_{rw,PCM-NF}^2\} = \epsilon_q^2 \eta_w^2 \sigma_x^2 \tag{7.54}$$

indicating a reduction over simple PCM given by the noise-shaping reduction factor γ_w^2. Indeed, such noise-feedback has been proposed to shift noise into frequency regions where it is less heavily weighted by $S_{ww}(e^{j\omega})$: for example, into the stopband region in oversampled systems [Spang and Schultheiss, 1962] [Noll, 1978] [Heuser and Noll, 1976]. ●

Table 7.1 provides a summary of the performance of selected coding schemes. The examples that follow provide further demonstrations of the benefits of noise weighting and noise feedback.

Table 7.1 Summary of performance of suboptimal coding systems which result as special cases of the NFC coder of Figure 7.1(c) [Noll;©1978, AT&T]. Without loss of generality, we can set $\sigma_w^2 = 1$ and hence $\eta_w^2 = \gamma_w^2$ in the last column.

Coding System	Characteristics	$\min\{\sigma_{rw}^2\}$
PCM	$A(z) = B(z) = 1;\quad F(z) = 0$	$\epsilon_q^2 \sigma_x^2 \sigma_w^2$
PCM-NF	$A(z) = B(z) = 1;\quad F(z) = F_{opt}(z)$	$\epsilon_q^2 \sigma_x^2 \eta_w^2$
DPCM	$A(z) = 1 - H_{opt}(z);\quad F(z) = H_{opt}(z)$	$\epsilon_q^2 \eta_x^2 \sigma_w^2$
NFC	$A(z) = 1 - H_{opt}(z);\quad F(z) = F_{opt}(z)$	$\epsilon_q^2 \eta_x^2 \eta_w^2$

Example 7.8. $S_{ww}(e^{j\omega}) \propto S_{xx}^{-1}(e^{j\omega})$ **for all** ω **(D*PCM); first-order Markov source**

The weighting function [Figure 7.5(b)] is

$$S_{ww}(e^{j\omega}) = c^2 S_{xx}^{-1}(e^{j\omega}) . \tag{7.55a}$$

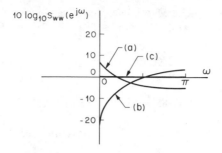

Figure 7.5 Frequency-weighting functions proportional to $S_{xx}^\lambda(e^{j\omega})$ with (a) $\lambda = 1/2$ (Example 7.10); (b) $\lambda = -1$ (Example 7.8); and (c) $\lambda = 0$. The input spectrum $S_{xx}(e^{j\omega})$ is that of an AR(1) process with $\rho = 0.9$ (Figure 2.16). The weighting functions have been normalized so that σ_w^2 is unity in each case.

and if $S_{ww}(\cdot)$ is normalized such that $\sigma_w^2 = 1$, it can be shown (Problem 7.5) that

$$c^2 = \sigma_x^2(1-\rho_1^2)/(1+\rho_1^2) \tag{7.55b}$$

We have seen in Chapter 2 that

$$\gamma_x^2 = \eta_x^2/\sigma_x^2 = 1 - \rho_1^2 \tag{7.56}$$

By straightforward mathematics (Problem 7.5)

$$\min\{\sigma_{rw}^2\} = \epsilon_q^2(1-\rho_1^2)(1+\rho_1^2)^{-1}\sigma_x^2 \tag{7.57}$$

The coding error variance is reduced by a factor $\gamma_x^2 = 1-\rho_1^2$ by means of optimal prediction and additionally by a factor $\gamma_w^2 = (1+\rho_1^2)^{-1}$ by means of optimal noise shaping. For $\rho_1 = 0.85$ (a long-term speech statistics model), the above gains are 5.6 dB and 2.4 dB, respectively. The total improvement is 8.0 dB for D*PCM or NFC, which is close to measured subjective gains of about 6 to 10 dB (see Example 7.5). ●

Example 7.9. NFC coder with one-tap filters

Consider the coder of Figure 7.6 with a one-tap feedback coefficient f and a one-tap predictor coefficient h_1:

$$F(e^{j\omega}) = f \exp(-j\omega) ; \qquad A(e^{j\omega}) = 1 - h_1 \exp(-j\omega) \tag{7.58}$$

Figure 7.6 One-tap NFC coder of Example 7.8 [Noll;©1978, AT&T].

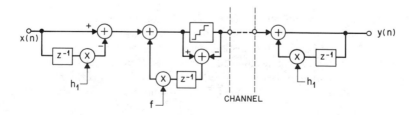

Further, assume an input with adjacent-sample correlation ρ_1. We have $B(e^{j\omega}) = A^{-1}(e^{j\omega})$ and the unweighted mse can be derived from (7.42) with $S_{ww}(e^{j\omega}) = 1$:

$$\sigma_r^2 = \epsilon_q^2 \frac{1+h_1^2-2h_1\rho_1}{1-h_1^2} (1+f^2 - 2h_1 f) \sigma_x^2 ; \quad h_1 < 1 ; \quad f \text{ arbitrary} \quad (7.59)$$

For $h_1 = 0$ and $f = 0$ we have the PCM result (7.9). For $h_1 = 0$ and finite f,

$$\sigma_r^2 = \epsilon_q^2 (1+f^2) \sigma_x^2 \quad (7.60)$$

i.e., noise feedback PCM increases the mse by a factor $(1+f^2)$ over that of PCM. For $f = 0$ and finite $h_1 < 1$, we have the case of D*PCM (prefiltering followed by quantization) with $\min\{\sigma_r^2\} = \epsilon_q^2 \sqrt{1-\rho_1^2}\sigma_x^2$ (Example 7.1). The best choice of f is $f = h_1$ if h_1 is given. The scheme then reduces to DPCM and attains its mmse $\min\{\sigma_r^2\} = \epsilon_q^2(1-\rho_1^2) \sigma_x^2$ for $h_1 = f = \rho_1$. ●

Example 7.10. Image coding using NFC and a first-order Markov model

As shown in Figure 2.9(b), an average image spectrum is flat for frequencies below the line rate and falls at about 6 dB/octave through the rest of the band. A proposed noise-weighting function for such a signal [Barstow and Christopher, 1962] [Bruce, 1964] [Brainard and Candy, 1969] [O'Neal, 1971] has a negative slope of 3 dB/octave. A mathematically tractable model with this property is the weighting model of Figure 7.5a:

$$S_{ww}(e^{j\omega}) = c^2 \sqrt{S_{xx}(e^{j\omega})} \quad (7.61)$$

For this function, the noise shaping reduction factor compared to PCM will be

$$\gamma_w^2 = \frac{\pi}{2F(\pi/2,\rho_1)} = \frac{1}{1 + \frac{1}{4}\rho_1^2 + \frac{9}{64}\rho_1^4 + ...} \quad (7.62)$$

where $F(\pi/2, \rho_1)$ has been defined in (7.30). Using $\rho_1 = 0.9625$ (a good model for video), we find a prediction gain of $(1-\rho_1^2)^{-1} = 11.3$ dB for optimal prediction, and a noise-shaping gain of $(\gamma_w^2)^{-1} = 2.4$ dB. This latter value is in good agreement with experimental subjective results [O'Neal, 1971] [Musmann, 1970]. ●

Example 7.11. Speech coding using APC and NFC (APC-NF)

Several types of noise-shaping can be realized by variation of a single parameter θ in the noise-feedback filter

$$F(z) = H(\theta z); \quad \theta \leqslant 1 \quad (7.63)$$

$H(\theta z)$ is the same transfer function that is obtained by replacing z^{-1} by θz^{-1} in $H(z)$. The special values of $\theta = 1$ and $\theta = 0$ correspond to noise spectra that are flat (DPCM) and speech-like (D*PCM). Intermediate designs have been found to be perceptually optimum in APC coding of speech at low bit rates ($1 \leqslant R \leqslant 2$ bits/sample) [Atal and Schroeder, 1979] [Makhoul and Berouti, 1979] [Atal, 1982]. For example, with (7.63), values of $\theta \sim 0.9$ and 0.73 are recommended for 2-bit and 1-bit coders, respectively. This value of θ

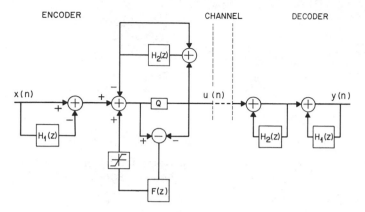

Figure 7.7 Block diagram of an APC-NF coder for speech. In addition to the components of Figure 7.1(c), this coder includes a limiter in the noise-feedback circuit and a pitch predictor $H_2(z)$ [Atal and Schroeder;©1979, IEEE].

increases the bandwidths of the zeros of $1-F(z)$ such that the noise peaks up in the formant regions where its audibility is least [Atal, 1982].

A block diagram of APC-NF appears in Figure 7.7. It includes a near-sample-based predictor $H_1(z)$, a distant-sample based pitch predictor $H_2(z)$, and a noise feedback filter $F(z) = H_1(\theta z)$. The noise feedback loop also includes a peak-limiter to ensure stability, especially in the presence of quantizer-overload effects, which have been neglected in our NFC analyses; the peak limiter limits noise feedback samples to a maximum value of about two times the rms value of the prediction error.

With the above system, and an entropy-coded 3-level quantizer, a representative value of unweighted average SNR is about 21 dB at a total bit rate of 19.2 kb/s. This is lower than the SNR of 23 dB in DPCM, but higher than the SNR of 13 dB in D*PCM, with all three coders operating at the same bit rate of 19.2 kb/s.

In all of the three coders above, the total bit rate includes 12.8 kb/s for the transmission of prediction error, and a bit rate of 6.4 kb/s for side information about the adaptive predictor. The 12.8 kb/s component is the result of sampling speech at 8 kHz, and coding the prediction error with 1.6 bits/sample. This rate is realized by coding error samples in blocks of 5, and representing each of the $3^5 = 243 < 2^8$ codewords of length 5 by 8 bits of information.

Subjectively, the quality of the reconstructed speech in APC-NF is much better than for either of the other two coders, DPCM and D*PCM. Comparisons with PCM-encoded speech show that the speech quality with the 3-level quantizer is close to that of 7 log-bit PCM which has an SNR of 32 dB. The noise shaping together with adaptive predictive coding thus produces a gain over PCM of about 12 dB in subjective SNR.

As mentioned in Chapter 6, a 16 kb/s APC-NF system that includes pitch prediction can provide an MOS score of nearly 4.0 [Daumer, 1982]. Adaptive spectrum prediction, adaptive pitch prediction and adaptive noise shaping are all factors that contribute to this result. Elimination of any one of these components for the sake of simplicity [Bastian, 1981] leads to noticeable degradation of performance at low bit rates in the order of 16 kb/s. On the other hand, as seen in Section 6.5.3, adaptive spectrum prediction alone can provide toll quality at 32 kb/s.   ●

Problems

(7.1) Verify the D*PCM equations (7.17) and (7.18).

(7.2) Consider a first-order Markov source with correlation $R_{xx}(k) = \rho^{|k|}\sigma_x^2$. Sketch

   (a) its psd,

   (b) its half-whitened psd and

   (c) $|A_{opt}(e^{j\omega})|^{-2}$, the magnitude-squared frequency response of the decoder filter.

   Compare with the magnitude-squared frequency response of the 1-tap D*PCM decoder filter for $\rho_1 = 0.85$ and the cases $h_1 = \rho_1$ and $h_1 = h_{1,opt}$ [see (7.18)].

(7.3) Verify (7.28).

(7.4) Verify the one-tap D*PCM result (*SNR* versus h_1) of Figure 6.35 for two-bit quantization of a Gaussian source ($\rho_1 = 0.85$) and a bit error rate of $p_e = 5\%$.

(7.5) A first-order Markov source is to be coded with the weighting $S_{ww}(e^{j\omega}) = c^2 S_{xx}^{-1}(e^{j\omega})$ for all ω.

   (a) Show that if σ_w^2 is to be normalized to unity, the value of c^2 is that in (7.55b).

   (b) Show that its weighted mse σ_{rw}^2 is that of (7.57), i.e., show that the noise-shaping reduction factor is $\gamma_w^2 = (1+\rho_1^2)^{-1}$.

   (c) Compare the improvements to be obtained for PCM with feedback and for DPCM.

   (d) Verify that the noise-weighting filter is a simple nonrecursive filter with coefficients $a_o = 0.762$ and $a_1 = -0.648$ (or vice versa).

References

B. S. Atal and M. R. Schroeder, "Predictive Coding of Speech Signals and Subjective Error Criteria," IEEE Trans. on Acoustics, Speech and Signal Processing, pp. 247-254, June 1979.

B. S. Atal, "Predictive Coding of Speech at Low Bit Rates," IEEE Trans. on Communications, pp. 600-614, April 1982.

J. M. Barstow and H. N. Christopher, "Measurement of Random Video Interference to Monochrome and Color TV," Trans. AIEE, Commun. and Electronics, pp. 313-320, November 1962.

R. Bastian, "Subjective Improvements in DPCM-AQ Performance Based on Adaptive Noise Shaping," IEEE Trans. on Acoustics, Speech and Signal Proc., pp. 1067-1071, October 1981.

T. Berger, *Rate Distortion Theory*, Prentice-Hall, Englewood Cliffs, N.J., 1971.

T. Berger and D. W. Tufts, "Optimum Pulse Amplitude Modulation: Parts I and II," IEEE Trans. on Information Theory, pp. 196-216, 1967.

J. V. Bodycomb and A. H. Haddad, "Some Properties of a Predictive Quantizing System," IEEE Trans. on Communication Technology, pp. 682-684, October 1970.

R. C. Brainard and J. C. Candy, "Direct-Feedback Coders: Design and Performance with Television Signals," Proc. IEEE, pp. 776-786, May 1969.

E. F. Brown, "A Sliding Scale Direct-Feedback Coder for Television," Bell System Tech. J., pp. 1537-1553, May-June 1969.

R. A. Bruce, "Optimum Pre-emphasis and De-emphasis Networks for Transmission of Television by PCM," IEEE Trans. on Communication Technology, pp. 91-96, September 1964.

K. W. Cattermole, *Principles of Pulse Code Modulation*, Iliffe Books, London, 1969.

D. Chan and R. W. Donaldson, "Optimum Pre- and Postfiltering of Sampled Signals with Application to Pulse Modulation and Data Compression Systems," IEEE Trans. on Communication Technology, pp. 141-156, April 1971.

K. Chang and R. W. Donaldson, "Analysis, Optimization and Sensitivity Study of Differential PCM Systems Operating on Noisy Communication Channels," IEEE Trans. on Communications, pp. 338-350, June 1972.

J. P. Costas, "Coding with Linear Systems," Proc. IRE, pp. 1101-1103, September 1952.

W. R. Daumer, "Subjective Evaluation of Several Speech Coders," IEEE Trans. on Communications, pp. 655-662, April 1982.

J. L. Flanagan, *Speech Analysis, Synthesis, and Perception*, 2nd ed., Heidelberg, Springer-Verlag, New York, 1972.

L. M. Goodman and P. R. Drouilhet, "Asymptotically Optimum Pre-emphasis and De-emphasis Networks for Sampling and Quantizing," Proc. IEEE, pp. 795-796, May 1966.

B. Heuser and P. Noll, "Error Feedback as a Means for Coloring Quantization Noise" (in German), Technical Report No. 191, Heinrich Hertz Institut, Berlin, 1976.

E. G. Kimme and F. F. Kuo, "Synthesis of Optimal Filters for a Feedback Quantization System," IEEE Trans. on Circuit Theory, pp. 405-413, September 1963.

J. Makhoul and M. Berouti, "Adaptive Noise Spectral Shaping and Entropy Coding in Predictive Coding of Speech," IEEE Trans. on Acoustics, Speech and Signal Proc., pp. 63-73, February 1979.

H. G. Musmann, "Redundancy Reduction by Linear Transforms" (in German), Nachrichtentechnischer Fachbericht, NTF Bd. 40, pp. 13-27, 1970.

P. Noll, "Some Properties of Differential PCM Schemes" (in German), Archiv für Elektronik und Übertragungstechnik (AEÜ), Bd. 30, pp. 125-130, 1976.

P. Noll, "On Predictive Quantizing Schemes," Bell System Tech. J., pp. 1499-1532, May-June 1978.

B. M. Oliver, "Efficient Coding," Bell System Tech. J., pp. 724-750, July 1952.

J. B. O'Neal, "Bounds of Subjective Performance Measures for Source Encoding Systems," IEEE Trans. on Information Theory, pp. 224-231, May 1971.

W. Schlink, "On Source Encoding of PCM Speech Signals" (in German), Thesis, TU Braunschweig, 1976.

H. A. Spang and P. M. Schultheiss, "Reduction of Quantizing Noise by Use of Feedback," IRE Trans. on Communication Systems, pp. 373-380, December 1962.

8

Deltamodulation

8.1 Introduction

An important member of the class of differential waveform coders is *one-bit* or *two-level* DPCM, better known as *Delta Modulation* or *Deltamodulation* (DM). The property of a one-bit codeword eliminates the need for word framing at the transmitter and receiver, and makes DM systems very attractive for many classes of digital communication. The simplicity of DM also makes it an important method for digital voice storage.

The subject of deltamodulation brings to the forefront at least two issues which were treated only in passing in the DPCM chapter. First, the properties of coarse quantization, and the perceptual ramifications thereof; and second, the effect of signal-oversampling. The oversampling is fairly critical in many applications where one is constrained to employ a two-level quantizer. The effect of a higher sampling rate is to increase the prediction gain by increasing neighboring sample correlations. Subsequent sections will give numerical examples of correlation coefficient ρ_1 and prediction gain G_P as functions of sampling rate.

The simplicity of DM has inspired numerous refinements and variations [Steele, 1975] of a basic invention [De Loraine, van Miero and Derjavitch, 1946]. We will cover several DM systems as we apply previously discussed principles of quantization and prediction to a one-bit coder. Except where mentioned, most of the DM systems to be discussed have been motivated by application to digitization of speech. At bit rates in the order of 32 to 48 kb/s, DM systems with adaptive quantizers provide reproduction of speech with very good quality, using extremely simple algorithms. For the DM example in Figure 5.14, the MOS rating at a bit rate of 48 kb/s was in the order of 4.3. Of particular importance are the so-called syllabically adaptive DM systems (Section 8.4) which also possess a remarkable degree of robustness to bit error rates in the order of 1%. This property holds at transmission bit rates as low as 9.6 kb/s and makes DM coders an important means for low bit rate speech digitization with communications quality.

Figure 8.1(a) depicts a DM coder in its simplest form, one that uses first-order prediction. Except for the inclusion of an output lowpass filter LPF, the circuit represents a special case of the more general DPCM schematic (Figure 6.1). The present quantizer is a two-level device by definition, with reconstruction levels of $\pm\delta(n)$ (also see Figure 4.9); and in *single-integration* DM, the predictor is a first-order device with $h_1 \leqslant 1$. The boxed portion of Figure 8.1(a) is often referred to in DM literature simply as an "accumulator" or "integrator". The $h_1 = 1$ design is called "ideal integration"; in this case, $\hat{x}(n)$ is simply a delayed version of the previous output $y(n-1)$. On the other hand, $h_1 < 1$ provides "leaky integration." Oversampling usually implies that the first normalized acf value $\rho_{xx}(1) \rightarrow 1$ so that a leaky integrator with $h_1 = \rho_{xx}(1)$ [see (6.23)] provides nearly ideal integration. Transmission error considerations (Section 8.5), however, may suggest a value of h_1 significantly less than 1. *Double-integration* DM systems are discussed separately in Section 8.3.

Emphasis in this book will be on DM systems with fairly simple nonadaptive predictors. The prediction error quantizer, on the other hand, will be invariably adaptive. Because of the special nature of one-bit quantization, algorithms for adapting the quantizer step size (Section 8.4) will be somewhat different from those of Section 4.10.

Figure 8.1 Block diagrams of single-integration DM: (a) standard DPCM notation; and (b) an "analog implementation" notation that is usual in DM literature.

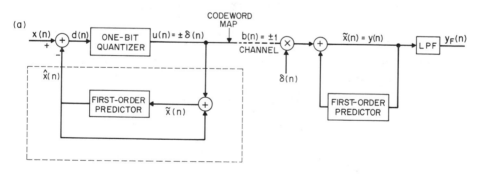

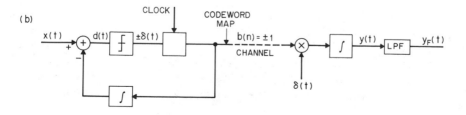

Figure 8.1(b) shows a single-integration DM coder in an "analog-implementation" notation that is very common in DM literature. Note that the coder input and output are now functions of continuous time t, and that the sampling clock appears *after* the two-level quantizer. The single integrator is a resistor-capacitor or charge-parceling network [Baldwin and Tewksbury, 1974], and the quantizer is a simple comparator. Outputs corresponding to $\hat{x}(n)$ and $\tilde{x}(n)$ in Figure 8.1(a) have not been indicated in Figure 8.1(b). These values, $\hat{x}(t)$ and $\tilde{x}(t)$, are realized at the output of the integrator in Figure 8.1(b) just *before* and just *after* each clock operation. The time-continuous notation in Figure 8.1(b) is very relevant for implementation. However, for analytical reasons and for uniformity of notation, we shall continue to use discrete-time notation in the rest of the DM chapter.

The function of the output filter in Figure 8.1 is in general fairly critical for DM coding. Practical DM coders typically oversample the input $\{x(n)\}$ to permit useful encoding under the constraint of the coarse two-level quantizer. As a result of this oversampling, the unfiltered output staircase function $y(n)$ is characterized by quantization noise and distortion components that extend beyond the input signal band of width W; and one requires a lowpass filter to reject out-of-band components between W and $f_s/2$ (see Figure 8.7; also, the region $(\Omega_W, \Omega_S/2)$ in Figure 3.7). The *oversampling ratio* F, which is the ratio of the sampling frequency to the Nyquist rate $2W$, is typically equal to 1 in multi-bit DPCM, or nominally higher, as discussed in Chapter 3; however, DM systems are characterized in general by

$$F = f_s/2W \gg 1 \qquad (8.1)$$

The transmission bit rate I in DM is numerically equal to the sampling rate f_s, because the number of quantization bits per sample R equals $\log_2 2 = 1$:

$$I|_{DM} = f_s R = f_s \quad \text{bits/second} \qquad (8.2)$$

In the absence of transmission errors, reconstruction error equals quantization error as in (6.12); quantization error $q(n)$, reconstruction error $r(n)$, and in-band reconstruction error $r_F(n)$ are defined by

$$r(n) = q(n) = x(n) - y(n) ; \qquad r_F(n) = x_F(n) - y_F(n) \qquad (8.3)$$

where $x_F(n)$ and $y_F(n)$ are the results of filtering $x(n)$ and $y(n)$, as in Figures 8.1 and 8.2.

Figure 8.2 suggests two ways of observing the in-band quantization noise $r_F(n)$; (a) by comparing the filtered output waveform $y_F(n)$ with the filtered version $x_F(n)$ of input $x(n)$; or, (b) by obtaining the unfiltered error waveform $r(n)$, and subsequently filtering it to obtain the signal-band error $r_F(n)$. In (a), the object of filtering $x(n)$ is to duplicate the delay introduced in the filtering of $y(n)$. The bandwidths of $x(n)$ and $x_F(n)$ are identical, or at least very nearly so. Figure 8.3 shows the effects of filtering the DM output $y(n)$, for the example of $F = 2$.

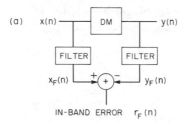

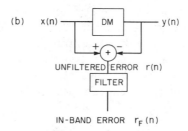

Figure 8.2 Two methods of measuring in-band errors in DM.

Figure 8.3 LDM coding of a speech input with $F = 2$, $f_s = 16$ kHz and $h_1 = 1$: (a) input $x(n)$, the waveform of Figure 1.4(a); (b) output $y(n)$; (c) filtered output $y_F(n)$; (d) reconstruction error $r(n)$; and (e) filtered reconstruction error $r_F(n)$. The input has a maximum magnitude of $|x|_{max} = 2048$. The LDM step size, a value that maximizes $SNRF$ (Section 8.2), is $\delta_{opt,F} = 96$ [Jayant, 1982].

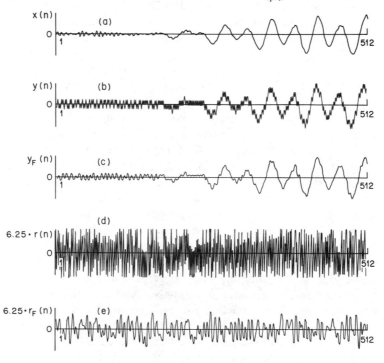

Defining Equations for Single-Integration DM. The important example of DM with first-order prediction is characterized by

$$b(n) = \text{sgn}[u(n)] = \text{sgn}[d(n)] = \text{sgn}[x(n) - h_1 y(n-1)] \qquad (8.4)$$

$$y(n) = h_1 y(n-1) + \delta(n) b(n) \qquad (8.5)$$

The binary quantity $b(n)$ in (8.4) is the sign of the quantized version $u(n)$ of the difference signal $d(n)$. It is the DM bit which determines the direction in which $y(n)$ is updated (8.5) at sampling instant n. The bit $b(n)$ is also the transmitted one-bit codeword in DM-based waveform transmission. The step size magnitude $\delta(n)$ is constant in non-adaptive DM, and it will simply be denoted by δ.

The definition of the DM bit in (8.4) is not empirical. It enables the updating process (8.5) to minimize waveform tracking error on an instantaneous basis, in the sense of picking the lesser of two possible reconstruction errors at time n. However, if one widens the scope of one-bit differential coding to include input anticipation (Chapter 9), one can meaningfully eschew the constraint (8.4) when appropriate.

Linear and Adaptive Deltamodulation. Sampling rates of interest in DM span a very wide range, say, $100 > F \geqslant 1$. The higher end of this range is of interest in using DM-based A/D converters of high precision [Goodman, 1969,I] (also see Appendix G); while DM coders meant for transmitting waveforms with reasonable quality, at minimal possible bit rates, tend to employ sampling rates characterized by the range $10 > F \geqslant 1$ [Schindler, 1970] [Steele, 1975].

The first of the above category of deltamodulators uses nonadaptive quantization wherever possible, because of a typical need for maximally simple signal processing. A good example would be a 256 kHz speech signal processor with $F = 32$, assuming that $2W = 8$ kHz. The second category of transmission-oriented coders tends to include the sophistication of adaptive quantization to minimize the distortion at bit rates suitable for transmission. The situation is similar to one in Chapter 5, where we noted that linear (uniformly quantized) PCM was more appropriate for signal processing, while companded PCM was more suitable for lower bit rate transmission. Good examples of transmission-oriented DM systems are 40 kHz and 6 MHz adaptive DM coders for high-quality coding of speech and low-resolution images, respectively. For input bandwidths of 4 kHz and 1 MHz, respective values of F are 5 and 3. Adaptive quantization may be needed in signal processing DM devices as well, if one cannot afford the sampling frequencies necessary for a nonadaptive device, as in high-speed video applications.

Nonadaptive or fixed step size deltamodulation is also known by the name of *linear deltamodulation* (LDM) because it essentially approximates the input with a sequence of linear ramp functions of slope $\pm \delta/T = \delta f_s$ where δ is the LDM step size and T is the sampling interval $1/f_s$. *Adaptive deltamodulation* (ADM) is a system where the step size is a time-variable quantity $\delta(n)$. [The symbol $\delta(n)$ is *not* the dirac-delta function in this chapter]. Section 8.4 describes specific adaptation algorithms using backward or forward estimations of step-size (DM-AQB or DM-AQF). If adaptation is not explicitly mentioned, the notation DM implies, in the literature as well as in this book, the nonadaptive case, LDM.

DM Noise Analyses. The dichotomy of unfiltered and filtered errors is one of the reasons why performance analyses of DM coders are more difficult than those for Nyquist-sampled multi-bit coders. A second factor that complicates DM studies is the particular importance of separating slope overload distortion and granular noise (Figure 6.3) components of reconstruction errors in one-bit coding. Recognizing the above difficulties, we have included, in Section 8.2, only simple (albeit sometimes approximate) formulas for noise power σ_r^2 and optimal step size δ, to provide rough-and-ready guidelines for DM design; and we have avoided for simplicity, many exact formulations and analyses which permit a deeper understanding of the DM process. As with all types of coders, satisfactory assessments of DM performance with inputs such as speech and video have to be based on extensive experimentation or simulation followed by perceptual tests.

Slope Overload and Granularity. In Figure 8.4(a) are shown LDM waveforms that result when the encoder is correctly tracking the input; in other words, when the step size δ is matched to the slope characteristics of the input $x(n)$. Notice how the average value of the DM bit sequence $\{b(n)\}$ tends to follow the local slope of the input waveform, which is negative in the segment for which the DM bits are shown. If the input slope statistics are not known, waveform encoding in LDM will be less accurate, with an arbitrarily selected step size being either too small, as in the *slope overload* example of Figure 8.4(b); or too large, as in the illustration of *granularity* in Figure 8.4(c). With speech and image inputs, even if the input statistics are known in an average or long-term sense, it is impossible to match the step size to the local input slope at all times, as was done in the case of the well-behaved, nearly sinusoidal waveform of Figure 8.4(a).

Figure 8.4 LDM waveforms when the step size δ is (a) well matched to input slope; (b) too small for the input slope; and (c) too large for the input slope.

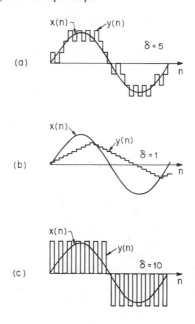

The slope-tracking problem with random waveforms is alleviated in ADM, where the step size is allowed to follow the variations in the input slope. With slowly adaptive or *syllabically adaptive* coders, the approach is to estimate the average slope of a waveform segment that is sufficiently well-behaved to be considered stationary, and to select for this waveform segment an "optimal" step size that may result in a waveform tracking similar to, if not as good as, the situation of Figure 8.4(a). With *instantaneously adaptive* encoders, the attempt will be to track the instantaneous or local input slope by appropriate, albeit abrupt, increases or decreases of the step size. In either type of ADM, in spite of step size adaptations, the coarseness of one-bit quantization results in instances of insufficient slope-tracking. Figure 8.5 illustrates slope overload distortion and granular noise for the examples of (a) a reasonably well-designed LDM and (b) instantaneously adaptive ADM. Slope-mistracking is more obvious in the LDM example, a fact well reflected by the highly structured sequence of five like bits in Figure 8.5(a). Structure in the bit sequence is in general less obvious in ADM.

A formal quantitative definition of slope overload is difficult. A succession of *more than* two like bits is one reasonable criterion. It takes into account the fact that clusters of exactly two like bits are very common and should therefore not be

Figure 8.5   Illustration of slope overload and granularity in (a) LDM and (b) instantaneous ADM.

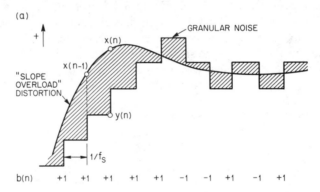

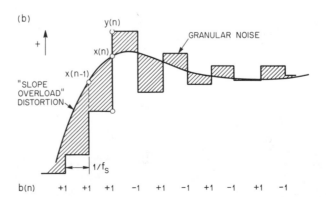

classified as slope overload; examples of two-bit clusters appear in Figures 8.4(a) and 8.5(b), or in many examples of ADM (Section 8.4). Another definition could be one that declares slope overload whenever the magnitude of input first difference $|d(n)|$ exceeds $\delta(n)$ at any instant n [Nielsen, 1970]. Still another empirical, but more conservative, definition is one that stipulates slope overload whenever δ (or an average value thereof in ADM) falls below $4\sigma_s$, where σ_s is the rms value of the adjacent sample difference $x(n) - x(n-1)$.

We shall see in Section 8.2 how the effect of step size on LDM performance can be predicted quantitatively, in terms of SNR formulas that apply to useful stationary waveform models; and in Section 8.4, we will indicate how to design slowly adaptive and instantaneously adaptive algorithms that maintain satisfactory levels of SNR in spite of local and long-term slope variations in nondeterministic and nonstationary waveforms. The intermediate Section 8.3 covers DM refinements based on higher order prediction (double-integration DM) and input pre-emphasis (Delta Sigma Modulation).

8.2 Quantization Noise in Single Integration DM

In this section, we develop simple approximate expressions for DM design and performance. Our approximations are shown to be useful for highly oversampled inputs $(F \gg 1)$, as seen by comparing them with well-known results from the LDM coding of sinusoidal signals and Gaussian signals with an integrated power spectrum. The simplicity of our analysis is due to two tacit, but experimentally supported assumptions. The first is the assumption that the best predictor coefficient is defined by $h_{1,opt} = \rho_{xx}(1) = \rho_1$; and the second is the assumption of a white or *all-pass* spectrum for the LDM quantization noise that includes components due to slope overload and granularity. The results of this section will be very useful for rule-of-thumb LDM designs in most situations of practical interest. The SNR results of this section will also be good predictors of the peak SNR performance of ADM coders.

Following DPCM analyses, the *unfiltered* error variance σ_r^2 is a function of prediction gain G_P and quantizer performance factor ϵ_q^2:

$$\sigma_r^2 = \sigma_q^2 = \epsilon_q^2 \sigma_d^2 = \epsilon_q^2 G_P^{-1} \sigma_x^2 \tag{8.6}$$

The *filtered* or in-band error variance in DM will be denoted by

$$\sigma_{rF}^2 = G_F^{-1} \sigma_r^2 \tag{8.7}$$

where G_F is the *filtering gain*. In the special case of Nyquist sampling $(F = 1)$, $G_F = 1$ as well.

If the quantizer performance factor is assumed not to change significantly in PCM and DM operation, the error variances above imply that

$$SNR\big|_{DM}(\text{dB}) = SNR\big|_{PCM}(\text{dB}) + 10 \log G_P \tag{8.8}$$

$$SNRF\big|_{DM}(\text{dB}) = SNR\big|_{PCM}(\text{dB}) + 10 \log (G_P G_F) \tag{8.9}$$

The product $G_P G_F$ can be interpreted as the SNR gain relative to PCM coding. The maximization of $SNRF$ requires a maximization of the product $G_P G_F$ with respect to quantizer step size δ and predictor coefficient h_1. The maximization of $G_P G_F$ is unfortunately not a mathematically tractable problem. One reason for this is that the error spectrum $S_{rr}(e^{j\omega})$, and hence G_F, are not simple functions of h_1 and δ. We therefore attempt a less ambitious DM design where we assume that $S_{rr}(e^{j\omega})$ is white in the neighborhood of optimum operation, so that

$$G_F = (f_s/2)/W = FW/W = F \qquad (8.10a)$$

$$SNRF \mid_{DM}(\text{dB}) = SNR \mid_{DM}(\text{dB}) + 10 \log F \qquad (8.10b)$$

The DM problem then simplifies to that of designing h_1 and δ for max$\{SNR\}$. With the further simplification (Chapter 6) that $h_{1,opt} = \rho_1$, the problem reduces to one of seeking a δ_{opt} that leads to a maximum SNR, i.e., a minimum σ_q^2. We emphasize that maximization of SNR is *not* a definitive criterion for maximization of $SNRF$. In fact, it is known from experimental results that $\delta_{opt,F}$, the step size that maximizes $SNRF$, is generally greater than the step size δ_{opt} that maximizes SNR. This is shown for the correlated Gaussian input example in Figure 8.6. The step size is shown as a fraction of the rms value of adjacent sample differences in the input, $\sigma_s = \sigma_x \sqrt{2(1-\rho_1)}$ (Problem 6.1). A parameter often used in DM literature is the *slope loading factor*, the ratio of step size to σ_s:

$$S = \delta/\sigma_s \qquad (8.11)$$

Figure 8.6 Measured DM performance versus step size δ for $F = 4$ and a correlated Gaussian input with $\rho_1 = 0.99$. (a) Variations of $SNRF$, SNR and G_F; and (b) variation of $\rho_{qq}(1)$ [Noll, 1976].

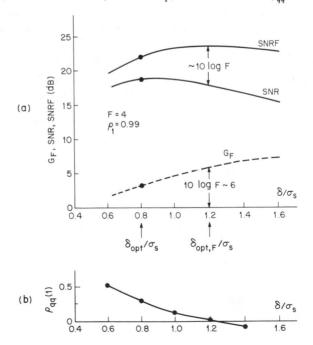

Note that in the range of step sizes used in the figure, G_F increases with step size δ. As δ increases, the noise becomes increasingly highpass, and this results in increased noise rejection due to the output lowpass filtering, as will be seen presently in Figure 8.7. The assumed equality $G_F = F$ [see (8.10a)] holds only in the region of $\delta \simeq \delta_{opt,F}$. [Also see (8.27)]. The simulation with the above input has also shown that the reconstruction noise is approximately an AR(1) process. As seen in Figure 8.6(b), its first-order acf value $\rho_{qq}(1)$ is positive for $\delta = \delta_{opt}$ and approximately zero for $\delta = \delta_{opt,F}$.

Optimization of DM coding involves the minimization of σ_{rF}^2 and the consequent maximization of $SNRF$:

$$\min\{\sigma_{rF}^2\} = \min\{\sigma_r^2/G_F\} \; ; \quad \max\{SNRF\} = \max\{SNR \cdot G_F\} \qquad (8.12a)$$

For analytical simplicity, however, the following approximation is often employed in DM literature and in this book:

$$\min\{\sigma_{rF}^2\} \simeq \min\{\sigma_r^2\}/F \; ; \quad \max\{SNRF\} \simeq \max\{SNR\} \, F \qquad (8.12b)$$

where all minimizations and maximizations will be with respect to the step size δ. As indicated quantitatively in Figure 8.7, the above is only an order-of-magnitude approximation.

Figure 8.7 Noise spectra with (a) allpass, (b) lowpass and (c) highpass characteristics. These spectra are also psd's for an AR(1) process with unit variance and adjacent sample correlation equal to (a)0, (b)1/3 and (c) = −1/3 [Jayant, 1978,II;©1978, IEEE].

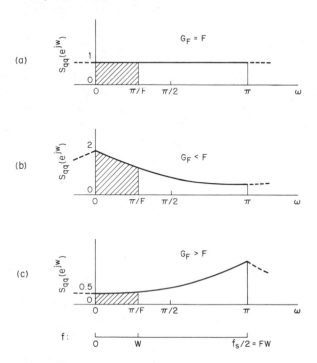

Unfiltered Error Variance σ_r^2. The following analysis, based for simplicity on Gaussian inputs to both coder and quantizer, discusses the minimization of unfiltered error variance σ_r^2 by appropriate design of both predictor and quantizer. The quantizer input $d(n)$ in single-integration LDM can be written in a form that explicitly reflects quantization error feedback (Problem 6.23):

$$d(n) = x(n) - h_1 y(n-1) = [x(n) - h_1 x(n-1)] - [h_1 q(n-1)] \quad (8.13)$$

Clearly, for perfect integration ($h_1 = 1$), the above expression is merely the sum of the input signal increment and the latest sample of quantization error. We have already noted in (6.64) that the mmse *predictor coefficient* is given by $h_{1,opt} = \rho_{xx}(1) = \rho_1$ for a first-order Gauss-Markov or AR(1) source. With this choice, the term in the first square brackets (8.13) is an *innovations* term

$$z(n) = x(n) - \rho_1 x(n-1) ; \quad \sigma_z^2 = (1-\rho_1^2)\sigma_x^2 \quad (8.14a)$$

that will be uncorrelated with the noise term $q(n-1)$ in the second square brackets. Therefore, squaring (8.13) and taking expected values, and setting $\sigma_q^2 = \sigma_r^2$, the variance of $d(n)$ for the above choice of h_1 can be written in the form

$$\sigma_d^2 = (1-\rho_1^2)\sigma_x^2 + \rho_1^2\sigma_r^2 \quad (8.14b)$$

Since $\sigma_r^2 = \sigma_q^2 = \epsilon_q^2 \sigma_d^2$, where ϵ_q^2 is the quantizer performance factor,

$$\sigma_d^2 = (1-\rho_1^2)(1-\epsilon_q^2\rho_1^2)^{-1}\sigma_x^2 \quad (8.15a)$$

$$\min\{\sigma_d^2\} = (1-\rho_1^2)(1-\rho_1^2\min\{\epsilon_q^2\})^{-1}\sigma_x^2 \quad (8.15b)$$

where the minimization is over step size δ.

Values of $\min\{\epsilon_q^2\}$ for different pdf's and $R = 1$ bit/sample have already been listed in the third column of Table 4.2. Note that σ_z^2 would be the variance of the difference signal $d(n)$ in a system without quantization error feedback (as in the D*PCM system of Chapter 7). Because of the presence of such feedback in DM, there is an increase in mean square error that is given by the factor $(1-\epsilon_q^2\rho_1^2)^{-1}$ (Problem 6.23). Note also that the minimization in (8.15b) is with respect to *quantizer step size*, which controls ϵ_q^2. The reconstruction error has a minimum variance [Nitadori, 1965]

$$\min\{\sigma_r^2\} = \min\{\epsilon_q^2\} \frac{1-\rho_1^2}{1-\min\{\epsilon_q^2\}\rho_1^2} \sigma_x^2 \quad (8.16)$$

This result has already been listed in (7.20), in a general form involving ϵ_q^2 rather than $\min\{\epsilon_q^2\}$. The minimum is obviously obtained only if the quantizer is chosen appropriately.

The relation (8.17) also holds for $h_1 \simeq \rho_1$ [Figure 7.3(a)], and is also useful for predicting performance with non-Gaussian processes.

The signal-to-noise ratio is simply the ratio of σ_x^2 to σ_r^2:

$$\max\{SNR\} = \frac{(\min\{\epsilon_q^2\})^{-1} - \rho_1^2}{1 - \rho_1^2} \simeq \frac{(\min\{\epsilon_q^2\})^{-1} - 1}{1 - \rho_1^2} \text{ if } \rho_1 \to 1 \qquad (8.17)$$

The above equation explicitly shows the effects on SNR of quantizer performance (the numerator terms) and the prediction gain (the denominator terms). For example, with $\min\{\epsilon_q^2\} = 0.363$ (Table 4.2) and $\rho_1 = 0.99$, the value of $\max\{SNR\}$ is 18.9 dB, which is indeed the experimental result of Figure 8.6.

Optimization of δ. From the theory of one-bit quantization, the optimum step size, the value that guarantees the minimum value of ϵ_q^2, is simply $\theta \, \sigma_d$ where θ is a pdf-specific constant. Values of θ have also been listed in the second column of Table 4.2. Thus,

$$\delta_{opt} = \theta \sigma_d = \theta (1 - \rho_1^2)^{1/2} (1 - \rho_1^2 \min\{\epsilon_q^2\})^{-1/2} \sigma_x \qquad (8.18a)$$

It will also be interesting to relate δ_{opt} to σ_z:

$$\delta_{opt} = \theta \ (1 - \rho_1^2 \min\{\epsilon_q^2\})^{-1/2} \sigma_z \qquad (8.18b)$$

Clearly, as $\rho_1 \to 1$,

$$\lim_{\rho_1 \to 1} \delta_{opt} = \theta \ (1 - \min\{\epsilon_q^2\})^{-1/2} \sigma_z \qquad (8.18c)$$

That is for ρ_1 values of usual interest, the best step size is simply proportional to the rms value of the innovations.

Example 8.1. Optimal step sizes for Gaussian inputs

By virtue of the summation in (8.13), if the quantization error is Gaussian [Arnstein, 1975], a Gaussian input to the DM coder implies a Gaussian input to the quantizer.

We therefore pursue the example of Gaussian inputs, and set $\min\{\epsilon_q^2\} = 0.363$ and $\theta = 0.796$. Table 8.1 shows δ_{opt} (normalized to σ_z) for several values of ρ_1. Notice that as ρ_1 increases, the extent of quantization error feedback increases as well. This in turn increases the quantizer input variance σ_d^2, and necessitates larger values of δ_{opt}, relative to σ_z.

Table 8.1 Values of $h_{1,opt}$ and δ_{opt} for a Gaussian input [Jayant, 1978].

ρ_1	1.00	0.98	0.95	0.90
$h_{1,opt}$	1.00	0.98	0.95	0.90
δ_{opt}/σ_z	1.01	0.98	0.96	0.95
δ_{opt}/σ_x	0.00	0.20	0.30	0.40

The limiting cases of $\rho_1 = 0$ and $\rho_1 = 1$ are interesting. For $\rho_1 = 0$, $h_{1,opt} = 0$ as well, and the DM coder degenerates into a non-differential one-bit quantizer whose input is σ_z (or σ_x, because $\sigma_x = \sigma_z$ if $\rho_1 = 0$); the optimum step size is simply $0.796\sigma_z$ as given by (8.18b) with $\theta = 0.796$. For $\rho_1 = 1$, on the other hand, the ratio δ_{opt}/σ_z approaches 1.01 as per (8.18c). It is also instructive to relate δ_{opt} to the variance of the coder input $x(n)$. This is done in the last row of Table 8.1. Note that although δ_{opt}/σ_z increases with increasing ρ_1 as noted earlier, the ratio δ_{opt}/σ_x decreases with increasing ρ_1. This is because σ_z/σ_x is a rapidly decreasing function of ρ_1. ●

Dependence of the $(1-\rho_1^2)$ Term on Input Spectrum and F. The foregoing theory applies strictly to first-order Gauss-Markov processes. It is tempting, however, to extend it to arbitrary input spectra. For many important characterizations of input psd, the first-order prediction gain term $G_P = (1-\rho_1^2)^{-1}$ can be shown to be proportional to the square of the sampling frequency, and thus to F^2. For example, with the bandlimited integrated power spectrum (2.159) of Example 2.8, using (2.161) for $F \gg 1$,

$$\rho_1 = \rho(T) = 1 - (\Omega_W \Omega_C/\pi) T^2 = 1 - \pi/[\psi(f_s/2W)^2] = 1 - \pi[\psi F^2]^{-1} \; ; \; F \gg 1 \quad (8.19a)$$

where

$$T = 1/(2WF) = \pi/F\Omega_W; \quad \psi = \Omega_W/\Omega_C \quad\quad (8.19b)$$

Recall from Examples 2.7 and 2.8 that Ω_W is the cutoff frequency in the input spectrum, and Ω_C is the corner frequency. As a consequence of (8.19), the square of the acf value and the prediction gain have the approximate forms

$$\rho_1^2 \simeq 1 - \frac{2\pi}{\psi F^2} \; ; \quad G_P = (1 - \rho_1^2)^{-1} \simeq \frac{\psi}{2\pi} F^2 \quad \text{for} \quad F \gg 1 \quad (8.20)$$

Application of (8.20) in (8.17) further yields the important result

$$\max\{SNR\} = \frac{\psi F^2}{2\pi} \frac{1-\min\{\epsilon_q^2\}}{\min\{\epsilon_q^2\}} = 0.28\psi F^2 \quad \text{for a Gaussian input} \quad (8.21)$$

For example, if $F = 4$ and $\psi = 20$, $\rho_1 \simeq 0.99$ as in Figure 8.6, and $\max\{SNR\} = 19.5$ dB, which is very close to the result obtained in that figure.

If quantization error feedback is neglected in (8.13), the SNR result (8.17) would involve $\min\{\epsilon_q^2\}^{-1}$ instead of $(\min\{\epsilon_q^2\})^{-1}-1$; and we would obtain $0.44\ \psi F^2$ in place of $0.28\ \psi F^2$ in (8.21) (Problem 8.4).

Recall from Chapter 6 that the prediction gain with perfect (ideal) integration ($h_1 = 1$) is $2(1-\rho_1)$, and not $(1-\rho_1^2)$. However, if $\rho_1 = 1-\epsilon \; ; \; \epsilon \to 0$,

$$1-\rho_1^2 \simeq 2(1-\rho_1) = 2\epsilon \quad\quad (8.22)$$

so that the SNR expression (8.21) could be used for ideal integration as well if $\rho_1 \to 1$.

Filtered Error Variance σ_{rF}^2. According to (8.12b) the mmse in DM is $\min\{\sigma_{rF}^2\} = \min\{\sigma_r^2\}/G_F$. We shall now make use of the white-noise model mentioned earlier. Besides being experimentally verifiable, the white-noise assumption [Figure 8.7(a)] has an important qualitative justification. One expects the spectrum of slope overload distortion errors to be lowpass in view of the low-frequency error bursts during overload. One also expects the spectrum of granular errors to be highpass, because of the high-frequency oscillations between positive and negative errors. It seems reasonable therefore that with a balanced mix of the above error types, the overall error spectrum $S_{rr}(e^{j\omega})$ should approach a neutral allpass, or white characteristic. In fact, the lowpass and highpass error spectra in Figures 8.7(b) and (c) correspond qualitatively to the slope overload and granular-error types dominant in Figure 8.4(b) and (c), respectively; while the allpass or white spectrum in Figure 8.7(a) is our proposed model for "optimal" operation, as depicted in Figure 8.4(a). Before proceeding with the filtered noise analysis, it is instructive to take a closer look at the spectra of Figure 8.7.

Example 8.2. AR(1) model for Q(n)
The specific plots in Figure 8.7 are psd functions (2.105)

$$S_{qq}(e^{j\omega}) = (1-\rho^2)(1+\rho^2-2\rho\cos\omega)^{-1} \tag{8.23}$$

of an AR(1) process model for $Q(n)$, with $\sigma_q^2 = 1$ and $\rho_{qq}(1) = \rho$.
For this process it can be shown (Problem 8.7) that the filtering gain is

$$G_F = \frac{\pi}{2}\left[\arctan\left[\frac{1+\rho}{1-\rho}\tan\frac{\pi}{2F}\right]\right]^{-1} \tag{8.24a}$$

$$= \frac{1-\rho}{1+\rho}F \text{ if } F \gg 1; \quad\text{and if}\quad F \gg \left[\frac{1+\rho}{1-\rho}\frac{\pi}{2}\right] \tag{8.24b}$$

Figure 8.7 illustrates (8.23) for $\rho = 0$, $\rho > 1$ and $\rho < 1$. Corresponding values of filtering gain are $G_F = F$, $G_F < F$ and $G_F > F$. Values of $\rho = 0$, 1/3 and $-1/3$ correspond from (8.24b) to asymptotic G_F values of F, $F/2$ and $2F$, respectively. The last value $2F$ has been noted explicitly in DM analyses with a zero slope overload assumption [Goodman, 1969,II] [Spilker, 1976]. Extreme values $\rho = \pm 1$ lead of course to G_F values of 1 and ∞. ●

As discussed in (8.10a) and also in the context of Figure 8.6(b) $[\rho_{qq}(1) = \rho = 0]$, we will be interested mostly in the white-noise case of $G_F = F$ [Figure 8.7(a)]. Using (8.12b) and the above white-noise result in the integrated power spectrum results (8.21),

$$\max\{SNRF\} = \max\{SNR\}F = 0.28\psi F^3 \text{ for a Gaussian input} \tag{8.25}$$

Example 8.3. $\psi = 4$ (speech model)

$$\max\{SNRF\} \text{ (dB)} = 0.5 + 30 \log_{10} F \tag{8.26a}$$

For a nominal bandwidth of 4 kHz and a bit rate of $I = 40$ kb/s, $F = 5$. For this example

$$\max\{SNRF\}(\text{dB}) = 21.5 \tag{8.26b}$$

This result will shortly be noted in the experimental speech results of Figure 8.8. With a bit rate of 48 kb/s, *SNRF* increases to 23.9 dB, implying a gain of 2.4 dB. On the other hand, in PCM coding, the expected gain in *SNR* in going from 40 kb/s ($R = 5$) to 48 kb/s ($R = 6$) is 6 dB, because of the $6R - 10$ dB formula for speech in Chapter 5. •

The above equations (8.25) and (8.26) have important physical interpretations. Firstly, they state that LDM (with single integration or first order prediction) has an error performance that improves as the *cube of the sampling frequency* and therefore as I^3, the *cube of bit rate*: that is, at a rate of *9 dB per octave*, or doubling of frequency. In the above result, the dependence of prediction gain G_P on F in (8.20) contributes 6 dB per octave, while the rejection of out-of-band noise contributes 3 dB/octave. These results are also valid for ADM coders with single integration. In fact, we shall demonstrate when appropriate that precise *SNRF* formulas such as (8.25) and (8.26), as well as a corresponding formula for sine-wave inputs (8.33), hold for ADM systems. The 9 dB/octave *SNRF* result for DM-SI (DM with single integration) is in contrast to the exponential improvement of performance with bit rate in the case of multi-bit quantization, as given by a term proportional to $2^{2R} = 2^{2I/f_s}$. A practical consequence of the above is that, while comparing DM and multi-bit coders, there is a crossover point in bit rate below which deltamodulation (which was originally considered only for its simplicity) can in fact outperform a multi-bit coder such as log-PCM [Zetterberg, 1955]. This is demonstrated by the crossover at 50 kb/s in the speech coding example in Figure 8.8. The example uses instantaneously adaptive DM [Section 8.4 and (8.58)] in anticipation of the non-stationarity of the speech input. As in DPCM, advantages over PCM at lower bit rates are subjectively even greater than what objective *SNR* comparisons suggest. Part of this is due to the fact that a significant portion of in-band DM noise is in the form of slope overload distortion which is perceptually less annoying than an equal amount of granular noise [Jayant

Figure 8.8 Comparison of DM-AQB with log PCM and DPCM-AQB by means of SNR versus bit rate characteristics for a bandlimited (200-3200 Hz) speech input. The DPCM-AQB algorithm uses a one-word memory (Section 4.10), and the DM-AQB algorithm uses a one-bit memory (Example 8.8). Both coders use an optimized first-order predictor [Rosenberg, 1973] [Jayant;©1974, IEEE].

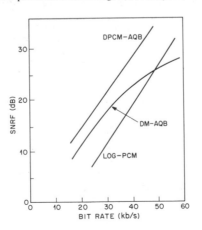

and Rosenberg, 1971]. It is necessary of course that the DM is operating with an optimal step size; this is usually ensured by the adaptive procedures in Section 8.4.

The SNR curves in Figure 8.8 also suggest that the performance gap between DM and DPCM decreases with bit rate I. This is intuitively expected because at 8 kb/s, DPCM (with $f_s = 8$ kHz and $R = 1$) is identical to 8 kb/s DM.

In all of Chapter 6, the oversampling parameter F was equal to 1; while in all of this chapter the number of bits per sample R equals 1. These special configurations follow DPCM and DM coding practice. The most general configuration is of course one where both F and R can be simultaneously greater than 1. It turns out, however, that there is only a narrow range of bit rates where this configuration is the best. Analytical models (Problem 8.13) as well as subjective experiments [Donaldson and Douville, 1969] indicate that if I is sufficiently high (say, 16 kb/s for telephone speech) it pays to design a coder with the maximum possible value of R, and hence the minimum possible (Nyquist) value of f_s. This is precisely the DPCM design of Chapter 6. When DM is used in preference to DPCM at the higher bit rates, it is in the interest of simplicity and greater robustness to channel errors (Section 8.5).

A second observation in the LDM performance equation relates to the factor ψ, which is the ratio of the highest input frequency to the corner frequency of the integrated spectrum. The proportionality of $SNRF$ (and SNR) to ψ suggests that the more lowpass the input spectrum (the larger the value of ψ), the better is the fidelity with which the input can be encoded using DM. This is expected because lowpass spectra suggest the presence of significant adjacent sample correlations, $\rho_1 \rightarrow 1$; which in turn implies that the LDM can track the input waveform with a reasonably small step size δ without running into severe slope overload. Practically, the dependence of SNR on ψ explains why image inputs ($25 < \psi < 100$; numbers in the first two rows in the first column of Table 2.4) can be deltamodulated even better (in an SNR sense) than speech inputs ($\psi \sim 4$) for a given F. Single integration DM performance is least impressive with bandlimited white noise ($\psi \simeq 1$) [Abate, 1967] and voiceband data waveforms [O'Neal, 1974].

In the case of bandlimited white noise, it is interesting to note that $G_P = 1$ if $F = 1$ (because $\rho_1 = 0$ for this psd with Nyquist sampling, see Problem 3.11). But with $F > 1$, positive values of ρ_1 result. Indeed if $F \gg 1$, the value of ρ_1 approaches 1 as shown by a si function (Figure A.1, $T \rightarrow 0$).

Example 8.4. $\psi = 25$ (Picturephone model)

Figure 8.9 illustrates experimental $SNRF$ results for the LDM encoding of a Gaussian input with an integrated power spectrum. The value of ψ is chosen to be about 25, to model videophone inputs whose frequency spectrum is typified by a truncation frequency that is approximately 25 times the corner frequency (Table 2.4). The performance of LDM is a function of F and δ. Note that the maximum values of $SNRF$, which occur at respective values of δ_{opt}, do indeed increase with frequency according to an F^3 (9 dB per octave) law, as predicted in (8.25). Furthermore, note that for $F = 8$, (8.25) predicts an SNR value of 35.6 dB for the given ψ. The corresponding maximum experimental value in Figure 8.9 is 32.5 dB. ●

A presumption in the foregoing $SNRF$ analysis is that the best step size δ_{opt} is nearly the same whether the performance criterion is the maximization of SNR, or

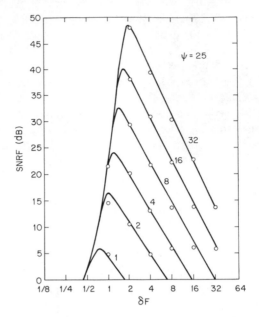

Figure 8.9 Variation of *SNRF* with step size for Gaussian inputs with $\sigma_x^2 = 1$ and an integrated power spectrum ($\psi=25$). Numbers next to the curves are values of oversampling ratio F [O'Neal;©1966, AT&T].

that of *SNRF*. The above supposition is strictly not true, as seen in the example of Figure 8.6. We do not have a simple theory that optimizes δ under an *SNRF* criterion. However, it should be noted that the possibility of filtering does allow the use of a step size that is larger than the value δ_{opt} that maximizes *SNR*. This is because the greater granularity introduced by the larger step size is reflected largely as high frequency noise, which is filtered out anyway. In one rule-of-thumb formula [Abate, 1967], the *SNRF*-optimal step size $\delta_{opt,F}$ in LDM is an F-dependent expression of the form

$$\log_e (2F)\sigma_s \; ; \quad S_{opt} = \log_e (2F) \text{ for } F \gg 1. \tag{8.27}$$

where σ_s is the rms value of adjacent sample differences in the DM input and S is the slope-loading factor (8.11).

Although $\log_e (2F)$ is an increasing function of frequency, $\delta_{opt,F}$ tends to be a decreasing function because σ_s is itself a decreasing function of sampling frequency. Using the value of ρ_1 in (8.19a), and the result $\sigma_s^2 = 2(1-\rho_1)\sigma_x^2$ (Problem 6.1), the optimum step size has a special explicit form for an input with the integrated power spectrum:

$$\delta_{opt,F} = \sigma_x (2\pi/\psi)^{\frac{1}{2}} \log_e (2F)/F \tag{8.28}$$

which is a decreasing function of oversampling ratio F. For example, if σ_x and ψ are fixed, the optimum step size with $F = 64$ is about three times smaller than that with $F = 16$. Also see Problem 8.11 and Figure 8.9.

Deltamodulation   8

In speech applications, step sizes that maximize segmental SNR or $SNRF$ are smaller than those maximizing conventional SNR or $SNRF$, by a factor of about 3. This is because segmental SNR is greatly influenced by the quality with which low-level and idle channel segments of speech are encoded; and this quality is increased by providing lower levels of granular and idle channel noise (that is, by decreasing δ), and the attendant increase of slope overload during the high-amplitude voiced segments of speech is not very objectionable from considerations of $SNRSEG$ (Appendix E) and perception [Jayant and Rosenberg, 1971]. Also, see [Aaron et al., 1969] and [Levitt, McGonegal and Cherry, 1970].

Example 8.5. Sine-wave input

With a sinusoidal input, the input to the quantizer in DM has the nature of a sinusoid (the derivative of the input) plus noise; let us model this approximately by assigning the value (Problem 4.3)

$$\min\{\epsilon_q^2\} = 0.19 \text{ for sine-wave input} \tag{8.29}$$

which characterizes the arcsine pdf [Cummiskey, 1975]. If the frequency of the sinusoid is f and the sampling frequency is f_s (Problem 8.12),

$$\rho_1 = \cos(2\pi f/f_s) \tag{8.30}$$

For an oversampled sine-wave input,

$$\rho_1 \to 1-2\pi^2 f^2/f_s^2 \;; \quad 1-\rho_1^2 \approx 4\pi^2 f^2/f_s^2 \;; \quad f \ll f_s \tag{8.31}$$

so that with (8.18) and the assumption of $G_F = F$,

$$\max\{SNRF\} = \max\{SNR\}F = \frac{4.2}{4\pi^2}\frac{Ff_s^2}{f^2} = 0.108\frac{Ff_s^2}{f^2}\;; \quad f \ll f_s \tag{8.32}$$

Since the oversampling ratio is defined as $F = f_s/2W$, where W is the width of the frequency band over which the DM noise is measured ($0 \leqslant f \leqslant W$),

$$\max\{SNRF\}_{(sine-wave)} = 0.054 f_s^3/(f^2 W) \tag{8.33} \quad \bullet$$

The result of (8.33) is within a factor of 1.25 from the sine-wave $SNRF$ derived by early researchers [deJager, 1952] [Tomozawa and Kaneko, 1968] using extremely different procedures. Also see (8.52). We shall note in Section 8.3 that DM-coding of sinusoidal signals using double integration is characterized by an $SNRF$ formula which is proportional to f_s^5.

The Generic SNR Curve for LDM. The results of this section have provided approximate results that are helpful in designing LDM coders and in predicting their SNR (or $SNRF$) performance. Our analysis has concentrated mostly on the optimum step size region, although we had one occasion to show SNR as a function of δ (Figure 8.9). An important feature of the SNR versus δ curve is an asymmetry mentioned already in the context of Figure 4.7. As δ falls below the value δ_{opt}, the SNR deteriorates more rapidly than if δ should take on values

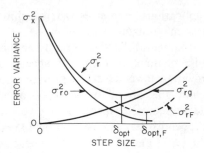

Figure 8.10 A generic error variance curve for DM. The terms σ_{ro}^2 and σ_{rg}^2 are normalized variances of slope overload and granular components of reconstruction error. The terms σ_r^2 and σ_{rF}^2 are unfiltered and filtered versions of overall reconstruction error variance.

greater than δ_{opt}. This is indicated in the qualitative error variance curves of Figure 8.10. The figure also shows how error filtering provides an improvement only in the granular-noise-dominated region, leading to a significant difference between σ_r^2 and σ_{rF}^2 values in that region.

We shall briefly comment on the shapes of the two shoulders of the performance curve in Figure 8.10. Exact analyses of DM, with one notable exception [Slepian, 1972], are based on the granularity-overload classification. We shall avoid exact analyses which are fairly involved (for example, [van de Weg, 1953] [Goodman, 1969,II] [Greenstein, 1973] [Steele, 1980]). Instead, we shall note useful quantitative approximations for error variance and qualitative representations of noise spectra, as in Figure 8.7.

Granular Noise. Assuming a uniform pdf of value $(1/2\delta)$ for granular noise r in the range $(-\delta, +\delta)$, the granular error variance is given by

$$\sigma_{rg}^2 = \frac{1}{2\delta} \int_{-\delta}^{\delta} r^2 dr = \frac{\delta^2}{3} \tag{8.34}$$

This variance simply increases as the square of the step size, as indicated by the granular error characteristic in Figure 8.10. Also see Problem 8.15. Granular noise spectra are highpass as expected by the alternating signs of consecutive granular noise samples. A typical illustration is that in Figure 8.7(c).

Slope Overload Distortion. We note without proof an approximate expression for overload noise power [Greenstein, 1973], one that gets decreasingly valid as the normalized step size S [the slope loading factor in (8.11)] approaches zero:

$$\sigma_{ro}^2 = kS^{-5}\exp(-S^2/2) \text{ unless } S \to 0 \; ; \quad S = \delta/\sigma_s \tag{8.35}$$

The constant k is input-spectrum dependent and given by:

$$k = \frac{243}{4\sqrt{2\pi}} \frac{D_1^2}{D_2} \tag{8.36}$$

where D_n is the nth *spectral moment* of the input psd:

$$D_n = \int_0^{2\pi W} \Omega^{2n} S_{xx}(\Omega) d\Omega \; ; \qquad (8.37)$$

$$D_1 = \int_0^{2\pi W} \Omega^2 S_{xx}(\Omega) d\Omega \; ; \qquad D_2 = \int_0^{2\pi W} \Omega^4 S_{xx}(\Omega) d\Omega \qquad (8.38)$$

The moment D_1 is related to the variance σ_s^2 of the adjacent sample difference s by a factor f_s^2 (Problem 8.10).

The expression (8.35) is a good approximation to the shape of the overload characteristic in Figure 8.10 if the step size is not too small. As $S \rightarrow 0$, however, (8.35) tends to overestimate the value of slope overload distortion. Note, for example, that overload noise power should tend to the input power σ_x^2 itself as $S \rightarrow 0$ (as in Figure 8.10), while (8.35) predicts a limiting noise power of infinity. A complicated expression for overload distortion, valid even for $S = 0$, is available elsewhere [Greenstein, 1973].

The spectrum of slope-overload distortion is lowpass as expected by the identical polarities of consecutive overload error samples. A typical spectrum is that in Figure 8.7(b).

Idle Channel Noise. When the DM input is zero (as during silences in speech, or constant luminance areas in images), it is said to be in the *idle channel* state, and the binary output sequence ideally consists of alternate *one*'s and *zero*'s:

$$... 10\ 10\ 10\ 10\ ... \qquad (8.39)$$

This "idle channel" or "zero signal" bit pattern is integrated by the DM decoder and the resulting signal is mostly rejected by the final filter. This rejection occurs because the fundamental frequency of the received binary signal is $(2T)^{-1} = f_s/2$; this is the lowest frequency W in the signal and none of its frequency components will be able to pass through a filter whose upper cutoff frequency is $W \ll f_s/2$ (assuming that $F \gg 1$). Practical filters do not have infinite attenuation at $f_s/2$ and consequently the output signal from the decoder in the idle channel condition will not be zero, but will be negligible.

If the encoding and decoding processes are asymmetrical, the idle channel bit pattern will occasionally have two adjacent *one*'s or *zero*'s, say

$$... 10\ 10\ 10\ \underline{11}\ 0\ ... \qquad (8.40)$$

and under certain circumstances, this will produce a distinct unwanted signal from the output filter, called *idle channel noise*. The cause for the above asymmetry can reside in the DM integrator or in the quantizer characteristic.

Figure 8.11 illustrates how ideal (8.39) and non-ideal (8.40) bit patterns result from (a) symmetrical and (b) asymmetrical quantization. The asymmetry in (b) is related to a constant difference between positive and negative steps δ_+ and δ_-:

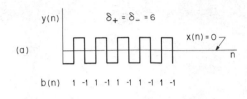

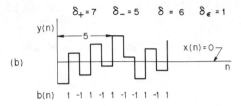

Figure 8.11 Idle-channel output patterns in (a) symmetrical and (b) asymmetrical quantization.

$$\delta_+ = \delta + \delta_\epsilon ; \qquad \delta_- = \delta - \delta_\epsilon \tag{8.41}$$

The characteristics of idle channel noise depend on the relative magnitudes of δ_ϵ and δ. These magnitudes control the periodicities of the sawtooth functions [Figure 8.11(b)] that characterize non-ideal DM tracking of a zero input. These sawtooth functions can generate objectionable idle channel noise components in the input frequency band.

The idle channel behavior of a DM coder with step size asymmetry is essentially equivalent to that of a symmetrical DM encoding an appropriate ramp input. Using this equivalence, one can quantify the nature of the idle channel noise spectrum [Iwersen, 1969] as follows.

Since the idle channel signal is periodic, it can be represented by a Fourier series, and the idle channel spectrum will then be a line spectrum. The discrete lines f_ℓ in the idle channel spectrum are given by

$$f_\ell = Q\left[\frac{\ell}{2}\left(1 - \frac{\delta_\epsilon}{\delta}\right)\right] f_s ; \qquad Q[\alpha] = |\alpha - n(\alpha)| \tag{8.42}$$

where $n(\alpha)$ is the integer nearest to α. The mean square value (noise power) associated with a frequency line f_ℓ is

$$\sigma_\ell^2 = 2\delta^2/\pi^2\ell^2 \sim \delta^2/5\ell^2 \tag{8.43}$$

Compare the above result with the frequency-independent $\Delta^2/4$ result mentioned for PCM (Chapter 5). As ℓ increases, the variance in (8.43) decreases; but this does *not* imply a monotonic behavior with frequency. For example, although the line f_1 has more power than lines corresponding to higher values of ℓ, the frequency f_1 may itself be a high or low frequency. If, as in Figure 8.11, the values of δ and δ_ϵ are 6 and 1 respectively, and $f_s = 50$ kHz, the values of $\ell = 1$ and, say, $\ell = 7$ imply:

$$f_1 = 20.8 \text{ kHz} \; ; \; \sigma_1^2 = 7.2 \qquad f_7 = 4.17\text{kHz} \; ; \; \sigma_7^2 = 0.14 \qquad (8.44)$$

The idle channel noise theory above can also be used to characterize the behavior of other coding systems such as PCM or multi-bit DPCM which suffer from quantizer asymmetry, as defined by minimum step size parameters that correspond to δ_+, δ_-, δ and δ_ϵ.

8.3 Double Integration, Second-Order Prediction and ΣDM

Double Integration (DM-DI). The basic principle of *double* integration DM (DM-DI) is to encode the input waveform using a difference signal $d(n)$ that follows the second derivative rather than the first derivative, as in single integration (DM-SI). This is done by cascading two single integrators in the decoding networks (Figure 8.12a) at both transmitter and receiver. Transmitted bits in DM-DI indicate changes in slope rather than actual values thereof. We shall comment presently on the additional gain loop in the coder part of Figure 8.12(a) and the gain factor G_0 in that loop; and on the close similarity between DM-DI with a non-zero gain factor G_0 and DM with a second-order predictor (DM-P2) [see Figure 8.12(b)]. The coder with $G_0 > 0$ will also be called a *mixed integration* system (DM-MI). The coder with $G_0 = 0$ will be called a *pure double integration* system. In both cases, we will be talking about *ideal* and *non-ideal* double integration networks, depending on whether constants A_1 and A_2, to be defined presently, are equal to 1 or less than 1.

Figure 8.13 provides a simple comparison of DM-SI and DM-DI with *ideal* double integration in the feedback network. The output of the DM-SI decoder in

Figure 8.12 Block diagram of DM systems with (a) double-integration (DM-DI) and (b) second-order prediction (DM-P2). In (a), the case of $G_0 = 0$ provides pure double integration. When $G_0 > 0$, the feedback network in (a) is characterized as mixed integration. In this case, the DM coder (DM-MI) will also have a non-trivial DM-P2 equivalent.

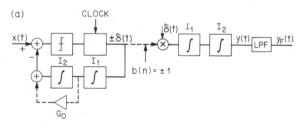

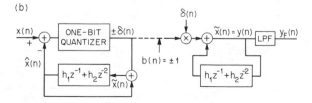

Figure 8.13(b) is the usual staircase output with step size δ. The output of the ideal DI decoder in Figure 8.13(c) is the integral of the staircase function; it is therefore a sequence of ramps. With a decoder input of like bits, as in the present example, the smooth version of the DM-SI output is a linear segment, while a smooth version of the DM-DI output is a parabolic segment. Note therefore that the DM-DI system can track an input waveform much faster than a DM-SI system, signifying lesser slope overload; equivalently, for a given slope capability, the DM-DI system can have a smaller minimum step size (signifying lower granular noise).

The fast-responding DM-DI just described has a tendency to be unstable [Nielsen, 1971] [Steele, 1975]. This is inherent in the parabolic approximations to input waveform segments, unlike the linear segments of DM-SI. Chapter 9 will discuss a tree coding approach to the stabilization of a DM-DI coder [Cutler, 1971]. A simpler stabilization procedure consists in a compromise or *mixed* type of integration in the feedback loop of the DM coder, resulting in a DM-MI coder. The effect of this kind of integration is typified by the dashed-line characteristic in Figure 8.13(c). The property of mixed integration is provided by the additional loop with gain G_0, shown by dashed lines in the *encoder* of Figure 8.12(a). Note that the DM-MI *decoder* is still a pure double integrator. The stabilizing influence of $G_0 > 0$ is illustrated by the qualitative comparison of waveforms (b) and (c) in Figure 8.14. As the DM coder attempts to track the input waveform, the

Figure 8.13 Response of (b) DM-SI and (c) ideal DM-DI decoders to a sequence (a) of four like bits. The step size is $\delta = 1$ [Steele, 1975. Reprinted with permission].

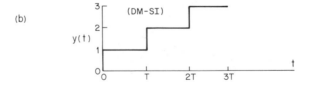

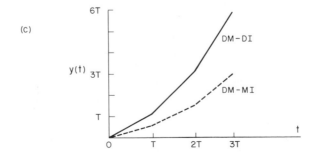

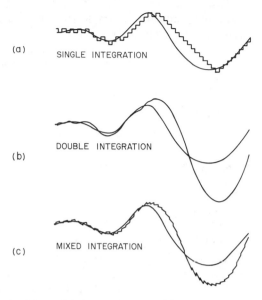

(a) SINGLE INTEGRATION

(b) DOUBLE INTEGRATION

(c) MIXED INTEGRATION

Figure 8.14 Waveforms in deltamodulation systems with (a) single integration; (b) double integration; and (c) mixed integration [Schindler;©1970, IEEE].

overshoots in the mixed-integration output waveform of (c) tend to be smaller than those in the double integration waveform (b). The stabilizing influence of a given value of $G_0 > 0$ can also be discussed quantitatively [Steele, 1975]. The example of $G_0 = 1$ will be discussed presently.

The following analysis refers to a time-discrete version of DM systems with double and mixed integration, and it will enable comparisons with DM-P2. Let us consider the transfer function $H_{DEC}(z)$ of the decoder. As in the prediction theory of Chapter 6, an optimal decoder is one with a decoder function $|H_{DEC}(e^{j\omega})|^2$ that resembles the input psd. The transfer function of the discrete-time equivalent of the pure DI decoder network is that of a tandem of two single-integrator networks:

$$H_{DEC}(z)|_{DI} = [Y(z)/U(z)]_{DI} = [(1-A_1z^{-1})(1-A_2z^{-1})]^{-1} , \qquad (8.45a)$$

where $Y(z)$ and $U(z)$ are the z- transforms of the sequences $y(n)$ and $b(n)\delta(n)$, and A_1 and A_2 are the component single-integrator constants. The decoder transfer function of the second-order prediction system DM-P2 is

$$H_{DEC}(z)|_{P2} = [Y(z)/U(z)]_{P2} = [1-(h_1z^{-1}+h_2z^{-2})]^{-1} = 1/[1-H(z)] \quad (8.45b)$$

Clearly, (8.45a) and (8.45b) are equivalent if

$$h_1 = A_1 + A_2 ; \qquad h_2 = - A_1A_2 \qquad (8.46)$$

It is instructive to note the special example of ideal double integration:

$$A_1 = 1, A_2 = 1 ; \qquad h_1 = 2, h_2 = -1 \qquad (8.47a)$$

Recall that this choice indicates a simple straight-line extrapolation in the decoder operation. The difference equation implied by (8.47a) is

$$y(n) = h_1 \, y(n-1) + h_2 \, y(n-2) + \delta(n) \, b(n) \qquad (8.47b)$$

This is precisely the difference equation implied in the waveform plot of Figure 8.13(c). Using the notion of

$$z = \exp(j\omega) = \exp(j2\pi f/f_s) \qquad (8.48)$$

one sees from (8.47a) that ideal DI has *two poles*, at frequencies f_1 and f_2, defined by

$$z_1 = A_1 = 1 \, ; \qquad z_2 = A_2 = 1 \, ; \qquad f_1 = f_2 = 0 \qquad (8.49)$$

The decoder networks in double integration and mixed integration systems are identical. Differences in the two systems, as provided by the parameter G_0 in Figure 8.12(a), can be seen by considering the transfer function of the feedback network $H_{FDBK}(z) = \hat{X}(z)/U(z)$ in the DM coders (Problems 8.18 and 8.19):

$$H_{FDBK}(z)|_{DI} = [(1-A_1 z^{-1})(1-A_2 z^{-1})]^{-1} , \qquad (8.50a)$$

which is identical to $H_{DEC}(z)|_{DI}$, and

$$H_{FDBK}(z)|_{MI} = [(1-A_1 z^{-1})(1-A_2 z^{-1})]^{-1}[1+G_0-G_0 A_2 z^{-1}] \qquad (8.50b)$$

Clearly the above transfer functions are identical when $G_0 = 0$. The corresponding transfer function in DM-P2 is

$$H_{FDBK}(z)|_{P2} = H(z)[1-H(z)]^{-1} = [1-h_1 z^{-1}-h_2 z^{-2}]^{-1}[h_1 z^{-1}+h_2 z^{-2}] \quad (8.50c)$$

For the special case of ideal double integration decoding (8.47a), note that

$$H_{FDBK}(z)|_{MI} = [(1-z^{-1})(1-z^{-1})]^{-1}[1+G_0-G_0 z^{-1}] \qquad (8.51a)$$

$$H_{FDBK}(z)|_{P2} = [(1-2z^{-1}+z^{-2})]^{-1}[2z^{-1}-z^{-2}] \qquad (8.51b)$$

If $G_0 = 1$, (8.51a) and (8.51b) are equivalent, correct to a delay factor z^{-1}. Similarly, (8.50b) and (8.50c) will be equivalent for appropriate settings of network parameters. On the other hand, the feedback transfer function in DM-DI is always different in that it lacks a numerator term, similar to the right-hand square-bracket terms of (8.51). The effect of the above difference is best seen in the magnitude-squared response $|H_{FDBK}(e^{j\omega})|^2$.

Figure 8.15 shows the magnitude-squared transfer function of the feedback network in DM-MI, and it illustrates how the "3 dB break points" f_1 and f_2 (corresponding to the two poles in earlier discussion) can be selected (by proper choices of A_1 and A_2) to provide a transfer function (coder overload characteristic) that can match the long-term spectrum of speech [Greefkes and Riemens, 1970]

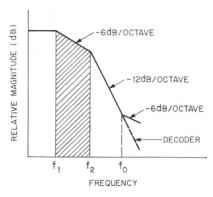

Figure 8.15 Transfer functions of the feedback network in DM-MI and DM-P2, with $A_1 \rightarrow 1$ and $A_2 \rightarrow 1$. In speech coding, the shaded area in the figure is typically designed to correspond to the lower half of the speech frequency band. Transfer functions of the decoder network are identical except for the absence of the f_0 discontinuity, i.e., $f_0 = \infty$ in the decoder. With pure double integration (DM-DI), the feedback and decoder responses are identical, and $f_0 = \infty$ by definition.

[Schindler, 1974]. The corresponding transfer function for DM-P2, which follows that of the AR(2) process with coefficients h_1 and h_2 [see (2.112)], can also be designed to have corners corresponding to f_1 and f_2. In the degenerate case of ideal DI, f_1 and f_2 are both zero [see (8.49)].

The corner frequencies f_1 and f_2 in Figure 8.15 are points at which two stages of 6 dB/octave roll-off are introduced in the transfer function, resulting in a total 12 dB/octave roll-off after f_2. These roll-offs are due to the contributions of $(1-fz^{-1})$-type terms, with $f \rightarrow 1$, in the denominators of $H_{FDBK}(z)$ (Problem 8.21). The effect of a similar term in the numerators of (8.51a) and (8.51b) is to introduce a stage of 6 dB/octave *increase*, resulting in a final roll-off, after f_0 (Figure 8.15), at 6 dB/octave rather than 12 dB/octave. This results in an increase in high frequency response, as in the waveform of Figure 8.14(c). Note that with pure DI, $f_0 = \infty$. Note also that $f_0 = \infty$ in all versions of the decoder function $|H_{DEC}(e^{j\omega})|^2$.

There is an important difference between the transfer functions of feedback networks in DM-MI and DM-P2. In the latter, there are only two degrees of freedom; parameters h_1 and h_2 which determine the three frequencies f_1, f_2 and f_0 (Problems 8.22 and 8.23). In the former, there is a third parameter G_0 that can be used to design f_0 independently of f_1 and f_2.

In speech and image coding, the benefits of DM-DI and DM-P2 are related to the better tracking of high input slope segments, which includes waveform components of high frequency. However, for very low sampling frequencies, the nature of the input acf can be such that the benefits of higher order prediction are negligible. In fact, for a pure sine-wave, DM-DI or DM-P2 coders can lead to negative gains over DM-SI coding if the sampling rate f_s is small enough. The cross-over point f_{cr} for f_s, below which DM-SI performs better than DM-DI, can be predicted by *SNR* formulas for a *sine-wave* of frequency f [deJager, 1952]:

$$SNRF|_{DM-SI} = 0.068 f_s^3/(f^2 W) ; \quad SNRF|_{DM-DI} = .0005 f_s^5/[f^2 W(f^2+f_2^2)] \quad (8.52a)$$

$$SNRF|_{DM-SI} > SNRF|_{DM-DI} \quad \text{if} \quad f_s < f_{cr} = 11.5\sqrt{f^2+f_2^2} \qquad (8.52b)$$

W is the bandwidth over which the noise power is measured, and it is usually about 3.2 kHz, the bandwidth of telephone speech. If $f = 0.8$ kHz and $f_2 = 1.2$ kHz, $f_{cr} = 18.4$ kHz. In an experimental study [Tomozawa and Kaneko, 1968], f_{cr} was indeed found to be nearly 18 kHz for these values of f and f_2. This is shown in Figure 8.16. Note that the $SNRF$ characteristics increase at 9 dB per octave and 15 dB per octave, for DM-SI and DM-DI, respectively. The behavior of $SNRF$ in DM-DI, as a function of f_s, can also be predicted by the approximate statistical approaches of Example 8.5. Briefly, the SNR term will now have an f_s^4 behavior because of two stages of prediction gain. Both of these stages involve sine-wave inputs (the original sine-wave and its cosinusoidal acf, Problem 2.9), and consequently realize prediction gains proportional to f_s^2 in each case; this, in conjunction with the out-of-band noise rejection factor $F = f_s/(2W)$, leads to an overall f_s^5 law or *15 dB per octave* law for double integration.

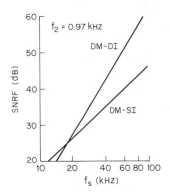

Figure 8.16 Comparison of DM-DI and DM-SI for a sine-wave input of frequency $f = 800$ Hz. The double-integration corner frequency (Figure 8.15) is $f_2 = 970$ Hz [Tomozawa and Kaneko;©1968, IEEE].

Nth Order DM. The DM coders discussed so far have certain basic limitations on the rate at which performance (SNR) increases with bit rate or sampling frequency f_s — for example, the 9- and 15 dB per octave limits for DM-SI and DM-DI. A method with a potential for further improving the SNR-versus-bit-rate behavior, without using multibit quantization, is N*th order DM* [Das and Chatterjee, 1967] [Chakravarthy and Faruqui, 1976]. This is one of the earliest examples of the explicit noise coding mentioned in Chapter 6, in the context of embedded coding. In the case of second-order behavior DM ($N = 2$), the quantization error signal from the first DM is filtered and encoded in a second DM. At the receiver, the decoded waveform from this second DM output is added to the decoded waveform from the first DM, in an attempt to provide a better approximation to the input being encoded. The procedure can be extended to any order; but there is usually an optimum value of N because, for a given total bit rate, increase of N implies a decrease in the bit rate at which the individual DM coders can operate, and hence a decrease in the SNR of the constituent DM coders (Problem 8.24).

Sigma Delta Modulation (ΣDM). Both DM-SI and DM-DI are suited for coding correlated waveforms with high values of adjacent sample correlation ρ_1, such as speech and image inputs which have psd functions resembling the integrated power spectrum. Voiceband data waveforms, on the other hand, do not exhibit the type of adjacent-sample correlations characteristic of integrated power spectra and this is directly reflected in corresponding values of quantization noise in the DM coding of data signals. The raised-cosine spectrum in Figure 2.23 is an example of a data signal spectrum. Other data waveforms also have spectra confined to the speech band, but located in different parts of this band with different shapes [O'Neal, 1974].

One way of adapting DM to encode such inputs is simply to integrate the input prior to DM coding. This pre-emphasizes the low frequencies in the input and increases adjacent sample correlations; the increase in ρ_1, for example, improves DM performance as given by a $(1-\rho_1^2)$ term for error variance, as in (8.15).

The procedure also simplifies DM decoding. The inverse signal emphasis (differentiation) at the receiver cancels with the conventional integration in DM-SI decoding, resulting in a decoder that is simply a lowpass (or bandpass) filter [Figure 8.17(a)].

The above arrangement is called *Delta Sigma Modulation*, or more precisely, *Sigma Deltamodulation* (ΣDM) [Inose, Yasuda and Marakami, 1962]. Further, the two integrators I_1 and I_2 in Figure 8.17 can be combined (in view of the linear operations involved), into a single integrator I_3 placed after the comparator, as in Figure 8.17(b). This version, besides being simpler, provides an interesting interpretation of ΣDM as being a "smoothed version" of one-bit PCM. The PCM interpretation relates to a lack of non-trivial prediction in the feedback network; and the smoothing refers to the integration of the comparator output prior to quantization. Such coding is appropriate to inputs that include segments with small values of adjacent sample correlation ρ_1; and as with nondifferential PCM, the overload characteristic (noise performance) of the coder is *frequency-independent* (Problem 8.25). This property of ΣDM makes it an ideal device for A/D conversion [Agrawal and Shenoi, 1983] (Appendix G).

Figure 8.17 Delta-sigma modulation or sigma DM (ΣDM).

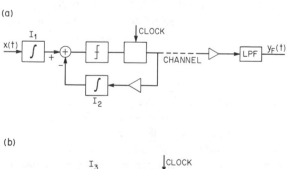

The benefits of the prefilter in Figure 8.17(a) are related to the processes of oversampling and subsequent rejection of out-of-band noise. Analyses in Chapter 7 will show that there is no advantage to be gained by prefiltering in a DPCM system with Nyquist sampling.

8.4 Adaptive Deltamodulation (ADM)

To deltamodulate speech and image waveforms at bit rates that are competitive with those of practical PCM and DPCM techniques, one needs to employ variable step size quantization. In speech coding, it is useful to distinguish between step size variations that are *instantaneous* [say, average step size change of one to several dB in the duration of one waveform sample, as in the ADM example of Figure 8.5(b)], or *syllabic* (say, a fraction of a dB change in one sample) [Kikkert, 1974] [Steele, 1975]. The benefits of instantaneous companding are versatility (for example, see [Jayant, 1973]) and suitability to signal-processing and digital code conversion applications (such as PCM-DM conversions) — contexts in which the DM encoder is expected to respond readily to instantaneous input variations; also, ADM coders for image coding are necessarily of the instantaneous type, in view of the abrupt variations that can occur in typical video material. Instantaneous ADM coders for image inputs have in fact been characterized as "edge-adaptive" coders [Jayant, 1976]. Syllabic adaptation is more appropriate for encoding speech waveforms which are characterized by relatively slowly varying envelopes. Properly designed instantaneous ADM coders can also track speech waveform variations quite smoothly; however, practical DM coders for speech are of the syllabic type because slowly adaptive algorithms are more robust in the context of transmission errors (Section 8.5). The instantaneous and syllabic coders to be discussed in Sections 8.4.1 and 8.4.2 are DM-AQB designs, implying adaptive quantization based on backward estimation using quantizer outputs. ADM systems that use *hybrid* adaptation logics, or combinations of instantaneous and syllabic algorithms, combine the fast response of instantaneous algorithms with the transmission error robustness of syllabic algorithms. Section 8.4.3 discusses one such hybrid system. Examples of DM-AQF are noted in Section 8.4.4. In these cases, the step size is computed using forward estimation based on buffered input samples.

Figure 8.18 defines DM-AQB and DM-AQF for both analog and discrete-time implementations. Single integration has been used, for purposes of illustration. The coders are therefore identical to those in Figure 8.1 except for the AQB and AQF components.

ADM systems can also be based on adapting parameters other than step size — for example, adapting output filter bandwidths or sampling rates to follow local bandwidths in speech [Smith and Allen, 1981] [Jayant, 1981] [Un and Cho, 1982], or switching to different sets of predicting pixels in image coding, to follow the changing nature of image material. The principles of these adaptive coders have already been mentioned in Chapter 6. Chapter 10 has an example of another kind of adaptation, deltamodulation with an instantaneously adaptive sampling rate. In the literature, ADM almost invariably stands for DM-AQ, as discussed earlier. This is also the meaning associated with ADM in the rest of this chapter.

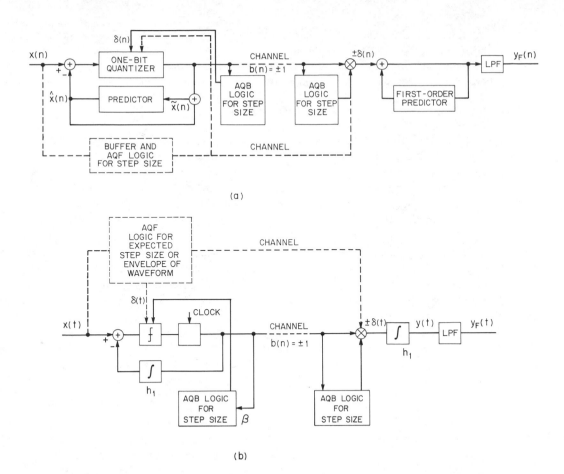

Figure 8.18 Block diagrams of ADM using AQB or AQF logics for step-size adaptations: (a) discrete-time implementation; and (b) "analog" implementation.

8.4.1 DM-AQB with Instantaneous Companding

In multibit quantization, output words carry both polarity and magnitude information explicitly. For this reason, the knowledge of only one codeword, that corresponding to the latest quantizer output, is adequate to provide overload and underload cues for AQB logics (Section 4.10.3). In one-bit quantization on the other hand, the (one-bit) codeword has only polarity information in explicit form; and overload and underload cues are provided by the occurrence, in recent quantizer output, of clusters of like and unlike bits. This was shown schematically in Figure 8.5(a) where the transmitted code sequence was a cluster of five *one*'s during slope overload. In DM-AQB, this clustering is used as a cue for increasing the DM step size, as in Figure 8.5(b).

The rest of this section will illustrate the above principle using several examples. Differences between algorithms are in terms of quantizer output memory used for adaptive cues, and recommended step size multipliers or increments. Some of the examples will also be input-specific, and matched specially to speech or image statistics. In the absence of channel errors, step size increases and decreases at coder and decoder will be synchronous.

Practical implementations of ADM algorithms presuppose appropriate constraints on maximum and minimum step size, as in Section 4.10:

$$\delta_{min} \leqslant \delta(n) \leqslant \delta_{max} \qquad (8.53a)$$

Certain types of adaptation processes also require an initial, or starting step size δ_{start}. This can be set to an arbitrary value in general. In speech coding, assuming that speech activity is preceded by silence, a more meaningful setting is $\delta_{start} = \delta_{min}$. Criteria for designing the limits in (8.53) are similar to those given in Chapter 4. The value of δ_{max} controls the amount of slope overload distortion, while the value of δ_{min} controls the amount of idle channel noise. A useful value of the ratio $\delta_{max}/\delta_{min}$ is in the order of 100 or 128 (a power of 2) for DM coding of nonstationary speech. The step size that is matched to a locally stationary segment of speech can be estimated using the expression for δ_{opt} in (8.28). In particular, the value of δ_{max} in (8.53) should be close to the value of δ_{opt} that is adequate to control the slope overload distortion in speech segments of maximum variance (Figure 8.27). Smaller values of $\delta_{max}/\delta_{min}$ are appropriate in the context of transmission errors, and/or in the coding of data signals or image inputs.

In the most general adaptation logic with an m-bit memory, step size $\delta(n)$ will be a function of the present bit $b(n)$, m preceding bits, and another step size δ', which is either the *minimum* step size δ_{min} or the *previous* step size $\delta(n-1)$:

$$\delta(n) = f[b(n), b(n-1),...,b(n-m), \delta'] \qquad (8.53b)$$

We recall that $b(n)$ also determines the sign of the step for sample n. A more useful form of the above logic is one that is based on the notion of a *step size multiplier* $M(n)$ that depends on the m preceding bits in the logic memory:

$$\delta(n) = M(n) \delta' \qquad (8.53c)$$

Depending on the allowed values of the multipliers, the step sizes changes during sustained increases or decreases can be either *linear* or *exponential*, or any other *arbitrary* function. If δ' is chosen to be the previous step size $\delta(n-1)$ [Winkler, 1963] [Jayant, 1970], a fairly small number of multipliers (sometimes as small as 2) can be sufficient to generate an adequate dictionary of $\delta(n)$ values. Also, in this case, sustained step size changes in a given direction will be strictly *exponential*.

It is appropriate to comment on the use of the most recent bit $b(n)$ in (8.53b). Note that this kind of information is not used in the one-word memory algorithm of Section 4.10. This is because that algorithm was designed for a multibit quantizer. The level information available in the output of such a quantizer is a powerful cue for step-size adaptation, although the information is that corresponding to the level of the *previous* sample, as in the $H(n-1)$ term of (4.185b). The non-availability of explicit level information in the one-bit quantizer makes the use of the *most recent* polarity $b(n)$ very valuable in ADM. The use of $b(n)$ for the coding of sample $x(n)$ also means that the quantization is really carried out in two steps. The first involves the determination of $b(n)$ as in (8.4), and the second is the application of this value in (8.53b) to determine $\delta(n)$ for the quantization itself. For simplicity, the block diagram of DM-AQB does not explicitly indicate these two separate processes. In some specific ADM designs, the most recent bit utilized for adaptation is $b(n-1)$, rather than $b(n)$ [Scheinberg and Schilling, 1976].

The following examples of ADM algorithms have been variously motivated by either speech coding of image coding; some of the algorithms are non-signal-specific, as indicated in respective discussions.

Example 8.6. High Information deltamodulation (HIDM)

This exponential adaptation algorithm [Winkler, 1963] is characterized by a step size control which multiplies the step size in each sampling period by a factor of 2, 1 or 0.5. Specifically, if the current time instant is n, and the step size multiplier is M, the adaptation rule is defined by

$$\delta(n) = M(n)\ \delta(n-1)\ ;$$

$$M(n) = \begin{cases} 2.0 \ \text{ if } b(n) = b(n-1) = b(n-2) \\ 0.5 \text{ if } b(n) \neq b(n-1) \\ 1.0 \text{ otherwise} \end{cases} \tag{8.54}$$

The fact that step sizes are powers of 2 is very useful from an implementation viewpoint in transmission applications, as well as in code conversion [Eggermont, 1975].

The HIDM algorithm can be characterized as ADM with a 2-bit memory, where the term 'memory' refers to the explicit utilization of the two bits $b(n-1)$ and $b(n-2)$ in (8.54). The implicit memory is of course infinite because of the $\delta(n-1)$ term in the adaptation logic. The algorithm also belongs in the class of so-called "constant factor" ADM logics, because the adaptations can be characterized in terms of the constant factors or values 2, 1 and 0.5, which the step size multiplier M assumes. ●

Example 8.7. An edge-adaptive algorithm for image inputs

An instantaneous adaptation logic that is well tailored to image material is one that returns the step size immediately to its minimum value δ_{min} upon the completion of an edge-encoding process [Bosworth and Candy, 1969]. A step size sequence with this property is

$$\{\delta(n)\} = \{1,1,2,3,5...,5,-1\}\delta_{min} \tag{8.55}$$

Notice that (8.55) not only lists the step size dictionary, but also shows the order in which the allowed step sizes are used in the adaptation process. Notice also the return to minimum step size when the polarity of the step is reversed (in this case, to $-\delta_{min}$) for the first time after a bit-cluster (in this case, of positive bits). The above step size sequence exhibits two desirable properties. First, no step size in the sequence exceeds the accumulated sum of previous step sizes, which guarantees a damping property to be discussed presently. Second, the sequence corresponds closely to a subjectively optimized sequence

$$\{\delta(n)\}_{opt} = \{1,1,2,3.6,4.7,...\}\delta_{min} \tag{8.56}$$

Each positive term in the curly braces in (8.55) is less than or equal to the sum of all

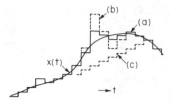

Figure 8.19 Comparison of DM waveforms with (a) critically damped, (b) underdamped and (c) overdamped (nonadaptive) step size [Steele, 1975. Reprinted with permission].

previous positive terms. Thus, as the step size grows in response to a cluster of like bits, the gradient in the step size evolution is bounded by the latest value of the step size. This implies that the step size growth is less than exponential. This adaptation algorithm is *critically damped* (Problem 8.26) as compared with the *underdamped* HIDM logic which has very abrupt step size changes, and the *overdamped* LDM logic, characterized by a complete absence of step size control. These comparisons are graphically brought out in Figure 8.19. In a 6.3 Mb/s ADM system based on (8.55) and an input bandwidth of $W = 1$ MHz, values of *equivalent SNR* (Appendix E) are in the order of 50 dB when ADM outputs are compared with images containing various extents of additive Gaussian noise with an integrated power spectrum (2.152) and corner frequency $f_c = 0.6$ MHz. •

Example 8.8. Constant-factor ADM (CFDM) with a one-bit memory

This is a minimally complex exponential logic which is also non-signal-specific [Jayant, 1970]:

$$\delta(n) = \begin{cases} M_1\delta(n-1) & \text{if} \quad b(n) = b(n-1) \\ M_2\delta(n-1) & \text{if} \quad b(n) \neq b(n-1) \end{cases} \tag{8.57}$$

A simple version of (8.57) has been found to be well-matched to typical speech and image inputs alike, over a wide range of sampling frequencies:

$$M_1 = M_2^{-1} = M \; ; \qquad M_{opt} = 1.5 \tag{8.58}$$

The use of $M = 1.2$ results in slightly smaller *SNR* values, but it is often perceptually better, owing to a decrease in the granular noise component of quantization noise. There also exists a theoretically predictable upper bound of $M_{opt} < 2$ for stability. In speech coding at bit rates of 20 to 60 kb/s, the ADM system in (8.58) realizes 5 to 10 dB *SNR* gains over optimum LDM, the case of $M = 1$.

One of the characteristics of this CFDM logic is a four-step *hunting* (or, oscillating) pattern while tracking some step inputs. This is a special case of a general result whereby a logic defined by $M_1^K M_2 = 1$, where K is an integer, produces a $(2K+2)$-step hunting pattern [Boyce, 1976]. These hunting patterns disappear in CFDM coders with an m-bit memory if $m > 1$.

As in multi-bit quantization, the reciprocal constraint (8.58) can be regarded as a special case of

$$M_1^{P_0} \cdot M_2^{1-P_0} = 1 \tag{8.59}$$

where P_0, the probability of overload $[b(n) = b(n-1)]$, or the probability of using multiplier M_1, is equal to 0.5. The probability of overload is indeed approximately 0.5 in at

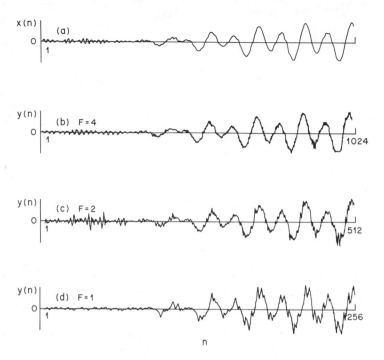

Figure 8.20 Adaptive deltamodulation of a speech waveform using the one-bit memory algorithm and $h_1 = 1$. (a) Input waveform (from Figure 1.4a), and (b)(c)(d) unfiltered outputs with $F = 4$, 2 and 1. The ratio of maximum to minimum step size is 128 in each case, but respective values of δ_{min} are 1, 2 and 16. The maximum magnitude of the input speech is $|x|_{max} = 2048$ [Jayant, 1982].

least one mathematically tractable situation, the steady-state DM encoding of a stationary Gaussian input [Jayant, 1978,I]. This is in sharp contrast to adaptive multi-bit quantization where the probabilities associated with different step size multipliers are clearly unequal. (Recall from Chapter 4 the 2:1 ratio of these probabilities in adaptive 2-bit quantization, corresponding to a 2:1 ratio for the probabilities that a stationary Gaussian input is in the outer or inner slots of a 4-level Max-quantizer).

Figure 8.20 illustrates the performance of (8.58) with the speech input of Figure 1.4, for F values of 4, 2 and 1. Corresponding sampling rates are 32, 16 and 8 kHz. The output waveforms in Figure 8.20 are unfiltered outputs $y(n)$. These waveforms exhibit the exponential adaptations due to (8.57). ●

Example 8.9.   Constant-factor ADM (CFDM) with a 2-bit memory

With a 2-bit memory logic [Kyaw and Steele, 1973], one can associate four multipliers M_1, M_2, M_3 and M_4. Table 8.2 shows a set of four multipliers, each of which is appropriate to a state described in column 4 of the table. If the first two states are merged into one, the remaining three states correspond exactly to the conditions in (8.54). If the last two states of Table 8.2 are also merged, the two states that remain correspond exactly to the conditions in (8.57).

The multiplier 0.4 in Table 8.2 provides the feature of overshoot suppression after sign reversal, as in Example 8.7. The ADM algorithm with a 2-bit memory therefore exhibits a rapidly converging step-input response (Problem 8.27). This is also seen in the coding of the waveform in Figure 8.21. However, increase of bit memory leads only to small *SNRF*

Table 8.2 Step-size multipliers for Constant-factor ADM with a two-bit memory [Steele, 1975. Reprinted with permission].

$b(n)$	$b(n-1)$	$b(n-2)$	State Description	Step size Multiplier $\delta(n)/\delta(n-1)$
-1	1	-1	Alternate	
1	-1	1	Polarity	0.9
-1	1	1	Sign	
1	-1	-1	Reversal	0.4
-1	-1	1	Semi-	
1	1	-1	Overload	1.5
-1	-1	-1		
1	1	1	Overload	2.0

differences in the coding of a waveform such as that in Figure 8.21. This is shown in the $SNRF$ comparisons of Figure 8.22 which refer to a bandlimited white input ($W = 3.2$ kHz) and the step size multipliers of Table 8.2. Notice that the unimodal SNR characteristic (a) for LDM is a direct reflection of the unimodal σ_r^2 characteristic in Figure 8.10. Differences between the dynamic range curves (b) and (c) are clearly negligible in comparison with differences from the LDM characteristic. Increase of quantizer memory is expected to be more beneficial with correlated inputs, although benefits are expected to cease when the quantizer memory exceeds the oversampling ratio F [Bello, Lincoln and Gish 1967].

As the length of memory used in step size adaptation increases, the determination of optimal multipliers becomes more difficult. Recommended values usually refer to results of experimentation with specific input material. With unknown inputs, best multipliers will need to be determined in a learning phase prior to subsequent coding, or in a continuous fashion; depending on whether the input is expected to be stationary or not [Castellino and Scagliola, 1977]. ●

Figure 8.21 Waveform tracking in (a) LDM and constant-factor ADM (CFDM) logics with (b) one-bit memory and (c) two-bit memory [Kyaw and Steele, 1973] [Steele, 1975. Reprinted with permission].

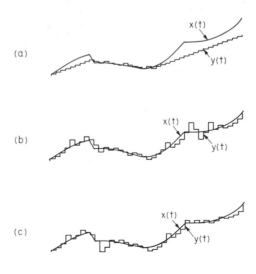

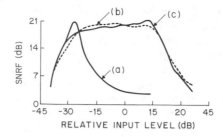

Figure 8.22 *SNRF* comparisons of (a) LDM and constant-factor ADM (CFDM) with (b) one-bit memory and (c) 2-bit memory, for a bandlimited white input ($W = 3.1$ kHz) and $f_s = 40$ kHz. In the ADM systems, $\delta_{max}/\delta_{min} = 167$ [Kyaw and Steele, 1973] [Steele, 1975. Reprinted with permission].

Example 8.10.   The Song deltamodulator

The step size logic [Song, Garodnick and Schilling, 1971] [Lei, Scheinberg and Schilling, 1977] is

$$\delta(n) = \delta_{min} \quad \text{if} \quad \delta(n-1) < \delta_{min} \tag{8.60a}$$

$$\delta(n) = \delta(n-1)\,|b(n) + b(n-1)/2| \quad \text{if} \quad \delta(n-1) \geqslant \delta_{min} \tag{8.60b}$$

Figure 8.23 ADM coding of a 3.75 MHz bandwidth image with the Song DM: (a) 10-bit PCM original, the coder input; (b) ADM output with $f_s = 15$ MHz; (c) reconstruction noise in (b); and (d) ADM output with $f_s = 7.5$ MHz [Lei, Scheinberg and Schilling;©1977, IEEE].

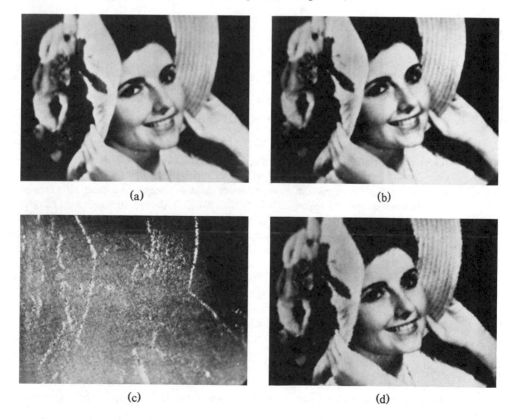

(a)

(b)

(c)

(d)

It can be seen that when step sizes exceed δ_{min}, the multipliers resulting from (8.60b) are similar to those from the one-bit memory logic (8.57) in Example 8.8. The multiplier magnitudes in (8.60b) are 1.5 and 0.5, while those in (8.58) are 1.5 and $1.5^{-1} = 0.666$. However, as mentioned earlier, the most recent bit utilized in (8.57) and (8.58) is $b(n)$, while the latest information used in (8.60) is that provided by $b(n-1)$. In any case, as in (8.58), (8.60) is not very signal-specific, and applications have been found both in speech and image coding. Figure 8.23 shows the results of using (8.60) in the ADM coding of a 3.75 MHz image with $F = 2$ ($f_s = 15$ MHz) and $F = 1$ ($f_s = 7.5$ MHz). The figure also shows how most of the reconstruction noise occurs in the edge-coding process. •

Example 8.11. The (J, K, L) algorithm

The utility of a simple one-bit memory logic suggests that although a longer memory may be desirable for reasons such as better step-response, an m-bit memory logic need not necessarily use 2^m distinct multipliers. Of special interest are the cases where m may be 2 or 3, but the number of distinct multipliers is limited to 2 for simplicity. A useful general model for such logics is the (J,K,L) algorithm [Jayant, 1976] [Noll, 1976]:

$$\delta(n) = \begin{cases} M_1\, \delta(n-1) & \text{if} \quad \alpha(n) = 1 \\ M_2\, \delta(n-1) & \text{if} \quad \alpha(n) = 0 \end{cases} \tag{8.61}$$

where $\alpha(n) = 1$ for L samples if K of the latest J bits are equal in sign, and $\alpha(n) = 0$ otherwise:

$$\alpha(n) = \begin{cases} 1 \;\; \text{for } L \text{ samples} & \text{if } \left| \sum_{j=0}^{J-1} b(n-j) \right| \geqslant 2K-J \\ 0 & \text{otherwise} \end{cases} \tag{8.62}$$

In the special case of $J = K$, the coincidence of $2K-K = K$ bits in (8.62) is simply detectable by the state of a logical function

$$[b(n) \cdot b(n-1) \cdot \;\; ... \;\; \cdot b(n-K+1)] \; \oplus \; [\overline{b(n)} \cdot \overline{b(n-1)} \cdot \;\; ... \;\; \cdot \overline{b(n-K+1)}]$$

A $(2,2,1)$ logic is a constant-factor one-bit memory scheme. The $(2,2,2)$ logic provides faster responses; the use of $L > 1$ implies that the step size increase state $\alpha(n) = 1$ is held over for an extra sample. This provides additional protection against overload and has been shown to provide a measurable performance gain in speech coding at bit rates of about 16 kb/s [Greefkes and Riemens, 1970] [Noll, 1976]. We shall discuss (J,K,L) algorithms at greater length for the case of syllabic adaptations.

Multiplier-based adaptations such as (8.57) and (8.61) provide *exponential* changes of step size. A useful generalization of (8.61) includes *linear* adaptations:

$$\delta(n) = \begin{cases} M_1\, \delta(n-1) + S_1 & \text{if} \quad \alpha(n) = 1 \\ M_2\, \delta(n-1) - S_2 & \text{if} \quad \alpha(n) = 0 \end{cases} \tag{8.63}$$

where S_1 and S_2 are appropriately chosen constant step sizes. Hybrid exponential and linear adaptations will be discussed again in the context of syllabic companding. •

Example 8.12. The space-shuttle (modified Abate) algorithm

This is a linear adaptation algorithm with a 7-bit memory, $\delta_{max} = 8\delta_{min}$, and instantaneous step size increases or decreases equal to 0 or δ_{min}. The algorithm [Auger et al., 1978] is defined in Table 8.3. Blank entries in the table represent bit values that are irrelevant to the choice of $\delta(n)$. The logic is a modified version of an earlier ADM algorithm [Abate, 1967]. The main modification is that in the present algorithm, the step size returns to the minimum value δ_{min} whenever the polarity is reversed (as also in the edge-adaptive image-coding system in Example 8.7). This feature eliminates limit cycles, and adds immunity to channel errors. Also contributing to the channel error resistance is the small step size ratio of $\delta_{max}/\delta_{min} = 8$, a value that is more than an order of magnitude smaller than the dynamic range of a speech signal. In spite of this, this ADM coder, while operating over noiseless channels, provides DRT scores (Appendix F) of 96.1, 93.5 and 89.8% at bit rates of 32, 24 and 16 kb/s respectively.

Table 8.3 Space Shuttle ADM Algorithm [Auger et al.;©1978, IEEE].

$b(n-7)$	$b(n-6)$	$b(n-5)$	$b(n-4)$	$b(n-3)$	$b(n-2)$	$b(n-1)$	$b(n)$	$\delta(n)/\delta_{min}$
1	1	1	1	1	1	1	1	8
−1	1	1	1	1	1	1	1	7
	−1	1	1	1	1	1	1	6
		−1	1	1	1	1	1	5
			−1	1	1	1	1	4
				−1	1	1	1	3
					−1	1	1	2
						−1	1	1
						1	−1	1
					1	−1	−1	2
				1	−1	−1	−1	3
			1	−1	−1	−1	−1	4
		1	−1	−1	−1	−1	−1	5
	1	−1	−1	−1	−1	−1	−1	6
1	−1	−1	−1	−1	−1	−1	−1	7
−1	−1	−1	−1	−1	−1	−1	−1	8

Implementation of Instantaneous ADM Algorithms. Many of the adaptation logics discussed so far imply a compact step size dictionary. In (8.55) for example, there are only 5 distinct step sizes. The more general examples allow a greater number of step sizes, but simplifications such as that in (8.58) $(M_1 = M_2^{-1})$ serve to make the step size dictionary very manageable [Schindler, 1970] [Cummiskey, 1975] [Steele, 1975]. In any case, a good assumption in implementation is that the number of needed step sizes be no more than a specified number, say 2^J, and to pick one of these for any given sample. This may be done, for example, using a J-bit up-down counter whose output addresses a ROM table or resistor bank. The input to the up-down counter would be the output of a step size logic using a memory of m bits, as stored in an m-bit buffer. Figure 8.24 shows such an implementation.

Figure 8.24 One approach to the implementation of instantaneous companding logics for ADM.

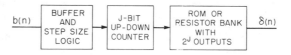

8.4.2 DM-AQB with Syllabic Companding

The adaptive algorithms used in many DM systems for speech coding adjust the step size magnitude at a rate much slower than the instantaneous variations in the speech signal. Typical adaptation rates (time constants) in such coders are in order of a pitch period (say, 5 to 10 ms). These "pitch-companded" algorithms are generally referred to as being *syllabically companded* (although a syllabic rate would strictly imply a period in the order of 100 ms or greater). The slowest of the syllabic algorithms are similar to locally stationary LDM schemes; and the success of these algorithms therefore hinges on an appropriate updating of the locally constant LDM step size. The rest of this section describes such adaptations to the locally stationary speech variance (or envelope), based on a memory of the quantizer output.

Continuous Deltamodulation. This was one of the earliest proposals for syllabic adaptation [Greefkes and deJager, 1968]. Step-size control is derived (both at the transmitter and receiver) in the AQB mode from the mean number of 1's in the bit stream. A 50:1 variation in δ is typically reflected by a variation in the proportion of 1's from about 1/3 to 1/2. The companding is rendered syllabic by a 100 Hz lowpass filter that operates on a signal that is proportional to the local mean number of 1's. The slow adaptation that characterizes this kind of companding has the effect of decreasing granular noise in the output speech, at the cost of a significant increase of slope overload distortion. This leads to a characteristic loss of "crispness" in syllabically companded speech in low bit rate DM systems. The slope overloading strategy, on the other hand, is a very useful means of providing a "clean-sounding" signal if one is constrained to operate at relatively low bit rates (say, below 24 kb/s) without significant increases of coder complexity.

Continuously Variable Slope Deltamodulation (CVSD). We next describe a class of syllabic algorithms with step-size changes that are based on observation times shorter than that in continuous DM, and therefore simpler to derive. The principle, which will be defined presently, has several variations. These differ in such issues as the time constants for step size adaptation and bit integration; the length of bit memory in the control logic; the ratio of maximum to minimum step size; the possible use of input signal shaping or slope clipping; and the possible use of Automatic Gain Control (in addition to the adaptation logic). These coders have been discussed in the literature as CVSD, or *Continuously Variable Slope Deltamodulation* systems. They are also known by the name *Digitally Controlled Deltamodulation* [Greefkes and Riemens, 1970].

A common characteristic of CVSD coders is that the cues for step size increase or decrease come out of observations on the most recent (3 or 4) DM bits; and the step size changes thus suggested are actuated with time constants in the order of 5 ms. Syllabic DM coding based on these principles can encode speech with 7-bit log-PCM (56 kb/s) quality at a DM bit rate of 40 kb/s; and the syllabic logic provides useful performance at bit rates as low as 16 kb/s [Greefkes and Riemens, 1970]. At lower bit rates, inferences based on bit patterns are rendered increasingly unreliable because of quantization noise feedback, and schemes using longer memory are recommended [such as continuous DM or AQF with a long block length (Section 8.4.4)]. The basic adaptation algorithm in CVSD can be expressed in a *linear adaptation* version of the (J,K,L) algorithm mentioned earlier in (8.61) and (8.62):

$$\delta(n) = \beta\,\delta(n-1) + \alpha(n)\,\delta_0\,;\qquad \beta = 1-\epsilon^2 \text{ with } \epsilon \to 0 \qquad (8.64a)$$

with $\alpha(n)$ following (8.62). The $\alpha(n) = 1$ condition (which signals a step size increase of δ_0) is signaled by the occurrence of at least K like bits (1's or -1's) in the most recent J bits. The holding of the $\alpha(n) = 1$ condition for L samples (irrespective of the state of the test sum for the next $L - 1$ samples) provides a supplementary means of overload protection. In the $\alpha(n) = 0$ state, the step size decreases at a rate given by β, but never below a positive minimum step size δ_{min}. When this step size is reached, the system degenerates to an LDM coder, until adaptations to an input cause the step size to increase again.

A specific but quite standard example of a CVSD coder is described in Figure 8.25(a). This system uses a (3,3,1) logic. A recommended value of δ_0 is $\delta_{min} = \delta_{max}/100$. The fact that such a resolution and step size range is adequate

Figure 8.25   CVSD using the (3, 3, 1) logic. (a) Decoder block diagram. (b) *SNRF* versus bit rate for sine-wave inputs. Numbers on curves show frequency of sinusoidal input with input level of -20 dBm0. The dashed line shows the performance of log-PCM [Dohrer, Metzger and Wimmer, 1979].

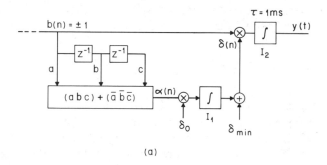

(a)

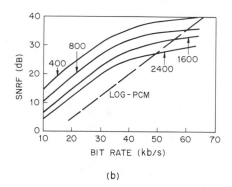

(b)

will be shortly demonstrated in the context of DM-AQF (Figure 8.27). Also, recall from Figure 4.46 that a step size ratio of 100 (or 40 dB) provides a dynamic range approaching 40 dB in coder performance. This value of 40 dB is also the dynamic range of one of the sentence-length speech signals in Figure 2.6. The performance of this CVSD coder will be described presently.

Adaptations described in (8.64a) are syllabic when the value of β is close to 1, and when the gain δ_0 (during step size increases) is typically a small fraction of the maximum value δ_{max}. If, on the other hand, δ_0 is sufficiently large, step size increases can be relatively rapid, and the result would be an adaptation logic that can be characterized as instantaneous for step sizes increases, and syllabic for step size decreases. Several such hybrid designs have been proposed for speech coding [Ahamed, 1978] [Steele, 1980]. In one proposal, for example, the instantaneous logic for step size increase is based on the Fibonacci sequence (1, 1, 2, 3, 5, 8, . . .) as in (8.55), and the decreases follow a syllabic exponential rule. In another hybrid approach, the adaptation follows two mutually exclusive rules, one providing fast changes in small step size regions, and the other providing slow changes in large step size regions [Chakravarthy and Faruqui, 1974]. The arrangement has perceptual advantages in speech coding especially in the context of transmission errors. Still another approach to hybrid companding is described in Section 8.4.3.

The CVSD logic (8.64a) implies a maximum step size (Problem 8.28):

$$\delta_{max} = \delta_0/(1-\beta) \tag{8.64b}$$

The constraint in (8.64b) can be avoided if the exponential decrease and linear increase of step size in (8.64a) are decoupled:

$$\delta(n) = \begin{cases} \beta\delta(n-1) & \text{if} \quad \alpha(n) = 0 \\ \delta(n) = \delta(n-1) + \delta_0 & \text{if} \quad \alpha(n) = 1 \end{cases} \tag{8.65}$$

Step-size waveforms in 16 kb/s ADM coding of a speech signal appear in Figure 8.26 for two values of β in (8.64a). The slower step size variation with $\beta = 0.995$ is more representative of a syllabically adaptive system. The rapid variations for $\beta = 0.9$ are quite similar, on the other hand, to the step size

Figure 8.26 Waveforms in syllabically companded DM based on a (3,3,1)-algorithm: (a) coder input $x(t)$; and waveforms of step size $\delta(t)$ with (b) $\beta = 0.9$ and (c) $\beta = .995$ [Noll, 1976].

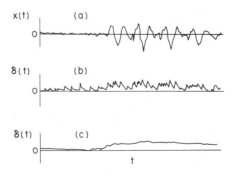

adaptations in an instantaneous scheme where the (J,K,L) configuration corresponds to $(2,2,2)$. The time-constants of step size decay corresponding to these values of β are 0.5 ms for $\beta = 0.9$ and 12 ms for $\beta = 0.995$ (Problem 8.29). The value of 0.5 ms is an untypical design for syllabic adaptations of step size. The time constant of the staircase function integrator, on the other hand, is usually in the order of 0.5 to 1.5 ms for sampling rates in the range of 8 to 32 kHz (Problem 8.20). Figure 8.18(b) has already shown the parts of the coder where the time constants implied by β and h_1 would be used. The step size logic in Figure 8.18(b) would of course be the (J,K,L) algorithm if that figure were to represent CVSD.

Example 8.13. CVSD coding of speech at 16 kb/s

A comparison of alternative CVSD designs for speech coding is afforded by Table 8.4. Results are for $f_s = 16$ kHz $(F = 2)$, $\beta = 0.995$ and single integration, with predictor coefficient $h_1 = 0.9$. The three columns show values of SNR, $SNRF$ and segmental $SNRF$. Note the importance of the $(3, 3, 1)$ and $(4, 4, 1)$ designs for maximizing SNR, as well as for maximizing the perceptually important parameter $SEGSNRF$. ●

Table 8.4 SNR comparisons of syllabic adaptation logics; $F = 2$, $h_1 = 0.9$ and $\beta = 0.995$ [Noll, 1976].

(J, K, L)	SNR (dB)	$SNRF$ (dB)	$SEGSNRF$ (dB)
2,2,1	7.0	12.3	10.7
3,3,1	8.5	12.8	13.1
4,4,1	9.1	12.6	13.4
5,5,1	8.9	12.4	12.3

The quality of speech digitized by 32 kb/s CVSD is very good, but less than toll quality. As seen already in Figure 5.14, attainment of a mean opinion score of 4.3 (the MOS score close to that of 64 kb/s log-PCM) requires an ADM bit rate in the order of 48 kb/s. The objective SNR at this bit rate would, however, be in the order of 26 dB (Figure 8.8), more than 10 dB below the 38 dB characteristic of 64 kb/s log-PCM. The attraction of ADM lies of course in the simplicity of a 1 bit/sample coding system, and the superior resistance of DM to bit errors on noisy channels (Figures 5.14 and 8.29).

CVSD Coding of Sinusoidal Signals. Figure 8.25(b) provides results on CVSD coding of sinusoidal signals using the $(3,3,1)$ algorithm and time constants of 4 ms and 1 ms for syllabic step size and staircase function integrators.

Figure 8.25(b) shows the $SNRF$ in the above CVSD algorithm as a function of bit rate. As in Figure 8.8, the 9 dB/octave improvement in $SNRF$ for DM-SI is contrasted with an exponential improvement for log-PCM (seen as a linear improvement on a dB scale). The crossover point is a decreasing function of input frequency. For a 2400 Hz input, the crossover point is about 50 kb/s, the crossover point for speech in Figure 8.8. In fact, the entire $SNRF$ versus bit rate characteristic for 2400 Hz in Figure 8.25(b) follows the characteristic for bandpass speech in Figure 8.8.

The *SNRF* value of 27 dB for the crossover mentioned above is very close to the analytical value that would result from using (8.33). Use of double integration in the above CVSD coder improves *SNRF* by 3 to 5 dB at 32 kb/s, as in Figure 8.16.

8.4.3 DM-AQB with Hybrid Companding

As indicated in previous sections, the primary motivation for syllabic companding is its resistance to transmission errors, a property that will be demonstrated in Section 8.5. In the absence of transmission errors, instantaneous algorithms perform extremely well, and in fact better than syllabic algorithms, at least from an *SNRF* viewpoint. Instantaneous algorithms are also less speech-specific, and examples in Section 8.4.1 have indeed referred to both speech and image coding.

Hybrid companding deltamodulation (HCDM) [Un and Lee, 1980] [Un, Lee and Song, 1981] includes both syllabic and instantaneous mechanisms for changing step size, to provide a combination of signal-tracking capability and transmission error robustness.

The basis for *syllabic* adaptation is provided by keeping track of a parameter the rms value $\sigma_{y'}$ of $y(n) - y(n-1)$, which is the first difference of the decoded signal. The parameter $\sigma_{y'}$ is obtained by measurements over a window in the order of 5 ms. The value is updated once for every 5 ms window and held constant for each such duration.

The basis for *instantaneous* adaptation is the two-bit memory HIDM scheme of Example 8.6, but with multiplier values $M(n) = 1,5, 0.66$ and 1.0, instead of those in (8.54).

The overall adaptation logic is defined by

$$\gamma(n) = M(n)\gamma(n-1) ; \qquad \delta_s = \alpha\sigma_{y'} ; \qquad \delta(n) = \delta_s\gamma(n) \qquad (8.66)$$

The components $\gamma(n)$ and δ_s respectively provide instantaneous and syllabic variations for the step size $\delta(n)$. The term α is a scaling constant with a recommended value of 0.8 for HCDM bit rates in the order of 16 and 24 kb/s.

Comparison of CFDM, CVSD and HCDM speech coders at 24 kb/s. The *SNRF* performance of 24 kb/s HCDM with 3.4 kHz speech inputs is shown in Figure 8.27 as a function of input level. The illustration includes characteristics for the instantaneous CFDM algorithm of (8.57) and (8.58), and the syllabic CVSD algorithm with a (3, 3, 1) logic. In this CVSD system, the 3-dB point in the transfer function of the step size integrator is 40 Hz. With 24 kHz sampling, this implies that $\beta = 0.985$ (Problem 8.22) and that the adaptation time constant is 3 ms (Problem 8.29). The staircase function integrators in the three systems are optimized separately, and the best values all correspond to a 3-dB point near 160 Hz. More exactly, the time-constants of these integrators (Problem 8.21) used are 1, 0.8, and 1.1 ms, respectively for CVSD, CFDM and HCDM. All adaptation

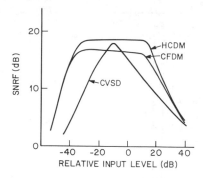

Figure 8.27 Comparison of instantaneous (CFDM), syllabic (CVSD) and hybrid (HCDM) adaptation algorithms for speech coding at 24 kb/s [Un, Lee and Song, 1981].

logics in Figure 8.27 have a step-size ratio of $\delta_{max}/\delta_{min} = 1000$. It is clear that both CFDM and HCDM have a much better dynamic range than CVSD. Further, the *SNRF* provided by the hybrid logic is always slightly better than that of the purely instantaneous algorithm. The gains over the instantaneous algorithm are much more dramatic with transmission error rates in the order of 10^{-3} or higher. At these error rates, both HCDM and CVSD are extremely robust; in fact, at least with an *SNRF* criterion, HCDM is again the better coder for all error rates [Un and Lee, 1980] [Un, Lee and Song, 1981].

8.4.4 Forward-Adaptive DM (DM-AQF)

Although less common than AQB logics in communication applications, DM-AQF coders have been discussed in several contexts: either to seek upper bounds in studies of ADM performance, or to provide explicit step size communication in practical applications where backward step-control is expected to be very unreliable because of excessive quantization or channel error effects.

DM-AQF with Periodic Adaptations. Periodic adaptations are perhaps less practical than the continuous adaptations to be discussed in the second half of this section. But a discussion of periodic adaptations provides an instructive link to the AQF theory of Chapter 4. As in the AQF systems of Chapter 4, DM-AQF (Figure 8.20) uses a buffer of N input samples to calculate the best step size for the (future) deltamodulation of that input block. The step size δ is recomputed exactly once, and explicitly transmitted to the receiver for every block of N samples.

As in Section 4.10.2, the criterion for step size computation can be the average absolute slope in the input, or the maximum or rms value thereof. A simple rule-of-thumb formula, appropriate to single-integration DM with bit rates in the range 16 to 32 kb/s [Jayant, 1975] is one based on the average absolute slope:

$$\delta = [4/(N-1)] \sum_{n=2}^{N} |x(n) - x(n-1)| \qquad (8.67)$$

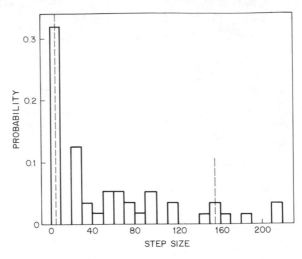

Figure 8.28 Histogram of step sizes in 24 kb/s DM-AQF. The maximum speech amplitude is given by $|x|_{max} = 2048$ [Jayant;©1975, AT&T].

A recommended buffer length is $N = 256$, which corresponds to 16 ms at 16 kb/s and 8 ms at 32 kb/s. This represents a compromise among considerations like encoding delay, the information rate in the step size transmitting channel, and the need to track the changing statistics of speech with an appropriate speed (say, a "syllabic" speed of 8 to 16 ms).

Figure 8.28 illustrates a histogram of step sizes that result from a utilization of (8.67) in a 24 kHz DM-AQF coder. It turns out that for a peak speech amplitude of $\pm$ 2048, the encoding is very tolerant to a minimum step size of 2, a maximum step size 157, and a step size resolution equal to about 5 bits — in other words, to a step size dictionary of only 32 steps (2,7,12,17, . . . ,157). Such finite resolution is desirable for implementation (Figure 8.24). It is also clearly critical for economies in step size transmission (Problem 4.32).

The maximum step size of about 200 in Figure 8.28 is indeed well matched to the input variance of high-level speech segments. This can be seen by assuming the simple Laplacian pdf for voiced speech to estimate σ_x from the nominal peak amplitude (2048 in this example), and by using this value of σ_x in the expression for δ_{opt} [see (8.28)].

DM-AQF with Continuous Adaptation. We conclude the discussion of ADM with a class of AQF coders which are not periodically adaptive. Rather, they are similar to the syllabic companded coders discussed earlier, except that the syllabic changes are no longer derived from the bit stream, but are explicitly transmitted. Such explicit transmissions can also be used as a supplementary means of step size control or step size protection in systems based on an AQB logic (for example, in a system with significant bit error rate p_e). When explicit transmissions are the only means of step size control, one may handle the step size waveform in a secondary low bit rate DM coder, and time-multiplex the primary (speech) and secondary (step size) DM bits. One example is the *two-channel DM* coder [Greefkes, 1973] for very low bit rate applications where syllabic AQB logics are rendered inefficient because of quantization error effects. With a 7.2 kb/s two-channel DM, appropriate bandwidths of the primary (speech) and secondary (speech slope envelope, or step size) channels are 2700 and 50 Hz respectively; and corresponding recommended bit rates are 6.8 and 0.4 kb/s, implying respective oversampling ratios of $F = 1.25$ and $F = 4$.

8.5 Transmission Error Effects

The total reconstruction noise variance in a DPCM system was shown in (6.125) to be

$$\sigma^2_{r,DPCM} = (\epsilon^2_q + \alpha\epsilon^2_c) \, G^{-1}_P \sigma^2_x \; ; \quad \epsilon^2_c = \xi p_e \qquad (8.68)$$

where the first and second terms refer to quantization noise and the reconstruction noise component due to a channel with random bit error probability p_e. The term α is the power transfer factor of the decoder loop, the value by which the channel error variance is changed by the network. The term ϵ^2_c is the channel error variance, and the channel coefficients ξ have been listed in Tables 4.11 and 4.12.

A *conservative* extension of (8.68) to oversampled DM is one that assumes that the channel noise spectrum, because of error propagation in the DM decoder, is lowpass; and that no noise rejection results due to output filtering. Rather, only the quantization noise gets reduced by the oversampling index F. As a result [Noll, 1976],

$$\sigma^2_{r,DM} = (\epsilon^2_q F^{-1} + \alpha\epsilon^2_c) \, G^{-1}_P \sigma^2_x \qquad (8.69a)$$

Expressions for α and G_P are given in (6.127) and (6.128) for a first-order predictor:

$$\alpha = (1-h^2_1)^{-1} \; ; \quad G_P = (1-2h_1\rho_1+h^2_1)^{-1} \; ; \quad \max\{G_P\} = (1-\rho^2_1)^{-1} \quad (8.69b)$$

If, in addition, the predictor is optimized for an error-free channel, $\alpha = \max\{G_P\}$ and the total channel error contribution will be $\epsilon^2_c\sigma^2_x$, that of PCM:

$$\sigma^2_{r,DM} = \epsilon^2_q\sigma^2_x/(F \max\{G_P\}) + \epsilon^2_c\sigma^2_x \qquad (8.69c)$$

However, Section 4.9.3 has shown that $\epsilon^2_c = \xi p_e$ is small since ξ is small for $R = 1$ bit/sample. The well-known channel error resistance of DM coders is therefore due not to oversampling, but to the fact that ξ decreases as the number of quantizer levels 2^R decreases (Table 4.12 and Figure 4.38).

Section 6.7.2 has also shown that when the reconstruction error variance is dominated by the channel noise term, the latter is minimized, in first-order prediction, by the choice

$$h_{1,opt} = \rho^{-1}_1 [1 - \sqrt{1-\rho^2_1}] \qquad (8.70)$$

However, as $\rho_1 \to 1$, $h_{1,opt} \to 1$ as well, and the reduction of channel noise variance, because of the optimization in (8.70), tends to vanish. This situation is typical of a highly oversampled DM coder.

Example 8.14.   Effect of 1% random errors on DM with $F = 4$

Assume first-order prediction, an oversampling ratio of $F = 4$ and an input with Gaussian pdf and an integrated power spectrum, with $\psi = 4$. From (8.19),

$$\rho_1 = 1 - \pi/\psi F^2 \simeq 0.95$$

From Table 4.11, $\epsilon_q^2 = 0.363$ and $\xi = 2.55$. Using these in (8.69a) and (8.69b), we can compute the *SNR* numerically for the following two settings of h_1:

(i) $h_1 = \rho_1 : \alpha = G_P = 10.26$; $\sigma_{r,DM}^2 = (0.01 + 0.0255)\sigma_x^2 = 0.034\sigma_x^2$; $SNRF = 14.6$ dB

(ii) $h_1 = h_{1,opt} = 0.724$; $\alpha = 2.10$; $G_P = 6.731$; $\sigma_{r,DM}^2 = 0.021\sigma_x^2$; $SNRF = 16.7$ dB

Thus, predictor reoptimization leads to an *SNRF* gain of 2.1 dB.   •

Section 4.9.3 has also shown that transmission errors suggest the use of a smaller quantization step

$$\delta_{opt} = \delta^*(1 - 2p_e) \, , \tag{8.71}$$

but that the gains due to step size redesign (8.71) are rather modest in one-bit quantization. The formula (8.71), however, reminds us that a potential source of channel error variance, in general, is an overly large step size and this is indeed taken into account in the design of adaptive quantizers, including those for DM. In fact, since DM is a one-bit system, many of the general strategies for increasing error resistance (such as protection of the most significant bit, or the use of FBC vs. NBC) do not apply to DM; and a careful design of step size adaptation procedures indeed becomes the single most important issue in DM error performance. Specifically, DM coders for noisy channels (in contrast to those intended for signal processing applications with negligible error rate) employ subdued adaptation logics for step size. The decrease in signal-handling capacity because of a slow logic is more than adequately compensated for by increased transmission error resistance (Problem 8.31).

Adaptation algorithms for DM coding of speech at high error rates. Subdued adaptations in DM coding of speech involve two procedures. One is the use of a longer bit memory before using a so-called slope overload cue for increasing the instantaneous step size, as in some of the (J,K,L) logics of Section 8.4. The second is the use of a syllabic time constant for the step size changes that finally affect the leaky integrator in the DM decoder.

DM-AQF systems possess an error resistance comparable to that of syllabic companded DM coders. In both cases the error resistance derives from the fact that the step size is relatively constant over a period of a few milliseconds.

Unwanted step size transitions are small in magnitude with syllabic companding, and in fact zero with DM-AQF. In fact, in one mobile telephony simulation [Jayant, 1975], DM-AQF outperformed syllabic DM-AQB at error rates of about 2 to 5%. The bit errors were due to correlated fading and therefore occurred in bursts. Permutation (within 1024-bit blocks) of transmitted DM bits had the equivalent effect of permuting or randomizing the channel error pattern, and this improved speech transmission quality. Also useful in this application was a leaky integrator characterized by $h_{1,opt} = 0.65$ as in (8.70), although the sampling frequency (24 kHz) suggested the use of $h_1 = \rho_1 \rightarrow 1$ for $p_e = 0$.

Perceptual Effects of Errors in Speech and Image Coding. As already noted in the DPCM section, the error propagation in a differential decoder has very different implications in image and speech coding.

In image coding, the error propagation takes the form of objectionable streaks, as in Figures 6.33(a) and (b), even at bit error rates as low as 10^{-6}. The quality of the DM output can be enhanced by techniques such as periodic PCM updates of pixel amplitudes, or replacement of a line m with a visible streak $[x(m,n); n=1,2,...,N]$ with interpolations using adjacent lines [Scheinberg and Schilling, 1976]:

$$\hat{x}(m,n) = 0.5\, x(m-1,n) + 0.5\, x(m+1,n); \quad n=1,2,...,N \qquad (8.72)$$

Also, as seen in Figure 5.14(b), the use of 2-D prediction leads to a significant improvement in transmission error performance, but error effects are still quite noticeable at error rates in the order of $5 \cdot 10^{-5}$ [Lei, Scheinberg and Schilling, 1975].

In speech coding, on the other hand, the combination of prediction gain and error propagation actually makes DM coding perceptually robust. This was already anticipated in the PCM and DPCM waveform comparisons in Figure 6.32; and more directly demonstrated in the PCM and DM subjective performance curves in Figure 5.14(a) [Daumer and Cavanaugh, 1978]. Note in that figure that even at an error rate of 1%, the DM coder retains a MOS rating of 3, as compared with the log-PCM score of 2. The MOS rating of the DM coder drops to less than 1.5 at an error rate of 10%, but the speech is still quite intelligible at this error rate, although quite noisy. Hybrid companding systems also perform extremely well at very high error rates, and in fact perform better than syllabic DM from an *SNR* viewpoint [Un and Lee, 1980] [Un, Lee and Song, 1981].

The error-robustness of syllabic DM coding is further illustrated in Figure 8.29. The figure refers to the example of a syllabically adaptive DM with a (3,3,1) logic as in Figure 8.25(a), but with a step size time constant of 50 ms that is appropriate for very high bit error rates. Notice that even the extreme case of a 7.2 kb/s DM coder retains a word intelligibility of 80% at bit error rates as high as 10% [Melnick, 1973]. In the communication of speech material with contextual redundancies, sentence intelligibility scores are expected to be greater than word intelligibility scores (Appendix F).

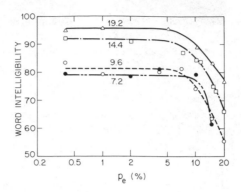

Figure 8.29 Illustration of the transmission error robustness of syllabic ADM. Numbers next to curves are respective bit rates in kb/s [Melnick;©1973, IEEE].

Problems

(8.1)   Consider the deltamodulation of the step input

$$x(n) = 0 \text{ for } n = 0 \text{ to } 7; \quad x(n) = 10.85 \text{ for } n = 8 \text{ to } 15.$$

with initial conditions $y(0) = 0.5$ and $b(0) = -1$. Sketch the output sequences $y(n)$, $b(n)$ and unfiltered error sequence $q(n)$ ($n = 1$ to 15) for

(a)   LDM with $\delta(n) = 1.0$.

(b)   ADM with a one-bit memory (8.57), $M_1 = M_2^{-1} = 2.0$, and initial step size $\delta_{start} = 1.0$.

(8.2)   Repeat Problem 8.1 for 4-level DPCM with quantizer step sizes of ± 0.5 and ± 1.5 ($\Delta = 1$ in the notation of Chapters 4 to 7).

(8.3)   Show that if $\rho_1 \rightarrow 1$, the σ_q^2 analysis in (8.18) implies [with Table (4.2)] that

(a) $\sigma_z^2 = 0.637 \min\{\sigma_d^2\}$; $\min\{\sigma_q^2\} = 0.363 \min\{\sigma_d^2\}$; $\delta_{opt} = 0.796\sigma_d = 0.997\sigma_z$ for a Gaussian input to the quantizer.

(b) $\sigma_z^2 = \min\{\sigma_q^2\} = 0.5\min\{\sigma_d^2\}$; $\delta_{opt} = 0.707\sigma_d = \sigma_z$ for a Laplacian input to the quantizer.

(8.4)   If quantization error feedback is neglected in the LDM theory for Gaussian inputs, show that the resulting SNR is $0.44 \, \psi F^2$ instead of $0.28 \, \psi F^2$, signifying an over-estimation of nearly 2 dB.

(8.5)   Show that the SNR corresponding to (8.21) for a lowpass uniform spectrum [$\Omega_l = 0$ in (2.164)] is $0.53 \, F^2$ which is less than that for an integrated power spectrum by a factor $0.53 \, \psi$. Also see Figure 8.22.

(8.6)   Consider the 12 dB per octave roll-off spectrum

$$S_{xx}(\Omega) = \begin{cases} \alpha_2 \dfrac{1}{1 + \left[\dfrac{\Omega}{\Omega_C}\right]^4} & ; \quad \Omega < 2\pi W \\[4mm] 0; & \quad \Omega \geqslant 2\pi W \end{cases}$$

where α_2 is an appropriate normalizing constant. For $\rho_1 \to 1$, obtain expressions for $(1 - \rho_1^2)$ and show that $G_P = (\psi/\pi)^2 F^2$ where $\psi = 2\pi W/\Omega_C$. Derive an expression for the corresponding SNR in DM. Compare with the results (8.19), (8.20) and (8.21) for the 6 dB per octave roll-off spectrum.

(8.7)   Refer to the in-band noise variance definition (8.8). Using the AR(1) noise spectrum model (8.23), and the large F assumptions (8.24b), derive the G_F expressions (8.24a).

(8.8)   Refer to the ρ_1 result (8.19) for a bandlimited integrated power spectrum.

(a)   Derive a corresponding result for a non-bandlimited input.

(b)   Determine the consequent dB loss in DM-SI SNR (8.21).

(8.9)   Assume a white noise model $S_{qq}(\Omega)$ and a non-ideal DM postfilter, with an integrated spectrum type characteristic, and corner frequency $f_c = W$ where W is the highest input frequency. Derive an expression for filtering gain G_F as a function of F.

(8.10)   The rms value σ_s of the input first difference is given by the product of the rms value of input time derivative $\sigma_{s'}$ with the sampling period $1/f_s$; show that $\sigma_{s'} = \sqrt{D_1}$ where D is the spectral moment defined in (8.38).

(8.11)   Consider a white input psd of bandwidth W

(a)   Using (8.27), show that

$$\delta_{opt,F} = \frac{\pi}{\sqrt{3}} \frac{\log_e(2F)}{F} \sigma_x$$

(b)   Thus, show that as F increases from 16 to 64, the optimum slope loading factor S_{opt} in (8.27) *increases* from 3.5 to 4.9, while δ_{opt} *decreases* from 0.4 σ_x to 0.14 σ_x.

(8.12)   Show that for a sinusoid of frequency f, sampled at f_s, the normalized acf is $\rho_1 = \cos(2\pi f/f_s)$.

(8.13)   Using the approximate formulation that $\rho(\tau) = 1 - A_1\tau^2$, where A_1 is a psd-specific constant, and a white spectrum model for quantization noise, show that the reconstruction quality $SNRF$ in I b/s DPCM coding is given by

$$SNRF = \alpha f_s^3 e^{2I/f_s} ; \quad \alpha = (4WA_1\epsilon_i^2)^{-1}$$

where ϵ_i^2 is the normalized quantizer performance factor defined in (4.21). Hence show that if $I > 8W$, the use of $f_s = 2W$ (Nyquist-sampled DPCM) is optimum; otherwise $f_s = I$ (oversampled DM) is optimum [Chang and Donaldson, 1972].

(8.14)   For a unit-variance bandlimited white input in $(0,W)$, show using (8.38), that

$$D_1 = (2\pi W)^2/3 ; \qquad D_2 = (2\pi W)^4/5$$

(8.15)   For the unit-variance integrated power spectrum, use (8.38) to show that

$$D_1 = (2\pi)^2 \left[\frac{W^2}{\psi^2}\right]\left[\frac{\psi}{\arctan\psi} - 1\right]$$

$$D_2 = (2\pi)^4 \left[\frac{W^4}{\psi^4}\right]\left[\frac{\psi^3-3\psi}{3\arctan\psi} + 1\right]$$

(8.16)   Use (8.34) and the results of Problem 8.14 in equations (8.35) and (8.36) to determine σ_{rg}^2 and σ_{ro}^2 for the bandlimited white input, with $\delta = \sigma_s$ and $\delta = 4\sigma_s$.

(8.17)   Consider a sine-wave input $x(n) = E \sin 2\pi fn/f_s$. Show that slope overload "just begins to occur" if $\Delta = E 2\pi f/f_s$ where f_s is the sampling frequency; while the DM is "completely overloaded" [the output $y(t)$ essentially becomes triangular and periodic with frequency f] if $\Delta = E \cdot 2\pi f/1.86 f_s$ [Steele, 1975].

(8.18)   Consider the mixed integration feedback network in Figure 8.12(a). If the individual integrators have coefficients A_1 and A_2 as in (8.45) and if the additional loop gain is G_0, show that the transfer function of the feedback network is

$$H(z) = \frac{(1+G_0) - (A_2G_0)z^{-1}}{(1-A_1z^{-1})(1-A_2z^{-2})}$$

(8.19)   Show that the transfer function of the feedback loop in the DM-P2 coder of Figure 8.12(b) is $[\hat{X}(z)/\Delta(z)] = H(z)[1-H(z)]^{-1}$.

(8.20)   Consider a DM-SI system with predictor coefficient h_1.

  (a)   Show that the time constant of the leaky integrator (the time needed for the output amplitude to decay by a factor e^{-1} in the absence of further inputs) is $\tau = [f_s \log_e (1/h_1)]^{-1}$.

  (b)   Hence show that if $h_1 = 0.81$, $\tau = 0.55$ ms; if $f_s = 20$ kHz and $h_1 = 0.95$, $\tau = 1.0$ ms; and if $f_s = 32$ kHz and $h_1 = 0.98$, $\tau = 1.6$ ms.

(8.21)   Show that as $A \rightarrow 1$, the magnitude of the transfer function $(1-Az^{-1})^{-1}$ has a -6 dB/octave characteristic for small frequencies.

(8.22)   (a)   Show that the corner frequency (3 dB point in transfer function) for the DM-SI integrator network is given by $f_c = f_s \omega_c/2\pi$ where $\cos \omega_c = (4h_1 - h_1^2 - 1)/2h_1$. [Alternatively, $h_1 = (2-\cos \omega_c) \pm (3+\cos^2\omega_c-4\cos \omega_c)^{1/2}$ for a given specification of corner frequency f_c or $\omega_c = 2\pi f_c/f_s$]. [Hint: set $|H(j2\pi f)|^2 = 1/2 |H(0)|^2$ with $H(z) = Y(z)/\Delta(z) = h_1z^{-1}/(1-h_1z^{-1})$; $z = \exp(j2\pi f/f_s) = \exp(j\omega_c)$].

  (b)   Hence show that if $f_s = 8$ kHz and $h_1 = 0.81$, $f_c = 270$ Hz.

(8.23)   Let $h_1 = 1.49$, $h_2 = -0.53$. Show that for a sampling frequency of $f_s = 16$ kHz, the 3 dB breakpoints f_1 and f_2 (Figure 8.15) of the DM-P2 network are located at 265 Hz and 1400 Hz while $f_0 = 2900$ Hz. Note that f_1 and f_2 contain the 'typical' speech frequency of 800 Hz, while the zero f_0 just clears the important portion of the speech band.

[Hint: Equate the transfer function of the DM-P2 network $H(z)[1-H(z)]^{-1}$ to $(1-a_3 z^{-1})$ $(1-a_1 z^{-1})^{-1}$ $(1-a_2 z^{-1})^{-1}$ and approximate the three points in question by the 3 dB breakpoints corresponding individually to $(a_1, a_2$ and $a_3)$, as in Problem 8.21(a)].

(8.24)   Consider a $D^N M$ system where the total bit rate is F_T and the bit rate per stage is $F_s = F_T/N$. Assume that the $SNRF$ for the first DM is cF_s^α where c is a constant, and that the $SNRF$ for subsequent error-coding DM stages is λcF_s^α, $\lambda < 1$. Show that the overall $SNRF$ is [Chakravarthy, 1977]

$$SNRF(N) = \lambda^{N-1} (cF_T^\alpha N^{-\alpha})^N$$

so that the $SNRF(N)$-maximizing value of N is

$$N_{opt} = e^{-1} F_T (c\lambda)^{\frac{1}{\alpha}}$$

Thus if $\alpha = 3$, $c = 0.01$, and $F_T = 40$ [$SNR(1)=28$ dB], show that λ values of 0.2 and 1 imply N_{opt} values of 2 and 3.

(8.25)   Consider a sine-wave input $E\sin 2\pi ft$. For a given step size and sampling frequency, show that the maximum amplitude E that can be coded without overload is proportional to

(a) f^0 in $\Sigma\Delta$M.

(b) f^{-1} in DM-SI.

(c) f^{-2} in DM-DI.

[Hint: The signals being quantized are essentially (i) the slope of the integrated input, (ii) the input slope and (iii) the slope of the input slope].

(8.26)   Sketch the responses of the step size logics in Examples 8.6 through 8.10 for the input of Problem 8.1. Assume as in Problem 8.1 an initial output value $y(0)=0$. Also assume that $\delta_{min} = 1$, $\delta_{max} = 100$; and, if needed, assume an initial step size δ_{start} equal to δ_{min}.

(8.27)   Sketch the step responses of the step size adaptation logics in Examples 8.8 and 8.9, using an input $x(n)=10.5$, $n=1$ to 20, initial output value $y(0)=0$ and initial step size $\delta_{start}=\delta_{min}=1$. Show that the one-bit memory logic has a 4-step oscillatory pattern.

(8.28)   Show that the CVSD logic (8.64a) implies a maximum step size of $\delta_{max} = \delta_0 /(1-\beta)$.

(8.29)   Consider the CVSD logic (8.64a).

(a)   Show that the time constant for step size decay (time taken for step size to decrease by a factor $1/e$) is $[f_s \log_e (1/\beta)]^{-1} \simeq [f_s (1-\beta)]^{-1}$ for $\beta \rightarrow 1$.

(b)   Hence show that if $f_s = 16$ kHz, $\tau = 0.5$ ms for $\beta = 0.9$, 1.2 ms for $\beta = 0.95$ and 12 ms for $\beta = 0.995$.

(8.30)   Assume a triangular pdf for the short-term bandwidth W' of speech [Jayant, 1981] [Smith and Allen, 1981], decreasing from a maximum value of

$2(W_2-W_1)^{-1}$ at $W' = W_1$ to a value of 0 at $W' = W_2$. Show that if the DM noise is assumed white, the average out-of-band noise rejection fact or $\overline{G}_F$ with adaptive lowpass filtering in DM coding with sampling rate $f_s = 2W_2$ is

$$\overline{G}_F = \frac{2W_2}{(W_2-W_1)} \log_e \left[\frac{W_2}{W_1} \right]$$

For $W_2 \gg W_1$, this implies a gain of $2 \log (W_2/W_1)$.

(8.31) Consider an AQB logic where an instantaneous increase of step size $\delta(n)$ occurs only when all of N bits $b(n), b(n-1), \ldots, b(n-N+1)$, are alike, and a step size decrease occurs otherwise.

(a) Show that with a random transmission error probability p_e, and an i.i.d. bit sequence at the coder output, the probability that the DM decoder at the receiver makes a step size change opposite to that at the transmitter is

$$2^{2-N} N p_e \quad \text{if} \quad N p_e \ll 1$$

(b) Hence show that this probability decreases by a factor of about 3 as the bit memory N is increased from 2 to 5.

(8.32) Refer to the step size histogram in Figure 8.28 for a speech input with a peak amplitude of $x_{max} = 2048$. Assume a Laplacian pdf model for the high-level voiced segments in the speech input, and estimate the standard deviation σ_x of their amplitudes by regarding 2048 as the value that is exceeded with a probability of $6 \cdot 10^{-5}$. (This is equivalent to the 4σ-assumption for a Gaussian pdf, see Example 2.1). Using this value of σ_x in (8.28) and using $\psi = 4$ and $F = 3$, estimate the optimum DM step size, and compare it with the value $\delta_{max} = 200$ in Figure 8.28.

References

M. R. Aaron, J. S. Fleischman, R. A. McDonald and E. N. Protonotarios, "Response of Deltamodulation to Gaussian Signals," Bell System Tech. J., pp. 1167-1195, May-June 1969.

J. E. Abate, "Linear and Adaptive Deltamodulation," Proc. IEEE, pp. 298-308, March 1967.

B. P. Agrawal and K. Shenoi, "Design Methodology for $\Sigma\Delta M$," IEEE Trans. on Communications, pp. 360-370, March 1983.

S. V. Ahamed, "Sequentially Companded Modulation for Low Clock Rate Speech Codec Application," Bell System Tech. J., pp. 765-778, March 1978.

D. Arnstein, "Quantization Errors in Predictive Coders," IEEE Trans. on Communications, pp. 423-429, April 1975.

A. L. Auger, M. W. Glancy, M. M. Gout ann and A. L. Kirsch, "The Space Shuttle Space Terminal Deltamodulation System," IEEE Trans. on Communications, pp. 1660-1670, November 1978.

G. L. Baldwin and S. K. Tewksbury, "Linear Delta Modulator Integrated Circuit with 17 Mb/s Sampling Rate," IEEE Trans. on Communications, pp. 977-985, July 1974.

R. H. Bosworth and J. C. Candy, "A Companded One-Bit Coder for Television Transmission," Bell System Tech. J., pp. 1459-1480, May 1969.

W. M. Boyce, "Step Response of an Adaptive Delta Modulator," Bell System Tech. J., pp. 373-393, April 1976.

P. Castellino and C. Scagliola, "Design of Instantaneously Companded Delta Modulators with m-Bit Memory," Proc. Int. Conf. on Acoustics, Speech and Signal Proc., Hartford, pp. 196-199, May 1977.

C. V. Chakravarthy and M. N. Faruqui, "Two Loop Adaptive Deltamodulation Systems," IEEE Trans. on Communications, pp. 1710-1713, October 1974.

C. V. Chakravarthy and M. N. Faruqui, "A Multidigit Adaptive Deltamodulation (ADM) System," IEEE Trans. on Communications, pp. 931-935, August 1976.

C. V. Chakravarthy, "Studies on Two Loop and Multidigit Adaptive Deltamodulators," Ph.D. Thesis, Indiana Institute of Technology, Kharagpur, 1977.

K.-Y. Chang and R. W. Donaldson, "Analysis, Optimization and Sensitivity Study of Differential PCM Systems Operating over Noisy Communication Channels," IEEE Trans. on Communications, pp. 338-350, June 1972.

P. Cummiskey, "Single-Integration, Adaptive Delta Modulation," Bell System Tech. J., pp. 1463-1474, October 1975.

C. C. Cutler, "Delayed Encoding: Stabilizer for Adaptive Coders," IEEE Trans. on Communication Technology, pp. 898-907, December 1971.

J. Das and P. K. Chatterjee, "An Optimized Δ-Δ Modulator," Electronics Letters, p. 286, 1967.

W. R. Daumer and J. R. Cavanaugh, "A Subjective Comparison of Selected Digital Codecs for Speech," Bell System Tech. J., pp. 3119-3166, November 1978.

F. deJager, "Deltamodulation — A New Method of PCM Transmission Using the 1-Unit Code," Philips Res. Rep., pp. 442-466, December 1952.

E. M. De Loraine, S. van Miero and B. Derjavitch, French Patent 932,140, 1946.

M. Dohrer, E. Metzger and G. Wimmer, "Digital-Übertragungssstem mit Deltamodulation für den mobilen Fernmeldedienst," Siemens Telcom Report No. 2, pp. 72-77, 1979.

R. W. Donaldson and R. J. Douville, "Analysis, Subjective Evaluation, Optimization and Comparison of the Performance Capabilities of PCM, DPCM, ΔM, AM and PM Voice Communication Systems," IEEE Trans. on Communication Technology, pp. 421-431, August 1969.

L. D. J. Eggermont, "A Single-Channel PCM Coder with Companded DM and Bandwidth-Restricting Digital Filtering," Proc. Int. Conf. on Communications, pp. 40-2 to 40-6, San Francisco, 1975.

D. J. Goodman, "The Application of Deltamodulation to Analog-to-PCM Encoding," Bell System Tech. J., pp. 321-343, February 1969.

D. J. Goodman, "Deltamodulation Granular Noise," Bell System Tech. J., pp. 1197-1218, May-June 1969.

J. A. Greefkes, "Code Modulation System for Voice Signals Using Bit Rates below 8 kb/s," Proc. Int. Conf. on Communications, pp. 46.8-46.11, Washington, D.C., June 1973.

J. A. Greefkes and F. deJager, "Continuous Deltamodulation," Philips Res. Rep. 23, pp. 233-246, 1968.

J. A. Greefkes and K. Riemens, "Code Modulation with Digitally Controlled Companding for Speech Transmission," Philips Tech. Rev., pp. 335-353, 1970.

L. J. Greenstein, "Slope Overload Noise in Linear Delta Modulators with Gaussian Inputs," Bell System Tech. J., pp. 387-421, March 1973.

H. Inose, Y. Yasuda and J. Marakami "A Telemetering System by Code Modulation, Delta-Sigma Modulation," IRE Trans. on Space, Electronics and Telemetry, SET-8, pp. 204-209, September 1962.

J. E. Iwersen, "Calculated Quantizing Noise of Single-Integration Deltamodulation Coders," Bell System Tech. J., pp. 2359-2389, September 1969.

N. S. Jayant, "Adaptive Deltamodulation with a One-Bit Memory," Bell System Tech. J., pp. 321-342, March 1970.

N. S. Jayant, "Deltamodulation of Pitch, Format, and Amplitude Signals for the Synthesis of Voiced Speech," IEEE Trans. on Audio and Electroacoustics, pp. 135-140, June 1973.

N. S. Jayant, "Digital Coding of Speech Waveforms — PCM, DPCM and DM Quantizers," Proc. IEEE, pp. 611-632, May 1974.

N. S. Jayant, "Step-Size Transmitting Differential Coders for Mobile Telephony," Bell System Tech. J., pp. 1557-1581, November 1975.

N. S. Jayant, unpublished work, Bell Laboratories, 1976.

N. S. Jayant (ed.), *Waveform Quantization and Coding,* IEEE Press, New York, 1976.

N. S. Jayant, "On the Deltamodulation of a First-Order Gauss-Markov Signal," IEEE Trans. on Communications, pp. 150-156, January 1978.

N. S. Jayant, "A First-Order Markov Model for Understanding Deltamodulation Noise Spectra," IEEE Trans. on Communications, pp. 1316-1318, August 1978.

N. S. Jayant, "Adaptive Post-Filtering of ADPCM Speech," Bell System Tech. J., pp 707-717, May-June 1981.

N. S. Jayant, unpublished work, Bell Laboratories, 1982.

N. S. Jayant and A. E. Rosenberg, "The Preference of Slope Overload to Granularity in the Deltamodulation of Speech," Bell System Tech. J., pp. 3117-3125, December 1971.

H. Jeong and C. K. Un, "A PCM/ADM and ADM/PCM Code Converter," IEEE Trans. on Communications, pp. 762-768, December 1979.

C. J. Kikkert, "Digital Companding Techniques," IEEE Trans. on Communication Technology, pp. 75-78, January 1974.

A. T. Kyaw and R. Steele, "Constant-Factor Delta Modulator," Electronics Letters, pp. 96-97, February 1973.

T.-L. R. Lei, N. Scheinberg and D. L. Schilling, "Adaptive Delta Modulation Systems for Video Encoding," IEEE Trans. on Communications, pp. 1302-1315, November 1977.

H. Levitt, C. A. McGonegal and L. Cherry, "Perception of Slope Overload Distortion in Delta Modulated Speech Signals," IEEE Trans. on Audio and Electroacoustics, pp. 240-247, September 1970.

M. Melnick, "Intelligibility Performance of a Variable Slope Delta Modulation," Proc. Int. Conf. on Communications, pp. 46.5-46.7, Seattle, June 1973.

P. T. Nielsen, "On the Stability of Double Integration Delta Modulation," IEEE Trans. on Communication Technology, pp. 364-366, June 1971.

K. Nitadori, "Statistical Analysis of DPCM," J. Inst. Electron. Commun. Eng. Japan, pp. 4-6, 1965.

P. Noll, unpublished work, Bell Laboratories, 1976.

J. B. O'Neal, Jr., "Delta Modulation Quantizing Noise: Analytical and Computer Simulation Results for Gaussian and Television Signals," Bell System Tech. J., pp. 117-141, January 1966.

J. B. O'Neal, Jr., "Delta Modulation of Data Signals," IEEE Trans. on Communications, pp. 334-339, March 1974.

E. N. Protonotarios, "Slope Overload Noise in Differential Pulse Code Modulation," Bell System Tech. J., pp. 2119-2162, November 1967.

A. E. Rosenberg, unpublished work, Bell Laboratories, 1973.

N. Scheinberg and D. L. Schilling, "Techniques for Correcting Transmission Errors in Adaptive Deltamodulation Channels," IEEE Trans. on Communications, pp. 1064-1069, September 1976.

H. R. Schindler, "Delta Modulation," IEEE Spectrum, pp. 69-78, October 1970.

D. Slepian, "On Delta Modulation," Bell System Tech. J., pp. 2101-2137, December 1972.

J. O. Smith and J. B. Allen, "Variable Bandwidth Adaptive Delta Modulation," Bell System Tech. J., May-June 1981.

C. L. Song, J. Garodnick and D. L. Schilling, "A Variable Step Size Robust Delta-Modulator," IEEE Trans. on Communication Technology, pp. 1033-1099, December 1971.

J. Spilker, *Digital Communications by Satellite,* Prentice-Hall, Englewood Cliffs, N.J., 1976.

R. Steele, *Delta Modulation Systems,* Halsted Press, New York, 1975.

R. Steele, "*SNR* Formula for Linear Deltamodulation with Bandlimited Flat and RC-Coupled Gaussian Signals," IEEE Trans. on Communications, pp. 1977-1984, December 1980.

A. Tomozawa and H. Kaneko, "Companded Delta Modulator for Telephone Transmission," IEEE Trans. on Communication Technology, pp. 149-157, February 1968.

C. K. Un and D. H. Cho, "Hybrid Companding DM with Variable-Rate Sampling," IEEE Trans. on Communications, pp. 593-599, April 1982.

C. K. Un and H. S. Lee, "A Study of the Comparative Performance of Adaptive Deltamodulation Systems," IEEE Trans. on Communications, pp. 96-101, January 1980.

C. K. Un, H. S. Lee and J. S. Song, "Hybrid Companding Delta Modulation," IEEE Trans. on Communications, September 1981.

H. van de Weg, "Quantizing Noise of a Single Integration Delta Modulation System with an N-Digit Code," Philips Res. Rep., pp. 367-385, October 1953.

M. R. Winkler, "High Information Modulation," IEEE Int. Conv. Rec., Pt. 8, pp. 260-265, March 1963.

L. H. Zetterberg, "A Comparison between Delta and Pulse Code Modulation," Ericsson Technics, pp. 95-154, 1955.

9

Delayed Decision Coding

9.1 Introduction

Chapters 1, 4 and 6 have introduced several systems that make use of encoding delay to provide efficient digitizations of analog inputs. Examples of such coding systems are those that employ AQF and APF algorithms for tracking the properties of nonstationary inputs. Chapters 10, 11 and 12 will provide examples of coding algorithms which employ encoding delay to provide run length measurement, subband filtering and linear transforms, respectively. These are functions that lead directly to the utilization of redundancy in the input signal. The techniques of the present chapter utilize encoding delay to provide the capability of a *multipath search*, a feature that will lead to efficient coding of redundant, as well as nonredundant inputs. These techniques will be described by the synonymous terms *Delayed Decision Coding* or *Multipath Search Coding*. Delayed Decision Coders can be used either directly as complete coding systems, or in combination with the coding systems described in other parts of this book. Both of these approaches will be discussed in this chapter.

While discussing amplitude quantization, we mentioned the interesting result that Delayed Coding of independent, identically distributed (i.i.d.) variables using vector quantization can provide a performance that is closer to the Rate Distortion bound than the minimum mean square error (mmse) of a zero-memory quantizer. We shall provide a demonstration of this result in the present chapter. A more important purpose of this chapter is to show the benefits of Delayed Decision Coding in the coding of correlated sources such as speech and video. The specific coding techniques discussed in this chapter are so-called *Codebook, Tree* and

Trellis Coding algorithms. The codebook coding algorithms are identical to the *vector quantization* algorithms used for encoding side-information vectors in Chapters 6 and 12. Those examples do not imply that the techniques of this chapter are useful only in the coding of side-information vectors. In fact, most of the discussion in this chapter is directed to the application of delayed decision coding directly to the original inputs to a coding system.

The benefits of delayed decision coding will be discussed mainly in terms of *SNR* gains over the techniques of earlier chapters, and sometimes in terms of the stabilizing action of delayed decision coding with otherwise unstable coder configurations. Examples of instability in conventional coding include those due to interactions between predictors and coarse quantizers, and those due to transmission error effects.

An interesting feature of delayed decision coding is that it provides a framework for realizing rates of $R < 1$ bit/sample, unlike systems based on conventional quantization, where $R \geqslant 1$. Fractional bit rates in the range $(0 < R < 1)$ have an obvious application in variable rate coding and embedded coding systems for very low bit rate systems. The possibility of $R < 1$ is a property that is also characteristic of the entropy coding schemes of Chapter 4 and the block quantizers of Chapter 12. Although we will discuss the cases of $R > 1$ and $R < 1$ as appropriate, emphasis in this chapter will be on the specific example of $R = 1$ bit/sample, for which many results are available for the performance of conventional coding systems. Delayed decision coding has the potential of improving this performance, although high quality coding may still require 2 bits/sample (Figure 1.5).

We begin by introducing three classes of delayed decision coders: Codebook Coders, Tree Coders and Trellis Coders (Section 9.2). We note that these classes are examples of coding with a *multipath search* that identifies the best possible output *sequence* out of a set of alternatives; while the conventional coders of Chapters 5 to 8, as well as the conventional systems in Chapters 10 to 12, are based on a *single-path search* characterized by a series of instantaneous and irrevocable choices for the component *samples* of output sequences. We go on to describe *deterministic*, *stochastic* and *iterative* means for populating codebooks, trees and trellises with candidate output sequences. We then describe *Search Algorithms* that look for the best entries or paths in a codebook, tree or trellis by using an appropriate criterion for the fidelity of source reproduction (Section 9.3). We shall subsequently describe applications to the encoding of i.i.d. sources (Section 9.4) and correlated sources including real speech and image inputs (Section 9.5).

Example 9.1. A simple but non-trivial example: slope-anticipating deltamodulation

The benefits of delayed decision coding are very simply illustrated with the examples of conventional DM and a *slope-anticipating* DM in Figure 9.1. At time $n=8$, although the DM bit should be $+1$ as in (8.4) and Figure 9.1(a), the slope-anticipating DM coder in Figure (b) emits a negative bit $b(8) = -1$, and the result is a significant reduction of slope overload distortion. Also see Problem 9.1. The anticipation period or encoding delay to realize this gain would be in the order of 0.5 ms for telephone-bandwidth speech coding [Newton, 1970]. At a sampling rate of 20 kHz, this would correspond to an anticipation

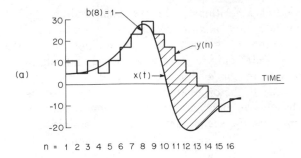

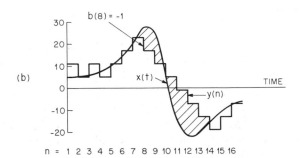

Figure 9.1 Linear DM with (a) conventional coding and (b) delayed decision coding.

window of 10 samples. The number of possible 10-sample binary sequences is $2^{10} = 1024$, and the idea of delayed decision coding is to select the best possible sequence (if the coding is based on an *exhaustive search*), or to localize encoder activity to a very small subset of these sequences, and to search for the best possible sequence in the subset. If the selections of the sequence subsets are based on reasonable criteria such as reduction of slope overload distortion, the performance of the delayed decision DM system, even when based on the suboptimal *non-exhaustive search*, will exceed that of a conventional DM system where selections of output sequence samples are instantaneous, and limited to no more than two choices at each sample. The improved waveform-tracking properties of the slope-anticipating DM are also reflected by better edge-tracking in image coding [Cutler, 1971] [Modestino, Bhaskaran and Anderson, 1981]. •

The input in Figure 9.1 is a slowly varying waveform, with a significant correlation between adjacent samples. We will note in Section 9.4 that delayed decision coding is also useful in the coding of uncorrelated sources. In either case, the benefits of delayed decision coding can be described objectively in terms of attainable values of reconstruction error variance σ_r^2. We shall note that asymptotic versions of the more complex types of delayed decision coding, using so-called *stochastic* and *iterative* approaches, provide a close approach to the distortion rate bound $\min\{\sigma_r^2\} = D(R)$ for stationary inputs. We will further note, where appropriate, that delayed decision coding also provides a natural framework for non-mmse distortion measures that may be more useful from a perception viewpoint.

Figure 9.2 is a general block diagram of a system using delayed decision coding. The candidate output sequences y_i; $i = 1,2,...,J$ are either stored, or generated as needed; and they are arranged as codebooks, trees or trellises, as explained in Section 9.2.4. The object of the search procedure is to pick the best possible output sequence using an appropriate window $\mathscr{W}$ for sequence observation, and an appropriate input-output difference criterion such as the reconstruction error energy:

$$E_i = (\mathbf{x}-\mathbf{y}_i)^T(\mathbf{x}-\mathbf{y}_i) \; ; \quad i = 1,2,...,J \tag{9.1a}$$

$$E_{i,opt} = \min_{\forall \, i}\{E_i\} \tag{9.1b}$$

Information about the index i_{opt} of the selected best sequence $y_{i,opt}$ is then transmitted to the receiver. The set of candidate output sequences should be chosen such that the expected reconstruction error variance in the overall procedure (the expected value of $E_{i,opt}$) is a minimum. The set will then consist of sequences which are typical for the input waveforms or segments thereof (Section 9.2.4).

If the observation window of length $\mathscr{W}$ is shifted by exactly $\mathscr{W}$ samples to continue the encoding process, the result is a *block mode* of operation. If the window displacement is less than its length, the result is an *incremental mode* of operation. In this case, only part of the information i_{opt} is transmitted in each stage of the process.

In conventional quantization with R bits/sample, the observation window $\mathscr{W}$ is one sample long, the output sequences are of length 1, and each of these output samples is one of 2^R possible quantizer output values.

The complexity of Delayed Decision Coding is essentially localized to the encoder which performs the search for the optimum sequence. Subsequent sections will quantify this complexity in terms of computational effort and memory requirements. The decoder in Figure 9.2 is much less complex, and in some cases, no more complicated than the conventional device in a corresponding single-path

Figure 9.2 Block diagram of a delayed decision coding system: (a) coder and (b) decoder. The candidate output vectors y_i are either stored, or generated as needed.

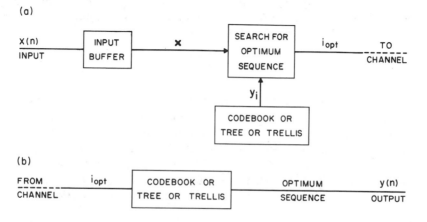

technique. For this reason, several applications, especially those involving waveform storage, can well afford the sophistication of Delayed Decision Coding.

9.2 Codebook, Tree and Trellis Coders

9.2.1 Codebook Coders

Consider an R-ary coder sequence of length N and rate R bits/sample. This implies a total of $J = (2^R)^N = 2^{NR}$ unique *codewords*. To each codeword, we assign a sequence of output samples, $\mathbf{y}_i$; $i = 1,2,...,2^{NR}$. The set of all these possible output sequences is the *codebook*. The values of the output samples are chosen from a reproducing alphabet, the nature of which will be discussed a little later, in Section 9.2.4. A *codebook coder* (also called *list coder* or *vector quantizer* [Buzo et al., 1980]) accepts a block $\mathbf{x}$ of N input samples, searches through the codebook with $J = 2^{NR}$ entries, finds the output sequence best matching the input block, as in (9.1), and transmits the corresponding codeword index i_{opt} to the decoder in the form of NR bits. The decoder looks up the corresponding codeword in its codebook and releases the N samples of $\mathbf{y}_{i,opt}$ as the output sequence. For $N > 1$, this represents a delayed decision procedure wherein a codeword is transmitted once for every block of N input samples. The codebook coder is therefore a *block coder* as well. The coder used by R-bit PCM is a block coder with $N = 1$: each input sample is quantized independently to one of the 2^R letters of the reproducing alphabet.

The number of codewords 2^{NR} in a codebook coder increases exponentially with N, implying that both storage and computation increase likewise. If the search for a best match to input waveform is based on an mse criterion, *the number of multiply/add operations per released sample is*

$$N_{OP} = 2^{NR} \qquad (9.2)$$

It is therefore impossible for an encoder of finite speed and storage capacity to employ a codebook of arbitrarily large N, which incidentally is necessary if the system is to approach the rate distortion limit of performance arbitrarily closely. A coder with $N \to \infty$ is termed *non-instrumentable* [Jelinek and Anderson, 1971] [Bodie, 1974].

9.2.2 Tree Coders

In *tree coders*, the output sequences cannot be chosen independently, but possess a particular structure, one that is easily illustrated with reference to the ideal-integration DM code trees of Figure 9.3, with $R = 1$ bit/sample. A *code tree* consists of a sets of nodes, one for each time index n. From each node at a given time, there are $2^R = 2$ branches [for example, branches with labels 1 or -1 in Figure 9.3(a)] which extend to nodes at the next time sample. Associated with each branch of the tree is one *branch letter* or *reconstruction value* chosen from a

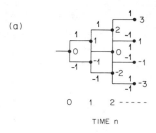

(a)

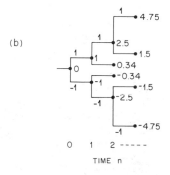

(b)

Figure 9.3 Code trees in DM: (a) the non-exponential tree of ideal-integration LDM; and (b) the exponential tree of ideal-integration ADM. Numbers on branches are possible innovations values $v(n)$ at time n. Numbers next to the nodes are reconstruction values $y(n-1)$.

reconstruction alphabet. These values are indicated next to the nodes at the ends of corresponding branches. For example, the reconstruction values at time instant 2 in Figure 9.3(a) are 3, 1, −1 and −3. The values of 1 and −1 on the branches of the code tree are DM bits, which carry information about the quantized prediction error, or the *innovations*, using the terminology in Chapters 2, 6 and 8. The code tree in Figure 9.3 therefore indicates the evolution of reconstruction values $y(n)$ as well as innovations values $v(n)$. When necessary, we shall refer to these evolutions as y-trees and v-trees.

Figure 9.3(a) has overlapping branches at all levels except 0, causing a less-than-exponential tree growth as a function of time. This is merely a consequence of ideal integration and of equal step sizes in positive and negative directions. More generally, as in the ADM example of Figure 9.3(b) [based on (8.58) with $M_{opt}=1.5$], the growth is indeed exponential. In this case, no two branches terminate on the same node, and there is thus a unique path consisting of a connected series of branches from the root of the tree (the one node at time 0) to *some other* given node. The number of time samples involved in any given stage of a path-selection process is called the *tree depth* $\mathscr{L}$. This parameter determines the encoding delay involved in the multipath tree search. The code tree in conventional PCM describes a memoryless, or zero-encoding delay situation. In this degenerate case, the nodes at each time sample are at a constant height such as zero.

The exponential code tree of Figure 9.3(b) can be generalized in two ways. First, there can be $2^{R'}$ branches out of every node, as in a code tree for DPCM with R'-bit quantization. Second, each branch of the tree can be associated with reconstruction or innovations values for a subsequence of $\beta > 1$ input samples; the resulting bit rate is R' bits per β samples, or $R = R'/\beta$ bits per sample. Such a configuration is a natural framework for coding with less than 1 bit per sample [Stewart, Gray and Linde, 1982]. For example, coding of 8 kHz-sampled speech at 4.8 kb/s needs $R = 0.6$ bits per sample. This can be realized with $R' = 3$ and $\beta = 5$. Unless otherwise mentioned, we assume that $\beta = 1$ in the rest of this chapter, implying the association of exactly one waveform sample per branch.

As with codebook decoders, the bits received by the decoder specify the output sequences to be generated. However, while codebook decoding is best described as a *table look-up* procedure, tree decoding can also be described geometrically. The decoder traces a path through the code tree, with each received bit specifying which of the 2^R branches extending from the node last reached is to be followed, in order to reach a node at the next time sample. These bits define a path through the tree. The encoder decides on the bits to be transmitted by means of a multipath search procedure which evaluates the fidelity criterion (9.1a) for the output sequences produced by a total number of paths J that could be as large as $2^{\mathscr{L}R}$ in an exhaustive search.

The amount of storage required to implement a tree coder is somewhat less than that for a codebook of equal encoding delay, due to the fact that the codewords of a tree code share certain letters; nonetheless, the storage in tree coding also increases exponentially with encoding delay. If, however, the decoder can *generate* reconstruction values as and when needed, from the received bits, the codebook can be entirely eliminated. This can be done for example, in DM, where the value of a particular reconstruction value $y(n)$ is just the sum of all previous values of $b(r)$, the summation being over the range $-\infty < r \leqslant n$. A decoder employing a code of this type need not store any reconstruction values, regardless of blocklength. In general, this is true of all conventional DPCM systems with an all-pole linear predictor of order P':

$$y(n) = \sum_{i=1}^{P'} h_i \, y(n-i) + v(n) \tag{9.3a}$$

If the coding system is to perform well, of course, it must be capable of generating codewords appropriate for the reproduction of any input block that the source may produce. In DM and DPCM, this is ensured by proper choice of decoder filter coefficients, and/or adaptive quantizer algorithms.

9.2.3 Trellis Coders

It is clear that the set of offered reconstruction values increases with tree depth $\mathscr{L}$ if the linear decoding filter is an all-pole structure. Indeed, for high values of $\mathscr{L}$, the reconstruction tree may exhibit unnecessary resolution. Consider, however, the case where reconstruction values are generated by an all-zero decoder filter of order P:

$$y(n) = \sum_{i=1}^{P} g_i \, v(n-i) + v(n) \qquad (9.3b)$$

as shown in Figure 9.4. In this case, the tree, after an initial fan-out characterized by an increasing number of possible output values, settles into a finite-state *trellis* with 2^{PR} output amplitudes per sample (Figure 9.5). For the DM tree with $R = 1$, and an all-zero filter with P taps, the number of distinguishable reconstruction values is 2^P (even for $N > P$) since each of the P coefficients g_i can have only two states, $\pm g_i$, depending on the DM bit $b(n-i)$.

In general, a trellis with 2^K allowed amplitudes is said to have an *intensity* of K. As in tree coding, the encoding delay is the number of successive time samples in the trellis used in any given stage of encoder decision. This is also the *trellis depth* $\mathscr{L}$.

The trellis structure in Figure 9.5 was developed in reference to DPCM coding, as in Figure 9.4. But it is important to stress that a trellis structure can be utilized in a non-DPCM context as well, as long as the generation of $y(n)$ values follows (9.3b). The trellis structure to be used in Section 9.4.3 will indeed be developed in the context of a non-DPCM situation. The $v(n)$ values in that discussion will be i.i.d. variables at the output of a random generator, rather than samples of a quantized prediction error sequence.

Figure 9.4 DPCM coder with an all-zero decoder filter: (a) coder and (b) decoder.

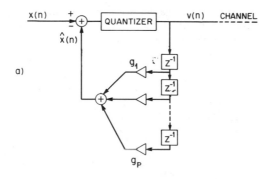

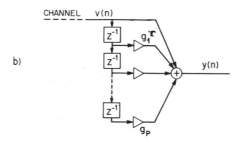

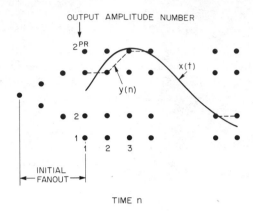

Figure 9.5 Trellis structure in a decoder with an *R* bits/sample input and an all-zero filter of order *P*.

Example 9.2. Structures for delayed decision coding with *R* = 1 and delay = 4

Figure 9.6 illustrates the coding structures utilized in the three delayed decision coding procedures that have been discussed, for the example of *R* = 1 bit/sample, and a delay of four samples. The delay is given by block length *N* in codebook coding [Figure 9.6(a)] and by tree- or trellis depth $\mathscr{L}$ in Figures 9.6(b) and (c). The output sequence is 1100 in each case, as shown by heavy pathmaps. ●

Figure 9.6 Three structures for delayed decision coding with *R* = 1 bit/sample. The delay equals four samples in each case. (a) Codebook coding; *N* = 4. (b) Tree coding; $\mathscr{L}$ = 4. (c) Trellis coding with intensity *K* = 2; $\mathscr{L}$ = 4 [Fehn and Noll, 1982].

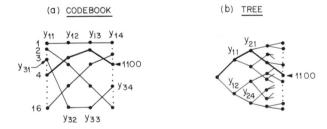

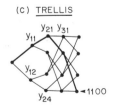

9.2.4 Deterministic, Stochastic and Iterative Populations

In the discussion of Figure 9.2, we pointed out the importance of offering appropriate output sequences as possible matches to an input sequence. The nature of these output sequences depends on the way that codebooks, trees or trellises are populated. There are at least three basic procedures for doing the same [Fehn and Noll, 1982]:

(i) *Deterministic* populations, such as those used in the generalized DPCM approaches of Figures 9.1 and 9.3; these populations are based on the use of an extremely restricted alphabet, such as the alphabet provided by conventional one-bit quantizers of LDM and ADM coders in Figure 9.3, and by conventional R-bit quantizers of DPCM coders in some future examples in this chapter.

(ii) *Stochastic* populations, which use r.v.'s that have carefully chosen statistics; for example, Gaussian and gamma r.v.'s with appropriate variance as in several examples in later sections of this chapter.

(iii) *Iterative* populations, obtained as the result of an optimization procedure that seeks to obtain candidate output sequences with a structure that best matches that of expected input sequences. Examples of this important approach will be mentioned in later discussions.

Techniques using deterministic populations are the simplest to implement, but they also provide the least gains over conventional coding procedures. There are applications, however, where these gains are quite useful, and these will be pointed out as appropriate. The simplicity of these schemes is due to the fact that output sequences can be generated as needed, and no storage is needed. Techniques using stochastic and iterative populations are more powerful, but also more complex in terms of computational effort and storage requirement. The latter problem can usually be alleviated significantly by limiting the amplitude resolution of the samples of candidate output sequences. For example, if the desired final coding rate R is 1 bit/sample, individual samples of candidate sequences may be specified with 3-bit accuracy in storage, without significant loss of overall performance [Fehn, 1981].

Techniques based on stochastic and iterative populations are also very sensitive to how well the populations are representative of the inputs being coded. The performances of these coding techniques depend critically on a training phase whose purpose is to realize the most effective populations of codebooks, characterized by the most typical candidate sequences. Adequate training may involve sequences of length 100,000 samples or more [Fehn and Noll, 1982] [Gray and Linde, 1982] [Stewart, Gray and Linde, 1982] [Cuperman, 1983]. There is also an interesting tradeoff between performance *within* the training sequence and *outside* the training sequence. As the length of the training sequence increases beyond a point, the quality of coding may continue to improve for inputs outside of the training sequence, but it may actually diminish for subsequences within the training sequence [Linde, Buzo and Gray, 1980]. In most applications, the criterion of performance is the quality of coding for inputs outside of the training sequence, and this quality tends to be a monotonically non-decreasing function of training effort.

For the example of codebook coding of i.i.d. gamma sequences, we will show that the iterative technique is significantly better than the stochastic technique, in terms of SNR gains over conventional coding for a given coding delay (Figure 9.8).

The Generalized Lloyd-Max Iterative Algorithm. An iterative technique that has been applied very successfully to codebook design is one that is based on a *clustering technique*, as in Pattern Recognition. This algorithm [Linde, Buzo and Gray, 1980] [Adoul, Debray and Dalle, 1980] is based on the following steps, where $\{x_j\}$; $j = 1,2,...,T$ is the training sequence of T input vectors, of length N each, and m is the level of iteration ($m = 0,1,2,...$):

(a) Given a codebook $\mathcal{Y}_m = \{y_{i,m}\}$; $i = 1,2,...,J$, find, for each i, all those input vectors that fall in a *minimum distance* partition $\mathcal{S}_i$ defined by

$$x_j \in \mathcal{S}_i \quad \text{if} \quad d(x_j, y_{i,m}) \leqslant d(x_j, y_{l,m}) \quad \text{for all} \quad l \tag{9.4}$$

where $d(x_j, y_{i,m})$ is a distortion measure [such as the error energy in (9.1a)]. This partition is defined by the fact that each training vector is associated with the *nearest neighbor* output vector.

(b) Determine the entry $y_{i,m+1}$ of codebook $\mathcal{Y}_{m+1}$ as the average over the T_i input vectors that belong to $\mathcal{S}_i$:

$$y_{i,m+1} = \frac{1}{T_i} \sum_j (x_j \in \mathcal{S}_i) \tag{9.5}$$

This codebook is defined by the fact that each of its elements is the centroid of a partition defined in (a).

(c) Use codebook $\mathcal{Y}_{m+1}$ in (a) and continue.

The design begins with an empirical but carefully chosen initial codebook $\mathcal{Y}_o$ and the iteration continues until the average distortion is below a specified threshold. If at iteration stage m, there is no vector x_j in a given cell $\mathcal{S}_i$ (the *empty cell* situation), a useful codebook vector $y_{i,m+1}$ will have to be defined; for example, a slightly perturbed version of another vector of that codebook.

The above procedure is a generalization of the Lloyd-Max quantizer discussed for scalar inputs in Chapter 4. In general, the designs in (a) and (b) represent necessary conditions for optimality, and the iterative approach based on these designs converges at least to a local optimum [Linde, Buzo and Gray, 1980].

Geometrical Interpretation. The partitions $\mathcal{S}$ that define the optimum codebook have a structure that depends on input statistics, the dimensionality N, and the number of bits/sample R [Gersho, 1977] [Sloane, 1981] [Fischer and Dicharry,

1983]. There are cases where the partition structure can be characterized in a useful geometrical fashion that also permits fast implementation. For example, for i.i.d. inputs with a uniform pdf, for very fine quantization, and for $N = 2$, the optimum partitions form a lattice of contiguous hexagons [Gersho, 1977, 1979]. If mmse scalar quantization is used for each of the two dimensions of the same input, the resulting partitions would be a suboptimal lattice of contiguous rectangles. Lattice structures are also known for higher dimensional quantizations of uniform pdf inputs [Sloane, 1981] [Conway and Sloane, 1982]. For the case of fine quantization, analytical results are available for a general pdf, in terms of lower and upper bounds on reconstruction error variance [Zador, 1966, 1982] [Gersho, 1979] [Yamada, Tazaki and Gray, 1980]. The upper bounds are N-dimensional generalizations of the results for large R in scalar quantization (Section 4.4.2).

Coding of Correlated Sources. There are two possible approaches for the coding of *correlated sources* with a multipath search. In the first approach, candidate sequences with appropriate correlation properties can be generated directly, and matched to a given input, as in vector quantization experiments with iteratively trained codebooks [Abut, Gray and Rebolledo, 1982]. An efficient version of this approach involves the use of vector quantization with memory: the output sequence used to code a given input vector is used to narrow down the choice of candidates considered for coding the next contiguous input vector. The scheme is called *finite state vector quantization* (FSVQ) [Foster, 1982] [Gray, 1984]. The second basic approach uses the *innovations* concept implied in differential coding. Matches to the input waveform then depend on choices of $v(n)$ values in an *innovations codebook*, or on an *innovations tree* or *innovations trellis*, as well as choices of proper filters that obtain a transformation from the v-domain to a y-domain. A technique that is related to the innovations codebook approach is *vector DPCM*, which combines vector quantization with vector prediction to realize a higher-dimensional generalization of conventional DPCM [Cuperman, 1982]. Most of the innovations coding techniques that we shall discuss retain the feature of scalar prediction. Consequently, they will need to use a sequential approach involving an innovation tree or an innovation trellis, rather than an innovations codebook. Sections 9.4 and 9.5 will discuss examples of efficient deterministic, stochastic and iterative systems for populating the innovations tree or trellis. The innovations trees implied hitherto in the book have been deterministically populated by the 2^R outputs of an R-bit memoryless quantizer.

9.3 Search Algorithms

Given that a codebook, tree or trellis is appropriately populated, the next function of the delayed decision coder is to select an output sequence that provides an adequate match to its input. An exhaustive search over all candidate output sequences will provide the best possible match, by definition. Many implementations of delayed decision coding in fact use such an exhaustive search. However, if the number of candidate output sequences is very large, computational constraints may suggest the use of non-exhaustive search procedures that only concentrate on the most promising portions of codebooks, trees or trellises. Such procedures can result in the final selection of an output sequence that is suboptimal. However, the attendant loss in performance can be made satisfactorily small if the non-exhaustive search follows certain well-designed algorithms. One example of a suboptimal, but very useful, non-exhaustive algorithm is the *binary tree search* mentioned in the context of vector quantization (codebook coding) in Chapter 6. In the present section, we will rediscuss this technique briefly. Another example of a useful non-exhaustive algorithm is the *M-algorithm* that is appropriate for tree and trellis coders.

Whatever the type of search algorithm used, the output at the conclusion of the search can consist of a complete block of samples corresponding to vector dimension N or the tree- or trellis depth L (the *block mode*), or part of such a block (the *incremental mode*, illustrated by the *delta sequence modulation* example to be mentioned in Section 9.5).

The complexity of a multipath search coding technique has two components, *computational complexity* $\mathscr{C}$ and *memory* $\mathscr{M}$. We define $\mathscr{C}$ as the number of branches whose path metrics must be examined to encode *one* input sample. (If the examination of each branch involves the squaring of S error components, the resulting number of multiply-add operations is $\mathscr{C}S$). The memory $\mathscr{M}$ is simply the total number of words that must be stored at any given time in the coding process. These words may represent either final reconstruction values $y(n)$ or intermediate quantities such as the innovations $v(n)$.

9.3.1 The Random Search

This is the degenerate example of a non-exhaustive algorithm: the encoder simply chooses a path at random, or equivalently, transmits randomly chosen channel digits. The *random search* algorithm [Bodie, 1974] is useless in practice, but it serves as a limiting case against which to compare the performance of a more intelligent algorithm. The computational complexity in the random search algorithm is

$$\mathscr{C} = 1 \qquad (9.6)$$

9.3.2 The Single-Path Search: PCM, DPCM and DM

The simplest search algorithm of practical value is the *single-path* algorithm. Having reached a node at some time sample, the algorithm examines the path error metrics of the 2^R branches extending from that node and follows the best branch to a node at the next level. This process is repeated until the end of the tree is reached; the bits defining the one path which the algorithm has traced through the tree are then transmitted to the decoder. The complexity $\mathscr{C}$ in a single-path search is

$$\mathscr{C} = 2^R \qquad (9.7a)$$

Once the algorithm has selected a branch at a given time, it is certain that the finally chosen path will include this branch, and the bit or bits defining the selected branch can be released to the decoder immediately, without considering the action of the algorithm at future instants. This search algorithm defines the operations of commonly used PCM, DPCM and DM systems. The major failing of the single-path search is that it completely disregards the possibility that *the best path up to a given time in the evolution of the tree may not extend from the best path up to an earlier time.* The multipath search algorithms are indeed designed to take this possibility into account.

The memory (in total number of samples) needed in the single-path search is formally given by

$$\mathcal{M} = 2^R \tag{9.7b}$$

the total number of candidate output levels at a given sampling instant. However, the single-path search used in memoryless quantization usually depends on short-form algorithms which do *not* need an explicit memory of 2^R samples.

9.3.3 The Exhaustive Search

An extreme example of a multipath search is the *exhaustive* search. In the incremental mode, where one sample is released after a search involving N input samples, the complexity in the exhaustive search is

$$\mathcal{C} = 2^{RN} \tag{9.8a}$$

The value of $\mathcal{C}$ decreases by a factor N in the block mode where the number of released samples after the search is N, rather than one. In either case, the computational complexity grows exponentially with N, and the search is non-instrumentable if $N \rightarrow \infty$.

The memory (in total number of samples) needed in the exhaustive search is

$$\mathcal{M} = N \, 2^{RN} \tag{9.8b}$$

which also grows rapidly with N.

For a tree or trellis search with depth $\mathcal{L}$, the computational complexity grows exponentially with $\mathcal{L}$.

9.3.4 The Binary Tree Search for Codebook Coding

If the number of candidate sequences in the codebook is $J = 2^{RN}$, the exhaustive search based on (9.1a) involves the computation of J dot products. The *binary tree search* is based on using a sequence of codebooks $\mathcal{Y}_j$ of increasing order $j = 1, 2, \ldots, \log_2 J = RN$ [Buzo et al., 1980]. The low-order codebooks are clustered versions of the final codebook, and the coding is performed in RN steps. Beginning with $j = 1$, the total population of J entries is partitioned into two regions of $J/2$ entries each. The centers of gravity of the two regions constitute a first-order codebook with two entries. The entry closer to the input is identified, and the corresponding partition is again split into two subpartitions, and the centers of gravity are compared to the input. The process is repeated until $j = RN$. The binary tree search is suboptimal, but the loss of performance is often very small compared with the savings in computational complexity [Gray and Abut, 1982] [Gray and Linde, 1982] [Gray, 1984]. The complexity $\mathscr{C}$ in a binary tree search is

$$\mathscr{C} = 2\log_2(2^{RN}) = 2RN \qquad (9.9a)$$

since the total number of binary partitions is the logarithm, to base 2, of the total number of codewords in the codebook; and each stage of selection, involving a pair of partitions, needs $2N$ products in (9.1a), or 2 products per sample. Therefore, $\mathscr{C}$ grows only linearly with N, unlike the exponential growth (9.8a) for an exhaustive search. However, the memory $\mathscr{M}$ for a binary search (in total number of stored samples) can be shown to be [Cuperman, 1983]

$$\mathscr{M} = N\sum_{i=1}^{RN} 2^i = N\,2(2^{RN}-1) \qquad (9.9b)$$

which is nearly two times the memory needed for the exhaustive search (9.8b).

9.3.5 Multipath Searches for Tree and Trellis Coders

The goodness of a tree- or trellis path is measured by a suitable distortion criterion E_p, or *path error metric* for path p, such as the error energy

$$E_p(n) = \sum_{r=n-\mathscr{W}+1}^{n} e_p^2(r) = \sum_{r=n-\mathscr{W}+1}^{n} [x(r) - y_p(r)]^2 \qquad (9.10a)$$

where $e_p^2(r)$ is the single-letter distortion associated with the path p at sampling instant r, and $\mathscr{W}$ is the number of samples in the error window.

A practical strategy is one where the window length $\mathscr{W}$ is a constant value that is independent of r. The path metric in this case follows the local average distortion as evaluated over $\mathscr{W}$. It is easy to see that the computation of the path error metric now follows a rule of the form [Koubanitsas, 1975]

$$E_p(n+1) = E_p(n) + e_p^2(n+1) - e_p^2(n-\mathscr{W}+1) \qquad (9.10b)$$

We shall see in the example of the next subsection that all the paths in contention at time r can be traced to a common predecessor node in the recent past. In such a situation, most of the earlier components in an infinite summation for error energy are common to the paths in contention. Therefore, the comparison of these paths can be simply accomplished by the use of a windowed error criterion such as (9.10a). Also, the squared distortion criterion $e_p^2(r)$ can be replaced in speech and image coding by a perceptually more meaningful function of $e_p(r)$, and the unweighted summation in (9.10a) can be refined into a time-weighted sum. The use of a weighted sum, however, prevents the use of a recursion such as (9.10b) in general; an exception is the case of one type of exponential weighting (Problem 9.2).

In any case, once a path error metric can be defined and computed, it is straightforward to talk about the best path metric in a tree; and an *exhaustive* search will always find this path. If the search involves a finite-state trellis, rather than a tree, the selection of the best path can be performed very efficiently using the *Viterbi Algorithm* [Forney, 1973] [Viterbi and Omura, 1974]. It is clear, however, that such a search becomes less feasible for tree codes of arbitrarily high values of tree depth or trellis depth. To allow longer block lengths, it is necessary to adopt a *non-exhaustive* search algorithm.

The M-algorithm. Non-exhaustive tree searches are well illustrated with the example of the *M-algorithm* [Jelinek and Anderson, 1971]. This algorithm proceeds through the error metric tree along M paths of equal length. At any time in the tree (except possibly at the very beginning of the encoding operation), there will be M nodes, called *saved nodes*, to which these paths have led. The algorithm examines the path error metrics of the $2^R M$ branches extending from M saved nodes, and follows once again, only the best M of these branches to nodes at the next sampling time instant. The process is repeated until the final time index is reached, and the bits defining the best of the M paths through the entire tree are then transmitted to the decoder. For a given number of search operations, this algorithm allows a greater value of tree depth $\mathscr{L}$ compared with an exhaustive search, where at any tree level, M simply equals the total number of available branches, $2^{\mathscr{L}R}$.

In the incremental mode where one output symbol is released after every search that involves $\mathscr{L}$ input samples, the complexity in the M-algorithm is

$$\mathscr{C} = 2^R M \; ; \quad \text{all } \mathscr{L} \qquad (9.11a)$$

Unlike in the exhaustive search, this complexity does not increase exponentially with delay or tree depth $\mathscr{L}$. The same property is shared by a trellis search, for which

$$\mathscr{C} = 2^{PR} = 2^K \qquad (9.11b)$$

is a depth-independent constant.

To reduce the memory requirements in this algorithm, we can make use of a typical characteristic of the paths generated by the M-algorithm: *the M paths retained at a given time usually stem from a single node not too many time instants back in the tree.* This implies that the bits defining the path leading to this single node have already been decided upon, and could be transmitted to the decoder without affecting the future operation of the algorithm. We can therefore modify the algorithm as follows: the best branch out of the $2^R M$ branches examined at each time instant is found, and the bit (or bits) L time samples back along the path leading to this branch are transmitted. This limits bit storage to a finite value $\leqslant \mathscr{L}MR$. Of course, the algorithm must choose the M branches to be followed to the next time instant from only those of the $2^R M$ examined which do stem from the node specified by the transmitted bit or bits. This requirement of a "legitimate" path may in fact occasionally limit the number of branches available to a value less than M.

Example 9.3. M-algorithm with $M = 4$, $R = 1$, $\mathscr{L} = 2$

Figure 9.7 illustrates the operation of the M-algorithm for the example of $M = 4$, $R = 1$ and $\mathscr{L} = 2$, with thick branches representing retained paths. Notice that at time $n = 4$, the number of paths retained is forced to be 3, i.e., less than M, because of the legitimacy problem mentioned earlier (viz., node labeled $N_{7,4}$ at time $n = 4$ does not emanate from node $N_{1,2}$ which at time $n = 4$ becomes a transmitted, or irrevocable node). Hence, $N_{7,4}$ and the branch leading to it are eliminated, although the corresponding path has the second best cumulative distortion at time n.   •

A DPCM-based delayed speech encoder, using an M-algorithm as above, is described at length in Section 9.4. Other nonexhaustive tree algorithms have been discussed and compared elsewhere [Anderson and Jelinek, 1973] [Knuth, 1973] [Mohan and Anderson, 1980].

Figure 9.7 Illustration of the M-algorithm for multipath searching ($M = 4$, tree depth $\mathscr{L} = 2$, $R = 1$). Unlike in earlier illustrations of trees, entries on branches are now instantaneous values of distortion [Jayant and Christensen, 1979].

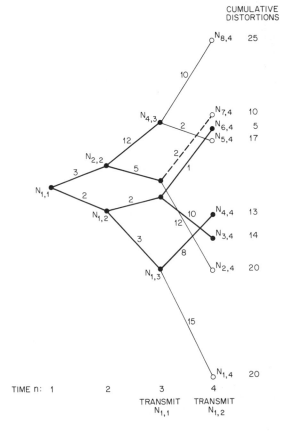

The Metric Tree. An interesting framework for comparing search algorithms is the notion of a *metric tree* where, associated with a given branch, is the value of a fidelity measure evaluated over the output sequence generated by the path leading to that branch. An 'exponential metric tree' for example, is an artificial metric tree generated probabilistically from an exponential distribution of path metric values. With the bit rate of $R = 1$ bit/sample, *random, single-path*, and *infinitely-complex multipath* searches yield the following values of relative distortion (Problem 9.3):

$$D_{random} = 1; \quad D_{single-path} = 0.5; \quad \min\{D_{multipath}\} = 0.22 \qquad (9.12)$$

More significantly, the M-algorithm approaches the minimum value of 0.22 faster than an exhaustive search, when distortion is determined as a function of complexity $\mathscr{C}$ [Bodie, 1974].

It must be emphasized that the exponential distribution for the samples of the above metric tree is nothing more than an analytically tractable model. Realistic distributions of the error metric are usually more complex. For example, if the samples $x(n)$ of an i.i.d. input and candidate output samples $y(n)$ are all described by Gaussian pdf's, the samples of the error metric based on (9.1a) will have a *chi-squared* distribution.

9.4 Delayed Decision Coding of Memoryless Sources; $R=1$

The specific example of $R = 1$ bit per sample is important in the coding of speech and image signals. The coding of memoryless sources is relevant to speech and image coding because prediction error sequences (unlike original speech or image sequences) can be modeled as i.i.d. sequences. The discussions in this section will be based entirely on the use of the mse criterion of coder performance.

As per rate distortion theory (Appendix D),

$$D(1)_G = 0.250 \ \sigma_x^2 \quad \text{for a Gaussian source}$$
$$D(1)_\Gamma = 0.139 \ \sigma_x^2 \quad \text{for a gamma source} \qquad (9.13)$$

On the other hand, as per the quantizer results of Chapter 4,

$$\min\{\sigma_q^2\}_G = 0.363 \ \sigma_x^2 \quad \text{for a Gaussian source}$$
$$\min\{\sigma_q^2\}_\Gamma = 0.667 \ \sigma_x^2 \quad \text{for a gamma source} \qquad (9.14)$$

For Gaussian and gamma inputs, equations (9.13) and (9.14) imply performance gaps of 1.6 dB and 6.8 dB, respectively, between $D(R)$ bounds and conventional one-bit quantization with a single-path search. As noted in Section 4.6, these SNR gaps can be reduced by entropy coding, but never totally bridged. The performance gaps between (9.13) and (9.14) can also be bridged by codebook coding or vector quantization with $N \rightarrow \infty$, and with tree and trellis coding with $\mathscr{L} \rightarrow \infty$.

9.4.1 Codebook Coding of Memoryless Sources; $R = 1$

The *SNR* gain in codebook coding is an increasing function of N, and the performance with finite N is shown in Figure 9.8 for the case of gamma sources. With stochastically populated codebooks, a gain of about 3 dB over conventional quantization can be obtained for gamma inputs with $N = 8$, and a positive gain of about 1.5 dB can be obtained even with $N = 3$. With $N = 1$ on the other hand, the performance of codebook coding is in fact *worse* than that for conventional quantization, since any deviation from a fixed optimum step size can only reduce performance in this case, and the stochastic population would fail to use that step-size with probability close to unity. The above results apply to codebooks populated stochastically, by i.i.d. r.v.'s of variance σ_y^2, and a pdf which follows that of the source pdf, but with a scaling of variance. The variance scaling factor σ_y^2 / σ_x^2 is given by an N-dependent value with an asymptote of nearly 2 for the gamma source [Fehn and Noll, 1982]. With a codebook populated by iterative techniques [Linde, Buzo and Gray, 1980], the performance gain over conventional quantization can increase to nearly 4 dB with $N = 8$. More significantly, the performance gain over conventional quantization is now non-negative even for small N, with a minimum gain of 0 dB at $N = 1$.

The highest level of performance in Figure 9.8 is given by the *SNR* value of about 6 dB at dimension $N = 8$, as obtained in the iterative codebook technique. A comparison with the rate distortion bound $\Gamma_{R(D)} = 10\log_{10}[\sigma_x^2 / D(1)_\Gamma]$ of (9.13) and the entropy coding bound Γ_{EC} (Section 4.6) shows that there is still a significant gap which can, however, be closed by delayed decision coding using higher input dimensions. This will be illustrated later in Figure 9.11 for a trellis coder with intensity $K = 8$ and trellis depth $\mathscr{L} = 1024$.

Figure 9.8 Codebook encoding of a memoryless gamma source with stochastically and iteratively populated codebooks and $R = 1$ bit/sample [Fehn, 1981]; and comparison with rate distortion bound (Appendix D), entropy coding bound and scalar quantization performance (Section 4.7).

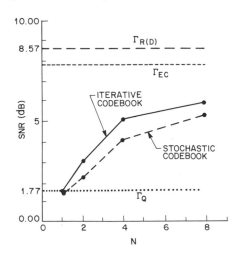

Table 9.1 lists *SNR* values for codebook coding of i.i.d. sources with $R = 1$ bit per sample, and compares them with RDF bounds (Table D.1) and scalar quantization results (Table 4.4). The values of Max-quantization are those from Table 4.4. As noted in Chapter 4, the 1.76 dB result for Max-quantization is not the best possible value for the memoryless quantization of the gamma pdf. In this case, non-symmetric quantization can yield an *SNR* of 2.23 dB [Brehm and Trottel, 1983]. The *SNR* values for codebook coding are rounded to the best values among sets of results that differ slightly because of different iterative procedures used in codebook design. As noted already in Figure 9.8, significant improvements are obtained only with gamma sources. For this specific source, very simple and highly structured codebooks that perform very close to the iterative designs of Figure 9.8 can be intuitively devised [Fehn and Noll, 1982]. Note also that with gamma sources, entropy coding may be attractive in terms of *SNR* gains, as well as in terms of implementation (Section 4.7) [Granzow and Noll, 1983]. Entropy coding techniques do not require the use of storage, or of a multipath search, but they do require the use of fairly long buffers.

Table 9.1   One bit per sample coding of stationary memoryless sources using scalar Max-quantizers, and codebook coding of input vectors of dimension N. Entries in the table are *SNR* values. Values for codebook coding are the best values among sets of results that differ slightly because of different iterative procedures used in codebook design. The entry in parenthesis is the result for a non-symmetric scalar quantizer. Also included are rate distortion bounds from Table D.1 [Fischer and Dicharry, 1983] [Granzow and Noll, 1983].

Input	Codebook Coding			Max-Quantization		RDF Bounds
	$N = 2$	$N = 4$	$N = 8$	$N = 1$		
U	6.0	6.0	6.0	6.02		6.79
G	4.5	4.7	4.8	4.40		6.02
L	3.8	4.6	4.9	3.01		6.62
Γ	3.2	5.4	6.4	1.76	(2.23)	8.53

9.4.2 Tree Coding of a Gaussian Source

Consider the problem of reproducing a sequence of source letters chosen independently from the normal distribution $N(0,\sigma_x^2)$. Table 9.1 has already demonstrated the modest improvements over scalar quantization when the input is coded using iteratively designed codebooks. We shall now consider the design of a 1 bit/sample tree coder based on stochastic populations.

A conventional code tree would be the two-level *zero-mean quantizer code tree* shown in Figure 9.9(a), in which the two branches extending from each node bear the reconstruction values δ and $-\delta$. Notice, however, that this tree is different from that in Figure 9.3(a), even if δ is set equal to 1. The reconstruction tree of Figure 9.3(a) implies a decoder with prediction coefficient $h_1 = 1$. On the other hand, it is assumed that $h_1 = 0$ for the decoders used for memoryless sources, whether the tree search is single-path or multipath. This assumption is implied in the *memoryless* trees of Figure 9.9.

As mentioned earlier, a single-path algorithm will search the tree in Figure 9.9(a) optimally and provide a conventional one-bit PCM encoding of the i.i.d.

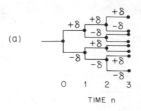

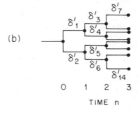

Figure 9.9 Code trees for $R = 1$: (a) two-level quantizer code tree; and (b) stochastically populated code tree.

source; it is well known that the performance of this system is described by the following relations (Chapters 4 and 8):

$$\delta_{opt} = (2/\pi)^{1/2}\sigma_x = 0.798\sigma_x; \quad \min\{\sigma_q^2\} = (1-2/\pi)\sigma_x^2 = 0.363\sigma_x^2 \qquad (9.15)$$

We have also noted in Chapter 4 that with entropy coding, we can attain lower values of reconstruction error variance. On the other hand, as per rate distortion theory, the minimum values of D are those in (9.13) for a Gaussian source of variance σ_x^2.

In the case of stochastically populated trees, reconstruction values on their branches are appropriate random variables δ' as in Figure 9.9(b); each r.v. is independent of all other, or at least most of the other, r.v.'s used to populate the tree or trellis. Delayed coders using these trees and trellises asymptotically reach the $D(R)$ bound of (9.13) for $\mathscr{L} \to \infty$.

One intuitively suggested code tree is a stochastically populated structure with branch letters chosen from the same $N(0,\sigma_x^2)$ distribution as the source letters. In fact, this tree is efficient and nearly optimal; on the other hand, a code tree based on the $N(0,0.75\sigma_x^2)$ distribution, when exhaustively searched, achieves the rate distortion bound of (9.13) for the asymptotic case of infinite tree depth ($\mathscr{L} \to \infty$) [Jelinek, 1969]. This is not surprising in view of the reconstruction-variance to input-variance ratio $\sigma_y^2/\sigma_x^2 = 1-D(1)_G = 0.75$ in the optimum x-y mapping of Figure D.2.

Figure 9.10(a) plots the results of computer simulation of ensembles of $N(0,\sigma_x^2)$ and $N(0,0.75\sigma_x^2)$ trees, exhaustively searched for small values of tree depth $\mathscr{L}$. Note that in this region, such trees are in fact worse than the conventional memoryless quantizer. Replacing the exhaustive search with the M algorithm allows the use of arbitrarily large $\mathscr{L}$, and produces the results of Figure 9.10(b). With $M = 8$, the complementary code trees in this figure achieve an SNR value of 4.8 dB, the value noted for $N = 8$ in codebook coding (Table 9.1).

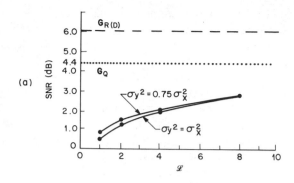

(a)

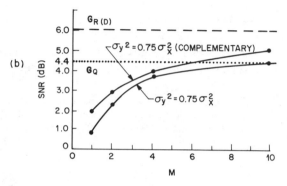

(b)

Figure 9.10 One-bit coding of the $N(0,\sigma_x^2)$ source with a stochastic code tree populated by $N(0,\sigma_y^2)$ samples: (a) SNR versus $\mathscr{L}$ with exhaustive search; and (b) SNR versus M in the M-algorithm search [Bodie, 1974].

Complementary Code Trees. The *complementary* trees in Figure 9.10(b) refer to pseudo-stochastic code trees in which the branch letters populating the branches extending from a given node are non-independent, and in fact quite dissimilar; in the binary case, this may mean that one of the branch letters out of a node is determined from the desired $N(0,\sigma_y^2)$ distribution (with $\sigma_y^2 = 1$ or 0.75), while the letter on the other branch is simply the negative of the former. For example, in Figure 9.9, $\delta_2' = -\delta_1'$, $\delta_4' = -\delta_3'$, and so on, with the r.v.'s δ_1', δ_3',... being mutually independent. This is indeed the population mechanism assumed for the complementary trees of Figure 9.10(b). It is interesting that such complementary trees perform better than trees where both branches out of a node are populated with independent random numbers. SNR values in excess of 5 dB can also been realized with a more practical discrete-alphabet stochastic tree, one in which reconstruction levels at each node are randomly selected as either $\pm A$, or $\pm B$. For example, with $M = 10$, one good design is given by $A = 0.4$, $B = 1.2$ [Bodie, 1974].

The fact that probabilistically generated code trees can perform better than a memoryless one-bit quantizer for an i.i.d. source is conceptually very significant.

As indicated earlier in this chapter, a qualitative explanation of this result is that the structure-free nature of the multipath-searched probabilistic code tree is more suited to the encoding of the i.i.d. source than a time-invariant two-level quantizer tree whose output sequences are hardly ever typical for the inputs being coded. Put differently, the probabilistic tree will always provide the encoder with a replicating waveform that matches the input waveform better, *on the average*, than a rigidly structured two-level waveform imposed by the one-bit PCM system, *provided that the population of the tree is adequate, the encoding delay is sufficient, and the search for the replicator is adequate.* The minimum encoding delay for a positive gain over conventional memoryless quantization is in fact expected to be less with iteratively designed tree populations. Recall that in the iterative codebook coding example of Figure 9.8, the gain over memoryless quantization was non-negative for all values of encoding delay, including zero.

9.4.3 Trellis Coding of Gaussian and Gamma Sources

Figure 9.11(a) shows the results for one-bit coding of unit-variance i.i.d. sources using a stochastically populated trellis; results are now a function of K, the trellis

Figure 9.11 Trellis encoding of memoryless Gaussian and gamma sources with $R = 1$ bit per sample: (a) *SNR* versus trellis intensity K, with trellis depth $\mathscr{L} = 1024$; and (b) waveforms of gamma input (i), and of reconstructions in (ii) single-path encoding and (iii) multipath (trellis) encoding with $K = 10$ and $\mathscr{L} = 1024$ [Fehn and Noll, 1982].

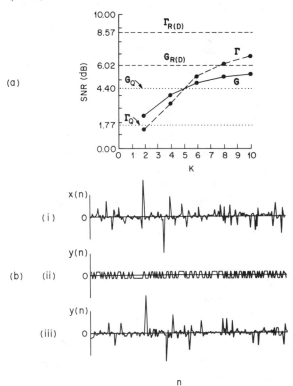

intensity. Recall that an intensity K implies a trellis with 2^K possible outputs for every time sample. Results in Figure 9.11 are based on coding in long blocks of $\mathscr{L} = 1024$ samples and use of a *block mode* release technique. The benefits of delayed decision coding are again more dramatic with the gamma source. Note also that for the gamma source, the gap between memoryless quantizer performance $[\min\{\sigma_q^2\}_\Gamma = 0.667\sigma_x^2]$ and RDF theory bound $[D(1)_\Gamma = 0.139\sigma_x^2]$ is much wider than the gap for the Gaussian source. Figure 9.11(a) also includes the asymptotic result for the Gaussian source $[D(1)_G = 0.25\sigma_x^2$, implying $\max\{SNR\} = 6.02$ dB]. The best performance for the Gaussian input, at $K = 10$, is slightly higher than 5 dB, and very close to the best performance of the complementary code tree in Figure 9.10(b).

Figure 9.11(b) shows a gamma-distributed input sequence (i) and corresponding outputs of binary digitizers with (ii) single-path and (iii) multipath coding. The single-path coder is one-bit PCM with optimal step size. The multipath coder is a stochastically populated trellis coder of Figure 9.11(a). The improvement due to multipath coding is dramatic. The price paid is increased complexity, storage, and encoding delay. Comparable results, in terms of waveform reproduction, have been obtained employing codebook coding using $N > 4$, and iteratively chosen codebooks. (Also see Figure 9.8).

9.5 Delayed Decision Coding of Correlated Sources

The benefits of delayed decision coding for i.i.d. sources, although well-demonstrated in Section 9.4, are intuitively not very obvious. In the coding of correlated sources, on the other hand, the benefits are easier to explain. For example, when DPCM is refined by delayed decision coding, one expects improvements because of several, not mutually exclusive, reasons: (a) the reduction of the effects of quantization error feedback, (b) improvement of performance due to an interpolative action provided by input-sample buffering, which is more powerful than extrapolative or predictive action; and (c) the possibility of noise shaping, by appropriate choices of error criteria used in the search. As a result of these effects, one expects delayed decision DPCM systems to perform closer to rate distortion bounds than conventional DPCM systems. We shall indeed demonstrate presently that this is true; we will further note how delayed decision coding is compatible with other coder features such as adaptive quantization and adaptive prediction; in fact, we shall demonstrate that delayed decision coding has the important property of stabilizing potentially unstable quantizer-predictor combinations.

When correlated sources are to be coded in a delayed decision system, it is necessary to seek typical correlated sequences, and to use the nearest neighbor of the input for reconstruction. There are two basic approaches for providing a set of typical correlated candidates $\mathbf{y}_i$: (i) population of the codebook, tree or trellis with correlated sequences, or (ii) use of an innovations codebook, tree or trellis, followed by a (linear) filter that introduces the desired statistical correlations. In this case, identical filters would be used at the encoder (to generate the set $\mathbf{y}_i$) and at the decoder (to generate $y_{i,opt}$, as specified by the received index i_{opt}). The filter parameters also need to be be adaptive for use with nonstationary inputs. The innovations sequences may once again be produced by processes that are deterministic, stochastic or iterative. The conventional DPCM coder uses the combination of a linear filter fed by an innovations that is described deterministically. In this case, there is no formal search involved in the encoder, since the prediction algorithm finds an almost optimum sequence. However, performance improvements can be obtained by searching through all innovations sequences (all possible quantizer output sequences within a given observation window). This deterministic approach can be called *delayed DPCM* [Aughenbaugh, Irwin and O'Neal, 1970], or *delayed decision DPCM*. It is also the approach implied in the DM example of Figure 9.1. Significantly better performances can be obtained by the use of stochastic and iterative innovations sequences with less restrictive elements.

Section 9.5.2 will discuss one example of codebook coding based on correlated candidate sequences for an AR(1) source. The disadvantages with this technique are the very rapid increase of codebook size with vector dimension N, and the fact that the concatenation of chosen typical sequences may create undesirable boundary effects in the coding of inputs such as speech or video. One solution to this problem is that of (ii) above. It involves the use of a *white* or *innovations* codebook or tree or trellis, and the coloring of its sequences by an appropriate linear filter to obtain correlated reconstruction values, as in Figures 9.3 and 9.4. Examples of this solution will also be discussed in this section.

9.5.1 AR(1) Processes

Consider a Gaussian AR(1) source with adjacent sample correlation ρ_1. According to rate distortion theory, the mean squared error is bounded by

$$D(R)_G = 2^{-2R} \min \{\sigma_d^2\} = 2^{-2R} (1-\rho_1^2)\, \sigma_x^2 \quad \text{if } R \geqslant \log_2 (1+\rho_1) \quad (9.16)$$

where $\min\{\sigma_d^2\}$ is the minimum value of prediction error variance, which equals the variance of the innovations process. For the example of $\rho_1 = 0.85$, $D(1)_G = 0.0694\,\sigma_x^2$, implying an *SNR* bound of 11.59 dB, which is 5.57 dB higher than the 6.02 dB bound for an i.i.d. Gaussian process. The difference is due, of course, to the $(1 - \rho_1^2)$ term.

A practical coding scheme for correlated sources is DPCM. We have seen that with a first-order predictor coefficient ρ_1, the DPCM quantization noise variance is

$$\sigma_q^2 = \epsilon_q^2\, \sigma_d^2 = \epsilon_q^2 \min\{\sigma_d^2\}(1 - \epsilon_q^2\, \rho_1^2)^{-1} \quad (9.17)$$

where the last term expresses the effect of quantization error feedback. With $R = 1$ bit/sample, the increase in noise variance due to this feedback is 1.96 dB for Gaussian innovations (Problem 8.4) and 2.9 dB for gamma innovations. The performances of practical DPCM schemes therefore fall short of rate distortion bound for two reasons: (i) the suboptimality of the DPCM quantizer for providing a representation of the innovations input into it [as shown in (9.13), and (9.14) for $R = 1$], and (ii) the effect of quantization noise feedback.

Experiments with one-bit DPCM and an AR(1) process with $\rho_1 = 0.85$ have shown how delayed decision coding can bridge the above performance gap; and in fact, compensate in part for the effects of quantization noise feedback as well [Fehn and Noll, 1982]. For Gaussian and gamma inputs with $\rho_1 = 0.85$, SNR values for one-bit DPCM with $h_1 = \rho_1$ are 8.6 dB and 4.2 dB respectively.

Codebook Coding. Figure 9.12(a) shows the results of codebook coding of a Gaussian AR(1) source using an iteratively determined codebook. Results are shown as a function of vector dimension N. The performance is better than that of DPCM (the 8.6 dB line) for $N \geqslant 4$. With $N = 7$, performance gains over DPCM are 1 dB for a binary tree search, and 1.6 dB for an exhaustive search (dashed curve) [Gray and Linde, 1982].

Figure 9.12 Multipath coding of correlated sources with $R = 1$ bit/sample: (a) codebook coding of Gaussian AR(1) source with acf $\rho_1 = 0.85$ [Gray and Linde, 1982]; (b) trellis coding of AR(1) sources with gamma innovations and acf $\rho_1 = 0.85$; and (c) waveforms of (i) input, (ii) DPCM output and (iii) trellis coder output [Fehn and Noll, 1982].

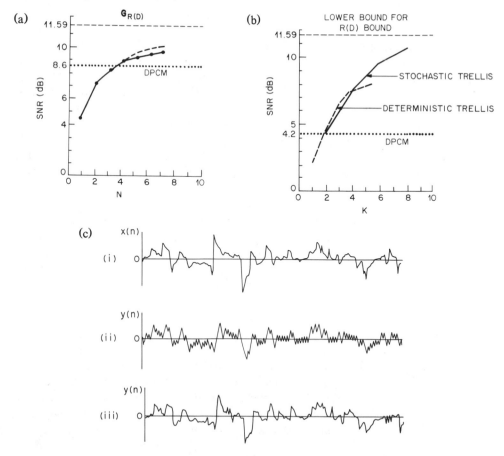

Tree and Trellis Coding. A deterministically populated DPCM tree with depth $\mathscr{L} = 4$ can lead to a performance gain of about 2.9 dB over DPCM with gamma innovations, a gain which effectively compensates for the 2.9 dB loss due to error feedback mentioned earlier [Fehn and Noll, 1982]. But the performance of the deterministically populated tree is still influenced by the use of a restrictive set of output sequences. Even better results can therefore be obtained with stochastically populated, or iteratively populated trees and trellises. Results in Figure 9.12(b) are for one-bit coding using both deterministic and stochastic trellises, with SNR shown as a function of trellis intensity K. In view of the exponential acf for the $AR(1)$ input, the coefficients of the all-zero filters in the encoder and decoder are chosen to follow an exponential decay, given by setting $g_i = g_0^{i-1}$ in (9.3b). As in the i.i.d. example, performance improves significantly when the innovations tree is stochastically populated. The delayed decision coder performs better than DPCM if $K \geqslant 3$. Even better results can be expected with iteratively optimized innovations trellises.

The 11.59 dB line in Figure 9.12(b) is a rate distortion lower bound (Appendix D). No precise $D(R)$ bound is known for gamma innovations; however, it is known that it is less than that for the Gaussian case:

$$D(R)_\Gamma < D(R)_G \qquad (9.18)$$

The trellis depth used in Figure 9.12(b) was $\mathscr{L} = 1024$ samples. However, a good deal of the delayed-encoding gain implied in Figure 9.12(b) can be realized with a shorter delay of $\mathscr{L} = 128$ samples. For example, with $K = 8$, the loss in performance in going from $\mathscr{L} = 1024$ to $\mathscr{L} = 128$ is only about 0.5 dB [Fehn and Noll, 1982].

Figure 9.12(c) demonstrates the improvements obtained with $K = 8$ in terms of reconstructed waveforms. The waveforms in (i), (ii) and (iii) are respectively the input, the output of conventional DPCM coder, and the output of a trellis coder with stochastic population. The improvement over conventional DPCM with $h_1 = 0.85$ is very evident.

Gaussian Signals with Speech-Like Spectrum. Figure 9.1 showed the benefits of delayed encoding with a single-integration deltamodulator. The combination of instantaneous step size adaptations and double integration can cause instability in deltamodulation, but this can be eliminated by the stabilizing action of a multipath tree search [Zetterberg and Uddenfeldt, 1974] [Uddenfeldt and Zetterberg, 1976]. The action of a double-integration DM with delayed decision is demonstrated in Figure 9.13. The example chosen is that of an ideal DI network ($h_1 = 2$; $h_2 = -1$) which was discussed in Chapter 8. The input used is Gaussian, with a psd similar to the long-time-averaged psd of speech in Figure 2.9. The results refer to a scheme called *delta sequence modulation* where, after each stage of exhaustive multipath search, the number of DM bits released to the channel is $\mathscr{W}_0$, with $1 \leqslant \mathscr{W}_0 \leqslant \mathscr{W}$, where $\mathscr{W}$ is the length of the error window. As expected, tree encoder performance is a decreasing function of $\mathscr{W}_0$, but surprisingly useful results are reported for the design $\mathscr{W}_0 = \mathscr{W}/2 = 3$ that was used in Figure 9.13. In

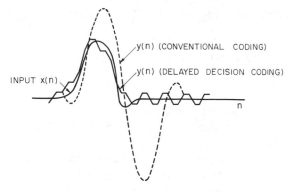

Figure 9.13 Comparison between conventional and delayed decision in DM-DI [Uddenfeldt and Zetterberg, 1976].

delayed DM with extremely high oversampling (say $F > 5$), an error criterion of the form

$$E_p(n) = \sum_{r=n-\mathscr{W}+1}^{n} e_p(r) \tag{9.19}$$

is preferable to the mse criterion (9.10a). The use of e_p in lieu of e_p^2 provides a simple way of emphasizing the contributions of low frequency (in-band) noise components in oversampled systems. More general versions of the path error metric can be used to provide noise-shaping [Wilson and Hussain, 1979]. In this sense, the multipath search technique can be regarded as a more general refinement for DM-DI than the mixed-integration concept mentioned in Chapter 8.

9.5.2 Speech Waveforms

Delayed Decision Coding is most useful for real speech waveforms at bit rates of 16 kb/s or less ($R \leqslant 2$ bits/sample, assuming 8 kHz samples). This is the region where the performance of single-path algorithms is known to be insufficient, even if the algorithms include adaptive quantization and/or adaptive prediction.

16 kb/s Tree Coding of Speech with DPCM and DM. We have already mentioned the utility of an all-zero filter for delayed decision DPCM. The approach to designing an all-zero filter is to start with an all-pole predictor $A(z)$, and to truncate the corresponding expression for $[1-A(z)]^{-1}$ (Problem 9.4) to an order that is higher (say two times) than that of $A(z)$; and finally, to trim the filter $G(z)$ used in (9.3b) in some kind of gradient-search procedure, using overall encoding performance (SNR) as the criterion. In this manner, the all-zero filter will be adequately matched to the other components of the tree encoding system, such as the coarse 2-bit quantizer and the search algorithm. The fine-trimming of the filter $G(z)$ is especially critical for non-exhaustive searches. The loss of performance due to truncating the order of $G(z)$ is also a function of search intensity: greater liberties can be taken with a multipath search [Anderson and Bodie, 1975] [Law,

1976] [Anderson and Law, 1977]. Recommended $\{g_i\}$ sequences mentioned for $M = 4$ are

$$\{0.79, 1.52, 1.63, 1.21, 0.50\} \quad \text{for } 16 \, kb/s \; DPCM-AQB\,; \quad R = 2 \; bits/sample$$

$$\{0.67, 1.51, 2.00, 2.10, 2.05, 1.96, 1.80, 1.51, 1.00, 49\} \quad \text{for } 16 \; kb/s \; DM-AQB \quad (9.20)$$

Gains due to multipath searching with the M-algorithm are comparable for the DM and DPCM coders, with a 4 dB increase showing for $M = 8$ compared with $M = 1$. This gain is input-dependent, and figures of up to 8 dB have been reported in some cases. However, the best performance of a DM-based tree code falls short of that of the DPCM-based tree-code by at least 3 dB. This difference is similar to that between conventional DM and DPCM at 16 kb/s (Figure 8.9). Multipath searching characterized by $M = 4$ is very appropriate to the above class of coding techniques; it ensures a useful and consistent gain of about 3 dB over $M = 1$, and it limits the searching intensity to a reasonable amount. For $M = 4$, the computation complexity $\mathscr{C} = 2^R M$ defined earlier in (9.9a) is equal to 16 branches per node for the DPCM tree and 4 branches per node for DM. An adequate design for tree depth is $\mathscr{L} = 7$ for DPCM and $\mathscr{L} = 14$ for DM [Anderson and Ho, 1977]. Recall that in the memoryless input example of Figure 9.10, the design of $M = 4$ was quite useless, and gains over conventional coding required values of M in excess of 6.

Earlier chapters have noted that coders for nonstationary signals invariably need some form of adaptive quantization. For 16 kb/s speech coding using DPCM, it has been shown explicitly that the benefits of adaptive quantization and delayed decision coding (using an M-algorithm tree search) are mutually exclusive [Jayant and Christensen, 1979]. The quality improvement in DPCM-AQ due to delayed decision coding is apparent both in terms of SNR gains and in terms of perceived quality, but coding noise is still discernible, suggesting the need for adaptive prediction as well. The deterministic techniques just discussed are not as effective as stochastic or iterative procedures, but they have the advantage that no storage is needed of the elements used for the population of the innovations tree.

APC with Tree Coding at $R \rightarrow 1$ bit/sample. As seen in an earlier section of Chapter 6, the combination of adaptive spectrum prediction and adaptive pitch prediction has the potential of providing useful, if not toll-quality speech waveform digitization at bit rates in the order of 9.6 kb/s or less. The quality of such a coder is limited sometimes by granular noise effects and by long-term loss-of-track effects [analogous to the short-term effect of slope overload in Figure 9.1(a)]. Tree encoding has the potential of mitigating both these effects. This has been demonstrated in a simulation of *Delayed Decision APC* [Becker and Viterbi, 1975] where the idea is to determine a better sequence of prediction errors (than in conventional APC) by means of an exhaustive trellis search. Unfortunately however, SNR-versus-time plots show that in the case of a deterministically populated tree or trellis, the effect of delayed decision coding is often to improve the SNR in frames where the conventional SNR itself is subjectively adequate, and not in frames that critically need improved rendition [Goldberg, 1977]. As a consequence, subjective gains due to delayed APC are less dramatic than average *SNR* gains.

Systems based on stochastic and iterative populations tend to produce more effective refinements of APC in speech coding [Fehn and Noll, 1980] [Schroeder and Atal, 1981] [Fehn and Noll, 1982].

Figure 9.14 shows results that apply to delayed one-bit DPCM encoding of speech with forward-adaptive prediction (DPCM-AQF-APF). Results refer to 1.5 second utterances of two speakers [Fehn and Noll, 1982].

Figure 9.14(a) refers to multipath coding using a tree that is populated *deterministically* by the i.i.d. outputs provided by an AQF algorithm (Section 4.10). Figure (i) shows segmental *SNR* versus all-pole predictor order P', with tree depth $\mathscr{L}$ as parameter. Note that the second-order predictor with tree search ($P' = 2$; $\mathscr{L} = 5$) has nearly the same performance as the tenth-order predictor without tree search ($P' = 10$; $\mathscr{L} = 1$), as shown by points A and B in Figure 9.14(a). On the other hand, the first-order predictor, even with the deepest search ($P' = 1$; $\mathscr{L} = 5$), falls well short of the conventional tenth-order scheme ($P' = 10$; $\mathscr{L} = 1$). The best scheme in Figure 9.14(a) ($P' = 10$; $\mathscr{L} = 5$) has a gain of nearly 6 dB over the worst ($P' = 1$; $\mathscr{L} = 1$). Figure (a) (ii) shows, however, that gains

Figure 9.14 Multipath coding of speech at 8 kb/s ($f_s = 8$ kHz; $R = 1$ bit/sample) with DPCM-APF-AQF, using (a) a deterministically populated tree and (b) a stochastically populated trellis. In each case, (i) shows segmental *SNR* versus predictor order P', with tree depth or trellis intensity as parameter (trellis depth $\mathscr{L} = 128$); while (ii) shows the time variation of *SNR* [Fehn and Noll, 1982].

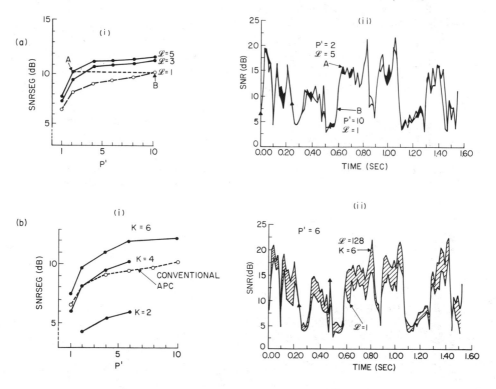

due to a deterministic tree search often occur in regions of the speech waveform where the conventional performance is already high.

Figure 9.14(b) shows results that apply to a more complex multipath coder, one that uses a *stochastically* populated trellis. The segmental *SNR* results in (i) are again a function of the all-pole predictor order P', but now the parameter is the trellis intensity K; the trellis depth is $\mathscr{L} = 128$ for all the results in Figure 9.14(b). The best values of *SNRSEG* and the best gains over conventional APC (the dashed curve) are comparable to the best values obtained with the deterministic tree in (a). However, unlike in Figure 9.14(a)(ii), the gains in the stochastic trellis scheme of Figure 9.14(b) (ii) are significant even in regions of the speech waveform where the conventional performance is relatively low. Low-amplitude, high-frequency speech segments are such regions; improved renditions of these segments are perceptually very significant because high-frequency reconstruction noise, unlike low-frequency reconstruction noise, is less liable to be masked by speech resonances.

Results for an *iteratively* populated trellis are also available, but not for the same input data as those in Figure 9.14. With a tenth-order predictor, the use of an iteratively populated trellis with an M-algorithm search can provide *SNR* values in the order of 10 dB for $R = 1$ bit/sample, and 6 dB for $R = 1/2$ bit/sample [Stewart, Gray and Linde, 1982]. These results include the side information used to convey predictor information to the receiver, using a codebook with 512 entries for the predictor coefficients.

Codebook Coding at a Rate of 1 bit/sample. Codebooks with correlated sequences can be directly generated using an iterative training procedure [Abut, Gray and Rebolledo, 1982]. At a rate of $R = 1$ bit per sample, this approach can be even more effective than DPCM-AQF-APF systems whose performance is limited by coarse quantization and error feedback. Table 9.2 compares results obtained from different coding procedures, based on a 5 second speech sample of one speaker [Noll, 1983] [Bochow and Noll, 1983]. The terms VQ and VQ-A refer to vector quantizers with fixed and blockwise-adaptive gain control, respectively. In VQ-A, waveform samples in every 128-sample block are scaled for constant block energy. It is seen from the table that this results in a significant gain in the segmental performance *SNRSEG*. The table also shows that VQ-A performs worse than ATC, but significantly better than DPCM-APF-AQF. However, the DPCM-APF-AQF system used in this example does not include pitch prediction.

Table 9.2 Comparison of several speech coders operating at $R = 1$ bit per sample [Noll, 1983].

Coder	SNR (dB)	SNRSEG (dB)
PCM	1.3	−10.8
PCM-AQF	4.2	4.1
DPCM	4.4	−3.0
DPCM-AQF	6.2	7.0
DPCM-AQF-APF	7.8	9.0
VQ (N = 8)	9.8	7.8
VQ-A (N = 8)	9.5	10.3
ATC	13.3	13.8

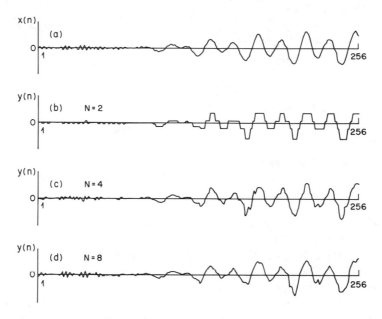

Figure 9.15 Input speech (a), and outputs of a block-adaptive vector quantization system with block lengths of (b) $N = 2$, (c) $N = 4$; and (d) $N = 8$. The input waveform is the same as that in Figure 1.4(a). [Bochow and Noll, 1983].

Figure 9.15 compares the input speech waveform of Figure 1.4(a) with the output of the adaptive vector quantizer system for dimensions $N = 2$, 4 and 8. The codebook used is an average design based on training sequences from four speakers. The improvement over scalar quantization [$N = 1$; Figure 5.4(d)] is obvious even with $N = 2$. With $N = 8$, many of the subtle features of the input waveform begin to appear in the vector quantizer output.

Multipulse-Excited APC. The examples of APC mentioned so far in this section are based on searching for an optimum sequence out of all output sequences obtained by passing innovations sequences $v(n)$ through an adaptive inverse prediction error filter. Depending on the mechanism for populating the innovations tree or trellis, the procedure places different kinds of restrictions on the amplitudes of innovations sequences.

The *multipulse* APC system [Atal and Remde, 1982] [Atal, 1983] is an innovations codebook approach that seeks an optimum sequence $v(n)$, based on a small number of intuitively determined key parameters. These parameters are the magnitudes, signs and locations of pulses that define the excitation signal for the inverse prediction error filter. The parametric nature of the candidate innovations sequences makes the approach very speech-specific, and effectively implies carefully selected classes of codebook populations.

Unlike in vocoding techniques, which are also very speech-specific, impulse parameters are not determined on the basis of pitch detection and voiced-unvoiced decisions, but on the basis of a more general search procedure that falls in the

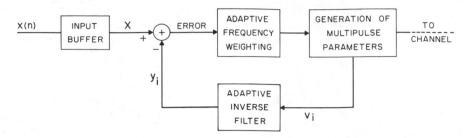

Figure 9.16 Block diagram of the coder in multipulse APC [Atal, 1982]. Parameters describing the multipulse excitation and inverse filter are both time-varying, and explicitly transmitted to the receiver.

framework of Figure 9.2. The procedure is an *analysis-by-synthesis* approach which generates the optimum innovations, rather than storing all candidates as in some of the earlier examples of this chapter.

A block diagram of multipulse APC appears in Figure 9.16. The search process that finds the optimum innovations is carried out in a succession of stages, each of which determines the amplitude and location of *one* pulse in the innovations process. The optimum amplitude is obtained by setting the derivative of an mse measure, with respect to the unknown amplitude, to zero. The error measure is then a function only of the pulse location. The optimum location is then found by computing the mse for all possible locations and by locating its minimum. A new error signal is then computed, and the process of locating additional pulses is continued until constraints on transmission rate or output quality indicate truncation of the iterative process.

The above procedure automatically produces quasi-periodic innovations sequences for voiced speech inputs, and random excitations during unvoiced speech inputs, and it yields high quality speech at coding rates in the range of 1 to 2 bits per sample if the mse measure is appropriately *frequency-weighted*, in a time-varying fashion, as in Example 7.10. In a 8 kb/s coder based on the multipulse APC algorithm, about 2 kb/s may be typically allocated to the transmission of APF (inverse filter) parameters (see Section 6.5), and the remaining 6 kb/s may be used for transmitting the parameters of 4 to 8 pulses once every 10 ms.

9.5.3 Image Waveforms

An important example for the tree encoding of images is in the context of deltamodulation [Candy, 1969] [Cutler, 1971] [Lei, Scheinberg and Schilling, 1977]. A quantitative comparison of ADM performance with and without delayed decision coding is available for ADM-DI coding at 6 MHz ($W = 1$ MHz, $F = 3$) [Cutler, 1971]. The ADM coder used is an instantaneously adaptive delta modulator with a one-bit memory (Section 8.5), and a double integration network. Delayed decisions are based on the local average (unsquared) error criterion (9.19) with delay $W = 2$. *SNR* improvements due to delayed coding are in the order 3 dB, but the most significant result is the stabilizing influence of delayed decision coding. This stabilizing action results in a reduction of perceived noise. With a single-path search, the one-bit adaptive quantizer and double integrator are nearly always incompatible. Also, the combination of adaptive quantization, double integration and multipath search performs significantly better than the multipath search with adaptive quantization alone, or with double integration alone.

The stabilizing influence of a multipath tree search extends to the more general example of 2D-DPCM, and to coding in the presence of channel errors [Lei, Schienberg and Schilling, 1977] [Modestino, Bhaskaran and Anderson, 1981] [Modestino and Bhaskaran, 1981]. For 2-D coding, the $(M, \mathscr{L})$ algorithm can be generalized to an $(M, \mathscr{L}_H, \mathscr{L}_V)$ algorithm, with $\mathscr{L}_H$ and $\mathscr{L}_V$ signifying horizontal and vertical separations between the current pixel and the pixel whose status is irreversibly encoded at that current time. The corresponding encoding delay is $k_S \mathscr{L}_H + \mathscr{L}_V$, where k_S is the number of pixels per scan line. With a recommended design of $M = 8$, $\mathscr{L}_H = \mathscr{L}_V = 2$ [Modestino, Bhaskaran and Anderson, 1981], significant improvements over single-path 2D-DPCM result even in the simple case of a deterministically populated tree. The use of a stochastic image model that accounts for the presence of edges leads to significant improvements in tree coder performance at a bit rate in the order of 1 bit/pixel [Modestino and Bhaskaran, 1981].

Delayed decision coding is expected to provide the basis for important new classes of image coding at bit rates of $R = 1$ bit/pixel or less. One of these classes is that of *adaptive-* or *switched vector quantization*, implying different sets of codebooks for different classes of sub-images [Gersho and Ramamurthi, 1982] [Ramamurthi and Gersho, 1983]. Features such as edges and continuous texture provide bases for sub-image classification, as in conventional coding. Efficient vector quantization configurations are possible at significant but not impractical levels of complexity, especially if the needed image quality is not necessarily broadcast quality [Gray, 1984], as in certain classes of image storage and display.

Problems

(9.1) Consider the conventional- and delayed-decision DM waveforms of Figure 9.1. Show by numerical inspection of $x(n)$, $r(n)$; $n=1$ to 16, that respective SNR values are approximately 4 and 8 dB.

(9.2) Consider a weighted error criterion $E_p(n) = \sum \alpha^{n-r} e_p^2(r)$ with the same range of r for summation as in (9.10a). Show that the path error metric $E_p(n)$ can be computed using the recursive form

$$E_p(n+1) = \alpha E_p(n) + e_p^2(n+1) - \alpha^{\mathscr{W}} e_p^2(n - \mathscr{W}+1)$$

(9.3) Consider the exponential metric-tree where each squared-error increment in the sum (9.10a) is chosen independently from the single-sided exponential pdf $p(x) = e^{-x}$. Show the following results of (9.12):

(a) $D_{random} = 1$.

(b) $D_{single\text{-}path} = 0.5$. [Hint: the average increase in error metric from one level to the next, in a single-path search, is the expected value of the minimum of two independent random variables, each with density $p(x)$].

As noted in (9.12), $\min\{D_{multipath}\} = 0.22$.

(9.4) The all-zero filter (9.3b) has a transfer function $G(z) = \sum g_i z^{-i}$, with summation over the range $0 \leqslant i \leqslant P$ and $g_o = 1$. Derive $\{g_i\}$ values for $P = 5$ so that $G(z)$ approximates the transfer function of the all-pole DPCM filter $[1 - A(z)]^{-1}$, for

(a) $A(z) = 0.85 \ z^{-1}$ and

(b) $A(z) = 1.1 \ z^{-1} -0.28z^{-2} -.08z^{-3}$.

References

H. Abut, R. M. Gray and G. Rebolledo, "Vector Quantization of Speech and Speech-like Waveforms," IEEE Trans. on Acoustics, Speech and Signal Proc., pp. 423-435, June 1982.

J. P. Adoul, J. L. Debray and D. Dalle, "Spectral Distance Measure Applied to the Optimum Design of DPCM Coders with L Predictors," Proc. ICASSP, pp. 512-515, 1980.

J. B. Anderson and J. B. Bodie, "Tree Encoding of Speech," IEEE Trans. on Information Theory, pp. 379-381, July 1975.

J. B. Anderson and C.-W. P. Ho, "Architecture and Construction of a Hardware Sequential Encoder for Speech," IEEE Trans. on Communications, pp. 703-707, July 1977.

J. B. Anderson and F. Jelinek, "A Two-Cycle Algorithm for Source Coding with a Fidelity Criterion," IEEE Trans. on Information Theory, pp. 77-92, January 1973.

J. B. Anderson and C.-W. Law, "Real-Number Convolutional Codes for Speech-Like Quasi-stationary Sources," IEEE Trans. on Information Theory, pp. 778-782, November 1977.

B. S. Atal, "Linear Predictive Coding of Speech," unpublished work, Bell Laboratories, 1983.

B. S. Atal and J. R. Remde, "A New Model of LPC Excitation for Producing Natural-Sounding Speech at Low Bit Rates," Proc. ICASSP, pp. 614-617, 1982.

G. W. Aughenbaugh, J. D. Irwin and J. B. O'Neal, "Delayed Differential Pulse Code Modulation," Proc. Second Annual Princeton Conf., pp. 125-130, October 1970.

D. W. Becker and A. J. Viterbi, "Speech Digitization and Compression by Adaptive Predictive Coding with Delayed Decision," Proc. Nat. Telecom. Conf., New Orleans, pp. 46-18 to 46-23, December 1975.

T. Berger, *Rate Distortion Theory, a Mathematical Basis for Data Compression*, Prentice-Hall, Englewood Cliffs, N.J., 1971.

B. Bochow and P. Noll, Technical University of Berlin, unpublished work, 1983.

J. B. Bodie, "Multi-path Tree Encoding for Analog Data Sources," McMaster University Report, Canada, June 1974.

H. Brehm and K. Trottel, "Vector Quantization of Spherically Invariant Random Processes," Proc. European Signal Processing Conference, pp. 383-386, 1983.

A. Buzo, A. H. Gray, Jr., R. M. Gray and J. D. Markel, "Speech Coding Based upon Vector Quantization," IEEE Trans. on Acoustics, Speech and Signal Proc., pp. 562-574, October 1980.

J. C. Candy, "Refinement of a Delta Modulator," Proc. Symp. on Picture Bandwidth Compression, M.I.T., Cambridge Tech. Rep., April 1969.

J. H. Conway and N. J. A. Sloane, "Fast Quantizing and Decoding Algorithms for Lattice Quantizers and Codes," IEEE Trans. on Information Theory, pp. 227-232, March 1982.

V. M. Cuperman, "Efficient Waveform Coding of Speech Using Vector Quantization," Ph.D. dissertation, University of California, Santa Barbara, February 1983.

C. C. Cutler, "Delayed Encoding: Stabilizer for Adaptive Coders," IEEE Trans. on Communications, pp. 898-904, December 1971.

H. G. Fehn, "Untersuchungen von Mehrwegesuchverfahren zur Codierung von Modell- und Sprachquellen" (in German), Dissertation, Universität Bremen, Germany, 1981.

H. G. Fehn and P. Noll, "Tree and Trellis Coding of Speech and Stationary Speech-like Signals," Proc. ASSP, Denver, pp. 547-551, April 1980.

H. G. Fehn and P. Noll, "Multipath Search Coding of Stationary Signals with Applications to Speech," IEEE Trans. on Communications, pp. 687-701, April 1982.

Th. R. Fischer and R. M. Dicharry, "Vector Quantization Design for Gaussian, Gamma and Laplacian Sources," Proc. Inter. Conf. on Communications, pp. 1085-1089, 1983.

G. D. Forney, Jr., "The Viterbi Algorithm," Proc. IEEE, pp. 268-278, March 1973.

J. Foster, "Finite State Vector Quantization for Waveform Coding," Ph.D. dissertation, Stanford University, November 1982.

A. Gersho, "Quantization," IEEE Communications Society Magazine, pp. 16-29, September 1977.

A. Gersho, "Asymptotically Optimal Block Quantization," IEEE Trans. on Information Theory, pp. 373-380, July 1979.

A. Gersho and B. Ramamurthi, "Image Coding Using Vector Quantization," Proc. ICASSP, pp. 428-431, April 1982.

A. J. Goldberg, "Predictive Coding with Delayed Decision," Proc. ICASSP, pp. 405-408, 1977.

W. Granzow and P. Noll, unpublished work, Technische Universität Berlin, Germany, 1983.

R. M. Gray, "Vector Quantization," IEEE ASSP Magazine, April 1984.

R. M Gray and H. Abut, "Full Search and Tree Search Vector Quantization of Speech Waveforms," Proc. ICASSP, pp. 593-596, May 1982.

R. M. Gray and Y. Linde, "Vector Quantizers and Predictive Quantizers for Gauss-Markov Sources," IEEE Trans. on Communications, pp. 381-389, February 1982.

N. S. Jayant and S. A. Christensen, "Tree Encoding of Speech Using the (M, L)-Algorithm and Adaptive Quantization," IEEE Trans. on Communications, pp. 165-170, January 1979.

F. Jelinek, "Tree Encoding of Memoryless Time-Discrete Sources with a Fidelity Criterion," IEEE Trans. on Information Theory, pp. 584-590, September 1969.

F. Jelinek and J. B. Anderson, "Instrumentable Tree Encoding of Information Sources," IEEE Trans. on Information Theory, pp. 118-119, January 1971.

D. E. Knuth, *The art of computer programming*, Vol. III: *Sorting and Searching*, Addison-Wesley, Reading, Mass., 1973.

T. S. Koubanitsas, "Application of the Viterbi Algorithm to Adaptive Delta Modulation with Delayed Decision," Proc. IEEE, pp. 1076-1077, July 1975.

C.-W. Law, "Code Design for Tree Speech Encoders," McMaster University Report, Canada, March 1976.

T.-L. R. Lei, N. Scheinberg and D. L. Schilling, "Adaptive Deltamodulation Systems for Video Encoding," IEEE Trans. on Communications, pp. 1302-1314, November 1977.

Y. Linde, A. Buzo and R. M. Gray, "An Algorithm for Vector Quantizer Design," IEEE Trans. on Communications, pp. 84-95, January 1980.

J. W. Modestino, V. Bhaskaran and J. B. Anderson, "Tree Encoding of Images in the Presence of Channel Errors," IEEE Trans. on Information Theory, pp. 677-696, November 1981.

J. W. Modestino and V. Bhaskaran, "Robust Two-Dimensional Tree Encoding of Images," IEEE Trans. on Communications, pp. 1786-1798, December 1981.

S. Mohan and J. B. Anderson, "Speech Encoding by a Stack Algorithm," IEEE Trans. on Communications, pp. 825-830, June 1980.

C. M. B. Newton, "Deltamodulation with Slope Overload Prediction," Electron. Letters, pp. 272-274, April 30, 1970.

P. Noll, "Trends in Speech Coding," Proc. of the European Signal Processing Conf., pp. 363-370, September 1983.

B. Ramamurthi and A. Gersho, "Image Coding Using Segmented Codebooks," Proc. International Picture Coding Symposium, pp. 105-106, March 1983.

M. R. Schroeder and B. S. Atal, "Rate Distortion Theory and Predictive Coding," Proc. ICASSP, April 1981.

N. J. A. Sloane, "Tables of Sphere Packings and Spherical Codes," IEEE Trans. on Information Theory, pp. 327-338, May 1981.

L. C. Stewart, R. M. Gray and Y. Linde, "The Design of Trellis Waveform Coders," IEEE Trans. on Communications, pp. 702-710, April 1982.

J. Uddenfeldt and L. H. Zetterberg, "Algorithms for Delayed Encoding in Deltamodulation with Speech-like Signals," IEEE Trans. on Communications, pp. 652-658, June 1976.

A. J. Viterbi and J. K. Omura, "Trellis Encoding of a Memoryless Discrete-Time Sources with a Fidelity Criterion," IEEE Trans. on Information Theory, pp. 325-332, May 1974.

S. G. Wilson and S. Hussain, "Adaptive Tree Encoding of Speech at 8000 Bits/s with a Frequency-Weighted Error Criterion," IEEE Trans. on Communications, pp. 165-170, January 1979.

Y. Yamada, S. Tazaki and R. M. Gray, "Asymptotic Performance of Block Quantizers with Difference Distortion Measures", IEEE Trans. on Information Theory, pp. 6-14, January 1980.

L. H. Zetterberg and J. Uddenfeldt, "Adaptive Deltamodulation with Delayed Decision," IEEE Trans. on Communications, pp. 1195-1198, September 1974.

P. Zador, "Topics in the Asymptotic Quantization of Continuous Random Vectors," unpublished Bell Laboratories memorandum, February 1966; also IEEE Transactions on Information Theory, pp. 139-149, March 1982.

10

Run-Length Coding

10.1 Introduction

Earlier chapters have discussed procedures for redundancy removal in the digitization of images. Two-level *graphics* or *facsimile* images, illustrated very simply in Figure 2.2, constitute an important special class. This class includes images of business documents, newspapers and weather maps. Because of their special importance, such images, and their transmission using either analog or digital methods, have been subjects of extensive research and international standardization [Arps, 1979] [Proceedings of the IEEE, 1980] [Brobst, 1982] [Stoffel, 1982]. Gray-level images are first approximated as arrays of black and white pixels in digital facsimile, and resulting two-level images exhibit a great potential for intraframe redundancy reduction by means of a subsequent operation called *run-length coding*.

Unlike the prediction process in DPCM coding, redundancy removal in digital facsimile occurs *after* quantization; specifically, after two-level quantization that results in black and white pixels. The raw input signal in monochrome facsimile is of course a multi-level input with infinite shades of gray. But in order to focus our attention on the run-length coding aspect, we shall regard the "input" process $\{X(n)\}$ in this chapter as the process at the output of an appropriate two-level quantizer, the input of which is amplitude-continuous [Huang, 1977]. This "input" process to the facsimile system is a binary-valued process with a random variable $X(n) \in (B, W)$, where the symbols B and W denote *black* and *white*. The two-level quantizer is typically not fixed; it is almost invariably an *adaptive-threshold* or *floating-threshold* device [Ting and Prasada, 1980] that filters out undesirable discontinuities or microscopic intensity variations that may be present in its input. The effect of such filtering will be to enhance the probability of long, unbroken runs of pixels of one kind in the two-level process $\{X(n)\}$.

The output quality in digital facsimile depends on the coding process, on digital channel quality, and on procedures that may be used for mitigating transmission error effects [Musmann and Preuss, 1977] [Proceedings of the IEEE, 1980] [Bodson and Schaphorst, 1983]. Unless otherwise mentioned, the rest of this chapter assumes the simple situation of *noiseless* or *exact* coding of the two-level input followed by error-free transmission of a lower-rate coder output.

Illustrative graphics inputs are shown in Figure 10.1 [Hunter and Robinson, 1980] [Kunt and Johnsen, 1980]. We shall refer back to these specific examples in the course of discussing the performance of run-length coding algorithms. The *normal resolution* CCITT facsimile standard [Proceedings of the IEEE, 1980] calls for a 1188 × 1728 pixel matrix with 1188 scan lines per frame and 1728 pixels per line. The 1188 scan lines correspond to a vertical scanning density of 3.85 lines/mm with a Standard A4 document of length 29.2 cm or 11.7 inches (and width 20.7 cm or 8.27 inches). The *higher-resolution* facsimile standard calls for a vertical scanning density of 7.7 lines/mm, and a 2376 × 1728 matrix. The total number of pixels is then 4 105 728, and this represents a number of pixels/frame that is about 10 times greater than in commercial television. The higher-resolution format is appropriate for intricate images such as the Japanese text in Figure 10.1(d). The horizontal resolution is about 8 pixels/mm in both of the above standards.

It is clear that with either of the above resolutions, all the documents of Figure 10.1 result in long *runs* or *clusters* or *bursts* of B and W pixels. It is precisely this property that is exploited in run-length coding — the two-valued input process $\{X(n)\}$ is transformed (non-linearly) to a many-valued run-length process $\{\beta(n)\}$, and the $\{\beta(n)\}$ process is subsequently coded for transmission purposes, as in Figure 10.2. Unless otherwise mentioned, the run-length process is considered as being *exactly coded*; so that the binary process $\{X(n)\}$ is replicated perfectly. Further, the coding of run-length invariably makes use of variable-length coding because longer runs in general are less probable than shorter runs. The shortest run of course is an isolated occurrence such as the isolated W in $BBWBBB$. It is sometimes convenient to talk about a run of length zero as well, as we shall see in Section 10.3.

Run-length coding constitutes a naturally appropriate technique for exploiting the redundancy in highly structured two-level inputs. The advantages due to a two-level input are obvious. A B-run is followed, by definition, with a W-run so that there is no need to transmit separate amplitude and timing information in a run-length-coding system. The quantization or reconstruction noise is zero if run lengths are correctly reproduced, so that exact replications of inputs are possible. Further, there is no need for real-time communication in facsimile, so that variable-rate coding of horizontal scan lines is no problem — there is no constraint on the time taken for encoding a line; the only criterion is an *average* one: for example, the average time of transmission for a document class over a given digital channel (Problem 10.3). Finally, unlike speech or gray-level images, facsimile

(a)

Deux éclatements de taille se sont produits en 1968, à Paris en mai, à Prague en août, l'un pour le socialisme dans la liberté, l'autre pour la liberté dans le socialisme. Une fois dépouillés de quelques apparences et oripeaux, les deux objectifs socialisme et liberté apparaissent bien ceux de la grande majorité de l'humanité évoluée. En dehors de l'Amérique du Nord, peu nombreux sont ceux qui osent les répudier ouvertement. Du moins personne ne se prononce-t-il contre la justice sociale, ni pour la mise en condition ou en tutelle des individus, ni même pour la société de classes.

Ceux qui ont peur du socialisme ne sont pas tous des propriétaires endurcis de grandes usines ou de centaines d'hectares, mais d'accablants précédents leur font craindre pour la plus précieuse des propriétés, celle de disposer de soi-même. Et ceux que n'enthousiasme pas l'expression "monde libre" ont bien présentes à l'esprit les exactions que recouvre ce beau drapeau.

Après deux siècles de recherches, de révolutions, de théories, d'expériences en tous sens, aucun point n'apparait sur la planète, aucun îlot, où les deux objectifs socialisme et liberté soient conciliés de façon satisfaisante.

Pendant un siècle ou presque, la démocratie, appelée dans la suite démocratie bourgeoise ou démocratie occidentale, selon le degré de sympathie qui lui est porté, a vécu sous la bannière de la liberté, mais avec le remords croissant de l'injustice sociale.

Depuis un demi-siècle, a été institué un nouveau régime dont l'objectif social a relégué la liberté des individus au second plan. Qui ne refuse franchement à ces deux régimes le droit de s'appeler dé-

(b)

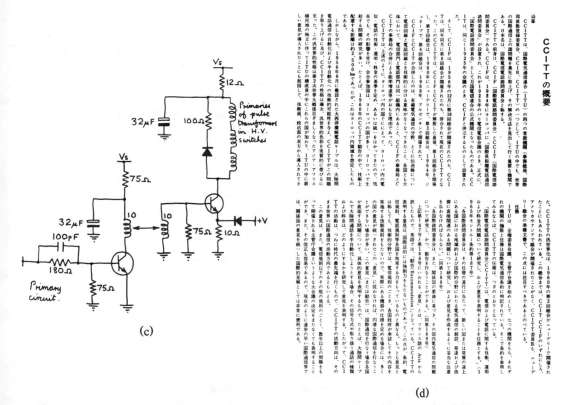

(c)

(d)

Figure 10.1 Illustrative two-level inputs: (a) weather map; (b) printed text [Kunt and Johnsen, 1980]; and CCITT documents (c) number 2 and (d) number 7 [Hunter and Robinson, 1980].

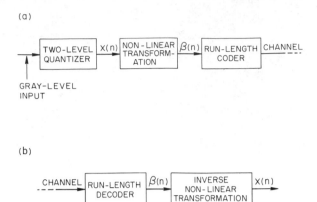

(a)

GRAY-LEVEL
INPUT

(b)

Figure 10.2 Block diagram of run-length coding (RLC): (a) coder; and (b) decoder.

inputs are indeed modeled as unknown waveforms with frequent runs of constant amplitude, a model best suited for the non-parametric approach that is typical of run-length coding systems; the run-length properties in two-level facsimile are also robust, as they are not affected by noise-induced transitions to a neighboring gray level. Problem 10.3 defines the goal of a one-minute transmission system for CCITT-recommended facsimile inputs. It is seen that for a 1-minute transmission time over a 4800 b/s switched telephone channel, the pixels in a high-resolution facsimile matrix need to be coded at an average rate of about 0.07 bit/pixel, implying a data compression factor of about 14 over an uncompressed 1 bit/pixel PCM version. Noiseless coding at 0.07 bit/pixel implies, of course, that the entropy of the source is no more than 0.07 bit/pixel. The Markov source of Example C.4 in Appendix C indeed shows that the entropy of a structured binary source can be much less than 1 bit/sample (in fact, 0.08 in Example C.4).

CCITT standards for high-resolution *analog* facsimile over telephone channels specify 3- and 6-minute transmissions rather than 1-minute transmission. The possibility of 1-minute transmission is a consequence of digitizing followed by redundancy removal. In fact, if a 64 kb/s digital transmission facility were to be available, as in evolving *Integrated Services Digital Network* (ISDN) systems, the high-resolution document, coded at a rate of 0.07 bits/pixel, can be transmitted almost instantaneously, in 4.5 seconds. Transmission of a newspaper page image [Usubuchi, Omachi and Iinuma, 1980] is more time-consuming, for a given channel and a given number of bits/pixel.

Section 10.2 discusses analytical principles of run-length coding, with special reference to a simple Markovian model. Section 10.3 discusses run-length coding systems in practical facsimile systems. This discussion includes a CCITT-approved modified Huffman code for variable-length coding of the run-length alphabet, as well as two-dimensional approaches that provide somewhat higher data compression. Section 10.4 provides a brief discussion of *Aperture Coding* and *Asynchronous Deltamodulation*; these systems can be regarded as attempts to extend run-length concepts to multi-level waveforms.

10.2 Principles of Run-Length Coding

In the section on Entropy Coding (Section 4.6), we saw the utility of representing *fixed-length-to-variable-length* mappings, in order to exploit the unequal probabilities of the input words. We shall now discuss a *variable-length-to-variable-length* mapping which is appropriate to the noiseless, or exact coding of clusters, or runs, of like input symbols. Run-length encoding can lead to significant data compression with redundant inputs characterized by long clusters of like symbols; for example, clusters of W's and B's in two-level facsimile. Applications of run-length coding have almost exclusively been in the facsimile field where such clustering is extremely obvious, although the concept is definitely applicable in principle for coding clusters of like bits in DPCM or DM outputs (Problem 10.1), or for coding clusters of different shades of gray in a continuous-tone picture.

A Markov Model for Two-Level Inputs. The output symbols of a binary source can be exactly encoded with $H(X)$ bits/symbol rather than with 1 bit/symbol, where $H(X)$ is the source entropy (Appendix C). The redundancy of a discrete-amplitude binary source is therefore defined as $1-H(X)$, where $H(X)$ is the source entropy. In the case of inputs where $H(X) \ll 1$, a useful property is the *maximum run-length coding gain* G_{RLC}, or the *maximum compression*, defined as the reciprocal of $H(X)$:

$$\max\{G_{RLC}\} = 1/H(X) \tag{10.1}$$

One of the purposes of this section is to relate $H(X)$, and therefore, $\max\{G_{RLC}\}$, to run-length statistics in a two-level input. We shall do so with the simple example of a first-order Markov model (Appendix C). The model, also called the *Capon model* [Capon, 1959], is realistic for certain classes of facsimile inputs such as weather maps [Kunt, 1974].

Figure 10.3(a) shows the first-order Markov model [Capon, 1959] that will be used to understand the statistics of the output from a binary waveform source. Although the model can be extended to general sources allowing for more states in the Markov chain, the properties of run-length distributions are best understood for the simple (and practically important) example of two states. These states are labeled W and B in Figure 10.3 in anticipation of *white* and *black* states in facsimile applications. The corresponding *transition probabilities* are t_W and t_B, or, in general, t_S for state S, where S is either W or B:

$$t_W = P\{X(n) = B \mid X(n-1) = W\}$$

$$t_B = P\{X(n) = W \mid X(n-1) = B\} \tag{10.2}$$

the *state probabilities* $P(W) = P\{X(n) = W\}$ and $P(B) = P\{X(n) = B\}$ are determined by the values of t_W and t_B (Problem 10.4 and Appendix D):

$$P(W) = 1 - P(B) = t_B(t_W+t_B)^{-1} \tag{10.3}$$

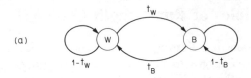

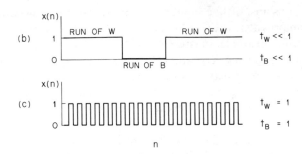

Figure 10.3 A first-order Markov model for the 1-D representation of two-level inputs. (a) Definition of states and transition probabilities. Waveform examples for (b) $t_W \ll 1$, $t_B \ll 1$, and for (c) $t_W = t_B = 1$.

Note that the state probabilities add up to 1 by definition while the sum of transition probabilities has no such constraint. In fact, in an input characterized by long runs of W's and B's [Figure 10.3(b)],

$$t_W \ll 1, \quad t_B \ll 1, \quad t_W + t_B \ll 1 \tag{10.4}$$

In the other extreme instance of $t_B = t_W = 1$, the maximum run length is also 1 [Figure 10.3(c)].

Run-Length Distributions. The probability of a run of β_k pixels in state S is

$$P(\beta_k|S) = t_S(1-t_S)^{\beta_k-1}; \quad \beta_k=1,2,...,\infty; \quad S = B, W \tag{10.5a}$$

where the term on the right is the probability of $(\beta_k - 1)$ non-transitions followed by a transition that ends the run. Using (10.4), the expected run length, the expectation of a r.v. β, conditioned on state S, can be shown to be simply the reciprocal of the corresponding transition probability (Problem 10.5):

$$E[\beta|S] = 1/t_S; \quad S = B, W \tag{10.5b}$$

It is instructive to rewrite (10.5a) using (10.5b):

$$P(\beta_k|S) = \frac{1}{E[\beta|S] - 1} \left[1 - (E[\beta|S])^{-1}\right]^{\beta_k} \tag{10.6}$$

This represents a *geometric* or *discrete-exponential* distribution for run-length β. This distribution is a consequence of the first-order Markov model.

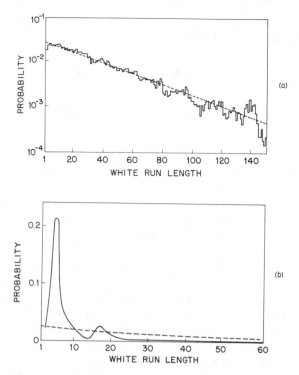

Figure 10.4 Measured distributions (solid curves) versus geometric run-length distributions (broken curves) for white runs in the inputs of (a) Figure 10.1(a); and (b) Figure 10.1(b) [Kunt, 1974].

Figure 10.4 shows measured distributions of W-runs for the facsimile examples of Figures 10.1(a) and (b). A linearly decreasing characteristic in Figure 10.4(a) signifies an exponential decay because of the use of log-probability on the y-axis. The geometric pdf, and hence the first-order Markov model, is remarkably appropriate to the weather map in Figure 10.1(a), but clearly inadequate for the printed text in Figure 10.1(b). The latter belongs to a class of highly structured facsimile inputs, models for which are discussed elsewhere [Kunt, 1974]. Clearly, one of the properties of this latter class is a pronounced peak in $P(\beta_k|S)$ at a small value of β_k [= 5 in the example of Figure 10.4(b)].

The distributions in Figure 10.4 refer to W-runs. The distributions of B-runs are qualitatively similar to the distributions of W-runs. However, expected run lengths are in general significantly different. For the usual case of *black-on-white* documents, the average length of white runs tends to be greater:

$$E[\beta|W] > E[\beta|B] \tag{10.7}$$

Entropy versus Average Run-Length. The entropy of the Markov process in Figure 10.3 is (Appendix C)

$$H(X) = P(W)\,H(X|S{=}W) + P(B)\,H(X|S{=}B) \tag{10.8}$$

where the conditional entropy terms are given in terms of the respective transition probabilities, and the *binary entropy function*

$$H(X|S=W) = \lambda(t_W); \quad H(X|S=B) = \lambda(t_B) \tag{10.9}$$

$$\lambda(p) = -p \log_2 p - (1-p) \log_2 (1-p) \tag{10.10}$$

Figure 10.5 shows contours of constant entropy $H(X)$ versus the expected run lengths [see (10.5b)]. Note that the least redundant source is one for which the expected run lengths are 2 for both W and B states. Corresponding transition probabilities are therefore 0.5 each, and from (10.3), the state probabilities are 0.5 as well. This is clearly the special case of an incompressible i.i.d. source (Problem 10.7). On the other hand, compressible sources [such as the example in Figure 10.1(b)] are characterized by long runs of W and B. For example, to achieve a compression of 10.0, or $H(X) = 0.1$ bit/sample, one needs a source in which $E[\beta|W] = E[\beta|B] = 75$; or following the $H(X) = 0.1$ contour into a more realistic region [see (10.7)], a source in which $E[\beta|W] = 100$ and $E[\beta|B] = 55$.

The relationship between entropy and run-length statistics, as shown in Figure 10.5, is clearly specific to a first-order Markov model with an exponential run-length pdf. It can be shown that, among all positive random variables with the same average run length, the r.v. with the geometrical pdf (10.6) has the maximum entropy [Capon, 1959] [Huang, 1972]. [See Problem (10.8)]. In other words, for given average run-lengths, non-Markov images are more compressible.

Figure 10.5 Contours of equal entropy $H(X)$ in the Markov model. The numbers next to the contours are values of $H(X)$. The x- and y-axes are expected run lengths $E[\beta|W]$ and $E[\beta|B]$ [Huang, 1977].

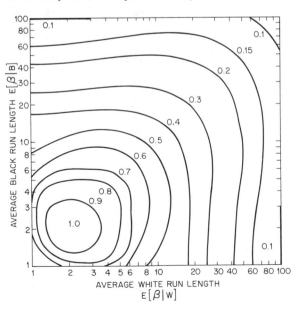

We have mentioned in (10.1) that the maximum compression due to run-length coding is equal to the reciprocal of $H(X)$. The equality is a result of the assumption that successive runs (in a given scan line) are independent, which is true in the first-order Markov source of Figure 10.3(a). Experimental measurements with practical non-Markov sources in facsimile also show that the effects of inter-run dependencies are very small; schemes that take these dependencies into account realize typical additional compressions of only about 10%. On the other hand, schemes that exploit two-dimensional redundancies realize more significant gains (in the order of 50% on the average), and this follows from the fact that the entropy computed from 2-D models is smaller than the 1-D entropy in (10.1) by a similar amount. We shall briefly discuss 2-D techniques in Section 10.3.

In 1-D run-length coding schemes, realization of the bound in (10.1) implies, in general, that separate run-length codes are used for states B and W, which are characterized by different pdf's. The use of a single code, optimized for the pooled statistics in the W and B states can be characterized by a lower performance bound [Huang, 1972]

$$G_{RLC} > [\lambda(p_0)]^{-1}; \quad p_0 = 2[E(\beta|W) + E(\beta|B)]^{-1} \tag{10.11}$$

Example 10.1. First-order Markov description of weather map and printed text
Table 10.1 shows first-order Markov descriptions that provide a close fit to experimentally obtained statistics of the images in Figures 10.1(a) and (b). It can be verified (Problem 10.9) that transition- and state-probabilities listed follow (10.3) and that the entropy follows (10.8). The theoretical white-run-length pdf's in Figure 10.4 result from the t_W values of Table 10.1 and (10.5). The $H_{2-D}(X)$ values in Table 10.1 are entropies obtained by taking into account 2-D redundancies. These values were obtained by dividing the image into (4×4) subimages, calculating the entropy per subimage assuming independent subimages, and dividing the subimage entropy by 16.

Table 10.1   First-order Markov description of the documents in Figures 10.1 (a) and (b) [Kunt, 1974].

Document	Weather Map	Printed Text
$P(W)$	0.887	0.935
$P(B)$	0.113	0.065
t_W	0.027	0.024
t_B	0.214	0.347
$H(X)$	0.241	0.215
$H_{2-D}(X)$	0.173	0.150

Variable-Length Coding of Run-length β. Table 10.2 shows two examples of Huffman coding (Appendix C) for a run-length alphabet with $\max\{\beta\} = 8$. In both cases, less probable values of β are coded with longer codewords. The distribution $P(\beta_k)$ is *exponential* in example (a). In this case, the length of the codeword increases *linearly* as we go down the table. In fact, the $P(\beta_k)$ values in (a) are of

Table 10.2 Variable-length coding schemes for run-length processes with (a) exponential and (b) slower-than-exponential run-length pdf $P(\beta_k)$ [Huang;©1975, IEEE].

<table>
<tr><td colspan="3" align="center">(a)</td><td colspan="3" align="center">(b)</td></tr>
<tr><td>β_k</td><td>$P(\beta_k)$</td><td>Codeword</td><td>β_k</td><td>$P(\beta_k)$</td><td>Codeword</td></tr>
<tr><td>1</td><td>1/2</td><td>1</td><td>1</td><td>1/4</td><td>1 1</td></tr>
<tr><td>2</td><td>1/4</td><td>0 1</td><td>2</td><td>1/4</td><td>1 0</td></tr>
<tr><td>3</td><td>1/8</td><td>0 0 1</td><td>3</td><td>1/8</td><td>0 1 1</td></tr>
<tr><td>4</td><td>1/16</td><td>0 0 0 1</td><td>4</td><td>1/8</td><td>0 1 0</td></tr>
<tr><td>5</td><td>1/32</td><td>0 0 0 0 1</td><td>5</td><td>1/16</td><td>0 0 1 1</td></tr>
<tr><td>6</td><td>1/64</td><td>0 0 0 0 0 1</td><td>6</td><td>1/16</td><td>0 0 1 0</td></tr>
<tr><td>7</td><td>1/128</td><td>0 0 0 0 0 0 1</td><td>7</td><td>1/16</td><td>0 0 0 1</td></tr>
<tr><td>8</td><td>1/128</td><td>0 0 0 0 0 0 0</td><td>8</td><td>1/16</td><td>0 0 0 0</td></tr>
</table>

the form 2^{-n} and corresponding codewords are n bits long. The pdf in example (b) is non-exponential; $P(\beta_k)$ values decay slower than in (a), and the codeword length consequently increases in a slower-than-linear fashion. In fact, if $P(\beta_k)$ can be modeled by a negative-power distribution, the codeword length can be shown to increase *logarithmically* as we go down a corresponding codeword table [Meyr, Rosdolsky and Huang, 1974] [Huang, 1975]. Facsimile documents such as weather maps [Figure 10.1(a)] are examples where $P(\beta_k)$ is exponential, and a linearly growing code is optimal. On the other hand, structured facsimile sources such as printed text [Figure 10.1(b)] are examples where $P(\beta_k)$ is non-exponential, and for these inputs, a slower-than-linear growth in codelength results when Huffman coding is employed. The CCITT- recommended modified Huffman code in Section 10.3 is less efficient (in terms of minimum average code length) than a Huffman code, but it is expected to be a good match for a broad class of $P(\beta_k)$ models. These distributions have a range, or support, equal to $\max\{\beta_k\} = 1728$ corresponding to the number of pixels in a scan line.

10.3 Run-Length Coding of Two-Level Graphics

One manifestation of redundancy in two-level graphics is the availability of easily exploitable runs of W and B pels on any given 1-D scan line; and the one-dimensional (1-D) CCITT scheme to be described next is a well-proven procedure for exploiting this redundancy. An even richer source of redundancy is the fact that facsimile inputs are composed of continuous black contours and areas on a white background, or vice versa; sophisticated 2-D encoding techniques such as *block coding* [Kunt and Johnsen, 1980], *contour coding* [Schreiber, Huang and Tretiak, 1972] [Morrin, 1976], and *blob encoding* [Frank, 1973] can provide extremely efficient utilizations of these 2-D redundancies. Some of these 2-D techniques have the additional property of providing *progressive transmission* [Frank, 1980]. This is a class of coding procedures which enable the receiver to obtain a rough but quick recognition of entire image content, to be followed, if needed, by higher-quality decoding. Clearly, this property is not possessed by 1-D coding methods that result in a line-by-line display. An adequate discussion of sophisticated 2-D techniques would take us beyond the scope of waveform coding, and possibly into the realm of pattern recognition. However, we shall note two examples where the simpler technique of run-length coding is extended to exploit two-dimensional redundancy, for additional compression gains in the order of 30 to 50%.

Modified Huffman Coding for 1-D Run-Length Coding. Table 10.3 is a CCITT-recommended variable-length coding system for a run-length alphabet with $\max\{\beta\} = 1728$, the scan length in the standard format mentioned earlier. The coding system regards a run-length β as a sum of two terms, so that runs longer than 63 are broken up into concatenations of shorter runs of maximum length 63:

$$\beta = 64\,m + n\;;\quad m = 0,1,2,...,27\;;\quad n = 0,1,2,...,63 \qquad (10.12)$$

The *terminating* codewords in Table 10.3 represent the value of n and the *make-up* codewords represent the value of $64\,m$. The zero-run codewords for W and B signify scan lines that begin with the opposite amplitude, B and W. The codeword for *end-of-line* (EOL) is a unique sequence which cannot be produced by a concatenation of other codewords. This is because none of them ends in a sequence of more than 3 zeroes or begins with a sequence of more than 6 zeroes; on the other hand, the EOL codeword has 11 zeros in it.

Table 10.4 shows the performance of the 1-D (modified Huffman) code when applied to CCITT documents of normal and high resolution. Documents numbered **2** and **7** have been shown in Figures 10.1(c) and (d). Note that for the low-activity document **2**, the output rate is 0.06 bit/pixel while for the high-activity document **7**, the output rate is 0.21 bit/pixel; these numbers are also essentially independent of image resolution. Recall from Problem 10.3 that a coding rate of 0.07 bit/pixel is needed for 1-minute transmission of a high-resolution image over a 4800 b/s channel. This goal is met in 1-D coding for only 2 of the 8 documents in the high-resolution table. On the other hand, the goal is met for 6 out of the 8 documents when the 2-D READ scheme is employed. This scheme will be described presently.

The performance of a 1-D code can be improved somewhat by pixel rearrangement procedures [Netravali and Mounts, 1980] [Yasuda, 1980] that enhance run-length statistics; the rearrangement information has to be explicitly transmitted to the receiver except in the case of systematic rearrangements such as those that take into account gaps between characters in printed text. Enhancement of 1-D system performances is desirable because 2-D schemes, although more bit-efficient, are more susceptible to transmission errors. Error effects can be confined to one scan line in 1-D schemes. Errors in digital facsimile are easy to detect; for example, by checking if the sum of received run lengths equals the sum line length. Error concealment is also straightforward. An erroneous line can be replaced by an all-W line, or by the pixel sequence on the previous scan line. When 2-D schemes are used for higher efficiency (this is usually important for the higher-resolution format), it is usual to revert periodically (once every K lines) to a 1-D procedure [Hunter and Robinson, 1980]. The 2-D scheme in Table 10.4 is a pure 2-D version with $K = \infty$.

Table 10.3 Modified Huffman Code Table [Hunter and Robinson;©1980, IEEE].

Terminating Codewords					
Run Length	White	Black	Run Length	White	Black
0	00110101	0000110111	32	00011011	000001101010
1	000111	010	33	00010010	000001101011
2	0111	11	34	00010011	000011010010
3	1000	10	35	00010100	000011010011
4	1011	011	36	00010101	000011010100
5	1100	0011	37	00010110	000011010101
6	1110	0010	38	00010111	000011010110
7	1111	00011	39	00101000	000011010111
8	10011	000101	40	00101001	000001101100
9	10100	000100	41	00101010	000001101101
10	00111	0000100	42	00101011	000011011010
11	01000	0000101	43	00101100	000011011011
12	001000	0000111	44	00101101	000001010100
13	000011	00000100	45	00000100	000001010101
14	110100	00000111	46	00000101	000001010110
15	110101	000011000	47	00001010	000001010111
16	101010	0000010111	48	00001011	000001100100
17	101011	0000011000	49	01010010	000001100101
18	0100111	0000001000	50	01010011	000001010010
19	0001100	00001100111	51	01010100	000001010011
20	0001000	00001101000	52	01010101	000000100100
21	0010111	00001101100	53	00100100	000000110111
22	0000011	00000110111	54	00100101	000000111000
23	0000100	00000101000	55	01011000	000000100111
24	0101000	00000010111	56	01011001	000000101000
25	0101011	00000011000	57	01011010	000001011000
26	0010011	000011001010	58	01011011	000001011001
27	0100100	000011001011	59	01001010	000000101011
28	0011000	000011001100	60	01001011	000000101100
29	00000010	000011001101	61	00110010	000001011010
30	00000011	000001101000	62	00110011	000001100110
31	00011010	000001101001	63	00110100	000001100111
Make-Up Codewords					
Run Length	White	Black	Run Length	White	Black
64	11011	0000001111	960	011010100	0000001110011
128	10010	000011001000	1024	011010101	0000001110100
192	010111	000011001001	1088	011010110	0000001110101
256	0110111	000001011011	1152	011010111	0000001110110
320	00110110	000000110011	1216	011011000	0000001110111
384	00110111	000000110100	1280	011011001	0000001010010
448	01100100	000000110101	1344	011011010	0000001010011
512	01100101	0000001101100	1408	011011011	0000001010100
576	01101000	0000001101101	1472	010011000	0000001010101
640	01100111	0000001001010	1536	010011001	0000001011010
704	011001100	0000001001011	1600	010011010	0000001011011
768	011001101	0000001001100	1664	011000	0000001100100
832	011010010	0000001001101	1728	010011011	0000001100101
896	011010011	0000001110010	EOL	000000000001	000000000001

Table 10.4 Data compression efficiency of one-dimensional (MH: modified Huffman) and two-dimensional (READ) facsimile codes. Entries are number of bits needed to code an image [Yasuda;©1980, IEEE].

CCITT Document Number	Normal Resolution (2 052 864 pixels)		Higher Resolution (4 105 728 pixels)	
	1-D MHC	2-D READ	1-D MHC	2-D READ
1	133 095	93 196	266 283	141 826
2	123 930	53 366	247 443	80 550
3	244 028	138 411	487 485	229 375
4	436 450	366 055	871 983	553 942
5	253 509	162 186	506 283	257 548
6	191 347	78 577	381 905	132 509
7	428 028	357 130	855 841	539 152
8	238 221	89 654	476 624	137 560
Average	256 076	167 322	511 731	259 058

Two-Dimensional Schemes. We have already discussed 2-D prediction for gray-level images. In the case of two-level images, the prediction error is also binary. Figure 10.6(a) is an original graphics input and Figure 10.6(b) is the two-level prediction error image resulting from a fourth-order predictor in which pixel A to be coded is predicted using one predicting pixel B from the current scan line and the three nearest pixels C, D and E from the previous scan line, in the notation of Figure 10.6(c). In the prediction error image, pixels that are correctly and incorrectly predicted are signified by white and black samples in corresponding pixel positions [Preuss, 1975] [Weber, 1975]. The resulting prediction error signal has longer runs of white than the original image. Consequently, run-length coding of the prediction error signal leads to greater compression factors.

The optimum prediction function is in general image-dependent. One set of experiments involving typical typewritten English and Japanese documents and a weather map shows that global efficient prediction functions for a third-order predictor is given by [Yasuda, 1980]

$$\hat{x}_A = x_B x_C + x_C x_E + x_E x_B \qquad (10.13)$$

in the notation of Figure 10.6(c). In (10.13), sum and product operations are both logical, and x_P is defined to be equal to 1 or 0, depending on whether pixel P ($P = A,B,C,D,$ or E) is white or black. Thus, (10.13) implies that the prediction of A is based on a majority count decision involving the observed values of the neighbors B, C and E. If B and C are white and E is black, the predicted value of A is still white, as in Figure 10.6(d). A majority count is obviously not possible with a prediction algorithm involving an even number of predicting pixels. For example, in the fourth order predictor used in Figure 10.6(b), the predicted state of

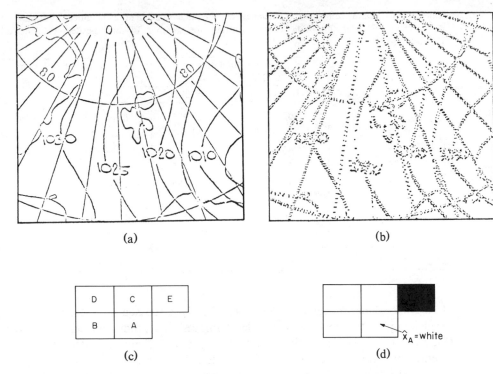

Figure 10.6 2-D prediction in facsimile systems: (a) an original image; (b) a prediction error image to be run-length-coded; (c) neighboring pixels used in a fourth-order prediction of pixel A and (d) result of typical prediction of a pixel A, based on (10.13) [Preuss, 1976].

A depends very strongly on the state of the same-line neighbor B. If B is black, A is predicted to be black in this algorithm even if all the other neighbors C, D and E are white. On the other hand, if B, C and D are white and E is black, A is predicted to be white, as in Figure 10.6(d).

The procedure described above can be made more efficient by higher-order predictions involving more than two rows, in general. However, a more efficient approach is differential coding applied to the run-lengths, rather than pixels, on successive scan lines [Yasuda, 1980]. For example, in Figure 10.7, the W-run of 7 on the lower scan line can be coded very efficiently by observing that it is a perturbation of the W-run of 6 on the upper elements. Specifically, in *relative address coding* (RAC), a transition element such as Q is coded in terms of its distance to one of two reference pixels — either a preceding transition element P on the same scan line, or in terms of a transition element Q' on a previous line, which has the same direction of transition as that of Q and is the nearest to P on its right side. The selection of P or Q' depends on which has a smaller distance from Q. When reference element P does not exist, it is replaced by the first element in the lower scan line. When reference element Q' does not exist, it is replaced by an imaginary pixel to the right of the last pixel on the upper scan line.

In *relative element address designate* (READ) coding, relative coding is performed similarly — but reference pixels and address changes are obtained by

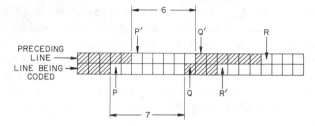

Figure 10.7 2-D pixel configurations utilized in relative address coding (RAC) and relative element address designate (READ) coding.

comparing codewords designating pixel positions rather than distances [Yasuda, 1980]. Both RAC and READ have the powerful feature that reference pels for encoding transition elements are adaptively selected. The resulting efficiency has already been demonstrated by the READ performance numbers in Table 10.4.

10.4 Extensions to Multi-Level Inputs

Multi-level waveforms inherently have less run-length structure than two-level images. The techniques to be described below recognize, however, that very slowly varying segments exist even in multi-level signals; and they utilize this feature for bit rate reduction procedures similar, if not identical, to run-length coding.

Asynchronous DM for Image Coding. Figure 10.8 shows the benefits of *asynchronous* DM systems where non-uniform sampling results in a lower output bit rate without obvious decrease of quality. Figure 10.8(a) depicts conventional linear DM. Figure 10.8(b) refers to an ideal asynchronous system where there is

Figure 10.8 Constant step size DM systems: (a) conventional DM; (b) ideal asynchronous DM; and (c) practical version of (b) [Hawkes and Simonpieri, 1974].

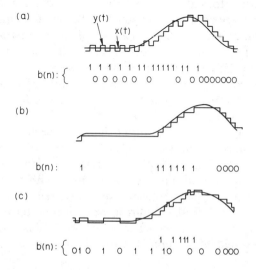

no modification of staircase output or transmitted bit $b(n)$ when the difference signal magnitude is less than an appropriate threshold. Figure 10.8(c) is a practical asynchronous system where information about sampling time need not be conveyed to the receiver. The sampling duration increases automatically during granularity $[b(n) \neq b(n-1)]$ and decreases automatically during slope overload $[b(n) = b(n-1)]$ [Hawkes and Simonpieri, 1974], in a fashion similar to automatic step size changes in instantaneous ADM.

Aperture Coding. Consider the scheme of Figure 10.9(a). The idea is to encode and transmit only the so-called *non-redundant* samples such as $x(0)$, $x(2)$, $x(7)$...; and to deem, as *redundant*, samples such as $x(1)$, $x(3)$, $x(4)$, $x(5)$, $x(6)$..., which fall within an appropriately wide *aperture* (hatched area of width $2\Delta x$) centered on the last transmitted value. The scheme is the simplest of a broad class of *aperture coding* techniques [Ehrman, 1967], and it has the following obvious advantages — a data compression potential because of the non-transmission of "redundant" samples; and explicit control of the aperture noise magnitude Δx. Note that reconstruction noise in this scheme has both aperture and quantization noise components, and many early applications of aperture coding [Kortman, 1967] have been characterized by aperture-noise-dominated reconstructions. Note also that in the special case of two-level facsimile, the aperture noise is zero by definition. The disadvantages of the scheme in Figure 10.9 are also clear: it is a variable-rate coding procedure, and therefore depends on the use of appropriate buffers and buffer management techniques, for employing a channel that expects a constant input bit rate; also, it needs, in its simplest form, transmission of both amplitude- and timing information; and the compression potential is strongly affected by noise either in the input waveform or in the quantization process, both of which tend to increase the frequency of aperture crossings.

The motivation of the aperture coding concept is greatest for applications where input statistics are unknown, and real-time coding is not crucial. With waveforms such as speech which have measurable statistics, especially in locally stationary segments, very formal and powerful data compression schemes exist, such as adaptive predictive coding (Chapter 6). Techniques similar to aperture coding may still be useful in such systems, especially if the prediction error signal has impulsive components [Atal and Schroeder, 1980]. Note finally that the scheme of Figure 10.9(a) is also "predictive", with coefficient $h_1 = 1$.

The attraction of aperture coding is also limited by the problem of conveying to the receiver information about the time of non-redundant samples (Problem 10.10). The overhead caused may be acceptable in high bit rate applications (Problem 10.2). But for low bit rate transmissions of speech or video, it is desirable to avoid explicit transmission of this information. We have already seen that two-level facsimile provides an ideal situation from this viewpoint. Implicit transmission of timing information is also possible with inputs with more than two levels; in general however, such implicit transmission [Murakami et al., 1976] [Jayant and Christensen, 1979] leads to direct penalties in terms of reconstruction fidelity. Implicit transmission of timing information is illustrated briefly in the truncated-aperture example of Figure 10.9(b). In this system, the maximum number of

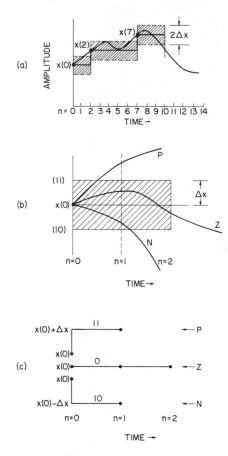

Figure 10.9 Aperture coding systems: (a) conventional floating-aperture method; (b) aperture scheme with no explicit transmission of crossing-time information; and (c) waveform updates corresponding to code choices P, Z and N from (b) [Jayant and Christensen;©1979, AT&T].

"redundant" samples per non-redundant sample is limited to a conveniently small value; this value is 2 in the present example. After transmitting a non-redundant sample $x(0)$ at $t = 0$, the encoder observes the waveform for two samples; it then transmits one of three codes Z, P and N. Codes P and N represent positive and negative aperture crossings before $t = 1$ while Z implies a segment of (zero) low activity, or a run of $\beta = n$ redundant samples, with $n = 2$ in the present example. Waveform inputs that are likely to lead to choices of codes P, N, Z are shown in Figure 10.9(b) while waveform reconstructions corresponding to these codes are shown in Figure 10.9(c). Note how the codes in this system carry both amplitude and time information. The aperture coding cycle repeats at $t = 1$ in the case of P and N codes, with apertures centered at $x(0) + \Delta x$ and $x(0) - \Delta x$ respectively; and at $t = 2$ in the case of the Z code, with an aperture centered again on $x(0)$. In the last case, one talks of a run of $\beta = 2$ redundant samples. The price paid for implicit time information representation with a given bit rate is obvious: certain types of waveform updates are simply not allowed [for example, the case of one redundant sample per transmitted sample in Figure 10.9(b)]. Nevertheless, the procedure has good potential for data compression when applied to structured waveform segments like silences in speech, or images with significant areas of constant brightness; especially in storage and multiplex situations where variable rate coding is more acceptable than in real-time and per-channel coding.

Problems

(10.1)   (a)   Let the output of an ADM coder be modeled by a run-length alphabet where allowable run lengths are $\beta = 1$ or $\beta = 2$, with equal probability. Show that a run-length coding scheme for this alphabet has a transmission rate of 0.75 bit/sample.

(b)   In contrast, show that a run-length coding of the more structured artificial facsimile output, with probabilities 0.4, 0.4, 0.1 and 0.1 for $\beta = 8$, 7, 6 and 5, has the much lower transmission rate of 0.144 bit/sample.

(10.2)   Consider the following sample-by-sample coding approach to a binary output characterized by a probability P_r of "redundant" samples. For each sample, the coding output consists of one bit that tells the receiver whether the sample is redundant or not; and in the case of a non-redundant sample, the above bit is followed by R bits of amplitude information. Show that this system results in data compression (less than R bits/sample on the average) only if $RP_r > 1$. Thus in DM or facsimile applications (where $R = 1$), the above approach will never provide data compression. On the other hand, it can be useful in an R-bit ($R > 1$, say 7) digital speech interpolation system [Campanella, 1976], where during channel overload, a perceptually acceptable "aperture" is used to obtain "redundant" samples with probability $P_r > 1/R = 1/7$.

(10.3)   Consider a 2376×1728 frame of two-level pixels.

(a)   Show that, without redundancy reducing coding, the frame can be transmitted over a 4800 bits/sec channel in 14.3 minutes.

(b)   Hence show that transmission of the above frame in 1 minute requires coding of the image with about 0.07 bit/pixel.

(10.4)   Show that for the stationary two-level source in Figure 10.3,

$$P(W) = t_B/(t_W + t_B) ; \qquad P(B) = t_W/(t_W + t_B)$$

(10.5)   (a)   Show that the run-length probability in the Markov model of Figure 10.3 is given by [Feller, 1968]

$$P(\beta_k | S) = t_S (1 - t_S)^{\beta_k - 1} ; \qquad \beta_k \geq 1 ; \qquad S = B, W$$

(b)   Hence show that the average run length is

$$E[\beta | S] = 1/t_S ; \qquad S = B, W$$

(10.6)   If successive run lengths can be assumed to be statistically independent, show that the entropy per run in state S is given as a product

$$H_{run} = E[\beta|S] \, H(X|S)$$

[Hint: If successive runs are independent, the desired entropy is simply $-\sum_{\beta_k} P(\beta_k|S) \log_2 P(\beta_k|S)$.]

(10.7)   Show that for a fixed $P(W)$, the minimum value of compression occurs when $t_W = 1 - P(W)$, and is given by

$$\min\{G_{RLC}(P(W))\} = [\lambda(P(W))]^{-1}$$

The global minimum occurs when $P(W) = 1/2$, and this minimum compression is simply equal to unity.

(10.8)   Show that among all positive-valued random processes with the same average value of run-length $E[\beta]$, the variable with the geometrical pdf (10.6) has the maximum entropy.

(10.9)   For the picture in Figure 10.1(a) a Capon model would be characterized by

$$t_W = 0.027, \quad t_B = 0.214$$

Using the numbers, show that

(a) $E[\beta|W] = 37, \quad E[\beta|B] = 4.7$;

(b) $H(X|W) = 0.18, \quad H(X|B) = .74; \quad H(X) = 0.24$ bit/pixel

(10.10) Consider a high resolution facsimile document with 2736×1728 pixels. Consider a 0.1 bit/pixel $1-D$ coding system in which transmission error effects do not propagate beyond one horizontal line. Show that if there is to be no more than 1 degraded line per document on the average, the acceptable value of random bit error probability is in the order of $2 \cdot 10^{-6}$.

(10.11) Let the probabilities of 11, 0, and 10 codes in Figure 10.9 corresponding to states P, Z, and N be p, $(1-p)/2$ and $(1-p)/2$, respectively, with $p \geqslant 1/2$. Show that with Huffman coding of the P, N, Z alphabet, the transmission rate approaches 0.5 bit/sample as $p \to 1$, and increases to 0.8 bits/sample if $p = 0.8$.

References

R. B. Arps, "Binary Image Compression," in *Image Transmission Techniques*, Academic Press, New York, pp. 219-276, 1979.

B. S. Atal and M. R. Schroeder, "Improved Quantizer for Adaptive Predictive Coding of Speech Signals at Low Bit Rates," Proc. 1980 Int. Conf. Denver, pp. 535-538, April 1980.

D. Bodson and R. A. Schaphorst, "Error Sensitivity of CCITT Standard Facsimile Coding Techniques," IEEE Trans. on Communications, pp. 69-81, January 1983.

P. L. Brobst, "The Subminute Digital Facsimile Explosion," Telecommunications, pp. 53-60, September 1982.

S. J. Campanella, "Digital Speech Interpolation," COMSAT Technical Review, pp. 127-158, Spring 1976.

J. Capon, "A Probabilistic Model for Run-Length Coding of Pictures," IRE Trans. on Information Theory, pp. 157-163, 1959.

L. Ehrman, "Analysis of Some Redundancy Removal Bandwidth Compression Techniques," Proc. IEEE, pp. 278-287, March 1967.

W. Feller, An Introduction to Probability Theory and Its Applications, John Wiley, New York, 1968.

A. J. Frank, "High Fidelity Encoding of Two-Level, High Resolution Images," Proc. Inter. Conf. on Communications, pp. 26.5-26.9, June 1973.

A. J. Frank, "Progressive Image Transmission Using a Growth-Geometry Coding," Proc. IEEE, pp. 897-909, June 1980.

T. A. Hawkes and A. Simonpieri, "Signal Coding Using Asynchronous Delta Modulation," IEEE Trans. on Communications, pp. 347-349, March 1974.

T. S. Huang, "Run-length Coding and Its Extensions," in Picture Bandwidth Compression, T. S. Huang and O. J. Tretiak, (eds.), Gordon and Breach, New York, 1972.

T. S. Huang, "Easily Implementable Suboptimum Run-Length Codes," Proc. Inter. Conf. on Communications, pp. 7.8-7.11, June 1975.

T. S. Huang, "Coding of Two-Tone Images," IEEE Trans. on Communications, pp. 1406-1424, November 1977.

R. Hunter and A. H. Robinson, "International Digital Facsimile Coding Standards," Proc. IEEE, pp. 854-867, July 1980.

N. S. Jayant and S. A. Christensen, "Adaptive Aperture Coding for Speech Waveforms - I," Bell System Tech. J., pp. 1631-1646, September 1979.

C. M. Kortman, "Redundancy Reduction — A Practical Method of Data Compression," Proc. IEEE, pp. 253-263, March 1967.

M. Kunt, "Comparaison de Techniques d'Encodage pour la Réduction de Redondance d'Images Facsimilé à Deux Niveaux," Ph.D. dissertation, Dept. Elec. Ecole Polytechnique Fédérale de Lausanne, Lausanne, Switzerland, 1974.

M. Kunt and O. Johnsen, "Block Coding of Graphics I: A Tutorial Review," Proc. IEEE, pp. 770-786, July 1980.

H. Meyr, H. G. Rosdolsky and T. S. Huang, "Optimum Run-Length Codes," IEEE Trans. on Communications, pp. 826-835, June 1974.

T. H. Morrin, "Chain-Link Compression of Arbitrary Black-White Images," Computer Graphics and Image Processing, 1976.

K. Murakami, K. Tachibana, H. Fujishita and K. Omura, "Variable Sampling Rate Coder," Technol. Report, Univ. of Osaka, Japan, pp. 499-505, October 1976.

H. G. Musmann and D. Preuss, "A Redundancy Reducing Facsimile Coding Scheme," Nachrichtentech. Zeitschrift, Vol. 26, No. 2, pp. 91-94, February 1973.

H. G. Musmann and D. Preuss, "Comparison of Redundancy Reducing Codes for Facsimile Transmission of Documents," IEEE Trans. on Communications, pp. 1425-1433, November 1977.

A. N. Netravali and F. W. Mounts, "Ordering Techniques for Facsimile Coding: A Review," Proc. IEEE, pp. 796-806, July 1980.

D. Preuss, "Comparison of Two-Dimensional Facsimile Coding Schemes," Proc. Inter. Conf. on Communications, pp. 7.12-7.16, June 1975.

Proceedings of the IEEE, Special Issue on Digital Encoding of Graphics, July 1980.

W. F. Schreiber, T. S. Huang, and O. J. Tretiak, "Contour Coding of Images," in *Picture Bandwidth Compression*, T. S. Huang and O. J. Tretiak, (eds.), Gordon and Breach, New York, 1972.

J. C. Stoffel, *Graphical and Binary Image Processing and Applications,* Artech House, Inc., Dedham, Massachusetts, 1982.

D. Ting and B. Prasada, "Digital Processing Techniques for Encoding of Graphics," Proc. IEEE, pp. 757-769, July 1980.

T. Usubuchi, T. Omachi and K. Iinuma, "Adaptive Predictive Coding for Newspaper Facsimile," Proc. IEEE, pp. 807-812, July 1980.

D. R. Weber, "An Adaptive Run-Length Coding Algorithm," Proc. Inter. Conf. on Communications, pp. 7.4-7.7, June 16-18, 1975.

Y. Yasuda, "Overview of Digital Facsimile Coding Techniques in Japan," Proc. IEEE, pp. 830-845, July 1980.

11

Sub-Band Coding

11.1 Introduction

In the class of *time domain* coding algorithms (Chapters 5 to 10), the input waveform is treated as a single full-band signal; and in predictive coders, redundancy is removed prior to encoding by prediction and inverse filtering. The main differences in the various algorithms are determined by the degree of prediction (Chapters 6 to 8) that is employed, and by whether schemes are adaptive or not. In delayed decision coding (Chapter 9), input structure is exploited by means of a multipath search.

In Chapters 11 and 12 another class of encoding algorithms will be discussed in which the approach is to divide the input signal into a number of separate frequency components, and to encode each of these components separately. This division into frequency components removes the redundancy in the input and provides a set of uncorrelated inputs to the channel. Recall that the action of a DPCM coder is also similar, if not identical. The encoder in that case, when fed by a redundant signal, outputs a sequence of prediction error components that tend to be uncorrelated. The *frequency domain* coding techniques have the advantage that the number of bits used to encode each frequency component can be variable, so that the encoding accuracy is always placed where it is needed in the frequency domain. In fact, bands with little or no energy may not be encoded at all. Variable bit allocation can in principle provide arbitrary forms of noise shaping, a feature that was realized to some extent by noise feedback in the time-domain methods of Chapter 7.

As in the case of time domain techniques, a large variety of frequency domain algorithms, from simple to complex, are available and the main differences are usually determined by the way in which source statistics are modeled, and the degree to which source redundancy is exploited, in the technique. We will begin by describing one technique of lower complexity called *Sub-Band Coding* (SBC) and then proceed to one of higher complexity called *Transform Coding* (TC) (Chapter 12). In the notation of Chapter 1, SBC with fixed bit allocation will be a *medium-complexity* coder and TC with variable bit allocation will be a *high-complexity* coder.

Unless otherwise mentioned, focus in this SBC chapter will be on speech waveforms. In the sub-band coder the speech band is divided into typically four or more sub-bands by a bank of bandpass filters. Each sub-band is, in effect, lowpass translated to zero frequency by a modulation process equivalent to single-side-band amplitude modulation. It is then sampled (or resampled) at its Nyquist rate (twice the width of the band) and digitally encoded with a PCM or DPCM encoder [Crochiere, Webber and Flanagan, 1976] [Esteban and Galand, 1978]. In this process, each sub-band can be encoded according to perceptual criteria that are specific to that band. On reconstruction, the sub-band signals are decoded and modulated back to their original locations. They are then summed to give a close replica of the original speech signal.

Encoding in sub-bands offers several advantages. By appropriately allocating the bits in different bands, the number of quantizer levels and hence reconstruction error variance can be separately controlled in each band, and the shape of the overall reconstruction error spectrum can be controlled as a function of frequency. In the lower frequency bands, where pitch and formant structure must be accurately preserved, a larger number of bits/sample can be used; whereas in upper frequency bands, where fricative and noise-like sounds occur in speech, fewer bits/sample can be used. Further, quantization noise can be contained within bands to prevent masking of a low-level input in one frequency range by quantizing noise in another frequency range. Section 11.2 gives a quantitative demonstration of objective (SNR) gains due to sub-band coding.

The most complex part of the coder is the filter bank [Bellanger, Bonnerot and Coudreuse, 1976] [Esteban and Galand, 1977]. With newer filter technologics such as CCD filters and digital filters, this complexity is rapidly being reduced. Also the design technique of *quadrature-mirror filters* (Section 11.4) affords distinct advantages in digital implementation of this coder.

Figure 11.1 illustrates a basic block diagram of the sub-band coder. The coder consists of a bank of M bandpass filters, followed by sub-band encoders which typically are PCM-AQB coders, and a multiplexer. The receiver has the inverse stages of demultiplexing, decoding and bandpass filtering prior to sub-band addition. Unlike the spectrum channel vocoder for synthetic speech [Flanagan et al., 1979] [Rabiner and Schafer, 1978] where the object of the filter-bank is only to preserve information about short-time energy as a function of frequency, the sub-band coder in Figure 11.1 transmits individual time waveforms $x_k(t)$; $k = 1, 2, ..., M$ and the receiver adds decoder versions $y_k(t)$ phase-synchronously to obtain $y(t)$. The sub-band coder is therefore a waveform-preserving coder.

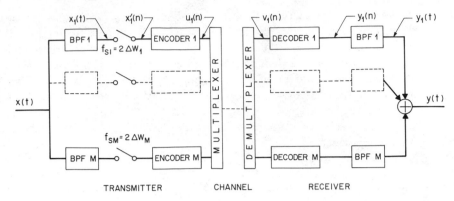

Figure 11.1 Block diagram of sub-band coding (SBC).

In Figure 11.1, sub-band width ΔW_k was a function of sub-band number k, implying *variable-width* sub-bands. The special case of *equal-width* sub-bands is important for implementation (Section 11.4) as well as analytical tractability (Section 11.2). Both types of arrangements will be considered for the sub-band coding of speech (Section 11.5). Figure 11.2 illustrates the two classes of arrangements for the example of $M = 4$. Shaded regions define sub-band number $k = 3$.

In the case of *equal-width* sub-bands

$$\Delta W_k = \Delta W = W/M ; \qquad k = 1,2,...,M$$

$$(11.1)$$

$$\Delta \Omega = 2\pi \Delta W = \Omega_W/M = 2\pi W/M$$

Figure 11.2 Division of input spectrum into $M = 4$ sub-bands of (a) constant and (b) variable width.

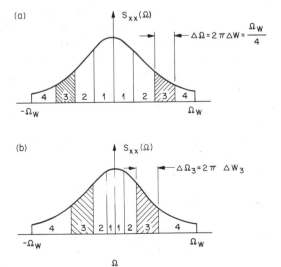

Sub-Band Coding   11

where W and Ω_W represent the total input bandwidth in Hz and radians/second, respectively. In the case of unequal sub-bands, they are typically made wider as k increases:

$$\Delta W_{k+1} > \Delta W_k \ ; \ k = 1,2,...,M-1 \tag{11.2}$$

The design in (11.2) suggests that the lower frequencies in the speech signal are more carefully isolated or observed than the higher frequencies. This provides a qualitative match to the long-time speech psd [Figure 2.9(a)] and the articulation-index function (Appendix E), both of which are lowpass functions that decrease as frequency increases. The above match is, however, not very critical in the presence of variable bit allocation, which offers the possibility of digitizing sub-bands with varying fidelity (Section 11.3). Indeed, an important filter-bank design (the quadrature-mirror filter bank, Section 11.4) has the defining characteristic that the input psd is split into equal sub-bands.

Figure 11.3 sketches filter-bank amplitude responses that may be appropriate to realize the band-splitting operations shown in Figure 11.2. The observations to be made with Figure 11.3 will also hold for the digital filter banks of Section 11.3, with $H(j\Omega)$ and Ω_W replaced by $H(e^{j\omega})$ and π, respectively. An important distinction in Figure 11.3 is between (a) equal-width and (b) variable-width filters. Another distinction is between filter characteristics that overlap, as in (a), and characteristics that are non-contiguous, as in (b). The in-between situation of exactly contiguous filters is academic because practical implementations involve amplitude responses with finite roll-off characteristics.

The approach in Figure 11.3(b) calls for extremely fast filter roll-offs that minimize inter-band gaps, but it offers the possibility of reduced sampling rates

Figure 11.3 Amplitude responses in filter-banks consisting of four individual bandpass characteristics of (a) equal width and (b) unequal width.

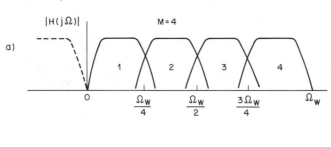

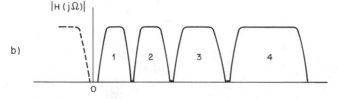

(smaller values of f_{sk}), and hence a lower coding rate I [see (11.3)] for given values of R_k. Inter-band frequency gaps will be non-zero in practical filter designs, and these gaps cause a reverberant quality in the output speech of low bit rate SBC designs, unless the sub-bands can adaptively track regions of significant speech energy, such as formant frequencies in voiced speech [Crochiere and Sambur, 1977]. Discussions of SBC in this book are confined to fixed bands and fixed bit allocations. Sub-band coding systems with adaptive bit allocation perform significantly better because of the dynamic noise-shaping that they provide [Esteban and Galand, 1978] [Grauel, 1980] [Ramstad, 1982] [Heron, Crochiere and Cox, 1983]. However, the higher processing involved in adaptive bit allocation makes it particularly appropriate in the higher-complexity approach of TC (Chapter 12).

11.2 Transmission Rate I, SNR and Gain Over PCM

In SBC, each sub-band waveform $x_k(t)$ is sampled at a rate f_{sk} and encoded using R_k bits per sub-band sample. The transmission rate in SBC is therefore the sum of the bit rates needed to code individual sub-bands:

$$I = \sum_{k=1}^{M} f_{sk} \, R_k \quad \text{b/s} \tag{11.3}$$

In the special case of *equal-width* sub-bands,

$$\Delta W_k = W/M \text{ for all } k \; ; \quad f_{sk} = 2\Delta W_k = 2W/M \tag{11.4a}$$

Since individual sub-band k can be sampled at the frequency $2\Delta W_k$ (Section 11.3), (11.3) simplifies to

$$I = \frac{2W}{M} \sum_{k=1}^{M} R_k \quad \text{b/s} \qquad \text{for equal-width bands} \tag{11.4b}$$

Note that (11.4b) reduces to the familiar form $I = 2WR$ for full-band coding if the total number of bits is expressed in the form

$$\sum_{k=1}^{M} R_k = MR \tag{11.5}$$

where R denotes the average number of bits used to encode a full-band sample. The simple equalities in (11.4b) and (11.5) imply that I is proportional to the sum of R_k values. This makes the design of variable bit allocation much simpler than in the general case of unequal-width sub-bands where the relationship between total bit rate I and the individual R_k values is less direct [see (11.3)].

In the following analysis, we assume non-overlapping equal-width sub-bands, so that the variances σ_{xk}^2 of sub-band inputs can be simply added to obtain the variance σ_x^2 of the full-band input. Similarly, variances σ_{rk}^2 of sub-band reconstruction errors can be added to obtain the variance σ_r^2 of signal reconstruction error.

The final reconstruction error variance is

$$\sigma_{r,SBC}^2 = \sum_{k=1}^{M} \sigma_{rk}^2 \qquad (11.6a)$$

We assume error-free transmission, and the use of PCM (or DPCM) coding of individual sub-bands. As a result, for any k, the sub-band reconstruction error variance is $\sigma_{rk}^2 = \sigma_{qk}^2$, a corresponding quantization error variance. Therefore,

$$\sigma_{r,SBC}^2 = \sum_{k=1}^{M} \epsilon_{*k}^2 \, 2^{-2R_k} \, \sigma_{xk}^2 \qquad (11.6b)$$

The reconstruction error variance of a conventional (full-band) PCM coder, with bit rate equal to the average bit rate R in (11.5), is given by

$$\sigma_{r,PCM}^2 = \epsilon_*^2 2^{-2R} \sigma_x^2 \qquad (11.6c)$$

where R is the number of bits/sample.

The *SNR* improvement G_{SBC} due to sub-band coding is the ratio of (11.6c) to (11.6b). Assuming for simplicity a *constant quantizer performance factor* ($\epsilon_{*k}^2 = \epsilon_*^2$; all k), we obtain a gain over PCM that depends *only* on the bit allocation algorithm:

$$G_{SBC} = \frac{2^{-2R} \, \sigma_x^2}{\sum_{k=1}^{M} \left[2^{-2R_k} \sigma_{xk}^2 \right]} = \frac{2^{-2\sum R_k / M} \sum_{k=1}^{M} \sigma_{xk}^2}{\sum_{k=1}^{M} \left[2^{-2R_k} \sigma_{xk}^2 \right]} \qquad (11.7a)$$

$$SNR \mid_{SBC} (\text{dB}) = SNR \mid_{PCM} (\text{dB}) + 10 \log G_{SBC} \qquad (11.7b)$$

With a flat spectrum, G_{SBC} can never exceed 1 (Example 11.1). In the case of non-flat spectra, values of $G_{SBC} > 1$ can be realized by *bit allocation* procedures where R_k values are matched to σ_{xk}^2 values in a sense that will be clear from Examples 11.1 and 11.2. The special case of σ_{xk}^2-independent and equal R_k simply leads to $G_{SBC} = 1$ in (11.7). In Chapter 12, we will fully develop a theory of optimum bit allocation.

The sub-band coding gain G_{SBC} is really analogous to the prediction gain G_P in that both of these gains result from the non-flatness of input spectrum. Sub-band coding gain increases as a function of number of bands M; and prediction gain increases with order of prediction. As in prediction, the greatest values of G_{SBC} are realized when spectrum-dependent bit allocation is allowed to be time varying [Stjernvall, 1977] [Esteban and Galand, 1978] [Grauel, 1980] [Ramstad, 1982] [Heron, Crochiere and Cox, 1983]. This will indeed be the approach of Adaptive Transform Coding in Chapter 12.

Example 11.1. Two-band coding of a flat spectrum input

We shall again consider the simple case of equally wide sub-bands of width $W/2$ each. As a result of the flat spectrum,

$$\sigma_{x1}^2 = \sigma_{x2}^2 = \sigma_x^2/2 \tag{11.8a}$$

Using this in (11.7a),

$$G_{SBC} = 2\,\frac{2^{-(R_1+R_2)}}{2^{-2R_1} + 2^{-2R_2}} \tag{11.8b}$$

Figure 11.4(a) plots G_{SBC} as a function of R_1 for the example of $R_1 + R_2 = 6$. The maximum value of $G_{SBC} = 1$ occurs for $R_1 = R_2 = 3$. This result can also be seen by identifying the above expression for G_{SBC} as the ratio of geometric mean and arithmetic mean of the terms 2^{-2R_1} and 2^{-2R_2}; this ratio is maximum when the terms are equal, i.e., when $R_1 = R_2$. •

Example 11.2. Two-band coding of the two-level spectrum of Figure 2.24 with $\alpha = 2/17$

From the results of Example 2.12,

$$\sigma_{x1}^2 = (16/17)\,\sigma_x^2\;;\qquad \sigma_{x2}^2 = (1/17)\,\sigma_x^2 \tag{11.9a}$$

Using this in (11.7a),

$$G_{SBC} = 17\,\frac{2^{-(R_1+R_2)}}{16\cdot 2^{-2R_1} + 1\cdot 2^{-2R_2}} \tag{11.9b}$$

Figure 11.4(b) plots G_{SBC} as a function of R_1 for the example of $2R = R_1 + R_2 = 6$. As in Example 11.1, equal bit allocation ($R_1 = R_2 = 3$) results in $G_{SBC} = 1$. But unlike in the flat-spectrum case, the maximum value of G_{SBC} is now 17/8. This maximum occurs if

Figure 11.4 G_{SBC} versus R_1 in two-band SBC schemes with $R = 3$ bits/sample, for (a) a flat-spectrum input, and (b) an input with the two-level psd of Figure 2.24 (with $\alpha = 2/17$).

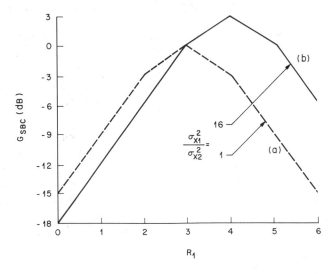

$R_1 = 4$ and $R_2 = 2$. Note that with this design, the error contributions in both sub-bands (denominator terms in the above expression for G_{SBC}) are equal. In fact, this maximum gain is the inverse of the spectral flatness measure γ_x^2 for the input (Problem 2.23):

$$\gamma_x^2 = [\alpha(2-\alpha)]^{1/2} = \left[\frac{2}{17} \cdot \frac{32}{17} \right]^{1/2} = \frac{8}{17}$$

The equality of maximum gain and γ_x^{-2} will be discussed again in Chapter 12. What is significant for the present discussion is that a two-band SBC procedure is sufficient to utilize all the spectral redundancy of a two-level psd: in other words, sufficient to realize $G_{SBC} = \gamma_x^{-2}$. The exact realization of the maximum possible gain is due to one other property of the input spectrum in question: the ratio of component variances, 16, is an integral power of 2.

The sufficiency of the two-band partition for the two-level spectrum is similar to a result in Chapter 6 where linear prediction of order N was adequate to utilize the *sfm* of an AR(N) process.   ●

The constraint on $\sum R_k$ used in Examples 11.1 and 11.2 is more meaningful with equal-width sub-bands [where I is directly proportional to $\sum R_k$ (11.4b)] than with variable-width sub-bands [where I is a weighted sum of the R_k (11.3)]. For equal-width sub-bands, the results of Example 11.2 can be generalized to the case of $M > 2$. The gain G_{SBC} in (11.7a) can again be maximized under the constraint of a given number of bits [see (11.5)]. This is equivalent to minimizing

$$\sigma_r^2 = \epsilon_*^2 \sum_{k=1}^{M} 2^{-2R_k} \sigma_{xk}^2$$

Using Lagrange multipliers,

$$\frac{\partial}{\partial R_k} \left[\epsilon_*^2 \sum_{k=1}^{M} 2^{-2R_k} \sigma_{xk}^2 - \lambda \left(MR - \sum_{k=1}^{M} R_k \right) \right] = 0$$

from which we can express R_k as a function of λ:

$$R_k = \frac{1}{2} \log_2 \left[2\epsilon_*^2 \log_e 2 \right] + \frac{1}{2} \log_2 \frac{\sigma_{xk}^2}{\lambda}$$

Using this result in $MR = \sum R_k$, the *optimum bit allocation* is

$$R_{k,opt} = R + \frac{1}{2} \log_2 \frac{\sigma_{xk}^2}{\left[\prod_{l=1}^{M} \sigma_{xl}^2 \right]^{1/M}} \tag{11.10}$$

and from the expression for σ_r^2 above, the *minimum mse* [Goodman, 1967] is

$$\min \{ \sigma_r^2 \} = M \, \epsilon_*^2 2^{-2R} \left[\prod_{l=1}^{M} \sigma_{xl}^2 \right]^{1/M} \tag{11.11}$$

and the *maximum gain* is the ratio of arithmetic mean and geometric mean of the sub-band variances σ_{xl}^2:

$$\max\{G_{SBC}\} = \frac{\sigma_x^2}{M\left[\prod_{l=1}^{M}\sigma_{xl}^2\right]^{1/M}} = \frac{\frac{1}{M}\sum_{l=1}^{M}\sigma_{xl}^2}{\left[\prod_{l=1}^{M}\sigma_{xl}^2\right]^{1/M}} \qquad (11.12)$$

The bit allocation in (11.10), which minimizes the mse σ_r^2, will also imply equal values of noise variance for different k, as a result of (11.6b) and (11.10); this is also shown formally in the analysis of Chapter 12. We will also see in Chapter 12 that specific forms of noise-shaping can be realized by bit allocations that minimize certain types of frequency-weighted mean square error.

In coding a signal such as speech whose psd can be approximated as an M-level psd with $M \gg 2$ (a generalization of Figure 2.24), SBC performance increases with increasing M. Very large values of M can also take into account the fine structure in the psd due to the pitch period, in the sense of maintaining a locally flat psd within each sub-band. The use of fairly small values such as $M = 4$ is therefore for simplicity, rather than because of a saturation of objective gain G_{SBC} as a function of M. In particular, 4-band SBC coding of speech is significantly better than 2-band SBC coding, both objectively and from a subjective quality viewpoint [Cox, 1981, II]. Improvement of performance with M is maintained at values as high as $M = 16$ [Ramstad, 1982] [Esteban and Galand, 1982].

11.3 The Integer-Band Filter Bank

An important feature in Figure 11.1 is that bandpass filter cutoffs are chosen such that each band can be sampled at twice the corresponding bandwidth

$$f_{sk} = 2\Delta W_k ; \qquad k = 1,2,...,M \qquad (11.13)$$

rather than at twice the highest frequency of the full-band signal. As discussed in Chapter 3, this is possible in the special situation of *integer-band sampling* [Crochiere and Rabiner, 1983] where the lower cutoff frequency W_{lk} in a sub-band k is an integral multiple of bandwidth (Figure 3.10):

$$W_{lk} = n\,\Delta W_k ; \qquad n = 0, 1,2,...; \qquad k' = 1,2,3,...,M \qquad (11.14)$$

The orders of bandpass filtering and sampling in Figure 11.1 can be reversed. Consider that discrete-time inputs $x(n)$ are available, sampled at the full-band Nyquist rate $f_s = 2W$ where $W = \sum \Delta W_k$, with summation from $k = 1$ to M, is the maximum frequency of the full-band signal.

Let the sub-band width be written in the form

$$\Delta W_k = W/\zeta_k ; \qquad k = 1,2,...,M \qquad (11.15)$$

$$\zeta_k = M \text{ for all } k \text{ with } \textit{equal-width} \text{ sub-bands}$$

With the sub-band partition of Figures 11.2(a) and 11.3(a), $\zeta_k = 4$ for all k. Some of the speech coding examples mentioned later in this chapter use unequal sub-bands. In these examples, the values of ζ_k range from 4 to 30 (Tables 11.1, 11.2 and 11.3).

Figure 11.5 shows the sequence of filtering and coding operations in SBC, using the general example of sub-band k in Figure 11.5(a) and the special case of $k = 3$ and $\zeta_3 = 4$ in Figure 11.5(b).

The ζ_k:1 *decimator* sub-samples the bandpass output $x_k(n)$ by a factor ζ_k, implying a sampling rate of $f_{sk} = 2W/\zeta_k = 2\Delta W_k$ for sub-band k. This decimation implies a repetition rate of its spectrum that is higher than that of the full-band spectrum by a factor ζ_k. As a result of this, the x-axes in the two figures of (b) differ by a factor $\zeta_k = 4$. One of the repetitions of the spectrum will be in the baseband, so that the decimation effectively translates the lower frequency edge of the bandpass signal band to zero frequency. The 1:ζ_k *interpolator* fills in ($\zeta_k - 1$) zeros in between every pair of incoming lowpass samples. The kth harmonic of the interpolated baseband is thus effectively bandpass-translated to the appropriate initial bandpass region. The explicit modulation processes mentioned in Section 11.1 are therefore replaced by simpler discrete-time processes of decimation and interpolation. It is assumed that the interpolation process includes an amplitude scaling factor of ζ_k. This maintains the original value of input variance in spite of the zero-valued amplitudes that are introduced in the interpolation process.

The amplitude spectra $|X_3(e^{j\omega})|$ and $|X'_3(e^{j\omega})|$ in Figure 11.5(b) refer to sub-band $k = 3$, with $\zeta_3 = 4$; the illustration is equivalent to the continuous-time case

Figure 11.5 Realization of integer-band sampling with a discrete-time input: (a) block diagram of SBC coding for sub-band k; and (b) original spectrum and resampled spectrum after decimation, for sub-band $k = 3$, with $\zeta_3 = 4$. The baseband spectrum resulting from the decimation is shifted back to the original frequency range of sub-band k after interpolation by a factor ζ_k.

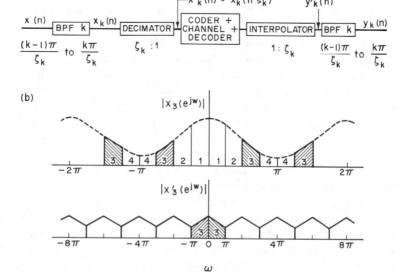

of Figure 3.9, which also used the example of $k = 3$. Note that the spectrum of the decimated sequence has its own frequency scaling. If the procedure of the last two paragraphs is repeated for an even-numbered sub-band ($k = 2$ or $k = 4$), it can be shown that the spectrum gets inverted in the process of lowpass translation to the baseband. This is, however, neutralized by a subsequent inversion in the interpolation process for even k [Crochiere and Rabiner, 1983].

The integer-band constraint in (11.14) is invariably assumed in SBC for the obvious reason of minimizing sub-band sampling frequencies and hence the overall information rate

$$I = \sum_{k=1}^{M} I_k = \sum_{k=1}^{M} f_{sk} R_k = \sum_{k=1}^{M} 2\Delta W_k \, R_k \ \text{bits/second} \qquad (11.16)$$

11.4 Quadrature-Mirror Filter Banks

The overlapping sub-band situation in Figure 11.3(a) suggests that aliasing effects can occur if sub-bands are sampled at $f_{sk} = 2W/M = \Omega_W/\pi M$. This problem is very elegantly tackled in the *quadrature-mirror filter bank* (QMFB) approach of Figure 11.6 [Esteban and Galand, 1977]. This figure shows the division of a full-band signal of maximum radian frequency π into two of equal width by using a constrained pair of lowpass and highpass filters. In the notation of (11.15), $\zeta_1 = \zeta_2 = M = 2$. By repeated subdivisions of resulting sub-bands using QMF filter banks, one can realize an SBC filter bank with M given by a power of 2, such as $M = 4$ as in Figure 11.3(a). Values of M that are not powers of 2 can also be realized by simply ignoring appropriate sub-band branches in the QMF tree (Table 11.3 and Problem 11.2).

The rest of the following discussion refers to the first stage of such a filter bank, involving two sub-bands as in Figure 11.6. When further stages of band-partitioning are introduced, each of the branches in Figure 11.6(a) will be split into further branches, and sampling frequencies will be reduced by factors of two at each stage; but the results of Figure 11.6(b) will apply repeatedly with appropriate redefinitions of the absolute frequencies represented by 0, π and $\pi/2$ in that figure.

Each of the sub-band signals $x_l(n)$ and $x_u(n)$ is resampled by a factor 2:1. This reduction of the sub-band sampling rates is necessary in order to maintain a minimal overall bit rate in encoding these signals. This reduction of sampling rate introduces aliasing terms in each of the sub-band signals because of the finite rate of roll-off in filter responses. For example, in the lower band the signal energy in the frequency range above $\pi/2$ is folded down into the range 0 to $\pi/2$ and appears as *aliasing distortion* in this signal, in the frequency range covered by the hatched region in the left half of Figure 11.6(b). In the above explanation, and in the rest of this section, π is *not* redefined as in Figure 11.5(b). Aliasing also occurs for the upper band in a similar fashion; any signal energy in the frequency range below $\pi/2$ is folded upward into its Nyquist band $\pi/2$ to π; this causes aliasing in the frequency range covered by the hatched area in the right half of Figure 11.6(b). This mutual aliasing of signal energy between the upper and lower sub-bands is

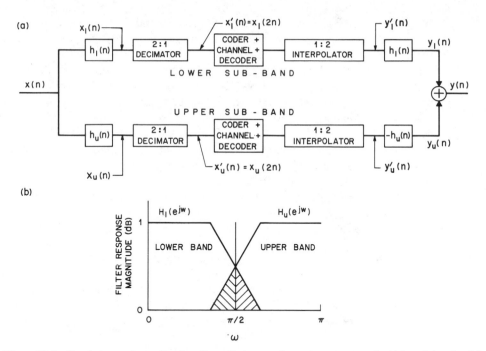

Figure 11.6 Quadrature-mirror filtering for splitting an input into two equal-width sub-bands: (a) implementation; and (b) qualitative illustration of a filter-bank response that provides alias-image cancellation [Esteban and Galand, 1978] [Crochiere, 1981].

sometimes called *interband leakage*. The amount of leakage that occurs between sub-bands is directly dependent on the degree to which the filters $h_l(n)$ and $h_u(n)$ approximate ideal lowpass and highpass filters, respectively.

In the reconstruction process, the sub-band sampling rates are increased by a factor 1:2 by filling in zero-valued samples between each pair of sub-band samples. This introduces a periodic repetition of the signal spectra in the sub-band. For example, in the lower band the signal energy from 0 to $\pi/2$ is symmetrically folded around the frequency $\pi/2$ into the range of the upper band. This unwanted signal energy, referred to as an *image* is mostly filtered out by the lowpass filter $h_l(n)$ in the receiver. This filtering operation effectively interpolates the zero-valued samples that have been inserted between the sub-band signals to values that appropriately represent the desired waveform [Crochiere and Rabiner, 1983]. Similarly, in the upper sub-band signal an image is reflected to the lower sub-band and filtered out by the filter $-h_u(n)$.

The degree to which the above images are removed by the filters $h_l(n)$ and $-h_u(n)$ is determined by the degree to which they approximate ideal lowpass and highpass filters. Because of the special relationship of the sub-band signals in the QMF filter bank, the remaining components of the images can be canceled by aliasing terms introduced in the analysis. This cancellation occurs *after* the addition of the two interpolated sub-band signals $y_l(n)$ and $y_u(n)$, and the cancellation is exact in the absence of coding errors. In the presence of coding, this cancellation is obtained to the level of quantization noise.

If S_l and S_u refer to lower-band and upper-band signals and subscripts A and I denote aliasing and imaging, the adder input $y_l(n)$ in Figure 11.6(a) will consist of the following main components, correct to filter attenuation effects: S_l and S_{uA} in the lower band and S_{lI} and S_{IuA} in the upper band. Similarly, input $y_u(n)$ will consist of components S_{ul} and S_{lIA} in the lower band and S_u and S_{lA} in the upper band. When $y_l(n)$ and $y_u(n)$ are added, components S_{uA} and S_{ul} cancel in the lower band, while components S_{lI} and S_{lIA} cancel in the upper band, leaving S_l and S_{ilA} in the lower band and S_u and S_{IuA} in the higher band. The components of S_{ilA} and S_{iuA} actually belong in the respective bands, and in the case of a QMF design with an allpass characteristic, these components exactly compensate for the in-band attenuations present in S_l and S_u.

One way of obtaining this cancellation property in the QMF filter bank is to use filters $h_l(n)$ and $h_u(n)$, which are respectively symmetrical and anti-symmetrical *finite impulse response* (FIR) designs with even numbers of taps, i.e.,

$$h_l(n) = h_u(n) = 0 \quad \text{for } 0 > n \geqslant N ; \tag{11.17}$$

$$h_l(n) = h_l(N - 1 - n) , \quad n = 0,1,...,N/2 - 1 ; \tag{11.18a}$$

$$h_u(n) = -h_u(N - 1 - n) , \quad n = 0,1,...,N/2 - 1 \tag{11.18b}$$

The cancellation of aliasing effects in the QMF filter bank further requires that the filters in Figure 11.6(a) satisfy the condition [Esteban and Galand, 1977] [Crochiere and Rabiner, 1983]

$$h_u(n) = (-1)^n h_l(n) , \quad n = 0,1,...,N - 1 \tag{11.19}$$

which is a *mirror image* relationship of the filters, implying symmetry about $\pi/2$, as in Figure 11.6(b). The coefficients of the filters are identical except that their signs alternate. Therefore, both filters can be realized using a single N-tap filter as the starting point.

Further, if the filter-bank output $y(n)$ is desired to be a delayed replica of input $x(n)$ (in the absence of coding errors), the filters $h_l(n)$ and $h_u(n)$ must also satisfy the condition

$$|H_l(e^{j\omega})|^2 + |H_u(e^{j\omega})|^2 = 1 , \tag{11.20}$$

where $H_l(e^{j\omega})$ and $H_u(e^{j\omega})$ are the Fourier transforms of $h_l(n)$ and $h_u(n)$, respectively; this is simply the condition for an *allpass* characteristic. If the allpass condition (11.20) is included in the mirror-image design (11.19), the point of intersection of the two filter functions in Figure 11.6(b) will be the -3 dB point for each transfer function.

The filter requirement in (11.20) cannot be met exactly by the mirror image filters of (11.19) except when $N = 2$ and when N approaches infinity. However, it can be very closely approximated for modest values of N. Filter designs which satisfy (11.18) and (11.19) and approximate the condition of (11.20) can be obtained with the aid of an optimization program [Johnston, 1980]. Resulting filter

Table 11.1 Quadrature Mirror Filters of order $N = 32$ and $N = 16$. Listed numbers are values of coefficients $h_l(n)$ for $N/2 \leqslant n \leqslant N$. Values of other coefficients follow (11.8) and (11.9) [Johnston, 1980] [Crochiere and Rabiner, 1983; Reprinted with permission].

| $N = 32$ | | $N = 16$ |
$h(16)$ to $h(23)$	$h(24)$ to $h(31)$	$h(8)$ to $h(15)$
4.6645830E-01	1.7881950E-02	.47211220E 00
1.2846510E-01	−1.7219030E-04	.11786660E 00
−9.9800110E-02	−9.3636330E-03	−.99295500E-01
−3.9244910E-02	1.4272050E-03	−.26275600E-01
5.2909300E-02	4.1581240E-03	.46476840E-01
1.4468810E-02	−1.2601150E-03	.19911500E-02
−3.1155320E-02	−1.3508480E-03	−.20487510E-01
−4.1094160E-03	6.5064660E-04	.65256660E-02

coefficients for N values in the range 8 to 64 have been tabulated [Crochiere, 1981] [Crochiere and Rabiner, 1983].

Table 11.1 lists representative designs for $N = 32$ and $N = 16$. In a QMF tree for $M = 4$ sub-bands, the first subdivision may use filters of order $N = 32$. In view of the 2:1 decimation, a matching design for the second stage of the QMF tree would then be $N = 16$.

Figure 11.7 shows the frequency response characteristics for a 32-tap filter design [Crochiere, 1981]. Figure 11.7(a) shows the magnitude of $H_l(e^{j\omega})$ and $H_u(e^{j\omega})$ expressed in dB as a function of ω. As in the schematic of Figure 11.6(b), note that the roll-off regions of the two responses intersect at the −3dB point for each characteristic. Figure 11.7(b) shows the magnitude of the expression $|H_l(e^{j\omega})|^2 + |H_u(e^{j\omega})|^2$ expressed in dB as a function of ω. As can be seen from Figure 11.7(b), the requirement of (11.20) is satisfied to within ±0.025 dB, which is more than satisfactory for good SBC performance. The reconstruction error in the 32-tap design of Table 11.1 is also ±0.025 dB, but the stop-band attenuation of this filter (measured at the first stop-band peak) is 52 dB, which is much greater than the 37 dB attenuation in the example of Figure 11.7(a). In the 16-tap example of Table 11.1, the reconstruction error is ±0.07 dB, and the stop-band attenuation is 30 dB.

The use of FIR filters has the advantage of linear-phase characteristics which eliminate the problems of group delay distortions. This feature also allows the 2-band design of Figure 11.6 to be conveniently cascaded in three structures (Example 11.5, Problem 11.2) without the need for phase compensation. However, effective FIR designs imply significant coding delays. For example, with the 32-tap design just mentioned, the coding and decoding delays due to the first level of the QMF tree are 4 ms each, assuming 8 kHz input sampling; and subsequent levels of the QMF partition introduce corresponding additional delays. In order to implement SBC systems with smaller values of delay, there has been at least one proposal for a QMF bank based on *infinite impulse response* (IIR) designs [Ramstad and Foss, 1980]. This proposal includes special procedures for mitigating the group delay distortions inherent in IIR designs.

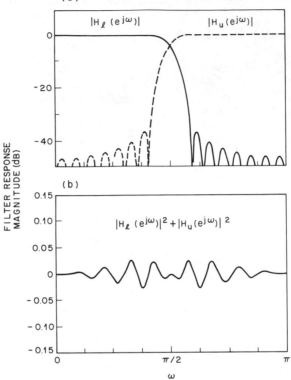

$|H_\ell(e^{j\omega})|$ $|H_u(e^{j\omega})|$

(b)

$|H_\ell(e^{j\omega})|^2 + |H_u(e^{j\omega})|^2$

Figure 11.7 Illustration of amplitude-frequency responses in a quadrature mirror filter bank using FIR filters: (a) lowpass and highpass characteristics of individual 32-tap FIR filters; and (b) approximately allpass characteristic of the combination [Crochiere, 1981].

11.5 Sub-Band Coding of Speech

The following examples illustrate the design of fixed bit-allocation SBC systems for speech at bit rates in the range of 9.6 kb/s to 32 kb/s. The 32 kb/s system with fixed bit allocation can provide very high subjective quality, with MOS scores in the order of 4.2, a necessary condition for *toll quality* reproduction of telephone speech, while fixed bit-allocation SBC systems at lower bit rates provide different grades of *communications quality* encoding. Example 11.5 also illustrates the use of the QMF systems discussed in Section 11.4.

Example 11.3. Sub-band coding of speech at 9.6 kb/s

Table 11.2 shows a sub-band partition for a 9.6 kb/s SBC system. The sub-band sampling rates are obtained from an original sampling rate of 9.6 kHz by using $\xi_k{:}1$ decimations, with ξ_k values of 20, 10, 9 and 5.

The PCM coders use adaptive quantization (for example, the AQB system with a one-word memory, Chapter 4); and ranges of step size are individually matched to the long-time-averaged variances of individual sub-band signals. This is indicated by the different Δ_{min} values in Table 11.2. Respective Δ_{max} values are typically 256 times greater.

Table 11.2 Sub-band coder designs for 9.6 kb/s [Crochiere, 1977]

Band	ζ_k Decimation Factor from 9.6 kHz	Band Edges (Hz)	Sub-band Sampling Rates (Hz)	Relative Δ_{min} Values (dB)	R_k (bits/sample)	I_k (kb/s)
1	20	240-480	480	0.0	3	1.44
2	10	480-960	960	−3.0	3	2.88
3	9	1067-1600	1067	−8.5	2	2.13
4	5	1920-2880	1920	−14.0	1.5	2.88
Sync						0.27
			Total Bit Rate I (kb/s)			9.60
			Typical SNR (dB)			10.8

The bit allocation of (3, 3, 2, 1.5) bits/sample is a perceptually optimized design; it codes lower frequency sub-bands with greater fidelity than the higher frequency sub-bands. The fractional value of $R_4 = 1.5$ bits/sample can be obtained in several ways [Crochiere, 1977]; for example, by the use of $R_4 = 1.0$ and $R_4 = 2.0$ for alternate samples, with appropriate modification of step size logics.

Notice that in Table 11.2, the transmission rate for each band is a rational fraction of total rate I so that sub-band data can be multiplexed into a repetitive framed sequence. The lowest common denominator of these rational fractions, including the fraction of transmission rate reserved for frame synchronization purposes (denoted by "Sync" in Table 11.2) determines the smallest possible frame size for the SBC transmission system [Crochiere, 1977]. In certain applications such as voice storage and computer voice response, synchronization procedures may be built-in, and there may not be any need for transmitting special "Sync" bits. This is indeed the situation assumed in Table 11.4.

The quality of the time-invariant 9.6 kb/s system is limited by a reverberant quality in the output $y(n)$ due to inter-band gaps. Designs without gaps involve smaller values of R_k, greater quantization noise, and even lower quality. On the other hand, 9.6 kb/s SBC systems, as a class, perform much better than full-band fixed-prediction speech coders at 9.6 kb/s; in particular, better than 9.6 kb/s ADM systems. In subjective tests, the 9.6 kb/s SBC system is judged to be equivalent to an ADM system at twice the coding rate, i.e., 19.2 kb/s [Crochiere, 1977]. This advantage is directly related to variable bit allocation, and the fact that the quantization noise in the coding of sub-band k with R_k bits/sample is contained within that band.   ●

Example 11.4.   SBC coding of speech at 16 kb/s

Table 11.3 refers to a 16 kb/s SBC system. The explanation of the numbers in this table is very similar to that for Table 11.2. In perceptual tests, this coder is comparable to 24 kb/s DPCM-AQB. The quality of 16 kb/s SBC with fixed bit allocation is useful for many communications applications, although this SBC output is clearly distinguishable from the original input in side-by-side comparisons.

A comparison of the Δ_{min} values in Tables 11.2 and 11.3 shows that the design of Table 11.3 is a better match to the long-time-averaged psd of speech. Note that in Figure 2.9(a), the psd peaks at a value of frequency that is non-zero, and so does the Δ_k versus k profile in Table 11.3. The behavior with respect to frequency k is monotonic in Table 11.2.   ●

Table 11.3 Sub-band coder design for 16 kb/s [Crochiere, 1977]

Band	ζ_k Decimation Factor from 10.67 kHz	Band Edges (Hz)	Sub-band Sampling Rates (Hz)	Relative Δ_{min} Values (dB)	R_k (bits/sample)	I_k (kb/s)
1	30	178-356	356	−2.0	4	1.42
2	18	296-593	593	0.0	4	2.37
3	10	533-1067	1067	−6.0	3	3.20
4	5	1067-2133	2133	−11.5	2	4.27
5	5	2133-3200	2133	−18.0	2	4.27
Sync						0.47
				Total Bit Rate I (kb/s)		16.00
				Typical SNR (dB)		13.6

Example 11.5. SBC coding of speech at 16, 24 or 32 kb/s

Table 11.4 shows a general sub-band partitioning framework that can be used for SBC coding at bit rates of 16, 24 or 32 kb/s. The sub-band partitioning is obtained by repeated use of the QMF partitioning principle (Problem 11.2). Note that the 16 and 24 kb/s systems use four sub-bands while the 32 kb/s system uses five sub-bands. The speech bandwidth allowed in this five-band system includes the 3 to 4 kHz range; this is a capability in excess of the 3.2 kHz limit assumed for telephone speech.

Figure 11.8 shows sub-band signals $x_k(n)$; $k = 1,2,3,4$ in a 4-band system which uses the four lower bands of Table 11.4. As shown in the table, respective sampling rates are $f_{sk} = 1000, 1000, 2000$ and 2000 Hz. These sampling rates are obtained from an original sampling rate of $f_s = 8000$ Hz by using ζ_k:1 decimations. Respective values of ζ_k, also listed in the table, are 8, 8, 4 and 4. Note that as we move the lowest sub-band (0-500 Hz) to the highest (2000-3000 Hz), the left half of the waveform becomes increasingly more prominent. This is because of the preponderance of high frequency energy in the left half of the original full-band waveform. Notice also that the waveforms in the lower two sub-bands do not look very different. This is because the original full-band waveform in this example has significant energies centered at about 700 Hz, and this is a strong common component in both of the lower two sub-bands, which happen to overlap significantly in the 700 Hz region.

Table 11.4 Sub-band coder designs for 16, 24 or 32 kb/s [Crochiere, 1981].

Band	ζ_k Decimation Factor From 8 kHz	Band Edges (Hz)	Sub-band Sampling Rates (Hz)	R_k (bits/sample) for I (kb/s) = 16	24	32
1	8	0-500	1000	4	5	5
2	8	500-1000	1000	4	5	5
3	4	1000-2000	2000	2	4	4
4	4	2000-3000	2000	2	3	4
5	4	3000-4000	2000	0	0	3

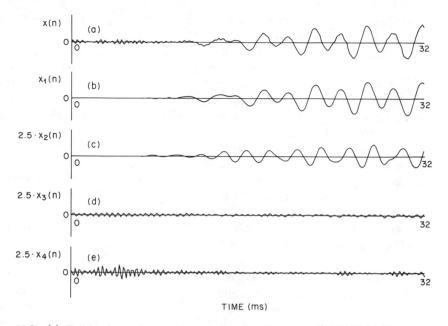

TIME (ms)

Figure 11.8 (a) Full-band speech waveform of duration 32 ms; and (b)(c)(d)(e) sub-band signals $x_k(n)$ for $k = 1,2,3,4$ in the SBC system of Table 11.4. The sub-band signals $x_2(n)$, $x_3(n)$ and $x_4(n)$ have been magnified by a factor of 2.5 [Cox, 1983].

The full-band signal corresponding to $x_n(k)$ waveforms is a voiced speech segment of duration 32 ms. At the respective Nyquist sampling rates f_{sk}, the sub-band signals exhibit much lower values of adjacent-sample correlation than a full-band speech waveform sampled at its Nyquist rate f_s. The entire waveform $x_1(n)$ in Figure 11.8(b), for example, is sampled only 32 times because of the decimation to 1 kHz. The lower correlations in sub-band signals can also be conjectured from Figure 11.2 where individual sub-bands are seen to have flatter psd's than the full-band speech. (Also, see Problem 11.7). This is the reason why PCM, rather than DPCM, is often assumed in SBC systems, although, with real speech spectra, non-negligible values of prediction gain can be realized even in the case of (individually optimized) fixed predictors of order one.

The nature of the long-time-averaged speech spectrum [Figure 2.9(a)] suggests that the long-term sub-band spectrum can be high-pass in the ranges of sub-bands 1 and 2 of Table 11.4. High-pass spectra in sub-bands can also result from high-frequency pre-emphasis in telephone systems. In fact, in an implementation of the coders of Table 11.4 with telephone speech that includes high-frequency pre-emphasis, the sub-band coders use DPCM-AQB with fixed first-order predictors that reflect highpass spectra in four out of five sub-bands. Recommended values of coefficient h_1, for pre-emphasized speech, are -0.71, -0.28, -0.31, 0.26 and -0.64 in sub-bands 1 through 5, respectively [Daumer, 1982]. ●

With fixed bit allocation, high quality coding with SBC requires a total bit rate in the order of 32 kb/s. In formal subjective testing, the SBC system of Table 11.4 obtains MOS scores (on a scale of 1 to 5), of 4.3, 3.9 and 3.1 at bit rates of 32, 24 and 16 kb/s [Daumer, 1982]. If the bit rate is at least 24 kb/s, there is an adequate margin of safety for accommodating tandem encodings of 2 to 3 SBC stages with useful final quality.

Although the results of Tables 11.2 to 11.4 refer to specific speech coding systems, they provide general design features that apply to other coding applications as well. An important example is in 9.6 kb/s SBC-TDHS (*time-domain harmonic scaling*) coding systems involving time-compression of input speech by a factor 2:1 prior to sub-band coding at a bit rate slightly under $2(9.6) = 19.2$ kb/s [Malah, 1979] [Malah, Crochiere and Cox, 1981] [Crochiere, Cox and Johnston, 1982]. This procedure can result in an improvement over direct SBC at 9.6 kb/s, but the improvement is obtained at the cost of additional complexity, needed for pitch computations that TDHS is based on. Another example of SBC application is the coding of FM-grade audio signals ($W = 20$ kHz) (Problem 11.3) and AM-grade audio signals ($W = 7$ kHz). For example, a two-band SBC system with the band partition [0-3500 Hz] [3500 Hz-7000 Hz] is a good digitizer for 7 kHz material at a coding rate of 56 kb/s [Johnston and Crochiere, 1979].

Comparison of DPCM, DPCM-AP, SBC and ATC. Figure 11.9 shows the performance of four speech coders as a function of bit rate I. The set of coders includes two time-domain coders (DPCM coders with and without adaptive prediction (prediction order equal to one and eight, respectively) and two frequency-domain coders, SBC and ATC (Chapter 12).

One significant comparison in the figure is between the *medium complexity* techniques, SBC (with fixed bit allocation) and DPCM (with fixed prediction). The DPCM coder degrades rapidly if $I < 16$ kb/s ($R < 2$ bits/sample) because of poor quantization performance, compounded by the effects of quantization error feedback. The other significant comparison is between the *high complexity* techniques, DPCM-AP (APC) and ATC. In this specific study, neither of the two techniques incorporated pitch structure. It is interesting that ATC has a consistent

Figure 11.9 Segmental *SNR* in time-domain and frequency-domain speech coders as a function of bit rate I [Tribolet et al.;©1979, AT&T].

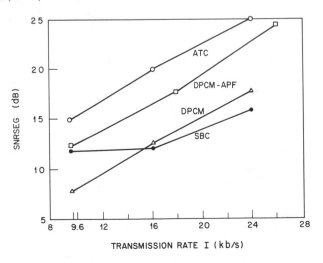

2 to 3 dB advantage. In another study, involving a subjective comparison of APC and ATC, both using pitch in formation, APC was in fact rated slightly better [Daumer, 1982]. Part of the reason for the very good performance of that APC system was a carefully designed algorithm for noise shaping.

The comparisons between DPCM and DPCM-APF, and between SBC and ATC, are less interesting in that the inferences are well expected in each case. The ATC system can be regarded crudely as the equivalent of an SBC system with two very significant refinements: (a) a much larger number of sub-bands M, and (b) adaptive bit-allocation $\{R_k\}$ that is matched to short-term rather than long-term-averaged speech spectrum. As a consequence of these refinements, ATC systems utilize the spectral non-flatness in speech more completely and adaptively, in a fashion similar to redundancy-removal in a full-fledged APC system with higher-order spectrum prediction. The nonadaptive SBC system utilizes spectral non-flatness only in a non-adaptive, and hence incomplete sense. A special, but academic, input for which SBC provides complete redundancy removal is one with a staircase-type psd, as in Figure 2.24. For that two-level psd example, SBC with $M = 2$ provides a complete utilization of spectral non-flatness (Example 11.3 and Problem 11.6).

Combinations of sub-band coding and adaptive prediction. The performance of sub-band coding can be significantly improved by supplementing it with the time-domain operation of adaptive prediction [Atal and Remde, 1981] [Honda, Kitawaki and Itakura, 1982]. The general philosophy of these hybrid techniques is to split the burden of redundancy removal between the frequency domain and the time domain. The hybrid approach also provides the possibility of noise shaping in both the frequency domain and the time domain. In one system, the latter is provided by dividing basic time blocks of duration in the order of one pitch period into sub-blocks, typically four in number; and allocating quantization bits on the basis of prediction error energy in each sub-interval. This is done separately for each of typically three to four sub-bands. The bit allocation in the time domain provides better encoding of the higher-valued prediction error samples during the onset of a pitch period and mitigates the problem of quantization error feedback, separately in each sub-band. With spectrum prediction of order four and pitch prediction, the sub-band coder with time-frequency bit allocation provides MOS quality scores in the order of 3.5 at 16 kb/s and 4.0 at 24 kb/s [Honda, Kitawaki and Itakura, 1982].

11.6 Transmission Error Effects

Bit errors in an individual sub-band will generate error contributions at the receiver output within that frequency band. Since the channel error contributions in different sub-bands are expected to be uncorrelated, the corresponding error variances will simply add. The results of Section 11.2 and Section 4.9 can therefore be used to derive an expression for channel error variance σ_c^2 in an SBC system. Also, explicit forms of error-protection can be used to mitigate channel error effects in SBC decoding. Error-protection systems can exploit not only the different sensitivities of various bits in transmitted codewords (as in Section 4.9), but also the different sensitivities of various sub-bands to transmission error effects. These points will be made more quantitative during the discussion of Transform Coding in Chapter 12.

Example 11.6. Transmission error effects in 24 kb/s SBC systems

Figure 11.10 describes the performance of three SBC systems at $I = 24$ kb/s and bit error rate p_e. In coder A, the adaptive quantizers use the one-word memory logic (4.185). In coder B, the adaptive quantizers use the robust version (4.199a) of the adaptation logic, with step size leakage factor $\beta = 31/32$. In coder C, the sign bit (most significant bit) as well as the most significant magnitude bit in the lowest frequency sub-band are ideally error protected. This protection requires an appropriate amount of bit-stealing from the quantizers, in order to maintain the total bit rate at the original value of $I = 24$ kb/s (Problem 11.8). However, the resulting increase of quantization noise is more than compensated for by reductions in channel noise if the error rate p_e is in the order of 10^{-2} or greater. The overall performance is so as to provide acceptable speech outputs at $p_e = 10^{-2}$, but not at $p_e = 10^{-1}$. •

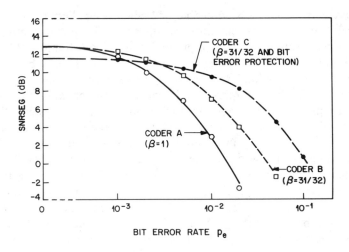

Figure 11.10 Transmission error performance of 16 kb/s SBC systems. Values of segmental SNR as a function of bit error rate p_e [Crochiere;©1978, AT&T].

Problems

(11.1)   Consider a 4-band SBC system where sub-band partitions are constrained by filter-bank considerations to be either (a) or (b) below:

(a) [0–800] [800–1600] [1600–2400] [2400–3200] Hz

(b) [225–450] [450–900] [1000–1500] [1800–2700] Hz

Ignoring side information for synchronization bits, show that bit allocations that provide 9.6 kb/s with the filter-banks above are respectively

(a) 3, 2, 1, 0   bits/sample

(b) 4, 3, 2, 1   bits/sample

Note that (b) is closer to the design recommended in Table 11.2.

(11.2) It is required to design a four-band filter-bank [0-0.5] [0.5-1.0] [1.0-2.0] [2.0-3.0] kHz for 16 kb/s coding of speech.

   (a) Show the band-division tree that realizes this partition using repeated quadrature mirror filtering of the [0-4.0] kHz band.

   (b) Assuming that $\max\{R_k\} = 5$ and $\min\{R_k\} = 2$ bits/sample, show that there are at least 2 bit assignments [5,3,2,2] [4,4,2,2] that realize a total bit rate $I = 16$ kb/s. Ignore side information considerations, as in Problem 11.1.

(11.3) Consider a 6-band SBC system for studio-grade music, with sub-bands [0-0.625] [0.625-1.25] [1.25-2.5] [2.5-5.0] [5.0-10.0] [10.0-20.0] kHz. Allowing 6 kb/s for synchronization information, show that the bit allocation (12, 10, 9, 8, 6, 5) bits/sample permits digital transmission over a 256 kb/s channel.

(11.4) Consider a SBC system with M bands of equal width ΔW. Consider the SBC input as a 1-second sequence of $2M\, \Delta W$ samples. Denote variances of individual samples of sub-band k by σ_{xk}^2 ; $k = 1,2,...,M$. Let each of these samples in sub-band k be quantized using R_k bits/sample. Because of a constant sampling rate $2\Delta W$, the total number of samples per second is independent of k. The optimum bit allocation for minimum mse, and the maximum gain G_{SBC} over single-band PCM, are given (on a *per sample* basis) by (11.10) and (11.12).

   It is also useful to give results on a *per second* basis. Define **R** as the total bit rate (bits/sec) in the SBC system, $\mathbf{R}_k = 2\Delta W\, R_k$ as the bit rate (bits/second) allocated to encode band k, and $\sigma_{xk}^2 = \sigma_{xk}^2\, 2\Delta W$ as the power in sub-band k. Show that the formulas (11.10) and (11.12) are equivalent to the pair of formulas

$$\mathbf{R}_{k,opt} = \frac{\mathbf{R}}{M} + \Delta W \log_2 \frac{\sigma_{xk}^2}{\left[\displaystyle\prod_{k=1}^{M}\sigma_{xk}^2\right]^{1/M}} \; ; \quad \max\{G_{SBC}\} = \frac{\dfrac{1}{M}\displaystyle\sum_{k=1}^{M}\sigma_{xk}^2}{\left[\displaystyle\prod_{k=1}^{M}\sigma_{xk}^2\right]^{1/M}}$$

(11.5) Refer to Problem 11.4 and the equal-width four-band partition of Problem 11.1(a). Equate the power $\sigma_{xk}^2 = \sigma_{xk}^2\, 2\Delta W$ to $S_k 2\Delta W$ where S_k represents the average value of input psd in sub-band k. Use the long-time psd of speech in Figure 2.9(a) together with the formula for $\mathbf{R}_{k,opt}$ in Problem 11.4 to show that the bit allocations in Problem 11.1(a) are indeed nearly optimal for a mmse criterion.

(11.6) Consider the highly structured two-level psd of Figure 2.24 and (2.168).

   (a) Consider SBC with $M = 2$ $\Delta\Omega = \Omega_W/2$, and band-edges at 0, $\Omega_W/2$ and Ω_W to follow the shape of the input psd. Use the result of Problem 11.4 to show that the maximum gain in 2-band SBC is

$$\max\{^2G_{SBC}\} = [\alpha(2-\alpha)]^{-\frac{1}{2}}$$

(b) Show that $\max\{^2G_{SBC}\} = \gamma_x^{-2} = \max\{G_{SBC}\}$, the reciprocal of the spectral flatness measure (Problem 2.22) of the process, i.e., SBC with $M = 2$ bands is sufficient to realize the maximum performance for this special psd.

(11.7) Consider the case of M equal-width sub-bands.

(a) Show that the adjacent sample correlation ρ_{1k} for the decimated signal in sub-band k vanishes if the psd in that sub-band is flat-topped.

(b) Determine the four values of ρ_{1k} for the 4-band partition of a signal with an integrated power spectrum and $\psi = 4$.

(11.8) Consider a 4-band SBC system for 24 kb/s speech coding, with the QMF partition [0, 1000] [1000, 2000] [2000, 3000] [3000, 4000] Hz, and with a normal bit allocation of (5, 4, 2, 1) bits/sample for quantization. Consider that this system is adapted to a noisy channel by protecting all bits in the first sub-band using a (12, 8) Hamming code (with 4 redundant bits for every 8 message bits). Show that if the bit allocation for quantization is changed to (4, 3, 2, 1) bits/sample, the total transmission rate is still 24 kb/s.

References

B. S. Atal and J. R. Remde, "Split-Band APC System for Low Bit Rate Encoding of Speech," Proc. ICASSP, April 1981.

H. G. Bellanger, G. Bonnerot, and M. Coudreuse, "Digital Filtering by Polyphase Network: Application to Sample-Rate Alteration and Filter-Banks", IEEE Trans. on Acoustics, Speech and Signal Proc., pp. 252-259, 1976.

R. V. Cox, unpublished work, Bell Laboratories, 1981.

R. V. Cox, "A Comparison of Three Speech Coders to Be Implemented on the Digital Signal Processor," Bell System Tech. J., pp. 1411-1421, September 1981.

R. V. Cox, unpublished work, Bell Laboratories, 1983.

R. E. Crochiere, "On the Design of Sub-Band Coders for Low Bit Rate Speech Communication," Bell System Tech. J., pp. 747-771, May-June 1977.

R. E. Crochiere, "An Analysis of 16 kb/s Sub-band Coder Performance: Dynamic Range, Tandem Connections, and Channel Errors," Bell System Tech., J., pp. 2927-2952, October 1978.

R. E. Crochiere, "Sub-band Coding," Bell System Tech. J., pp. 1633-1654, September 1981.

R. E. Crochiere, R. V. Cox and J. D. Johnston, "Real Time Speech Coding," IEEE Trans. on Communications, pp. 621-634, April 1982.

R. E. Crochiere and L. R. Rabiner, "Interpolation and Decimation of Digital Signals — A Tutorial Review," Proc. IEEE, pp. 300-331, March 1981.

R. E. Crochiere and L. R. Rabiner, *Multirate Digital Processing,* Prentice Hall, 1983.

R. E. Crochiere and M. R. Sambur, "A Variable-Band Coding Scheme for Speech Encoding at 4.8 kb/s", Bell System Tech. J., pp. 771-780, May-June 1977.

R. E. Crochiere, S. A. Webber and J. L. Flanagan, "Digital Coding of Speech in Sub-bands," Bell System Tech. J., pp. 1069-1085, October 1976.

W. R. Daumer, "Subjective Evaluation of Several Efficient Speech Coders," IEEE Trans. on Communications, pp. 662-665, April 1982.

D. Esteban and C. Galand, "Application of Quadrature Mirror Filters to Split Band Voice Coding Schemes," Proc. ICASSP, pp. 191-195, May 1977.

D. Esteban and C. Galand, "32 kb/s CCITT-Compatible Split Band Coding Scheme," Proc. ICASSP, pp. 320-325, 1978.

J. L. Flanagan et al., "Speech Coding", IEEE Trans. on Communications, pp. 710-737, April 1979.

C. Galand and D. Esteban, "16 kb/s Sub-band Coder Incorporating Variable Overhead Information," Proc. ICASSP, pp. 1684-1687, April 1982.

L. M. Goodman, "Channel Encoders," Proc. IEEE, pp. 127-128, 1967.

C. Grauel, "Sub-band Coding with Adaptive Bit Allocation," Signal Proc., 1980.

C. D. Heron, R. E. Crochiere and R. V. Cox, "A 32-Band Sub-Band/Transform Coder Incorporating Vector Quantization for Dynamic Bit Allocation," Proc. ICASSP, pp. 1276-1279, April 1983.

M. Honda, N. Kitawaki and F. Itakura, "Adaptive Bit Allocation Scheme in Predictive Coding of Speech," Proc. ICASSP, pp. 1672-1675, May 1982.

J. D. Johnston, "A Filter Family Designed for Use in Quadrature Mirror Filter Banks," Proc. ICASSP, pp. 291-294, April 1980.

J. D. Johnston and R. E. Crochiere, "An All-Digital 'Commentary-Grade' Sub-band Coder," Audio Eng. Soc. Conv., AES preprint, May 1979.

D. Malah, "Time Domain Harmonic Scaling Algorithms for Bandwidth Reduction and Time Scaling of Speech Signals," IEEE Trans. on Acoustics, Speech and Signal Processing, pp. 121-133, April 1979.

D. Malah, R. E. Crochiere and R. V. Cox, "Performance of Transform and Sub-Band Coding Systems Combined with Harmonic Scaling of Speech," IEEE Trans. on Acoustics, Speech and Signal Proc., pp. 273-283, April 1981.

L. R. Rabiner and R. W. Schafer, *Digital Processing of Speech Signals,* Prentice-Hall, Englewood Cliffs, N.J., 1978.

T. A. Ramstad, "Sub-band Coder with a Simple Bit Allocation Algorithm: A Possible Candidate for Digital Mobile Telephony," Proc. ICASSP, pp. 203-207, May 1982.

T. A. Ramstad and O. Foss, "Sub-band Coder Design Using Recursive Quadrature Mirror Filters," Proc. EUSIPCO, pp. 747-752, 1980.

J. E. Stjernvall, "On Rate and Frequency Allocation in Sub-band Coding of Gaussian Sources", Dept. of Elec. Eng. Report No. 1977-12-05, Linkoping University, Sweden, 1977.

J. M. Tribolet, P. Noll, B. J. McDermott and R. E. Crochiere, "A Comparison of the Performance of Our Low Bit Rate Speech Waveform Coders," Bell System Tech. J., pp. 699-713, March 1979.

12

Transform Coding

12.1 Introduction

We have seen in Chapter 6 that a stationary random sequence $\{X(n)\}$ can be efficiently encoded by predictive coding (DPCM) if its psd $S_{xx}(e^{j\omega})$ is not flat. Specifically, the reconstruction error in predictive encoding is upper-bounded in the form

$$\sigma_r^2 = \epsilon_q^2 \sigma_d^2 \geqslant \epsilon_q^2 \gamma_x^2 \sigma_x^2 \tag{12.1a}$$

where ϵ_q^2 is the quantizer performance factor, σ_d^2 is the variance of the difference (prediction error) signal, and γ_x^2 is the spectral flatness measure:

$$\gamma_x^2 = \exp\left[\frac{1}{2\pi}\int_{-\pi}^{\pi} \log_e S_{xx}(e^{j\omega})\,d\omega\right]/\sigma_x^2 \tag{12.1b}$$

For the example of first-order Gauss-Markov sources (Chapter 2), (12.1b) takes on the special values $(1-\rho^2)$ and $(1-\rho^2)^2$ in one- and two-dimensional cases, respectively, and the prediction gains (gains over PCM), given by the reciprocal of γ_x^2 values, are realized by an optimal first-order predictor in the one-dimensional example (6.24c), and by an optimal three-element predictor in the separable two-dimensional case (6.36d). With higher-order processes, we have seen that the predictor order should be correspondingly higher in order to approach the performance bound (12.1). Finally, we recall that the γ_x^2 bound applies to systems which exploit linear dependencies between input samples. DPCM is an example of such a system, and the first-order Markov source (with $\rho \rightarrow \pm 1$) is an example where linear dependencies can be simply observed, in terms of very significant correlations between adjacent input samples, or, equivalently, a psd that is lowpass or highpass.

The techniques of the present chapter will represent another approach for the utilization of linear dependencies for efficient digitization, called *Transform Coding* (TC). Its performance will be characterized by a performance gain over PCM, denoted by G_{TC}:

$$SNR \ (\text{dB})|_{TC} = SNR \ (\text{dB})|_{PCM} + 10 \log G_{TC} \qquad (12.2)$$

The gain G_{TC} will be a function of the source statistics, the type of linear transform and the transform length N to be defined presently. Later sections of this chapter will include closed-form expressions for G_{TC} for certain model sources, as well as experimental values of G_{TC} for speech and image inputs.

The asymptotic mse performance is theoretically the same for DPCM and TC [Nitadori, 1970]. In the latter case, this performance is expressed by the asymptotic gain $^{\infty}G_{TC}$; and its maximum value is equal to the maximum value of $^{\infty}G_P$ for a given source. However, important differences exist between DPCM and TC, especially at low bit rates: in terms of subjective quality, matching of algorithm to input statistics, and effects of transmission errors. In the case of video inputs, TC is more robust than DPCM with regard to input statistics and channel errors [Netravali and Limb, 1980]. In the case of an ideal channel and a known source, TC offers a more direct approach to $R(D)$ bounds, in both image and speech applications. The price paid for these advantages is increased encoding delay which, in TC, is proportional to transform length N and, in the case of TC with adaptive bit assignment (ATC), an encoding complexity comparable to that of fully adaptive APC.

Transform coding is a "frequency-domain" approach like SBC; however, the problem of bit allocation, introduced in Chapter 11, will be considered much more carefully in this chapter; and in the case of speech signals, the number of sub-bands, or equivalently, the number of transform coefficients, will be much greater than four, which was typical in the discussion of Chapter 11. The *number of transform coefficients* will be called N; it will also be referred to as the *order of the transform*; transform coding is also referred to as *block quantization* [Huang and Schultheiss, 1963] and input blocks used for an Nth order transform will in fact be N samples long. By using appropriate values of N and appropriate bit allocation strategies, transform coding procedures for speech and images will be shown to provide *high quality* digitizations at an average rate of $R = 2$ bits/sample (Figures 1.5 and 1.6) and *acceptable* digitizations at $R = 1$ bit/sample.

Variable bit allocation is always assumed in this chapter; and for simplicity, the resulting *average bit rate R* will be referred to simply as the *bit rate R*.

Transform Coding may also be used for the efficient encoding of sequences which are not successive samples of a waveform, but samples of N correlated sources: for example, the outputs of N parallel filters in a speech vocoder [Kramer and Mathews, 1956]. In all of the rest of this chapter, however, we will be concerned with the use of TC for encoding sequences of successive samples of a single waveform.

The efficiency of a transform coding system will depend on the type of linear transform (Sections 12.5 and 12.6) and the nature of bit allocation for quantizing transform coefficients (Section 12.4). Most practical systems will be based on sub-optimal approaches for transform operation as well as bit allocation.

Figure 12.1(a) is a block diagram of transform coding. It is a waveform digitizing procedure where a block of N input samples $x(n)$ is linearly transformed into a set of N *transform coefficients* $\theta(n)$ (for example, a set of Fourier coefficients). The coefficients are then quantized for transmission, and a reconstruction of $x(n)$ is obtained at the receiver using an inverse transform operation on quantized coefficients. Figure 12.1(b) shows how the above coding scheme is implemented. The input block could be one of high resolution PCM samples; for example, 8-bit resolution for images, and 12-bit resolution for speech. The output of the coder is the combination of the outputs of N PCM coders that convey quantized coefficient information, typically with a much lower total bit rate than what is present at the coder input.

In principle, the set of N transform coefficients can be quantized with lower average mse by the use of vector quantization or the related methods of Chapter 9. In the rest of this chapter, however, we shall follow the simpler practice of a scalar quantizer bank as in Figure 12.1. We will however briefly consider simple differential techniques for efficient quantization of correlated sets of coefficients in so-called hybrid coding systems (Section 12.6.5).

A crucial part of Transform Coding is a bit-allocation algorithm that provides the possibility of quantizing some coefficients "frequency components" more finely

Figure 12.1 (a) Block diagram of transform coding (TC); and (b) implementation of the encoder with a bank of PCM coders.

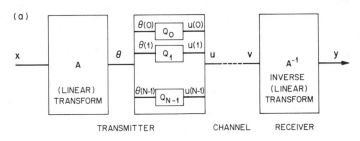

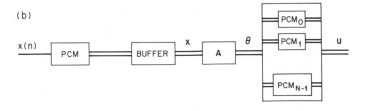

than others. The criterion for bit allocation can be the minimization of the mean squared value of reconstruction error. More generally, procedures may involve frequency-weighted reconstruction errors and adaptive bit-allocation for nonstationary inputs.

12.2 Linear Transforms of Order $N = 2$

A simple way of introducing transform coding or block quantization is with reference to the deterministic "lowpass" input sequence $\{x(n)\}$ of Figure 12.2:

$$x(0) = 2 ; \quad x(1) = 3 \tag{12.3}$$

Clearly, this sequence $\{2,3\}$ can be *approximately* represented in the form $\{2.5, 2.5\}$. For reasons that will be apparent as formalism develops, we shall write the approximating sequence in the form

$$\{2.5, 2.5\} = \frac{5}{\sqrt{2}} \{\frac{1}{\sqrt{2}}, \frac{1}{\sqrt{2}}\} = \frac{5}{\sqrt{2}} \{b_{00}, b_{01}\} \tag{12.4}$$

Figure 12.2 (a) Input sequence of length two; and (b) a set of two basis sequences used to represent (a); (c) and (d) are matrix representations of (a) and (b).

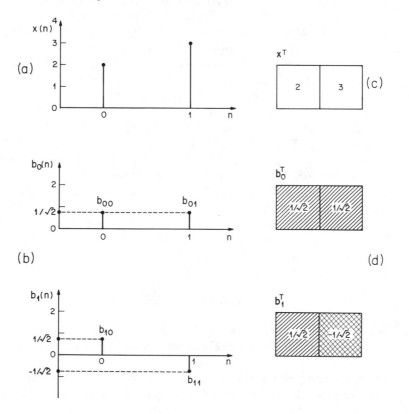

The input $\{x(n)\}$ can be *exactly* described if (12.4) is corrected by adding to it a sequence $\{-0.5, +0.5\}$:

$$\{-0.5,+0.5\} = \frac{-1}{\sqrt{2}}\{\frac{1}{\sqrt{2}},\frac{-1}{\sqrt{2}}\} = \frac{-1}{\sqrt{2}}\{b_{10},b_{11}\} \qquad (12.5)$$

The b-sequences in (12.4) and (12.5) can be regarded as *basis sequences* or *basis vectors* $\mathbf{b}_0$ and $\mathbf{b}_1$ used to represent $\{x(n)\}$ by a weighted linear combination, and the *weights*, or *transform* coefficients $5/\sqrt{2}$ and $-1/\sqrt{2}$, can be expressed in the form

$$\theta(0) = \frac{5}{\sqrt{2}} = \frac{1}{\sqrt{2}}\left[x(0)+x(1)\right]; \quad \theta(1) = \frac{-1}{\sqrt{2}} = \frac{1}{\sqrt{2}}\left[x(0)-x(1)\right] \quad (12.6a)$$

The values of transform coefficients indicate the similarity (in sign as well as in relative magnitude) between the input $\{x(n)\}$ and the two basis vectors.

The input $\{x(n)\}$ can be recovered by an inverse operation

$$x(0) = \frac{1}{\sqrt{2}}\left[\theta(0)+\theta(1)\right]; \quad x(1) = \frac{1}{\sqrt{2}}\left[\theta(0)-\theta(1)\right] \qquad (12.6b)$$

Note that $\theta(0)$ and $\theta(1)$ represent the sum and difference of the two input samples, and hence the powers of low frequency and high frequency components in $\{x(n)\}$. For minimizing the mean squared error in the reconstruction of the lowpass signal (12.3), one expects that the coefficient $\theta(0)$ is more crucial than $\theta(1)$ (Problem 12.5). This isolation of low and high frequency components is precisely the motivation for the *transform* representation (12.6).

Succeeding sections will show that transform representations such as (12.6) can be a basis for utilizing linear redundancies for the efficient coding of inputs with non-flat spectra, and that the upper bound for transformation *(transform coding)* gain is the same spectral flatness measure γ_x^2 that bounds *prediction gain*. A significant point of difference is that predictive systems utilize input dependencies in a recursive fashion while transform systems do so in a nonrecursive fashion, based on observations of N-blocks of $\{x(n)\}$. For speech and image sources, which can be described best by autoregressive models, predictive systems approach asymptotic performance faster (in terms of the order of prediction) than transform systems (in terms of order of transform, or block length).

In addition to providing components with variances that are different in general, transform operations such as (12.6) provide a representation in terms of uncorrelated coefficients. It is easy to see in fact that for a stationary random sequence $\{X(n)\}$ transformed by (12.6a),

$$E[\Theta(0)\Theta(1)] = E[X(0)^2] - E[X(1)^2] = 0 \qquad (12.7)$$

Recall that predictive encoding also aims to represent correlated inputs in terms of less correlated, ideally uncorrelated prediction error sequences.

A geometric interpretation. The decorrelation provided in a transform representation is well illustrated geometrically. Consider the sequence (12.3) as a point in the two-dimensional (x_0, x_1) domain of Figure 12.3. Also shown in the figure are *orthogonal* vectors $\mathbf{b}_0$ and $\mathbf{b}_1$ corresponding to the basis sequences of (12.4) and (12.5). We will see presently [in (12.22)] that these vectors are also *orthonormal*. The vectors $\mathbf{b}_0$ and $\mathbf{b}_1$ are along axes on which $x_0 = x_1$ and $x_0 = -x_1$, respectively. They define a new (θ_0, θ_1) domain obtained by rotating and reflecting the (x_0, x_1) domain. The input point $(2,3)$ can be represented in the

Figure 12.3 Geometrical interpretations for (a) the transform representation of the input $\{2,3\}$; and (b) a population of positively correlated input sequences of length 2.

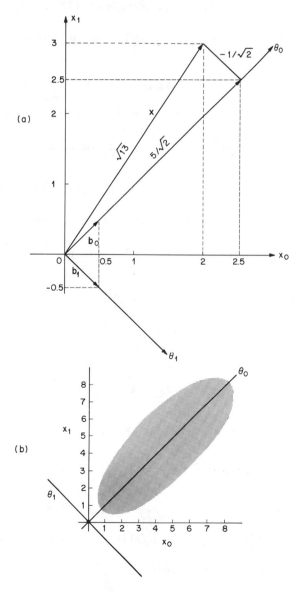

(θ_0, θ_1) domain by traversing $\theta(0) = +5/\sqrt{2}$ units in the $\mathbf{b}_0$ direction (starting from the origin), and traversing $\theta(1) = -1/\sqrt{2}$ unit in the $\mathbf{b}_1$ direction.

Let us now consider a population or ensemble of input sequences of length 2. Assume for illustration that each of these sequences exhibits a positive adjacent sample correlation as in Figure 12.2(a). The members of such an ensemble of $(x(0), x(1))$-pairs will occupy the shaded ellipse-like region of Figure 12.3(b). Points in this region have the property that their (x_0, x_1) coordinates are highly correlated, while the (θ_0, θ_1) coordinates are not. Given the θ_0 coordinate $\theta(0)$ of a sample point, one expects the $\theta(1)$ value to be smaller in magnitude, but one cannot predict the sign of $\theta(1)$. In other words, $x(1)$ can be greater or less than $x(0)$ with equal probability. In the specific example of (12.6a), $\theta(1)$ was of course negative.

Vector and marix notations. The following notation is very useful in representing transforms of arbitrary order N:

$$\boldsymbol{\theta} = \mathbf{A}\mathbf{x} \; ; \quad \mathbf{x} = \mathbf{B}\boldsymbol{\theta} \; ; \quad \mathbf{B} = \mathbf{A}^{-1} \qquad (12.8)$$

where $\mathbf{A}$ is a *transform matrix* and $\mathbf{B}$ is the *inverse transform matrix* (Section 12.3).

Input and coefficient vectors are represented as $(1 \times N)$ matrices for 1-D sequences

$$\mathbf{x}^T = \left[x(0), x(1), ..., x(N-1) \right] \; ; \quad \boldsymbol{\theta}^T = \left[\theta(0), \theta(1), ..., \theta(N-1) \right] , \quad (12.9)$$

as $(N \times N)$ matrices for 2-D sequences, and as appropriate tensors for higher dimensions.

For $N = 2$ we will see (Section 12.5) that, most generally,

$$\mathbf{A} = \mathbf{B} = \begin{bmatrix} a & \sqrt{1-a^2} \\ \sqrt{1-a^2} & -a \end{bmatrix} \qquad (12.10a)$$

For the important special case of $a = 1/\sqrt{2}$ (Problem 12.1), the inverse transform $\mathbf{B}$ equals $\mathbf{A}$:

$$\mathbf{A} = \mathbf{B} = \frac{1}{\sqrt{2}} \begin{bmatrix} 1 & 1 \\ 1 & -1 \end{bmatrix} \qquad (12.10b)$$

The basis vectors $\mathbf{b}_0$ and $\mathbf{b}_1$ are the columns of $\mathbf{B}$:

$$\mathbf{b}_0^T = (b_{00}, b_{10}) = \left[\frac{1}{\sqrt{2}}, \frac{1}{\sqrt{2}} \right] \; ; \quad \mathbf{b}_1^T = (b_{01}, b_{11}) = \left[\frac{1}{\sqrt{2}}, \frac{-1}{\sqrt{2}} \right] \quad (12.11)$$

The inverse transform $\mathbf{x} = \mathbf{B}\boldsymbol{\theta}$ has an explicit interpretation

$$x(0) = b_{00}\theta(0) + b_{01}\theta(1) \; ; \quad x(1) = b_{10}\theta(0) + b_{11}\theta(1) \qquad (12.12)$$

or, the *basis vector* interpretation

$$\mathbf{x} = \theta(0)\mathbf{b}_0 + \theta(1)\mathbf{b}_1 \qquad (12.13)$$

which tells us that $\mathbf{x}$ is the weighted sum of the two basis vectors, and that the weights are just the transform coefficients. In the example of Figure 12.2,

$$\mathbf{x} = \begin{bmatrix} 2 \\ 3 \end{bmatrix} ; \quad \theta = \frac{1}{\sqrt{2}} \begin{bmatrix} 1 & 1 \\ 1 & -1 \end{bmatrix} \begin{bmatrix} 2 \\ 3 \end{bmatrix} = \frac{1}{\sqrt{2}} \begin{bmatrix} 5 \\ -1 \end{bmatrix} ; \qquad (12.14a)$$

$$\mathbf{x} = \frac{5}{\sqrt{2}} \mathbf{b}_0 - \frac{1}{\sqrt{2}} \mathbf{b}_1 \qquad (12.14b)$$

However, *transform coding* implies the use of quantized versions $u(i) = Q[\theta(i)]$ of the coefficients, and hence an output

$$\mathbf{y} = Q[\theta(0)]\mathbf{b}_0 + Q[\theta(1)]\mathbf{b}_1 = u(0)\mathbf{b}_0 + u(1)\mathbf{b}_1 \qquad (12.14c)$$

which will be different from $\mathbf{x}$. This will cause a reconstruction error $\mathbf{r} = \mathbf{x} - \mathbf{y}$ (Section 12.3).

The example of $N = 2$ is too simple to be of practical significance in typical speech and image applications. But the discussion of this simple case has already provided significant insight. It has shown that Transform Coding is different in structure from Sub-band Coding but yet similar to it in the qualitative sense that different frequency components in the input are separated. The example of $N = 2$ has also shown the importance of bit allocation, and the fact that the channel input, as in the case of DPCM and SBC, is a sequence of quantities that are less correlated than the input samples themselves.

Section 12.3 will formalize an $N \times N$ transform in greater detail, and Section 12.4 will discuss variances, which leads in turn to the important issue of error-minimizing bit allocation. Sections 12.5 and 12.6 will discuss optimum (input decorrelating) and several suboptimum transforms. For the special case of $N = 2$, all of these transforms reduce to the one defined in (12.10). Section 12.7 will discuss adaptive bit allocation and resulting techniques for adaptive transform coding (ATC), and Section 12.8 will describe the effects of transmission errors.

12.3 $N \times N$ Transforms

Basic transform definitions have been introduced in Chapter 2 and in Sections 12.1 and 12.2. This section will provide a recapitulation, and also point out classes of one- and two-dimensional transforms that are important for digital coding of waveforms.

12.3.1 One-Dimensional Transforms

We extend the notation of Section 12.2 to define the Nth order linear transform of a one-dimensional sequence

$$\{x(n)\} ; \quad n = 0,1,...,N-1 \qquad (12.15)$$

The transform is given by

$$\theta(k) = \sum_{n=0}^{N-1} x(n)a(k, n) \qquad \text{for } k = 0,1,...,N - 1 \qquad (12.16a)$$

where $a(k,n)$ is a *forward transformation kernel*, and $\theta(k)$ are the *transform coefficients*. The inverse transform that recovers the input sequence is

$$x(n) = \sum_{k=0}^{N-1} \theta(k)b(k, n) \qquad \text{for } n = 0,1,...,N - 1 \qquad (12.16b)$$

where $b(k, n)$ is the *inverse transformation kernel* (see Appendix A).
    In matrix notation (Appendix B),

$$\boldsymbol{\theta} = \mathbf{A}\mathbf{x} ; \qquad \mathbf{x} = \mathbf{B}\boldsymbol{\theta} ; \qquad \mathbf{B} = \mathbf{A}^{-1} \qquad (12.17)$$

with $\mathbf{x}$ and $\boldsymbol{\theta}$ as in (12.9) and

$$\mathbf{A} = \{a(m, n)\}_{m, n=0,1,...,N-1} ; \qquad \mathbf{B} = \{b(m, n)\}_{m, n=0,1,...,N-1} \qquad (12.18)$$

For simplicity, we use the notation

$$\mathbf{B} = \{\mathbf{b}_k\}_{k=0,1,...,N-1} ; \qquad \mathbf{b}_k = \{b(m, k)\}_{m=0,1,...,N-1} \qquad (12.19)$$

where the $\mathbf{b}_k$ are *basis vectors*. We also note, as a generalization of (12.13), that

$$\mathbf{x} = \mathbf{B}\boldsymbol{\theta} = \sum_{k=0}^{N-1} \theta(k)\mathbf{b}_k \qquad (12.20a)$$

Hence $\mathbf{x}$ is *the weighted sum of basis vectors, where the weights are just the values of the transform coefficients* ($\mathbf{x}$ can also be considered as a point in an N-dimensional $\boldsymbol{\theta}$-space, generalizing on Figure 12.2). In *transform coding*, output $\mathbf{y}$ will also be a weighted sum of basis vectors. But the weights will be quantized versions of $\theta(k)$ (Section 12.4):

$$\mathbf{y} = \sum_{k=0}^{N-1} u(k)\mathbf{b}_k; \qquad u(k) = Q[\theta(k)] \qquad (12.20b)$$

    The matrix $\mathbf{A}$ can be complex in general, as in some later subsections. For the time being, let $\mathbf{A}$ be real; the class of *orthogonal* transforms is defined by

$$\mathbf{A}^{-1} = \mathbf{A}^T \qquad (12.21)$$

which implies that

$$\mathbf{A}^T\mathbf{A} = \mathbf{A}\mathbf{A}^T = \mathbf{I} \qquad (12.22)$$

where $\mathbf{I}$ is the identity matrix of order N. A real matrix is orthogonal if and only if its columns and rows form an *orthonormal* set (Problem 12.1). From the above, we find that the inverse transform is just the transpose of **A**:

$$\mathbf{B} = \mathbf{A}^{-1} = \mathbf{A}^T \qquad (12.23)$$

This implies that the basis vectors are rows of **A** (see Figure 12.4) and that

$$\mathbf{b}_i^T \cdot \mathbf{b}_j = \delta_{ij} \qquad (12.24)$$

For example, with the basis vectors in (12.11),

$$\mathbf{b}_0^T \cdot \mathbf{b}_0 = \mathbf{b}_1^T \cdot \mathbf{b}_1 = 1 \; ; \qquad \mathbf{b}_0^T \cdot \mathbf{b}_1 = \mathbf{b}_1^T \cdot \mathbf{b}_0 = 0 \qquad (12.25)$$

Orthogonality is clearly a necessary property for basis vectors that are used to decompose an input into uncorrelated components in an N-dimensional space, as in Figure 12.2 for $N = 2$. *Orthonormality* of basis vector is a stronger property; it leads to transforms which are necessary in transform coding to make the average sum of the variances of the elements of $\boldsymbol{\theta}$ equal to σ_x^2, the variance of the elements of **x**; this also means that the average reconstruction error variance equals the error variance introduced in the quantization of transform coefficients (Section 12.3).

Figure 12.5 shows basis vectors for several one-dimensional transforms of order $N = 8$. In each of the four sets of basis vectors, all vectors except those in the first row are zero-mean sequences. The basis vectors in the first row are constant-amplitude sequences in all cases except the *Karhunen Loeve Transform* (KLT). The basis vectors in the *Discrete Fourier Transform* (DFT) are simply sines and cosines (fundamental frequency and multiples thereof) appropriate to $N = 8$. The basis vectors in the *Discrete Walsh Hadamard Transform* (DWHT) are square waves of different *sequencies* (Section 12.6), while the *Discrete Cosine Transform* (DCT) basis vectors are cosine functions with special phase and amplitude patterns (Section 12.6). The basis vectors in DFT, DWHT and DCT are input-signal-

Figure 12.4 Transform matrix **A**, inverse $\mathbf{B} = \mathbf{A}^{-1} = \mathbf{A}^T$, and basis vectors $\mathbf{b}_k$.

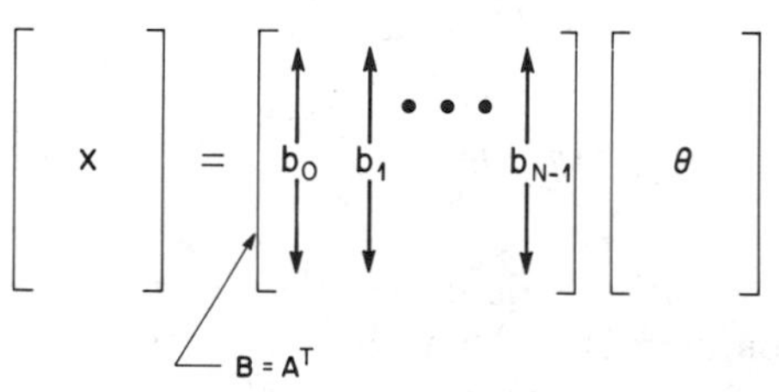

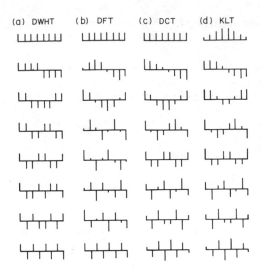

Figure 12.5 Basis vectors for $N = 8$ in (a) DWHT, (b) DFT, (c) DCT and (d) KLT. The input-dependent KLT set in (d) is derived from an AR(8) modeling of long-time-averaged speech statistics [Zelinski and Noll, 1975. Reprinted with permission].

independent. By contrast, the KLT basis vectors, also called *eigenvectors*, are defined by input statistics, as described in Section 12.5. In the specific example of Figure 12.5, the KLT basis vectors are appropriate to long-term speech statistics. Basic vectors for other values of N can be found in coding literature (for example, [Campanella and Robinson, 1971]).

Input-dependent transforms are the hardest to implement, but they also have the best input-decorrelating and variance-ordering properties, as explained in Section 12.4. KLT basis vectors also exhibit the greatest possible resemblance to waveform segments that are typical of the input class whose statistics are used in the KLT derivation. This will be reflected in the fact that the dimensionality N needed for a given representation error is least when the representation is in terms of KLT basis vectors (eigenvectors). Section 12.4 will discuss representations based on retaining only a small fraction of eigenvectors for the reconstruction in (12.16b).

12.3.2 Two-Dimensional Transforms

Let us begin with a straightforward generalization of (12.16):

$$\theta(k, l) = \sum_{m=0}^{N-1} \sum_{n=0}^{N-1} x(m, n) \, a(k, l, m, n) \; ;$$

$$x(m, n) = \sum_{k=0}^{N-1} \sum_{l=0}^{N-1} \theta(k, l) \, b(k, l, m, n) \tag{12.26}$$

The above equations describe the transform of N^2-point sequences with transformation kernels $a(\cdot)$ and $b(\cdot)$ that are described by N^4 elements in general. For a 2-dimensional image input, the N^2 values of $x(m,n)$ are usually the elements

Transform Coding   12

of a square array, a subimage of size $N \times N$. Typical arrays in image coding use $N = 4$, 8 or 16. The partitioning into subimages is particularly efficient in cases where correlations are localized to neighboring pixels, and where structural details tend to cluster. Equation (12.26) does not preclude the arrangement of the same N^2 input points as a single $(1 \times N^2)$ vector.

Separable Two-Dimensional Transforms. The image transforms that we will study will invariably assume a $N \times N$ square sub-image. In addition, we will only consider the simple case where the transform kernels $a(\cdot)$ and $b(\cdot)$ are *separable* into kernels signifying separate horizontal (row) and vertical (column) operations:

$$a(k, l, m, n) = a_v(k, m) \, a_h(l, n) ;$$

$$b(k, l, m, n) = b_v(k, m) \, b_h(l, n) \tag{12.27}$$

The two-dimensional transform to obtain $\theta(k,l)$ [Equation (12.26)] can now be conveniently performed in two steps, each of which involves a one-dimensional transform operation. The first step uses $a_h(\cdot)$ for operation on row m to obtain the lth transform coefficient $\theta[m,l]$ [compare with (12.16a)], while the second step uses $a_v(\cdot)$ to provide the one-dimensional transform of column l:

$$\theta(k, l) = \sum_{m=0}^{N-1} a_v(k, m) \sum_{n=0}^{N-1} x(m, n) \, a_h(l, n) = \sum_{m=0}^{N-1} a_v(k, m) \, \theta(m, l) \tag{12.28}$$

X and **Θ** are arrays which have as their elements $x(m, n)$ and $\theta(k, l)$, respectively. We may write

$$\mathbf{A_h} = \{a_h(m,n)\}_{m,n=0,1,\ldots,N-1} ; \quad \mathbf{A_v} = \{a_v(m,n)\}_{m,n=0,1,\ldots,N-1} \tag{12.29}$$

so that

$$\mathbf{\Theta} = \mathbf{A_v X A_h}^T \tag{12.30}$$

For *symmetrical* kernels,

$$\mathbf{A_v} = \mathbf{A_h} = \mathbf{A} ; \quad \mathbf{\Theta} = \mathbf{AXA}^T \tag{12.31}$$

and with $\mathbf{A}^{-1} = \mathbf{A}^T$,

$$\mathbf{X} = \mathbf{A}^T \mathbf{\Theta A} \tag{12.32}$$

Note that **A** is simply the 1-D transform (12.31) and that the matrix operation of (12.32) is possible only with separable transforms. With general non-separable transforms, 2-D operations would involve tensor operations, rather than the matrix operations of (12.32). Also, as a result of a separable $b(\cdot)$ kernel, image **X** can be expressed as a superposition of *basis images* $\mathbf{B_{kl}}$ [see (12.26)]:

$$\mathbf{X} = \sum_{k=0}^{N-1} \sum_{l=0}^{N-1} \theta(k, l) \mathbf{B_{kl}} ; \quad \mathbf{B_{kl}} = \mathbf{b_k b_l}^T \tag{12.33a}$$

The second part of (12.33a) is a good working definition for a separable transform.

The basis image is the two-dimensional counterpart of the basis vector in (12.20a). In *transform coding*, the reconstructed image **Y** will be superposition of basis images $\mathbf{B}_{kl}$ which have been weighted by quantized versions of $\theta(k,l)$:

$$\mathbf{Y} = \sum_{k=0}^{N-1} \sum_{l=0}^{N-1} Q[\theta(k,l)]\mathbf{B}_{kl} = \sum_{k=0}^{N-1}\sum_{l=0}^{N-1} u(k,l)\mathbf{B}_{kl} \qquad (12.33b)$$

Figure 12.6(a) is an example of a (2×2) image [Problem 12.6(a)] and Figure 12.6(b) is a separable (2×2) transform with a set of four basis images $\mathbf{B}_{00}$, $\mathbf{B}_{01}$, $\mathbf{B}_{10}$ and $\mathbf{B}_{11}$. By assigning amplitude levels of 1/2 and −1/2 with single-hatched and cross-hatched areas in Figure 12.6(b), the 2×2 basis images $\mathbf{B}_{00}$, $\mathbf{B}_{01}$, $\mathbf{B}_{10}$ and $\mathbf{B}_{11}$ are seen to be those in (12.34):

$$\mathbf{B}_{00} = \frac{1}{2}\begin{bmatrix} 1 & 1 \\ 1 & 1 \end{bmatrix} \qquad \mathbf{B}_{01} = \frac{1}{2}\begin{bmatrix} 1 & -1 \\ 1 & -1 \end{bmatrix}$$

$$\mathbf{B}_{10} = \frac{1}{2}\begin{bmatrix} 1 & 1 \\ -1 & -1 \end{bmatrix} \qquad \mathbf{B}_{11} = \frac{1}{2}\begin{bmatrix} 1 & -1 \\ -1 & 1 \end{bmatrix} \qquad (12.34)$$

Note that the basis images are given by $\mathbf{B}_{kl} = \mathbf{b}_k \mathbf{b}_l^T$, as in (12.11) and (12.30).

Figure 12.6 2-D transforms: (a) is a 2×2 input and (b) is a set of four basis images that may be used to represent (a); (c) is the image of "cameraman," which may be represented by sets of (16×16) basis images in (d) DWHT or (e) KLT [Wintz;©1972, IEEE].

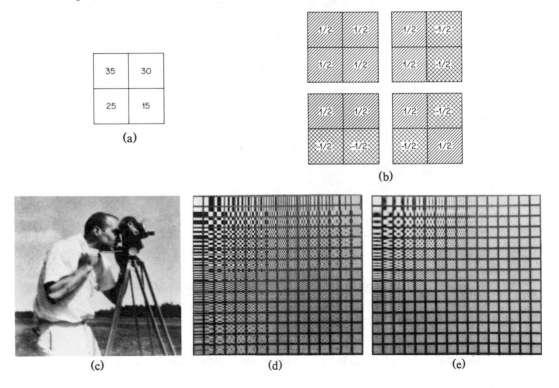

(a)

(b)

(c)   (d)   (e)

The intensity levels of binary images are usually assigned values of 1 (for *white*) and 0 (for *black*). This is in fact the explicit notation of Figure 2.2 and Chapter 10. However, if binary intensities are associated with basis images, the two intensity levels are 1 and −1, as in (12.34).

Higher order transforms are useful in the representation of real images such as that in Figure 12.6(c) (Problem 12.2). Basis images of (16×16) arrays are shown in Figure 12.6(d) and (e). If the (256×256) image of Figure 12.6(c) is divided into 256 sub-images of size (16×16) each, these subimages can be described as a superposition of the basis images in Figures 12.6(d) or (e). The basis images in DWHT have black-or-white components as in Figure 12.6(b), while the basis images in KLT have elements representing all shades of gray. In each superposition, the intensities of the basis images add in proportion to the weighting provided by the respective transform coefficient (see 12.33a). Since the values of these coefficients are not constrained to be binary, the above process can generate *gray* levels of intensity even if the sub-images have only two levels of intensity (white and black), as in DWHT.

Consider next the DWHT basis vectors $\mathbf{b}_k$ of length $N = 8$ in Figure 12.5. We can obtain the first $8 \times 8 = 64$ basis images of Figure 12.12 [a lower-dimensional version of Figure 12.6(d)] by using these 8 vectors in $\mathbf{b}_k \mathbf{b}_l^T$ (12.33) (Problem 12.3).

KLT basis images are also called *eigenimages*. They are specific to a given description of input statistics. In the example of Figure 12.6(e), they are derived from a two-dimensional $AR(2)$ modeling of the input process in Figure 12.6(c). This model uses measured correlation coefficients of 0.883 and 0.780 in the horizontal and vertical directions. We will see shortly that for a given input process, out of all basis image sets, the eigenimage set leads to the smallest reconstruction error for a given dimensionality $(N \times N)$ of representation, i.e., a given number of basis images. Section 12.5 will demonstrate image reconstructions based on retaining only a small fraction of eigenimages in the representation (12.33).

12.3.3 Complex Transforms

Complex kernels and coefficients will be treated at some length in the DFT discussion of Section 12.5. For completeness, however, we note the following generalization rightaway. *Unitary* transforms (Appendix B) are described by

$$\mathbf{B} = \mathbf{A}^{-1} = \mathbf{A}^{*T} ; \quad \boldsymbol{\theta} = \mathbf{A}\mathbf{x} ; \quad \mathbf{x} = \mathbf{A}^{*T}\boldsymbol{\theta} \qquad (12.35)$$

and they are the counterpart of orthogonal transforms in the real-valued case. As in that case, columns and rows of the $\mathbf{A}$ and $\mathbf{B}$ matrices in (12.35) are orthonormal. Separable two-dimensional transforms with symmetrical kernels are described in general by

$$\boldsymbol{\Theta} = \mathbf{A}\mathbf{X}\mathbf{A}^{*T} ; \quad \mathbf{X} = \mathbf{A}^{*T}\boldsymbol{\Theta}\mathbf{A} \qquad (12.36)$$

12.4 Optimum Bit Allocation and Zonal Sampling

This section will show two results basic to Transform Coder (TC) performance. We first show that for orthogonal (in general, unitary) transforms, the reconstruction error variance for an input block is the sum of error variances in the coding (quantization) of individual transform coefficients. We then show that Transform Coding, which is based on the quantization of these coefficients, can provide an *SNR* gain over PCM, denoted by G_{TC}, whose maximum value is equal to the ratio of arithmetic to geometric means of transform coefficient variances. Sections 12.5 and 12.6 will describe transforms that seek to make this ratio as large as possible. The maximum gain over PCM is achieved in the case of *optimum bit allocation* for the quantization of transform coefficients. We will also discuss one example of suboptimum bit allocation, called *zonal sampling*.

12.4.1 Optimum Bit Allocation

Reconstruction Error. We will begin with a one-dimensional input for simplicity. Refer to the Transform Coder block diagram of Figure 12.1. We arrange N successive signal samples $\{x(n)\}$; $n=0,1,...,N-1$ into a block or vector $\mathbf{x}$. The vector $\mathbf{x}$ is linearly transformed using an orthogonal (in general, unitary) matrix $\mathbf{A}$. The elements of $\boldsymbol{\theta} = \mathbf{Ax}$, i.e., the transform coefficients, are *independently* quantized using a bank of N quantizers Q_i; $i = 0,1,...,N-1$. The vector $\mathbf{u} = Q[\boldsymbol{\theta}]$ of quantized coefficients is transmitted to the receiver and its received version $\mathbf{v}$ (which equals $\mathbf{u}$ with error-free transmission) is inverse-transformed using $\mathbf{A}^{-1}$:

$$\mathbf{y} = \mathbf{A}^{-1}\mathbf{u} = \mathbf{A}^T\mathbf{u} = \sum_{k=0}^{N-1} u(k)\mathbf{b}_k \tag{12.37}$$

The elements of $\mathbf{y}$ are the reconstructed output samples. It can be shown [Huang and Schultheiss, 1963] that $\mathbf{A}^{-1}$, which was assumed for $\mathbf{B}$ in (12.17), is in fact the best inverse transform in the mse sense for Gaussian inputs and Max-quantizers.

We will now compute error variances. In order to do so, we assume that $\mathbf{x}$ is taken from a zero-mean stationary scalar source. Successive vectors thus constitute a random vector source $\mathbf{X}$ whose elements are random variables $X(n)$; $n = 0,1,...,N - 1$.

As noted in Section 12.2, orthogonal transforms are variance-preserving. We will hence show that if $\mathbf{A}$ is orthogonal ($\mathbf{A}^{-1}=\mathbf{A}^T$), the average sum of variances $E[\Theta^2(k)] = \sigma_k^2$ of the transform coefficients $\theta(k)$ equals the variance of the input:

$$\frac{1}{N} \sum_{k=0}^{N-1} \sigma_k^2 = \frac{1}{N} \sum_{k=0}^{N-1} E[\Theta^2(k)] = \frac{1}{N} E[\boldsymbol{\Theta}^T\boldsymbol{\Theta}] = \frac{1}{N} E[\mathbf{X}^T\mathbf{A}^T\mathbf{AX}]$$

$$= \frac{1}{N} E[\mathbf{X}^T\mathbf{X}] = \frac{1}{N} \sum_{k=0}^{N-1} E[X^2(k)] = \frac{1}{N} \sum_{k=0}^{N-1} \sigma_x^2 = \sigma_x^2 \tag{12.38}$$

We will next relate the total reconstruction error between input $\mathbf{X}$ and output $\mathbf{Y}$ to the errors introduced by the individual quantizers Q_i. Let

$$\sigma_{rk}^2 = E[(X(k)-Y(k))^2]; \qquad k = 0,1,\ldots,N-1 \tag{12.39}$$

be the mse of element k of $\mathbf{X}$. The average reconstruction error variance is

$$\sigma_r^2 = \frac{1}{N}\sum_{k=0}^{N-1}\sigma_{rk}^2 = \frac{1}{N}E[(\mathbf{X}-\mathbf{Y})^T(\mathbf{X}-\mathbf{Y})] \tag{12.40}$$

Clearly, $\mathbf{r} = \mathbf{x} - \mathbf{y}$ is the N-block of error samples and (12.40) is the variance, as averaged over that block. Using (12.37), the corresponding relation $\mathbf{x} = \mathbf{A}^{-1}\boldsymbol{\theta}$ for unquantized quantities, and assuming that $\mathbf{A}^{-1} = \mathbf{A}^T$, (12.40) can be rewritten as

$$\sigma_r^2 = \frac{1}{N}E[(\boldsymbol{\Theta}-\mathbf{U})^T(\boldsymbol{\Theta}-\mathbf{U})] = \frac{1}{N}E[\mathbf{Q}^T\mathbf{Q}] = \frac{1}{N}\sum_{k=0}^{N-1}\sigma_{qk}^2 = \sigma_q^2 \tag{12.41}$$

where $\mathbf{q} = \boldsymbol{\theta} - \mathbf{u}$ is the block of quantization errors, and $\sigma_{qk}^2 = E[(\Theta(k)-U(k))^2]$. In other words, *for orthogonal transforms, the reconstruction error variance in TC equals that introduced by the set of coefficient quantizers.*

We may also describe the reconstruction error vector $\mathbf{r}$ as a superposition of basis vectors weighted by the corresponding quantization errors. From (12.20a) and (12.37),

$$\mathbf{r} = \sum_{k=0}^{N-1} q(k)\mathbf{b}_k \tag{12.42}$$

The result $\sigma_r^2 = \sigma_q^2$ can also be established from (12.42).

The results in (12.40) and (12.41) can be straightforwardly extended to include complex entries in $\mathbf{A}$ and to two-dimensional signals where (12.40) and (12.41) generalize to averages taken over N^2 elements.

The error components in (12.41) can be explicitly written, as in Chapter 4, in the form

$$\sigma_{qk}^2 = \epsilon_{qk}^2\sigma_k^2 \approx \epsilon_*^2 2^{-2R_k}\sigma_k^2 \tag{12.43}$$

where $\sigma_k^2 = E[\Theta^2(k)]$ is the variance of the input to quantizer k, and ϵ_{qk}^2 is the corresponding quantizer performance factor. This factor depends on the pdf of the input (kth transform coefficient) and on the quantizer characteristic, especially on the number of levels therein. However, ϵ_{qk}^2 is approximately reduced by a factor of four if the number of levels is doubled, which leads to the approximation in (12.43). The quantity ϵ_*^2 can be regarded as a variable correction factor that takes into account the performance of practical quantizers. We recall from Chapter 4 that minimum values of ϵ_*^2, for sufficiently fine quantization without entropy coding, are respectively 1.0, 2.7, 4.5 and 5.7 for Max quantizers with uniform, Gaussian, Laplacian and gamma distributions at the input. We also recall that ϵ_*^2 values less than 1 can be realized by entropy coding under certain conditions. We shall use the approximation in (12.43) in the rest of this chapter, although it is quite coarse for low values of R_k.

Rewriting (12.43) as

$$R_k = \frac{1}{2}\log_2\epsilon_*^2 + \frac{1}{2}\log_2\frac{\sigma_k^2}{\sigma_{qk}^2}; \qquad k = 0,1,\ldots,N-1 \tag{12.44}$$

provides an expression for the rate R_k (bits/sample) needed for coefficient $\theta(k)$ of variance σ_k^2 if an average MSE σ_{qk}^2 is not to be exceeded. The second term in the right-half of (12.44) is a minimum rate from rate distortion bounds for statistically independent Gaussian random variables (Appendix D), and the first term is the above mentioned correction for practical quantizers.

Values of σ_k^2 are in general different and so are the individual rates R_k. In fact, the problem of optimizing a Transform Coding scheme can be stated as that of finding an orthogonal (in general, unitary) matrix, and then of finding a distribution (allocation) of bits R_k such that the average coefficient error variance

$$\sigma_q^2 = \frac{1}{N} \sum_{k=0}^{N-1} \sigma_{qk}^2 \tag{12.45}$$

is minimized with the constraint of a given *average* bit rate

$$R = \frac{1}{N} \sum_{k=0}^{N-1} R_k = \text{constant} \tag{12.46}$$

A later subsection will generalize (12.45) to include frequency-weighted (k-weighted) error criteria.

Bit Allocation for $N = 2$. Assuming an appropriate transform, the problem is to minimize

$$\sigma_r^2 = \sigma_q^2 = \frac{1}{2} (\sigma_{q0}^2 + \sigma_{q1}^2) \tag{12.47}$$

given that

$$R_0 + R_1 = 2R \tag{12.48}$$

The problem reduces to one of minimizing σ_r^2 with respect to R_0 because $R_1 = 2R - R_0$. Using (12.43) and (12.47),

$$\sigma_r^2 = \frac{1}{2} \epsilon_\theta^2 [2^{-2R_0} \sigma_0^2 + 2^{2R_0 - 4R} \sigma_1^2] \tag{12.49}$$

To minimize (12.49) using bit allocation, we set its (partial) derivative with respect to R_0 to zero:

$$\frac{\partial \sigma_r^2}{\partial R_0} = 2[-\sigma_0^2 \, 2^{-2R_0} + \sigma_1^2 \, 2^{2R_0 - 4R}] = 0 \tag{12.50}$$

so that

$$\sigma_0^2 / 2^{2R_0} = \sigma_1^2 / 2^{2R_1} ; \quad 2R_0 = \log_2 \sigma_0^2 + c ; \quad 2R_1 = \log_2 \sigma_1^2 + c \tag{12.51}$$

where c is a constant. From (12.48),

$$R = \frac{1}{2} \log_2 (\sigma_0 \sigma_1) + \frac{c}{2} \tag{12.52}$$

We express c in terms of R using (12.52), and use it to rewrite (12.51) as

$$R_0 = R + \frac{1}{2} \log_2 \frac{\sigma_0}{\sigma_1} ; \quad R_1 = R - \frac{1}{2} \log_2 \frac{\sigma_0}{\sigma_1} \tag{12.53}$$

which expresses the desired *bit allocation*. The second derivative of σ_q^2 with respect to R_0 is always positive so that the extremum provided by (12.53) is indeed a minimum (not maximum) value of σ_q^2. (Also see Problem 12.5 for a numerical example).

Inspection of (12.51) and (12.43) reveals that

$$\sigma_{q_0}^2 = \sigma_{q_1}^2 \tag{12.54}$$

so that the bit allocation procedure that minimizes σ_r^2 also provides equal quantization errors in the quantizing of the individual transform coefficients. This implies a reconstruction noise spectrum that is independent of coefficient index k. [In DFT (Section 12.6.2) this provides a reconstruction noise spectrum that is flat as a function of frequency.] Finally, setting (12.53) in (12.43),

$$\sigma_{q1}^2 = \epsilon_*^2 2^{-2R} (\sigma_0 \sigma_1)$$

and because of (12.43), (12.47) and (12.53),

$$\sigma_{r,TC}^2 = \sigma_q^2 = \sigma_{q0}^2 = \sigma_{q1}^2 = \epsilon_*^2 2^{-2R} (\sigma_0 \sigma_1) \tag{12.55}$$

We will now compare this with the average reconstruction error in PCM [R-bit quantization of $x(n)$]. Assuming an identical quantizer performance factor ϵ_*^2,

$$\sigma_{r,PCM}^2 = \sigma_q^2 = \epsilon_*^2 \, 2^{-2R} \sigma_x^2 \tag{12.56}$$

Also, from (12.38), $\sigma_x^2 = (\sigma_0^2 + \sigma_1^2)/2$, so that the gain due to Transform Coding with $N = 2$ is

$$\max\{^2G_{TC}\} = \frac{\sigma_{r,PCM}^2}{\sigma_{r,TC}^2} = \frac{(\sigma_0^2 + \sigma_1^2)/2}{(\sigma_0^2 \sigma_1^2)^{1/2}} = \frac{\sigma_x^2}{(\sigma_0^2 \sigma_1^2)^{1/2}} , \tag{12.57}$$

the *ratio of arithmetic to geometric means of the coefficient variances* σ_0^2 and σ_1^2. This is a crucial result in Transform Coding theory and it will be generalized to $N > 2$ in the next subsection. Unless otherwise mentioned, maximum values of G_{TC} imply maximization with respect to bit allocation, as in (12.57), and not maximization with respect to linear transform type.

Bit Allocation for $N > 2$. The problem once again is to minimize, by means of an optimum bit allocation R_k; $k = 0,1,...,N - 1$, the reconstruction error (12.45) subject to the constraint (12.46). Using the Lagrange multiplier method,

$$\frac{\partial}{\partial R_k} \left[\sigma_q^2 - \lambda (R - \frac{1}{N} \sum_{k=0}^{N-1} R_k) \right] = 0; \quad k = 0, 1, ..., N-1 \quad (12.58)$$

with

$$\sigma_q^2 = \frac{1}{N} \sum_{k=0}^{N-1} \sigma_{qk}^2 = \frac{1}{N} \epsilon_*^2 \sum_{k=0}^{N-1} 2^{-2R_k} \sigma_k^2 , \quad (12.59)$$

we arrive at an optimum bit allocation given by

$$R_k = R + \frac{1}{2} \log_2 \frac{\sigma_k^2}{\left[\prod_{j=0}^{N-1} \sigma_j^2 \right]^{1/N}} \quad (12.60)$$

that depends only on the distribution of coefficient variances, as with $N = 2$. Clearly, (12.60) reduces to (12.53) for that special case. Note, from both of these equations, that the number of quantizer levels 2^{2R_k} is proportional to the variance σ_k^2 [Huang and Schultheiss, 1963] [Segall, 1976]. We will shortly note a graphical interpretation of (12.60) in Figure 12.8. This will also suggest a simple way of implementing the optimal bit allocation.

As with $N = 2$, we find that the bit allocation (12.60) also implies identical error variances in coefficient quantization:

$$\min\{\sigma_r^2\} = \min\{\sigma_q^2\} = \sigma_{qk,opt}^2 = \epsilon_*^2 2^{-2R} \left[\prod_{j=0}^{N-1} \sigma_j^2 \right]^{1/N} ; \quad k = 0,1,...,N-1 \quad (12.61)$$

The above result can be easily interpreted for the example of uniform quantizers operating without overload. Identical quantization error variances result if *all quantizers have the same step size* Δ, and hence the same $\sigma_q^2 = \Delta^2/12$. But then a coefficient with higher variance (Figure 12.7b) needs *more levels* than a coefficient of lower variance (Figure 12.7a), for a match in each case, of dynamic ranges of quantizer and input; and this is indeed guaranteed by the bit allocation result (12.60).

An orthogonal transform implies [see (12.38)] that

$$\sigma_x^2 = \frac{1}{N} \sum_{k=0}^{N-1} \sigma_k^2 \quad (12.62)$$

so that the gain over PCM is

$$\max\{^N G_{TC}\} = \frac{\sigma_{r,PCM}^2}{\min\{\sigma_{r,TC}^2\}} = \frac{\frac{1}{N} \sum_{k=0}^{N-1} \sigma_k^2}{\left[\prod_{k=0}^{N-1} \sigma_k^2 \right]^{1/N}} ; \quad (12.63a)$$

$$SNR \mid_{TC} (\text{dB}) = SNR \mid_{PCM} (\text{dB}) + 10 \log {}^N G_{TC} \quad (12.63b)$$

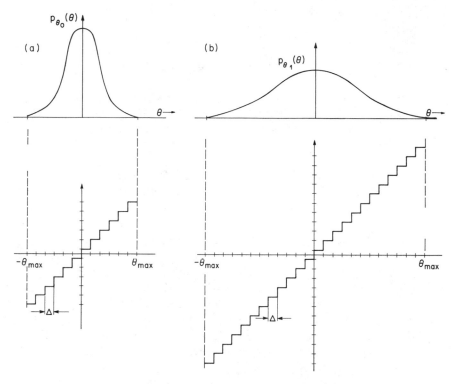

Figure 12.7 Uniform quantization of coefficients (a) θ_0 and (b) θ_1 without overload. The identical step size Δ ensures identical error variances σ_{q0}^2 and σ_{q1}^2, and the differing numbers of quantization levels ensure a match, in each case, of dynamic ranges of quantizer and input.

If we retain the possibility of different quantization performance factors, the above expression will be modified by a term $\epsilon_{*,PCM}^2/\epsilon_{*,TC}^2$. For example, if the effect of transforming is one of changing a uniform distribution to one that is Laplacian, the effect on G_{TC} would be a factor of $(1/4.5)$, or about 6.5 dB less than what an arithmetic-to-geometric mean ratio in (12.63) would suggest. The situation of uniformly distributed $X(k)$ and Laplacian $\Theta(k)$ is a good model for image coding (however, see [Murakami, Hatori and Yamamoto, 1982]). Although each $\theta(n)$ is a weighted sum of N values of $x(n)$; $n = 0$ to $N-1$, the pdf of the transform coefficients tends to be non-Gaussian because the $x(n)$-components in the sum are not statistically independent. At any rate, the 6.5 dB loss above relates to the fact that inputs with a nonuniform pdf are more difficult to quantize than those with a uniform pdf. There are two cases where $\epsilon_{*,PCM}^2 = \epsilon_{*,TC}^2$. One is if $X(k)$ is Gaussian, in which case $\Theta(k)$ is Gaussian as well. The other case is if quantization is logarithmic; in this case the pdf is irrelevant.

It is interesting to compare (12.63) to the maximum gain in DPCM (6.19)

$$\max\{G_{DPCM}\} = \sigma_x^2/\eta_x^2 = (\gamma_x^2)^{-1} \tag{12.64}$$

where σ_x^2 is identical to the arithmetic mean in (12.63) assuming unitary transforms, η_x^2 is the minimum prediction error variance and γ_x^2 is the spectral flatness measure. We will show in Section 12.5 that

$$\max\{G_{TC}\} = \max\{G_{DPCM}\} \qquad (12.65)$$

where the first maximum is over all bit allocations and transform types, and the second maximum is over all prediction algorithms. The maximum values are also those reached with infinite values, in general, for length of transform and order of prediction.

The Non-Negative Integer Constraint for R_k. Practical quantizers for coefficient quantization have the constraint of having to use non-negative integers for the number of bits R_k obtained in the bit allocation procedure (12.60) (Problems 12.5 and 12.7). A weaker but generally less practical constraint is to allow values of R_k for which corresponding values of 2^{R_k}, the number of quantizer *levels*, is an integral value.

Particularly significant is the possibility of negative R_k values for coefficients whose variances are sufficiently smaller than the geometric mean, as given by (12.60). A typical bit reassignment procedure consists in setting $R_k = 0$ in these cases, implying no transmission of the corresponding coefficient, and a corresponding typical error of $\sigma_{qk}^2 = \sigma_k^2$. Clearly, when negative R_k values are increased to zero, the nonzero values of R_j; $j \neq k$ will also have to be altered to maintain a given value of R. Several re-optimization procedures are possible [Huang and Schultheiss, 1963] [Wintz, 1972] [Zelinski and Noll, 1975] [Segall, 1976]. In some of these, use is also made of the fact that R_k values exceeding an appropriate $R_{\max}$ are unwarranted from perceptual considerations, leading to a second type of reassignment, that of surplus quantizer bits. These bits can, of course, be used to transmit coefficients that would otherwise never be coded, or merely to round negative R_k values to zero.

Zero-level quantization of transform coefficients ($R_i = 0$) is reminiscent of an information theoretical result, the RDF for i.i.d. Gaussian samples given by

$$R_k = \max\{0, (1/2)\log_2(\sigma_k^2/D)\} \qquad (12.66)$$

and the *water-filling procedure* (Figure D.4) whereby input (spectral) components lower in variance than an average distortion D are excluded from transmission. The points of difference are that (a) Gaussian samples cannot be quantized with $(1/2)\log_2(\sigma_k^2/D)$ bits, but with a number of bits defined by a practical quantizer, and that (b) water-filling procedures in Transform Coding are generally not implemented on eigenvalues (coefficients of the optimum KLT, Section 12.5), but on coefficients from suboptimal transformations (Section 12.6).

A Graphical Interpretation. We conclude this section with a graphical description of a practical bit allocation rule that is based on adjusting the value of σ_q^2 such that the sum of R_i values equals NR. The dashed horizontals in Figure 12.8(a) represent allocation thresholds κ_k for choosing the bit allocation R_k. For example, if $\log_2\sigma_k^2$ lies between κ_3 and κ_4, we assign $R_k = 4$. The thresholds are spaced 6 dB

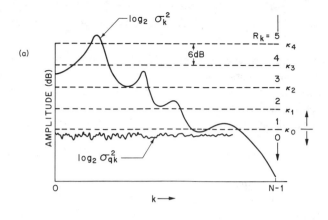

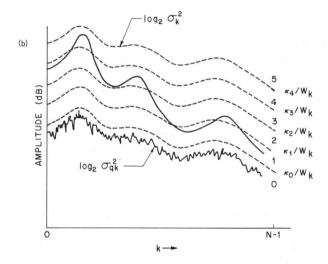

Figure 12.8 A graphical illustration of bit allocation for obtaining (a) white and (b) frequency-weighted quantization noise spectra [Tribolet and Crochiere;©1979, IEEE].

apart. Thus for every 6 dB that σ_k^2 is increased, one more bit is added to the quantizer. Clearly, the noise also remains flat across k values ($\sigma_{qk}^2 = \sigma_{ql}^2$). Two exceptions to the rule occur. Values of $\log_2\sigma_k^2$ below κ_0 are assigned zero (not negative) bits in this example, and all values of $\log_2\sigma_k^2$ above, say κ_4, are assigned $R_{max} = 5$ bits in this example. If the resulting total number of bits assigned in this way is less (or greater) than NR, then the levels of the thresholds κ_k (proportional to σ_{qk}^2) are uniformly decreased (or increased), respectively, while always maintaining the 6 dB spacings. The process is repeated until $\sum R_k = NR$. A somewhat similar procedure for bit allocation is described in [Ramstad, 1982].

White Noise Property of the Reconstruction Error. We have shown that the variance σ_r^2 of the reconstruction error is

$$\sigma_r^2 = \frac{1}{N} E[(\mathbf{\Theta}-\mathbf{U})^T(\mathbf{\Theta}-\mathbf{U})] = \frac{1}{N} E[\mathbf{Q}^T\mathbf{Q}] = \sigma_q^2 \qquad (12.67)$$

provided that $\mathbf{A}^T\mathbf{A} = \mathbf{I}$ [see (12.41)]. We show now that the individual reconstruction errors for $x(n)$ samples within the input N-blocks are not correlated, i.e., the reconstruction error is white noise as in PCM or DPCM. The block of quantization errors $\mathbf{Q}$ is inversely transformed at the decoder to $\mathbf{A}^T\mathbf{Q}$. Therefore, the covariance matrix of the reconstruction error is

$$\mathbf{R}_{rr} = E[\mathbf{A}^T\mathbf{Q}(\mathbf{A}^T\mathbf{Q})^T] = \mathbf{A}^T E[\mathbf{Q}\mathbf{Q}^T]\mathbf{A} = \mathbf{A}^T\mathbf{R}_{qq}\mathbf{A} \qquad (12.68a)$$

$\mathbf{R}_{qq}$ has as its elements the crosscorrelation between quantization errors and these crosscorrelations can be considered to be zero since even for correlated samples, quantization errors tend to be much less correlated. This was illustrated in Figure 4.24(b) for the example of an AR(1) input to the quantizer. In the present context, the transform coefficients are much less correlated than the inputs (and not correlated at all in the case of an optimum KLT transform; see Section 12.5). Hence $\mathbf{R}_{qq}$ is diagonal. In the case of an *optimum* bit allocation (12.61) we have seen that all quantization error variances are to be of the same value σ_q^2. Hence

$$\mathbf{R}_{qq} = \sigma_q^2\mathbf{I} \quad \text{and} \quad \mathbf{R}_{rr} = \sigma_q^2\mathbf{A}^T\mathbf{I}\mathbf{A} = \sigma_q^2\mathbf{I} \qquad (12.68b)$$

All reconstruction errors in a block have the same variance σ_q^2 and are not correlated. Note that this result is not obvious since $\mathbf{Q}$ is actually linearly transformed by $\mathbf{A}^T$. A later section will show that the quantizer inputs, or the coefficients, are themselves uncorrelated within a block if the transform $\mathbf{A}$ is of a special form called the KLT (Section 12.5).

Bit Allocations That Minimize Frequency-Weighted Reconstruction Error. Figure 12.8(a) depicted a bit allocation framework that is appropriate to a flat reconstruction error spectrum as in (12.61). Figure 12.8(b) refers to a similar bit allocation algorithm, but with the important difference that the decision thresholds are no longer flat with respect to frequency (coefficient number). In other words, each threshold κ_k is weighted by a certain W_k in anticipation of an overall error spectrum that is desired to be non-flat, specifically a spectrum whose shape follows the quantity W_k^{-1}; $k=0,1,...,N-1$. The error weighting provided by W_k is referred to in general as *frequency-weighting*, although the latter term is precise only in the special case of DFT (Section 12.6), where each index k corresponds to a specific *frequency* component. Frequency-weighted TC algorithms have been beneficial in speech coding [Zelinski and Noll, 1975, 1977] [Tribolet and Crochiere, 1979] as well as image coding [O'Neal and Natarajan, 1977].

The optimum bit allocation is obtained (Problem 12.9) by replacing the σ_k^2 terms in (12.60) by $W_k\sigma_k^2$ terms; and the error spectrum is described by a constant $W_k\sigma_{qk}^2$ rule. In place of (12.61), the weighted-noise contributions are now equal for all coefficients. We have noted a similar result in NFC (Chapter 7).

An interesting class of weighting functions (Appendix E) [Tribolet and Crochiere, 1979] is

$$W_k = (\sigma_k^2)^\lambda \tag{12.69}$$

The case of $\lambda = 0$ provides a white error spectrum $(\sigma_{qk}^2 = \sigma_{ql}^2)$ as noted earlier, while $\lambda = -1$ provides a constant bit assignment $(R_k = R_l)$ (Problem 12.10). In this case, we find that the ratio of input signal variance and error variance is constant for each coefficient, i.e., the error spectrum has the shape of the input spectrum itself (Figure 12.25).

12.4.3 Zonal Sampling

Bit allocation as discussed hitherto is a complex strategy, especially if it is adaptive. It involves quantizers with different numbers of levels. It also involves reassignment procedures in general, because of the nonzero constraint for R_k.

A simpler strategy is possible in the case of inputs where coefficient variance distributions are known, a priori, to have significant structure. This strategy, known as *zonal sampling*, can be implemented very simply if the input psd is highly structured, as in the two-level example of Figure 2.24. This is exactly what was done in the SBC coding of a two-band signal (Example 11.1) with $R_2 = 0$. More generally, in the case of an input that is expected to be lowpass, if basis vectors are chosen so that low indices of vectors indicate low frequencies, it is possible to obtain useful bit rate reduction by simply retaining $n < N$ coefficients in the transform representation. In reconstructing an approximation to the input, coefficients not included in this subset or zone are set to zero in the simplest case. The term *zonal sampling* originates from 2-D coding where only transform coefficients in a certain geometric zone [for example, the upper left quadrant; see Figure 12.6(d) and (e)] are retained. In keeping with the intent of simplicity, zonal sampling procedures employ a single quantizer with a fixed number of levels for the n in-zone coefficients, and are associated with a straightforward bit rate reduction by a factor of N/n.

We shall now derive an expression for the truncation error in a zonal sampling transform coder. In an actual zonal sampling system, this truncation error will be only one of the components of final reconstruction error. The other component will be the sum of quantization errors for the n retained coefficients.

Let $\mathbf{x}$ be described by a superposition of orthonormal basis vectors $\mathbf{b}_k$ as in (12.20):

$$\mathbf{x} = \sum_{k=0}^{N-1} \theta(k) \mathbf{b}_k \tag{12.70}$$

Let $\mathbf{x}_{zs}$ be the approximation obtained by superposing a subset of $n < N$ basis vectors with the same weights (coefficients) that they had in (12.70):

$$\mathbf{x}_{zs} = \sum_{k=0}^{n-1} \theta(k) \mathbf{b}_k \tag{12.71}$$

The quantities $\mathbf{x}$ and $\mathbf{x}_{zs}$ can be interpreted as points in N- or n-dimensional space, and they can be viewed as realizations of random vectors $\mathbf{X}$ and $\mathbf{X}_{zs}$, respectively.

The mean-square truncation error or zonal sampling error is

$$\sigma_{zs}^2 = E\left[\frac{1}{N}(\mathbf{X}-\mathbf{X}_{zs})^T(\mathbf{X}-\mathbf{X}_{zs}) \right] \qquad (12.72)$$

However,

$$\mathbf{x} - \mathbf{x}_{zs} = \sum_{k=0}^{N-1} t(k)\mathbf{b}_k \ ;$$

$$t(k) = \begin{cases} 0 & k = 0,1,...,n-1 \\ \theta(k) & k = n,n+1,...,N-1 \end{cases} \qquad (12.73)$$

and assuming an orthonormal basis vector set

$$\mathbf{b}_k^T \cdot \mathbf{b}_l = \delta_{kl} \ , \qquad (12.74)$$

we obtain

$$\sigma_{zs}^2 = \frac{1}{N} E\left[\sum_{k=0}^{N-1} T^2(k) \right] = \frac{1}{N} \sum_{k=n}^{N-1} \sigma_k^2 \qquad (12.75)$$

where $\sigma_k^2 = E[\Theta^2(k)]$. Thus the total truncation error $N\sigma_{zs}^2$ of the N-block equals the sum of the variances of the discarded coefficients.

A generalization to two dimensions leads to the results

$$\sigma_{zs}^2 = \frac{1}{N^2} \sum_{k=n}^{N-1} \sum_{l=n}^{N-1} \sigma_{kl}^2 \ ; \qquad \sigma_{kl}^2 = E[\Theta^2(k,l)] \ . \qquad (12.76)$$

The transform which minimizes the mean square error is the one that packs the maximum amount of variance in the first n coefficients in one-dimensional TC, and the first n^2 coefficients in two-dimensional TC. The KLT of Section 12.5 possesses this important property.

Figure 12.9 shows the effect of 4:1 zonal sampling for image inputs on the signal-to-prefiltering-distortion ratio $10\log(\sigma_x^2/\sigma_{zs}^2)$, as a function of subimage size $N \times N$, for sizes ranging from (4×4) to (256×256). Note that the results show a substantial loss due to 4:1 prefiltering when the subimage size is as small as 4×4, and also predict a further rapid loss in truncation error performance in (2×2) coding. (Also see Problem 12.12). Results are based on a first-order Markov process model with equal vertical and horizontal adjacent sample correlations $\rho_v = \rho_h = 0.95$. The ranking of the four alternative transform procedures in Figure 12.9 anticipates a similar observation in Sections 12.5 and 12.6.

The asymptotes in Figure 12.9 range from 20 dB to 24 dB. Perceptually, the degradations represented by these values tend to be less serious than objectively equivalent degradations due to quantization noise. This is because zonal sampling

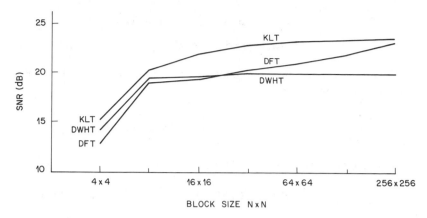

Figure 12.9 Signal-to-truncation error ratio with 4:1 zonal sampling $(n = N^2/4)$ in $N \times N$ image transforms, as a function of block size $N \times N$, for an image with $\rho_v = \rho_h = 0.95$ [Pratt, 1978. Reprinted with permission].

is essentially a controlled prefiltering distortion; and unless n is too small, this degradation is perceptually more acceptable than noise that is external to the signal. The nature of prefiltering distortion was in fact discussed earlier in the speech example of Figure 3.16.

In the zonal sampling results of Figure 12.9, the reconstruction error does not include the effect of quantizing retained coefficients. Instead, it is assumed that $R_k = 0$ for rejected coefficients and $R_k = \infty$ for retained coefficients. In *zonal coding*, one assumes that retained coefficients are appropriately quantized. A simple numerical example of zonal coding appears in Problem 12.7. Results for real images will appear in Section 12.5 for DWHT and DFT procedures.

Best results are obtained when the n retained coefficients are not fixed a priori as in zonal sampling, but are adaptively chosen to match input statistics. One form of such adaptive coding is *threshold coding* [Pratt, 1978] [Wintz, 1972] where a coefficient has to exceed a pre-specified or adaptively determined threshold before being included in the transmitter output. This is very closely related to the adaptive bit allocation procedures of Section 12.7. In both threshold coding and adaptive bit allocation coding, one needs side information that informs the receiver about transmitted coefficient indices k and corresponding quantization bits used, R_k.

12.5 Optimum Transform (KLT)

Equations (12.57) and (12.63) show that an optimum matrix **A** is one that distributes coefficient variances σ_k^2 in such a way as to minimize their geometric mean. The minimum geometric mean result extends to two dimensions with coefficient variances σ_{kl}^2. We will now describe a matrix **L** with that property.

For any **A**, the coefficient variances are the diagonal elements of $\mathbf{R}_{\theta\theta} = \{R_{\theta\theta}(k,l)\}$; $k, l = 0, 1, ..., N - 1$:

$$\sigma_k^2 = E[\Theta^2(k)] = R_{\theta\theta}(k,k) \tag{12.77}$$

$$\mathbf{R}_{\theta\theta} = E[\boldsymbol{\Theta}\boldsymbol{\Theta}^T] = E[\mathbf{A}\mathbf{X}\mathbf{X}^T\mathbf{A}^T] = \mathbf{A}\mathbf{R}_{xx}\mathbf{A}^T \tag{12.78}$$

We are interested in the product of the diagonal elements of $\mathbf{R}_{\theta\theta}$. From matrix theory [Bellman, 1960],

$$|\mathbf{R}_{\theta\theta}| \leqslant \prod_{k=0}^{N-1} \sigma_k^2 \tag{12.79}$$

for any matrix, while for an orthogonal matrix $\mathbf{A}$,

$$|\mathbf{R}_{\theta\theta}| = |\mathbf{A}\mathbf{R}_{xx}\mathbf{A}^T| = |\mathbf{R}_{xx}||\mathbf{A}\mathbf{A}^T| = |\mathbf{R}_{xx}||\mathbf{I}| = |\mathbf{R}_{xx}| \tag{12.80}$$

and hence

$$\left[\prod_{k=0}^{N-1} \sigma_k^2\right]^{1/N} \geqslant |\mathbf{R}_{\theta\theta}|^{1/N} = |\mathbf{R}_{xx}|^{1/N} \tag{12.81}$$

Minimization of the geometric mean of coefficient variances is provided by a (unitary) matrix $\mathbf{A}$ that leads to an equality in (12.79). We shall now describe this optimum transform matrix. We have already shown that corresponding to any $\mathbf{R}_{xx}$, there is a set of *eigenvalues* λ_k; $k=0,1,...,N-1$, and *eigenvectors* $\mathbf{l}_k$; $k=0,1,...,N-1$, defined by

$$\mathbf{R}_{xx}\mathbf{l_k} = \lambda_k\mathbf{l_k} \tag{12.82}$$

Since $\mathbf{R}_{xx}$ is a real symmetric matrix, it follows that the eigenvalues are real, and that there are exactly N eigenvectors which are orthogonal and can be chosen to be orthonormal:

$$\mathbf{l}_k^T \cdot \mathbf{l}_l = \delta_{kl} \tag{12.83}$$

The (discrete) *Karhunen-Loeve Transform* $\mathbf{L}$ (*KLT-* or *eigenvector-* or *Hotelling* transform [Hotelling, 1933] [Karhunen, 1947]) is defined by the fact that its *rows* are the above eigenvectors of $\mathbf{R}_{xx}$:

$$\mathbf{b_k} = \mathbf{l_k} \quad \text{for} \quad \mathbf{L} \tag{12.84}$$

It follows that $\mathbf{L}$ is orthogonal, and we have (see 12.20a)

$$\boldsymbol{\theta} = \mathbf{L}\mathbf{x} \; ; \quad \mathbf{x} = \mathbf{L}^T\boldsymbol{\theta} = \sum_{k=0}^{N-1} \theta(k)\mathbf{l_k} \tag{12.85}$$

Note that input vector $\mathbf{x}$ is a superposition of eigenvectors which are derived from the statistics of the input (via $\mathbf{R}_{xx}$), and which represent "typical" sequences of the given input sequence. (See the examples of Figures 12.5 and 12.6). Since these basis vectors are signal-dependent, fewer of these vectors can be used on the average, to approximate the given input, as compared to representations using signal-independent basis vectors. Recall from (12.78) that

$$\mathbf{R}_{\theta\theta} = \mathbf{L}\mathbf{R}_{xx}\mathbf{L}^T \tag{12.86}$$

From (12.82) and (12.84),

$$\mathbf{R}_{\theta\theta} = \begin{bmatrix} \mathbf{l}_0^T \\ \mathbf{l}_1^T \\ \cdot \\ \cdot \\ \cdot \\ \mathbf{l}_{N-1}^T \end{bmatrix} [\lambda_0 \mathbf{l}_0 \quad \lambda_1 \mathbf{l}_1 \quad ...\lambda_{N-1}\mathbf{l}_{N-1}]$$

$$= [\lambda_j \mathbf{l}_i^T \cdot \mathbf{l}_j^T]_{i,j} = [\lambda_j \delta_{ji}]$$

$$= \begin{bmatrix} \lambda_0 & 0 & 0 & . & . & 0 \\ 0 & \lambda_1 & 0 & . & . & . \\ 0 & 0 & \lambda_2 & & & \\ . & & & & & \\ . & & & & & \\ 0 & . & . & . & . & \lambda_{N-1} \end{bmatrix} = \lambda \tag{12.87}$$

and, from (12.86) and (12.82),

$$\mathbf{L}\mathbf{R}_{xx} = \lambda \mathbf{L} \tag{12.88}$$

Note that the elements of $\mathbf{R}_{\theta\theta}$ are $E[\Theta(i)\Theta(j)]$. Therefore, it turns out that the KLT diagonalizes $\mathbf{R}_{\theta\theta}$, i.e., the transform coefficients are uncorrelated. This supports our approach to quantize these coefficients independently. Note that the uncorrelated nature of the transform coefficients does not imply that their variances are unrelated. For example, the magnitudes of adjacent transform coefficients tend to exhibit closeness in speech and image transforms; this will be illustrated later in the short-time spectra of Figure 12.22a.

Note also that

$$E[\Theta^2(k)] = \lambda_k ; \qquad k = 0,1,...,N-1 \tag{12.89}$$

i.e., *the eigenvalues are the variances of the transform coefficients* in the case of KLT. In this ideal case, the individual quantizers of Figure 8.1 quantize linearly independent random variables $\Theta(k)$ of variances λ_k.

The transform $\mathbf{L}$ not only diagonalizes $\mathbf{R}_{\theta\theta}$ but also minimizes the geometric mean of the variances. Indeed, since $\mathbf{R}_{\theta\theta}$ is diagonal, its determinant is just the product of the elements on the main diagonal:

$$|\mathbf{R}_{\theta\theta}| = \prod_{k=0}^{N-1} \lambda_k \tag{12.90}$$

which is the equality in (12.79). Therefore, the KLT results in the least value of the geometric mean of coefficient variances and corresponds to a maximum transform gain, for a given N, of

$$\max_{A}\{^{N}G_{TC}\} = {}^{N}G_{KLT} = \frac{\frac{1}{N}\sum_{k=0}^{N-1}\lambda_k}{\left[\prod_{k=0}^{N-1}\lambda_k\right]^{1/N}} = \frac{\sigma_x^2}{\left[\prod_{k=0}^{N-1}\lambda_k\right]^{1/N}} \qquad (12.91a)$$

From (12.61),

$$\min\{\sigma_r^2\} = \epsilon_*^2 2^{-2R}\left[\prod_{k=0}^{N-1}\lambda_k\right]^{1/N} \qquad (12.91b)$$

Compare this result with the rate distortion bound for transmitting correlated Gaussian variables in N-blocks:

$$D = 2^{-2R}\left[\prod_{k=0}^{N-1}\lambda_k\right]^{1/N}$$

The geometric mean is the entropy power of Gaussian N-blocks. It turns out that the KLT coding scheme is close to the bound, the difference being zero if a quantizer could be realized with $\epsilon_*^2 = 1$, conditions for which were discussed in Chapter 4 and Section 12.4. We note finally that the denominator in (12.91) can be determined from the correlation matrix $\mathbf{R}_{xx}$ directly from (12.90) and (12.80):

$$\left[\prod_{k=0}^{N-1}\lambda_k\right]^{1/N} = |\mathbf{R}_{\theta\theta}|^{1/N} = |\mathbf{R}_{xx}|^{1/N} \qquad (12.92)$$

We will show presently (12.112b) that $|\mathbf{R}_{xx}|$ can be determined from prediction error variances.

Determination of Eigenvalues and Eigenvectors. Let $\mathbf{l}$ be an eigenvector of $\mathbf{R}_{xx}$. The corresponding eigenvalue λ is then defined by (12.82):

$$\mathbf{R}_{xx}\mathbf{l} = \lambda\mathbf{l} \qquad \text{or} \qquad (\mathbf{R}_{xx} - \lambda\mathbf{I})\mathbf{l} = 0 \qquad (12.93a)$$

This is a linear homogeneous system of equations for the unknown λ. In order to have a nonzero eigenvector it is both necessary and sufficient that

$$|\mathbf{R}_{xx} - \lambda\mathbf{I}| = 0 \qquad (12.93b)$$

Equation (12.93b) is called the *characteristic equation* of $\mathbf{R}_{xx}$. The determinant above, when expanded, is a polynomial in λ of degree N, and it will have N zeros λ_i with corresponding eigenvectors $\mathbf{l}_i$. The eigenvectors are of course determined only to within a scalar multiple. $\mathbf{R}_{xx}$ is a real symmetric matrix. It can be shown then that the characteristic equation has N distinct and real zeros (in general, there may be multiplicities), and consequently it has exactly N distinct eigenvectors. In general, it is very difficult to find eigenvalues of a matrix and numerical techniques have to be used. Also, in many cases $\mathbf{R}_{xx}$ is singular, and eigenvectors cannot be uniquely defined [Landau and Slepian, 1971]. What is more significant is that, if $\mathbf{R}_{xx}$ is not known a priori, estimation of its elements requires observations and computations involving an input block of length N' that is an order of magnitude greater than N, for reliable acf estimation. Examples listed below represent relatively simple inputs for which closed-form solutions are available.

Determination of KLT Basis Vectors from $\mathbf{R}_{xx}$. As in Section 12.2, we begin with the simple example of a transform of order 2.

Example 12.1. The case of $N = 2$

Consider a stationary source with variance of unity and normalized autocorrelation ρ between neighboring samples

$$\mathbf{R}_{xx} = \begin{bmatrix} 1 & \rho \\ \rho & 1 \end{bmatrix} \tag{12.94}$$

As shown in Example 2.2, the eigenvalues λ are obtained from the characteristic equation $|\mathbf{R}_{xx} - \lambda \mathbf{I}| = 0$:

$$\begin{vmatrix} 1-\lambda & \rho \\ \rho & 1-\lambda \end{vmatrix} = 0 ; \tag{12.95}$$

$$\lambda_0 = 1 + \rho ; \quad \lambda_1 = 1 - \rho \tag{12.96}$$

so that

$$\prod_{i=0}^{N-1} \lambda_i = \lambda_0 \lambda_1 = 1 - \rho^2 = |\mathbf{R}_{xx}| \tag{12.97}$$

and

$$\mathbf{R}_{\theta\theta} = \begin{bmatrix} \lambda_0 & 0 \\ 0 & \lambda_1 \end{bmatrix} = \begin{bmatrix} 1+\rho & 0 \\ 0 & 1-\rho \end{bmatrix} \tag{12.98}$$

The transform coding gain is

$$G_{KLT} = \frac{[(1+\rho)+(1-\rho)]/2}{[(1+\rho)(1-\rho)]^{1/2}} = \frac{1}{\sqrt{1-\rho^2}} \tag{12.99}$$

To find the eigenvectors, $\mathbf{b}_i = \mathbf{l}_i$, we use (12.82). For $i = 0$,

$$\begin{bmatrix} 1 & \rho \\ \rho & 1 \end{bmatrix} \begin{bmatrix} l_0(0) \\ l_0(1) \end{bmatrix} = (1+\rho) \begin{bmatrix} l_0(0) \\ l_0(1) \end{bmatrix} ; \quad l_0(0) = l_0(1) \tag{12.100a}$$

Similarly for $i = 1$,

$$l_1(0) = -l_1(1) \tag{12.100b}$$

However, $\mathbf{l_0}$ and $\mathbf{l_1}$ are the rows of $\mathbf{L}$ and for orthonormality, $\mathbf{LL}^T = \mathbf{I}$. Therefore,

$$l_0^2(0) + l_0^2(1) = l_1^2(0) + l_1^2(1) = 1 \tag{12.101}$$

From (12.100) and (12.101), the optimum transform is given by

$$^2\mathbf{L} = {}^2\mathbf{L}^T = {}^2\mathbf{L}^{-1} = \frac{1}{\sqrt{2}}\begin{bmatrix} 1 & 1 \\ 1 & -1 \end{bmatrix} \tag{12.102}$$

Note that (12.102) also results from setting $a = 1/\sqrt{2}$ in the matrix of (12.10a). ●

We have already noted in earlier sections that a matrix $\mathbf{A}$ of the form (12.102) leads to a transform coding gain (12.99). It is significant that the gain noted in these earlier sections is indeed the maximum possible gain for $N = 2$. Recall, from Section 12.2, that it is the sum and the difference of neighboring samples which are to be quantized. It is also significant (Section 12.6) that properties (12.99) and (12.102) are shared by so-called suboptimum transforms, for $N = 2$. Finally, it is interesting to note that for $N = 2$, the KLT is input-independent, in that the matrix $\mathbf{L}$ has no entries depending on ρ. In general, however, for $N > 2$, the basis vectors in $\mathbf{L}$ are input- or $\mathbf{R}_{xx}$-dependent.

KLT Basis Vectors for $N > 2$. The computations of KLT basis vectors for $N > 2$ are invariably tedious. In the following, we will simply mention two examples where the eigenvectors can be derived explicitly.

Example 12.2. Moving Average process
Consider the MA(1) process (2.122):

$$X(n) = Z(n) + a_1 Z(n-1) \tag{12.103}$$

The process has a psd (2.126)

$$S_{xx}(e^{j\omega}) = (1 + 2\rho \cos\omega)\sigma_x^2 ; \tag{12.104}$$

$$\rho = a_1/(1+a_1^2) \tag{12.105}$$

and the eigenvalues (2.127) are simply values of the psd at equidistant *eigenfrequencies* in the interval $(0,\pi)$ given by $(k+1)\pi/(N+1); k = 0,1,...,N-1$. The eigenvectors (2.129a) are samples of sine waves with these eigenfrequencies. ●

Example 12.3. Autoregressive process
Consider the AR(1) process as in (2.96):

$$X(n) = \rho X(n-1) + Z(n) ; \tag{12.106}$$

It can be shown for $\rho \to 1$ that the eigenfrequencies Ω_k are asymptotically uniformly distributed in $(0,\pi)$ and the eigenvalues are the psd values at these eigenfrequencies. The

Ω_k values can be obtained as roots of a polynomial [Bellman, 1960]. In addition, it can be shown that the eigenvectors are sampled sine waves with unequal frequency spacing (except if $\rho \to 1$), and phases ϕ_k depending on Ω_k:

$$\lambda_k = S_{xx}(e^{j\Omega_k}) = \frac{(1-\rho^2)\sigma_x^2}{1 + \rho^2 - 2\rho \cos \Omega_k} \quad k = 0,1,...,N-1 \tag{12.107}$$

$$\mathbf{l}_k = \{\cos n \, \Omega_k - \phi_k\}_{n=1,2,...,N} \quad \text{for} \quad k = 0,1,...,N-1 \tag{12.108}$$

$$\phi_k = \arctan \frac{1 - \rho \cos \Omega_k}{\rho \sin \Omega_k} \tag{12.109}$$

The Ω_k values are obtained as roots of the polynomial

$$\frac{\sin(\Omega_k(N+1))}{\sin \Omega_k} - 2\rho \frac{\sin(\Omega_k N)}{\sin \Omega_k} + \rho^2 \frac{\sin(\Omega_k(N-1))}{\sin \Omega_k} = 0 \quad \text{for } k = 0,1,...,N-1 \tag{12.110}$$

Table 12.1 Eigenvectors and eigenvalues for KLT coding of an AR(1) process; $N = 8$ and $\rho = 0.95$.

Eigenvector Matrix								Eigenvalues
−.3383	−.3512	−.3599	−.3642	−.3642	−.3599	−.3512	−.3383	7.030
.4809	.4204	.2860	.1013	−.1013	−.2860	−.4204	−.4809	0.575
.4665	.2065	−.1789	−.4557	−.4557	−.1789	.2065	.4665	0.168
.4226	−.0854	−.4865	−.2783	.2783	.4865	.0854	−.4226	0.082
.3602	−.3468	−.3558	.3513	.3513	−.3558	−.3468	.3602	0.051
−.2833	.4882	−.0942	−.4154	.4154	.0942	−.4882	.2833	0.037
.1952	−.4623	.4603	−.1904	−.1904	.4603	−.4623	.1952	0.030
.0996	−.2786	.4156	−.4896	.4896	−.4156	.2786	−.0996	0.027

Table 12.1 shows the eigenvectors and eigenvalues for an AR(1) process with $\rho = 0.95$, for a block length of $N = 8$. Note that the first eigenvalue λ_0 is much larger than the remaining ones. The eigenvalues for $N = 2$ are simply $1 + \rho = 1.95$ and $1 - \rho = 0.05$. Respective values of $^N G_{TC}$ are 5 dB for $N = 2$ and 7 dB for $N = 8$ (Problem 12.19). ●

Example 12.4. AR(10) modeling of speech

The first 10 long-time-averaged acf values for a speech signal can be used to develop an AR(10) model. Its maximum prediction gain $^\infty G_P = {}^{10}G_P$ is 9.5 dB. The model can then be used to compute $\mathbf{R}_{xx}$ for any N. KLT basis vectors and transform codings gains can then be computed. Values of $^N G_{TC}$ are shown in Figure 12.10 as a function of N. Transform coding results have also been shown for the suboptimum transforms to be discussed in Section 12.6. Note that the KLT gain G_{KLT} is upper-bounded by the maximum value of optimum prediction gain, 9.5 dB.

The basis vectors for this example have already been shown for $N = 8$ in Figure 12.5. Note that the basis vectors, especially the first basis vector $\mathbf{b}_0$, differ considerably from one transform to another. For example, the eigenvector $\mathbf{l}_0$ ($\mathbf{b}_0$ for KLT) is more typical, by definition, for any block of eight successive speech samples $\mathbf{X}$ than the $\mathbf{b}_0$ vector of DFT, DCT, or DWHT, implying that $\mathbf{X}$ usually has no zero-frequency component.

Results from real speech are similar to those of Figure 12.10. Note from this figure that the increase in gain in going from $N = 2$ to $N = 8$ is about 5 dB. A similar gain results for an AR(1) process of adjacent sample correlation $\rho = 0.95$ (Problem 12.19). Also, in Figure 12.10, the gain at $N = 8$ is only 2.5 dB short of the maximum possible gain of 9.5 dB. ●

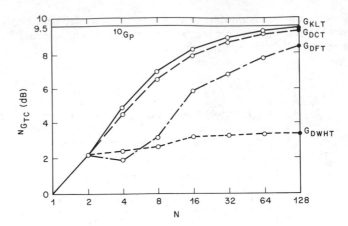

Figure 12.10 Transform coding gain $^N G_{TC}$ versus N from an AR(10) model of speech signals. The DFT and DWHT are, respectively, frequency-ordered and sequency-ordered transforms [Zelinski and Noll, 1975. Reprinted with permission].

We shall now discuss the effect of N analytically. Results will only apply for KLT, although suboptimal transforms can approach KLT performance, as seen in the example of Figure 12.10.

G_{KLT} as a Function of N. Recall from (12.63), with $\epsilon_{*,PCM}^2 = \epsilon_{*,TC}^2$ that

$$\sigma_{r,TC}^2 = \sigma_{r,PCM}^2 / G_{TC}$$

We have seen in (12.91) that

$$\max_{\mathbf{A}}\{^N G_{TC}\} = {}^N G_{KLT} = \frac{\sigma_x^2}{|^N\mathbf{R}_{xx}|^{1/N}} \qquad (12.111)$$

where $^N G_{KLT}$ is assumed to include the results of optimum bit allocation for any given N. Also, from linear prediction theory (6.48),

$$\frac{|^N\mathbf{R}_{xx}|}{|^{N-1}\mathbf{R}_{xx}|} = \min\{^{N-1}\sigma_d^2\} ; \qquad (12.112a)$$

and hence [Davisson, 1972]

$$|^N\mathbf{R}_{xx}| = \prod_{k=0}^{N-1} \min\{^k\sigma_d^2\} = \prod_{k=0}^{N-1} \left(\sigma_x^2 / {}^k G_P\right) \qquad (12.112b)$$

where left superscripts refer to covariance matrix or prediction order, and $\min\{\sigma_d^2\}$ and G_P denote prediction error variance and prediction gain, with $^0 G_P = 1$. Using (12.112b) in (12.111),

$$\max_{\mathbf{A}}\{^N G_{TC}\} = {}^N G_{KLT} = \left[\prod_{k=0}^{N-1} {}^k G_P\right]^{1/N} \qquad (12.113)$$

This relation shows that *the maximum performance of TC is the geometric mean of the first N prediction gains.* Clearly, from (12.113),

$$\max_{\mathbf{A}}\{^N G_{TC}\} = {}^N G_{KLT} < {}^N G_P \qquad (12.114)$$

For example, with a first-order Markov source with adjacent correlation ρ [Noll, 1977],

$$^1 G_P = {}^2 G_P = \ldots = {}^\infty G_P = (1-\rho^2)^{-1} \qquad (12.115a)$$

$$^N G_{KLT} = \left[\prod_{k=1}^{N-1} (1-\rho^2)^{-1} \right]^{1/N} = (1-\rho^2)^{-\frac{N-1}{N}} \qquad (12.115b)$$

As special cases of (12.115b),

$$^1 G_{KLT} = 1 \;\; ; \;\; {}^2 G_{KLT} = (1-\rho^2)^{-1/2} \qquad (12.116)$$

The above results show that transform coding gain (as a function of block length) increases more slowly than the prediction gain in DPCM (as a function of predictor order). A similar observation holds in the adaptive coding of speech signals using TC (Figure 12.26) and DPCM (Figure 6.20). PCM performance is represented by $^0 G_P = {}^1 G_{TC} = 1$.

The above comparison of TC and DPCM has a simple qualitative explanation. In a DPCM coder with explicit memory (predictor order) N, the effective memory is much greater than N, because of the propagation of memory in the prediction loop. In TC, however, the effective memory is no greater than the explicit memory (block length) N. Thus, in order to utilize a given extent of memory in the speech process, DPCM needs a much smaller explicit memory than TC. The containing of memory within a block in TC is, however, an advantage in the context of transmission errors (Section 12.8).

Asymptotic Performance. Because of a preponderance of asymptotic terms in (12.113) as $N \to \infty$, the limiting value of (12.113) is

$$\max \{G_{TC}\} = \lim_{N \to \infty} {}^N G_{KLT} = {}^\infty G_{KLT} = {}^\infty G_P = \frac{\sigma_x^2}{\min\{^\infty \sigma_d^2\}} = (\gamma_x^2)^{-1} \quad (12.117)$$

where $\min\{^\infty \sigma_d^2\}$ is the minimum prediction error and γ_x^2 is the spectral flatness measure.

This result can also be derived by noting that

$$\left[\prod_{i=0}^{N-1} \lambda_i \right]^{1/N} = e^{1/N \sum \log_e \lambda_i} \qquad (12.118)$$

and that (2.65)

$$\lim_{N \to \infty} \frac{1}{N} \sum_{i=0}^{N-1} \log_e \lambda_i = \frac{1}{2\pi} \int_{-\pi}^{\pi} \log_e S_{xx}(e^{j\omega}) d\omega$$

The above integral is simply $\gamma_x^2 \sigma_x^2$ and (12.117) follows.

In summary, for any block-size N, the KLT is optimum. This transform also yields uncorrelated transform coefficients. However, successive transform coefficients of the same index are still correlated, although there is no correlation *within* a block. Finally, in order to realize the spectral flatness measure bound, an infinite block length $N \to \infty$ is needed, in general, in the KLT.

The Optimum Transform for Zonal Sampling. We have noted that the KLT maximizes transform coding performance for any N. It can be shown that the KLT also minimizes zonal sampling error σ_{zs}^2 for any block length N and any value $n \leqslant N$ for the number of coefficients included in the zonal sampling process. Assuming zero mean inputs, the average zonal sampling truncation error is (12.75)

$$\sigma_{zs}^2 = \frac{1}{N} \sum_{k=n}^{N-1} E[\Theta^2(k)] \tag{12.119}$$

Let us minimize (12.119) with respect to transform $\mathbf{A}$ subject to the constraint of orthonormality. We minimize

$$\sigma^2 = \sigma_{zs}^2 + \sum_{k=n}^{N-1} \lambda'_k (\mathbf{a}_k^T \mathbf{a}_k - 1) \tag{12.120}$$

where λ'_k's are Lagrange multipliers. From (12.119) and (12.78)

$$\sigma^2 = \frac{1}{N} \sum_{k=n}^{N-1} \mathbf{a}_k^T \mathbf{R}_{xx} \mathbf{a}_k + \sum_{k=n}^{N-1} \lambda'_k (\mathbf{a}_k^T \mathbf{a}_k - 1) \tag{12.121}$$

The gradient $\nabla \sigma^2$ of (12.121) with respect to $\mathbf{a}_k$ has to be set to zero, the gradient being

$$[\nabla \sigma^2]^T = \left[\frac{\partial \sigma^2}{\partial a_k(0)}, \frac{\partial \sigma^2}{\partial a_k(1)}, \cdots, \frac{\partial \sigma^2}{\partial a_k(N-1)} \right] \tag{12.122}$$

Note that for any $\mathbf{f}$ and $\mathbf{F}$,

$$\nabla (\mathbf{f}^T \mathbf{F} \mathbf{f}) = \mathbf{F} \nabla (\mathbf{f}^T \mathbf{f}) = 2 \mathbf{F} \mathbf{f} \tag{12.123}$$

Applying (12.123) with $\mathbf{F} = \mathbf{R}_{xx}$ and $\mathbf{f} = \mathbf{a}$, and carrying out the operation $\nabla \sigma^2 = 0$, we find that

$$\mathbf{R}_{xx} \mathbf{a}_k = \lambda_k \mathbf{a}_k \tag{12.124}$$

By definition, (12.124) can hold only for

$$\lambda'_k = \lambda_k; \qquad \mathbf{a}_k = \mathbf{l}_k \tag{12.125}$$

where λ_k are the eigenvalues of $\mathbf{R}_{xx}$, and $\mathbf{l}_k$ are the eigenvectors of $\mathbf{R}_{xx}$. Thus the minimization of zonal sampling error is obtained for any n and N with $\mathbf{A} = \mathbf{L}$, the eigenvector (KLT) matrix. The minimum value of zonal sampling error is

$$\min\{\sigma_{zs}^2\} = \frac{1}{N} \sum_{k=n}^{N-1} \mathbf{l}_k^T \mathbf{R}_{xx} \mathbf{l}_k = \frac{1}{N} \sum_{k=n}^{N-1} \lambda_k \tag{12.126}$$

The KLT packs most of the energy into the lower-index coefficients so that the error due to truncation is smaller than with other transforms.

Two-Dimensional KLT. As noted in (12.30), the case of interest is a separable transform of the form

$$\boldsymbol{\Theta} = \mathbf{L}_v \mathbf{X} \mathbf{L}_h^T \tag{12.127}$$

The matrices $\mathbf{L}_v$ and $\mathbf{L}_h$ are computed as in the one-dimensional case, via the KLT basis vector definition (12.88)

$$\mathbf{R}_h = \mathbf{L}_h^T \lambda_h \mathbf{L}_h ; \qquad \mathbf{R}_v = \mathbf{L}_v^T \lambda_v \mathbf{L}_v , \tag{12.128}$$

assuming that horizontal and vertical statistics can be separated in the form

$$R_{xx}(k,l) = R_h(k) R_v(l) \tag{12.129}$$

as in the first-order Markov model with separable acf (2.136):

$$\mathbf{R}_h = \{\rho_h^{|i-j|}\}_{i,\,j=0,1,\dots,N-1} \quad ; \quad \mathbf{R}_v = \{\rho_v^{|i-j|}\}_{i,\,j=0,1,\dots,N-1} \tag{12.130}$$

When the acf is separable as above, eigenmatrices can be formed from outer products of eigenvectors of the acf in horizontal and vertical directions [Habibi, 1971] [Wintz, 1972].

The above model has been used in deriving the basis images of size 16×16 for the cameraman example in Figure 12.6. Figure 12.11 shows the distribution of variances of coefficients of index 1 to 256, the distributions being statistics taken over 256 subimages of the cameraman image. The monotonic decrease of coefficient variance σ_k^2 with index k is quite evident. It implies that the lowpass basis images (Figure 12.6) get relatively greater weights in image reconstruction. Notice that the packing of energy into low-order coefficients is maximal for the KLT. However, all the transforms in Figure 12.11 have this energy-packing property to different extents, and we will see further examples of zonal coding where this property is utilized. If only 128 coefficients are retained (2:1 zonal sampling), the mse is between 0.34% (KLT) and 0.49% (DWHT), implying respective signal-to-zonal-sampling-error ratios of 25 and 23 dB. In both cases, no visible degradation occurs. If only 64 coefficients are retained (4:1 zonal sampling),

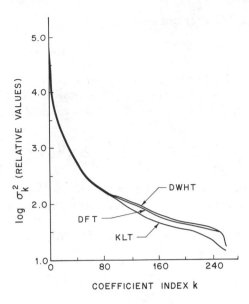

Figure 12.11 Distribution of coefficient variances in 16×16 transform coding of the cameraman of Figure 12.6. Variances are averaged over the 256 sub-images and ordered according to their magnitudes [Wintz;©1972, IEEE].

a blurring effect is visible with all transforms. The hierarchy of coefficients implied in the variance-ordering process is also useful in *embedded coding* and *progressive transmission* systems [Knowlton, 1980]. In these systems, although all coefficients are transmitted to a receiver under ideal conditions, greater priority is given to the transmission of the more important coefficients in the coefficient hierarchy.

12.6 Suboptimum Transforms (DHT, DWHT, DFT, DCT)

The KLT computations (12.85) and (12.86) requires N^2 multiply/add operations. The two stage transform (12.127) needs $2N^3$ multiply-add operations, with each stage needing N^3 (N^2 linear products involving N elements each). The computational problem gets to be simpler with the suboptimum transforms to be discussed next; indeed, the KLT is usually used only to bound the performances of these suboptimal but practical algorithms.

We have already compared the performance of KLT with that of other transforms in Figures 12.9 to 12.11. It is clear that the KLT always performs best. However, for large transform sizes N, the performance of the DFT approaches that of the KLT in both 1-D and 2-D examples; and for very small transform sizes, the mse performances of different transforms do not differ very significantly. Indeed, as seen in Figure 12.10, all mse values are identical for $N = 2$. In this case, all transform matrices, including the input-dependent KLT matrix, simplify to the very familiar matrix (12.10b). Large values of N (say, $N = 128$ or 256) are necessary to realize significant gains in speech coding (as suggested in Figure 12.10).

Transform coding gains saturate faster with N in 2-D image coding. Objective SNR gains tend to saturate after the transform size exceeds (8×8). However, from subjective considerations, a (4×4) transform is in general quite adequate [Netravali and Limb, 1980].

The input-independent suboptimum transforms of this section do not diagonalize covariance matrices. By the same fact, as explained in Section 12.4, they do not minimize the geometric mean of coefficient variances, or provide the best possible distribution of variances for zonal sampling with a given proportion of retained coefficients. However, the input independence of these transforms also makes them simpler in that their basis vectors are predetermined; fast algorithms (such as FFT) exist and aid the implementation of these transforms; and finally, although the gains over PCM for these transforms are strictly upper-bounded by those of the KLT, the gains are often significant enough to warrant their use in digital coding, especially if these applications include refinements such as zonal sampling or adaptive bit allocation. Note that although the design of these transforms is input-independent, their performance (as given by $\mathbf{R}_{\theta\theta}$) will depend on $\mathbf{R}_{xx}$.

The *Discrete Walsh Hadamard* and *Discrete Hadamard* transforms (DWHT and DHT), the *Discrete Fourier* transform (DFT) and the *Discrete Cosine* transform (DCT) are important examples of suboptimal transforms. Several fast algorithms are known for implementing them efficiently [Singleton, 1969] [Ahmed and Rao, 1975] [Elliott and Rao, 1982]

Before we proceed to discuss the suboptimal transforms, let us note for completeness that PCM coding is equivalent to quantization of transform coefficients resulting from the *identity transform*

$$\mathbf{I} = \begin{bmatrix} 1 & 0 & 0 & . & . \\ 0 & 1 & 0 & & \\ 0 & 0 & 1 & & \\ . & . & . & & \\ . & . & . & . & 1 \end{bmatrix} = \{\delta_{ij}\}_{i,j=0,1,\dots,N-1} \qquad (12.131)$$

None of the basis vectors in $\mathbf{I}$ can be expected to be typical for an input sequence. All basis vectors will have to be used to reconstruct an input. The weights (transform coefficients) have equal variances, and hence $G_{TC} = 1$ in this case.

12.6.1 Discrete Hadamard and Walsh Hadamard Transforms (DHT and DWHT)

Walsh Hadamard and Hadamard transforms are characterized by symmetrical orthogonal matrices with unit magnitude elements and orthonormal rows (basis vectors). *Discrete Hadamard Transform* (DHT) and *Discrete Walsh Hadamard Transform* (DWHT) are denoted by matrices $\mathbf{H}$ and $\mathbf{H}'$ respectively:

$$\text{DHT: } \boldsymbol{\theta} = \mathbf{H}\mathbf{x} ; \quad \mathbf{x} = \mathbf{H}\boldsymbol{\theta}$$

$$\text{DWHT: } \boldsymbol{\theta} = \mathbf{H}'\mathbf{x} ; \quad \mathbf{x} = \mathbf{H}'\boldsymbol{\theta}$$

$$(12.132)$$

Note that forward and inverse transforms **A** and **B** are equal in both cases of (12.132), and equal to **H** and **H'** respectively.

The *Hadamard transform* of order 2 is

$$^{2}\mathbf{H} = \frac{1}{\sqrt{2}} \begin{bmatrix} 1 & 1 \\ 1 & -1 \end{bmatrix} \tag{12.133}$$

which is identical to the KLT matrix for $N = 2$. It is also the familiar matrix (12.10b).

Hadamard matrices of higher order are given by the recursive rule [Shum, Elliot and Brown, 1973]

$$^{2N}\mathbf{H} = \frac{1}{\sqrt{2}} \begin{bmatrix} {}^{N}\mathbf{H} & {}^{N}\mathbf{H} \\ {}^{N}\mathbf{H} & -{}^{N}\mathbf{H} \end{bmatrix} \tag{12.134}$$

This rule ensures Hadamard matrices of size 2^p for positive integral p, although Hadamard matrices of other orders (size 0 modulo 4) may exist. From (12.133) and (12.134),

$$^{4}\mathbf{H} = \frac{1}{2} \begin{bmatrix} 1 & 1 & 1 & 1 \\ 1 & -1 & 1 & -1 \\ 1 & 1 & -1 & -1 \\ 1 & -1 & -1 & 1 \end{bmatrix} \tag{12.135a}$$

Walsh transforms, which differ from $^{N}\mathbf{H}$ with regard to ordering of rows, exist for any integral N. But N is invariably a power of 2 in most applications and the term Walsh Hadamard transform is generally used in such cases to describe any transform that has basis vectors with elements ± 1. Let us consider a *sequency-ordered Walsh Hadamard* matrix $^{4}\mathbf{H}'$ that differs from $^{4}\mathbf{H}$ in terms of row ordering:

$$^{4}\mathbf{H}' = \frac{1}{2} \begin{bmatrix} 1 & 1 & 1 & 1 \\ 1 & 1 & -1 & -1 \\ 1 & -1 & -1 & 1 \\ 1 & -1 & 1 & -1 \end{bmatrix} \tag{12.135b}$$

The *sequency* of a ± 1 sequence is defined as half the number of sign changes in one period of the sequence [Harmuth, 1972]. If the period of a basis vector is considered to be the transform size N, the matrices $^{4}\mathbf{H}$ and $^{4}\mathbf{H}'$ are characterized by basis vector sequencies of $(0,3/2,1/2,1)$ and $(0,1/2,1,3/2)$. Similarly, the DWHT basis vectors in Figure 12.5(a) have sequencies in the range 0 to 7/2. The term *sequency* (of a rectangular basis waveform $\mathbf{b}_j$) has a connotation that is similar to *frequency* (of a trigonometric sine or cosine waveform, as in DFT).

With a lowpass input and a DWHT matrix of the type $^4\mathbf{H}'$, one expects transform coefficient variances that monotonically decrease with coefficient index. Recall that the jth coefficient reflects the correlation between the input and the jth basis vector. The coefficients would not be monotonically ordered with a Hadamard transform of the type $^4\mathbf{H}$, but the coding performances of $^4\mathbf{H}$ and $^4\mathbf{H}$ would be identical because the geometric means of coefficient variances would be identical.

Note also that the matrices (12.135a) and (12.135b) are both symmetric. This property extends to all higher-order matrices $^N\mathbf{H}$ and $^N\mathbf{H}'$.

Figure 12.12 shows a set of 64 basis images appropriate to the DWHT matrix $^8\mathbf{H}'$. These subimages can also be derived from the rectangular basis waveforms given in Figure 12.5(a) (Problem 12.3).

The sequency-ordered Hadamard transform DWHT and its inverse can be explicitly described in the form

$$\theta(k) = \sum_{n=0}^{N-1} x(n)h(k,n) ; \quad x(n) = \sum_{k=0}^{N-1} \theta(k)h(k,n) \qquad (12.136)$$

with forward and inverse transformation kernels that are equal, and given by

$$h(m,n) = a(m,n) = b(m,n) = \frac{1}{\sqrt{N}}(-1)^{\alpha(m,m)} \qquad (12.137)$$

where $\alpha(m,n)$ is a function of m and n, assuming values ± 1 [Wintz, 1972] [Pratt, 1978].

Figure 12.12 The set of 64 basis images in 8×8 DWHT. White and black areas represent intensities of $+1/8$ and $-1/8$ [Habibi and Robinson;©1974, IEEE].

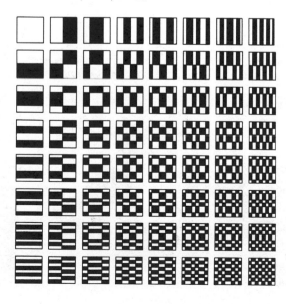

The comparison of transforms in Figures 12.9 and 12.10 has shown that DWHT is not as effective as transforms with sine-cosine (DFT) and DCT basis vectors. In fact, DWHT performance is not even asymptotically optimum. The suboptimality of the transform is reflected in the fact that it does not diagonalize covariance matrices which are Toeplitz. However, the Hadamard transform does diagonalize a *dyadic* matrix (Problem 12.23). Although suboptimal from the point of view of mse, the rectangular bases in DHT and DWHT suggest that these transforms should be particularly effective in digitizing images which have many edges and discontinuities. In the specific example of intrafield composite coding of color images, simple examples of 2-D DWHT provide better performance than third-order 2-D DPCM (Chapter 6) if the bit rates are in the order of $R = 2$ bits/pixel or less [Murakami, Hatori and Yamamoto, 1982].

Coding systems based on two-dimensional DHT and DWHT have been extensively studied because of the simplicity that is related to the fact that all elements in $^N\mathbf{H}$ and $^N\mathbf{H}'$ are ± 1; resulting multiply operations are therefore simply additions with sign changes when appropriate.

2-D DWHT Coding. A discussion of 2-D DWHT coding was already provided in Figure 12.9, in the specific context of zonal sampling. This section will consider this transform in some more detail, with special reference to 2 bits/sample coding.

Example 12.5.   4 × 4 DWHT coding

We have mentioned earlier that 4×4 is an adequate transform size from a perceptual viewpoint. Results from 4×4 DWHT coding are shown in Figure 12.13. Figure 12.13(a) is an original 10-bit PCM representation. Figure 12.13(b) shows a reconstruction based on 16:1 zonal sampling ($R_i = 0$; $0 < i \leqslant 15$), and Figure 12.13(c) is the result of DWHT coding using the bit allocation procedure shown in Table 12.2, with $R = 2$ bits/sample.

Figure 12.13   Results from 4×4 coding: (a) original 10-bit PCM picture; (b) reconstruction using only the first coefficient $\theta(0)$ in a 4×4 transform (16:1 zonal sampling); and (c) reconstruction based on the bit-allocation procedure of Table 12.2, with $R = 2$ bits/sample [Landau and Slepian;©1971, AT&T].

| (a) | (b) | (c) |

Table 12.2 Bit allocation in a 4×4 DWHT coding system with $R = 2$ bits/sample [Landau and Slepian;©1971, AT&T].

Coefficient Number i	Coefficient Variance σ_i^2	Quantizer Bits R_i
0	1.000	6
1	0.098	4
2	0.087	4
3	0.035	3
4	0.038	3
5	0.051	3
6	0.048	3
7	0.034	2
8	0.024	2
9	0.024	2
10	0.020	0
11	0.022	0
12	0.019	0
12	0.015	0
14	0.016	0
15	0.014	0

The dynamic range of coefficient variances in the second column of Table 12.2 is 10 log (1.000/0.014) = 18.4 dB. This is less than the dynamic range of variances to be expected in a KLT. The smaller the dynamic range, the smaller is the ratio of arithmetic mean to geometric mean in (12.63a), and therefore the smaller is the transform coding gain G_{TC}. The same result is true in speech coding. With AR(10) modeling of speech, the dynamic range of coefficient variances is about 30 dB for the DWHT, and about 40 dB for the KLT and the DCT [Zelinski and Noll, 1975].

12.6.2 Discrete Fourier Transform (DFT)

This transform is defined by

$$\theta(k) = \frac{1}{\sqrt{N}} \sum_{n=0}^{N-1} x(n) e^{-j2\pi kn/N} ; \quad k = 0, 1, 2, ..., N-1$$

$$(12.138)$$

$$x(n) = \frac{1}{\sqrt{N}} \sum_{k=0}^{N-1} \theta(k) e^{j2\pi kn/N} ; \quad n = 0, 1, 2, ..., N-1$$

or $\boldsymbol{\theta} = \mathbf{Fx} ; \quad \mathbf{x} = \mathbf{F^*\theta} ; \quad \mathbf{F} = \left\{ \frac{1}{\sqrt{N}} e^{-j2\pi kn/N} \right\}_{k,n\,=\,0,1,...,N-1}$ $\qquad$ (12.139)

The inverse transformation kernel is the conjugate transpose of the forward kernel [as in (12.35)]. In addition, because of the symmetry of $\mathbf{F}$,

$$\mathbf{F}^{-1} = \mathbf{F}^{*T} = \mathbf{F}^*$$

$$(12.140)$$

For $N = 2$,

$$^2\mathbf{F} = \frac{1}{\sqrt{2}} \begin{bmatrix} e^0 & e^0 \\ e^0 & e^{-j\pi} \end{bmatrix} = \frac{1}{\sqrt{2}} \begin{bmatrix} 1 & 1 \\ 1 & -1 \end{bmatrix} \tag{12.141}$$

which is identical to the KLT matrix of size 2. For $N = 4$,

$$^4\mathbf{F} = \frac{1}{2} \begin{bmatrix} 1 & 1 & 1 & 1 \\ 1 & -j & -1 & j \\ 1 & -1 & 1 & -1 \\ 1 & j & -1 & -j \end{bmatrix} ; \quad ^4\mathbf{F}^{-1} = {}^4\mathbf{F}^* = \frac{1}{2} \begin{bmatrix} 1 & 1 & 1 & 1 \\ 1 & j & -1 & -j \\ 1 & -1 & 1 & -1 \\ 1 & -j & -1 & j \end{bmatrix} \tag{12.142}$$

The columns of $\mathbf{F}^{-1}$ are the unitary basis vectors of the DFT:

$$\mathbf{b}_k = \left\{ \frac{1}{\sqrt{N}} e^{j2\pi kl/N} \right\}_{l=0,1,...,N-1} ; \quad \mathbf{b}_k^{*T} \cdot \mathbf{b}_l = \delta_{kl} \tag{12.143}$$

Note that (12.142) is symmetric, as in the case of the DWHT matrices $^4\mathbf{H}$ and $^4\mathbf{H}'$. The general matrix $^N\mathbf{F}$ is also symmetric.

Although $\mathbf{F}$ and $\mathbf{F}^*$ have complex elements of the form $(a+jb)$, a *conjugate symmetry* property applies to the DFT of *real-valued inputs*, and as a consequence the DFT representation involves a total of only N (not $2N$) elements. The conjugate symmetry is described by

$$\theta(k) = \theta^*(N-k) ; \quad k = 1,2,...,(N/2)-1 \tag{12.144}$$

so that

$$\mathrm{Re}\{\theta(k)\} = \mathrm{Re}\{\theta(N-k)\} ; \quad k = 1,2,...,(N/2)-1 \tag{12.145}$$

$$\mathrm{Im}\{\theta(k)\} = -\mathrm{Im}\{\theta(N-k)\} ; \quad k = 1,2,...,(N/2)-1 \tag{12.146a}$$

$$\mathrm{Im}\{\theta(0)\} = \mathrm{Im}\{\theta(N/2)\} = 0 \tag{12.146b}$$

In the case of even N, the total number of nonredundant real-valued numbers in the DFT representation is simply N, since $\theta(0)$ and $\theta(N/2)$ are real-valued, and the remaining $N-2$ components have a total of $N-2$ nonredundant numbers. Therefore, for N input samples, there are exactly N unique numbers, representing the transform coefficients that have to be quantized and transmitted.

Example 12.6. 1-D DFT; $N = 4$

$$\mathbf{x}^T = (3, -1, 4, 2) ; \quad \ell = (4, -1/2 + 3j/2, 3, -1/2 - 3j/2) \tag{12.147}$$

The DFT representation has $N = 4$ non-redundant numbers, $-1/2$, $3/2$, 4 and 3. The DFT pair (12.147) is shown in Figure 12.14(a). Notice that the *amplitude spectrum* $|\theta(k)|$, and hence the *energy spectrum* $|\theta(k)|^2$, is symmetrical about $k = N/2 = 2$, except for the $k = 0$ term. •

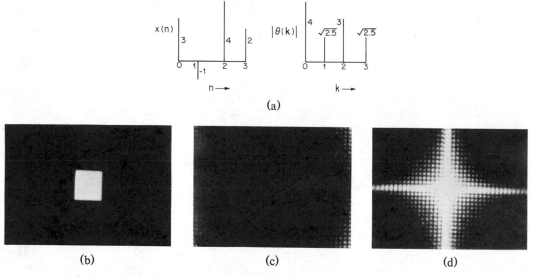

(a)

(b)   (c)   (d)

Figure 12.14 DFT examples: (a) 1-D input $x(n)$ and DFT coefficients $\theta(k)$; (b) 2-D input; and DFT coefficient images (c) without spectrum shifting, and (d) with spectrum shifting [Gonzalez and Wintz, 1977. Reprinted with permission].

Example 12.7. A 2-D square input

The square input in Figure 12.14(b) has a $\sin x/x$-type DFT in both spatial dimensions. In the left part of Figure 12.14(c), the origin for the DFT is in the upper left corner of the image, and this is consistent with matrix notation. In Figure 12.14(d), the origin of the DFT, i.e., the zero frequency, has been shifted to the geometric center of the image. This makes the $\sin x/x$ behavior more visible. Both representations include symmetries about $N/2$ as in Example 12.6. Also, in both DFT representations, the luminance of the DFT image has been displayed to be $\log|1+\theta(k,l)|$ rather than $\theta(k,l)$; this is done to accommodate the dynamic range of the DFT terms, which is much larger than the dynamic range of luminance that can be effectively displayed in the illustration. •

The complex basis vectors $\mathbf{b}_k$ in DFT can be decomposed into sine and cosine components. For example, the vector $(1,j,-1,-j)$ in $^4\mathbf{F}$ can be decomposed into real and imaginary components $(1,0,-1,0)$ and $(0,1,0,-1)$, which can be interpreted as a sine-cosine basis pair. This observation leads to the possibility of a slightly different Fourier transform $\mathbf{F}'$.

Frequency-Ordered and Real-Valued Fourier Matrix $\mathbf{F}'$. We briefly discuss a transform DF'T which provides only real components in

$$\boldsymbol{\theta}' = \mathbf{F}'\mathbf{x} \qquad (12.148)$$

We use the mapping

$$\theta'(0) = \text{Re}\{\theta(0)\} = \theta(0); \quad \theta'(1) = \sqrt{2}\text{Im}\{\theta(1)\}; \quad \theta'(2) = \sqrt{2}\text{Re}\{\theta(1)\};$$
$$\ldots\ldots\, \theta'(N-3) = \sqrt{2}\text{Im}\{\theta((N/2)-1)\}; \quad \theta'(N-2) = \sqrt{2}\text{Re}\{\theta((N/2)-1)\};$$

$$\theta'(N-1) = \mathrm{Re}\{\theta(N/2)\} = \theta(N/2) \qquad (12.149)$$

The scaling factors and the ordering have been chosen such that the basis vectors are orthonormal and frequency-ordered [Zelinski and Noll, 1975]. For computation purposes, θ' can be obtained via an FFT that yields θ followed by rescaling and ordering.

The basis vector $\mathbf{b}'_k$ corresponding to (12.149) form a real-valued Fourier matrix $\mathbf{F}'$ which does not have the redundancies caused by the conjugate symmetry of the DFT. Furthermore, the set $\mathbf{b}'_k$ is ordered in accordance with the familiar notion of increasing frequency, beginning with a zero frequency vector $\mathbf{b}'_0$. This has already been shown in Figure 12.5 for the example of $N = 8$.

Example 12.8. 1-D DF'T; $N = 4$

$$^4\mathbf{F}' = \frac{1}{2} \begin{bmatrix} 1 & 1 & 1 & 1 \\ 0 & -\sqrt{2} & 0 & +\sqrt{2} \\ \sqrt{2} & 0 & -\sqrt{2} & 0 \\ 1 & -1 & 1 & -1 \end{bmatrix}$$

$$\mathbf{x}^T = (3, -1, 4, 2) \; ; \quad \theta'^T = (4, +3/\sqrt{2}, -1/\sqrt{2}, 3) \qquad (12.150) \quad \bullet$$

Implementation of the DFT and IDFT. DFT representations have two important advantages. The first is that a sine-cosine basis space is a very familiar concept. It provides a natural framework for optimizations of transform coder design with inputs where the perceptual effects of signal distortion are best understood in the frequency domain. A second advantage has to do with computation. A direct evaluation of an N-point DFT requires about N^2 complex multiply-add operations; but if N is a power of 2, the Fast Fourier Transform (FFT) method needs in the order of $N \log_2 N$ operations [Elliott and Rao, 1982]. With $N = 1024$, the FFT is about one hundred times faster than a direct computation. The savings in computation time are approximately 32 and 18 for $N = 256$ and 128, respectively.

In the case of real-valued inputs, further reductions are possible by exploiting the symmetry properties of the DFT. Two N-point real sequences can be considered real and imaginary parts of a complex sequence and the $2N$-point sequence can be transformed with a single transform. A simple even-odd separation recovers the real and imaginary parts of the two spectra. This procedure involves a total number of operations in the order of $(N \log_2 N)/4$ [Narasimha and Peterson, 1978].

The FFT algorithm can also be used to evaluate the inverse (IDFT) operation $\mathbf{x} = \mathbf{F}^*\theta$. Indeed, by computing the DFT of the complex conjugate of θ, i.e., the DFT of θ^*, we obtain $\mathbf{x}^* = \mathbf{F}\theta^*$, and we obtain $\mathbf{x}$ by complex-conjugating the result. We finally note that FFT's usually compute a DFT that has no scaling factor and an IDFT that has a scaling by $1/N$. Resulting basis vectors are orthogonal but not orthonormal.

Performance of DFT, KLT and DCT with an AR(1) Input. Figure 12.15 illustrates transform coder performance for a first-order Gauss Markov or AR(1) input. With such an input, since transform coefficients are also Gaussian, the quantizer

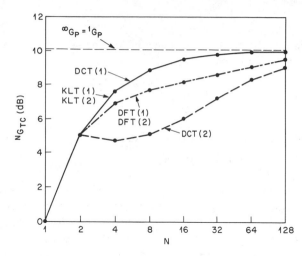

Figure 12.15 Transform coding gains for a first-order Gauss-Markov source with (1) $\rho = 0.95$; and (2) $\rho = -0.95$ [Zelinski and Noll, 1975. Reprinted with permission].

performance factor $\epsilon_{\tilde{*}}^2$ indeed does not have to be modified, and gains based on coefficient variance distributions, as derived in Sections 12.3 and 12.4, are true gains over PCM. The maximum performance in Figure 12.15 corresponds to $^{\infty}G_P = {}^{1}G_P = (1-\rho^2)^{-1} = \gamma_x^{-2}$ [see (12.115a)]. For $\rho = +0.95$, this value is 10.25, or approximately 10.11 dB. This is the upper bound for any transform. For $N = 2$, the transform coding gain is $^{2}G_{TC} = (1-\rho^2)^{-1/2}$ or 5.06 dB (12.116).

Note that the gap between G_P and G_{TC} becomes smaller with increasing N but the approach to G_P depends on the transform. The increase of gain in DFT is slower than that in KLT, which in the example of a positive $\rho = 0.95$ almost equals that of DCT, with a difference of less than 0.1 dB. With a negative $\rho = -0.95$, however, DFT is significantly better than DCT. It is interesting that the performance of DFT does not depend on the sign of ρ, but only on its magnitude. The KLT performance is identical for positive and negative ρ's, but note that the KLT matrix has to be reoptimized accordingly. We recall that the eigenvectors of an AR(1) process are sines (or cosines) of appropriate frequency and phase given by (12.109a). DFT basis vectors are suboptimum; they have frequencies which are multiples of a fundamental frequency. For $N \to \infty$, the eigenfrequencies in the KLT are uniformly distributed, as if they were multiples of a fundamental, and the DFT is therefore asymptotically optimum. For finite N it can be shown [Pearl, 1973] that

$$G_{KLT} - G_{DFT} \sim 1/\sqrt{N} \qquad (12.151)$$

The suboptimality of the DFT is related to the fact that it does not diagonalize covariance matrices which are Toeplitz. However, the DFT does diagonalize a *circular* acf matrix where all rows are circularly shifted versions of the first row (Problem 12.29). The above result is not surprising. The DFT representation introduces periodicities with period N in all sequences (input as well as transform coefficients). The inverse DFT generates a sequence

$$c(n) = x(n); \qquad n = 0,1,...,N-1 \qquad (12.152)$$

which equals the original sequence within the N-block but which does not equal the input outside the block. Instead,

$$c(n) = c(n+N) \tag{12.153}$$

As a result of this periodicity,

$$\mathbf{R}_{cc}(k) = E[C(n)C(n+k)] = E[C(n+N)C(n+k)|$$
$$= R_{cc}(N-k) \; ; \; k = 0,1,...,N-1 \tag{12.154}$$

which is a *circular* acf of with period N. Clearly, as N increases, the period in the acf function $\mathbf{R}_{cc}$ becomes longer, the non-Toeplitz structure in $\mathbf{R}_{xx}$ becomes less evident, and the suboptimality of the DFT for a Toeplitz covariance matrix becomes less, as suggested in (12.151). The effect can be explained in terms of end effects induced by forced periodicities and consequent discontinuities at the beginning and end of each N-block. Similar (end) effects limit the performance of DCT transforms. In the case of DCT, it will be shown (Section 12.6.3) that end effects are less harmful than in DFT for a given N. DWHT transforms do not have deviations from Toeplitz at the ends of the matrix but within the matrix. Larger N's do not shift effects to the ends. Therefore, there is no asymptotically optimum performance.

Two-Dimensional DFT. In general, a 2-D transform requires premultiplication of the input with a fourth-order tensor. However, the DFT kernel

$$\frac{1}{N}e^{-j2\pi(km+ln)/N} \; ; \quad k,l = 0,1,...,N-1 \tag{12.155}$$

is separable and symmetric (see Section A.2.1), so that, with (12.36) and (12.140),

$$\mathbf{\Theta} = \mathbf{FXF} \; ; \quad \mathbf{X} = \mathbf{F^*\Theta F^*} \tag{12.156}$$

The operations in (12.156) can be performed with $2N^2\log_2 N$ instead of $2N^3$ complex multiply/add operations if an FFT algorithm is applied. ($N \log_2 N$ operations for one row of X, $N^2\log_2 N$ operations for $\mathbf{XF}$, and $2N^2\log_2 N$ operations for $\mathbf{FXF}$). Also, as in the one-dimensional case, although complex elements are involved in the matrix $\mathbf{F}$, the two-dimensional representation requires only N^2 numbers that have to be quantized and transmitted (Problem 12.25). Redundant components are indicated by cross-hatched regions in the $N = 256$ example of Figure 12.16.

As in the one-dimensional case, there is a suboptimality in DFT performance that can be described in terms of un-diagonalized covariances or, equivalently, in terms of end effects due to DFT-induced periodicities in the IDFT output. These end effects refer, in general, to all four edges of a subimage and the intensity of these effects diminishes with increasing subimage size.

Example 12.9. 16×16 DFT coding of images

Figure 12.17 shows examples of 16×16 coding using the image in Figure 12.6(c) as input. The distribution of variances has already been given in Figure 12.11. Figures

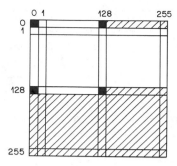

Figure 12.16 Nonredundant (blank), redundant (crosshatched), and real (darkened) areas in two-dimensional DFT with $N = 256$ [Pratt, 1978. Reprinted with permission].

Figure 12.17 An example of 16×16 DFT coding with the image of Figure 12.7(c) as input: (a) reconstructed image in zonal sampling (retaining of $n = 128$ out of 256 coefficients); (b) error in (a) versus the original, scaled by a factor of eight (black refers to zero error and white to an error of 32 gray levels); (c) reconstruction based on coding the 128 coefficients in zonal sampling with a set of 4-level nonuniform quantizers, optimized for the pdf of each transform coefficient ($R = 2$ bits/sample); and (d) reconstruction based on a quantizing system that uses variance-adaptive bit allocation (Section 12.7.2) and an average bit rate of $R = 2$ bits/sample [Wintz;©1972, IEEE].

12.17(a) and (b) show the output and the errors in a 2:1 zonal sampling scheme where only 128 of the most important coefficients are retained. For lowpass images (which are typical) the coefficients with the higher variances are those found in the upper left corner of an unshifted coefficient image array such as Figure 12.14(c). Figure 12.17(b) shows how high frequency edge-information is lost due to the truncation error caused by zonal sampling; the variance of this error is 0.45% ($SNR = 23.5$ dB). Figures 12.17(c) and (d) show the effect of coding the 128 retained coefficients with a total of 256 bits, using a set of 128 mmse four-level quantizers in (c), and a variance-adaptive bit allocation system (Section 12.7.2) in (d). The quantization error variances in (c) and (d) are 2.1% and 0.78% ($SNR = 17$ dB and 21 dB, respectively). Note that in (c), the quantization error variance is an order of magnitude higher than the zonal sampling error variance in (a) and (b). With adaptive bit allocation, the variances of zonal sampling and quantization errors are in the same order of magnitude. The quantization error variance can be lowered by at least another order of magnitude by the use of entropy coding [Wintz, 1972]. •

12.6.3 Discrete Cosine Transform (DCT)

The DCT is an orthonormal transform

$$\boldsymbol{\theta} = \mathbf{C}\mathbf{x} ; \qquad \mathbf{x} = \mathbf{C}^{-1}\boldsymbol{\theta} \tag{12.157a}$$

defined by [Ahmed, Natarajan and Rao, 1974] [Ahmed and Rao, 1975]

$$\theta(k) = \sqrt{\frac{2}{N}}\, \alpha(k) \sum_{n=0}^{N-1} x(n)\cos\frac{(2n+1)k\pi}{2N} ; \qquad k = 0,1,...,N-1 \tag{12.157b}$$

$$\alpha(0) = 1/\sqrt{2} \text{ and } \alpha(k) = 1; \qquad k \neq 0$$

$$x(n) = \sqrt{\frac{2}{N}} \sum_{k=0}^{N-1} \alpha(k)\theta(k)\cos\frac{(2n+1)k\pi}{2N} ; \qquad n = 0,1,...,N-1 \tag{12.157c}$$

Note that correct to a scaling factor, forward and backward (inverse) transforms have identical transformation kernels. A comparison of the last equation with (12.20a) shows that the basis vectors are sampled cosines which have phase shifts that are not given by an alternating 0 and $\pi/2$ pattern as in (the sines and cosines of) DFT. Comparing (12.157c) and (12.20a), the DCT basis vectors are

$$\mathbf{b}_k = \left\{ \sqrt{\frac{2}{N}}\, \alpha(k)\cos\frac{(2n+1)k\pi}{2N} \right\}_{n=1,2,...,N-1} \qquad \text{for } k = 0,1,...,N-1 \tag{12.158}$$

With $\Omega_k = k\pi/N$ in (12.108), the basis vectors can be rewritten to be just the eigenvectors of an AR(1) process with correlation approaching unity. The DCT is thus close to the optimum for AR(1) processes with correlation $\rho \rightarrow 1$ [Jain, 1976]. For $N = 2$, the DCT is identical to the optimum KLT in (12.102):

$$^2\mathbf{C} = \begin{bmatrix} \dfrac{1}{\sqrt{2}} & \dfrac{1}{\sqrt{2}} \\ \cos\dfrac{\pi}{4} & \cos\dfrac{3\pi}{4} \end{bmatrix} = \frac{1}{\sqrt{2}} \begin{bmatrix} 1 & 1 \\ 1 & -1 \end{bmatrix} = {}^2\mathbf{L} \tag{12.159}$$

For $N = 4$

$$^4\mathbf{C} = \frac{1}{2}\begin{bmatrix} 1 & 1 & 1 & 1 \\ a & b & -b & -a \\ 1 & -1 & -1 & 1 \\ b & -a & a & -b \end{bmatrix} \quad ; \quad \begin{array}{l} a = \sqrt{2}\cos\dfrac{\pi}{8} = 1.306 \\[2mm] b = \sqrt{2}\cos\dfrac{3\pi}{8} = 0.541 \end{array} \qquad (12.160)$$

Note that $^4\mathbf{C}$ is *not* symmetric, unlike $^4\mathbf{H}$ in (12.135) and $^4\mathbf{F}$ in (12.142).

The near-optimality of DCT for AR(10)-modeled speech statistics has been seen from the KLT and DCT basis vectors of Figure 12.5 for $N = 8$; and its optimality for an AR(1) process with $\rho = 0.95$ has been seen in Figure 12.15.

The attractiveness of the DCT is two-fold: (a) it is nearly optimal for AR(1) processes with high positive values of adjacent-sample correlation, and (b) it can be computed via the DFT using an FFT algorithm [Ahmed and Rao, 1975] [Chen, Smith and Fralick, 1976] [Elliott and Rao, 1982].

The feature (a) is very important since many signals can be described fairly accurately by AR(1)-statistics. In all other cases, the DCT does not diagonalize Toeplitz matrices; but it diagonalizes matrices whose elements at the end of the *main* diagonal are slightly perturbed (i.e., they deviate from the Toeplitz structure). The suboptimality of the DCT for negatively correlated sequences is shown in Figure 12.15 and Problem 12.31.

The fast computation procedure mentioned in (b) consists of extending the input block of N samples to a $2N$-block with even symmetry, taking a $2N$-point DFT, and saving N terms in it. The DFT of a real and symmetric sequence contains only real coefficients corresponding to the cosine terms of the series. The extension is defined as

$$x'(n) = \begin{cases} x(n) & n = 0,1,...,N-1 \\ x(2N-1-n) & n = N, N+1,...,2N-1 \end{cases} \qquad (12.161\text{a})$$

as shown in Figure 12.18. The $2N$-DFT of $x'(n)$ is

$$\theta'(k) = \frac{1}{\sqrt{2N}}\sum_{n=0}^{2N-1} x'(n)e^{-j(2\pi kn/2N)}$$

$$= \frac{1}{\sqrt{2N}}e^{jk\pi/2N}\sum_{n=0}^{N-1} x(n)\cos\left[\frac{(2n+1)k\pi}{2N}\right] \qquad (12.161\text{b})$$

By comparing it with (12.157b), it can be seen that

$$\theta(k) = \alpha(k)e^{-jk\pi/2N}\theta'(k) \qquad (12.161\text{c})$$

Notice that periodic extensions which are inherent in DFT operations have smaller end-effects (caused by discontinuity at the border of one block and its repetition) in the case of the $2N$-extension than DFT operations based on the N-block. In DFT, quantization effects cause an exchange of distortion components between the left

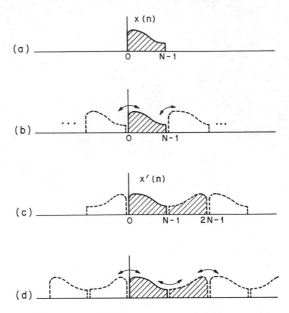

Figure 12.18 Illustration of end effects in DFT and DCT: (a) input block of length N; (b) end effects in DFT analysis/synthesis; (c) equivalent $2N$-point data block for DCT; and (d) end effects in DCT analysis/synthesis [Tribolet and Crochiere;©1979, IEEE].

and right boundaries. In DCT, such an exchange does not occur [Tribolet and Crochiere, 1979].

From the above discussion, it also follows that the DCT can be obtained with $2N \log_2 N$ multiply-add operations. Slightly more efficient procedures are described in the literature [Chen, Smith and Fralick, 1976] [Wang, 1983].

Two-Dimensional DCT. In two dimensions, the DCT can be expressed in the form [Pratt, 1978] [Gonzalez and Wintz, 1977]

$$\theta(k,l) = \frac{2}{N}\alpha(k)\alpha(l)\sum_{m=0}^{N-1}\sum_{n=0}^{N-1} x(m,n)\cos\frac{\pi k(2m+1)}{2N}\cos\frac{\pi l(2n+1)}{2N} \qquad (12.162a)$$

$$x(m,n) = \frac{2}{N}\sum_{k=0}^{N-1}\sum_{l=0}^{N-1}\alpha(k)\alpha(l)\theta(k,l)\cos\frac{\pi k(2m+1)}{2N}\cos\frac{\pi l(2n+1)}{2N} \qquad (12.162b)$$

where $x(m,n)$ is a $N \times N$ field, k, l, m, n all range from 0 to $N - 1$, and $\alpha(0) = 1/\sqrt{2}$; $\alpha(j) = 1$; $j \neq 0$. Note that the transformation kernels are separable, so that the 2-D DCT can be conveniently performed in two steps, each of which involves a 1-D DCT. As in the one-dimensional case (Figure 12.18), DCT coding with an even-symmetry end extension has fewer edge-effect problems than DFT image coding.

12.6.4 Three-Dimensional Transform Coding of Images

Moving images can be represented as a sequence of still images presented at adequately frequent intervals (for example, 30 frames or 60 interlaced fields). There is a high *temporal* correlation between successive frames that can be exploited to reduce the bit rate beyond what is possible in schemes that only utilize *spatial* correlations within single frames. Such *interframe* coding, of course, necessitates the storage of one or more frames, as well as the use of special vector processing algorithms [Natarajan and Ahmed, 1977]. To keep the total number of transformed pixels down to a manageable value, it is usual to employ 4 × 4 (rather than, say an 8 × 8 or 16 × 16) subimages in any given frame. An interframe transform coder using 4 frames will then involve a pixel-cube containing 4×4×4 = 64 elements.

Formally, a 3-D transform, which is a generalization of the 2-D version (12.26), can be described as follows. A sequence of image frames $X(k,l,m)$ is 3-D transformed in blocks of $K \times L \times M$ pixels with transform coefficients

$$\theta(u, v, w) = \sum_{k=0}^{K-1} \sum_{l=0}^{L-1} \sum_{m=0}^{M-1} x(k, l, m) a(u, v, w; k, l, m) \qquad (12.163)$$

and inverse-transformed by

$$x(k, l, m) = \sum_{k=0}^{K-1} \sum_{l=0}^{L-1} \sum_{m=0}^{M-1} \theta(u, v, w) b(u, v, w; k, l, m) \qquad (12.164)$$

In the case of separable transforms,

$$a(u, v, w; k, l, m) = a(u, k) a(v, l) a(w, m) \qquad (12.165)$$

where the $a(\cdot, \cdot)$ are *transform kernels,* elements of basis vectors of 1-D transforms (see Section 12.3). As an example, using the DCT is nearly equivalent to the optimum (KLT) if the statistics of the image can indeed be described by separable first-order Markov processes with correlations $\rho \rightarrow +1$, along rows, columns and temporal axes. A $(K \times L \times M)$ transform with 32:1 zonal sampling and an 8-bit representation for in-zone coefficients ($R = 0.25$ bit/pixel) provides SNR values of 13 and 18 dB with 4×4×4 and 32×32×4 transforms [Roese, Pratt and Robinson, 1977].

12.6.5 Hybrid Schemes involving TC and DPCM Coding

Both TC and DPCM are based on source decorrelation prior to quantization, suggesting that in a J-dimensional approach ($J > 1$), both of these techniques can be used in different dimensions to exploit respective correlations. The use of DPCM in a given dimension can alleviate storage requirements, and also provide more efficient decorrelation. We recall that $AR(M)$ processes can be decorrelated by Mth order predictors. Other advantages of a hybrid approach can include implementation advantages and robustness to transmission errors. A general block diagram of a hybrid TC/DPCM coder appears in Figure 12.19.

The diagram shows that hybrid coding can be applied to both intraframe and interframe systems. We will presently discuss one example of each of these types of systems. The interframe hybrid coder is in general more complex, but it offers advantages in bit rate compression as well as transmission error robustness [Roese, Pratt and Robinson, 1977] [Kamanagar and Rao, 1981] [Ploysongsang and Rao, 1982]. The intraframe hybrid coder with DPCM in the vertical direction has the traditional problem of transmission error streaks that is characteristic of 1-D DPCM (Chapter 6).

The intraframe TC/DPCM coder [Habibi, 1974] [Habibi and Robinson, 1974] [Habibi, 1981] uses an N-block 1-D transform along an image line l, and the transform coefficients $\theta_l(k)$; $k = 0,1,...,N-1$, are separately DPCM-encoded with a bank of N first-order DPCM coders which use respective reconstructed coefficients $\tilde{\theta}_{l-1}(k)$ from the previous line $l-1$ for predictions. The predicted value is $\hat{\theta}_l(k)$ and the quantized quantity is the interline difference

$$d_l(k) = \theta_l(k) - h(k)\tilde{\theta}_{l-1}(k) \quad ; \quad k = 0,1,...,N-1 \qquad (12.167)$$

where $h(k)$ is an appropriate predictor coefficient chosen as described in the DPCM section. The reconstructed values $\tilde{\theta}_l(k)$ are used at the receiver for the inverse transform operations. The DPCM encoder utilizes interline image correlations, as reflected in correlations between successive transform coefficients of identical index. The number of bits assigned to the DPCM encoders are ideally set proportional to the logarithm of the respective difference signal variances:

$$\sigma_{dk}^2 = \sigma_k^2(1-\rho_k^2) \quad ; \quad k = 0,1,...,N-1 \qquad (12.168)$$

where σ_k^2 and ρ_k are the variance and adjacent-line correlation for transform coefficient of index k.

Figure 12.19 Block diagram of hybrid TC/DPCM coder. The upper row of symbols represents the case where 1-D transform coding of a segment of an image line is followed by DPCM coding of the coefficient vector, based on coefficients of an adjacent line. The lower row of symbols represents the case where 2-D transform coding of a subimage is followed by DPCM coding of the coefficient matrix, using coefficients of an adjacent frame.

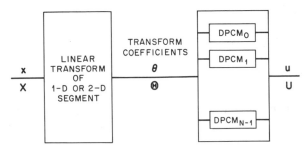

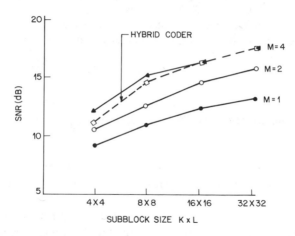

Figure 12.20 Comparison of 3-D DCT and hybrid coding based on 2-D DCT/DPCM. The input is a 3-D Markov source with equal acf values of $\rho = 0.95$ in all three dimensions. The average bit rate in both schemes is 0.25 bits/sample [Roese, Pratt and Robinson;©1977, IEEE].

In the interframe TC/DPCM coder, spatial correlations are utilized by a 2-D transform, and temporal correlations by first-order DPCM, thus avoiding one-step transform processing of $N \times N \times N$ blocks (Figure 12.19). Figure 12.20 provides a comparison of two interframe approaches—one based on 3-D DCT and the other based on a hybrid approach, with 2-D DCT followed by DPCM [Roese, Pratt and Robinson, 1977]. The input is a 3-D Markov source with equal acf values of $\rho = 0.95$ in horizontal, vertical and temporal directions. With 32:1 zonal sampling and 8-bits per retained coefficient, all the schemes represent an average bit rate of $R = 0.25$ bit/pixel. The 3-D DCT coder requires a $16 \times 16 \times 4$ transform $(K = L = 16, M = 4)$, i.e., a storage of 4 frames for an SNR of about 17 dB. The hybrid coder with $K = L = 16$ reaches this performance with an explicit memory of only one frame for DPCM prediction. The $M = 1$ characteristic in the figure describes the performance of an intraframe zonal-sampling DCT system.

With real images, the SNR performances of the 3-D TC and 2-D TC/DPCM coders are in general very different for a given dimensionality. The hybrid approach has the advantage that adaptive bit allocation (see Section 12.7.4) is simpler to optimize in 2-D transform coding and also in the 1-D DPCM stage. A $16 \times 16 \times 16$ 2-D TC/DPCM coder can provide high quality digitizations of (256×256) black-and-white images at bit rates in the order of 0.5 to 1 bit/pixel (Example 12.11).

12.7 Adaptive Transform Coding of Speech and Images

We will now re-examine the components of Figure 12.1 with emphasis on quantization and adaptive bit allocation. Although transform coding systems can be made adaptive in many different ways [Habibi, 1977], the term *Adaptive Transform Coding* (ATC) in this book will be reserved for systems that use adaptive bit allocation. The use of adaptive bit allocation will lead to significant increases in *SNR* as well as perceived quality for both speech and images. Important limits on ATC performance are those set by boundary effects due to the block operations inherent in Transform Coding. We will discuss these effects as and when appropriate.

12.7.1 Quantization and Bit Allocation Strategies

Earlier chapters have discussed quantization systems at length. We have seen that quantizer performance can be maximized by means of nonuniform quantizer characteristics, adaptive logics for step size, entropy coding or a suitable combination of such features.

A transform coefficient can be regarded as a random variable. The coefficient is a linear combination of N^J random variables, where J is the transform dimensionality. The pdf of the coefficient therefore depends on input statistics, the type of transform, its size N^J, and in general, also on coefficient index. We note, however, that the pdf's will be strictly Gaussian for Gaussian inputs, while for other inputs, there is a Gaussian tendency for $N \to \infty$.

In *image coding* with finite N, Gaussian or Laplacian models have been found to be adequate for all except the first coefficient for which several alternative models have been proposed [Tescher, 1979] [Murakami, Hatori and Yamamoto, 1982]. Information about coefficient pdf can be utilized fully only if the quantizer bank of Figure 12.1 consists of a multiplicity of quantizers.

In *speech coding* systems, adaptive step size quantizers are usually critical to handle nonstationarity. As discussed in earlier sections [Figures 4.40(b) and (c)], there are two equivalent approaches, one based on scaling quantizer inputs to provide unit variance, and one based on explicit adaptations of the quantizer step size. In either approach, the scaling depends on information about input variance. This information is either explicitly transmitted (AQF) or recovered reliably from examining a recent sequence of quantizer outputs (AQB). The AQB procedure is very appropriate in the context of sub-band coding (Chapter 11). But ATC systems for speech depend on explicit transmission of variance information anyway, because of the need for adaptive bit allocation; and therefore AQF procedures become a more natural choice for step size adaptation.

An important design parameter in both speech and image coding is the number of quantizer levels as a function of coefficient index. In zonal sampling, where the emphasis is on simplicity, the number of quantizer levels is usually held constant; this leads to a simple system, involving a single shared quantizer. The coefficients can, of course, be scaled to unit variance before quantization, provided that individual variances are known a priori or can be reliably estimated. In a zonal coding or variable bit allocation system, the number of quantizer levels is variable. But if these numbers are constrained to be powers of 2, a shared-quantizer procedure is still possible; all coefficients are first quantized to $2^{R_{max}}$ levels where R_{max} is the maximum number of bits allowed in the allocation procedure; subsequently, for coefficient k, the least significant $(R_{max} - R_k)$ bits in its representation are simply discarded.

12.7.2 Adaptive Bit Allocation

We have already discussed one class of approaches to variable bit allocation — a procedure called *zonal coding*, which uses a priori bit allocations based on log-variance [see (12.60)]; or a simpler procedure based on a priori allocations of zero bits to out-of-zone coefficients in *zonal sampling*, and a constant number of bits to in-zone coefficients. The latter approach can be made more efficient by basing the in-zone coefficient selections on observed magnitudes of coefficients in a particular image rather than a priori. This adaptive procedure, which prevents the suppression of significant frequency components that may lie outside predetermined zones, would be called *threshold sampling*. It is more complex than zonal sampling in that the indices of chosen coefficients have to be transmitted to the decoder, by means of some form of addressing such as run-length coding. It is also possible to keep the total number of bits per block constant by using a variable threshold for transmitted coefficient magnitudes.

In the most general design, the matrix $\mathbf{A}$ can also be adaptive [Tasto and Wintz, 1971]. However, in most image work, and in the discussions of this chapter, the term ATC will signify variable bit allocation only. If the input is nonstationary, the bit allocation procedure will have to be adapted to local statistics, especially because the transform type, i.e., matrix $\mathbf{A}$, itself is usually fixed. Adaptive bit allocation plays a role in TC systems that is comparable to that of adaptive prediction in DPCM (APC). As in that context, adaptations can be accomplished in three ways — partial adaptation as provided by (a) input classifications followed by switching to one of a small number of typical bit allocation rules [Tasto and Wintz, 1971] [Zelinski and Noll, 1975] [Guinlett, 1975]; or fully adaptive bit allocation based on a formal tracking of input spectra (coefficient variances, in general) by (b) *backward* or (c) *forward* estimation procedures.

In the *backward* estimation procedure, the variance of the kth coefficient is estimated either (i) from a time history of the quantized value of *that coefficient over successive blocks*, or (ii) from a recursive relation, *within a given block*, involving the variance estimate for the $(k-1)$th coefficient and its actual quantized value $u(k-1)$. The first coefficient $k = 0$, or the first k_1 coefficients in general, may be nonadaptively quantized, for example, with a very high number of bits, say eight. To start off the recursive estimation procedure reliably, the success of procedure (ii) implies that the variances show a smooth variation with respect to k. Frequency-ordered DFT's and sequency-ordered DWHT's are very helpful in achieving this goal. In image coding, this may involve converting the 2-D coefficients into a specially scanned 1-D array [Cox and Tescher, 1976]. An adaptive procedure of type (ii) above is the following:

$$\hat{\sigma}_k^2 = w\hat{\sigma}_{k-1}^2 + (1-w)u^2(k-1) ; \qquad k = 2,3,...,N^2-1 \qquad (12.169)$$

$\hat{\sigma}_k^2$ is the estimated variance of quantized coefficient $u(k)$ and w is a weighting term such as 0.75 [Habibi, Samulon and Fultz, 1977]. The average brightness coefficient $\theta(0)$ is quantized nonadaptively with an 8 bit uniform quantizer, $\hat{\sigma}_1^2$ is computed as the mean-squared value of the next four coefficients [$\hat{\sigma}_1^2 = \{\theta^2(1) + \theta^2(2) + \theta^2(3) + \theta^2(4)\}/4$] and serves as a starting value of the above recursion. Since this recursion has to be done both at coder and decoder, side information about $\hat{\sigma}_1^2$ has to be explicitly transmitted. Bit allocations follow rules of Section 12.3. Gains over a nonadaptive bit allocation procedure are in excess of 3 dB for $R = 1$ and 2 bits/pixel in 16 × 16 WHT coding [Habibi, Samulon and Fultz, 1977].

In *forward* estimation schemes for variable bit allocation, the actual variance distributions cannot be transmitted if the side information is to be kept small. Instead, the *envelope of the variance distribution*, as described by a few parameters, is used as a coarse description. The envelope parameters are quantized and transmitted as side information; variances are approximately recalculated from this envelope (both at the transmitter and receiver) to compute log-variance-based bit allocations as in Section 12.4. This method is described in detail in the next section.

12.7.3 Adaptive Transform Coding of Speech

A block diagram of an ATC coder with a side information branch appears in Figure 12.21 [Zelinski and Noll, 1977] [Tribolet and Crochiere, 1979] [Cox and Crochiere, 1981] [Crochiere, Cox and Johnston, 1982]. The side information can additionally be used to compute information about the step sizes of different coefficient quantizers, an important requirement in the coding of nonstationary inputs such as speech.

Figure 12.21 Block diagram of an ATC coder with side information transmission for bit allocation and quantizer step size [Zelinski and Noll;©1977, IEEE].

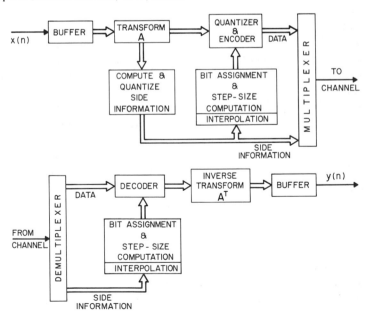

Bit Allocation. Figure 12.22(a) illustrates the squared magnitude of transformed coefficients as a function of coefficient index. Note that although an efficient linear transform decorrelates the coefficients, the actual magnitudes of adjacent coefficients are not unrelated. Rather, they exhibit a slowly varying envelope, perturbed by local, but uncorrelated variations of magnitude.

In one example of speech coding with $N = 128$, sets of 8 to 16 neighboring transform coefficients are therefore squared and averaged, and the averaged values (the L values in Figure 12.22b) are used as support values of an envelope, and recalculations of intermediate individual values $\hat{\sigma}_i^2$ use geometric interpolations, which are equivalent to linear interpolations in the log-domain. The interpolation in the log-domain ensures that low-level coefficients, which are perceptually important, are properly encoded. The encoding of side information requires at least 2 kb/s. A more efficient, but also more complex way of transmitting side information results from using predictor coefficients, or equivalents thereof. These can specify the variance distribution via an autoregressive model (Chapter 6).

Figure 12.22 Adaptive bit allocation in transform coding of speech using forward estimation of variance: (a) actual squared amplitudes of transform coefficients; (b) support values of envelope obtained by averaging sets of N/L adjacent squared values of (a); and (c) envelope obtained from straight-line interpolation in the log-domain between support values [Zelinski and Noll;©1977, IEEE].

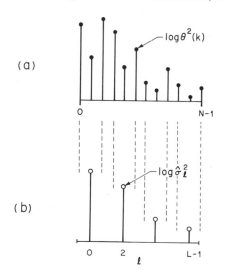

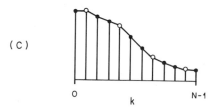

The benefits of adaptive bit allocation are seen in terms of *SNR* results in Figure 12.23, measured with a speech input of duration 1.6 seconds, and a bit rate of $R = 3$ bits/sample.

The figures compare (a) the time-dependence of short-term variance $\sigma_x^2(m)$, where m is the segment number, with (b)(c)(d) the *SNR*-versus-time performance *SNR(m)* of three different TC schemes. The segment length is 16 ms in each case. Part (b) shows that a fixed quantizer, even with logarithmic characteristics, leads to a relatively poor performance. The TC-AQF coder of part (c) employs a forward-

Figure 12.23 Illustration of the benefits of adaptive bit allocation in transform coding of speech at 24 kb/s. Plots of (a) short-time segment variance and short-time *SNR* with (b) TC and log-quantizer, (c) TC-AQF and (d) ATC-AQF [Zelinski and Noll;©1977, IEEE].

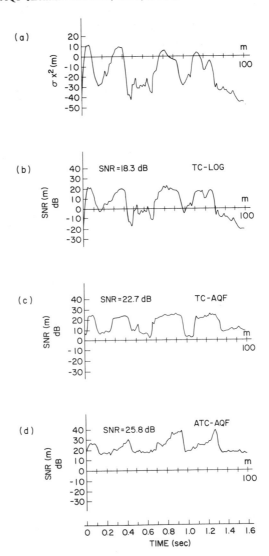

adaptive quantizer, again with a fixed bit allocation and achieves an *SNR* gain of over 4 dB. A further increase of 3 dB in *SNR* is obtained with the fully adaptive scheme of part (d), which includes variable bit allocation. These results can be compared with the DPCM-AQF-APF (APC) result (SNR = 22.5 dB) of Figure 6.19 for the same speech input. Note that TC-AQF has an *SNR* very similar to that of DPCM-AQF-APF, but ATC-AQF is 3 dB better. Neither the APC coder nor the ATC coder in question employ pitch prediction. The benefits of pitch prediction in DPCM have been discussed in Chapter 6. The benefits of pitch information in ATC will be discussed in the next section.

Side Information Algorithms for ATC Coding of Speech. Figure 12.24 shows a voiced-speech DCT spectrum, two procedures for bit allocation and corresponding reconstructed spectra.

In the first procedure, the side information is based on a smooth spectrum that does not include the effect of pitch-induced fine structure in the input spectrum. This smooth spectrum is obtained following the procedure of Figure 12.22, and it is shown by the dashed lines in Figure 12.24(b)(ii). A consequence of such smoothing is increased zero bit allocation at high frequencies [>2.2 kHz in Figure 12.24(b)], with all available bits getting used to describe the low frequencies. There are many efficient techniques for the derivation of such a smooth spectrum; for example, techniques based on all-pole models.

If, on the other hand, the side information includes the fine structure due to pitch, there are more zero-bit allocations at lower frequencies corresponding to gaps between pitch teeth, and this releases bits that get allocated to high frequency parts in the spectrum [for example, the frequencies in the 2.7 to 3.3 kHz range in Figure 12.24(c)]. The best results in ATC are obtained using this more 'speech-specific', unsmoothed-spectrum-based procedure in Figure 12.24(c), although the greater amount of side information needed in this procedure decreases the value of R, the average number of bits/sample for the quantization of transform coefficients. The 'speech-specific' procedure is also more complex. It involves pitch determination, generation of a pitch pattern in the frequency domain, and multiplication with the smooth spectrum. The resulting spectrum with fine structure is seen in Figure 12.24(c)(ii). The dashed line spectrum in this figure is used for bit allocation as well as for the determination of quantizer step sizes. The improvement due to this method is seen in the reconstructed spectra of Figures 12.24(b) and (c). The speech-specific procedure can be realized very efficiently in systems which transmit a crude version of the so-called *cepstrum* information for providing bit allocation information [Cox and Crochiere, 1981] [Crochiere, Cox and Johnston, 1982] [Zelinski, 1982].

At 16 kb/s and above, both of the above techniques have a similar, if not identical quality. At bit rates under 16 kb/s, the speech-specific algorithm shows significant gains in perceptual performance.

The nature of bit allocation can also be manipulated with a frequency-weighted error criteria as in Figure 12.8(b). Best results for speech are obtained when the error weighting parameter λ in (12.69) is in the order of -0.3; this represents a situation that is midway between the extremes of $\lambda = 0$ [Figure 12.8(a) with white

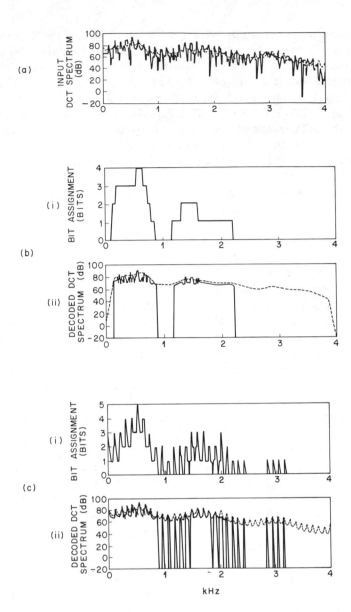

Figure 12.24 (a) Example of DCT spectrum in voiced speech; and bit allocations based on (b) smoothed and (c) unsmoothed short-time spectra. The dashed lines in b(ii) and c(ii) describe the coefficient variance distribution that is used for bit allocation [Tribolet and Crochiere;©1979, IEEE].

error spectrum] and $\lambda = -1$ [constant bit assignment, input psd-type error spectrum]. Indeed, the $\lambda = -0.3$ shaping is very close to that of Figure 12.8(b). The result of optimum error weighting is sketched in Figure 12.25. The non-zero error-weighting is a convenient way of utilizing masking phenomena in perception. One such phenomenon is that the human ear does not perceive noise in a given frequency band if it is more than 20 dB below the signal level in that band.

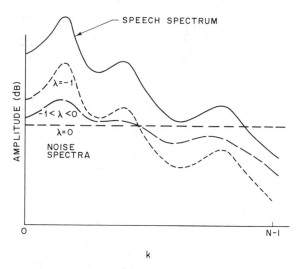

Figure 12.25 The psd of transform coding noise as a function of error-weighting parameter λ in (12.69) [Tribolet and Crochiere;©1979, IEEE].

Switched Bit Allocation. A simpler procedure for bit allocation is one based on *switching*, once for every block, to one of B possible predetermined bit assignment patterns. This approach is similar to switched prediction and vector quantization search techniques, as discussed in the context of APC (Section 6.5.1). The approach has been used in image coding [Tasto and Wintz, 1971] as well as speech coding [Zelinski and Noll, 1979]. The switching may be based on a simple block-classification procedure such as the number of zero crossings per block. With $B = 8$, this type of bit allocation provides a gain over TC-AQF that is about 2 dB, as against the 3 dB gain in ATC-AQF [Zelinski and Noll, 1979]. With a greater value of B, such as $B = 32$, and a more sophisticated classification procedure such as the matching of short-term spectrum to one of B predetermined typical spectral templates, it is possible to obtain a performance that is extremely close to that of ATC-AQF [Heron, Crochiere and Cox, 1982].

Choice of Transform. Figure 12.26 shows the performance of an adaptive coder with different transforms for the three speech sounds (m, $ü$, sch). It demonstrates once again the near-optimality of the DCT, especially for a voiced input (with adjacent sample correlation $\rho_1 \to +1$). The results in Figure 12.26 are for no error weighting ($\gamma = 0$) and the smooth-spectrum-based bit allocation procedure in Figure 12.24(b). The maximum TC gains $\max\{G_{TC}\}$ refer to KLT with $N \to \infty$. Note that the greatest value of G_{TC} (for a nasal sound m) is equivalent to more than a 4-bit gain over PCM, and the worst case gain (for sound sch) is nearly equivalent to a 1-bit advantage.

We have noted earlier that DCT coding offers better end-effect performance than DFT. In speech coding, the choice of the analysis window for the DCT is important in further controlling periodic block-boundary effects which tend to cause a characteristic *burbling distortion* at low bit rates. Trapezoidal windows have

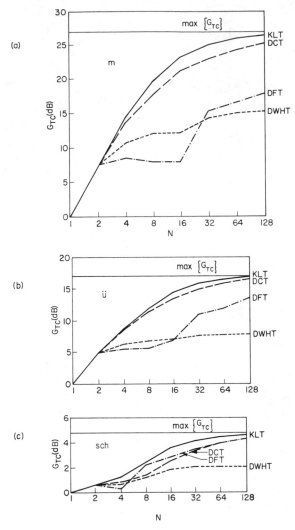

Figure 12.26 Adaptive transform coding gain G_{TC} with different speech inputs [Zelinski and Noll;©1977, IEEE].

been found very useful for low bit rate transform coding of speech [Tribolet and Crochiere, 1979]. By allowing a small overlap between the successive blocks, such that the sum of the overlapped window heights is always unity, an additional reduction of end effect noise is achieved without significantly lowering the number of bits available for encoding each block. As the number of quantizer bits approaches values of $R = 1$ or less, DCT coding degradation takes the form of a *tonal noise*. This is due to the perceptually conspicuous nature of rapid block-to-block changes in bit allocations to adjacent frequency bands.

Figure 11.9 has demonstrated the excellent performance of ATC as compared with other redundancy-removing coders for speech waveforms, on the basis of the segmental measure *SNRSEG*. The performance of ATC as a function of bit rate is further described by the waveforms in Figure 12.27 for $R = 3$, 2 and 1 bit/sample (bit rates $I = 24$, 16 and 8 kb/s, not including side information). The 2-bit output in part (c) of this figure is seen to reproduce the input much better, for example, than the 2-bit DPCM-AQB waveform of Figure 6.12(d). In fact, the noise power in 2-bit ATC is very similar to that in 3-bit DPCM-AQB [Figures 12.27(f) and 6.12(f)]. In addition, the greater speech-like structure in the ATC noise waveform leads to an additional perceptual advantage in the ATC system. Although the reconstruction waveform in 1-bit ATC looks very smooth [Figure 12.27(d)], its quality is limited by distortions that are perceptually extremely obvious.

The error waveform of 24 kb/s ATC implies a value of SNR that is much less than that of 8-bit log-PCM. This can be seen from the relative magnitudes in respective waveforms of reconstruction error [Figures 12.27(b) and 1.4(b)]. It is also clear from the SNR results of Figure 12.23, which are more than 12 dB lower

Figure 12.27 Adaptive transform coding of speech waveforms: (a) input $x(n)$; (b) (c) (d) reconstruction error waveforms $r(n)$ with (b) $R = 3$, (c) $R = 2$ and (d) $R = 1$ bit per sample. The error waveforms are magnified by a factor of 6.25. The input (a) is the same as that in Figure 1.4 [Cox, 1981].

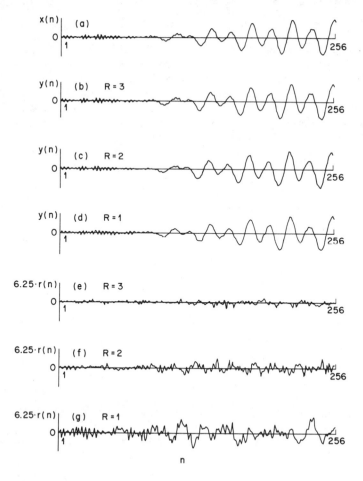

than the 38 dB *SNR* (Figures 5.7 and 5.10) of 8-bit log-PCM. Subjectively, however, 24 kb/s or 3 bit/sample ATC is very close to 8 bit/sample log-PCM. This is confirmed by MOS quality measurements. With the speech-specific design of Figure 12.24(c), the MOS, on a scale of 1 to 5, was found to be 4.1 at a total bit rate of 24 kb/s, 3.8 at at 16 kb/s and 2.4 at 9.6 kb/s [Daumer, 1982]. This is very close to the variation of MOS with bit rate for the *high complexity* coder of Figure 1.5.

12.7.4 Adaptive Transform Coding of Images

Previous sections have shown examples of transform coded images, including illustrations of zonal coding and/or adaptive bit allocation (Figures 12.13 and 12.17). With adaptive bit allocation and DCT, high quality digitizations (*SNR* approaching 30 dB) are possible in the coding of still images at average rates of $R \simeq 2$ bits/sample, and medium-quality (*SNR* in the range 20 to 25 dB) digitizations are possible at R values of about 1 bit/sample [Mauersberger, 1980]. As in DPCM, interframe techniques are needed to produce high-quality reconstructions of moving images at bits rates in the order of 2 bits/sample and less [Natarajan and Ahmed, 1977].

Example 12.10. Interframe 3-D DCT coding with 1 bit/sample
Figure 12.28 shows the distribution of coefficient variances in a 3D-DCT example. The transformed subimages are chosen to be $4 \times 4 \times 4$ blocks (four frames with 16 pixels each), and in Figure 12.28, coefficients with indices 16 to 63 represent temporal information. Table 12.3 gives a bit allocation procedure. Note that the total number of bits, with summation over 16 coefficients and four frames, is 64, resulting in an average bit rate of 1 bit/sample. The quantizers used for the 64 coefficients have pdf-optimized nonuniform characteristics, with a Laplacian pdf model for all except the first coefficient, which is modeled by a uniform pdf. Figure 12.29 shows original images and reconstructions for

Figure 12.28 Interframe transform coding; DCT coefficient variances in four successive frames [Natarajan and Ahmed;©1977, IEEE].

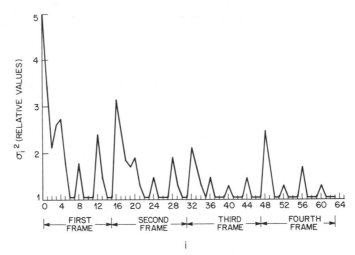

Table 12.3 Bit allocation in a 4×4×4 DCT coder with $R = 1$ bit/pixel. Each column represents R_i values for the 16 coefficients of a given frame [Natarajan and Ahmed; ©1977, IEEE].

Frame Number			
1	2	3	4
7	5	3	2
4	3	0	0
2	0	0	0
3	0	0	0
5	4	3	0
3	2	0	0
2	0	0	0
2	0	0	0
3	3	2	0
2	0	0	0
0	0	0	0
0	0	0	0
2	0	0	0
0	0	0	0
2	0	0	0
0	0	0	0

Figure 12.29 Interframe transform coding; (a)(b) frames one and four; (c)(d) the same frames reconstructed using 1 bit/pixel DCT [Natarajan and Ahmed; ©1977, IEEE].

(a)

(c)

(b)

(d)

frames 1 and 4. The measured *SNR* is 23 dB with the low-activity image represented in Figure 12.29, and less with an image with more violent motion [Natarajan and Ahmed, 1977]. But in each case, there are no visible distortions or motion degradations in the reconstructed moving images, based on comparison with black-and-white originals with 6 bit PCM samples.

Example 12.11   Interframe 2-D DCT/DPCM coding.

We discussed a nonadaptive hybrid coder in Section 12.6.5 with special reference to Markov inputs. The performance of this coder at low bit rates is less impressive with real images because of their nonstationarity and temporal characteristics. However, with adaptive bit allocation in the 2-D TC system, and adaptive prediction in the temporal DPCM system, a 16×16×16 hybrid coder realizes *SNR* values as high as 37 dB at $R = 1$ bit/pixel, with no degradation of perceived image quality. Coder performance is however image-and-motion-dependent, and certain classes of moving images in broadcast-standard color television may require bit rates as high as 2 bits/sample for high-quality encoding [Kamanagar and Rao, 1981]. The coder is robust with random bit error rates of up to 10^{-4} [Roese, Pratt and Robinson, 1977]. •

12.8 Transmission Error Effects

As in the case of earlier chapters, we shall consider transmission error effects on mse performance as well as on the subjective quality of digitized speech and images.

12.8.1 Effect on Reconstruction Error Variance

Recall that in PCM (Chapters 4 and 5), the reconstruction error in the presence of transmission errors had the form $r(n) = q(n) + c(n)$, with a variance

$$\sigma^2_{r,PCM} = \sigma^2_q + \sigma^2_c = (\epsilon^2_q + \epsilon^2_c)\sigma^2_x \; ; \quad \epsilon^2_c = \xi p_e \text{ with single errors} \quad (12.170\text{a})$$

provided that $c(n)$ and $q(n)$ are uncorrelated (as with Max-quantizers). We recall that p_e is the bit error rate and ξ is the channel coefficient, a function of bit rate R, pdf of the quantizer input, and the binary code.

In DPCM (Chapter 6), the reconstruction error was $r(n) = q(n) + c(n)*g(n)$ with a variance

$$\sigma^2_{r,DPCM} = (\epsilon^2_q + \alpha\epsilon^2_c)\sigma^2_x/G_P \; ; \quad \alpha = \sum_{k=0}^{\infty} h^2_{DEC}(k) \geqslant 1 \quad (12.170\text{b})$$

where $h_{DEC}(k)$ is the impulse response of the decoder filter. The term α reflects error propagation; but the channel error contribution $\sigma^2_{c,DPCM} = \alpha\epsilon^2_c/G_P$ equals $\sigma^2_{c,PCM}$ if one uses a mmse predictor for which max$\{G_P\} = \alpha$ [see (6.132)]:

$$\sigma^2_{c,DPCM} = \sigma^2_{c,PCM} \quad \text{with mmse prediction} \quad (12.170\text{c})$$

We will now show that a similar result holds in the case of TC.

The reconstructed output **y** in TC can be described as a superposition of weighted basis vectors (or images) in the form (12.20b):

$$\mathbf{y} = \sum_{k=0}^{N-1} v(k)\mathbf{b}_k \tag{12.171}$$

where $v(k)$ are received versions of quantized transform coefficients. With channel errors, $v(k) = u(k) - c(k)$ and the output will differ from the intended output $\sum u(k)\mathbf{b}_k$ by a term

$$\mathbf{r} = \mathbf{x} - \mathbf{y} = \sum_{k=0}^{N-1} q(k)\mathbf{b}_k + \sum_{k=0}^{N-1} c(k)\mathbf{b}_k \tag{12.172}$$

i.e., by a superposition of basis vectors weighted by the sum of quantization error and channel error components in $v(k)$. The summations in (12.172) indicate that channel errors propagate beyond a single sample; they affect, to different extents, all the reconstructions within a block of length N (or subimage of size $N \times N$ in a 2-D transform).

Assuming uncorrelated error components $q(k)$ and $c(k)$ and orthonormal basis vectors $(\mathbf{b}_i^T\mathbf{b}_j = \delta_{ij})$, the reconstruction error variance is

$$\sigma_{r,TC}^2 = \frac{1}{N} E[(\mathbf{X} - \mathbf{Y})^T(\mathbf{X} - \mathbf{Y})] = \sigma_q^2 + \sigma_c^2 \tag{12.173}$$

with σ_q^2 following (12.61) and with

$$\sigma_{c,TC}^2 = \frac{1}{N} \sum_{k=0}^{N-1} E[C^2(k)] = \frac{1}{N} \sum_{k=0}^{N-1} \sigma_{ck}^2 \tag{12.174}$$

The channel error variance σ_{ck}^2 that is added to the kth transform coefficient $\theta(k)$ of variance σ_k^2 can be given (as in 12.170a) by

$$\sigma_{ck}^2 = \xi p_e \sigma_k^2 \quad \text{for all } k \tag{12.175}$$

Here we have assumed that all channel coefficients ξ are of same value, i.e., they do not depend on the bit rate R_k for the given sample. Earlier results (Chapter 4) show that this approximation is valid *as long as R_k is not very small*. From (12.174) and (12.175), we obtain the result [Zelinski, 1979]

$$\sigma_{c,TC}^2 = \frac{1}{N} \xi p_e \sum_{k=0}^{N-1} \sigma_k^2 = \xi p_e \sigma_x^2 = \sigma_{c,PCM}^2 \tag{12.176}$$

i.e., channel errors in TC produce the same error variance in the output as in PCM. This result is the counterpart of (12.170c). There, as in the derivation leading to (12.176), it is assumed that all ξ values are equal. Note also that the assumption of a constant ξ leads to an expression for $\sigma_{c,TC}^2$ that is independent of bit allocation and transform matrix. The above result should be carefully interpreted; as in DPCM, the channel error variance, *relative* to quantization error variance, has actually *increased*; in TC, this increase is by a factor G_{TC}.

12.8   Transmission Error Effects

12.8.2 Results for Speech and Images

Subjectively, TC is more robust to transmission errors than PCM, in both speech and image coding. Tolerable random error rates are in the order of 10^{-3} and 10^{-4} for low bit rate speech and video in the absence of explicit error protection.

In ATC coding of speech, the error-sensitive part of the coder output is the side information that carries bit allocation information. In low bit rate ATC (say, at 16 kb/s), the side information can constitute up to about 20% of the total coder output. If this side information is not error-protected, output speech is poor in quality at $p_e = 10^{-3}$ [Cox, 1980]. The speech is intelligible, but is degraded by screeches, clicks, pops and other loud sounds. With $p_e = 10^{-2}$, there is significant loss of intelligibility as well. On the other hand, in a system where about 1 kb/s (Problem 12.33) is dedicated to protection of side information, output speech quality is good at $p_e = 10^{-3}$ and acceptable even at $p_e = 10^{-2}$.

With nonadaptive transform coders, the effect of a bit error does not propagate beyond the block because only the samples within a transform subblock depend on a wrongly decoded coefficient. The exact nature of the degradation depends upon the type of transform used and the coefficients that are received in error.

In image coding, errors in lower frequency coefficients are more visible than higher frequency coefficients due to the fact that above a certain frequency the sensitivity of the eye decreases with frequency. Also, the probability of errors occurring in the lower frequency coefficients is higher due to larger number of bits that are required to code them. As the block size decreases, the averaging property (i.e., spreading of error over the entire block) decreases, and the transmission errors appear as blotches in the picture. Results for 16×16 DFT coding with 2:1 zonal sampling and $R = 1$ appear in Figure 12.30 for $p_e = 10^{-3}$ and $p_e = 10^{-2}$. Note

Figure 12.30 Effects of random transmission errors in 2-D transform coding with DFT-based 2:1 zonal sampling, $R = 1$ bit/sample and p_e values of (a) 10^{-3} and (b) 10^{-2}. The uncoded 8-bit PCM image is shown in Figure 12.6(c) [Wintz;©1972, IEEE].

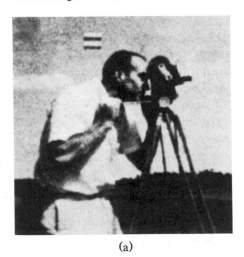
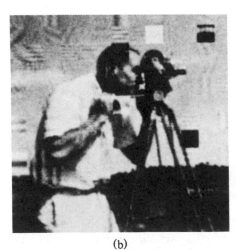

(a)   (b)

the effects of superimposed basis vectors as indicated by (12.172). Note also that effects do not propagate beyond the transform sub-block. Error visibility is much less than the streaks that result in 1-D DPCM (Figure 6.33) at similar error rates, but it is comparable to the error visibility in well-designed 2-D DPCM (Figure 6.34). Also, as in DPCM, error concealment procedures can be devised that significantly enhance reconstructed quality with only a slight increase of total transmission rate; or with no increase of total transmission rate in the case of techniques that exploit the natural redundancies in images [Wong and Steele, 1978].

Effect of Error-Protection on TC and PCM. The result (12.176) indicates that TC has no advantage over PCM with noisy channels. However, we will show next that TC has an advantage over PCM if explicit error-protection is employed. The advantage comes out of the possibility of protecting the more important coefficients more carefully, a possibility already noted in Section 11.6.

Consider a PCM system where the most significant bits are ideally error-protected. Let e be the number of protected bits per sample. An analysis of channel coefficients [Zelinski, 1979] shows that channel error variance is approximately reduced by a factor of 4 for each protected bit:

$$\sigma_{c,PCM}^2 \simeq \xi 2^{-2e} p_e \sigma_x^2 ; \quad e = 0,1,...,R \quad (12.177)$$

This result holds for the NBC and Gray code, and also for the FBC code with the exception of its first bit. The above PCM system needs a side information for error protection that depends on e. In a TC system with an identical fraction of side information, Ne bits per *block* are available to protect the transform coefficients. However, instead of allocating e of these protection bits to each coefficient, we can now make use of the hierarchy of coefficient variances σ_k^2 and assign e_k bits to coefficient of index k; and we can thereby minimize

$$\sigma_{c,TC}^2 = \frac{1}{N} \xi p_e \sum_{k=0}^{N-1} 2^{-2e_k} \sigma_k^2 \quad (12.178a)$$

under the constraint

$$e = \frac{1}{N} \sum_{k=0}^{N-1} e_k = \text{constant} \quad (12.178b)$$

The derivation of optimum bit allocation for error protection as well as the gain over an error-protected system follow arguments very similar to those used for deriving the bit allocation that minimized quantization error variance in Section 12.4. The end results are also very similar. The optimum number of protection bits [Zelinski, 1979] is

$$e_k = e + \frac{1}{2} \log_2 \frac{\sigma_k^2}{\left[\prod_{j=0}^{N-1} \sigma_j^2 \right]^{1/N}} \quad (12.179)$$

Using (12.178a),

$$\frac{\sigma_{c,PCM}^2}{\sigma_{c,TC}^2}\bigg|_{e > 0} \sim G_{TC} \qquad (12.180)$$

The channel error variance in TC can be made smaller than that in a comparable PCM scheme by a factor of G_{TC} if the same (average) number of bits is error-protected. An ideally error-protected TC system can therefore reduce both quantization error and channel error by the same factor G_{TC}, so that

$$\sigma_r^2 = (\epsilon_q^2 + \epsilon_c^2)\sigma_x^2/G_{TC} \qquad (12.181)$$

The analytical discussion above has assumed nonadaptive coding and an mse criterion for simplicity. It has been shown that, in the absence of error protection, the mse due to channel errors is the same in TC and PCM, while with ideal error protection, TC offers significantly better transmission error performance [Zelinski, 1979]. The following example shows that the results also apply to adaptive schemes.

Example 12.12. Error-protected ATC and PCM systems for speech

Figure 12.31 compares SNR-versus-p_e results with a real speech input, for 32 kb/s PCM-AQF and 16 kb/s ATC, both of which use a block length of $N = 128$. The measured value of G_{TC} is 12 dB. Without error protection, both schemes perform within 1 dB of each other. But with error protection of 1 bit/sample (PCM) and of 128 bits/block [ATC with optimum protection allocation (12.179)], PCM performance improves by about 6 dB as expected from (12.177), while TC performance improves by an *additional* 10.8 to 12.5 dB as predicted by (12.180). Note that Figure 12.31 has assumed error-free transmission of side information for simplicity. Results are therefore optimistic representations of performance. •

Figure 12.31 SNR versus p_e in PCM-AQF and ATC-AQF speech-coding systems (a) with error protection and (b) without error protection. In (a), the protection is provided for 1 bit in each sample in PCM, and for a total of 128 bits in a 128-sample block in ATC [Zelinski and Noll, 1975].

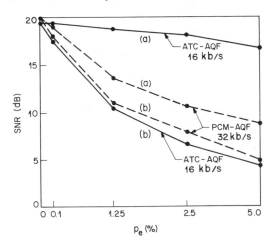

Problems

(12.1)   Show that for $N = 2$ the most general orthonormal transform is that given by (12.10a).

(12.2)   Consider the (2×2) subimage

$$\mathbf{X} = \begin{bmatrix} x(0,0) & x(0,1) \\ x(1,0) & x(1,1) \end{bmatrix}$$

and the separable transform based on (12.30) with $\mathbf{A}_v$ and $\mathbf{A}_h$ based on (12.10b).

(a)   Show that the coefficient matrix is

$$\boldsymbol{\theta} = \frac{1}{2} \begin{bmatrix} x(0,0)+x(0,1)+x(1,0)+x(1,1) & x(0,0)-x(0,1)+x(1,0)-x(1,1) \\ x(0,0)+x(0,1)-x(1,0)-x(1,1) & x(0,0)-x(0,1)-x(1,0)+x(1,1) \end{bmatrix}$$

Note that the coefficients can be interpreted respectively as scaled values of average pixel intensity, average intensity difference between columns, average intensity difference between rows, and finally, a difference between row and column differences.

(b)   Use (12.33a) to show that the basis images implied by $\mathbf{A}_v$ and $\mathbf{A}_h$ above are those in (12.34) and Figure 12.6(b).

(12.3)   It has been stated in Section 12.3 that the first 64 DWHT basis images of Figure 12.12 can be obtained by using the 8 DWHT vectors from Figure 12.5(a) in (12.33a). Show this result for the basis image B_{43} (column 5, row 4) of Figure 12.12.

(12.4)   Consider the orthogonal transform in (12.10). Assume that $\sigma_x^2 = 1$.

(a)   Show that for an adjacent sample correlation of $\rho_{xx}(1) = \rho$, the geometric mean of coefficient variances is $[1 - 4a^2(1-a^2)\rho^2]^{1/2}$.

(b)   Show that the geometric mean is minimized [and therefore $^2G_{TC}$ in (12.57) is maximized] when $a = 1/\sqrt{2}$, which leads to the well-known transform (12.10b).

(c)   For the above value of a, show that

$$^2G_{TC} = (1-\rho^2)^{-1/2}$$

Compare the TC gain above with DPCM and D*PCM gains for a first-order predictor:

$$^1G_{DPCM} = (1-\rho^2)^{-1} ; \quad ^1G_{D*PCM} = (1-\rho^2)^{-1/2}$$

(12.5)   Consider the transform (12.10b), and an input with variance σ_x^2 and $\rho_{xx}(1) = \rho = 0.85$.

(a)   Show that the coefficient variances are

$$\sigma_0^2 = E[\Theta^2(0)] = \sigma_x^2(1+\rho) = 1.85\sigma_x^2 ; \quad \sigma_1^2 = E[\Theta^2(1)] = \sigma_x^2(1-\rho) = 0.15\sigma_x^2 .$$

(b)   Show that $E[\Theta(0)\Theta(1)] = 0$.

(c)   For an average rate $R = 1.5$, and $\sigma_x^2 = \epsilon_z^2 = 1$, show that a minimum reconstruction error variance of 0.065 is realized with $R_0 = 2.41$ and $R_1 = 0.59$, and that this corresponds to max$\{G_{TC}\} = 2.78$ dB.

(d)   Show that if $\sigma_x^2 = 1$, the values of error variances corresponding to $R_0 = 3,2,1,0$ and $R_1 = 3 - R_0$, are 0.089, 0.077, 0.236 and 0.926, respectively.

(12.6)   (a)   Consider a two-dimensional image source with adjacent sample correlation ρ in both horizontal and vertical directions. Show that with a "half-transform" $\Theta = AX$ where A is the matrix (12.10b), the ratio of arithmetic and geometric means of coefficient variances is $(1-\rho^2)^{-\frac{1}{2}}$, the one-dimensional result $^2G_{TC}$ in Problem 12.4.

(b)   Show that the arithmetic to geometric mean ratio increases to $(1-\rho^2)^{-1}$ with a "full-transform" $\Theta = AXA^T$ as in (12.31), assuming a separable acf model (with a the correlation ρ^2 between diagonally opposite elements of X).

(c)   Show that for $\rho = 0.95$, the arithmetic-to-geometric mean ratios in (a) and (b) are $\sqrt{10.26}$ and 10.26 respectively.

(d)   Consider the transform $\Theta = AXA^T$ as in (b) but an isotropic acf model with a correlation between diagonally opposite elements of $\rho^{\sqrt{2}}$. Show that the arithmetic-to-geometric mean ratio for $\rho = 0.95$ is 6.4, reflecting a 2 dB loss in performance compared to the separable acf case.

(12.7)   Assume a quantizer performance factor of $\epsilon_z^2 = 1$, an average rate of $R = 2$, $\sigma_x^2 = 1$ and $\rho = 0.95$ for a (2×2) image. Show that error-minimizing bit assignments for the examples (a), (b) and (d) in Problem 12.6 are

$$\begin{bmatrix} 3 & 3 \\ 1 & 1 \end{bmatrix} \quad \begin{bmatrix} 4 & 2 \\ 2 & 0 \end{bmatrix} \quad \text{and} \quad \begin{bmatrix} 3 & 2 \\ 2 & 1 \end{bmatrix}$$

with corresponding reconstruction error variances of (a) 22/1024, (b) 8/1024 and (c) 20/1024. The bit allocation (b) above implies that $\theta(0,0)$ is quantized using 4 bits, $\theta(0,1)$ and $\theta(1,0)$ with 2 bits each, and $\theta(1,1)$ is not transmitted at all.

(12.8)   Consider the two-level psd of Figure 2.24. Show that the transform-coding gain with $N = 2$ would be

$$^2G_{TC} = \left[1 - \left[\frac{2}{\pi}(1-\alpha) \right]^2 \right]^{-\frac{1}{2}}$$

Note that this is less than the asymptotic gain $[\alpha(2-\alpha)]^{-\frac{1}{2}}$ [Problem 2.22(c)] for all $0 < \alpha < 1$. Discuss the special cases of $\alpha = 0$ and $\alpha = 1$.

(12.9)   Consider the problem of minimizing a frequency-weighted reconstruction error variance

$$\sigma_q^2 = \frac{1}{N} \sum_{k=0}^{N-1} W_k \sigma_{qk}^2$$

subject to an average bit rate constraint R as in (12.46). Show that the bit allocation that minimizes the above expression is

$$R_k = R + \frac{1}{2} \log_2 \frac{W_k \sigma_k^2}{\left[\prod_{j=0}^{N-1} W_j \sigma_j^2\right]^{1/N}} ; \quad k = 0,1,...,N-1$$

with an error spectrum described by

$$W_k \sigma_{qk}^2 = W_l \sigma_{ql}^2 ; \quad k,l = 0,1,...N-1$$

In the above design, the *weighted*-noise variances are equal for all coefficients.

(12.10)   (a)   Show that, with $W_k = (\sigma_k^2)^\lambda$ in (12.69) and $N = 2$, the optimum bit allocation is given by

$$R_0 = R + \frac{\lambda+1}{2} \log_2 \frac{\sigma_0}{\sigma_1}$$

(b)   For the example of Problem 12.5, show that $\lambda = -0.5$ leads to a bit assignment $(R_0=1.96, R_1 = 1.04)$, while $\lambda = +0.5$ leads to $(R_0 = 2.88, R_1 = 0.12)$.

(12.11)   Consider the four-sample input sequence

$$\{x(n)\} = \{17,19,21,18\}$$

Determine the output sequence of a transform coding system based on the Discrete Walsh Hadamard transform $^4\mathbf{H}'$, and a zonal coding procedure where the first two transform coefficients are quantized with zero error, and the last two coefficients are discarded, and replaced by zero values at the decoder.

(12.12)   Consider the 2×2 image $\mathbf{X}$ of Figure 12.6(a):

$$\mathbf{X} = \begin{bmatrix} 35 & 30 \\ 25 & 15 \end{bmatrix}$$

and the two-dimensional transform (12.30) $\boldsymbol{\Theta} = \mathbf{A}_v \mathbf{X} \mathbf{A}_h^T$ where $\mathbf{A}_v$ and $\mathbf{A}_h$ are defined by (12.10b). Assume a zonal sampling procedure that zeroes second-column coefficients a priori, and represents the first-column coefficients with negligible quantization error:

$$\hat{\boldsymbol{\theta}} = \begin{bmatrix} \Theta(0,0) & 0 \\ \Theta(1,0) & 0 \end{bmatrix}$$

(a)   Show that the reconstructed image is

$$\hat{\mathbf{X}} = \begin{bmatrix} 32.5 & 32.5 \\ 20.0 & 20.0 \end{bmatrix}$$

(b)   Show that the average reconstruction error is 15.625, or nearly 28% of input variance, assuming a mean of 26.25 for **X**. Derive that result by a direct comparison of **X** and $\hat{\mathbf{X}}$.

(c)   Derive the above value of σ_{zs}^2 by using (12.76).

While the above example illustrates the nature of zonal sampling in a simple fashion, it should be recognized as a purely deterministic illustration. The average reconstruction error of 15.625, for example, is simply an average of the error in representing the four components of the specific inputs **X** of that problem, not an expectation over a statistically characterized ensemble of (2×2) images.

(12.13)   Assume a separable image model and adjacent sample correlation ρ in both horizontal and vertical directions. With $\sigma_x^2 = 1$, show that the variances of coefficients in a 2×2 transform based on (12.31) and (12.10b) are the entries in

$$\begin{bmatrix} (1+\rho)^2 & 1-\rho^2 \\ 1-\rho^2 & (1-\rho)^2 \end{bmatrix}$$

(12.14)   Assuming that the quantizer performance given by $\sigma_{qi}^2 = 2^{-2R_i}\sigma_i^2$, and a value of $\rho = 0.95$, derive the bit allocations and reconstruction error variances given in the following table, for PCM, TC-ZS (2:1 zonal sampling) and ATC, using the image transform of Example 12.13. (The first two values of R in each set refer to the bits allocated to the first column coefficients).

Coding Scheme	$(R = 2)$		$(R = 1)$	
	R_i-Values	$mse = \sigma_q^2$	R_i-values	$mse = \sigma_q^2$
PCM	(2,2,2,2)	64/1024	(1,1,1,1)	256/1024
2:1 Zonal Sampling with $n = N/2 = 2$	(4,4,0,0)	30/1024	(2,2,0,0)	88/1024
Optimum Bit Allocation	(4,2,2,0)	8/1024	(3,1,0,0)	48/1024

For $R = 1$, show also that 4:1 zonal sampling with a bit allocation of (4,0,0,0) gives an mse of (56/1024) as against (88/1024) for 2:1 zonal sampling.

(12.15)   For inputs of block length $N = 2$, consider 2:1 zonal sampling in the *time domain*: $y(0) = x(0)$; (a) $y(1) = 0$, or (b) $y(1) = y(0)$, i.e., the untransmitted sample is set at the receiver either (a) to zero, or (b) to the value of its predecessor. Show that the respective reconstruction error variances are (a) $\sigma_x^2/2$ and (b) $\sigma_x^2(1-\rho)$, where $\rho = R_{xx}(1)/\sigma_x^2$.

Now use **A** of (12.10b), set $\theta(0) = \theta(0)$ and set (c) $\theta(1) = \theta(0)$, or (d) $\theta(1) = 0$ (2:1 zonal sampling in the *transform domain*). Show that the respective error variances are σ_x^2 and $\sigma_x^2(1-\rho)/2$.

Note that the results hold for any input with variance σ_x^2 and acf $\rho_{xx}(1) = \rho$. Note also that with the zonal coding in (d), a gain over (a) and (b) results for any $\rho > 0$. In particular, with $\rho = 0.95$, show that the schemes (a), (b), (c), (d) have *SNR* values of 3, 13, 0 and 16 dB, respectively.

(12.16)   Consider inputs of block length $N = 2$, assume 2:1 zonal sampling, and a process with a two-level psd (Figure 2.24). Verify that the error variance is

$$\sigma_{zs}^2 = \frac{1}{2}\left[1 - \frac{2}{\pi}(1-\alpha)\right]\sigma_x^2$$

Note that for the 2:1 zonal sampling of a white input ($\alpha = 1$), $\sigma_{zs}^2 = \sigma_x^2/2$.

(12.17) Consider the non-Toeplitz matrix

$$\begin{bmatrix} 1 & 2 \\ 4 & 3 \end{bmatrix}$$

(a) Show that its eigenvalues are $\lambda_0 = -1$ and $\lambda_1 = 5$.

(b) Compute the orthonormal eigenvectors.

(12.18) Simplify the results (12.108), (12.109) and (12.110) for the case of $N = 2$.

(12.19) Show that the transform coding gain for the numbers in Table 12.1 for $N = 8$ exceeds that for $N = 2$ in (12.99) by 4 dB. Also see Figure 12.10.

(12.20) Consider an MA(1) source.

(a) Compute the KLT matrix for $N = 3$.

(b) Verify that the transform coefficient variances are

$$\sigma_0^2 = \sigma_x^2(1 + \sqrt{2}\rho) ; \quad \sigma_1^2 = \sigma_x^2; \quad \sigma_2^2 = \sigma_x^2(1 - \sqrt{2}\rho)$$

(c) Hence show that the transform coding gain is $(1 - 2\rho^2)^{-1/3}$.

(12.21) Use the results of Example 12.1 and Table 12.1 to discuss the effects of 2:1 zonal sampling for $N = 2$ and 8, and 4:1 zonal sampling for $N = 8$. Calculate the value of $SNR = \sigma_x^2/\sigma_{zs}^2$ in each case.

(12.22) Consider an input with $\sigma_x^2 = 1$ and acf values $\rho_{xx}(n) = \rho_n$; $n = 0,1,2,3$, and a linear transform of it using ${}^4\mathbf{H}$ (12.135a).

(a) Show that the coefficient variances are $(\rho_0+1.5\rho_1+\rho_2+0.5\rho_3)$, $(\rho_0-1.5\rho_1+\rho_2-0.5\rho_3)$, $(\rho_0+0.5\rho_1-\rho_2-0.5\rho_3)$ and $(\rho_0-0.5\rho_1-\rho_2+0.5\rho_3)$.

(b) Show therefore that G_{TC} values for a (i) speech input (ρ_0=1.0, ρ_1=0.825, ρ_2=0.562 and ρ_3=0.31) and a (ii) voiceband data signal (ρ_0=1.0, ρ_1=0.15, ρ_2=−0.75 and ρ_3=−0.26) are 2.0 and 1.6, respectively.

(c) Show also that corresponding gains are (i) 1.77 and (ii) 1.01 for the ${}^2\mathbf{H}$ transform (12.132).

(12.23) Consider the transform ${}^4\mathbf{H}$ in (12.135a).

(a) Show that ${}^4\mathbf{H}$ does not diagonalize the Toeplitz matrix defined by $\mathbf{R}_{xx}(i,j) = \rho^{|i-j|}$.

(b) Show, however, that ${}^4\mathbf{H}$ diagonalizes a *dyadic* covariance matrix

$$\mathbf{R}_{dd} = \begin{bmatrix} \rho_0 & \rho_1 & \rho_2 & \rho_3 \\ \rho_1 & \rho_0 & \rho_3 & \rho_2 \\ \rho_2 & \rho_3 & \rho_0 & \rho_1 \\ \rho_3 & \rho_2 & \rho_1 & \rho_0 \end{bmatrix}$$

and that diagonal elements in the output acf are $(\rho_0+\rho_1+\rho_2+\rho_3)$, $(\rho_0-\rho_1+\rho_2-\rho_3)$, $(\rho_0+\rho_1-\rho_2-\rho_3)$ and $(\rho_0-\rho_1-\rho_2+\rho_3)$.

(12.24)   Show that in DFT representation

$$\sum_{k=0}^{N-1} |\theta(k)|^2 = \sum_{k=0}^{N-1} x^2(k)$$

Note that the right-hand term defines the energy in the sequence $x(n)$.

(12.25)   Show the following property of conjugate symmetry for 2-D DFT:

$$\theta(k,l) = \theta^* (mN-k, nN-l)$$

with $m,n = 0,1,2....$ Show that there are $(N^2/2)+2$ non-redundant complex coefficients and N^2 non-redundant numbers in the 2-D DFT representation.

(12.26)   Use the mmse rule (12.60) to derive the optimum bit allocation $\{R_k\}$ for the coefficient variances listed in Table 12.2. Compare the result with the bit-allocation rule used in Table 12.2.

(12.27)   Give the form of the basic vectors $\mathbf{b}_k'$ corresponding to the real-valued Fourier matrix $\mathbf{F}'$ and show their orthonormality.

(12.28)   Consider the input of Problem 12.23. Assume that a DFT (12.142) is used instead of the DWHT.

   (a)   Show that the coefficient variances $E[\Theta^2(k)]$ are $(4+6\rho_1+4\rho_2+2\rho_3)$, $(4-4\rho_2)$, $(4-6\rho_1+4\rho_2-2\rho_3)$ and $(4-4\rho_2)$.

   (b)   Hence show that the variance geometric means for the (i) speech and (ii) voiceband data examples are 0.57 and 0.64, respectively, corresponding to G_{TC} values of 1.75 and 1.6. Note that in the speech example, the performance of $^4\mathbf{F}$ is worse than that of $^4\mathbf{H}$ and nearly equal to that of $^2\mathbf{F}$. (The $N = 2$ transform $^2\mathbf{H} = {}^2\mathbf{F}$ had gains of 1.7 and 1.01 for speech and data signal statistics).

(12.29)   (a)   Show that $^4\mathbf{F}$ in (12.142) does not diagonalize the Toeplitz matrix defined by $\mathbf{R}_{xx}(i,j) = \rho^{|i-j|}$.

   (b)   Show, however, that $^4\mathbf{F}$ diagonalizes a *circular* covariance matrix $\mathbf{R}_{cc}$ in the form

$$\mathbf{R}_{cc} = \begin{bmatrix} \rho_0 & \rho_1 & \rho_2 & \rho_1 \\ \rho_1 & \rho_0 & \rho_1 & \rho_2 \\ \rho_2 & \rho_1 & \rho_0 & \rho_1 \\ \rho_1 & \rho_2 & \rho_1 & \rho_0 \end{bmatrix}$$

Show that resulting diagonal elements in the coefficient acf matrix are $(\rho_0+2\rho_1+\rho_2)$, $(\rho_0-\rho_2)$, $(\rho_0-2\rho_1+\rho_2)$ and $(\rho_0-\rho_2)$. Note that $\mathbf{R}_{cc}$ is not Toeplitz; the deviation is in the top right and bottom left corners. Note also that all rows are circularly shifted versions of the first row.

(12.30)   Consider the input of Problem 12.22 with $\sigma_x^2 = 1$, and the transform $^4\mathbf{C}$ in (12.160).

(a) Show that coefficient variances are $(4+6.3\rho_1+3.4\rho_2+1.1\rho_3)$, $(4+2.6\rho_1-3.4\rho_2-2.6\rho_3)$, $(4-2.6\rho_1-3.4\rho_2+2.6\rho_2)$ and $(4-6.3\rho_1+3.4\rho_2-1.1\rho_3)$.

(b) Hence show that the gains G_{TC} for the (i) speech and (ii) data signal examples in Problem 12.22 are 2.2 and 1.4, respectively. Note that the performance of DCT exceeds that of DHT and DFT for the speech example. Note also that the acf values of speech resemble an AR(1)-acf sequence ρ^n; $n = 0,1,2,3$ (with $\rho=0.825$), while the acf values of the data signal do not.

(12.31) Show that 2-D DCT can be obtained by sequential row and column operations involving 1-D transforms in the form $\boldsymbol{\Theta} = \mathbf{C}\mathbf{X}\mathbf{C}^T$ where $\mathbf{C}$ is that defined in (12.157a).

(12.32) Assume that the short-term spectrum of a speech signal can be approximately reconstructed by specifying pitch, spectral envelope and absolute spectrum level information using 32 bits of information, once every 16 ms. The spectral envelope information may be conveyed in one of several equivalent ways, such as AR-parameter, or *parcor* values.

(a) Consider that the above specification is used as side information for predictor updates in a 1 bit/sample DPCM-APF system. If the total bit rate I of the system should be 8 kb/s, and further, if the speech bandwidth W is to be 0.45 f_s, where f_s is the sampling rate, determine the maximum permissible value of W in the above system.

(b) Consider next that the short-term spectral representation is used for bit allocation updates in a DFT-ATC system. Let the bit rate I be 8 kb/s as in (a), but let the values of bandwidth and sampling rate be constrained to be full-bandwidth designs $W = 3.2\text{kHz}$ and $f_s = 8\text{kHz}$. Determine the maximum permissible value of R, the average number of bits available to quantize the DFT coefficients.

(12.33) Consider a 16 kb/s ATC coder. Assume that side information is transmitted in a total of 88 bits per 30 ms block of speech [Cox, 1980].

(a) Show that at $p_e = 10^{-3}$, the probability of one or more bit errors per side-information block is 0.0843. Assuming that any error can result in a lost block, show that one in every 12 blocks (or approximately 3 blocks per second) are effectively lost. Show also that if an error correcting code could correct 3 or fewer errors per block, the probability of losing a block is about 10^{-5}, or one lost block per hour. A coding theory bound says that 28 parity bits will suffice to correct up to 3 errors if there are 88 information bits. If a (116,28) code is employed for the side information, show that check bits account for 933 bps, and the bit rate available for coefficient quantization drops from 13.1 to about 12.1 kb/s.

(b) At $p_e = 10^{-2}$, show that about 3% of all side information will be lost with the (116,28) scheme in (a). If up to 7 errors can be corrected, side information will once again be well protected. From a coding theory bound, use of 61 parity bits will protect at least 7 errors. Show that the resulting (149,61) code for side information reduces the bit rate available for coefficient quantization to about 11.0 kb/s.

References

N. Ahmed and K. R. Rao, *Orthogonal Transforms for Digital Signal Processing,* Springer-Verlag, New York, 1975.

N. Ahmed, T. Natarajan and K. Rao, "Discrete Cosine Transform," IEEE Trans. on Computers, pp. 90-93, January 1974.

R. Bellman, *Introduction to Matrix Analysis*, McGraw-Hill, New York, 1960.

T. Berger, *Rate Distortion Theory*, Prentice-Hall, Englewood Cliffs, N.J., 1971.

S. J. Campanella and G. S. Robinson, "A Comparison of Orthogonal Transformations for Digital Speech Processing," IEEE Trans. on Communication Technology, pp. 1045-1049, December 1971.

W. Chen, C. H. Smith and S. Fralick, "A Fast Computational Algorithm for the Discrete Cosine Transform," IEEE Trans. on Communications, pp. 1004-1009, September 1977.

R. V. Cox, unpublished work, Bell Laboratories, 1980.

R. V. Cox, unpublished work, Bell Laboratories, 1981.

R. V. Cox and R. E. Crochiere, "Real-Time Simulation of Adaptive Transform Coding," IEEE Trans. on Acoustics, Speech and Signal Proc., pp. 147-154, April 1981.

R. V. Cox and A. G. Tescher, "Generalized Adaptive Transform Coding," Proc. Picture Coding Symposium, Asilomar, Calif., January 1976.

R. E. Crochiere, R. V. Cox and J. D. Johnston, "Real-Time Speech Coding," IEEE Trans. on Communications, pp. 621-634, April 1982.

W. R. Daumer, "Subjective Evaluation of Several Efficient Speech Coders," IEEE Trans. on Communications, pp. 655-662, April 1982.

L. D. Davisson, "Rate Distortion Theory and Applications," Proc. IEEE, pp. 800-808, July 1972.

D. F. Elliott and K. R. Rao, *Fast Transforms — Algorithms, Analyses and Applications,* Academic Press, New York, 1982.

R. C. Gonzalez and P. Wintz, *Digital Image Processing*, Addison-Wesley, Reading, Mass., 1977.

J. I. Guinlett, "Use of Activity Classes in Adaptive Transform Image Coding," IEEE Trans. on Communications, pp. 785-786, July 1975.

A. Habibi, "Comparison of nth Order DPCM Encoder with Linear Transformations and Block Quantization Techniques," IEEE Trans. on Communication Technology, pp. 948-956, February 1971.

A. Habibi, "Hybrid Coding of Pictorial Data," IEEE Trans. on Communications, pp. 614-624, May 1974.

A. Habibi, "Survey of Adaptive Image Coding Techniques," IEEE Trans. on Communications, pp. 1275-1284, November 1977.

A. Habibi, "An Adaptive Strategy for Hybrid Image Coding," IEEE Trans. on Communications, pp. 1736-1753, December 1981.

A. Habibi and G. S. Robinson, "A Survey of Digital Picture Coding," IEEE Computer, pp. 22-34, May 1974.

A. Habibi, A. S. Samulon and G. L. Fultz, "Adaptive Coding of MSS Imagery," Proc. Nat. Telecom. Conf., pp. 10.2.1-10.2.8, 1977.

H. Harmuth, *Transmission of Information by Orthogonal Functions*, Springer-Verlag, New York, 1972.

C. Heron, R. E. Crochiere and R. V. Cox, "A 32-band Sub-band/Transform Coder Incorporating Vector Quantization for the Transmission of Side Information," Proc. ICASSP, April 1983.

H. Hotelling, "Analysis of a Complex of Statistical Variables into Principal Components," J. Educational Psychology, pp. 417-441, 498-520, 1933.

Y. Huang and P. M. Schultheiss, "Block Quantization of Correlated Gaussian Random Variables," IEEE Trans. on Communication Systems, pp. 289-296, September 1963.

A. Jain, "A Fast Karhunen-Loeve Transform for a Class of Random Processes," IEEE Trans. on Communications, pp. 1023-1029, September 1976.

F. A. Kamanagar and K. R. Rao, "Interfield Hybrid Coding of Component Color Television Signals," IEEE Trans. on Communications, pp. 1740-1753, December 1981.

H. Karhunen, "Uber lineare Methoden in der Wahrscheinlichkeitsrechnung," Ann. Acad. Sci. Fenn., Ser. A.I.37, Helsinki, Finland, 1947.

K. Knowlton, "Progressive Transmission of Grey-Scale and Binary Pictures by Simple, Efficient and Lossless Encoding Schemes," Proc. IEEE, pp. 885-896, July 1980.

H. P. Kramer and M. V. Mathews, "A Linear Encoding for Transmitting as Set of Correlated Signals," IRE Trans. on Information Theory, pp. 41-46, September 1956.

H. J. Landau and D. Slepian, "Some Computer Experiments in Picture Processing for Bandwidth Reduction," Bell System Tech. J., pp. 1525-1540, May-June 1971.

W. Mauersberger, "Adaptive Transformationskodierung von digitalisierten Bildsignalen," Thesis, RWTH Aachen, 1980.

H. Murakami, Y. Hatori and H. Yamamoto, "Comparison between DPCM and Hadamard Transform Coding in the Composite Coding of the NTSC Color TV Signal," IEEE Trans. on Communications, pp. 469-479, March 1982.

M. J. Narasimha and A. M. Peterson, "On the Computation of the Discrete Cosine Transform," IEEE Trans. on Communications, pp. 934-936, June 1978.

T. R. Natarajan and N. Ahmed, "On Interframe Transform Coding," IEEE Trans. on Communications, pp. 1323-1329, November 1977.

A. N. Netravali and J. O. Limb, "Picture Coding: A Review," Proc. IEEE, pp. 366-406, March 1980.

K. Nitadori, "Linear transform coding and predictive coding" (in Japanese), Trans. IECE Japan, February 1970.

P. Noll, "Adaptive Transform Coding of Speech Signals," Proc. Int. Conf. on Communications, pp. 13.5-306—13.5-309, 1977.

J. B. O'Neal and T. R. Natarajan, "Coding Isotropic Images," IEEE Trans. on Information Theory, pp. 697-707, November 1977.

J. Pearl, "On Coding and Filtering Stationary Signals by Discrete Fourier Transforms," IEEE Trans. on Information Theory, pp. 229-232, March 1973.

A. Ploysongsang and K. R. Rao, "DCT/DPCM Processing of NTSC Composite Video Signal," IEEE Trans. on Communications, pp. 541-549, March 1982.

W. Pratt, Digital Image Processing, John Wiley, New York, 1978.

W. K. Pratt, J. Kane and H. C. Andrews, "Hadamard Transform Image Coding," Proc. IEEE, pp. 58-68, January 1969.

J. A. Roese, W. K. Pratt and G. S. Robinson, "Interframe Cosine Transform Image Coding," IEEE Trans. on Communications, pp. 1329-1339, November 1977.

A. Segall, "Bit Allocation and Encoding for Vector Sources," IEEE Trans. on Information Theory, pp. 162-169, March 1976.

F. Shum, A. Elliot and W. Brown, "Speech Processing with Walsh-Hadamard Transforms," IEEE Trans. on Audio and Electroacoustics, pp. 174-179, June 1973.

M. Tasto and P. A. Wintz, "Image Coding by Adaptive Block Quantization," IEEE Trans. on Communications, pp. 957-971, December 1971.

A. G. Tescher, "Transform Image Coding," in *Advances in Electron Physics,* Supplement 12, Academic Press, New York, 1979.

J. Tribolet and R. E. Crochiere, "Frequency Domain Coding of Speech," IEEE Trans. on Acoustics, Speech and Signal Proc., pp. 512-530, October 1979.

Z. Wang, "Reconsideration of a Fast Computational Algorithm for the Discrete Cosine Transform," IEEE Transaction on Communications, pp. 121-123, January 1983.

P. A. Wintz, "Transform Picture Coding," Proc. IEEE, pp. 809-820, July 1972.

W. C. Wong and R. Steele, "Partial Correction of Transmission Errors in Walsh Transform Image Coding Without Recourse to Error Correction Coding," Electronics Lett., pp. 298-300, May 1978.

R. Zelinski, "On Some Asymptotic Properties of Orthogonal Transforms for Diagonalizing of Toeplitz Matrices," (in German), Technical Report No. 190, Heinrich Hertz Institut, Berlin, 1976.

R. Zelinski, "Effects of Transmission Errors on the Mean-Squared Performance of Transform Coding Systems," IEEE Trans. on Acoustics, Speech and Signal Proc., pp. 121-133, April 1979.

R. Zelinski, "An Adaptive Transform Coding System Based on Cepstral Control and Entropy Coding," Frequenz, pp. 193-198, 1982.

R. Zelinski and P. Noll, "Adaptive Block Quantization of Speech Signals" (in German), Technical Report No. 181, Heinrich Hertz Institut, Berlin, 1975.

R. Zelinski and P. Noll, "Adaptive Transform Coding of Speech Signals," IEEE Trans. on Acoustics, Speech and Signal Proc., pp. 299-309, August 1977.

R. Zelinski and P. Noll, "Approaches to Adaptive Transform Speech Coding at Low Bit Rates," IEEE Trans. on Acoustics, Speech and Signal Processing, pp. 89-95, February 1979.

Computer Projects

(1) **Generation and Analysis of an AR(1) Sequence**

Consider the i.i.d. Gaussian process $\{Z(n)\}$ with mean zero and variance 10000.

(a) Using a Gaussian random number generator program, simulate and plot the random sequence

$$\{Z(n)\} ; \quad n = 1,2,...,640$$

(b) Compute and plot the AR(1) sequence defined by

$$X(n) = 0.9X(n-1) + Z(n)$$

Compare with Fig. 2.16(a)(i).

(c) Compute and plot the acf $R_{xx}(k)$ for $k = 1,2,...,50$. Compare with Fig. 2.16(a)(ii).

(d) Use the approximation $R_{xx}(k) = 0$ for $k > 50$; use this to compute and plot the psd $S_{xx}(e^{j\omega})$. Compare with Figure 2.16(a)(iii).

(e) Compute the psd using (i) the periodogram (2.7) and (ii) the average of 5 periodograms, one for each of 5 nonoverlapping segments of $Z(n)$. Compare with Figure 2.16(a)(iii).

(f) Compute the spectral flatness measure using the results of (e). Compare with the theoretical value of $(1-0.9^2) = 0.19$ for the AR(1) process.

(2) **Design and Analysis of a 2-bit Max-Quantizer**

(a) Write an iterative program to design a mmse non-uniform quantizer for a Laplacian pdf input, with $R = 2$ bits/sample. Verify that the results are those of Table 4.3.

(b) Using the decision and reconstruction values from the iterative design, evaluate the *SNR*, and verify that the value is the result of Table 4.4.

(3) Quantization with Entropy Coding

Simulate the uniform-threshold quantization of a gamma pdf input. Use large values of L (both odd and even) and optimum reconstruction values given by (4.45b).

(a) Plot the entropy H_Q versus step size Δ.

(b) Plot the normalized error variance σ_q^2/σ_x^2 versus step size Δ.

(c) Plot the entropy as a function of normalized error variance. Compare with Figure 4.19(b).

(d) Repeat (a) (b) and (c) for a Laplacian input.

(4) Statistical Properties of Quantization Error

Quantize the samples of the AR(1) sequence in Project (1)(b) using mmse Max-quantizers with number of levels $L = 2$, 4 and 32. ($R = 1$, 2 and 5 bits per sample).

(a) Plot the reconstruction error sequences $r(n) = q(n)$ scaled by a factor 2^R, as in Figure 4.30.

(b) Compute, in each case, the error variances σ_r^2, σ_{rg}^2 and σ_{ro}^2, where g and o stand for granular noise and overload distortion. Also, compute the probabilities of overload.

(c) Compute the pdf of reconstruction error in each case. Compare with Figure 4.22.

(d) Compute and plot the normalized acf $\rho_{rr}(n)$ for the case of $L = 2$. Compare with the result of Figure 4.24(b). [Note that $\rho_{xx}(1) = 0.95$ in that example].

(e) Determine the values of the normalized crosscorrelation $\rho_{rx}(0)$ for $L = 2$ and 4. Compare with the values for $L = 2$ and $\rho_{xx}(1) = 0.9$ in Figure 4.24(c).

(f) Repeat (a) (d) and (e) for the case of $L = 2$ and a dithered quantization system. Use a dither signal with a uniform pdf in the range $(-\Delta/2, \Delta/2)$, and assume that the dither signal is eventually subtracted at the receiver.

(g) Repeat (a) (d) and (e) for the case of $L = 2$ and an oscillating two-level dither sequence $\{-3\Delta/8, \Delta/8, -\Delta/8, 3\Delta/8,...\}$.

(5) Comparison of 2-bit Quantizers

(a) Compute and plot a locally stationary Gauss-Markov sequence of length 640 samples, with $\rho_1 = 0.85$ and σ_x values of 1, 10, 100, 50 and 10 for five continuous segments of 128 samples each.

(b) Consider a 2 bit/sample Lloyd-Max nonuniform quantizer based on the long-time (640 sample-) averaged input variance, and the quantizer design of Table 4.3. Compute and plot the quantized output waveform, and the reconstruction error waveform magnified by a factor of 5. Determine the *SNR*, the five values of local *SNR* (one for each segment of 128 samples), and the overall segmental *SNR*, *SNRSEG*.

(c) Repeat (b) for a coding system based on μ-law companding ($\mu = 255$; $x_{max} = 200$) and a 2 bit/sample uniform quantizer designed by assuming a uniform pdf in $(-x_{max}, x_{max})$.

(d) Repeat (b) for an adaptive quantizer with a one-word memory, with $M_1 = 0.8$, $M_2 = 1.6$, and initial step size of 1.

(e) Repeat (b) for a forward-adaptive quantization system with a block length of 128 samples and an mmse step-size given by $0.996 \, \sigma_x(m)$; $m = 1,2,...,5$.

(6) Effects of Transmission Errors on 4-bit Quantizers

(a) Simulate an AR(1) sequence, as in Project 1(b), but for $n = 1, 2, \ldots ,64000$.

(b) Quantize the input using a 4 bit/sample AQB system with the multipliers of Table 4.14, a uniform quantization characteristic, an initial step-size of 1, and minimum and maximum step sizes of 1 and 512. Compute the values of SNR and $SNRSEG$, and plot the output $y(n)$.

(c) Repeat (b) for bit error rates of 10^{-4}, 10^{-3}, 10^{-2} and 10^{-1}, assuming an FBC code in each case. Compare with the characteristic of Figure 4.33(a) for $R = 2$.

(d) Repeat (b) and (c) using the robust adaptive quantizer of (4.199a) with $\beta = 31/32$.

(7) Toll Quality PCM Coding

(a) Simulate the digitally linearizable 8 bit/sample $A\,87.56$ PCM coding system of Table 5.3 for the 640-sample Gauss-Markov input of Project 5(a). Compute the SNR, the five values of local SNR (one for each segment of 128 samples), and the overall segmental $SNR, SNRSEG$. Plot the output and reconstruction error magnified by a factor of 100, as in Figure 1.4.

(b) Repeat (a) with a bit error rate of 10^{-2}.

(c) Enhance the output by (b) by using the following procedure for error detection followed by interpolation. For error detection, declare the sample at time n to be in error if the difference $y(n) - y_c(n-1)$ exceeds $\lambda\sigma_{y'}$ where $y_c(n-1)$ is the correct (or corrected) previous sample, and $\sigma_{y'}$ is the standard deviation of the difference signal in the error-free condition (a). Use the first-order interpolation algorithm $y_c(n) = 0.5 \, y(n-1) + 0.5 \, y(n+1)$ to correct a sample suspected to be in error. Determine the SNR-maximizing value of λ, and compare the corresponding output, SNR and $SNRSEG$ with the results of (a) and (b).

(8) Analysis of Linear Prediction
Consider the acf data in the last column of Table 2.2.

(a) Compute optimum prediction- and parcor- coefficients $\mathbf{h}$ and $\boldsymbol{\pi}$ for mmse linear prediction of order $N = 1, 2, \ldots ,8$.

(b) Compute the corresponding values of prediction gain $^N G_P$.

(c) Use the predictors of (a) to compute a set of autoregressive estimates of the psd that correspond to the acf data of Table 2.2. Compare with the long-time-averaged speech spectra in Figure 2.9(a).

(9) Comparison of 2-bit DPCM Techniques

(a) Compute and plot a locally stationary Gauss-Markov AR(1) sequence of length 640 samples, with $\sigma_x = 100$ and ρ_1 values of 0.9, 0.95, 0.85, 0 and -0.5 for five continuous segments of 128 samples each.

(b) Consider a 2 bit/sample adaptive quantizer with a one-word memory with $M_1 = 0.8$, $M_2 = 1.6$, a uniform quantization characteristic, an initial step-size of 10, and minimum and maximum step sizes of 1 and 512. Compute and plot the quantized 2-bit PCM output $y(n)$ and the reconstruction error waveform magnified by a factor of 5. Determine the SNR, the five values of local SNR (one for each segment of 128 samples), and the overall segmental SNR, SNRSEG.

(c) Repeat (b) for 2-bit DPCM-AQB with $h_1 = 0.85$.

(d) Repeat (b) for 2-bit DPCM-AQB-APF assuming that h_1 is known and set equal to the appropriate ρ_1.

(e) Repeat (b) for 2-bit DPCM-AQB-APB based on the polarity-correlation gradient search

$$h_1(n+1) = h_1(n) + c \ sgn \ d(n) \ sgn \ y(n-1)$$

and a value of c that maximizes SNRSEG.

(f) Repeat for a 4 bit/sample DPCM-AQB-APB system. Use the AQB system of Table 4.14 and the APB system of Section 6.5.3.

(10) Comparison of Intraframe Predictors

(a) Generate a 32×32 2-D field based on an autoregressive model and a separable acf with $\rho_v = \rho_h = 0.95$, and a unit-variance innovations process (2.138).

(b) Simulate a 3 bit/sample DPCM system based on first order prediction, using the previous horizontal neighbor and prediction coefficient 0.95. Compute the SNR.

(c) Repeat with first-order prediction based on the previous vertical neighbor.

(d) Repeat with 2-D prediction of order three, with coefficients 0.95, 0.95 and -0.95^2 (Example 6.5; case of $J = 2$) for horizontal, vertical and diagonal neighbors. Compare the SNR (dB) gain over (b) or (c) with the factor of two improvement expected in the separable acf model.

(11) Noise Feedback Coding
Consider the AR(1) input of Project 1(b).

(a) Simulate a 3 bit/sample DPCM-AQF-APF coder with $\Delta = 0.996$ $\sigma_z = 99.6$ (which is the mmse step size, ignoring quantization error feedback), and first-order prediction with $h_1 = 0.9$. Compute the SNR and plot the psd $S_{rr}(e^{j\omega})$ of reconstruction noise.

(b) Repeat (a) for D*PCM with an mmse design of h_1 (7.18).

(c) Repeat (a) for the one-tap NFC coder of Figure 7.6.

(12) Deltamodulation with F=2
Consider the AR(1) input of Project 1(b).

(a) Use a lowpass filter program to bandlimit the sequence to a frequency slightly less than one-half of the sampling rate. Oversample the output of the filter by a factor 2.

(b) Determine SNRF-maximizing step-size in LDM coding, assuming that the LDM staircase output is filtered by the lowpass filter in (a).

(c) Plot $y(n)$, $y_F(n)$, $r(n)$ and $r_F(n)$ using the best design in (b), as in Figure 8.3.

(d) Compute the values of SNR and $SNRF$. Compare the value of filtering gain G_F with the theoretical estimate of $10 \log F = 3$ dB.

(e) Repeat (c) for a bit error rate of 10^{-2}.

(f) Repeat (c) and (d) for ADM with a one-bit memory, with multiplier $M_1 = M_2^{-1} = 1.2$, an initial step size of 10, and minimum and maximum step sizes of 1 and 512.

(13) Generalized Lloyd-Max Vector Quantizer

(a) Write an iterative, generalized Lloyd-Max program to design a vector quantizer for a Gaussian pdf input, with $N = 8$ and $R = 1$ bit/sample. Compute the SNR. Verify that the result is that of Table 9.1.

(b) Repeat for $N = 2$ and $R = 1,2,...$ for a uniform pdf in $(0,1)$. Verify that the partitioning of the 2-D space by the VQ algorithm evolves toward a hexagonal lattice for large values of R.

(14) Sub-band Coding (M=4; R=2 bits/sample)
Simulate a four-band, 2 bit/sample SBC system for the input of Project 5(a), using a QMF tree with 32-tap and 16-tap filter components of Table 11.1 for the first and second stages of the tree. Use the AQB system of Project 5(d) for the quantization of the sub-band signals.

(a) Compute the SNR for each band and the overall SNR.

(b) Plot the input $x(n)$, and the output $y(n)$, as well as the sub-band outputs $y_k(n)$; $k = 1$ to 4.

(c) Compute the variances and normalized adjacent sample correlations in individual sub-band signals $x_k(n)$.

(d) Use the variances in (c) to obtain a mmse bit allocation. Use this to repeat (a) and (b). Compare the SNR gain over the fixed bit allocation system with the theoretical maximum gain of 0.19^{-1} mentioned in Project 1(f).

(15) Eigenvectors and Eigenvalues
Consider a zero-mean AR(1) process with $\rho = 0.95$ and variance $\sigma_x^2 = 1$. Use an eigenvector computation program to compute eigenvectors and eigenvalues for $N = 2$ and 8 (See (12.102) and Table 12.1). Note that the sum of eigenvalues is equal to $N\sigma_x^2 = N$ in each case.

(16) Transform Coding (R=2 bits/sample)
Simulate a 2 bit/sample TC system for the input of Project 1(b), using the DCT, uniform quantizers and values of block length $N = 4$, 32 and 128.

(a) Compute the SNR and $SNRSEG$, and plot the output $y(n)$ for each value of N.

(b) Compute the variances of the transform coefficients and determine the mmse bit allocation for each value of N.

(c) Repeat (a) for a zonal coding system that retains the first $N/2$ coefficients and quantizes them using 4 bits/sample.

(d) Repeat (a) for an ATC system using the mmse bit allocation obtained in (b).

Compare the gain in *SNR* with the theoretical value obtained from the variance distribution in (b).

(17) Speech input

Repeat relevant parts of Projects 1 through 16 for the speech input of Table CP.1. Compare the 16 kb/s speech outputs in Projects 2, 5, 9 and 12 with those resulting from simulations of the toll-quality systems in Projects 7 and 9(f). [In the projects involving adaptive quantization, maintain the ratio of 512 between maximum and minimum step size, but change the values of initial, minimum and maximum step sizes as needed, to provide a good match to the amplitude levels in Table CP.1].

(18) Image input

Repeat relevant parts of Projects 10, 13(a) and 16 for the image input of Table CP.2. Assume a (8×8) 2D approach in the ATC and VQ projects.

Table CP.1   The speech sequence of Figure 1.4(a). The eight columns represent contiguous segments of 4 ms duration. The total duration is 32 ms (256 samples at 8 kHz).

−120	−166	144	−1381	−3150	418	1860	−3690
186	1087	363	−899	3013	−603	2621	−3565
−348	−497	−341	−1012	−2460	−2202	2790	−2645
−517	−991	−203	−637	−2001	−3100	3551	−1439
555	1034	373	−73	−1129	−3740	3473	−79
−5	606	106	−1	−5	−4572	1997	1097
−434	−1205	−98	594	1023	−5140	837	1682
17	523	86	1112	1795	−4530	380	2373
595	644	227	867	2596	−3996	−1169	3352
−225	−706	54	1369	3491	−3005	−3620	3431
−473	205	88	1585	3482	−1731	−4224	3091
189	320	37	968	3114	−308	−5309	3414
237	−642	−136	1164	2508	1260	−6060	2477
−3	512	337	1420	2256	2898	−5987	450
−188	294	359	709	1581	4169	−5841	−891
117	−892	−281	403	231	5079	−4288	−1903
−249	3	−4	402	−612	5698	−3035	−3887
12	688	772	181	−666	5376	−1301	−5615
617	−525	317	105	−1222	4730	703	−5664
−932	−298	−34	220	−1628	3589	2439	−6152
−92	412	427	540	−1490	2403	4205	−6432
970	−9	610	882	−980	760	5564	−5684
−497	−331	296	693	−747	−658	6520	−4636
−592	9	318	538	−402	−1734	6693	−2713
873	−79	90	503	284	−2531	5896	−569
−175	11	−192	304	827	−3103	4825	1284
−314	80	−17	−296	1530	−3249	3262	3138
178	−505	−583	−1051	2143	−2651	1413	4577
−249	−200	−1108	−1640	2147	−1758	−429	5609
149	449	−863	−2066	2117	−870	−1887	6757
451	−196	−946	−2706	1361	−17	−2974	7069
−884	−538	−1505	−3267	1078	659	−3409	6248

Table CP.2 The 32×32 image sequence of Figure CP.1(b). The 32 rows represent scan lines with 32 pixels per scan line. Intensity levels of 255 and 0 represent pure white and pure black [R. Baker, 1983].

```
118 113  85 101 161 151 151 163 177 174 165 167 131 124 147 158 181 189 166 148 144 147 145 123 128 129 138 143 148 149 148 156
118  85 101 151 140 144 157 162 178 173 176 169 134 108 159 173 183 170 154 140 138 141 125 129 134 134 144 147 151 152 154 154
 89  90 141 146 140 138 145 166 178 172 176 172 149 107 159 180 172 153 141 133 127 128 128 131 135 139 146 149 147 153 153 158
 84 141 158 134 138 138 143 155 176 177 173 174 163 134 167 169 148 148 135 126 134 140 134 133 139 140 147 150 150 152 154 160
129 161 140 144 147 137 140 156 179 181 172 177 167 162 170 160 148 132 126 134 138 140 138 139 141 143 148 157 153 152 156 155
171 145 152 160 153 141 138 157 177 179 177 178 170 169 164 124  84  97 113 120 127 135 139 141 144 149 153 153 156 158 156 155
154 147 162 170 151 133 129 155 179 183 185 180 179 159  80  42  58  74  81  95 104 106 114 128 141 147 151 157 160 157 153 154
150 161 174 180 143 133 138 168 179 186 186 185 144  72  67  75  75  69  64  66  54  63  75  86 109 130 145 155 162 156 154 154
163 170 186 174 135 133 149 174 180 186 183 131  91 101 116 114 114 105  93  81  61  34  36  36  53  70 106 130 150 152 153 157
168 183 188 155 129 144 166 182 188 179 113  84 102 115 123 117 113 130 127 109  88  74  54  45  36  32  41  67 112 138 145 145
178 190 179 141 135 159 181 189 173  94  82  93  93 107 105 106  72 118 131 117  90  97  63  63  56  50  47  51  71 104 138 138
186 190 167 147 150 174 192 158  74  66  74  70  73  79  80  75  26  67 116  80  61  66  68  88  68  76  65  69  68  91 116 126
129 186 170 157 169 190 155  55  54  55  51  59  37  34  35  31  16  30  47  24  20  25  52  87  65  92  85  81  82  89 102 116
190 178 174 170 189 133  43  33  38  32  22  27  23  22  20  19  21  25  26  25  16  11  14  28  85 106  92  91  89  93 104 111
186 179 179 182 141  42  32  31  19  20  21  23  25  19  15  17  16  38  67  57  28  18  14  13  27  75 102  97  90  92 100 107
187 179 188 145  42  41  33  23  18  21  20  20  19  18  16  25  28  70 151 150  88  36  13  12  14  42  88  99  89  90  99 101
187 192 154  55  52  43  26  18  12  27  50  30  35  28   9  30  48  57 174 188 168 127  43  25  59  41  79  88  82  86  96 101
192 172  70  65  54  34  22  19  15  35  73  49  47  63  27  41  67  40 174 191 189 176 110  38  76  65  64  82  76  84  90 100
177  90  71  83  73  56  50  27  14  38  72  89  39  54  59  55  31  98 199 199 197 193 148  65  54  83  58  72  74  80  84  94
 92  78  84  95  93  89  81  60  17  25  69  87  83  47  31  43  95 177 193 193 189 178 136  95  66  87  75  75  86  78  84  94
 82  86  82  87 105 106  99  84  54  50  64  81 101  97  90 117 167 184 191 196 191 159 109 115  92  78  95  81  78  85  91  91
 88  90  96  91 107 114 110 104  94  72  67  69  83 100 116 128 139 156 164 164 158 158 133 113  95  95  95  87  81  81  90  93
 95  94 100  99 106 110 111 112 107  92  99  91  71  82  62  91 103 102 110 100 126 145 151 155 141 110  87  87  86  90  88  93
 98 101 110 104 110 112 112 110 113 113 113  99  84  90  70  97 106  99  89  92 124 120 130 131 118 103  86  84  92  96  89  89
 98 103 114 111 115 116 120 113 108 112 119 107 107 104  95  99 106 107 106 120 126 129 124 118 122 119  89  87  97  99  92  90
102 111 117 122 122 119 122 123 124 121 117 110 114 111 108 111 113 122 125 131 136 137 133 135 137 111  95  95 100 100  92  87
 98 108 118 122 124 125 132 133 132 132 129 121 124 129 124 131 135 139 142 145 140 144 134 141 132 107  93  99 106  99  88  90
102 105 117 119 126 127 135 142 135 139 148 148 140 139 141 140 150 151 148 145 140 147 139 141 124 106 102 111 107  99  93  91
104 103 112 120 125 127 133 145 135 141 148 153 148 143 142 144 148 148 145 143 148 147 142 131 121 109 104 110 102  96  89  92
 97 105 111 121 120 127 132 142 145 144 150 153 149 156 153 151 148 144 145 153 153 151 140 129 120 114 107 110 107  99  91  96
100 105 112 119 119 126 132 141 147 148 149 158 151 145 156 155 157 155 151 152 154 149 143 133 120 115 118 112 108 100  95  95
 95 102 112 111 121 126 131 140 143 148 150 157 156 154 154 155 153 154 155 156 150 142 135 128 126 117 113 111 108 103  94  94
```

Figure CP.1 (a) the "woman with hat" image; and (b) a subimage which includes the woman's left eye, eyebrow and a nice diagonal edge formed by a portion of the brim of her hat [R. Baker, 1983].

(a)

(b)
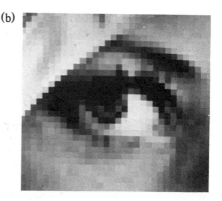

Appendix A

Deterministic Signals and Linear Systems

In this book we deal with deterministic and stochastic signals, both in continuous-time and discrete-time representations. The continuous-time versions, however, are mainly of interest in discussing sampling and certain results in DM coding; and unless otherwise mentioned, we shall assume *discrete-time* signals obtained by sampling a continuous-time signal, a sample function of a random process. In the amplitude domain, waveforms such as speech are either strictly continuous, or as is usual in processing and computer simulations of coding, regarded to be so, in view of a very fine quantization (say, to 4096 levels) of uncoded inputs.

A.1   Fourier Representation

In discrete-time systems [Oppenheim and Willsky, 1983], we are concerned with sequences $\{x(n)\}$ where $x(n)$ denotes its nth sample. Let $\{x(n)\}$ be absolutely summable, i.e.,

$$\sum_{n=-\infty}^{\infty} |x(n)| < \infty \tag{A.1}$$

Then $\{x(n)\}$ has a Fourier representation given by the *Fourier Transform*

$$X(e^{j\omega}) = \sum_{n=-\infty}^{\infty} x(n) \, e^{-jn\omega} \tag{A.2a}$$

and the *Inverse Fourier Transform* is then

$$x(n) = \frac{1}{2\pi} \int_{-\pi}^{\pi} X(e^{j\omega}) \, e^{jn\omega} d\omega \qquad (A.2b)$$

which can be easily proved by inserting $x(n)$ in (A.2a). $X(e^{j\omega})$ is a measure of the frequency content of the signal $x(n)$. For example, $X(0)$, which is the sum of all signal samples, is simply a zero frequency- or dc term. Also, $X(e^{j\omega})$ is periodic with 2π since $\exp[j(n+2\pi)\omega] = \exp(jn\omega)$; thus $X(\cdot)$ can be viewed as a Fourier series representation where the Fourier coefficients are the samples of the sequence. Another way of representing sequences is given by the two-sided z-transform, where z is a complex variable:

$$X(z) = \sum_{n=-\infty}^{\infty} x(n)z^{-n} \qquad (A.3a)$$

$$x(n) = \frac{1}{2\pi j} \int X(z) \, z^{n-1} dz \qquad (A.3b)$$

We note that $X(z)$ is an infinite power series in the variable z^{-1}. Sequence $\{x(n)\}$ is z-transformable if $X(z)$ converges, which will be the case for z values within a region of convergence. In (A.3b), the integration path can be any closed path in the region of convergence within the z-plane. Evaluating the z-transform on a circle of unit radius, i.e., $z = e^{j\omega}$, yields the Fourier transform.

A.1.1 The Discrete Fourier Transform

The *Discrete Fourier Transform* (DFT) is another representation of interest. If $\{x(n)\}$ is a sequence that is periodic with a period of N samples,

$$x(n) = x(n+N) \qquad (A.4)$$

it has a DFT

$$\theta(k) = \frac{1}{\sqrt{N}} \sum_{n=0}^{N-1} x(n)e^{-j2\pi kn/N} \; ; \qquad k = 0, 1, ..., N-1 \qquad (A.5a)$$

where $\theta(k)$ is the kth *Fourier or* DFT *coefficient*. The *inverse transform* (IDFT) is

$$x(n) = \frac{1}{\sqrt{N}} \sum_{k=0}^{N-1} \theta(k) \, e^{+j2\pi kn/N} \qquad (A.5b)$$

[In digital signal processing literature, the scaling factor $1/\sqrt{N}$ in (A.5a) is usually left out, and the factor $1/\sqrt{N}$ in (A.5b) replaced by $1/N$]. The DFT and IDFT form a so-called *unitary transform* pair (Appendix B and Chapter 12). Note that $\{x(n)\}$ is represented by a finite sum of sinusoids and that the DFT is a periodic repetition of a sequence of N spectral lines $\theta(k)$, the DFT coefficients. These coefficients are the equally spaced points $e^{j2\pi k/N}$ of $X(z)$ on the unit circle scaled by $1/\sqrt{N}$. This implies that they correspond to samples of the continuous transform at values $0, 2\pi/N, 4\pi/N, ..., 2\pi(N-1)/N$. Time sampling with T implies that the spectral samples are multiples of the angular frequency $2\pi/NT$.

The DFT is also unique for describing a finite duration sequence $\{x(n)\}$ that is zero for $n < 0$ and $n \geq N$ as long as only the values within the interval are taken into account. It is important, however, to bear in mind that when using the DFT representation *all sequences behave as if they were periodic.* It is easy to see that

$$\theta(N/2 + l) = \theta^*(N/2 - l) ; \quad l = 0, 1, 2, ..., (N/2 - 1) \qquad (A.6)$$

for real-valued $x(\cdot)$ and even N, with * denoting a *complex conjugate*. The magnitude of the Fourier transform, $|\theta(k)|$, is the *amplitude spectrum*, $\tan^{-1}[\text{Im}\{\theta(k)\}/\text{Re}\{\theta(k)\}]$ is the *phase spectrum*, and $|\theta(k)|^2$ is the *energy spectrum*, representing the energy contributed by the spectral line k. Equation (A.6) shows that amplitude and energy spectra are even about $N/2$ and that the phase spectrum is odd. Representations of (A.5) by matrices and basis vectors were introduced in Chapter 12.

A.1.2 Other Discrete Transforms

We should note at this point that the DFT is one of many possible transforms. A *general discrete transform* can be expressed as

$$\theta(k) = \sum_{n=0}^{N-1} x(n)\, a(k,n) \qquad (A.7)$$

where $a(k,n)$ is the *forward transformation kernel*. The *general inverse transform* is

$$x(n) = \sum_{k=0}^{N-1} \theta(k)\, b(k,n) \qquad (A.8)$$

where $b(k,n)$ is the *inverse transformation kernel*. We use various transforms and their basis vector interpretations in Transform Coding (Chapter 12).

A.2 Two-Dimensional (2-D) Signals

Two-dimensional (2-D) representations of signals are a useful tool for studying problems in image processing and image coding. In fact, we shall call a 2-D representation an *image* (for example, a luminance field). We are mainly concerned with *discrete images* which have been obtained by spatially sampling points of a space-continuous image. Such a sampling can be based on a 2-D procedure or on line-scanning (Chapter 3). Moving images are actually three-dimensional (3-D) signals; they are sampled in time in addition to being sampled in space.

Let $x(m,n)$ be a sample amplitude of a discretized 2-D monochromatic image. It represents the intensity or luminance value, or *gray level* at spatial coordinates m,n (m is the row, n is the column). As in 1-D notation, we use the term $\{x(m,n)\}$ to describe a sequence that spreads out spatially in two directions. Thus, this 2-D sequence is a function of two integer variables. The intensity may be amplitude-continuous or may be discretized itself. In the latter case we use the term *digital image* [Rosenfeld and Kak, 1976] [Gonzalez and Wintz, 1977]. Indeed, processing and encoding of images are usually based on digital images (with, say, 64 to 256 grey levels). These finely quantized intensities will often be considered as being amplitude-continuous.

A.2.1 The Two-Dimensional DFT

If the 2-D sequence $\{x(m,n)\}$ is absolutely summable [see (A.1)]:

$$\sum_{m=-\infty}^{\infty} \sum_{n=-\infty}^{\infty} |x(m,n)| < \infty \qquad \text{(A.9)}$$

then it can be represented by a 2-D Fourier transform with spatial frequencies

$$X(e^{j\omega_1}, e^{j\omega_2}) = \sum_{m=-\infty}^{\infty} \sum_{n=-\infty}^{\infty} x(m,n) e^{-j\omega_1 m} e^{-j\omega_2 n} \qquad \text{(A.10)}$$

where we have assumed a grid with unity distances in both directions. $X(\cdot,\cdot)$ is periodic in both ω_1 and ω_2 with period 2π in each. Formally, we may also define a two-dimensional z-transform [Oppenheim and Schafer, 1975] [Rabiner and Gold, 1975] [Merserau and Dudgeon, 1975] in a hyperplane; the Fourier transform is then equal to the z-transform evaluated on the surface $e^{j\omega_1}$, $e^{j\omega_2}$:

$$X(z_1, z_2) = \sum_{m=-\infty}^{\infty} \sum_{n=-\infty}^{\infty} x(m,n) \, z_1^{-m} z_2^{-n} \qquad \text{(A.11)}$$

As in the 1-D case, $X(e^{j\omega_1}, e^{j\omega_2})$ is a measure of the frequency content of the signal. In the case of $\omega_1 = \omega_2 = 0$, we find that $X(0,0)$ is just the sum of all image elements, i.e., it represents the zero frequency- or dc term. Slowly varying signals will have Fourier transforms which are mostly concentrated near the origin of the (ω_1, ω_2) plane and rapidly varying sequences have a higher content for ω_1 and ω_2 close to π. (Note that the Fourier transform is periodic, with period 2π in both frequency directions. This is rediscussed in the example of Figure 12.14).

The original sequence samples $x(m,n)$ can be recovered by the inverse operation

$$x(m,n) = \frac{1}{4\pi^2} \int_{-\pi}^{\pi} \int_{-\pi}^{\pi} X(e^{j\omega_1}, e^{j\omega_2}) \, e^{j\omega_1 m} e^{j\omega_2 n} d\omega_1 d\omega_2 \qquad \text{(A.12)}$$

As in the 1-D case, transforms (A.10) and (A.12) suffer from the computational disadvantage that they are functions of continuous variables. One can also define a

2-D *Discrete Fourier Transform* for a (square) array of $N \times N$ image elements:

$$\theta(k,l) = \frac{1}{N} \sum_{m=0}^{N-1} \sum_{n=0}^{N-1} x(m,n) e^{-j2\pi(km+ln)/N} \; ; \quad k,l = 0,1,...,N-1 \quad \text{(A.13)}$$

where $\theta(k,l)$ is a *Fourier or DFT coefficient* and its inverse is

$$x(m,n) = \frac{1}{N} \sum_{k=0}^{N-1} \sum_{l=0}^{N-1} \theta(k,l) \; e^{j2\pi(km+ln)/N} \quad \text{(A.14)}$$

Also, as in the 1-D case, the image and transform are both periodic, in spatial and (two) frequency domains, respectively.

The transform $\theta(k,l)$ can also be expressed in the *separable form*

$$\theta(k,l) = \frac{1}{\sqrt{N}} \sum_{m=0}^{N-1} e^{-j2\pi km/N} \frac{1}{\sqrt{N}} \sum_{n=0}^{N-1} x(m,n) \; e^{-j2\pi ln/N} \quad \text{(A.15)}$$

A comparison with (A.5a) shows that the second term is just a 1-D DFT yielding $\theta(m,l)$ — it is the 1-D DFT of row m. A second step is to obtain

$$\theta(k,l) = \frac{1}{\sqrt{N}} \sum_{m=0}^{N-1} \theta(m,l) \; e^{-j2\pi km/N} \quad \text{(A.16)}$$

which is again a 1-D DFT operation along columns. Therefore a 2-D DFT can be carried out by successive computations of 1-D DFT's. In practice, row and column operations can be interchanged and DFT redundancies and fast DFT (FFT) algorithms can be utilized for efficient computation.

A.2.2   General 2-D Transforms

As in the 1-D case, the 2-D DFT is only a special transform. Very generally, a 2-D transform has the form

$$\theta(k,l) = \sum_{m=0}^{N-1} \sum_{n=0}^{N-1} x(m,n) \, a(k,l,m,n) \quad \text{(A.17)}$$

For *separable* transforms,

$$a(k,l,m,n) = a_1(k,m) \, a_2(l,n) \quad \text{(A.18)}$$

A.3   Linear Systems

A.3.1   1-D Linear Systems

A linear, time-(or shift-) invariant, time-discrete system is specified by its *impulse response or weighting function* $\{h(n)\}$, which is the response to a unit-sample sequence $\{\delta(n)\}$ with

$$\delta(n) = \begin{cases} 1 & n=0 \\ 0 & n \neq 0 \end{cases} \tag{A.19}$$

The system is *causal* if $\{h(n)\} = 0$ for $n < 0$ and it is *stable* if $\{h(n)\}$ is absolutely summable. It can be described in the frequency domain by its *frequency response*

$$H(e^{j\omega}) = \sum_{n=-\infty}^{\infty} h(n) e^{-jn\omega} \tag{A.20}$$

and in the z-domain by its *system function* or *transfer function*

$$H(z) = \sum_{n=-\infty}^{\infty} h(n)z^{-n} \tag{A.21}$$

Output $\{y(n)\}$ and input $\{x(n)\}$ of the system are related by the following equations:

$$y(n) = x(n) * h(n) = \sum_{k=-\infty}^{\infty} x(k) h(n-k) = \sum_{k=-\infty}^{\infty} h(k)x(n-k) \tag{A.22}$$

$$Y(e^{j\omega}) = X(e^{j\omega}) H(e^{j\omega}) ; \quad Y(z) = X(z) H(z) \tag{A.23}$$

The energy of the impulse response is

$$\alpha = \sum_{k=-\infty}^{\infty} h^2(k) \tag{A.24}$$

and it can be shown, by using the orthogonality of exponential functions and (A.2b), that

$$\alpha = \frac{1}{2\pi} \int_{-\pi}^{\pi} |H(e^{j\omega})|^2 d\omega \tag{A.25}$$

which is a form of *Parseval's theorem*.

We will sometimes use the fact that white noise of variance σ_z^2 at the input of a linear system of frequency response $H(e^{j\omega})$ produces a process variance $\alpha\sigma_z^2$ at its output. Indeed, since

$$S_{zz}(e^{j\omega}) = \sigma_z^2 \text{ and } S_{xx}(e^{j\omega}) = S_{zz}(e^{j\omega}) |H(e^{j\omega})|^2 , \tag{A.26}$$

we obtain

$$\sigma_x^2 = \frac{1}{2\pi} \int_{-\pi}^{\pi} S_{xx}(e^{j\omega}) d\omega = \alpha\sigma_z^2 \tag{A.27}$$

The factor α will be called the *power transfer factor*.

A generalization of (A.25) is worth noting:

$$\sum_{k=-\infty}^{\infty} h_1(k)\, h_2(k) = \frac{1}{2\pi} \int_{-\pi}^{\pi} H_1(e^{j\omega})\, H_2(e^{j\omega})\, d\omega \qquad (A.28)$$

Any time-invariant linear system can also be described by a difference equation

$$y(n) = \sum_{k=0}^{M} a_k x(n-k) + \sum_{k=1}^{N} b_k y(n-k) \qquad (A.29)$$

Taking the z-transform we obtain the system function

$$H(z) = \frac{Y(z)}{X(z)} = \frac{\displaystyle\sum_{k=0}^{M} a_k z^{-k}}{1 - \displaystyle\sum_{k=1}^{N} b_k z^{-k}} \qquad (A.30)$$

as the ratio of two polynomials. By determining the zeros of the polynomials,

$$H(z) = a_0\, z^{N-M} \frac{\displaystyle\prod_{k=1}^{M} (z - z_{0k})}{\displaystyle\prod_{k=1}^{N} (z - z_{\infty k})} \qquad (A.31)$$

$H(z)$ can thus be specified by the zeros z_{0k} and the poles $z_{\infty k}$ (these are the zeros of the denominator polynomial) in the z-plane. Special cases of importance are the *all-zero filters* without poles (except those for $z=0$), given by setting $b_k = 0$; $k = 1,2,...,N$:

$$H(z) = \sum_{k=0}^{M} a_k z^{-k} \qquad (A.32)$$

and the *all-pole filters* given by setting $a_0 = 1$; $a_k = 0$; $k = 1, 2, ..., M$:

$$H(z) = \frac{1}{1 - \displaystyle\sum_{k=1}^{N} b_k z^{-k}} \qquad (A.33)$$

The impulse response of the all-zero filter is finite for finite M-values. Thus it is absolutely summable and the filter is stable. The impulse response of the all-pole system is typically infinite. Stability is obtained if the zeros of the denominator polynomial $D(z) = 1 - \sum b_k z^{-k}$ lie inside the unit circle of the z-plane. The all-zero and all-pole filters are therefore called *finite impulse response* (FIR) and *infinite impulse response* (IIR) filters, respectively.

Example A.1. All-pole filter of order $N = 2$

Consider an all-pole filter

$$H(z) = (1 - b_1 z^{-1} - b_2 z^{-2})^{-1} \qquad (A.34)$$

Using $H(e^{j\omega})$, we can show that the power transfer factor is

$$\alpha = \frac{1 - b_2}{(1 + b_2)(1 - b_1 - b_2)(1 + b_1 - b_2)} \qquad (A.35)$$

We note that the above transfer function is an inverse prediction error filter, a DPCM decoder loop of second order (Chapter 6). ●

A.3.2 2-D Linear Systems

A linear shift-invariant *two-dimensional* (2-D) system is given by its impulse response $\{h(m,n)\}$. In image processing, $\{h(m,n)\}$ is called a *point spread function*. This impulse response $\{h(m,n)\}$ is the output of the system when the input is a two-dimensional *point source*, the unit-sample sequence $\{\delta(m,n)\}$ given by

$$\delta(m,n) = \begin{cases} 1 & m = n = 0 \\ 0 & otherwise \end{cases} \qquad (A.36)$$

Impulse response and *frequency response* are again a Fourier transform pair

$$H(e^{j\omega_1}, e^{j\omega_2}) = \sum_{m=-\infty}^{\infty} \sum_{n=-\infty}^{\infty} h(m,n) \, e^{-jm\omega_1} e^{-jn\omega_2} \qquad (A.37a)$$

$$h(m,n) = \frac{1}{4\pi^2} \int_{-\pi}^{\pi} \int_{-\pi}^{\pi} H(e^{j\omega_1}, e^{j\omega_2}) e^{jm\omega_1} e^{jn\omega_2} d\omega_1 d\omega_2 \qquad (A.37b)$$

The *system* or *transfer function* is

$$H(z_1, z_2) = \sum_{m=-\infty}^{\infty} \sum_{n=-\infty}^{\infty} h(m,n) z_1^{-m} z_2^{-n} \qquad (A.38a)$$

and the *power transfer factor* is

$$\alpha = \sum_{m=-\infty}^{\infty} \sum_{n=-\infty}^{\infty} h^2(m,n) = \frac{1}{4\pi^2} \iint |H(e^{j\omega_1}, e^{j\omega_2})|^2 d\omega_1 d\omega_2 \qquad (A.38b)$$

The output $y(m,n)$ for any given input $x(m,n)$ is again a convolution sum:

$$y(m,n) = \sum_{k=-\infty}^{\infty} \sum_{l=-\infty}^{\infty} x(k,l) h(m-k, n-l) = \sum_{k=-\infty}^{\infty} \sum_{l=-\infty}^{\infty} h(k,l) x(m-k, n-l) \quad (A.39)$$

Also,

$$Y(e^{j\omega_1}, e^{j\omega_2}) = X(e^{j\omega_1}, e^{j\omega_2}) \, H(e^{j\omega_1}, e^{j\omega_2}) \tag{A.40}$$

An important issue is the stability of 2-D filters. *A bounded input* should lead to a *bounded output* for (BIBO) stability. It can be shown [Shanks, Treitel and Justice, 1972] that this condition is equivalent to the requirement that the impulse response is absolutely summable:

$$\sum_{m=-\infty}^{\infty} \sum_{n=-\infty}^{\infty} |h(m,n)| < \infty \tag{A.41}$$

For FIR filters, $h(m,n)$ has only a finite number of nonzero terms, and stability is guaranteed. For IIR filters, stability is a very important design constraint [Huang, 1972] [Shanks, Treitel and Justice, 1972].

Example A.2. 2-D DPCM filter
Consider the transfer function

$$H(z_1, z_2) = \frac{1}{1 - bz_1^{-1} - cz_2^{-1} - dz_1^{-1}z_2^{-1}} \tag{A.42}$$

which plays an important role in 2-D DPCM as an inverse prediction error filter (Chapter 6). Use of $H(e^{j\omega_1}, e^{j\omega_2})$ shows that its power transfer factor is that given in (6.134):

$$\alpha = \frac{1}{[(1+b)^2-(c-d)^2]^{1/2}[(1-b)^2-(c+d)^2]^{1/2}} \tag{A.43}$$

Conditions for stability are given in (6.135). ●

A.4 Continuous-Time Signals and Systems

A continuous-time signal $x(t)$ has a Fourier representation

$$X(j\Omega) = \int_{-\infty}^{\infty} x(t)e^{-j\Omega t}\,dt \tag{A.44}$$

provided that $x(t)$ is absolutely integrable, i.e.,

$$\int_{-\infty}^{\infty} |x(t)|\,dt < \infty \tag{A.45}$$

The inverse Fourier transform is

$$x(t) = \frac{1}{2\pi} \int_{-\infty}^{\infty} X(j\Omega)e^{j\Omega t}\,d\Omega \tag{A.46}$$

Let $h(t)$ be the impulse response of a time-invariant linear system whose stability is guaranteed if $h(t)$ is absolutely integrable; the frequency response is then defined as

$$H(j\Omega) = \int_{-\infty}^{\infty} h(t)e^{-j\Omega t}dt \qquad (A.47)$$

Output and input are related by

$$y(t) = x(t)*h(t) = \int_{-\infty}^{\infty} x(\tau)h(t-\tau)d\tau$$

$$Y(j\Omega) = X(j\Omega)H(j\Omega) \qquad (A.48)$$

Example A.3. Rectangular time and frequency functions

Consider the rectangular time function shown in Figure A.1. We adopt the notation

$$x(t) = \text{rect}\left(\frac{t}{T}\right) = \begin{cases} 1 & |t| \leqslant T/2 \\ 0 & \text{otherwise} \end{cases} \qquad (A.49)$$

Its Fourier transform is

$$X(j\Omega) = T\,\frac{\sin \Omega\ T/2}{\Omega\ T/2} = T\text{si}\,(\Omega\ T/2) \qquad (A.50)$$

The si($\cdot$) function is invoked many times in this book, in the context of both continuous and discrete representations, and in both 1- and 2-D examples.

Figure A.1 A continuous-time signal and its Fourier transform.

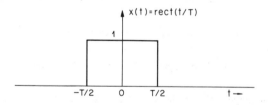

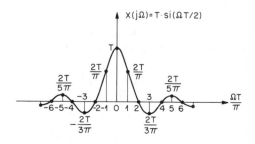

Consider next the rectangular frequency function

$$H(j\,\Omega) = \text{rect}\left[\frac{\Omega}{2\,\Omega_W}\right] \tag{A.51}$$

which is the ideal lowpass frequency response with angular cutoff frequency Ω_W radians, or $\Omega_W/2\pi$ Hz. Its impulse response is

$$h(t) = \frac{\Omega_W}{2\pi}\,\text{si}\left[\frac{\Omega_W t}{2}\right] \tag{A.52}$$

and it is discussed at length in Chapter 3. ●

Example A.4. Dirac delta time function

Consider a Dirac delta impulse $x(t) = \delta(t)$ defined by

$$\int_{-\infty}^{\infty} \delta(t)\,\phi(t)dt = \phi(0) \qquad \text{for } any \ \ \phi(t) \tag{A.53}$$

$\delta(t)$ exists only for $t = 0$. When setting $\phi(t) = e^{-j\Omega t}$, we may interpret this integral as a Fourier-integral of $\delta(t)$. Hence, $X(j\,\Omega) = 1$, i.e., the spectrum is constant for all frequencies. Alternatively, we have $X(j\,\Omega) = 2\pi\delta(\Omega)$ for $x(t) = 1$, i.e., a constant input is represented by a spectral line at zero frequency. ●

References

R. C. Gonzalez and P. Wintz, *Digital Image Processing,* Addison-Wesley, Reading, Mass., 1977.

T. S. Huang, "Stability of Two-Dimensional Recursive Filters," IEEE Trans. on Audio and Electroacoustics, pp. 159-163, June 1972.

R. M. Merserau and D. E. Dudgeon, "Two-Dimensional Digital Filtering," Proc. IEEE, pp. 610-623, April 1975.

A. V. Oppenheim and R. W. Schafer, *Digital Signal Processing,* Prentice-Hall, Englewood Cliffs, N.J., 1975.

A. V. Oppenheim and A. S. Willsky (with I. T. Young), *Signals and Systems,* Prentice-Hall, Englewood Cliffs, N.J. 1983.

L. R. Rabiner and B. Gold, *Theory and Application of Digital Signal Processing,* Prentice-Hall, Englewood Cliffs, N.J., 1975.

A. Rosenfeld and A. C. Kak, *Digital Picture Processing,* Academic Press, New York, 1976.

J. L. Shanks, S. Treitel and J. H. Justice, "Stability and Synthesis of Two-Dimensional Recursive Filters," IEEE Trans. on Audio and Electroacoustics, pp. 115-128, June 1972.

Appendix B

Matrix Operations

An $(M \times N)$ *matrix* is a rectangular array of MN numbers arranged in M rows and N columns. When $M = N$, the matrix is called a *square matrix*, and the number M, equal to N, is called its *order*.

A *column matrix* or *column vector* is a *rectangular matrix* defined by N elements

$$\mathbf{x} = \begin{bmatrix} x_0 \\ x_1 \\ \vdots \\ \vdots \\ x_{N-1} \end{bmatrix} = \{x_j\}_{j=0,1,\dots,N-1} \qquad (\text{B.1})$$

and its *transpose* is another rectangular matrix, a *row matrix* or *row vector*

$$\mathbf{x}^T = \begin{bmatrix} x_0 & x_1 & \cdots & x_{N-1} \end{bmatrix} \qquad (\text{B.2})$$

A *scalar* or *dot product* of two vectors $\mathbf{x}$ and $\mathbf{y}$ is

$$\mathbf{x}^T \cdot \mathbf{y} = \sum_{j=0}^{N-1} x_j y_j = \text{trace} \ (\mathbf{x}\mathbf{y}^T) = \text{trace} \ (\mathbf{A}) \qquad (\text{B.3})$$

where the *trace* is the sum of the elements of the main diagonal of a matrix.

A *dyad product* of two N-element vectors is a square matrix

$$\mathbf{x}\mathbf{y}^T = \mathbf{A} = \{x_i y_j\}_{i,j=0,1,...,N-1} \qquad (B.4)$$

Example B.1. Row and column matrices

$$\mathbf{x} = \begin{bmatrix} 2 \\ 3 \end{bmatrix} ; \mathbf{y} = \begin{bmatrix} 2 \\ 5 \end{bmatrix}$$

$$\mathbf{x}^T \cdot \mathbf{y} = [2 \quad 3] \cdot \begin{bmatrix} 2 \\ 5 \end{bmatrix} = 4 + 15 = 19$$

$$\mathbf{x}\mathbf{y}^T = \mathbf{A} = \begin{bmatrix} 2 \\ 3 \end{bmatrix} [2 \quad 5] = \begin{bmatrix} 4 & 10 \\ 6 & 15 \end{bmatrix}$$

$$\text{trace } (\mathbf{A}) = 4+15 = \mathbf{x}^T \cdot \mathbf{y} \qquad \bullet$$

An $N \times N$ *square matrix* is an ordered set of elements

$$\mathbf{A} = \begin{bmatrix} a_{00} & a_{01} & ... & a_{0,N-1} \\ a_{10} & a_{11} & ... & a_{1,N-1} \\ \cdot & & & \\ \cdot & & & \\ \cdot & & & \\ a_{N-1,0} & a_{N-1,1} & ... & a_{N-1,N-1} \end{bmatrix} = \{a_{ij}\}_{i,j=0,1,...,N-1} \qquad (B.5)$$

where i is the *row* index and j is the *column* index. Exchanging these indices yields the *transpose*

$$\mathbf{B} = \mathbf{A}^T = \{b_{ij}=a_{ji}\}_{i,\,j=0,\,1,\,...,\,N-1} \qquad (B.6)$$

Example B.2. Transpose

$$\mathbf{A} = \begin{bmatrix} 4 & 10 \\ 6 & 15 \end{bmatrix} ; \quad \mathbf{B} = \mathbf{A}^T = \begin{bmatrix} 4 & 6 \\ 10 & 15 \end{bmatrix} \qquad \bullet$$

$\mathbf{A}$ is called *symmetric* if $\mathbf{A}^T = \mathbf{A}$. Covariance and correlation matrices of stationary processes (Chapter 2) are always symmetric. A special case of a symmetric matrix is the *identity matrix*

$$\mathbf{I} = \begin{bmatrix} 1 & \cdot & \cdot & \cdot & 0 \\ \cdot & 1 & & & \cdot \\ \cdot & & 1 & & \cdot \\ \cdot & & & 1 & \cdot \\ 0 & \cdot & \cdot & \cdot & 1 \end{bmatrix} = \{\delta_{ij}\}_{i,\,j=0,\,1,\,...,\,N-1} \qquad (B.7)$$

where δ_{ij} is the *Kronecker delta* function ($\delta_{ij}=0$ if $i \neq j$; $\delta_{ij}=1$ if $i=j$). The identity matrix is also a special case of a *diagonal matrix*, which is a square matrix in which all elements outside the main diagonal are zero. **I** is also a special case of a *triangular* matrix, one in which all elements to the left or right of the main diagonal are zero.

The *transpose* possesses the following properties:

$$(\mathbf{A}^T)^T = \mathbf{A} ; \quad (\mathbf{A} + \mathbf{B})^T = \mathbf{A}^T + \mathbf{B}^T ; (\mathbf{AB})^T = \mathbf{B}^T \mathbf{A}^T \tag{B.8}$$

If **A** has complex elements, the *transpose conjugate* of **A**, denoted by $\mathbf{A}^{*T}$, is the matrix obtained from **A** by taking the transpose of the matrix whose elements are the complex conjugates of the elements of **A**. If $\mathbf{A} = \mathbf{A}^{*T}$, **A** is a *Hermitian* matrix. A real symmetric matrix is a special case.

A multiplication of two $N \times N$ matrices **A** and **B** leads to a *product matrix*

$$\mathbf{C} = \mathbf{AB} = \{c_{mn}\}_{m,n=0,1,\ldots,N-1} = \left\{ \sum_{k=0}^{N-1} a_{mk} \, b_{kn} \right\}_{m,n=0,1,\ldots,N-1} \tag{B.9}$$

Note that the element c_{mn} is the dot product of the mth row of **A** and the nth column of **B**.

Example B.3.   Multiplication

$$\mathbf{A} = \begin{bmatrix} 2 & 1 \\ -1 & 3 \end{bmatrix} ; \quad \mathbf{B} = \begin{bmatrix} 4 & 0 \\ 1 & 2 \end{bmatrix}$$

If **A** *premultiplies* **B**, $\mathbf{AB} = \begin{bmatrix} 9 & 2 \\ -1 & 6 \end{bmatrix}$

If **A** *postmultiplies* **B**, $\mathbf{BA} = \begin{bmatrix} 8 & 4 \\ 0 & 7 \end{bmatrix}$ ●

Matrix multiplication is not *commutative* ($\mathbf{AB} \neq \mathbf{BA}$) in general. One important exception is that

$$\mathbf{AI} = \mathbf{IA} = \mathbf{A} \tag{B.10a}$$

Also, the *cancellation* law *does not hold* in matrix multiplication

$$\mathbf{AB} = \mathbf{AC} \quad \text{does not imply} \quad \mathbf{B} = \mathbf{C} \tag{B.10b}$$

However, matrix multiplication is *associative*:

$$\mathbf{A}(\mathbf{BC}) = (\mathbf{AB})\mathbf{C} \tag{B.11}$$

and *distributive* with respect to addition:

$$\mathbf{A}(\mathbf{B+C}) = \mathbf{AB} + \mathbf{AC} \tag{B.12}$$

If **B** is a vector **b** (i.e., a one-column matrix),

$$C = AB = Ab = c \qquad (B.13)$$

is also a vector. Equation (B.13) can be looked at as a set of linear equations (see Examples B.5 and B.6).

Associated with every matrix **A** is a *determinant* $|A|$. It is a scalar whose value is defined as the sum of the products of elements in any row or column of **A** with respective *cofactors* c_{ij}. A cofactor of an element a_{ij} is defined as $(-1)^{i+j} m_{ij}$ where the *minor* m_{ij} is the determinant of the $(N-1) \times (N-1)$ submatrix obtained by removing the ith row and jth column in **A**. The determinant of an $(N \times N)$ matrix is thus defined in terms of the determinants of N square matrices, each of order $(N-1)$. The value of each m_{ij} is in turn defined in terms of appropriate submatrices of order $(N-2)$. The recursion is carried over until one encounters a 1×1 submatrix whose element is a_{ij}; its determinant is simply the scalar a_{ij}.

The determinant $|A|$ has the following properties:

$$(i) \quad |A| = 0 \quad \begin{array}{l} \text{if one row is zero or if} \\ \text{two rows are identical} \end{array} ; \quad (ii) \quad |A^T| = |A|$$

$$(B.14a)$$

$$(iii) \quad |A\,B| = |A|\,|B| \quad \begin{array}{l} \text{if } A \text{ and } B \text{ are} \\ \text{of same size} \end{array} ; \quad (iv) \quad |A^{-1}| = |A|^{-1}$$

For an $(N \times N)$ matrix **A**,

$$|\alpha A| = |\{\alpha a_{i,j}\}| = \alpha^N |A| \quad \text{for scalar } \alpha \qquad (B.14b)$$

$$|A| = \pm 1 \text{ if } A \text{ is orthogonal (or only } \pm 1) \qquad (B.14c)$$

$$|A| = \prod_{i=0}^{N-1} a_{ii} \quad \text{if } A \text{ is } diagonal \text{ or } triangular \qquad (B.14d)$$

Example B.4. Determinant

$$A = \begin{bmatrix} 2 & 1 \\ -1 & 3 \end{bmatrix} ; \quad |A| = a_{00}(-1)^{0+0} a_{11} + a_{01}(-1)^{0+1} a_{10} = 7$$

$$B = \begin{bmatrix} 3 & 1 & 0 \\ -1 & 2 & 4 \\ 5 & 6 & -2 \end{bmatrix} ; \quad |B| = 3(-28) - 1(-18) + 0() = -66 \qquad \bullet$$

The *inverse of a matrix* is defined by

$$A^{-1}A = AA^{-1} = I ; \quad A^{-1} = \frac{1}{|A|} \cdot A^a \qquad (B.15a)$$

The matrix A^a is the *adjoint matrix*, the transpose of the *cofactor matrix* $A^c = \{c_{ij}\}$. The inverse A^{-1} exists if $|A| > 0$ (*invertible* or *nonsingular* **A**).

Techniques of finding the inverse are described in the References. The properties of inverse matrices include:

$$(i)\ (\mathbf{A}^{-1})^{-1} = \mathbf{A}\ ; \qquad (ii)\ (\mathbf{AB})^{-1} = \mathbf{B}^{-1}\mathbf{A}^{-1}$$

$$(iii)\ (\mathbf{A}^{-1})^T = (\mathbf{A}^T)^{-1}\ ; \qquad (iv)\ (\mathbf{ABC})^{-1} = \mathbf{C}^{-1}\mathbf{B}^{-1}\mathbf{A}^{-1} \tag{B.15b}$$

For $N = 2$,

$$\mathbf{A}^{-1} = \frac{1}{|\mathbf{A}|}\begin{bmatrix} a_{11} & -a_{01} \\ -a_{10} & a_{00} \end{bmatrix} \tag{B.16}$$

Finally, a symmetric $\mathbf{A}$ implies a symmetric $\mathbf{A}^{-1}$.

Example B.5.   Inverse

$$\mathbf{A} = \begin{bmatrix} 2 & 1 \\ -1 & 3 \end{bmatrix}\ ; \qquad |\mathbf{A}| = 6+1 = 7\ ; \qquad \mathbf{A}^{-1} = \frac{1}{7}\begin{bmatrix} 3 & -1 \\ 1 & 2 \end{bmatrix}$$

$$|\mathbf{A}^{-1}| = \frac{1}{49}(6+1) = \frac{1}{7} = \frac{1}{|\mathbf{A}|} \qquad\qquad \bullet$$

If we have a set of linear equations

$$\mathbf{c} = \mathbf{A}\,\mathbf{b} \tag{B.17}$$

where $\mathbf{b}$ is unknown, the solution is

$$\mathbf{b} = \mathbf{A}^{-1}\mathbf{c} \tag{B.18}$$

by simple premultiplication with $\mathbf{A}^{-1}$. Solution of linear equations is a very important application for the inverse of a matrix.

Example B.6.   Linear equations

$$\mathbf{A} = \begin{bmatrix} 2 & 1 \\ -1 & 3 \end{bmatrix} \qquad \mathbf{c} = \begin{bmatrix} 7 \\ 4 \end{bmatrix}$$

so that

$$\begin{bmatrix} 7 \\ 4 \end{bmatrix} = \begin{bmatrix} 2 & 1 \\ -1 & 3 \end{bmatrix}\begin{bmatrix} b_0 \\ b_1 \end{bmatrix} \qquad \text{or} \qquad 7 = 2b_0 + 3b_1\ ; \qquad 4 = -1b_0 + 3b_1$$

Therefore,

$$\mathbf{b} = \mathbf{A}^{-1}\mathbf{c} = \frac{1}{7}\begin{bmatrix} 3 & -1 \\ 1 & 2 \end{bmatrix}\begin{bmatrix} 7 \\ 4 \end{bmatrix} = \frac{1}{7}\begin{bmatrix} 17 \\ 15 \end{bmatrix} \qquad\qquad \bullet$$

A matrix is called *orthogonal* if

$$A^T A = I \tag{B.19}$$

Postmultiplying by A^{-1} yields

$$A^T = A^{-1} \tag{B.20a}$$

with $I A^{-1} = A^{-1}$. We find that the inverse matrix is just the transpose of A.

Let A be described by column vectors in the form

$$A = \{a_k\}_{k=0,1,\ldots,N-1} \tag{B.20b}$$

Then, in the case of orthogonal matrices, the column vectors (and rows, if they are considered as vectors) are *orthonormal*:

$$a_j^T a_k = \delta_{jk} \tag{B.20c}$$

Also, in the case of orthogonal matrices A,

$$\text{if } c = Ab, \quad \text{then} \quad c^T c = b^T A^T Ab = b^T b \tag{B.21}$$

Finally, orthogonality of A implies that A^T (and hence A^{-1}) are orthogonal.

If the elements of A are complex, then A is a *unitary* matrix if

$$A^{*T} A = I \tag{B.22}$$

where A^{*T} is the transpose conjugate. The columns of a unitary matrix form an orthonormal set.

Consider a square matrix A. A nonzero vector l is an *eigenvector* if there exists a scalar λ such that

$$Al = \lambda l \quad \text{or} \quad (A - \lambda I)l = 0 \tag{B.23}$$

λ is an *eigenvalue* of A. Examples for the determination of eigenvectors are given in Chapters 2 and 12. We simply note here that (B.23) leads to a non-trivial eigenvector only if

$$|A - \lambda I| = 0 \tag{B.24}$$

This is the *characteristic equation* of A and its roots are the eigenvalues. An $(N \times N)$ matrix can have *at most* N linearly independent eigenvectors. Eigenvectors corresponding to distinct eigenvalues are linearly independent. Eigenvectors x_1 and x_2 are linearly independent if the only solution to $\alpha_1 x_1 = \alpha_2 x_2 = 0$ is given by $\alpha_1 = \alpha_2 = 0$. Properties of eigenvalues include

$$(i) \text{ trace } (A) = \sum_{j=0}^{N-1} \lambda_j ; \quad (ii) \ |A| = \prod_{j=0}^{N-1} \lambda_j \tag{B.25}$$

Also, if $\mathbf{A}$ has an eigenvalue λ, $\mathbf{A}^T$ also has an eigenvalue λ, and $\mathbf{A}^{-1}$ has an eigenvalue λ^{-1} if $|\mathbf{A}| > 0$. Properties of eigenvectors are listed in Chapter 2.

Example B.7. Eigenvectors and eigenvalues

$$\mathbf{A} = \begin{bmatrix} 1 & 2 \\ 4 & 3 \end{bmatrix} \text{ has eigenvectors } \quad \mathbf{l}_0 = \begin{bmatrix} -1 \\ 1 \end{bmatrix} ; \quad \mathbf{l}_1 = \begin{bmatrix} 1 \\ 2 \end{bmatrix}$$

Both eigenvectors are given correct to within a scalar constant (i.e., $\alpha \, \mathbf{l}_0$ is also an eigenvector). The eigenvalues are

$$\lambda_0 = -1 ; \quad \lambda_1 = 5$$

Also,

$$\prod_{j=0}^{N-1} \lambda_j = -5 = |\mathbf{A}| ; \quad \text{trace } (\mathbf{A}) = 1 + 3 = \lambda_0 + \lambda_1 = 4 \qquad \bullet$$

References

R. Bronson, *Matrix Methods, an Introduction*, Academic Press, New York, 1969.

F. R. Gantmacher, *The Theory of Matrices*, Vols. 1 and 2, Chelsea, New York, 1960.

A. Ralston and P. Rabinowitz, *First Course in Numerical Analysis*, McGraw-Hill, New York, 1978.

D. I. Steinberg, *Computational Matrix Algebra*, McGraw-Hill, New York, 1974.

Appendix C

Information Theory of Sources and Channels

Consider a discrete-time and ergodic *source* which generates sequences $\{x(n)\}$, $n = 0 \pm 1, \pm 2,...$ of *source symbols*. The sequences can be considered as realizations of a random sequence $\{X(n)\}$, $n = 0, \pm 1, \pm 2,...$. Each r.v. $X(n)$ assumes a value from a *source alphabet* A_x which is either a finite set of amplitudes (or *letters*) x_k, $k = 1,2,...,K$, or an infinite set given by the real line. The source is said to be *amplitude-discrete* if the size of the alphabet is finite, and is said to be *amplitude-continuous* otherwise. Additionally, the source is *memoryless* if successive samples are statistically independent. A *channel* is said to be *discrete* if input and output U and V (see Figure 1.2) are chosen from finite-size *code alphabets*, A_u and A_v, respectively. The channel may be noisy and hence must be viewed as a probabilistic mapping between input and output. A *discrete memoryless channel* (DMC) is characterized by the fact that each output letter $v(n)$ in the channel output sequence depends only on the corresponding input $u(n)$. The *binary symmetric channel* (BSC) of Figure 1.8(b) is a special case of a DMC. All sources and channels will be assumed to be stationary; that is, the statistical dependencies between the r.v.'s do not depend on time.

The purpose of this section is to develop basic information-theoretical descriptions of sources and channels [Slepian, 1973] [Berlekamp, 1974] [Viterbi and Omura, 1979]. These descriptions will be useful in defining two fundamental quantities, *source entropy* and *channel capacity*, and later in the development of *rate distortion functions* (Appendix D) that bound the performance of practical source coding systems. The development in this appendix is neither complete nor rigorous, and examples of excellent treatments of the subject appear in the list of references. Our purpose will be to develop notions of *entropy* and *mutual information* fairly rapidly, starting with the simple notion that associated with any random event with prior probability p is an amount of information given by $-\log_2 p$ bits. Note that this information is zero if $p = 1$ (a certain event conveys no information when it occurs), and that the less probable the event, the greater is the information conveyed when it does occur.

The entropy $H(X)$ will have the following interpretations. For discrete-amplitude sources, $H(X)$ equals the minimum average bit rate R that a coding system must have if the source symbols are to be transmitted without distortion: $\min\{R\} = H(X)$. For continuous-amplitude sources, the *differential entropy* $h(X)$ lower-bounds the mean square distortion of any coding system. This minimum is $D \geqslant (2\pi e)^{-1}2^{2h(X)}2^{-2R}$, with equality if $R \gg 1$.

The relevance of channel capacity C is given by the fact that data can be transmitted over the channel at any rate below C with arbitrarily small error probability if the data are appropriately encoded. The encoding implies, in general, the use of large blocks of input data, with resulting penalties in terms of encoding delay and complexity.

C.1 Discrete-Amplitude Memoryless Sources

Discrete-amplitude sources are specified by the fact that each source symbol $x(n)$ can only assume one of the K *letters* of a source alphabet A_x; i.e., we have $x(n) \in \{x_1, x_2, \ldots, x_K\}$ for all n. Memoryless sources are defined by the fact that its source samples are statistically independent of each other. With each possible outcome x_k at time n of the stationary source is associated a probability of occurrence $P\{X(n) = x_k\} = P(x_k) = P_k$ and a *self-information*

$$I(x_k) = -\log_2 P_k \text{ bits} \tag{C.1}$$

$I(x_k)$ is a measure of the information received if one is informed that the r.v. $X(n)$ has assumed a value x_k at time instant n. This information is related to the uncertainty of messages, and a partial description of the source is given by the average information content, the *entropy*

$$H(X) = E[I(X)] = -\sum_{k=1}^{K} P_k \log_2 P_k \text{ bits/symbol} \tag{C.2}$$

$H(X)$ is the average information received if one is informed about the value the r.v. $X(n)$ has assumed at time instant n. It is also the average of uncertainty about the source output before one is informed about it. It can be shown that

$$0 \leqslant H(X) \leqslant \log_2 K \tag{C.3}$$

The left-side equality holds only if all letter probabilities except one are zero. In this case, non-zero probability is unity, implying a totally predictable source. The right-side equality holds if and only if all probabilities are equal, as in the case of the most unpredictable source. The quantity $\log_2 K$ is the maximum value of the entropy and is sometimes called the *capacity* of the alphabet. The *redundancy* $\Re(X)$ of the source is the difference between the capacity and the entropy:

$$\Re(X) = \log_2 K - H(X) \qquad (C.4)$$

Example C.1.   Binary source *(K = 2); P(x$_1$) = P$_1$ and P(x$_2$) = 1 – P$_1$*

$$H(X) = \lambda(P_1) = - P_1 \log_2 P_1 - (1-P_1) \log_2 (1-P_1) \quad \text{bits/symbol} \qquad (C.5a)$$

$$\Re(X) = \log_2 2 - \lambda(P_1) = 1 - \lambda(P_1) \qquad (C.5b)$$

The convex and concave curves in Figure C.1 are plots of entropy $\lambda(P_1)$ and redundancy $1 - \lambda(P_1)$, respectively. Note the special cases

$$\lambda(0.5) = 1 \; ; \quad \lambda(0) = \lambda(1.0) = 0 \qquad (C.5c)$$

Note also the symmetry about $P_1 = 0.5$. For example,

$$H(X) = 0.72 \quad \text{if } P_1 = 0.2 \text{ or if } P_1 = 0.8 \qquad (C.6) \quad \bullet$$

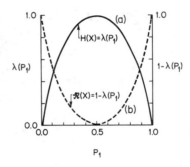

Figure C.1   Plots of (a) binary source entropy function $H(X) = \lambda(P_1)$ and (b) binary source redundancy function $\Re(X) = 1 - \lambda(P_1)$.

Example C.2.   Quaternary source *(K = 4); P(x$_k$) = P$_k$; k = 1,2,3,4*
If the symbol probabilities P_k $(k=1$ to 4) are *equal*:

$$P_1 = P_2 = P_3 = P_4 = 0.25 , \qquad (C.7a)$$

we obtain a maximum possible entropy of

$$H(X) = - 4(0.25 \log 1/4) = \log_2 4 = 2 \quad \text{bits/symbol} \qquad (C.7b)$$

Unequal symbol probabilities reduce $H(X)$. For example, if

$$P_1 = 0.5, P_2 = 0.25, P_3 = 0.125 \text{ and } P_4 = 0.125 , \qquad (C.7c)$$

the entropy decreases to

$$H(X) = - \sum_{k=1}^{4} P_k \log_2 P_k = 1.75 \quad \text{bits/symbol} \qquad (C.7d) \quad \bullet$$

C.2 Discrete-Amplitude Sources with Memory

Sources with memory exhibit statistical dependencies between successive samples. To take these dependencies into account, we arrange N successive samples $x(n)$, $x(n+1)$, ..., $x(n+N-1)$ into a block or sourceword written as a vector $\mathbf{x}(n) = \mathbf{x}$. The probability of a specific source word $\mathbf{x}$ is $P(\mathbf{x})$. This probability does not depend on time instant n since we have assumed stationary sources. Any vector $\mathbf{x}$ can now be viewed as a realization of a vector r.v. $\mathbf{X} = \{X(n), X(n+1), ..., X(n+N-1)\}$, and the entropy per symbol of this joint ensemble of N r.v.'s is

$$H_N(X) = \frac{1}{N}E[-\log_2 P(\mathbf{X})] = -\frac{1}{N} \sum \sum_{\text{all } \mathbf{x}} \cdots \sum P(\mathbf{x}) \log_2 P(\mathbf{x}) \ bits/symbol \quad \text{(C.8)}$$

$H_N(X)$ will be called N-*block entropy*, and the limit

$$H(X) = \lim_{N \to \infty} H_N(X) \quad \text{(C.9)}$$

is the entropy of the source. Another approach is based on conditional probabilities. Let $H[X(n)|X(n-1),...,X(n-N+1)]$ be the *conditional entropy* of the symbol at time instant n given the $N-1$ preceding symbols. It is defined by corresponding conditional probabilities, and its value is a measure of the remaining average uncertainty about the outcome at time n if $N-1$ preceding outcomes are already known. It can be shown that

$$H(X(n)|X(n-1),...,X(n-N+1)) \leqslant H_N(X) \quad \text{(C.10)}$$

Both the N-block entropy and the conditional entropy are non-increasing with N. The limits of these entropies exist and are indeed equal [Gallager, 1968] to the source entropy (C.9):

$$H(X) = \lim_{N \to \infty} H(X(n)|X(n-1),...X(n-N+1)) \quad \text{(C.11)}$$

Two special cases are worth noting:

(i) A *memoryless* source produces outcomes that are statistically independent of each other; that is, for any time instant n, say $n = 1$,

$$P(\mathbf{x}) = \prod_{k=1}^{N} P(x_k) \quad \text{(C.12a)}$$

where x_k is the kth component of $\mathbf{x}$, with K possible values for each k. From (C.8) and (C.2),

$$H_N(X) = H(X) = -\sum_{k=1}^{N} P(x_k) \log_2 P(x_k) \quad \text{(C.12b)}$$

(ii) A *Markov* source which has a *finite memory* has the property that the limiting value $H(X)$ is reached for finite N. The source entropy will have a simple formulation as a weighted average of conditional entropies: the entropies are conditioned on a *state* that the source is in, and the weighting is the *probability* of the state.

It can also be shown in general that for two sources with identical alphabets and letter probabilities,

$$H(X)\big|_{\text{source with memory}} < H(X)\big|_{\text{source without memory}} \qquad (C.13)$$

Example C.3.　Binary first-order Markov source

Consider the source described in Figure C.2 with *state probabilities* $P(x_1)$ and $P(x_2)$, and *transition probabilities*

$$P\{(X(n) = x_2|X(n-1) = x_1)\} = P(x_2|x_1) = 0.1 \;;$$
$$P\{(X(n) = x_1|X(n-1) = x_2)\} = P(x_1|x_2) = 0.4$$

The memory consists in the fact that a source output x_1 is more likely to be followed by another x_1 than with a x_2. This is expressed by the value of transition probability $P(x_2|x_1) = 0.1$. The symbol x_1 will not only be more probable [see (C.16)] than x_2 (as in Example C.5), but also the x_1's (and the x_2's) in the source output occur in *clusters*, or *runs*.

The entropy of the Markov source is

$$H(X) = P(x_1)H(X|x_1) + P(x_2)H(X|x_2) \qquad (C.14)$$

where $H(X|x_1)$ and $H(X|x_2)$, the conditional entropies in states x_1 and x_2, are the binary source entropy functions $\lambda[P(x_2|x_1)]$ and $\lambda[P(x_1|x_2)]$ that correspond to transition probability values $P(x_2|x_1)$ and $P(x_1|x_2)$. That is,

$$H(X|x_1) = H(X(n)|X(n-1) = x_1) = \lambda(P(x_2|x_1)$$
$$H(X|x_2) = H(X(n)|X(n-1) = x_2) = \lambda(P(x_1|x_2))$$

The state probabilities $P(x_1)$ and $P(x_2)$ satisfy the equations

$$P(x_1) = P(x_1)(1-P(x_2|x_1)) + P(x_2)P(x_1|x_2) \qquad (C.15a)$$
$$P(x_1) + P(x_2) = 1 \qquad (C.15b)$$

Figure C.2　Binary Markov source.

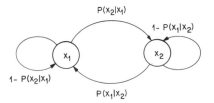

Information Theory of Sources and Channels　　C

Note that the right hand side of (C.15a) is the average probability that the process *goes to* state x_1, beginning from states x_1 and x_2. This, by definition, equals the left hand side of (C.15a), the probability that the process *is* in state x_1. From (C.15a) and (C.15b), and with $P(x_2|x_1) = 0.1$ and $P(x_1|x_2) = 0.4$ (Figure C.2),

$$P(x_1) = 0.8; \quad P(x_2) = 0.2 \tag{C.16a}$$

Using (C.14),

$$H(X) = (0.8) \, \lambda(0.1) + (0.2) \, \lambda(0.4) = 0.58 \ \text{bits/symbol} \tag{C.16b}$$

Note that this is less than the entropy of the binary memoryless source with the same letter probabilities 0.8 and 0.2. See Example C1. •

Comparison of (C.5), (C.6) and (C.16b) shows how discrete source entropy can be less than the maximum possible value $\log_2 K$ because of two factors: unequal letter probabilities and source memory.

Example C.4. Binary first-order Markov source with equal letter probabilities
Consider the first-order Markov source statistics

$$P(x_1) = P(x_2) = 0.5 \; ; \quad P(x_2|x_1) = P(x_1|x_2) = 0.01 \tag{C.17a}$$

These values indeed satisfy the general constraint (C.15a) and the source entropy will be

$$H(X) = \lambda \, (0.01) = 0.08 \ \text{bit/symbol} \tag{C.17b}$$

which is once again less than that of the memoryless source with the same (equal) letter probabilities, 0.5 and 0.5. This Markov example is used again in Chapter 10 on two-level graphics. •

C.3   Noiseless Coding of Discrete-Amplitude Sources

Examples of discrete-amplitude sources in this book are either quantizer outputs or two-level graphics sources. In the former case, and to a great extent in the latter case as well, we assume *noiseless* or *distortionless* coding of the discrete-amplitude source symbols. Practical procedures that realize noiseless coding are sometimes known as procedures that provide *entropy coding*. The following constructive examples illustrate how distortionless coding is attained or approached when the input is discrete in amplitude.

Example C.5.   Memoryless binary source; $P(x_1) = 0.8$; $P(x_2) = 0.2$
The entropy (C.6) is $H(X) = 0.72$. A simple binary code which assigns a bit "1" to output x_1 and "0" to output x_2 can provide a distortionless representation of the source, but its average bit rate R is 1 bit/symbol, which is greater than $H(X)$ [Table C.1(a)].

Table C.1 Entropy Coding of a memoryless binary source $[P(x_1) = 0.8, P(x_2) = 0.2]$ with (a) $R = 1$ bit/symbol and (b) $R = 0.78$ bit/symbol.

	Source Word	Probability			Code
(a)	x_1	0.8 ----			1
	x_2	0.2			0
(b)	$x_1 x_1$	0.64 ---			1
	$x_1 x_2$	0.16	0.16 ---		0 1
	$x_2 x_1$	0.16	0.16	0.16 ---	0 0 1
	$x_2 x_2$	0.04	0.04	0.04	0 0 0

A rate closer to $\min\{R\} = R(0) = H(X)$ can be obtained by a combination of *encoding delay* and *variable-length coding*. We look at all possible source sequences of length 2, and assign short codewords to the more probable sequences and long codewords to the less probable sequences, and realize an average encoding rate R of 0.78 bit/symbol [see Table C.1(b)]. ●

The coding scheme of Table C.1(b) is a simple illustration of *Huffman Coding* or *variable length entropy coding*. The procedure consists in arranging source words in decreasing order of probability; successively partitioning them into groups of approximately equal total probability (as shown by dashed horizontals); and assigning at each of the three stages (i), (ii) and (iii), binary code letters "1" and "0" to members that are above and below the partition, respectively.

The code of Table C.1(b) has an important *prefix condition* property whereby no codeword is a prefix or an initial part of another codeword. Thus codewords can be readily concatenated (in a *comma free* fashion) and can still be uniquely (unambiguously) decoded. This property is related to the fact that every codeword corresponds to one at the free end of a code tree whose branches always emanate from all-zero nodes. The codewords of Table C.1(b) are thus the boxed-in codewords in the *code tree* of Figure C.3.

For binary encoding, the efficiency [closeness of R to $H(X)$] of entropy coding is related to how well source letter or source word probabilities can be approximated by negative exponents of 2. In the example of Figure C.3, such a structure was realized by considering letter-pairs, rather than individual letters, as source symbols. In the next example, individual source letters have probabilities that are exactly negative exponents of 2. There is no need for considering letter-

Figure C.3 Code tree that relates to coding method in Table C.1(b).

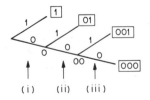

pairs in this case; the special input probability structure facilitates direct (memoryless) entropy coding with perfect efficiency: $R = \min\{R\} = H(X)$.

The performances of variable-length entropy coding schemes can be described by the *noiseless coding theorem* [Shannon, 1948]:

$$\min\{R\} = H(X) + \epsilon \text{ bits/symbol} \tag{C.18}$$

where R is the transmission rate and ϵ is a positive quantity that can be made arbitrarily close to zero by means of sophisticated coding procedures utilizing, in general, an appropriate amount of encoding delay.

Example C.6. Memoryless Quaternary source; $P(x_1) = 0.5$, $P(x_2) = 0.25$, $P(x_3) = P(x_4) = 0.125$

The entropy (C.7b) is $H(X) = 1.75$ bits/symbol. Following the variable coding procedure of Figure C.3, we assign codewords 1, 01, 001 and 000 to the four letters (not letter-pairs) of the source. The average transmission rate will then be $R = 1.75$ bits/symbol $= H(X)$. This is an example where the lower bound of distortionless coding is very simply attained. ●

Mismatch of Code and Source. The above coding procedures are tailored to source statistics, and performance degrades in general if the source is nonstationary, or has statistics different from those assumed in code design.

Example C.7. Use of code in Table C.1 for a mismatched binary source with $P(x_1) = 0.5$

The transmission rate will increase to 1.125 bits/symbol. This is very inefficient in comparison to $R = 0.78$. In addition, if a buffer is designed to accommodate the output of the source in Table C.1, with a negligible overflow probability, use of the mismatched source will significantly increase the probability of overflow. ●

Discrete Sources with Memory. The consequences of memory (non-independent source letters) are in general twofold. The entropy $H(X)$ is smaller than that of a memoryless source with identical (unconditional) letter probabilities; and the role of encoding delay in realizing efficient entropy coding is more significant.

Example C.8. Binary Markov source of Example C.3

The entropy of this source has been shown to be $H(X) = 0.58$ bit/symbol. A letter-pair-based entropy code in the fashion of Table C.1(b) leads to codewords 1, 01, 001 and 000 with probabilities 0.72, 0.12, 0.08 and 0.08 for letter-pairs x_1x_1, x_2x_2, x_1x_2 and x_2x_1. These probabilities result from the general expression $P(x_r)P(x_s|x_r)$ for the probability of letter pair x_rx_s. Thus, for example, with $x_r = x_s = x_1$, the probability of the letter pair x_1x_1 is $0.8 (1-0.1) = 0.72$. The average transmission rate R will be 0.72 bits/symbol $> H(X)$, suggesting the need for observing longer input strings for encoding, unlike in the parallel memoryless case of Table C.1(b) where observation of letter pairs led to an average rate $R = 0.78$ which is quite close to $H(X) = 0.72$. ●

Various chapters in the book will describe many examples of noiseless entropy coding. These procedures use both fixed-length-to-variable-length and variable-length-to-fixed-length mappings of codewords. We will also discuss non-exact mappings (coding with distortion) that are motivated by constraints on either transmission rate and/or buffer considerations.

C.4   Continuous-Amplitude Memoryless Sources

We consider zero-mean memoryless stationary sources $\{X(n)\}$ with pdf $p_x(x)$, variance $\sigma_x^2 = E[X^2(n)]$, and an acf $R_{xx}(k) = \sigma_x^2 \delta(k)$ that is zero for $k \neq 0$. In the case of continuous-amplitude sources, the probability $P(x_k)$ is zero for any specific amplitude x_k, and $X(n)$ has infinite absolute entropy. Nevertheless, we can define an average self-information

$$h(X) = E[-\log_2 p_x(X)] = -\int_{-\infty}^{\infty} p_x(x) \log_2 p_x(x) \, dx \qquad (C.19)$$

which is called *differential entropy*. Unlike in the example of a discrete source where $H(X)$ is always positive (C.3), the differential entropy $h(X)$ in (C.19) can be positive, negative or zero, depending on amplitude-scaling factors; hence the term *differential* (rather than *absolute*) entropy.

Example C.9.   Uniform pdf; $p_x(x) = 1/A; 0 \leqslant x \leqslant A$

$$h(X) = -\int_0^A (1/A) \log_2 (1/A) \, dx = \log_2 A \qquad (C.20)$$

This entropy is greater than, less than or equal to zero, depending on whether A is greater than, less than or equal to 1.   •

Example C.10.   Maximum entropy with constrained variance
Using Lagrange multipliers with the constraints that the integrals of $p_x(x)$ and $x^2 p_x(x)$ over all x are 1 and σ_x^2, it can be shown that the maximal differential entropy for any memoryless source of specified variance σ_x^2 is that for the $N(0,\sigma_x^2)$ source, i.e., for

$$p_x(x) = (2\pi\sigma_x^2)^{-1} \exp(-x^2/2\sigma_x^2) \qquad (C.21a)$$

This maximum entropy is

$$h(X)_G = \log_2 \sqrt{2\pi e \, \sigma_x^2} \qquad (C.21b) \quad •$$

Table C.2 lists differential entropies of various sources together with the *entropy power* defined by

$$Q = (2\pi e)^{-1} 2^{2h(X)} \qquad (C.22)$$

For a *Gaussian* source the entropy power Q equals the source variance σ_x^2. For *non-Gaussian* sources, $Q < \sigma_x^2$, suggesting that these sources have lesser information content per unit of variance.

Table C.2 Differential entropy and entropy power of memoryless sources (C = Euler's constant = 0.5772).

pdf	$h(X)$	Q/σ_x^2
Uniform	$2^{-1} \cdot \log_2 (12\, \sigma_x^2)$	0.703
Gaussian	$2^{-1} \cdot \log_2 (2\pi\, e\, \sigma_x^2)$	1.000
Laplacian	$2^{-1} \cdot \log_2 (2e^2\, \sigma_x^2)$	0.865
Gamma	$2^{-1} \cdot \log_2 (4\pi e^{1-C} \sigma_x^2/3)$	0.374

C.5 Continuous-Amplitude Sources with Memory

Definitions follow those of the last sections. Each source word $\mathbf{x}$ of N successive symbols is described by a joint probability density $p_\mathbf{x}(\mathbf{x})$ and the differential entropy per symbol of such a source word is

$$h_N(X) = \frac{1}{N} E[-\log_2 p_\mathbf{x}(\mathbf{X})] = -\frac{1}{N} \int_{-\infty}^{\infty} \int_{-\infty}^{\infty} \cdots \int_{-\infty}^{\infty} p_\mathbf{x}(\mathbf{x}) \log_2 p_\mathbf{x}(\mathbf{x})\, d\mathbf{x} \quad \text{(C.23)}$$

It is almost always impossible to calculate these entropies. However, for a zero-mean Gaussian source with pdf (2.51)

$$p_\mathbf{x}(\mathbf{x}) = \frac{1}{(2\pi)^{N/2}} \frac{1}{|\mathbf{R}_{\mathbf{xx}}|^{1/2}} \exp[-\frac{1}{2} \mathbf{x}^T \mathbf{R}_{\mathbf{xx}}^{-1} \mathbf{x}] \quad \text{(C.24)}$$

where $\mathbf{R}_{\mathbf{xx}}$ is the Nth order autocorrelation matrix of the process,

$$h_N(X) = \frac{1}{2} \log_2(2\pi\, e\, |\mathbf{R}_{\mathbf{xx}}|^{1/N}) \quad \text{(C.25)}$$

The differential entropy per symbol is

$$h(X) = \lim_{N \to \infty} h_N(X) = \lim_{N \to \infty} |\mathbf{R}_{\mathbf{xx}}|^{1/N} \quad \text{(C.26a)}$$

and, therefore, the entropy power for this source is

$$Q = \lim_{N \to \infty} |\mathbf{R}_{\mathbf{xx}}|^{1/N} \quad \text{(C.26b)}$$

Using the results (2.67), (2.74) and (C.22),

$$Q = \gamma_x^2\, \sigma_x^2 = \eta_x^2 \quad \text{(C.27)}$$

This result states that the entropy power of a Gaussian source with memory is equal to the product of the variance σ_x^2 and the *spectral flatness measure* γ_x^2. For a white (memoryless) Gaussian source, $\gamma_x^2 = 1$, leading to the earlier entropy formula (C.22). We note also that the entropy power $\gamma_x^2 \sigma_x^2$ is equal to the *minimum one-step-ahead prediction error variance* η_x^2. We finally note that as in Table C.2, the entropy power of non-Gaussian sources with memory is smaller than that of the Gaussian source with the same memory, i.e. the same value of γ_x^2. Also, as in (C.13b), a memoryless source has higher values of entropy and entropy power than a source of same variance with memory. Indeed, $\gamma_x^2 \leqslant 1$ with equality only if the process is not predictable [see (2.75)].

Example C.11.   Gaussian AR(1) source

Let the source have variance σ_x^2 and adjacent-sample correlation ρ. The spectral flatness measure (2.104) is $\gamma_x^2 = 1 - \rho^2$. Therefore, $Q = (1-\rho^2)\sigma_x^2$. Comparison with (2.102) shows that $Q = \sigma_z^2$. Thus, the entropy power equals the variance of the innovations process.   •

The coding of discrete-amplitude sources was discussed at some length in Section C.3. The coding of continuous-amplitude sources will not be discussed in this appendix, as this subject is indeed the main topic of most of this book.

C.6   Channel Capacity

Discrete-Amplitude Channels. *Discrete-amplitude channels* have inputs and outputs that are sequences of r.v.'s, $\{U(n)\}$ and $\{V(n)\}$, respectively, taking values in the corresponding code alphabets A_u and A_v. We assume that these alphabets are of the same size, say M. Thus we have $A_u = (u_1, u_2, ..., u_M)$ and $A_v = (v_1, v_2, ..., v_M)$. Transmission over noisy channels can be interpreted as a probabilistic mapping between symbols chosen from the letters of input and output alphabets. We use the conditional probability $P(v_j|u_i)$ to describe the probability of the reception of v_j if u_i is transmitted. Implicit in this description is the assumption that the channel is memoryless, i.e. each output depends only on the corresponding input; hence the notation DMC (*discrete memoryless channel*).

Assume that we are given an input sequence of N successive inputs, $\mathbf{u} = \{u(1), u(2), ..., u(N)\}$, and a corresponding output sequence $\mathbf{v}$, both being realizations of respective random vectors $\mathbf{U}$ and $\mathbf{V}$. A memoryless channel is then defined by the fact that there is a transition probability assignment such that

$$P(\mathbf{v}|\mathbf{u}) = \prod_{k=1}^{N} P(v(k)|u(k)) \qquad (C.28)$$

Figure C.4   Transition probabilities in (a) M-ary discrete memoryless channel and (b) binary symmetric channel.

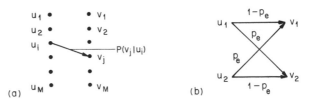

where $v(k)$ and $u(k)$ are the kth components of $\mathbf{v}$ and $\mathbf{u}$, respectively, with M possible values in each case. Note that, since the channel is assumed to be memoryless, the time index n has been dropped. The total set of transition probabilities can be displayed as an $M \times M$ *channel matrix*

$$
\mathbf{T} =
\begin{bmatrix}
P(v_1|u_1) & P(v_2|u_1) & \cdots & P(v_M|u_1) \\
P(v_1|u_2) & P(v_2|u_2) & \cdots & P(v_M|u_2) \\
\vdots & & & \\
P(v_1|u_M) & P(v_2|u_M) & \cdots & P(v_M|u_M)
\end{bmatrix}
\tag{C.29}
$$

Ideally, i.e., for error-free transmission, this channel matrix $\mathbf{T}$ should be the identity matrix $\mathbf{I}$. Practical channels, however, are noisy, and in these cases, the non-diagonal elements of $\mathbf{T}$ will be nonzero. Figure C.4(a) is a graphical representation of the DMC.

We are interested in the average amount of information that is transferred from channel input to channel output. The *mutual information* is defined by the relation

$$
I(u_i;v_j) = \log_2 P(v_j|u_i) - \log_2 P(v_j)
\tag{C.30}
$$

It is a measure of the information that the reception of symbol v_j supplies about the value u_i. Note that this mutual information is zero if the outcome v_j does not depend on u_i since $P(v_j|u_i) = P(v_j)$ in this case. On the other hand, $I(u_i;v_j)$ is a maximum when $P(v_j|u_i) = 1$, that is, when the channel is error-free for this specific pair of input and output symbols. Then the mutual information is just $I(v_j) = I(u_i)$, the self-information of the symbols. The information (C.30) is termed *mutual* because, on the basis of simple conditional probability relations,

$$
I(u_i;v_j) = \log_2 \frac{P(v_j|u_i)}{P(v_j)} = \log_2 \frac{P(u_i|v_j)}{P(u_i)} = I(v_j;u_i)
\tag{C.31}
$$

The third expression in (C.31) also gives another physical interpretation. It shows that as a result of using the transmission channel, the a posteriori probability of source symbol u_i changes from the a priori value $P(u_i)$ to the a posteriori value $P(u_i|v_j)$. The latter pdf is expected to be *peakier* than the former at the point value u_i.

The *average* mutual information $I(U;V)$ per sample is a measure of the average information that a reception of an output symbol supplies about the input symbol. It is defined as the expected value of $I(u_i;v_j)$ with respect to the joint probability $P(u_i;v_j)$:

$$
I(U;V) = \sum_{i=1}^{M} \sum_{j=1}^{M} P(u_i,v_j) \log_2 \frac{P(v_j|u_i)}{P(v_j)} = \sum_{i=1}^{M} \sum_{j=1}^{M} P(u_i,v_j) \log_2 \frac{P(u_i|v_j)}{P(u_i)}
\tag{C.32}
$$

The average mutual information $I(U;V)$ is a nonnegative quantity and it is zero only if the events of channel input and output are statistically independent $[P(v_j|u_i) = P(v_j); P(u_i|v_j) = P(u_i)]$. Also, $I(U;V)$, unlike source entropy $H(X)$, is a property of the entire communication system.

An important application of the average mutual information concept will be in Rate Distortion Theory [Berger, 1971]. We will see in Appendix D that the minimum value of $I(X;Y)$, with respect to an appropriate class of transition probabilities $P(y_j|x_i)$, defines the minimum rate R at which information about the sources must be supplied to the user in order that the user may reproduce it with a prescribed fidelity D.

In the present context we shall use the quantity $I(U;V)$ to define the *capacity* of an discrete-amplitude memoryless channel. Observe that $I(U;V)$ not only depends on the channel statistics which define the channel matrix **T** but also on the a priori probabilities of the channel input symbols. This input distribution $P(u_i)$ can be adjusted by the coder. Therefore, it is reasonable to define *channel capacity* as the maximum of the average information that can be transferred to the receiver:

$$C = \max_{P(u_i)}\{I(U;V)\}; \quad i = 1,2,...,M \tag{C.33}$$

where the search for maximum is over all input probability assignments subject to the constraints $P(u_i) \geqslant 0$ and $\sum P(u_i) = 1$. The significance of channel capacity C is given by *Shannon's noisy channel coding theorem*, which states that (for a broad class of communication channels) data can be transmitted over the channel at any rate below channel capacity *reliably*, or *with arbitrarily small error probability* [Shannon, 1948]. The data have to be appropriately coded in order to obtain such practically error-free transmission, and this implies the use of large blocks **u** of input data and this, in turn, introduces complexity into the channel encoder and decoder. The rate at which the error probability p_e can be made to approach zero with increasing block length is a function of transmission rate R and the channel in question.

Following (C.31) and extending the entropy definition (C.2) to conditional pdf's and *conditional entropies*, the average mutual information can also be expressed in the form

$$I(U;V) = H(V) - H(V|U) = H(U) - H(U|V) \tag{C.34}$$

The conditional entropies $H(V|U)$ and $H(U|V)$ have the following physical interpretations. $H(V|U)$ is a *noise entropy* added in the channel. $H(U|V)$, the *equivocation*, is the average remaining uncertainty about the channel input after its output has been observed.

An important result [Gallager, 1968] is that the maximum value (C.33) is obtained only if the inputs are *statistically independent* and also have the probability assignment that maximizes $I(U;V)$ in (C.33). This statistical independence of source encoder outputs is a *necessary* condition for optimal coding; a *sufficient* condition is that the number of output symbols per second is minimum.

Nothing can be said in general about the input probability assignment that maximizes $I(U;V)$. However, there is an important result for *symmetric channels* which are defined by the simplifying property that all rows *and* columns of the channel matrix $\mathbf{T}$ are identical except for permutations. In this special case [Thomas, 1968],

$$C = \log_2 M + \sum_{j=1}^{M} P(v_j|u_i) \log_2 P(v_j|u_j) \quad \text{for any } i \quad (C.35)$$

and this capacity of the symmetric channel is achieved by using *independent and identically distributed* (*i.i.d.*) inputs with equal probability [Gallager, 1968].

Example C.12. Binary Symmetric Channel

This is a special case of the discrete memoryless channel, with $M = 2$ and a channel matrix [Figure C.4(b)]

$$\mathbf{T} = \begin{bmatrix} 1-p_e & p_e \\ p_e & 1-p_e \end{bmatrix} \quad (C.36a)$$

where p_e is the *bit error probability*. From (C.35), the channel capacity, achieved with identically distributed independent inputs, is

$$C(p_e) = 1-\lambda(p_e) \quad (C.36b)$$

where $\lambda(p_e)$ is the binary entropy function sketched in Figure C.1. In fact, the dashed-line curve in that figure describes $C(p_e)$ if the abscissa is p_e. Note that a 10% error probability reduces channel capacity by a factor of about 2.

If one of the two input symbols has a probability $q \neq 0.5$, the average mutual information is

$$I(U;V) = \lambda[(p_e q+(1-p_e)(1-q)] - \lambda(p_e) \quad (C.37a)$$

The reader may verify that $I(U;V)$ is maximum for $q = 0.5$. If the channel is error-free,

$$I(U;V) = \lambda(1-q) \quad \text{if } p_e = 0 \quad (C.37b)$$

The quantity $\lambda(1-q)$ is now simply the entropy of the channel input [or channel output since $v(n) = u(n)$ if $p_e = 0$]. From Figure C.1, note that reducing q from 0.5 to 0.1 decreases $I(U;V)$ from 1 to 0.48 bit/symbol. ●

For a symmetric non-binary DMC, (C.37b) can be generalized in the form

$$I(U;V) = H(V) = H(U) \quad \text{for } p_e = 0$$
$$\simeq H(U) \quad \text{for } p_e \to 0 \quad (C.38)$$

The conditions for p_e in (C.38) are interesting channel characterizations for most waveform communications. In these cases, maximization of $I(U;V)$ is realized by maximizing $H(U)$, which in turn calls for an *i.i.d.* sequence at the channel input.

Discrete channels with memory are described by noting that each letter in the output sequence depends statistically both on the corresponding input *and* on past inputs and outputs (as in the Markov source model of Figure C.2). Capacity depends heavily on the initial state of the channel (which is a description of input and output sequences up to a given point) and on the channel encoder's knowledge of it. Simplifications are possible if the channels are such that the effect of an initial state dies away with time. Fairly simple models, such as the Markov model in Figure C.2, can be given for correlated or burst-error-channels (discrete-time equivalent of slowly fading channels), which have a tendency to persist in a given state [Gallager, 1968]. In general, the effect of such memory is to increase channel capacity beyond that for the DMC, for a given average error rate p_e.

Continuous-Amplitude Channels. *Continuous-amplitude channels* have input and output alphabets of infinite size. Accordingly, random variables U and V have infinite absolute entropy. However, as in Section C.4, we can define entropies that are analogous to discrete entropies. Many of the basic properties of discrete entropy as given above carry over to the continuous amplitude case. *Additive noise continuous channels* are of great importance in communication theory. The output of an additive noise channel is the sum of the channel input and a statistically independent r.v. which is called the *channel noise*.

Example C.13. Memoryless additive Gaussian noise channel

Consider a time-discrete physical channel whose input and output samples are amplitude-continuous, and the channel noise N is additive, white, Gaussian and of variance σ_n^2. This additive noise channel is described by the conditional pdf

$$p_{v|u}\,(v|u) = (2\pi\sigma_n^2)^{-1} \exp\left[-\,(v-u)^2/2\,\sigma_n^2\right] \tag{C.39}$$

For input-independent noise, the average mutual information can be written in the form

$$I(U;V) = h(V) - h(V|U) = h(V) - h(N) \tag{C.40}$$

For a given constraint σ_u^2 on input variance, this will be maximized if V and hence the channel input $U = V - N$ are also *Gaussian* and *memoryless*. Using the Gaussian entropy expression (C.21b), the capacity is

$$C_G = \log_2 \sqrt{2\pi\,e\,\sigma_v^2} - \log_2 \sqrt{2\pi\,e\,\sigma_n^2}$$

$$= \frac{1}{2}\,\log_2\,(\sigma_v^2/\sigma_n^2) = \frac{1}{2}\,\log_2\,(1+\sigma_u^2/\sigma_n^2)\ \text{bits/symbol} \tag{C.41}$$

where σ_u^2/σ_n^2 is the *signal-to-channel-noise ratio*. Higher capacities apply to non-Gaussian additive channels of identical noise variance σ_n^2. Gaussian noise is the worst kind of additive noise from a capacity standpoint.

The capacity (C.41) has another well-known version that applies to a bandlimited time-continuous communication system [Shannon, 1949]

$$C_G = W \log_2 \left[1 + \frac{P}{N_0 W}\right]\ \text{bits/sec} \tag{C.42}$$

which is obtained by multiplying (C.41) by the number of samples/second $2W$ that is appropriate to a W Hz system. In (C.42), P is the transmitted signal power and $N_0/2$ is the two-sided spectral density of the Gaussian noise. The formula (C.42) shows that the capacity C_G increases linearly with bandwidth but only logarithmically with the signal-to-noise ratio term. A very significant limiting condition is recognized by rewriting (C.42) in the form

$$\frac{C_G}{W} = \log_2 \left(1 + \frac{P}{N_0 C_G} \frac{C_G}{W}\right) \text{ bits/sec/Hz} \qquad (C.43)$$

The term $P/N_0 C_G$ can be interpreted as the *signal-to-channel-noise ratio per bit*, the ratio of signal energy per bit to power spectral density of channel noise. By noting that $\ln(1+x) \rightarrow x$ if $x \ll 1$, and letting $W \rightarrow \infty$ in (C.43),

$$\lim_{W \rightarrow \infty} \frac{P}{N_0 C_G} = \ln 2 = 0.69 \leftrightarrow -1.6 \text{ dB} \qquad (C.44)$$

This is the limiting value of signal-to-noise-ratio per bit at which one can operate at capacity; i.e., the smallest value of that ratio at which it is possible to communicate over an additive Gaussian noise channel with an error probability arbitrarily close to zero. This -1.6 dB value is indeed the *Shannon limit* of Figure 1.8(c).   ●

References

T. Berger, *Rate Distortion Theory*, Prentice-Hall, Englewood Cliffs, N.J., 1971.

E. R. Berlekamp (ed.), *Key Papers in the Development of Coding Theory*, IEEE Press, New York, 1974.

R. G. Gallager, *Information Theory and Reliable Communication*, Halsted Press, John Wiley, New York, 1968.

C. E. Shannon, "A Mathematical Theory of Communication," Bell System Tech. J., pp. 379-423 (Part I) pp. 623-656 (Part II), 1948.

C. E. Shannon, "Communication in the Presence of Noise," Proc. IRE, pp. 10-21, 1949.

D. Slepian (ed.), *Key Papers in the Development of Information Theory*, IEEE Press, New York, 1973.

J. B. Thomas, *An Introduction to Statistical Communication Theory*, John Wiley, New York, 1968.

A. J. Viterbi and J. K. Omura, *Principles of Digital Communication and Coding*, McGraw-Hill, New York, 1979.

Appendix D

Distortion Rate Functions

D.1 Introduction

The globally *minimum average distortion function* introduced in Chapter 1 is impossible to evaluate since the class of possible coders is infinitely large. However, if the source is *stationary* and *ergodic*, there exists a monotonically non-increasing *distortion rate function* (DRF), $D(R)$, which provides a *lower bound* D on the average distortion for a given rate R, and hence an *upper bound* on the performance of practical waveform coders [Shannon, 1948, 1959] [Kolmogorov, 1956] [Berger, 1971] [Slepian, 1974] [Davisson and Gray, 1976] [Wyner, 1981].

The function $D(R)$ is based on the concept of mutual information as a measure of the transmission of information from source to user. The function $D(R)$ has an inverse, the *rate distortion function $R(D)$*, which is equal to the minimum value of *average mutual information* $I(X;Y) = \lim I_N(X;Y)$ as $N \rightarrow \infty$, where X and Y respectively represent source vectors and corresponding reconstruction vectors that imply a specified distortion D. In fact, the *source coding theorem* states, in essence, that there *exists* a mapping (which we shall call the *optimal mapping*) from the source letters to codewords such that for a given D, $R(D)$ bits per sample are sufficient to reconstruct the samples with an average distortion that is arbitrarily close to D. In particular, for perfect reproduction $(D = 0)$, $R(0) = H(X)$, *the source entropy* or *average self-information*. As noted in Figure 1.10 and Appendix C, $H(X) = R(0)$ is finite for discrete-amplitude sources and infinite for continuous-amplitude sources. The function $I(X;Y)$ will depend in general on the conditional pdf $p(y|x)$, a mapping which can be used to define a so-called *test channel*.

Practical schemes for communication of *continuous-amplitude* sources assume a coder-decoder structure, a bit rate of R bits/sample, and yield the mean-squared reconstruction error $D' = \min\{\sigma_r^2\}$ as a design objective. With varying R, we then obtain a practical distortion function $D'(R)$. Information Theory, on the other hand, provides the function $D(R)$ where D is the minimum obtainable mse for any coder-decoder structure for a given bit rate R. Therefore, $D \leqslant \min\{\sigma_r^2\} = D'$, and the function $D(R)$ can be used to calibrate the performance of practical coder-decoder structures. In the case of discrete-amplitude sources, where distortion-free coding can be obtained, it is more useful to use the inverse functions $R'(D)$ (for a given coder-decoder structure) and $R(D)$ (for the best structure), with $R'(D) \geqslant R(D)$ and $R'(0) \geqslant R(0) = H(X)$.

An important purpose of this appendix is to note (mostly without proof) the quantitative nature of $D(R)$ for simple models of continuous-amplitude sources, including those with non-flat spectra; and in one case, the nature of a related function $D_N(R)$, the minimum average distortion when the block length of *vectors* $\mathbf{X}$ and $\mathbf{Y}$ is limited to a finite number N. The function $D_N(R)$ will be monotonically non-increasing as a function of N, and the function $D(R)$ is in fact the asymptotic value based on the assumption of coding in very long blocks $(N \to \infty)$. The use of these long blocks in coding implies that the corresponding coding delay does not significantly affect the relevance of the information presented to the user. However, practical communication networks do impose limits on the maximum allowable value of such delay.

Even though $N \gg 1$ in many coding schemes, the average distortion criterion itself will be based on a *single-letter distortion* measure: in particular, the squared error between a source sample and its representation at the destination.

The emphasis in this appendix will be on the *existence* of $D(R)$ bounds, rather than on the *construction* of codes that approach or attain such bounds. The $D(R)$ bounds will provide a way of characterizing waveforms for the coding problem, and they will serve as calibrators of performance for coders which digitize these waveforms.

D.2 Summary of Source Entropy Results

Before developing the notion of average mutual information $I(\mathbf{X};\mathbf{Y})$ that defines $D(R)$, it will be useful to repeat the formalism for *average self-information* or *source entropy* $H(X)$. A longer discussion is provided in Appendix C.

For *discrete-amplitude memoryless sources*,

$$H(X) = E\,[I(X)] = -\sum_{k=1}^{K} P(x_k)\,\log_2 P(x_k) \qquad (\text{D}.1)$$

and for *discrete-amplitude sources with memory*,

$$H(X) = \lim_{N \to \infty} H_N(X) = \lim_{N \to \infty} \left[-\frac{1}{N} \sum \sum \cdots \sum_{all\,\mathbf{x}} P(\mathbf{x})\,\log_2 P(\mathbf{x}) \right]; \qquad (\text{D}.2)$$

$$H(X)|_{\text{with memory}} < H(X)|_{\text{without memory}} \leqslant \log_2 K \qquad \text{(D.3)}$$

The *source redundancy*, which is the positive difference between $\log_2 K$ and source entropy $H(X)$, is due to two reasons in general: a *nonuniform* distribution of probabilities $P(x_k)$ and the presence of *memory*. For a *memoryless source* with $P(x_k) = 1/K$, $H(X) = \log_2 K$ and the redundancy is zero.

For *continuous-amplitude memoryless sources*,

$$h(X) = E\ [-\log_2 p_x(X)] = -\int_{-\infty}^{\infty} p_x(x)\ \log_2 p_x(x)\ dx \qquad \text{(D.4)}$$

and for *continuous-amplitude sources with memory*,

$$h(X) = \lim_{N \to \infty} h_N(X) = \lim_{N \to \infty} \left[-\frac{1}{N} \int_{-\infty}^{\infty} \int_{-\infty}^{\infty} \cdots \int_{-\infty}^{\infty} p_\mathbf{x}(\mathbf{x}) \log_2 p_\mathbf{x}(\mathbf{x})\ d\mathbf{x} \right] \qquad \text{(D.5)}$$

It can be shown that

$$h(X)|_{\text{with memory}} < h(X)|_{\text{without memory}} \leqslant \frac{1}{2} \log_2 (2\pi\ e\ \sigma_x^2) \qquad \text{(D.6)}$$

For a given source variance σ_x^2, the entropy in (D.4) is maximum, and equal to the bound in (D.6), for a Gaussian pdf; entropies lower than this value, and corresponding *redundancies*, are again due to two reasons: a *non-Gaussian* pdf, and the presence of *memory* (as indicated, for example, by a non-flat spectrum). We also note that the continuous-amplitude source entropies $h(X)$ are formally called *differential entropies*, and that it is useful to define an *entropy power*

$$Q = (2\pi\ e)^{-1}\ 2^{2h(X)} \qquad \text{(D.7)}$$

which has a maximum value, equal to σ_x^2, for a *memoryless Gaussian source*, with *independent identically distributed* (i.i.d.) outputs. For a Gaussian source with memory (a colored Gaussian source), the entropy power is equal to $\gamma_x^2\ \sigma_x^2$, where γ_x^2 is the *spectral flatness measure* (Chapter 2).

D.3 Discrete-Amplitude Sources

Appendix C has discussed several examples of *noiseless coding* for discrete-amplitude sources characterized by finite average bit rates R and a finite minimum rate $\min\{R\} = R(0) = H(X)$ [see (C.18)]. The constructive techniques for such coding make use of *encoding delay* as well as *variable length coding*, and examples in Appendix C showed that this could lead to coding procedures with perfect efficiency, i.e., procedures with an average transmission rate of $R'(0) = H(X)$. This book includes other examples of such noiseless coding. One example is the *variable length entropy coding* of quantizer outputs, which are discrete-amplitude sources by definition.

A second example of a discrete-amplitude source in this book is two-level graphics. This is also a discrete source with memory. As shown in the Markov model of Appendix C, the consequences of such memory are two-fold: the source entropy is less than that for a memoryless source with identical letter probabilities $P(x_k)$; and with $R'(0) = H(X)$, the requirements in terms of encoding delay are greater than with a memoryless source (Example C.8). We pursued this topic in Chapter 10. We also note that although in principle all discrete-amplitude sources can be coded with zero distortion, implementation considerations may require coding with non-zero, albeit imperceptible, distortion.

It is good to emphasize once again the distinction between transmission rate $R'(D)$ in an actual communication scheme with the *best possible* $R(D)$ which is the rate distortion function for the same distortion D. Comparison of $R'(D)$ and $R(D)$ — or of the inverse functions $D'(R)$ and $D(R)$ — is indeed one of the objectives of this book. This is done for amplitude-continuous sources in most of the chapters of the book, and for a simple discrete-amplitude source in Example D.1.

Example D.1.   Memoryless binary source; $P(x_1) = P(x_2) = 0.5$

Consider an *i.i.d. binary source* with *equiprobable* letters 1 and 0. Let the distortion measure be the *Hamming distance*, the distance $d(x,y)$ between a transmitted letter and the received version y (1 if $x \neq y$ and 0 if $x = y$). Consider a coding scheme where 1 out of M letters is *not transmitted* at all but *guessed* at the receiver based on the tossing of an unbiased coin. The rate R' and average distortion D are

$$R' = \frac{M-1}{M} = 1 - \frac{1}{M} \; bits/symbol \tag{D.8a}$$

$$D = \frac{1}{M}\left[\frac{1}{2}\cdot 0 + \frac{1}{2}\cdot 1\right] = \frac{1}{2M} \tag{D.8b}$$

$$D(R') = \frac{1-R'}{2} \quad ; \quad R'(D) = 1-2D \tag{D.8c}$$

The 0 and 1 in (D.8b) are distances (distortions) that apply to correct and incorrect guesses of the untransmitted letter. The factors 1/2 signify that the two types of guesses are equiprobable. The rate-versus-distortion function $R'(D)$ (D.8c) for this scheme is shown in curve (a) of Figure D.1.

Figure D.1   Coding of a memoryless binary source with equiprobable letters: (a) the function $R'(D)$ for the artificial coding scheme of Example D.1, and (b) the bound $R(D)$ [Berger, 1971].

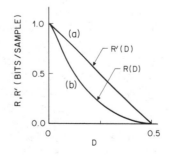

Also shown in Figure D.1 is the $R(D)$ bound [Berger, 1971]

$$R(D) = \lambda(1/2) - \lambda(D) ; \quad \lambda(p) = -p \log_2 p - (1-p)\log_2(1-p) \qquad (D.9)$$

where $\lambda(p)$ is the entropy function defined in Appendix C.

Note that in Figure D.1,

$$R(0) = H(X) = 1 \; bit/symbol$$

Distortionless coding is indeed attained by our artificial coding system asymptotically for $M \to \infty$. Several practical schemes exist for coding the binary memoryless source at rates of $R < 1$ with adequately low values of distortion; many of these are more sophisticated than our simple 1-out-of-M procedure. •

D.4 Continuous-Amplitude Sources

We shall now quantify the $R(D)$ or $D(R)$ curve, the lowermost curve in Figure 1.9, for examples of continuous-amplitude sources. The $R(D)$ results of this section will refer to an ergodic and stationary Gaussian source. These results, however, will also serve as lower bounds on performance when the source is non-Gaussian.

We will use *mean square error* (mse) as the distortion measure. The mse, sometimes refined by one or more of *amplitude -, time -* and *frequency -* weighting procedures, is the most widely used distortion measure, in spite of inadequacies for real-signal coding, as pointed out in this book wherever appropriate. The mse is mathematically tractable, and it does provide a guideline by which speech and image coder designs can be assessed (if not strictly optimized) from a perceptual viewpoint.

Although $R(D)$ and $D(R)$ formulations are mathematically equivalent, the $D(R)$ approach is more relevant to this book. Typically, our coding systems will have constraints on the rate R (reflecting available digital channel capacity) rather than constraints on distortion D. Given R, together with constraints on encoding delay and complexity, the problem will be to realize a coder performance that is as close as possible to the minimum D.

D.4.1 Mutual Information and Distortion

We consider a stationary, discrete-time, continuous-amplitude source $\{X(n)\}$, $n=0, \pm 1, \pm 2,...$. We arrange N source symbols (samples) into a *source vector* $\mathbf{x}$. Any of these vectors can be viewed as a realization of a vector random variable $\mathbf{X}$ with joint pdf $p_\mathbf{x}(\mathbf{x})$. *Reconstruction vectors* at the receiver are denoted by $\mathbf{y}$, a realization of another vector random variable $\mathbf{Y}$. In general $\mathbf{y}$ differs from a corresponding $\mathbf{x}$. The alphabet in each case will be the real line, reflecting a continuous-amplitude model. The basic distortion component is the single-letter squared error measure

$$d_1[x(n),y(n)] = [x(n) - y(n)]^2 \qquad (D.10)$$

Considering the case of $n = 1$ for convenience, the distortion per sample for the N-tuple $\mathbf{x}$ is

$$d_N(\mathbf{x},\mathbf{y}) = \frac{1}{N} \sum_{k=1}^{N} d_1[x(k),y(k)] \qquad \text{(D.11)}$$

Its average value, the average distortion per symbol

$$E[d_N(\mathbf{X},\mathbf{Y})] = \int_{-\infty}^{\infty}\int_{-\infty}^{\infty} \cdots \int_{-\infty}^{\infty} d_N(\mathbf{x},\mathbf{y}) p(\mathbf{x},\mathbf{y}) \, d\mathbf{x} \, d\mathbf{y} \qquad \text{(D.12)}$$

depends on both *source statistics* and *transition probability*. Since the joint pdf is $p(\mathbf{x},\mathbf{y}) = p(\mathbf{y}|\mathbf{x})p_\mathbf{x}(\mathbf{x})$, it can be minimized by choosing an appropriate mapping subject to a constraint on the rate.

In Appendix C, we have introduced the average mutual information per symbol between channel input and output as a measure of the average information that a reception of a discrete-amplitude output symbol supplies about a discrete-amplitude input symbol. A generalization of this definition to a continuous-amplitude N-tuple vector source that generates statistically independent vectors has the form

$$I_N(\mathbf{X};\mathbf{Y}) = (1/N)\int_{-\infty}^{\infty}\int_{-\infty}^{\infty} \cdots \int_{-\infty}^{\infty} p(\mathbf{x},\mathbf{y}) \, \log_2\left[p(\mathbf{y}|\mathbf{x})/p(\mathbf{y})\right] d\mathbf{x} \, d\mathbf{y}$$

$$\text{(D.13)}$$

$$= (1/N)\int_{-\infty}^{\infty}\int_{-\infty}^{\infty} \cdots \int_{-\infty}^{\infty} p(\mathbf{x},\mathbf{y}) \, \log_2\left[p(\mathbf{x}|\mathbf{y})/p(\mathbf{x})\right] d\mathbf{x} \, d\mathbf{y}$$

It depends on source statistics as well as transition probabilities between $\mathbf{X}$ and $\mathbf{Y}$, and it describes the information flow between vectors $\mathbf{x}$ and $\mathbf{y}$ as the average mutual information *per symbol*. Its asymptotic value is $I(X;Y) = \lim_{N\to\infty} I(\mathbf{X};\mathbf{Y})$ (see Chapter 1). We consider, for a given $p_\mathbf{x}(\mathbf{x})$, all transmission schemes (mappings) with transition probabilities $p(\mathbf{y}|\mathbf{x})$. We denote by

$$\mathbf{S} = \left\{ p(\mathbf{y}|\mathbf{x}) : I_N(\mathbf{X};\mathbf{Y}) \leqslant R \right\} \qquad \text{(D.14)}$$

the set of schemes (mappings) $p(\mathbf{y}|\mathbf{x})$ with the property that the average mutual information *per symbol* does not exceed a given rate R. Each of the schemes in this set has an average distortion given by (D.12). We search for the minimum of this distortion, within the set $\mathbf{S}$, and define

$$D_N(R) = \min_{p(\mathbf{y}|\mathbf{x}) \in \mathbf{S}} \{E[d_N(\mathbf{X},\mathbf{Y})]\} \qquad \text{(D.15)}$$

This function is the minimum possible distortion subject to the requirement that the information rate must not exceed a given R, provided that successive vectors of the source are statistically independent. The mapping $p(\mathbf{y}|\mathbf{x})$ that realizes $D_N(R)$ is the *optimal mapping*. If successive vectors are statistically dependent, longer blocks can be considered such that successive vectors are *almost* independent. The function $D_N(R)$ is called the *N-block distortion rate function*. The *distortion rate function* (DRF) $D(R)$ is defined as

$$D(R) = \lim_{N \to \infty} D_N(R) \tag{D.16}$$

It is the minimum possible distortion for a given rate R, a lower bound on the distortion that can be realized in any possible scheme.

The proof that the limit exists for stationary sources and the proof that $D(R)$ is indeed the minimum possible distortion for a given R can be found elsewhere [Berger, 1971].

The inverse of (D.16) is $R(D)$, the minimum information rate needed to be able to reconstruct the signal at the receiver with a value D. Therefore $R(D)$ also gives the channel capacity needed for a transmission subject to the requirement of a reconstruction with fidelity D. Since an almost error-free transmission is possible as long as the rate is below the capacity of the channel (*Noisy-Channel Coding Theorem* (Section C.6) [Shannon, 1948]), we interpret $R(D)$ as the minimum rate at the output of the source coder. This *source coder* will thus lead to an *irreversible mapping* which causes an average distortion D for a given rate R.

Recall once again the qualitative nature of Figure 1.9, and note that $R(0) = \infty$ for continuous-amplitude sources. This is the uninteresting case of zero data compression, and maximum mutual information corresponding to $[p(\mathbf{y}|\mathbf{x}) = 1$ for $\mathbf{y} = \mathbf{x}$; and $p(\mathbf{y}|\mathbf{x}) = 0$ otherwise] in (D.13):

$$D = 0 ; \quad H(X) = H(Y) = I(X;Y) = \infty \tag{D.17}$$

Interesting mappings for waveform communication are described by

$$D > 0 ; \quad I(X;Y) < \infty \tag{D.18}$$

D.4.2 Memoryless Sources

For a memoryless zero-mean Gaussian source $N(0,\sigma_x^2)$ [Berger, 1971],

$$R(D)_G = \max\{0, \frac{1}{2} \log_2 \frac{\sigma_x^2}{D}\} = \begin{cases} \frac{1}{2} \log_2 \frac{\sigma_x^2}{D} ; & 0 \leqslant D \leqslant \sigma_x^2 \\ 0; & D \geqslant \sigma_x^2 \end{cases} \tag{D.19a}$$

$$D(R)_G = 2^{-2R} \sigma_x^2 \tag{D.19b}$$

It is obvious that no information needs to be transmitted $[R(D)_G = 0]$ *for a given* $D \geqslant \sigma_x^2$ since $D = \sigma_x^2$ can be obtained by using zeros for the reconstruction [reconstruction error $r(n) = x(n) - y(n) = x(n) - 0 = x(n)$]; and $D > \sigma_x^2$ can be realized by using x-independent zero-mean noise samples $e(n)$ of variance $(D - \sigma_x^2)$ for reconstruction $[r(n) = x(n) - e(n);\ E[R^2(n)] = \sigma_x^2 + (D - \sigma_x^2) = D]$. Another interesting conclusion from (D.19b) is that *the mse is reduced by a factor of 4 for each bit additionally spent in the transmission; the SNR in dB is 6.02 times the bit rate R.* In Chapter 4, we note a very similar result in the description of quantizer performance.

The statistics of the optimal mapping that realizes (D.19) can be given explicitly [Berger, 1971]:

$$p(y|x) = \frac{1}{\sqrt{2\pi\beta D}} \exp\left[-(y-\beta x)^2/2\beta D\right] ; \qquad \beta = 1 - D/\sigma_x^2 \qquad \text{(D.20)}$$

signifying that the output is an $N(\beta x, \beta D)$ Gaussian source for a given input x. An optimum *test channel* that provides the x-y mapping in (D.20) is shown in Figure D.2. Note that in this test channel, the *input $x(n)$ is scaled* and the *additive noise is also Gaussian, and $x(n)$-independent.* This implies that the reconstruction error is also Gaussian and input-independent.

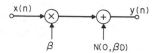

Figure D.2 The optimal x-y mapping for memoryless Gaussian sources; $\beta = 1 - D/\sigma_x^2$.

We note in Chapter 4 that the reconstruction error in the mapping provided by a certain practical system, a memoryless quantizer, is x-dependent and non-Gaussian, for Gaussian x. Such a system is suboptimal; and indeed more sophisticated coding systems (delayed decision coders) strive to achieve the x-independent Gaussian noise ideal implied in the $R(D)$-optimal mapping (D.20). This is accomplished by coding the input in long blocks although the source is memoryless (Section 4.6 and Chapter 9).

The non-zero $R(D)_G$ in (D.19a) can also be rewritten as

$$R(D)_G = \frac{1}{2} \log_2 \frac{\sigma_x^2}{D} = \frac{1}{2} \log_2 2\pi e\ \sigma_x^2 - \frac{1}{2} \log_2 2\pi e\ D \qquad \text{(D.21)}$$

This has the interesting interpretation that the bit rate needed for reproducing the source with distortion D is the difference in entropies (see Appendix C) of the source and the noise, which are two zero-mean Gaussian r.v.'s, with variances of σ_x^2 and D.

Memoryless Non-Gaussian Sources. There are no explicit DRF results for non-Gaussian memoryless sources but upper and lower bounds are available in the form

$$^L D(R) \leqslant D(R) \leqslant D(R)_G \qquad \text{(D.22a)}$$

The upper bound is the DRF of the zero-mean memoryless Gaussian source, with equality if $p_x(x)$ is $N(0, \sigma_x^2)$: *the DRF of any zero-mean memoryless non-Gaussian source lies below* that of *the Gaussian source*; the lower bound is the *Shannon lower bound* (for an mse criterion)

$$^L D(R) = (2\pi e)^{-1} 2^{-2[R - h(X)]} = 2^{-2R} Q \qquad (D.22b)$$

or, alternatively,

$$^L R(D) = h(X) - (1/2) \log_2 2\pi e D , \qquad (D.22c)$$

where the differential entropy $h(X)$ and entropy power Q are those defined in Appendix C and in Section D.2. Recall that Q is the variance of a Gaussian source that has the same differential entropy as the given non-Gaussian source; for a Gaussian source, $Q = \sigma_x^2$ and $^L D(R)$ is equal to the true DRF. In fact, at high rates, $^L D(R)$ converges to the true DRF for a rather broad class of distributions. For lower bit rates, say $R = 1$ to 3 bits/sample, $^L D(R)$ bounds are too optimistic; and numerical calculation of the DRF via the Blahut algorithm [Blahut, 1972] is more informative (Chapters 4 and 9). Table D.1 lists the maximum obtainable *SNR* values $\max\{SNR\} = 10\log(\sigma_x^2/D)$ for various memoryless sources [Noll and Zelinski, 1978]. Figure D.3 shows the numerically determined DRF of a memoryless gamma-distributed source, together with lower and upper bounds $^L D(R)$ and $D(R)_G$.

Table D.1 Maximum obtainable *SNR* values $\max\{SNR\}$ (dB) = 10 log (σ_x^2/D) for memoryless sources (U: Uniform, G: Gaussian, L: Laplacian and Γ: Gamma) [Noll and Zelinski, 1978].

R (bits per sample)	U	G	L	Γ
1	6.79	6.02	6.62	8.53
2	13.21	12.04	12.66	15.21
3	19.42	18.06	18.68	21.59

Figure D.3 Distortion rate function for memoryless sources with (a) Gaussian pdf and (b) gamma pdf. $D(R)_G$, which is the function (a), is an upper bound for (b), and $^L D(R)$ is a lower bound for (b) [Noll and Zelinski, 1978].

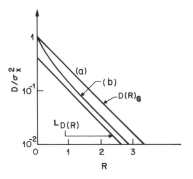

D.4.3 Sources with Memory

Sources with memory permit greater data compression than memoryless sources for a given D and we shall now note some results in the Gaussian case. The $D(R)$ function reflects this higher data compression or entropy compression through expressions that measure the *non-flatness* of the *source psd*. Recall that the entropy power of a Gaussian source with memory is simply $\gamma_x^2 \sigma_x^2$, where γ_x^2 is the spectral flatness measure. The existence of $\gamma_x^2 < 1$ is explicitly exploited in DPCM and Transform Coding. Even greater compressions are possible with non-Gaussian sources. But in this case, the coding systems would require more information than that provided by the source psd or acf.

The $D(R)$ function for a general (colored) zero-mean Gaussian source is given parametrically in the form [Kolmogorov, 1956] [Berger, 1971]:

$$D(\phi)_{\mathbf{G}} = \frac{1}{2\pi} \int_{-\pi}^{\pi} \min \{\phi, S_{xx}(e^{j\omega})\} d\omega \qquad \text{(D.23a)}$$

$$R(\phi)_{\mathbf{G}} = \frac{1}{2\pi} \int_{-\pi}^{\pi} \max \left\{0, \frac{1}{2} \log_2 \frac{S_{xx}(e^{j\omega})}{\phi}\right\} d\omega \qquad \text{(D.23b)}$$

Note that $D(\phi)_{\mathbf{G}}$ and $R(\phi)_{\mathbf{G}}$ depend only on the psd $S_{xx}(e^{j\omega})$ of the Gaussian sequence. A memoryless source has a white spectrum, i.e., $S_{xx}(\cdot) = $ const., and the above result equals that of (D.19). The result of (D.23) has the interpretation of the "water-filling" procedure of Figure D.4 [McDonald and Schultheiss, 1964] [Berger, 1971]. The frequency axis can be divided into two sets A and B:

$$\omega \in A \text{ if } S_{xx}(e^{j\omega}) \geqslant \phi; \quad \omega \in B \text{ if } S_{xx}(e^{j\omega}) < \phi \qquad \text{(D.24)}$$

Set B is simply obtained conceptually by filling water into a container whose bottom is the $(-\pi, \pi)$ range of the x-axis of the figure, and whose top surface is in the shape of $S_{xx}(\cdot)$; and noting that the water does not come up to the level of the dashed horizontal in areas where the top surface of the container is not high enough. The results of (D.23) imply that the spectral contributions of the set B are not transmitted at all since they do not contribute to the rate. An ideal scheme attempts only to reproduce the spectrum of the frequency set A. Thus the frequency band is divided into *passbands* (set A) and *stopbands* (set B).

The parametric representation of the DRF as given above can also be interpreted differently by defining the spectrum $S_{rr}(e^{j\omega})$ of the reconstruction error $r(n) = x(n) - y(n)$ as

$$S_{rr}(e^{j\omega}, \phi) = \min \{\phi, S_{xx}(e^{j\omega})\} \qquad \text{(D.25)}$$

so that [Kolmogorov, 1956]

$$D(\phi)_{\mathbf{G}} = \frac{1}{2\pi} \int_{-\pi}^{\pi} S_{rr}(e^{j\omega}, \phi) d\omega \qquad \text{(D.26)}$$

$$R(\phi)_G = \frac{1}{2\pi} \int_{-\pi}^{\pi} \frac{1}{2} \log_2 \frac{S_{xx}(e^{j\omega})}{S_{rr}(e^{j\omega},\phi)} d\omega \qquad \text{(D.27)}$$

A comparison with (D.23) and (D.24) reveals that the error spectrum is

$$S_{rr}(e^{j\omega},\phi) = \begin{cases} \phi = constant & \omega \in A \\ S_{xx}(e^{j\omega}) & \omega \in B \end{cases} \qquad \text{(D.28)}$$

The fact that the error spectrum equals the source spectrum in the set B is clear from the statement that the information contained in that frequency region is not transmitted at all. The error spectrum in the set A must be constant, and it turns out that the optimal error spectrum is that of the shaded area in Figure D.4. In the ideal coding scheme, frequency bands with higher power are coded with higher signal-to-distortion ratios than other bands.

For the example of a monotonically decreasing input spectrum $S_{xx}(e^{j\omega})$, our results imply that the source should be lowpass filtered such that the region B is an ideal stopband. This does *not* mean that the lowpass filter has to be ideal, with $H(e^{j\omega}) = 1$ for $\omega \in A$, and it does *not* mean that the optimum mapping from the source to the destination can be modeled by such an ideal lowpass filter followed by the addition of white noise of psd $\phi = $ const. in the region A. It is true that the error spectrum in A must be $\phi = $ const. However, this constant spectrum is realized by a combination of a *non-ideal* lowpass-filter $H(e^{j\omega},\phi)$ and a *non-white* Gaussian additive noise which is input-independent. For any nonwhite Gaussian sequence (not only for those with monotonically decreasing spectra), the filter and additive noise components of the optimal mapping are [Berger, 1971]

Figure D.4 Optimal error spectrum, shown by the shaded region, with (a) unweighted errors; and (b) frequency-weighted errors [Kolmogorov, 1956].

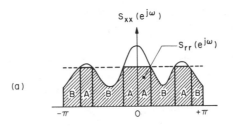

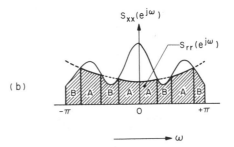

$$H(e^{j\omega},\phi) = \min\left\{0, 1 - \frac{\phi}{S_{xx}(e^{j\omega})}\right\}; \quad S_{nn}(e^{j\omega},\phi) = \min\left\{0, \phi\left(1 - \frac{\phi}{S_{xx}(e^{j\omega})}\right)\right\} \quad \text{(D.29)}$$

The optimal mapping is shown in Figure D.5. This is a generalization of Figure D.2 which referred to a memoryless Gaussian input, and was therefore frequency-invariant. The error sequences $r(n) = x(n) - y(n)$ in the filter structure of Figure D.5 have a psd

$$S_{rr}(e^{j\omega},\phi) = S_{xx}(e^{j\omega})|1 - H(e^{j\omega},\phi)|^2 + S_{nn}(e^{j\omega},\phi) \qquad \text{(D.30)}$$

if the additive noise and the input signal are uncorrelated. Upon combining (D.28), (D.29) and (D.30),

$$S_{rr}(e^{j\omega},\phi) = \begin{cases} \dfrac{\phi^2}{S_{xx}(e^{j\omega})} + \phi\left[1 - \dfrac{\phi}{S_{xx}(e^{j\omega})}\right] \ ; \quad \omega \in A \\ S_{rr}^{(1)}(e^{j\omega}) + S_{rr}^{(2)}(e^{j\omega}) \end{cases}$$

$$\text{(D.31)}$$

This is indeed the optimal shape of the reconstruction error spectrum in frequency band A. Note that this error spectrum consists of two terms; the first term is caused by *suppressing* signal contributions [the lowpass or bandpass filters of (D.29) are *non-ideal*], and the second term is due to *non-white* Gaussian additive noise.

Figure D.6(b) uses a lowpass input example to demonstrate that a significant part of the distortion in an optimal system is caused by a suppression of source contributions and as such is not additive at all. The two terms $S_{rr}^{(1)}(\cdot)$ and $S_{rr}^{(2)}(\cdot)$ are those that apply to the passband region A, as in (D.31). The term $S_{rr}^{(3)}(\cdot)$ refers to the stopband region B. In the literature we often find the interpretation that $S_{rr}^{(3)}$ is the "bandlimiting noise" and that the in-band noise is "coding noise". In this book, all the three distortion components in Figure D.6(b) will be regarded as components of *coding noise*. In many coder examples, the bandlimiting noise component is zero; these will constitute a convenient but sub-optimal design. The bit-allocation procedures in Transform Coding will constitute a practical recognition of stop-band region B, the associated water-filling procedure, and hence a non-zero bandlimiting noise component in $S_{rr}(e^{j\omega})$. Figure D.6(a) shows optimal spectra in the coding of a white source. The result is, of course, that of Figure D.2: the source samples are first scaled by a factor $(1 - D/\sigma_x^2)$, causing error spectrum $S_{rr}^{(1)}(e^{j\omega})$; and then, additive Gaussian noise $N(0, \beta D)$ is introduced, causing the error spectrum $S_{rr}^{(2)}(e^{j\omega})$.

Figure D.5 The optimal x-y mapping for non-white Gaussian sources.

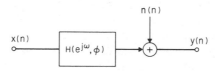

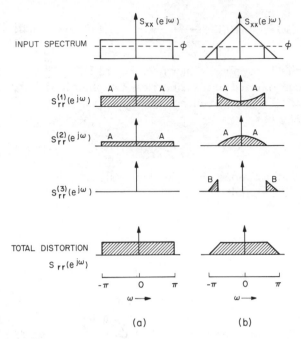

Figure D.6 Error spectra in the optimal x-y mapping which achieves the DRF bounds for (a) a white Gaussian source and (b) a colored Gaussian source.

Small Distortions. A simpler form of the DRF of a Gaussian source is obtained for *small distortions* defined by $\phi \leqslant \min_{\omega} \{S_{xx}(e^{j\omega})\}$. The DRF is then

$$D(R)_G = \gamma_x^2 \, 2^{-2R} \, \sigma_x^2 \; ; \quad \gamma_x^2 = \exp\left[\frac{1}{2\pi} \int_{-\pi}^{\pi} \log_e S_{xx}(e^{j\omega}) \, d\omega\right]/\sigma_x^2 \quad \text{(D.32)}$$

where γ_x^2 is the *spectral flatness measure (sfm)* of the process $\{X(n)\}$. *It is also the normalized one-step-ahead prediction error variance of the process with psd $S_{xx}(\cdot)$; and its inverse is the maximally obtainable prediction gain.* For an AR source, the variance $\gamma_x^2\sigma_x^2$ in (D.32) is just the variance of the innovations process that generates the source $\{X(n)\}$; all the information contained in the correlated source sequence is also contained in the innovations sequence. It can be shown that this result is not restricted to stationary sources.

Chapter 2 has shown that $\gamma_x^2 \leqslant 1$, with equality only for memoryless sources $[S_{xx}(e^{j\omega}) = \sigma_x^2 = \text{constant}]$. Hence, a comparison of (D.32) with (D.19b) reveals that, for a given rate R, the distortion can be reduced by γ_x^2 in the range of small distortions:

$$D(R)_G|_{\text{correlated source}} = \gamma_x^2 \, D(R)_G|_{\text{white source}} \quad \text{(D.33)}$$

Example D.2. First-order Markov source with $\rho = 0.95$

We shall explain some of the results for a Gaussian first-order Markov source of zero mean and with acf and psd

$$R_{xx}(k) = \rho^{|k|}\sigma_x^2 ; \quad S_{xx}(e^{j\omega}) = \frac{1-\rho^2}{1+\rho^2 - 2\,\rho\,\cos\omega}\sigma_x^2 \tag{D.34}$$

For $\rho \geqslant 0$, its minimum is given for $\omega = \pi$:

$$\min_{\omega}\,\{S_{xx}(e^{j\omega})\} = \frac{1-\rho^2}{(1+\rho)^2}\sigma_x^2 = \frac{1-\rho}{1+\rho}\,\sigma_x^2 \tag{D.35}$$

For $\rho = 0.95$,

$$\min_{\omega}\,\{S_{xx}(e^{j\omega})\} = 0.0256\,\sigma_x^2 \tag{D.36}$$

The *small distortion* region is defined by $D/\sigma_x^2 \leqslant 0.0256$ [or $R \geqslant \log_2(1+\rho) = 0.964$]. For this region,

$$D(R)_{\mathbf{G}} = (1-\rho^2)2^{-2R}\sigma_x^2 \tag{D.37}$$

since

$$\gamma_x^2 = 1 - \rho^2 \tag{D.38}$$

Figure D.7 shows the DRF plot. The curve parallels the bound $D(R)_{\mathbf{G}}$ for $R > 0.964$. For $R < 0.964$, the values for the curve are obtained by parametric expressions (D.23). ●

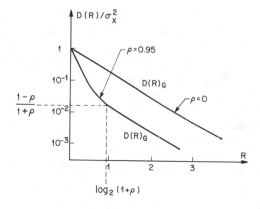

Figure D.7   DRF plots for a first-order Gauss-Markov [AR(1)] source with $\rho = 0.95$ and $\rho = 0.0$.

N-Block DRF.   In equation (D.15), we introduced the notion of $D_N(R)$, the DRF of a source that produces *statistically independent blocks* of N symbols. For a Gaussian source it can be shown [Berger, 1971] that

$$D_N(\phi) = \frac{1}{N}\sum_{k=0}^{N-1}\min\{\phi,\lambda_k\} \tag{D.39a}$$

$$R_N(\phi) = \frac{1}{N}\sum_{k=0}^{N-1}\max\{0,\tfrac{1}{2}\log_2\frac{\lambda_k}{\phi}\} \tag{D.39b}$$

where λ_k is the kth eigenvalue of the source process $\{X(n)\}$. Upon applying the Toeplitz distribution theorem, the DRF results of (D.23) are obtained for $N \rightarrow \infty$. We are also interested, however, in the case of finite N.

First, note that the rate R_N can be interpreted as the average of N rates R_k resulting from coding Gaussian memoryless sources with variances λ_k [see (D.19)]. However, the distortion contributions are optimal and are given by $D_k = \min\{\phi, \lambda_k\}$. The interesting result is that the distortion contributions of those r.v.'s whose variances λ_k are not smaller than a given value of ϕ are all equal, and that the values of the other distortion contributions equal the eigenvalues. This implies that these latter r.v.'s need not be transmitted at all (or, equivalently, they are of no use for reproducing the vector for a given distortion); consequently, $R_k = 0$ for $\phi \geqslant \lambda_k$.

Let us briefly discuss the special case of *small distortions*. If $\phi \leqslant \min \{\lambda_k\}$; where the minimum is over all k for $k = 0,1,...,N-1$, we have $D_N = \phi$, and the N-block DRF (for a given rate R) is

$$D_N(R) = 2^{-2R} \left[\prod_{k=0}^{N-1} \lambda_k \right]^{1/N} \tag{D.40}$$

It is easy to see that the DRF $D_N(R)$ of sources with memory is upper-bounded by the DRF of the memoryless source (D.19). Indeed, since the variance σ_x^2 of the source equals the arithmetic mean of the N eigenvalues λ_k, a comparison of (D.19) and (D.39) reveals that

$$D_N(R) \leqslant D(R)_G|_{\text{white source}} = 2^{-2R} \sigma_x^2 \tag{D.41}$$

The equality applies if all eigenvalues are equal, which is only true for memoryless sources. This statement is based on the fact that the geometric mean of N variables does not exceed the corresponding arithmetic mean. We conclude that sources with memory can be encoded and transmitted with smaller distortions than memoryless sources.

We next use the result (2.63a):

$$|^N\mathbf{R_{xx}}| = \prod_{k=0}^{N-1} \lambda_k \tag{D.42}$$

where $|^N\mathbf{R_{xx}}|$ is the determinant of the Nth order correlation matrix of the source process, and λ_k is the kth eigenvalue. The entropy power of the process, as defined by (C.26b), is

$$Q_N = |^N\mathbf{R_{xx}}|^{1/N} \tag{D.43}$$

From (D.42) and (D.40),

$$D_N(R) = 2^{-2R} Q_N = {}^L D(R) \tag{D.44}$$

That is, the DRF equals its Shannon lower bound for small distortions. A coding scheme called Transform Coding, (based on the Karhunen-Loeve transform) operates in a manner that is conceptually close to the above results. This scheme is described in Chapter 12. There, however, successive vectors, taken from a scalar source, are not statistically independent of each other, and (D.39a) only holds for large N.

Frequency-Weighted Distortions. Frequency weighting of the error spectrum is an important means for obtaining a subjectively more relevant distortion measure (Chapters 7, 11 and 12, and Appendix E). Let $S_{ww}(e^{j\omega})$ be such a weighting function; a small value of $S_{ww}(\cdot)$ indicates that a high error variance is acceptable in that frequency region, and vice versa. $S_{ww}(\cdot)$ can be interpreted as the square-magnitude frequency response of a noise-weighting filter, as in Figure D.8. Earlier results for Gaussian sources extend in the form

$$D(\phi)_G = \frac{1}{2\pi} \int_{-\pi}^{\pi} \min \{\phi, S_{xx}(e^{j\omega}) S_{ww}(e^{j\omega})\} \, d\omega \tag{D.45}$$

$$R(\phi)_G = \frac{1}{2\pi} \int_{-\pi}^{\pi} \max \left\{0, \frac{1}{2} \log_2 \frac{S_{xx}(e^{j\omega}) S_{ww}(e^{j\omega})}{\phi}\right\} \tag{D.46}$$

For a given ϕ, the spectrum separates again into two frequency sets A and B such that

$$\omega \in A \quad \text{for} \quad \phi \leqslant S_{xx}(e^{j\omega}) S_{ww}(e^{j\omega})$$

$$\omega \in B \quad \text{for} \quad \phi > S_{xx}(e^{j\omega}) S_{ww}(e^{j\omega}) \tag{D.47}$$

and it is easy to see that the *weighted* error spectrum must be constant for the frequency set A, which is the only set contributing to the rate R. We noted similar results in *Noise Feedback Coding* (Chapter 7). [The unweighted error spectrum for the frequency set B is $S_{xx}(\cdot)$, corresponding to zero outputs]. Finally, the optimal unweighted error spectrum in set A is inverse to the weighting function, i.e., relatively large error contributions occur where the weight $S_{ww}(\cdot)$ is small. In the example of Figure D.4(b), the large error contributions are at higher frequencies. This implies a *lowpass $S_{ww}(\cdot)$ function.*

Figure D.8 Frequency weighting of error.

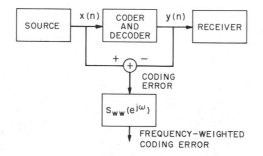

For *small distortions*,

$$D(R)_G = \gamma_x^2 \, \gamma_w^2 \, \sigma_x^2 \, 2^{-2R} \tag{D.48}$$

where γ_w^2 is the spectral flatness measure for the weighting spectrum $S_{ww}(\cdot)$, which is assumed to be normalized so that $\sigma_w^2 = 1$. Compare (D.48) with the special cases (D.19b) and (D.32).

Two-Dimensional Sources. For a Gaussian random field $\{X(m,n)\}$ with acf $R_{xx}(k,l)$ and psd

$$S_{xx}(e^{j\omega}, e^{j\omega_2}) = \sum_{-\infty}^{\infty} \sum_{-\infty}^{\infty} R_{xx}(k,l) e^{-j(k\omega_1 + l\omega_2)}, \tag{D.49}$$

$$D(\phi)_G = \left[\frac{1}{2\pi}\right]^2 \int_{-\infty}^{\infty} \int_{-\infty}^{\infty} \min\{\phi, S_{xx}(e^{j\omega_1}, e^{j\omega_2})\} \, d\omega_1 d\omega_2 \tag{D.50a}$$

$$R(\phi)_G = \left[\frac{1}{2\pi}\right]^2 \int_{-\infty}^{\infty} \int_{-\infty}^{\infty} \max\left\{0, \frac{1}{4} \log_2 S_{xx}(e^{j\omega_1}, e^{j\omega_2})\right\} \, d\omega_1 d\omega_2 \tag{D.50b}$$

Non-Gaussian Sources. As in the case of memoryless sources (D.22),

$$^L D(R) \leqslant D(R) \leqslant D(R)_G \tag{D.51}$$

where $^L D(R)$ is the Shannon lower bound as defined in (D.22b). Again, as in the memoryless case, the Gaussian source is the most difficult one to reproduce, for a fixed second moment and the mse criterion.

D.4.4   Continuous-Time Sources

DRF results for continuous-time sources are formally very close to those for discrete-time sources. Specifically, let $S_{xx}(\Omega)$ be the source psd, R the rate in *bits/second* (instead of *bits/symbol*), and D the mse, also on a per second basis:

$$D = E\left[\frac{1}{T} \int_0^T [X(t) - Y(t)]^2 \, dt\right] \tag{D.52a}$$

where $\{X(t)\}$ and $\{Y(t)\}$ are the stationary, time-continuous and amplitude-continuous processes describing the source and reconstruction signals. The parametric DRF equations are

$$D(\phi) = \frac{1}{2\pi} \int_{-\infty}^{\infty} \min\{\phi, S_{xx}(\Omega)\} \, d\Omega \tag{D.52b}$$

$$R(\phi) = \frac{1}{2\pi} \int_{-\infty}^{\infty} \max\left\{0, \frac{1}{2} \log_2 \frac{S_{xx}(\Omega)}{\phi}\right\} d\Omega \tag{D.52c}$$

The DRF results are now for non-bandlimited spectra, in general. For a given R, these results provide lower bounds on the distortion obtainable in communication schemes which may include subsequent bandlimiting or not. Here the distortion includes contributions due to bandlimiting as well as encoding. In the case of spectra that monotonically decrease with ω, the DRF defines a cut-off frequency (depending on distortion D) above which the spectrum should not be transmitted. Obviously, an optimal encoding is partly based on lowpass filtering of the source signal. The bandlimiting that is tacitly assumed in waveform communication does not typically reflect the knowledge of results such as (D.52), but depends on simple subjective criteria (such as articulation as a function of lowpass filter cutoff for speech, see Chapter 3).

Example D.3.   Bandlimited Gaussian source
Consider the psd

$$S_{xx}(\Omega) = \begin{cases} \sigma_x^2/2W & \text{for } |\Omega| \leqslant 2\pi \, W \\ \\ 0 & \text{for } |\Omega| > 2\pi \, W \end{cases} \tag{D.53}$$

Use of this in (D.52) yields

$$R(D)_G = W \log_2 (\sigma_x^2/D) \; ; \quad 0 \leqslant D \leqslant \sigma_x^2 \tag{D.54a}$$

$$D(R)_G = 2^{-R/W} \sigma_x^2 \tag{D.54b}$$

which is Shannon's classic formula. It can also be derived directly from (D.19b) since $\{X(t)\}$ can be exactly represented by i.i.d. $N(0,\sigma_x^2)$ samples taken $1/2W$ seconds apart, as per the sampling theorem (Chapter 3). $\bullet$

References

T. Berger, *Rate Distortion Theory*, Prentice-Hall, Englewood Cliffs, N.J., 1971.

R. E. Blahut, "Computation of Channel Capacity and Rate Distortion Functions," IEEE Trans. on Information Theory, pp. 460-473, July 1972.

L. D. Davisson and R. M. Gray (eds.), *Data Compression,* Halsted Press, John Wiley, New York, 1976.

A. N. Kolmogorov, "On the Shannon Theory of Information Transmission in the Case of Continuous Signals," IRE Trans. on Information Theory, pp. 102-103, September 1956.

R. A. McDonald and P. M. Schultheiss, "Information Rates of Gaussian Signals under Criteria Constraining the Error Spectrum," Proc. IEEE, pp. 415-416, April 1964.

P. Noll and R. Zelinski, "Bounds on Quantizer Performance in the Low Bit Rate Region," IEEE Trans. on Communications, pp. 300-304, February 1978.

C. E. Shannon, "A Mathematical Theory of Communication," Bell System Tech. J., pp. 379-423 (Part I) and pp. 623-656 (Part II), 1948.

C. E. Shannon, "Coding Theorems for a Discrete Source with a Fidelity Criterion," IRE National Convention Record, part 4, pp. 142-163, 1959; also in *Information and Decision Processes* (R. E. Machol, ed.), pp. 93-126, McGraw-Hill, New York, 1960.

D. Slepian (ed.), *Key Papers in the Development of Information Theory*, IEEE Press, 1974.

A. D. Wyner, "Fundamental Limits in Information Theory," Proc. IEEE, pp. 239-251, February 1981.

Appendix E

Objective Measurement of Coder Performance

The purpose of this appendix is to summarize certain objective measures of coder quality used many times in this book. All of these measures have the general nature of a *signal-to-noise ratio (SNR)*. These measures have been used either in the computer simulations of coders, or in analytical examples, or both. Some of these measures are also used in standardized evaluations of coder hardware, and these examples will be pointed out, as and when appropriate. The *SNR* refinements discussed in this appendix are motivated to a great extent by speech work. Extensions and generalizations to image coding are mentioned as appropriate.

E.1 Signal-To-Noise Ratio, *SNR*

As discussed in Section 1.1.2, the reconstruction error $r(n)$ in digital coding is defined as the difference between coder input $x(n)$ and coder output $y(n)$; and the *signal-to-noise ratio* $SNR = \sigma_x^2/\sigma_r^2$, the ratio of input signal variance to reconstruction error variance, is the single most utilized descriptor of coder performance. The input signal used in measurements of coder quality is either the intended input (as in most of the speech coding illustrations in this book), or — in the interest of standardization and repeatability — *sine-wave signals* or *narrow-band noise* [CCITT, 1981] (as in Figures 5.9 and 5.10). In any case, coder designs that maximize the *SNR* do so by minimizing σ_r^2. They are *minimum mean square error* (mmse) designs.

In an ongoing quest for a *subjectively meaningful objective measure* of coder quality, several refinements of the conventional *SNR* have been proposed and used in speech and image work. We will now discuss some of these refinements — not necessarily in order of importance, but perhaps in order of increasing complexity. An ideal measure is a *single* number that would be *valid, meaningful, reliable, easy to obtain* and *diagnostic*. No single measure satisfies all these requirements. All of the *objective measures* in this section, as in the case of conventional *SNR*, should be regarded therefore as partial descriptors of coder performance; with signals such as speech and video, the above measurements are either supplemented by secondary objective measurements (for example, measurements with a *pulse-and-bar* input in image work [Mallon, 1970]) or by the use of the *subjective measures* of Appendix F.

E.2 Segmental Signal-to-Noise Ratio, *SNRSEG*

An important class of *SNR* refinements, used widely in speech coding, are those that recognize the fact that the speech signal is nonstationary and that the same amount of noise has different perceptual values depending on the ambient signal level.

The *Q measure* [Richards, 1968] [Cattermole, 1969] [Richards, 1973] uses an experimental pdf for the varying *root mean square* (rms) input level in the segments of a (single-talker) speech signal (Figure 2.6), and it computes an average coder performance by integrating performance over the range of the above pdf. The conventional *SNR* measure does not penalize the bad rendition of weak signals as much as *Q* does.

The *segmental SNR* (*SNRSEG*) [Noll, 1974] measure is similar in that it compensates for the under-emphasis of weak-signal performance in conventional *SNR* calculation. However, unlike the *Q* measure which is a fixed time-invariant amplitude-weighting, the segmental *SNR* is based on dynamic time-weighting: specifically, a log-weighting that converts component *SNR* values to dB values prior to averaging, so that very high *SNR* values corresponding to well-coded large-signal segments do not camouflage coder performance with the weak segments, as in conventional *SNR*. The segmental *SNR* is defined as

$$SNRSEG \text{ (dB)} = E[SNR(m) \text{ (dB)}] \tag{E.1}$$

where $SNR(m)$ is the conventional *SNR* for segment m, and the expectation is in practice a time average over all segments of interest in an input sequence. An appropriate segment length in speech work would be in the order of 16 ms. Segments representing silences in speech may be considered as either important or not by the user of (E.1). In the latter case, such segments can be detected by setting an input power threshold in the order of −40dB (relative to long-term power level) and excluded from the expectation or summation operation. When the proportion of silent segments in the input is very small, say less than 5%, the isolation of such segments will not make a significant difference in the value of *SNRSEG*. The above is true for most of the sentence-length speech waveforms illustrated in this book.

The fact that *SNRSEG* reflects weak-signal rendition better than the conventional *SNR* is illustrated by the simple two-segment example in Table E.1. The conventional value of *SNR* (dB) = 17 is primarily influenced by *SNR* (1) (dB) = 20, the value for the higher energy segment, while *SNRSEG* (dB) = 10 shows equal weighting of the component values *SNR* (1) (dB) and *SNR* (2) (dB). In non-logarithmic units, the segmental *SNR* is also 10, and it is the *geometric mean* of component *SNR* (*m*) values 100 and 1. An even greater weighting of the low energy segment would be provided if the final quality is defined as the *harmonic mean* of the component values [Ramamoorthy, 1978]. In this example, the value of such a measure would be $[0.5(1^{-1} + 100^{-1})]^{-1} \sim 2$, or 3 dB.

The subjective relevance of *SNRSEG* has been investigated in several experiments. The measure is particularly relevant in situations where a significant number of weak segments exist, and they are indeed poorly coded [McDermott, Scagliola and Goodman, 1978] [Nakatsui and Mermelstein, 1982].

Table E.1 *SNRSEG* and Conventional *SNR*

Segment Number *m*	1	2
Input rms signal	10	1
Input rms noise	1	1
SNR (*m*)	100	1
SNR (*m*) (dB)	20	0
Signal-to-noise ratios		
Conventional *SNR*	$\dfrac{100+1}{2} = 50.5 \quad \longrightarrow$	17 dB
SNRSEG	$\dfrac{20\ \text{dB}+0\ \text{dB}}{2} \quad \longrightarrow$	10 dB

E.3   Frequency-Weighted *SNR* and Reconstruction Error

This refinement recognizes that noise in certain frequency bands is less harmful than that in other bands of an input signal, suggesting an effective, or frequency-weighted error variance (Chapter 7 and Figure D.8) of the type

$$\sigma_{rw}^2 = \frac{1}{2\pi} \int_{-\pi}^{\pi} S_{rr}(e^{j\omega}) S_{ww}(e^{j\omega}) d\omega \qquad (E.2)$$

A smaller value of the *error spectrum* weighting function $S_{ww}(e^{j\omega})$ at a given frequency indicates a greater perceptual tolerance of errors at that frequency.

Error-weighting functions proposed for speech and image coding appear in Figure E.1.

The *C-message weighting* function for speech represents the frequency response of the 500 type telephone set, as well as the hearing characteristics of the average telephone user [Members of Technical Staff, Bell Laboratories, 1971]. The

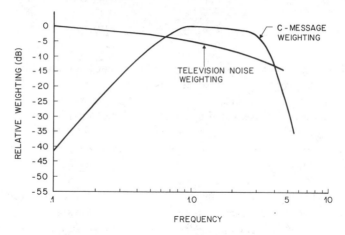

Figure E.1 Frequency-weighting functions proposed for measuring error variances in speech and image coding. The frequency axis is in kilohertz for the speech weighting function, and in megahertz for the television weighting function [Members of Technical Staff, Bell Laboratories, 1971. Reprinted with permission] [Barstow and Christopher, 1962].

psophometric weighting function, the European (CCITT) standard, is very similar to the C-message weighting function; but it has a peak at about 900 Hz rather than at 1000 Hz as in Figure E.1. The implication of these weighting functions is that in the important region between 100 and 1000 Hz, error perception in a speech coding system *increases* as a function of increasing frequency. Note that in the second half of this frequency region, the average input speech spectrum $S_{xx}(e^{j\omega})$ [Figure 2.9(a)] *decreases* with frequency.

The weighting function $S_{ww}(e^{j\omega})$ for images implies that error perception *decreases* monotonically as a function of frequency [Barstow and Christopher, 1962], although at a rate much slower than the decrease of average input spectrum $S_{xx}(e^{j\omega})$ with frequency (Figure 2.9).

Powerful as the procedure (E.2) is, it must be recognized as a static, time-invariant weighting. Dynamic frequency-weighting, where $S_{ww}(e^{j\omega})$ follows local input spectra, can lead to error variances that are perceptually even more meaningful. This is because such dynamic weightings can provide a more realistic simulation of noise-masking in perception.

Weighting functions proportional to $S_{xx}^{-1}(e^{j\omega})$ and $S_{xx}^{1/2}(e^{j\omega})$. The error-weighting functions in Figure E.1 are not very tractable for analytical work. Further, the weighting functions in Figure E.1 do not reflect short-term phenomena in perception. Model weighting functions that are more useful for dynamic frequency-weighting are those that are related to short-term input spectra; for example, noise-weighting functions that are proportional to (a) $S_{xx}^{1/2}(e^{j\omega})$ for images, and to (b) $S_{xx}^{-1}(e^{j\omega})$ for speech. Such error-weighting functions are illustrated for the examples of an AR(1) input spectrum ($\rho = 0.9$) in Figure 7.5. This input spectrum was already shown in Figure 2.16(a)(iii). The weighting functions are scaled so that

$$\sigma_w^2 = \frac{1}{2\pi} \int_{-\pi}^{\pi} S_{ww}(e^{j\omega}) \, d\omega = 1 \tag{E.3}$$

The figure also shows (c) the frequency-independent, constant weighting function $S_{ww}(e^{j\omega}) = 1$. Use of this function in (E.2) leads to the conventional, unweighted error variance σ_r^2.

Chapter 7 discusses coding examples based on noise-weighting functions of the form $S_{ww}(e^{j\omega}) = S_{xx}^{\lambda}(e^{j\omega})$ with $\lambda = -1$ and $1/2$ [O'Neal, 1972]. Chapter 12 discusses the case of $\lambda = -1/2$, which is useful for short-term noise weighting in speech coding.

Articulation Index. A good example of frequency-weighted SNR is the *Articulation Index* (AI) used in early speech work [French and Steinberg, 1947] [Beranek, 1947] [Kryter, 1969]. The speech signal is observed in 20 sub-bands, described in Table E.2, and component SNR values SNR_i; $i = 1, 2, ..., 20$ (limited to a maximum allowable $SNRMAX = 30$ dB), are averaged:

$$AI = 0.05 \sum_{i=1}^{20} [\min\{SNR_i, 30\}/30] \tag{E.4}$$

The frequency-weighting is a result of the fact that the sub-bands are of increasing width. For example, sub-band 16 (the last sub-band of interest in telephone quality work) is 380 Hz wide, while sub-band 1 is 130 Hz wide; but both of these contribute, at their best, an equal amount 0.05 to the Articulation Index. Note that the frequency-weighting for SNR, implied by (E.5), has a corresponding, although not obvious, frequency-weighting $S_{ww}(e^{j\omega})$ for reconstruction errors.

Table E.2 Frequency bands of equal contribution to the Articulation Index (all entries are in Hz)

Number	Limits	Mean	Number	Limits	Mean
1	200 to 330	270	11	1660 to 1830	1740
2	330 to 430	380	12	1830 to 2020	1920
3	430 to 560	490	13	2020 to 2240	2130
4	560 to 700	630	14	2240 to 2500	2370
5	700 to 840	770	15	2500 to 2820	2660
6	840 to 1000	920	16	2820 to 3200	3000
7	1000 to 1150	1070	17	3200 to 3650	3400
8	1150 to 1310	1230	18	3650 to 4250	3950
9	1310 to 1480	1400	19	4250 to 5050	4650
10	1480 to 1660	1570	20	5050 to 6100	5600

Although the Articulation Index was originally used in the context of additive noise impairments in analog speech systems, the notion is still useful in the context of digital coding, such as in estimating the intelligibility of coded speech (Figure F.3). Chapter 3 has already noted another significant *AI* result: the fact that the 3.2 kHz bandwidth assumed tacitly in this book provides a value of *AI* = 90% [Figure 3.16(b)].

E.4 *SNRMAX, SNRMIN* and Non-mmse Measures

SNRMAX and *SNRMIN*. In the coding of physical signals such as speech and video, *SNR* values that exceed a certain number *SNRMAX* may indicate an enhanced quality of coding that is perceptually irrelevant. It would be meaningful then to define a perceptual limit *SNRMAX*. Typical *SNRMAX* values for speech and image signals may be in the order of 35 and 50 dB, respectively. Information about *SNRMAX* can prevent over-designs of coders. This can be especially significant where a bit-assignment procedure is involved (Chapter 12), and *SNRMAX* directs the designer to transfer irrelevant bits to coefficients that can benefit from finer quantization.

There may be applications where *SNR* may also be meaningfully lower-bounded to a minimum value *SNRMIN*. This is very useful, for example, when *SNR* is computed over short signal segments for subsequent averaging, as in (E.1); in such instances, an occasional all-zero input block may imply a local $SNR = -\infty$ dB, or in practice, an extremely large negative value; this will obviously over-penalize the average dB measurement; while a more reasonable "default" value of *SNRMIN* (in the range of 0 to −20 dB, for example) will not be so obviously reflected in the final measurement. Computer programs for evaluating *SNRSEG* usually have this default feature built in; alternatively, they detect and eliminate all-zero segments and compute *SNRSEG* as an average over the non-zero speech segments.

SNR Measurements Based on a Non-Mmse Criterion, $E[E|R(n)|^p]$; $p \neq 2$. Conventional noise measurement involves the mean square error (mse) $E[R^2(n)]$. The main attractions of the mse criterion are its simplicity and analytical tractability. There are situations where the mse measure can also be a reasonably good indicator of perceived quality: for example, in the coding of flat gray areas in image inputs [Netravali and Limb, 1980]. The alternative of mean absolute error $E[|R(n)|]$ has sometimes been used, the corresponding signal-to-noise ratio being defined as $20 \log \{E[|X(n)|]/E[|R(n)|]\}$ dB. This form is not only simpler to evaluate but it has also been suggested as more appropriate in situations where very large errors are not perceptually harmful enough to warrant over-emphasis by a squaring procedure: for example, in computing distortion during slope overloaded segments in DM [Fletcher, 1971]. In speech coding, a measure that is based on *perceived loudness* (of appropriately defined signal and noise stimuli) is in fact obtained by a one-fourth power operation [Schroeder, Atal and Hall, 1979]. Similar non-mmse measures have been proposed in image work as well [Musmann, 1979] [Netravali and Limb, 1980].

E.5 Signal-to-Uncorrelated Noise Ratio, SNR_u

Reconstruction errors in digital coding have input-dependent components in general. These signify a *distortion* that has a different (very often, a significantly lesser) annoyance value than the *noise* that signal-independent errors constitute. It is therefore useful to isolate or identify these noise components. A practical approach to noise identification is a partial one that filters out the error components that have *linear correlations* with the input. This can be done by passing the input through a variable linear filter and varying the transfer function of the filter to obtain a minimum mse between filtered input and coder output. This minimum mse is a residual uncorrelated noise power, $E[R_u^2(n)]$, with a corresponding signal-to-uncorrelated-noise ratio $SNR_u = E[X^2(n)]/E[R_u^2(n)]$ [Aaron et al, 1969] [Crochiere et al, 1978]. Isolation of input-correlated and input-uncorrelated errors can be approximated, in principle, by appropriate frequency weighting of the error spectrum, as in (E.2).

A good example of input-correlated errors is that during slope overload distortion in differential coding of speech and image signals (Chapters 6 and 8). Slope overload distortion often contributes significantly to the total error variance $\sigma_r^2 = E[R^2(n)]$; but perceptually, slope overload is often much less perceptible than granular noise that tends to be input-uncorrelated. Isolation of granular errors provides an approximation to the isolation of $E[R_u^2(n)]$, and therefore provides an objective measurement SNR_u that is perceptually more meaningful than conventional total error variance σ_r^2 [Jayant and Rosenberg, 1971].

References

M. R. Aaron, J. S. Fleischman, R. W. McDonald and E. N. Protonotarlos, "Response of Deltamodulation to Gaussian Signals," Bell System Tech. J., pp. 1167-1195, May-June 1969.

J. M. Barstow and H. N. Christopher, "Measurement of Random Video Interference to Monochrome and Color TV," AIEE Trans. (Commun. Electron.), pp. 313-320, November 1962.

L. L. Beranek, "The Design of Communications Systems," Proc. IRE, pp. 880-890, September 1947.

K. W. Cattermole, *Principles of Pulse Code Modulation,* Iliffe, London, 1969.

CCITT, Recommendation G712, Yellow Book, III-2, Line Transmission, Geneva, Switzerland, 1981.

R. E. Crochiere, L. R. Rabiner, N. S. Jayant and J. M. Tribolet, "A Study of Objective Measures for Speech Waveform Coders," Proc. Int. Zurich Seminar on Digital Communications, pp. H1.1-H1.7, March 1978.

H. Fletcher, unpublished work, Bell Laboratories, 1971.

N. R. French and J. C. Steinberg, "Factors Governing the Intelligibility of Speech Sounds," J. Acoust. Soc. Am., pp. 90-119, January 1947.

N. S. Jayant and A. E. Rosenberg, "The Preference of Slope Overload to Granularity in the Deltamodulation of Speech", Bell System Tech. J., pp. 3117-3125, December 1971.

K. D. Kryter, "Methods for the Calculation of the Articulation Index," ANSI S3.5-1969, American National Standards Institute, New York, 1969.

R. E. Mallon, "Application of K-Rating to USA NTSC Systems," J. Soc. Motion Pict. Telev. Eng., pp. 16-19, January 1970.

B. J. McDermott, C. Scagliola and D. J. Goodman, "Perceptual and Objective Evaluation of Speech Processed by Adaptive Differential PCM," Bell System Tech. J., pp. 1597-1618, May-June 1978.

Members of Technical Staff, Bell Laboratories, *Transmission Systems for Communications,* Western Electric Company Technical Publications, Winston-Salem, N.C., 1971.

H. G. Musmann, "Predictive Image Coding," in *Advances in Electronics and Electron. Physics,* Suppl. 12, pp. 73-112, Academic Press, 1979.

M. Nakatsui and P. Mermelstein, "Subjective Speech-to-Noise Ratio as a Measure of Speech Quality for Digital Waveform Coders," J. Acoust. Soc. Am., 72, pp. 1136-1144, 1982.

A. N. Netravali and J. O. Limb, "Picture Coding: A Review," Proc. IEEE, pp. 366-406, March 1980.

P. Noll, "Adaptive Quantization in Speech Coding Systems," Proc. Int. Zurich Seminar on Digital Communications, pp. B3.1 to B3.6, October 1974.

J. B. O'Neal, Jr., "Bounds on Subjective Performance Measures for Source Encoding Systems," IEEE Trans. on Information Theory, pp. 224-231, 1971.

V. Ramamoorthy, unpublished work, University of Linköping, Sweden, 1978.

D. L. Richards, "Transmission Performance of Telephone Networks Containing PCM Links," Proc. IEEE, pp. 1245-1258, 1968.

D. L. Richards, *Telecommunication by Speech*, Halsted Press, John Wiley, New York, 1973.

M. R. Schroeder, B. S. Atal and J. L. Hall, "Optimizing Digital Speech Coders by Exploiting Masking Properties of the Human Ear," J. Acoust. Soc. Am., pp. 1647-1652, December 1979.

Appendix F

Subjective Measurement of Coder Performance

In the coding of communications signals such as speech and video, the definitive mechanism for noise measurement is the human perception mechanism; therefore, perceptual and subjective testing procedures should constitute an integral part of coder design and evaluation. Even in situations where perceptually meaningful objective measures are known, some amount of subjective testing is needed to supplement, verify or calibrate the objective data.

Unfortunately, however, subjective tests for determining quality or intelligibility are very time consuming. For reliable results, these tests require several versions of a single stimulus class (for example, several talkers speaking through a speech coder, or several scenes digitized by an image coder). Besides, experiments may involve several coders that are to be graded or compared. An important requirement in the design of these experiments is one of presenting the totality of the above stimuli with maximal randomness of order to protect against possible effects of presentation order; and with sufficient redundancy for averaging out noise or variability in subjects' decisions. Finally, subjects in these tests may be either untrained or experienced, depending on whether users of the coding system in question are expected to be untrained or experienced. In either case, it is important that the number of subjects be large enough, so that the variability in the results be adequately small: for example, if the Mean Opinion Score (Section F.1) is considered as the mean value of a random variable, the standard deviation about the mean will be inversely proportional to $\sqrt{n_s}$, where n_s is the number of subjects. The size of the test of course increases linearly with n_s. In view of the time-consuming nature of the above procedures, formal subjective testing is invariably preceded by *pilot*, or *informal* tests whose results can be used to design the formal test in the most economical and useful fashion.

The result of the subjective testing procedure may be a single number such as a *mean opinion score*, or a set of data that also reflects *differences in judgement* as in *multidimensional scaling*; the nature of the testing procedure will be correspondingly different. Testing procedures also differ depending on whether the issue is the *quality* or the *intelligibility* of the digitized signal. A high quality output implies very good intelligibility, but the converse is not true.

F.1 Quality Measurements

Binary Decision Tasks. The subjects' basic task is easiest when the decision to be made is binary: as with a two-point scale (e.g., *acceptable, not acceptable*). A more interesting example of a binary task is an *A-B preference* test where stimuli *A* and *B* occur in pairs, and the subject is required to indicate a preference for either *A* or *B*. Non-binary *rankings* and *ratings* of stimuli can be derived from such binary data, provided all possible coder pairs are compared against each other.

Subjective *SNR*. Binary preference judgements can also be the basis for determining the *equivalent SNR*. A given coded stimulus is compared against a reference signal with, say, additive noise and the amount of this noise increased (or decreased) until subjects prefer the coded stimulus in 50% of the comparisons. The signal-to-noise ratio of the resulting additive-noisy stimulus, say SNR_A, is then defined as the *equivalent additive-noise SNR*, or *subjective SNR* of the coded stimulus [Bosworth and Candy, 1969]. Additive white noise is a usual reference in such experiments, although signal-dependent noise sources may be perceptually more meaningful. For example, consider the signal [Schroeder, 1968]

$$\hat{s}(n) = (1+\alpha^2)^{\frac{1}{2}} [s(n)+\alpha u(n)] \qquad (F.1)$$

where $u(n)$ is a *multiplicative* noise process derived from a signal $s(n)$ by multiplying its samples by a signal-independent binary i.i.d. source with outputs ± 1; this signal has a well-defined SNR_A value of α^{-2}; and in many coding applications, $\hat{s}(n)$ is perceptually more similar to a coded stimulus $s_c(n)$ than a white-noise corrupted version $s_w(n)$ of the signal. Preference tests involving $\hat{s}(n)$ and $s_c(n)$ are therefore easier, and produce more consistent results, than those involving $s_c(n)$ and $s_w(n)$. When the subject decides on a value of α for which the quality of coded stimulus is equal to that of the reference $s(n)$, the equivalent *SNR* of the former is simply α^{-1}.

Speech quality measurement using the *Modulated Noise Reference Unit* (MNRU) [Law and Seymour, 1962] [CCITT, 1967, 1969, 1976] is also based on the use of the *equivalent multiplicative noise* method. In the case of 8-bit log-PCM coding of speech, the MNRU provides a 38dB result, a figure identical to the objective SNR of that coder (Chapter 5).

Mean Opinion Score (MOS). A quality test involves the recruitment of an ensemble of subjects, each of whom classifies a stimulus (coder output) on an *N*-point quality scale; for example, on a 5-point adjectival scale for signal *quality* or signal *impairment*. These scales are shown in the second and third columns of Table F.1. The words in parentheses represent alternative labels (as in the last row), or supplementary labels (as in the middle three rows). In any case, these adjectives are used as though they are reliable values on a well-calibrated meter. Quality tests such as the above have been standardized for image quality assessment [CCIR, 1974, 1978, 1980] [Pearson, 1972], and they are also very useful in speech work [Daumer, 1982].

An alternative, or often a supplement, to adjectival description consists in associating numbers with categories, as in the first column of Table F.1. Judgements can thus be on a scale of, say, 1 to 5. The final results from these tests, in the simplest form, is a pooled average judgement called the *Mean Opinion Score* (MOS) for the ensemble of listeners or viewers. MOS ratings can also be estimated as normalized scores of tournament-type tests where the basic task is a binary comparison, rather than a category identification.

Unimpaired and extremely high-quality signals tend to get an MOS rating in between 4 and 5 in these tests (Figure 1.5). This is due to the fact that subjects may sometimes award a score such as 4 to a stimulus that ideally deserves a 5; or, in an A-B comparison, they may occasionally rank a very slightly impaired stimulus higher than the original.

MOS values are very difficult to duplicate in repetitions of an experiment, and several factors can contribute to its variability. A number that is very useful in assessing the value of a given MOS rating is the *standard deviation* of the rating obtained by the stimulus across the population of subjects and talkers. For example, 64 kb/s PCM coding of speech produces an output with a representative MOS value of 4.53 and a standard deviation of 0.57 [Daumer, 1982].

In digital communication systems, *toll quality* speech and *broadcast-quality* images cannot always be defined by means of an MOS requirement alone. In speech work, for example, a network-oriented definition of *toll quality* may also imply the satisfaction of further requirements such as adequate performance with non-speech inputs. As long as this qualification is kept in mind, an MOS score in the range of 4.0 to 4.5 is a very useful indicator of high quality digitization. This criterion is indeed used repeatedly in this book. In fact, this criterion is used for both speech and image coding examples.

The use of a *mean* or *average* quality statistic is particularly appropriate if the distribution of quality across the subject ensemble can be described by a *symmetrical* pdf. In this case, the mean score is also identical to the *median* score

Table F.1 Five-point adjectival scales for quality and impairment, and associated number scores.

Number Scores	Quality Scale	Impairment Scale
5	Excellent	Imperceptible
4	Good	(Just) Perceptible but not Annoying
3	Fair	(Perceptible and) Slightly Annoying
2	Poor	Annoying (but not Objectionable)
1	Unsatisfactory (Bad)	Very Annoying (Objectionable)

(which is the score exceeded in 50% of the cases) or the *modal* score (which is the most probable score). When the pdf of subject scores is *asymmetrical*, or *skewed*, the mean, median and mode of the pdf are no longer the same; and any one or more of these descriptions of central tendency may be useful.

Isopreference Curves. A good example of statistically-aided coder design is the use of so-called *isopreference curves* [Munson and Karlin, 1962] which allow coder designers to select alternative combinations of coder parameters for a given level of quality. In the simplest case the number of independent parameters in question would be two, P_1 and P_2. A typical intermediate step in constructing isopreference contours is the generation of so-called *psychometric* functions; these may define, for example, the level λ of uncorrelated noise that is equivalent to a coder-parameter pair, in the opinion of 50% of the subjects. By repeating the equivalent-noise measurement for a number of parameter pairs that is adequate to span the interesting range of λ, and by appropriate interpolation, one can display a family of isopreference curves; the X and Y axes in these figures represent values of P_1 and P_2 and each curve of constant preference refers to a specific target value of λ (Figure F.1).

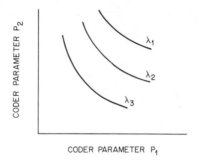

Figure F.1 Isopreference curves.

A good example of the use of isopreference methods is in the understanding of DPCM coders for speech. In one study, P_1 was the sampling rate and P_2 was the number of bits per sample [Chan and Donaldson, 1971]. In another, P_1 described the static performance of the adaptive quantizer and P_2 described the dynamic performance of the quantizer [McDermott, Scagliola and Goodman, 1978]. In both cases, designers had, in principle, an infinity of (P_1, P_2) pairs for a given level of digital speech quality. In the first example, the transmission rate (product of P_1 and P_2) was an obvious design constraint as well.

Quality Measurements That Include Differences of Judgement. Multidimensional Scaling (MDS) procedures [Kruskal and Wish, 1978] [Shepard, Romney and Nerlove, 1972] provide a more complete framework for modeling subjective judgements of coder conditions which in general constitute multivariate stimuli (because there is a multiplicity of coder parameters or *physical variables* that define the coder quality to a given human receiver). The versatility of the MDS procedures stems from the fact that no assumptions are made about the number or

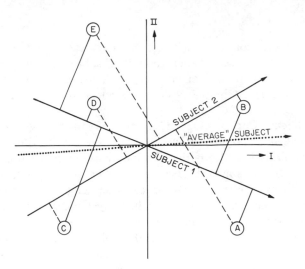

Figure F.2 Output from an MDS procedure for testing five coders (A, B, C, D and E), with two subjects (1 and 2) [McDermott, Scagliola and Goodman, 1978].

nature of the relevant *subjective variables*. Furthermore, typical MDS results preserve differences in individual subject judgements. Specifically, a typical MDS solution displays coder conditions (or types) as points in a suitably dimensioned space, and individual listeners or viewers appear as vectors in the same space. Projections of the coder conditions onto a subject vector display the rank-ordering of coder condition (or type) by that subject. If the vectors are tightly clustered and essentially coincident, the space is unidimensional and the scaling of the points on that dimension represents the average subject. Projections on a typical or an average vector determine a typical or an average rank-ordering. This is the kind of average rank-ordering that would also result by displaying MOS scores as a function of coder.

Figure F.2 illustrates a solution for the example of five coder points, two subjects, and two dimensions for displaying test results (either coder distances or differences in coder preferences, depending on the MDS procedure used). When the points are projected onto the vector representing subject 1, they are ordered ABCDE; but when they are projected onto the vector representing subject 2, they are ordered BAEDC. The average subject vector (the dashed-line vector) is almost coincident with the subjective dimension I in this case, showing that *on the average*, coder ranking follows a one-dimensional assessment. For example, dimension I may correspond to granular noise level in ADPCM coding, and dimension II to slope overload distortion. It is well known that granularity is a perceptually more important feature than slope overload distortion, at least for the average listener [Jayant and Rosenberg, 1971] [McDermott, Scagliola and Goodman, 1978].

F.2   Intelligibility Tests

When the coder bit rate is very low, and/or when the transmission context is exacting (for example, multiple encoding, or very noisy channels), *intelligibility* of the coder output can be a serious issue. In these situations, the intent will not be to measure quality which will be quite low anyway, but rather to measure features that preserve information-bearing contrast — for example, edges in pictures, and consonants in speech. An important class of intelligibility tests in speech work are the so-called *Rhyme Tests*, where the subject's task would be to recognize one of several possible consonants in a closed *rhyming* set (such as *meat*, *feat*, *heat*, *seat*, *beat*, *neat*). The insistence on a known, compact *closed* set of possible stimuli relieves the subject from attempting guesses based on a priori probabilities of words in the language. In this form, the test is actually called a *Modified Rhyme Test* (MRT) [House et al., 1965], in contrast with the original version, where the subject had to make consonant decisions from an unknown open set [Fairbanks, 1958]. In the *Diagnostic Rhyme Test* (DRT) [Voiers, 1977] the subject's basic task is to recognize one of two possible stimuli in each of 96 rhyming pairs. In so doing, the subject tries to diagnose the presence or extent of each of six elementary attributes of consonant phonemes (for example: the attribute of voicing in *v*ast versus *f*ast, the attribute of nasality in *m*oot versus *b*oot). One may also use *phonetically balanced*, rather than rhyming, word stimuli; but in this case, recognition scores, for a given level of speech impairment, depend critically on the number of words in the test repertoire. This is seen in Figure F.3 [Kryter, 1970], where different types of intelligibility scores, including phonetically balanced- or

Figure F.3 Speech intelligibility versus articulation index *AI* [Kryter, 1970].

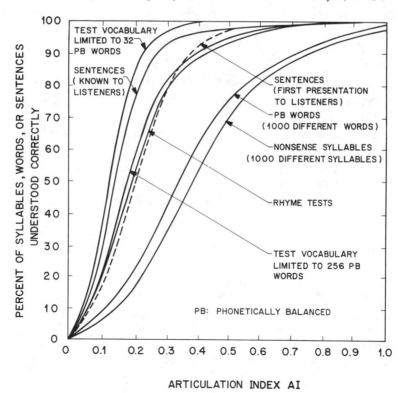

PB-stimuli scores and MRT scores, are shown as a function of the Articulation Index (AI) defined in Appendix E. In subjective assessments of digital coders, it is more relevant of course to show plots of intelligibility versus coder type, or coder parameter, or bit rate. Common to all these testing procedures is the observation that the intelligibility of the whole input (for example, a spoken sentence or a complete image of an object) is in general higher than the average intelligibility of its parts (for example, spoken words or sub-images). Figure F.3 demonstrates, for example, differences between word and sentence intelligibility scores. When the word intelligibility score from the Rhyme Test is 50% (at $AI = 0.2$), the intelligibility of sentences previously known to listeners is 80%. This increase in the score is a result of the higher redundancy in sentence stimuli.

References

R. H. Bosworth and J. C. Candy, "A Companded One-Bit Coder for Television Transmission," Bell System Tech. J., pp. 1459-1480, May-June 1969.

CCIR, "Method for the Subjective Assessment of the Quality of Television Pictures," 13th Plenary Assembly, Rec 500, pp. 65-68, 1974.

CCIR, "Method for the Subjective Assessment of the Quality of Television Pictures," Recommendation (500-1), 14th Plenary Assembly, 1978.

CCIR, "Subjective Assessment of the Quality of Television Pictures — Method Recommended by the EBU," Doc. 11/17-E28, Annex 1, May 1980.

CCITT, Study Group XII — Contribution No. 84 (Transmission Performance of PCM Systems), August 1967.

CCITT, White Book, Vol. V**, Question 21/XII, published by the Int. Telecom. Union, 1969.

CCITT, Study Group XII, "Transmission Quality of Digital Systems," Contrib. COM XVI, Annex 2, 1976.

D. Chan and R. W. Donaldson, "Subjective Evaluation of Pre- and Post-filtering in PAM, PCM and DPCM Voice Communication Systems," IEEE Trans. on Communications, pp. 601-612, October 1971.

W. R. Daumer, "Subjective Evaluation of Several Efficient Speech Coders," IEEE Trans. on Communications, pp. 655-662, April 1982.

G. Fairbanks, "Test of Phonemic Differentation: The Rhyme Test," J. Acoust. Soc. Am., pp. 596-600, 1958.

A. S. House, C. E. Williams, M. H. L. Hecker and K. D. Kryter, "Articulation Testing Methods: Consonated Differentation with a Closed-Response Set," J. Acoust. Soc. Am., pp. 158-166, January 1965.

N. S. Jayant and A. Rosenberg, "The Preference of Slope Overload to Granularity in the Deltamodulation of Speech," Bell System Tech. J., pp. 3117-3125, December 1971.

J. B. Kruskal and M. Wish, "Multidimensional Scaling," Sage University Paper No. 11. Series on Quantitative Applications in the Social Sciences (E. M. Uslaner, ed.), Sage Publications, Beverly Hills, Calif., 1978.

K. D. Kryter, "Masking and Speech Communication in Noise," Chapter 2 in The Effects of Noise on Man, Academic Press, New York, 1970.

H. B. Law and R. A. Seymour, "A Reference Distortion System Using Modulated Noise," IEE, Paper No. 3992E, November 1962.

B. McDermott, C. Scagliola and D. Goodman, "Perceptual and Objective Evaluation of Speech Processed by Adaptive Differential PCM," Bell System Tech. J., pp. 1597-1618, May-June 1978.

W. A. Munson and J. E. Karlin, "The Isopreference Method for Evaluating Speech Transmission Systems," J. Acoust. Soc. Am., p. 763, 1962.

A. N. Netravali and J. O. Limb, "Picture Coding: A Review," Proc. IEEE, pp. 366-406, March 1980.

D. E. Pearson, "Methods for Scaling Television Picture Quality," in *Picture Bandwidth Compression* (T. S. Huang and O. J. Tretiak, eds.), Gordon and Breach, New York, pp. 47-95, 1972.

M. R. Schroeder, "Reference Signal for Signal Quality Studies," J. Acoust. Soc. Am., pp. 1735-1736, 1968.

R. N. Shepard, A. Romney and S. B. Nerlove (eds.), *Multidimensional Scaling*, Vols. 1 and 2, Seminar Press, New York, 1972.

W. D. Voiers, "Diagnostic Evaluation of Speech Intelligibility," in *Speech Intelligibility and Speaker Recognition*, M. Hawley (ed.), Dowden Hutchinson Ross, Stroudsburg, Pa., 1977.

Appendix G

A/D and D/A Conversion

This appendix will describe the principles behind important techniques [Schmid, 1970] [Sheingold, 1972] [Hnatek, 1976] used in the A/D and D/A stages of Figure 5.1. These conversion principles apply not only to PCM but also to other coders discussed in this book. Appropriate A/D and D/A stages are in fact tacitly assumed in all chapters. There are two qualifications to be made, however, right at the outset.

First, in the case of these other coders, the input to the A/D (and the output of the D/A) will not be PAM waveform samples, in general; for example, they may be samples of a prediction error waveform in DPCM (Chapter 6), samples of a narrow-band filter output in SBC (Chapter 11), or transform coefficients in TC (Chapter 12).

A second point of difference relates to the relative merits of several conversion types that will be described and compared in this appendix. These comparisons are in general a function of R, the number of bits/sample; and as R decreases, the importance of the distinctions and comparisons to be made in this appendix may also decrease. For example, the distinction between a slow *digit-at-a-time* A/D and a fast *word-at-a-time* A/D is much more important if $R = 12$ or $R = 8$ than if $R = 4$ or 2; an extreme case is deltamodulation $(R = 1)$ in which case very specific A/D and D/A techniques may come into play.

For simplicity, our discussions will be limited to A/D and D/A operations that correspond to uniform quantization characteristics. Extension to nonuniform characteristics will be noted where possible. In the important case of log-quantization of speech, conversion between uniform and logarithmic formats can be done digitally, as in Section 5.3. Recent PCM implementations are almost invariably based on direct digital conversion between uniform and logarithmic formats (Figure 5.8). The A/D/A problem in this case is simply one of an initial 13-bit or 12-bit A/D and a final 13-bit or 12-bit D/A, both based on uniform quantization. This configuration is typical of time-shared as well as per-channel PCM coder implementations [Cecil, Solomon and Moyer, 1976] [Gray et al, 1975]. Incidentally, PCM codecs may realize all of Figure 5.1, including multiplexing in the case of a shared codec, on no more than two integrated circuit chips. One of these chips is usually dedicated to pre- and post-filtering operations.

The conversion principles to be described in this appendix will not be signal-specific, although it will be clear that some classes of techniques will be more suited to speech than to video (in view of the higher sampling frequencies in the latter context), and vice versa.

G.1 Analog-to-Digital Conversion

It will be useful to distinguish three classes of techniques, termed *digit-at-a-time*, *level-at-a-time*, and *word-at-a-time*. Level-at-a-time converters are simple, but involve a large number of sequential operations that restrict their use to relatively slow speed applications. Word-at-a-time converters are complex but fast, and therefore suitable for high speed application. Digit-at-a-time converters provide a compromise between speed and complexity. In all cases, overall A/D accuracy is also controlled by the quality of associated sample-and-hold circuitry [Hnatek, 1976].

G.1.1 Digit-at-a-time Conversion: Successive Approximation

Also known as the sequential-comparison method, this technique is analogous to the process of *successive approximation weighing* with a mechanical balance using an unknown weight W_x on one side, and a number of reference weights on the other; the problem is to find that specific combination of R reference weights whose total approximates W_x best.

The procedure is illustrated for $R = 4$ bits/sample in Figure G.1(a) where the analog input (corresponding to W_x above) is 9.14, and the reference 'weights' are 8, 4, 2 and 1. These numbers are chosen to be powers of 2, in order to facilitate the decimal-to-binary relation implied in the NBC code (also, the magnitude part of the FBC code), [see (4.141)]. Figure G.1 also shows how the best combination is one that includes weights 8 and 1 ($b_1 = b_4 = 1$) and excludes weights 4 and 2 ($b_2 = b_3 = 0$); and how these bits, or digits, are determined *one at a time* as the staircase function y makes a sequence of four approximations. The equation for final approximation $y(n)$ follows the NBC code for $R = 4$, together with a correction factor of 0.5 necessary for a midrise quantizer format (with step size $\Delta = 1$ and output levels equal to multiples of $\Delta/2 = 0.5$).

Notice that the A/D converter in Figure G.1(b) includes a D/A converter in the feedback loop. In the example just given, the D/A uses an NBC code to convert binary information to decimal, or analog versions of y (for example, 12 at stage 2).

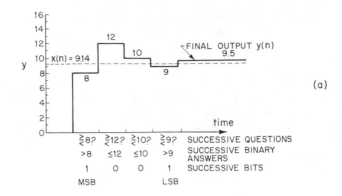

(a)

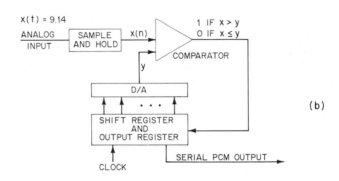

(b)

$$y(n) = 0.5 + (2^3 \cdot 1 + 2^2 \cdot 0 + 2^1 \cdot 0 + 2^0 \cdot 1) = 9.5$$

Figure G.1   Successive approximation A/D converter ($R = 4$ bits/sample).

The circuit of Figure G.1(b) has been used as a basis for integrated circuit implementations for 13-bit uniform PCM [for example, Gray et al., 1975]. By including a stage-specific gain factor G in this D/A conversion (in addition to the factor of 2 implied in the uniform quantizer/NBC format), the circuit of Figure G.1 can also be adapted to realize at least one type of non-uniform quantization characteristic directly — the case where successive quantization intervals are related by a (not necessarily constant) ratio G. Realizations of A/D conversion appropriate to segmented μ- and A-laws, as well as non-NBC formats, are discussed elsewhere [Damann, McDaniel and Maddox, 1972] [Marsh et al., 1981].

G.1.2   Level-at-a-time Conversion: Ramp-Comparison

A simple but slow level-at-a-time A/D results if the NBC coded D/A in the feedback loop of Figure G.2 is replaced by a counter (and an appropriately small gain, say, unity). This arrangement is shown in Figure G.2. The staircase function is now ramp-like with a step size much smaller than the expected input $x(n) (= 9.14)$. The A/D process halts when the ramp function crosses the input

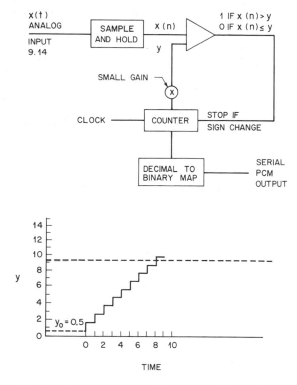

Figure G.2 Counting or ramp-type A/D converter ($R = 4$ bits/sample).

level. The decimal state of the counter is then mapped to a binary word which is the converter output. In the present example, the word is 1001, corresponding to counter state 9; this is the crossing state ($y = 9.5$), assuming a midrise starting state of $y_0 = 0.5$. In certain realizations of the above circuit, the conversion is made faster by using a time-continuous linear ramp, such as that obtained in the linear portion of the charging curve of a resistor-capacitor circuit. High-precision implementations [for example, Duttweiler, 1977], however, do use a time-quantized ramp, because timing accuracy is easier to guarantee than component (resistor-capacitor) accuracy. Unlike the y-function in Figure G.1, which makes a total of R updates, the y-function in ramp-comparison counting makes up to 2^R updates/input sample, depending on its amplitude level. The level-at-a-time device is therefore very slow for large R, and consequently may not be well suited to high-speed applications such as image coding.

G.1.3 Level-at-a-time Conversion: Interpolation

The resolution in the A/D conversion of Figure G.2 is no better than the gain in the feedback loop, which was 1.0 in that example. Accurate small gains will be difficult to realize beyond a point. For illustration, let us say that gains or amplitude resolutions smaller than 1.0 pose accuracy problems. The idea of the interpolative coder in Figure G.3 is to realize resolutions much less than 1.0

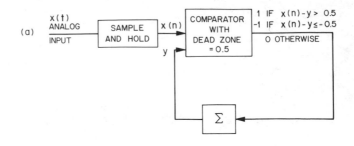

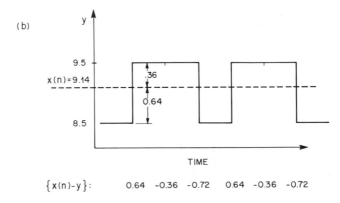

Figure G.3 Illustration of the concept behind interpolative A/D conversion.

although the fundamental physical resolution in the circuit is limited to 1.0. This is done by an *oversample-interpolate* procedure. The arrangement of Figure G.3 is *not* a complete A/D converter. Rather, it illustrates the way in which the class of interpolative A/D devices [Candy, 1974] [Candy and Wooley, 1974] [Wooley and Henry, 1979] exchange speed for accuracy, and realize additional R_f-bit resolutions with an oversampling in the order of 2^{R_f}. For example, a 256 kHz rather than a 8 kHz A/D for speech implies $2^{R_f} = 32$; it can provide a resolution gain of five bits [Candy, 1974].

The y-function in Figure G.3 oscillates around $x(n) = 9.14$ with the step size of 1. Moreover, it spends more time at the level 9.5, which is closer to 9.14 than the other allowed level 8.5. In the illustration of Figure G.3, the higher probability of the 9.5 level is ensured by the combination of difference-integration and comparator dead zone (in the comparator input range of -0.5 to 0.5); this causes y to stay in the 9.5 level for two (high frequency) samples before the integrated difference magnitude (0.36 + 0.36 = 0.72) exceeds 0.5. When $y = 8.5$, the difference magnitude 0.64 is greater than 0.5, and therefore adequate to flip the y-function, without further integration of the difference $x(n)-y$.

The best output or estimate $\hat{x}$ that is possible in the above process is a weighted linear combination of 8.5 and 9.5, with probabilities $P\{y = 8.5\} = 1/3$ and $P\{y = 9.5\} = 2/3$. The result is $8.5/3 + 2(9.5)/3 = 9.17$, which represents a much higher resolution than either 8.5 or 9.5. In the simplified illustration of Figure G.3, the probabilities of the two device levels emerge after only 3 high frequency samples. In the presence of practical non-idealities (such as those in a deltamodulator used to provide reference levels such as 8.5 and 9.5), the estimation of level probabilities improves with the number of high frequency samples used in the conversion, and therefore with the amount of oversampling.

DM/PCM Converters. An A/D device based on oversampling and interpolation is essentially a *DM-to-PCM converter* [Goodman, 1969] [Eggermont, Hofelt and Salters, 1977] [Everhard, 1978] [Candy, Wooley and Benjamin, 1981]. The deltamodulation provides the oversampled discrete-amplitude output, and decimation and digital filtering stages convert this to a Nyquist-rate output of high amplitude resolution. The sampling rate that is needed is a function of desired final resolution, and the type of deltamodulator employed. Converters based on *sigma deltamodulation* [Misawa et al., 1981] [Agrawal and Shenoi, 1983] have the particular advantage of a frequency-independent performance characteristic (Chapter 8).

G.1.4 Word-at-a-time Conversion: Parallel A/D

This is the fastest class of A/D methods. Historically, word-at-a-time coding was realized in a cathode-ray beam-coding tube [Members of Technical Staff, Bell Laboratories, 1971]. Here, a codeplate with 2^R patterns of "holes" and "no holes" (1's and 0's) stored all possible codewords. Input signal levels $x(n)$ controlled the deflection of a ribbon beam which in turn connected to the appropriate R-bit codeword, causing R electron current "bits" (1 for current or 0 for no current).

More recent implementations of word-at-a-time coding use *multiple threshold* circuits. Logic circuitry senses the highest threshold triggered by the unknown sample, and produces the appropriate codeword. Figure G.4 shows a parallel 4-bit converter with output levels 1/2, 3/2, . . . , 31/2. It has $2^4 - 1 = 15$ comparators, whose thresholds V_k; $k = 1$ to 15, are spaced by 1, with the lowest threshold V_1 being zero. For a zero input, all comparators are in the *off* state. As the input increases, it causes an increasing number of comparators to switch to the *on* state. By using an appropriate binary table, a multiple threshold circuit can generate any desired binary code at the output, such as the NBC or the Gray code. With electronic threshold devices such as diodes, the use of a Gray code has the property that the devices tend to stay in sustained *on* or *off* states with a slowly changing analog input. This is because of the gradual bit transition pattern in the Gray code dictionary (Figure 4.35).

The evident advantage of the above approach is that conversion occurs in parallel, with speed limited only by the switching time of the comparators and gates. Parallel A/D conversion is therefore very appropriate for high-speed applications such as video A/D conversion at 10 MHz. Unfortunately, the number of circuit elements increases exponentially with resolution. For example, with R bits, one needs 2^R-1 comparators. The multiple-threshold A/D converter is thus impractical for large R, although the limits of practicality tend to increase with the availability of integrated circuit elements of higher complexity.

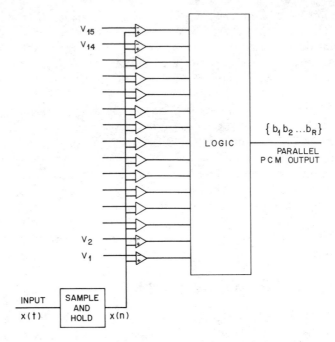

Figure G.4 Parallel A/D conversion ($R = 4$ bits/sample).

G.2 Digital-to-Analog Conversion

It will be useful to distinguish two classes of techniques, termed *parallel* D/A, characterized by fast operation, and *serial* D/A, characterized by simple circuitry.

G.2.1 Parallel D/A Conversion — The Weighted Resistor D/A

The weighted resistor D/A, illustrated for $R = 4$ in Figure G.5, is the most straightforward procedure for generating an analog output corresponding to an NBC codeword (4.141). The D/A uses one resistor per bit to realize the weighted sum (4.141), or more general versions thereof, for non-uniform quantization.

If in Figure G.5, $\mathcal{R}_L \ll \mathcal{R}/8$, currents with magnitudes $V/\mathcal{R}$, $2V/\mathcal{R}$, $4V/\mathcal{R}$ and $8V/\mathcal{R}$ can be generated through the resistors $\mathcal{R}$, $\mathcal{R}/2$, $\mathcal{R}/4$ and $\mathcal{R}/8$ upon closure of respective switches. No current flow is possible if a corresponding switch is open or connected to ground. Switches S_i are driven directly by bits b_i and S_i is closed only if $b_i = 1$; $i=1$ to 4. When a given b_i equals 1, the corresponding current through resistor $\mathcal{R}_i$ provides a voltage contribution $\mathcal{R}_i 2^i V/\mathcal{R}$ across $\mathcal{R}_L$. The total output voltage across $\mathcal{R}_L$ is therefore a sum of four such voltages, each with weight $b_i = 0$ or 1. This total output is the NBC analog output (4.141) correct to a factor $V\mathcal{R}_L/\mathcal{R}$.

The range of resistor values in Figure G.5 was 8. In general in an R-bit D/A of that type, the range would be 2^{R-1}. This is also the range of capacitor values in equivalent circuits based on capacitor switching rather than resistor switching. For

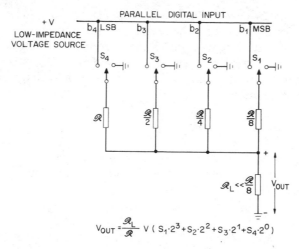

$$V_{OUT} = \frac{\mathcal{R}_L}{\mathcal{R}} V (S_1 \cdot 2^3 + S_2 \cdot 2^2 + S_3 \cdot 2^1 + S_4 \cdot 2^0)$$

Figure G.5 Weighted resistor D/A converter ($R = 4$ bits/sample).

large R, this represents a serious problem in terms of precision component availability or economy. A solution that is based on only two precision components is the $\mathcal{R}-2\mathcal{R}$ (or $\mathcal{C}-2\mathcal{C}$) ladder D/A converter.

G.2.2 Parallel D/A Conversion — The $\mathcal{R}$-2$\mathcal{R}$ Resistor Ladder

The resistor ladder D/A of Figure G.6 avoids the problem of widely varying resistor values, and uses only two precision values, say, $\mathcal{R}$ and $2\mathcal{R}$, although at the cost of using more units of these components in one converter. The resistor ladder is by far the most widely used arrangement for D/A conversion.

The crucial property of the ladder is that the impedances of the three branches of any node N are equal, and that a current I, flowing into a node through one

Figure G.6 The $\mathcal{R}$-2$\mathcal{R}$ resistor ladder D/A converter ($R = 4$ bits/sample).

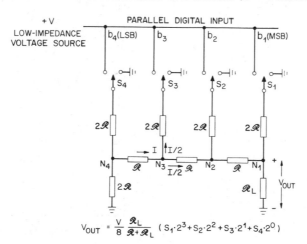

$$V_{OUT} = \frac{V}{8} \frac{\mathcal{R}_L}{\mathcal{R} + \mathcal{R}_L} (S_1 \cdot 2^3 + S_2 \cdot 2^2 + S_3 \cdot 2^1 + S_4 \cdot 2^0)$$

branch, causes currents of $I/2$ to flow out through the other two branches. The current flow due to the closure of a given switch depends therefore on the relative position of that switch and the point where current flow is measured. The switches S_i and bits b_i have the same significance as in Figure G.5, and the D/A output follows the NBC formula (4.141) correct to a scaling factor $V\mathcal{R}_L/8(\mathcal{R} + \mathcal{R}_L)$. Also see Problem 5.9.

G.2.3 Serial D/A Conversion

Parallel D/A converters are fast, but they require many components; and in applications where the speed is not critical, or where the speed of the parallel converter cannot be exploited due to other reasons, there is a motivation to use much slower, but compact serial techniques. The historical Shannon-Rack decoder [Members of Technical Staff, Bell Laboratories, 1971] is a serial D/A converter.

The general principle of serial D/A conversion is illustrated in Figure G.7. The serial-binary input $\{b_i\}$ controls the operation of the converter on a bit-by-bit basis. If $b_i = 1$ during clock period T_i ($i=1$ to R), a reference voltage V is added to a voltage V_i, stored on a capacitor, and the resulting sum is reduced to one-half; if $b_i = 0$, V_i alone is reduced to one-half. The result of this operation is a voltage V_{i+1}, which is stored on a capacitor, so that it will be available during the next clock period T_{i+1}. Mathematically, this implies the recursion

$$V_{i+1} = (V_i + b_i V)/2$$

Note that the above equation is essentially the recursive realization of weighted sums such as that in the NBC representation (4.141).

The voltage stored on the capacitor during the last bit interval T_R represents the output of the D/A converter. Since this output is available only for a short

Figure G.7 Serial D/A conversion.

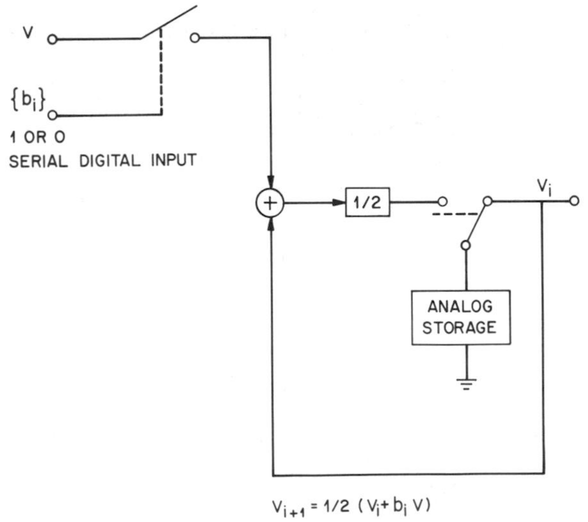

$$V_{i+1} = 1/2 \, (V_i + b_i \, V)$$

interval during each word time, a sample/hold circuit must be added to provide a constant output voltage.

The negative feature of this D/A technique is the fact that the conversion of an R-bit word requires R operation cycles, each of which takes up one clock pulse interval. However, serial D/A converters are very simple. In multiplex situations, the circuit of Figure G.7 is simple enough to be used on a per-channel basis.

References

B. P. Agrawal and K. Shenoi, "Design Methodology for $\Sigma\Delta M$," IEEE Trans. on Communications, pp. 360-370, March 1983.

J. C. Candy, "Interpolative A/D Converters with Uniform or Segmented Companding," Proc. Int. Conf. Commun., pp. 13E.1 to 13E.3, June 1974.

J. C. Candy and B. A. Wooley, "An A/D Converter with Segmented Companding," Proc. NTC, pp. 388-390, 1974.

J. C. Candy, B. A. Wooley and O. J. Benjamin, "A Voiceband Codec with Digital Filtering," IEEE Trans. on Communications, pp. 815-830, June 1981.

J. B. Cecil, J. E. Solomon and J. C. Moyer, "Trends in Monolithic A/D and D/A Converter Art," Proc. Nat. Telecom. Conf., pp. 10.3-1 to 10.3-5, Dallas, November 1976.

C. L. Damann, L. D. McDaniel and C. L. Maddox, "D2 Channel Band: Multiplexing and Coding," Bell System Tech. J., pp. 1675-1699, October 1972.

D. L. Duttweiler, "A $\mu 255$ Encoder Requiring No Precision Components," IEEE Trans. on Communications, pp. 297-303, March 1977.

L. D. J. Eggermont, M. H. H. Hofelt and R. H. W. Salters, "A deltamodulation to PCM Converter," Philips Technical Review, pp. 313-329, December 1977.

J. D. Everhard, "A single-channel PCM codec," IEEE J. Solid State Circuits, pp. 25-38, February 1979.

D. J. Goodman, "The application of delta modulation to analog-to-digital PCM encoding," Bell System Tech. J., pp. 321-343, February 1969.

P. R. Gray, D. A. Hodges, J. P. Tsividis and J. Chacko, Jr., "Companded PCM Voice Codec Using Monolithic Weighted Capacitor Arrays," IEEE Jour. Solid State Circuits, pp. 497-501, December 1975.

E. R. Hnatek, *A User's Handbook of D/A and A/D Conversions*, John Wiley, New York, 1976.

D. G. Marsh, B. K. Ahuja, T. Misawa, M. R. Dwarakanath, P. E. Fleischer and V. R. Saari, "A Single-Chip CMOS PCM Codec with Filters," IEEE Jour. of Solid State Circuits, pp. 308-315, August 1981.

Members of Technical Staff, Bell Laboratories, *Transmission Systems for Communications,* Western Electric Company, Technical Publications, Winston-Salem, N.C., 1971.

T. Misawa, J. E. Iwersen, L. J. Loporcaro and J. G. Ruch," Single-chip per channel codec with filters utilizing Δ-Σ Modulation," IEEE Jour. of Solid State Circuits, pp. 333-341, August 1981.

H. Schmid, *Electronic Analog/Digital Conversions,* Van Nostrand Reinhold, New York, 1970.

D. H. Sheingold (ed.), "Analog-Digital Conversion Handbook," 1972. Also, "Analog-Digital Conversion Notes," November 1977, Analog Devices Inc., Norwood, Mass. 02062.

B. A. Wooley and J. L. Henry, "An Integrated Per-Channel PCM Encoder Based on Interpolation," IEEE Trans. on Communications, pp. 272-278, February 1979.

Index

Error protection, (*cont.*)
  with natural redundancy, 247, 337
  in PCM, 246, 247
  of quantizer output, 185, 187, 188, 214
  in SBC, 506, 508
  in TC, 578–80
Error streaks in images, 327, 419
Estimators of input variance, 196, 198
Exchange of spatial and temporal resolution, 322
Exhaustive search, 430, 441
Explicit coding of reconstruction noise, 290, 398
Exponential adaptation, 402–6

Facsimile, 2, 9, 322, 465–85
Fast Fourier transform (FFT), 554, 559
Filtered reconstruction error, 375
Filtering gain, 379–81
Fine quantization, 257, 278, 279
Finite impulse response (FIR), 498, 604
Finite state vector quantizer (FSVQ), 439
First-order interpolation, 247, 248, 265
First-order Markov source, 63, 620 (*also see* AR(1) process)
First-order prediction:
  in delayed decision, 457
  in DM, 373, 417
  in DPCM and D*PCM, 261, 262, 278, 283, 316, 327, 330, 335, 358, 359
  in SBC, 503
Five-point quality scale, 660
Fixed bit allocation, 487
Fixed predictor, 252, 271, 272, 276, 287, 293, 295
Folded binary code (FBC), 177, 187, 215
Forward-adaptive prediction (APF), 292, 295, 307
Forward transformation kernel, 518
Fourier transform, 598
Four-sigma loading, 45, 125
Fourth-order image prediction, 264, 477
Fractional bit rates, 429
Frame period, 15, 30, 39, 101, 320
Frequency division multiplex (FDM), 113
Frequency domain coding, 16, 58, 486, 511
Frequency-ordered Fourier matrix, 553
Frequency response, 603, 605
Frequency weighted reconstruction error:
  ATC coding of speech, 569–70
  in delayed decision, 460

  in NFC, 351, 355, 366–68
  rate distortion theory, 642–47, 652
  in transform coding, 532
Frequency weighted *SNR,* 652
Frequency weighting function, 363

Gain over PCM:
  in DM, 295, 379–81, 386, 411
  in DPCM, 253, 259, 271, 272, 282, 294, 295, 335, 386
  in SBC, 491, 494
  in TC, 511, 527, 543, 572
Gamma source, 34, 154, 156, 157, 182, 445, 446, 450, 454, 640
Gaussian source, 24, 34, 151, 154, 162, 182, 445, 447, 450, 452, 454, 640
Generalized Lloyd-Max quantizer, 438
Geometric interpretation of TC, 515
Geometric interpretation of VQ, 438
Geometric pdf of run length, 470
Granular noise, 121
  in DM, 377, 390
  in DPCM, 258, 282, 283, 285
  in RLC, 480
Graphical interpretation of bit allocation, 531
Graphics, 2, 9, 322, 465–85
Gray code, 177, 215, 671
Gray level image, 30

Half-whitening, 357, 358, 360
Hamming distance, 179, 214, 635
High complexity coder, 11, 13, 317, 324, 369, 487, 504, 574
High detail image, 30, 37, 38, 41
High information deltamodulation (HIDM), 403
Highpass filter, 497, 500
Highpass signal, 40, 41, 64, 70, 273, 277, 381
High quality coding, 13, 376, 429, 511, 576
  (*also see* Broadcasting quality; Toll quality
Hotelling transform, 536
Huffman coding, 148, 622
Hybrid coding:
  APC/SBC, 505
  DPCM/PCM, 328, 336
  intraframe/interframe, 322
  TC/DPCM, 561–63, 576
Hybrid companding, 400, 412, 414

and reconstruction error in DPCM, 257
and reconstruction error in NFC, 353
and reconstruction error in TC, 525
statistics with AR(1) input, 162
unconditional mean of, 132
variance, 119, 133, 137, 166, 179
waveform, 161
Quantization error feedback, 260, 278, 279,
    285, 334, 353, 358, 411, 451, 453,
    504, 505
Quantization interval, 116
Quantizer-input mismatch, 128, 139, 140, 146
Quantizer loading factor, 124, 125, 139, 208
Quantizer performance factor, 120, 257, 259,
    491, 525
Quantizer reoptimization, 182, 184

_R-2R_ resistor ladder D/A, 673
Raised cosine spectrum, 70, 78, 399
Ramp comparison A/D converter, 668
Random field, 43
Random processes, 27, 43, 52, 55, 70
Random search, 440
Random sequence, 43
Random variables, 43, 47, 48
Raster scanning, 101
Rate distortion bound, 365, 428, 430
Rate distortion function (RDF), 21, 628, 632,
    639
  and entropy coding, 154, 155, 157
  qualitative curves, 22
  and quantizer performance, 121
  and water filling, 530
$R(D)$, RDF (_see_ Rate distortion bound and
    function)
Real-valued Fourier matrix, 553
Reconstruction error, 6
  in DM, 375, 381, 407
  in DPCM, 257, 260, 279, 280–82, 312
  filtered, 375
  images, 407
  in PCM, 8
  in quantization, 118, 122, 165, 172, 177
  spectra, 260, 381, 532, 642, 644
  speech waveforms, 280, 375, 573
  in TC, 573
Reconstruction error variance, 6
  in continuous time, 111
  in DM, 379, 381, 382

with DM transmission errors, 417
in DPCM, 253, 259
with DPCM transmission errors, 329, 330
in D*PCM, 357
with D*PCM transmission errors, 361
in NFC, 365
with PCM transmission errors, 243
and prefiltering error variance, 87
in SBC, 491, 493
in TC, 525, 527
with TC transmission errors, 577
with transmission errors, 180–86
Reconstruction filtering, 3, 86
  casual, 92
  continuous time, 111
  ideal lowpass, 92, 93
Reconstruction level, 116, 134
Redundancy, 16, 17, 428, 618, 634
  of discrete-amplitude source, 147
  explicit, 246
  and irrelevancy, 16, 17
  natural, 247
  and spectral flatness, 58
  temporal, 322
  use in error protection, 246, 247
Reflected binary code (RBC), 177
Relative address coding (RAC), 478
Relative element address designate (READ)
    coding, 478
Re-optimization for noisy channels, 182, 184,
    334
RLC (_see_ Run length coding)
Robust adaptive quantizer, 283, 506
Robust LMS algorithm, 306
Root mean square (rms) value, 31, 44
Run-length coding, 37, 322, 465–85

Sample-and-hold, 87–88
Sampling, 3, 26, 86–114
  of bandpass signals, 96–98
  errors in, 102
  ideal, 92
  integer-band, 97, 98
  of moving images, 101
  nonuniform, 94
  rate, 5
  theorems, 89, 90–91, 94, 98, 101
  of 3-D signals, 101–2

Truncation error, 535
Two-channel DM, 416
Two-dimensional DCT, 560
Two-dimensional DFT, 556, 601
Two-dimensional linear system, 605
Two'dimensional prediction, 264–66, 287, 327, 331, 477
Two-dimensional transform, 520
Two-dimensional z-transform, 601
Two-level images (*see* Graphics)
Two-level psd, 79, 492
Two's complement code, 177, 215
Two-sided polarity correlation, 298, 306, 318, 342

Uniform pdf source, 34, 123, 125, 176, 187, 447, 640
Unitary transform, 523
Unit delay predictor, 257
Unvoiced speech, 28, 40, 41, 277, 292, 316

Variable bit allocation, 59, 322, 486, 551, 557, 571
Variable-length coding, 289, 323, 469, 473, 622
Variable-width sub-bands, 488, 489
Variance, 6, 31, 44
Vector DPCM, 439
Vector quantization, 16, 301, 303, 428–64
Video, 2, 9, 101
Videoconferencing, 324
Videophone, 9, 13, 77, 321–24, 387
Viterbi algorithm, 443
Vocoders, 10

Voiceband data, 78, 204, 273, 274, 399
Voiced speech, 28, 40, 41, 68, 277, 291, 316
Voice storage, (*see* Storage)

Water-filling procedure, 530, 641
Waveform coding, 1–25
Waveform decoder, 3
Waveform encoder, 2
Waveform-preserving coder, 9, 487
Waveforms, 2, 26–85
  amplitude versus time plots, 27
  gray-level image, 30
  multi-dimensional, 31
  properties, 15
  speech, 28
  two-level image, 29
Weighted resistor D/A, 672
Whitening filter, 59, 275, 357, 358, 359
White noise, 57, 60, 78, 275, 387
Wiener Hopf equation, 269, 303
Wiener Khinchine theorem, 56
Wiener process, 66
Word-at-a-time A/D, 671

Yule-Walker equations, 269

Zero-mean signal, 6, 31, 33, 49
Zero-memory quantization, 1, 16, 115–46, 428
Zero-order extrapolation, 247
Zonal coding, 565
Zonal sampling, 533, 535, 544, 550, 557, 565
z-transform, 599